Conditional Relations
Paṭṭhāana
(2 Parts)

MLBD

SACRED BOOKS OF THE BUDDHISTS SERIES

Reprinted Under License from **Pali Text Society**

- **A Buddhist Manual of Psychological Ethics** : Translation of the First Book in Abhidhamma Piṭaka entitled Dhammasaṅgaṇī—With Introductory Essay and Notes by *C.A.F. Rhys Davids.*
- **The Book of the Gradual Sayings** : Translation of Anguttara Nikāya, the Fourth Collection of Sutta Piṭaka **(5 Vols.)**—Tr. by *F.L. Woodward* and *E.M. Hare.*
- **The Book of the Kindred Sayings** : Translation of Saṁyutta-Nikāya **(5 Vols.)**—Tr. ,Ed. & Introduction by *C.A.F. Rhys Davids,* Tr. by *F.L. Woodward.*
- **The Collection of the Middle Length Sayings** : Translation of Majjhima Nikāya, the Second Collection of the Sutta Piṭaka containing 152 suttas. **(3 Vols.)**—Tr. from the Pali by *I.B. Horner.*
- **Compendium of Philosophy** : Translation of Abhidhammattha-Saṅgaha)—With Tr., Introductory Essay and Notes by *Shwe Zan-Aung,* Rev. & Ed. by *C.A.F. Rhys Davids.*
- **Culavaṁśa** : Translation from German Translation by Wilhelm Geiger. A Continuation of *Great Chronicle of Ceylon* (Mahāvaṃśa) : **(2 Pts. in One)**—by *C. Mabel Rickmers.*
- **Dialogues of the Buddha** : Dīgha Nikāya, the First Collection of Sutta Piṭaka **(3 Vols.)**—Translation from the Pali by *T.W. Rhys Davids* and *C.A.F. Rhys Davids.*
- **Dictionary of Pali Proper Names (2 Vols.)**—*G.P. Malalasekera.*
- **English-Pali Dictionary** —*Venerable A.P. Buddhadata.*
- **The Expositor** : Translation of Atthaśālinī, Buddhaghoṣa's Commentary on Dhammasaṅgaṇī, the First Book of Abhidhamma Piṭaka—Tr. by *Pe Maung Tin,* Rev. & Ed. by *C.A.F. Rhys Davids.*
- **Conditional Relations [Paṭṭhāna] (2 Pts.)** Part I : Guide, Part II : Translation of Caṭṭasaṅgāyana Text of the Seventh Book of Abhidhamma Piṭaka—Tr. by *U. Narada Mula Patt Thana Sayadow,* Assisted by *U. Thein Nyun.*
- **The Jātaka or Stories of the Buddha's Former Births (6 Vols. in 3 Pts.)**: Translation from the Tenth Book of Khuddaka Nikāya of Sutta Piṭaka—Ed. by *E.B. Cowell,* Tr. by *Robert Chalmers, W.H.D. Rouse, H.T. Francis* and *R.A. Neil.*
- **Pali-English Dictionary**—*T.W. Rhys Davids* and *William Stede.*
- **Pali Metre** : A Contribution to the History of Indian Literature—*A.K. Warder.*
- **Points of Controversy** (Subjects of Discourse) : A Translation of the Kathāvathu from the Fifth Book of Abhidhamma Piṭaka—Tr. by *S.Z. Aung* and *C.A.F. Rhys Davids.*
- **The Sutra of Golden Light** : Translation of Suvarnabhasottamasūtra—*R.E. Emmerick.*

Pali Text Society
Translation Series No. 42

CONDITIONAL RELATIONS

Paṭṭhāna

(2 Parts)

Part I Being a guide to pages 1-12 of Conditional Relations (*Paṭṭhāna*). An explanation of the conditions and of the methods for working out the answers in the 6 chapters of the Faultless triplet Paṭṭhāna where only the numbers of answers are given in Conditional Relations.

Part II The *Chaṭṭhasaṅgāyaya* Text of the Seventh Book of the *Abhidhamma-piṭaka*

A Translation by
U NARADA MULA PATTANA SAYADAW
Aggamahāpaṇdita of Rangoon, Burma
Originator of Abidhamma Charts

Assisted by
THEIN NYUN

MOTILAL BANARSIDASS PUBLISHERS
PRIVATE LIMITED • DELHI

First Indian Edition: Delhi, ***2016***
First Published (Part I): Wiltshire, (UK),1979 (2013)
First Published (Part II): Wiltshire, (UK),1981 (1993, 1998, 2011)

ISBN: 978-81-208-4037-9

Also available at
MOTILAL BANARSIDASS
41 U.A. Bungalow Road, Jawahar Nagar, Delhi 110 007
8 Mahalaxmi Chamber, 22 Bhulabhai Desai Road, Mumbai 400 026
203 Royapettah High Road, Mylapore, Chennai 600 004
236, 9th Main III Block, Jayanagar, Bengaluru 560 011
8 Camac Street, Kolkata 700 017
Ashok Rajpath, Patna 800 004
Chowk, Varanasi 221 001

MLBD Cataloging-in-Publication Data
Guide to Conditional Relations [Paṭṭhāna] (2 Parts)
Part I : Guide, Part II : *Translation by*
U Narada Mula Pattana Sayadaw
Assisted by Thein Nyun
in *MLBD Sacred Books of the Buddhists Series*
Includes *Catthasaṅgāyan* Text of the Seventh
Book of the *Abhidhamma-Piṭaka*
ISBN : 978-81-208-4037-9
I. Buddhism II. Paṭṭhāna
III. Chaṭṭhasaṅgāyana IV. Nyun, Thein

Published by
Motilal Banarsidass Publishers Private Limited
www.mlbd.com • mlbd@mlbd.com
Printed by Replika Press Pvt. Ltd.

General Contents

FOREWORD

In 1969 the Pali Text Society published, as No. 37 in its Translation Series, a translation by U Nārada Mūla Paṭṭhāna Sayadaw of Vol. I of the Chaṭṭhasaṅgāyana edition of Paṭṭhāna, the seventh book of the Abhidhamma-Piṭaka, under the title of *Conditional Relations* (*C.R.*), Vol. I. In my Foreword to this translation I spoke (p. x) of the "vast complexities and unique content" of this difficult and intricate work, to be grasped and more fully studied only by the provision of a guide to Paṭṭhāna. The results of the Ven. Sayadaw's many years of intensive scrutiny, research, and reflection are contained in this companion volume to Conditional Relations I, which accordingly is named *Guide to Conditional Relations* (*G.C.R.*). But as it covers no more than the first twelve pages of *C.R.*, it has been called Vol. I, Part 1. At this stage it can only be said that, though at some future date the Society no doubt will do its best to publish *G.C.R.* in full, a more immediate publication of a further part will depend largely on the response to this present part and on the interest it arouses.

The production of this Part 1 of *G.C.R.* presented a number of typographical problems. These included so arranging the charts as to enable them to fit the normal size of P.T.S. book-pages. Also, as usual, some alterations had to be made after the work was in proof. Such matters have added to the expenses and are in part responsible for the high cost of this little volume.

We owe much gratitude to Mr K. D. Somadasa for reading the proofs, and above all for his invaluable assistance in sorting out these alterations which the author sent to us from Rangoon in order to bring this guide to his own high standard and lucidly clear comprehension of Paṭṭhāna. Without Mr Somadasa's determination and acumen some unfortunate muddles and misunderstandings might well have resulted. We also wish to express our indebtedness to Mrs Reba Lawless for the sustained, intelligent and most able and helpful assistance she has given in a variety of ways. And, of course, specially warm thanks are offered to U Thein Nyun for the copious and unstinted part he has played in the preparation of this volume as well as of the succeeding ones, not yet published.

In the belief that interest in Abhidhamma is increasing in various parts of the world, we hope that *Guide to Conditional Relations*, Vol. I, part 1, may be a welcome addition to the P.T.S. books ancillary to the study of Pāli. We also hope that it will promote research and an understanding of a subject of which U Nārada is an acknowledged master and authority, now never to be superseded since the prolonged, severe, and thorough training he received is no longer prescribed.

London, 1978

I.B. Horner

PREFACE

WHY THE GUIDE TO CONDITIONAL RELATIONS IS COMPILED

In *Discourse on Elements*, a translation of Dhātukathā, issued by the Pali Text Society in 1962, I included explanations and methods together with charts and also the states of the Triplets and Couplets of the Dhammasaṅgaṇī so that the reader could, on his own, understand this subject. As a result many good reviews of the book were received. Besides, I received a letter from a reader stating that "I cannot express too highly my admiration for the charts which you prepared on the Dhātukathā. Is there any hope that you will place us even more in debt to you for similar charts presenting comprehensively the content of the Paṭṭhāna? This is our greatest need."

With the idea of translating Paṭṭh on the same lines, a portion of Paṭṭh was translated giving all the explanations, methods, and analytical states involved therewith, consisting of more than 300 pages of typescript. When the P.T.S. was informed of this, a reply was received from the Secretary pointing out the fact that this was not in line with the policy of the Society and that the text should first be translated as a whole and, later, a supplement provided in which all details could be given. Therefore, the work being carried out at the time had to be stopped and the whole text of Volume I of Paṭṭh translated. This has been issued by the Society as *Conditional Relations*. But by simply reading through the translation without the explanations, methods and analytical states being given, the reader or Pāli scholar will not understand Paṭṭh. That is why an Introduction covering over 100 pages was provided in *Conditional Relations* to enable the reader to get some idea of the translated text and also have a general idea of what is expounded in the 24 divisions comprising Paṭṭh.

Even then only a very superficial idea of Paṭṭh will be acquired because, although there are only 24 main divisions, there are in all 129,232 Paṭṭh sections under them. So for the benefit of readers, *Guide to Conditional Relations* has been painstakingly compiled and is now offered for publication. Only when this *Guide* is read along with

Conditional Relations will the reader understand Paṭṭh and realise how causes and effects are related in all animate and inanimate things.

The Difficulty of Abhidhamma

With regard to the Abhidhamma expounded by the Buddha, the analyses of the states involved are difficult and the individual characteristics (*sabhāva*) of the states are deep and profound. That is why, even for *devas* and *brahmās* who have swift, intuitive knowledge, the Buddha, in expounding Abhidhamma to them in the Tāvatiṃsa world of *devas*, always provided methods wherever necessary in order to make them understand certain portions. This is pointed out in *The Expositor* 440 as follows: "Indeed, the Supreme Buddha is never known to have missed the right occasion on which to use method when he came to Abhidhamma." Therefore, for one who desires to understand Abhidhamma, the essential thing is to know the analytical states involved in a particular Abhidhamma text. For a knowledge of such states is indispensable for a thorough understanding of that particular text. That this is so can be seen from the Dhammasaṅgaṇī, the first book of Abhidhamma, where the four chapters beginning with "The Genesis of Thoughts" (*cittuppādakaṇḍa*) deal with the analytical states.

Western Pāli scholars may be well enough versed in Pāli to be able to read the Abhidhamma texts but there are very few who are conversant with the analytical states involved in them. Although there are many who know some of the analytical states from a study of *Compendium of Philosophy*. There are very few who understand Dhs when it is studied later. The reason is that no one has written a book to show how the analytical states given in Dhs correspond with those in *Cpd.* So I have heard it said that those who are interested in Abhidhamma read through the Dhs translation, find it difficult to understand and so put it aside. Then they make another attempt, again fail to understand what is read and put it aside again and so it goes on. Even the translator of Dhs cannot give definitive decisions on certain matters. For example, on p. 36 of the translation dealing with the Third Type of Thought, right intention (*sammādiṭṭhi*) is included and a footnote on it given thus: "*Sammādiṭṭhi* should have been omitted in the text, just as it was rightly omitted at the place of the second mention between *avyāpādo* and *hiri*." *Sammādiṭṭhi* was included by mistake in the Pāli text which was translated. It is not included in the Burmese edition. So it shows that the translator, not being conversant with the analytical states, dared not exclude *sammādiṭṭhi* but had to have a footnote on it. Besides, with regard to the Supplementary Digest appended to the Dhs and entitled in the commentary the Aṭṭhakathākaṇḍa (Expositional Division) or Atthuddhāra (Elucidation), the translator of Dhs stated on p. 361, "I have not thought it worth while to translate them." But this portion is of great importance in Abhidhamma as the analytical states are provided. That is why *Expos*. 519, which calls this portion "The Commentarial Chapter", stated, "But why has this chapter come to be called Commentarial? Because it is established by elucidating the meaning of the three Piṭakas, the Buddha's Word. For the special doctrine which does not come in the three Piṭakas, being defined and determined by the Commentarial Chapter, becomes well determined. It behoves the Abhidhamma student who cannot note the method of procedure in the entire Abhidhamma-Piṭaka, the framing of queries, and the numerical series in the Great Book (Paṭṭh) to compare or bring them together from the Commentarial Chapter only."

Why Abhidhamma Thrives in Burma

The reason why Abhidhamma thrives in Burma is that the *akauks* concerned with Abhidhamma: (1) the analytical states (*akauks*) of the Table of Contents of Dhātukathā, (2) the analytical states of Yamaka and (3) the analytical states of Paṭṭh, were compiled by Burmese Sayadaws of old. These analytical states are known only in Burma and in no other Theravada country. These *akauks* are detailed compilations based on the analytical states given in the cty and Subcomy. of the different states expounded in the Pāli Canon. For they are given very briefly in the cty and Subcomy. and the Pāli scholar going through them cannot know all the analytical states.

But even though the *akauks* give the analytical states completely, the methods of taking the appropriate ones in the text concerned are not given and, therefore, only the very few who have deep knowledge of Abhidhamma understand these *akauks*. Otherwise anyone who can read Burmese would understand them. So it shows that the methods to understand these *akauks* are lacking. That is why, for those who desire to understand the methods easily, I have written books in Burmese entitled (1) Abhidhammatthasaṅgaha with charts concerned not only with this text but also with those of Paṭṭh so that one who has studied this book will find no difficulty with the study of Paṭṭh, (2) Expertise on the Table of Contents of Dhātukathā, (3) Expertise on Yamaka, (4) Supplement to the Expertise on Yamaka, and (5) Expertise on Paṭṭhāna. In all these books charts are provided and methods given so that they are easily understood even though the analytical states of Yamaka and Paṭṭh are very difficult to know. As a result the methods are known all over Burma.

At my suggestion, the Abhidhamma Propagation Society was formally established in Rangoon about twenty-five years ago. Since then I, along with some of my old pupils, have been teaching Abhidhamma every year. Those attending these classes are workers who have to attend to their official duties during the day and so the classes are held twice a week in the evenings for an hour and a half starting at five o'clock. Even though the pupils spend only a short time in learning, they are capable of passing oral examinations on the Table of Contents of Dhātukathā, Yamaka, and Paṭṭh, and written examinations on the individual characteristics of the states of Abhidhamma. The reason for this is that they first learn the analytical states and then acquire the methods. Therefore, in Abhidhamma, the most essential thing is to know the analytical states first.

The Difficulty of Knowing the Individual Characteristics

The difficulty of knowing the individual characteristics of the states can be overcome by referring to what the cty and Subcomy. say and to the pronouncements of the Sayadaws of old and then thinking over the decisions given by them. Even one who is studying the three Piṭakas cannot know them from the texts. First of all, reference has to be made to the cty to understand the difficult portions, and, if the cty does not provide the explanations, reference to the Subcomy. has to be made. This shows the difficulty of knowing the individual characteristics of the states. But in this *Guide to Conditional Relations* all such difficulties are not met with because the analytical states and explanations of each chapter are given, and so it is hoped that the reader will find it interesting.

Paṭṭhāna Is Understood if the Table of Contents of the Dhammasaṅgaṇī Is Understood

In the Table of Contents (*matika*) of Dhs, the Triplets and Couplets are expounded such as: "Faultless states, faulty states, indeterminate states" for the Faultless Triplet. With this knowledge of the Triplets and Couplets, Vibh, Dhātukathā, and Paṭṭh can be understood. For in (1) Vibh they are expounded in the Catechism, (2) Dhātukathā, those concerned in each method, and (3) Paṭṭh the Faultless Triplet in the Faultless Triplet Paṭṭh, the Feeling Triplet in the Feeling Triplet Paṭṭh, and so on. Paṭṭh, which is the first portion of the Buddha's teaching to decay, is found to be difficult, not only by laymen, but even by bhikkhus who are constantly studying the three Piṭakas.

While I was residing in Upper Burma about thirty-five years ago, I taught Abhidhamma to young girls. At first I taught Abhidh-s and then, after giving them the analytical states of the Faultless Triplet, the Faultless Triplet Paṭṭh, I succeeded in making them understand this Paṭṭh. Later, I taught them the Triplets and Couplets and then told them the method of filling up the elisions in all the 24 divisions of Paṭṭh, which they were able to do on their own. The girls did not learn

Abhidhamma as a pastime. They had to sit for an examination lasting twenty days. Although young, they were capable of understanding what was taught and of acquiring the methods because they obtained over 80 per cent marks. These girls only knew the analytical states of the Triplets and Couplets but had never seen the book of Dhs, or ever heard of Vibh and Dhātukathā. What I am driving at is that, since Paṭṭh is concerned with the Triplets and Couplets that form the Table of Contents of Dhs, if the latter is understood one can take up the study of Paṭṭh without having to learn Vibh and Dhātukathā, the texts that come before Paṭṭh. The bhikkhus, laymen and laywomen attending Paṭṭh classes held by the Abhidhamma Propagation Society mentioned above, appear for oral and written examinations on Yamaka and Paṭṭh without having any knowledge of Vibh and Dhātukathā.

PAṬṬHĀNA IS THE TEACHING OF *ANATTA*

If one considers the teaching of Abhidhamma starting with Dhs and ending with Paṭṭh, it will be seen that aggregates, bases, elements, and so on are expounded in them. This shows that the realities, with which Abhidhamma deals, consist of aggregates, bases, and elements that behave according to their own natures and, therefore, are not dependent on one's wishes. In other words, the realities behave according to the principle of *anatta*. But there are many people who believe there is *atta*, soul, etc., i.e. an ego-entity, and are so attached to this wrong view that they cannot easily give it up.

The so-called being consists of materiality-mentality (the five aggregates) and nothing else besides. This is what Vajira told Mara:

> "Being"! Why dost thou harp upon that word?
> 'Mong false opinions, Māra, hast thou strayed.
> Mere bundle of conditioned factors, this!
> No "being" can be here discerned to be.
> For just as, when the parts are rightly set,
> The word "chariot" ariseth [in our minds],
> So doth our usage convenant to say,

"A being" when the aggregates are there (*K.S.* I 170).

But there are teachers who imagine that something exists where none does, such as the Burmese sayings: "The hare's horns", "The turtle's hair", "The prawn's blood", "The dog's flea's white wings". For the hare has no horns, the turtle has no hair, the prawn has no blood and the dog's flea has no white wings.

It is in the nature of human beings to cling to one's views so that they cannot be easily given up. For once there is the belief that something is true, one becomes attached to this belief and so simple reasoning and argument to prove it to be false are of no avail. That is why it is said that "The hardest thing in the world to open is a closed mind". And in the Sutta-Piṭaka there are many instances where even the Buddha could not get some of his hearers to forsake certain views upheld in his time although he put forward ample reasons and arguments to prove them wrong.

In the Anatta Sutta the Buddha expounded, "Body, monks, is not self" (*rūpaṃ bhikkhave anattā*) and so on (B.D. IV, 20). But he also expounded that

Oneself is the guardian of oneself;
What other guardian would there be?
With oneself fully controlled,
One obtains a refuge which is hard to gain.

(Dhammapada, v. 160)

Some who have read this verse of the Buddha have taken the view that *atta* exists. But if this utterance is considered with reference to the context, it will be seen that the reason for this utterance was that the son, Venerable Kumāra-Kassapa, was very much attached to his mother, a Bhikkhunī, and so he was advised by the Buddha to depend upon himself. In such cases, of course, conventional language such as "oneself" cannot be avoided but it should not be taken literally.

In essence, Paṭṭh deals with the conditioned (*sappaccaya*) and formed (*saṅkhata*) states that arise and cease at every instant without a break and which make up what are said to be animate and inanimate things. These states arise dependent on root and the other conditions and are not at the will and mercy of any being. They do so, not from one cause alone, but from many causes such as the conditioning forces given in the Analytical Exposition of the Conditions. So Paṭṭh is the teaching of *anatta*.

The materiality-mentality, which constitute the human being, is not willed nor incited by *atta* or by any abiding entity, but is due to many causes. For example, when visible objects are seen daily, the seeing is due to four causes: (1) visible object, (2) sensitive eye, (3) light, and (4) attention. For it is only when these four causes are present at the same time that eye-consciousness arises to see or know a visible object. But with the arising of eye-consciousness with a very great object a mental process takes place according to the fixed nature of the mind (*citta-niyāma*). This process[1] consists of: (1) past life-continuum, (2) vibrating life-continuum, (3) arresting life-continuum, (4) five-door advertence, (5) eye-consciousness, (6) recipient consciousness, (7) investigating consciousness, (8) determining consciousness, (9) seven impulsions and (10) two registering consciousnesses. Again, the states involved in the process of seeing: eye-consciousness, visible object and sensitive eye arise due to many causes as shown below:

Eye-consciousness. When eye-consciousness arises it never arises alone. As expounded in Dhs, the seven primary mental states, the associated states, arise together with it. When eye-consciousness and the seven primary mental factors are classified under the aggregates as shown in the Discourse on Elements, they are the four mental aggregates. These four mental aggregates are mutually related to one another by the forces of seven conditions: conascence, mutuality, dependence, resultant, association, presence, and non-disappearance. Also, eye-

---

[1]The mental processes were not made up by the Commentators. They took them from proximity condition of Paṭṭh expounded by the Buddha. These mental processes are dealt with in the proximity condition of this guide.

consciousness is related to the seven primary mental factors by the forces of two conditions: nutriment and faculty.

Of the seven primary mental factors, contact is related to the others by the force of nutriment condition, feeling by that of faculty condition, volition by those of *kamma* and nutriment conditions, one-pointedness by that of faculty condition (although one-pointedness is related also by the forces of *jhāna* and path conditions, these forces are not included here because they are not concerned with eye-consciousness), psychic life-faculty by that of faculty condition. Perception and attention are not included in the minor conascence group of conditions and so their forces are not given.

Five-door advertence is related to eye-consciousness and the seven primary mental factors, i.e. eight mental states, by the forces of five conditions: proximity, contiguity, proximity-strong-dependence, absence, and disappearance.

The faultless and faulty *kamma* done in past existences are related respectively to the rootless faultless resultant eye-consciousness and rootless faulty-resultant eye-consciousness by the forces of two conditions: natural strong dependence and asynchronous *kamma*.

Visible Object. Visible object is related to eye-consciousness and the rest of the eight mental states by the forces of four conditions: object, object-prenascence, object-prenascence-presence, and object-prenascence-non-disappearance.

Sensitive eye. Sensitive eye is related to eye-consciousness and the rest of the eight mental states by the forces of six conditions: base-prenascence-dependence, base-prenascence, base-prenascence-faculty, base-prenascence-dissociation, base-prenascence-presence, and base-prenascence-non-disappearance.

From the above it will be seen that when the group of mental states including eye-consciousness arises, it does so by the forces of eighteen conditions exclusive of root, predominance, postnascence, repetition, *jhāna*, and path which are not concerned with eye-consciousness.

Therefore, these mental states are neither willed nor planned by *atta* which does not really exist but is imagined to exist by certain sects.

In the discourse on the Six Sixes (*M.L.S.* III 333) it is stated: "If anyone should say, 'Eye is self', that is not fitting. For the arising of the eye is to be seen and its decaying. Since its arising and decaying are to be seen, one would thus be brought to the stage of saying, 'Self arises in me and passes away.' Therefore if anyone should say, 'Eye is self', that is not fitting; in this way eye is not self," and so on. This shows in detail the *anatta* nature of materiality-mentality. So when it is said that a being sees, and so on, it is really the functions of materiality-mentality and, according to Paṭṭh as shown above, the functions of the conditioning forces. It is not the functions of *atta*.

Some do accept the *anatta* nature of materiality-mentality but say that this combination cannot see, hear, etc., and is, therefore, as useless as dried leaves. Instead, they say that it is the *atta*, existing in the body of each individual, that carries out those functions. This, of course, is not correct. For all such acts are due to the functionings of materiality-mentality and not to those of beings or persons. And only one who does not know the nature of materiality-mentality will assume that their functions are those of a person or *atta*.

The so-called being has six senses: that of (1) sight by means of which objects are seen, (2) hearing by which sounds are heard, (3) smell by which odours are smelt, (4) taste by which savours are tasted, (5) touch by which objects are felt and (6) the mind, based on the heart-base, which plans and thinks. Of these, the seeing or knowing of visible objects is due to the sensitive eye, the materiality, as cause and eye-consciousness, the mentality, as effect. It is not at all due to *atta*. For it is only when there is sensitive eye that seeing takes place. And when this cause is not present as in the case of the blind, no seeing can take place. If there were an *atta* in the body that could see or know, then because of it, the blind would be able to see. But since this does not happen, the *atta* is of no use in this case. So is it in the cases of hearing, smelling, etc.

The above shows that *atta* does not exist like materiality-mentality and that it has no functions of its own. All the functions are those of materiality-mentality which are dependent on many conditions such as root and so on for its arising. So Paṭṭh, which deals with all these conditions, is the teaching of *anatta*.

If one reflects on the teaching of Paṭṭh it will be concluded that only material and mental states are expounded. If one is able to distinguish between materiality and mentality, one acquires Purity of Views (*diṭṭhi-visuddhi*). With regard to this it is stated that:

> The mental and material are really here,
> But here there is no human being to be found,
> For it is void and merely fashioned like a doll —
> Just suffering piled up [void] like grass and sticks.
>
> (*P.Pfn.*, 689)

Again, Paṭṭh deals with materiality-mentality as the cause, the effect, and the conditioning force. So if one really knows materiality-mentality in these three ways one acquires Purity of Overcoming Doubt (*kaṅkhāvitaraṇa-visuddhi*), is freed from rebirth in the lower regions and is sure of one's destiny. This is given as: "When a man practising insight has become possessed of this knowledge he has found comfort in the Buddha's dispensation, he has found a foothold, he is certain of his destiny, he is called a 'Lesser Stream-enterer' " (*P.Pfn.*, 703).

After this stage is reached it is not so difficult to advance to the knowledge of the three general characteristics (*sammasana-ñāṇa*) and the other knowledges of insight for the attainment of Path and Fruition. It is only the above two Purifications that are difficult to acquire. Therefore, it is fervently hoped that those who are studying Paṭṭh will be able to reflect properly so as to acquire these two purifications and then contemplate further to attain Path and Fruition.

Reference in Connection with *Atta*

I would like those who wish to know more about *atta* to refer to the book *The Buddha's Teaching of Egolessness* (Anatta) by Nyanatiloka

Mahāthera where many explanations are given and quotations provided. One of the remarks made there is: "There are, however, to be found various would-be Buddhists in the West who are attached to an imaginary Great Self and who uphold that the Buddha did in no way reject the view of an eternal Ātman or soul, behind and independent of the phenomena of existence, and who believe that the Mahāyāna texts teach such a doctrine." This *Guide to Conditional Relations* explains in this Part and in Part II (forthcoming) the Twenty-four Conditions, the Analytical Exposition of the Conditions, and the six Chapters of the Faultless Triplet Paṭṭh which are given in pp. 1–141 of *Conditional Relations*. It has been compiled according to the method that I have adopted for teaching Paṭṭh, the method which is based on the commentary, subcommmentary, Burmese *akauks* of Paṭṭh, and other Burmese works. The explanation of the Investigation Chapter needs a separate volume of its own.

My thanks are due to U Kassapa, Dr Thein Maung, Ma Than Aye, Maung Tun Thwin, the Abhidhamma Propagating Society, and Dr I.B. Horner for help given in various ways.

U Nārada

Mūla Paṭṭhāna Sayadaw

INTRODUCTION

Guide to Conditional Relations, Part I, deals with the first twelve pages of *Conditional Relations*. It explains the Enumeration of the Conditions, the Analytical Exposition of Conditions, the Question Chapter, and the first six Chapters of the Faultless Triplet included therein. In this Introduction brief accounts of the matter treated in this Guide are given.

I. CONDITIONAL RELATIONS

At first a general idea of the subject matter of Conditional Relations (Paṭṭh) is given. It is mentioned that the states of the 22 Triplets and 100 Couplets (as given in Dhs) and of their combinations are involved as actual causes (known as conditioning states) and actual effects (known as conditioned states) which are related by the 24 conditions. It is also pointed out that the conditioning states possess various conditioning forces and that these forces, which bring about the conditioned states, are involved as well. So in this teaching on cause and effect, the conditioning forces are also taken into account. Incidentally, it is shown how this method of teaching on cause and effect in Paṭṭh differs from the methods in the Noble Truths and Dependent Origination and so it is pointed out that these three methods have to be considered separately as they are not connected in any way.

In Conditional Relations the actual conditioning and conditioned states, which are the rudiments of Paṭṭh, are not given, but these must be known in order to understand this subject. That is why it is stressed that the conditioning, conditioned, and non-conditioned states of each condition must first be learnt and thoroughly digested. In this Guide these states are given for the Faultless Triplet Paṭṭh section which is the first of the 129,232 Paṭṭh sections dealt with in the whole of Paṭṭh. The definitions of the terms involved, the order of the Paṭṭh exposition and a general idea of Paṭṭh were given in the Introduction to Conditioned Relations.

II. Brief Explanations of the 24 Conditions

The Buddha expounded Paṭṭh after he completed the Yamaka. In doing so he began by enumerating the 24 conditions. The reason for this is that he had to deal with these 24 conditions in the innumerable methods to be given in the 24 divisions of Paṭṭh. It will be seen from *C.R.* that the 24 conditions are expounded as required for (i) the Analytical Exposition of the Conditions, (ii) the Classification Chapters of the six Chapters and Investigation Chapter, and (iii) the Enumeration Chapters of the seven Chapters. Besides, the causes and effects are expounded with reference to these 24 conditions. For example, it is said that such-and-such a state is the cause of root condition and such-and-such a state is the effect of root condition and that such states as cause and effect are related by the force of root condition.

Here, in the Brief Explanations of the 24 Conditions, the definitions of the conditions together with the analogies and explanations are given. In the case of the conditions like predominance, the kinds of predominance condition and so on are also considered. Moreover, wherever the conditions appear to be alike, because they have the same conditioning and conditioned states, the actual differences between them are given. So the reader will come to know why the conditions are so named and thereby come to have the basic idea behind Paṭṭh. Besides, the conditioning and conditioned states of each condition are given and also, wherever necessary, the reasons why they are so, and why certain states are never conditioning or conditioned states of a particular condition. This should give some idea of what is dealt with under this head in the 74 pages of the Guide and to which reference should be made for the details. But in the cty root condition is the only condition which is treated somewhat in detail and the analogies are given fully only for root, object, conascence, mutuality, dependence, postnascence, and repetition conditions.

III. Explanation of the Single Enumerations (Chart No. 1)

Before going on to the explanation of the Analytical Exposition of the Conditions (which comes after the Enumeration of the Conditions in Conditional Relations), an explanation of the Single Enumerations is first given. Here the conditioning and conditioned states of each condition, as given in the Analytical Exposition, are taken according to the method of the Classification Chapter of the Investigation Chapter in order to explain about conditioning forces and common conditions. For these have to be considered in the explanation of the Analytical Exposition.

Single Enumerations mean the enumerations or numbers of answers obtained from the conditioning and conditioned states of the single conditions, i.e. when the conditions are taken "By Ones" or "Singly". As pointed out above, these conditioning and conditioned states are the fundamentals of Paṭṭh, just as alphabets are for a language. If the conditioning and conditioned states of the conditions in the Faultless Triplet Paṭṭh section, which is dealt with here, are known, this portion of Paṭṭh will be easily understood. This holds true, likewise, for all the Paṭṭh sections.

Root condition is treated in great detail (1) to explain what is meant by "common conditions" and to give the method of determining them and (2) to show that a conditioning force occurs either "completely" amongst those of the common conditions or "completely" in some and "appropriately" in the rest. When this matter is grasped, the commons (*sabhāga*) and combinations (*ghaṭanā*), the difficult portions of Paṭṭh, will be easily understood. So the reader is advised to study this Explanation of the Single Enumerations which covers over 30 pages.

IV. Explanation of the Analytical Exposition of the Conditions (Chart No. 2)

It is pointed out that the Buddha expounded the Faultless Triplet Paṭṭh, the first Paṭṭh section, in detail in order to provide the methods so that all the other Paṭṭh sections, given briefly, could be expanded by application of those methods. That is why the Enumeration of the Conditions and the Analytical Exposition of the Conditions are expounded only in this Faultless Triplet Paṭṭh. But an example of this application is given with the Feeling Triplet Paṭṭh to show that only 21 out of the 24 conditions are to be enumerated and that materiality is to be excluded in the relations given for these 21 conditions in the Analytical Exposition of the Conditions in the Faultless Triplet Paṭṭh.

The Analytical Exposition is not as brief as the Enumeration of the Conditions nor as exhaustive as the Classification Chapter of the Investigation Chapter. That is why it is said to be a teaching which is neither too brief nor too detailed (*nātisaṅkhepa-nātivitthāra*).

1. Root Condition

The Analytical Exposition, just like the Classification Chapter of the Investigation Chapter, gives (i) the conditioning states, (ii) the conditioned states and (iii) the conditioning forces involved in the relations. For root condition the relation is given as: "The roots are related to the states which are associated with roots, and the matter produced thereby, by root condition." Here (i) the roots are the conditioning states, (ii) the states associated with roots and the matter produced thereby are the conditioned states, and (iii) by (the force of) root condition is the conditioning force. But this general statement, the only information provided in the text, is not sufficient for knowing all about this relation. One has to know (i) what the roots are, i.e. the analytical states of the conditioning states, (ii) what the states associated with roots and the matter produced thereby are, i.e. the analytical states of the conditioned states, and (iii) the conditioning forces that are involved. That is why explanations about them are given. For easy reference the analytical states, which are the conditioning and conditioned states of the conditions, are given in the Single Enumeration and Analytical Exposition charts.

As regards the conditioning force, only the number of common conditions in which this force occurs completely and appropriately is given in the chart. Therefore, explanations about these conditioning forces are given under each condition. Besides, the occurrence of each condition in planes and in beings is given.

2. Object Condition

The conditioning and conditioned states, conditioning force, and the occurrence of the condition in planes and in beings are explained for each condition as in root condition. So this fact will not be mentioned again for the other conditions.

With regard to the relation: "All states are related to mind-consciousness element and its associated states by object condition", all the conditioning and conditioned states concerned must be known and so they are given in the detailed chart of Object Condition (Chart no. 3) with the exception of the objects which are the conditioning states of rebirth consciousness. That is why extracts from the Vibh and Vism commentaries on this matter are given.

On examination of the objects of fine-material, immaterial, and super-knowledge consciousnesses given in the chart, it will be found that they are the causes for developing the mind. So if the inhabitants of the world were to practise to develop their minds, there would be peace for the individual and the world. The Buddha expounded about these consciousnesses in the Pāli Canon. In *The Path of Purification* the methods of practice are given in detail for acquiring such developed minds, particularly for super-knowledge consciousnesses which are dealt with in two chapters. As for supramundane consciousnesses, they take Nibbāna as object and when this object can be taken there will be release from every kind of suffering.

3. Predominance Condition

Of the two kinds: (a) conascence-predominance and (b) object-predominance, the four predominant realities of (a) and the conditioning and conditioned states of (b) are analysed. The latter, which are given in the chart, are not easy to know from the simple relation in the text which is: "Taking any state as estimable object, these states, consciousness and mental factors, arise; those [former] states are related to those [latter] states by predominance condition."

Also, it is pointed out that the predominant realities, desire, effort, etc., give results depending upon their degree of predominance, which is classed as (1) inferior, (2) medium and (3) superior. The different results produced by these three classes are shown with the first *jhāna* as an example. Besides, the Buddha explained that it is due to the degree of predominance with which *kamma* was performed in past existences that there are differences in the status of the same class of human beings. This degree of predominance holds good not only with the sensuous states but also with the lofty and supramundane states which are far superior.

4.–5. Proximity and Contiguity Conditions

In these conditions the mental processes are involved. To understand why a particular consciousness follows another in a mental process, the functions of the various consciousnesses must first be known. These are given in Chart no. 4 and explained. Moreover, since the relations are between consciousnesses and mental factors, these mental states are briefly explained.

In the Analytical Exposition chart all the conditioning and conditioned states are taken together and the relations, faultless-faultless, etc., shown in a general way. But proper selection of the faultless states, etc., must be made in order to know the relations in detail. For the latter the detailed chart of Proximity Condition (Chart no. 5) is provided and the appropriate relations taken from it. Here all the mental processes concerned with the Faultless Triplet are given, but they will be dealt with in greater detail in the Guide to *C.R.*, Part III, when the Investigation Chapter will be explained and the relations between one consciousness and another shown.

6.–7. Conascence and Mutuality Conditions

In the relation: "The four immaterial (i.e. mental) aggregates are mutually related to one another by conascence condition", it is pointed out why all the four mental aggregates cannot be taken as either conditioning or conditioned states. It is shown that when one of the four mental aggregates is the conditioning state, the other three mental aggregates are the conditioned states and so on. Also, that when the specific aggregates are taken into account, there are in all fourteen ways of taking this relation.

Mutuality condition is a part of conascence condition and is included in the latter.

8. Dependence Condition

There are two kinds: (a) conascence-dependence, which is the same as conascence condition above, and (b) base-prenascence-dependence. In dealing with (b) it is pointed out that the fivefold consciousnesses are dependent on the five bases of medium duration and not on the other two kinds, slow and quick durations. The eye-door mental process is taken as the example to prove this. Then the remaining base, heart-base, is dealt with and shown how the brain is affected by the mind which is dependent on the heart-base.

9. Strong-dependence Condition

There are three kinds: (a) object-strong-dependence, (b) proximity-strong-dependence and (c) natural strong-dependence. But no differentiation is made of them in the nine relations given in the text which are: "Preceding faultless states are related to subsequent faultless states by strong-dependence condition", and so on. So the analytical states of the conditioning and conditioned states are given, and it is shown that there are twenty-three relations in all, seven for (a), seven for (b), and nine for (c). These analytical states are not given in the cty although the three kinds of strong-dependence condition are mentioned.

10. Prenascence Condition

There are two kinds: (a) base-prenascence and (b) object-prenascence. Kind (a) occurs during life. As for (b) it is not given completely, for in this incomplete (*sāvasesa*) teaching, the relations involved in the five-door mental process but not in the mind-door process are considered.

The cty also remarks that object-prenascence condition is not given completely.

11. Postnascence Condition

The conditioning and conditioned states of this condition are given in a general way in the Analytical Exposition chart, and so a few examples are worked out to show how these states have to be taken to know the relation in detail. Also, it is explained why certain states do not belong to this condition.

12. Repetition Condition

The totals of the analytical states which are the conditioning and conditioned states of this condition are given in the Analytical Exposition chart. So it is shown how the analytical states concerned have to be taken to know the relation in detail. It is pointed out that beings attain Paths and Fruitions because of the force of this condition which brings about acute faculties of knowledge, effort, and so forth. That is why the Buddha, although he had great compassion on all beings, instructed only those who had acquired such faculties for the attainments of Paths and Fruitions. Specific instances are given to show that in the other cases the Buddha did not so instruct beings because the relation by repetition condition was so weak that they were not ripe for such attainments.

13. *Kamma* Condition

There are two kinds: (a) asynchronous *kamma* and (b) conascence-*kamma*. In the Asynchronous *Kamma* chart (Chart no. 6), the conditioning and conditioned states, given in the Analytical Exposition chart, are selected to give the relation in detail. In the detailed chart of Asynchronous *Kamma* Condition (Chart no. 7), the results produced at rebirth and during life by the faultless and faulty *kamma* are shown and explanations provided wherever necessary. As *kamma* condition is of fundamental importance in the Buddha's teaching, extracts from Buddhist literature are given to show (1) the different kinds of *kamma*, (2) that there is no doer apart from *kamma* and its result, and (3) that the Noble Eightfold Path, the supramundane Path, is to be practised for the destruction of *kamma*. The explanation of this condition covers several pages.

14. Resultant Condition

Consciousnesses are classed as four kinds (with regard to both effort and quiet) to show how resultant consciousness differs from faulty, faultless, and functional consciousnesses.

15. Nutriment Condition

There are two kinds: (a) physical nutriment and (b) conascence-nutriment. With regard to (a) it is shown how the relations with nutritive essence and the twenty-one groups of matter have to be taken. Also, it is pointed out that sensuous beings, since they cannot exist without food, have to undergo various kinds of hardship in seeking food or earning money to buy food and that the killing of creatures on this account is one of the causes for rebirth in the lower regions. With regard to (b) explanations are given about contact, volition and consciousness, the mental nutriments. Then the similes from *K.S.* regarding each of these four nutriments are given where in each case it is stated that when it is well understood, *Arahatta* Fruition is attained.

16. Faculty Condition

There are three kinds: (a) base-prenascence-faculty, (b) physical life-faculty, and (c) conascence-faculty. It is pointed out that these three kinds of faculty condition are not dealt with in the same order as the Investigation Chapter but in accordance with that in the Vibh cty, from which extracts are given. In (b) it is shown how the relations with physical life-faculty and each of the nine groups of *kamma*-produced matter have to be taken. In (c) the functions of the five conascence-faculties (confidence, effort, mindfulness, one-pointedness and knowledge) and the similes in this connexion, taken from the cty on S, are given.

17. *Jhāna* Condition

The nine *jhāna* factors given in the Dhs come under five realities, and that is why only five *jhāna* factors are taken. At first, the meaning of *jhāna* and its difference from *jhāna* factors are given. Then the functions of the five *jhāna* factors are explained in detail. It is also pointed out that *jhāna* is so called because it suppresses the hindrances, and explanations as to why the *jhāna* factors do so are provided. Finally, the two kinds of *jhāna* are mentioned.

18. Path Condition

The eight supramundane path factors are explained. It is pointed out that right view is the most important of them, that there are only two conditions for bringing it about so as to become a Sotāpanna, and that right view has to be forwarded by five factors so as to become an Arahant. The cty on the Mahāvedalla Sutta, which deals with this matter, is included.

19. Association Condition

In this condition both the conditioning and conditioned states are consciousnesses and mental factors. The number of mental states associated with each consciousness, given in Dhs, are different from the number of mental factors associated with each consciousness given in Abhidh-s (*Cpd.*). So one who has first studied the latter gets confused when the study of the former is taken up. Therefore, Chart no. 8 is provided giving all the associated mental states and the mental factors of these two texts. As for the "or-whatever" (*yevā panaka*) states of Dhs which are given, the appropriate ones to be taken for each consciousness are mentioned.

The chart is explained with the first pair of great faultless consciousnesses by means of red squares in the chart. All the other consciousnesses are dealt with by taking the associated mental states of Dhs and working out the associated mental factors of Abhidh-s.

20. Dissociation Condition

In the text, the relations, given in a general way, are: "The material states are related to the immaterial states by dissociation condition", and "The immaterial states are related to the material states by dissociation condition". But in the Analytical Exposition chart the conditioning and conditioned states of three kinds of dissociation condition are given, those of (a) conascence-dissociation and base-prenascence-dissociation that come under (i) above and (b) conascence-dissociation and postnascence-dissociation that come under (ii) above. Extracts from *P.Pfn.* are given to show that materiality and mentality are separate but interdependent entities and that, besides them, there is no being, person, *deva* or *brahmā*.

21. Presence Condition

It is pointed out that presence condition is not completely expounded in this Analytical Exposition of the Conditions where the teaching is neither too brief nor too detailed. So, of the nine kinds of presence condition, postnascence-presence, physical nutriment-presence, physical life-faculty-presence and the three kinds of mixed conditions are left out. Also, the reason is given why Nibbāna, which is eternal, is not included in this condition.

22.–23. Absence and Disappearance Conditions

These two conditions are the same as proximity condition, but they are not expounded in detail as that condition was. It will be seen from the chart that only the totals of the conditioning and conditioned states are given.

24. Non-disappearance Condition

This is the same as presence condition.

V. The Commentary on Chapter I and II and Its Explanation

The Order in the Commentary

The cty, after explaining the 24 conditions enumerated in Chapter I of *C.R.*, deals with the decisions regarding (i) State (*dhamma*), (ii) Period (*kāla*), (iii) Manifold Division (*nānappakāra*), and (iv) Conditioned States (*paccayuppannato*) in order to have a full understanding of these conditions. Again, after explaining the Analytical Exposition of the Conditions, which forms Chapter II of *C.R.*, the cty, for the purpose of acquiring clear and deep knowledge of this portion, treats of the Miscellaneous Decisions (*pakiṇṇaka vinicchaya*) which consist of the following ten items:

(i) Several States [in] One Condition (*aneka dhamma eka paccaya*);
(ii) One State [in] Several Conditions (*eka dhamma aneka paccaya*);
(iii) One Condition [common with] Several Conditions (*eka paccaya aneka paccaya*);
(iv) Common Conditions (*paccaya sabhāga*);
(v) Not Common Conditions (*paccaya visabhāga*);
(vi) Pairs (*yugaḷaka*);
(vii) Production and Non-production (*janakājanaka*);
(viii) Causes or Not Causes of All Formations (*sabbaṭṭhānikā-sabbaṭṭhānika*);
(ix) Materiality to Materiality (*rūpaṃ rūpassa*), etc.;
(x) Divisions of Existence (*bhava-bheda*).

The Order in the Guide

In this Guide a different order is taken. This has been done so as to enable the reader to understand the cty easily and to avoid the use of many charts. Besides the contents of the cty, additional information is provided with regard to the analytical states concerned and the conditions that occur during life and at the moment of conception, etc. So the order here is:

1. Manifold Division with one chart;
2. Conditioned States with several charts;
3. One State (in) Several Conditions with one chart, i.e. number (ii) below of the Miscellaneous Decisions of the cty;

4. One Condition (common with) Several Conditions with one chart, i.e. (iii) of the Miscellaneous Decisions of the cty;
5. The rest under the heading of Miscellaneous Decisions with one chart. They are:

(i) State;
(ii) Period;
(iii) Several States in One Condition;
(iv) Common Conditions;
(v) Not Common Conditions;
(vi) Pairs;
(vii) Production and Non-production;
(viii) Causes or Not Causes of All Formations;
(ix) Materiality to Materiality, etc.;
(x) Divisions of Existence;
(xi) During Life and at the Moment of Conception;
(xii) Concept, Mentality, Materiality, Nibbāna as Conditioning States.

1. Manifold Division (Chart No. 9)

Here the conditioning states of the conditions are distinguished by classes and planes. A chart of the conditions together with classes and planes of the conditioning states is provided and explained, at first, in a general way, where the conditioning states of the conditions under the groups are taken as given in the Single Enumeration charts in the Intro. to *C.R.* Then, as in the cty, the conditioning states of each condition, taken in the usual order and so given in the chart, are dealt with in detail. The information provided in the cty is based on the conditioning states in the Single Enumeration charts referred to above, and, if the appropriate ones are referred to while reading, this portion will be easily understood. If the Pāli scholar knows these conditioning states and also the methods provided in the chart, he will have no difficulty in understanding all that is contained in the cty.

2. Conditioned States

The cty on the 24 conditions deals with the conditioned states at the end of each condition. Here also, similar to the conditioning states in the Manifold Division, the conditioned states are distinguished by classes and planes, i.e. by categories. The conditioning states concerned, also taken by classes and planes, have to be given because the kinds of conditioned states that arise as effect in a particular relation are dependent on them as cause. But the cty does not give the analytical states of the conditioned states and the specific relations (which have to be taken from the Classification Chapter of the Investigation Chapter) that are involved. They are given in the Guide in order to help readers understand the cty. Although the cty treats each of the 24 conditions in detail in serial order, here the conditions are taken according to their groups. For only in this way will the non-Pāli reader readily understand and remember the facts of the cty. As for the Pāli scholar, it will be of great help to a systematic understanding of the cty.

Object Group (Chart No. 10)

The cty on object condition begins thus: "Sensuous faultless [object] is related to sensuous faultless, fine-material faultless, faulty, sensuous resultant, sensuous functional, and fine-material functional, i.e. to six categories, by object condition." The number of each of these conditioned states is not given. Here, the chart, giving these numbers, is explained. Besides, in the last column, the number of the conditioned states, which always or occasionally take a particular kind of object, is given in the way shown under "Of Object of Consciousness" in Part III of *Cpd.*, pp. 119–22. In the chart, which is based on the cty, it is shown that two super-knowledges take Nibbāna as object. The remarks in the subcty are provided to show that this is not possible and also the author's opinion in the matter is given along with quotations to support his arguments. But what is more interesting is that the relations concerned, expounded by the Buddha in the Investigation Chapter, are quoted. For example, when sensuous faultless is related to sensuous faultless by object condition, the relation quoted is: "After having offered the offering, having undertaken the precept, having fulfilled the duty of observance, [one] reviews it. [One] reviews such acts formerly well done" and so on. All the items in the chart are dealt with and the quotations for the relations are either given or referred to. Moreover, a chart on Objects of Super-knowledges (Chart no. 11) is provided. It will be very useful when this subject is considered again in Volume II and others of Paṭṭh where the objects concerned are so complicated that it is difficult to know the object which is related to a particular super-knowledge. The cty deals very briefly with this matter. Finally, an example of the way to read the chart is given as is done for the charts of other conditions.

Object-predominance and Object-prenascence (Charts Nos. 12 and 13)

The figures and quotations provided here are not given in the cty. The above three charts are for the Object Group of Conditions.

Conascence Group (Chart No. 14)

The cty deals with each of the fifteen conditions of the conascence group in their serial order. But here, for quick and ready reference, the contents of the cty are compiled in a single chart by taking the conditions according to groups as was the case with the object group. The chart is used to explain the seven Minor conascence, the four Major conascence and the four Medium conascence conditions. Quotations are also given for the relations.

Conascence Group in Detail (Chart No. 15)

The cty given above deals very briefly with the conditions of the conascence group. So a detailed chart of the Conascence Group of Conditions is provided and explained. It gives all the details necessary to have a thorough understanding of the Minor, Medium, and Major conascence conditions. Quotations are also given for the relations.

Proximity-strong-dependence Group

The group of conditions, which follows in serial order after the object and conascence groups, is the proximity-strong-dependence group, and so this is next considered. It must be borne in mind that the figures in all the charts are provided by the author, for they are never given in the cty. Besides, the author, with the fervent desire that the reader may understand Paṭṭh completely, has provided quotations for faultless-faultless and other relations. And this selection of the appropriate quotations is not an easy matter except for one who is well-versed in Paṭṭh.

Proximity Condition (Chart No. 16)

The five conditions in the group starting with proximity condition (proximity group) have the same conditioning and conditioned states, and so, when proximity condition is dealt with, the others are known as well. Proximity condition is treated in detail so that the reader will understand the mental processes involved.

Repetition Condition (Chart No. 17)

It is pointed out that repetition condition is a part of proximity condition where only the impulsions in them are involved. So, if proximity condition is understood there will be no difficulty about this condition.

As for proximity-*kamma* condition, the remaining condition of this group, it is not dealt with in the cty, but it can be easily worked out from its conditioning and conditioned states using the above method.

Natural Strong-dependence Group

Of the three kinds, (a) object-strong-dependence and (b) proximity-strong-dependence are respectively the same as object-predominance of the object group and proximity condition of the proximity-strong-dependence group. So only (c) natural strong-dependence condition is here considered. This condition and strong asynchronous *kamma* condition come under the natural strong-dependence group of conditions.

Natural Strong-dependence Condition (Chart No. 18)

The relations in the chart are explained in detail. The remarks of the cty and subcty on these relations are given, one of which is that Arahatta Fruition is not related to the faultless. In this condition, (1) matter by the Suttanta method and (2) some of the concepts, such as person in the Analytical Exposition, are included.

Strong Asynchronous *Kamma* Condition (Chart No. 19)

It is pointed out that in the cty the two kinds of *kamma* condition, conascence-*kamma* and asynchronous *kamma*, are dealt with together, but here, where the conditions are taken according to groups, they are treated separately as they belong to different groups. The remarks made in the cty and subcty are also included. Besides, the results that this condition produces at rebirth and during life and the planes where these results take place are given.

Base-prenascence Group, etc. (Charts Nos. 20–22)

The charts of the conditions of (i) base-prenascence group, (ii) postnascence group, (iii) physical nutriment group and (iv) physical life-faulty group are easy to understand and, as they take up very little space, they are given on the same page. The charts are explained and the remarks in the subcty on physical life-faculty condition are included.

The mixed conditions are not dealt with in the cty and so they are not given here. But in the Explanation of the Single Enumerations they have been given in detail.

Proximity Condition Cycle (Chart No. 23)

The proximity condition cycle is drawn up from the detailed chart of Proximity Condition (Chart no. 5) where the way to read that chart is given. The cycle has to be read in the same way to understand it. It gives the analytical states of proximity condition dealt with in detail in the Explanation of the Analytical Exposition and also shows how repetition, base-prenascence, and postnascence conditions have to be known in detail. Examples are given of the ways of reading the cycle for these conditions. The purpose of providing this cycle is to let the reader know that when the relation by proximity condition no longer takes place at the death of a person, there will be eternal peace because the round of rebirths is ended. But so long as there is this relation by proximity condition there is no escape from the round of rebirths.

At the end of this explanation of "Conditioned States" it is pointed out that when the methods employed above for determining the conditioning and conditioned states of the relations are known, the rest of Paṭṭh will be easily understood. As a matter of fact, the cty has provided these methods in the Faultless Triplet Paṭṭh for the purpose of applying them to all the 24 divisions of Paṭṭh.

3. One State in Several Conditions (Chart No. 24)

This deals with the number of conditions in which a particular state is a conditioning state. This shows that a conditioning state arises due to many conditions and not simply to one condition alone. The cty deals with the conditioning states of the 24 conditions taken in serial order. If a chart were to be drawn up for each state according to the cty it would be a very big one, there would be so much to explain, and it would not be properly understood. So in order to understand readily and remember easily all the information given in the cty, a special chart is provided. But in order to know easily and readily the number of conditions in which a particular consciousness, mental factor, or matter is a conditioning state without the aid of the chart, rules are provided and applied. For example, those for any one of the eighty-nine consciousnesses are:

1. Exclude root, prenascence, *kamma*, *jhāna*, and path, and take the other nineteen conditions as reference;
2. If it is delusion-rooted consciousness or body-consciousness accompanied by pain, exclude predominance;
3. If it is not a resultant consciousness, exclude resultant;
4. If it is an immaterial resultant consciousness, exclude post-nascence and dissociation;

5. If it is not a mundane impulsion, exclude repetition.

If these rules are learnt and applied it will only take about a minute to work out the answer for any consciousness, and this answer can then be checked with that in the chart. Similarly, rules are given for mental factor and matter.

4. One Condition Common with Several Conditions (Chart No. 25)

This deals with the number of conditions which are common with each of the 24 conditions. In the Explanation of the Single Enumerations, each condition is taken according to the group to which it belongs, and the total of the common conditions is worked out for each condition taken as a whole, i.e. taking all the conditioning states of a condition together. For example, it is given there that root condition is common with eleven conditions where the six roots, the conditioning states of root condition, are taken together. These common conditions are given in the Single Enumerations chart. Here each condition is dealt with in serial order, and each of the conditioning states is taken separately to find the common conditions. For example, the conditions common with non-greed, non-hate, non-delusion, greed, hate, and delusion are worked out separately. And in finding out these common conditions, the methods are provided and explanations given wherever necessary. The common conditions are tabulated in the chart.

5. Miscellaneous Decisions (Chart No. 26)

This deals with the conditions considered under the following heads: (1) State, (2) Period, (3) Several States in One Condition, (4) Common Conditions, (5) Uncommon Conditions, (6) Pairs, (7) Production and Nonproduction, (8) Causes of All Formations, etc., (9) Materiality to Materiality, etc., (10) Planes of Existence, (11) During Life and At Rebirth, and (12) Concept, Mentality, Materiality, Nibbāna. All these are explained and summarised in a chart. The remarks of the subcty are included and the Pāli verse, given in the cty on Period, explained.

End of the Analytical Exposition of the Conditions.

VI. Question Chapter

After the Analytical Exposition of the Conditions the Buddha expounded the Question Chapter. It is pointed out that the Analytical Exposition is given in the Faultless Triplet Paṭṭh (which is the first Paṭṭh section) to provide the methods so that they could be applied to the other 129,231 Paṭṭh sections. Also, the Question Chapter, which is Chapter III of *C.R.*, is given just to provide the method of arriving at the questions and is, therefore, dealt with briefly. Although only the answers that can be given are provided in each of the seven chapters: (1) Dependent Chapter, (2) Conascent Chapter, (3) Conditioned Chapter, (4) Supported Chapter, (5) Conjoined Chapter, (6) Associated Chapter and (7) Investigation Chapter, that come under the Triplets, Couplets, etc., in the 24 divisions of Paṭṭh with regard to the questions, all the questions have to be provided whether there are answers for them or not.

In *C.R.* only the questions of Dependent Chapter in the Faultless Triplet for the conditions taken "By Ones" to "By Twenty-four" are given. All the questions are not provided but only those that are just sufficient to show the method which will serve as a model for arriving at the questions of the other chapters of the Faultless Triplet Paṭṭh as well as for the rest of Paṭṭh.

Questions of Paṭṭh

The total number of questions in Paṭṭh can be calculated when (1) the total number of Paṭṭh sections and (2) the number of questions in each of those sections are known.

Detailed Paṭṭh Sections (Chart No. 27)

As regards (1) above, although there are only 24 Paṭṭh divisions, when each Triplet and Couplet and each of their combinations are considered, there are, as explained, 129,232 Paṭṭh sections which are summarised in the detailed Paṭṭh Sections chart.

Model of Paṭṭh Questions (Chart No. 28)

As regards (2) above, the method of exposition of the questions in each of the sections must be known. Although the method of asking questions is provided for Dependent Chapter of the Faultless Triplet, the method has to be modified for the other sections. That is why models of Paṭṭh questions for Dependent Chapter of the Feeling Triplet and the rest of the six Paṭṭhs of the Positive Division and also for that of the six Paṭṭhs each of the Negative, Positive-Negative and Negative-Positive Divisions are provided. The states that are involved in the above model questions are not given in the Model of Paṭṭh Questions chart.

It must be remembered, however, that the questions are asked, not only for the Positive conditions, but also for the Negative, Positive-Negative and Negative-Positive conditions taken "By Ones", "By Twos", etc., as in the case of the questions for Dependent Chapter given in *C.R.* Besides, similar questions are asked for the rest of the seven chapters where the wordings are different depending on the chapter under consideration.

The cty deals with the first portions of the Question Chapter in detail and gives verses to get the total of the questions in them. The reason is that the method provided can be applied to work out the rest so as to arrive at the grand total. As for the subcty, verses are given completely to arrive at the grand total.

Number of Questions (cty) (Chart No. 29)

Based on the method given in the cty the author has worked out the grand total of questions which is 404,948,533,248. All the details are explained and shown in the chart.

Number of Questions (subcty) (Chart No. 30)

Based on the method given in the subcty the author has worked out the grand total of questions which is 388,788,713,344. All the details are explained and shown in the chart.

The subcty has supplied verses at the end of the book giving the totals for the different items. But the Pāli scholar may find them difficult to understand and so they are translated to show the totals they denote.

It will be noted that the grand totals of the cty and the subcty are different. This is due to some difference in the method of calculation and the reason for this is pointed out.

If 100,000 questions were to be recited in a day, it would take over 10,000 years to complete the questions of Paṭṭh. The cty states that the Buddha expounded all the Paṭṭh questions to his audience of *devas* and Brahmās in the Tāvatiṃsa world of *devas*. This amply shows the Omniscience of the Buddha.

This Question Chapter is very important for the whole of Paṭṭh, and that is why it is treated in detail here. If the method of asking questions in the examples provided is understood, it will not be necessary to remember the questions, for one will be able to recite them without end. The reader is requested to find out for himself if this is so.

VII. Preliminaries to the six Chapters

After expounding the method of asking questions in the Question Chapter, the Buddha gave the answers in Chapter IV of *C.R.* It will be seen that all the questions do not have answers. For example, root condition of Dependent Chapter of the Faultless Triplet has forty-nine questions, but only nine of them have answers, and so these nine answers are given while the rest of the questions are set aside. Before dealing with the methods of finding the answers given in Chapter IV of *C.R.*, preliminary explanations are given about (1) how the conditioning and conditioned states (single enumerations for short) of the Positive conditions in the six chapters are obtained and (2) how, based on them, the answers in the Classification Chapters and the enumerations in the Enumeration Chapters are obtained. The final chapter of the Faultless Triplet, the Investigation Chapter, is not dealt with here as it requires a separate volume of its own.

Single Enumerations of the Positive Conditions in the Six Chapters (Chart No. 31)

The single enumerations of the conditions in the chapters concerned must be known in order to understand those chapters. That is why before each chapter is studied, the single enumerations of the conditions in that chapter must first be found. Only then will the Classification and Enumeration Chapters of Dependent, Conascent, and the rest of the six chapters be understood. Therefore, a chart of the Single Enumerations of the Positive Conditions for the Six Chapters (CSEP6) is provided. Of these chapters, Dependent and Conascent deal with conascence condition, Conditioned and Supported with dependence condition, and Conjoined and Associated with association condition.

From the above it will be seen that Dependent and Conascent Chapters will be understood only if the conditioning and conditioned states of conascence condition are known. That is why these states of conascence condition are given completely. For the same reason the conditioning and conditioned states of dependence and association conditions are given completely.

The cty and subcty do not explain why conascence condition is dealt with in Dependent and Conascent Chapters, dependence condition in Conditioned and Supported Chapters, and association condition in Conjoined and Associated Chapters. But the author has provided a plausible explanation. It is also pointed out that, although three different conditions are dealt with in the six chapters, actually it is conascence condition of Dependent and Conascent Chapters (i) to which base-prenascence-dependence condition is included in Conditioned and Supported Chapters and (ii) from which materiality is excluded in Conjoined and Associated Chapters.

In the chart mentioned above, all the conditioning and conditioned states of the twenty-three Positive conditions (postnascence is excluded) for all the six chapters are given. All these conditioning and conditioned states are worked out. The conditioned states (which, as the subcty points out, are given prominence in the six chapters) are taken from the relations given in the Analytical Exposition previously expounded. Then the conditioning states which are related to those conditioned states by conascence, dependence, and association conditions, dealt with in the six chapters, are found. In the *akauks* only the conditioned states are given, but for a clear understanding of this portion this is not sufficient, for the corresponding conditioning states must be known in order to be able to determine the enumerations, the numbers of answers. That is why the conditioning states are worked out, otherwise the reader will have to take the trouble of finding the conditioning states by himself and not be sure whether they are correct or not.

How the Answers are Obtained

In the text each of the six chapters gives the answers for the conditions under the four heads in the following order:

1. Conditions: Positive (i) Classification Chapter;
1. Conditions: Positive (ii) Enumeration Chapter;
2. Conditions: Negative (i) Classification Chapter;
2. Conditions: Negative (ii) Enumeration Chapter;
3. Conditions: Positive-Negative (Enumeration Chapter);
4. Conditions: Negative-Positive (Enumeration Chapter).

But here in the Preliminaries where the six chapters are taken for explanations, they are dealt with in the order below so as to avoid repetitions:

1. Classification Chapters of all the Positive Conditions in the six chapters;
2. Classification Chapters of all the Negative Conditions in the six chapters;
3. Enumeration Chapters of all the Positive, Negative, Positive-Negative and Negative-Positive Conditions in the six chapters.

After this portion is studied, the reader will get a good idea of how the text is expounded, be able to follow the explanations, given later, about how the answers in the text are obtained, and also be able to fill in the many elisions in the text.

First of all, the method of determining the direct answers from the conditioning and conditioned states is explained, and then it is shown how the classified answers are obtained from them. For the direct and classified answers form the Classification Chapter in the text. These classified answers, quoted from the text, are summarised in text charts.

Classification Chapters of All the Positive Conditions in the Six Chapters

(a) Dependent and Conascent Chapters

The Dependent Chapter, the same as the Conascent Chapter, is first dealt with. Since in this chapter conascence condition, which has all the conditioning and conditioned states, is considered, these conditioning and conditioned states are taken to find the direct and classified answers for this condition. Once this is understood, the answers for the other conditions can be found, for they are only parts of conascence condition, i.e. their conditioning and conditioned states are parts of those of conascence condition. The first direct answer, faultless-faultless, and its classified answer are worked out, and the items in the text which give such answers are referred to, mentioning the fact that they are elided in chapters which are the same. Then the other answers are also worked out. In the case of the indeterminate-indeterminate answer, the classified answers are given under three heads, depending on the conditioning and conditioned states involved. They are: (1) during life, (2) at the moment of conception and (3) materiality. All the details are provided so that the reader will (i) clearly see how the conditioning and conditioned states of conascence condition, worked out and given in the chart of the Single Enumerations of the Positive Conditions for the Six Chapters (CSEP6), have to be taken to determine the enumerations and (ii) know how the answers, given in the Classification Chapter of the text, are obtained. The classified answers, as worked out, are summarised in Chart no. 32, the text chart for the Positive conditions in Dependent, Conascent, Conjoined, and Associated Chapters. With the other Positive conditions only the indeterminate-indeterminate answers are dealt with, as all the other answers for them are the same as those for conascence condition, even though their conditioning and conditioned states are slightly different. For dissociation condition, there are additional answers at the end of the usual classified answers, and so the reasons why they are expounded and the type of answer to be taken in each case are given. In addition, a summary is provided of the enumerations that are possible from the particular conditioning and conditioned states of the Positive conditions of Dependent Chapter.

(b) Conditioned and Supported Chapters

Next, the Positive conditions in the Conditioned Chapter, the same as the Supported Chapter, are dealt with. The difference from the Dependent Chapter is that, besides conascence-dependence condition (which is the same as conascence condition of Dependent Chapter) base-prenascence-dependence condition is included. So in the explanation of this chapter only the enumerations for base-prenascence-dependence condition together with the direct and classified answers for them are considered. As in the case of Dependent Chapter, the conditioning and conditioned states of conascence condition are taken as the example. For the indeterminate-indeterminate answer there is another head "Bases", and so only the classified answer for this is dealt with. Also, the other eight answers, besides the nine of Dependent Chapter, are worked out. The classified answers are summarised in Chart no. 33, the text chart for Conditioned and Supported Chapters. The other Positive conditions, which are parts of conascence condition, are also dealt with. In addition, a summary is provided of the enumerations that are possible from the particular conditioning and conditioned states of the Positive conditions of Conditioned Chapter.

(c) Conjoined and Associated Chapters

Finally, the Positive conditions in Conjoined Chapter, the same as Associated Chapter, are dealt with. There is no difficulty here because the only difference from Dependent Chapter is that materiality is excluded from both the conditioning and conditioned states of the conditions.

In conclusion, a summary is provided of the enumerations that are possible in Dependent, Conditioned, and Conjoined Chapters, depending upon the particular conditioning and conditioned states (Chart no. 34).

2. Classification Chapters of All the Negative Conditions in the Six Chapters

The non-conditioned states, which are those states that are not conditioned states of the Positive conditions, are the conditioned states of the Negative conditions. The conditioning states which are related to those conditioned states by conascence, dependence, and association conditions are found in the same way as for the Positive conditions. All the conditioning and conditioned states of the Negative conditions of the six chapters are provided in Chart no. 35, the chart of the Single Enumerations of the Negative Conditions for the Six Chapters (CSEN6), and the classified answers, as worked out, are summarised in Chart nos. 36 and 37, the text charts for the Negative conditions in (1) Dependent, Conascent, Conjoined and Associated Chapters and (2) base-prenascence-dependence condition in Conditioned and Supported Chapters.

There are only twenty Negative conditions because the four Major conascence conditions have all the conditioned states, and so there are no non-conditioned states to be taken for their Negative conditions. All these Negative conditions are dealt with in detail. Special note must be taken about not-prenascence and not-repetition conditions because they have mind-produced matter as conditioned state. So the conditioning states to be taken for this conditioned state are the conditioning states of positive prenascence and positive repetition conditions which arise together with this matter.

Not-prenascence. Positive prenascence condition has all the mental states that occur during life in the five-aggregate planes as conditioned states. So the remaining states (which are the states of the immaterial plane, the mental states at the moment of conception in the five-aggregate planes, and all the seven kinds of matter) are the conditioned states of not-prenascence condition. Since matter is not concerned with the states of the immaterial plane, in the answers, faultless-faultless, faulty-faulty, and indeterminate-indeterminate (during life) for those states, specific mention is made of this plane as "In the immaterial plane" at the beginning of the classified answers for them. With regard to mind-produced matter, the conditioned state, the mental states which arise together with it during life in the five-aggregate planes have to be taken also as the conditioning states of not-prenascence condition. It should be noted that those states are also the conditioning states of Positive prenascence condition. That is why twenty-one faultless consciousnesses and twelve faulty consciousnesses during life in the five-aggregate planes are taken with mind-produced matter for the answers, faultless-indeterminate, faulty-indeterminate. Besides the classified answer for the states of the immaterial plane in the indeterminate-indeterminate answer mentioned above, there is also another answer for the states in the five-aggregate planes, i.e. resultant and functional indeterminate states with mind-produced matter. Also, there is a classified answer for, at the moment of conception, with the states of the five-aggregate planes. Since the conditioning and conditioned states of not-prenascence condition are somewhat complicated, they are shown very clearly in the chart.

Not-repetition. As in prenascence, repetition condition has only mental states that occur during life as conditioned states but not all of them. Therefore, the remaining mental states during life, the mental states at the moment of conception, and all the seven kinds of matter are the conditioned states of not-repetition condition. Here also, mind-produced matter is a conditioned state and so the mental states which arise together with it during life in the five-aggregate planes have to be taken as the conditioning states. It should be noted that these mental states are also the conditioning states of the Positive repetition condition. Not-repetition condition is not so complicated as not-prenascence condition where, because the states in the immaterial and five-aggregate planes have to be distinguished, separate classified answers have to be given for the different planes.

In the case of the Negative conditions in Conditioned and Supported Chapters, there are answers for base-prenascence-dependence condition besides those for conascence given in Dependent and Conascent Chapters. Therefore only classified answers for base-prenascence-dependence condition are worked out and provided in a separate text chart already mentioned. As for the Negative conditions in Conjoined and Associated Chapters, the classified answers that are obtained are the same as those of Dependent and Conascent Chapters but with all materiality excluded. Here there are only ten Negative conditions involved, i.e. those which have mental states as both conditioning and conditioned states. At the end a summary is provided of the enumerations that are special to the conditioning and conditioned states of the Negative conditions.

3. Enumeration Chapters in the Six Chapters

In the Classification Chapters of this Guide it is shown (1) how the enumerations, faultless-faultless, etc., the direct answers, are obtained for the single conditions, i.e. single enumerations, from the conditioning and conditioned states of each condition which are worked out and given in the two Single Enumeration charts, CSEP6 and CSEN6 and (2) how the classified answers are obtained from the enumerations. The direct and classified answers so obtained form the Classification Chapters of the text. But in the Enumeration Chapters of the text only the figures denoting the enumerations are given for the Positive, Negative, Positive-Negative, and Negative-Positive conditions taken also "By Twos", "By Threes", etc. Here, for the purpose of explanation, the six chapters are taken together. This means that when the conditioning and conditioned states are obtained for determining the enumerations, the enumerations are determined for the six chapters. In this way repetition is avoided and the reader will be able to have a clear understanding of this portion. Only examples are given to show (1) how the common conditioning and conditioned states of two or more conditions are obtained for determining the enumerations and (2) how the classified answers are obtained from those conditioning and conditioned states. For both the direct and classified answers have to be given to provide complete answers to the questions in the way shown in the text in the Classification Chapters of the single conditions.

The Classification Chapters are not given in the Enumeration Chapters of the text but they must be either the same as or parts of those of the single conditions. For the common conditioning and conditioned states of two or more conditions can only be either those of one of the conditions or parts of them. So there is no difficulty in finding the classified answers as all that is necessary is to select the appropriate ones from those in the Classification Chapter concerned. The working out of the complete answers in the Enumeration Chapters makes these chapters very interesting, for the figures by themselves appear to be meaningless.

Positive Conditions

By Ones

This is dealt with in the Classification Chapters of the Positive conditions as shown above. In the Enumeration Chapters, the enumerations are given under each chapter.

By Twos

Here each Positive condition is taken as the reference and each of the other Positive conditions is taken as the variant. So two conditions are taken together. The conditioning and conditioned states of the two conditions, given in the CSEP6, are compared and those which are common to both are selected. Then from the common conditioning and conditioned states the enumerations and classified answers are obtained. Examples are worked out with root condition as reference and a few variants.

By Threes, etc.

In the case of "By Threes", two Positive conditions are taken together as reference conditions and each of the other Positive conditions as variant. So three conditions are taken together. Since the common conditioning and conditioned states of the two reference conditions were previously found in "By Twos", all that is necessary is to compare these conditioning and conditioned states with those of the variant in the CSEP6 to find the common states of three conditions. This is also the method employed to find the common states of four conditions, etc. in "By Fours", etc. And from these common states the enumerations and classified answers are obtained. A few examples are worked out.

Negative Conditions

By Ones, etc.

"By Ones" are expounded in the Classification Chapters. As for "By Twos", etc., the method of determining the commons is the same as that given for the Positive conditions. Here reference has to be made to the CSEN6. Examples of "By Twos" are worked out.

Positive-Negative Conditions

By Twos, etc.

There are no enumerations for "By Ones" because here a Positive condition is taken as the reference and a Negative condition as the variant. So the enumerations start with "By Twos". Examples of these are worked out. For "By Threes", two Positive conditions are taken as reference conditions (in the same way as in "By Threes" of the Positive conditions) with a Negative condition as variant. Similarly for "By Fours", etc.

Negative-Positive Conditions

By Twos, etc.

Here also, there are no enumerations for "By Ones" as a Negative condition is the reference and a Positive condition is the variant. So the enumerations start with "By Twos". Examples of "By Threes", where two Negative conditions are taken together as reference conditions (in the same way as in "By Threes" of the Negative conditions) with a Positive condition as the variant are worked out.

As a summary of the Enumeration Chapters of the six chapters, it is pointed out that the common conditioning and conditioned states have to be found first with the aid of the charts CSEIP6 and CSEIN6. For it is from these states that (1) the enumerations are determined and (2) the analytical states are selected to obtain the classified answers. For the classified answers have to be known in order to work out the Classification Chapters in these Enumeration Chapters.

Actually, the text should give all the Classification Chapters as in "By Ones". But this is impossible as there are so many of them, and, as a matter of fact, it is not necessary for, as shown above, they can be worked out easily. For the same reason, in the explanation of the six chapters of the text that follow, the classified answers are not dealt with but only the methods of determining the common conditioning and conditioned states concerned. For once these states are known, it is a simple matter to determine the enumerations and classified answers according to the procedure given in these Preliminaries.

VIII. Analytical States for the Answers in the six Chapters

Here the six Chapters of the Faultless Triplet Paṭṭh are explained. The main thing is to select the analytical states from the conditioning and conditioned states that are involved so as to find the enumerations which are given in *C.R.* and then work out the classified answers. For only then will Paṭṭh be understood. The cty and subcty, however, do not give all the analytical states. Here the analytical states are not dealt with in accordance with the order in *C.R.* because many of them are the same in many places. In order to avoid repetitions, therefore, the order taken is as follows:

1. Classification Chapters of the Positive Conditions in the Six Chapters.
2. Classification Chapters of the Negative Conditions in the Six Chapters.

3. Enumeration Chapters of the Positive Conditions in the Six Chapters.
4. Enumeration Chapters of the Negative Conditions in the first Four Chapters.
5. Enumeration Chapters of the Negative Conditions in the remaining Two Chapters.
6. Enumeration Chapters of the Positive-Negative Conditions in the Six Chapters.
7. Enumeration Chapters of the Negative-Positive Conditions in the first Four Chapters.
8. Enumeration Chapters of the Negative-Positive Conditions in the remaining Two Chapters.

Paṭṭh deals with three kinds of analytical states. They are those of (1) the conditioning states, (2) the conditioned states, and (3) the conditioning forces. They are determined for each answer.

1. Classification Chapters of the Positive Conditions in the Six Chapters

I. Dependent Chapter

Root Condition 9

First of all, the cty remarks on the fact that, although there are forty-nine questions for root condition and others, all these questions do not have answers. But the subcty points out that in certain cases there are forty-nine answers. So the reason for giving all the possible questions is that such general sets of questions are applicable to the whole of Paṭṭh and for a particular case only those questions that have answers need to be considered.

For root condition it is shown in detail how the analytical states from the conditioning and conditioned states of root condition in the Dependent Chapter have to be selected to get the nine answers, faultless-faultless and so on. These analytical states are then tabulated. As for the conditioning forces it is explained how they are obtained for each answer. Remarks of the cty and subcty are also provided in several places together with Pāli quotations as footnotes. This portion of the

Guide should be looked up to know the details and the general methods of obtaining the answers for the other conditions. They cannot be given here.

Object, Predominance

The conditioning forces, which are given in detail for each answer of object condition, are taken from the detailed chart of Object Condition. As for the answers of predominance condition, the conditioning forces of object-predominance and conascence-predominance are taken as required.

Proximity, Contiguity

It is explained why there are only three answers in the Dependent Chapter although the Analytical Exposition and the Investigation Chapter have seven answers each. The conditioning forces, also given in detail, are obtained from "How to read the chart" of the detailed chart of Proximity Condition.

Conascence, Mutuality

Where the analytical states for the answers are the same as those already met with, only references are made. The subcty points out why the classified answer — "Dependent on one aggregate and [heart-]base, arise three aggregates" and so on — have to be taken in mutuality condition.

Dependence, Strong-dependence

Quotations from the cty and subcty are given to point out the fact that, since conascence condition is dealt with in the Dependent Chapter, eye-base, etc., are not included here as in the dependence condition of the Analytical Exposition. Also, it is shown that heart-base is distinguished depending upon the mental states to which it is related. In connexion with strong-dependence condition, the cty points out that, since materiality is not included, there are only three answers, and so it is said to be the same as object condition. Of course, the conditioning forces are different.

Prenascence, Postnascence

Here the cty gives the reason why only base-prenascence condition (but not the other kind, object-prenascence) is expounded and the subcty explains why "base by prenascence condition" is mentioned in the classified answer but not in the cases of root condition and others. As for postnascence condition, the reasons are given why it is not expounded in the Positive conditions.

Repetition, *Kamma*

The analytical states for the answers of repetition condition are tabulated. As for the conditioning forces in detail, they are taken from "How to read the chart" of the detailed chart of Proximity Condition. In the case of *kamma* condition, the analytical states are referred to when they are the same as those already met with. As for the conditioning forces in detail, they are taken from the detailed chart of Asynchronous *Kamma* Condition. Besides, remarks on this condition in the cty are given.

Resultant to Association

All the analytical states and conditioning forces for these conditions are given. In the cases of (1) nutriment condition, two kinds of forces and (2) faculty condition, three kinds of forces are dealt with. Also, remarks in the cty on some of these conditions are provided.

Dissociation

Here "base by dissociation condition" and "aggregates by dissociation condition" are specifically included, where appropriate, at the end of the classified answers. In this connexion, explanations are given as well as the remarks in the cty.

Presence

The text states that presence condition is the same as conascence condition. But this refers to the analytical states as the conditioning forces are different. As the four kinds of forces were dealt with previously, only references to them are made.

End of the Dependent Chapter.

II. Conascent Chapter

The Conascent Chapter is the same as the Dependent Chapter.

III., IV. Conditioned and Supported Chapters

Where the analytical states for the answers and the conditioning forces in the Conditioned Chapter are the same as those in the Dependent Chapter, only references are made. Therefore, only the bases in the indeterminate-indeterminate answers and others which are special to these two chapters are dealt with.

Root Condition, etc.

The analytical states which are the conditioning and conditioned states for (1) the bases in prenascence-dependence and (2) mixed conascence-prenascence are selected and tabulated for each condition concerned. Remarks in the cty on some of these conditions are also provided. Under nutriment condition, a concise method is given for determining the conditioning and conditioned states to be taken for the bases. The Supported Chapter is the same as the Conditioned Chapter.

V., VI. Conjoined and Associated Chapters

In these two chapters, which are the same, only mental states are involved as association condition is dealt with. So all that has to be done is to exclude materiality from both the conditioning and conditioned states of the conditions in Dependent Chapter.

Root Condition, etc.

There is nothing new in these conditions because only the mental states of the same conditions in Dependent Chapter are taken.

If a proper study is made of the twenty-three Positive conditions in the six chapters, as explained in the Guide, and the reader is able to select the proper conditioning and conditioned states, then it can be said that the reader has understood the principles of Paṭṭh.

End of Classification Chapter of the Positive
Conditions in the Six Chapters.

2. Classification Chapters of the Negative Conditions in the Six Chapters

Dependent Chapter

Not-root (fty-fty)

It will be seen from the chart of the Single Enumerations of the Negative Conditions for the Six Chapters (CSEN6) that the conditioning and conditioned states of the conditions are those which are not included in the chart of the Single Enumerations of the Positive Conditions for the Six Chapters (CSEP6). As in the case of the Positive conditions, the conditioning and conditioned states of the Negative conditions are analysed and selected for the answers, faultless-faultless and so on. All these analytical states for the answers are given completely. But the conditioning forces are given differently from the Positive conditions. In the latter the conditioning states that are related to the conditioned states are given as the conditioning forces. But if it were to be given in this way with the Negative conditions it would be very complicated. So only the Positive conditions which contain those conditioned states are given. "By [the force of] not-root condition" means that root condition is excluded, and only the other Positive conditions which are appropriate have to be taken. These Positive conditions are those that are given in CSEP6.

The Method. "Not-root condition" means that it is not root condition, and so the other twenty-two Positive conditions have to be considered. So in the faulty-faulty answer where doubt-accompanied and restlessness-accompanied delusion are the conditioned states, the conditioning forces are the Positive conditions which contain these conditioned states. These are found in object, proximity, and other conditions, but not in predominance and resultant conditions. So two conditions are excluded from twenty-two and only twenty conditions are taken. Actually, the conditioning states in these conditions which are related to those conditioned states should be given as the conditioning forces as were given for the Positive conditions. But the reader will realise how complicated this is going to be. Again, in (1) repetition condition, only the second to the seventh impulsions of the conditioned states and (2) prenascence and dissociation conditions, the conditioned states in the five-aggregate planes have to be taken. So the conditioned states of these three conditions are here taken appropriately. That is why the conditioning forces of faulty-faulty are given as the conditioning states of the twenty conditions taken appropriately when they are related to their conditioned states, doubt-accompanied, or restlessness-accompanied delusion. In the other answers only the conditions are given as the conditioning forces.

Not-root (ind-ind)

Here also the conditioning and conditioned states and the conditioning forces are given completely for the three classified answers that come under the three heads: (1) during life, (2) at the moment of conception and (3) mere materiality. The cty does not give any of these. So, by simply studying the text and looking up the cty, one will not understand Paṭṭh. For this purpose the analytical states of the conditioning and conditioned states and the conditioning forces must be known. These are given completely in this Guide to *C.R.*

As for the conditioning forces, which are of not-root condition, root condition is excluded, as was done above, and the other conditions which contain the conditioned states are taken. For example, in the case of rootless mind-produced matter, which is a conditioned state of mere materiality in the answer indeterminate-indeterminate, the conditions which contain this matter as conditioned state are taken. On examination of the twenty-two conditions that have to be considered, object, proximity, contiguity, strong-dependence, repetition, absence and disappearance conditions are excluded because they have only mental states as conditioned states. As for path condition this is excluded because it has rooted (and not rootless) mind-produced matter as conditioned state. In the case of mutuality, it has only rootless mind-produced great primaries, which is part of rootless mind-produced matter, as conditioned states and so it is taken appropriately. Therefore, conascence, mutuality, dependence, *kamma*, resultant, nutriment, faculty, *jhāna*, dissociation, presence, and non-disappearance (eleven conditions) taken appropriately are the conditioning forces when they are related to rootless mind-produced matter. This is the method of determining the conditioning forces of the Negative conditions. Another method is to examine the single enumerations of the Investigation Chapter and take those conditions that contain the conditioned states.

Note. If the conditions have all the conditioned states concerned, the conditioning forces occur completely, but if they have only part of the conditioned states concerned, the conditioning forces occur appropriately. It will be seen from the examples given above that, although "appropriately" is mentioned, there are conditioning forces which occur completely. So, because all the conditioning forces do not occur completely, "appropriately" has to be mentioned.

Not-object, etc.

The details about these Negative conditions can be looked up in the Guide.

The General Method. The general method is to analyse the conditioning and conditioned states given in CSEN6 and select the analytical states for arriving at the answers, fls-fls, etc. Although the method is brief, it suffices for general application to the Negative conditions. So only some special cases are considered below.

Not-predominance

In this condition there are cases when predominance condition is (1) obtained and (2) not obtained. (1) is possible only when the predominant realities are the conditioned states and (2) is taken when there are other conditioned states. With regard to the predominant realities mentioned in (1), these are the conditioned states of not-predominance because they were excluded from the conditioned states of predominance condition. As for the other conditioned states mentioned in (2), they are those that are not the conditioned states of predominance condition. The conditioning states of the predominant realities are the fifty-two predominant impulsions which are conascent with them. These impulsions are faultless, faulty, lofty, or supramundane. But, as pointed out so often in the Guide, the sensuous impulsions are occasionally predominant whereas the lofty artd supramundane are always predominant.

It will be noted from the tables for the answers that whenever non-predominant mind-produced matter is the conditioned state, predominance condition is not obtained. But in the case of the answer, indeterminate-indeterminate during life, both the cases are taken.

Note. By means of a question and answer it is explained why the classified answer with the predominant realities as the conditioned states is not given separately in the text. Quotations are provided in support of the argument. It is a clarification of the remarks made in the cty.

Not-conascence, etc.

It is again pointed out why such Negative conditions are not obtained.

Not-mutuality, etc.

The conditioning and conditioned states of not-mutuality are almost the same as not-object condition. The only difference is with the indeterminate-indeterminate answer for (1) at the moment of conception and (2) mere materiality where in the latter only derived matter is taken as the conditioned state.

Not-prenascence

It was pointed out above when dealing with the Preliminaries, that the conditioned states of not-prenascence are (1) the mental states of the immaterial plane, (2) the mental states at the moment of conception in the five-aggregate planes and (3) the seven kinds of matter. For these are the non-conditioned states of Positive prenascence condition. Since mind-produced matter is a conditioned state, the mental states that arise with this matter have to be taken as the conditioning states, and it will be found that these mental states are also the conditioning states of Positive prenascence condition. So, when the relations are between (1) mental states only, these states are of the immaterial plane and (2) mental states and matter, as in the faultless-indeterminate and faulty-indeterminate answers, the mental states in the five-aggregate planes, that belong also to prenascence condition, are taken as the conditioning states. This will be clear from the tables referred to. Faultless-faultless, indeterminate, etc. are Not Obtained. The reason is that the mental states of the immaterial plane have to be taken, but they cannot be taken with indeterminate materiality which is of the five-aggregate plane.

As for indeterminate-indeterminate during life, there are two separate answers: (1) for mental states of the immaterial plane and (2) for mental states and mind-produced matter of the five-aggregate planes. This is shown clearly in the table for this answer. That is why two classified answers are given in the text.

Not-postnascence

It is pointed out that the conditioning and conditioned states of not-postnascence condition are the same as those of Positive conascence condition which has all the mental and material states. The conditioning forces are given separately.

Not-repetition

Although the text points out that not-repetition condition has the same enumerations and the same classified answers as not-predominance condition, the conditioning and conditioned states, however, cannot be the same. Since only mental states are involved in Positive repetition condition, mind-produced matter is a conditioned state of not-repetition condition, and, therefore, like not-prenascence, the mental states of Positive repetition condition which arise with that matter are also the conditioning states of not-repetition condition. But, unlike not-prenascence, there are no separate states of the immaterial plane and so all the states concerned are taken, not separately by planes, but where appropriate.

In this condition, the first impulsions of the states which are excluded in the conditioned states of repetition condition, the second to seventh impulsions of the states of repetition condition that arise with mind-produced matter, and the seven kinds of matter are involved. In the table for the answer, indeterminate-indeterminate during life, it is clearly shown that there are two separate answers for the analytical states but there is only one classified answer in the text, and so the reason for this is given. Also, the cty's remark is given that, although the first impulsions only are involved in not-repetition condition, the classified answers have to be expanded, like not-predominance where all the impulsions are involved.

Not-*kamma*

The conditioning and conditioned states of not-*kamma* condition are analysed and the analytical states selected for the answers. Resultant volition is not included in not-*kamma* condition, and the reason for this, given in the cty, is quoted.

Not-resultant to Not-association

There is nothing special to be said about these conditions. The remarks of the cty on not-nutriment, not-*jhāna* and not-path are given.

Not-dissociation

Only the mental states of the immaterial plane are here involved. So mind-produced matter is not a conditioned state of not-dissociation condition and, therefore, the mental states that arise with it do not have to be taken as in not-prenascence condition. In the Dependent and Conjoined Chapters, dealt with in the Preliminaries, the reason is given why a separate classified answer for the four immaterial resultant consciousnesses at the moment of conception is not expounded.

End of Dependent Chapter.

Conditioned Chapter

Not-root, etc.

The difference from Dependent Chapter is that there are classified answers for "Bases". The analytical states for them are provided in the tables. Although the text states that not-predominance is the same as Positive conascence, the analytical states are different and so they are provided. There is nothing special to say about the other conditions.

End of Conditioned Chapter.

Conjoined Chapter

Not-root, etc.

The ten Negative conditions which have only mental states as both conditioning and conditioned states have to be considered. These mental states are analysed and selected for finding the answers. The explanation is given for the remark in the subcty that there is no need for taking "conception" in not-dissociation.

End of Classification Chapters of the Negative Conditions in the Six Chapters.

3. Enumeration Chapters of the Positive Conditions in the Six Chapters

By Ones

Here the Positive conditions are taken "By Ones", "By Twos", etc. The enumerations and classified answers for "By Ones" have already been dealt with in the Classification Chapters of the Positive conditions in the six chapters. The cty states that there are three different enumerations in the Dependent Chapter and gives the number of conditions having each of these enumerations. It is mentioned that this is also dealt with for the enumerations in the Conditioned and Conjoined Chapters.

Root by Twos

The method of determining the common of the conditions taken "By Twos" is given. Then, taking an example with root condition as the reference and object condition as the variant, it is shown how the common conditioning and conditioned states are obtained, how they have to be analysed to determine the direct answers, faultless-faultless and so on, i.e. the enumerations, and how the classified answers are obtained from the analytical states. All these details for the above two conditions taken together in "By Twos" are given for all the six chapters so that the reader will know how to find the enumerations, the analytical states, and the classified answers in the Enumeration Chapters. For in the Guide only the common conditioning and conditioned states of the conditions taken together "By Twos", "By Threes", etc., are worked out and tabulated for finding the answers. The reason is that it is impossible to give all such details for all the enumerations in the text.

The common conditioning and conditioned states of root condition as the reference and each of the other conditions, predominance, conascence, etc., as the variant are worked out and tabulated in full. The only remark made in the cty on "By Twos" is that with resultant as the variant the enumeration is 1.

Root By Threes

It is explained that in the case of the conditions taken "By Threes", there is no need to find the common of three conditions at the same time. For root and object, the next conditions in serial order, are taken as the reference conditions here, and so the common conditioning and conditioned states of these two conditions, already found in "By Twos", are compared with the conditioning and conditioned states of each of the other conditions, predominance and so on, as the variant to find the common of three conditions. The method of finding the commons of the conditions taken together "By Fours", "By Fives", etc. is the same.

Root "By Fours" to "By Elevens"

"By Fours" to "By Elevens" are elided in the text because the enumerations for the common states of the reference conditions and the variants are all the same as "By Threes". But the common states from which these enumerations are determined are not always the same. This depends on the conditioning and conditioned states of the conditions taken as references. The elisions are dealt with so as to (1) show how to find out what they are and (2) note the differences in the common states.

It will be seen that in "By Fours" predominance becomes another reference condition and so the common of the reference conditions and the common states with the variant are given according to that condition. Also, from the determination of the common states with prenascence, repetition, *kamma*, resultant and dissociation as references or variants, it will be noted how the common states are altered. For example, in "By Elevens" when prenascence, which occurs only in the five-aggregate planes, becomes another reference condition, it is pointed out that special mention must be made of the fact that the common of the reference conditions, i.e. the reference states, as well as the common states with the variants are of the five-aggregate planes.

Root By Twelves (with repetition condition)

Here repetition is taken as another reference condition for "By Twelves". It is shown how the common conditioning and conditioned states of the reference conditions, i.e. the reference states, are obtained and how the common of the reference states and the states of the variant can be found. The reason given for specifying "with repetition condition" in "By Twelves" is that resultant condition has no common state with the reference states in which repetition is included. Therefore, in such cases resultant cannot be taken as a reference condition with repetition or as a variant with repetition as reference. That is why another series with resultant condition included as reference is expounded.

Root By Thirteens, etc.

"By Thirteens" to "By Twenty-ones", elided in the text, are dealt with to show what they are and to explain how the common states and enumerations are obtained. "By Twenty-two" (with repetition condition), given in the text, is explained.

Root By Twelves

This is not included in the text but is given in the Guide to show that, instead of taking repetition as a reference condition as above, the next condition, *kamma*, is here taken for "By Twelves". In this case resultant is taken as a variant and is also included as another reference condition for "By Thirteens". This time, where resultant is a reference condition, repetition cannot be taken as a variant.

Root By Thirteens (with resultant condition)

In "By Twelves" above, the common states of eleven reference conditions and resultant, taken as the variant, are given and these are the reference states here. It is shown that these reference states are also the common states with the variants.

Root By Fourteens to by Twenty-two

"By Fourteens" to "By Twenty-ones" are elided in the text because they are the same as "By Thirteens". "By Twenty-two" has only one variant but it is given to show that it is the last in this series.

In conclusion, the author gives an outline of the method employed above for root condition in determining (1) the common conditioning and conditioned states of the reference conditions and the variants and (2) the enumerations from those common states. This method by the author is applicable to both the Positive and Negative conditions whereas the method in the cty is not reliable with the Negative conditions. As the method is fully explained for root condition, its application to the rest of the conditions is briefly given in the Guide.

Object, etc., by Twos

"Etc." includes proximity and the other conditions which are taken together in CSEP6 because they have the same conditioning and conditioned states. Since object condition has all the mental states, the common states with the variants are the mental states of the latter. Heart-base (six bases), as the conditioning states, are taken when they are common with the variants. It must be borne in mind that in the Faultless Triplet Paṭṭh, whenever resultant is either a reference or a variant condition, the enumeration is always 1. This enumeration 1 with resultant as variant in Object "By Twos" is the exception because those with the other variants are 3.

Object By Threes, etc.

Here object and root are the reference conditions and are also the reference conditions in Root "By Threes". So Object "By Threes" is the same as Root "By Threes". Therefore, "By Threes" to "By Twenty-two", including those with repetition and with resultant, are all the same as root condition.

Predominance By Twos

With predominance and the variants (1) root and (2) object conditions were met with before when (1) root was the reference and predominance the variant and (2) object was the reference and predominance the variant. They are just interchanges of references and variants, so only the common states with the other variants are dealt with.

Predominance by Threes, etc.

It is shown that this is the same as "By Twos" above and that "By Fours" to "By Twenty-two", including those with repetition and with resultant, are the same as root condition.

Proximity, Contiguity

Although "By Twos" of these conditions are mentioned in the text, it is pointed out that "By Twos" and the rest are the same as object condition.

Conascence by Twos, etc.

Since conascence condition has all the mental and material states as both conditioning and conditioned states, the common states with the variants are those of the latter. It is shown that "By Threes" to "By Twenty-two" are the same as root condition.

Mutuality, etc.

The method of determining the common conditioning and conditioned states are explained in full, wherever necessary, for mutuality and the rest of the conditions. The common states are then classified as faultless-faultless, etc. for the six chapters and the analytical states are selected for the classified answers in the way shown with root condition above.

End of the Enumeration Chapters of the Positive Conditions in the Six Chapters.

4. Enumeration Chapters of the Negative Conditions in the First Four Chapters

By Ones

These are given in the Classification Chapters of the Negative conditions in the Dependent, Conascent, Conditioned, and Supported Chapters, the first four chapters. The Conjoined and Associated Chapters, where only mental states are involved, are not included here because all the Negative conditions cannot be taken in serial order as reference and variant conditions as in the case of the others. For example, not-root, which has mental states, has no common states with not-object which has only material states. That is why only the first four chapters are taken together.

Not-root By Twos, etc.

The method employed here is the same as that for the Positive conditions, the only difference being that CSEN6 has to be referred to for finding the common conditioning and conditioned states. Not-root "By Twos" is explained in detail in order to show how the common states are analysed as faultless-faultless, etc., and how those analytical states are selected to work out the classified answers. It is pointed out again that (1) the classified answers are the same as or parts of those in the Classification Chapters of the Negative conditions and (2) both the direct and classified answers must be given after the enumerations are found as provided in the Classification Chapters of the single conditions. By knowing the method the reader will be able to follow the rest, i.e. "By Threes" to "By Twenty", of this condition.

In this Guide (1) detailed explanations are given of those portions which are likely to be difficult to understand, (2) the elisions in the text are worked out giving all the details as well as the reasons for the elisions, (3) the classified answers are given where there may be some difficulty in working them out, and (4) the remarks in the cty and subcty are provided in full wherever necessary. So the reader is requested to make a careful study of the Guide because the rest of its contents can only be briefly given in this Introduction.

Not-object By Twos, etc.

Not-object "By Twos" is given in detail. It is pointed out that Not-object "By Threes" is the same as Not-root"By Threes" because in each case the reference conditions are not-root and not-object. So all the others are the same as not-root condition.

Not-predominance by Twos, etc.

Not-predominance "By Twos" is given in detail. It is shown that "By Threes" to "By Twenty" are the same as not-root condition.

Not-proximity, etc.

It is pointed out that these conditions are the same as not-object condition.

Not-mutuality by Twos, etc.

In "By Twos" details are given where the common states are different from the reference states. "By Threes" to "By Twenty" are given, mentioning the fact that from "By Sevens" they are the same as not-root condition.

Not-prenascence, etc.

Not-prenascence condition and the rest are dealt with giving all details, wherever necessary, for "By Twos", "By Threes", etc. At the end a concise method for the four chapters is given. It is an outline of the method employed in the above Negative conditions and is the same as that given for the Positive conditions.

End of Enumeration Chapters of the Negative Conditions in the First Four Chapters.

5. Enumeration Chapters of the Negative Conditions in the Remaining Two Chapters

By Ones

These are given in the Classification Chapters of Conjoined and Associated Chapters. Since association condition, where the conditioning and conditioned states are mental states only, is dealt with in these two chapters, it is pointed out that there are only ten conditions involved and that whatever material states they contain are excluded.

Not-root by Twos, etc.

Not-object has only material states as conditioned states, and so this condition cannot be taken as a variant with not-root, where only mental states are taken, because there is no state common to both. That is why the commons with only nine variants, which have mental states as conditioned states, are taken. The common mental states, given in the form of analytical states, for "By Twos" to "By Nine" are provided in the tables together with the necessary quotations from the cty.

Not-predominance, etc.

Not-predominance and the rest of the nine Negative conditions are dealt with, giving all details, wherever necessary, for "By Twos" to "By Nine". It will be seen that not-*jhāna* cannot be taken as a variant when not-prenascence, not-*kamma*, not-resultant and not-dissociation are reference conditions. That is why when not-*jhāna* is the reference condition there are only "By Twos" to "By Six".

End of Enumeration Chapters of the Negative
Conditions in the Remaining Two Chapters.

6. Enumeration Chapters of the Positive-Negative Conditions in the Six Chapters

As in the case of the Positive conditions, the six chapters are taken together in these Positive-Negative conditions. But it has to be borne in mind that when the conditioned states are materiality only, Conjoined and Associated Chapters are not involved. Here "By Ones" cannot be taken because there must be at least two conditions, one Positive condition as the reference and one Negative condition as the variant, so the enumerations start with "By Twos". This is also the case with the Negative-Positive conditions.

The Method. It is similar to that for the Positive and Negative conditions dealt with above. The only difference is that the conditioning and conditioned states of the Positive and Negative conditions are compared to find the common states for determining the enumerations and working out the classified answers. The method of the cty for determining the enumerations is to take the smaller enumeration of the conditions concerned. But the subcty points out that this is not always applicable and cites the case of "With mutuality condition, not-object 1", where mutuality has enumeration 3 and not-object 5, and, according to the cty, it should be 3. However, the Anuṭīkā explains that the method of the cty is generally applicable. The safe method is to determine the enumerations from the common states given above and adopted all along.

Root by Twos

The common states of root and the Negative condition as variant are provided together with explanations wherever necessary. It is pointed out that the Negative conditions, not-nutriment, not-faculty, not-*jhāna*, and not-path, cannot be taken as variants because they have no state common with root condition. In this connection, the remark in the cty about the Negative conditions which cannot be taken as variants with some of the Positive conditions is provided.

Root by Threes

Here the reference conditions are root and object, the same as those taken for Root "By Threes" in the Positive conditions. Therefore, the common conditioning and conditioned states of these two conditions, which were found there, are compared with the conditioning and conditioned states of the variants, the Negative conditions, to find the common of three conditions. It is shown how all these common states are found.

Root by Fours, etc.

The common states for "By Fours" to "By Twenty-threes" are worked out. Here the reference conditions for them are the same as those in the Positive conditions where the commons of the reference conditions, the reference states, were found. So it is only necessary to find the common states of those reference states and the states of the variants, the Negative conditions, for determining the enumerations and working out the classified answers. And, as in the Positive conditions, the reference conditions are taken separately "with repetition" and "with resultant" and also explained.

Object by Twos, etc.

Since object condition has all the mental states, the common states with the Negative conditions as variants for "By Twos", are the mental states of the latter. So, for these common states, reference is made to the items of the Negative conditions in CSEN6. Object "By Threes" is the same as Root "By Threes", and, therefore, the rest, including those "with repetition" and "with resultant", being the same as root condition above, are elided in the text.

Predominance, etc.

All the conditions from predominance to non-disappearance are explained in detail wherever necessary, and the elisions are worked out with the sole purpose that the reader easily understands how to find the common states in order to obtain the enumerations which are either given or elided in the text.

End of Enumeration Chapters of the Positive-Negative Conditions in the Six Chapters.

7. Enumeration Chapters of the Negative-Positive Conditions in the First Four Chapters

Here, as in the Negative conditions, the first four chapters are treated separately from the remaining two chapters.

The Method. The difference from the Positive-Negative conditions is that the conditioning and conditioned states of the Negative conditions (which are taken as reference here) and the Positive conditions are compared to find the common states. So, here also, there are no "By Ones".

Note. "By Twos" of the Negative-Positive conditions are included in "By Twos" of the Positive-Negative conditions already dealt with. For the two conditions taken in them are just interchanges of reference and variant. For example, "With not-root condition, object" of the Negative-Positive conditions "By Twos" is the same as "With object condition, not-root" of the Positive-Negative conditions "By Twos". A chart is provided showing the same enumerations for "By Twos" of the Positive-Negative and Negative-Positive conditions for the four chapters and another chart for the remaining two chapters. When the charts are read horizontally, they are Positive-Negative and vertically, Negative-Positive. That is why, although the text gives all the "By Twos", they are simply referred to in the Guide.

Not-root by Threes, etc.

The Method. The reference conditions taken for "By Threes", etc., are the same as those in the Negative conditions where the commons of these reference conditions, the reference states, were found. So all that is needed here is to find the common states of those reference states and the states of the variants, the Positive conditions, for determining the enumerations and working out the classified answers. The common states in "By Threes" to "By Twenty-ones" are all dealt with.

Not-object, etc.

All the conditions from Not-object to Not-disappearance are explained in detail wherever necessary.

End of Enumeration Chapters of the Negative-Positive Conditions in the First Four Chapters.

8. Enumeration Chapters of the Negative-Positive Conditions in the Remaining Two Chapters

Not-root, etc.

All the "By Twos" were dealt with in the Positive-Negative conditions, the difference here being that the reference and the variant are interchanged. All the conditions concerned are dealt with.

End of Enumeration Chapters of the Negative-Positive Conditions in the Remaining Two Chapters.

IX. Summary of the Method of the Six Chapters

A summary table is provided to show how the Classification and Enumeration Chapters of the six chapters in the Faultless Triplet Paṭṭh, as dealt with above, can be arrived at by the shortest possible method. For, as it will have been observed, this Faultless Triplet Paṭṭh itself is so expansive that one is likely to forget what was learnt at the earlier stages when the later stages are taken up. The great value of the table is that one will not forget what was learnt because the whole subject is summarised in it. The table gives the analytical states of the three sections of the Faultless Triplet as expounded in Dhs. So the Faultless Triplet, briefly dealt with in that text, is expanded to the Faultless Triplet Paṭṭh in Paṭṭh.

It is pointed out that all the details for the conditions can be worked out from this table. An example is given with root condition of the Positive conditions to work out the enumeration 9 in the Dependent Chapter, 17 in the Conditioned Chapter, and 3 in the Conjoined Chapter. Also, another with not-root condition of the Negative conditions to work out the enumeration 2 in the Dependent Chapter, 4 in the Conditioned Chapter and 2 in the Conjoined Chapter. As for the Enumeration Chapters, the method is provided. This will enable the reader to find the enumerations for all the Positive, Negative, Positive-Negative, and Negative-Positive conditions in the six chapters of the Faultless Triplet Paṭṭh.

In a similar way the Paṭṭhs for the rest of the Triplets and all the Couplets can be known from the tables giving their analytical states, all of which are provided in *Disc. on Elem.* As for the Paṭṭhs for the Triplet and Couplet combinations, the author has compiled the analytical states for them (which are not provided anywhere) so as to know their Paṭṭhs.

X. Permutations and Combinations of the Aggregates

There is no mention made of these permutations and combinations of the aggregates in the cty and subcty, but if they are known, it will be understood how the classified answers are obtained for the Classification Chapters in the six chapters. The numbers of classified answers that can be obtained for each direct answer in both the Positive and Negative conditions are worked out and given in two charts, one for the Positive, and the other for the Negative conditions. Although the Faultless Triplet Paṭṭh section deals with all the four mental aggregates, in the other sections there are many cases where only one, two, or three mental aggregates have to be taken, but the classified answers for them can be obtained in the ways shown here.

ADDENDA

The Abhidhamma is difficult for one who does not know the exact analytical states involved. So, to understand Dhs and Vibh the analytical states involved must be known. For the Dhātukathā, the analytical states involved are provided by the translator in *Discourse on Elements*, the translated text. In this Guide, dealing with the six chapters of the Faultless Triplet Paṭṭh, all the analytical states are provided by the author. The analytical states are not given in the PTS translations of Dhs and Vibh, so it is hoped that someone will come forward to supply these analytical states in these two texts so that they will be properly understood. As regards Yamaka, which has not been translated as yet, there will be no difficulty in making a literal translation of the text. But the subject cannot be understood unless methods are provided to know the analytical states which are, indeed, more difficult and complicated than those in Paṭṭh.

At the end of this Guide two charts are provided: (1) of the various types of consciousnesses and (2) of the consciousness associated with mental factors (showing the mental factors which are associated with each consciousness) and of the mental factor associated with consciousnesses (showing the consciousnesses which are associated with each mental factor). They are meant for the reader who is not conversant with them so that he will know what they are when he comes across their numbers in the Guide. For it is these 89 consciousnesses (121 as expanded), 52 mental factors, and the 28 material states that carry out their respective functions in the world at large and not I, being, person, man, woman, or thing that do not really exist but are mere objective concepts taken by mental states. This was explained in the Contemplation of Presence Condition given under the Brief Explanations of the 24 Conditions. So that is why these conditioned, impermanent mental and material states and the unconditioned, permanent state of Nibbāna, the only realities, are the subject of Abhidhamma and also of the Four Noble Truths, the essence of Buddhism.

Thein Nyun

Abbreviations

	PĀLI TEXTS	TRANSLATIONS
B.D.	Vinaya-piṭaka	*Book of the Discipline*
Cpd.	Abhidhammatthasaṅgaha	*Compendium of Philosophy*
C.R.	Paṭṭhāna	*Conditions Relations*
Dhs	Dhammasaṅgaṇī	*Buddhist Psychological Ethics*
Dial.	Dīgha-nikāya	*Dialogues of the Buddha*
Expos.	Atthasālinī	*The Expositor*
Disc. on Ele.	Dhātukathā	*Discourse on Elements*
Dhp-a	Dhammapada-aṭṭhakathā	*Buddhist Ledgends*
G.S.	Aṅguttara-nikāya	*The Book of the Gradual Sayings*
K.S.	Saṃyutta-nikāya	*The Book of the Kindred Sayings*
M.L.S.	Majjhima-nikāya	*The Middle Length Sayings*
P.Pfn.	Visuddhimagga	*The Path of Purification*
Paṭṭh-a	Paṭṭhāna-aṭṭhakathā (Burmese edition)	
Ppk-a	Pañcappakaraṇa-aṭṭhakathā[2]	
Vism	Visuddhimagga	
Vism-mhṭ	Visuddhimagga-mahāṭīkā (= Paramatthamañjūsā)	
Vibh	Vibhaṅga	*The Book of Analysis*
Vibh-a	Vibhaṅga-aṭṭhakathā (= Sammohavinodanī)	

CONDITIONS IN SERIAL ORDER

Ro	Root
Ob	Object
Ob-pd	Object-predominance
Ob-pm-pd	Object-prenascence-predominance
Ba-ob-pm-pd	Base-object-prenascence-predominance
Cn-pd	Conascence-predominance
Px	Proximity
ct	Contiguity
Cn	Conascence
Mu	Mutuality
Dp	Dependence
Ba-ob-pm-dp	Base-object-prenascence-dependence
Cn-dp	Conascence-dependence

---

[2]The cty on Tika-Paṭṭh from this text is published with the text in the PTS edition.

Ba-pm-dp	Base-prenascence-dependence
Mixed Cn-pm	Mixed conascence-prenascence
S.D.	Strong-dependence
Ob-S.D.	Object-strong-dependence
Px-S.D.	Proximity-strong-dependence
Na S.D.	Natural Strong-dependence
Prn	Prenascence
Ob-prn	Object-prenascence
Ba-prn	Base-prenascence
Pon	Postnascence
Rp	Postnascence
Kam	*Kamma*
Cn-kam	Conascence-*kamma*
Px-kam	Proximity-*kamma*
S. asy. kam	Strong asynchronous *kamma*
S.& W. asy. kam	Strong-and-Weak asynchronous *kamma*
Rs	Resultant
Nu	Nutriment
Cn-nu	Conascence-nutriment
Phy-nu	Physical nutriment
Fa	Faculty
Cn-fa	Conascence-faculty
Ba-pm-fa	Base-prenascence-faculty
Phy life-fa	Physical life-faculty
Jha	*Jhāna*
Pa	Path
Asn	Association
Dss	Dissociation
Ba-ob-pm-dss	Base-object-prenascence-dissociation
Cn-dss	Conascence-dissociation
Ba-prn-dss	Base-prenascence-dissociation
Pon-dss	Postnascence-dissociation
Ps	Presence
Ob-pm-ps	Object-prenascence-presence
Cn-ps	Conascence-presence
Ba-pm-ps	Base-prenascence-presence
Pon-ps	Postnascence-presence
Phy-nu-ps	Physical nutriment-presence
Phy life-fa-ps	Physical life-faculty-presence
Mixed Cn-pm-ps	Mixed conascence-prenascence-presence
Mixed Pon-nu-ps	Mixed postnascence-nutriment-presence
Mixed Pon-fa-ps	Mixed postnascence-faculty-presence
Ab	Absence

Dsp	Disappearance
N.D.	Non-disappearance

Sigla and Abbreviations

AEC	Chart of the Analytical Exposition of the Conditions
AECO	Analytical Explanation of Conditions
AECo	Analytical Exposition of the Conditions
assoc.	associated
CdS	Conditioned State or States
cty, cties	commentary, commentaries
cons.	consciousness
CS	Conditioning State or States
der.mat.	derived matter
excl.	excluding
fls	faultless
fty	faulty
func	functional
gr.pr.	great primaries
ind	indeterminate
Intr.	Introduction
m.agg.	mental aggregates
m.f.	mental factors
res	resultant
SE	Single Enumerations
SEC	Chart of the Single Enumerations of the Conditions
subcty	subcommentary
subcties	subcommentaries
5-agg.	five-aggregate

The other sigla and abbreviations are given along with the charts.

CHARTS

The Guide to the Paṭṭhāna
Contents in Detail

Guide to Conditional Relations (Paṭṭhāna)
Part I (Chapters I–IV)

Guide to Conditional Relations
Part I

(dealing with pp. 1–12 of *Conditional Relations*, Vol. I)

I. Conditional Relations

1. The Subject of Conditional Relations

Conditional Relations is the subject which deals with: (1) the 22 Triplets and 100 Couplets of Dhs, both singly and in combinations, with reference to the 24 conditions to show how the causes and their effects are related (see Intr. to *C.R.*, p. xi). In other words, it deals with the 24 conditions in the 24 divisions of Paṭṭh which, when subdivided, are the 129,232 Paṭṭh sections as shown in the chart on the Question Chapter; (2) the various conditioning forces such as root, object, predominance and so on, and the conditioning states such as the six roots and so on, which possess these conditioning forces. For instance, the root, non-delusion, a conditioning state of root condition, possesses as many as twelve conditioning forces, namely: root, predominance, conascence, mutuality, dependence, resultant, faculty, path, association, dissociation, presence and non-disappearance. Since in root condition alone there are six roots as the conditioning states, it will be seen that there are numerous conditioning forces; (3) actual causes and actual effects. There are two kinds of effects: actual effects and incidental effects. Actual effects are direct effects which are invariably produced from causes and incidental effects are indirect effects which may or may not follow from causes. In *C.R.* only actual effects produced from actual causes are considered. For example, suppose a man desires to acquire paddy. At that time greed has arisen. Here greed is the actual cause and greed-consciousness, the mental factors and mind-produced matter which arise together with greed at the time are the actual effects. Later, the man may go to a suitable place in the countryside and cultivate paddy. As a result, he acquires paddy by means of which he supports himself and his family. Besides, he performs meritorious deeds with the hope that he will get good results from them. These are the incidental effects.

2. The Three Methods of Teaching on Cause and Effect

There are three methods of teaching on cause and effect, namely: (1) Noble Truths method, (2) Dependent Origination method and (3) Conditional Relations method.

(1) Noble Truths Method

Here craving, Origin Truth, is the cause, and Suffering Truth is the effect. See *K.S.* III, p. 30: "He who takes delight, brethren, in body, feeling, perception, the activities, consciousness ... is not released from suffering." Thus, if there is the cause — the delight in the five aggregates which is craving — Origin Truth, then the effect, Suffering Truth — which consists of all kinds of suffering — will take place. When viewed with the eye of Truth Knowledge (*sacca-ñāṇa*) and Insight Knowledge (*vipassanaā-ñāṇa*), all the aggregates in the three planes of existence are all suffering.

The common worldling cannot lay down this burden of suffering, so all kinds of peril and suffering have to be endured. Only when this burden of suffering is completely laid down will there be freedom from all peril and suffering and true happiness thereby attained. See the Burden Sutta, *K.S.* III, p. 24.

Again, the Noble Eightfold Path, which consists of Right Understanding and the rest, is Path Truth. This is the cause of release or deliverance, Nibbāna, Cessation Truth, which is the effect. Since there are different kinds of cessation, that which is Cessation Truth needs to be explained.

The cessation of craving is due to: (1) its arising on account of conditions and then ceasing. This is known as cessation after arising (*uppanna-nirodha*); (2) its non-arising because the conditions for its arising are absent. This is known as cessation without arising (*anuppanna-nirodha*). Of the latter, there are five types, namely:

(i) Cessation by the Opposite (*tadaṅga-nirodha*). Craving does not arise at the moment when great faultless consciousness arises;

(ii) Cessation by Repression (*vikkhambhana-nirodha*). Craving ceases for some time when lofty faultless consciousnesses arise;

(iii) Cessation by Destruction (*samuccheda-nirodha*). Craving is eradicated when Path-consciousness arises;

(iv) Cessation by Tranquillisation (*paṭippassaddhi-nirodha*). Craving which, after eradication, ceases forever when Fruition-consciousness arises;

(v) Cessation by Deliverance (*nissaraṇa-nirodha*). This is Nibbāna.

The third and fourth types bring about final cessation of craving so that it does not arise again. They are not like the fifth type, which is permanent deliverance from craving. This is Nibbāna, Cessation Truth. This explains the Noble Truths method of teaching on cause and effect.

(2) Dependent Origination Method

Dependent Origination is the teaching about all that happens in one existence. Therefore, it teaches about:

(i) the causes for coming into this present existence. These are ignorance and formations of past existences;

(ii) the causes for the change to another existence. This is *kamma*-becoming which brings about birth, decay, and death in another existence;

(iii) the present existence. These are consciousness, mentality-materiality, six bases, contact, feeling, craving, and attachment.

Just as the taste of the water in the ocean can be known by tasting a drop of water in it, so also, what happens in each and every existence can be known when everything that happens in one existence is known. In this Dependent Origination, the primary cause of the round of rebirths is ignorance. And so the causes and effects are here expounded in this manner: Ignorance is the cause, and formations are the effect, and so on.

(3) Conditional Relations Method

In the Conditional Relations method all the states are treated with reference to 24 conditions to show how the causes and their effects are related. Here it is expounded that such-and-such a state, as cause, is related to such-and-such a state, as effect, by such-and-such a conditioning force.

Note. The cause and effect expounded in these three methods of teaching must be considered separately, each in its own way. If they are taken together and any interrelation between them is sought there will be doubt and perplexity. This is illustrated by the following examples:

(i) Take the case of feeling and craving. In the Noble Truths method, craving, Origin Truth, is the cause, and feeling, as Suffering Truth, is the effect. But in the Dependent Origination method, feeling is the cause and craving is the effect;

(ii) Take the case of visible object and craving. In the Conditional Relations method when there is craving for visible object, visible object, the conditioning state of object condition, is the cause, and craving, the conditioned state, is the effect. But in the Noble Truths method, craving, Origin Truth, is the cause, and visible object, Suffering Truth, is the effect.

Thus the three methods of teaching must be understood so as to be clear as to which method is applicable in any particular case of cause and effect.

3. The Rudiments of Conditional Relations

One who is desirous of understanding Conditional Relations must know the conditioning, conditioned, and non-conditioned states of the conditions in each of the Triplets, Couplets and their combinations. For these are the things that are dealt with in the 24 divisions of Paṭṭh. They are the rudiments of Conditional Relations which must first be learnt and thoroughly digested — just as one has to learn and digest the alphabet first in order to learn a language. Thus all the methods and explanations provided in this Guide must, of necessity, deal with these states. So, however clearly and precisely the methods are described and explanations given, it will not be easy to acquire knowledge of Conditional Relations if these states are not known. But if they are known, this subject will be readily grasped.

Each of the 129,232 Paṭṭh sections deals first with the conditions concerned (i.e. Enumeration of Conditions) and the conditioning and conditioned states, neither too brief nor too detailed (i.e. Analytical Exposition), of those conditions. Therefore, to help the reader to understand the Faultless Triplet section, which is the first Paṭṭh section, brief explanations of the 24 conditions concerned, enumerated in Chapter I of *C.R.*, p. 1, are given below, and later, an explanation of the Analytical Exposition of the Conditions — see items 1–24 in Chapter II, pp. 2–12. The definitions of the terms involved are given in the Intro. to *C.R.*, pp.xi–xiii.

II. Brief Explanations of the 24 Conditions

Here the 24 conditions enumerated in Chapter I of *C.R.* are briefly explained.

1. Root Condition (*hetu-paccaya*)

Definition. The condition where a conditioning state, functioning like a root, relates by causing the associated states, the conditioned states, to arise together and keep them firmly fixed together is known as root condition.[3]

Analogy. It is called (a) "root" because it functions like the roots of a tree and (b) "condition" because it relates as cause to produce the effect. So the roots are related to conditioned states just like the roots to trees.

The roots are useful to the trees because they carry out various functions. The roots, which are firmly fixed to the ground, (1) take up water and soluble nutriments and constantly feed the trees for their growth and development and (2) keep the trees firmly fixed to the ground to prevent them from falling when they are blown about by winds or pushed against. As long as the roots are firm and functioning, the trees grow and develop. So, just as the roots are related to the trees as the basis for existence, growth, development, and stability, the six roots are related to the states associated with them by bringing them about and keeping them firmly fixed together.

Good and bad actions performed by beings in the world are like trees, and the six roots are like the roots of trees. All actions in thought, word, and deed originate from these six roots. When the causes of the origin of those that are faultless and those that are faulty are sought, it will be found that, of these six roots, three are for the former and three for the latter.

The Conditioning States. These are the six roots, three faulty and three faultless.

---

[3]See AEC for the conditioning and conditioned states of the conditions.

The Three Faulty Roots. These are greed, hate, and delusion. All bad actions are due to one of them.

The Three Faultless Roots. These are non-greed, non-hate, and non-delusion. All good actions are due to one of them.

These causes of the origin of actions are given in *G.S.* I, p. 241.

Just as trees grow and expand with the increase in the size and strength of their roots, so also the population of the four woeful worlds increases with the increase of the three faulty roots, and the population of the happy worlds increases with the increase of the three faultless roots. For the three faulty roots bring about unpleasantness, anxiety, vexation, and suffering as fruits and flowers in the woeful worlds, while, on the other hand, the three faultless roots bring about pleasantness, wonderful and delightful states of happiness, and prosperity as different fruits and flowers in the happy worlds. But just as, when there are no roots, the trees die, so also, when the six roots as causes are absent, there is cessation from the round of rebirths.

Also, it is stated in *G.S.* I, p. 196 that: "Passion is the cause of blindness, of not seeing, of not knowing, of loss of insight; it is joined with vexation, it does not conduce to Nibbāna", and so on for malice and delusion as well, and "seeing this disadvantage in passion (greed), malice (hate) and delusion, we preach the abandoning of them", the practice for which is the Ariyan eightfold way.

2. Object Condition (*ārammaṇa-paccaya*)

Definition. The condition where a conditioning state, as object, relates by causing other states, the conditioned states, to arise is known as object condition.

Analogy. The six kinds of objects, the conditioning states, are the sources of enjoyment of consciousness and mental factors, the conditioned states of object condition. These objects can be compared to a pleasant garden which has many kinds of fruit trees, flowering plants, ponds, streams, roads, and seats. The consciousness and mental factors can be compared to the people who are freely moving about in the garden and enjoying themselves. And just as the garden is a source of delight to the people in the garden, so the six kinds of objects are sources of delight to consciousness and mental factors.

Another Analogy. Again, just as a weak or old man has to depend on a rope or staff to get up or walk, so consciousness and mental factors have to depend on the six kinds of objects for their existence. And just as the weak or old man gathers strength from the rope or staff, so consciousness and mental factors gather strength from the six kinds of objects.

The Conditioning States.[4] These are the six kinds of objects: (1) visible object, (2) sound, (3) odour, (4) taste, (5) tangible object consisting of hardness, heat, and motion, (6) cognizable object consisting of the remaining twenty-one states of materiality, eighty-nine consciousnesses, fifty-two mental factors, Nibbāna, and concept. Of these latter objects, materiality, consciousness, and mental factors are either of the past, present, or future, but Nibbāna and concept are time-freed.

So, in this object condition there is no state that cannot be an object of consciousness and mental factors. This object condition pervades the teaching in the Pāli Canon. The details about it will be found in the Analytical Exposition of the Conditions and the Investigation Chapter that are dealt with later.

The Conditioned States. These are consciousness and mental factors. Consciousness takes and knows objects and cannot arise without them. Even during sleep, the life-continuum takes the object which was taken in the dying process of the previous existence and is one of three kinds: (1) past action (*kamma*), (2) Sign of action (*kamma-nimitta*), and (3) Sign of destiny (*gati-nimitta*). But in the non-percipient plane of existence and during the period of Attainment of Extinction (*nirodha-samāpatti*) no objects are taken because consciousness and mental factors are absent.

It must be specially noted that objects are known only by consciousness and the associated mental factors that always arise together

---

[4]Refer to the conditioning and conditioned states of object condition in AEC.

with it. So consciousness and mental factors, which are mentality, are conditioned states of object condition. Materiality is never a conditioned state of object condition because it cannot take and know objects.

The awareness of objects by consciousness and mental factors concerns living beings.[5] It is not the concern of inanimate things such as trees.[6] For they cannot take and know objects, do not possess the states by which they could be called life, and are not consciousness and mental factors. They are simply material states. That is why it is expounded in Dhs that "All matter (form) is that which is void of taking objects (ideas).[7]

3. Predominance Condition (*adhipati-paccaya*)

Definition. The condition where a conditioning state relates by dominating over the states with which it is concerned, the conditioned states, is known as predominance condition.

Kinds. There are two kinds of predominance condition, namely: (a) object-predominance (*ārammaṇādhipati*) and (b) conascence-predominance (*sahajātādhipati*). Object-predominance belongs to the object group of conditions, and conascence-predominance belongs to the conascence group of conditions. Although they both come under predominance condition, they belong to different groups, and so there are no common states between them. It is just like two persons with different beliefs living in the same house. This matter will become clear in the Enumeration Chapter of the Investigation Chapter where it is dealt with.

---

[5]Actually there is no life, but it is so-called when *kamma*-produced heat, life-continuum, physical, and psychic life are present.

[6]The inclination of trees towards the sun, the blossoming of flowers during sunlight or moonlight, the folding of leaves after sunset as if asleep, and other similar occurrences are due to temperature.

[7]*sabbaṃ rūpaṃ anārammaṇaṃ*.

3 (a) Object-Predominance Condition

The objects of object-predominance condition are those of object condition which are greatly desired and esteemed by beings.

Definition. The condition where a conditioning state, as an object, relates by causing mental states, the conditioned states, to arise and dominates them overwhelmingly is known as object-predominance condition.

Analogies. Just as a master can make his slaves obey his wishes, and can exert his influence to make them respect and serve him constantly, so also the conditioning state of object-predominance can make the conditioned mental states, which take it as object, obey its wishes and can exert its influence to make them respect and serve it constantly.

Also, it is just like gold which will enslave a person who earnestly desires it. Although that person undergoes a great deal of suffering in the search for it, he cannot hate it, cast it away or give it up. It is the same with a person who earnestly desires merit from charitable deeds, merit from observance of the precepts, and so on.

Two Types of Objects. These are (a) ordinary and (b) predominant. Ordinary objects possess the force of object condition only, whereas predominant objects possess both the forces of object and predominance conditions. The esteemed predominant objects, which are the conditioning states, are likened to the master and the conditioned mental states, which take those predominant objects, are likened to the slave. And as the object, the master, commands, so the mind, the slave, has to obey. This is illustrated in the following examples:

(i) In the Kusa Jātaka, Pabhāvatī's visible object, as the conditioning state of object-predominance, became the condition for King Kusa's successive minds of greed. Here, Pabhāvatī's visible object is the master, and King Kusa's mind is the slave. And, therefore, at the behest of Pabhāvatī, because of her visible object, King Kusa had to weave mats, make pots and so on.

(ii) On his wedding day Prince Nanda was called away by his elder brother, the Buddha, to carry his almsbowl. Princess Janapadakalyāṇī knew about it, and from the palace window she spoke in request, "Prince, please return quickly." The sound of her voice, as the conditioning state of object-predominance, became the object of attachment for Prince Nanda's successive minds of greed.

(iii) The taste of human flesh, as the conditioning state of object-predominance, became the condition for the arising of greed in Prince Porisāda and so he gave up his kingdom.

Conditioning States of Object-predominance. These are objects which are estimable, i.e. objects which are highly valued and revered and which, when taken, cannot be given up, ignored or treated with scorn.

States which are Never Conditioning States of Object-predominance.[8]

(i) *Materiality.* These are the ten non-produced kinds of matter (*anipphanna-rūpa*).[9] These states do not possess the intrinsic characteristics for attachment to them. They are just signs resulting from the eighteen produced kinds of matter and are not easily discernible. So they are never conditioning states of object-predominance.

---

[8]See AEC.

[9]These are not directly produced by any one of the four causes: *kamma*, mind, temperature, and food. They consist of (1) space, (2) two intimations, (3) three distinctive conditions of matter, (4) four salient marks.

(1) *Space.* This is the intervening space between the groups of matter produced by one or more or all of the four causes given above and come into being on its own whenever such groups of matter are produced.

(2) *Two Intimations.* These are bodily and vocal. They are bodily gestures and speech respectively by which one's intention is apprehended. Bodily intimation is a special characteristic of mind-produced motion element, and vocal intimation is that of mind-produced hardness element.

(3) *Three Distinctive Conditions.* These are lightness, pliancy, and wieldiness of matter produced by mind, temperature, and food and are special characteristics which distinguish them from the normal conditions.

(4) *Four Salient Marks.* These are integration, continuation (of integration), decay, and impermanence of matter produced by one or more or all of the four causes and are conceptual marks.

These ten kinds of non-produced matter are not separate ultimate realities and are, therefore, not considered in the Investigation Chapter where only ultimate realities are dealt with.

(ii) *Mentality*. These are: (a) two hate-rooted consciousnesses, (b) two delusion-rooted consciousnesses and (c) body-consciousness accompanied by painful feeling. These consciousnesses are the undesirable states which bring about anxiety, grief, etc., in persons. Hence they are not estimable objects. In the case of (a) there is dislike of persons seen, and so these states are worthless and undesirable; (b) there is either restlessness or wavering due to doubt and (c) there is suffering from pain. So these states are never conditioning states of object-predominance.

(iii) *Concepts*. Concepts do not possess intrinsic characteristics. As only ultimate realities with such characteristics are dealt with here, concepts are never conditioning states of object-predominance.

(a) In the PTS publication, Mohavicchedanī, p. 333, it is stated: "*tattha ca ārammaṇādhipati-ārammaṇūpanissaya-pakatūpanissayesu paññatti pi saṅgahita ti*." This shows that concepts are conditioning states of object-predominance and object-strong-dependence conditions.

(b) Again, on p. 336, "*rūpārūpa-paññatti hutvā arūpass' eva paccayo pi atthi*; *so ārammaṇa-upanissaya-vasena duvidho*." This states that materiality, mentality, and concepts are related to the conditioned states of mentality by the two conditions, object and strong-dependence.

So with regard to concepts as conditioning states, the two statements above, made in the same book, do not agree.

(c) Also, on p. 323, where the conditioning states of object-predominance condition are considered, Nibbāna is included but not concepts.

(d) On p. 333 it is also stated: "*sesā ārammaṇādhi-upanissya-paccayā tayo pi tekālikā pi*; *nibbānapaññattivasena kālavimuttā pi*." This means that the three conditions, object, predominance, and strong-dependence are either of the past, present, or future and that Nibbāna and concepts, which are included in them, are time-freed.

In the Paṭṭh cty, p. 352, statement (a) above is not to be found, but on pp. 360 and 370 statements (b) and (c) regarding object and strong-dependence are found respectively, and on p. 352 statement (d) is found.

The question now arises as to whether (a) is correct or not.

The Answer. (a) is not correct if (b) and (c) are considered. As regards (d) it is explained as follows:

(1) *Object condition.* The conditioning states are consciousness, mental factors, materiality, Nibbāna, and concepts. Of these, the first three are either of the past, present, or future; and the other two, Nibbāna and concepts, are time-freed;

(2) *Predominance condition.* It does not state whether it is conascence-predominance or object-predominance. But since Nibbāna and concepts are never conascence-predominance conditions, object-predominance condition must be taken here. In this case the conditioning states are consciousness, mental factors, materiality, and Nibbāna, the first three, as above, being either of the past, present, or future; and Nibbāna is time-freed. And according to (c) concepts are not included;

(3) *Strong-dependence condition.* Of the three kinds, natural strong-dependence must be taken. Here the conditioning states are consciousness, mental factors, materiality, and concepts, the first three being either of the past, present, or future; and concepts are time-freed.

It clearly shows, therefore, that Nibbāna is a conditioning state of both object and object-predominance conditions, and concepts are conditioning states of object and strong-dependence conditions, this latter fact being in agreement with (b).

(iv) *Counterpart Signs* (*paṭibhāga-nimitta*). Counterpart signs as objects are capable of bringing about *jhāna*, but being concepts they are not conditioning states here.

Being, Time, Plane of Existence. This object-predominance condition takes into account: (1) being, (2) time, and (3) plane of existence. For example:

(1) A visible object, as conditioning state, may be highly valued by some beings but not by others.

(2) The eight greed-rooted consciousnesses may sometimes be greatly attached to, as being very desirable, and sometimes only nominally so.

(3) In the human plane of existence, a visible object may be highly valued but in the *deva* plane it is not. Also, in the same human plane, things which have never been seen or heard about in villages may be attractive and of importance to a villager, whereas to a townsman they are quite ordinary.

Thus such states, as objects, are conditioning states of object-predominance occasionally.

Conditioned States of Object-predominance. The conditioned states of this condition are given in the Investigation Chapter as "After having offered the offering, having undertaken the precept, having fulfilled the duty of observance, [one] esteems and reviews it", and so on. These consist of eight greed-rooted consciousnesses; eight great faultless consciousnesses and four great functional consciousnesses associated with knowledge that carry out the function of review, change-of-linage, or purification; four Path- and four Fruition-consciousnesses that take Nibbāna as object. These are the twenty-eight consciousnesses which function as impulsions only.

Of these, the eight supramundane consciousnesses that take Nibbāna as object, which is always a predominant conditioning state, are always conditioned states of object-predominance. The remaining twenty conditioned states, which take objects that are dependent on being, time, or plane of existence for being predominant, as was shown above, are not always object-predominance but only occasionally.

States which are Never Conditioned States of Object-predominance. The remaining sixty-one consciousnesses are never conditioned states of object-predominance. For two hate-rooted consciousnesses, two delusion-rooted consciousnesses, thirty-two mundane resultant consciousnesses, and three rootless functional consciousnesses do not carry out the function of delight or review. Also, eighteen lofty impulsions, although they are *jhāna* consciousnesses, do not carry out such functions. The reason given in Atthāsalinī "*attano mahaggatatāya*" is that the lofty impulsions, being themselves exalted, do not regard Path-consciousnesses as estimable.

Why Great Functional Consciousnesses Dissociated from Knowledge are Never Conditioned States. Although these four consciousnesses function as impulsions in the Arahatta's continuity and also carry out the function of review, they do not take predominant objects but only ordinary ones. For the Arahats only esteem Arahatta Path-consciousness, Arahatta Fruition-consciousness, and Nibbāna, and these are taken as objects only by great functional consciousnesses associated with knowledge.

3(b) Conascence-Predominance

Definition. The condition where a conditioning state, on arising, relates by causing the associated states, the conditioned states, to arise together with it and by dominating over them absolutely is known as conascence-predominance.

Analogy. This condition is like the universal monarch who, with regard to influence and authority, has no rival and reigns with absolute sovereignty over the four islands. So if one of the four predominant states is a conditioning state, the remaining three, together with all the associated mental states and mind-produced matter, have to follow it as conditioned states.

Conditioning States of Conascence-predominance. These are the four predominant realities: predominant desire, predominant effort, predominant investigating-wisdom, and predominant consciousness.

The mental factor, desire, which is associated with the fifty-two co-predominant impulsions[10] is known as predominant desire. The mental

[10]There are altogether fifty-five impulsions: twelve faulty consciousnesses, twenty-one faultless consciousnesses, eighteen functional consciousnesses exclusive of the two advertences, four Fruition-consciousnesses. With the

factor, effort, which is associated with the fifty-two co-predominant impulsions, is known as predominant effort. The mental factor, wisdom, which is associated with the thirty-four three-rooted impulsions, is known as predominant investigating-wisdom. The fifty-two co-predominant impulsions are known as predominant consciousness.

Why Only Desire and the Others are Predominant. The four states, desire and the others, have the required potency and basic features for carrying out the function of predominance. It is primarily due to these states that deep and profound knowledge is acquired, herculean tasks are accomplished, high moral character is developed, things of which the majority are incapable. As instances: (1) With regard to worldly affairs, *dhamma*, good or bad morality or anything else for that matter, it is only when there is an inordinate and sustained desire for it, for acquiring it, and for success in it that such a desire can be fulfilled either quickly or in the long run. (2) In cases where efforts are required to accomplish great works, whether faultless or faulty, and such efforts are not regarded as burdensome, the tasks can be accomplished. (3) In performing great works, whether faultless or faulty, they can be accomplished only with strong, resolute minds. (4) When difficult and complicated tasks are undertaken, they can be accomplished by wise planning and execution. In short, however colossal the tasks may be, they will be successfully accomplished when desire and so on function predominantly. So it is due to these predominant states that the world is either good or bad, and persons become Enlightened Buddhas or Silent Buddhas. Predominant desire associated with faultless states brings about a good world, and that associated with faulty states brings about a bad world.

Why the Remaining States are Never Predominant. Although it was pointed out that the four states mentioned above can function

---

exclusion of two delusion-rooted consciousnesses of the twelve faulty consciousnesses and Arahatta's smile-consciousness of the eighteen functional consciousnesses, the remaining fifty-two are known as co-predominant impulsions.

predominantly, it must be understood that, in the past, the mind had to be trained to incite those states to make them predominant. In the case of contact and the other states, they do not possess the required potency and basic features whereby, on incitement, they could become predominant, for their functions cannot be extended beyond the normal ones of contact and so on.

States which are Always Conascence-predominance. These are:

(1) *Wrong Views with Fixed Destiny.*[11] These arise in the sensuous plane and are as powerful as *Jhāna* impulsions. Therefore, they are said to be always conascence-predominance.

(2) *Lofty and Supramundane Impulsions. Jhāna*, Path, and Fruition can be attained only by one of the four predominant states. Since they cannot be attained apart from predominance, they are always conascence-predominance.

(3) *Fruition Impulsions.* These are the only resultant consciousnesses which are conascence-predominance, for this condition functions strongly and is applicable only to active and powerful consciousnesses. Except for Fruition-consciousnesses, all the other resultant consciousnesses are very weak. Although these mundane resultant consciousnesses are caused by volitions, they take effect after long periods of time, separated by existences and worlds. Therefore, they do not inherit the full forces of the volitions of the impulsions that brought them about as in the case of proximity force. In short, mundane resultant consciousnesses are weak because the volitions of the impulsions are not related to them by proximity force. With Fruition-consciousness, however, this resultant consciousness takes effect immediately after the volition associated with Path impulsion which is the cause, thereby occurring in the same mental process and taking the same object. Thus Fruition-consciousness inherits the full force of the volition of the Path impulsion (which is the proximity force), and, therefore, although it is a resultant consciousness, it performs the function of impulsion. That is why it is always conascence-predominance. And because the volition

[11]Paṭṭh II 363.

associated with Path impulsion gives immediate results without any interval of time, one of the specific virtues of *Dhamma* is stated as "*akālika*".

States which do Not Belong to Conascence-predominance. These are the rootless and one-rooted impulsions. Although they function as impulsions, the rootless impulsion, which is the Arahatta's smile-consciousness, is weak because it is devoid of roots; and one-rooted impulsions, which are the two delusion-rooted consciousnesses, are weak because no other root is associated with the delusion in them. Since this predominance function is concerned with strong impulsions, these weak ones do not belong to conascence-predominance.

Co-predominant (sādhipati) and Non-predominant (nirādhipati) Consciousness. The consciousness which arises together with predominant desire or any of the other three predominant states is said to be co-predominant consciousness; that which does not arise together with any of these predominant states is said to be non-predominant consciousness.

Predominant Matter and Non-predominant Matter. Matter produced by co-predominant consciousness is known as predominant mind-produced matter; that produced by non-predominant consciousness is known as non-predominant mind-produced matter.

This conascence-predominance condition is expounded in detail in Roads to Psychic Power of Vibh (Abhidhamma-Piṭaka) and the Saṃyutta-piṭaka (Sutta-Piṭaka).

4. Proximity Condition (*anantara-paccaya*)

5. Contiguity Condition (*samanantara-paccaya*)

Definitions. The condition where a mental state, the conditioning state, relates by causing the next mental state, the conditioned state, to arise immediately after its ceasing, so that no other mental state can intervene between them, is known as proximity condition.

The condition where a mental state, the conditioning state, relates by causing the next mental state, the conditioned state, to arise immediately after its ceasing in accordance with the fixed order of the mental process is known as contiguity condition.

Proximity and Contiguity Conditions are the Same. There is no difference between these two conditions as regards the states involved and the conditioning forces which bring about the relations. They differ only in terms as stated in *P.Pfn.*, p. 614: "The difference here is only in the letter (word), there is none in the meaning."

The reason for expounding them separately as two conditions is that some among the audience come to understand this condition by stating that, although the preceding mental state ceases, there is no chance for a break in the sequence of mental states because it causes a subsequent mental state to arise immediately after. Here the preceding mental state is related to the subsequent mental state by the force of proximity condition. But there are others who understand this condition by stating that, although the subsequent mental state arises, there is no chance for it to arise as it likes, but it does so in accordance with the fixed order of the mental process with respect to function and stage so that there is no break between the cessation of the preceding mental state and the arising of the subsequent mental state. Here the preceding mental state is related to the subsequent mental state by the force of contiguity condition. Therefore, it is only for the benefit of the audience that the two conditions are expounded separately.

The Meaning of the Term saṃ" in samanantara (*Contiguity*). With material states, which collect together as groups (*kālapa*), there are shapes (*saṇṭhāna*) and intervening spaces between the groups. So the locations of these groups can be said to be above or below, on the right or left. But with mental states, which do not collect together as groups, shapes and intervening spaces are absent. Moreover two or three consciousnesses cannot take the same object simultaneously. One consciousness follows another in the right or proper way, although they do so in such rapid succession that they appear to be one and the same. Here *saṃ* means "right" or "proper".

Proximity Force is Not Destroyed by the Intervention of Materiality. When the Anāgāmīs and Arahats enter the Attainment of Extinction,[12] there is total suspension of consciousness, mental factors, and mind-produced matter. But matter produced by *kamma*, temperature, and nutriment continues to arise as usual in the case of beings in the human plane, and matter produced by *kamma* and temperature only in the case of beings in the Brahmā plane. Since the nutriment from one meal lasts for seven days in the human plane, this Attainment can be entered into by human beings only for that length of time, but in the Brahmā plane, where there is no need for nutriment, Brahmā beings can enter into it for as long as desired.

In the mental process of the Attainment of Extinction of the Anāgāmī,[13] the total suspension of consciousness, mental factors, and mind-produced matter takes place after the cessation of faultless neither-perception-nor-non-perception impulsion and only matter produced by *kamma*, etc., continues to arise. Then, after emerging from this Attainment, the Anāgāmī Fruition-consciousness arises. Although materiality has intervened between the two mental states, faultless neither-perception-nor-non-perception impulsion is related to Anāgāmī Fruition-consciousness by proximity condition. This is stated in the Investigation Chapter of the Faultless Triplet[14] as: "having emerged from the attainment of Extinction, faultless neither-perception-nor-non-perception is related to the attainment of Fruition by proximity condition". With the Arahat the relation is between functional neither-perception-nor-non-perception and Arahatta Fruition-consciousness. So, no matter how many material states may succeed one another to intervene between two mental states, they have no power to cut off the succession of such mental states with which proximity condition is concerned.

---

[12]Details about this are given in *P.Pfn.*, pp. 824–33.

[13]All mental processes are described in proximity condition in the explanation of the AEC given later.

[14]*C.R.*, pp. 148–49, items 417 (ii) and (v).

Another example is that of one who attains the fifth *jhāna* in the sensuous plane and dies. Rebirth takes place in the non-percipient plane where there is materiality only and which lasts for 500 worlds. Then after death there is rebirth in the sensuous plane. The death-consciousness in the sensuous plane (prior to rebirth in the non-percipient plane) is related to rebirth consciousness in the sensuous plane (after death in the non-percipient plane) by proximity condition without the intervention of any other mentality. Here the proximity force is not destroyed, although materiality lasting for 500 worlds intervenes.

When Other Mentality Intervenes, Proximity Force is Destroyed. In the eye-door mental process, the following sequence of mental states takes place: past life-continuum, vibrating life-continuum, arresting life-continuum, five-door advertence, eye-consciousness, recipient consciousness, investigating consciousness, determining consciousness, seven impulsions, two registering consciousnesses. Here past life-continuum is related to vibrating life-continuum, vibrating life-continuum to arresting life-continuum, arresting life-continuum to five-door advertence by proximity condition without any interval of time. Similarly with the others. But if, for example, five-door advertence is not related to eye-consciousness but by-passes it and is related to recipient consciousness, the force of proximity condition is destroyed because eye-consciousness intervenes. This, of course, never happens.

According to the fixed order of the mental process, the preceding consciousnesses are related to the subsequent consciousnesses by the force of proximity condition. This is expounded as "Preceding states are related to subsequent states". Also, it is only after the preceding consciousness ceases that the subsequent consciousness arises. Therefore, the former is of the past, and the latter is of the present. This difference in time of the two thought-moments is expounded as "Past state is related to present state by proximity condition". All such knowledge can be ascribed only to omniscience.

Round of Rebirths (*saṃsāra*). The beginning of the round of rebirths cannot be known, as stated in *K.S.* II, p. 118: "Incalculable is the beginning, brethren, of this faring on." The ultimate realities of *saṃsāra* and the kind of ocean it is are given in *Expos.* I, p.13.

During the passage through *saṃsāra*, the successive consciousnesses arise continually without a break. After rebirth consciousness ceases, life-continuum and other successive consciousnesses constantly arise with respect to object, door, and function, last for their span of one thought-moment, and cease. This arising and ceasing goes on without stopping even for an instant. As the subsequent consciousness arises immediately after the preceding consciousness ceases, these consciousnesses are not the same. But because there is no interval of time between them, this difference in the consciousnesses is not discerned and so it appears that it is one and the same consciousness that thinks throughout the day and lasts throughout life. That is why beings hold firmly to the wrong view that consciousness is permanent. Conditioning and Conditioned states. With the exception of the Arahatta's death-consciousness, the preceding eighty-nine consciousnesses and fifty-two mental factors are the conditioning states. The Arahatta's death-consciousness together with the subsequent eighty-nine consciousnesses and fifty-two mental factors are the conditioned states. It will be seen that all the conditioning states are also conditioned states. But the reverse is not the case. For the Arahatta's death-consciousness is a conditioned but never a conditioning state.

In the dying mental process of the Arahat, the mind-door advertence, impulsions and registering consciousnesses do not produce kammic results and, therefore, unlike other dying mental processes, past action (*kamma*) or a sign of *kamma* (*kamma-nimitta*) is not taken as object. And since there is no future existence for the Arahat, a sign of destiny (*gati-nimitta*) cannot be taken as object. The object is either a mundane materiality, mentality, or concept. But the Arahatta's death-consciousness takes the same object, which is *kamma*, *kamma-nimitta* or *gati-nimitta*, that was taken at rebirth consciousness. If this death-consciousness follows impulsion or life-continuum, as the case may be, then the impulsion or life-continuum is the conditioning state, and the

Arahatta's death-consciousness is the conditioned state. And since there is no rebirth after the Arahatta's death-consciousness, the latter can never be a conditioning state. That is why, although the beginning of *saaṃsāra* cannot be known, as pointed out above, there is an end to it. This is the Arahatta's death-consciousness.

Proximity: Condition can be Known Only by the Mental Processes. Since proximity condition deals with the mental processes, the latter must be understood in order to know the nature of this condition. Also, the functions of the consciousnesses —given under "Function" in *Cpd.*, pp. 114–17 — involved in the mental processes must be understood. The mental processes and functions are given in charts of the Explanation of the Analytical Exposition of Conditions.

How Proximity and Contiguity Conditions can be Distinguished. Proximity condition is like the Universal Monarch who has gone forth into the homeless life, and contiguity condition is like the Universal Monarch who has died. Each is the condition for the eldest son to become the monarch.

6. Conascence Condition (*sahajāta-paccaya*)

Definition. The condition where a conditioning state, on arising, relates by causing the associated states, the conditioned states, to arise simultaneously with it is known as conascence condition.

Analogy. It is like the flame of an oil lamp which, when it appears, is related to the light, colour and heat which are produced simultaneously with it. The light, etc., produced by the flame are not present before it appears or after it dies out. So also, the conditioned states arise simultaneously with the conditioning state and do not arise before or after the latter. Therefore, in this conascence condition, the conditioning state is related to the conditioned states which arise simultaneously with it — at the nascent phase of its arising (according to the cty) or at the static phase (subcty).

Conditioning and Conditioned States. These are given in the Single Enumeration of conascence condition.[15] The relations between them can be classified under five heads: (1) mentality to mentality, (2) mentality to materiality, (3) mentality to mentality-materiality, (4) materiality to materiality, (5) materiality to mentality.

(1) *Mentality to Mentality*. In the Consciousness Chapter of Dhs it is stated that consciousness never arises alone but always simultaneously with its associated mental factors. This mental group is classified under the four mental aggregates as given in the Dhs trsl. pp. 26, 32, 37, 40, etc. "Now, on that occasion the *khandhas* are four ...". (The method of classification of the ultimate realities under the aggregates, bases, and elements is shown in detail, with charts, in *Disc. on Elem.*)

Example. When a visible object is seen, eye-consciousness, which carries out its function of seeing, arises, and simultaneously with it arise its associated mental factors: contact, feeling, perception, volition, one-pointedness of mind, psychic life, and attention. When these are classified under the aggregates, the feeling mental factor comes under the feeling aggregate, the perception mental factor comes under the perception aggregate, the other five mental factors come under the mental formation aggregate, and eye-consciousness comes under the consciousness aggregate, i.e. the four mental aggregates.

Now, if the feeling aggregate, one of the four mental aggregates, is taken as the conditioning state, the remaining three aggregates are the conditioned states; if the perception aggregate is taken as the conditioning state, the remaining three aggregates are the conditioned states, and so on. Thus, if each aggregate is taken as the conditioning state by turns, this can be done in four ways. The Investigation Chapter gives this as: "One aggregate is related to three aggregates by conascence condition" (*C.R.* 419, p. 150).

Also, if three aggregates — feeling, perception, and the mental formation — are taken together as the conditioning states, the remaining

---

[15]See *C.R.*, chart (II) E, facing p. lxiv. Also see SEC.

consciousness aggregate is the conditioned state; if the perception, mental formation, and consciousness aggregates are the conditioning states, the remaining feeling aggregate is the conditioned state, and so on. Here also it can be taken by turns in four ways. The Investigation Chapter gives this as: "Three aggregates are related to one aggregate by conascence condition".

Again, if two aggregates (feeling and perception) are taken as the conditioning states, the remaining two aggregates are the conditioned states and so on. Here it can be taken by turns in six ways. The Investigation Chapter gives this as: "Two aggregates are related to two aggregates by conascence condition".

The above shows how the four mental aggregates are both conditioning and conditioned states. But in the Analytical Exposition of the Conditions it is briefly stated as: "The four immaterial (i.e. mental) aggregates are mutually related to one another by conascence condition" (*C.R.* 6, p. 5). Here the relation is between mentality and mentality.

It is to be noted, therefore, that in this process of seeing, it is not I, you, man, or woman that sees but merely the mental aggregates carrying out their functions. It is the same with the processes of hearing, smelling, tasting, touching, and thinking.

(2) *Mentality to Materiality*. The conditioning states are the mental aggregates; and the conditioned states, which are materiality, are *kamma*-produced matter at rebirth and mind-produced matter during life.

Why the Other Kinds of Materiality are Not Conditioned States. Although nutriment-produced and temperature-produced matter also arise simultaneously with consciousness at its nascent phase[16] in a being's continuity, they are not mind-produced and they do not have any connection whatsoever with the mind. Therefore, mentality cannot be related to such matter by conascence condition. Again, in the five-

[16]One thought-moment (*cittakkhaṇa*), the period occupied by any single state of consciousness (*cittuppāda*), consists of three phases: nascent (*uppāda*), static (*ṭhiti*) and cessant (*bhaṅga*).

aggregate planes during life, *kamma*-produced matter — which arises simultaneously with rebirth consciousness at its static phase in the continuity of a being and then arises successively with each phase of consciousness during life — is also not connected with the mind. As a case in point, take that of the entry of Attainment of Extinction dealt with in proximity condition above. There is no consciousness at the time, but there are successive arisings during life of *kamma*-produced matter. So mentality cannot be related to this kind of matter by conascence condition.

Mentality to Mind-produced Matter. Although the conditioning states are mentality, the four immaterial resultant consciousnesses, the twice fivefold consciousnesses, an Arahatta's death-consciousness, and rebirth consciousness in the five-aggregate planes are excluded because they do not produce matter. The reasons are:

(i) The four immaterial resultant consciousnesses, which function at rebirth and during life in the immaterial plane, do not produce matter because it is absent in that plane.

(ii) Twice fivefold consciousnesses can carry out the functions of seeing, hearing, etc., only, and as they are very weak, they do not perform the function of *jhāna*. Thus they cannot produce matter.

(iii) The death-consciousness of the Arahat, who has no more rebirth, is very subtle and, being dependent on the last heart-base, is too weak to produce matter.

(iv) Rebirth consciousness in the five-aggregate planes, which is dependent on the first heart-base that arises together with it, is too weak to produce matter.

Note. The Arahatta's death-consciousness in (iii) above consists of one of the following: 4 great resultant consciousnesses associated with knowledge, 5 fine-material resultant consciousnesses, and 4 immaterial resultant consciousnesses, i.e. 13. Rebirth consciousness in the five-aggregate planes in (iv) above consists of one of the following: 2 investigating consciousnesses accompanied by indifferent feeling, 8 great resultant consciousnesses, and 5 fine-material resultant consciousnesses, i.e. 15. All these states perform the functions of rebirth, life-continuum and death. Though they do not produce matter at rebirth and death, they do so as life-continuum (i.e. during life), and, as such, these states are included. Therefore, even though rebirth consciousness, also the Arahatta's death-consciousness, in the five-aggregate planes are excluded, the number of consciousnesses excluded is not 16 but only 14, i.e. (i) + (ii).

The conditioning states are, therefore, 75 (i.e. 89 -14) consciousnesses and the 52 mental factors, all of which are classified under the four mental aggregates. So, during life in the five-aggregate planes, one of these four mental aggregates is related to the matter produced by it and which arises together with it; two aggregates, three aggregates, and four aggregates are related to the respective matter produced by them and which arises together with them. The Investigation Chapter gives this as: "Faultless (also faulty) aggregates are related to mind-produced matter". Since the numbers of aggregates are not specified they must be taken in separate lots of one, two, three (i.e. taken partly), and the total of four aggregates (i.e. taken wholly).

Mentality to Rebirth Kamma-produced Matter. The conditioning states are 15 rebirth consciousnesses, 35 mental factors which are the mentality at the moment of conception in the five-aggregate planes. They are also classified under the four mental aggregates. So, at rebirth in the five-aggregate planes, one of the four mental aggregates is related to *kamma*-produced matter which arises together with it by conascence condition, and so on. Here, too, the aggregates must be taken in separate lots of one, two, three, and four aggregates.

The Relation is Not Mutual. Here mentality and materiality are not mutually related. Just as the mother assists the new-born baby by providing it with milk and so on, but it can be of no assistance to the mother in return, so when mind (consciousness and its associated mental factors) and mind-produced matter arise together, mind is related to mind-produced matter, but the latter is not related to the former, i.e. they are not mutually related. Similarly, rebirth consciousness in the five-aggregate planes is related to *kamma*-produced matter (with heart-base excluded) that arises together with it but not conversely.

(3) *Mentality to Mentality-materiality*. During life in the five-aggregate planes, one mental aggregate is related to the remaining three mental aggregates and mind-produced matter; three mental aggregates are related to the remaining mental aggregate and mind-produced matter; two mental aggregates are related to the remaining two mental aggregates and mind-produced matter by conascence condition. Similarly, for rebirth consciousness in the five-aggregate planes, one mental aggregate is related to the remaining three mental aggregates and *kamma*-produced matter, and so on.

Example. When a person speaks to another about things that are interesting and delightful, the listener is pleased and happy and this mood is expressed in his features. But when the subject is changed to things that cause grief and anxiety, the expression on his face changes immediately, and he appears sad and worried. Here only the change in the physical manifestations can be observed but not the minds that caused them. So the change in mind-produced matter, which arises together with the mind, can be observed with every change of mind. It is by means of the eye- and mind-doors that the changes and impermanence of mind-produced matter, due to the impermanence of the mind, can be distinctly seen and known. This is how mentality is related to mentality-materiality.

(4) *Materiality to Materiality*. Materiality is related to materiality in two ways: (1) the mutual relations between the great primaries and (2) the relation between the great primaries and derived matter.

Great Primaries to Great Primaries. Although the great primaries consist of hardness, cohesion, heat, and motion, they are differentiated as seven kinds in Paṭṭh: those which are (i) mind-produced, i.e. produced by mind, (ii) rebirth *kamma*-produced, i.e. produced by *kamma* at rebirth, (iii) external, i.e. in inanimate things such as trees, mountains, oceans and earth, (iv) nutriment-produced, i.e. produced by food in a being's continuity, (v) temperature-produced, i.e. produced by temperature in both animate and inanimate things, (vi) non-percipient beings' *kamma*-produced, i.e. produced by past *kamma* at rebirth and during life in the non-percipient *brahmā*'s continuity, and (vii) during life *kamma*-produced, i.e. produced by *kamma* at the static phase of rebirth consciousness and at every phase of consciousness during life in the five-aggregate planes. The four great primaries always arise together in a group[17] of the inseparable material qualities (*avinibbhoga*) and, like the four mental aggregates, they cannot be separated individually.

Of the seven kinds of great primaries, take the case of those that are mind-produced. If one of the four great primaries that arise together in a group is the conditioning state, then the remaining three are the conditioned states. Also if three or two of them are the conditioning states, the remaining one or two are, respectively, the conditioned states. They have to be taken by turns as in the case of the four mental aggregates. It is the same with the other kinds of great primaries.

The Arising of the Four Great Primaries.[18] With regard to the arising of the four great primaries in the physical body: if hardness is prominent, motion is not prominent, cohesion is weak, and heat is normal; if cohesion is prominent, motion is not prominent, hardness is weak, and heat is normal; if heat is prominent, cohesion is not prominent, hardness is weak, and motion is indifferent; if motion is prominent, cohesion is not prominent, hardness is weak, and heat is indifferent. Of these four great primaries, if cohesion which is weak can be activated, it will become so prominent as to make the whole body a mass of flowing water; if heat which is weak can be activated, it will become so prominent as to make the whole body a mass of burning flame; if motion which is weak can be activated, it will become so prominent as to make the whole body gaseous.

---

[17] *Cpd.* p. 164 gives four kinds of matter and their groupings: 9 that are *kamma*-produced, 6 that are mind-produced, 4 that are temperature-produced, and 2 that are nutriment-produced = 21 groups (*kālapa*).

[18] Ledi Sayadaw's pamphlet on "Characteristics" (*Lakkhaṇa-dīpanī*, 1906).

Great Primaries to Derived Matter. Like the great primaries, there are seven kinds of derived matter. When the great primaries are related to derived matter by conascence condition, both of them must belong to the same kind but not to other kinds. Here one, three, two, and all the four great primaries are respectively related to derived matter which are in the same group.

Note. Unlike the great primaries, which are mutually related, the great primaries and derived matter are not mutually related by conascence condition, i.e. derived matter is not related to the great primaries. So derived matter is always the conditioned state.

Great Primaries to Great Primaries and Derived Matter. A red flower has (1) a red colour which is the visible object element, (2) a fragment odour which is the odour element, (3) a bitter or hot taste which is the taste element, and (4) nutriment which is the nutritive essence element. These derived matter are present in addition to the four great primaries. Such inanimate things consist of at least these eight material elements. Of these, if one great primary is the conditioning state, the remaining three great primaries and derived matter are the conditioned states; if three great primaries are the conditioning states, the remaining great primary and derived matter are the conditioned states; if two great primaries are the conditioning states, the remaining two great primaries and derived matter are the conditioned states. This applies to each of the twenty-one material groups.

(5) *Materiality to Mentality*. Beings who have not become Arahats and attained Parinibbāna will certainly be reborn[19] according to their *kamma* in some existence after death-consciousness ceases. Of the nineteen rebirth consciousnesses,[20] the four immaterial resultant consciousnesses that function as rebirth consciousness, life-continuum, and death-consciousness in the immaterial plane, are the only ones which

---

[19] *Dhātu* chapter of Anusaya Yamaka and Proximity Condition of Paṭṭh.

[20] 2 investigating consciousnesses accompanied by indifferent feeling, 8 great resultant consciousnesses, 5 fine-material resultant consciousnesses, 4 immaterial resultant consciousnesses = 19.

are not dependent on and do not arise with materiality. The remaining fifteen always arise with materiality as explained below:

At the moment of conception of a being in the mother's womb in the sensuous plane, there arise together with rebirth consciousness at its nascent phase, thirty-three mental factors and *kamma*-produced matter consisting of the body-decad, sex-decad, and base-decad, i.e. thirty material states. Of these three material groups, the heart-base of the base-decad is related to sensuous rebirth consciousness, and the latter is related to the former, i.e. the two are mutually related, by conascence condition. The Analytical Exposition of the Conditions gives this as "At the moment of conception, mentality and materiality are mutually related to one another by conascence condition" and the Investigation Chapter as "aggregates are related to [heart-]base by conascence condition; [heart-]base is related to aggregates by conascence condition." Since the mutual relation between materiality and mentality is being considered, only the heart-base, out of the thirty material states that arise together, can be taken as the conditioning state. The rest are always conditioned states of conascence condition.

At the moment of conception of a spontaneous (*opapātika*) or moisture-born (*saṃsedaja*) being in the sensuous plane, the difference from the above is that, instead of three, there are seven *kamma*-produced material groups: eye-decad, ear-decad, nose-decad, tongue-decad, body-decad, sex-decad, and base-decad. And at the moment of conception in the fine-material plane, there arise four *kamma*-produced material groups: vital-nonad, eye-decad, ear-decad, and base-decad.

The Relations at the Moment of Conception. Suppose a person is reborn in the human plane with the first great resultant consciousness as rebirth consciousness. At the moment of conception there arise that rebirth consciousness, thirty-three mental factors, which together are classified under the four mental aggregates, and the three *kamma*-produced material groups given above. The relations that take place at the moment of conception are: (1) one mental aggregate is related to the remaining three mental aggregates, and so on, i.e. mentality is mutually related to mentality; (2) four mental aggregates are related to the three *kamma*-produced material groups, i.e. mentality is related to materiality; (3) one mental aggregate is related to the remaining three mental aggregates and the three *kamma*-produced material groups, and so on, i.e. mentality is related to mentality-materiality; (4) one great primary is related to the remaining three great primaries of the same *kamma*-produced material group, and so on. Also, the great primaries are related to derived matter of the same *kamma*-produced material group, i.e. materiality is related to materiality; (5) heart-base of the base-decad is related to the mental aggregates, i.e. materiality is related to mentality.

It will be noted that the relation where the mental aggregates are related to mind-produced matter is not included in (2) above. This is because such matter arises only during life and not at the moment of conception.

7. Mutuality Condition (*aññāmañña-paccaya*)

Mutuality condition belongs to the conascence group of conditions and forms part of conascence condition. Under the Selection of the Conditions for Negative in the Investigation Chapter (Intr. to *C.R.*, p. lviii), the 24 conditions are grouped according to kind. These various groups together with the conditions in each group are given in the charts facing p. lxiv of the Intr. to *C.R.* It will be seen that there are fifteen conditions in the conascence group. Four of them, conascence, conascence-dependence, conascence-presence, and conascence-non-disappearance in chart II E) are known as Major conascence because the conditioning and conditioned states that are involved are numerous; another four, mutuality, resultant, association, and conascence-dissociation in chart II (D) are known as Medium conascence because the conditioning and conditioned states involved are not so numerous; the remaining seven, root, conascence-predominance, conascence-*kamma*, conascence-nutriment, conascence-faculty, *jhāna*, and path in chart II (C) are known as Minor conascence because the conditioning states involved are ultimate realities which are so few in number that they cannot be classified under the four mental aggregates.

Definition. The condition where a conditioning state relates by causing the associated states, the conditioned states, to arise simultaneously with it and which are all mutually dependent is known as mutuality condition.

Analogy. A tripod has three legs because, when it is set up, it will stand on account of the interdependence of these legs. But if one of them is broken, the remaining two legs cannot make it stand. Similarly, in this condition, (1) the mental aggregates are mutually related, (2) the great primaries of the same material group are mutually related, and (3) the mental aggregates at rebirth in the five-aggregate planes and the heart-base are mutually related.

The Nature of Conascence and Mutuality. In conascence condition, the conditioning state is simply related to the associated states that arise simultaneously with it. On the other hand, in mutuality condition, the conditioning state is not only related to the associated states that arise simultaneously with it, but also each of the states is mutually related to the other. According to the subcty "*attano-upakārakassa upakārakatā*", in mutuality condition, a conditioning state gives its force to the conditioned state and also receives the force of the conditioned state.

The Difference between Conascence and Mutuality. On examination of the conditioning and conditioned states, it will be found (i) that those of conascence are numerous, whereas those of mutuality are few; (ii) that those of conascence are not always of mutuality. For example, consciousness and mental factors are related to mind-produced matter, and also great primaries are related to derived matter by conascence condition but not by mutuality condition; (iii) that those of mutuality are always of conascence.

8. Dependence Condition (*nissaya-paccaya*)

Definition. The condition where a conditioning state, as base or dependence, relates by causing other states, the conditioned states, to arise is known as dependence condition.

Analogy. Just as the soil, as base, is related to the tree, and the canvas, as dependence,[21] is related to the painting, so also, the conditioning states, either as base or dependence, are related to the conditioned states.

The Four Kinds of Dependence Condition.[22] These are (a) base-object-prenascence-dependence, (b) conascence-dependence, (c) base-pre-nascence-dependence, (d) mixed conascence-prenascence.

8. (a) Base-Object-Prenascence-Dependence

Definition. The condition where a conditioning state (which must (i) be a material base, (ii) be an object of the conditioned states, (iii) have arisen and be at its static phase before the conditioned states arise, (iv) be the dependence by dependence force) relates by causing mental states, the conditioned states, to arise is known as base-object-pre-nascence-dependence condition.

The Conditioning State. Heart-base is the only conditioning state that satisfies all the above. It is of two kinds: (a) that which arises at the time of dying and (b) that which arises during life.

(a) Counting backwards to the seventeenth thought-moment from death-consciousness, *kamma*-produced matter (which includes the heart-base) has not the strength to arise again. So the successive consciousnesses (the mind-door advertence, dying impulsions, register-ing consciousnesses, and death-consciousness that arise when this dying mental process takes place) have to depend on that one and only heart-base which had already arisen before them. In this condition it is this

---

[21]The great primary, hardness, as base, is related to the remaining three great primaries. This is conascence-dependence condition, which has the nature of base. The six bases, as dependence, are related to eye-consciousness and others. This is base-prenascence-dependence condition, which has the nature of dependence (subcty, p.171).

[22]See this condition in SEC.

heart-base that is taken as object by all the dying impulsions even if there is delight, grief, doubt, or restlessness at the time;

(b) When the present heart-base is taken as object and either insight practice into impermanency, suffering, and impersonality are carried out or there is lust for it, the heart-base is related to great faultless consciousness in the former case and to greed-consciousness in the latter. This is stated in Paṭṭh, Vol. II, Internal Triplet, p. 442, as "[One] practises insight into impermanency, suffering, impersonality ... enjoys and delights in the internal [heart-]base. Taking it as object, arises lust, arises wrong views, arises doubt, arises restlessness, arises grief. "

This condition is not treated separately in the Investigation Chapter but is included in item 444 (*C.R.*, p. 182) as a common condition with object: "With object condition and dependence 3, prenascence 3, dissociation 3", and in item 445 (3) as a combination with other conditions: "Combination of object, dependence, prenascence, dissociation, presence and non-disappearance 3." This condition is a part of base-prenascence-dependence condition which occurs during life only.

Analogy. This condition is like the Buddha who was the first to attain supramundane states; and human beings, *devas*, and *brahmās* who, not being rid of defilements, had to depend on him for preaching the Dhamma, for taking refuge in him and for taking him as object. This is the analogy given by teachers of old.

8. (b) Conascence-Dependence

Definition. The condition where a conditioning state, on arising, relates by causing other states, the conditioned states, to arise simultaneously with it and be dependent on it is known as conascence-dependence condition.

Conascence-dependence and Conascence Conditions are the Same. In both these conditions, hardness, a great primary, is related to the remaining three great primaries and derived matter. Here hardness not only relates by causing the remaining three great primaries and derived matter to arise simultaneously with it (which is the nature of conascence), but also relates as base or dependence for the arising of the remaining three great primaries and derived matter (which is the nature of dependence). Similarly, when those three great primaries are related to hardness and derived matter, the three great primaries have the nature of conascence and base or dependence. It is only when the conditioning state has the nature of base or dependence that the relation can be that of conascence-dependence condition and also of conascence condition. Thus these two conditions are the same. In the cases of derived matter (which arises with the great primaries) and mind-produced matter or rebirth *kamma*-produced matter (which arises with the four mental aggregates) they do not have the nature of base or dependence and, therefore, cannot be conditioning states but only conditioned states of conascence-dependence and conascence conditions. So a state must not only arise together with other states but must also be the base or dependence of those states to be a conditioning state of these two conditions.

8. (c) Base-Prenascence-Dependence

Definition. The condition where a conditioning state (which must (i) be a material base, (ii) have arisen and be at its static phase before the conditioned states arise, and (iii) be the dependence of mentality) relates by causing mental states, the conditioned states, to arise, is known as base-prenascence-dependence condition.

The Conditioning States. These are the six material bases. With regard to (i), (ii) and (iii) above:

(i) The six material bases during life in the five aggregate planes, which arise prior to the seven consciousness elements, are related to those consciousnesses by dependence force. The consciousnesses in this plane cannot arise without dependence on a base. Even during sleep, when life-continuum arises, it does so dependent on a base. That is why eye-base and the rest of the five bases are related to eye-consciousness and the other fivefold consciousnesses by base-prenascence-dependence condition. The Analytical Exposition of the Conditions gives this as: "Eye-base is related to eye-consciousness element and its associated states by dependence condition", and so on.

(ii) The five bases. The fivefold consciousnesses, which are dependent on the five bases which have not yet ceased, take as objects the five sense-objects which have not yet ceased.[23] Therefore, the five bases must be those which are present states. Also, in base-prenascence-presence condition, which is one kind of presence condition, the five bases, as present states, are the conditioning states. This shows that, although the five bases must arise before the conditioned states which are eye-consciousness and the rest of the fivefold consciousnesses, those bases that have ceased and are not present when these consciousnesses arise, cannot be conditioning states of base-prenascence-dependence condition. (This will be clear from the mental process given in proximity condition in the explanation of the Analytical Exposition of the Conditions.)

Heart-base. There are three kinds: (1) that which arises together with the preceding rebirth consciousness and other consciousnesses, (2) that which arises at about one thought-moment before emergence from the Attainment of Extinction, (3) that which arises with the seventeenth thought-moment counted backwards from death-consciousness in the dying mental process.

(1) For beings who are not Arahats and, therefore, have not ended rebirths, rebirth consciousness arises, without any interval of time, after death-consciousness. After that rebirth consciousness there arise, according to the fixed order of the mental process, sixteen life-continuums, mind-door advertence, seven impulsions of craving for the new existence. At the nascent phase of rebirth consciousness in the five-aggregate planes, heart-base also arises. Here that heart-base is related to rebirth consciousness that arises with it, not by prenascence condition, but by conascence condition as pointed out above where it was stated that "[At the moment of conception] aggregates are related to [heart-]base by conascence condition; [heart-]base is related to aggregates by conascence condition". In the other cases the consciousnesses are related to the heart-base that arose together with each of the

[23] *pañca viññāṇā asambhinna-vatthukā asambhinnārammaṇā.* (Vibh, p. 323).

preceding consciousnesses by base-prenascence-dependence condition. So, with the sixteen life-continuums that arise after rebirth consciousness, the first life-continuum is dependent on the heart-base which arose together with rebirth consciousness that precedes it. Here that heart-base is the base-prenascence-dependence conditioning state, and the first life-continuum is the conditioned state. And the second life-continuum is dependent on the heart-base that arose together with the first life-continuum, and so on for the rest of the sixteen life-continuums. Then mind-door advertence is dependent on the heart-base that arose together with the sixteenth life-continuum, and so on. *P.Pfn.*, p. 714, states this as: "The second life-continuum arises with the prenascent physical [heart] basis as its support, which has already reached presence and arose at the rebirth-linking consciousness's instant of arising. The third life-continuum arises with the prenascent physical basis as its support, which has already reached presence and arose together with that [second life-continuum consciousness]. The occurrence of consciousness can be understood to happen in this way throughout life." Also, in eye-door mental process, the heart-base which arose together with the past life-continuum, is the conditioning state, and the vibrating life-continuum, the consciousness that follows, is the conditioned state. Thus the arising of consciousness during life is dependent on the heart-base that arose together with the consciousness immediately preceding it.

(2) During the entry into the Attainment of Extinction, the heart-base is continually arising and ceasing like the water in a flowing river. But since there are no consciousnesses and mental factors during this period, those heart-bases are not base-prenascence-dependence conditioning states. Only when the Anāgamī and the Arahat emerge from this Attainment is it that Anāgamī Fruition- or Arahatta Fruition-consciousness arises, dependent on the heart-base which had arisen about one thought-moment before them. That heart-base is related to those consciousnesses by base-prenascence-dependence condition.

(3) It was pointed out, in dealing with base-object-prenascence-dependence condition above, that, at the time of dying, all the con-

sciousnesses in the mental process depend on one heart-base. This is given in the *P.Pfn.*, p. 714, as: "But in one who is facing death, sixteen consciousnesses arise with a single prenascent physical [heart] basis as their support, which has already reached presence". (In the above 16 consciousnesses death-consciousness is not included, only in 17 is it included).

At the time of dying, the consciousnesses and mental factors, which are mind-element and mind-consciousness element, depend on one heart-base. It is like many persons sitting astride an old man who is very weak. For the heart-base at the time of dying is very weak and many consciousnesses have to depend on it, and it ceases with the ceasing of death-consciousness. The simultaneous ceasing of this materiality with consciousness is known as death. (Note that the simultaneous arising of this materiality with consciousness is known as birth in the five-aggregate planes.)

(iii) It was stated that mentality in the five-aggregate planes cannot arise without depending on a material base. But why does mentality depend, not on the base that arises together with it, but on the preceding one? The reason is that materiality is very weak at the nascent phase of its arising, and only at the static phase is it strong enough to be the dependence of mentality. If that is the case, why is it that rebirth consciousness is dependent on the conascent heart-base, i.e. that which arises together with it? The explanation is that at the time of arising of rebirth consciousness there is no prenascent heart-base, i.e. there is no heart-base present prior to its arising, and since consciousness in the five-aggregate planes cannot arise without dependence on a base, it has to depend on the one and only available conascent heart-base, i.e. that which arises together with it.

Analogy. Base-prenascence-dependence condition is like the sun and moon which appeared at the beginning of the world, and on which beings existing at the present time are dependent.

Base-prenascence-dependence Condition Occurs During Life Only. At the time rebirth consciousness arises in beings born of the mother's womb, the eye-base and the rest of the five bases do not arise. They do so only on the seventy-seventh day after conception. In the case of beings that are moisture-born or spontaneously born, the eye-base and so on do arise with rebirth consciousness, but they are not as yet the causes of eye-consciousness and so on. And the heart-base which arises with rebirth consciousness of such beings is not a prenascent force but a conascence force. Therefore, this condition occurs during life only, never at the moment of conception.

8. (d) Mixed Conascence-Prenascence

Conascence-dependence and base-prenascence-dependence conditions, which were expounded separately in this dependence condition, are dealt with together as mixed conascence-prenascence condition in the Classification Chapter of the Investigation Chapter but not in the Analytical Exposition of the Conditions where the teaching is neither too brief nor too detailed. Although there are only 24 conditions, when they are treated in detail and grouped under various kinds, as shown in chart II (A) in the Intr. to *C.R.*, p. liii, there are: 8 for object, 15 for conascence, 7 for proximity-strong-dependence, 2 for natural strong-dependence, 6 for base-prenascence, 4 for postnascence, 1 for strong-and-weak asynchronous *kamma*, 3 for physical nutriment, 3 for physical life-faculty and 3 mixed conditions of the Faultless Triplet.

In this condition, since base is included, it is not pure conascence condition; and since mental aggregates are included, it is not pure prenascence condition. Because the conascent mental aggregates and prenascent base are taken together as the conditioning states, it is known as mixed conascence-prenascence condition. This is given in chart II (H) in the Intr. to *C.R.*, facing p. lxiv. It will also be seen from this chart that in presence and non-disappearance conditions, there are (1) this mixed condition, (2) mixed postnascence-nutriment where postnascence and physical nutriment conditions are mixed and (3) mixed post-nascence-faculty where postnascence and physical life-faculty conditions are mixed. In this connection it may be mentioned that there are altogether eight mixed conditions in the 24 divisions of Paṭṭh. In addition to the above three there are: mixed (4) object-prenascence/base-prenascence, (5) conascence-faculty/base-prenascence-faculty, (6) conascence/postnascence, (7) postnascence/nutriment/faculty, (8) object-prenascence/base-prenascence/conascence.

The relations between the different conditioning and conditioned states of the mixed conditions always take place in the present and simultaneously. For example, in (8) above:

(i) visible object is related to the seven primary mental factors that arise together with eye-consciousness by object-prenascence condition;

(ii) eye-base is related to those seven mental factors by base-prenascence condition;

(iii) eye-consciousness is related to those seven mental factors by conascence condition.

Here the states are all present states and the relations between them take place simultaneously. This is dealt with in Paṭṭh, Vol. II, p. 488,[24] where it is stated that the above three conditioning states, visible object, eye-base, and eye-consciousness, are related to the conditioned states, the seven primary mental factors, by presence condition.

9. Strong-Dependence Condition (*upanissaya-paccaya*)

This is not like the normal dependence in dependence condition, for here, the conditioning states are related to the conditioned states by dependence which is strong and powerful. Therefore it is known as strong-dependence condition.

Analogy. This condition is like the rain on which trees depend for their growth and beings for their well-being. Here the trees and beings depend greatly on the rain. Similarly, in strong-dependence condition, the conditioned states depend strongly on the conditioning states.

The Difference between Dependence and Strong-dependence. The condition where dependence is primary for the conditioned states is strong-dependence condition, and the condition where dependence is

---

[24] *rūpāyatanaṃ ca, cakkhāyatanaṃ ca, cakkhu-viññāṇaṃ ca cakkhu-viññāṇa-sahagatānaṃ khandhānaṃ atthi-paccayena paccayo.*

necessary only at the time for the same conditioned states to arise is dependence condition. The following illustration is provided for a better understanding. For obtaining cooked rice, there must, first of all, be rice. So paddy seeds, a plot of land and rain are the primary things to produce rice. This is primary dependence. But once rice is obtained it is only necessary to depend on the cooking pot, fuel, fire, water, and the cook to get cooked rice. This is ordinary dependence. In a similar way, eye-consciousness, a resultant consciousness that arises in a being's continuity is primarily dependent on past *kamma*, which is, therefore, a strong-dependence conditioning state. But for the actual arising of eye-consciousness, it is necessarily dependent on the eye-base at the time and which, therefore, is a dependence conditioning state. In Paṭṭh, dependence condition is given as: "Eye-base is related to eye-consciousness [a resultant] by dependence condition", and strong dependence as: "Faultless (or faulty) *kamma* is related to [its] resultant (e.g. eye-consciousness) by strong-dependence condition".

The Three Kinds of Strong-dependence. These are (a) object-strong-dependence, (b) proximity-strong-dependence, (c) natural strong-dependence.

9. (a) Object-Strong-Dependence

Definition. The condition where a conditioning state as object (which is not of the ordinary type but is very desirable and pleasing) relates by causing the subjective mental states, the conditioned states, which are strongly dependent on it, to arise, is known as object-strong-dependence condition.

Difference from Object-predominance. Object-strong-dependence is the same as object-predominance with respect to the states involved, but there is a slight difference in the forces by which they are related. The force which attracts and governs the subjective conditioned states of mentality that are concerned, so that they cannot refrain from taking the object as the conditioning state, is the object-predominance force. But the force where the arising of the subjective conditioned states of mentality depends strongly on the object as the conditioning state is the object-strong-dependence force.

9. (b) Proximity-Strong-Dependence

Definition. The condition where a mental state, as the conditioning state, relates by causing the next mental state, the conditioned state, which is strongly dependent on it, to arise, is known as proximity-strong-dependence condition.

Difference from Proximity. Proximity-strong-dependence is the same as proximity condition with respect to the states involved, but there is a slight difference in the forces by which they are related. The force which causes the subsequent conditioned states of mentality to arise immediately after the ceasing of the preceding states, the conditioning states, is known as proximity force. But the force which causes the subsequent conditioned states of mentality to arise because they are strongly dependent on the ceasing of the preceding states, the conditioning states, is known as proximity-strong-dependence force.

9. (c) Natural Strong-Dependence

Definition. The cty gives two definitions: (i) *pakato upanissayo pakatūpanissayo* and (ii) *pakatiyā yeva vā upanissayo pakatūpanissayo*.

(i) *Pakata* means "done properly". Here, the condition where a conditioning state relates by causing the conditioned states which are strongly dependent on it to arise because it was done properly is known as natural strong-dependence condition.

It is said to be "done properly" when, at the proper time, it is certain to produce results from causes such as (a) greed or confidence brought about in one's internal continuity or (b) persons associated with, food eaten, or lodging-place in external continuity.

(ii) *Pakati* means "naturally". Here the condition where a conditioning state relates by causing the conditioned states which are strongly dependent on it to arise naturally is known as natural strong-dependence condition.

It is said to occur "naturally" when the cause is naturally strongly dependent, i.e. originally by itself without mixing with or without the assistance of either object-strong-dependence or proximity-strong-dependence, the other two kinds of strong-dependence condition.

The Three Kinds of Natural Strong-dependence. There are three kinds because it is unmixed-or mixed with one of the other two kinds of strong-dependence condition.

(a) This is natural strong-dependence (ii) above. It is not mixed with and does not need the assistance of the other two kinds of strong-dependence condition. For instance, a person has to have confidence first so that, based on it, he will perform other good deeds subsequently. Confidence does not possess object and proximity forces, and, therefore, it cannot be related by object and proximity conditions. And such conditions are not at all necessary since confidence, by its nature and of its own accord, is a very strong cause for the good deeds performed later. The Investigation Chapter gives this as "By the strong-dependence of confidence, [one] offers the offering, undertakes the precept ...".

(b) In the Path Object Triplet (Paṭṭh II 403), natural strong-dependence condition is mixed with object-strong-dependence condition.

(c) In the Faultless Triplet where it is stated "Path is related to Fruition", natural strong-dependence condition is mixed with proximity-strong-dependence condition.

So, natural strong-dependence, which is naturally strong by itself, becomes much stronger when it is assisted by another kind of strong-dependence condition mixed with it.

Strong (balava) Conditioning States. Upa of *upanissaya*, the Pāli term for this condition, means strong and powerful, and, therefore, the term "strong" is employed for the conditioning states. The power of dependence on the conditioning states for the arising of the conditioned states, consciousness, and mental factors, is not of the normal kind but very strong (*balava*) and that is why the conditioning states are said to be so. For instance, when *kamma* is performed, it may be of two kinds: (1) that which is so strong that it cannot be interfered with by another *kamma*. This is strong (*balava*) *kamma*; (2) that which can be interfered with and become ineffectual by another *kamma*. This is weak (*dubbala*) *kamma*. In strongdependence condition, the former kind of *kamma* must be taken.

Concepts. In the Investigation Chapter, where only ultimate realities involved in the 24 conditions are dealt with, concepts are not taken as conditioning states. In the Analytical Exposition of the Conditions, although they are included, those which are the subjects of concentration (*samādhi*) such as foulness, *kasiṇas*, and others are not considered.

Why Materiality can Never be a Conditioned State. In strong-dependence condition, materiality is a conditioning state but never a conditioned state. However, there are cases where it appears to be so. As examples, take the cases of (1) materiality in external continuity such as grasses and trees where their growth, yields of flowers, and fruits are dependent on the soil, water, and so on; (2) physical health and well-being in the internal continuity of persons where freedom from disease is dependent on herbs and medicines. Could it be said that these are related by strong-dependence force where materiality is a conditioned state?

Answer. Of the two kinds of continuity, materiality, and mentality, there is no volition in the case of the former, and so it does not possess the nature of performing anything. Since *pakata*, as stated above, means "done properly" in the past so that it is certain to produce results as conditioned states at the proper time, materiality, which is incapable of this, can never, therefore, be conditioned states of this condition. On the other hand, mentality, the other kind of continuity, has the nature of volition and, therefore, of *pakata*. Thus it can produce results as mentality to become a conditioned state of this condition.

Natural Strong-dependence according to the Sutta Method. Although, as explained above, materiality can never be a conditioned state according to the Abhidhamma method, they are so according to the Sutta method, where the method employed is "If this is the cause, that is the effect. If there is no cause, there is no effect." Here are a few examples:

The weather in April is related to the blossoming of *gangaw*; rain is related to the greenness and freshness of withering trees; the cold in winter is related to the solidification of crude petroleum and other liquids; the cold in the Himalaya mountains is related to the solidification of water; heat is related to the melting of wax, iron, silver, gold, and other solids; good medicine is related to the physical well-being of sick and diseased persons. These are cases where materiality is the conditioned state in the relation by strong-dependence force according to the Sutta method. Another example can be taken from Dependent Origination which is "Conditioned by consciousness, mentality-materiality arises." Here consciousness is related to *kamma*-produced matter (the conditioned state) of the non-percipient and the twenty-six five-aggregate planes.

10. *Prenascence Condition* (*purejāta-paccaya*)

Definition. The condition where a conditioning state (having arisen previously and reached the static phase) relates by causing mental states, the conditioned states, to arise after it, is known as prenascence condition.

Analogy. This condition is like the sun and moon which appeared at the beginning of the world and which do not disappear but give light, heat, and cold to the people who come after. Similarly, the conditioning states, which appear previously and do not cease as yet but remain at the static phase, are related to the consciousness and mental factors, the conditioned states, that arise after them.

The Two Kinds of Prenascence Condition. These are: (a) object-prenascence, (b) base-prenascence.

10. (a) Object-Prenascence

Conditioning States.[25] These must be objects which have arisen prior to and are still present before the conditioned states arise. They are the present eighteen types of produced matter. The other ten types of non-produced matter cannot be said to be present states because they are not pure ultimate realities. As for consciousness and mental factors, their

[25] See SEC.

existence is of extremely short duration and, therefore, their static phases do not last long enough to be present states. In the case of Nibbāna, which is time-freed, i.e. freed from past, present, and future time, it cannot be said to be a present state.

Conditioned States.[26] The fifty-four sensuous consciousnesses that can take the eighteen types of present produced matter as objects are conditioned states. The lofty consciousnesses (which take *kasiṇa* concepts and other lofty objects) and supramundane consciousnesses (which take Nibbāna as object) can never be conditioned states.

Superknowledge (*abhiññā*).[27] The five super-knowledges: (1) Divine-eye, (2) Divine-ear, (3) Knowledge of supernormal power, (4) Knowledge of remembrance of past existences, and (5) Knowledge of future existences, take materiality as object. (Knowledge of penetration into others' minds and Knowledge of rebirths according to one's *kamma* take mentality as object.) See the chart on the Objects of Super-knowledges given later. Of the five above, (4) and (5) take past and future objects respectively and not present objects, and so they cannot be conditioned states; (1) and (2) are dealt with as conditioned states in the Investigation Chapter. So it is only necessary to consider (3).

(3) *Knowledge of Supernormal Power.* One who has attained this power can, by resolution, such as "Let my body be as swift as the mind", bring it about. At the time of the resolution, one of the previously arisen and present produced types of matter existing in the body is the object as the conditioning state, and knowledge of supernormal power is the conditioned state of object-prenascence condition.[28]

Object-conascence.[29] It must not be concluded that the eighteen types of produced matter can only be object-prenascence and never conascence

---

[26]See SEC

[27]See *P.Pfn.*, Chaps. XII and XIII.

[28]*cittavasena kāyaṃ pariṇāmayato iddhividhābhiññāya ca aṭṭhārasasu yaṃ kiñci ārammaṃa-purejātaṃ hoti ti daṭṭhabbaṃ* (subcty, p. 188).

[29]*abhiññā-ñāṇassa pana kadāci sahajātam pi ārammaṇa-paccayo hoti yeva. appacurabhāvato apākaṭabhāvato ca na gahitaṃ* (Anuṭīkā, p. 303).

conditioning states. There are rare instances when, as objects, they are not prenascence but conascence conditioning states. Then they are said to be object-conascence, i.e. both object and conascence conditioning states. For example, when, by knowledge of supernormal power, manifold images are created, they arise together with and are, therefore, conascent with that knowledge. At that time the images are taken as objects and as conascent materiality are related to knowledge of supernormal power by object force. But since such cases are exceptional and abstruse they are not taken into account.

Sensuous Rebirth Consciousness is Never Object-prenascence. It might appear that sensuous rebirth consciousness comes under object-prenascence when it takes present objects such as the sign of *kamma* and the sign of destiny. But in prenascence condition this consciousness is not a conditioned state, and as such it cannot be a conditioned state in this case. Moreover, since it is not included in base-prenascence condition, it cannot be included in object-prenascence condition[30] because only those that are the former can also be the latter. Therefore, although rebirth consciousness takes a present sign (*nimitta*) as object, it is not an object-prenascence conditioned state. Then, what kind of object is this present object that is taken? As it is one that was taken at the time of dying in a previous existence, it is of a different existence and, therefore, it is not prominent but just an ordinary one. So such objects are related to sensuous rebirth consciousness by object force only.

This object-prenascence condition comes from object condition.

10. (b) Base-Prenascence

Base-prenascence condition comes from dependence condition, and it is exactly the same as base-prenascence-dependence condition dealt with above. But it is treated separately in order to show that the conditioning states of dependence and object conditions dealt with are those which had arisen before the conditioned states.

---

[30] *ārammṇa-purejatam pi hi vatthupurejāte avijjamāne na labbhati* (subcty, p. 209).

11. Postnascence Condition (*pacchājāta-paccaya*)

Definition. The condition where a conditioning state relates by supporting the conditioned states that had arisen before it is known as postnascence condition.

Note. Since the cause arises after the effect in this condition, this will appear to be strange and bewildering.

Analogy. This condition is like the volition of appetite (*āhārāsācetanā*) for food, which is the condition that supports the bodies of young vultures so that they do not die even though they have no food to eat. This needs further explanation. It is customary for vultures, unlike other birds, to eat all the food they find and not bring back any to the young ones left in the nests. The young ones, however, expect the mother to bring back food for them and ask for it when she returns. They are put off with the reply that no food was brought but that she will do so tomorrow. This is the reply given by the mother to the young ones until they have acquired wings to fly and search for food by themselves.

Here the volition which is associated with the craving for taste, i.e. with the desire for and expectancy of tasting food, is related to the young vultures by supporting them so that they do not die of hunger. In a similar way, the conditioning states of mentality which arise later are related to the matter produced by the four causes that had already arisen by supporting that matter so that they continue to produce similar materiality successively.

Another Analogy. Owing to the annual rains which fall later, the young trees that already exist grow up gradually and eventually form a forest of such trees. Similarly, there exists matter produced by the four causes: *kamma*, mind, temperature, and nutriment (which constitute the matter of beings) that arise at every phase of consciousness beginning with that at the moment of conception. Owing to the conditioning states, consciousness and mental factors (which are first life-continuum and so on) that arise later, the conditioned states, the matter produced by the four causes, gradually develop and arise successively till death.

How Postnascence Condition Supports. The seedling has to be watered so that it will not die. The water supports the seedling. Also, the child at birth has to be provided with milk so that it will not die. Milk supports the child. Similarly, postnascent mentality supports the matter produced by the four causes so that, although the preceding ones cease, the subsequent ones that arise remain fresh and active while they last.

Mentality possesses such powerful force that, although it depends on the heart-base (which is dependent on the blood inside the heart that is a very small part of the body), it is related to the matter produced by the four causes present in the whole body by postnascence condition.

The Relation by Postnascence Condition. At the nascent phase of rebirth consciousness there arises only *kamma*-produced matter and this is known as one-cause-produced matter. Since there is no matter prior to rebirth consciousness the latter cannot be related to matter by postnascence condition. Then, at the static phase of rebirth consciousness, temperature-produced matter arises. When this is taken together with the *kamma*-produced matter already present, the matter is said to be two-cause-produced matter. At this time the *kamma*-produced matter which arose with rebirth consciousness has reached the static phase. But since the next consciousness, the first life-continuum, has not arisen and is, therefore, not present, it cannot be related to the *kamma*-produced matter which had reached the static phase. The reason is that in presence condition, where postnascence-presence is dealt with, the relation takes place only when the states are present at that very instant. When life-continuum arises, however, it is related to the above two-cause-produced matter present at the time by postnascence condition. Then at the nascent phase of this life-continuum, mind-produced matter arises. So with the previous two-cause-produced matter, the matter present is said to be three-cause-produced matter. The second life-continuum, which arises after the first life-continuum ceases, is related to the three-cause-produced matter by postnascence condition. As for nutriment-produced matter, this arises (1) in the case of womb-born beings, two or three weeks after conception when the food taken by the mother penetrates the embryo and (2) in the cases of moisture-born and spontaneously born beings, when saliva is swallowed or when some food is taken. When this matter arises, the matter that is present is said to be four-cause-produced matter. Then each of the consciousnesses that arise later is related to the four-cause-produced matter that precede it by postnascence condition.

12. Repetition Condition (*āsevanna-paccaya*)

Definition. The condition where a conditioning state relates by causing similar states, the conditioned states, to arise repeatedly after it ceases is known as repetition condition. Or, the condition where a conditioning state relates by habitually causing states similar to itself, the conditioned states, to arise after it ceases is known as repetition condition.

Analogy. When clothes are kept in a sandalwood casket or box, the fragrant odour of the sandalwood is given to the clothes. This is an example of a thing which has the tendency of giving its attribute to another and strengthening the latter's attribute. Also, when the study of a subject is taken up, it is difficult at the beginning but as time goes on and progress is made, it becomes easier by repetition. What was learnt earlier helps to make the study become gradually easier later on. Similarly, in this condition, the preceding impulsion relates by causing the subsequent impulsion of the same class to arise and strengthen it.

States which are Not of Repetition Condition. Repetition condition has the nature of making efforts deliberately, so this applies only to faultless, faulty, and functional impulsions. Therefore, the other states are not of repetition condition. These are: five-door advertence which has no other function than that of attention; mind-door advertence, though it can arise two or three times in succession, is very weak and cannot make efforts to increase or reduce the power of its successive states; mundane resultants, which are the result of past *kamma*, arise in the present existence without effort; Path impulsions can destroy the corruptions at the first time of arising; Fruition consciousnesses, although they perform the function of impulsion and can make efforts, are caused by volitions of the Path impulsions concerned and being dependent on the latter, cannot make efforts for their own arising. Moreover, Path impulsion is faultless and Fruition impulsion that follows is resultant and, therefore, the former cannot be related to the latter by repetition condition because they are not of the same class. From the above it will be seen that only the forty-seven (55 -8) mundane impulsions are conditioning states of repetition condition.

Only Impulsions of the Same Class are Related by Repetition Condition. In the five-door mental process, determining consciousness is related to the first impulsion by proximity force. So also, in the mind-door process, mind-door advertence is related to the first impulsion by proximity force. But since determining consciousness and mind-door advertence do not function as impulsions, they are not related to the first impulsion by repetition condition. Thus the first impulsion cannot be a conditioned state of repetition condition. On the other hand, the seventh impulsion, which is the last impulsion, is related to registering consciousness or life-continuum (depending on the mental process) by proximity force but not by repetition force. The reasons are that they are not of the same class of consciousness and the force of repetition is exhausted at this last impulsion. Thus the seventh impulsion cannot be a conditioning state of repetition condition. But the impulsions between the first and the last are both conditioning and conditioned states of repetition condition.

Seven and Five Impulsions. Sensuous impulsions generally arise seven times and *jhāna* impulsions five times in their respective mental processes. In the case where there are seven impulsions, the repetition conditioning force of the first impulsion is received by the second impulsion, which thus becomes stronger than the first. Similarly, that of the second impulsion is received by the third and that of the latter by the fourth. Through this gradual increase in strength, the force reaches its maximum at the middle impulsion, which is the fourth. Then, although the force of the fourth impulsion is given to the fifth and this in turn to the sixth and this in turn to the seventh, the strength of the force gradually decreases and is exhausted at the seventh impulsion so that there is no strength to produce another impulsion. Thus the repetition of impulsions comes to an end with the seventh impulsion. That is why this latter impulsion is not a repetition conditioning state.

In the case of *jhāna* there are five impulsions for a beginner. The first four are sensuous impulsions (preparation, approximation, adaptation, and change-of-lineage) and the fifth is a *jhāna* impulsion which is the last. After that, life-continuum arises. As regards the attainment of *jhāna* process, although as many *jhāna* impulsions take place as desired, the strength of the repetition conditioning force is exhausted with the last impulsion, life-continuum arising after it.

Repetition Condition when the Object Taken is Not the Same. It was pointed out that the states are related by repetition condition only when they are of the same class. That is why in *C.R.*, p. 168, item 426 (i) it is given that "Adaptation [is related] to change-of-lineage; adaptation [is related] to purification [by repetition condition]". Here all the three impulsions are of the same sensuous class and plane, but adaptation takes a state of mundane formation as object whereas the other two take Nibbāna as object. So, although the states take different objects, they are related by repetition condition.

Repetition Condition when the Plane is Not the Same. In the same reference given above it is also stated that "change-of-lineage [is related] to Path; purification is related to Path by repetition condition". Here, all the three impulsions are of the same faultless class, take the same object, Nibbāna, but change-of-lineage and purification are of the sensuous plane whereas Path is of the supramundane plane.

The Difference between Natural Strong-dependence and Repetition. The arising of faultless and faulty states at any time or in any existence is due to natural strong-dependence condition but the increase in the powers of these states is due to repetition condition. In this world, all the great and wonderful discoveries, *jhāna*, supernormal power, Attainment, Path, Fruition, and the practice of the Perfections to become a

Buddha — such as charity and the rest — are not possible without repetition condition.

13. *Kamma* Condition (*Kamma-paccaya*)

Definition. The condition where a conditioning state relates by encouraging (i) itself to make efforts to accomplish its function and (ii) the other states, the conditioned states, to accomplish their individual functions (which is the distinctive feature of volition) is known as *kamma* condition.

Note. Just as the distinctive feature of the body is bodily intimation, and that of speech is verbal intimation, so that of the mind is volition.

Analogy. This condition is like the chief disciple or chief carpenter who encourages (1) himself to make efforts to complete his own task and (2) the younger disciples or assistant carpenters to make efforts to complete their individual tasks.

The Four Kinds of Kamma Condition.[31] These are: (a) proximity-*kamma*, (b) conascence-*kamma*, (c) strong-asynchronous-*kamma*, (d) strong-and-weak-asynchronous-*kamma*.

13. (a) Proximity-*Kamma*

This is not a separate condition by itself. It is only taken as such when the common states of proximity and *kamma* conditions are selected and when the combinations of conditions are considered. The conditioning states are the volitions associated with the four Path-consciousnesses, and the immediate results they give without any interval of time, the corresponding four Fruition-consciousnesses, are the conditioned states. This is one of the qualities of Dhamma, known as *akālika*, ascribed to the four Path-consciousnesses. For they are the only ones out of all the eighty-nine consciousnesses which, apart from other properties, have the force to give immediate results.

---

[31]See SEC.

13. (b) Conascence-*Kamma*

This is like root condition where the six roots, which are the conditioning states of conascence condition, are taken separately in that condition. Here volition, which is a conditioning state of conascence condition, is taken separately. And when it is related to the associated states which arise together with it, it is said to be a conditioning state of conascence-*kamma* condition.

13. (c) Strong Asynchronous *Kamma*

The three kinds of *kamma* condition given above, (a) proximity-*kamma*, (c) strong-asynchronous *kamma* and (d) strong-and-weak-asynchronous *kamma*, are taken together in the Analytical Exposition of the Conditions as asynchronous *kamma*. Here they are distinguished to show that they belong to different groups of conditions.[32] Strong asynchronous *kamma* belongs to the natural strong-dependence group of conditions whereas strong-and-weak asynchronous *kamma*, as the only condition, belongs to a separate group of its own, independent of all the other groups.

Asynchronous Kamma. The volition which produces a result at a different instant of time, unlike conascence-*kamma*, is known as asynchronous *kamma*. Just as the seed supported by the soil and water grows into a tree, so also asynchronous *kamma* supported by the four causes — destiny (*gati*), time (*kāla*), substratum of birth (*upadhi*) and effort (*payoga*) — will result in (i) various kinds of resultant mental aggregates and *kamma*-produced matter in the thirty-one planes; (ii) different kinds of bodies (*nānatta-kāya*), perceptions, and the rest of the nine existences (*upapatti-bhava*); (iii) four different kinds of birth: womb-born, and so on.

The Two Functions of Volition. When volition arises, it can carry out two functions, namely: (i) to make efforts for the conascent states that

---

[32]See Intr. to *C.R.*, chart II (A), p. liii, for the groups of conditions and to the charts facing p. lxiv for the conditioning and conditioned states of the conditions so grouped.

arise together with it to perform their individual functions and which is the conascence-*kamma* function, (ii) to leave behind a force, like the seed or germ, which will produce resultant mental aggregates and *kamma*-produced matter in the future and which is the asynchronous *kamma* function. The eighty-nine volitions associated with the eighty-nine consciousnesses carry out the former function, and the thirty-three volitions associated with the thirty-three faultless and faulty consciousnesses carry out the latter function. It will be seen from this that the thirty-three volitions in the thirty-three faultless and faulty consciousnesses carry out both functions, whereas those remaining out of the eighty-nine, the fifty-six in the resultant and functional consciousnesses, carry out only the former function of conascence-*kamma*.

Analogy. The two kinds of function of volition, which take place simultaneously, may be compared to a flame which at the same time destroys darkness and gives light.

The Force Left Behind Produces Results. Although an asynchronous faultless or faulty volition arises for one thought-moment and then ceases, this is not the end of it. For a special force is left behind in the mind's successive continuity so that at some time in the future, the appropriate result of that volition will be produced when the proper conditions are satisfied. It is due to the presence of this force that results appear. However, this force does not manifest itself like the mind with its nascent, static, and cessant phases but is present like the latent tendencies. And just as the latter are not concepts, so also this special force of asynchronous *kamma* condition is not a concept. It is a special force of the ultimate realities.

Examples of this Force. (i) The knowledge that was acquired in youth does not remain fixed within the body. In fact, some of it is actually forgotten. But based upon such knowledge, higher knowledge is acquired with the advancing years. Here the knowledge that was acquired in youth and which had ceased to be is related to the knowledge acquired when grown up. (ii)[33] A person borrows money from another. This act of borrowing is finalised and ceases as soon as the money is received by the borrower. But because the money was borrowed, there is the indebtedness to repay the loan either in a lump sum or in instalments. The borrower has to abide by his promise to repay, and this cannot be avoided by any means. The main concern here is not whether there has been the past act of borrowing or not, but the responsibility to repay the loan. Only when the whole amount has been paid will there be relief from this responsibility.

In a similar way, when an act of *kamma* is performed, the *kamma*, before it ceases, leaves behind a special force of asynchronous *kamma* condition which will, at some time in the future, produce an appropriate result when the conditions for its arising are satisfied. And so long as the result is not produced, this indebtedness to *kamma* in the round of rebirths is ever present. The main concern here is not whether there has been the past act of *kamma* or not, but the indebtedness which will surely produce a result. But once a result is produced, the indebtedness to *kamma* no longer holds and no other result will be brought about because of this particular *kamma*. But if there is no opportunity for a result to be produced, i.e. *kamma* is no longer effective (*ahosi kamma*), then the force of volition ceases.

When Asynchronous Kamma Produces Results. Some asynchronous *kamma* (volitions) produce results in the present existence, some in the next existence, and some in the others beginning from the third existence right up to Parinibbāna, whenever opportunities for such results occur. Such volitions can produce results either at birth or during life in an existence separated by 4 æons and 100,000 worlds.

Volitions which are Ineffective Asynchronous Kamma. The sensuous and lofty faultless volitions in the learner's continuity of the Vehapphala, Akaniṭṭha, and Neither-perception-nor-non-perception planes do not produce results by way of rebirth in another plane; the many

[33]Paṭiccasamuppada-vibh. cty, p. 156.

faultless volitions in lofty attainments (which are the results of the practice of *jhānas*), will not produce results; and faulty and mundane faultless volitions of beings for whom it is going to be the last existence do not produce rebirth as result. So these volitions are not asynchronous *kamma* conditioning states.

Being's are Born of this Condition. Just as various kinds of trees result from various kinds of seeds, so also, in this round of rebirths, countless kinds of beings and the planes in which they are born result from this condition. The happiness and sorrow experienced by beings, all kinds of dwelling places, water, soil, forests, mountains, and the rest are the incidental results of this condition.

How Wrong Views are Held. Those who do not accept the above views about this condition or are opposed to them will (i) discard the ten right views starting with the one that there is no merit in charity, and others; (ii) hold to wrong views with fixed destiny; (iii) believe in a creator. So in future existences in the round of rebirths they, like animals, will not know what is faulty and faultless, what are woeful and happy existences.

The Strange Results Produced by Asynchronous Kamma. There is no place where materiality and mentality are stored for their continual arising and ceasing in succession. Just as when a match is struck a flame appears from nowhere and then disappears, so also, when object and base coincide, consciousness and mental factors arise from nowhere, last for a thought-moment, and then cease and vanish altogether. In this condition, volition, which is an ultimate reality, also arises and ceases in the same fashion. However, the force which is left behind after volition ceases is not destroyed and may be present for countless worlds in the successive continuity of a being — bound by craving, conceit, and wrong views — to produce a result suddenly. The result cannot be foreseen and seems to be spontaneous. Indeed, these forces give strange results. As instances, all of a sudden (i) a poor man wins a lottery and becomes rich and (ii) presidents, prime ministers, and national leaders are assassinated or gaoled.

Materiality is Never a Conditioned State. Strong asynchronous *kamma* condition belongs to the natural strong-dependence group of conditions and, as in the case of natural strong-dependence condition, where it has already been explained, materiality can never be a conditioned state.

13. (d) Strong-and-Weak Asynchronous *Kamma*

Both strong and weak asynchronous *kamma* are involved in this condition. If sensuous faultless and faulty volitions give strong, sensuous resultants, they are strong asynchronous *kamma*, but if they give weak ones, they are weak asynchronous *kamma*. Lofty and supramundane volitions are always strong asynchronous *kamma*. In the five-aggregate planes when the faultless and faulty volitions, which are related to *kamma*-produced matter, are (i) sensuous ones, they can be either strong or weak asynchronous *kamma*, and (ii) fine-material ones, they are always strong asynchronous *kamma*.

14. Resultant Condition (*vipāka-paccaya*)

Definition. The condition where a conditioning state relates by making the associated states, the conditioned states, that arise together with it as passive, calm, and peaceful as itself — and which is so because it is the result of *kamma* — is known as resultant condition.

Analogy. This condition is like fruits which have ripened and flowers which have bloomed. Since energy was expended to reach these stages, they have now become weak and are, therefore, passive and calm.

The Resultant Consciousnesses are Calm. In the continuity of a person who is asleep, the resultant life-continuum, taking as object either *kamma*, a sign of *kamma*, or a sign of destiny, successively arises and ceases like the water in a flowing river. During this time of sleep no efforts are made for action in thought, word, or deed, and the life-continuum is so calm that there is no awareness that the mind is functioning at all. On awaking, it cannot cause the mind to know and perceive anything. Also, in the five-door mental process, the fivefold consciousnesses and the other resultant consciousnesses arise without having to make efforts when the objects and bases coincide. So, if these were the only consciousnesses, there would be no awareness of objects. It is only when the impulsions arise that objects are known. This shows how calm the resultant consciousnesses are.

The Difference between Resultant Consciousnesses and the Others. The faultless and faulty consciousnesses have to make efforts in two directions: (i) for the production of resultant consciousnesses and (ii) for physical, verbal, and mental actions to take place. With functional consciousnesses efforts for (i) are not necessary but only for (ii). So the functional consciousnesses, which arise and cease in the continuity of the Arahat, are calm whereas faultless and faulty consciousnesses are not. With resultant consciousnesses, however, the above two efforts are not necessary and so they are very calm and, as it were, soothe the associated states to become calm like them. Therefore, the materiality in the continuity of a being, which is troubled and restless on account of the efforts that have to be made by the mind, can be made calm and peaceful by this resultant condition, i.e. by sleep when there is only resultant life-continuum.

15. Nutriment Condition (*āhāra-paccaya*)

Definition. The condition where a conditioning state relates by maintaining the existence of and supporting the growth and development of the conditioned states is known as nutriment condition.

Analogy. This condition is like the prop which supports an old house to prevent it from falling down and being destroyed.

The Two Kinds of Nutriment Condition. These are (a) physical nutriment and (b) mental nutriment.

The Force of Support is the Essential Function. Although nutriment condition has two functions, that of support and that of production, the former is its essential function.

How Physical Nutriment Supports. When food is taken, the nutritive essence in it not only produces nutriment-produced matter but also supports *kamma*-produced matter, mind-produced matter, and temperature-produced matter in the whole body by keeping them strong and fresh. That is why these three kinds of matter continue to arise successively.

When there is no support by physical (i.e. external) nutriment because food is not taken, the nutritive essence in each of the types of matter produced by the four causes in the whole body (i.e. internal nutriment) carries out the function of support only. But when food is taken, the nutritive essence from external food carries out the other function of production, i.e. producing nutriment-produced matter. Human beings commonly can go without food for seven days only, but some of the *devas*, *petas*, and those in the lower regions (*apāya*), who have strong *kamma*-produced matter in their bodies, can do so for long periods of time. The reason is that their bodies can exist for a long time supported only by internal nutriment. Therefore, in this condition, the essential function is that of support because this is the only function when external nutriment, which has the function of production, is absent.

The Three Mental Nutriments. These are: (i) contact, (ii) volition, (iii) consciousness.

How Contact Nutriment Supports. Contact strongly supports the mental factors, the chief of which is feeling experienced concerning objects. Beings continue from one existence to another in this prolonged manner in the round of rebirths because of this contact nutriment. For if this did not arise, the three kinds of feeling would not arise, and, therefore, there being no craving, there would be an end of the round of rebirths. But contact does arise, e.g. when visible object and sensitive-eye coincide, contact arises. Since Dependent Origination states "Conditioned by contact, feeling arises", and so on, feeling experienced concerning desirable and undesirable objects arises, and then craving for desirable objects arises and increases. Then, to be able to experience pleasant feelings again, faultless and faulty *kamma* are performed, and since they give results in the future, there is a prolongation of the round of rebirths. So it will be seen that contact supports and maintains the prolongation of the round of rebirths.

How Volition Nutriment Supports. Since Dependent Origination states, "Conditioned by formation, consciousness arises", the faultless or faulty volition nutriment, as formation, causes the arising of rebirth consciousness and other resultant consciousnesses in future existences. So volition supports the three types of existence.

How Consciousness Nutriment Supports. Here also, since Dependent Origination states, "Conditioned by consciousness, mentality-materiality arises", consciousness causes mental factors and materiality to grow and develop. So consciousness supports and maintains the continuation of the successive arisings of the aggregates.

Note. In the Abhidhamma method, the three mental nutriments, as conditioning states, relate by supporting their associated states.

Physical Nutriment Conditioning State. The nutritive essence in each of the types of matter produced by the four causes in the internal continuity and the temperature-produced nutritive essence in external continuity such as rice, butter, and other foods, are the physical nutriment conditioning states.

How Physical Nutriment Condition is Related. The external nutritive essence is related to (i) the new nutriment-produced matter produced by it in the body by the force of production; (ii) the nutriment-produced matter produced by nutritive essence present in the other physical nutriment groups by the force of support, and (iii) the remaining kinds of matter produced by three causes by the force of support. Then internal nutritive essence in a physical nutriment group is related to (i) the other matter in that group by the forces of production and maintenance and (ii) the other material groups by the force of maintenance. Also, nutritive essence in each of the other material groups is related to (i) the other matter in that same group by the forces of production and maintenance and (ii) the other material groups by the force of maintenance (cty, p. 378).

Note. It will be seen from the above that the relations are with (i) external nutritive essence, (ii) internal nutritive essence in nutriment-produced matter and (iii) internal nutritive essence in each of the groups produced by the other three causes.

It must be understood, however, that when internal nutritive essence is related by the force of production, this is possible only when it is supported by external nutritive essence. Otherwise it is related by the force of support only. The way internal nutritive essence functions for production is explained as follows: When the external nutritive essence in rice and other foods — which have been digested by the heat of *kamma*-produced matter and then distributed throughout the whole body by the motion element — is mixed with the internal nutritive essence in each of the types of matter produced by the four causes, then only the force of production functions and there is produced nutriment-produced matter. In this material group of nutriment-produced matter, heat is strong, and uniform and it produces temperature-produced matter. The latter, therefore, has nutritive essence as its cause.

How Nutritive Essence Supports to Produce Temperature-produced Matter. Nutritive essence serves as fuel to support heat so as to keep it uniform throughout and then increase it. By this support heat becomes vigorous and produces fresh temperature-produced matter.

How Nutritive Essence Supports Womb-born Beings, etc. Before the nutritive essence in the food taken by the mother is distributed throughout the fœtus, the latter is supported by the nutritive essence in each of the types of matter produced by the three causes. But when it is distributed, nutriment-produced matter is produced for the first time, and from then onwards nutritive essence in foods supports the body for the whole period of an existence. Also, spontaneously-born *devas* in the sensuous plane are supported at birth by the nutritive essence in each of the types of matter produced by the three causes before they take *deva* food. Then nutriment-produced matter is produced to support their bodies for life.

Why Physical Nutriment is Taken Separately. All animate and inanimate materiality has to depend on heat (*tejo*). It exists because of heat and is greatly dependent on it. All materialities are at the will and mercy of heat for they are essentially governed by it. But this heat, in turn, has to depend on nutritive essence as the fuel and has to be maintained by the food taken. Thus nutritive essence is the source of heat. That is why nutritive essence, as physical nutriment, is taken separately in nutriment condition.

16. Faculty Condition (*indriya-paccaya*)

Definition. The condition where a conditioning state relates by having great control over the states concerned with it, the conditioned states, is known as faculty condition.

Analogy. This condition is like each of the four ministers of state who, by not interfering with one another, has freedom of control in governing respectively the northern, southern, eastern, and western divisions with which each is concerned.

The Three Kinds of Faculty Condition. These are (a) conascence-faculty, (b) base-prenascence-faculty, (c) physical life-faculty.

16. (a) Conascence-Faculty Definition.

Definition. The condition where a conditioning state relates by controlling the states of materiality and mentality, the conditioned states, which arise together with it, is known as conascence-faculty condition.

The Nature of Control. Control means that only the conditioning states are prominent but not their associated states, the conditioned states. For example, when bodily pain arises, pain is prominent while its associated states, consciousness, contact, and the rest are not.

What the Faculties Control. The eight ultimate realities of the states concerned in conascence-faculty condition are: psychic life, consciousness, feeling, confidence, effort, mindfulness, one-pointedness of mind, and wisdom. The following shows what each controls:

Psychic Life-faculty. This controls the life of the four mental aggregates. Life of the four mental aggregates, in the sense taken here, means their continual arising in succession. Since psychic life is present in every mental group, mentality appears to have life. And the states which psychic life controls are the mentality and materiality that arise together with it.

Consciousness (*Mind-faculty*). Consciousness, which is aware of or takes different objects, controls its associated mental factors.

Feeling. There are five states of feeling as faculties which control.

(a) Bodily-pleasure faculty controls the pleasure experienced by the body;

(b) bodily-pain faculty controls the pain experienced by the body;

(c) mental-joy faculty controls the pleasure experienced by the mind;

(d) grief faculty controls the grief experienced by the mind;

(e) indifference faculty controls the indifferent (neither painful nor pleasant) feeling experienced by the mind.

The respective ultimate realities of these different faculties are (a) feeling present at bodily-pleasure consciousness, (b) feeling present at bodily-pain consciousness, (c) feeling present at sixty-two mental-joy consciousnesses, (d) feeling present at two hate-rooted consciousnesses, and (e) feeling present at fifty-five indifferent consciousnesses. Since they are all feeling, they are taken under the one ultimate reality of feeling. Feeling controls the consciousness and mental factors that arise together with it.

Confidence Faculty. This controls the confidence in the qualities of the Buddha, Dhamma, Saṅgha, precepts, and others.

Effort Faculty. This controls the effort in the four Right Efforts.

Mindfulness Faculty. This controls the mindfulness in the four Applications of Mindfulness.

Concentration Faculty. This controls the concentration in *jhāna* and the Attainments. It is the ultimate reality of one-pointedness of mind.

Wisdom Faculty. This controls wisdom and the realisation of the four Noble Truths.

The above five faculties control the three kinds of action performed in thought, word and deed, for, without them, these actions cannot be performed. Of these, the confidence, mindfulness, and wisdom faculties control the faultless actions performed; and the remaining two, the effort and concentration faculties, control both the faultless and faulty actions performed.

I-shall-know-what-I-did-not-know Faculty. This controls the purity of knowledge at the moment of Stream-winner (*sotāpatti*) Path-consciousness.

Higher Realisation Faculty. This controls the purity of knowledge at the moment of each of the three Higher Path-consciousnesses and the three Lower Fruition-consciousnesses.

He-who-has-known Faculty. This controls the purity of knowledge at the moment of Arahatta Fruition-consciousness.

The wisdom faculty and the three supramundane faculties given above come under the ultimate reality of wisdom.

16. (b) Base-Prenascence-Faculty

Definition. The condition where a conditioning state (which is a dependence base that has previously arisen and is still present) relates by controlling the functions of the states concerned — the conditioned states that arise after it — is known as base-prenascence-faculty condition.

Analogy. This condition is like the four Deva Kings (*Catu-Mahārājika-deva*) who, by not interfering with one another, have freedom of control in governing Kumbhaṇḍas, Yakkhas, and others respectively that come later.

What the Faculties Control. The conditioning states concerned in base-prenascence-faculty condition are the five sense-faculties such as eye-faculty and so on. The following shows what each controls:

Eye faculty. This is the sensitive-eye which controls eye-consciousness that has the function of seeing and is dependent on it.

Explanation about the Process of Seeing. Depending on the age of a person he is said to have good or bad eye-sight. But there is no difference in the way eye-consciousness arises. Nevertheless, in order to account for the difference in eye-sight, it is sometimes explained that eye-consciousness is associated with more mental factors and has longer life when there is clear vision and that eye-consciousness is associated with less mental factors and has a shorter life when the vision is not clear. But this is not tenable for, in both cases, eye-consciousness is always associated with seven mental factors and always lasts for three phase-moments of thought.

The true explanation is that the difference in the sensitive-eye, which controls eye-consciousness, brings about this distinction between good and bad eye-sight. An old man's vision is not clear because the sensitive-eye has been affected by age, and so the eye-consciousness, which is dependent on it, does not give clear vision. This is what is meant by bad eye-sight. In the case of a young man, the sensitive-eye has not been so affected, and eye-consciousness gives a clear vision. Even then, when he reads too much, the sensitive-eye is affected and vision is bad. In brief, sensitive-eye controls eye-consciousness, and so the latter has no alternative but to obey its command. Thus good or bad eye-sight depends upon the difference in the sensitive-eye. But in both cases the way of arising of eye-consciousness is the same.

Ear-faculty. This is the sensitive-ear which controls ear-consciousness that has the function of hearing and is dependent on it.

Nose-faculty. This is the sensitive-nose which controls nose-consciousness that has the function of smelling and is dependent on it.

Tongue-faculty. This is the sensitive-tongue that controls tongue-consciousness that has the function of tasting and is dependent on it.

Body-faculty. This is the sensitive-body that controls body-consciousness that has the function of touching and is dependent on it.

Why Heart-base is Never a Conditioning State. As shown above, five of the six bases are the conditioning states of base-prenascence-faculty condition, but the remaining base, heart-base, is never so. The reasons for this are

(i) Heart-base arises before the mind-element and mind-consciousness element which are dependent on it. In this respect it is similar to the other five bases. But unlike them, the strength or weakness of the consciousness is not dependent on it. Because, whether the heart-base is clear or not, the mind-element and mind-consciousness element are not affected accordingly. Thus the heart-base does not control the consciousness dependent on it.

(ii) The five bases and the five corresponding sense-objects are respectively the receivers and impingers. But this is not so with heart-base and cognizable object. Instead, cognizable object impinges on the mind-door (life-continuum) and appears in it. Hence, heart-base is not a door. and so it can never be a conditioning state of base-prenascence-faculty condition.

16. (c) Physical Life-Faculty

Definition. The condition where physical life-faculty, the conditioning state, relates by controlling *kamma*-produced matter (that was caused by past *kamma*) so as to prolong its life (i.e. to bring about the succession of *kamma*-produced matter), although there is no cause for it by present *kamma*, is known as physical life-faculty condition.

At rebirth and during life, the physical life-faculty, which is present in every *kamma*-produced material group that arises, controls that group by its functions of maintaining life and of making that group arise in continuous succession. That is why *kamma*-produced matter appears to have life and is said to be "live materiality". On the other hand, physical life-faculty is not present in mind-produced, nutriment-produced, and temperature-produced matter. and so they are said to be "dead materiality". The bodies of beings appear to have life or to be alive because of this power of physical life-faculty.

Analogy. This condition is like the muddy water which controls the lotus plant by keeping it fresh and green and so prolonging its life although the seed from which it had grown is destroyed.

What Physical Life-faculty Controls. Physical life-faculty maintains the other *kamma*-produced matter which arises together with it so that they last for forty-nine thought-phases. In the cases of the other types of cause-produced matter such as nutriment-produced matter, it arises only when the nutriment, the cause, exists. But with *kamma*-produced matter, although the cause, *kamma*, does not exist, it goes on existing because physical life-faculty maintains it. So nutriment-produced, temperature-produced, and mind-produced matter may each be compared to the child with the mother alive, and *kamma*-produced matter, which is maintained by physical life-faculty, to the motherless child maintained by a wet-nurse.

Why Physical Life-faculty is Taken Separately. The mental faculties are related to their associated states at the nascent phase of their arising. Physical life-faculty, however, is related to the *kamma*-produced matter of the same group that arises together with it, but only at the static phase by the forces of control and maintenance. Since it does not relate by the force of production, it does not possess the characteristic of conascence and, therefore, cannot be included in conascence-faculty condition. Thus it is taken separately in faculty condition.

The Conditioning States of Faculty Condition. When life-faculty, one of the twenty-two faculties, is distinguished as psychic life-faculty and physical life-faculty, there are twenty-three faculties. Of these, fifteen are the mental faculties: psychic life, mind, five feelings, confidence, effort, mindfulness, concentration, wisdom, I-shall-know-what-I-did-not-know, Higher Realisation, and He-who-has-known. They are all conascence-faculty conditioning states. The remaining eight are the physical faculties. Of these, the five sense-faculties (eye-faculty, ear-faculty, nose-faculty, tongue-faculty, and body-faculty) are base-prenascence-faculty conditioning states, and physical life-faculty is physical life-faculty conditioning state. The other physical faculties, the sex faculties, are not conditioning states of faculty condition.

Why the Two Sex Faculties are Never Faculty Conditioning States. The distinctive characteristics of a woman are due to the female sex, which is the feminine faculty. These are:

(i) Feminine features (*itthi-liṅga*). This is the form of a woman's body. Since this is distinct from the form of a man's body, people recognize a woman by her bodily form.

(ii) Feminine signs (*itthi-nimitta*). The signs of a woman are different from those of a man. For a woman's hands and feet are small and delicate, the face is without beard or moustache, and so on.

(iii) Feminine occupation (*itthi-kutta*). From youth a woman plays, enjoys herself and works in a womanly fashion which are actions different from those of a man.

(iv) Feminine deportment (*itthi-ākappa*). The frail manner of walking, the way of using her hands and feet, the smile and speech, etc., of a woman are manners which are different from those of a man.

The distinctive characteristics of a man are due to the male sex which is the masculine faculty. The masculine features, etc. are the opposite of the feminine faculty.

Since the distinctive characteristics of a man and a woman are due to the sex faculties, the question arises as to whether these faculties control those characteristics and are, therefore, faculty conditioning states. The sex materiality of beings born in the sensuous plane arises at the nascent phase of rebirth consciousness. But the distinctive characteristics do not appear simultaneously at that time. Now, a conditioning state of faculty condition is always that of presence condition and, accordingly, the conditioning and conditioned states must arise together either at the nascent or static phase. As pointed out above, the distinctive sexual characteristics do not arise together with the sex materiality and, therefore, the latter cannot be a conditioning state of presence condition. As such it cannot be that of faculty condition which controls those characteristics. Furthermore, sex materiality is not capable of controlling either the nine states of materiality that arise together with it in a materiality group (male- or female-decad) or the states of materiality belonging to another materiality group.

Another Explanation. According to the Paṭṭh method, the requirements of a condition are satisfied when a conditioning state is related either by the force of (i) producing the conditioned states, such as proximity condition and others or (ii) supporting the conditioned states so that they continue to exist and develop, such as postnascence condition or

(iii) maintaining the conditioned states so that they continue to arise successively, such as physical life-faculty condition. The sex faculties do not possess any of these three forces and so they cannot be conditioning states of faculty condition or, indeed, of any other condition.

Why the Two Sex Materialities are Themselves Faculties. The male and female sex materialities have their own independent power to bring about the bodily form and other distinctive characteristics of a man or woman respectively, and because of this control or domination they are faculties.

The Difference between Predominance and Faculty Conditions. Predominance condition is like the universal monarch who is the absolute ruler and has no rival, whereas faculty condition is like the kinglets who are rivals among themselves. Or, predominance condition is like the king, and faculty condition is like the ministers and government officials. For in predominance condition, two predominant states are never associated together as conditioning states, whereas in faculty condition, many mental faculty states can be associated with one another as conditioning states so that one of them is assisted by the others in carrying out its function.

17. *Jhāna* Condition (*jhāna-paccaya*)

Definition. The condition where a conditioning state, like applied thought and others, relates by making its associated states, the conditioned states, fix themselves firmly to pleasant or unpleasant objects, just as it does, is known as *jhāna* condition.

Analogy. This condition is like a person who goes to the top of a tree or hill and not only sees for himself the pleasant and unpleasant objects down below but also tells them to those who are on the ground.

Another Analogy. The hunter has to take proper aim first and then hold the arrow firmly towards the bird or animal he is going to shoot with his bow and arrow. This condition is like directing the aim and holding the arrow firmly because it has to direct itself to and hold firmly to the object.

The Conditioning States. These are the *jhāna* factors, the ultimate realities of which are applied thought, sustained thought, rapture, feeling, and one-pointedness of mind. (i) Applied thought has the characteristic of directing the mind straight towards the object it desires; (ii) sustained thought has the characteristic of taking the object repeatedly; (iii) rapture has the characteristic of interest in the object; (iv) feeling has the characteristic of experiencing the object. Although each of them carries out its own function, it is (v) one-pointedness of mind which has the characteristic of fixing the mind firmly on the object. For even in the case of hate which offends, it is one-pointedness of mind that firmly fixes the mind on the unpleasant object although painful feeling is experienced with that object.

No Action can be Performed Without Jhāna Condition. It is due to *jhāna* condition that a faultless or faulty action in thought, word, or deed can be completely performed from the beginning right through to the end. Without *jhāna* condition it would not be possible (i) to shoot birds and animals, (ii) to clearly distinguish what and whose form it is, (iii) to take one straight step forward correctly, for, if at the beginning the foot was pointed eastwards, it would point southwards in the middle and westwards at the end of the step. Or else, while taking the step forward, the mind would take another object and forget about the step altogether, (iv) and it would not be possible to pronounce one word correctly. This shows how swiftly the mind is distracted and changed. So the mind may be compared to a young, wild bull and *jhāna* condition to the rope, post, grass, and water which keeps the bull under control and prevents it from wandering away.

18. Path Condition (*magga-paccaya*)

Definition. The condition where a conditioning state relates by causing the associated states, the conditioned states, to function as a path to happy or woeful existences, to freedom from the round of rebirths, Nibbāna, is known as path condition.

Analogy. This condition is like the path taken by the cart, boat, steamer, train, or plane on which one gets to the right or wrong destination.

The Conditioning States. These are the twelve path factors: right view and the rest of the Noble Eightfold Path, wrong view, wrong applied thought, wrong effort, and wrong concentration. They come under nine ultimate realities: wisdom, applied thought, right speech, right action, right livelihood, effort, mindfulness, one-pointedness of mind, and wrong view. Of these, applied thought (which is either right or wrong applied thought), effort (which is either right or wrong effort), and one-pointedness of mind (which is either right or wrong concentration), are either faultless or faulty; wrong view is purely faulty; the rest are right path factors.

The Remaining Four Wrong Path Factors are Not Conditioning States. Wrong speech, wrong action, wrong livelihood, and wrong mindfulness are the remaining four wrong path factors. They are faulty volitions or faulty mental aggregates which do not come under any of the ultimate realities of path condition mentioned above. Thus they are not conditioning states of path condition.

Why It is Called Path. Path means a route leading to a place of destination. In order to go on a journey to near or distant places in all the four or eight directions, there are many and various routes. The cart, car, boat, train, and plane are the vehicles, means of conveyance, that take one along the route to the desired destination. Similarly, wrong path factors are the states which take one along the path to woeful existences, and right path factors to happy existences and Nibbāna. Therefore they are called paths.

How Woeful and Happy Existences are Reached. Wrong view is the great highway to woeful existences. Wrong applied thought, wrong effort, and wrong concentration are the vehicles that go on this road to woeful existences. For it is by means of these four wrong path factors, going on the wrong track, that faulty actions, such as murder, are committed to reach woeful existences. On the other hand, right view is the great highway to happy existences and Nibbāna. The remaining seven right path factors are the vehicles that go on this road to happy existences and Nibbāna. For it is by means of these eight right path factors, going on the right track, that charity, precepts, and mental development are undertaken to reach happy existences and Nibbāna.

Indeterminate Path Factors. If the path can lead to happy and woeful existences, it is reasonable to ascribe this to faultless and faulty path factors respectively. But indeterminate path factors, which are resultant and functional states, do not lead to such existences, and, therefore, it is questionable whether they possess path conditioning forces.

The Explanation. Although the path factors present at the rooted resultant consciousnesses are themselves results and cannot lead to happy existences, they were caused by the faultless states which functioned as path conditioning states, so, likewise, these resultant consciousnesses are also path conditioning states. With the path factors present at the rooted functional consciousnesses, although they can lead to happy existences, they do not do so because they arise only in the continuity of the Arahat who has ended the round of rebirths.

The Difference between Jhāna and Path Conditions. Jhāna condition fixes the mind directly and firmly on the object so as to lead to *jhāna*. Path condition (i) fixes the volition directly and firmly on the path to existences in the round of rebirths so that full courses of action and their increase and development are brought about and (ii) fixes the mental development *kamma* directly and firmly on the path to Nibbāna so that special planes are reached.

How Full Courses of Action are Brought About. The volition in (i) above which brings about the fulfilment of conditions for the completion of faultless actions such as offerings, etc., and faulty actions such as killing, etc., to give results as rebirth in existences, is said to bring about the full courses of action.

How Special Planes are Reached. The mental development *kamma* in (ii) above which brings about the various steps in mental development by which it is possible to go by stages from the sensuous plane to the lofty and supramundane planes in one posture is said to reach special planes.

19. Association Condition (*sampayutta-paccaya*)

Definition. The condition where a conditioning state relates by causing the other states, the conditioned states, to arise and be associated in a group so that they are inseparable and cannot be singled out as contact, feeling, etc., because they possess the four characteristics of association, i.e. of arising and ceasing together, of taking the same object and of depending on the same base, is known as association condition.

Analogy. This condition is like the four sweets (*catu-madhura*) where all the ingredients are so thoroughly and inseparably mixed together that the taste cannot be distinguished as that of butter, honey, etc. Or, it is like the water in the ocean where the waters from the five rivers and 500 rivulets are so thoroughly and inseparably mixed together that it cannot be distinguished as water from the Ganges, Yamuna, and the other rivers.

How the States are Associated in a Group. Eye-consciousness and the seven primary mental factors, a total of eight states, are inseparably associated together in a group. And although it is conventionally said that it is the eye-consciousness which sees, it cannot do so without the rest of the group. Actually, therefore, it should not be definitely stated that a particular state of that group sees. Moreover, it is impossible to separate the states in the group to know them individually.

Materiality is Not of Association Condition. Although material states form material groups such as octad, nonad, etc., which arise and cease together, they are not mental states, and so they do not possess the four characteristics of association given above. Hence, materiality does not belong to association condition. Only mental states can be conditioning and conditioned states of association condition.

20. Dissociation Condition (*vippayutta-paccaya*)

Definition. The condition where a conditioning state relates by making the other states, the conditioned states, arise together with it according to the nature of conascence only, but are not associated according to the characteristics of association, is known as dissociation condition.

Analogy. This condition is like a mixture of the six flavours: sweet, sour, hot, salty, astringent, and bitter, which, although they are together, remain separate, i.e. the sweet taste does not become sour but remains sweet, nor does the sour taste become sweet but remains sour, and so on. Or, it is like a mixture of water and mercury where, although they are together, they remain separate.

The Four Kinds of Dissociation Condition. These are: (a) base-object-prenascence-dissociation, (b) conascence-dissociation, (c) base-prenascence-dissociation, (d) postnascence-dissociation.

20. (a) Base-Object-Prenascence-Dissociation

This is the same as base-object-prenascence-dependence condition given under Dependence Condition.

20. (b) Conascence-Dissociation

In this condition, if the conditioning state is mentality, the conditioned state is materiality and vice versa.

Mentality as Conditioning and Materiality as Conditioned State. During life, mind (the conditioning state) and mind-produced matter (the conditioned state) arise together according to the nature of conascence but not of association. So this is dissociation. Similarly, at rebirth, rebirth consciousness and *kamma*-produced matter arise together at the nascent phase of rebirth consciousness. This is not association but dissociation. Again, in the five-aggregate planes, rebirth consciousness and heart-base arise together. This is not association but dissociation.

Materiality as Conditioning and Mentality as Conditioned State. In the five-aggregate planes, heart-base and rebirth consciousness arise together. This is not association but dissociation.

This dissociation condition was expounded so as to leave no doubt as to whether materiality and mentality, when they arise together as in conascence condition, are associated or not. Also, in conascence condition, the great primaries, which arise together, are mutually related by conascence condition. They are further related to derived matter by conascence condition as they all arise together. The question arises as to whether these come under dissociation condition. As already pointed out, only mentality and materiality can be related by dissociation condition, and so the above relations between materiality and materiality are not of dissociation condition.

20. (c) Base-Prenascence-Dissociation

Definition. The condition where a conditioning state (which must (i) be a material base, (ii) have arisen and be at the static phase before the conditioned states arise, and (iii) be the dependence of mentality) relates by causing mental states, the conditioned states, to arise but which is not associated with them, is known as base-prenascence-dissociation condition. It is the same as base-prenascence-dependence condition given under Dependence Condition.

Why this Dependence Condition is Expounded Again as Dissociation Condition. Here the six bases are the conditioning states and eye-consciousness element and the rest of the seven consciousness elements are the conditioned states. The conditioning state is materiality, and the conditioned state is mentality. For instance, eye-base is the materiality and eye-consciousness is the mentality which depends on that base for its arising. This consciousness is not originally present on the eye-base. It arises only when visible object-base and eye-base coincide. But since it appears to arise from within the eye-base, this dissociation condition is expounded to dispel any doubt as to whether the eye-base and eye-consciousness are associated or not. Actually they are not associated. The analogy is that of a white insect fluttering about in red-coloured water. The insect can be observed distinctly, existing separately in the water. So also, eye-consciousness, like the white insect, is distinct and arises separately in the prenascent eye-base, like the coloured water. This also applies to the other five bases. So the materiality and the mentality which arises dependent on it are separate and apart from each other, and hence they are not associated.

The Relation between the Five Sense-objects and the Fivefold Consciousnesses is Not a Case of Dissociation. If materiality and mentality are dissociated, as in the examples given above, it might be assumed that, since the five sense-objects are materiality and the respective fivefold consciousnesses which arise taking them as object are mentality, the relation between them is also a case of dissociation. In Paṭṭh, however, dissociation condition is expounded only in those cases where there is the likelihood that it might appear to be associated. Here the sense-objects are external to the fivefold consciousnesses, and, being just subject-object relations, the relation between them is not that of dissociation, and, therefore, the question does not arise as to whether they are associated or not. That is why they are not expounded here.

20. (d) Postnascence-Dissociation

This condition was expounded to dispel any doubt that may arise as to whether mentality, the conditioning state, and materiality, the conditioned state, of postnascence condition are associated or not. For in this case it might be regarded as associated because the nascent phase of mentality, the conditioning state which arises later, coincides with the static phase of materiality, the conditioned state that had arisen earlier. This condition is the same as postnascence condition.

21. Presence Condition (*atthi-paccaya*)

Definition. The condition where a conditioning state, at the moment of its presence, relates by supporting the other states, the conditioned states, which have also arisen at that moment, is known as presence condition.

Analogy. This condition is like the earth, Mount Meru, and the Himalaya mountains which, by their presence, support the trees, herbs, etc., growing on them by keeping those trees, etc., fresh and green and increasing their nutritive power.

Forces of Presence Condition. Presence condition has two forces, that of production and of support. The conditioning state, which possesses these two forces, is not prominent at its nascent and cessant phases but only at the static phase. Therefore, although the force of production functions at the nascent phase, that of support at the static phase is its essential function.

Nibbāna is Not a Conditioning State of Presence Condition. Since in presence condition, the conditioning state which relates is one that is present at the moment then, Nibbāna, the ultimate reality which is always present, could be regarded as a conditioning state. But it is only as the object of Path- and Fruition-consciousness, etc., that Nibbāna is a conditioning state. And Nibbāna is a state that is unconditioned, permanently present and time-freed, i.e. void of the nascent, static, and cessant phases. But this permanent presence is not the kind intended here. For in this condition a state can be a conditioning state only when it is a presently arisen one, otherwise it is not. So the states concerned are those that are impermanent and conditioned by the four causes, i.e. those that arise and cease. Therefore, Nibbāna, which does not arise and cease but is eternally present, is not a conditioning state of presence condition.

Kinds of Presence Condition. There are 5, 6, 9, and 14 kinds as shown below:

The 5 kinds. These are (1) conascence-presence, (2) prenascence-presence, (3) postnascence-presence, (4) physical nutriment-presence, (5) physical life-faculty-presence.

The 6 kinds. When (2) prenascence-presence condition above is differentiated as (i) object-prenascence-presence and (ii) base-prenascence-presence, there are 6 kinds.

The 9 kinds. When the 3 mixed conditions of the Faultless Triplet: (i) conascence-prenascence-presence, (ii) postnascence-nutriment-presence, (iii) postnascence-faculty-presence, are taken with the 6 above, there are 9 kinds.

The 14 kinds. When, in addition, the other 5 mixed conditions of the 24 divisions of Paṭṭh: (i) object-prenascence-base-prenascence, (ii) conascence-faculty-prenascence-faculty, (iii) conascence-postnascence,

(iv) postnascence-nutriment-faculty, (v) object-prenascence-base-prenascence-conascence are taken, there are 14 kinds.

Since Faultless Triplet is dealt with here, only those 9 kinds of presence condition that belong to it will be considered.

21. (a) Object-Prenascence-Presence

This is the same as object-prenascence condition given under Prenascence Condition.

How the Conditioning and Conditioned States are Related. Take the case of an eye-door mental process which occurs with a very great visible object that arises with past life-continuum. There arise and cease in succession: five-door advertence, eye-consciousness, recipient consciousness, investigating consciousness, determining consciousness, seven impulsions, and two registering consciousnesses. At the time each of them is present the visible object is related to that particular one present by the force of object-prenascence condition. Here, the external visible object is the conditioning state, and each kind of consciousness such as five-door advertence which is present at that moment is the conditioned state.

When Registering Consciousness is Not a Conditioned State. In the cases of the other eye-door mental processes which occur with great visible object and others, visible object is related to each of the consciousnesses as shown above with the exception of the two registering consciousnesses. The reason is that the span of existence of the visible object, the conditioning state, ends before those consciousnesses can arise, and since the latter are no longer present they cannot be conditioned states.

21. (b) Conascence-Presence

This is the same as conascence condition.

21. (c) Base-Prenascence-Presence

This is the same as base-prenascence-dependence condition.

21. (d) Postnascence-Presence

This is the same as postnascence condition.

21. (e) Physical Nutriment-Presence

This is the same as physical nutriment condition.

21. (f) Physical Life-Faculty-Presence

This is the same as physical life-faculty condition.

21. (g) Mixed Conascence-Prenascence-Presence

Conascence and base-prenascence conditions are dealt with together as conascence-prenascence-presence condition.

21. (h) Mixed Postnascence-Nutriment-Presence

Postnascence and physical nutriment conditions are dealt with together as postnascence-nutriment-presence condition.

21. (i) Mixed Postnascence-Faculty-Presence

Postnascence and physical life-faculty conditions are dealt with together as postnascence-faculty-presence condition.

The three mixed conditions above are treated in the Classification Chapter of the Investigation Chapter.

Contemplation on Presence Condition. The states of materiality and mentality, which arise together to carry out their respective functions and are present at every moment, are related to one another by presence condition. But these states are not permanent, for they cease soon after they have arisen. However, the successive arisings and ceasings take place so rapidly that they appear to be present all the time. Thus they give rise to the concepts of continuity, collection, form, and action in the mind. As a consequence, various forms, images, and the drama of life are visualised in the mind. Of course these concepts do exist, but only in the realm of the mind, i.e. not independent of or outside the mind as are the momentary material and mental states from which they are derived. These operations of the mind are similar to those that take place whereby forms, images, and the drama of a story are visualised and mentally projected on the cinema screen when one watches the momentarily present shadows that are projected in rapid succession on that screen.

It has to be realised, therefore, that such forms, images, and the drama of life of oneself or of another are due to the activities of the mind on the past and present states of materiality and mentality and are not real like them but simply conceptual objects of mind-consciousness element and its associated states (subjective mind for short) that had arisen along with the subjective materiality at that moment. Then when there is awareness that it is the subjective mind which takes those concepts as objects and attention is directed to the subjective mind:

(i) Those concepts will disappear because they are no longer taken as objects at such moments. This may be compared to a self-destructive machine with all its parts connected together and which, remaining at a standstill, is calm and quiet. However, once the switch for its operation is turned on, all the various parts start to break into small pieces which scatter in all directions and the machine disappears because it is destroyed.

(ii) Greed and the other corruptions cannot arise because no images are taken. For it has to be remembered that corruptions arise only when unwise reflection is made on images. For although the image may be discriminated as beautiful, pleasant, cultured, estimable, or lovable, unless there is unwise reflection on it there can be no delight for it for greed to arise.

Moreover, there cannot be any self-existent entity present because, according to presence condition, one state is present because another state is present or for one state to be present there must be another state related by presence condition. So, at any moment, there must be at least two states present. Therefore, it will be realised that the states of materiality and mentality of presence condition are collectively taken as a unit for the purpose of communicating about them in the briefest way possible since the image derived from them is worded as "I", "self", "being", "person", "man", "woman", and these are then further distinguished as "John", "Mary", etc. Being ignorant of the presence of the subjective mind that takes those words as objects when they are recalled to mind, spoken, or written (for only mentality can take words as objects) those words, which are really objective states, are taken as unitary, subjective states. Besides, these words are taken to be the subject in grammar. This is how wrong view of words has come about, i.e. of the view that they are subjective states which correspond with reality. Also, not being aware of the fact that words were coined in the mind of man for the purpose of expressing ideas of the various forms, images and actions in the briefest possible way, repeated use of them with the view that they represent reality has brought about deep attachment to that view. Hence, there was no need to enquire whether the view held was correct or not.

Other Types of Contemplation. Due to the force of:

(i) object-prenascence-presence condition, visible object, as the conditioning state, brings about the conditioned states of mentality, which are eye-consciousness and the seven primary mental factors, that see visible object. It is simply the result conditioned by the cause. Here the force of the above condition brings about the process of seeing. So it is not "I" that sees. Similarly, in the cases of hearing, smelling, tasting, touching, and thinking, "I" has no part in them;

(ii) conascence-presence condition, materiality, and mentality arise together in succession and are momentarily present. So it is not "I" that is present;

(iii) postnascence-presence condition, mentality, as the conditioning state, supports the four cause-produced matter so that, though the preceding ones cease, the succeeding ones which arise do not decay but remain fresh and active while they exist for their respective periods of existence. So it is not "I" that exists;

(iv) physical nutriment-presence condition, nutritive essence, as the conditioning state, supports the four cause-produced matter so that they are strong, fresh, and lively. So it is not "I" that is strong, fresh, and lively;

(v) physical life-faculty-presence condition, physical life-faculty, as the conditioning state, maintains the life of *kamma*-produced matter and makes it arise in continuous succession. So it is not "I" that has life and continues to exist.

It will be seen, from the above contemplation on presence condition, that the only things which presently arise at any moment are the states of materiality and mentality, the latter, of course, with an object. These states arise to carry out their respective functions and then cease. This is the natural state of affairs at any moment. But when there is ignorance of presence condition or there is no practical realisation of the nature of presence condition, the presence of the states of mentality (which arise when the functions of the subjective states of materiality and mentality that had ceased are recalled as objects and those states are then unified and personified) are entirely overlooked. So the unified or personified object is taken to be the only state present and to be subjective. Here are just two examples to show what is meant:

(i) After the ceasing of the eye-consciousness element and the associated seven primary mental factors which see the visible object, the mind-consciousness element and its associated states arise, sometimes, to recall the function of seeing of eye-consciousness (that had just ceased) as the object, and then another group of mentality takes that eye-consciousness element and its seven primary factors as "I", "person", "man", "woman", etc. For it is supposed that it is "I", "person", etc. that sees. Here a group of mental states is unified or personified as "I", "person", etc. Although these words are objects of the subjective states of mentality, the presence of the mental states is overlooked and so it is believed that "I", or "person", and so on, is the only state present and that it is subjective. This is how the wrong view that "I", "person", etc., exists has come about. At such times the subjective mind-consciousness element and its associated mental factors including wrong view arise with the reality of "I", "person", and so on, taken as the object. But it must be noted, however, that this wrong view of "I", "person", etc., is not taken after each and every natural process of seeing.

(ii) After the ceasing of the mind-consciousness element and its associated states which recalled the functions of the subjective states of materiality that had ceased, another group of mentality unifies those states as a solid body and takes it as object. Again, another group of mentality arises, sometimes, to recall the past body that was taken as object and regards it as "one's own" or "my" body. Here also, the presence of the group of mental states, which takes the words "one's own" or "my" as object, is overlooked, and so it is believed that "one's own" or "my" is the only state present and that it is subjective. This is how the wrong view that "one's own" or "my" exists has come about. At such times the subjective mind-consciousness element and its associated mental factors including wrong view arise with the reality of "one's own" or "my" taken as the object. But, as pointed out above, this wrong view is not taken every time.

So "I", "person", "my", etc. are merely objects taken by the subjective states of mentality present at that moment (the fundamental states that are generally overlooked) and such words exist only in the mind. They do not have separate existences in or apart from the states of materiality and mentality on which they are based. Nor are these states at the beck and call of an "I" or "Self" or whatnot at the back of them. For besides these mundane states, which are conditioned and impermanent and which appear at each moment owing to presence condition and disappear soon after, there is nothing else but the supramundane, unconditioned, eternal state of Nibbāna. As Nibbāna does not appear and disappear, it is, therefore, a signless, infinite state of peace that does not belong to presence condition and has no connection, whatsoever, with the mundane states of that condition.

22. Absence Condition (*natthi-paccaya*)

Definition. The condition where a mental state, the conditioning state, which, by its cessation, relates by giving the opportunity for the next mental state, the conditioned state, to arise, is known as absence condition.

Analogy. This condition is like the flame which, by its dying out, gives the opportunity for darkness to arise.

Conditioning and Conditioned States. These are the same as proximity condition.

Presence and Absence Conditions are Opposites. In presence condition the conditioning states are still present when the conditioned states arise. But in absence condition the conditioning states are absent and belong to the past when the conditioned states arise. This shows that the two conditions are the opposite of each other.

23. Disappearance Condition (*vigata-paccaya*)

Definition. The condition where a mental state, the conditioning state, which, by its disappearance, relates by giving the opportunity for the next mental state, the conditioned state, to arise, is known as disappearance condition.

Analogy. This condition is like sunlight which, by its disappearance, gives the opportunity for darkness to set in.

Conditioning and Conditioned States. These are the same as proximity condition.

The Difference between Absence and Disappearance Conditions.[34] When the conditioning states which relate are absent because they have ceased after going through the nascent, static and cessant phases, they are those of absence condition. But when the conditioning states which relate have disappeared after ceasing, they are those of disappearance condition.

24. Non-Disappearance Condition (*avigata-paccaya*)

Definition. The condition where a conditioning state, which has not disappeared but is still present, relates by supporting the other states, the conditioned states, which are also present at that moment, is known as non-disappearance condition.

---

[34] *natthitā ca nirodhānantara-suññatā. vigatatā nirodhappattatā. ayam etesaṃ viseso* (subcty, p. 175).

Analogy. This condition is like the ocean in which the fish, turtles, etc., can live coolly and comfortably as long as it has not disappeared.

The Nine Kinds of Non-disappearance Condition. These are the same as presence condition.

Disappearance and Non-disappearance Conditions are Opposites. In disappearance condition the conditioning states have disappeared when the conditioned states arise. But in non-disappearance condition the conditioning states have not disappeared when the conditioned states arise. This shows that the two conditions are the opposite of each other.

The Difference between Presence and Non-disappearance Conditions.[35] When the conditioning state which relates is an ultimate reality that is present at that moment and exhibiting its characteristic, it is that of presence condition. But when a conditioning state which relates is an ultimate reality that has not disappeared and ceased, it is that of non-disappearance condition.

Note. See *P.Pfn*., pp. 61122, for the explanations of the 24 conditions as given in the cty.

---

[35] *atthitāya sasabhāvatāya upakārakatā atthipaccayatā. sabhāvāvigamanena nirodhassa appattiyā upakārakatā avigata-paccayatā ti paccayabhāva-viseso dhammāvisese pi veditabbo* (subcty, p. 175).

III. Explanation of the Single Enumerations

Before going on to the explanation of the Analytical Exposition of the Conditions which forms Chapter II of *C.R.*, explanations are given about conditioning forces and common conditions as these are to be dealt with there. For this purpose the conditioning and conditioned states of the Single conditions and the enumerations obtained from them — known as Single Enumerations (*suddha-saṅkhyā*) — taken according to the method of the Classification Chapter of the Investigation Chapter have to be known. They are given in the Single Enumerations chart (SEC for short).[36]

It needs to be emphasised again that one who is desirous of understanding Paṭṭh should, first of all, acquire a thorough knowledge of the conditioning and conditioned states. For they are the fundamentals of Paṭṭh, just as the alphabet is for a language. And this Faultless Triplet Paṭṭh, the first Paṭṭh section, deals with the conditioning and conditioned states of the conditions concerned with the Faultless Triplet. Similarly, the remaining 129,231 Paṭṭh sections deal with the conditioning and conditioned states of the conditions concerned. Thus all the methods and explanations provided in this Guide must, of necessity, be concerned with these states. Therefore, the reader is requested to make a proper study of the conditioning and conditioned states given in the SEC.

[36]The Single Enumerations are the numbers of answers for the conditions taken "Singly" or "By Ones". Since these answers can be obtained only from the conditioning and conditioned states, the SEC gives these states. So this chart must be referred to for the conditioning and conditioned states of the condition concerned.

FAULTLESS TRIPLET — METHOD OF INVESTIGATION CHAPTER

I. CHART OF SINGLE ENUMERATIONS OF THE CONDITIONS* (SEC)

Conds.** Ser. No.	Kind	Conditioning States	Conditioned States	Enu.	Com. Conds. Comp.	App.
1. Ro		6 roots	71 rooted cons., 52 m.f. excluding delusion from 2 delusion-rooted cons.; rooted mind- and rooted rebirth *kamma*-produced matter	7		12***
2. Ob		89 cons., 52 m.f., 28 matter, Nibbāna, (concept)	89 cons., 52 mf.	9	1	
3. Pd	(a) Ob-pd	Predominant 18 produced matter; 84 cons. exclusive of 2 hate-rooted cons., 2 delusion-rooted cons., and bodily-pain cons. (i.e. 89 -5 = 84); 47 m.f. exclusive of hate, envy, stinginess, worry, and doubt (i.e. 52 -5 = 47); Nibbāna	Predominating 8 greed-rooted cons., 8 great functional cons. 4 great functional cons. assoc. with knowledge, 8 supramundane cons., 45 m.f. exclusive of hate, envy, stinginess, worry, doubt, and 2 illimitables (i.e. 52 -7 =45)	7	3	
	(b) Ob-prn-pd	Predominant 18 present produced matter	Predominating 8 greed-rooted cons.	1	6	
	(c) Ba-ob-prn-pd	At the dying process, the predominant last heart-base arising at the nascent phase of the 17th thought-moment reckoned backwards from death-cons.	Predominating 5 thought-moments of greed-rooted dying impulsions	1	8	
	(d) Cn-pd	One of the predominant factors, namely: desire, cons., effort, investigating-wisdom	52 predominant impulsions, 51 m.f. exlusive of doubt; predominant mind-produced matter	7		13
4. Px		Preceding 89 cons., 52	Subsequent 89 cons.,	7	5	

* Compare with those in Intro to *C.R.*, facing p. lxiv.

** Abbreviations: Conds. = Conditions; Com. = Common; Ser. = Serial; Enu. = Enumeration; Comp. = Completely; App. = Appropriately.

*** 12 includes root condition. It is the same for the other conditions.

Conds. Ser. No. Kind	Conditioning States	Conditioned States	Enu.	Com. Conds. Comp. App.
5. Ct	m.f. excluding Arahatta's death-cons.	52 m.f. including Arahatta's death-cons.		
6. Cn	(1) 4 m.agg. during life and at the moment of conception	4 m. agg. (mutually); mind- and rebirth *kamma*-produced matter	9	4
	(b) 4 gr.pr. of mind-produced, rebirth *kamma*-produced, external, nutriment-produced, temperature-produced, non-percipient beings' *kamma*-produced and during life *kamma*-produced matter	4 gr. pr. (mutually) and 24 derived matter	9	4
7. Mu	(a) 4 m.agg. during life and at the moment of conception	4 m.agg. (mutually) and heart-base	3	5
	(b) 4 gr. pr.	4 gr. pr. (utually)	3	5
	(c) 4 rebirth m.agg. and heart-base at the moment of conception in 5-agg. planes	4 rebirth m.agg. and heart-base (mutually)	3	5
8. Dp (a) Ba-ob-prn-dp	At the dying process, the last heart-base arising at the nascent phase of the 17th thought-moment reckoned backwards from death-cons.	Mind-door advertence, 5 sensuous dying impulsions, 11 registering cons.	3	6
(b) Cn-dp	Same as conascence condition		9	4
(c) Ba-prn-dp	6 bases during life in 5-agg. planes	7 cons. elements excluding 4 immaterial resultants, 52 m.f.	3	5
(d) Mixed Cn-prn	21 fls cons., 12 fty cons., 52 m.f. which are taken separately as 1, 3, 2, aggregates hearty-base which had arisen together with the preceding determining or mind-door advertence, etc., in 5-agg. planes	21 fls cons., 12 fty cons., 52 m.f. (mutually)	2	3

Conds. Ser. No. Kind	Conditioning States	Conditioned States	Enu.	Com. Conds. Comp.	App.
9. S.D. (a) Ob-S.D.	Same as object-predominance condition		7	3	
(b) P-S.D.	Same as proximity condition		7	5	
(c) Na S.D.	Natural strong 89 cons., 52 m.f., 28 matter and some concepts*	89 cons., 52 m.f.	9	1	
10. Prn (a) Ob-prn	18 present produced matter	54 sensuous cons., 52 m.f., Divine-eye and Divine-ear superknowledges	3	4	
(b) Ba-prn	Same as base-prenascence-dependence condition		3	5	
11. Pon	4 m.agg., i.e. subsequent first life-continuum, etc., excluding 4 immaterial resultants, during life in 5-agg. planes	Matter due to 1, 2, 3 or 4 causes (i.e. *kamma*, mind, temperature, nutriment) which had arisen together with the preceding rebirth-cons., etc., and reached the static phase	3	4	
12. Rp	47 preceding mundane impulsions exluding the last (impulsions)	Subsequent 51 impulsions excluding the first, and Fruition impulsions	3	6	
13. Kam (a) Cn-kam	Volition assoc. with 89 cons.	89 cons., 52 m.f. eclusive of volition; mind- and rebirth *kamma*-produced matter	7		10
(b) Px-kam	Volition assoc. with 4 Path cons.	4 Fruition cons. after Paths	1	6	
(c) S. asy. kam.	Strong faultless and faulty volition	36 resultant cons., 38 m.f.	2	2	
(d) S.&W. asy. kam.	(a) Weak asynchronous volition assoc. with great faultless and faulty cons.	23 sensuous resultant cons., 33 m.f.	2	1	

*Concepts are not considred in the enumeration.

Conds. Ser. No. Kind	Conditioning States	Conditioned States	Enu.	Com. Conds. Comp.	App.
	(b) Both strong and weak faultless and faulty volition in 5-agg. planes	*Kamma*-produced matter			
14. Rs	(a) 4 resultant m.agg. during life and at the moment of conception	4 resultant m.agg. (mutually); mind- and rebirth *kamma*-produced matter	1	5	
	(b) 4 rebirth m.agg. at the moment of conception in 5-agg. planes	hear-base			
15. Nu (a) Cn-nu.	Contact, volition, and cons.	89 cons., 52 m.f.; mind- and rebirth *kamma*-produced matter	7		12
(b) Phy-nu	Nutritive essence produced by 4 causes, namely: *kamma*, mind, temperature, and nutriment	Matter produced by 4 causes which are (i) in the same group by excluding nutritive essence and (ii) in the different groups	1	3	
16. Fa (a) Cn-fa	8 factors of mental faculty, namely: psychic life, cons., feeling, confidence, effort, mindfulness, one-pointedness and knowledge	89 cons., 52 m.f.; mind-and rebirth *kamma*-produced matter	7		14
(b) Ba-prn-fa	5 sentient faculties which had arisen at the static phase of past life-continuum	twice fivefold cons., 7 primary m.f.	1	6	
(c) Phy life-fa	Physical life-faculty	All the 9 groups of *kamma*-produced matter excluding physical life from the same group	1	3	
17. Jha	5 *jhāna* factors, namely: applied thought, sustrained thought, rapture, feeling, and one-pointedness	79 cons. exclusive of twice fivefold cons., 52 m.f.; mind- and rebirth *kamma*-produced matter	7		11
18. Pa	9 path factors, namely: knowledge, applied	71 rooted cons., 52 m.f., rooted mind-	7		13

Conds. Ser. No. Kind	Conditioning States	Conditioned States	Enu.	Com. Conds. Comp. App.
	thought, 3 abstinences, effort, mindfulness, one-pointedness and wrong view	and rooted rebirth *kamma*-produced matter		
19. Ass	4 m.agg. during life at the moment of conception	4 m.agg. (mutually)	3	6
20. Dss (a) Ba-ob-prn-dss	Same as base-object-prenascence-dependence condition		3	6
(b) Cn-dss	(i) 75 cons. exclusive of 4 immaterial result-tant cons. twice five-fold cons.andArahatta's death cons. (i.e. 89 - 14 = 75), 52 m.f. which are 4 m.agg. during life and at the moment of conception in 5-agg. planes	Mind- and rebirth *kamma*-produced matter		
	(ii) 4 rebirth m.agg. and heart-base at the moment of conception in 5-agg. planes	4 rebirth m.agg. and heart-base in 5 agg. planes (mutually)		
(c) Ba-prn-dss	Same as base-prenascence-dependence condition		3	5
(d) Pon-dss	Same as postnascence condition		3	4
21. Ps (a) Ob-prn-ps	Same as object-prenascence condition		3	4
(b) Cn-ps	Same as conascence condition		9	4
(c) Ba-prn-ps	Same as base-prenascence condition		3	5
(d) Pon-ps	Same as postnascence condition		3	4
(e) Phy-nu-ps	Same as physical nutriment condition		1	3
(f) Phy life-fas-ps	Same as phsycial life-faulty condition		1	3

Conds. Ser. No.	Kind	Conditioning States	Conditioned States	Enu.	Com. Conds. Comp.	App.
	(g) Mixed Cn-prn-ps	Same as mixed conascence-prenascence-dependence condition		2		3
	(h) Mixed Pon-nu-ps	21 faultless cons., 12 fault cons., 52 m.f. which are aggregates taken separately as 1, 3, 2, a d all 4 + nutriment present in matter which ahd arisen together with the preceding determining cons. or mind-door advertence, etc., and reached the static phase in 5-agg. planes	Matter due to 3 or 4 causes which had arisen together with the preceding determining cons. or mind-door advertence, etc. and reached the static phase at the same time together	2		2
	(i) Mixed Pon-fa-ps	... + physical life ... as above	Matter due to *kamma* which ... (as above)	2		2
22. Ab		Same as proximity condition		7		5
23. Dsp						
24. N.D.		Same as presence condition		13	19*	

1. Root Condition (*hetu-paccayo*)

How to Read the SEC. The 6 roots are related to 71 rooted consciousnesses, 52 mental factors excluding delusion from the 2 delusion-rooted consciousnesses; rooted mind- and rooted rebirth *kamma*-produced matter by root condition; enumeration 7; common conditions 12 completely and appropriately. This is the way to read the rest of the chart. (When the figure for common conditions is given under "completely", "appropriately" does not apply.)

Explanation

Conditioning States (*paccaya-dhammā*). These are the 6 roots: greed, hate, delusion, non-greed, non-hatenon-delus, non-delusion.

---

*Exclusive of proximity, contiguity, repetition, absence, and disappearance conditions.

Conditioned States (*paccayuppanna-dhammā*). Root condition belongs to the conascence group of conditions as shown in chart II (A) on Grouped Conditions in the Intr. to *C.R.*, p. liii.[37] It was already mentioned in the Brief Explanations of the Conditions given above (where the definition of conascence condition was dealt with) that, in this condition, the conditioning states must be related to the mental and material states, the conditioned states, that arise together with them. Therefore, for root condition also (which is of the conascence group) the 6 roots, the conditioning states, must be related to the mental and material states, the conditioned states, that arise together with them.

Conditioned Mental States. The mental states which arise together with the 6 roots are the conditioned mental states. These are 71 rooted consciousnesses and 52 mental factors excluding delusion from the 2 delusion-rooted consciousnesses. Delusion from each of the 2 delusion-rooted consciousnesses is excluded because it is not associated with another root, and, being the only root present, it can only be a conditioning state but never a conditioned state in these cases. But this does not reduce the number of mental factors from 52 to 51. The reason is that delusion is a conditioned state in the other cases. For when greed (of greed-rooted consciousnesses which has 2 roots, greed and delusion) or hate (of hate-rooted consciousnesses which has 2 roots, hate and delusion) is a conditioning state, delusion is a conditioned state. As for the remaining 18 (89 -71) rootless consciousnesses, they have no roots and, therefore, they can never be conditioned states of root condition.

Conditioned Material States. They are also known as conascent matter (*sahajāta-rūpa*). These are rebirth *kamma*-produced matter at the moment of conception and mind-produced matter during life. The nascent phase of rebirth consciousness is known as the "moment of conception", and the matter produced at that moment is known as rebirth *kamma*-produced matter. The period from the static phase of rebirth-consciousness to death-consciousness is known as "during life",

---

[37]See chart to know the group to which a condition belongs.

and the matter produced by each consciousness during this period is known as mind-produced matter. Here, they are said to be rooted mind- and rooted rebirth *kamma*-produced matter because they arise together with rooted mentality.

The detailed classification of the conditioning and conditioned states is given in the explanation of the Analytical Exposition of the Conditions which follows.

Enumeration (*saṅkhyā*) 7. This is the number of answers that can be given for the set of 49 questions with root condition (see Intr. to *C.R.*, pp. xlix–li).

What the 7 answers are. These are obtained from the conditioning and conditioned states of root condition.

Conditioning States. The 6 roots, which are the conditioning states, are classified under three heads: faultless, faulty, and indeterminate. Non-greed, non-hate, and non-delusion are the 3 faultless roots; greed, hate, and delusion are the 3 faulty roots; non-greed, non-hate, and non-delusion are the 3 indeterminate (resultant and functional) roots. So the conditioning states can be faultless, faulty, or indeterminate.

Relations with the Conditioned States. The possible relations are:

(i) When the 3 faultless roots are related to 21 faultless consciousnesses and 38 mental factors (the faultless conditioned states) which arise together with them, it is said that faultless state is related to faultless state, i.e. fls-fls. This is one answer.

(ii) When the 3 faultless roots are related to mind-produced matter (the indeterminate conditioned state) which arises together with them, it is said that faultless state is related to indeterminate state, i.e. fls-ind. This is another answer. From what has been explained above about this matter, it will be noted that this relation occurs during life.

(iii) When the 3 faultless roots are related to 21 faultless consciousnesses and 38 mental factors (the faultless conditioned states) and mind-produced matter (the indeterminate conditioned state) that arise together with them, it is said that faultless state is related to faultless (state) and indeterminate state, i.e. fls-fls, ind. This is another answer. So, with the faultless roots as the conditioning states there are three answers.

Occurrence of the Above Relations in the Planes. Of the 3 relations with the faultless given above, (i) has faultless states as conditioned states, and so, the relation being between mental states, it occurs in 30 out of 31 planes. The remaining plane, the non-percipient plane, where only matter arises, is excluded; (ii) and (iii) have matter as conditioned states, and so they occur in the 26 five-aggregate planes. The 4 immaterial planes are excluded because matter does not arise in them, and the non-percipient plane is excluded because only matter arises in that plane. It will be seen, therefore, that root condition does not occur in the non-percipient plane. The occurrence of the 24 conditions in the different planes, as given in the cty, is shown later by charts; (iv)–(vi) When the 3 faulty roots are the conditioning states, they are related like the faultless roots, i.e. (iv) fty-fty, (v) fty-ind, (vi) fty-fty, ind. So, with the faulty roots as conditioning states, there are three answers also. The faulty conditioned states are 12 faulty consciousnesses and 27 mental factors excluding delusion from the 2 delusion-rooted consciousnesses. The reason for excluding this delusion was given above. (vii) The 3 indeterminate roots, non-greed, non-hate, and non-delusion are the conditioning states both during life and at the moment of conception. When, during life, the 3 resultant and 3 functional roots are related to (1) 21 rooted resultant consciousnesses, 17 rooted functional consciousnesses, and 38 mental factors or (2) rooted mind-produced matter or (3), both (1) the mentality and (2) the materiality together — as in the cases of the faultless and faulty — all of them are indeterminate conditioned states. Thus indeterminate state is related to indeterminate state, i.e. ind-ind. Here, there is only one relation and not three as with the faultless and faulty roots.

Also, at the moment of conception, the 3 rebirth (resultant) roots are related to (1) 17 rooted rebirth (resultant) consciousnesses and 35 mental factors, (2) rooted rebirth *kamma*-produced matter and (3) both (1) the mentality and (2) the materiality together. All of them are indeterminate conditioned states. Thus indeterminate state is related to indeterminate state. So here also there is only one relation, ind-ind. Therefore, with the indeterminate roots as conditioning states there is only one answer.

When the separate relations are determined from the appropriate conditioning and conditioned states of root condition, in the manner shown above, it is found that only 7 are possible. In other words, there are only 7 answers, i.e. the enumeration is 7. This method of determining the enumeration from the conditioning and conditioned states of root condition has to be applied not only from those of the other conditions in this Faultless Triplet Paṭṭh section, but also from those of the conditions in all the other 129,231 Paṭṭh sections.

Common Conditions (*sabhāga-paccaya*). The reason why root condition has 12 common conditions (as shown under the "Common Conditions" column of the SEC and the Minor Conascence Group chart, chart II (C),[38] facing p. lxiv in the Intr. to *C.R.*) needs to be given. As mentioned before, root condition belongs to the conascence group of conditions. This group consists of 15 conditions divided under three heads: (1) Major conascence, of which there are 4: conascence, conascence-dependence, conascence-presence, conascence-non-disappearance; (2) Medium conascence, of which there are 4: mutuality, resultant, association, conascence-dissociation; (3) Minor conascence, of which there are 7: root, conascence-predominance, conascence-*kamma*, conascence-nutriment, conascence-faculty, *jhāna*, path. The conditions that are common with root condition will be found only in this group of 15 conditions and not in a different group such as the object group. For the conditions are grouped together according to certain features which are common to them, and so one group is separate and distinct from the other. This may be compared to different beliefs held by persons and which have nothing in common.

For root condition (which is the particular condition under consideration), there are 12 conditions out of the 15 in the conascence

[38]See appropriate Group chart in the case of the other conditions.

group which are common. That is to say, all or parts of the conditioning and conditioned states of root condition are included in these 12 conditions. This is what is meant by saying that root condition has 12 common conditions. Of course, root condition is included in the 12. So it now remains to show that all or parts of the conditioning and conditioned states of root condition are included in the other 11 conditions, i.e. that root condition is common with the other 11 conditions.

(1) *Root and Predominance Conditions.* On examination of the conditioning and conditioned states of root and predominance (conascence-predominance) conditions given in the SEC, it is found that non-delusion, one of the roots of root condition, and investigating-wisdom predominance of predominance condition, which are conditioning states, come under the same reality, knowledge. But whereas the former is associated with 47 three-rooted consciousnesses, the latter is associated with 34 three-rooted predominant impulsions. From this it will be seen that the conditioning and conditioned states of investigating-wisdom predominance are common to the two conditions. So investigating-wisdom is the common conditioning state and 34 three-rooted predominant impulsions, 37 mental factors exclusive of investigating-wisdom, and predominant mind-produced matter are the common conditioned states. Thus parts of the conditioning and conditioned states of root condition are included in those of predominance condition, i.e. root condition is common with predominance condition. The method of determining the commons of the conditions was given briefly in the Intr. to *C.R.*, pp. li–liv. They will be dealt with in detail in the Explanation of the Investigation Chapter.

(2) *Root and Conascence Conditions.* Conascence condition has all the conditioning and conditioned states, and, therefore, all those of root condition, which are included in them, are common, i.e. root condition is common with conascence condition.

(3) *Root and Mutuality Conditions.* All the mental states are both conditioning and conditioned states of mutuality condition, and, there-

fore, those of root condition are the common mental states. But with regard to the material states in the conditioned states, mind-produced matter is not a conditioned state of mutuality condition, and only heart-base, which is rebirth *kamma*-produced matter, is common to both the conditions. Thus the common conditioning states are the 6 roots, and the common conditioned states are 71 rooted consciousnesses, 52 mental factors excluding delusion from the 2 delusion-rooted consciousnesses and heart-base. So all the conditioning states and part of the conditioned states of root condition are included in those of mutuality condition, i.e. root condition is common with mutuality condition.

(4)–(6) *Root, Dependence, Presence, and Non-disappearance-conditions.* As in the case of conascence condition, dependence, presence and non-disappearance conditions have all the conditioning and conditioned states, and, therefore, all the conditioning and conditioned states of root condition are included in those of each of these three conditions, i.e. root condition is common with the dependence, presence, and non-disappearance conditions.

(7) *Root and Resultant Conditions.* The common conditioning states are the 3 resultant roots, and the common conditioned states are 21 rooted resultant consciousnesses, 38 mental factors, resultant rooted mind- and rooted rebirth *kamma*-produced matter. Thus parts of the conditioning and conditioned states of root condition are included in those of resultant condition, i.e. root condition is common with the resultant condition.

(8)–(9) *Root, Faculty, and Path Conditions*. Non-delusion, a root of root condition, knowledge of faculty (conascence-faculty) condition, and knowledge of path condition, which are conditioning states, come under the same reality, knowledge. And each is associated with 47 three-rooted consciousnesses. So the common conditioning state is non-delusion and the common conditioned states are 47 three-rooted consciousnesses, 37 mental factors exclusive of non-delusion, rooted mind- and rooted rebirth *kamma*-produced matter. Thus parts of the conditioning and conditioned states of root condition are included in those of the 2 conditions, i.e. root condition is common with faculty and path conditions.

(10) *Root and Association Conditions*. Materiality is not included in the association condition, but all the mental states are both conditioning and conditioned states. So the 6 roots are the common conditioning states, and all the mental states of root condition are the common conditioned states. Thus all the conditioning states and part of the conditioned states of root condition are included in those of association condition, i.e. root condition is common with the association condition.

(11) *Root and Dissociation Conditions*. When mental states are conditioning states in dissociation (conascence-dissociation) condition, there are no mental states as conditioned states. In this case there are no mental states as common conditioned states. So the 6 roots are the common conditioning states, and rooted mind- and rooted rebirth *kamma*-produced matter are the common conditioned states. Thus all the conditioning states and part of the conditioned states of root condition are included in those of dissociation condition, i.e. root condition is common with the dissociation condition.

Root Condition is not Common with 3 Conditions. Volition of *kamma* (conascence-*kamma*) condition; contact, volition, and consciousness of nutriment (conascence-nutriment) condition; 5 *jhāna* factors of *jhāna* condition are the mental states which are the conditioning states of these 3 remaining conditions of the conascence group. As the roots are not included as conditioning states, the roots of root condition cannot be common with them. Therefore, root condition is not common with *kamma*, nutriment, and *jhāna* conditions of the conascence group.

The above shows that root condition is common with itself and with the other 11 conditions, i.e. root condition has 12 common conditions. This method of determining the commons with root condition has been given in detail so that it can be applied to the other conditions which will be dealt with briefly.

Completely (*paripuṇṇa*)[39] *and Appropriately* (*yathārahaṃ*). In the AEC[40] it is stated that "The roots are related to the states which are associated with roots, and the matter produced thereby, by root condition." From this it would appear that the relation applies only to root condition. But this is not so. For, as shown above, the roots are related to their associated states and matter, not only by root condition alone, but also by the other 11 conditions. And it will be noted that in the case of each of: (1) the 5 conditions: root, conascence, dependence, presence, and non-disappearance, all the conditioning and conditioned states of root condition are included, i.e. the whole of root condition is included. Therefore, it is said that root condition occurs "completely" in these 5 conditions; (2) the remaining 7 conditions: predominance, mutuality, resultant, faculty, path, association, and dissociation, only parts of the conditioning and conditioned states of root condition or the whole of either of them are included but not all of them as in (1) above, i.e. the appropriate parts of root condition. Therefore, it is said that root condition occurs "appropriately" in these 7 conditions. This can be seen from the Common under Root Condition, *C.R.*, p. 180, item 440, where the 5 conditions in which root condition occurs completely have the same enumeration 7 as root condition, and the remaining 7 have less. So root condition (i.e. the conditioning and conditioned states of root condition) occurs completely and appropriately in the 12 common conditions.

Here the particular condition dealt with is root condition and so only the conditioning force of root condition present amongst those of the 12 common conditions in which it occurs completely and appropriately is taken into account. This goes to show that a particular conditioning force never acts alone but always in combination with those of

---

[39]The translation of *nissesa* in *akauk* is "simultaneously" as given in the charts facing p. lxiv in Intr. to *C.R.* But this is somewhat misleading because it will be found from the explanations given that the conditions in which root condition occurs appropriately also occur simultaneously.

[40]AEC = Analytical Exposition of the Conditions.

the other conditions which are common with it. That is why the Investigation Chapter deals with the commons and combinations.

2. Object Condition (*ārammaṇa-paccayo*)

Conditioning and Conditioned States. These are given in the SEC. They are different from those given in chart II (B) facing p. lxiv in Intr. to *C.R.* There, the Investigation Chapter is considered, and since it deals only with ultimate realities, concept is not taken as a conditioning state and the 21 consciousnesses: 15 fine-material, 3 infinity of space, and 3 nothingness, which take concept as object, are excluded from the conditioned states. But in the AEC, where concept is dealt with, the above states are included.

Enumeration 9. The conditioning states which are faultless, faulty, and indeterminate are selected just as in the case of the 6 roots, the conditioning states of root condition. Then the relations with the conditioned states are found. Since faultless state can take faultless state as object, there is the relation, (i) fls-fls.[41] Also, faulty state can take faultless state as object, i.e. (ii) fls-fty. And indeterminate state can take faultless state as object, i.e. (iii) fls-ind. So there are 3 answers for the faultless section. Similarly, there are 3 relations each for the faulty and indeterminate sections, i.e. (iv) fty-fty, (v) fty-fls, (vi) fty-ind, (vii) ind-ind, (viii) ind-fls, (ix) ind-fty. So there is a total of 9 answers, i.e. enumeration 9.

Common Condition 1. The object group[42] consists of the following 8 conditions: (1) object, (2) object-predominance, (3) base-object-prenascence-dependence, (4) object-strong-dependence, (5) object-prenascence (6) base-object-prenascence-dissociation, (7) object-prenascence-presence, (8) object-prenascence-non-disappearance. When the

---

[41]How faultless states, etc. can take faultless states, etc., as objects, as given later in the detailed chart on Object Condition, will be understood when the Classification Chapter of the Investigation Chapter is explained.

[42]See Grouped Conditions chart II (A) on p. liii and chart II (B) facing p. lxiv of *C.R.*

conditioning and conditioned states of these conditions in the object group are examined, it will be found that object condition has the greatest number of them. Therefore, it is the leader of this group. So object condition is the only condition in that group which occurs completely. That is why it is said to have 1 common condition.[43] Thus when object condition is the particular condition under consideration, there is no other common condition in which it occurs completely, and so there is no combination with it. The other two cases where the common condition is 1 are (1) natural strong-dependence condition which is the leader of the group of 2 conditions and (2) strong-and-weak asynchronous *kamma* which is the only condition in the group.

In object condition the objective states (*ārammaṇa-dhammā*) are related to the subjective states (*ārammaṇika-dhammā*), i.e. the relation is between subject and object. The objective states can be of the present, past, or future. The classification of the 24 conditions according to period (*kāla*) is given later in the chart on Miscellaneous Decisions.

3. Predominance Condition (*adhipati-paccayo*)

From the SEC it will be seen that there are four kinds: (a) object-predominance, (b) object-prenascence-predominance, (c) base-object-prenascence-predominance, (d) conascence-predominance.

3. (a) Object-Predominance (*ārammaṇādhipati*)

This condition belongs to the object group. It is dealt with after conascence-predominance in the AEC. But in the Investigation Chapter this order is reversed and, since the method of this Chapter is being considered here, the latter order is taken. This is in accordance with the

---

[43]Object condition is common with the other conditions of the object group, but it occurs appropriately in them. But this is not considered here because the particular condition dealt with is object condition, i.e. all the conditioning and conditioned states of object condition, and no other condition in the group has all of them. In the case of root condition, however, it does not have all the conditioning and conditioned states of the conascence group, and, therefore, those conditions in the group with which it is common and in which it occurs both completely and appropriately have to be taken.

sequence in the "Selection of the Conditions for Negative" chart, Intr. to *C.R.*, p. lviii. But this reason for the difference in the sequence is not mentioned either in the cty or subcty.

Enumeration 7. From the detailed chart on object-predominance given later, it can be found that there are 7 answers, i.e. enumeration 7. Unlike object condition with enumeration 9, the 2 answers (i) fty-fls and (ii) ftyind are not possible. For (i) the faulty states cannot be related to faultless states in this condition since one cannot esteem and review with faultlessness the faulty acts that one has done, and (ii) faulty states cannot be related to indeterminate states since no indeterminate state esteems and reviews faulty states. The indeterminate states, which are the conditioned states of this condition, are the 4 great functional consciousnesses associated with knowledge which esteem and review Arahatta Path, Arahatta Fruition or Nibbāna; and the 4 Fruitions (of the 8 supramundane consciousnesses) take Nibbāna as estimable object.

Common Conditions 3. As pointed out above, object condition is the leader of the object group because it has the greatest number of conditioning and conditioned states of the conditions in that group. Therefore, the conditioning and conditioned states of the other 7 conditions in the group are included in those of object condition. Since object-predominance, which is considered here, is one of the conditions in this group, all its conditioning and conditioned states are included in those of object condition, i.e. it is common with and occurs completely in object condition. Also, object-predominance and object strong-dependence of the group have the same conditioning and conditioned states,[44] and so the former is common with and occurs completely in the latter. Thus object-predominance, which is a kind of predominance condition, occurs completely in the 3 common conditions: object, predominance, and strong-dependence. And it is based on this fact that the combination "Combination of object, predominance and strong-dependence [there are] 7 [answers]" is given in *C.R.*, p. 182, item 445.1.

---

[44]See object group, chart II (B), facing p. lxiv in *C.R.* The appropriate charts to be referred to in *C.R.* will be known by now.

3. (b) Object-Prenascence-Predominance (*ārammaṇa-purejātādhipati*) This is not expounded as a separate kind of predominance condition. It is included in the object group[45] so as to be able to determine the common "With predominance condition and prenascence 1" and the combination "Of predominance, object, strong-dependence, prenascence, presence, and non-disappearance 1" in *C.R.*, p. 183, items 446 and 448.5.

Conditioning and Conditioned States. When a comparison is made of the conditioning and conditioned states of object-prenascence-predominance and object-predominance conditions given in the SEC, it will be found that both have predominant 18 present produced matter as the conditioning states and predominating 8 greed-rooted consciousnesses as the conditioned states. The other conditioned states of object-predominance — the predominating 8 great faultless consciousnesses and the 4 great functional consciousnesses associated with knowledge — are not included in object-prenascence-predominance. What is the reason for this?

Answer. This is not given in the cty. But it is obvious from *C.R.*, p. 148, item 416 (x) which shows that only greed-rooted consciousnesses (lust and wrong views) arise when matter is taken as estimable object, i.e. ind-fty. And in the relations, ind-ind and ind-fls, given on the same page for object-predominance, it is not stated that great functional (indeterminate) or great faultless consciousnesses arise with matter taken as estimable object. So these 2 relations are not possible. Moreover, in the common and combination quoted above, the answer is 1 and not 3. Therefore, when one takes the visible object (matter) of the Buddha as estimable object, faultless consciousness does not arise but a greed-rooted one. For example, in Dhp-a III 53, it is stated:

> When the season of the rains had passed and the Terminal Festival had been celebrated, the Teacher informed Sakka, "Great King, it is my intention to return to the path of men." Thereupon Sakka created three ladders, one of

[45]See chart II (B), facing p. lxiv in *C.R.*

> gold, one of jewels, and one of silver. The feet of these ladders rested against the gate of the city Saṅkassa, and their tops against the summit of Mount Sineru. On the right side was the ladder of gold for the deities (*devas*), on the left side the ladder of silver for Mahā-Brahmā and his train, and in the middle the ladder of jewels for the Tathagata. On the occasion of the Descent of the Gods (*devas*), the Teacher, standing on the summit of Mount Sineru, performed the "Twin-miracle" and looked up. There was a clear view of the nine worlds of Brahmā. As he looked down he had a clear view as far as the Avīci Hell. Then he looked forth to the four cardinal points and to the four intermediate points, and there was a clear view of countless thousands of worlds. Gods (*devas*) looked upon men, and men looked upon gods (*devas*); in all that assembly, thirty-six leagues in circuit, not one looked upon the glory of the Buddha that day but desired for himself the estate of a Buddha.

Here desire, which is greed, arises when the glory of the Buddha which is visible object is taken as estimable object. Thus only greed-consciousness arises when matter is taken as estimable object.

Enumeration 1. There is only one relation, as explained above, between produced matter (indeterminate) and greed-rooted consciousness (faulty), i.e. ind-fty. So there is only one answer, i.e. enumeration 1.

Common Conditions 6. Object-prenascence-predominance belongs to the object group and is part of object-prenascence condition and also of object-prenascence-presence and object-prenascence-non-disappearance, which are all the same. So it is common with 4 conditions: object, prenascence, presence, and non-disappearance. It is also part of object-predominance and, therefore, of object-strong-dependence as they are the same. So it is also common with predominance and strong-dependence conditions. Thus object-prenascence-predominance condition occurs completely in 6 common conditions.

3. (c) Base-Object-Prenascence-Predominance (*vatthārammaṇa-purejātādhipati*)

This is not expounded as a separate kind of predominance condition. It is included in the object group so as to be able to determine the common "With dependence condition and strong-dependence 1" (*C.R.*, p. 188, item 461) and the combination "Of dependence, object, predominance, strong-dependence, prenascence, dissociation, presence, and non-disappearance 1" (*C.R.*, p. 189, item 463.9). For this condition is common with object-strong-dependence and base-object-prenascence-dependence conditions.

Enumeration 1. Here heart-base, the conditioning state, is related to 5 greed-rooted consciousnesses, the conditioned states, i.e. ind-fty. So there is only one answer, i.e. enumeration 1.

Common Conditions 8. This condition is part of object-prenascence-predominance condition which, as shown above, has 6 common conditions. And since "base" is included, it is also part of base-object-prenascence-dependence and of base-object-prenascence-dissociation as both of them are the same, i.e. the conditioning and conditioned states are the same. Therefore, it is also common with dependence and dissociation conditions. Thus base-object-prenascence-predominance condition occurs completely in the 8 common conditions.

3. (d) Conascence-Predominance (*sahajātadhipati*)

Conditioning States. The 4 predominant conditioning states were dealt with in the Brief Explanations of the Conditions. They occur during life only, and so there are no answers for "at the moment of conception". It was already learnt that out of the total of 55 impulsions that were listed, 52 are predominant impulsions. The remaining 3, 2 delusion-rooted consciousnesses and the Arahatta's smile-consciousness, do not perform the function of predominance as they do not require preliminary preparations. In the case of the former there are wavering and restlessness; and of the latter, great deeds are not involved with it. Predominant desire and predominant effort are each associated with 52 predominant impulsions; predominant consciousnesses are the 52 predominant impulsions; predominant investigating-wisdom is associated with 34 three-rooted predominant impulsions.

Conditioned States. In accordance with the nature of conascence — since this condition belongs to the conascence group — the 52 predominant impulsions and 51 mental factors exclusive of doubt (because delusion-rooted consciousnesses are excluded) which arise together with the 4 predominant conditioning states are the conditioned mental states. As regards the material states, predominant mind-produced matter which arises together with the predominant impulsions is the conditioned state. Rebirth *kamma*-produced matter is not included because, as stated above, the conditioning states do not occur at the moment of conception, and it is only then that this matter arises.

Enumeration 7. Apply the method given with root condition to determine that there are 7 answers.

Common Conditions 13. Like root condition, conascence-predominance is a Minor conascence condition and so it is common completely[46] with the 4 Major and appropriately with the 4 Medium conascence conditions. Next, the commons with the Minor conascence conditions have to be found. Predominating investigating-wisdom is common with non-delusion of root condition; predominant consciousness is common with consciousness of nutriment (conascence-nutriment) condition; predominant consciousness, effort, and investigating-wisdom are common with consciousness, effort, and knowledge respectively of faculty (conascence-faculty) condition; predominant effort and investigating-wisdom are common with effort and knowledge respectively of path

[46]The 4 Major conascence conditions: (i) conascence, (ii) conascence-dependence of dependence condition, (iii) conascence-presence of presence condition, and (iv) conascence-non-disappearance of non-disappearance condition, contain all the conditioning and conditioned states of the conditions in the conascence group. Therefore, those of all the other conditions in the group are common with and occur completely in them. In the case of the 4 Medium conascence conditions, the other conditions of the group are also common with but occur completely or appropriately depending on their conditioning and conditioned states.

condition. Thus it is common appropriately with the 4 Minor conascence conditions: root, nutriment, faculty, and path. Thus conascence-predominance condition occurs in 13 common conditions — completely in 5 conditions: predominance and 4 Major conascence, and appropriately in 8 conditions: 4 Medium and 4 Minor conascence.

Predominance Condition: *Total Enumeration 10*. When the different answers of all the kinds of predominance condition are totalled, it will be found that these are 7 of object-predominance and 3 (fls-fls, ind and fty-fty, ind) of conascence-predominance. So the total enumeration is 10.

4, 5, 22, 23. Proximity, Contiguity, Absence, Disappearance Conditions (*anantara-*, *samanantara-*, *natthi-*, *vigata-paccayā*)

Sufficient explanations about these conditions were given in the Brief Explanations of the Conditions and so only the enumerations and common conditions will be dealt with.

Enumeration 7. The conditioning and conditioned states are the 89 consciousnesses that are faultless, faulty, and indeterminate. As a faultless impulsion arises immediately after the ceasing of the preceding faultless impulsion, there is the relation (i) fls-fls. But a faulty impulsion cannot arise after a faultless impulsion, and so the relation fls-fty is not possible. For in a mental process where 7 sensuous impulsions generally occur, if the first impulsion is faultless, the second and the rest are the same faultless ones. Thus no faulty impulsion can occur here. Besides, the faultless or faulty state performs not only the function of impulsion but also that of *kamma*, and two opposite kinds of *kamma* cannot take place in one mental process. Then, after the last faultless impulsion, either registering consciousness, life-continuum, or Fruition consciousness, which are indeterminate states, arises as fully expounded in the Classification Chapter of the Investigation Chapter. Therefore, there is the relation (ii) fls-ind.

Similarly, for the faulty impulsions, there are 2 relations: (iii) fty-fty, (iv) fty-ind. As for the indeterminate states, there are 3 relations:

(v) ind-ind, (vi) ind-fls, (vii) ind-fty, because an indeterminate state is followed by an indeterminate, faultless, or faulty state in a mental process. Thus the enumeration is 7. There cannot be more than 7 answers for each of these conditions in the Faultless Triplet.

Common Conditions 5. Out of the 7 conditions of the proximity-strong-dependence group of conditions (see the appropriate chart in *C.R.*), 5 of them (proximity, contiguity, proximity-strong-dependence, absence, and disappearance, known as the proximity group) have the same conditioning and conditioned states. So each one of them occurs completely in these 5 common conditions.

6. Conascence Condition (*sahajāta-paccayo*)

Enumeration 9. It will be seen from the SEC that the conditioning and conditioned states of conascence condition are divided under three heads: (a), (b), (c).

(a) *Conditioning States*. These are given as 4 mental aggregates. They are 89 consciousnesses and 52 mental factors. For the 89 consciousnesses come under the consciousness aggregate, and of the 52 mental factors, feeling mental factor comes under the feeling aggregate, perception mental factor under the perception aggregate, and the remaining 50 mental factors under mental formation aggregate. Again, the 4 mental aggregates are differentiated as (i) 4 faultless mental aggregates (21 faultless consciousnesses and 38 mental factors), (ii) 4 faulty mental aggregates (12 faulty consciousnesses and 27 mental factors) and (iii) 4 indeterminate mental aggregates (36 resultant consciousnesses, 20 functional consciousnesses and 38 mental factors).

Conditioned states. These are the same 4 mental aggregates, mind-produced matter during life and rebirth *kamma*-produced matter at the moment of conception.

It was pointed out that when 1, 2, and 3 of the 4 mental aggregates are taken as the conditioning states, the remaining 3, 2, and 1 respectively are the conditioned states. If the mental aggregates taken as the conditioning states are faultless, the mental aggregates as the conditioned states are also faultless. For the consciousness and mental factors, the mental aggregates, arise together according to the characteristics of conascence and association. So there is the relation (i) fls-fls. This relation between mental aggregates is not possible in the non-percipient plane.

Mutually Related. When the 4 mental aggregates are related to one another in turns, as 1 to 3, 3 to 1, 2 to 2, as shown above, they are said to be mutually related.

Further, when a faultless consciousness arises in the five-aggregate planes, it does not arise alone but always together with mind-produced matter as was shown in root condition. So 1, 2, 3, and 4 mental aggregates are respectively related to mind-produced matter. So there is the relation (ii) fls-ind. And when the 2 relations above are taken together, faultless mental aggregates are related to faultless mental aggregates and mind-produced matter and there is relation (iii) fls-fls, ind and fty-fty, ind. Thus there are 3 answers for the faultless mental aggregates.

Similarly, there are 3 answers for the 4 faulty mental aggregates: (iv) fty-fty, (v) fty-ind, (vi) fty-fty, ind.

With regard to the 4 indeterminate mental aggregates and mind-produced matter that arise during life, the relations between them are similar to those for the faultless and faulty mental aggregates. In addition, the 4 rebirth (resultant indeterminate) mental aggregates at the moment of conception are related to the same 4 mental aggregates and rebirth *kamma*-produced matter that arises together with them. Since the states are all indeterminate states, there is only one relation (vii) ind-ind. So for (a) the enumeration is 7 just as in the case of root condition.

(b) *Conditioning and Conditioned States.* These are materiality (indeterminate) and there is only one relation, ind-ind. (The 4 great primaries are mutually related.)

(c) *Conditioning and Conditioned States.* These are indeterminate states. For the 4 rebirth (resultant indeterminate) mental aggregates in the five-aggregate planes and heart-base are mutually related, i.e. when the former are the conditioning states, the latter is the conditioned state and vice versa. So there is only one relation, ind-ind. This relation does not apply to beings (i) in the non-percipient plane where there is no mentality and (ii) in the immaterial plane where there is no materiality and, therefore, no heart-base. It only applies to beings at the moment of conception in the five-aggregate planes where consciousness has to arise dependent on a base. So when a being is born into a new existence in this plane, rebirth consciousness has to depend on a base for its arising. Since no previous base existed before then, it has to depend on the lone heart-base that arises together with it. So far, the total of the different relations for (a), (b), and (c), which were taken separately, is 7. But there are other relations when (a) and (b) are taken together. For when the 4 faultless mental aggregates that arise during life of (a) and the 4 great primaries of mind-produced matter of (b) are taken as the conditioning states, mind-produced matter is the conditioned-state. Here faultless aggregates and great primaries (indeterminate) are related to mind-produced matter, and so there is the relation (viii) fls, ind-ind. For example, when a faultless consciousness, which performs the function of impulsion, arises as the first impulsion in the five-aggregate planes, the matter produced by this consciousness, mind-produced matter, also arises together with it. Then this first faultless impulsion and the great primaries of mind-produced matter as the conditioning states are related to the remaining mind-produced matter as the conditioned states. This also holds true for the 4 faulty mental aggregates, and so there is another relation (ix) fty, ind-ind.

Question. But does this apply to the indeterminate mental aggregates as well? Are (i) the 4 resultant or functional mental aggregates that arise during life and the great primaries of mind-produced matter related to the remaining mind-produced matter and (ii) the 4 rebirth (resultant indeterminate) mental aggregates that arise at the moment of conception and the great primaries of rebirth *kamma*-produced matter related to the remaining rebirth *kamma*-produced matter?

Answer. Yes, it does apply to them and they are so related. But there is no need to specify these relations as they come under ind-ind, which was already obtained above. It is not a separate answer to the rest of the 49 questions between the sections and sub-sections of the Faultless Triplet. But where it is so, as in the Resultant Triplet, *C.R.*, p. 408, item 99 (x) and others, the relations are given.

Conascence Condition: *Total Enumeration 9*. When the different answers are totalled as above, there are nine of them, i.e. enumeration 9.

Common Conditions 4. The 4 Major conascence conditions: conascence, conascence-dependence of dependence condition, conascence-presence of presence condition, and conascencenon-disappearance of non-disappearance condition, have the same conditioning and conditioned states. Thus conascence condition occurs completely in the 4 common conditions: conascence, dependence, presence, and non-disappearance. This fact is useful when dealing with the combinations of conditions.

As pointed out in the case of object condition, conascence condition, which is the particular condition under consideration here, contains all the conditioning and conditioned states of the conascence group, and, therefore, only those conditions in the group that contain all those states are taken into account, i.e. the 4 common conditions above. Of course, conascence condition also occurs appropriately in the remaining 11 conditions of the conascence group.

7. Mutuality Condition (*aññamañña-paccayo*)

Enumeration 3. Here, too, as in conascence condition, the conditioning and conditioned states are divided under three heads. It will be observed that the difference between these two conditions is that the conditioned material states in mutuality are the great primaries and heart-base only. In (a) where the mental aggregates are mutually related to one another, there are 3 relations: (i) fls-fls, (ii) fty-fty, (iii) ind-ind. As for heart-base, the conditioned state, rebirth resultant mental aggregates at the moment of conception are the conditioning states related to it. This is also ind-ind. In (b) and (c) the conditioning and conditioned states are all indeterminate and so the relations are also ind-ind. Thus the enumeration is 3.

Common Conditions 5. Next to the 4 Major conascence conditions, mutuality condition has the greatest number of conditioning and conditioned states of the conditions in the conascence group. So this particular condition occurs completely in 5 common conditions: conascence, mutuality, dependence, presence, and non-disappearance.

8. Dependence Condition (*nissaya-paccayo*)

There are four kinds: (a) base-object-prenascence-dependence, (b) conascence-dependence, (c) base-prenascence-dependence, (d) mixed conascence-prenascence.

8. (a) Base-Object-Prenascence-Dependence (*vatthārammaṇa-purejāta-nissaya*)

Enumeration 3. This condition is not expounded as a separate condition but is derived, as shown earlier, from the common of object and dependence conditions (see base-object-prenascence-predominance). In the relations here, heart-base (indeterminate) is always the conditioning state. When the conditioned states are mind-door advertence, 5 functional dying impulsions or 11 registering consciousnesses, which are all indeterminate, the relations are ind-ind. But when the conditioned states are 5 faultless or faulty dying impulsions, the relations are ind-fls and ind-fty. Thus the enumeration is 3.

Common Conditions 6. This condition belongs to the object group and so it is common with object condition. As it is a part of object-prenascence which is the same as object-prenascence-presence and object-prenascence-non-disappearance, it is common with prenascence, presence and non-disappearance conditions. Moreover, it is the same as base-object-prenascence-dissociation and so it is common with dissociation condition. So base-object-prenascence-dependence condition, which is a kind of dependence condition, occurs completely in the 6 common conditions: object, dependence, prenascence, dissociation, presence, and non-disappearance.

8. (b) Conascence-Dependence (*sahajāta-nissaya*)

This is exactly the same as conascence condition.

8. (c) Base-Prenascence-Dependence (*vatthupurejāta-nissaya*)

Enumeration 3. The conditioning states are the 6 bases which are all indeterminate states. The 4 immaterial resultant consciousnesses, which perform the functions of rebirth, life-continuum, and death in the immaterial plane, are excluded from the conditioned states as they do not depend on a material base for their arising. For in the immaterial plane there is no matter. Therefore, the conditioned states are the 7 consciousness elements exclusive of the 4 immaterial resultants, i.e. 85 consciousnesses and 52 mental factors. They are faultless, faulty, and indeterminate states. So the relations are (i) ind-ind, (ii) ind-fls, (iii) ind-fty. Thus the enumeration is 3.

Common Conditions 5. Of the 6 conditions of the base-prenascence group (see the appropriate chart in *C.R.*), base-prenascence of prenascence condition, base-prenascence-dependence of dependence condition, base-prenascence-dissociation of dissociation condition, base-prenascence-presence of presence condition and base-prenascence-non-disappearance of non-disappearance condition have the same conditioning and conditioned states. So base-prenascence-dependence condition occurs completely in the 5 common conditions: dependence, prenascence, dissociation, presence and non-disappearance.

8. (d) Mixed Conascence-Prenascence (*sahajāta-purejātamissaka*)

Here the two kinds of dependence condition (b) and (c) above, i.e. conascence-dependence and base-prenascence-dependence conditions, are taken together.

Enumeration 2. From the SEC it will be seen that the conditioning states are 21 faultless consciousnesses, 12 faulty consciousnesses, 52 mental factors, and heart-base, and the conditioned states are the same mental states (heart-base is not included). The mixed condition can be illustrated in the case of a mental process. Suppose a mind-door process takes place with a great faultless impulsion. The sequence of the thought-moments is as follows: vibrating life-continuum, arresting life-continuum, mind-door advertence, 7 great faultless impulsions of the same kind, and 2 registertng consciousnesses. The first great impulsion (as with each of the rest) consists of 1 great faultless consciousness and 38 mental factors, i.e. 4 faultless mental aggregates. At the moment when this first impulsion arises: (a) 1 of the aggregates is related to the other 3, 3 of them to the remaining 1, and 2 of them to the other 2. This is conascence or conascence-dependence condition which are the same; (b) the aggregates, the conditioned states, arise depending on the heart-base which had already arisen together with the preceding mind-door advertence. This is base-prenascence-dependence condition. By taking these two conditions together it is said to be mixed conascence-prenascence. In this case the conditioning states are faultless, indeterminate and the conditioned states are faultless, i.e. the relation is fls, ind-fls. This applies to each of the 21 faultless consciousnesses. With the 12 faulty consciousnesses the relation is fty, ind-fty. Thus the enumeration is 2.

Common Conditions 3. In this Faultless Triplet, there are 3 conditions in the mixed conascence-prenascence group: mixed conascence-prenascence of this dependence condition, mixed conascence-prenascence-presence of presence condition, and mixed conascence-prenascence-non-disappearance of non-disappearance condition, and they have the same conditioning and conditioned states as can be seen from chart II (H) in *C.R.* So mixed conascence-prenascence condition occurs completely in the 3 common conditions: dependence, presence and non-disappearance.

Dependence Condition: *Total Enumeration 13*. The different kinds of answers for the four kinds of dependence condition are totalled: (a) base-object-prenascence-dependence has 3 answers, and with the 8 of (b) conascence-dependence which are different, there are 11 answers; (c) base-prenascence-dependence has the same 3 answers as (a) above and there is no addition; (d) mixed conascence-prenascence has 2 other answers. So the total enumeration is 13.

9. Strong-Dependence Condition (*upanissaya-paccayo*)

There are three kinds: (a) object-strong-dependence, (b) proximity-strong-dependence, (c) natural strong-dependence. (a) and (b) are respectively the same as object-predominance and proximity conditions, as shown in the SEC, and which were dealt with already.

9. (c) Natural Strong-Dependence (*pakatūpanissaya*)

Enumeration 9. As both the conditioning and conditioned states are faultless, faulty and indeterminate, like object condition, the enumeration is 9.

Common Condition 1. Like object condition, it is the only condition which has the maximum number of conditioning and conditioned states in the group, and, therefore, it has 1 common condition.

Strong-dependence: *Total Enumeration 9.* The different kinds of answers for the three kinds of strong-dependence condition are those of natural strong-dependence because those of the other two conditions are included in it. Thus the total enumeration is 9.

10. Prenascence Condition (*purejāta-paccayo*)

There are two kinds: (a) object-prenasence, (b) base-prenascence.

10. (a) Object-Prenascence (*ārammaṇa-purejāta*)

Enumeration 3. The conditioning states, 18 present produced matter, are indeterminate. As for the conditioned states, 23 sensuous resultant consciousnesses, 11 sensuous functional consciousnesses, functional divine-eye and divine-ear are indeterminate; 8 great faultless consciousnesses, faultless divine-eye and divine-ear are faultless; 12 faulty consciousnesses are faulty. So the relations are (i) ind-ind, (ii) ind-fls, (iii) ind-fty. Thus the enumeration is 3.

Common Conditions 4. It belongs to the object group of conditions and it is common with object condition. And since it is the same as object-prenascence-presence and object-prenascence-non-disappearance (because they have the same conditioning and conditioned states), it is common with presence and non-disappearance conditions. Therefore, object-prenascence condition occurs completely in the 4 common conditions: object, prenascence, presence, and non-disappearance.

10. (b) Base-Prenascence (*vatthu-purejāta*)

From the SEC it is seen that this condition is the same as base-prenascence-dependence condition already dealt with.

Prenascence: *Total Enumeration 3*. Since the two kinds of prenascence condition have the same three answers, the total enumeration is also 3.

11. Postnascence Condition (*pacchājāta-paccayo*)

Enumeration 3. The conditioning states, the 4 mental aggregates exclusive of the 4 immaterial resultants, are 85 consciousnesses and 52 mental factors. They are faultless, faulty and indeterminate. The conditioned states are materiality which is indeterminate. So the relations are (i) fls-ind, (ii) fty-ind, (iii) ind-ind. Thus the enumeration is 3.

Common Conditions 4. This condition belongs to the postnascence group of 4 conditions which, it will be seen from chart II (G) in *C.R.*, have the same conditioning and conditioned states. The others are postnascence-dissociation of dissociation condition, postnascence-presence of presence condition and postnascence-non-disappearance of non-disappearance condition. So postnascence condition occurs completely in the 4 common conditions: postnascence, dissociation, presence and non-disappearance.

12. Repetition Condition (*āsevana-paccayo*)

Enumeration 3. This condition belongs to the proximity-strong-dependence group. Here the impulsions of the same class are related. The conditioning states are 17 mundane faultless, 12 faulty, and 18 functional impulsions. The last of each of these impulsions in the mental process is excluded because it is not related to the same impulsion but to the registering consciousness or life-continuum that arises after it, the relation being that of proximity condition. The conditioned states are 21 faultless (including the 4 Path impulsions), 12 faulty, and 18 functional impulsions. The first of each of these mundane impulsions is excluded because the preceding state is not an impulsion but either determining consciousness or mind-door advertence which is related to the first impulsion by proximity condition. Also, each of the 4 Fruition impulsions are excluded from the conditioned states because the Path impulsion that precedes each one of them is not of the same class. Since the faultless, faulty, and indeterminate impulsions are related only to the same class, the relations are (i) fls-fls, (ii) fty-fty, (iii) ind-ind. Thus the enumeration is 3.

Common Conditions 6. This condition, which belongs to the proximity-strong-dependence group of 7 conditions, has less of the conditioning and conditioned states of the 5 conditions, proximity, etc., of the proximity group, but more than proximity-*kamma* with which there is no common conditioning and conditioned state. So repetition condition occurs completely in the 6 common conditions: proximity, contiguity, strong-dependence, repetition, absence, and disappearance.

13. *Kamma* Condition (*kamma-paccayo*)

There are four kinds: (a) conascence-*kamma*, (b) proximity-*kamma*, (c) strong asynchronous *kamma*, (d) strong-and-weak asynchronous *kamma*.

13. (a) Conascence-*Kamma* (*sahajāta-kamma*)

Enumeration 7. This condition, like root condition, belongs to the Minor conascence group. Determine the enumeration in the way given there.

Common Conditions 10. Since this condition belongs to the Minor conascence group it is common completely with the 4 Major conascence and appropriately (as all the conditioned states of this condition are not included in them) with the 4 Medium conascence conditions. Besides, it is common completely with conascence-nutriment of nutriment condition being a condition of the Minor conascence group which has all the conditioning and conditioned states of conascence-*kamma*. Therefore, conascence-*kamma* condition occurs in the 10 common conditions: completely in 6 (4 Major conascence, *kamma*, and nutriment), and appropriately in 4 (4 Medium conascence).

13. (b) Proximity-*Kamma* (*anantara-kamma*)

Enumeration 1. The conditioning states are the volitions associated with the 4 Paths (faultless), and the conditioned states are the 4 Fruitions (indeterminate). The only relation is fls-ind. Thus the enumeration is 1.

Common Conditions 6. This condition belongs to the proximity-strong-dependence group, 5 of which (the proximity group of conditions) have, as pointed out before, the maximum number of conditioning and conditioned states. So proximity-*kamma* condition occurs completely in the 6 common conditions: proximity, continguity, strong-dependence, *kamma*, absence, and disappearance.

13. (c) Strong Asynchronous *Kamma* (*balava nanākkhaṇika-kamma*)

Enumeration 2. The conditioning states are strong faultless, and faulty volitions and the conditioned states are resultant consciousnesses and associated mental factors which are indeterminate. So the relations are fls-ind and fty-ind. Thus the enumeration is 2.

Common Conditions 2. This condition, which is one of the two conditions in the natural strong-dependence group, has the lesser number of conditioning and conditioned states. So strong asynchronous *kamma* condition occurs completely in the 2 common conditions: strong-dependence and *kamma*.

13. (d) Strong-and-Weak Asynchronous *Kamma*
(*balava-dubbala nanākkhaṇika-kamma*)

Enumeration 2. Lofty and supramundane volitions are always strong and so they are included in strong asynchronous *kamma* condition above. That is why in the SEC the conditioning states of (a), the sensuous faultless and faulty volitions, which are weak in comparison, are said to be weak. The conditioned states are the sensuous resultants. So the relations in (a) are fls-ind and fty-ind. As for (b), both the strong faultless and faulty volitions of strong asynchronous *kamma* above and the weak asynchronous volitions of (a) give results as rebirth, and if this takes place in the five-aggregate planes, rebirth *kamma*-produced matter, the conditioned state, arises together with them. Therefore, these volitions are taken together in order to show that they have the same relation with materiality. The relations are of the same kind as (a). Thus the enumeration is 2.

Common Condition 1. This condition is distinct and separate from all the other conditions and is, therefore, the only one in the group. So the common condition is 1. It was already explained why object and natural strong-dependence conditions have also common condition 1.

14. Resultant Condition (*vipāka-paccayo*)

Enumeration 1. As its name implies, the conditioning states are resultant mental aggregates as shown in (a) of the SEC. Since it belongs to the conascence group, the conditioned states, which arise together, are the same resultant mental aggregates (as they are mutually related), mind-produced matter which occurs during life and rebirth *kamma*-produced matter at the moment of conception. So the relation here is ind-ind. Also in (b) the resultant mental aggregates at the moment of conception in the five-aggregate planes are related to heart-base on which they are dependent. But they are not mutually related as in conascence condition. Here also, the relation is ind-ind. Thus the enumeration is 1.

Common Conditions 5. This condition belongs to the Medium conascence group and it will be seen that resultant condition occurs completely in the 5 common conditions: 4 Major conascence and resultant.

15. Nutriment Condition (*āhāra-paccayo*)

There are two kinds: (a) conascence-nutriment, (b) physical nutriment.

15. (a) Conascence-Nutriment (*sahajātāhāra*)

Enumeration 7. According to Dhs and Vibh there are 4 nutriments: contact, volition, consciousness, and nutritive essence. The first three, which are mental nutriments, are the conascence-nutriments, and the last is physical nutriment. They are the conditioning states of nutriment condition. With regard to the 3 conascence-nutriments, contact and volition are each associated with 89 consciousnesses, and consciousness consists of 89 consciousnesses. Thus they are faultless, faulty, and indeterminate states. The conditioned states are 89 consciousnesses and 52 mental factors associated with the mental nutriments, mind- and rebirth *kamma*-produced matter. They are also faultless, faulty, and indeterminate states. Since this condition belongs to the Minor conascence group, determine that the enumeration is 7 as was done with root condition.

Common Conditions 12. This condition, which belongs to the Minor conascence group, is common completely with the 4 Major and appropriately with the 4 Medium conascence conditions. As for the commons with those within its own group, consciousness nutriment is common with predominant consciousness of predominance condition and consciousness faculty of faculty condition; volition nutriment is common with volition of *kamma* condition. So conascence-nutriment condition occurs in the 12 common conditions: completely in 5 (4 Major conascence and nutriment) and appropriately in 7 (4 Medium conascence, predominance, *kamma*, and faculty).

15. (b) Physical Nutriment (*rūpāhāra*)

Enumeration 1. As both the conditioning and conditioned states are materiality, the relation is ind-ind. Thus the enumeration is 1. The exclusion of nutritive essence in the same materiality group of the conditioned states was already explained in the Brief Explanations of the Conditions.

Common Conditions 3. This condition is one of the 3 in the physical nutriment group, all of which have the same conditioning and conditioned states. The others are physical nutriment-presence of presence condition and physical nutriment-non-disappearance of non-disappearance condition. So physical nutriment condition occurs completely in the 3 common conditions: nutriment, presence, and non-disappearance.

16. Faculty Condition (*indriya-paccayo*)

There are three kinds: (a) conascence-faculty, (b) base-prenascence-faculty, (c) physical life-faculty.

16. (a) Conascence-Faculty (*sahajātindriya*)

Enumeration 7. This condition belongs to the Minor conascence group. Determine that the enumeration is 7 as was done with root condition.

Common Conditions 14. From the conditioning and conditioned states of this Minor conascence condition it will be seen that it is common completely with the 4 Major and appropriately with the 4 Medium conascence conditions. As for the commons with those within its own group, it can be found that it is common with root, predominance, and nutriment as these have already been dealt with. It is also common with feeling and one-pointedness of *jhāna* condition, and knowledge, effort, mindfulness, and one-pointedness of path condition. So conascence-faculty condition occurs in the 14 common conditions: completely in 5 (4 Major conascence and faculty) and appropriately in 9 (4 Medium conascence, root, predominance, nutriment, *jhāna*, and path).

16. (b) Base-Prenascence-Faculty (*vatthupurejātindriya*)

Enumeration 1. Both the conditioning states, the 5 sentient faculties, and the conditioned states, twice fivefold consciousnesses, are all indeterminate states. So the relation is ind-ind. Thus the enumeration is 1.

Common Conditions 6. This condition belongs to the base-prenascence group. As shown in the case of base-prenascence-dependence, it is common completely with the 5 conditions: dependence, prenascence, dissociation, presence, and non-disappearance. So base-prenascence-faculty condition occurs completely in the 6 common conditions: the 5 above and faculty.

16. (c) Physical Life-Faculty (*rūpajīvitindriya*)

Enumeration 1. Both the conditioning and conditioned states are materiality and so the relation is ind-ind. Thus the enumeration is 1.

Common Conditions 3. This condition is one of the 3 in the physical life-faculty group, all of which have the same conditioning and conditioned states. The others are physical life-faculty-presence of presence condition and physical life-faculty-non-disappearance of non-disappearance condition. So physical life-faculty condition occurs completely in the 3 common conditions: faculty, presence and non-disappearance.

17. *Jhāna* Condition (*jhāna-paccayo*)

Enumeration 7. This condition belongs to the Minor conascence group. Determine that the enumeration is 7 as was done with root condition. It will be noted that all the conditions of this group have the same enumeration 7.

Common Conditions 11. This Minor conascence condition is common completely with the 4 Major and appropriately with the 4 Medium conascence conditions. As for the commons with those within its own group, it was shown in conascence-faculty that it is common with faculty condition. Also, it is common with applied thought and one-pointedness of path condition. So *jhāna* condition occurs in the 11 common conditions: completely in 5 (4 Major conascence and *jhāna*) and appropriately in 6 (4 Medium conascence, faculty. and path).

18. Path Condition (*magga-paccayo*)

Enumeration 7. Determine the enumeration as in the case of *jhāna* condition.

Common Conditions 13. Refer to conascence-faculty. The difference here is that it is not common with nutriment condition. So path condition occurs in the 13 common conditions: completely in 5 (4 Major conascence and path) and appropriately in 8 (4 Medium conascence, root, predominance, faculty and *jhāna*).

19. Association Condition (*sampayutta-paccayo*)

Enumeration 3. Both the conditioning and conditioned states are the 4 mental aggregates. Therefore, as was shown in conascence and mutuality conditions, the relations are fls-fls, fty-fty, ind-ind. Thus the enumeration is 3.

Common Conditions 6. This condition belongs to the Medium conascence group. So it is common completely with the 4 Major conascence conditions. As for the commons with those within the same group, it is common completely with mutuality condition. So association condition occurs completely in the 6 common conditions: 4 Major conascence, mutuality, and association.

20. Dissociation Condition (*vippayutta-paccayo*)

There are four kinds: (a) base-object-prenascencedissociation, (b) conascence-dissociation, (c) base-prenascence-dissociation, (d) postnascence-dissociation.

20. (a) Base-Object-Prenascence-Dissociation (*vatthārammṇa-purejāta-vippayutta*)

As pointed out in the SEC this condition is the same as base-object-prenascence-dependence condition.

20. (b) Conascence-Dissociation (*sahajāta-vippayutta*)

Enumeration 3. In the Brief Explanations of the Conditions, where dissociation condition was dealt with, it was stated that when mentality and materiality arise together they are not associated but dissociated. In (i) the conditioning states are mentality, and the conditioned states are materiality. The consciousnesses which do not produce materiality are excluded from the conditioning states, and this leaves 75 consciousnesses which are faultless, faulty, and indeterminate. The conditioned states, materiality, are indeterminate. So the relations here are fls-ind, fty-ind, ind-ind. Thus the enumeration is 3. In (ii) the conditioning and conditioned states — which are mentality and materiality respectively and vice versa — are all indeterminate states. Refer to the explanation above under (c) of conascence condition with which it is the same. The relation, ind-ind, is already included in (i) above, and so there is no addition to be made to the enumeration already obtained.

Common Conditions 5. This condition belongs to the Medium conascence group and so it is common with the 4 Major conascence conditions. So conascence-dissociation occurs completely in the 5 common conditions: 4 Major conascence and dissociation.

20. (c) Base-Prenascence-Dissociation (*vatthupurejāta-vippayutta*)

As pointed out in the SEC this condition is the same as base-prenascence-dependence condition already dealt with.

20. (d) Postnascence-Dissociation (*pacchajāta-vippayutta*)

This is the same as postnascence condition.

Dissociation Condition: *Total Enumeration* 5. In the four kinds of this condition, (a) and (c) have the same answers, ind-ind, ind-fls, ind-fty, and (b) and (d) also have the same answers, fls-ind, fty-ind, ind-ind. Therefore the total of the different answers is 5, i.e. enumeration 5.

21. Presence Condition (*atthi-paccayo*)

There are nine kinds as shown in the SEC: (a) object-prenascence-presence (*ārammaṇa-purejātatthi*), (b) conascence-presence (*sahajātatthi*), (c) base-prenascence-presence (*vatthu-purejātatthi*), (d) postnascence-presence (*pacchājātatthi*), (e) physical nutriment-presence (*rūpāhāratthi*), (f) physical life-faculty-presence (*rūpajīvitindriyatthi*), (g) mixed conascence-prenascence-presence (*sahajāta-purejātatthi missaka*), (h) mixed postnascence-nutriment-presence (*pacchājātāhāratthi missaka*), (i) mixed postnascence-faculty-presence (*pacchājātindriyatthi missaka*). The first seven are the same as the conditions pointed out in the SEC and which have been dealt with.

21. (h) Mixed Postnascence-Nutriment-Presence
(*pacchājātāhāratthi missaka*)

Enumeration 2. The relations can be explained, as was done with mixed conascence-prenascence of dependence condition, by means of the mental process. Taking the first faultless impulsion as an example, this arises after determining consciousness in the five-door mental process and after mind-door advertence in the mind-door process. Here the conditioning states are the first faultless impulsion (1 faultless consciousness and 38 mental factors) and the nutritive essence present in the 3 or 4 cause-produced matter, all the matter which had arisen with the preceding determining consciousness or mind-door advertence and had reached the static phases. The conditioned states are the above-mentioned 3 or 4 cause-produced matter (indeterminate) which had reached the static phases at the same time together. When the first faultless impulsion is related to the conditioned states above, it is post-nascence condition. When nutritive essence is related to the same conditioned states it is nutriment condition. By taking these 2 conditions together there is the relation fls, ind-ind and fty, ind-ind. Similarly for the faulty states, there is the relation fty, ind-ind. Thus the enumeration is 2.

Common Conditions 2. The other condition in this mixed postnascence-nutriment group is mixed postnascence-nutriment-non-disappearance of non-disappearance condition. So mixed postnascence-nutriment-presence condition occurs completely in the 2 common conditions: presence and non-disappearance.

21. (i) Mixed Postnascence-Faculty-Presence (*pacchājātindriyatthi missaka*)

The difference from the above is that, instead of nutritive essence, physical life-faculty is taken as the conditioning state. And since physical life-faculty is *kamma*-produced matter, it is related to the other *kamma*-produced matter which are the conditioned states in this case as shown in the SEC.

Enumeration and Common Conditions. They are the same as in (h) above.

Presence Condition: *Total Enumeration 13*. When the different answers for the various kinds of presence condition are totalled, the number is found to be 13 just as in dependence condition. So the total enumeration is 13.

22, 23. Absence and Disappearance Conditions (*natthi-paccayo, vigata-paccayo*)

They are the same as proximity condition.

24. Non-Disappearance Condition (*avigata-paccayo*)

This is the same as presence condition.

Note. All the conditioning and conditioned states of non-disappearance condition as a whole are also those of presence condition. So, when non-disappearance condition, which has the maximum number of conditioning and conditioned states, is the particular condition under consideration, it occurs completely in the 2 common conditions: presence and non-disappearance. But parts of the conditioning and conditioned states of non-disappearance condition are found in root, object, predominance, conascence, mutuality, dependence, strong-dependence, prenascence, postnascence, *kamma*, resultant, nutriment, faculty, *jhāna*, path, association, and dissociation conditions, i.e. non-disappearance condition occurs appropriately in the above 17 common conditions. So it can be said that non-disappearance condition occurs completely and appropriately in the 19 common conditions (see *C.R.*, p. 214, item 523). But here only the 2 conditions that occur completely are taken into account. This was also explained in object condition. So it will now be understood why the figure 19 under "appropriately" is given in the SEC.

IV. Explanation of the Analytical Exposition of the Conditions

After the 24 conditions are enumerated as root condition, object condition and so on, they are treated again at some length, which is neither too brief nor too detailed, in the AECo. It is only in the Investigation Chapter that the conditions are exhaustively dealt with.

The Analytical Exposition of the Conditions (*paccaya-niddesa*). Here the exposition is confined to the Paṭṭh on the Faultless Triplet which is just one section of Paṭṭh. It is given in full so that the method used here can be applied to the remaining 129,231 sections for determining the AECo of each of them and which are not provided in the text. For instance, in the case of proximity condition of the Faultless Triplet, it is stated that "Preceding faultless states are related to subsequent faultless states by proximity condition", and so on. So that of the Feeling Triplet will be "Preceding states associated with pleasant feeling are related to subsequent states associated with pleasant feeling by proximity condition", and so on. Also, in the cases of root condition and others of the Feeling Triplet, materiality is left out as it is not included in that Triplet. Therefore, the Analytical Exposition will be "Roots are related to the states which are associated with roots by root condition", and so on.

The Buddha Provided the Methods in Abhidhamma. The Abhidhamma is very comprehensive and if the entire teaching were to be given in full it would be very voluminous. But by providing the method as a model in one particular case, the rest, which is abbreviated, can be known by simply applying that method. So the Buddha always provided the method when he expounded the Abhidhamma. This is pointed out in *Expos.*, p. 440: "Indeed, the Supreme Buddha is never known to have missed the right occasion on which to use the method when he came to Abhidhamma."

Enumeration of the Conditions (*paccayuddesa*). Although there are 24 conditions in the Faultless Triplet and they are so enumerated in Chapter I, there are fewer conditions in the Feeling Triplet and others where only mentality is concerned and also in some of the other Paṭṭh sections where only materiality is concerned. Thus the number of conditions which are to be enumerated depends upon the particular Triplet or Couplet that is under consideration. The enumerations of the conditions for the other 129,231 sections are not given in the text.

An Example. In the SEC it will be seen that materiality is a conditioning state of prenascence condition and a conditioned state of postnascence condition. Also, materiality is a conditioning state of dissociation condition when mentality is the conditioned state, and it is a conditioned state when mentality is a conditioning state of that condition. These three conditions, where materiality is included as a conditioning or conditioned state, are not included in the Feeling Triplet, which is concerned only with mentality. Therefore, for the enumeration of the conditions in the Feeling Triplet there are only 21 conditions.

From the above example it will be seen that, by application of the method given in the Faultless Triplet, the other Triplets and Couplets can be known regarding the enumeration of the conditions, the analytical exposition, the six Chapters, Investigation Chapter, common conditions and the combinations of conditions as required for each of their sections.

Explanation of the Method of the Analytical Exposition[47]

1. Root Condition

The conditioning and conditioned states, the enumerations, and the common conditions were explained in the Explanation of the Single Enumerations and summarised in the SEC. There, the enumerations were considered because the method of the Investigation Chapter was dealt with. But here in the Analytical Exposition the enumerations are not required, and so only the conditioning and conditioned states, as given in the chart, and the conditioning forces that are concerned are considered.

---

[47]Reference to the Analytical Exposition in *C.R.* and the chart given here must be made whenever necessary.

2. Chart of the Analytical Exposition of the Conditions (AEC)

Conds.* Ser. No. Kind	Item** No.	Conditioning States	Conditioned States	Com.Conds. Comp.	Com.Conds. App.
1. Ro		6 roots, namely: greed, hate, delusion, non-greed, non-hate, non-delusion	71 rooted cons., 52 m.f. excluding delusion from 2 delusion-rooted and rooted rebirth *kamma*-produced matter		12
2. Ob	(i)	Visible object-base	2 eye-cons. elements, 7 primary m.f.	4	
	(ii)	Sound-base	2 ear-cons. elements, 7 primary m.f.	4	
	(iii)	Odour-base	2 nose-cons. elements, 7 primary m.f.	4	
	(iv)	Taste-base	2 tongue-cons. elements 7 primary m.f.	4	
	(v)	Tangible object-base	2 body-cons. elements, 7 primary m.f.	4	
	(vi)	Visible object-base, sound-base, odour-base, taste-base, tangble object-base	3 mind-elements, 7 primary and 3 secondary m.f. exclusive of effort, rapture, and desire	4	
	(vii)	All the 6 kinds of objects which are 89 cons., 52 m.f., 28 matter, Nibbāna and concept	76 mind-cons. elements, 52 m.f.		8
	(viii)	Any of the 6 kinds of objects which are 89 cons., 52 m.f., 28 matter, Nibbāna and concept	Any of the conditioned states which are 89 cons., 52 m.f.		
		Specific 6 kinds of objects (as above)	Specific 89 cons., 52 m.f.		8

* Abbreviations: Conds. = Conditions; Com. = Common; Ser. = Serial; Comp. = Completely; App. = Appropriately.

** Items are those under the conditions in Analytical Exposition of the Conditions, pp. 2–12 of *C.R.*

Conds. Ser. No.	Kind	Item No.	Conditioning States	Conditioned States	Com.Conds. Comp. App.
3. Pd	Cn-pd	(i)	Predominant desire which is assoc. with 52 predominant impulsions	52 predominant impulsions, 50 m.f. exclusive of desire and doubt; predominant mind-produced matter	9
		(ii)	Predominant effort which is assoc. with 52 predominant impulsions	52 predominant impulsions, 50 mf. exclusive of desire and doubt; predominant mind-produced matter	11
		(iii)	Predominant cons. which are 52 predominant impulsions	51 m.f. exclusive of doubt; predominant mind-produced matter	11
		(iv)	Predominant investigating wisdom which is assoc. with 34 predominant three-rooted impulsions	34 predominant three-rooted impulsions, 37 m.f. exclusive of investigating wisdom; predominant mind-produced matter	12
	Ob-pd	(v)	6 kinds of objects which are predominant 18 desirable produced matter; 84 cons. exclusive of 2 hate-rooted cons., 2 delusion-rooted cons. and bodily pain cons., 47 m.f. exclusive of hate, envy, stinginess, worry, and doubt; doubt; Nibbāna	Any of the predominating 8 greed-rooted cons., 8 great faultless cons., 4 great functional cons. assoc. with knowledge, 8 supramundane cons., 45 m.f. exclusive of hate, envy, stinginess, worry, doubt, and 2 illimitables	
			Specific 6 kinds of objects (as above)	Specific conditioned states (as above)	
4. Px		(i)	2 eye-cons. elements, 7 primary m.f.	2 recipient cons., 7 primary and 3 secondary m.f. exclusive of effort, rapture, and desire	5
			2 recipient cons., 7 primary and 3 secondary m.f. exclusive of effort, rapture, and desire	3 investigating cons., 7 primary and 4 secondary m.f. exclusive of effort and desire	5

Conds. Ser. No. Kind	Item No.	Conditioning States	Conditioned States	Com.Conds. Comp. App.
	(ii) to (v)	As above for ear-cons., nose-cons., tongue-cons., and body-cons.	As above	5
	(vi)	Preceding 7 mundane faultless impulsaions excluding the last impulsions, 38 m.f.	Subsequent 17 mundane faultless impulsions excluding the first impulsions, and 4 Path-cons., 38 m.f.	6
	(vii)	Preceding last impulsions of 17 mundane faultless cons., 4 Path cons., 38 m.f.	Subsequent 11 registering cons., 9 Lofty resultant cons., 4 Fruition cons., 38 m.f.	6
	(viii)	Preceding 12 faulty impulsions excluding the last impulsions, 27 m.f.	Subsequent 12 faulty impulsions excluding the first impulsions, 27 m.f.	6
	(ix)	Preceding last impulsions of 12 faulty cons., 27 m.f.	Subsequent 11 registering cons., 9 Lofty resultant cons., 35 m.f.	5
	(x)	Preceding 36 resultant cons. excluding Arahatta's death cons., 20 functional cons., 38 m.f.	Subsequent 36 resultant cons. including Arahatta's death cons., 20 functional cons., 38 m.f.	
	(xi)	Preceding determining cons. excluding Arahatta's death cons., 20 functional cons., 38 m.f.	Subsequent first impul-cons. including Arahatta's death cons., 20 functional cons. 38 m.f.	5
	(xii)	As (xi)	Subsequent first impulsions of 12 faulty cons., 27 m.f.	5
	(xiii)	Any of the preceding 89 cons. excluding Arahatta's death cons., 52 m.f.	Any of the conditioned states which are subsequent 89 cons. including Arahatta's death cons., 52 m.f.	
		Specific preceding 89 cons. excluding Arahatta's death cons., 52 m.f.	Subsequent 89 cons. including Arahatta's death cons., 52 m.f.	

Conds. Ser. No.	Kind	Item No.	Conditioning States	Conditioned States	Com.Conds. Comp. App.
6. Cn		(i)	1 of the 4 m.agg. 3 of the 4 m.agg. 2 of the 4 m.agg.	Remaining 3 of the 4 m.agg. Remaining 2 of the 4 m.agg. Remaining 2 of the 4 m.agg.	7
		(ii)	1 of the 4 great primaries 3 of the 4 gr. pr. 2 of the 4 gr. pr.	Remaining 3 of the 4 gr.pr. Remaining 1 of the 4 gr.pr. Remaining 2 of the 4 gr. pr.	5
		(iii)	At the moment of conception, 15 rebirth cons., 35 m.f. and heart-base in 5-agg. planes	15 rebirth cons., 35 m.f. and heart-base (mutually)	6
		(iv)	75 cons. exclusive of 4 immaterial resultant cons., twice fivefold cons. and Arahatta's death cons., 52 m.f. during life in 5-agg. planes	Mind-produced matter	5
		(v)	4 gr.pr.	24 derived matter	4
		(vi)	Heart-base Heart-base at the moment of conception But heart-base during life	15 rebirth cons., 35 m.f. in 5-agg. planes is related to the above cons. by conascence condition is not related to the above cons. by conascence condition	6
7. Mu		(i) (ii) (iii)	The same as conascence condition (i)–(iii)		
8. Dp	Cn-dp	(i) to (v)	The same as conascence condition (i)–(v)		
	Prn-dp	(vi)	Eye-base	2 eye-cons. elements, 7 primary m.f.	6
		(vii)	Ear-base	2 ear-cons. elements, 7 primary m.f.	6
		(viii)	Nose-base	2 nose-cons. elements, 7 primary m.f.	6
		(ix)	Tongue-base	2 tongue-copns. elements, 7 primary m.f.	6

Conds. Ser. No.	Kind	Item No.	Conditioning States	Conditioned States	Com.Conds. / Comp. App.
		(x)	Body-base	2 body-cons. elements, 7 primary m.f.	6
		(xi)	(a) Any heart-base which had arisen together with the preceding rebirth cons., etc.	3 mind-elements, 72 mind-cons., elements (exclusive of 4 immaterial resultant cons.) which are first life-continuum, etc., in 5-agg. planes	
			(b) Having emerged from the Attainment of Extinction, preceding heart-base which had arisen about one thought-moment before	Anāgāmī- and Arahatta Fruition	
			(c) At the dying process, the last heart-base which had arisen at the nascent phase of the 17th thought-moment reckoned backwards from death cons.	15 life-continuums, 2 advertences, 2 recipient cons., 3 investigating cons., determining cons., 5 dying impulsions, registering cons. and death cons. in 5 -agg. planes	
			Specific heart-base (of the 3 above)	3 mind-elements, 72 mind-cons. elements exclusive of 4 immaterial resultant cons., 52 m.f.	
9. S.D.	Ob-S.D.	(i)	(a) Predominant 20 faultless cons. exclusive of Arahatta's Path cons., 38 m.f.	Predominating 8 great faultless cons., 33 m.f. exclusive of 3 abstinences and 2 illimitables	3
	Px-S.D.		(b) The same as proximity condition (vi)		6
	Na S.D.		(c) 20 strong faultless cons. exclusive of Arahatta's Path cons., 38 m.f.	21 faultless cons., 38 m.f.	1
	Ob-S.D.	(ii)	(a)* Predominant 17 mundane faultless cons., 38 m.f.	Predominating 8 greed-rooted cons., 22 m.f.	3

*(a) = Ob-S.D.; (b) = Px-S.D.; (c) = Na S.D.

Conds. Ser. No.	Kind	Item No.	Conditioning States	Conditioned States	Com.Conds. Comp.	App.
	Na S.D.		(c) 17 strong mundane faultless cons., 38 m.f.	12 faulty cons., 27 m.f.	1	
	Ob-S.D.	(iii)	(a) Predominant Arahatta's Path cons. 36 m.f. exclusive of 2 illimitables	Predominating 4 great functional cons. assoc. with knowledge, 33 m.f. exclusive of 3 abstinences and 2 illimitables	3	
	Px-S.D.		(b) The same as proximity condition (vii)			6
	Na S.D.		(c) 21 stong faultless cons., 38 m.f.	36 resultant cons., 20 functional cons., 38 m.f.		6
	Ob-S.D.	(iv)	(a) Predominant 8 greed-rooted cons., 22 m.f.	Predominating 8 greed-rooted cons., 22 m.f.	3	
	Px-S.D.		(b) The same as proximity condition (viii)			6
	Na S.D.		(c) 21 strong faultless cons., 27 m.f.	12 faulty cons., 27 m.f.		6
	Ob-S.D.	(v)	As Na S.D.	21 faultless cons.,	1	
	Px-S.D.	(vi)	(b) The same as proximity condition (ix)		5	
	Na S.D.		(c) 12 strong faulty cons., 27 m.f.	36 resultant cons., 20 functional cons., 38 m.f.		2
	Ob-S.D.	(vii)	(a) Predominant Arahatta's Fruition cons., 36 m.f., Nibbāna Nibbāna	Predominating 4 great functional cons. assoc. with knowledge, 33 m.f. 4 Fruition cons., 36 m.f.	3	
	Px-S.D.		(b) The same as proximit condition (x)			6
	Na S.D.		(c) 36 strong resultant cons., 20 functional cons., 38 m.f., 38 matter	36 resultant cons., 20 functional cons., 38 m.f.	1	
	Ob-S.D.	(viii)	(a) Predominant 3 lower Fruition cons., 36 m.f., 38 matter	Predominating 4 great faultless cons. assoc. with knowledge, 33 m.f.	3	
	Px-S.D.		(b) The same as proximity condition (xi)		5	
	Na S.D.		(c) 35 srong resultant cons. exclusive of Arahatta's Fruition cons., 20 functional cons., 38 m.f., 38 matter	21 faultless cons., 38 m.f.	1	

Conds. Ser. No. Kind	Item No.	Conditioning States	Conditioned States	Com.Conds. Comp. App.
Ob-S.D.	(ix)	(a) Predominant 18 desirable produced matter; 31 mundane resultant cons. exclusive of bodily pain cons., 20 functionarl cons., 35 m.f.	Predominating 8 greed-rooted cons., 22 m.f.	
Px-S.D.		(b) The same as proximity condition (xii)		5
Na D.S.		(c) 32 strong mundane resultant cons., 20 functional cons., 35 m.f., 28 matter.	12 faulty cons., 27 m.s.	1
Na S.D.	(x)	Suitable or unsuitable weather and food, good or bad friends, suitable or unsuitable lodging-place		Na Na Na
10. Prn	(i) to (xi)	(i)–(v) are the same as dependence condition (vi)–(x) (vi–xi) are the same as object condition (i)–(vi)		
	(xii)	(a), (b), and (c) are the same as dependence condition (xi) (a), (b), and (c)		
		Specific heart-base	3 mind-elements, 10 m.f.	5
	(xii)	Specific heart-base	72 mind-cons. elements exclusive of 4 immaterial resultant cons., 52 m.f.	
		Heart-base during lif	is related to the above cons. by prenascence condition	
		Heart-base at the moment of conception	is not related to the above cons. by prenascence condition	
11. Pon		Subsequent 4 m.agg. which are first life-continuum, etc. (excluding the 4 immaterial resultant cons.) during life in 5-agg. planes	Matter due to 1, 2, 3, or 4 causes which arose together with the preceding rebirth cons., etc., and reached the the static phase	2[*]
12. Rp	(i)	The same as proximity condition (vi)		6
	(ii)	The same as proximity condition (viii)		6
	(iii)	Preceding 18 functional impulsions excluding the last impulsions, 35 m.f.	Subsequent 18 functional impulsions exluding the first impulsions, 35 m.f.	6

[*] According to the text, there is no Pon-pa. and Pon-N.D. so the common conditions are 2.

Conds. Ser. No.	Conds. Kind	Item No.	Conditioning States	Conditioned States	Com.Conds. Comp.	Com.Conds. App.
13. Kam	Asy kam	(i)	21 faultless volitions, 12 faulty volitions	36 resultant cons., 38 m.f. and *kamma*-produced matter[*]		6
	Cn-kam	(ii)	Volition assoc. with 89 cons.	89 cons., 51 m.f. exclusive of volition, mind- and rebirth *kamma*-produced matter		10
14. Rs			1 of the 4 resultant m.agg. 3 of the 4 resultant m.agg. 2 of the 4 resultant m.agg.	3 of the 4 resultant m.agg. 1 of the 4 resultant m.agg. 2 of the 4 resultant m.agg.	7	
15. Nu	Phy-nu	(i)	Nutritive essence produced by 4 causes, namely: *kamma*, mind, temperature, and nutriment	Matter produced by 4 causes which are (i) in the same group but excluding nutritive essence, and (ii) in the different groups	1[**]	
	Cn-nu	(ii)	Mental nutriments, namely: contact, volition, cons.	89 cons., 52 m.f.; mind-mind- and rebirth *kamma*-produced matter		12
16. Fa	Ba-	(i)	Eye-faculty	2 eye-cons. elements, 7 primary m.f.	6	
		(ii)	Ear-faculty	2 ear-cons. elements, 7 primary m.f.	6	
		(iii)	Nose-faculty	2 nose-cons. elements, 7 primary m.f.	6	
		(iv)	Tongue-faculty	2 tongue-cons. elements, 7 primary m.f.	6	
		(v)	Body-faculty	2 body-cons. elements, 7 primary m.f.	6	
	Phy life-fa	(vi)	Physical life-faculty	All the 9 groups of *kamma*-produced matter exluding physical life-faculty from the same group	1[***]	
	Cn-fa	(vii)	8 mental faculties, namely: psychic life, cons., feeling, con-	89 cons., 52 m.f.; mind- and rebirth *kamma*-produced matter		14

[*] Rebirth *kamma*-produced matter, during life-*kamma*-produced matter, non-percipient beings' *kamma*-produced matter.

[**] Similar to Pon, there is no Phy-nu-ps and Phy-nu-N.D.

[***] The same reason as Phy-nu.

Conds. Ser. No. Kind		Item No.	Conditioning States	Conditioned States	Com.Conds. Comp.	App.
			fidence, effort, mindfulness, one-pointedness, and knowledge			
17. Jha			5 *jhāna* factors, namely: applied thought, sustained thought, rapture, feeling, and one-pointedness	79 cons. exclusive of twice fivefold cons., 52 m.f.; mind- and rebirth *kamma* produced matter		11
18. Pa			9 path factors, namely: knowledge, applied thought, 3 abstinences, effort, mindfulness, one-pointedness and wrong views	71 rooted cons., 52 m.f.; rooted mind- and rooted rebirth *kamma*-produced matter		13
19. Ass			The same as conascence condition (i)			7
20. Dss	Cn-dss	(i)	(a) Heart-base	15 rebirth cons., 35 m.f. in 5 agg. planes	6	
	Prn-dss		(b) 6 bases during life	7 cons. elements excluding 4 immaterial resultant cons., 52 m.f.		9
	Cn-dss	(ii)	(a) 75 cons. exclusive of 4 immaterial resultant cons., twice fivefold cons. and Arahatta's death cons., 52 m.f. during life and at the moment of conception in 5-agg. planes	Mind- and rebirth *kamma*-produced matter	5	
	Pon-dss		(b) The same as postnascence condition			
21. Ps		(i) to (x)	The same as dependence condition (i) to (x)			
		(xi) to (xvi)	The same as object condition (i) to (vi)			
		(xvii)	The same as dependence condition (xi)			
22. Ab			Just ceased 89 cons. excluding Arahatta's death cons., 52 m.f.	Present 89 cons. including Arahatta's death cons., 52 m.f.		7
23. Dsp			Just disappeared 89 cons. excluding Arahatta's death cons. 52 m.f.	Present 89 cons. including Arahatta's death cons., 52 m.f.		7
24. N.D.			The same as presence condition			

Explanation of the Chart. The chart gives the analytical states of the conditioning and conditioned states involved in the relation by root condition and points out the number of conditions where the conditioning force of root condition occurs, i.e. the common conditions where this particular root conditioning force acts. So, for the relation "The roots are related to the states which are associated with roots, and the matter produced thereby, by root condition" as given in the text:

(i) the conditioning states are the roots. These are the 6 roots, namely: greed, hate, delusion, non-greed, non-hate, and non-delusion as given in the chart;

(ii) the conditioned states are the states which are associated with roots and the matter produced thereby. These are the 71 rooted consciousnesses, 52 mental factors excluding delusion from the 2 delusion-rooted consciousnesses, rooted mind-produced matter, and rooted rebirth *kamma*-produced matter as given in the chart;

(iii) "by root condition" means the conditioning force of root condition. Here it shows that this particular force is under consideration. But since this force never occurs alone (and no force ever does) it is pointed out that this particular force of root condition is present amongst those of the 12[48] common conditions: root, predominance, conascence, mutuality, dependence, resultant, faculty, path, association, dissociation, presence, and non-disappearance where it occurs either completely or appropriately.

Completely and Appropriately.[49] Root condition belongs to the conascence group of conditions and, therefore, its conditioning and conditioned states are to be found also in those of the conditions in that group. These are the 12 conditions given above. When all the conditioning and conditioned states of root condition are included in those of the other conditions in that group, the force of root condition occurs completely. This is the case with root and the 4 Major conascence

---

[48]See Explanation of the Single Enumerations. It will now be clear why such explanations had to be given before dealing with the AECo.

[49]See Explanation of the Single Enumerations.

conditions, conascence, dependence, presence, and non-disappearance. So it is said that the force of root condition occurs completely in these 5 conditions. But when only parts of the conditioning and conditioned states of root condition are included in those of the other conditions in that group, the force of root condition does not occur completely but only appropriately. This is the case with the 4 Medium conascence conditions: mutuality, resultant, association, dissociation, and with the 3 Minor conascence conditions: predominance, faculty, path. So it is said that the force of root condition occurs appropriately in those 7 conditions. As an example of the latter, take the case of predominance condition where only investigating-wisdom, which is non-delusion, one of the 6 roots, is included in its conditioning states and only part of the conditioned states of root condition are included in its conditioned states. So the force of non-delusion only is present in predominance, but not those of the other roots. What this means is that the conditioning forces of all the 6 roots of root condition do not occur completely but only appropriately in predominance condition.

The above shows how the relation by root condition given in the text is explained in the chart. It serves as an example for the relations by the other conditions. So explanations in this connection will be given only in special cases.

How the 6 Roots, the Conditioning States, have to be Taken Separately. The root greed, a mental factor, is associated with 8 greed-rooted consciousnesses and 21 other mental factors. These latter states are the states associated with the root, greed. The root hate, a mental factor, is associated with 2 hate-rooted consciousnesses and 21 other mental factors, the states associated with the root hate. The root delusion, a mental factor, is associated with 12 faulty consciousnesses (8 greed-rooted, 2 hate-rooted, and 2 delusion-rooted) and 26 other mental factors, the states associated with the root delusion. As regards "the matter produced thereby", since these 3 roots arise only during life, only mind-produced matter arises together with them, and so this is the matter to be taken.

Similarly, for the remaining 3 roots, non-greed, nonhate, and non-delusion, the associated consciousnesses and mental factors, the states associated with each of these roots have to be taken. These are given in *Cpd.* As regards "the matter produced thereby", since these 3 roots, as faultless and indeterminate, arise during life and, as resultant indeterminate, arise at rebirth, mind-produced and rebirth *kamma*-produced matter respectively arises together with them and so these are the matter to be taken.

By taking the conditioning and conditioned states of each of the 6 roots separately in the manner given above, it will readily be seen why the Couplet Paṭṭh states that "Greed is related to delusion and its associated aggregates and mind-produced matter by root condition", and "Delusion is related to greed and its associated aggregates and mind-produced matter by root condition", and so on. This is the reason why, when the method given in the Faultless Triplet Paṭṭh is known, all that are expounded in the 24 divisions of Paṭṭh can be understood.

An Illustration of Root Condition in a Mental Group. Suppose a young man comes across a beautiful woman when he goes out for a walk. As is the case with most persons of his age, greed naturally arises. He is attracted by the beautiful appearance (visible object) of the woman, takes pleasure and delight in it, and becomes attached to it. So he cannot take his eyes off her and gazes joyfully (this is the matter produced by the greedy mind) at this object. Here, as explained in Abhidhamma, the first type of greed-rooted consciousness, its 19 associated mental factors including greed and mind-produced matter, had arisen.

According to root condition, greed, which is one of the 19 associated mental factors, is the conditioning state and greed-rooted consciousness, the remaining 18 associated mental factors and mind-produced matter, are the conditioned states. Although greed, the root, is related to greed-rooted consciousness and its associated mental factors, i.e. related to the states which are associated with greed, they are all mental states and so it is difficult to know them. But the matter which arises with that consciousness and mental factors, i.e. the mind-produced matter, the remaining conditioned state, is visibly manifested in the features of the person having greed. So, judging from the physical manifestation, the greedy mind can be inferred.

It can also be similarly explained in the cases where the other faulty roots, hate and delusion, arise; also with the faultless roots associated with great faultless states, lofty states and Path-consciousnesses, and with the indeterminate roots associated with rooted resultant and rooted functional states. But only a brief explanation is given here because, if all the 6 roots as conditioning states and the 71 consciousnesses associated with them as conditioned states were to be treated in detail, there would be so much to explain. However, the details regarding the conditioning and conditioned states of root condition and others of the 15 conditions of the conascence group are given in the Single Enumeration charts in the Intr. to *C.R.*

With Reference to Planes. The cty on this and others is given later in the form of charts. Here it will be briefly explained.

Conditioning States. All the 6 roots are possible in the sensuous plane, but hate is not possible in the fine-material and immaterial planes because hate does not arise in the beings of those planes.

Conditioned States. Both the mental and material aggregates arise in the sensuous and fine-material planes, but only the mental in the immaterial plane where there is no materiality. So in the latter plane, mind-produced and rebirth *kamma*-produced matter do not arise as conditioned states.

With Reference to Beings. All the 6 roots arise in all the 12 types of beings; the 3 faulty roots do not arise in the beings at the 4 Path-moment and the Arahat; hate does not arise in the Anāgāmī.

2. Object Condition

(*i*)–(*vi*)[50] *of the Chart.* Visible object-base is the conditioning state, and one of the 2 eye-consciousness elements and 7 primary mental factors are the conditioned state, and so on.

Conditioning Force. All the above conditioning and conditioned states are included in those of object-prenascence, object-prenascence-presence and object-prenascence-non-disappearance of the object group of conditions (see the chart in *C.R.*). So there are 4 common conditions. Here the conditioning force of object condition occurs completely in these 4 common conditions.

(*vii*) Here all the conditioning states cognized by 76 mind-consciousness elements and 52 mental factors are summarily grouped together. The details are given in the Detailed Chart of Object Condition where items 3 to 25 are to be considered. As pointed out in the footnote there, the faultless and functional super-knowledge consciousnesses must be taken separately. So if the faultless ones are the conditioned states, the Arahatta Path- and Arahatta Fruition-consciousnesses are to be excluded from the conditioning states. But if the functional ones are the conditioned states, there is no need for exclusion of those consciousnesses.

[50] All these items correspond with those of the AECo in *C.R.*

3. Detailed Chart of Object Condition

	Conditioning States	Object	Conditioned States
1.	Present visible object-base ...	Present matter	2 eye-consciousnesses ...
	Present tangible object-base		2 body-consciousnesses
2.	Present fivefold sense object	Present matter	3 mind-elements
3.	54 sensuous consciousnesses, 52 mental factors, 28 matter	6	11 registering consciousnesses, 1 smile cons. of the Arahat
4.	81 mundane consciousnesses, 52 mental factors, 28 matter 28 matter, Nibbāna, and concepts	6	12 faulty cons., 8 great associated with knowledge
5.	87 cons. excl. Arahatta's Path- and Fruition-cons., 52 mental factors, 28 matter, Nibbāna, and concepts	6	4 great faultless cons. associated with knowledge
6.	89 cons., 52 mental factors, 28 matter, Nibbāna, and concepts	6	1 mind-door advertence, 4 great functional cons. associated with knowledge
7.	Present visible object which is far, hidden, soft, or subtle	Visible	Faultless and functional Superknowledge of Divine-Eye
8.	Present sound which is far, hidden, soft, or subtle	Sound	Faultless and functional Superknowledge of Divine-Ear
9.	Fine-material faultless 5th *Jhāna* as basis, 100 or 1000 of created images	6	Faultless knowledge of suprnormal power
10.	Fine-material functional 5th *Jhāna* as basis, 100 or 1000 of created images	6	Functional knowledge of supernormal power
11.	89 cons., 52 mental factors of other beings which arose 7 days in the past, which arise in the present and which will arise during 7 days in the future	Cognizable	Faultless or functional knowledge of penetration into others' minds
12.	5 aggregates of past lives which are the past 89 cons., 52 mental factors and 28 matter; Nibbāna from examination of the 5 aggregates; concepts of name and race	6	Faultless or functional knowledge of remembrance of past existences

	Conditioning States	Object	Conditioned States
13.	Past mundane faultless and faulty *kamma*	Cogn.	Faultless or functional knowledge of rebirths according to one's *kamma*
14.	5 aggregates in future lives … (Same as past lives in 12)	6	Faultless or functional knowledge of future existences
15.	25 kinds of concepts which are 10 *kasiṇas*, 10 impurities (*asubha*), mindfulness regarding the body (*kāyagatāsati*), mindfulness regarding breathing in and out (*ānāpānā-sati*), 3 illimitables which are loving-kindness (*mettā*), compassion (*karuṇā*), and sympathetic joy (*muditā*)	Cogn.	3 fine-material first *Jhāna*
16.	14 kinds of concepts which are 10 *kasiṇas*, mindfulness regarding breathing in and out, 3 illimitables which are loving-kindness, compassion, and sympathetic joy	Cogn.	3 each of the fine-material second, third, or fourth *Jhāna*
17.	12 kinds of concepts which are 10 *kasiṇas*, mindfulness regarding breathing in ahd out, and one of the illimitables which is equanimity	Cogn.	3 fine-matrial fifth *Jhāna*
18.	Space (*ākāsa*) left by discarding the other 9 *kasiṇas*	Cogn.	3 infinity of space consciousnesses
19.	Faultless infinity of space consciousness which arises in internal continuity in this existence or past existence	Cogn.	Faultless infinity of consciousness
20.	Faultless infinity of space consciousness which arises in internal continuity in the past existence	Cogn.	Functional infinity of consciousness
21.	Functional infinity of space consciousness which arises in internal continuity in this existence; faultless infinity of space consciousness which arises in internal continuity in this existence or past existence	Cogn.	Functional infinity of consciousness

	Conditioning States	Object	Conditioned States
22.	Nothingness of faultless and functional infinity of space consciousness	Cogn.	3 nothingness consciousnesses
23. 24. 25.	Similar to 19, 20, and 21; Infinity of space is substituted by nothingness	Cogn.	Faultless, resultant and functional neither-perception-nor-non-perception
26.	Nibbāna	Cogn.	8 supramundane consciousnesses

Note : In the case of faultless super-knowledges, exclude Arahatta's Path-and Fruition-cons. from the conditioning states.

(*viii*) *Take the conditioning and conditioned states as in the chart. Conditioning Force*. As pointed out in the explanation of the SE, object condition has the largest number of conditioning and conditioned states of the 8 conditions in the object group, and the other 7 (predominance, dependence, strong-dependence, prenascence, dissociation, presence, and non-disappearance) have parts of those of object condition. So this particular conditioning force of object condition under consideration is present amongst those of the 8 common conditions and it occurs completely in object condition and appropriately in the other 7.

Since the relation by object condition is considered here, this particular force of object condition is taken as the reference with those of the common conditions in which it is included. This was also pointed out in root condition and applies to all the other conditions.

The 6 Kinds of Objects. These are (i)–(v) and (vii) of the chart.[51] The appropriate ones arise and cease at every moment in the continuity of a being in every plane except the non-percipient plane. When one of them, such as visible object-base, is taken as object, eye-consciousness with the 7 primary mental factors arise. The presently arisen visible object-base, as the conditioning state, is the cause and eye-conscious-

[51]Note that these are bases that exist independent of consciousness and mental factors, and it is only when the latter are aware of them that they become objects.

ness, etc., which take it as object, as the conditioned states, are the subjective results. This Paṭṭh method of showing that results cannot arise without causes, and so on, can be realised only by one who studies this text. With the exception of twice fivefold consciousnesses and the 3 mind-elements (which arise at the 5 doors) all the other numerous consciousnesses (which are sensuous, fine-material, immaterial, supramundane, super-knowledge and so on) arise at the mind-door. And just as there is such a wide variety of consciousnesses, so also there is a wide variety of the objects that they take. The Omniscient Mind of the Buddha can take all objects, i.e. there is nothing that cannot be taken as an object of that Mind.

With regard to the details of object condition given in the detailed chart, those about (1) concepts and lofty objects taken by the fine-material and immaterial *jhāna* consciousnesses are dealt with in Dhs and Vism, (2) the objects taken by super-knowledge consciousnesses are dealt with in Vibh-a and Vism (for details see *P.Pfn.*, chaps. XII and XIII), (3) how materiality-mentality of the distant past, of past existences, of past worlds, of past round of rebirths, which have ceased and are no more, and those which will arise in the future are related by object conditioning force to the consciousness and mental factors of recluses and bhikkhus in the present existence who have attained super-knowledge; how the present worlds of humans, *devas* and *brahmās* are related by object conditioning force to the superknowledge consciousnesses concerned are dealt with in Vism and Ps, (4) how Path-and Fruition-consciousness arise and why Nibbāna has to be taken as object are dealt with in the Abhidhamma, its Commentaries, and Vism.

Since all the mentality, i.e. 89 consciousnesses and 52 mental factors, are the conditioned states of object condition, an object must be taken by a consciousness. In other words, consciousness cannot arise without an object.

The Objects of Rebirth-consciousness. No one can deny the fact that death will certainly take place for any being that is born. Of course, there is a difference in the span of life, depending on the being and the plane of existence. So death is the inevitable consequence of birth. And it is only in the case of a Buddha or an Arahat that, after death (Parinibbāna death-consciousness), there is no more rebirth. As for all other beings who have not destroyed the latent tendencies (*anusaya*). they will be reborn. In the Latent Tendencies section of the Yamaka text, mention is made of the 81 ways by which all common worldlings and learners in the 31 planes are reborn into new existences after death. The following is cited as an example: "One who, after passing away from the Sensuous plane is reborn in the Sensuous plane, may have 7 latent tendencies (the worldling), or 5 latent tendencies (Sotāpanna and Sakadāgaāmī), or 3 latent tendencies (Anāgāmī)."

As the objects of rebirth-consciousness have not been shown in the Detailed Chart of Object Condition, extracts from Vibh-a and Vism-a on this matter are given below:

The three kinds of objects of rebirth-consciousness are: (i) *kamma*, (ii) sign of *kamma*, (iii) sign of destiny, i.e. of future existence. Of these:

(i) when a past faultless or faulty volition is taken as object it is a *kamma* object;

(ii) when a thing involved in the performance of a *kamma* is taken as object it is a sign of *kamma* object.

These two kinds of objects, which appear at the time of death, can be those that had been taken 100,000 worlds ago or earlier.

Illustration of the Sign of Kamma Object. A person by the name of Gopaka Sīvali built a pagoda in the Tālapiṭṭhika Monastery. When he was lying on his death-bed, the image of the pagoda appeared in his mind. As the pagoda was the sign of *kamma* object, he was reborn in a *deva* world.

One of these two kinds of objects is always taken by the mind:

(*a*) *In the unconscious state.* As instances, when a person's head is cut off suddenly by a very sharp sword from behind and when a person is forcibly drowned in water;

(*b*) *When death occurs suddenly.* As an example take the case when a fly, resting on the handle of a chisel, is hammered with a mallet and then crushed. The mind-door process taking place at the time is not broken off but has to be completed. For no mental process can be broken off before its completion. So after mind-door advertence, the impulsions follow and then life continuums. It is only after this process that the life-continuum is arrested and the body-door process (due to the hammering and crushing) takes place. Here the five-door advertence is followed by body-consciousness, recipient consciousness, investigating consciousness, determining consciousness, the 7 impulsions and life-continuums. Then another mind-door process (the dying process) occurs with the mind-door advertence and the impulsions taking one of the two objects, *kamma* or sign of *kamma*, followed by life-continuums. It is only at the last life-continuum (death-consciousness) of this process that death takes place. This shows how rapidly mental states arise and cease.

(iii) when an image which indicates the existence in which one will be reborn after death is the object, it is the Sign of destiny object. One who will be reborn (a) in hell will see the image of a red-hot iron pot, (b) in the human world will see the image of a mother's womb, (c) in the *deva* world will see the image of a celestial mansion or a *deva* bed (Vibh-a, p.148).

One of the three objects above, which is taken in the dying process, is also the object taken at rebirth-consciousness.

Objects of Rebirth-consciousness (*according to Vism*).

> Briefly rebirth-linking (consciousness) has three kinds of objects, namely, "past", "present", and "not-so-classifiable". Non-percipient rebirth-linking has no object.
>
> Herein, in the base consisting of boundless consciousness and the base consisting of neither perception nor non-perception, the object of rebirth-linking is past. That of the ten kinds of sense-sphere rebirth-linking is past or present. That of the rest is not-so-classifiable. But while the rebirth-linking consciousness occurs thus with three kinds of objects, the death consciousness, next to which it occurs, has only a "past" or a "not-so-classifiable" object, there being no death consciousness with a "present" object. Consequently it should be understood how it occurs in the happy destinies and the unhappy destinies as follows, that is to say, how rebirth-linking

consciousness with one of three kinds of objects occurs next to death consciousness with one of two kinds of objects.

(*From Happy to Unhappy Destiny.*)

For example, firstly in the case of a person in the happy destinies of the sense-sphere who is an evil-doer, when he is lying on his death-bed, his evil *kamma* according as it has been stored up, or its Sign, comes into focus in the mind-door. For it is said, "Then [the evil deeds that he did in the past] ... cover him [and overspread him and envelop him]" and so on. Then next to the cognitive series of impulsions ending in registration that arose contingent upon that (*kamma* or its sign), death consciousness arises making the life-continuum's objective field its object. When it has ceased, rebirth-linking consciousness arises contingent upon that same *kamma* or *kamma* sign that had come into focus, and it does so located in the unhappy destiny, being driven there by the force of defilements that have not been cut off. This is the kind of rebirth-linking that has a past object and comes next to death consciousness with a past object (*P.Pfn.*, pp.631-2, Vibh-a, p.149).

(*From Happy to Happy Destiny.*)

In another's case, relatives present (objects to him) at the five sense-doors, such as a visible datum as object, perhaps flowers, garlands, flags, banners, etc., saying "This is being offered to the Blessed One for your sake, dear, set your mind at rest"; or a sound as object, perhaps, preaching of the *Dhamma*, offerings of music, etc.; or an odour as object, perhaps incense, scents, perfumes, etc.; or a taste as object, perhaps honey, molasses, etc., saying "Taste this, dear, it is a gift to be given for your sake"; or a tangible datum as object, perhaps Chinese silk, silk of Somara, saying, "Touch this, dear, it is a gift to be given for your sake". Now when that visible datum, or whatever it may be, as object has come into focus for him and the consciousnesses ending in determining have arisen in due succession, there arise in him impulsion numbering five because of slowing down due to the nearness of death, and two registrations; after that, one death consciousness, making the life-continuum's objective field its object. At the end of that, having that same object, which lasts only a single conscious moment, rebirth-linking consciousness arises. This also is the kind of rebirth-linking with a *present* object and comes next to a death consciousness with a *past* object (*P.Pfn.*, p. 634, Vibh-a, p. 151).

The objects of the remaining rebirth consciousnesses and how rebirth occurs are given in *P.Pfn*.

With Reference to Planes. The conditioning states are present in the 31 planes and also in inanimate things such as forests, mountains, oceans, etc. In the 11 sensuous planes all the 6 kinds of objects, i.e. all the conditioning states, are present; in the 15 fine-material planes exclusive of the non-percipient plane odour-base, taste-base, and tangible object-base are absent; in the 4 immaterial planes all the 5 sense-objects are absent. As regards the conditioned states, they are present in the 30 planes exclusive of the non-percipient plane.

With Reference to Beings. Non-percipient beings cannot take the 6 kinds of objects; beings at the moments of 4 Path-consciousnesses and at the attainments of *jhānas* and Fruitions do not take the 5 sense-objects but only cognizable object; the Anāgāmīs and Arahats abiding in the Attainment of Extinction do not take any of the 6 kinds of objects; beings in the present existence who took *kamma* object at death in a previous existence and *brahmās* do not take the 5 sense-objects as objects of rebirth-consciousness, life-continuum, and death-consciousness.

3. Predominance Condition

(a) Conascence-predominance

Conditioning and Conditioned States. (i)–(iv) in the chart.

(i) *Conditioning Force of Predominant Desire.* In the Explanation of the Single Enumerations it was shown that conascence-predominance — where the 4 predominant realities are taken together — has 13 common conditions. Since only desire is here dealt with, the conditions where desire is not a conditioning state have to be excluded. These are the 4 conditions: root, nutriment, faculty, and path. Thus predominant desire has only 9 common conditions. Or, taking the conditions of the conascence group to which conascence-predominance belongs, it will be seen that desire is a conditioning state of the 4 Major and 4 Medium conascence conditions and of conascence-predominance, the only one of the 7 Minor conascence conditions. Thus predominant desire has 9 common conditions.

Completely and Appropriately. All the conditioning and conditioned states of predominant desire are found in predominance and the 4 Major conascence conditions. So the conditioning force of predominant desire occurs completely in these 5 common conditions. But only some of the conditioned states of predominant desire are found in the 4 Medium conascence conditions, and, therefore, the conditioning force of predominant desire occurs appropriately in these 4 conditions. So predominant desire has 9 common conditions, and its conditioning force occurs completely in 5 (predominance and 4 Major conascence) and appropriately in 4 (4 Medium conascence). That is why 9 is given under "appropriately" in the chart.

(ii) *Conditioning Force of Predominant Effort.* Effort is also a conditioning state of faculty and path conditions and so only 2 conditions, root and nutriment (instead of the 4 as was the case with predominant desire) are excluded from the 13 common conditions of conascence-predominance condition. So predominant effort has 11 common conditions and its conditioning force occurs completely in 7 (the 5 as in predominant desire, faculty and path) and appropriately in 4 (4 Medium conascence).

(iii) *Conditioning Force of Predominant Consciousness.* Consciousness is also a conditioning state of nutriment and faculty conditions of the Minor conascence group and so only 2 conditions, root and path, are excluded from the 13 common conditions of conascence-predominance. Therefore, predominant consciousness has 11 common conditions and its conditioning force occurs completely in 7 (the 5 as above, nutriment and faculty) and appropriately in 4 (4 Medium conascence).

(iv) *Conditioning Force of Predominant Investigating-wisdom.* Investigating-wisdom comes under the ultimate reality, knowledge, which is associated with 34 three-rooted impulsions. Since knowledge is also a conditioning state of root, faculty, and path conditions of the Minor conascence group, only nutriment is excluded from the 13 common conditions of conascence-predominance. So predominant investigating-wisdom has 12 common conditions, and its conditioning force occurs completely in 8 (the 5 as above, root, faculty, and path) and appropriately in 4 (4 Medium conascence).

Why Some Mental Factors are Excluded from the Conditioned States (see Chart). When desire, effort, or investigating-wisdom is the conditioning state, it must be excluded from the conditioned states. Since 2 delusion-rooted consciousnesses can never be predominant impulsions, doubt (which is associated with one of them) is always excluded. As regards consciousness, when it is a conditioning state it cannot be a conditioned state as well because 2 consciousnesses cannot be associated. So in this case the conditioned states are the associated mental factors. With investigating-wisdom as the conditioning state, doubt is never a conditioned state and so, in this case, there is no need for its exclusion.

(b) Object-predominance

(v) *Conditioning and Conditioned States*. As in the chart and the same as in the SEC.

Conditioning Force. On examination of the conditioning and conditioned states it will be found that all or some of them are included in those of the 8 conditions of the object group. On reference to the Explanation of the Single Enumerations, it will be seen that object-predominance occurs completely in object, predominance, and strong-dependence conditions because all the states are included in them. But in the remaining 5 conditions of the object group, only some of the states are included, and, therefore, object-predominance occurs appropriately in them. So the conditioning force of object-predominance, which is present amongst those of the 8 common conditions, occurs completely in the 3 conditions above and appropriately in 5 (dependence, prenascence, dissociation, presence, and non-disappearance).

All the great and wonderful things in this world can be performed owing to the conditioning force of conascence-predominance which consists of the predominant factors, desire, effort, consciousness, and investigating-wisdom. On the other hand, since greed-rooted and hate-rooted impulsions are included in predominant consciousness, their conditioning forces can bring about suffering and destruction in manifold ways to oneself, to the inhabitants of the world and to the world itself. As an example, take the case of an angry person. It will be seen that his eyes are bulging out almost to the point of bursting as if he were about to devour someone. Here the hate-rooted impulsions, the conditioning states, are functioning predominantly, and so the conditioned states, the associated mental factors and predominant mind-produced matter — the physical manifestation of anger described above — arise.

Results Depend Upon the Degree of Predominance. Faultless sensuous and lofty impulsions (Dhs 69; Dhs trsl., p. 76) are classed as (1) inferior (*hīna*), (2) medium (*majjhima*), and (3) superior (*paṇīta*), and the results produced by them are different. For instance, when the first *jhāna* developed functions as predominance which is: (1) inferior, rebirth takes place in the plane of Brahmā's retinue, (2) medium, rebirth takes place in the plane of Brahmā's ministers, (3) superior, rebirth takes place in the plane of great Brahmās (Vibh 439). So it must be understood that desire, effort, etc., give results graded according to their degree of predominance.

Also in the human world it will be observed that, although there is only the same class of human beings, there are differences in their status. For the latter depends upon the degree of predominance with which *kamma* was performed in past existences. This was expounded in many Suttas, one of which is in *M.L.S.* III 248, given below:

> Now, good Gotama, what is the cause, what the reason that lowness and excellence are to be seen among human beings while they are in human form? For, good Gotama, human beings of short life-span are to be seen and those of long life-span; those of many and those of few illnesses; those who are ugly, those who are beautiful; those who are of little account, those of great account; those who are poor, those who are wealthy; those who are of lowly families, those of high families; those who are weak in wisdom, those who are full of wisdom. Now what, good Gotama, is the cause, what the reason that lowness and excellence are to be seen among human beings while they are in human form?
>
> Deeds (*kamma*) are one's own, brahman youth, beings are heirs to deeds, deeds are matrix, deeds are kin, deeds are arbiters. Deed divides beings, that is to say by lowness and excellence.

4., 5. *Proximity and Contiguity Conditions*

It was mentioned earlier that the functions of the different consciousnesses would be shown by a chart when proximity condition is dealt with. These functions are given in *Expos.* as, for example, p. 352:

> And the second (element of mind cognition known as investigating consciousness) becomes a result on five occasions. How? At the time when the blind, the deaf, the foolish, the mad, a hermaphrodite, or a neuter takes conception in the world of men, such consciousness takes effect as conception; after that as long as such a person lives, it takes effect as life-continuum; in the fivefold object process with respect to the moderately desirable, it takes effect as receiving (investigating), in a vivid object at the six doors, at the moment of death, registration and decease respectively. Thus it results on five occasions.

And also in Vibh-a 145 and *P.Pfn.*, p. 629: The remaining nineteen occur in the three kinds of becoming, either in the course of an existence or at rebirth-linking, as appropriate. How?

> Firstly in — one who has been reborn by means of either profitable result or unprofitable result; according as his faculties mature, so the five profitable-resultant eye, etc., consciousnesses occur accomplishing the respective functions of seeing, hearing, smelling, tasting, and touching contingent respectively upon a desirable or desirable-neutral visible datum, etc., as objects that have come into the focus of the eye, etc., and having the sensitivity of the eye, etc., as [material] support. And likewise the five unprofitable-resultant consciousnesses; the only difference being this, that the visible data, etc., as object for these are undesirable or undesirable-neutral. And these ten are invariable as to their door, object, physical basis, and position [in the cognitive series], and invariable as to their functions....

All these functions are summarized in *Cpd.*, pp.114–17.

Based on the knowledge of these various functions, it is possible to determine the consciousness that can arise after a consciousness of known function. Therefore, the consciousnesses that must succeed one another in a particular mental process can be known. For example, greed-rooted consciousness performs the function of impulsion, and so; after these impulsions take place, registering consciousness, life-continuum, or death-consciousness must arise in such mental processes.

Of the 11 registering consciousnesses, 19 life-continuums, 10 sensuous death-consciousnesses, and 8 greed-rooted impulsions which are possible, there are, actually, only 28 different consciousnesses. For the 2 investigating consciousnesses accompanied by indifference and the 8 great resultant consciousnesses of the 11 registering consciousnesses and the 10 sensuous death-consciousnesses are included in the 19 life-continuums. This leaves 1 of registering consciousness, 19 life-continuums and 8 greed-rooted impulsions, a total of 28 consciousnesses.

The various mental processes, which are here given in full in the Detailed Chart of Proximity Condition, must be understood in order to have a good grasp of this condition. Those who have not studied Paṭṭh, or, if they have and did not understand it, are of the opinion that these mental processes were not expounded by the Buddha but made up by the Commentators. It can be proved, however, that they were expounded by the Buddha because there is ample evidence provided in the Investigation Chapter of this Faultless Triplet (and which will be pointed out when that chapter is dealt with) and of other Triplets and Couplets.

Functions of Consciousnesses. The Chart of the Fourteen Functions is provided. The chart is read as follows:

1–3. The 19 consciousnesses, namely: 2 investigating consciousnesses accompanied by indifference, 8 great resultants, 9 lofty resultants, perform the functions of rebirth, life-continuum and death;

4. The 2 advertences, namely: five-door and mind-door advertences, perform the function of adverting;

5–9. Twice fivefold consciousnesses, of which 2 eye-consciousnesses perform the function of seeing; 2 eye-consciousnesses perform the function of hearing, etc. The rest of the chart can be read off.

The last two lines of the chart summarize the number of functions performed by the consciousnesses: 55 impulsions (12 faulty consciousnesses, etc.), twice fivefold consciousnesses, 3 mind-elements (five-door advertence and 2 recipient consciousnesses), i.e. 68 (the total of the numbers with asterisks in the last line) consciousnesses perform 1 function (the line above); investigating consciousness accompanied by pleasure performs 2 functions of investigating and registering; mind-door advertence performs 2 functions of adverting and determining. In the same way read off the consciousnesses which perform 3, 4 and 5 functions.

4. Proximity Condition

In proximity condition, where only mental states are involved, the relations between them are: (1) consciousness to consciousness, (2) consciousness to mental factor, (3) consciousness to consciousness and mental factor, (4) mental factor to mental factor, (5) mental factor to consciousness, (6) mental factor to consciousness and mental factor, (7) consciousness and mental factor to consciousness, (8) consciousness and mental factor to mental factor, (9) consciousness and mental factor to consciousness and mental factor. These are given in the Consciousness Couplet and Mental Factor Couplet of the Couplet Paṭṭh as: "Consciousness is related to consciousness by proximity condition", and so on.

Of consciousness and mental factor, the former is known as (i) *citta* because it is strange and wonderful and cannot be conceived, (ii) *viññaṇa* because it has the characteristic of knowing, (iii) *mano* because it is non-substantial and is just a property of knowing. Such descriptions of consciousness are given in Dhs. So this consciousness, which is subtle and abstruse, cannot be known by ordinary persons but only by those who are deeply wise and intelligent.

4 CHART OF FOURTEEN FUNCTIONS

14 functions	Fty 12	Rootless consciousnesses 18											Sen-su-ous 24		Lof-ty 27		Supra 8	
	Faulty consciousnesses 12	Eye-consciousnesses 2	Ear-consciousnesses 2	Nose-consciousnesses 2	Tongue-consciousnesses 2	Body-consciousnesses 2	Recipient consciousnesses 2	Investigating cons. acc. by pleasure 1	" " " indiff. 2	Five-door Advertence 1	Mind-door Advertence 1	Arahatta's smile-cons. 1	Great faultless and functional cons. 16	Great resultant cons. 8	Lofty fls. and functional cons. 18	Lofty resultant cons. 9	Supra-mundane consciousnesses 8	Total
1-3 Rebirth, life-continuum, death									"					"		"		19
4 Advertence										("	")							2
5-9 Seeing,* hearing, smelling, tasting, touching		* "	"	"	"	"												2 each
10 Receiving							"											2
11 Investigating								("	")									3
12 Determining											"							1
13 Impulsion	"											"	"		"		"	55
14 Registering								("	")					"				11
No. of functions	1	1					1	2	5	1	2	1	1	4	1	3	1	
Functioning consciousness	*12	*10					*2	1	2	*1	1	*1	*16	8	*18	9	*8	

Since consciousness possesses just the characteristic of knowing an object, it is neither faultless like non-greed nor faulty like greed. So it does not produce results as do non-greed and greed, which are the faultless and faulty mental factors respectively. An analogy to illustrate the difference between consciousness and mental factors is that of drinking a solution of poison in water. The spreading of the solution throughout the whole body is the function of the water, and the poisoning of the whole body is the function of the poison. The water cannot poison the body. This is due to the poison. So also, the knowing of an object is the function of consciousness, and the performance of the faulty actions to produce faulty results such as birth in a woeful existence are the functions of greed, hate, and delusion, which are the faulty mental factors associated with consciousness. Here, too, consciousness cannot perform faulty actions to produce faulty results as birth in a woeful existence. These are due to greed, hate, and delusion. This also applies to non-greed and so on, the faultless mental factors associated with consciousness which produce good results.

Although it is said that greed and non-greed perform their respective functions, they cannot do so unless consciousness is the forerunner. So the faultless and faulty mental factors can carry out their functions only when consciousness is associated with them and acts as the forerunner. Actually, consciousness is neither faultless nor faulty, but when it is associated with faultless or faulty mental factors and acts as their forerunner, it has to accede to their wishes and become like them. That is why consciousness is called faultless or faulty. Therefore, consciousness and mental factors which arise together with (i) greed and the like are stated as "these are the states that are faulty" and (ii) non-greed and the like as "these are the states that are faultless" in Dhs.

Just as water when mixed with poison acts as the leader of the poison, so also consciousness when associated with faultless and faulty mental factors acts as their leader. This is stated as "Monks, whatsoever things are evil, have part in evil, are on the side of evil — all such have mind (consciousness) for their causing. First arises mind as the forerunner of them and these evil things follow after" (*G.S.* I 9). So unless the mind is tamed it will produce evil results. That is why in the Suttas there are many statements in this connection such as: "The mind that is untamed conduces to great loss; the mind that is tamed conduces to great profit" (*G.S.* I 5). Also

> This mind, monks, is luminous, but it is defiled by taints (corruptions) that come from without (adventitious). But this the uneducated manyfolk understands not as it really is. Wherefore for the uneducated manyfolk there is no cultivation of the mind, I declare. That mind, monks, is luminous, but it is cleansed of taints that come from without. This the educated Ariyan disciple understands as it really is. Wherefore for the educated Ariyan disciple there is cultivation of the mind, I declare (*G.S.* I 8).

Full accounts of the meaning and nature of (i) consciousness are given in Dhs, Consciousness Yamaka, Dhammapada, Saṃyutta- and Aṅguttara-nikāya, and (ii) mental factors in Dhs.

(i)–(v)[52] Indeterminate-indeterminate

Conditioning and Conditioned States. The ear-consciousness elements, etc., must be taken in the same way as shown above with the 2 eye-consciousness elements.

Conditioning Force. The 5 common conditions are those of the proximity group, i.e. proximity, contiguity, strong-dependence, absence, and disappearance, which belong to the proximity-strong-dependence group of 7 conditions. They are common because all the conditioning and conditioned states concerned in each of the above relations are contained in them. The other 2 conditions: (i) repetition condition where only the impulsions are related to one another and (ii) proximity-*kamma* where only the volitions associated with the 4 Path consciousnesses are related to the Fruition consciousnesses, are excluded because those states concerned are not contained in them. This is why these 2 conditions are excluded wherever 5 common conditions are given in the chart for the relations by proximity condition. The 5 conditions of the proximity group always occur together completely because they have the same conditioning and conditioned states. So the particular conditioning force in each of the ind-ind relations above, which is present amongst those of the 5 common conditions, occurs completely in them.

---

[52]These items in the chart correspond with those in *C.R.*

(vi) Faultless-faultless

Conditioning States. The preceding 17 mundane faultless impulsions are the conditioning states. The last of each of these impulsions is excluded because, in the mental process, it is followed, not by a faultless state, but by an indeterminate state which is either registering consciousness or life-continuum. Since in this relation a faultless state must be followed by a faultless state, such impulsions cannot be conditioning states here. Similarly, Path impulsions are excluded from the conditioning states because they are followed by Fruition consciousnesses which are indeterminate states. (Refer to the Detailed Chart of Proximity Condition.)

Conditioned States. The subsequent 21 faultless impulsions are the conditioned states. The first of each of the 17 mundane impulsions is excluded because, in the mental process, it is preceded, not by a faultless state, but by an indeterminate state which is either determining consciousness or mind-door advertence. Since in this relation a faultless state must precede a faultless state, such impulsions cannot be conditioned states here. In the case of the 4 Path impulsions (faultless), which occur only once, each of them is preceded by either change-of-lineage or purification, which are great faultless states, and so they are included as conditioned states. This is why there are 21 faultless conditioned states.

It is to be noted that all the conditioning and conditioned states are here taken together and the relation shown in a general way. But proper selection of these faultless states must be made, as done in the Detailed Chart of Proximity Condition to which reference will have to be made, to know the relations in detail.

5 DETAILED CHART OF PROXIMITY CONDITION

Processes	Preceding cons. = Conditioning state								Subsequent cons. = Conditioned state									
	Slight								Very great, great, clear or obscure									
									Sensuous impulsions 29									Life Continuums
	Rebirth	Life-Continuum 16	Md-door adv	5-door-adv	2 x 5 cons	Recipient	Investigating	Md-door adv Determining	First	Second	Third	Fourth	Fifth	Sixth	Seventh	Registering	Registering	Sensuous 10
Sensuous		5 agg. pl. 15	"					2nd	Greed rooted, delusion rooted, great fls cons							11		Life-continuum 19
		Imm 4	"		5 agg.pl. L.C.			15	Hate-rooted cons							Indf	6	Sensuous indf L.C. 6
									Arahatta's smile cons							pls	5	5 agg. three rooted 9
									Great func accompanied by pleasure							pls	5	Three-rooted 13
									" indifference							Indf	6	Three-rooted 13

Processes	Vibrating L.C.	Arresting L.C.	Md-door adv	Preparation	Approximation	Adaptation	Change of lineage	Lofty fls jh		Lofty func jh		Jhāna	Jhāna	Jhāna	
Jhāna								pls	indf	pls	indf				
								4	5	4	5				Life-Continuums

Attainments								Preceding Lofty faultless, functional impulsions Fine-mat fls, func. / Inf. S	Similar subsequent Lofty faultless, functional impulsions Inf. C / Nothingness / Neither..	5-agg 3-root 9	Inf. S 10	Inf. C 11	Not 12	Neither 13
Path	"	"	"	"	"	"	" Puri.	Path: pls 16, indf 4 Fruition (Fine-mat fls, func. / Inf. S)	Fruition (Inf. C) Fruition (Nothingness / Neither..)	Three-rooted life-continuums 13				
Fruition Attainment	"	"	"	Adaptation	Adaptation	Adaptation	Adaptation	Fruition: pls 12 4, indf 3 1 Fruition: Preceding 4 Fruition impulsions	Fruition: Similar subsequent 4 Fruition impulsions	"				
Extinction Attainment	"	"	"	Preparation	Approximation	Adaptation	Change of lineage	Fls Neither .... * Func Neither ... * Extinction	Non-returner's * Fruition Arahatta's Fruition *	"				

Dying		Sensuous death cons	death cons	3-rooted death cons	
	After				"
	Registering	10			
	Fty imp / gr.fls imp / gr.func imp	10	19	13	
	Life-continuum		19		

Rebirth After death cons.	Death consciousness	Rebirth consciousness: Rootless 2	2-rooted 4	3-rooted 4	Fine-mat 5	Inf.S.1	Inf.C.1	Not....1	Neither..1	Total
	2-rooted, rootless	"	"	"						10
	Sensuous 3-rooted	"	"	"	"	"	"	"	"	19
	Fine-material	x								17
	Infinity of Space			"		"	"	"	"	8
	Infinity of Cons.			"			"	"	"	7
	Nothingness			"				"	"	6
	Neither-perception-nor-non-perception			"					"	5

How to Read the Chart

1. Sensuous Processes

I. (1) Rebirth consciousness is related to first life-continuum;

(2) preceding first life-continuum, etc. are related to subsequent second life-continuum, etc.;

(3) 15 five-aggregate life-continuums are related to 2 advertences;

(4) 4 immaterial life-continuums are related to mind-door advertence;

(5) five-door advertence is related to twice fivefold consciousnesses;

(6) twice fivefold consciousnesses are related to recipient consciousness;

(7) recipient consciousness is related to investigating consciousness;

(8) investigating consciousness is related to determining consciousness;

II. (9) If the process is slight (*paritta*), first determining consciousness is related to second determining consciousness;

(10) second determining consciousness is related to 15 five-aggregate life-continuums;

III. (11) If the processes are very great (*atimahanta*), great (*mahanta*) , clear (*vibhūta*) or obscure (*avibhūta*), determining consciousness or mind-door advertence is related to first impulsion (of the 29 sensuous impulsions);

(12) first impulsion is related to second impulsion ... sixth impulsion is related to seventh impulsion;

IV. (13) If registering consciousness arises after greed-rooted, delusion-rooted or 8 great faultless impulsions, the last greed-rooted impulsions, etc. are related to 11 registering consciousnesses; if it does not arise, the last greed-rooted impulsions, etc., are related to 19 life-continuums;

(14) If registering consciousness arises after hate-rooted impulsions, the last hate-rooted impulsions are related to 6 registering consciousnesses accompanied by indifference; if it does not arise, the last hate-rooted impulsions are related to 6 sensuous life-continuums accompanied by indifference;

(15) If registering consciousness arises after Arahatta's smile impulsion, the last Arahatta's smile impulsion is related to 5 registering consciousnesses accompanied by pleasure; if it does not arise, the last Arahatta's smile impulsion is related to 9 five-aggregate three-rooted life-continuums;

(16) If registering consciousness arises after the great functional impulsions accompanied by pleasure, the last great functional impulsions accompanied by pleasure are related to 5 registering consciousnesses accompanied by pleasure; if it does not arise, it is related to 13 three-rooted life-continuums;

(17) If registering consciousness arises after the great functional impulsions accompanied by indifference, the last great functional impulsions accompanied by indifference are related to 6 registering consciousnesses accompanied by indifference; if it does not arise, it is related to 13 three-rooted life-continuums;

V. (18) first registering consciousness is related to second registering consciousness; second registering consciousness is related to 10 sensuous life-continuums;

2. *Jhāna*, Path and Fruition Attainment Processes

VI. (19) First pair of great faultless consciousnesses, functioning as change-of-lineage, purification or adaptation, is related to 4 Lofty faultless consciousnesses accompanied by pleasure, 16 Path consciousnesses accompanied by pleasure and 12 lower Fruition consciousnesses accompanied by pleasure;

(20) third pair of great faultless consciousnesses, functioning as change-of-lineage, purification or adaptation, is related to 5 Lofty faultless consciousnesses accompanied by indifference, 4 Path consciousnesses accompanied by indifference and 3 lower Fruition consciousnesses accompanied by indifference;

(21) first pair of great functional consciousnesses, functioning as change-of-lineage or adaptation, is related to 4 Lofty functional consciousnesses accompanied by pleasure and 4 Arahatta's Fruition consciousnesses accompanied by pleasure;

(22) third pair of great functional consciousnesses, functioning as change-of-lineage or adaptation, is related to 5 Lofty functional consciousnesses accompanied by indifference and 1 Arahatta's Fruition consciousness accompanied by indifference;

3. Attainments Processes

VII. (23) In the Attainments processes, preceding Lofty faultless or functional impulsions are related to similar subsequent Lofty faultless or functional impulsions;

(24) the last fine-material faultless or functional impulsions are related to 9 five-aggregate three-rooted life-continuums;

(25) the last faultless or functional infinity of space impulsions are related to 9 five-aggregate three-rooted life-continuums and infinity of space life-continuum, i.e. 10 life-continuums;

(26) the last faultless or functional infinity of consciousness impulsions are related to 11 life-continuums, i.e. 9 five-aggregate three-rooted, infinity of space and infinity of consciousness;

(27) the last faultless or functional nothingness impulsions are related to 12 life-continuums, i.e. 9 five-aggregate three-rooted, infinity of space, infinity of consciousness and nothingness;

(28) the last faultless or functional neither-perception-nor-non-perception impulsions are related to 13 life-continuums, i.e. 9 five-aggregate three-rooted, infinity of space, infinity of consciousness, nothingness and neither-perception-nor-non-perception;

4. Extinction Attainments

VIII. (29) Having emerged from the Attainment of Extinction, the last faultless or functional neither-perception-nor-non-perception impulsion is related to Non-returner's Fruition or Arahatta's Fruition;

5. Path

IX. (30) Stream-winner's Path is related to Stream-winner's Fruition; Once-returner's Path is related to Once-returner's Fruition; Non-returner's Path is related to Non-returner's Fruition; Arahatta's Path is related to Arahatta's Fruition;

6. Fruition Attainment Processes

X. (31) Preceding 4 Fruition impulsions are related to similar subsequent 4 Fruition impulsions;

(32) the last 4 Fruition impulsions are related to 13 three-rooted life-continuums;

7. Dying Processes

XI. (33) In the dying process, if death consciousness arises after registering consciousness, the second registering consciousness is related to 10 sensuous death consciousnesses;

(34) if death consciousness arises after faulty impulsions the last (the fifth) faulty impulsion is related to 10 sensuous death consciousnesses;

(35) if death consciousness arises after great faultless impulsions, the last (the fifth) great faultless impulsion is related to 19 death consciousnesses;

(36) if death consciousness arises after great functional impulsions, the last (the fifth) great functional impulsion is related to 13 three-rooted death consciousnesses;

(37) if death consciousness arises after life-continuum, 19 life-continuums are related to 19 death consciousnesses;

8. Rebirth After Death Consciousness

XII. (38) 4 two-rooted and 2 rootless death-consciousnesses are related to 10 sensuous rebirth-consciousnesses;

(39) 4 sensuous three-rooted death consciousnesses are related to 19 rebirth consciousnesses;

(40) 5 fine-material death consciousnesses are related to 17 rooted rebirth consciousnesses;

(41) infinity of space death consciousness is related to 4 three-rooted sensuous and 4 immaterial rebirth consciousnesses;

(42) infinity of consciousness death consciousness is related to 4 three-rooted sensuous, infinity of consciousness, nothingness and neither-perceptionnor-non-perception rebirth consciousnesses;

(43) nothingness death consciousness is related to 4 three-rooted sensuous, nothingness, and neither-perception-nor-non-perception rebirth consciousnesses;

(44) neither-perception-nor-non-perception death consciousness is related to 4 three-rooted sensuous and neither-perception-nor-non-perception rebirth consciousnesses.

Relations in Detail to Show the Conditioning States. First great faultless impulsion is related to second impulsion; second impulsion is related to third impulsion ... sixth impulsion is related to seventh impulsion. (This is read from the sensuous impulsions in the Detailed Chart.)

First pair of great faultless consciousnesses (i.e. associated with knowledge), functioning either as change-of-lineage or purification, is related to 4 Lofty faultless consciousnesses and 16 (as expanded) Path consciousnesses accompanied by pleasure. Third pair of great faultless consciousnesses, functioning either as change-of-lineage or purification, is related to 5 Lofty faultless consciousnesses and 4 Path consciousnesses accompanied by indifference. (This is read from the change-of-lineage and purification columns of the Detailed Chart.)

In the process of Attainment (*samāpajjana-vīthi*) preceding 9 Lofty faultless impulsions are related to similar subsequent 9 Lofty faultless impulsions.

Conditioned States. It will be seen from the above that these are second great faultless impulsions, etc., 9 Lofty faultless consciousnesses and 20 (as expanded) Path-consciousnesses.

Conditioning Force. All the above conditioning and conditioned states are included in those of the 5 conditions of the proximity group as well as in repetition condition. So the particular conditioning force in this fls-fls relation, which is present amongst those in the 6 common conditions, occurs completely in them.

(vii) Faultless-indeterminate

Conditioning and Conditioned States. See AEC.

In Detail: *Conditioning States*. If registering consciousness arises after the impulsions, the last great faultless impulsion (which is the seventh of one[53] of the 8 great faultless consciousnesses) is related to (one of) the 11 registering consciousnesses (indeterminate). Otherwise the last great faultless impulsion is related to (one of) the 19 life-continuums (indeterminate) arising after it.

The first pair of great faultless consciousnesses, functioning as adaptation, is related to 12 (as expanded) lower Fruitions accompanied by pleasure; the third pair of great faultless consciousnesses, functioning as adaptation, is related to 3 (as expanded) lower Fruitions accompanied by indifference. This is read from the Fruition attainment process.

The last fine-material faultless impulsion is related to the 9 three-rooted life-continuums in five-aggregate planes; the last faultless infinity of space impulsion is related to 10 life-continuums (the 9 above and infinity of space); the last faultless infinity of consciousness impulsion is related to 11 life-continuums (the 10 above and infinity of

[53] Although the total of the states is given, they have to be taken singly in every case.

consciousness); the last faultless nothingness impulsion is related to 12 life-continuums (the 11 above and nothingness); the last faultless neither-perception-nor-non-perception impulsion is related to 13 life-continuums (the 12 above and neither-perception-nor-non-perception), having emerged from the Attainment of Extinction, the last faultless neither-perception-nor-non-perception is related to the Non-Returner's Fruition; 4 Path-consciousnesses are related to the corresponding 4 Fruition-consciousnesses.

In the Dying Process. The last (usually the fifth) great faultless impulsion is related to 19 death-consciousnesses (which are the same as life-continuums).

Conditioned States. From the above it is seen that these are the subsequent 11 registering consciousnesses, 9 Lofty resultant consciousnesses, 4 Fruitions, and 38 mental factors.

Conditioning Force. All the above conditioning and conditioned states are included in those of the 5 conditions of the proximity group and parts of them in proximity-*kamma* condition. So the particular conditioning force in this fls-ind relation, which is present amongst those of the 6 common conditions, occurs completely in the 5 proximity group conditions and appropriately in *kamma* condition. For in proximity-*kamma*, only the volitions of the Path impulsions, as the conditioning states, and the 4 Fruitions, as the conditioned states, are included amongst those in this relation.

(viii) Faulty-faulty

In Detail: Conditioning States. First faulty impulsion is related to second impulsion; second impulsion is related to third impulsion ... sixth impulsion is related to seventh impulsion.

Conditioned States. From the above it is seen that these are second faulty impulsions, etc.

Conditioning Force. The same as faultless-faultless above.

(ix) Faulty-indeterminate

In Detail: *Conditioning States*. If registering consciousness arises after the impulsions in the cases of (i) 8 greed-rooted and 2 delusion-rooted impulsions, the last faulty impulsion (which is the seventh) is related to 11 registering consciousnesses; otherwise this last impulsion is related to 19 life-continuums and (ii) 2 hate-rooted impulsions, the last faulty impulsion is related to 6 registering consciousnesses accompanied by indifference; otherwise this last impulsion is related to 6 sensuous life-continuums accompanied by indifference.

In the Dying Process. The last (usually the fifth) faulty impulsion is related to 10 sensuous death-consciousnesses.

Conditioned States. These are the subsequent 11 registering consciousnesses, 9 Lofty resultant consciousnesses and 35 mental factors.

Conditioning Force. It occurs completely in the 5 conditions of the proximity group.

(x) Indeterminate-indeterminate

Conditioning and Conditioned States. See AEC.

In Detail: *Conditioning States*. Rebirth-consciousness is related to first life-continuum; preceding first life-continuum is related to subsequent second life-continuum; preceding second life-continuum is related to subsequent third life-continuum, and so on; 15 life-continuums in the five-aggregate planes are related to 2 advertences (these are to be found in the sensuous process of the Detailed Chart); 4 immaterial life-continuums are related to mind-door advertence; five-door advertence is related to twice fivefold consciousnesses; twice fivefold consciousnesses are related to recipient consciousness; recipient consciousness is related to investigating consciousness; investigating consciousness is related to determining consciousness.

In the Slight Object Process (*parittārammaṇa-vīthi*). The first determining consciousness is related to the second determining consciousness; the second determining consciousness is related to 15 life-continuums in the five-aggregate planes.

In the Very Great (atimahanta), Great (mahanta), Clear (vibhūta) and Obscure (avibhūta) Object Processes. Determining consciousness or mind-door advertence is related to the Arahatta's smile-consciousness or 8 great functional impulsions; the first great functional impulsion is related to the second impulsion; the second impulsion is related to the third impulsion ... the sixth impulsion is related to the seventh impulsion.

If registering consciousness arises after the impulsions, (i) the last (the seventh) impulsion of Arahatta's smile-consciousness is related to 5 registering consciousnesses accompanied by pleasure; otherwise it is related to 9 three-rooted life-continuums in the five-aggregate planes; (ii) the last great functional impulsion accompanied by pleasure is related to 5 registering consciousnesses accompanied by pleasure; otherwise it is related to 13 three-rooted life-continuums; (iii) the last great functional impulsion accompanied by indifference is related to 6 registering consciousnesses accompanied by indifference; otherwise it is related to 13 three-rooted life-continuums.

The first registering consciousness is related to the second registering consciousness; the second registering consciousness is related to 10 sensuous life-continuums.

The first pair of great functional consciousnesses, functioning as change-of-lineage or adaptation, is related to 4 Lofty functional consciousnesses and 4 Arahatta's Fruition-consciousnesses accompanied by pleasure; the third pair of great functional consciousnesses, functioning as change-of-lineage or adaptation, is related to 5 Lofty functional consciousnesses and 1 Arahatta's Fruition-consciousness accompanied by indifference.

In the Process of Attainments. Preceding Lofty functional impulsions are related to similar subsequent Lofty functional impulsions.

The last fine-material functional impulsion is related to 9 three-rooted life-continuums in the five-aggregate planes; the last functional infinity of space impulsion is related to 10 life-continuums (the 9 above and infinity of space); the last functional infinity of consciousness impulsion is related to 11 life-continuums (the 10 above and infinity of consciousness); the last functional nothingness impulsion is related to 12 life-continuums (the 11 above and nothingness); the last functional neither-perception-nor-non-perception impulsion is related to 13 life-continuums (the 12 above and neither-perception-nor-non-perception); having emerged from the Attainment of Extinction, the last functional neither-perception-nor-non-perception impulsion is related to the Arahatta's Fruition-consciousness.

The preceding 4 Fruition impulsions are related to similar subsequent 4 Fruition impulsions. The last 4 Fruition impulsions are related to 13 three-rooted life-continuums.

In the Dying Process. If death-consciousness arises: (i) after registering consciousness, the second registering consciousness is related to 10 sensuous death-consciousnesses; (ii) after great functional impulsions, the last (the fifth) great functional (dying) inpulsion is related to 13 three-rooted death-consciousnesses; (iii) after life-continuum, 19 life-continuums are related to 19 death-consciousnesses.

In the Rebirth Process. The different relations are:

(1) 4 two-rooted and 2 rootless death-consciousnesses are related to 10 sensuous rebirth-consciousnesses;

(2) 4 sensuous three-rooted death-consciousnesses are related to 19 rebirth-consciousnesses;

(3) 5 fine-material death-consciousnesses are related to 17 rooted rebirth-consciousnesses;

(4) infinity of space (immaterial) death-consciousness is related to 4 three-rooted sensuous and 4 immaterial rebirth-consciousnesses;

(5) infinity of consciousness (immaterial) death-consciousness is related to 4 three-rooted sensuous, infinity of consciousness, nothingness and neither-perception-nor-non-perception rebirth-consciousnesses;

(6) nothingness (immaterial) death-consciousness is related to 4 three-rooted sensuous, nothingness and neither-perception-nor-non-perception rebirth-consciousnesses;

(7) neither-perception-nor-non-perception (immaterial) death-consciousness is related to 4 three-rooted sensuous and neither-perception-nor-non-perception rebirth-consciousnesses.

Conditioned States. From the above it will be seen that these are 36 resultant consciousnesses including the Arahatta's death-consciousness, 20 functional consciousnesses, 38 mental factors.

Conditioning Force. All the above conditioning and conditioned states are contained in those of the 5 conditions of the proximity group, and parts of them in repetition condition. So the particular conditioning force here, which is present amongst those of the 6 common conditions, occurs completely in the 5 conditions of the proximity group and appropriately in repetition condition.

(xi), (xii) Indeterminate-faultless, Indeterminate-faulty

Conditioning and Conditioned States. See AEC.

Conditioning Forces. They occur completely in the 5 conditions of the proximity group.

(xiii)

Conditioning and Conditioned States. See AEC. Here the total of the conditioning and conditioned states of proximity condition as a whole are given.

Conditioning Force. All the above conditioning and conditioned states are contained in those of the 5 conditions of the proximity group, and parts of them in the repetition and *kamma* conditions, the remaining 2 of the 7 that belong to the proximity-strong-dependence group. So the particular conditioning force, which is present amongst those of the 7 common conditions, occurs completely in the 5 proximity group conditions and appropriately in repetition and *kamma* conditions.

It will be seen from the Detailed Chart of Proximity Condition, where the analytical units of the conditioning and conditioned states are given, that all the mental processes which are concerned with the Faultless Triplet are included. The relations between one consciousness and another in these mental processes will be considered again when dealing with the Investigation Chapter where textual references will be given.

So long as Parinibbāna has not taken place after becoming an Arahat, there is an uninterrupted succession of consciousnesses, each preceding consciousness ceasing and a subsequent one arising, without a break, in the continuity of a being in the round of existences excepting (i) during existence in the non-percipient plane and (ii) during the Attainment of Extinction. Of course, when consciousness is mentioned it means a group of mentality comprising one consciousness and its associated mental factors. Now, two groups of mentality cannot arise at the same time in the continuity of a being. One group has to cease before another group of the same or another kind can arise. But since the arisings of these groups of mentality take place with such rapidity that it defies description, it appears that they arise simultaneously. However, a new group of mentality can arise only after the previous one has ceased and is no longer in existence. Thus, with the momentary awareness each time of the same or new object, a new group of mentality arises, the old group having ceased to exist.

This continual change from old to new groups of mentality is known as succession of consciousnesses. It is only when this succession is analysed in order to observe the changes of consciousness that impermanence will be properly comprehended. It is such succession that acts as a stumbling block for perceiving impermanence. This is why the cty states that continuity of the successive consciousnesses masks impermanence.

On casual observation it appears that the flowing water in the river is a stretch of still water and the flame of a lamp is one and the same still flame. But on careful examination it is found that movement takes place in both the cases. This movement is due to the change from old to new materiality in the flowing water and burning flame. It is because of these changes that the water flows and the flame burns. Similarly, mentality is repeatedly changing from old to new but these changes are so subtle and rapid that it appears to be unbroken and continuous.

Proximity condition shows that the consciousnesses, which are separate and discontinuous, are impermanent. Also, that the consciousnesses in the continuity of a being are arising and ceasing at every instant, i.e. the mental life of a being lasts for an instant. Here the cause, the preceding consciousness, ceases for the effect, the subsequent consciousness, to arise. Thus this kind of causality is quite different from that recognized by scientists.

Planes. This condition occurs in 30 planes but not in the remaining non-percipient plane where there is only materiality.

Persons. This condition occurs in all the 12 types of persons.

5. Contiguity Condition

It is shown in the chart that all the conditioning and conditioned states of this condition are the same as proximity condition.

6. Conascence Condition

(i) *Conditioning and Conditioned states*. These are 89 consciousnesses and 52 mental factors. It was already explained that they are classified under the 4 mental aggregates and that these aggregates have to be taken in turns as shown in the chart. All the 4 mental aggregates cannot be taken together as the conditioning and conditioned states for, if they were, there would be no mental aggregate as conditioned and conditioning state respectively.

Although the aggregates are taken in turns as 1, 3, 2 for the conditioning states to show that there are 3 general ways of doing so, when the specific aggregates are taken into account, there are 14 ways in all as shown below:

(1) *One Aggregate in Turns*: *4 Ways*. When the conditioning state is (i) feeling, the conditioned states are the remaining 3; (ii) perception, the conditioned states are the remaining 3; (iii) mental formation, the conditioned states are the remaining 3; (iv) consciousness, the conditioned states are the remaining 3. Thus there are 4 ways here.

(2) *Three Turns*: *4 Ways*. When the conditioning states are (i) feeling, perception, and mental formation, the conditioned state is con-

sciousness; (ii) perception, mental formation, and consciousness, the conditioned state is feeling; (iii) mental formation, consciousness, and feeling, the conditioned state is perception; (iv) consciousness, feeling, and perception, the conditioned state is mental formation. There are also 4 ways here.

(3) *Two Aggregates in Turns*: *6 Ways*. When the conditioning states are (i) feeling and perception, the conditioned states are mental formation and consciousness; (ii) feeling and mental formation, the conditioned states are perception and consciousness; (iii) feeling and consciousness, the conditioned states are perception and mental formation; (iv) perception and mental formation, the conditioned states are feeling and consciousness; (v) perception and consciousness, the conditioned states are feeling and mental formation; (vi) mental formation and consciousness, the conditioned states are feeling and perception. There are 6 ways here. Thus there is a total of 14 ways.

This has to be applied to the 4 great primaries and others. They have to be taken in these ways in the six Chapters and in the conascence and base-prenascence groups of conditions in the Investigation Chapter. The details about these different ways, including those with both mentality and materiality together, are given at the end of *G.C.R.* Pt II and summarized in a chart of the Permutations and Combinations of the Aggregates.

Conditioning Force. All the mental states are both the conditioning and conditioned states. This is so in the 6 conditions: conascence, mutuality, dependence, association, presence, and non-disappearance. But only resultant mental states (where the faultless, faulty, and functional states are not included) are those of resultant condition. So this particular conditioning force, which is present amongst those[54] of the 7 common

[54]This stresses the fact that a conditioning force never acts alone but always in combination with those of the common conditions concerned. This will not be mentioned again but it should be so understood when the common conditions are given.

conditions of the conascence group, occurs completely in the 6 conditions above and appropriately in resultant condition.

(ii) *Conditioning and Conditioned States.* The 4 great primaries have to be taken in the same way as the 4 mental aggregates. See the chart.

Conditioning Force. It occurs completely in the 5 common conditions: conascence, mutuality, dependence, presence, and non-disappearance.

(iii) *Conditioning and Conditioned States.* 15 rebirth-consciousnesses, 35 mental factors, and heart-base in the five-aggregate planes are both the conditioning and conditioned states. If the consciousnesses and mental factors are the conditioning states, heart-base is the conditioned state and vice versa.

Conditioning Force. It occurs completely in the 6 common conditions: conascence, mutuality, dependence, dissociation, presence, and non-disappearance. It also occurs appropriately in resultant condition according to the detailed teaching in the Investigation Chapter of *C.R.*, p. 169, item 428(b). But in this Analytical Exposition, where the relation is given as "The four immaterial resultant aggregates are mutually related to one another by resultant condition", materiality is neither a conditioning nor conditioned state. So heart-base is excluded here, and, therefore, the force of resultant condition is not taken and there are only 6 common conditions.

(iv) *Conditioning and Conditioned States.* See the chart. The conditioning and conditioned states are the same as those of conascence-dissociation (see this in the chart) but with this difference that they are taken during life only and not at the moment of conception as well. Therefore, rebirth *kamma*-produced matter is not a conditioned state. However, it is given as such in conascence condition of the Investigation Chapter, *C.R.*, pp. 15152, item 419 (vii) (b), which, as stated before, is a detailed teaching. It must be noted that when materiality is a conditioning or conditioned state, the condition concerned occurs only in the five-aggregate planes.

Conditioning Force. It occurs completely in the 5 common conditions: conascence, dependence, dissociation, presence, and non-disappearance. If rebirth *kamma*-produced matter is taken into account as in the Investigation Chapter, this conditioning force also occurs appropriately in mutuality and resultant conditions.

(v) *Conditioning and Conditioned States*. They are clear from the chart.

Conditioning Force. It occurs completely in the 4 common conditions: conascence, dependence, presence, and non-disappearance (the 4 Major conascence).

(vi) "This matter", mentioned in dependence condition and elsewhere in the Analytical Exposition, is the heart-base. For at the moment of conception of a being in the five-aggregate planes, rebirth-consciousness has to depend on the only heart-base which arises together with it. This is the only case where the heart-base is related to consciousness by conascence condition. In this connection the cty states: "*rūpino dhammā arūpīnaṃ dhammānan ti hadaya-vatthu catunnaṃ khandhāṇaṃ*", i.e. [of] the material states, heart-base is related to the immaterial states, the 4 [mental] aggregates. Also, it raises the question as to the occasion when heart-base is related to rebirth-consciousness in the five-aggregate planes and answers that it is only at the moment of conception and not during life.

Two Types of Continuity. All the relations (i)\-(vi) by conascence condition occur in the internal continuity of a being. But only (ii) — where the great primaries of the same group are mutually related to one another — and (v) — where the great primaries are related to derived matter (relations in which mental states are not included) — occur in external continuity, i.e. in inanimate things.

Planes. All the relations by conascence condition occur in the 26 five-aggregate planes. It must be noted, however, that (1) only relation (i), where the mental states are mutually related to one another, occurs (a) when eye-consciousness and the rest of the fivefold consciousnesses arise because they do not produce matter and cannot, therefore, be related to mind-produced matter and (b) in the 4 immaterial planes because materiality is absent in them; and (2) only relations (ii) and (v), where the relations are between material states, occur in the non-percipient plane because mentality is absent in it just as in the case of external continuity above.

Persons. All the relations occur in the 12 types of persons. But (1) only (ii) and (v) occur in persons during the Attainment of Extinction; and (2) only (i), (ii), and (v) occur at Arahatta's death-consciousness.

Period. All the relations by conascence condition occur in the present, and, therefore, the cause and effect are related at the time both are present. Thus it is unlike proximity condition where the cause has to cease before the effect can arise.

7. Mutuality Condition

Mutuality condition, which belongs to the conascence group of conditions, is a part of conascence condition as indicated in the chart.

8. Dependence Condition

There are two kinds: (a) conascence-dependence, (b) prenascence-dependence.

(a) Conascence-dependence

(i)–(v) They are the same as conascence condition.

(b) Prenascence-dependence

(vi) *Conditioning and Conditioned States.* See the chart.

Conditioning Force. This condition belongs to the base-prenascence group of 6 conditions and since the above conditioning and conditioned states are included in each of them, the conditioning force occurs completely in those 6 common conditions: dependence, prenascence, faculty, dissociation, presence and non-disappearance.

(vii)-(x) Similar to the above.

In Paṭṭh it is expounded that the 5 bases are related to fivefold consciousnesses by dependence condition. The cty has no remarks on this, but beginning from the Abhidhammāvatāra subcty the later teachers have pointed out that there are three kinds of each of these 5 bases, namely: (1) slow duration (*mandāyuka*), (2) quick duration (*amandāyuka*) and (3) medium duration (*majjhimāyuka*), and that the fivefold consciousnesses are dependent only on the 5 bases of medium duration and not on those of the other durations. They definitely state that the 5 bases of medium duration are the conditioning states of base-prenascence-dependence condition.

The Three Kinds of Duration. These durations will be explained with eye-base to serve as an example for the remaining 4 bases. Eye-base (sensitive eye), which is *kamma*-produced matter, arises without any break whatsoever at every phase-moment of thought, i.e. the nascent, static, and cessant phases of a thought-moment, and exists for 51 phase-moments of thought.[55] Since each of the nascent and cessant phases of an eye-base lasts for a thought-phase; its static phase lasts for 49 thought-phases. At each of these thought-phases a new eye-base arises. Therefore, at the cessant phase of an eye-base there are 49 eye-bases which have reached the static phases. Of these 49, which is the one:

(1) on which eye-consciousness is dependent?

(2) where visible object impinges on it?

(3) which performs the function of door in the eye-door mental process?

Answers. In all the three cases, it is that eye-base which arises together with past life-continuum. For this eye-base and the visible object which impinges on it cease together after their durations of 17 thought-moments which is also the duration of the eye-door mental process.

From the above it will be seen that the eye-base, on which eye-consciousness depends, must be chosen from the ones that had reached the static phases. The method of selection is given below with the eye-door mental process which is involved here.

---

[55]See *Disc. on Elem.*, p. xxvii, for the durations of mental and material elements. A thought-moment consists of 3 phase-moments. To distinguish these phases from the material ones they are called thought-phases.

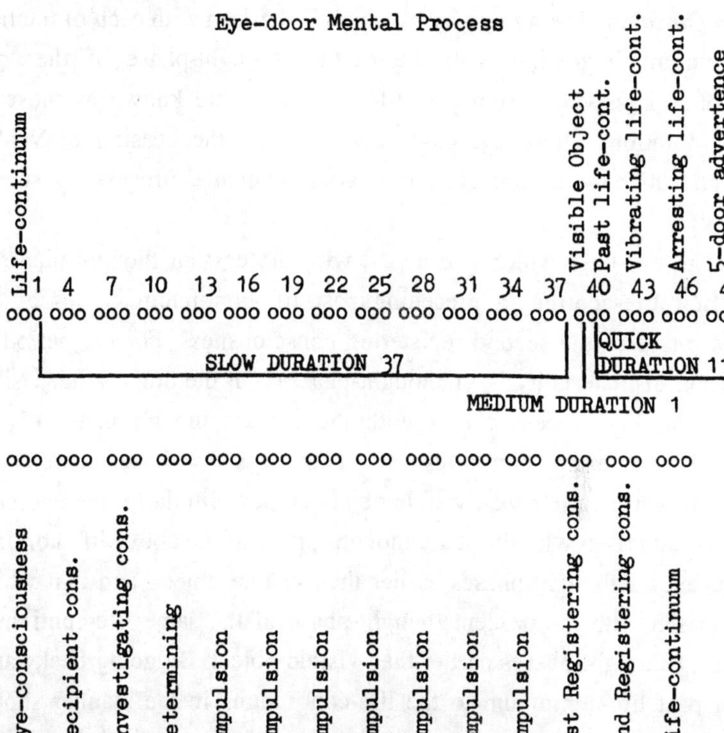

The eye-bases which had arisen with the life-continuum starting from the cessant thought-phase of the 13th reckoned backwards from past life-continuum right up to the cessant thought-phase of five-door advertence (the 49 eye-bases that arose during this period of 49 thought-phases) have not ceased but are still at the static phases when eye-consciousness is at its nascent thought-phase. These are the eye-bases that must be taken into account. For (i) at the time when eye-consciousness arises, the eye-base which arises together with it at its nascent thought-phase is at the nascent phase and not at the static phase,and (ii) the eye-base that arose with the static thought-phase of the 13th life-continuum reckoned backwards from past life-continuum is at its cessant phase and those prior to it have all ceased. So these eye-bases and those that will arise after the nascent thought-phase of eye-consciousness need not be considered in this mental process.

Slow Duration. The 37 eye-bases which had arisen with each of the life-continuums beginning with the cessant thought-phase of the 13th reckoned backwards from past life-continuum are known as those of slow duration. These eye-bases cease before the ceasing of visible object, which is the object of the eye-door mental process, as shown below:

The eye-base which had arisen with the cessant thought-phase of the first life-continuum preceding past life-continuum ceases at the static phase of the second registering consciousness. For the period of duration of materiality is 51 thought-phases. On the other hand, visible object in this process ceases with the cessant thought-phase of the second registering consciousness. Thus this eye-base ceases one thought-phase earlier than visible object ceases. Similarly, the eye-base which had arisen with the static thought-phase of the above life-continuum ceases 2 thought-phases earlier than visible object, and that which had arisen with the nascent thought-phase of the same life-continuum ceases 3 thought-phases earlier than visible object. By going backwards from past life-continuum to the life-continuums in the manner shown above for the eye-bases, it will be found that the one which had arisen with the cessant thought-phase of the 13th life-continuum preceding past life-continuum ceases at the static thought-phase of eye-consciousness, i.e. 37 thought-phases earlier than visible object. Since all these 37 eye-bases do not cease at the same time as visible object but earlier, they are known as slow duration eye-bases.

Quick Duration. The 11 eye-bases which arise with every thought-phase, beginning with the static thought-phase of past life-continuum and ending with the cessant thought-phase of five-door advertence, are known as eye-bases of quick duration. They cease after the ceasing of visible object. For example, the eye-base which arises with the static thought-phase of past life-continuum ceases at the nascent thought-phase of the first life-continuum that comes after second registering consciousness, i.e. one thought-phase later than visible object. Similarly, it will be found that the other 10 eye-bases cease much later than visible object, the last being 11 thought-phases later. So they are known as quick duration eye-bases.

Medium Duration. The eye-base which arises with the nascent thought-phase of past life-continuum is known as the eye-base of medium duration. This is the one and only eye-base which ceases at the same time as visible object, and not earlier or later than it as with the ones above. Here both the eye-base and visible object cease at the cessant thought-phase of the second registering consciousness, the stage at which the eye-door mental process ends. As mentioned earlier, the later teachers state that it is on this eye-base, which is the medium duration eye-base, that eye-consciousness is dependent.

This example with eye-base in the eye-door mental process also holds true for the other 4 bases that are involved in the five-door mental process. Normally, the fivefold consciousnesses are dependent on the 5 bases of medium duration during life. But in the dying process these consciousnesses are dependent on the 5 bases that arise with the nascent phase of the 17th thought-moment reckoned backwards from death-consciousness. The reason is that no more *kamma*-produced matter arises after this thought-moment in the dying process.

This method of selection of the bases of medium duration applies only to the Very Great, Great, and Slight Object mental processes (details of which are given in *Cpd.*, pp. 27–32, 124–28). For it is only in these cases that fivefold consciousnesses arise in them. The example given above is for the Very Great Object (*atimahantārammaṇa*) mental process. Those for the other two are given below:

Great Object (*mahantārammaṇa*) *Process.* There are two kinds: (i) first and (ii) second great object processes. In (i) the first, there are two past life-continuums preceding vibrating life-continuum instead of one as in the Very Great Object process. By applying the method given in the latter it will be found that there are 37 -3 = 34 bases of slow duration and 11 + 3 = 14 of quick duration. This is due to the extra past life-continuum where 3 additional bases arise with each of its thought-phases. So there is a decrease of 3 in those of slow and an increase of 3 in those of quick durations. Of course, there is only one base of medium duration but it has shifted one place behind. In (ii) the second, there are 3 past life-continuums and so there are 31 bases of slow duration and 17 of quick duration. The base of medium duration has again shifted one place behind.

Slight Object (*parittārammaṇa*) *Process*. There are six kinds. In the first there are 28 of slow and 20 of quick durations. Those for the others are: second = 25 and 23, third = 22 and 26, fourth = 19 and 29, fifth = 16 and 32, sixth = 13 and 35. In each of these cases an extra past life-continuum intervenes before vibrating life-continuum so that there is an arithmetical progression of 3 in these durations, and the one of medium duration shifts accordingly. Here, the complete stages in the Great Object and the other mental processes are not given but only the additional past life-continuums that are necessary for selection of the durations.

Heart-base. This is the sixth base. Some comments on it are given below:

> Heart. This is the heart flesh. As to colour, it is the colour of the back of a red-lotus petal. As to shape, it is the shape of a lotus bud with the outer petals removed and turned upside down; it is smooth outside, and inside it is like the interior of a *kosātakī* (loofah gourd). In those who possess understanding it is a little expanded; in those without understanding it is still only a bud. Inside it there is a hollow the size of a punnaga seed's bed where half a *pasata* (handful) measure of blood is kept, [and where the heart-base pervades and][56] with which as their support the mind element and mind-consciousness element occur.... As to location, it is to be found in the middle between the two breasts, inside the body ... (*P.Pfn.*, p. 275).
>
> The heart-basis has the characteristic of being the [material] support for the mind-element and for the mind-consciousness-element. Its function is to subserve them. It is manifested as the carrying of them. It is to be found in dependence on the blood, of the kind described in the Treatise on Mindfulness of the Body, inside the heart. It is assisted by the primaries with their functions of upholding, etc.; it is consolidated by temperature, consciousness, and nutriment; it is maintained by life; and it serves as physical basis

[56]Text within brackets is left out in *P.Pfn.*

for the mind-element and mind-consciousness-element, and for the states associated with them (*P.Pfn.*, pp. 496-97).

"The heart-basis ... the support for the mind-element and for the mind-consciousness-element": how is that to be known? (i) From scriptures and (ii) from logical reasoning.

(i) The scripture is this: "The materiality dependent on which the mind-element and mind-consciousness element occur is a condition, as support-condition, for the mind-element and the mind-consciousness-element and what is associated therewith" (Paṭṭh 1.5). If that is so, why is it not mentioned in the *rūpakaṇḍa* of Dhs (pp. 583*ff.*)? Its not being mentioned there is for another reason. What is that? Non-inconsistency of the teaching. For while eye-consciousness, etc., have the eye, etc., as their respective supports absolutely, mind-consciousness does not in the same way have the heart-basis as its support absolutely. And the teaching in the physical-basis dyad (*vatthu-duka*) is given by way of the material supports thus, "There is matter that is the physical basis of eye-consciousness; there is matter that is not the physical basis of eye-consciousness" (Dhs 585), and so on; and if the dyads were stated by way of what had the heart-basis absolutely as its support thus, "There is matter that is the physical basis of mind-consciousness", and so on, then the object dyads (*ārammaṇa-duka*) do not fall into line: for one cannot say, "There is matter that is the object of mind-consciousness; there is matter that is not the object of mind-consciousness." So the physical-basis and object dyads being thus made inconsistent, the teaching would lack unity (*ekasāra*), and the Master's wish was to give the teaching here in a form that has unity. That is why the heart-basis is not mentioned, not because it is unapprehendable.

(ii) But the logical reasoning should be understood in this way. In the five-constituent becoming, [that is, in the sense sphere and fine-material sphere,] these two elements have as their support produced (*nipphanna*) derived matter. Herein, since the visible-data base, etc., and nutritive essence, are found to occur apart from what is bound up with faculties, to make them the support would be illogical. Since these two elements are found in a continuity that is devoid of the femininity and masculinity faculties (i.e. in the Brahmā world), to make them the support would be illogical too. In the case of the life-faculty, that would have to have another function, so to make it the support would be illogical too. So it is the heart-basis that remains to be recognized as their support.

For it is possible to say that these two elements have as their support produced derived matter, since existence is bound up with matter in the five-constituent becoming. Whatever has its existence bound up with matter is found to have as its support produced derived matter, as the eye-consciousness element does. The distinction "in the five-constituent becoming" is made on account of the mind-consciousness-element; in the four-constituent becoming, (i. e. the immaterial sphere) there is no mind-element.

Does there not follow contradiction of the middle term (*hetu*) because of establishing faculties as their support? No; because that is disproved by what is seen. For these two elements are not, as in the case of eye-consciousness, controlled by the slackness and keenness, etc., of their physical basis; and accordingly it is not said in the texts that they have the faculties as their condition. Hence their having faculties as their support, in other words, their being controlled by them, is disproved.

Granted that these two elements have as their support the derived matter consisting of the heart-basis, how is it to be known that it is *kamma*-originated, has an invariable function, and is to be found located in the heart? It may be said to be *kamma*-originated because, like the eye, it is the materiality of a physical basis; and because of that it has an invariable function; because it is the materiality of a physical basis and because it is a support for consciousness, is the meaning. It is known that its location is there because of the heart's exhaustion (*khujjana*) in one who thinks of anything, bringing it to mind intently and directing his whole mind to it (Vism-mhṭ, 449–50).

The word *hadaya* (heart), used in a purely mental and not physical sense, occurs in the definitions of the mind-element and mind-consciousness-element in the Vibh (pp. 88–89). The brain (*matthaluṅga*), which seems to have been first added as the 32nd part of the body in Ps I 7, was ignored, and the Vism is hard put to it to find a use for it. The Piṭakas (e.g. Paṭṭh 1.5 quoted above) connect the mind with the matter of the body without specifying (*P.Pfn.*, pp. 497–98).

Some references from the cties and subcties about the heart-base have been given. and now the author's views will be briefly expressed. "Heart-base" is not specifically mentioned in the Pāli Canon, but "base" is expounded in Paṭṭh in the Dependent and Conditioned Chapters and in the dependence, prenascence, dissociation, presence, and non-disappearance conditions of the Investigation Chapter. Although it occurs frequently in them, only one example from each is provided here.

Dependent Chapter. "Dependent on aggregates, [heart-]base arises; dependent on [heart-]base, aggregates arise." This takes place at the moment of conception. It is also given in the Conditioned Chapter.

Conditioned Chapter. "Conditioned by [heart-]base, resultant indeterminate or functional indeterminate aggregates arise"; "Conditioned by [heart-]base, faultless aggregates arise"; "Conditioned by [heart-]base, faulty aggregates arise".

Investigation Chapter: *Dependence Condition.* "[Heart-]base is related to resultant indeterminate or functional indeterminate aggregates by dependence condition"; "[Heart-]base is related to faultless aggregates by dependence condition"; "[Heart-]base is related to faulty aggregates by dependence condition." These are also given for prenascence and the other conditions mentioned above.

Question. Why is it that the general term "base" expounded in Paṭṭh is specified as "heart-base" by the Commentators when this is not mentioned anywhere in the Pāli Canon?

Answer. It is clear to many that eye-consciousness, etc., are dependent and based on eye-base, etc. But in the case of the material base in question, "heart" is prefixed to it so that there will be no doubt as to which base is meant. For mind-element and mind-consciousness element are dependent on the material base which is situated within the heart and is, therefore, called "heart-base". Thus "base" and "heart-base" are one and the same.

Material Base Located Within the Heart. When some difficult problem is being pondered over or when some cause for grief is encountered, the heat caused by the anxious mind is transmitted to the material base on which the mind depends. Again, the heat of the base is transmitted to the heart's blood on which the base is dependent and thence to the heart. That is why the chest is heated on those occasions. Also, when a loud and frightful sound is heard or a frightful object is seen, the mind is upset and there is rapid throbbing of the heart and chest. There are times when, because of deep and crushing grief, death occurs of a broken heart. On the other hand, when joy is experienced there is a quaint feeling in the chest. These examples show that the material base on which the mind — i.e. mind-consciousness as distinguished from eye-consciousness, etc. — depends is located within the heart.

How the Brain is Affected. The blood and the air that is breathed in are circulating in the body and so the blood of the heart also goes to the brain. When there is great disappointment or displeasure, the mind is inflamed with anger. So the heart-base, on which the mind depends, gets heated and also the heart-blood. Then this hot blood and air also get to the brain, which is thereby heated. Therefore, this gives rise to the expression "the brain is dried up".

(*xi*) (*a*), (*b*), (*c*). These show that there are three ways of dependence on the heart-base.

(a) *Conditioning States.* At the moment of conception of beings in the five-aggregate planes, rebirth-consciousness with its associated mental factors, the base-decad and other *kamma*-produced matter always arise simultaneously. This is given in the rebirth mental process in the Detailed Chart of Proximity Condition. After rebirth-consciousness, 16 life-continuums arise and cease one after another. The first life-continuum is dependent on the heart-base that had arisen together with rebirth-consciousness; the second life-continuum is dependent on the heart-base which had arisen together with the first life-continuum, and so on, where the consciousness that arises is dependent on the heart-base that had arisen together with the preceding consciousness. It will be seen from the Detailed Proximity Chart that, with the exception of the twice fivefold consciousnesses, every other consciousness that arises during life in the five-aggregate planes is dependent on the heart-base, which had arisen together with the preceding consciousness. That is why the conditioning states are given in this Analytical Exposition Chart as "Any heart-base which had arisen together with the preceding rebirth-consciousness, etc."

Conditioned States. The 4 immaterial resultants are excluded because they only perform the functions of rebirth, life-continuum, and death in the immaterial planes, where there is no materiality and which, therefore, are not dependent on a material base.

(b) *Conditioning and Conditioned States.* At the Attainment of Extinction heart-base, which is *kamma*-produced matter, goes on arising and ceasing. But it cannot be a conditioning state of base-prenascence-dependence condition at that time because there is no consciousness to depend upon it. However, on the emergence from the Attainment of Extinction, Anāgāmī Fruition (in the case of Anāgāmī) or Arahatta Fruition (in the case of the Arahat) arises. These consciousnesses are dependent on the heart-base which had arisen about one thought-moment before them.

(c) *Conditioning and Conditioned States.* See the chart. This dependence on the heart-base in the dying process was explained in the Brief Explanations of the Conditions.

Specific Heart-base. The term "this" (*yaṃ*) in the text denotes all the heart-bases in the relations (xi) (a), (b), and (c) and is, therefore, indefinite. To make them specific, the term "that" (*taṃ*), is employed and each of the above relations confirmed. The former term is similar to a plan which has been drawn up, such as the draft of a code of laws, and the latter to the approval of the plan. Here the total conditioning and conditioned states of (a), (b), and (c) are given.

Conditioning Force. This condition belongs to the base-prenascence group of conditions, and since all its conditioning and conditioned states are included in those of the 5 base-prenascence conditions, the conditioning force occurs completely in the 5 common conditions: dependence, prenascence, dissociation, presence, and non-disappearance. Besides, since the heart-base in the dying process is a conditioning state, base-object-prenascence-dependence and base-object-prenascence-predominance conditions of the object group have to be taken into account. These are common with all the 8 conditions of the object group. So the above conditioning force also occurs appropriately in object, predominance and strong-dependence conditions, the other 5 of the object group being already accounted for above. Thus this conditioning force occurs completely and appropriately in 8 common conditions as explained above.

Planes. Although this condition occurs in the 26 five-aggregate planes, it is only in the 11 sensuous planes that all the 6 bases arise. For in the 15 fine-material planes, only 3 bases — eye-base, ear-base and heart-base — arise. The four-aggregate (4 immaterial) planes are excluded because there is no materiality on which the consciousnesses that arise there have to depend.

Persons. This condition occurs in all the 12 types of persons. But for the 4 Path individuals there is only heart-base at those Path-moments. And this condition does not occur in the Anāgāmī and Arahat at the Attainment of Extinction.

9. Strong-Dependence Condition

23 Relations. There are three kinds of strong-dependence condition: (a) object-strong-dependence, (b) proximity-strong-dependence, (c) natural strong-dependence. But there is no differentiation made of these in the 9 relations given in the text (*C.R.*, p. 6, item 9). So the states are analysed and the various relations between the analytical units are given in the chart. It will be seen that there are 3 for (i) fls-fls, 2 for (ii) fls-fty, 3 for (iii) fls-ind, 3 for (iv) fty-fty, 1 for (v) fty-fls, 2 for (vi) fty-ind, 3 for (vii) ind-ind, 3 for (viii) indfls, and 3 for (ix) ind-fty, i.e. a total of 23 relations. Also, that of the 23, 7 are object-strong-dependence, 7 are proximity-strong-dependence and 9 are natural strong-dependence conditions.

In the object group of conditions, object-predominance of predominance condition and object-strong-dependence (which is now being considered) are shown to have the same conditioning and conditioned states. But in the chart of the Analytical Exposition (AEC), which is in accordance with the text, it will be observed that for the former condition the totals of the conditioning and conditioned states are given, whereas for the latter they are analysed. The conditioning and conditioned states so analysed for the latter are given in the chart below so as to show how the different relations for this condition are obtained.

CHART OF OBJECT-PREDOMINANCE AND OBJECT-STRONG-DEPENDENCE CONDITIONS

ITEM	CONDITIONING STATES	CONDITIONED STATES
1.	Predominant 18 desirable produced matter; 76 mundane cons. exclusive of 2 hate-rooted cons., 2 delusion-rooted cons., and bodily-pain cons., 47 m.f. exclusive of hate, envy, stinginess, worry, and doubt	Predominating 8 greed-rooted cons., 22 m.f.
2.	Predominant 17 mundane faultless cons., 38 m.f.	Predominating 4 great faultless cons. dissociatred from knowledge, 32 m.f. exclusive of knowledge
3.	Predominant 17 mundane fautless cons., 3 lower Paths, 3 lower Fruitions and Nibbāna	Predominating 4 great faultless cons. associated with knowledge, 33 m.f.
4.	Predominant Arahatta's Path Arahatta's Fruition and Nibbāna	Predominating 4 great functional cons. associated with knowledge, 33 m.f.
5.	Nibbāna	8 supramundane cons, 36 m.f.

(i)[57] Faultless-faultless

(a)[58] *Object-strong-dependence*:

Conditioning and Conditioned States. See the AEC. They are the faultless states in items 2 and 3 of the above chart of two conditions.

Conditioning Force. It was shown in the Explanation of the Single Enumerations that this force occurs completely in the 3 common conditions: object, predominance, and strong-dependence.

(b) *Proximity-strong-dependence*. As referred to in the AEC, the explanation of which has already been given.

(c) *Natural Strong-dependence*: [59]

[57]This is also the item in *C.R*

[58]This distinguishes the three kinds of strong-dependence in the AEC.

[59]When no explanations are necessary about the conditioning and conditioned states, they will not be mentioned as they can be found from the AEC.

Conditioning Force. It occurs completely in natural strong-dependence condition only, there being only one common condition.

(ii) Faultless-faulty

(a) *Object-strong-dependence*:

Conditioning States. Just as a fly never goes near a vigorously burning flame, so also a faulty state never arises based on a supramundane state. So the latter is never related to a faulty state by any condition whatsoever. Thus the conditioning states are mundane faultless states.

Conditioned States. These can only be greed-rooted consciousnesses as given in the chart.

Conditioning Force. The same as (i) (a) above.

(c) *Natural Strong-dependence*:

Conditioning Force. The same as (i) (c) above. No other force is involved as this relation is not concerned with proximity-*kamma* or proximity-strong-dependence of the proximity-strong-dependence group of conditions. For the former deals with supramundane states and the latter cannot have a faulty impulsion following a faultless impulsion in one mental process.

(iii) Faultless-indeterminate

(a) *Object-strong-dependence*:

Conditioning Force. The same as (i) (a).

(b) *Proximity-strong-dependence.* As referred to in the chart.

(c) *Natural Strong-dependence*:

Conditioning and Conditioned States. All the faultless states are the conditioning states and all the indeterminate (resultant and functional) states are the conditioned states.

Conditioning Force. In this relation the volitions associated with the 4 Path-consciousnesses are included in the conditioning states and the corresponding 4 Fruition-consciousnesses in the conditioned states. These are the conditioning and conditioned states of proximity-*kamma* condition, and so this condition must be taken into account. All the conditioning and conditioned states of this relation are contained in those of the 5 conditions of the proximity group. So this force occurs in 6 common conditions: completely in proximity, contiguity, strong-dependence, absence, and disappearance (the 5 of the proximity group) and appropriately in *kamma* condition.

(iv) Faulty-faulty

(a) *Object-strong-dependence*:

Conditioning and Conditioned States. Both are 8 greed-rooted consciousnesses.

Conditioning Force. The same as (i) (a) because the states are all mental. It will be different only when the conditioning states include matter.

(b) *Proximity-strong-dependence.* As referred to in the chart.

(c) *Natural Strong-dependence*:

Conditioning Force. The same as (i)(c).

(v) Faulty-faultless

(c) *Natural Strong-dependence*:

Conditioning Force. The same as (i) (c).

Note. Object-strong-dependence is not possible here because the act of reviewing a faulty state (the object) with esteem can never be a faultless one. Also, proximity-strong-dependence is out of the question because a faulty impulsion is never followed by a faultless impulsion in a mental process.

(vi) Faulty-indeterminate

(a) *Object-strong-dependence.* This is not possible for a similar reason as above and is not included in the chart.

(b) *Proximity-strong-dependence.* As referred to in the chart.

(c) *Natural Strong-dependence*:

Conditioning Force. Here the faulty volitions, part of the conditioning states, are related to the 7 faulty-resultants, part of the conditioned states, as in the case of strong asynchronous *kamma*, the other condition in the natural strong-dependence group. Therefore, this force occurs completely in natural strong-dependence condition and appropriately in *kamma* condition.

(vii) Indeterminate-indeterminate

(a) *Object-strong-dependence*:

Conditioning States. These are Arahatta's Fruition-consciousness and Nibbāna, objects which are taken with esteem.

Conditioned States. These are the 4 great functional consciousnesses associated with knowledge and the 4 Fruition-consciousnesses. But the relations are given separately, as in the chart, because Fruition-consciousnesses take Nibbāna only as object.

Conditioning Force. The same as (i) (a).

(b) *Proximity-strong-dependence.* As referred to in the chart.

(c) *Natural Strong-dependence*:

Conditioning Force. The same as (i)(c).

(viii) Indeterminate-faultless

(a) *Object-strong-dependence*:

Conditioning and Conditioned States. Here, too, they are given as two separate relations because Path-consciousnesses take Nibbāna only as object.

Conditioning Force. The same as (i) (a).

(b) *Proximity-strong-dependence.* As referred to in the chart.

(c) *Natural Strong-dependence*: *Conditioning Force.* The same as (i) (c).

(ix) Indeterminate-faulty

(a) *Object-strong-dependence*:

Conditioning and Conditioned States. This is the only case where matter is included in the conditioning states, and, as pointed out, the conditioning force will be different this time.

Conditioning Force. It will be seen that the conditioning and conditioned states of base-object-prenascence-predominance of the object group are included. As shown in the Explanation of the Single Enumerations, it has 8 common conditions: object, predominance, dependence, strong-dependence, prenascence, dissociation, presence, and non-disappearance. So this force occurs completely, as usual, in object, predominance, and strong-dependence (the 3 of the 8 above) and appropriately in the rest.

(b) *Proximity-strong-dependence.* As referred to in the chart.

(c) *Natural Strong-dependence*:

Conditioning Force. The same as (i) (c).

(x) Weather, etc.

Weather, food, friend, and lodging-place are strong causes for the occurrence of natural strong-dependence condition. The conditioned states are not given, however, because the teaching here is neither too brief nor too detailed. In the case of weather and food, the chart is to be read as "Suitable or unsuitable weather and food are the conditioning states. The conditioning force is natural strong-dependence force." Similarly for good and bad friends and for suitable and unsuitable lodging-places.

Analytical Units in Brief. (1) Select the ones desired for object-strong-dependence from those given in the object-strong-dependence chart; (2) those of proximity-strong-dependence are the same as proximity condition; (3) when the conditioned states of natural strong-dependence are (a) faultless, Arahatta's Path- and Fruition-consciousnesses are excluded from the conditioning states, and (b) faulty, the conditioning states are mundane.

Strong-dependence condition was dealt with briefly in the Brief Explanations of the Conditions but will be treated in detail in the Investigation Chapter.

Planes. This condition occurs in all the 31 planes.

Persons. This condition occurs appropriately in the 12 types of persons.

10. Prenascence Condition

(i)–(xi) As referred to in the chart.

(xii) *Conditioning and Conditioned States.* The difference from dependence condition is that the relation between heart-base, the conditioning state, and the 3 mind-elements, the conditioned states, is taken separately. The reason for this is given below.

Conditioning Force. This base-prenascence condition belongs to the base-prenascence group of conditions, and, as shown in the Explanation of the Single Enumerations, it occurs completely in the 5 common conditions: dependence, prenascence, dissociation, presence, and non-disappearance.

As for the relation between the heart-base and mind-consciousness element by prenascence condition, this occurs during life only and not at the moment of conception. But there is also the relation between heart-base and mind-consciousness element (rebirth-consciousness) by conascence condition which takes place only at the moment of conception. Therefore, to distinguish this relation between heart-base and mind-consciousness element, the word "sometimes" (*kiñcikāle*), is employed in both these conditions where in conascence it is meant that it occurs only at the moment of conception and in prenascence that it occurs only during life. But in the case of the relation between heart-base and the mind-elements it always occurs during life. That is why this latter relation is taken separately.

Although the two kinds of prenascence condition, object-prenascence and base-prenascence, are dealt with here, in this incomplete (*sāvasesa*) teaching, the relations involved in the five-door mental process but not in the mind-door process are given in object-prenascence. This was pointed out in the Brief Explanations of the Conditions. Planes. This condition occurs in the 26 five-aggregate planes as the conditioning states are materiality. It does not occur in (a) the 4 immaterial planes because there is no materiality there and (b) the non-percipient plane because there is no mentality to take the appropriate materiality present there as object or dependence.

Persons. Object-prenascence condition occurs in the 8 types of persons exclusive of the 4 Path individuals. As for base-prenascence this is the same as base-prenascence-dependence of dependence condition.

11. Postnascence Condition

Conditioning and Conditioned States. From the chart it will be seen that the conditioning states are the mentality which arise after materiality, the conditioned states which had arisen and existed before that mentality. Since the conditioned states are materiality, this condition does not occur in the immaterial plane where there is no materiality; and since the conditioning states are mentality, this condition does not occur in the non-percipient plane where there is no mentality. That is why mentality in the five-aggregate planes have to be taken and why the 4 immaterial resultants, which occur only in the immaterial plane, have to be excluded.

Conditioning Force. The 4 conditions in the postnascence group have the same conditioning and conditioned states. So this force occurs completely in the 4 common conditions: postnascence, dissociation, presence, and non-disappearance. But in the AEC only 2 conditions are given. The reason is that in the Analytical Exposition postnascence-presence and postnascence-non-disappearance are not included, and so the conditioning force occurs completely in the 2 common conditions: postnascence and dissociation.

Here the conditioning and conditioned states are given in a general way. In order to know them in detail reference to the Detailed Chart of Proximity Condition must be made for the succession of mental states. Of course, the 4 immaterial resultants given there have to be excluded.

Relation in Detail: A Few Examples. Rebirth-consciousness is not a conditioning state of postnascence condition because there is no materiality as the conditioned state which had arisen before it. First life-continuum is related to (i) *kamma*-produced matter which had arisen together with the preceding rebirth-consciousness at its nascent thought-phase and (ii) temperature-produced matter which had arisen together with the preceding rebirth-consciousness at its static thought-phase. So first life-continuum is related to two-cause-produced matter, which had reached their static phases, by the force of postnascence condition. Second life-continuum is related to *kamma*-produced matter, temperature-produced matter and mind-produced matter (which had arisen together with first life-continuum at its nascent thought-phase), i.e. three-cause-produced matter, which had reached their static phases by the force of postnascence condition. Then, when nutriment-produced matter arises and reaches the static phase, the consciousness that immediately arises after is related to the four-cause-produced matter, which had reached their static phases by the force of postnascence condition. The 2 advertences are related to 3 or 4[60] cause-produced matter which had arisen together with (one of the) 15 life-continuums in the five-aggregate planes and had reached the static phases; recipient consciousness is related to 2 or 3[61] cause-produced matter which had arisen together with fivefold consciousnesses and reached the static phases. The rest of the consciousnesses must be taken in the order given in the Detailed Proximity chart with the exclusion of the 4 immaterial resultants as pointed out above.

It has to be noted that after emergence from the Attainment of Extinction, the Anāgāmī Fruition and Arahatta Fruition-consciousnesses are related to 2 or 3 cause-produced matter which had arisen about one thought-moment before and reached the static phases. For at the time of this Attainment, consciousness does not arise, and, therefore, mind-produced matter is not present. Also, in the dying process, (i) if death-consciousness follows impulsion, the 15 death-consciousnesses in the five-aggregate planes are related to 2 or 3 cause-produced matter which had arisen together with the fifth and last dying impulsion and reached

---

[60]With the Brahmās in the fine-material plane, nutriment-produced matter does not arise. Therefore, 3-cause-produced matter is meant for the Brahmās and 4-cause-produced matter for sensuous beings.

[61]Mind-produced matter is excluded because fivefold consciousnesses do not produce matter and so the cause-produced matter is reduced by one in both cases.

the static phases. For at the time of death, *kamma*-produced matter does not arise; (ii) if death consciousness follows registering consciousness, the 10 sensuous death-consciousnesses are related to 3 cause-produced matter which had arisen together with the second registering consciousness and reached the static phases. Here also *kamma*-produced matter does not arise, but since registering consciousness does not arise in the fine-material plane, the 3 cause-produced matter is meant for the sensuous plane. In all the other cases, 3 or 4 cause-produced matter are the conditioned states.

Note. The relations are given with materiality which had reached the static phases because it is at this stage that materiality is strongest. But consciousness is also related to the preceding materiality at the nascent and cessant phases.

When the relation is given with "matter which had arisen together with the preceding consciousness and reached the static phase", this must not be taken to mean just the consciousness immediately preceding. The teachers of old stated it in this way for easy recital. The time interval between the first life-continuum and rebirth-consciousness, which is the only consciousness that precedes it, is not even a thought-moment. So when the second life-continuum arises, there exists matter which had arisen together with rebirth-consciousness and with the first life-continuum. From the statement above it would appear that this second life-continuum is not related to the matter which had arisen together with rebirth-consciousness. But it should not be understood as such. For the consciousness that follows is related to the matter which had arisen with all the preceding consciousnesses so long as that matter has not ceased. That is why the text gives this relation as "The states, postnascent consciousness and mental factors, are related to this prenascent body by postnascence condition" (*C.R.*, p. 8, item 11).

States which are Not of Postnascence Condition. These are: (i) the consciousnesses in the immaterial plane where there is no materiality, (ii) rebirth-consciousness in the five-aggregate planes where there is no preceding materiality, (iii) the materiality in the non-percipient plane where there is no mentality, (iv) mind-produced matter which had arisen together with the last impulsion of neither-perception-nor-non-perception at the Attainment of Extinction, and also, from that instant, all the *kamma*-produced, temperature-produced, and nutriment-produced matter which arise and cease before Anāgāmī Fruition- or Arahatta Fruition-consciousness arises, (v) the non-produced matter which are never conditioned states of postnascence condition. Of these, (a) space, which has the characteristic of delimiting matter, has no actual quality for mentality to become a force of postnascence condition, (b) the 2 intimations which cease together with the consciousnesses that produced them, (c) integration and continuity (which are, in the real sense, the same as origination of matter), and impermanence (which is the cessation of matter).

Planes. This condition occurs only in the five-aggregate planes.

Persons. This condition occurs in the 12 types of persons but only in internal continuity.

12. Repetition Condition

(*i*)–(*ii*) *Contitioning and Conditioned States*. As referred to in the chart.

(*iii*) *Contitioning and Conditions States*. See the chart.

This repetition condition deals specifically with the relations between the impulsions which are included in the states related by proximity condition. So the details of (i) and (ii) can be referred to as they have already been given, but those of (iii), obtained from the Detailed Proximity chart, are as follows:

In Detail: *Conditioning States*. The first impulsion of the Arahatta's smile-consciousness and of the 8 great functional consciousnesses is related to second impulsion, ... sixth impulsion is related to seventh impulsion.

First pair of great functional consciousnesses, functioning as change-of-lineage or adaptation, is related to 4 Lofty functional consciousnesses accompanied by pleasure; third pair of great functional consciousnesses, functioning as change-of-lineage or adaptation, is related to 5 Lofty functional consciousnesses accompanied by indifference.

In the process of Attainment, the preceding 9 Lofty functional impulsions are related to similar subsequent 9 Lofty functional impulsions.

Conditioned States. These are Arahatta's smile-consciousness, 8 great functional consciousnesses which are second impulsions, etc., 9 Lofty functional impulsions, 35 mental factors.

Conditioning Force. Repetition condition belongs to the proximity-strong-dependence group and so this particular conditioning force occurs completely in the 6 common conditions: proximity, contiguity, strong-dependence, repetition, absence, and disappearance.

Paths and Fruitions. Beings attain Path and Fruition because of the force of this condition which brings about acute faculties of knowledge, effort, and so forth. For when the first impulsion associated with knowledge, etc., is related to the second impulsion, the latter acquires the force of the knowledge, etc., of the former and becomes stronger. In the same way, the third and fourth impulsions acquire stronger forces of knowledge, etc., by degrees till these faculties become acute.

In the section of Ps dealing with the different kinds of Buddha knowledge, the knowledge of the faculties and intentions of others is mentioned, such as "The Buddha saw beings with little dust in their eyes, with much dust in their eyes; with acute faculties, with dull faculties; of good dispositions, of bad dispositions; docile, indocile; few seeing fear in sins (faults), and few not seeing fear in sins". This knowledge is the prerogative of the Buddha, unattainable by any of his disciples.

Although the Buddha had great compassion on all beings, he could not make them all attain Paths and Fruitions. Only those beings who had practised and acquired ripe knowledge, etc., were immediately instructed for such attainments. In other cases he had to bide his time till they became proficient. For instance, when the King of Devas wanted to worship the Buddha, he was not allowed to do so because he was not ripe for the Path at the time, and so the Buddha abided in Fruition. This is given in Sakkapanha Suttanta (*Dial.* II, p. 305) as follows:

> Now at that time, lord, the Exalted One was seated, rapt in some stage of meditation, and Bhuñjatī, wife of Vessavaṇa, was waiting on him, worshipping with clasped hands. Then I said to Bhuñjatī, "Madam, do you salute the Exalted One for me and say, 'Sakka, Lord, ruler of gods, with ministers and suite, does homage at the feet of the Exalted One," And Bhuñjatī replied, "'Tis not the right time, sir, for seeing the Exalted One; he is in retreat."

Again, the Buddha could not make his younger brother, Ānanda, attain Arahatship during his lifetime as Ānanda's knowledge, etc., were not ripe enough for that purpose. However, Ānanda earnestly wanted to become an Arahat. For he had heard other monks telling the Buddha that they had become Arahats after they had practised meditation on the five aggregates as instructed by the Buddha, and Ānanda wanted to emulate them. So he requested the Buddha to give him instructions for meditative practices on the five aggregates. Although the Buddha knew that Ānanda would not be able to destroy the corruptions by the 3 Higher Paths at the time, he did so just to satisfy Ānanda and to bring about Arahatship later on (Spk II 307).

Also, in connection with the kind of sorrow that is permissible, it is related (in the cty on the Sakka-pañha Suttanta, ? ? 320) that Mahāsiva Thera, who thought he would attain Arahatship after practising for 2 or 3 days, cried at the end of each year when he failed to do so. It was only in the thirtieth year of practice that he succeeded. This shows how a person can attain Path and Fruition by repetition if he is not at present fully developed.

The above examples show that Path and Fruition cannot be attained if the relation by repetition condition is weak. Therefore, one who is practising to attain Path and Fruition must realise that, for the many, they are difficult to attain. That is why in *B.D.* IV 6 it is stated, "This Dhamma won to by me is deep, difficult to understand, peaceful, excellent, beyond dialectic, subtle, intelligible to the learned." Thus repetition condition is of great importance in this regard. But just because Path and Fruition are difficult to attain, it does not mean that one should be disheartened and not practise at all. For if success is not achieved by practice in the present life, repetition will be the cause for success in some future existence.

Planes. This condition occurs in 30 planes, the remaining non-percipient plane being excluded because there is no mentality in that plane.

Persons. This condition occurs in 8 types of persons. The 4 Path individuals are excluded because Path-consciousnesses are only conditioned states. Also excluded are the Anāgāmīs and Arahats when they are at the Attainment of Extinction.

13. *Kamma* Condition

There are two kinds: (a) asynchronous *kamma*, (b) conascence-*kamma*.

(a) Asynchronous *Kamma*

(i) *Conditioning and Conditioned States.* The totals of these states are given in the AEC. They are detailed in the Asynchronous *Kamma* chart which is read as follows:

Faulty Volition. The 12 faulty volitions are related to 7 faulty-resultants, rebirth *kamma*-produced — and during life — *kamma*-produced matter by asynchronous *kamma* condition.

Faultless Volition. The 4 three-rooted higher class (*ukkaṭṭha*) great faultless volitions are related to 8 rootless faultless resultants, 8 great resultants, rebirth *kamma*-produced — and during life — *kamma*-produced matter by asynchronous *kamma* condition.

The 4 three-rooted lower class (*omaka*) and 4 two-rooted higher class great faultless volitions are related to 8 rootless faultless-resultants, 4 great resultants dissociated from knowledge, rebirth *kamma*-produced — and during life — *kamma*-produced matter by asynchronous *kamma* condition. The rest can be read off.

Conditioning Force. The 4 Path volitions and the 4 Fruition-consciousnesses, which are included as conditioning and conditioned states respectively of this condition, are those of proximity-*kamma* condition. The latter belongs to the proximity-strong-dependence group, and, as was shown in the Explanation of the Single Enumerations, it has 6 common conditions. So this conditioning force occurs completely in *kamma* condition and appropriately in proximity, contiguity, strong-dependence, absence, and disappearance conditions.

(b) Conascence-*kamma*

(ii) *Conditioning and Conditioned States*. See the AEC.

Conditioning Force. Refer to this condition in the Explanation of the Single Enumerations. This force occurs completely in the 4 Major conascence, *kamma* and nutriment and appropriately in the 4 Medium conascence conditions.

Importance of *Kamma* Condition

Kamma condition is of fundamental importance in the Buddha's teaching. In the case of:

(1) *Conascence-kamma*, the volition is associated with each of the 89 consciousnesses; and so every action in thought, word, and deed performed by a being at every second, minute, and hour of the day comes under conascence-*kamma* condition. For no action can be performed without volition. When people say that a man is good-natured, kind-hearted, or well-intentioned, it is to this *kamma* that they refer.

(2) Asynchronous *Kamma*, the necessary information about it, provided below, is taken from the Pāli texts and commentaries:

1. Herein, *kamma* is fourfold: (i) to be experienced here and now (*diṭṭha-dhamma-vedanīya*), (ii) to be experienced on rebirth (*upapajja-vedanīya*), (iii) to be experienced in some subsequent becoming (*aparāpariya-vedanīya*), and (iv) lapsed *kamma* (*ahosi*).

6 ASYNCHRONOUS KAMMA CHART

Volitions		Faulty-resultant 7	Rootless fls-res 8	Great res diss. fr. knl 4	Great res ass. with knl 4	First Jhāna resultant 1	Second " 1	Third " 1	Fourth " 1	Fifth " 1	Infinity of Space res 1	" Cons. res 1	Nothingness res 1	Neither perception ... res 1	Stream-winner's Fruition 1	Once-returner's " 1	Non-returner's " 1	Arahatta's " 1	Rebirth kamma-prod. matter	During life "	Non-percipient beings ... "
Faulty	12	"																	"	"	
3-rooted higher class great faultless	4		"		"														"	"	
3-rooted lower and 2 rooted higher class great faultless	4		"	"															"	"	
2-rooted lower class great faultless	4		"																"	"	
First Jhāna faultless	1					"													"	"	
Second ...	1						"												"	"	
Third ...	1							"											"	"	
Fourth ...	1								"										"	"	
Fifth ...	1									"									"	"	"
Infinity of Space faultless	1										"										
Infinity of Cons. faultless	1											"									
Nothingness faultless	1												"								
Neither perception ... fls	1													"							
Stream-winner's Path	1														"						
Once-returner's Path	1															"					
Non-returner's Path	1																"				
Arahatta's Path	1																	"			

[(i) "*To be experienced here and now*" means *kamma* whose fruit is to be experienced in this present selfhood; (ii) "*to be experienced on rebirth*" means *kamma* whose fruit is to be experienced (in the becoming) next to the present becoming; (iii) "*to be experienced in some subsequent becoming* (*existence*)" means *kamma* whose fruit is to be experienced in some successive selfhood other than either that here and now or next to that here and now; (iv) "*lapsed kamma*" is *kamma* of which it has to be said, "There has been *kamma*, but there has not been, is not, and will not be, *kamma*-result."]

Of these, (i) the volition, either profitable or unprofitable, of the first of the seven impulsion consciousnesses in a single cognitive series of impulsions is called *kamma to be experienced here and now*; it gives its result in this same selfhood. But if it cannot do so, it is called (iv) *lapsed kamma* (*ahosi-kamma*), according to the triad described thus: "There has been (*ahosi*) *kamma*, there has been no *kamma*-result, there will be no *kamma*-result." (ii) The volition of the seventh impulsion that accomplishes its purpose is called *kamma to be experienced on rebirth*; it gives its result in the next selfhood. If it cannot do so, it is called (iv) lapsed *kamma* in the way already described. (iii) The volition of the five impulsions between these two is called *kamma to be experienced in some subsequent becoming*; it gives its result in the future when it gets the opportunity, and however long the round of rebirths continues, it never becomes lapsed *kamma*.

[The volition of the first impulsion, which has efficient power by not being prevented by opposition and by having acquired the distinction of a condition, and which has definitely occurred as a prior *kamma*-formation of the appropriate kind, giving its fruit in this selfhood, is called "*to be experienced here and now*". For while that first-impulsion volition, being effective in the way stated, is helpful to what is associated with its special qualities in the impulsion continuity, yet because it wields little power over aspects and because it has little result owing to lack of repetition, it is not, like the other two kinds, *kamma* that looks beyond the occurring continuity and looks to obtain an opportunity; it gives its fruit here only as mere result during the course of becoming, like a mere flower. "*But if it cannot do so*": *kamma*'s giving of result comes about only through the due occurrence of conditions consisting of (suitable) essentials of becoming, means, etc., failing which it is unable to give its result in that selfhood. "*That accomplishes its purpose*": that fulfils its purpose in giving, etc., and in killing, and so on. For the seventh impulsion to which this refers is the final impulsion in the series, and when it has acquired distinction in the way already stated and has acquired the service of repetition by the previous impulsions, it gives its result in the next selfhood and is called "to be experienced on rebirth".]

2. Another fourfold classification of *kamma* is this: (v) weighty (*garuka*), (vi) habitual (*bahula*), (Vii) death-threshold (*maraṇāsanna*), and (viii) *kamma* (stored up) by being performed (*kaṭattā-kamma*).

[(v) "*Weighty*" *kamma* is very reprehensible unprofitable *kamma* and very powerful profitable *kamma*. (vi) "*Habitual*" *kamma* is what is habitually, continually done and repeated. (vii) "*Death-threshold*" *kamma* is what is remembered with great vividness at the time next before death; what is meant is that there is no question about what is done at the time of death.]

Herein, (v) when there is weighty and unweighty *kamma*, the *weightier*, whether profitable or unprofitable, whether *kamma* consisting in matricide or *kamma* of the exalted spheres, takes precedence in ripening. (vi) Likewise when there is habitual and unhabitual *kamma*, the *more habitual*, whether consisting in good or bad conduct, takes precedence in ripening. (vii) *Death-threshold kamma* is that remembered at the time of death; for when a man near death can remember (*kamma*), he is born according to that. (viii) *Kamma* not included in the foregoing three kinds that has been often repeated is called *kamma (stored up) by being performed*. This brings about rebirth-linking if other kinds fail.

["*That has been often repeated*": he draws a distinction between this kind of *kamma* as stated and the "habitual" kind, and he likewise excludes *kamma* to be experienced here and now from it because the bringing on of rebirth-linking is admitted; for the tetrad beginning with the "weighty" is stated as productive of rebirth-linking.

Herein, the weighty ripens first of all, and that is why it is so called. When weighty *kamma* is lacking, what has been much done ripens. When that is lacking, death-threshold *kamma* ripens. When that too is lacking, then *kamma* done in previous births, which is called "*kamma (stored up) by being performed*", ripens. The last three when produced can be strong or weak (Vism-a, 769–71). This cty then cites various Birth Stories (Jātakas) and M Sutta 136 in order to show how, for various reasons, the result of one kind of *kamma* may be delayed or displaced by the result of another and concludes, "This is the province of the Tathāgata's knowledge of the Great Exposition of *Kamma*", in other words, the mastery of the order of ripening of such-and-such *kamma* for such-and-such reasons.]

3. Another fourfold classification of *kamma* is this: (ix) productive (*janaka*), (x) consolidating (*upatthambhaka*), (xi) frustrating (*upapīḷaka*), and (xii) supplanting (*upaghātaka*).

[(ix) "*Productive*" *kamma* is what produces resultant continuity by providing rebirth-linking and so on. (x) "*Consolidating*" *kamma* prolongs the occurrence of the continuity of pleasure or pain, or the endurance of materiality. (xi) "*Frustrating*" *kamma* slowly diminishes the endurance of pleasure or pain when they occur. It cuts off the result of other *kamma* without giving any result of its own. (xii) "*Supplanting*" *kamma*, however, cuts off weak *kamma* and makes its own result arise. This is their difference (Vism-a 771).]

Herein, (ix) what is called *productive* is both profitable and unprofitable. It produces the material and immaterial aggregates both at rebirth-linking and during the course of an existence. (x) *Consolidating kamma* cannot produce result, but when result has already been produced in the provision of rebirth-linking by other *kamma*, it consolidates the pleasure or pain that arises and makes it last. (xi) When result has already been produced in the provision of rebirth-linking by other *kamma*, *frustrating kamma* frustrates and obstructs the pleasure or pain that arises and does not allow it to last. (xii) *Supplanting kamma* is itself both profitable and unprofitable; it supplants other, weaker, *kamma*;

prevents its resulting; and usurps that *kamma*'s opportunity in order to cause its own result. But when the opportunity has thus been furnished by the (other) *kamma*, it is that (supplanting *kamma*'s) result that is called arisen (*P.Pfn.*, pp.696–98).

There is No Doer Apart from Kamma and Its Result. In all kinds of becoming, generation, destiny, station, and abode there appears only mentality-materiality, which occurs by means of the linking of cause with fruit. He sees no doer over and above the doing, no experiencer of the result over and above the occurrence of the result. But he sees clearly with right understanding that the wise say "doer" when there is doing and "experiencer" when there is experiencing simply as a mode of common usage. Hence the Ancients said:

There is no doer of a deed
Or one who reaps the deed's result;
Phenomena alone flow on —
No other view than this is right.

And so, while *kamma* and result
Thus causally maintain their round,
As seed and tree succeed in turn,
No first beginning can be shown.

Nor in the future round of births
Can they be shown not to occur:
Sectarians, not knowing this,
Have failed to gain self-mastery.

They assume a being, see it as
Eternal or annihilated,
Adopt the sixty-two wrong views,
Each contradicting one another.

The stream of craving bears them on
Caught in the meshes of their views:
And as the stream thus bears them on
They are not freed from suffering.

A monk, disciple of the Buddha,
With direct knowledge of this fact
Can penetrate this deep and subtle
Void conditionality.

There is no *kamma* in result,

Nor does result exist in *kamma*;
Though they are void of one another,
There is no fruit without the *kamma*.

As fire does not exist inside
The sun, a gem, cowdung, nor yet
Outside them, but is brought to be
By means of its component parts,

So neither can result be found
Within the *kamma*, nor without;
Nor does the *kamma* still persist
[In the result it has produced].

The *kamma* of its fruit is void;
No fruit exists yet in the *kamma*;
And still the fruit is born from it,
Wholly depending on the *kamma*.

For here there is no Brahmā God,
Creator of the round of births,
Phenomena alone flow on
Cause and component their condition.

(*P.Pfn.*, pp.700–701)

2. The following account of *kamma* is given in *G.S.* III 294:

Monks, it is said: "Action (*kamma*) must be discerned, its tie-source, variety, fruit, ending, and the steps leading thereto" — and wherefore is this said?

Monks, I say that determinate thought (volition) is action. When one determines, one acts by deed, word, or thought.

And what is action's tie-source? Contact, monks.

And what is action's variety? There is action that is experienced (ripens) in hell, in a beast's womb, in the realm of the departed (*peta* world), in the world of man, and in the *deva* world.

And what is action's fruit? I say that it is threefold: It may either rise here now [in the present existence] or at another time [in the next existence] or on the way [in some subsequent existence].

And what is action's ending? Contact's ending, monks.

And just in this Ariyan eightfold Way are the steps leading to action's ending: right view, and so forth. And when the Ariyan disciple thus knows action, its tie-source, variety, fruit, ending, and the steps leading thereto; he knows the penetrative godly life as action's ending.

3. In *Expos.*, pp.117*f.*, it is stated that *kamma* is volition as well as some states associated therewith.

And that states associated with volition are also *kamma* has been shown by the fourfold classification of *kamma*. It has been said, "Bhikkhus, there are four, which I have realized and understood by my own higher [intuitive] knowledge. Which are the four? There is, bhikkhus, *kamma* which is impure and productive of impurity; there is, bhikkhus, *kamma* which is pure and productive of purity; there is, bhikkhus, *kamma* which is both impure and pure, and productive of both impurity and purity; there is, bhikkhus, *kamma* which is neither impure nor pure, productive of neither impurity nor purity, and which, though itself *kamma*, conduces to the destruction of *kammas*. And which, bhikkhus, is *kamma* which is neither impure nor pure, and is productive of neither impurity nor purity? How does it, though itself *kamma*, lead to the destruction of *kamma*s? The seven factors of wisdom (*bojjhaṅga*): — mindfulness, etc., may be said to be *kamma* which, being neither impure nor pure, productive of neither impurity nor purity, lead to the destruction of *kammas*. [The same is repeated substituting the Ariyan eightfold path for the seven factors of wisdom (see *G.S.* II, Suttas 231–36, pp. 238*f.*)]. Thus these fifteen states, factors of wisdom and of the Path, have been shown by the fourfold classification of *kamma*.

The twenty-one states, viz., these fifteen together with the six [covetousness, ill-will, wrong view, noncovetousness, good-will, right view] should be understood as states associated with volition.

4. The following is part of the conversation between Prince Pāyāsi and the Venerable Master Kassapa on rebirth and *kamma* (*Dial.* II 351).

"I, Master Kassapa, am of this opinion, of these views: Neither is there another world, nor are there beings reborn not of parents, nor is there fruit or result of deeds well-done or ill-done."

[At the beginning of the Suttanta this is said to be an evil view of things.]

"I, Prince, have neither seen or heard of anyone holding such a view, such an opinion. How then can you declare, as you do, that 'there neither is another world, nor rebirth as inheritor of the highest heavens, nor fruit or result of deeds well-done or ill-done'? Wherefore, Prince, I will cross-question you herein, and do you reply in what way you may approve. What think you, yon moon and sun, are they in this world or in another world, are they divine or human?"

"This moon and sun, Master Kassapa, are in another world, not in this, they are gods, not human."

> "Then, Prince, let this be taken as evidence that there is both another world, and rebirth as inheritor of the highest heavens, and fruit and result of deeds done well or ill."

Note. The cty on the Sudhābhojana Jātaka, p. 398, states that the Buddha expounded that there are *devas* on the moon and on the sun.

The faultless and faulty actions do not produce results at the time they are performed. If they did, a man would become a *deva* while he carried out a faultless action which produces rebirth in the *deva* world. But this is not so. For the instant after *kamma* is performed it has ceased and is no longer in existence. However, because of the performance of *kamma*, it can give results later, either in the present existence or the next or some subsequent one, when causes other than that of that *kamma* provide the opportunity for doing so (Paṭṭh-a, p. 374). This was already mentioned in the Brief Explanations of the Conditions.

Detailed Explanation of Asynchronous *Kamma*

The Detailed Asynchronous *Kamma* chart, here provided, explains in detail the relation: "Faultless and faulty *kamma* is related to resultant aggregates and *kamma*-produced matter by *kamma* condition" given in the Analytical Exposition, *C.R.*, p. 8, item 13 (i). The resultant aggregates are the 36 resultant consciousnesses, and the different kinds of *kamma*-produced matter are rebirth *kamma*-produced, during life *kamma*-produced, and non-percipient beings' *kamma*-produced matter. The way the items in the chart have to be read and the explanations connected therewith are given below:

1. The 11 faulty volitions exclusive of restlessness produce results at rebirth in the 4 lower planes as faultyresultant investigating consciousness accompanied by indifference and rebirth *kamma*-produced matter.

2. The 12 faulty volitions produce results during life in the 26 (11 + 15) five-aggregate planes as 7 faulty-resultant consciousnesses and during life *kamma*-produced matter.

Restlessness Does Not Produce Rebirth Result. This is known from item 1 above. *Expos.* 347, states:

But when action is put forth by these twelve classes of immoral consciousness, excepting the one accompanied by distraction (restlessness), the remaining eleven involve rebirth. When the kind that is accompanied by doubt, being weak and without obtaining resolve, involves rebirth, why does not the one accompanied by distraction, which is strong and has obtained resolve, do so? Because of its not being a state "removable by the path of insight (*dassanena pahātabba*)". Did it carry rebirth, it would come in the division named "removable by the path of insight". [But it does not so come], hence, excepting it, the remaining eleven involve rebirth. Moreover when action is put forth by any of the eleven, there is rebirth in the four places of suffering by that volition, and rebirth is got by the unconditioned element of mind-cognition (investigating consciousness) accompanied by indifference as an immoral result. There would also be a getting of rebirth in the four places of suffering by the kind of consciousness accompanied by distraction. If so, there should then be removal by the path of insight. But because there is to this kind of consciousness no getting of rebirth in purgatory, therefore it does not come in that Division.

Non-inclusion in the Triplet of States Eradicated by the First Path. Restlessness is not included as given in *Psych. Eth.*, p. 256: "Which are the states that are to be put away by insight? The three Fetters, to wit, the theory of individuality, perplexity (doubt), and the contagion of mere rule and ritual."

7 **DETAILED CHART OF ASYNCHRONOUS KAMMA CONDITIONS**

	Sensuous volitions	At rebirth	During life	Planes		Faulty-resultant investigating cons. accompanied by indifference 1	The remaining rootless fty-res 6	Faultless resultant investigating cons. accompanied by indifference 1	The remaining rootless fls-res 7	Great resultant cons. diss. from knowledge 4	Great resultant cons. assoc. with knowledge 4	Total
1	11 faulty volitions exclusive of restlessness	"		Lower planes	4	1						1
2	12 faulty volitions		"	Sensuous Fine-material	11 15	"						7
3	8 great faultless volitions	"		Happy sensuous	7			"		"		9
			"	" "	7					"		8
			"	5-aggregate	26			"				8
4	4 three-rooted higher class great faultless volitions	"		Happy sensuous	7						"	4
			"	5-aggregate	26			"		"		16
5	4 three-rooted lower class or 4 two-rooted higher class great faultless volitions	"		Happy sensuous	7					"		4
			"	5-aggregate	26			"		"		12
6	4 two-rooted lower class great faultless volitions	"		Human world and demon world of suffering	2			"				1
			"	5-aggregate	26			"				8

Lofty and Supra-mundane volitions	1st Jhāna resultant	2nd "	3rd "	4th "	Vital monad	4th Jhāna resultant	"	"	"	"	4 Immaterial resultants	4 Fruitions
	3 planes of first Jhāna	" second "	" third "	The realm of Great reward	Non-percipient plane	The realm of Avihā- Brahmās	" Atappā- "	" Sudassā- "	" Sudassī- "	" Akaniṭṭha- "	4 Immaterial planes	17, 21, 26 planes
7 The minor, medium or major faultless first Jhāna	•											
8 ... faultless second Jhāna		"										
9 ... faultless third Jhāna			"									
10 The ordinary faultless fourth Jhāna				"								
11 The faultless fourth Jhāna attained by non-attachment to consciousness					"							
12 The faultless fourth Jhāna of non-returner with surpassing confidence						"						
... with surpassing effort							"					
... with surpassing mindfulness								"				
... with surpassing concentration									"			
... with surpassing knowledge										"		
13 4 Immaterial faultless											"	
14 4 Paths												"

Volition Associated with Restlessness Produces Results During Life. In the Vibhaṅga section of Ps, p. 113, it is stated, "*yasmiṃ samaye akusalaṃ cittaṃ uppannaṃ hoti upekkhā-sahagataṃ uddhacca sampayuttaṃ ... imesu dhammesu ñāṇaṃ dhammapaṭisambhidā*", and so on. This means that the knowledge of the results produced by the arising of faulty consciousness accompanied by indifference and associated with restlessness is known as *atthapaṭisambhidā.* It shows, therefore, that volition associated with the above consciousness does produce results. Now, results are of two kinds: (i) rebirth and (ii) during life. But since the Stream-winner, who has not eradicated this faulty consciousness associated with restlessness, is never reborn in the lower regions, which is mentioned in the Suttanipāta as "freedom from the four hells", this faulty consciousness gives faulty results during life only. And although the 12 faulty volitions produce faulty results during life as given in item 2 above, in the fine-material plane the three faulty-resultants, nose-, tongue-, and body-consciousness, are not produced as they are absent there.

For Consideration. When the volitions which produce faultless-resultants, given in the chart, are examined, it is found that (i) three-rooted volitions produce three-rooted resultants, two-rooted resultants, or rootless resultants; (ii) two-rooted volitions produce two-rooted resultants or rootless resultants. It could be assumed from (ii), therefore, that two-rooted faulty volitions present in greed-rooted and hate-rooted consciousnesses produce two-rooted falllty-resultants. But why is it that only rootless faulty-resultants are produced?

The Answer. In the first place, it is to be noted that there are no rooted falllty-resultants but only rooted faultless-resultants. The volitions associated with the rooted faulty consciousnesses are violent. So, after such volitions arise and cease, they cannot produce results which are associated with faultless roots that are calm and unruffled. Let alone these faulty volitions, even in the case of the three-rooted or two-rooted faultless volitions, if they are hemmed in by faulty consciousnesses, they do not produce results which are associated with the roots of the volitions that caused them. Hence, two-rooted faulty volitions cannot produce rooted resultants.

Another Answer. Faulty-resultant consciousnesses are always indeterminate. Faulty roots are always faulty. Therefore, faulty roots must always be associated with faulty consciousnesses but never with indeterminate consciousnesses. Again, resultants produced from faultless consciousnesses can be associated with faultless roots such as non-greed and so on, but the resultants produced from faulty consciousnesses are never associated with such faultless roots. Hence, two-rooted faulty volitions can never produce two-rooted resultants but only rootless faulty ones.

3. The 8 great faultless volitions produce results (i) at rebirth in the 7 happy sensuous planes as faultless-resultant investigating consciousness accompanied by indifference, 8 great resultants — i.e. a total of 9 rebirth resultants — and rebirth *kamma*-produced matter; (ii) during life in the 7 happy sensuous planes as 8 great resultants, and during life *kamma*-produced matter; (iii) during life in the 26 five-aggregate planes as 8 rootless faultlessresultants, and during life *kamma*-produced matter.

The 8 Great Resultants in (ii) above. It was shown, when the functions were dealt with in proximity condition, that the 8 great resultants perform the functions of rebirth, life-continuum, death, and registration. But they do not function as such in the fine-material and immaterial planes, for other resultants perform the first three functions in those planes; and the other function is concerned only with sensuous beings, sensuous impulsions, and sensuous objects. Of the remaining 11 planes, which are sensuous, these great resultants do not occur in beings of the 4 lower planes where rebirth is inferior. That is why the 7 happy sensuous planes are specifically mentioned here.

The 8 Rootless Faultless-Resultants in (iii) above. It will not be denied that great faultless volitions can bring about desirable *kamma*-produced matter and rootless-faultless eye-consciousness and others in the 7 sensuous and 15 fine-material planes of the 26 five-aggregate planes. But it will appear strange that such results are also produced in the 4 lower planes. In these planes there are comforts and luxuries enjoyed by the king of dragons and king of mythical birds; some of the other beings, such as elephants and horses, have beautiful bodies; and others have enchanting voices and so on, all of which provide the opportunity for rootless faultless eye-consciousness and others to arise.

One Faultless-Resultant Investigating Consciousness Accompanied by Indifference in (i) above. If faulty consciousnesses precede and follow any of the 8 great faultless volitions, these volitions become degraded and weak and so produce rebirth with this rootless consciousness.

4. The 4 three-rooted higher class great faultless volitions produce (i) at rebirth in the 7 happy sensuous planes as 4 great resultants associated with knowledge and rebirth *kamma*-produced matter, (ii) during life in the 26 five-aggregate planes as 8 great resultants, 8 rootless faultless resultants, and during life *kamma*-produced matter.

Three-rooted Faultless Volitions. When a faultless-deed is performed with knowledge that *kamma* is one's property, i.e. with confidence in *kamma* and its result, or with insight knowledge, i.e. that all material and mental states are impermanent, suffering, or impersonal, the volition is associated with the 3 roots, non-greed, non-hate, and non-delusion, and is known as three-rooted volition. Otherwise, the volition is associated with only 2 roots, non-greed and non-hate, and is known as two-rooted volition.

Higher and Lower. Suppose that it has been decided to perform an act of charity, and at this time of prior (*pubba*) volition, there is pleasure in the thought and great determination to carry it out, many faultless impulsions arise and cease. Then after the deed is performed, and at this time of later (*apara*) volition, there is great satisfaction at having completed the deed and great pleasure at having done a deed that ought to be done by good men. Such a faultless action, which is preceded and followed by faultless volitions is very strong and, being highly estimable, is known as higher class faultless action. So for the three-rooted being who performs a deed in the above manner, it is said to be a three-rooted higher class faultless action, and for the two-rooted being, a two-rooted higher class faultless action.

But if, at the time of prior volition, there is no pleasure but stinginess or dissatisfaction for one reason or another, or the deed is going to be performed for gaining fame, this is a faulty action preceding the actual deed. Then after the deed is performed, at the time of later volition, there is sorrow and regret at having done it, this is a faulty action. Such a faultless action, which is preceded and followed by faulty volitions is weak and, being degrading, is known as lower class faultless action. So for the three-rooted being who performs a deed in the above manner, it is a three-rooted lower class faultless action, and for the two-rooted being, a two-rooted lower class faultless action.

Also, faultless actions will produce results depending upon the degree of predominance of desire, effort, consciousness, or investigating-wisdom with which they were performed. Besides, there are cases where the prior volition is faulty and the later volition is faultless or vice versa and the results will depend upon the forces of these volitions.

5. The 4 three-rooted lower class great faultless volitions or 4 two-rooted higher class great faultless volitions, a total of 8 volitions, produce results (i) at rebirth in the 7 happy sensuous planes as 4 great resultants dissociated from knowledge and rebirth *kamma*-produced matter, (ii) during life in the 26 five-aggregate planes as 4 great resultants dissociated from knowledge, 8 rootless faultless-resultants, and during life *kamma*-produced matter.

6. The 4 two-rooted lower class great faultless volitions produce results (i) at rebirth in the human plane and the demon world of suffering (*vinipātika asura*), i.e. 2 sensuous planes, as rootless faultless-resultant investigating consciousness accompanied by indifference and rebirth *kamma*-produced matter, (ii) during life in the 26 five-aggregate planes as 8 rootless faultless-resultants, and during life *kamma*-produced matter.

7. The minor faultless first *jhāna* (volition) produces results (i) at rebirth in the realm of Brahmā's retinue as first *jhāna* resultant and rebirth *kamma*-produced matter, (ii) during life as first *jhāna* resultant and during life *kamma*-produced matter.

The medium faultless first *jhāna* produces results (i) at rebirth in the realm of Brahmā's ministers as first *jhāna* resultant and rebirth *kamma*-produced matter, (ii) during life as first *jhāna* resultant and during life *kamma*-produced matter.

The major faultless first *jhāna* produces results (i) at rebirth in the realm of Great Brahmās as first *jhāna* resultant and rebirth *kamma*-produced matter, (ii) during life as first *jhāna* resultant and during life *kamma*-produced matter.

Minor, Medium, and Major Jhānas. It was shown in predominance condition that the *jhānas*, Paths, and Fruitions cannot be obtained without predominance. But although predominant states are powerful, they can still be graded as low, average, and exalted. Therefore, if the first *jhāna* was obtained with low grade predominance, it is minor first *jhāna*; with average predominance, it is medium first *jhāna*; with exalted predominance, it is major first *jhāna*. So, although rebirth takes place in the first *jhāna* plane, there is a difference in the lifespan and supernormal power. It must be noted that, with the exception of Nibbāna, every state has these three grades.

8. and 9. These can be read off from the chart. The 3 second *jhāna* planes are the realms of (i) Minor Lustre, (ii) Infinite Lustre, (iii) Radiant Lustre, and the 3 third *jhāna* planes are the realms of (i) Minor Aura, (ii) Infinite Aura, (iii) Steady Aura.

10. The ordinary faultless fourth *jhāna* produces results (i) at rebirth in the realm of Great Reward as fourth *jhāna* resultant and rebirth *kamma*-produced matter, (ii) during life as fourth *jhāna* resultant and during life *kamma*-produced matter.

There is only one fourth *jhāna* plane, the realm of Great Reward, and so whether the fourth *jhāna* is minor, medium, or major, the lifespan here is 500 worlds. But there are differences in the supernormal powers and comforts depending on the grades. (The fourth *jhāna* method is here given as expounded in Paṭṭh.)

11. The faultless fourth *jhāna* attained by non-attachment to consciousness (mental states) produces result at rebirth in the non-percipient plane as vital nonad non-percipient rebirth *kamma*-produced matter.

When the worldling in the sensuous plane has attained the fourth *jhāna* he comes to realise that perception is the cause of longing and anxiety about things and of other kinds of suffering. So, with the idea that perception is like a boil or a bad disease, he enters and abides in the fourth *jhāna* and on emergence takes up the practice of mental development on disgust for perception (*saññāgantho saññārogo*) till there is sufficient disgust. Then when he abides in the fourth *jhāna* already attained, this element of disgust of perception is included. As a result he gets what was desired, i.e. rebirth in the plane where there is no perception, which is the non-percipient plane. Of course, although perception alone is mentioned, all the other mental states are also included.

12. The faultless fourth *jhāna* of the Non-Returner (Anāgāmī) with surpassing confidence produces results (i) at rebirth in the realm of Avihā Brahmās as fourth *jhāna* resultant and rebirth *kamma*-produced matter, (ii) during life as fourth *jhāna* resultant and during life *kamma*-produced matter.

The Non-Returner is reborn in one of the 5 Pure Abodes in accordance with the degrees of the five faculties as shown in the chart. So the rest can be read off.

13. The 4 faultless immaterial volitions, infinity of space and so on, and the results they produce are given in a condensed form in order to save space.

14. Here, also, the 4 faultless Path volitions and the Fruition-consciousnesses they produce are condensed. This item should be read as follows:

Volition associated with the Path-consciousness of the Stream-winner produces Fruition-consciousness of the Stream-winner in the 7 happy sensuous planes and the 10 fine-material planes up to the realm of Great Reward, i.e. 17 planes.

Volition associated with the Path-consciousness of the Once-Returner produces Fruition-consciousness of the Once-Returner in the 7 happy sensuous planes, 10 fine-material planes up to the realm of Great Reward and the 4 immaterial planes, i.e. 21 planes.

Volition associated with the Path-consciousness of the Non-Returner produces Fruition-consciousness of the Non-Returner in the 21 planes given above.

Volition associated with the Path-consciousness of the Arahat produces Fruition-consciousness of the Arahat in 22 five-aggregate planes (exclusive of the 4 lower planes) and the 4 immaterial planes, i.e. 26 planes.

Planes. Asynchronous *kamma* condition occurs in 30 planes exclusive of the non-percipient plane. The sensuous and Lofty volitions in the continuity of the Learner in (i) the realm of Great Reward, (ii) the highest realm of the Pure Abodes (*akaniṭṭha*) and (iii) the plane of neither-perception-nor-non-perception are excluded. The reason is that the Learners in these three planes are reborn in the same plane and not in another. Also, the mundane faultless and faulty volitions of beings for whom it is going to be their last birth are excluded because they are sure to be Arahats in their present existence, and so there is no more rebirth for them. Again, excepting the one faultless Lofty volition which will produce results, all the other countless faultless Lofty volitions are excluded.

Persons. This condition occurs in 11 types of persons exclusive of the Arahat who is without faultless and faulty volitions.

14. Resultant Condition

(i) *Conditioning and Conditioned States*. These are the 36 resultant consciousnesses and 38 mental factors which, when classified under the aggregates, are the 4 mental aggregates. They have to be taken in parts as shown in the chart. This has to be done for the conditions of the conascence group to which resultant condition belongs.

Conditioning Force. In this Analytical Exposition where the Teaching is not given in full, mind-produced and rebirth *kamma*-produced matter are not included as conditioned states as in the Investigation Chapter. So conascence-dissociation in the same Medium conascence group is not common. Thus the conditioning force occurs completely in the 7 common conditions: conascence, mutuality, dependence, resultant, association, presence, and non-disappearance. This will be readily seen from the charts of the Major and Medium conascence groups in the Intr. to *C.R.*

Additional Information. In explaining the nature of resultant, the cty on p. 349 states: "A resultant state that, by effortless quiet, relates by bringing about effortless quiet [in other states] is a resultant condition." Based on this statement, Maṇisāramañjūsā, p. 313, classifies both effort and quiet taken together as four kinds:

(i) *sa-ussāha asanta sabhāva citta*, i.e. consciousness with effort and without quiet;

(ii) *sa-ussāha santa sabhāva citta*, i.e. consciousness with effort and with quiet;

(iii) *nir-ussāha santa sabhāva citta*, i.e. consciousness without effort and with quiet;

(iv) *nir-ussāha santa sabhāva, sa-ussāha santa sabhāva citta*, i.e. consciousness without effort and with quiet, with effort and with quiet.

In the case of: (i) they are the faulty consciousnesses. For the efforts in them bring about acts in thoughts, words, and deeds that produce results later on. Also, since these consciousnesses arise, excited by the corruptions, they are not calm and quiet; (ii) they are the faultless consciousnesses. For, like the faulty ones, the efforts in them bring about acts in thoughts, words, and deeds that will produce results later on. But, unlike the faulty, these consciousnesses are not excited by the corruptions, and, therefore, they are calm and quiet; (iii) they are the resultant consciousnesses in resultant condition. For no efforts are required to bring them about. Moreover, the corruptions are absent and, therefore, they are calm and quiet; (iv) they are the functional consciousnesses. For, being functional, they do not produce results later on, i.e. there are no efforts in this direction. But efforts have to be made by them to bring about acts in thoughts, words, and deeds. And since the corruptions are absent, they are calm and quiet.

Planes. This condition occurs in 30 planes exclusive of the non-percipient plane. Persons. This condition occurs in 8 types of persons exclusive of the 4 Path individuals.

15. Nutriment Condition

There are two kinds: (a) physical nutriment, (b) conascence-nutriment.

(a) Physical Nutriment

(i) *Conditioning and Conditioned States*. See the chart.

In Detail. Edible food, the conditioning state which is produced by 4 causes, means the nutritive essence which is present in each of the 9 groups produced by *kamma*, the 6 groups produced by mind, the 4 groups produced by temperature and the 2 groups produced by nutriment, i.e. 21 groups of matter. These groups are given in *Cpd.*, *P.Pfn.*, and *Expos.* They are detailed below:

The 9 Groups Produced by Kamma (*kammaja kālapa*). (i) The vital nonad = physical life vitality + inseparable matter,[62] (2) the eye-decad = vital nonad + sensitive eye. Similarly, there are with the vital nonad, (3) the ear-decad = 9 + sensitive ear, (4) the nose-decad = 9 + sensitive nose, (5) the tongue-decad = 9 + sensitive tongue, (6) the body-decad = 9 + sensitive body, (7) the femininity-decad = 9 + femininity, (8) the masculinity-decad = 9 + masculinity, (9) the base-decad = 9 + heart-base.

The 6 Groups Produced by the Mind (*cittaja kalāpa*). The pure octad = 8 inseparable matter, (2) the nonad of bodily intimation = 8 + bodily

[62]Consists of hardness, heat, cohesion, motion (the 4 great primaries); and colour, odour, taste, nutritive essence. They are also known as the pure octad.

intimation, (3) the decad of vocal intimation = 8 + sound + vocal intimation, (4) the undecad of lightness = 8 + buoyancy, plasticity, and wieldiness of matter, (5) the dodecad of bodily intimation and lightness = the above undecad + bodily intimation, (6) the tridecad of sound, vocal intimation and lightness = the above undecad + sound + vocal intimation.

The 4 Groups Produced by Temperature (*utuja kalāpa*). (1) the pure octad, (2) the sound nonad = 8 + sound, (3) the undecad of lightness, (4) the dodecad of sound = undecad of lightness + sound.

The 2 groups Produced by Nutriment (*āhāraja kalāpa*). (1) the pure octad, (2) the undecad of lightness.

Of the 9 groups produced by *kamma*, the nutritive essence in the vital nonad is related to the remaining 8 *kamma*-produced matter in that group and the remaining 20 groups by physical nutriment condition. In this manner the nutritive essence in each of the 21 groups must be taken as the conditioning state by turns. If there are 8, 9, and 10 material states in a group, the nutritive essence in that group is related respectively to the remaining 7, 8, and 9 material states in that group and to the remaining 20 groups. It must be noted that the remaining 20 groups are always conditioned states.

Conditioning Force. Physical nutriment condition occurs completely in one common condition, i.e. nutriment.

(b) Conascence-nutriment

(ii) *Conditioning and Conditioned States*. See the chart.

Conditioning Force. In the Explanation of the Single Enumerations it was shown that this force occurs in 12 common conditions, completely in 5 (4 Major conascence and nutriment) and appropriately in 7 (4 Medium conascence, predominance, *kamma*, and faculty).

Explanation of Physical Nutriment

Sensuous beings cannot exist without food. Apart from the time that they are asleep, most of the day is spent by such beings of the land, water, and air in efforts at obtaining food. In doing so, however, they have to undergo various kinds of hardship. As a matter of fact, countless beings have died because of the dangers met with in searching for food or making money to buy food.

The fires of greed, hate, and delusion often oppress beings when (i) they desire and long for food to keep themselves alive, (ii) they are making efforts to obtain food, (iii) they meet with failures and disappointments in the search for food, (iv) they have to store and look after the food obtained. Greater faults are committed in the world because of earning a living than from any other cause. As most of the beings of the land, water, and air are carnivorous, they kill for food. It is on account of killing, the greatest of faults, that beings are daily making causes for rebirth in the lower regions. In fact, most of the beings are in the lower regions because they committed faults in seeking food or earning a livelihood.

Then when food is eaten it turns into urine, excrement, eye-dirt, ear-dirt, snot, spittle, phelgm, etc. If it has been properly digested, it produces the various kinds of ordure consisting of head hairs, body hairs, body odours, sweat, etc. But if it is not properly digested, it produces various diseases such as those of the eye, ear, chest, skin, throat, etc., resulting, very often, in death. Moreover, when the stomach is full, lust and the rest of the 1,500 corruptions are aroused. But with an empty stomach, even the king of the Tāvatiṃsa *devas* has no desire to take delight in and find pleasure with his queens. A detailed account of the repulsiveness of food is given in *P.Pfn.* under "Perception of repulsiveness in nutriment".

Explanation of Conascence-nutriment

The Sequence. After physical nutriment, which is the most prominent of the 4 nutriments, was expounded, the other 3 were expounded in the following sequence: contact nutriment, which impinges on material objects; volition nutriment, which is a consequence of contact; and consciousness nutriment. For contact holds fast to what is desirable or undesirable in an object; volition is the constant exertion of the associated states on account of an object which is desirable or undesirable; consciousness is the awareness of an object.

Contact Nutriment

Contact exerts great influence. If, in the continuity of a being, there were only consciousness but no contact, he would only be aware of the fires burning in hell, but not experience suffering due to the intense heat. As there is contact, suffering is experienced. On the other hand, if there were only contact and no consciousness he would not even be aware of the heat of the fires in hell, just as is the case with a log of wood. Again, if there were contact and consciousness but no volition, then, although bodily suffering will be greatly experienced, he would not be able to express it in thought, word, or deed. For it is volition that brings about actions in thought, word, and deed. Also, because of these 3 nutriments, humans, *devas*, and *brahmā*s are aware of, experience, and express happiness. On consideration of the above, therefore, it will be seen that all happiness and suffering originate from contact. So if there were no contact, there would be no happiness and suffering. When there is no happiness there cannot be greed (craving); when there is no suffering there cannot be hate; and where there is neither greed nor hate, there cannot be delusion and the rest of the 1,500 corruptions.

Volition Nutriment

Consciousness and its associated states cannot remain still because volition is inciting them to run after the object they take. This is why the minds of people are never still but always agitated. For instance, when an object of greed is encountered, volition is continually exciting greed, urging one to get to the object of greed so as to experience that object. This is similar with the objects of hate and delusion.

For the common worldling, the volitions are very weak and sluggish in the cases for good such as confidence, knowledge, charity, the precepts, and mental development. He has to find many reasons and incentives to induce himself to perform such good acts, such as the dread of suffering to be experienced if he is reborn in hell or if he has to continue in the round of rebirths, and the happy results which will accrue from doing good.

Illustration of Volition. Suppose that at a port there are 49 barges of cargo and only one tug-boat and that the latter tows each of the barges to various ports at various times. The people at that port will remark, "The tug-boat is towing such-and-such a barge and sailing out of the river to such-and-such a port." Similarly, at times, volition (which is dependent on heart-base) tows greed and comes out of the heart to go to the object of greed; at times, volition tows hate and comes out of the heart to go to the object of hate. This is also the case with each of the remaining mental states, all totalling 49 which come under mental formation aggregate. Volition does not function for one existence only, nor does it end at death. For after the *kamma*-produced matter ceases at death, the volition just before that time acts to bring about a new existence with new *kamma*-produced matter. It ends only at pari-nibbāna, the final death, because there is no more rebirth since all the corruptions had been eradicated, i.e. at the death of the Arahat.

Consciousness Nutriment

There are six kinds of consciousness nutriment: eye-consciousness, ear-consciousness, nose-consciousness, tongue-consciousness, body-consciousness and mind-consciousness. When the sensitive eye coincides with any visible object, the consciousness that arises is eye-consciousness. Similarly, when the sensitive ear coincides with any sound, ear-consciousness arises, and so on. In the case of cognizable objects such as confidence, precepts, learning, charity, knowledge, etc., that are faultless; and greed, hate, delusion, etc., that are faulty, the consciousness that arises in each case at the heart-base is known as mind-consciousness. It is due to this consciousness nutriment that people seek visible objects, sounds, and other sense-objects for enjoyment and pleasure; that they are greedy and, therefore, invent luxuries, desire to become millionaires, kings, ministers of state, etc.; that they perform charity and other good deeds for better existences in the future; that they make plans and efforts to acquire worldly possessions, and so on.

But in the course of seeking such worldly comforts, honours, and sensual pleasures, many dangers and misfortunes are encountered, corruptions increase, and all kinds of faulty actions are committed.

The 4 Nutriments Explained by Similes

K.S. II, pp. 68–70, explains the 4 nutriments by similes and states that when they are well understood, Arahatta Fruition is attained.

Physical Nutriment, Simile of the Child's Flesh.

"And how, brethren, is material food to be considered?

"It is as if two parents who had taken slender provisions were on their way in the path through the jungle, and theirs was an only child dear and sweet. Now suppose that the scanty provisions of those parents in the jungle came to an end, used up. And suppose that there was yet a portion of the jungle untraversed. Then those parents might say, 'What scanty provisions we had are come to an end, are used up, and there is this remainder of the jungle to traverse. What if we were to slay this our only child, sweet and dear, and make both dried pieces and juicy pieces, and so, eating flesh of child, might traverse that remainder of the jungle. Let us not all three perish!' And so those two parents slew that only child sweet and dear, and made both dried pieces and juicy pieces, and so, eating flesh of child they could traverse that remainder of the jungle. They would both eat child-flesh and smite on their breasts crying, 'Where is our only child? Where is our only child?'

"Now what think you, brethren? Would they take the food for sport? Or would they take the food from indulgence? Or would they take the food for personal charm? Or would they take the food for plumpness?"

"Not so, lord."

"Would they not take the food, brethren, in order that they might last till the jungle was crossed?"

"Even so, lord."

"Even so, brethren, I declare should solid food be regarded. When such food is well understood, the passions of the five senses are well understood. When the passions of the five senses are well understood, the fetters do not exist, bound by which, the Ariyan disciple could come again to this world."

Contact Nutriment. Simile of the Cow with a Sore Hide.

"And how, brethren, is the food that is contact to be regarded?

"It is as if, brethren, a cow with a sore hide should stand leaning against a wall. The creatures that live on the wall would bite her; if she stood leaning against a tree, the creatures that live on the tree would bite her; yea, whatever she stood leaning against, whatever creatures lived thereon would bite her. If she stood buoyed up by water, the creatures that live in the water would bite her; if she stood buoyed up by the air, the creatures that live in dependence on the air would bite her; yea, whatever she stood up against, whatsoever creatures that lived in dependence thereon would bite her.

"Even so do I declare that the food which is contact should be regarded. When such food is well understood, the three feelings are well understood. When the three feelings are well understood, I declare that there is nothing further which the Ariyan disciple has to do."

Volition Nutriment. Simile of the Pit of Live Charcoal.

"And how, brethren, is the food that is will of mind (volition) to be regarded? It is as if, brethren, there were a pit of charcoal, deeper than a man is high, filled with clear, glowing, smokeless charcoal. And a man were to come by, loving his life, not loving death, loving happiness, and loathing pain. And two strong men seizing him by each arm were to drag him up to the pit. Now to be far from that, brethren, would be the will of that man, to be far would be his wish, to be far would be his aspiration. Why so? Verily the man would think: I shall fall on that heap of charcoal; through that I shall come in for death or for mortal pain.

"Even so, brethren, I declare that the food which is will of mind should be regarded. When that food is well understood, the three cravings are well understood. When these are well understood, I declare that there is nothing further that the Ariyan disciple has to do."

Consciousness Nutriment. Simile of the Hundred Darts.

"And how, brethren, is the food that is consciousness to be regarded?

"It is as if, brethren, they were to seize a robber, an evildoer, and were to show him to the king, saying, 'This man, sire, is a robber, an evildoer. Inflict on him such punishment as is desired.' And the king should pronounce this concerning him, "Go, masters, smite this man at dawn with a hundred darts (or lances, or spears, or javelins)." And they were to do so. Then at noon the king should declare this, "Ho, masters, how is that man? "

" 'At this moment, sire, he is alive.'

"And the king should pronounce this concerning him, 'Go, masters, smite this man at noon with a hundred darts.' And they were to do so. Then at eventide the king should declare this, 'Ho, masters, how is that man? '

" 'At this moment, sire, he is alive.'

"And the king should pronounce this concerning him, 'Go, masters, smite this man at eventide with a hundred darts.' And they were to do so.

"What think you, brethren? Would that man, smitten during the day by three hundred darts, suffer there from pain and sorrow? "

"Were he smitten, lord, by but one dart, he would therefrom suffer pain and sorrow; what need to speak of being smitten by three hundred? "

"Even so, brethren, do I declare that the food called consciousness should be regarded. When consciousness, brethren, is well understood, name-and-shape (mentality-and-materiality) is well understood. When name-and-shape is well understood, I declare that there is nothing further that the Ariyan disciple has to do."

(The Sustenance Suttas and others in this volume of *K.S.* deal with the 4 nutriments in detail.)

Planes. Physical nutriment occurs in 27 planes exclusive of the 4 immaterial planes; the mental nutriments (conascence-nutriment) occur in 30 planes exclusive of the non-percipient plane.

Persons. This condition occurs in the 12 types of persons.

16. Faculty Condition

There are three kinds: (a) base-prenascence-faculty, (b) physical life-faculty, (c) conascence-faculty.

(a) Base-prenascence-faculty

(i)–(v) *Conditioning and Conditioned States*. See the chart.

Conditioning Force. This condition belongs to the base-prenascence group, and, as shown in the Explanation of the Single Enumerations, the force occurs completely in the 6 common conditions: dependence, prenascence, faculty, dissociation, presence, and non-disappearance.

(b) Physical Life-faculty

(vi) *Conditioning and Conditioned States*. See the chart.

In Detail. All the 9 groups of *kamma*-produced matter must be taken. They were given under physical nutriment condition above.

Example of the Method. Of the 9 groups of *kamma*-produced matter, take that of the eye-decad. The physical life-faculty of the eye-decad is related to the remaining 9 *kamma*-produced matter of that decad by the force of physical life-faculty condition. So also for the physical life-faculty in ear-decad and the rest of the 9 groups. Since physical life-faculty is always *kamma*-produced matter it is related only to *kamma*-produced matter of the same group.

Conditioning Force. In this Analytical Exposition physical life-faculty-presence and physical life-faculty-non-disappearance are not included, and so the force occurs completely in faculty condition.

(c) Conascence-faculty

(vii) *Conditioning and Conditioned States*. See the chart.

Conditioning Force. Refer to the Explanation of the Single Enumerations where it was pointed out that this condition belongs to the Minor conascence group and occurs in the 14 common conditions, conascence-*kamma* alone of the group being excluded. So this force occurs in 14 common conditions: completely in 5 (4 Major conascence and faculty) and appropriately in 9 (4 Medium conascence, root, predominance, nutriment, *jhāna*, and path).

Explanation. In the Investigation Chapter the three kinds of faculty condition are not dealt with in the same order as in this Analytical Exposition. Here the sequence is in accordance with that in Vibh as pointed out below:

> *As to order* (*kamato*): this too is only the order of teaching. Herein,
>
> (a) the noble plane [the stages of Stream Entry, etc.,] is attained through the full-understanding of internal states, and so the eye-faculty and the rest included in the selfhood are taught first (i.e. base-prenascence-faculty); then the femininity faculty and masculinity faculty, to show on what account that selfhood is called "woman" or "man".
>
> (b) Next, the life-faculty, to make it known that although that selfhood is twofold, still its existence is bound up with the life-faculty (i.e. physical life-faculty).
>
> (c) Next, the [bodily-]pleasure faculty, etc., to make it known that there is no remission of these feelings as long as that [selfhood] continues, and that all feeling is [ultimately] suffering. Next, the faith (confidence) faculty, etc., to show the way, since these things are to be developed in order to make that [suffering] cease. Next, the I-shall-come-to-know-the-unknown faculty to show that the way is not sterile, since it is through this way that this state is first manifested in oneself. Next, the final-knowledge faculty, because it is the fruit of the last-mentioned faculty and so must be developed after it. Next, the final-knower faculty, the supreme reward, is taught last to make it known that it is attained by development, and that when it is attained, there is nothing more to be done (i.e. conascence-faculty). This is the order here (Vibh-a, p. 119, given in *P.Pfn.*, pp. 560–61).

Functions. The functions of the faculties were dealt with in the Brief Explanations of the Conditions. As regards the 5 faculties — confidence, effort, mindfulness, one-pointedness of mind and knowledge — *K.S.* V 171, states, "But from what point of view, monks, should the controlling power of faith (confidence) be regarded? From that of the four limbs of stream-winning...." This shows that confidence and the rest of the 5 faculties are controllers of their own functions and the following simile given in S-a, p. 265, illustrates this:

> Once five friends, a king and four rich men, went to take part in the celebrations of the appearance of the constellations. On their way they reached the house of one of the rich men. The owner gave the order, "Provide the guests with refreshment, perfumes and ornaments, etc.", while the other four remained silent. Similarly, when they reached the houses of the other rich men, only the owner of the house gave the order while the other four remained silent. Finally, when they reached the house of the king, who was the ruler of the country, he also gave the order while the four rich men remained silent.
>
> In the same way, just like the five friends who took to the road, confidence and the rest of the five faculties together take the same object. As in the case of the first rich man, who, on reaching his house, gave the order for entertaining his four friends who remained silent, so also, when the Path of Stream-winner is reached, confidence faculty, which has the characteristic of trusting, takes the lead and the other four faculties follow it. Also, when the house of the second rich man is reached, he gave the order while the other four remained silent, so also, when the four right efforts are reached, the effort faculty, which has the characteristic of exerting, takes the lead and the other faculties follow it. Then when the house of the third rich man is reached, he gave the order while the other four remained silent, so also, when the applications of mindfulness are reached, mindfulness faculty, which has the characteristic of recollection, takes the lead and the other four faculties follow it. Next, when the house of the fourth rich man is reached, he gave the order and the other four remained silent, so also, when *jhāna* or deliverance (*vimokkha*) is reached, one-pointedness of mind faculty, which has the characteristic of non-distraction, takes the lead and the other four faculties follow it. Finally, when the house of the king is reached, he gave the order and the other four remained silent, so also, when the Four Noble Truths are reached, the knowledge (wisdom) faculty, which has the characteristic of knowing from all aspects, takes the lead and the other four faculties follow it.

The Teaching on faculty condition is given in detail in Faculty Yamaka of the Abhidhamma. In the Suttas it is given under *K.S.* on the Faculties. The restraint of the sense faculties which the bhikkhu has to practise belongs to this faculty condition.

Planes. The faculties of eye, ear, nose, tongue, body, femininity, masculinity, pleasure, pain, and grief occur in the sensuous planes only. Mind-faculty, life-faculty, indifference faculty, and the faculties of confidence, effort, mindfulness, one-pointedness, and knowledge (wisdom) occur in 4 planes: sensuous, fine-material, immaterial, and supramundane. Joy faculty occurs in 3 planes: sensuous, fine-material, and supramundane. The remaining 3 faculties occur in the supramundane plane only.

Persons. The 3 supramundane faculties occur in the 8 types of Noble beings. The rest occur in all the 12 types of persons.

17. *Jhāna* Condition

Conditioning and Conditioned States. See the chart.

Conditioning Force. From the Explanation of the Single Enumerations it will be seen that this force occurs in 11 common conditions: completely in 5 (4 Major conascence and *jhāna*) and appropriately in 6 (4 Medium conascence, faculty, and path).

The 5 Jhāna Factors. In Dhs 9 *jhāna* factors are given, namely: (1) wrong applied thought, (2) right applied thought, (3) sustained thought, (4) rapture, (5) joy, (6) grief, (7) indifference, (8) wrong one-pointedness of mind, (9) right one-pointedness of mind. Of these, (1) and (2) come under the reality of applied thought; (5), (6) and (7) under the reality of feeling; (8) and (9) under the reality of one-pointedness of mind. Thus, when the different realities are taken, there are only 5 *jhāna* factors.

Jhāna. Consciousness is restless because the new ones that successively arise and cease do not remain fixed to one object but take different objects. And when consciousness is made to concentrate on a particular object to the exclusion of all the others so that it remains firmly fixed to that object, this is known as *jhāna*.

Jhāna and Jhāna Factors. When two or more *jhāna* factors are taken together as a group, it is known as *jhāna*, but when each of them is taken separately it is known as a *jhāna* factor. The *jhāna* factors may be compared to the several parts, wheels, hub, etc., of a chariot (*rathaṅga*), and *jhāna* to the chariot itself which is assembled from those parts.

Explanation of the Functions of the Jhāna Factors. In this world there are objects and actions which bring about either gradual development or degeneration of character. For there are (i) those which bring about gradual decrease of the corruptions and which lead to a lofty path and (ii) those which bring about increase of corruptions and which lead to a low path just like the water in the river flowing to a lower level.

Applied Thought. Wrongly applied thought may be compared to the storm which violently blows the water downwards; consciousness to the boat; knowledge to the helmsman; wise reflection to the helm; effort to the oarsman; right applied thought to the oars. Only when consciousness — the boat — is rowed strongly with right applied thought — the oars — will it travel upstream to the objects and actions for the removal of the corruptions. If there is no rowing, then wrong applied thought — the storm — will blow it downstream for increase of the corruptions. Thus it will be seen that right applied thought — the oars — is the *jhāna* factor which has to be used with great force in order that consciousness — the boat — will become lofty, i.e. go upstream.

Sustained Thought. Once right applied thought has carried out its function of directing consciousness to its object and an object such as a *kasiṇa* has been taken, then sustained thought performs its function of occupation with the object so that consciousness will not turn away but remain fixed on it. If there is no such fixing on the object, then, however strongly right applied thought is used, it will be like a tortoise climbing up a hill where it takes one step forward but falls back two steps.

Rapture. Rapture then performs its function of enjoying the object and action so that consciousness will not be disgusted or bored. For if there is no enjoyment, but dislike and boredom, consciousness will not be able to remain fixed on the object but will be compelled to withdraw and turn away from the object.

Bliss. Next, bliss performs its function of great relish so that consciousness cannot turn away from the object which it enjoys. For although consciousness enjoys the object, unless the relish is very great, the object will not be dear enough for consciousness to fasten on to it. Because the delight, which takes place for a short while owing to the novelty of the object, will soon turn into disgust and eventually consciousness will turn away from the object.

One-pointedness of Mind. Finally, one-pointedness of mind performs its function of keeping consciousness firmly rooted to the object. For consciousness had been accustomed to thrive on filthy sensual pleasures in past existences and had taken great delight therein. So, although it now experiences lofty delight with the object and action of mental development, yet, it cannot forget the past delights of sensual pleasures and is ever eager to taste them again. That is why one-pointedness of mind has to, as it were, chain consciousness to the object. Consciousness may be compared to a dog which, originally, had been accustomed to living on excreta in the village and taken great delight in it. Later on, it was brought up by kings and rājas who provided it with meat and rice that it could partake of at pleasure. But even then it cannot forget the delight of the taste of nasty and foul excreta that it had a natural liking for when young. So if it got the odour of excreta it would go after such things, preferring it to the meat and rice. That is why the dog had to be chained so that it could not go back to the old way of feeding on excreta.

These 5 states, which keep consciousness firmly rooted to the object of mental development with great delight, are known as *jhāna*. And when consciousness is thus concentrated, the corruptions are suppressed hour by hour, day by day, till they no longer arise. Thereby consciousness becomes pure and luminous. This is the meaning of *jhāyati upanijjhāyati ti jhānaṃ*.

Another Explanation. Jhāna is so-called because it burns and destroys its opposite states, the hindrances, and so prevents them from arising, i.e. suppresses them but does not eradicate them. Sloth and torpor are the opposites of applied thought. Applied thought, which constantly drives consciousness to take an object of mental development, forcibly burns and destroys sloth and torpor, which are respectively mental laziness and backwardness, and, thereby, suppresses them. Doubt is the opposite of sustained thought. Sustained thought, which repeatedly reflects on the object and gradually makes the act of mental development (*bhāvanā-kamma*) clearer and clearer, forcibly burns and destroys doubt, which makes consciousness waver, muddled and depressed, and, thereby, suppresses it. Ill will is the opposite of rapture. Rapture, which makes consciousness refreshed, forcibly burns and destroys ill will, which makes consciousness bored and disgusted, and, thereby, suppresses it. Restlessness and worry are the opposites of bliss. Bliss, which gives peace and satisfaction, forcibly burns and destroys restlessness and worry, which make consciousness distracted and ill at ease, and thereby suppresses them. Lust is the opposite of one-pointedness of mind. One-pointedness of mind, which keeps consciousness firmly fixed to the object, forcibly burns and destroys lust, which makes consciousness excited and agitated, and, thereby, suppresses it. In *P.Pfn.*, p. 147, it is stated:

> For the hindrances are the contrary opposites of the *jhāna* factors; what is meant is that the *jhāna* factors are incompatible with them, eliminate them, abolish them. And it is said accordingly in the Peṭaka "Concentration (one-pointedness of mind) is incompatible with lust, happiness (rapture) with ill will, applied thought with stiffness and torpor, bliss with agitation (restlessness) and worry, and sustained thought with uncertainty (doubt)." This is what is meant by *paccanīka-dhamme jhāpetī ti jhānaṃ*.

Two Kinds of Jhāna. These are: (1) *Jhāna* which is attained by the practice of concentration on the *kasiṇas* and other objects. It is known as *pa~ipada-siddha* and (2) *Jhāna* attained by Ānanda; by the 500 bhikkhus in Mahāsamaya Sutta; by those who attained the 6 super knowledges when they were called "Come, O Bhikkhus" by the Buddha after hearing his teaching for the first time; and, automatically, by those when they attained the Path after insight practice. It is known as *magga-siddha*.

The teaching on *jhāna* condition is given in *Jhāna* Vibh of the Abhidhamma and in the mental development of concentration in the various Suttas.

Planes. This condition occurs in 30 planes exclusive of the non-percipient plane.

Persons. This condition occurs in the 12 types of persons.

18. Path Condition

Conditioning and Conditioned States. See the chart.

Conditioning Force. From the Explanation of the Single Enumerations it will be seen that this force occurs in 13 common conditions: completely in 5 (4 Major conascence and path) and appropriately in 8 (4 Medium conascence, root, predominance, faculty and *jhāna*).

Explanation. In the Brief Explanations of the Conditions it was pointed out that although there are also 8 wrong path factors, 4 of them (which are wrong speech, wrong action, wrong livelihood, and wrong mindfulness) are not separate realities but come under the faulty group of consciousness and associated mental factors, and, therefore, there are only 12 path factors. These are then reduced to 9 when the different realities are taken as was the case with the *jhāna* factors. Here a brief explanation of the 8 path factors, the supramundane states, is provided.

First of all, these supramundane states must be differentiated from the mundane states. For example, in the case of right view as a mundane state, there are many kinds, one of which is that concerning *kamma*. Here the knowledge that all faultless and faulty actions performed by oneself to produce results exists in one's continuity throughout the many existences and worlds in this round of rebirths and are, therefore, one's property, is right view of *kamma*. It is also known as "straightening one's views" (*diṭṭhujukatā*), one of the items of the ten meritorious actions (*puñña-kiriya-vatthu*). In this connection *G.S.* III 59, states, "I am the result of my own deeds; heir to deeds; deeds are matrix; deeds are kin; deeds are foundation; whatever deed I do, whether good or bad, I shall become heir to it." Then there is right view of the ten kinds of subjects (*dasa-vatthuka-sammādiṭṭhi*) as given in *M.L.S.* I 347–48:

> (1) There is [result of] gift. (2) There is [result of] offering on a large scale (*yiṭṭha*). (3) There is [result of] offering on a small scale (*hutā*). (4) There is fruit and ripening of deeds well done and ill done. (5) There is this world. (6) There is a world beyond (other worlds). (7) There is [result of] good and evil deeds done to one's mother. (8) There is [result of] good and evil deeds done to one's father. (9) There are spontaneously uprising beings. (10) There exists in this human world, recluses and brahmans who practise the true *dhamma* and possess tranquillity of mind and who, having seen and realised this very world and other worlds by their own super-knowledge, impart their knowledge to others.

The Supramundane 8 Path Factors. P.Pfn., pp. 582–84, gives them briefly as:

Right View. "When a meditator is progressing towards the penetration of the four truths, his eye of understanding with Nibbāna as its object eliminates the inherent tendency to ignorance, and that is right view."

Right Thinking (Applied Thought). "When he possesses such view, his directing of the mind on to Nibbāna, which [directing] is associated with that [right view], abolishes wrong thinking, and that is right thinking."

Right Speech. "And when he sees and thinks thus, his abstinence from wrong speech, which abstinence is associated with that [right view], abolishes bad verbal conduct, and that is called right speech."

Right Action. "When he abstains thus, his abstinence from killing living things, which abstinence is associated with that [right view], cuts off wrong action, and that is called right action."

Right Livelihood. "When his right speech and right action are purified, his abstinence from wrong livelihood, which abstinence is associated with that [right view], cuts off scheming, etc., and that is called right livelihood."

Right Effort. "When he is established on that plane of virtue called right speech, right action, and right livelihood, his energy, which is in conformity and associated with that [right view], cuts off idleness, and that is called right effort.

Right Mindfulness. "When he exerts himself thus, the non-forgetfulness in his mind, which is associated with that [right view], shakes off wrong mindfulness, and that is called right mindfulness."

Right Concentration. "When his mind is thus guarded by supreme mindfulness, the unification of mind, which is associated with that [right view], abolishes wrong concentration, and that is called right concentration."

Further, on pp. 589–90 of the above text (or M-a II 361), it is stated:

> [T]he Noble Eightfold Path is included by the three aggregates. (1) Any right speech, any right action, any right livelihood: these are included in the virtue aggregate. (2) Any right effort, any right mindfulness, any right concentration: these are included in the concentration aggregate. (3) Any right view, any right thinking: these are included in the understanding aggregate....
>
> As to the three beginning with right effort, concentration cannot of its own nature cause absorption through unification on the object; but with energy accomplishing its function of exerting and mindfulness accomplishing its function of preventing wobbling, it can do so. Here is a simile: three friends [thinking], "We will celebrate the festival", entered a park. Then one saw a champak (*campaka*) tree in full blossom, but he could not reach the flowers by raising his hand. The second bent down for the first to climb on his back. But although standing on the other's back, he still could not pick them because of his unsteadiness. Then the third offered his shoulder [as support]. So standing on the back of the one and supporting himself on the other's shoulder, he picked as many flowers as he wanted, and after adorning himself, he went and enjoyed the festival.
>
> And so it is with this. For the three states beginning with right effort, which are born together, are like the three friends who enter the park together. The object is like the champak tree in full blossom. Concentration, which cannot of its own nature bring about absorption by unification on the object, is like the man who could not pick the flowers by raising his arm. Effort is like the companion who bent down, giving his back to mount upon. Mindfulness is like the friend who stood by, giving his shoulder for support. Just standing on the back of the one and supporting himself on the other's shoulder he could pick as many flowers as he wanted, so too, when energy accomplishes its function of exerting and when mindfulness accomplishes

its function of preventing wobbling, with the help so obtained concentration can bring about absorption by unification on the object. So here in the concentration aggregate, it is only concentration that is included as of the same kind. But effort and mindfulness are included because of their action [in assisting].

Also as regards right view and right thinking, understanding cannot of its own nature define an object as impermanent, painful, not-self. But with applied thought giving [assistance] by repeatedly hitting [the object] it can. How? Just as a money changer, having a coin placed in his hand and being desirous of looking at it on all sides equally, cannot turn it over with the power of his eye only, but by turning it over with his fingers he is able to look at it on all sides, similarly, understanding cannot of its own nature define an object as impermanent, and so on. But [assisted] by applied thought with its characteristic of directing the mind on to [the object] and its function of striking and threshing, as it were, hitting and turning over, it can take anything given and define it. So here in the understanding aggregate it is only right view that is included as of the same kind. But right thinking is included because of its action [in assisting].

So the path is included by the three aggregates. Hence it was said that it is of three kinds classed according to the three aggregates.

Right View is the Most Important. Right view is the most important of the 8 path factors because it is not possible to attain Path and Fruition without it. How right view can be acquired and how, if right view is properly supported, it leads to Arahatta Fruition are given in Mahāvedalla Sutta, *M.L.S.* I 353:

"But how many conditions are there, your reverence, for bringing right understanding (view)[63] into existence?"

"There are two conditions, your reverence, for bringing right understanding into existence: the utterance of another (person)[64] and wise attention. Your reverence, these are the two conditions for bringing right understanding into existence."

---

[63]The right understanding through vision, the right understanding of the Way (M-a II 346).

[64]Herein, what is *another's utterance*? It is any teaching, advice, instruction, talk about truth, in conformity with truth, from another. The Truths are four: they are Suffering, Origin, Cessation, and the Path. Any teaching, showing, divulging, analysing, exhibiting, displaying these four Truths is called another's utterance in conformity with truth (*Piṭ. Discl.*, p. 1).

"If right understanding is forwarded, by how many factors, your reverence, does there come to be the fruit of freedom of mind and the advantage of the fruit of freedom of mind, and the fruit of freedom through intuitive wisdom and the advantage of the fruit of freedom through intuitive wisdom?"

"Your reverence, if right understanding is forwarded by five factors there comes to be the fruit of freedom of mind and the advantage of the fruit of freedom of mind, and the fruit of freedom through intuitive wisdom and the advantage of the fruit of freedom through intuitive wisdom: in this case, your reverence, right understanding is forwarded by moral habit, and it is forwarded by hearing, and it is forwarded by discussion, and it is forwarded by calm and it is forwarded by vision. Your reverence, if right understanding is forwarded by these five factors, there comes to be the fruit of freedom of mind and the advantage of the fruit of freedom of mind, and there comes to be the fruit of freedom through intuitive wisdom and the advantage of the fruit of freedom through intuitive wisdom."[65]

Mahāvedalla Commentary. Right View. These are Insight Right View and Path Right View. Even such a great disciple as Sāriputta Thera required the above two conditions for bringing about right view. Although he practised the perfections for 1 æon and 100,000 worlds, he could not destroy even a minute trace of the corruptions by himself. It was only when he heard the stanza beginning with "Dhammas arise from causes" from Assaji Thera that he acquired right view and became a Sotāpanna. As for Silent Buddhas and Omniscient Buddhas, they do not require the utterance of another person but become so by their own wise attention (reflection).

Forwarded by Calm. Calm consists of the eight Attainments based on insight. They are the four fine-material *jhānas* and the four immaterial *jhānas*.

Forwarded by Vision. Vision consists of the seven Contemplations (*sattānupassana*). These are the contemplations of: (1) impermanence (*anicca*), (2) suffering (*dukkha*), (3) not-self (*anattā*), (4) dispassion (*nibbheda*), (5) fading away (*virāga*), (6) cessation (*nirodha*), (7) relinquishment (*paṭinissagga*).

[65]For, the Way to Arahantship coming into being as a result of practising these five factors, gives the fruit (M-a II 346).

The Five Factors. After having perfected the four precepts of purity (*catupārisuddhi-sīla*), listened to the appropriate teaching, discarded wrong practices by discussion, and practised the eight attainments based on insight, the seven contemplations are developed for the arising of the Arahatta Path which gives Arahatta Fruition as result. This may be compared to a person who wants to partake of sweet and ripe mangoes. He has to (1) make a round hollow space around the young mango plant for retaining the water, (2) water the plant with a watering-pot occasionally, (3) make a firm mound around the plant to prevent water from draining away after watering, (4) remove the weeds, creepers, dried branches, ants' hills, and cobwebs near the plant, (5) turn over the soil with a spade occasionally. If these five actions are performed, the mango plant will thrive and bear fruit, the sweet and ripe mangoes. Here, the mango plant is like right view and (1) is like the precepts, (2) is like listening to the appropriate teaching, (3) is like the attainments of *jhāna*, (4) is like discarding wrong practices by discussion, (5) is like the seven contemplations. For when these five actions are performed, these actions which support right view result in Arahatta Fruition just as the five actions which support the mango plant result in sweet and ripe mango fruits.

Planes. This condition, in which only mental states are involved, occurs in 30 planes exclusive of the non-percipient plane.

Persons. This condition occurs appropriately in the 12 types of persons.

19. Association Condition

Conditioning and Conditioned States. Conditioning Force. As stated in the chart they are the same as conascence condition (i).

Explanation. Both the conditioning and conditioned states are consciousnesses and mental factors, i.e. mental aggregates. On no occasion does consciousness arise by itself. It always arises together with the other mental states associated with it. Besides, consciousness and its associated mental states cannot arise without an object. They always take one of the six kinds of objects. Also, they always depend on a base for their arising in the five-aggregate planes. The occasions when the 89 consciousnesses arise and the mental states associated with each of them are given in detail under "The Genesis of Thoughts (*cittuppāda-kaṇḍa*)" of Dhs. The reason why they are given at the very beginning of the first book of Abhidhamma is that one who desires to understand this subject must, first of all, know these facts. There, the subject-matter is treated in a different way from that of Abhidh-s (*Cpd.*) and, therefore, many who have only studied the latter cannot understand the former. Therefore, a chart is provided on consciousnesses and the mental states associated with them[66] as given both in Dhs and Abhidh-s so that some idea about the differences between these two texts will be obtained and also because it forms the subject-matter of association condition dealt with here. Although the author has charts summarizing the whole of each of the above texts, they cannot be provided here where Paṭṭh is being dealt with.

Planes. This condition is one kind of conascence condition where only mental states are involved. As such it occurs in 30 planes exclusive of the non-percipient plane.

Persons. This condition occurs in all the 12 types of persons.

[66]For the non-Pāli reader, all information about these states can be obtained from *Psych. Eth.* and its cty, *Expos.*

8 CLASSIFICATION OF THE MENTAL STATES OF THE DHAMMASAṄGANĪ UNDER THE REALITIES OF ABHIDHAMMATTHA-SAṄGAHA

18 groups			Consciousness and associated mental states																				
			Contact	Greed	Hate	Delusion	Non-greed	Non-hate	Right applied thought	Wrong applied thought	Sustained thought	Rapture	Confidence	Right effort	Wrong effort	Mindfulness	Right concentration	Wrong concentration	Bliss (Happiness)	Pain	Mental joy (Pleasure)	Mental displeasure	Indifference
1 Contact quintet*	1	5	"																		F		
2 Jhāna factors*	1	7							A-T 1		" 2	" 3					One 7				B 4	" 5	" 6
3 Faculties*	1	15											" 1	" 2		3	" 4		" 7	" 8	" 9	" 10	" 11
4 Path factors*	1	12							" 2	" 10				6	" 11	" 7	8	" 12					
5 Strengths*	1	9											"	"		"	"						
6 Roots*	1	6		"	"	"	"	"															
7 Ways of action*	1	6		A	I		NA	NI															
8 Guardians of the world	1	2																					
9 Destroyers* "	1	2																					
10 The six pairs	6	12																					
11 The Helpers	1	2														"							
12 The Pairwise Combination*	1	2															T						
13 The Last Dyad*	1	2												D	"		U	"					
	18																						
Realities			Contact	Greed	Hate	Delusion	Non-greed	Non-hate	Applied thought		Sustained thought	Rapture	Confidence	Effort		Mindfulness	One-pointedness		Feeling				

Abbreviations: F = Feeling; C = Consciousness; One = One-pointedness; A-T = Applied thought; B = Bliss; A = Avarice

Consciousness and associated mental states														The or-whatever state 15 Yevāpanaka										
Perception	Volition	Faculty of mind	Faculty of Vitality	3 Abstinences 3	Faculty of knowledge	I-shall-know-what-I-did not-know faculty	Higher realization faculty	He-who-has-known faculty	Wrong views	Shame, Fear 2	Shamelessness, Fearlessness 2	Doubt (Delusion)	The six pairs 12	Desire 1	Decision 1	Attention 1	Equanimity 1	3 Abstinences 3	Compassion, Sympathetic joy 2	Restlessness (Delusion) 1	Conceit 1	Sloth, Torpor 2	Envy, Stinginess, Worry 3	Realities
"	"	C																						5
																								5
		"6	"12		"5	"13	"14	"15																16
				3"5	Right views 1				"9															9
					Power of Knl					"	"													9
					Non-delusion							"								"				6
					Right-views				"															6
										"														2
											"													2
													"											12
					C.C																			2
					Insight																			2
																								2
Perception	Volition	Consciousness	Mental vitality (psychic life)	3 Abstinences	Knowledge				Wrong views	Shame, Fear	Shamelessness, Fearlessness	Doubt	The six pairs	Desire	Decision	Attention	Equanimity	3 Abstinences	Compassion, Sympathetic joy	Restlessness	Conceit	Sloth, Torpor	Envy, Stinginess, Worry	

I = Ill-will
N.A = Non-avarice
N.I = Non-ill-will
C.C = Clear comprehension
T = Tranquillity
D = Determination
U = Undistractedness

Mental States of Dhs and the Realities of Abhidh-s

Explanation of the Chart. This single chart gives all the information about the associations of the 89 consciousnesses with their mental states as provided in Dhs. All the states involved are listed at the top of the chart and the realities to which those states belong are listed at the bottom. The serial numbers in the first column give the serial order in which the states are to be taken. The shaded squares show the states that are included in the first pair of great faultless consciousnesses. This serves as an example to show how the other consciousnesses and their associated states are to be taken.

The 18 Groups. There are altogether 18 groups starting with the Contact quintet in serial order.

The Six Pairs. The six pairs, which is serial no. 10, form 6 groups: (1) Tranquillity of mental factors, Tranquillity of consciousness, (2) Agility of mental factors, Agility of consciousness, (3) Pliancy of mental factors, Pliancy of consciousness, (4) Adaptability of mental factors, Adaptability of consciousness, (S) Proficiency of mental factors, Proficiency of consciousness, (6) Uprightness of mental factors, Uprightness of consciousness.

Asterisks for Faulty States. The asterisks show that 10 groups are involved in the faulty states. Serial nos 12 and 13 are taken together as "Final Pairs" in *Expos.* 335, and in that case there are 9 such groups.

Groups Involved. Serial no. 9, Destroyers of the world, applies only to faulty states but all the other 17 groups are involved in the faultless and indeterminate states.

The Or-whatever (*ye-vā-panakā*). In addition to the states mentioned under the various groups there are, according to the cty, 16 of "the or-whatever states" but only those that are applicable to the consciousness in question are taken.

Great Faultless Consciousnesses

First Pair. By taking the shaded squares horizontally with the group, it will be seen that there are: (1) Contact quintet 5, (2) *Jhāna* factors 5, (3)

Faculties 8, (4) Path factors 5, (5) Strengths 7, (6) Roots 3, (7) Ways of action 3, (8) Guardians of the world 2, (10) The six pairs 12, (11) The Helpers 2, (12) The Pairwise Combination 2, (13) The Last Dyad 2. These are the 56 states mentioned in Dhs. In addition, desire, decision, attention, equanimity, 3 abstinences, and 2 illimitables (compassion and sympathetic joy) — the 9 under "the or-whatever" states — have to be taken. So the total number of associated states which arise with each faultless consciousness of the first pair is 56 + 9 = 65.

In Abhidh-s only the separate realities of the above 65 states are taken. The realities corresponding to them can be read off by taking the shaded squares vertically. For the 56 states there are 30 realities, but consciousness has to be excluded, and so there are 29. As for the 9 "or-whatever" states, they are separate realities. So the total number of associated mental factors (*cetasika*) which arise with each faultless consciousness of the first pair is 29 + 9 = 38 as given in Abhidh-s.

Note. In what follows (1) "associated states" indicate those states given in Dhs, and "associated mental factors" those in Abhidh-s; (2) only the variations in the states mentioned and the corresponding realities will be pointed out because the states under "or-whatever" are also the realities taken in Abhidh-s.

Second Pair. Since these consciousnesses are dissociated from knowledge, all the 7 states represented by shaded squares under knowledge reality are excluded. Thus there are 56 -7 + 9 = 58 associated states. As for the associated mental factors, knowledge is excluded from the realities and so there are 29 -1 + 9 = 37.

Third Pair. Since these consciousnesses are accompanied by indifference instead of mental joy as with the first pair, rapture of the *Jhāna* factors is excluded and indifference is substituted for mental joy in the Faculties. As there is a decrease of 1 due to the exclusion of rapture, there are 56 -1 + 9 = 64 associated states. Similarly, rapture is excluded from the realities and there are 29 -1 + 9 = 37 associated mental factors.

Fourth Pair. Since these consciousnesses are dissociated from knowledge as with the second pair but accompanied by indifference as with the third pair, the 7 states under knowledge reality together with rapture are excluded. Thus there are 56 -7 -1 + 9 = 57 associated states and 29 -1 -1 + 9 = 36 associated mental factors.

Fine-material Faultless Consciousnesses (Fourfold System of *Jhāna*)

First Jhāna. These are the same 56 associated states as with the first pair of great faultless consciousnesses. All of them are not given in the text. In addition, 6 under "the or-whatever" states have to be taken. These are the 9 for the faultless consciousnesses with the 3 abstinences excluded. Thus there are 56 + 6 = 62 associated states and 29 + 6 = 35 associated mental factors.

Second Jhāna. Applied thought and sustained thought are excluded from the 56 above and so there are 56 -2 + 6 = 60 associated states and 29 -2 + 6 = 33 associated mental factors.

Third Jhāna. Rapture is excluded from the above and so there are 59 associated states and 32 associated mental factors.

Fourth Jhāna. Since this consciousness is accompanied by indifference, the latter is substituted for bliss but this does not change the number of states. But 2 illimitables from the 6 under "the or-whatever" states have to be excluded. So there are 59 -2 =57 associateed states and 32 -2 = 30 associated mental factors.

Fine-material Faultless Consciousnesses
(Fivefold System of *Jhāna*)

First Jhāna. This is the same as the First *Jhāna* of the Fourfold System. So there are 62 associated states and 35 associated mental factors.

Second Jhāna. Only applied thought is excluded from the above. So there are 61 associated states and 34 associated mental factors.

Third Jhāna. Since applied thought and sustained thought are excluded, this is the same as the Second *Jhāna* of the Fourfold System. So there are 60 associated states and 33 associated mental factors.

Fourth Jhāna. This is the same as the Third *Jhāna* of the Fourfold System. So there are 59 associated states and 32 associated mental factors.

Fifth Jhāna. This is the same as the Fourth *Jhāna* of the Fourfold System. So there are 57 associated states and 30 associated mental factors.

Immaterial Faultless Consciousnesses

All the 4 immaterial faultless consciousnesses are the same as the Fourth *Jhāna* of the Fourfold System or the Fifth *Jhāna* of the Fivefold System. So there are 57 associated states and 30 associated mental factors.

Supramundane Faultless Consciousnesses

First Path (Path of Stream-winner). I-shall-know-what-I-did-not-know faculty is included in the Faculties group and the 3 abstinences of "the or-whatever" states are included here. For the latter are always associated with supramundane consciousnesses. Thus there are 60 states mentioned instead of 56 as with the first pair of great faultless consciousnesses. Also desire, decision, attention, equanimity — the 4 under "the or-whatever" states — are included. The 2 illimitables are excluded because they take beings as objects whereas supramundane consciousnesses always take Nibbāna as object. Thus there are 60 + 4 = 64 associated states. As for the realities, since the I-shall-know-what-I-did-not-know faculty comes under the reality of knowledge, which is already included, there is no addition to be made for this faculty. So only the 3 abstinences have to be added to the 29 given for the first pair of great faultless consciousnesses along with the 4 under "the or-whatever" states. So there are 29 + 3 + 4 = 36 associated mental factors.

The 3 Higher Paths. In the Faculties group the Higher Realization or, in the case of the Arahatta Path, He-who-has-known is substituted for I-shall-know-what-I-did-notknow faculty of the First Path above. Since there is no difference in the number of states from the above, there are 64 associated states and 36 associated mental factors.

Faulty Consciousnesses; Greed-rooted Consciousnesses

First Consciousness. The states mentioned in Dhs are: (1) Contact quintet 5, (2) *Jhāna* factors 5, (3) Faculties 5 (confidence, mindfulness, and knowledge, which are not concerned with faulty states, are excluded), (4) Path factors 4 (the 4 wrong path factors), (5) Strengths 4 (wrong effort, wrong concentration, shamelessness, fearlessness), (6) Roots 2 (greed, delusion), (7) Ways of action 2 (avarice, wrong view), (9) Destroyers of the world 2, (12) Pairwise combination 1 (wrong tranquillity), (13) The Last Dyad 2 (wrong determination, wrong distraction), a total of 32 states. In addition, desire, decision, attention, and restlessness, the 4 under "the or-whatever" states, have to be taken. So there are 32 + 4 36 associated states.

The realities of the above 32 states in the groups are: contact, greed, delusion, applied thought, sustained thought, rapture, effort, one-pointedness, feeling, perception, volition, mental vitality (psychic life), wrong view, shamelessness, and fearlessness, i.e. 15, and with the 4 of the "or-whatever" states given above, there are 15 + 4 = 19 associated mental factors.

Second Consciousness. Since this is prompted, sloth and torpor of "the or-whatever" states have to be added to the above. So there are 32 + 6 = 38 associated states and 15 + 6 = 21 associated mental factors.

Third Consciousness. Since this is dissociated from wrong view, this state in the Path factors and Ways of action groups is excluded. Therefore, instead of 32 above, there are 32 -2 = 30. And conceit under "the or-whatever" states has to be added to the 4 for the first consciousness. So there are 30 + 5 = 35 associated states. Also, wrong view is excluded from the 15 realities and so there are 15 -1 + 5 = 19 associated mental factors.

Fourth Consciousness. Since this is prompted third consciousness, sloth and torpor of "the or-whatever" states are included as with the second consciousness. So there are 30 + 7 = 37 associated states and 15 -1 + 7 = 21 associated mental factors.

Fifth Consciousness. This differs from the first consciousness in that it is accompanied by indifference instead of mental joy. Therefore rapture is excluded from the *jhāna* factors group and indifference is substituted for bliss. So there are 32 -1 + 4 = 35 associated states and 15 -1 + 4 = 18 associated mental factors.

Sixth Consciousness. As this is prompted fifth consciousness, sloth and torpor of "the or-whatever" states are included in the above. So there are 32 -1 + 6 = 37 associated states and 15 -1 + 6 = 20 associated mental factors.

Seventh Consciousness. This differs from the third consciousness in that it is accompanied by indifference instead of mental joy. Therefore, rapture is excluded from the *jhāna* factors group and indifference is substituted for bliss. So there are 30 -1 + 5 = 34 associated states and 15 -1 -1 + 5 = 18 associated mental factors.

Eighth Consciousness. This is prompted seventh consciousness, and so sloth and torpor are added to the above. So there are 34 + 2 = 36 associated states and 18 + 2 = 20 associated mental factors.

Hate-rooted Consciousnesses

First Consciousness. The differences from the first greed-rooted consciousness will be pointed out. With regard to the states mentioned in Dhs, they are: (1) Contact quintet 5, (2) *Jhāna* factors 4 (rapture is excluded because this consciousness is accompanied by mental displeasure), (3) Faculties 5 (substitute mental displeasure for mental joy), (4) Path factors 3 (wrong view is excluded), (5) Strengths 4, (6) Roots 2 (substitute hate for greed), (7) Ways of action 1 (ill will), (9) Destroyers of the world 2, (12) and (13) Final pairs 3, i.e. 29. Then envy, stinginess, and worry, 3 of "the or-whatever" states, have to be added to the 4 of the first greed-rooted consciousness. So there are 29 + 7 = 36 associated states.

The realities are: contact, hate, delusion, applied thought, sustained thought, effort, one-pointedness, feeling, perception, volition, mental vitality, shamelessness, and fearlessness, i.e. 13, and 7 of "the or-whatever" states = 20. So there are 20 associated mental factors.

Second Consciousness. Since this is prompted, sloth and torpor are added. So there are 36 + 2 = 38 associated states and 20 + 2 = 22 associated mental factors.

Delusion-rooted Consciousnesses

Consciousness Associated with Doubt. This is accompanied by indifference and so the latter is taken in the *Jhāna* factors and Faculties groups. The states mentioned in Dhs are: (1) Contact quintet 5, (2) *Jhāna* factors 4 (rapture is excluded), (3) Faculties 4 (concentration is excluded), (4) Path factors 2 (wrong thought, wrong effort), (5) Strengths 3 (concentration is excluded), (6) Roots 2 (doubt and delusion are taken together in one column), (9) Destroyers of the world 2, (12) and (13) Final pairs 1 (determination), i.e. 23. Then attention and restlessness, the 2 under "the or-whatever" states, are to be added. So there are 23 + 2 = 25 associated states.

The realities are: contact, delusion, applied thought, sustained thought, effort, one-pointedness, feeling, perception, volition, mental vitality, shamelessness, fearlessness, and doubt, i.e. 13, and the 2 of "the or-whatever" states = 15. So there are 15 associated mental factors.

Consciousness Associated with Restlessness. This is also accompanied by indifference, but it differs from the above in that concentration is included. Thus there are: (1) Contact quintet 5, (2) *Jhāna* factors 4, (3) Faculties 5 (concentration is included), (4) Path factors 3 (wrong concentration is included), (5) Strengths 4, (6) Roots 2 (restlessness and delusion are taken together in one column under "the or-whatever" states but in this case the states are mentioned), (9) Destroyers of the world 2, (12) and (13) Final pairs 3, i.e. 28. Then decision and attention, the 2 under "the or-whatever" states, have to be added. So there are 28 + 2 = 30 associated states.

The realities are 13 also as in the above but the difference is that restlessness is substituted for doubt, and 2 of "the or-whatever" states 15. So there are 15 associated mental factors.

Faultless-Resultant Fivefold Consciousnesses

Eye-consciousness. This is accompanied by indifference, and the latter has to be included as pointed out above. The states mentioned are: (1) Contact quintet 5, (2) *Jhāna* factors 2 (indifference and one-pointedness only, applied thought, sustained thought and rapture being excluded), (3) Faculties 3 (mind, indifference and mental vitality), i.e. 10. Then with attention under "the or-whatever" states = 11. So there are 11 associated states.

The realities are: contact, one-pointedness, feeling, perception, volition, mental vitality, and also attention of "the or-whatever" states = 7. So there are 7 associated mental factors.

Ear-, Nose-, Tongue-consciousness. The same as above.

Body-consciousness. As this is accompanied by pleasure, substitute bodily pleasure for indifference in the *Jhāna* factors and mental joy for indifference in the Faculties groups. Here also there are 11 associated states and the same 7 associated mental factors.

Other Faultless-Resultant Consciousnesses

Faultless-Resultant Mind-element (*Recipient Consciousness*). This is accompanied by indifference. It differs from eye-consciousness in that applied thought and sustained thought of the *Jhāna* factors and the decision under "the or-whatever" states are included. So there are 11 + 3 = 14 associated states and 7 + 3 = 10 associated mental factors.

Faultless-Resultant Mind-consciousness Element Accompanied by Pleasure (*Investigating Consciousness Accompanied by Pleasure*). Since this is accompanied by pleasure, it differs from the above in that, instead of indifference, rapture and bliss are included in the *Jhāna* factors and mental joy in the Faculties groups. As rapture is the only additional state, there are 14 + 1 = 15 associated states and 10 + 1 = 11 associated mental factors.

Faultless-Resultant Mind-consciousness Element Accompanied by Indifference (Investigating Consciousness Accompanied by Indifference). This is the same as faultless-resultant mind-element (recipient consciousness).

Great Resultant Consciousnesses

First Pair. Only the first and the last states are mentioned in the text. But it is the same 56 states as the first pair of great faultless consciousnesses. And of the 9 under "the or-whatever" states, the 3 abstinences and 2 illimitables are excluded and only 4 (desire, decision, attention, and equanimity) are taken. So there are 56 + 4 = 60 associated states and 29 + 4 = 33 associated mental factors.

Second Pair and Others. They differ from the corresponding pairs of great faultless consciousnesses in that only 4 out of the 9 "the or-whatever" states, as in the first pair above, are taken. So there are respectively: 58 -5 = 53, 64 -5 = 59, 57 -5 = 52 associated states and 37 -5 = 32, 37 -5 = 32, 36 -5 = 31 associated mental factors.

Fine-material Resultant and Immaterial Resultant Consciousnesses

They are the same as Fine-material Faultless and Immaterial Faultless ones.

Supramundane Resultant Consciousnesses

The only difference from the supramundane faultless consciousnesses is that, instead of I-shall-know-what-I-did-not-know faculty in the Faculties group, Higher Realization is taken till the third consciousness (Anāgāmī Fruition) and he-who-has-known for the last consciousness (Arahatta Fruition).

Faulty-Resultant Fivefold Consciousnesses

Eye-consciousness, etc. With the exception of substituting pain for bodily pleasure in the faculties group for body-consciousness accompanied by pain, they are the same as the faultless-resultant ones.

Fault-resultant Mind-element (*Recipient Consciousness*), *Faulty-Resultant Mind-consciousness Eleement* (*Investigating Consciousness*), *Functional Mind-element* (*Five-door Advertence*). These three are the same as faultless-resultant mind-element.

Functional Mind-consciousness Element Accompanied by Pleasure (*Arahatta's Smile-consciousness*). The states mentioned are (1) Contact quintet 5, (2) *Jhāna* factors 5 (includes bliss), (3) Faculties 5 (mindfulness and knowledge are excluded), i.e. 15. Then decision and attention — the 2 under "the or-whatever" states — are taken. So there are 15 + 2 = 17 associated states.

The realities are: contact, applied thought, sustained thought, rapture, effort, one-pointedness, feeling, perception, volition, mental vitality, i.e. 10 and 2 of "the or-whatever" states = 12. So there are 12 associated mental factors.

Functional Mind-consciousness Element Accompanied by Indifference (*Mind-door Advertence*). The states mentioned are (1) Contact quintet 5, (2) *Jhāna* factors 4 (rapture is excluded), (3) Faculties 5 (as above but substitute indifference for mental joy). The difference from the above is that rapture is excluded. So there are 17 -1 = 16 associated states and 12 -1 = 11 associated mental factors.

Great Functional Consciousnesses

First Pair. The difference from the first pair of great faultless consciousnesses is that the 3 abstinences are excluded. So there are 65 -3 = 62 associated states and 38 -3 = 35 associated mental factors. Second Pair and Others. Here also the 3 abstinences are excluded from the corresponding pairs of great faultless consciousnesses. So there are respectively: 58 -3 = 55, 64 -3 = 61, 57 -3 = 54 associated states and 37 -3 = 34, 37 -3 = 34, 36 -3 = 33 associated mental factors.

Fine-material Functional and Immaterial Functional Consciousnesses

They are the same as fine-material faultless and immaterial faultless ones.

20. Dissociation Condition

In this Analytical Exposition of the Conditions the Buddha expounded materiality and mentality of dissociation condition in a simple way so that the audience could easily understand. For when materiality is the conditioning state, mentality is the conditioned state and vice versa. It is only in the Investigation Chapter that the different kinds of dissociation condition are treated in detail. Of the three kinds of dissociation condition: (1) conascence-dissociation has (a) mentality as conditioning state and materiality as conditioned state and (b) materiality as conditioning state and mentality as conditioned state, (2) base-prenascence-dissociation has materiality as conditioning state and mentality as conditioned state, (3) postnascence-dissociation has mentality as conditioning state and materiality as conditioned state.

From the above it will be seen that: (1) (b) conascence-dissociation and (2) base-prenascence-dissociation have materiality as conditioning state and mentality as conditioned state; (1) (a) conascence-dissociation and (3) postnascence-dissociation have mentality as conditioning state and materiality as conditioned state. This is how they are separated in the chart.

Materiality as Conditioning State and
Mentality as Conditioned State

(i) (a) *Conditioning and Conditioned States*. See the chart.

Conditioning Force. Conascence-dissociation belongs to the Medium conascence group. And when the Major and Medium conascence conditions are examined to find out the conditions where heart-base is the conditioning state and rebirth-consciousnesses in the five-aggregate planes are the conditioned states, it will be seen that these are the 4 Major conascence and 2 of Medium conascence, i.e. mutuality and dissociation. So this force occurs completely in these 6 common conditions.

(i) (b) *Conditioning and Conditioned States*. See the chart.

Conditioning Force. In the Explanation of the Single Enumerations it was pointed out that this condition belongs to the base-prenascence group and occurs completely in the 5 conditions: dependence, prenascence, dissociation, presence, and non-disappearance. Since (1) heart-base is a conditioning state, this condition is also base-object-prenascence-dissociation in which base-object-prenascence-predominance is included. From the Object Group chart in Intr. to *C.R.* it will be seen that this latter condition occurs in all the 8 common conditions of the object group, i.e. object, predominance, dependence, strong-dependence, prenascence, dissociation, presence and non-disappearance; (2) the other 5 bases (sentient faculties) are also conditioning states, this condition is also the base-prenascence-faculty of faculty condition. So this force occurs in 9 common conditions: completely in 5 (dependence, prenascence, dissociation, presence, and non-disappearance) and appropriately in 4 (object, predominance, strong-dependence, and faculty).

Mentality as Conditioning State and
Materiality as Conditioned State

(ii)(a) *Conditioning and Conditioned States*. See the chart. It will be seen that they are the same as the first part of conascence-dissociation given under dissociation condition in the SEC. It includes the 4 mental aggregates at the moment of conception (rebirth-consciousnesses) in the five-aggregate planes as conditioning states and heart-base as conditioned state.

Conditioning Force. This condition belongs to the Medium conascence group of conditions. So this force occurs in 6 common conditions: completely in 5 (the 4 Major conascence and dissociation) and appropriately in mutuality.

(ii)(b) It is the same as postnascence condition to which the chart refers.

Planes. Dissociation condition occurs only in the 26 five-aggregate planes.

Persons. This condition occurs appropriately in the 12 types of persons.

Explanation. In dissociation condition although (1) mentality and materiality arise together (conascence-dissociation); (2) mentality depends on materiality for its arising (base-prenascence-dissociation); (3) subsequent mentalities are related to preceding materialities (postnascence-dissociation), yet materiality and mentality are separate entities. If mentality and materiality are seen as they really are and also that, besides them, there is no person, being and so on, this is purity of view. In this connection, the following extracts from *P.Pfn*. are given:

> (1) [H]e concludes that over and above mere mentality-materiality there is nothing else that is a being or a person or a deity (*deva*) or a Brahmā.

After defining mentality-materiality thus according to its true nature, then in order to abandon this worldly designation of "a being" and "a person" more thoroughly, to surmount confusion about beings and to establish his mind on the plane of non-confusion, he makes sure that the meaning defined, namely, "This is mere mentality-materiality, there is no being, no person", is confirmed by a number of Suttas (pp. 687–88).

(2) Therefore, just as a marionette is void, soulless and without curiosity, and while it walks and stands merely through the combination of strings and wood, yet it seems as if it had curiosity and interestedness, so too, this mentality-materiality is void, soulless and without curiosity, and while it walks and stands merely through the combination of the two together, yet it seems as if it had curiosity and interestedness. This is how it should be regarded. Hence the Ancients said,

> The mental and material are really here, But here there is no human being to be found, For it is void and merely fashioned like a doll Just suffering piled up [void] like grass and sticks.

And this [interdependence of mentality and materiality] should be explained not only by means of the simile of the marionette, but also by means of the analogies of the sheaves of reeds and so on. For just as when two sheaves of reeds are propped one against the other, each one gives the other consolidating support, and when one falls the other falls, so too, in the five-constituent becoming mentality-materiality occurs as an interdependent state, each of its components giving the other consolidating support, and when one falls owing to death, the other falls too. Hence the Ancients said:

> The mental and material
> Are twins and each supports the other,
> When one breaks up, they both break up
> Through interconditionality (pp.689–90).

(3) Furthermore, mentality has no efficient power; it cannot occur by its own efficient power. It does not eat, it does not drink, it does not speak, it does not adopt postures. And materiality is without efficient power; it cannot occur by its own efficient power. For it has no desire to eat, it has no desire to drink, it has no desire to speak, it has no desire to adopt postures. But rather it is when supported by materiality that mentality occurs; and it is when supported by mentality that materiality occurs. When mentality has the desire to eat, the desire to drink, the desire to speak, the desire to adopt a posture, it is materiality that eats, drinks, speaks and adopts a posture.

But for the purpose of explaining this meaning they give this simile as an example: a man born blind and a stool-crawling cripple wanted to go somewhere. The blind man said to the cripple, "Look, I can do what should be done by legs, but I have no eyes with which to see what is rough and smooth." The cripple said, "Look, I can do what should be done by eyes, but

I have no legs with which to go and come." The blind man was delighted, and he made the cripple climb up on his shoulder. Sitting on the blind man's shoulder the cripple spoke thus, "Leave the left, take the right, leave the right, take the left" (pp. 690–91).

21. Presence Condition

It was already pointed out that presence condition is not completely expounded in this Analytical Exposition where the teaching is neither too brief nor too detailed. So postnascence-presence, physical nutriment-presence, physical life-faculty-presence and the 3 mixed conditions are left out. But in the Investigation Chapter, except for the conditions of the strong-dependence group and strong-and-weak asynchronous *kamma* group, those of the remaining 9 groups are included in presence condition. This can be seen from chart II (A) in the Intr. to *C.R.*

Conditioning and Conditioned States. The chart refers to the conditions where the relations are the same and, therefore, the forces are also the same.

Nibbāna is Not Included in Presence Condition. The reason for this was given in the Brief Explanations of the Conditions. "Presence" here means "presence after having arisen". For only when a state arises and is present does it belong to presence condition, not when it has not arisen and is not present. In the case of Nibbāna it is not a state that can be present on one occasion and absent on another because it eternally exists. Thus it is not included in presence condition.

Planes. This condition occurs in 30 planes exclusive of the non-percipient plane in this Analytical Exposition and in all the 31 planes in the Investigation Chapter.

Persons. This condition occurs appropriately in the 12 types of persons.

22., 23. Absence, Disappearance Conditions

Conditioning and Conditioned States. See the chart. The states are not analysed as in proximity condition — with which each is the same — but only the totals are given.

Conditioning Force. This condition belongs to the proximity-strong-dependence group of 7 conditions. So this force occurs in 7 common conditions: completely in 5 (proximity, contiguity, strong-dependence, absence, disappearance) and appropriately in 2 (repetition and *kamma*).

In Detail. This is the same as that given for proximity condition and the way of recitation is the same. Planes and Persons. The same as proximity condition.

24. Non-Disappearance Condition

The chart points out that this condition is the same as presence condition.

Part 2

CONDITIONAL RELATIONS

Paṭṭhāna

The *Chaṭṭhasaṅgāyaya* Text of the
Seventh Book of the *Abhidhamma-piṭaka*

GENERAL CONTENTS

CONDITIONAL RELATIONS VOL. II

FOREWORD

In 1969 the Pali Text Society published important translations of two Abhidhamma works: *Conditional Relations*, being Vol. I of the Chaṭṭhasaṅgāyana (ChS) text of Paṭṭhāna, and No. 37 in the Translation Series (T.S.) by U Nārada Mūla Paṭṭhāna Sayadaw; and *The Book of Analysis*, Vibhaṅga, translated also from the ChS edition by Paṭhamakyaw Ashin Thiṭṭila, No. 39 in the T.S. A third, and revised edition, of Mrs Rhys David's translation of Dhammasaṅgaṇī, *Buddhist Psychological Ethics*, was published in 1974, No. 41 in the T.S. These had been preceded by U Nārada's *Discourse on Elements*, his translation of Dhātukathā, 1962, reprinted in 1977, and No. 34 in the T.S. The demand for these Abhidhamma works, though small, has been steady, and has grown steadily as the years have gone by. There is now a study of the first few pages of Paṭṭhāna by U Nārada called *Guide to Conditional Relations*, vol. I. He wished to write it to make explicit and intelligible many of the difficulties in the highly complex Paṭṭhāna, the seventh and last of the Abhidhamma works. Here again U Nārada's knowledge is due to the long period of study he has devoted to this work and to the early comprehensive, solid and precise Abhidhamma training he received, a training no longer existing even in Burma.

As I said in my Foreword to *Conditional Relations*, vol. I (as it should now be called), it had not been expected that the same translator would translate the ChS vols. II, III, IV, or V. But the unexpected happened and the present book is the result.

The preparation of the typescript and of most of the proof-reading have been done by U Nārada and U Thein Nyun, his zealous assistant of many years' standing. The Pali Text Society offers sincere gratitude to them both.

I. B. HORNER

London.
June 1979.

INTRODUCTION

The Introduction to Conditional Relations Vol. I (C.R. I) gives (1) a brief account of the methods and how to apply them in order to arrive at the answers in the 7 Chapters of the Faultless Triplet Paṭṭhāna section; (2) the states of the other 4 Triplets also dealt with therein; (3) a general idea of the remaining 23 Paṭṭhānas which make up the last 3 of the 5 volumes of Paṭṭhāna. Also, it states that the remaining 17 Triplets, like the Clinging and Corrupt Triplets of Vol. I, are treated very briefly in Vol. II, the present volume. This completes the Triplet Paṭṭhāna, the first of the 6 Paṭṭhānas in the Positive Method Division.

Among the Triplets in Vol. II, the Applied Thought Triplet not only includes many states but they are also complicated and difficult to understand. With regard to all the 6 Chapters of each Triplet in this volume, it will be found that in the Enumeration Chapters (1) of the Positive and Negative conditions, in most cases only "By Ones" are given and (2) of the Positive-Negative and Negative-Positive conditions, only "By Twos" are given. As for "By Threes", "By Fours" and so on, it is directed that they be worked out according to the method given in the Faultless Triplet. As for the Investigation Chapters, it will be found that, as in the preceding 6 Chapters, only "By Ones" and "By Twos" are given and the reader is then directed to "Enumerate the enumerations of Investigation Chapter without confusion" and so forth in order to obtain the rest. And it is only in the last Triplet, the Visible and Impinging Triplet, that the common of root condition and one ordinary combination are given. The rest of the commons, combinations and others are not given for any Triplet but it is directed that they be found in order to know them in detail.

Even in the Faultless Triplet, which is given in detail, there are many elisions. So it is no wonder that the Triplets in this volume, which are given briefly, should have so many elisions. How, then, can these elisions be determined? Even in Burma, where Abhidhamma flourishes, no one has, in times past, worked out what those elisions are. The reason, of course, is that this is no easy matter at all. Although it may be possible, when the method is known, to find what the elisions are in the first two

Paṭṭhānas, i.e. the Triplet and Couplet Paṭṭhānas of the Positive Method Division, it is extremely difficult to know what the elisions are in the remaining 22 Paṭṭhānas. For, sometimes, it takes 15–20 minutes of deep thought to be able to work out an answer that is elided. That is why the translator painstakingly determined the elisions for the benefit of persons who wish to have complete understanding of all the 24 Paṭṭhānas. Also, wherever necessary, the elisions were determined for the Sixth Synod Editions, especially those in Vols. IV and V.

Paṭṭhāna is, indeed, deep and profound and so it is really difficult to conceive of it completely on one's own. But the Buddha provided a method so that, on that basis, there would be no difficulty in grasping the subject. That method is none other than the Table of Contents (the Triplets and Couplets) expounded at the beginning of Dhammasaṅgaṇī. As examples, the Faultless, Faulty and Indeterminate states of the Faultless Triplet were expounded to form the Faultless Triplet Paṭṭhāna Section; the states of the Feeling Triplet were expounded to form the Feeling Triplet Paṭṭhāna Section. Therefore, when the appropriate states of the Triplets are taken as references (1) from the Single Enumerations (the conditioning and conditioned states of the conditions) of the Positive and Negative conditions, as given in Guide to C.R., Part II, the 6 Chapters can be easily understood and (2) from the Single Enumerations of the Investigation Chapter, as given in the Introduction to C.R. I, the Investigation Chapters can be easily understood.

In this volume the enumerations "By Ones" of the conditions in Dependent Chapter and others are given completely in the Enumeration Chapters but not in the Classification Chapters. Therefore, in places where difficulties may be encountered, the enumerations in the elisions are worked out. But the reason for obtaining them from the appropriate single enumerations must be borne in mind. Since it is not possible to give everything completely, the reader must apply the method to determine the enumerations in the other elisions on his own.

6. Applied Thought Triplet

Triplet States

Reference (R)	Variant (V)
1. 55 cons. with applied thought and sustained thought, 50 m.f. exclusive of applied thought and sustained thought.	1. 55 cons. with applied thought and sustained thought, 50 m.f. exclusive of applied thought and sustained thought.

2. 11 second Jhāna cons., 36 m.f. exclusive of applied thought and sustained thought; 55 applied thought m.f. present at 55 cons. with applied thought and sustained thought.	2. 11 second Jhāna cons., 36 m.f. exclusive of applied thought and sustained thought; 55 applied thought m.f. present at 55 cons. with applied thought and sustained thought.
3. 55 cons. without applied thought and sustained thought, 36 m.f. exclusive of applied thought and sustained thought; 11 sustained thought m.f. present at 11 second Jhāna cons.; 28 matter; Nibbāna.	3. 55 cons. without applied thought and sustained thought, 36 m.f. exclusive of applied thought and sustained thought; 11 sustained thought m.f. present at 11 second Jhāna cons.; 28 matter; Nibbāna.

Abbreviations: cons. = consciousness; m.f. = mental factors

The above states are taken from Discourse on Elements pp. 36–7. Please see this text also for the sections (given as footnotes in this volume) and states of the other Triplets (given in this Introduction). Since 55 sustained thought mental factors—present at 55 consciousnesses with applied thought and sustained thought—are not included in this Triplet, they are Triplet-freed. Therefore, there is no need to consider them here as they are not concerned with this Triplet.

One who is versed in the Compendium of Philosophy will know what the above states are, but for one who is not and has no knowledge of them, some explanation is provided below:

1. The first section is "States with applied thought and sustained thought." These are (a) 55 consciousnesses with applied thought and sustained thought—made up of 44 sensuous consciousnesses exclusive of twice fivefold consciousnesses and 11 (3 fine-material and 8 supramundane) first Jhāna consciousnesses; (b) 50 associated mental factors exclusive of applied thought and sustained thought.

2. The second section is "States without applied thought but with sustained thought." These are (a) 11 second Jhāna consciousnesses; (b) 36 associated mental factors exclusive of applied thought and sustained thought; (c) 55 applied thought mental factors—those that were excluded in the first section because they were associated with the 55 applied thought consciousnesses. (Since each applied thought consciousness is associated with applied thought mental factor and there are 55 of the former, there are 55 of the latter.)

Note (i): The fact that 55 consciousnesses with applied thought and sustained thought—the reference states in the first section—are conascent with 55 applied thought mental factors—the variant states in the second section—must be kept in mind.

3. The third section is "States without applied thought and sustained thought." These are (a) 55 consciousnesses without applied thought and sustained thought—made up of 11 third Jhāna, 11 fourth Jhāna, 23 (3 fine-material + 12 immaterial + 8 supramundane) fifth Jhāna consciousnesses and twice fivefold consciousnesses; (b) 36 associated mental factors exclusive of applied thought and sustained thought; (c) 11 sustained thought mental factors which were not concerned with the second section and, therefore, excluded from the 11 second Jhāna consciousnesses in the second section; (d) 28 matter; (e) Nibbāna.

Note (ii): The fact that 11 second Jhāna consciousnesses—the reference states in the second section—are conascent with 11 sustained thought mental factors—the variant states in the third section—must be kept in mind.

The Triplet-freed states have already been given. Since matter and Nibbāna are not involved in the first and second sections they are included in the third section. Particular note must be made of the fact that Nibbāna is never taken into account in the 6 Chapters but only in the Investigation Chapter and, even then, only in object, object-predominance and object-strong-dependence conditions.

Now it will be clearly shown why the Classification Chapters of Dependent Chapter in the text are so expounded. Of course, it will not be possible to deal with all the conditions. So only one, as the reference condition, in each Triplet will be considered in order to provide the method. Then, based on that method, those for the other conditions can be found.

6. APPLIED THOUGHT TRIPLET — I. "DEPENDENT" CHAPTER

1. Conditions: Positive (i) Classification Chapter

Root Condition

Please refer to the chart. The states of root condition are all rooted mentality and materiality. The answers given here must be compared with those in the text.

With the reference states of section 1, which are all mentality, there are:

(i) (*1-1*).[1] Here the mentality of the reference (R for short) states and of the variant (V for short) states of section 1 are related both during life ("dl" for short) and at the moment of conception ("mc" for short). (Since the states with applied thought and sustained thought, as the reference states, arise both during life and at the moment of conception, these have to be stated every time and so abbreviations are used for them.)

(ii) (*1-2*). R 1 and 55 applied thought m.f. of V 2 are conascent—which had to be kept in mind in note (i) above—both "dl" and "mc".

(iii) (*1-3*). R 1 and mind-produced matter "dl" and also kamma-produced matter "mc" of V 3 are conascent.

(iv) (*1-1,3*). R 1 and the mentality of V 1 + matter of V 3 are conascent. Wherever both "dl" and "mc" apply they will not be indicated, but must be assumed.

(v) (*1-2,3*). R 1 and 55 applied thought m.f. of V 2 + matter of V 3 are conascent, i.e. (1–2) and (1–3) above are combined.

(vi) (*1-1,2*). Mentality of R 1 and that of V 1 + 55 applied thought m.f. of V 2 are conascent, i.e. (1–1) and (1–2) are combined.

(vii) (*1-1,2,3*). Mentality of R 1 and that of V 1 + 55 applied thought m.f. of V 2 + matter of V 3 are conascent, i.e. (1–2,3) and (1–1,2) are combined.

Thus, with the reference states of section 1, there are 7 answers. With the reference states of section 2 there are:

(viii) (*2-2*). Here the mentality of R 2 and that of V 2 are conascent. (Since conascence condition is expounded in this Chapter, the fact that the states are conascent is to be understood and so this will not be mentioned again.)

(ix) (*2-1*). Just as the answer (1–2) was obtained above, here the reverse also holds true, i.e. 55 applied thought m.f. of R 2 and mentality of V 1.

(x) (*2-3*). Unlike (1–3) above where only matter of V 3 was taken, here 11 sustained thought m.f. of V 3, which are conascent with the mental aggregates of R 2—which had to be kept in mind in

---

[1] The figure or figures before the dash denote the appropriate reference states of the section or sections and those after denote the appropriate variant states of the section or sections that are selected for an answer. This is to be understood for all the answers. As the answers will be given in this way, the word "answer" will be left out.

note (ii) above—are also taken. In (1–3) above, the mental aggregates of R 1 are not conascent with these sustained thought m.f. and so the latter were not taken there. Also, 55 applied thought m.f. of R 2 are conascent with matter of V 3.

(xi) (*2–1,3*). 55 applied thought m.f. of R 2 and the mental aggregates of V 1 + matter of V 3.

(xii) (*2–2,3*). Mentality of R 2 and that of V 2 + 11 sustained thought m.f. of V 3 + matter of V 3.

Why (2–1,2) and (2–1,2,3) are not obtained. The mental aggregates of R 2 and those of V 1 are not conascent and so (2–1,2) is not obtained. Consequently, (2–1,2,3) is not obtained as well.

Thus, with the reference states of section 2, there are 5 answers.

With the reference states of section 3 there are:

(xiii) (*3–3*). "dl": mentality of R 3 and that of V 3 + mind-produced matter of V 3; also 11 sustained thought m.f. of R 3 and mind-produced matter of V 3 as they are conascent;

"mc": similar to "dl" above: mentality of R 3 and that of V 3 + kamma-produced matter of V 3; also, 11 sustained thought m.f. of R 3 and kamma-produced matter of V 3; also, the usual relations between (heart-)base and mental aggregates, i.e. (a) mental aggregates of R 3 and (heart-)base of V 3 and (b) (heart-)base of R 3 and mental aggregates of V 3; again, 11 sustained thought m.f. of R 3 and (heart-)base of V 3 and the reverse, i.e. (heart-) base of R 3 and 11 sustained thought m.f. of V 3; furthermore, the relations between matter of R 3 and V 3 which consists of the 2 kinds above as given in the single enumeration of root condition.

Note: Matter "dl" is mind-produced matter and matter "mc" is kamma-produced matter.

(xiv) (*3–1*). (Heart-)base has wide application but in this Dependent Chapter it applies only to "mc". Therefore, whenever (heart-)base is taken it is meant for "mc". Here (heart-)base of R 3 and mental aggregates of V 1 are taken to give (3–1).

(xv) (*3–2*). 11 sustained thought m.f. of R 3 and mental aggregates of V 2 for "dl" and "mc"; also, (heart-)base of R 3 and mental aggregates of V 2; again, (heart-)base of R 3 and 55 applied thought m.f. of V 2 for "mc".

(xvi) (*3–1,3*). (Heart-)base of R 3 and mental aggregates of V 1; great primaries of R 3 and kamma-produced matter of V 3. Here (3–1) and part of (3–3) are combined to give (3–1,3).

(xvii) (*3-2,3*). 11 sustained thought m.f. of R 3 and mental aggregates of V 2 + matter of V 3 for "dl" and "mc"; also, like (3–1,3) above, (heart-)base of R 3 and mental aggregates of V 2 and great primaries of R 3 and matter of V 3 to give (3–2,3); again, (heart-) base of R 3 and 55 applied thought m.f. of V 2; great primaries of R 3 and matter of V 3; besides, (heart-)base of R 3 and mental aggregates of V 2 + 11 sustained thought m.f. of V 3. All these states are contained in the chart.

(xviii) (*3-1,2*). (Heart-)base of R 3 and mental aggregates of V 1 + 55 applied thought m.f. of V 2.

(xix) (*3-1,2,3*). (Heart-)base of R 3 and mental aggregates of V 1 + 55 applied thought m.f. of V 2; great primaries of R 3 and matter of V 3.

Thus, with the reference states of section 3, there are 7 answers.

With the reference states of sections 1 and 3 taken together there are:

(xx) (*1,3-1*). Here the reference states are the mental aggregates of R 1 and (heart-)base of R 3. As (heart-)base is taken it is for "mc". The variant states are the mental aggregates of V 1.

(xxi) (*1,3-2*). The above reference states and 55 applied thought m.f. of V 2.

(xxii) (*1,3-3*). Here the reference states are the mental aggregates of R 1 and great primaries of R 3. The variant is matter of V 3. This occurs "dl" and "mc".

(xxiii) (*1,3-1,3*). This is a combination of (1,3–1) and (1,3–3). As (heart-)base is taken it is for "mc".

(xxiv) (*1,3-2,3*). This is a combination of (1,3–2) and (1,3–3).

(xxv) (*1,3-1,2*). The reference states are the mental aggregates of R 1 and (heart-)base of R 3. The variant states are the mental aggregates of V 1 and 55 applied thought m.f. of V 2.

(xxvi) (*1,3-1,2,3*). This is a combination of (1,3–1,2) and (1,3–3) above.

Now that the method has been provided up to this stage, it is left to the reader to find the other answers by making use of the knowledge gained. That is why they are purposely left out. The 37 answers must be compared with those expounded in the text. Then, from the chart it will be seen why they are so expounded.

1. Conditions: Positive (ii) Enumeration Chapter

By Ones

In the Classification Chapter of the Dependent Chapter root, object and dissociation conditions[1] are given in detail but the other 20 conditions are just referred to. In the Enumeration Chapter, however, the enumerations "By Ones" of all the conditions are given. How they are obtained is shown below because the reader will not find them easy.

It has already been shown in the Single Enumerations in C.R. I that (1) object, proximity, contiguity, strong-dependence, association, absence and disappearance have the same enumerations; (2) conascence, dependence, presence and non-disappearance have the same enumerations. Although there is more matter in the Major conascence group of conditions, i.e. (2) above, than in root for the answer (3–3), there is no difference in the enumerations. Therefore, the conditions which have the same enumerations as root and object respectively—the 2 that have been dealt with in detail—will not be considered but only the other conditions.

Predominance 23. The Single Enumeration of this condition shows that it occurs during life only and not at the moment of conception. But because predominant mind-produced matter is a conditioned state, only the 14 answers which have only "at the moment of conception", have to be excluded[2] from those for root condition. These are:

(1) With 3 as reference: (3–1), (3–1,3), (3–1,2), (3–1,2,3), i.e. 4;

(2) With 1,3 as reference: all except (1,3-3), i.e. 6;

(3) With 2,3 as reference: (2,3–1), (2,3–1,3), i.e. 2;

(4) With 1,2,3 as reference: (1,2,3–1), (1,2,3–1,2), i.e. 2.

Therefore, the enumeration is 37 – 14 = 23. This can be proved to be so from the text.

Mutuality 28. The conditioning and conditioned states contain all the mentality. As for materiality, only (heart-)base of kamma-produced matter at the moment of conception and all the great primaries are included but not derived matter and mind-produced matter. The 9 answers not obtained are: (3–1,3), (3–1,2,3), (1,3–3), (1,3–1,3),

---

[1] When there is no doubt that "condition" or "conditions" is meant, such words will be left out.

[2] Also those from the other answers so that only "during life" are taken.

(1,3-2,3), (2,3-1,3), (1,2-1,3), (1,2,3-3) and (1,2,3-1,3). Therefore the enumeration is 37 – 9 = 28.

Prenascence 11, Repetition 11. These 2 conditions have mentality as conditioning and conditioned states which occur during life. There is no materiality. The 11 answers obtained are: (1–1), (1–2), (1–1,2), (2–2), (2–1), (2–3), (2–2,3), (3–3), (3–2), (2,3–2) and (1,2–1).

These answers should be checked with those in the text to find whether they are correct or not. By doing so knowledge will be acquired to enable one to fill in the elisions. Of course, the chart giving the states of the Triplet must always be referred to.

By Twos

They are all the same as "By Ones". That is why, after the elisions, it is noted that they are abbreviated. And it must be understood that when the enumerations are not given later, this is because there are no differences.

2. Conditions: Negative (i) Classification Chapter

Root condition was taken as the example in the Positive conditions to explain the Classification Chapter and now not-object 7 is taken in the Negative conditions. The conditioning states of not-object are the mentality in the five-aggregate planes and all the great primaries while the conditioned states are all materiality. Since materiality is included only in the third section of the Triplet, the variant, materiality, is invariably V 3.

The 7 answers for not-object apply to both "dl" and "mc". For "dl" they are:

(i) (*1-3*). Mental aggregates of R 1 + matter of V 3;

(ii) (*2-3*). Mental aggregates of R 2 + matter of V 3;

(iii) (*3-3*). Mental aggregates of R 3 and matter of V 3 + all materiality;

(iv) (*1,3-3*). Mental aggregates of R 1 + great primaries of R 3 and matter of V 3;

(v) (*2,3-3*). Mental aggregates of R 2 + 11 sustained thought m.f. of R 3 and, since it is "dl", mind-produced matter of V 3; also, like (1,3–3) above, mental aggregates of R 2 + great primaries of R 3 and matter of V 3; again, 55 applied thought m.f. of R 2 + great primaries of R 3 and matter of V 3;

(vi) (*1,2-3*). Mental aggregates of R 1 + conascent 55 applied thought m.f. of R 2 and matter of V 3;

(vii) (*1,2,3-3*). Mental aggregates of R 1 + 55 applied thought m.f. of R 2 + great primaries of R 3 and matter of V 3.

For "mc" the 7 answers have to be taken in a similar way to "dl". The last 3 answers for "mc" are elided in the text.

The answers obtained for the other conditions should be compared with those in the text.

2. Conditions: Negative (ii) Enumeration Chapter

By Ones

Not-root 33. This is given fully in the Classification Chapter of the text.

Not-path 33. The only difference from not-root is that delusion is excluded.

Not-object 7. This is given fully in the Classification Chapter of the text.

Not-proximity and others 7. They have the same enumeration as not-object.

Not-predominance and others 37. They are the same as those given under Positive root condition.

Not-kamma 7. This is given fully in the Classification Chapter of the text.

Not-resultant 23. This needs to be explained. Since not-resultant has no resultant states, those states which occur "mc" and kamma-produced matter are not obtained. But as there is mind-produced matter, this condition is similar to predominance in the Positive conditions and has the same enumeration.

Not-nutriment and Not-faculty 1. These are 1 because only materiality is involved to give (3-3).

Not-jhāna 1. It is 1 because twice fivefold consciousnesses are included in section 3 and only (3-3) is obtained.

Not-dissociation 11. This is given fully in the Classification Chapter of the text.

3. Conditions: Positive-Negative (ii) Enumeration Chapter

Root By Twos

In the Enumeration Chapters of the Positive-Negative and Negative-Positive conditions, only "By Twos" are given. So "By Threes" and others must, as repeatedly directed, be found by applying the method given in the Faultless Triplet. This is meant for the reader who wishes to understand Paṭṭhāna completely.

The text for the Positive-Negative conditions is: "With root condition, but not-object 7 . . . not-disappearance 7." How will one know what the elisions are? Not-nutriment, not-faculty, not-jhāna and not-path have no common states with root condition 37 as reference and so they are not included as variants. As for the other conditions, the enumerations are the same as those shown above in "By Ones" of the Negative conditions.

4. Conditions: Negative-Positive (ii) Enumeration Chapter

Not-root By Twos

With not-root 33 as reference, those variant conditions with 33 are all the same as not-root.

Object, etc. 14. These are: (1–1), (1–2), (1–1,2), (2–2), (3–3), (3–1), (3–2), (3–1,2), (1,3–1), (1,3–2), (1,3–1,2), (2,3–1), (1,2–1), (1,2,3–1). Here the common conditioned states are delusion from 2 delusion-rooted consciousnesses and 18 rootless consciousnesses and so the answers for the enumeration are taken from those states in not-root condition.

Mutuality 22. Rootless mind-produced matter is not common and so the answers with these states, not being obtained in those for root condition, give this enumeration.

Prenascence 6. The common conditioned states are delusion from 2 delusion-rooted consciousnesses and 18 rootless consciousnesses during life in the five-aggregate planes. These states have to be looked for in the States chart given above to obtain the answers. These are: (1–1), (1–2) where 2 is for applied thought, (1–1,2), (2–1), (3–3) for there are twice fivefold consciousnesses, (1,2–1), i.e. enumeration 6. (2–2) is not obtained because only applied thought is involved and it cannot be conascent with itself.

Repetition 5. The common conditioned states are delusion at the second impulsion of 2 delusion-rooted consciousnesses and second to seventh impulsions of the smile-consciousness of the Arahat. Here the states of section 3 are not involved and so the answer (3–3) is not obtained. Therefore, this answer not being included in the 6 above, the enumeration is 5.

Path 3. The common conditioned state is delusion from 2 delusion-rooted consciousnesses and so the answers are: (1-1), (1-2) and (1-1,2). (2-2) and others are not obtained.

Method. In the Enumeration Chapters, the enumerations "By Twos", "By Threes" and so on are obtained by first determining the common states and then getting the answers for the enumerations from these states in the States chart. Now that the method has been provided the reader should, from now on, find the enumerations by himself. Of course, it does take time but once they are found there will be great satisfaction and delight.

6. Applied Thought Triplet III. "Conditioned" Chapter

1. Conditions: Positive (i) Classification Chapter

The 7 answers with the reference states of 1 and the 5 answers with the reference states of 2 are stated to be the same as those given in the Dependent Chapter above for root condition. The reason is that there are no bases and so they are just conascence-dependence. It is only when base-prenascence-dependence is expounded that classified answers for the bases are given. Even then, the enumerations are usually the same as in the Dependent Chapter. The text notes that the differences are predominance 37, prenascence and repetition 21 each.

Predominance 37. This is taken in the same way as root condition.

Prenascence 21, Repetition 21. These are the conditions that have mentality which occur during life as their states. The answers are: (1-1), (1-2), (1-1,2); (2-2), (2-1), (2-3), (2-2,3); (3-3), (3-1), (3-2), (3-2,3), (3-1,2); (1,3-1), (1,3-2), (1,3-1,2); (2,3-1), (2,3-2), (2,3-2,3); (1,2-1), (1,2-3); (1,2,3-1). To know how these answers are obtained reference must be made to the chart.

2. Conditions: Negative (i) Classification Chapter

Not-root

In not-root 33, although the Classification Chapter has to include answers for the 6 bases wherever they are relevant, the enumeration is the same as that in the Dependent Chapter. What is special here is the instruction to extract the 7 kinds of delusion in 7 places. This is not easy for the reader to do and so they are extracted below. It is to be noted that delusion is included in the first section and, therefore, the variant, delusion, is always 1.

The 7 kinds of delusion are:

1. (*1-1*). Conditioned by doubt-accompanied or restlessness-accompanied aggregates, arises doubt-accompanied or restlessness-accompanied delusion;
2. (*2-1*). Conditioned by doubt-accompanied or restlessness-accompanied applied thought, arises doubt-accompanied or restlessness-accompanied delusion;
3. (*3-1*). Conditioned by (heart-)base, arises doubt-accompanied or restlessness-accompanied delusion;
4. (*1,3-1*). Conditioned by aggregates with applied thought and sustained thought, and (heart-)base, arises doubt-accompanied or restlessness-accompanied delusion;
5. (*2,3-1*). Conditioned by applied thought and (heart-)base, arises doubt-accompanied or restlessness-accompanied delusion;
6. (*1,2-1*). Conditioned by aggregates with applied thought and sustained thought, and applied thought, arises doubt-accompanied or restlessness-accompanied delusion;
   Conditioned by doubt-accompanied or restlessness-accompanied aggregates and applied thought, arises doubt-accompanied or restlessness-accompanied delusion;
7. (*1,2,3-1*). Conditioned by aggregates with applied thought and sustained thought, applied thought and (heart-)base, arises doubt-accompanied or restlessness-accompanied delusion.

Not-object, etc. Just as in the Positive conditions where object, proximity and so on are the same, it is to be noted that in the Negative conditions not-object, not-proximity, not-contiguity, not-strong-dependence, not-absence and not-disappearance are always the same. Their enumerations are the same as those in the Dependent Chapter.

2. Conditions: Negative (ii) Enumeration Chapter

By Ones, etc.

In "By Ones", etc., the enumeration 37 is the same as that given in the Positive conditions. There are not many differences in the enumerations which should all be known by now. "By Twos" of Positive-Negative conditions are not different from those of the Dependent Chapter. As for "By Twos" of Negative-Positive conditions, repetition 13 and path 5 are the ones that are slightly different. They can be found according to the method provided.

6. APPLIED THOUGHT TRIPLET V. "CONJOINED" CHAPTER

1. Conditions: Positive

If only mentality, with which this Chapter is concerned, is selected from the chart for the answers, the enumeration for each of the conditions is 11 as shown for root condition. That is why the text states that they are all 11.

2. Conditions: Negative

The Classification Chapter of the Negative conditions is not given at all. The Text directs the reader to "Do the Negative without confusion" and then goes on to deal with the enumerations "By Ones". Paṭṭhāna is difficult because (1) the classification answers are not given but only the enumerations, (2) elisions are included and (3) references are made. Yet, when the states are selected from those states contained in the chart for the particular Chapter concerned, the enumerations that are given in the text and those that are not given can be known. This method of selecting the states will now be shown. But this cannot be done every time for there are so many and there will be no end to them. Besides, it is desired that the reader acquire his own knowledge by carrying them out on his own.

By Ones

In "By Ones" the enumeration 11 for the conditions is the same as that shown for root condition.

Not-root 6, Not-path 6. The 6 answers are: (1-1), (1-2), (1-1,2), (2-1), (3-3), (1,2-1). The difference with not-path is that, according to its single enumeration, delusion is excluded.

Not-kamma 7. This is the 6 above and (2-2).

Not-jhāna 1. This is (3-3).

Whether these are correct or not must be checked by the reader to improve his knowledge.

3. Conditions: Positive-Negative (ii) Enumeration Chapter

Root By Twos

There is nothing special here.

mental states remain. This is, therefore, the same as association which, as shown earlier, has the 11 answers: (1-1), (1-2), (1-1,2); (2-2), (2-1), (2-3), (2-2,3); (3-3), (3-2); (2,3-2) and (1,2-1). But since these are also the answers for object condition and others, there is no increase in the number of answers.

(3) *Not-prenascence-dissociation.* The answers for mixed conascence-prenascence are not obtained.

(4) *Not-postnascence-dissociation.* The answers for the 2 mixed conditions are not obtained.

So the answers for the remaining conditions, i.e. object and others, must be taken. The answers for object are those included for strong-dependence with enumeration 25 together with those not included, i.e. the 2: (1-1,3) and (1-1,2,3) for kamma and so the total is 27, the enumeration for not-dissociation.

Not-presence 27, Not-disappearance 27. These are the 25 of strong-dependence and the 2 of kamma as given above.

Remaining Conditions. In the remaining conditions there is no need to deduct any answer and so the enumeration for each of them is 35.

Based on the method that has now been provided, the charts for the Selection of the Negative Conditions for the remaining Triplets can be drawn up by the reader. Then, from them, the enumerations "By Ones" can be found and checked with the text to find whether they are correct or not. It is not possible to deal with every one of them because it would take up so much space.

3. Conditions: Positive-Negative (ii) Enumeration Chapter

Root by Twos

The enumeration with root and each of the variant conditions, not-object and others, is 11, the same as Positive root condition. And in the case of not-predominance, where investigating-wisdom predominance and so on, the common states with predominance, are excluded, there is no decrease in the enumeration.

Not-mutuality 3, Not-association 3. Only materiality remains as conditioned states so that the answers are: (1-3), (2-3), (3-3).

Not-dissociation 7. Only mentality remains and those variant mental states, which are contained in root condition, give the answers: (1-1), (1-2), (1-1,2); (2-2), (2-3), (2-2,3); (3-3), i.e. a total of 7, the enumeration.

SELECTION OF THE CONDITIONS FOR NEGATIVE 35

Conditions	1 = 7							2 = 6						3 = 5					1,3 = 4				2,3 = 5					1,2 = 6						1,2,3=2		Enumerations
	1	2	3	1,3	2,3	1,2	1,2,3	2	1	3	1,3	2,3	1,2	3	1	2	2,3	1,2	1	2	3	1,2	1	2	3	2,3	1,2	1	2	3	1,3	2,3	1,2	1	3	
	1	"	"	"	"	"	"	2	"	"	"	"	"	3	"	"	"	"	1,3	"	"	"	2,3	"	"	"	"	1,2	"	"	"	"	"	1,2,3	"	
1. Object	"	"	"			"		"	"	"			"	"	"	"	"	"					"	"	"		"	"	"	"			"			21
2. Conascence	"	"	"	"	"	"	"	"	"	"	"	"		"	"	"	"	"	"	"	"	"	"	"	"	"		"		"	"			"	"	30
3. Strong-dependence	"	"	"		"	"		"	"	"		"	"	"	"	"	"	"					"	"	"	"	"	"	"	"		"	"			25
4. Prenascence														"	"	"	"	"																		5
5. Postnascence			"							"				"																						5
6. Kamma	"	"	"	"	"	"	"			"		"		"																						10
7. Nutriment														"																						1
8. Faculty														"																						1
9. Conascence-prenascence																			"	"		"	"	"	"	"								"		8
10. Postnascence-nutriment																					"				"										"	3
11. Postnascence-faculty																					"				"										"	3

when "reviews", "knows" or "practises insight" is expounded, it must be understood that great faultless states are meant. They are explained in great detail in Guide to C.R., Part III which is under preparation.

1. Conditions: Positive (ii) Enumeration Chapter

All the "By Ones" are given. But the commons and combinations are not given as they were in the Faultless Triplet. The text merely directs that they be found according to the method in the Faultless Triplet. It must be noted that the text never directs that things be known briefly but always fully. Therefore, in order to know the commons and combinations they will, later, be shown briefly so that they can be expanded to know them fully.

1. Conditions: Negative (ii) Enumeration Chapter

Selection of the Negative Conditions

The Negative conditions of the Investigation Chapter are deep and difficult to understand. For, unlike the 6 Chapters, no direct and classified answers are given but only the enumerations. Therefore, the Synod authorities provided a section on the selection of the conditions—which was not expounded by the Buddha—in order to make the Negative conditions more understandable. This is of great value; for, by this means, it can be known how the enumerations, including those that are elided, are obtained.

As it stands, the chart for the Selection of the Conditions for Negative (see facing page) does not provide a large amount of information. All that it gives are the enumerations of object condition and others which were expounded in the Classification Chapter. Similar enumerations have to be provided for such charts in the Triplets that follow. So, the reader, by applying the method given here, can prepare his own charts in those cases and they will not be provided.

Note: In "By Ones" of the Faultless Triplet (C.R. I, p. 217) not-conascence, not-mutuality, not-dependence, not-prenascence, not-association, not-dissociation, not-presence and not-non-disappearance have different enumerations. All the others have the same, i.e. 15. In this Triplet not-strong-dependence and those given above, with the exception of not-prenascence, have different enumerations. Not-prenascence has the same enumerations as the rest, i.e. 35. As for not-root condition and others there cannot be differences because they are parts of the group conditions.

How to Read the Chart

Before explaining how the different enumerations of the Negative conditions are obtained, it will first be shown how the chart has to be read along with the text on the Selection of the Negative Conditions. In the chart prenascence is base-prenascence; kamma is strong and weak asynchronous kamma; nutriment is physical nutriment; faculty is physical faculty and Nos. 9, 10 and 11 are mixed conditions. If the answer (1–1) in the column is read against the conditions, it will be seen from the "ditto" signs that this answer is obtained for object, conascence, strong-dependence and kamma conditions. Similarly, read off the conditions for the answer (1–2) and the rest of the 35 answers.

Particular Conditions

Not-conascence 29. Please see the chart. Since it is not-conascence, the answers for conascence and mixed conascence-prenascence are not obtained. So where the answers are solely for these conditions they are excluded. And when the different answers are taken the total is 29, the enumeration.

Not-mutuality 29. When the answers for mutuality are deducted from those of conascence, there are more answers but they are not different ones and so the enumeration is 29.

Not-dependence 29. The answers for base-prenascence are not excluded because they are obtained for object condition and others and so the different answers total 29 just like conascence.

Not-strong-dependence 34. When the columns against strong-dependence are examined, it will be found that there is only one answer (1,2–2,3) which belongs solely to this condition. Therefore, for not-strong-dependence this is the only answer to be excluded and so the total is 34, the enumeration.

Not-association 29. This is the same as not-mutuality.

Not-dissociation 27. There are 4 kinds of dissociation: (1) base-object-prenascence-dissociation, (2) conascence-dissociation, (3) prenascence-dissociation and (4) postnascence-dissociation. For (1) there are no answers to be deducted. As for the others:

(2) *Not-conascence-dissociation.* When the answers for conascence-dissociation are deducted from those of conascence, the answers with

mental states remain. This is, therefore, the same as association which, as shown earlier, has the 11 answers: (1-1), (1-2), (1-1,2); (2-2), (2-1), (2-3), (2-2,3); (3-3), (3-2); (2,3-2) and (1,2-1). But since these are also the answers for object condition and others, there is no increase in the number of answers.

(3) *Not-prenascence-dissociation.* The answers for mixed conascence-prenascence are not obtained.

(4) *Not-postnascence-dissociation.* The answers for the 2 mixed conditions are not obtained.

So the answers for the remaining conditions, i.e. object and others, must be taken. The answers for object are those included for strong-dependence with enumeration 25 together with those not included, i.e. the 2: (1-1,3) and (1-1,2,3) for kamma and so the total is 27, the enumeration for not-dissociation.

Not-presence 27, Not-disappearance 27. These are the 25 of strong-dependence and the 2 of kamma as given above.

Remaining Conditions. In the remaining conditions there is no need to deduct any answer and so the enumeration for each of them is 35.

Based on the method that has now been provided, the charts for the Selection of the Negative Conditions for the remaining Triplets can be drawn up by the reader. Then, from them, the enumerations "By Ones" can be found and checked with the text to find whether they are correct or not. It is not possible to deal with every one of them because it would take up so much space.

3. Conditions: Positive-Negative (ii) Enumeration Chapter

Root by Twos

The enumeration with root and each of the variant conditions, not-object and others, is 11, the same as Positive root condition. And in the case of not-predominance, where investigating-wisdom predominance and so on, the common states with predominance, are excluded, there is no decrease in the enumeration.

Not-mutuality 3, Not-association 3. Only materiality remains as conditioned states so that the answers are: (1-3), (2-3), (3-3).

Not-dissociation 7. Only mentality remains and those variant mental states, which are contained in root condition, give the answers: (1-1), (1-2), (1-1,2); (2-2), (2-3), (2-2,3); (3-3), i.e. a total of 7, the enumeration.

4. Conditions: Negative-Positive (ii) Enumeration Chapter

Not-root By Twos

The enumerations are the same as those given in "By Ones" of the Positive conditions and so there is nothing special here. One thing to be noted, however, is that the states of the common conditions, as variants, which are common with root condition, have to be excluded. There is no need to consider the conditions that are not common.

In this difficult Triplet many methods and explanations have been provided. Since these hold true for the remaining Triplets, from now on only those portions that need special mention will be briefly considered.

END OF APPLIED THOUGHT TRIPLET

7. RAPTURE TRIPLET

Triplet States

Reference (R)	Variant (V)
1. 51 cons. accompanied by rapture, 46 m.f. exclusive of rapture, hate, envy, stinginess, worry and doubt.	1. 51 cons. accompanied by rapture, 46 m.f. exclusive of rapture, hate, envy, stinginess, worry and doubt.
2. 63 cons. accompanied by pleasure, 46 m.f. exclusive of feeling, hate, envy, stinginess, worry and doubt.	2. 63 cons. accompanied by pleasure, 46 m.f. exclusive of feeling, hate, envy, stinginess, worry and doubt.
3. 55 cons. accompanied by indifference, 46 m.f. exclusive of feeling, rapture, hate, envy, stinginess and worry.	3. 55 cons. accompanied by indifference, 46 m.f. exclusive of feeling, rapture, hate, envy, stinginess and worry.

6 Chapters

1. Conditions: Positive (i) Classification Chapters

The chart shows that, as in the Feeling Triplet, the states are all mentality. Here the Triplet-freed states are: 12 pleasurable feeling present at 1 bodily happiness and 11 fourth Jhāna consciousnesses, 55 indifferent feeling, 3 painful consciousnesses, 22 mental factors, 28 matter and Nibbāna.

As the states involved are all mentality, all the other 5 Chapters are the same as for the Dependent Chapter. When the states of the first and second sections are compared it will be found that those in the first section are contained in the second which has, in addition, 1 bodily happiness and 11 fourth Jhāna consciousnesses. Therefore, the common states in these two sections are those of the first. The rest are just as in the Feeling Triplet. There is nothing extraordinary here. When the text is read with the chart everything should be clear. As for the enumerations there are no special differences. In "By Ones" they are all 10.

2. Conditions: Negative (i) Classification Chapters

Not-predominance, etc. The text notes (1) under not-predominance: "In not-predominance, at the moment of conception is to be completed." The reason is that the single enumeration of not-predominance contains all the mentality at the moment of conception. Also, (2) under not-prenascence: "Remember (to take) immaterial and at the moment of conception." The reason is that the single enumeration of not-prenascence contains the states of the immaterial plane and all the mentality at the moment of conception.

Not-resultant. The text notes under not-resultant: "Complete. No conception." The reason is that the single enumeration of not-resultant contains only faultless, faulty and functional states and is, therefore, not concerned with conception. So whatever the text notes can be easily understood because they can be found from the single enumerations.

Not-jhāna, etc. The text notes (1) under not-path: "The same as not-root condition. No delusion." For in the single enumeration of not-path, delusion is excluded. Also, (2) under not-dissociation: "Only immaterial question." For in the single enumeration of not-dissociation there is only mentality in the immaterial plane.

Note: As such notes in the text refer to the single enumerations concerned, they will not be considered again except in special cases.

(ii) Enumeration Chapters

By Ones of Negative; Root By Twos of Positive-Negative and Not-root By Twos of Negative-Positive are not difficult and can now be understood. In the Negative-Positive "(With not-root,) path 1" the common conditioning states are 2 delusion-rooted consciousnesses and the common conditioned state is delusion from 2 delusion-rooted consciousnesses. Since they belong to the third section of the Triplet, the only answer obtainable is (3–3).

"Investigation" Chapter

There should be no difficulty about the Classification and Enumeration Chapters. As for the Selection of the Negative Conditions, this will be clear when the reader prepares his own chart according to the method given in the Applied Thought Triplet. This Rapture Triplet is easy because the only difference from the Feeling Triplet is that it includes "States accompanied by rapture."

END OF RAPTURE TRIPLET

8. Triplet of (State) Eradicated by First Path

Triplet States

Reference (R)	Variant (V)
1. 8 greed-rooted cons., 2 hate-rooted cons., 1 doubt-accompanied cons., 27 m.f.	1. 8 greed-rooted cons., 2 hate-rooted cons., 1 doubt-accompanied cons., 27 m.f.
2. 4 cons. dissociated from wrong view, 2 hate-rooted cons., 1 restlessness-accompanied cons., 25 m.f. exclusive of wrong view and doubt.	2. 4 cons. dissociated from wrong view, 2 hate-rooted cons., 1 restlessness-accompanied cons., 25 m.f. exclusive of wrong view and doubt.
3. 21 faultless cons., 36 resultant cons., 20 functional cons., 38 m.f., 28 matter, Nibbāna.	3. 21 faultless cons., 36 resultant cons., 20 functional cons., 38 m.f., 28 matter, Nibbāna.

6 Chapters

1. Conditions: Positive

The states of this Triplet are similar to those of the Faultless Triplet. The only difference from that Triplet is that the first section consists of faulty states instead of faultless. That is why the Classification and Enumeration Chapters of the 6 Chapters are expounded in exactly the same way as in the Faultless Triplet.

2. Conditions: Negative

In the Negative conditions of the 6 Chapters all the conditions, except not-root, are expounded in the same way as for the Faultless Triplet. The difference with not-root is that doubt and restlessness are not taken together as in the Faultless Triplet but separately. Therefore, the answers for not-root (1) in Dependent Chapter are: (1–1), (2–2) and (3–3); (2) in Conditioned Chapter are, besides the 3 above, another 4: (3–1), (3-2), (1,3–1) and (2,3–2); (3) in Conjoined Chapter are the same as the 3 answers in Dependent Chapter.

By Twos (i.e. of Positive-Negative and Negative-Positive conditions) are not difficult.

"Investigation" Chapter

1. Conditions: Positive

Here, also, the Investigation Chapter is expounded according to the chart. The enumerations for all the conditions, except object and strong-dependence, are the same as for those in the Faultless Triplet. The difference with these 2 conditions is that here the enumeration for each of them is 8 instead of 9 as in the Faultless Triplet. The reason is that the answer (1–2) is not obtained. For the states of the first section are not related to the states of the second section by any condition whatsoever. This is stated in the Comy. p. 488 as "State eradicated by First Path is never related to state eradicated by Higher 3 Paths by any of the conditions."[1] Why are they not related? It is because the states of the first section are the attributes of the ignorant worldling whereas the states of the second section are those of the Stream-winner and others and it is impossible for the states that arise in a person of a lower grade to be related to the states that arise in a person of a higher grade.

Selection of the Conditions for Negative

Here, also, (1–2) is not obtained and so the total enumeration is 14. Otherwise, they are the same as for the Faultless Triplet.

2. Conditions: Negative

By Ones, etc.

Since (1–2) is not obtained, the enumerations are reduced by 1 in the enumerations of all the Negative conditions of the Faultless Triplet.

---

[1] Dassanena pahātabbo dhammo bhāvanāya pahātabbassa dhammassa ekena pi paccayena paccayo na hoti. (Tikp 353).

Positive-Negative and Negative-Positive

By Twos

The Positive-Negative conditions have exactly the same enumerations as in the Faultless Triplet. The Negative-Positive conditions have the same enumerations as given by "By Ones" of the Positive conditions.

END OF TRIPLET OF (STATE) ERADICATED BY FIRST PATH

9. TRIPLET OF (STATE) TOGETHER WITH ROOT ERADICATED BY FIRST PATH

Triplet States

Reference (R)	Variant (V)
1. 8 greed-rooted cons., 2 hate-rooted cons., 1 doubt-accompanied cons., 27 m.f. excluding delusion present at doubt-accompanied cons.	1. 8 greed-rooted cons., 2 hate-rooted cons., 1 doubt-accompanied cons., 27 m.f. excluding delusion present at doubt-accompanied cons.
2. 4 cons. dissociated from wrong view, 2 hate-rooted cons., 1 restlessness-accompanied cons., 25 m.f. exclusive of wrong view, doubt and delusion present at restlessness-accompanied cons.	2. 4 cons. dissociated from wrong view, 2 hate-rooted cons., 1 restlessness-accompanied cons., 25 m.f. exclusive of wrong view, doubt and delusion present at restlessness-accompanied cons.
3. 21 faultless cons., 36 resultant cons., 20 functional cons., 38 m.f., delusion present at 2 delusion-rooted cons., 28 matter, Nibbāna.	3. 21 faultless cons., 36 resultant cons., 20 functional cons., 38 m.f., delusion present at 2 delusion-rooted cons., 28 matter, Nibbāna.

Dependent Chapter

1. Conditions: Positive (i) Classification Chapter

Root 17

The chart shows that this Triplet is similar to that of (State) Eradicated by First Path above. The difference from that Triplet is that delusion at doubt-accompanied consciousness of the first section and delusion at restlessness-accompanied consciousness of the second section are excluded from those sections and included in the third section of this Triplet. On account of that (1) doubt-accompanied consciousness as reference of section 1 and delusion at doubt-accompanied consciousness as variant of section 3 and (2) restlessness-accompanied consciousness as reference of section 2 and delusion at restlessness-accompanied consciousness as variant of section 3—which are conascent states—give additional answers such as (1-3) and so on to give enumeration 17. Also, it must be noted that delusion-rooted consciousnesses and delusion are conascent with mind-produced matter. These will be clearly known when the text is read with the chart.

Object 11, Predominance 9. The enumerations 11 for object condition and others are found in the same way as above because they include the delusions. As for predominance, where delusions are not involved, the enumeration 9 is the same as that of Triplet of (State) Eradicated by First Path. The others are easy.

2. Conditions: Negative

Not-root 3. Since the conascent states with delusion, as given above, are included, there are 2 more answers (1-3) and (2-3) besides (1-1) to give enumeration 3.

Not-object 5. The conditioned states of not-object are materiality only. So, although the conascent delusions given above are also included, here they are conascent with mind-produced matter only. This gives additional classified answers but the enumeration remains the same.

Not-predominance 17, etc. Not-predominance, not-postnascence and other conditions have enumeration 17 each. As for not-prenascence 13, not-kamma 7 and not-dissociation 11, they are given fully in the text.

3-4. Conditions: Positive-Negative and Negative-Positive

By Twos

These are easy. All the Positive-Negative conditions have the same enumerations as Negative "By Ones". All the Negative-Positive conditions, except resultant and path, have the same enumeration 3 as not-root. In the case of path there is a slight difference. Its enumeration is 2 because delusion from 2 delusion-rooted consciousnesses is the common state. On looking up the chart in this connection, it will be found that there are 2 answers (1-3) and (2-3).

As these "By Twos" of the above conditions are easy they will not be dealt with in the other Triplets unless there is something special to note.

Conditioned and Conjoined Chapters

These 2 Chapters can be known when the text is read with the chart. Owing to limitations of space they cannot be dealt with here.

Investigation Chapter

1. Conditions: Positive

The Classification Chapter and "By Ones" of the Enumeration Chapter can be known. With the knowledge that the answers (1-3) and (2-3) are obtained because the reference and variant states, denoted by the figures, are conascent, it will be clear, with the aid of the chart, how the classified answers for root condition and others are expounded. So, however comprehensive and complicated such answers may seem, they can always be found from the chart because all the states, necessary for finding the answers, are contained in it.

This is the case with all the 24 Paṭṭhānas. In the first 2 Paṭṭhānas, Triplet and Couplet Paṭṭhānas, the states involved in them are expounded in the Dhammasaṅgaṇī and are easy to know. But when it comes to the remaining 22 Paṭṭhānas, Couplet-Triplet Paṭṭhāna and others, the states involved in them have to be found by oneself (see Intr. C.R. I, pp. lxxxiii ff.) and tabulated in charts. Then, knowing what the single enumerations of the Chapters concerned are, it will not be so difficult to select the states in order to arrive at the answers. And once these answers are obtained, the direct and classified answers can be found. This is the method for all the 24 Paṭṭhānas.

Selection of the Conditions for Negative

Although it was stated that such charts would not be provided again, it is done here because this is a special case. For it is rather complicated and there are so many things that have to be noted. So it will be shown how the reader, by examining the chart, can find for himself the reasons why certain things have to be noted and what the answers ought to be. The Comy. is silent about these notes and the Subcomy. stops short at Applied Thought Triplet.

Please see item 111.(xiv) of the Selection of the Conditions for Negative where it is noted that mixed conascence-prenascence also has the answer (1,3-1) which is shown in the chart. It is also noted that mixed conascence-prenascence has the answers (1,3-1,3) of item 111.(xvi),

SELECTION OF THE CONDITIONS FOR NEGATIVE 21

Conditions	1-1	" -3	" -1,3	2-2	" -1	" -3	" -1,3	" -2,3	3-3	" -1	" -2	" -1,3	" -2,3	1,3-1	" -3	" -1,3	2,3-1	" -2	" -3	" -1,3	" -2,3	Enumerations
Ob	"	"	"	"	"	"	"	"	"	"	"	"	"	"	"	"	"	"	"	"	"	21
Cn	"	"	"	"		"		"	"	"	"	"	"	"	"	"		"	"		"	17
S.D.	"	"	"	"	"	"	"	"	"	"	"	"	"	"	"	"	"	"	"	"	"	21
Prn									"	"	"	"	"									5
Pon		"							"					"								5
Kam		"							"													2
Nu									"													1
Fa									"													1
Cn-prn														"	"	"		"	"		"	6
Pon-nu															"				"			2
Pon-fa															"				"			2

(2,3-2) of item 112.(xviii) and (2,3-2,3) of item 112.(xxi) which are shown in the chart.

Again, it is noted that object and strong-dependence have the answer (1,3-3) of item 111.(xv) which is not given in the text. The chart shows not only that these 2 conditions have these 2 answers but also that all the answers for their enumeration number 21. This is also the case with the answer (2,3-3) of item 112.(xix). All the notes about these answers in the Selection of the Conditions for Negative are in entire agreement with what is given in the chart.

For Reflexion. Why is it that when the chart, based on the Classification Chapter, gives everything completely, the text does not do so?

Answer. The Comy. has nothing to say on this matter. Here is the translator's opinion. In the Guide to C.R., Part III it is pointed out that there is a total of 8 mixed conditions in all the 24 Paṭṭhānas. They are expounded in the text as follows:

1. Mixed conascence-prenascence as conascence-prenascence.

2. & 3. Mixed postnascence-nutriment and mixed postnascence-faculty are either combined as postnascence-nutriment-faculty or separately as postnascence-nutriment and postnascence-faculty.

4. Mixed conascence-postnascence as conascence-postnascence.

5. Mixed postnascence-nutriment-faculty as postnascence-nutriment-faculty.

6. Mixed conascence-base-prenascence-faculty as conascence-prenascence.

7. Mixed object-prenascence and base-prenascence as prenascence.

8. Mixed conascence, object-prenascence-base-prenascence as conascence-prenascence.

On consideration of the above it will be seen that all the mixed conditions are expounded with nasal consonants to show that the conditions are mixed. Even when conascence, which is not a mixed condition, is expounded along with mixed conditions as conascence, postnascence-nutriment-faculty, a nasal consonant is employed and the word "condition" is left out. That is why in item 111.(xiv) above, if all the conditions having the answer (1,3–1) were to be expounded according to the note given there, it would include the mixed condition. So it would have to be expounded as "object, conascence, strong-dependence, conascence-prenascence" or "By object condition, conascence condition, strong-dependence condition, conascence-prenascence". As such this could not be easily recited and there is a possibility of some confusion. Also, in item 111.(xv), if all the conditions having the answer (1,3–3) were to be expounded it would be "By object condition, strong-dependence condition, conascence-prenascence, postnascence-nutriment-faculty". As such the conditions would not be in proper sequence and there is a possibility of some confusion. So this explains why all the conditions that should be included are not given in the text.

2. Conditions: Negative (ii) Enumeration Chapter

By Ones

The chart shows that object and strong-dependence have all the 21 answers. Therefore, for not-object, all the 21 answers are not excluded because strong-dependence has them. Similarly, for not-strong-dependence, all the 21 answers are not excluded becaus object has them.

"By Twos" of Positive-Negative and Negative-Positive conditions are easy.

END OF TRIPLET OF (STATE) TOGETHER WITH ROOT ERADICATED BY FIRST PATH

10. Triplet of (State) Leading to Rebirth and Death

Triplet States

Reference (R)	Variant (V)
1. 12 faulty cons., 17 mundane faultless cons., 52 m.f.	1. 12 faulty cons., 17 mundane faultless cons., 52 m.f.
2. 4 Path cons., 36 m.f.	2. 4 Path cons., 36 m.f.
3. 36 resultant cons., 20 functional cons., 38 m.f., 28 matter, Nibbāna.	3. 36 resultant cons., 20 functional cons., 38 m.f., 28 matter, Nibbāna.

1. Conditions: Positive

6 Chapters

The arrangement of the states in the chart is similar to that for the Faultless Triplet. Since all the Positive conditions of the 6 Chapters are similar to those of the Faultless Triplet, there is nothing to note here. They are also abbreviated in the text.

2. Conditions: Negative

Dependent Chapter

All are the same as in the Faultless Triplet except not-predominance 6 and not-repetition 7.

Not-predominance 6. 4 Path consciousnesses in section 2 are always predominant and are, therefore, not conascent with non-predominant mind-produced matter, the only conditioned state in the single enumeration. That is why (2-3) and (2-2,3) and, likewise, (2,3-3) are not obtained. Thus the enumeration 9 in the Faultless Triplet is reduced by 3 to 6.

Not-repetition 7. From the text it will be found that (2-2) and

(2–2,3) are not obtained. Thus the enumeration 9 in the Faultless Triplet is reduced by 2 to 7.

"By Twos" of the Positive-Negative and Negative-Positive conditions can be known.

Conditioned Chapter

The text shows in full how enumeration 12 for not-predominance and 11 for not-repetition are obtained. Mind-produced matter, which was not included in the Positive repetition condition, is expounded here. That is why the 4 Path consciousnesses, which arise with mind-produced matter, are expounded here although they are not included in the single enumeration of not-repetition. This is explained in great detail in Guide to C.R., Part II, under preparation.

Conjoined Chapter

The reason why not-repetition has only 2 answers is that (2–2) is not obtained and this leaves (1–1) and (3–3). In this Chapter the states are all mentality and the enumerations are found from the single enumerations of the conditions.

"By Twos" have nothing of note.

Investigation Chapter

The text must be read with the chart in order to understand how this Chapter is expounded.

Object 7. 4 Path consciousnesses, the states of variant 2, cannot take the states of reference 1 as object but only Nibbāna. So (1–2) is not obtained. Again, 4 Path consciousnesses cannot take one another as object and so (2–2) is not obtained. When these 2 answers are left out from the 9 of the Faultless Triplet, the enumeration is 7.

Proximity, etc. 6. 4 Path consciousnesses, which are the only states of reference 2, are followed by their corresponding Fruition consciousnesses. So Path consciousnesses are not related by proximity condition and (2–2) is not obtained. When this answer is left out from the 7 of the Faultless Triplet, the enumeration is 6.

The other enumerations are the same as those of the Faultless Triplet.

Selection of the Conditions for Negative and By Ones

As for the Faultless Triplet the total enumeration is 15. All the "By

Ones" are the same as for the Faultless Triplet except not-strong-dependence which is 14.

Not-strong dependence 14. If the Selection Chart is examined, it will be seen that only strong-dependence has the answer (1–2). Therefore, this answer, not being obtained for not-strong-dependence, the enumeration is 14.

Positive-Negative and Negative-Positive

By Twos

In the Positive-Negative conditions, not-mutuality, not-association, not-dissociation have the same enumeration 3 just as for the Faultless Triplet. The Negative-Positive conditions have the same enumerations as Positive "By Ones".

END OF TRIPLET OF (STATE) LEADING TO REBIRTH AND DEATH

11. LEARNERS TRIPLET

Triplet States

Reference (R)	Variant (V)
1. 7 supramundane cons. exclusive of Arahatta Fruition, 36 m.f.	1. 7 supramundane cons. exclusive of Arahatta Fruition, 36 m.f.
2. 1 Arahatta Fruition cons., 36 m.f.	2. 1 Arahatta Fruition cons., 36 m.f.
3. 81 mundane cons., 52 m.f., 28 matter, Nibbāna.	3. 81 mundane cons., 52 m.f., 28 matter, Nibbāna.

Conditions: Positive 6 Chapters

Dependent Chapter

The states of the first and second sections, as with those of the Faultless Triplet, are mentality and those of the third section contain materiality. So it is exactly the same as in the Faultless Triplet. The conditions have the same enumerations as for the Faultless Triplet, the exceptions being repetition and resultant.

Repetition 2. The states of the second section are not included in the single enumeration of this condition and so the answer (2–2) of the Faultless Triplet, not being obtained, the enumeration is 2.

Resultant 9. In the Faultless Triplet the resultant states are included in the third section only and so the enumeration is 1. Here they are included in all the three sections and, therefore, the enumeration is 9.

Conditioned Chapter

Here the differences from the Faultless Triplet are:

Repetition 4. Besides the 2 answers of the Dependent Chapter there are 2 others, (3–1) and (1,3–1), to give enumeration 4.

Resultant 17. As the Dependent Chapter has 9 answers, here there are 17.

Conjoined Chapter

Here the differences from the Faultless Triplet are:

Repetition 2. This is the same as for the Dependent Chapter above.

Resultant 3. This is elided. There are three answers: (1–1), (2–2), (3–3).

The text should be read along with the chart in order to know how it is expounded.

Conditions: Negative 6 Chapters

Dependent Chapter

The enumerations of the conditions are the same as for the Faultless Triplet, the exceptions being:

Not-root 1. The states of the single enumeration of the condition concerned must be selected from the chart. For not-root the states are contained in section 3 only and so the only answer is (3–3).

Not-predominance 3. Non-predominant mind-produced matter of this condition in section 3 is involved only "when predominance condition is not obtained". But here the supramundane consciousnesses in sections 1 and 2 are always predominant and so they are not conascent with matter in section 3. Therefore the 6 answers with matter: (1–3), (1–1,3), (2–3), (2–2,3), (1,3–3) and (2,3–3), not being obtained, the enumeration is 3.

Not-kamma 2. Since in section 2 there is only Arahatta Fruition consciousness, a resultant state, there are no conascent faultless, faulty and functional volitions. So (2–2) is not obtained and the enumeration is 2.

Not-resultant 5. As Arahatta Fruition consciousness is not included in the single enumeration of not-resultant, the answer (2–2) is not obtained. Consequently, (2–3), (2–2,3), (2,3–3) are not obtained. That is why the enumeration is 5.

Conditioned Chapter

The differences from the Faultless Triplet are:

Not-root 1. Although the 6 bases are included, they are contained in section 3 and so the only answer is (3–3).

Not-predominance 7. Since (heart-)base is included there are 4 more answers: (3–1), (3–2), (1,3–1), (2,3–2), besides the 3 of the Dependent Chapter, to give enumeration 7.

Not-kamma 4. Here also there are 2 more answers: (3–1), (1,3–1), besides the 2 of the Dependent Chapter, to give enumeration 4.

Not-resultant 9. Here, too, there are 4 more answers: (3–1), (1,3–1), (1,3–3), (1,3–1,3), besides the 5 of the Dependent Chapter, to give enumeration 9.

Conjoined Chapter

Some differences from the Faultless Triplet:

Not-kamma 2. This is the same as for the Dependent Chapter above.

Not-resultant 2. The 2 answers are: (1–1), (3–3). It was pointed out above that the answers with section 2 are not obtained.

Positive Negative and Negative-Positive
By Twos

The Enumeration Chapters of the Positive-Negative and Negative-Positive conditions "By Twos" of the 6 Chapters are straightforward.

Investigation Chapter

In this Investigation Chapter, just as in that of the Faultless Triplet, the states of the single enumeration of the condition concerned must be selected from those in the chart.

The conditions have the same enumerations as for the Faultless Triplet, the exceptions being:

Object 5. Since supramundane consciousnesses take only Nibbāna as object and not one another, the 4 answers: (1–1), (1–2), (2–2), (2–1) are not obtained and so the enumeration is 5.

Predominance 9. (1–1) is not an answer for object, as shown above, and therefore it is not for object-predominance; but, nevertheless, it is for conascence-predominance and so it is not excluded. In the case of the states of sections 1 and 2, they are never conascent states in any predominant condition and this answer: (1–2), being the only one not obtained, the enumeration is 9.

Proximity, etc. 8. As Arahatta Path consciousnesses of section 1 is related to Arahatta Fruition consciousness of section 2, the additional answer: (1–2), makes the enumeration 8.

Strong-dependence 8. Although natural strong-dependence of strong-dependence condition has wide application, in this Triplet the answer (2–1) is not obtained. For Arahatta Fruition consciousness of reference section 2 cannot be the cause of any of the 7 supramundane consciousnesses of variant section 1. That is why the Comy. (p. 489) remarks: "State appertaining to Arahatta is never related to state appertaining to Learners by any of the conditions."[1] So the enumeration is 8.

Repetition 2. Path consciousnesses but not Fruition consciousnesses are included in the single enumeration of repetition condition. And because only change-of-lineage and purification are related to Path but not Path to Path, the answers (1–1) and so on are not obtained. So there are only 2 answers: (3–3), (3–1).

Kamma 8. Conascence-kamma has, like root, enumeration 7. And for asynchronous kamma there is the additional answer: (1–2), to make the enumeration 8.

Resultant 7. Since resultant states are included in all the 3 sections of this Triplet, there are 7 answers.

Selection of the Conditions for Negative

The total enumeration is 14. Not-root condition and others have 14. They are just like those in the Faultless Triplet except that, apart from not-strong-dependence and not-resultant, they do not have the answer: (2–1). So the enumeration, reduced by 1, is 14.

Not-strong-dependence 13. Since the answer (1–2) is solely for strong-dependence, it is excluded for not-strong-dependence and so the enumeration is 13.

Not-resultant 12. In the previous Triplets there were no special differences with the enumerations for not-resultant condition. But here

---

[1] Asekkho dhammo sekkhassa dhammassa na kenaci paccayena paccayo. (Tikp 354).

there is. For it will be seen from the Selection of the Conditions for Negative that the answers are: (1-1,3), (2-2,3), where the reference states, which are related by conascence condition, include resultant states. Therefore, for not-resultant, these 2 answers not being obtained, the enumeration is 12.

Positive-Negative and Negative-Positive "By Twos" are easy.

END OF LEARNERS TRIPLET

12. Limited Triplet

Triplet States

Reference (R)	Variant (v)
1. 54 sensuous cons., 52 m.f., 28 matter.	1. 54 sensuous cons., 52 m.f., 28 matter.
2. 27 Lofty cons., 35 m.f.	2. 27 Lofty cons., 35 m.f.
3. 8 Supramundane cons., 36 m.f., Nibbāna.	3. 8 Supramundane cons., 36 m.f., Nibbāna.

Conditions: Positive

Dependent Chapter

Root 13. In this Triplet there is materiality in section 1 and Lofty resultant states in section 2. Therefore, the arrangement of the states is different from in the Faultless Triplet but similar to the Clinging Triplet. The materiality in section 1 contains (heart-)base and, therefore, the answers for "at the moment of conception" are obtained. These are: (1-2), because (heart-)base of section 1 and resultant states of section 2 are conascent. But of the Lofty resultant states in section 2, immaterial resultants are excluded because they are not concerned with materiality and only fine-material resultants are taken. Similarly, there are answers: (1-1,2), (1,2-2), (1,2-1,2). So, with the increase of 4 answers to the 9 of Faultless Triplet the enumeration is 13.

Object 5. Here there are 2 more answers: (1-2), (1,2-2) to the 3 of Faultless Triplet to give enumeration 5.

Predominance 9. Since this condition occurs during life only, there is no increase in the enumeration and so it is the same as Faultless Triplet.

Mutuality 7. The 4 extra answers for root above are included with the 3 of Faultless Triplet to give enumeration 7.

Other Conditions. Their enumerations are easily found.

Conditioned Chapter

Root and Others 17. They are just as for the Faultless Triplet and can be easily known.

Mutuality 9. With 2 more answers: (1–3), (1–1,3), besides the 7 of Dependent Chapter, the enumeration is 9. This is the special difference here.

Conjoined Chapter

There is nothing special here. The enumerations are 3.

Conditions: Negative

Dependent Chapter

Not-predominance 10, not-prenascence 12, not-resultant 9. They are given fully in the text and, based on the method given there, the others can be understood.

Conditioned Chapter

Not-predominance 12. This difference from Faultless Triplet is given in the text.

Conjoined Chapter

There is nothing complicated here.

Investigation Chapter

Object 7. Supramundane consciousnesses take Nibbāna only as object, not sensuous nor Lofty states. So the 2 answers: (1–3), (2–3), not being obtained, the enumeration is 7 instead of the 9 in the Faultless Triplet.

Predominance 7. In object condition the superknowledges of variant 2 take the states of reference 1 as object to give the answer (1–2). But here there are no superknowledges and so answer (1–2) and others are not obtained. With this fact kept in mind, the way the other conditions are expounded can be known with the help of the chart.

Selection of the Conditions for Negative and By Ones

The total enumeration is 15.

Not-conascence, etc. 12. When the Selection chart is examined it will be found that: (a) (3–1,3) is the answer for conascence only; (b) (1,3–3) and (1,2–2) are the answers for conascence-prenascence only. These answers are not obtained for not-conascence and, therefore, the enumeration is 12 instead of 15.

Not-strong-dependence 14. Since (2–3) is the answer for strong-dependence only, it is not obtained for not-strong-dependence and so the enumeration is 14.

Not-prenascence 14. As shown above, (1,3–3) and (1,2–2) are the answers for conascence-prenascence only and so it might be thought that by simply deducting these 2 answers the enumeration would be 13. But of these, (1,2–2) is also the answer for conascence alone and, therefore, the only answer not obtained is (1,3–3). That is why the enumeration is 14. This will be clear from the Selection chart which should be easy to prepare because the method for doing so has been given.

Not-dissociation, not-presence, not-non-disappearance 10. When the answer for kamma: (2–1,2), which was not obtained for strong-dependence, is included, the enumeration is 10 instead of the 9 in the Faultless Triplet.

"By Twos"[1] are straightforward.

END OF LIMITED TRIPLET

13. LIMITED OBJECT TRIPLET

Triplet States

Reference (R)	Variant (V)
1. 54 sensuous cons., 2 superknowledges, 52 m.f.	1. 54 sensuous cons., 2 superknowledges, 52 m.f.
2. 12 faulty cons., 1 mind-door advertence, 8 great faultless cons., 8 great functional cons., 3 infinity of cons., 3 neither-perception-nor-non-perception cons., 2 superknowledges, 47 m.f. exclusive of 3 abstinences and 2 illimitables.	2. 12 faulty cons., 1 mind-door advertence, 8 great faultless cons., 8 great functional cons., 3 infinity of cons., 3 neither-perception-nor-non-perception cons., 2 superknowledges, 47 m.f. exclusive of 3 abstinences and 2 illimitables.

[1] This is always meant for Positive-Negative and Negative-Positive conditions, and will not be pointed out again.

3. 1 mind-door advertence, 4 great faultless cons. assoc. with knowledge, 4 great functional cons. assoc. with knowledge, 2 superknowledges, 8 supramundane cons., 36 m.f. exclusive of 2 illimitables.	3. 1 mind-door advertence, 4 great faultless cons. assoc. with knowledge, 4 great functional cons. assoc. with knowledge, 2 superknowledges, 8 supramundane cons., 36 m.f. exclusive of 2 illimitables.

The chart shows that there are many states involved. They are given in the Mnemonic of the Compendium of Philosophy p. 122 as: "Lower objects to twenty-five; exalted objects to six" and so on. But they can be more easily remembered by noting that in (1) sensuous objects are always (taken by) 25 and occasionally (taken by) 31; (2) Lofty objects always by 6 and occasionally by 31; (3) Nibbāna object always by 8 and occasionally by 11. In this Triplet materiality and Nibbāna are not involved and so, just as for the Feeling Triplet, the states are all mentality.

6 Chapters

Conditions: Positive

In Dependent and the other 5 Chapters there are 3 answers: (1–1), (2–2) and (3–3). There are answers for "at the moment of conception" in sections 1 and 2 but not in section 3. As all the 23 conditions have enumeration 3, there are elisions in "By Ones" of the text.

Conditions: Negative

Not-jhāna 1. The answer is (1–1). This is different from the other conditions which have enumeration 3.

"By Twos" are easy.

Investigation Chapter

Root 3. It can be seen how these answers are obtained.

Object 7. When limited and Lofty objects are taken, Incomparable states do not arise. So the answers: (1–3) and (2–3), not being obtained, the enumeration is 7 instead of the 9 in the Faultless Triplet. Of these 7 answers it can be known how (1–1) is expounded. But when it is considered why (1–2) is expounded as: "(One) reviews Divine-eye" and so on, it will be observed that this is due to the fact that there are superknowledges in section 1 and great faultless states in section 2. This applies similarly to (2–2) and others. But it is difficult to know which superknowledge is included in the answer. This can be known, however, by referring to the chart on Superknowledges given in Guide to C.R., Part II. The rest must be compared with the text.

Predominance 7. Enumeration 7, just like that for object, is for object-predominance; enumeration 3, just like that for root, is for conascence-predominance. Taking the distinctive ones, the enumeration is 7.

Proximity 9. The 2 extra answers: (1–2), (2–1), besides the 7 of object, make the enumeration 9.

Conascence, etc. These can be seen.

Kamma 5. Conascence-kamma, like conascence, has enumeration 3. And 2 additional answers: (2–1), (3–1), make it 5. The answer (3–1) is expounded as: "Volition with Incomparable object is related to its resultant aggregates with limited object by kamma condition." Here "volition with Incomparable object" is the volition of Learner's change-of-lineage. It can also be volition of review. The fact that volition which precedes Path can give rebirth results is pointed out in the Comy, p. 489.[1]

The rest can be seen.

Selection of the Conditions for Negative and By Ones

The text shows that in "By Ones" the enumeration is 9 for all the conditions except not-strong-dependence.

Not-strong-dependence 7. Since (1–3) and (2–3) are the answers for strong-dependence only, these 2 answers are not obtained for not-strong-dependence and so the enumeration is 7.

"By Twos" are straightforward.

END OF LIMITED OBJECT TRIPLET

14. Low Triplet

Low Triplet is the same as Corrupt Triplet.

---

[1] **Appamāṇārammaṇā cetanā ti sekkhānaṁ gotrabhu-cetanā. Paccavekkhaṇa-cetanā ti pi vattuṁ vaṭṭati. Ye pana gotrabhu-cittena natthi paṭisandhī ti vadanti, te iminā suttena paṭisedhetabbā. (Cf. Tikp 354).**

15. TRIPLET OF (STATE) WITH FIXED DESTINY DUE TO WRONG VIEWS

Triplet States

Reference (R)	Variant (V)
1. Seventh impulsions of 4 cons. assoc. with wrong view, seventh impulsions of 2 hate-rooted cons., 25 m.f. exclusive of conceit and doubt.	1. Seventh impulsions of cons. assoc. with wrong view, seventh impulsions of 2 hate-rooted cons., 25 m.f. exclusive of conceit and doubt.
2. 4 Path cons., 36 m.f.	2. 4 Path cons., 36 m.f.
3. 12 faulty cons. excepting seventh impulsions of (1) above, 17 mundane faultless cons., 36 resultant cons., 20 functional cons., 52 m.f., 28 matter, Nibbāna.	3. 12 faulty cons. excepting seventh impulsions of (1) above, 17 mundane faultless cons., 36 resultant cons., 20 functional cons., 52 m.f., 28 matter, Nibbāna.

6 Chapters

Conditions: Positive

The chart shows that the states are similar to those of Faultless Triplet. There is nothing special to note here. Everything is clear.

Conditions: Negative

Dependent Chapter

The enumerations that are different from those of the 6 Chapters of the Faultless Triplet are dealt with below:

Not-root 1. The states in the single enumeration of not-root are contained in section 3 and so there is only one answer: (3–3).

Not-predominance 3. The states of sections 1 and 2 are always predominant states and so they are not related to non-predominant mind-produced matter. That is why the answers: (1–3), (2–3), not being obtained, there are only 3 answers: (1–1), (2–2), (3–3).

Not-prenascence 6. This is not given in the text. The answers are: (1–3), (2–2), (2–3), (3–3), (1,3–3), (2,3–3). Of these, (1–3) and (2–3) are obtained, not from the single enumeration of this Negative condition, but from the mere mentality of the Positive conditions which are

In this volume there are 8 Triplets, namely: (1) the Applied Thought Triplet, (2) the Rapture Triplet, (3) the Limited Object Triplet, (4) the Path Object Triplet, (5) the Arisen Triplet, (6) the Past Triplet, (7) the Past Object Triplet, (8) the Internal Object Triplet, that do not contain certain states. These, being Triplet-freed, are not taken into account. The remaining Triplets contain all the ultimate realities.

Single Enumerations

The Triplet Paṭṭhāna cannot be understood without knowing the single enumerations, i.e. the conditioning and conditioned states of the conditions, of the Triplets concerned. So the first thing to do is to know what the single enumerations are. This can be done by applying the method given in the Faultless Triplet. How is this done? In each Triplet the states of the 3 sections of the Triplet are given and it is from these states—excluding Nibbāna for the 6 Chapters and including Nibbāna for the Investigation Chapters—that the single enumerations are found. In the case of the Triplets without Triplet-freed states, the conditioning and conditioned states of the conditions are the same as those contained in the single enumerations of the Faultless Triplet; but for those Triplets with Triplet-freed states, the freed states are simply excluded.

6 Chapters

After knowing what the single enumerations are, the states in the Triplets have to be examined, as has been repeatedly pointed out, to find (1) whether they are conascent or not for the Dependent and Conascent Chapters, (2) whether the 6 bases are involved for the Conditioned and Supported Chapters, (3) whether they are associated or not for the Conjoined and Associated Chapters. Then from the answers for the states so selected the enumerations of the single Positive and Negative conditions can be obtained. As for the Enumeration Chapters "By Twos", "By Threes" and so on, the common states of the Positive, Negative, Positive-Negative and Negative-Positive conditions are found and from them the enumerations for the Triplet concerned are determined. Although the method is given concisely, it will be seen, when it is applied, that everything is included for the 6 Chapters. Examples of the method were given in the Intr. to C.R. and summarized on p. xlvii.

prenascence." This will be understood from the answer: (3-1), of prenascence condition expounded in the text.

(5) "When mundane consciousnesses, which are states with no fixed destiny, are taken as object, wrong views with fixed destiny arise." For this the answer: (3-1), of object condition must be referred to.

(6) "When the states with fixed destiny other than wrong views are taken as object, wrong views with fixed destiny do not arise." Here, also, the answer: (3-1), in the text must be referred to.

(7) "States with fixed destiny due to wrong views cannot be taken as estimable objects." This is clear from the answers: (1-1), (1-3) and (1-1,3), of predominance which do not include object-predominance.

(8) "Faultless states are not related to states with fixed destiny due to wrong views by strong-dependence condition." This is clear from strong-dependence condition in the text.

Conditions: Positive—By Ones

These can be known from (1) the text where they are given fully and (2) the above Comy. remarks and discussions. So there is no need to go into details.

Selection of the Conditions for Negative and By Ones

The total enumeration, being 13, is 2 answers less than that of Faultless Triplet. Therefore, the enumeration for each of the conditions in Faultless Triplet have to be reduced by 2. There is nothing else to note.

"By Twos" are easy.

END OF TRIPLET OF (STATE) WITH FIXED DESTINY DUE TO WRONG VIEWS

16. Path Object Triplet

Triplet States

Reference (R)	Variant (V)
1. 1 mind-door advertence, 4 great faultless cons. assoc. with knowledge, 4 great functional cons. assoc. with knowledge, 2 superknowledges, 33 m.f. exclusive of 3 abstinences and 2 illimitables.	1. 1 mind-door advertence, 4 great faultless cons. assoc. with knowledge, 4 great functional cons. assoc. with knowledge, 2 superknowledges, 33 m.f. exclusive of 3 abstinences and 2 illimitables.
2. 4 Path cons., 36 m.f.	2. 4 Path cons., 36 m.f. exclusive of 2 illimitables.

3. **4 great faultless cons. assoc. with knowledge, 4 great functional cons. assoc. with knowledge, 4 Path cons., 36 m.f. exclusive of 2 illimitables.**	3. **4 great faultless cons. assoc. with knowledge, 4 great functional cons. assoc. with knowledge, 4 Path cons., 36 m.f. exclusive of 2 illimitables.**

The chart shows that (1) section 1 has 9 sensuous consciousnesses and 2 superknowledges, a total of 11 states; (2) section 2 has 4 Path consciousnesses; (3) section 3 has 8 sensuous consciousnesses and 4 Path consciousnesses. All the other states are Triplet-freed. It will be seen that only mental states are involved and so all the 6 Chapters are the same.

In these 3 sections, the states of 1 and 2 are not conascent and so they cannot be taken together for an answer. But the states of 1 and 3 and those of 2 and 3, being conascent, can be taken together for answers.

6 Chapters

Conditions: Positive

Root 17. As given in the method above, the conascent states have to be considered. Those conascent with (a) reference 1 are (1–1), (1–3), (1–1,3) giving 3 answers; (b) reference 2 are (2–2), (2–3), (2–2,3) giving 3 answers; (c) reference 3 are (3–3), (3–1), (3–2), (3–1,3), (3–2,3) giving 5 answers. Also, because the states of 1 and 3 are conascent, with them as reference states there are (1,3–1), (1,3–3), (1,3–1,3) giving 3 answers. Similarly, with the states of 2 and 3 as reference states there are (2,3–2), (2,3–3), (2,3–2,3) giving 3 answers. Thus the enumeration is 17.

Object and All the Others. Their enumerations are also 17.

Conditions: Negative

Not-root 1, not-path 1. The single enumerations of both these conditions contain mind-door advertence which is a state of section 1. So there is the answer: (1–1).

Not-predominance 17. This is given fully in the text. In this condition Lofty and Supramundane impulsions always contain predominant realities. Here Path is included in sections 2 and 3 but not in 1. Therefore, with: (a) reference 1 there are 3 answers without predominant realities; (b) reference 2 there are 3 answers with predominant realities because Path is included in them; (c) reference 3, where there are Path and other consciousnesses, there is 1 answer: (3–3), divided under 2 heads, 1 for Path and 1 for the other consciousnesses. With the answer (3–1) there are no predominant realities because they are not contained in variant 1 but with (3–2) there are because variant 2 has them. With (3–1,3) there are none but with (3–2,3) there are. Again, with 1 and 3 as reference states there are no predominant realities in the 3 answers but with 2 and 3 as reference states there are in the 3 answers.

Not-repetition 9. As Path is not included in the single enumeration of this condition, the 3 answers with reference 2, the 2 with reference 3, i.e. (3–2), (3–2,3), and the 3 with reference 2 and 3, i.e. 8 answers, are not obtained. So the enumeration is 9.

The Other Conditions. Their enumerations are 17.

Note: This Triplet, like the Feeling Triplet, has no material states and, therefore, not-object condition and others, which contain them, are not expounded.

"By Twos" are easy.

Comy. p. 489 (Tikp 354). "Resultant condition and asynchronous kamma of kamma condition are not included in the Positive conditions of Dependent Chapter." The reason for this can be known from the chart where resultant states are not included. The Comy. also points out that asynchronous kamma is not included in Arisen and Past Triplets.

Investigation Chapter

Root 17. This is the same as for the Dependent Chapter.

Object 9. The states of section 1 are those that arise in the continuity of a Noble person when Path is taken as object. In the chart the appropriate states are taken together and so they are specified below:

The States of Section 1. (1) 1 mind-door advertence, 4 great faultless consciousnesses associated with knowledge and faultless superknowledge of the Stream-Winner who takes Stream-Winner's Path as object; (2) 1 mind-door advertence, 4 great faultless consciousnesses associated with knowledge and faultless superknowledge of the Once-Returner who takes Stream-Winner's and Once-Returner's Paths as objects; (3) 1 mind-door advertence, 4 great faultless consciousnesses associated with knowledge and faultless superknowledge of the Non-Returner who takes Stream-Winner's, Once-Returner's and Non-Returner's Paths as objects; (4) 1 mind-door advertence, 4 great functional consciousnesses associated with knowledge and functional superknowledge of the Arahat who takes the 4 Paths as objects.

The States of Section 3. These are the 4 Paths together with (1) 4 great faultless consciousnesses associated with knowledge of the Stream-Winner who takes Stream-Winner's Path as estimable object;[1] (2) 4 great faultless consciousnesses associated with knowledge of the Once-Returner who takes Once-Returner's Path as estimable object; (3) 4 great faultless consciousnesses associated with knowledge of the Non-Returner who takes Non-Returner's Path as estimable object; (4) 4 great functional consciousnesses associated with knowledge of the Arahat who takes Arahatta's Path as estimable object.

Refer to the text. The states of reference (R) 1 take Path as object but as Path is not included in variant (V) 1, the answer (1-1) and so on are not obtained for any condition whatsoever. So the states of R 1 are never conditioning states. The states of R 2 are Paths and these are taken by (a) mind-door advertence, sensuous faultless and functional consciousnesses and superknowledge of V 1 to give the answer (2-1); (b) great faultless and functional consciousnesses of V 3 which, as shown above, take the Path concerned as estimable object, to give the answer (2-3). Here, in object condition, the states of V 3 take objects with esteem. So when it is expounded as "The Noble persons, having emerged from Path, esteem and review the Path" this belongs to object-predominance. But in object condition ordinary objects as well as estimable objects of object-predominance are taken. Again, with R 2 and the variants 1 and 3, the answer (2-1,3) is given in the same way as (2-3) because the states of 1 and 3 are conascent. The states of R 3 with V 3 give the answer (3-3) and with V 1 the answer (3-1) which, it must be known, is expounded like (2-1). By knowing this method it will be understood how the text is expounded. The enumeration 9 for object condition consists of 3 answers with R 2, 3 with R 3 and 3 with R 2 and 3. As explained above there is no answer with R 1.

Predominance 21. Conascence-predominance, like root, has enumeration 17. When the 4 answers: (2-1), (2-1,3), (2,3-1), (2,3-1,3), which are those of object-predominance, are added the enumeration is 21. The way these answers are expounded can be seen.

Proximity 9. R 2 has Path only and so there is no answer with V 2.

---

[1] When it is said that an object is taken with esteem, only one's Path is taken as such, not another's. See the single enumeration of object-predominance.

As for the sensuous faultless and functional consciousnesses of V 1 and V 2, which take Path as object, they are not related to Path by this condition. And sensuous faultless change-of-lineage and purification, which arise before Path, take Nibbāna as object. Since they take different objects, they are not related here and so there are no answers with V 1 and V 2. But there are 3 answers each with R 1, R 3, R 2 and 3, i.e. enumeration 9.

Strong-dependence 21. It can be known how enumeration 21 is obtained. In this condition it is specially expounded as "Reviewing is related to reviewing." Why is it so expounded? When Path is taken as object in the mental process of review, the conditioning and conditioned states are great faultless or functional consciousnesses associated with knowledge, the states that are included in sections 1 and 3. So when the conditioning or conditioned states are the above consciousnesses it is expounded as reviewing; when they are Paths it is expounded as "First Path to second Path" and so on. This has to be briefly noted for natural strong-dependence.

The other conditions can be known.

Selection of the Conditions for Negative and By Ones

The text shows that, apart from not-object 17, the other conditions have enumeration 21. The text notes in not-object condition (item 54) that "When not-object is taken, both natural object and strong-dependence object are excluded." The wording here is entirely different from that in the previous Triplets. So what are natural object and strong-dependence object? How are they expounded in the text? Besides these two what is the other strong-dependence? Only when these are known will it be clearly understood why not-object has enumeration 17. Both the Comy. and Subcomy. are silent on this matter. But this will now be clarified.

(1) *Natural object.* This is given in the text as "Reviewing is related to reviewing." At the time Path is taken as object in the mental process of reviewing the Path, great faultless or functional consciousnesses associated with knowledge arise. So in this Triplet object and strong-dependence are expounded together. Since it is not purely object it is not expounded in object condition.

(2) *Strong-dependence object.* This is given in the text as "The Noble persons, having emerged from Path, esteem and review the Path". This is object-predominance.

SELECTION OF THE CONDITIONS FOR NEGATIVE 21

Conditions	1	"	"	2	"	"	"	"	3	"	"	"	"	1,3	"	"	2,3	"	"	"	"	Enumerations
	1	3	1,3	2	1	3	1,3	2,3	3	1	2	1,3	2,3	1	3	1,3	1	2	3	1,3	2,3	
Ob					"	X	X		X	"		X					"		X	X		9
Cn	"	"	"	"		"		"	"	"	"	"	"	"	"	"		"	"		"	17
S.D.	*	*	*	"	X	"	X	"	"	*	"	*	"	*	*	*	X	"	"	X	"	21

(3) *Natural strong-dependence.* This is given in the text as "First Path to second Path" and so on.

With the knowledge of these three terms and with the aid of the chart for the Selection of Conditions for Negative, the above note in the text will be clearly understood.

In the columns against strong-dependence the 8 answers, shown by asterisks, are natural object; the 4, shown by crosses, are strong-dependence object; the remaining 9, shown by ditto signs, are natural strong-dependence. In the columns against object the answers, shown by crosses, are strong-dependence object.

Not-object 17. In accordance with the above note in the text, the answers for natural object and strong-dependence object are not obtained but only the 9, shown by ditto signs, of natural strong-dependence. But since these 9 are also obtained in the 17 answers of conascence, no addition is necessary and so the enumeration for not-object is 17.

Not-strong-dependence 21. This is conascence 17 + 4 from object, which are not included in 17, to give enumeration 21.

All the Other Conditions 21. This is the 21 of strong-dependence.

"By Twos" are easy.

END OF PATH OBJECT TRIPLET

17. ARISEN TRIPLET

Triplet States

Reference (R)	Variant (V)
1. 89 present cons., 52 m.f., 28 matter.	1. 89 present cons., 52 m.f., 28 matter.
2. 12 future faulty cons., 21 faultless cons., 20 functional cons., 52 m.f., 17 mind-produced matter, 15 temperature-produced matter, 14 nutriment-produced matter.	2. 12 future faulty cons., 21 faultless cons., 20 functional cons., 52 m.f., 17 mind-produced matter, 15 temperature-produced matter, 14 nutriment-produced matter.
3. 36 future resultant cons., 38 m.f., 20 kamma-produced matter.	3. 36 future resultant cons., 38 m.f., 20 kamma-produced matter.

In this Triplet and the Past Triplet, which follows, Nibbāna is Triplet-freed.

Comy. p. 490 (Tikp 355): In this Triplet and the Past Triplet, the Dependent Chapter and the rest of the 6 Chapters are not expounded but only the Investigation Chapter. What is the reason for this? It is because there are only conascence and prenascence conditions in the 6 Chapters. For in these 2 Triplets past and future states are mixed. Why are proximity and other conditions not included in the Arisen Triplet? The reason is that this Triplet does not contain past states (there are only present and future states as can be seen from the chart). "States arisen and not arisen are never related to states arisen and not arisen by any of the conditions. States not arisen and bound to arise are related to states arisen by object-strong-dependence."

As stated in the Comy. above, it must be noted that the 6 Chapters are not expounded in this Triplet.

Investigation Chapter

Conditions: Positive

Root, etc. 1. Root and the rest of the 15 conditions of the conascence group, prenascence, postnascence, nutriment and faculty conditions, which occur in the present, have the answer (1–1).

Note: Whether the conditions occur in the present or whether they occur in the past or future, the conditioned states must always be present states. This can be known from this Triplet and the Past Triplet that follows.

Object, etc. 3. Object has the answers: (1-1), (2-1), (3-1). In predominance, object-predominance has 3 answers. In strong-dependence, both object-strong-dependence and natural strong-dependence have 3 answers each. These conditions occur in the above 3 periods of time.

The proximity group of conditions and asynchronous kamma are not expounded. For these conditions have past states as conditioning states and in this Triplet there are no such states.

In this way all the conditions can be known.

Selection of the Conditions for Negative

The answer (1-1) is obtained by all the conditions that are concerned with the present. (2-1) and (3-1) are obtained by object and strong-dependence only.

Conditions: Negative

By Ones

Not-presence 2, not-non-disappearance 2. These are somewhat difficult. In order to consider this matter so that it agrees with the text, reference must be made to the way the answer (1-1) is expounded for object condition. How does it differ from that expounded for object-prenascence-presence of presence condition? It will be seen that "aggregates arisen" is given only in object condition and these being 18 produced matter, there is nothing special here. Also, in object condition, "knowledge of supernormal power" is included but not in object-prenascence-presence. But it is explained in Guide to C.R., Part II, however, that, although this knowledge is not specifically expounded in object-prenascence-presence, it should be included. That being the case, the nature of object and object-prenascence-presence is the same and, therefore, the answer (1-1) is not obtained. That is why not-presence and not-non-disappearance have 2 answers.

Again, when natural strong-dependence is considered, the conditioned states in the answer (1-1) are all the 89 consciousnesses which have the nature of conascence. That being so, (1-1) is not obtained for strong-dependence and, therefore, there are only 2 answers for not-presence and not-non-disappearance. The teachers of old stated that (1-1), being of the present, is not obtained. What they actually meant was that present states are all included in conascence condition. In the Negative conditions of Past Triplet, the next Triplet, the same line of reasoning holds for not-presence 2, not-non-disappearance 2.

"By Twos" are easy.

END OF ARISEN TRIPLET

18. PAST TRIPLET

Triplet States

Reference (R)	Variant (V)
1. 89 past cons., 52 m.f., 28 matter.	1. 89 past cons., 52 m.f., 28 matter.
2. 89 future cons., 52 m.f., 28 matter.	2. 89 future cons., 52 m.f., 28 matter.
3. 89 present cons., 52 m.f., 28 matter.	3. 89 present cons., 52 m.f., 28 matter.

Investigation Chapter

As the states of this Triplet belong to the three periods of time, all the 24 conditions are expounded. As with the Arisen Triplet, the conditions which are concerned with present states only have only 1 answer (3-3). For proximity and the other conditions which have past conditioning states and present conditioned states, there is the answer (1-3); for kamma condition, which is concerned with both past and present states, there is the answer (1-3) with past states and (3-3) with present states. The text should be referred to in order to know how the conditions are expounded. The Negative conditions are like those of the Arisen Triplet dealt with above.

Comy. p. 490 (Tikp 355): In this Triplet present is never related to past and future nor past and future to past and future by any of the conditions.

END OF PAST TRIPLET

19. PAST OBJECT TRIPLET

Triplet States

Reference (R)	Variant (V)
1. 1 mind-door advertence, 29 sensuous impulsions, 11 registering cons., 2 superknowledges, 3 infinity of cons., 3 neither-perception-nor-nonperception cons., 47 m.f. exclusive of 3 abstinences and 2 illimitables.	1. 1 mind-door advertence, 29 sensuous impulsions, 11 registering cons., 2 superknowledges, 3 infinity of cons., 3 neither-perception-nor-nonperception cons., 47 m.f. exclusive of 3 abstinences and 2 illimitables.
2. 1 mind-door advertence, 29 sensuout impulsions, 11 registering cons., 2 superknowledges, 50 m.f. exclusive of 2 illimitables.	2. 1 mind-door advertence, 29 sensuous impulsions, 11 registering cons., 2 superknowledges, 50 m.f. exclusive of 2 illimitables.
3. 10 twice fivefold cons., 3 mind-element, 1 mind-door advertence, 29 sensuous impulsions, 11 registering cons., 2 superknowledges, 50 m.f. exclusive of 2 illimitables.	3. 10 twice fivefold cons., 3 mind-element, 1 mind-door advertence, 29 sensuous impulsions, 11 registering cons., 2 superknowledges, 50 m.f. exclusive of 2 illimitables.

6 Chapters

Conditions: Positive

As materiality is not included in this Triplet, the 6 Chapters are all the same. And when the states are selected to determine the enumerations it is found that all the 23 conditions have the same enumeration 3 which are (1-1), (2-2), (3-3). This is straightforward.

Conditions: Negative

Only 10 Negative conditions are expounded. On examining the single enumeration of not-jhāna it will be seen that there is only 1 answer: (3-3). But not-dissociation does not give this answer. From this it will be known that the states of the immaterial plane which take present object cannot be conascent with one another. If this is the case with not-dissociation why does not-prenascence have this answer? The reason is that this is not due to the states of the immaterial plane but to rebirth consciousness in the five-aggregate planes. For the classified answer given in the text for (3-3) is "At the moment of conception, dependent on one aggregate with present object . . . two aggregates . . ." All the other conditions have enumeration 3.

"By Twos" are easy.

Investigation Chapter

Conditions: Positive

When there is only mentality in the Triplet prenascence, postnascence and dissociation conditions are never included in the Investigation Chapter. The reason for this can be known by examination of their single enumerations. This, of course, applies to all the preceding Triplets of this nature.

Root, etc. 3. The conditions of the conascence group have 3 answers: (1-1), (2-2), (3-3).

Object 9. The text gives "(One) reviews infinity of consciousness" and so on and, therefore, from the states that are involved in them, determine the answers (1-1) and so on. How enumeration 9 is obtained can also be found from the text.

Predominance 7. As shown above, conascence-predominance has 3 answers. Object-predominance has (1-1) and (1-2). But (1-3) is not obtained because the conditioned states of object-predominance do not contain superknowledges whereas this answer (1-3) is concerned with them. For the same reason the answer (2-3) is not obtained. So when these 2 answers in object condition are not obtained the enumeration is 7. This will be clearly understood by referring to the way object condition is expounded.

Proximity 7. This condition is expounded in an unusual way. But if the mental process, which is dealt with to some extent in Guide to C.R., Part II, is understood there should be no difficulty at all.

Strong-dependence 9. It will be seen that "Contemplation of impermanence" and so forth are taken as the essential things in natural strong-dependence. As for the Faultless Triplet there are 3 answers each with R 1, R 2 and R 3 to give enumeration 9.

Kamma 9. As shown above, conascence-kamma has 3 answers. The enumeration 9 is due to asynchronous kamma. In this Triplet asynchronous kamma is expounded in a peculiar way. For the results that are obtained are stated thus: "Asynchronous volition with past object is related to (its) resultant aggregates (a) with past object, (b) with future object, (c) with present object; asynchronous volition with future object is related to (its) resultant aggregates (a) with future object, (b) with past object, (c) with present object; asynchronous volition with present object is related to (its) resultant aggregates (a) with present object, (b) with past object, (c) with future object.

The Other Conditions. These are straightforward.

As for "By Twos" there is nothing special to note.

Selection of the Conditions for Negative and By Ones

Not-Object, Not-Strong-dependence, Not-Kamma 9. Some of the 9 answers are different but the total enumeration for each of them is 9.

"By Twos" are easy.

END OF PAST OBJECT TRIPLET

20. Internal Triplet

Triplet States

Reference (R)	Variant (V)
1. 89 cons., 52 m.f., 28 matter.	1. 89 cons., 52 m.f., 28 matter.
2. 89 cons., 52 m.f., 28 matter, Nibbāna.	2. 89 cons., 52 m.f., 28 matter, Nibbāna.

Unlike the other Triplets only 2 sections, instead of the usual 3, are taken because the internal and external states of section 3 are not expounded. The Comy. p. 490 (Tikp 355) gives the following explanation: In the Internal Triplet the section of internal and external states should not be taken. The reason is that these 2 sections cannot exist together as conditioning or conditioned states at the same time. It is just as when a mustard fruit is laid on the palm of the hand, the colour of the mustard fruit and that of the palm of the hand cannot exist together as one object at the same time. Likewise, the Internal Object Triplet has only 2 sections.

6 Chapters

Conditions: Positive

Dependent Chapter

The chart shows that section 1 has all the states except Nibbāna and section 2 has all the states including Nibbāna. For the 6 Chapters, which do not take Nibbāna into account, the 2 sections have all the states for these Chapters. All that needs to be done is to select the states from the single enumerations of the 23 conditions. But since the internal and external states are not conascent, each of the conditions has only 2 answers: (1–1), (2–2), i.e. enumeration 2.

Conditioned Chapter

Here base-prenascence-dependence is included and so the 6 bases have to be taken. But since external states are not dependent on internal bases, there are the same 2 answers as for the Dependent Chapter.

Conjoined Chapter

Here the difference is that materiality is excluded but the enumeration is also 2 for each condition.

Conditions: Negative

The Negative conditions of the 6 Chapters, like the Positive conditions, have enumeration 2.

"By Twos" are straightforward and all of them have enumeration 2.

Investigation Chapter

Root condition and others are expounded fully and should be looked up in the text. Here those with special enumerations are considered.

Object 4. Root condition and others have 2 answers: (1–1), (2–2), i.e. enumeration 2. But in object condition, where the reference and variant can be taken both ways, there are 2 more answers: (1–2), (2–1), to give enumeration 4.

Predominance 4. Conascence-predominance has only 2 answers: (1–1), (2–2). But object-predominance, like object, has the 2 answers: (1–2), (2–1). Thus the enumeration is 4.

Strong-dependence 4. Proximity-strong-dependence has only 2 answers: (1–1), (2–2). But object-strong-dependence and natural strong-dependence have another 2: (1–2), (2–1). So the enumeration is 4.

Prenascence 6. Base-prenascence has only 2 answers: (1–1), (2–2). Object-prenascence has another 2: (1–2), (2–1). Mixed object-prenascence-base-prenascence has another 2: (1,2–1), (1,2–2). So the total enumeration is 6.

Nutriment 6. Conascence-nutriment, like conascence above, has only

2 answers: (1-1), (2-2). But physical nutriment, like prenascence above, has 6. So the enumeration is 6. Nutriment condition was explained in detail in Guide to C.R., Part I.

Presence 6. Here, like prenascence, there are mixed conditions. Also, like nutriment, there is physical nutriment. Therefore the enumeration is 6.

All the Other Conditions. Each has enumeration 2.

Selection of the Conditions for Negative and By Ones

Not-presence 4. In the Selection of the Conditions for Negative the total enumeration is 6. Presence condition contains prenascence and nutriment which have the 2 answers: (1,2-1), (1,2-2). So these answers are not obtained for not-presence and that is why its enumeration is 4.

"By Twos" are easy.

END OF INTERNAL TRIPLET

21. Internal Object Triplet

Triplet States

Reference (R)	Variant (V)
1. 54 sensuous cons., 2 superknowledges, 3 infinity of cons., 3 neither-perception-nor-non-perception cons., 49 m.f. exclusive of envy and 2 illimitables.	1. 54 sensuous cons., 2 superknowledges, 3 infinity of cons., 3 neither-perception-nor-non-perception cons., 49 m.f. exclusive of envy and 2 illimitables.
2. 54 sensuous cons., 2 superknowledges, 15 fine-material cons. excluding 2 superknowledges, 3 infinity of space, 8 supramundane cons., 51 m.f. exclusive of stinginess.	2. 54 sensuous cons., 2 superknowledges, 15 fine-material cons. excluding 2 superknowledges, 3 infinity of space, 8 supramundane cons., 51 m.f. exclusive of stinginess.

6 Chapters

Conditions: Positive

Since (1) there are only mental states because materiality is excluded and (2) only the first 2 sections have to be taken, it will be clear that all the 23 conditions have enumeration 2.

Conditions: Negative

Since 54 sensuous consciousnesses, etc. are included in both the sections, the 10 Negative conditions, like the Positive conditions above, have enumeration 2.

"By Twos" are clear.

Investigation Chapter

In this Triplet there are only mental states and so root condition and others of the conascence group have only 2 answers: (1–1), (2–2), i.e. enumeration 2. Here only those conditions with special enumerations are considered.

Object 4. As in the Internal Triplet above, the 2 answers: (1–2) and (2–1) are included to give enumeration 4.

Predominance 3. It is clear that conascence-predominance has enumeration 2. For object-predominance the 2 answers: (1–2), (2–2), are not obtained but only (2–1). Therefore the enumeration is 3. Why are the above 2 answers not obtained? If the way object condition is expounded is examined, it will be found that the single enumeration of object-predominance is not involved in these answers.

Proximity 4. This is clear from the text.

Strong-dependence 4. There are 4 answers for proximity-strong dependence and natural strong-dependence and so the enumeration is 4. In natural strong-dependence "Contemplation of impermanence" and so forth are expounded.

Repetition 3. Here (2–1) is not obtained. The reason for this can be seen by referring to proximity condition. There the relations are between (1) death-consciousness and rebirth-consciousness; (2) life-continuum and advertence; (3) aggregates and emergence. The relations between impulsions, which belong to repetition condition, are not included.

Kamma 4. It is clear that conascence-kamma has enumeration 2. But asynchronous kamma has all the 4 answers. So the enumeration is 4.

The Other Conditions. Their enumeration is 2.

Selection of the Conditions for Negative and By Ones

The Selection of the Conditions for Negative shows that the total enumeration is 4. As object, strong-dependence and kamma are included in all these enumerations, all the 24 conditions in Negative "By Ones" have enumeration 4.

"By Twos" are easy.

END OF INTERNAL OBJECT TRIPLET

22. VISIBLE AND IMPINGING TRIPLET

Triplet States

Reference (R)	Variant (V)
1. Visible object	1. Visible object
2. 11 gross matter exclusive of visible object	2. 11 gross matter exclusive of visible object
3. 89 cons., 52 m.f., 16 subtle matter, Nibbāna.	3. 89 cons., 52 m.f., 16 subtle matter, Nibbāna.

This Triplet contains all the states and so there is no state that is Triplet-freed. Sections 1 and 2 consist of materiality only. In the former there are no great primaries but just one derived matter and in the latter 3 great primaries (cohesion is not included) and 8 derived matter. Section 3, however, consists of all mentality and subtle matter. It will be seen, therefore, that materiality, of one kind or another, is included in the 3 sections. So it is only in this Triplet that: (1) the 18 produced matter are expounded fully and (2) cohesion and so on, which were not expounded in the other Triplets, are expounded.

Conditions: Positive

Dependent Chapter

Root, etc. 21. R 1 has visible object only and so the answers (1-1) and so on are not obtained. With R 2, R 3 and R 2 and 3 there are 7 answers each to give enumeration 21. Whenever the conditions contain both great primaries and derived matter the enumeration is 21. Of course, only those material states concerned in each case are to be taken.

Object, etc. 1. With object condition and others, which have only mentality, there is only 1 answer: (3-3). So, wherever the enumeration is 1, it shows that the conditions have only mentality.

Mutuality 6. The single enumeration of mutuality has great primaries but no derived matter. Therefore, there are (a) 3 answers: (2–2), (2–3), (2–2,3) with R 2;(b) 2 answers: (3–3), (3–2) with R 3 and (c) 1 answer: (2,3–2) with R 2 and 3 to give enumeration 6.

Conditioned Chapter

The text does not give the Conditioned and the Conjoined Chapters for both the Positive and Negative conditions. They are simply referred to at the end of the Dependent Chapter pointing out that they are the same as for that Chapter. But in the Conditioned Chapter, eye-base and the rest of the 5 bases in section 2 and (heart-)base in section 3 have to be taken into account and classified answers for them must be known. The text states that the Conditioned Chapter is the same as the Dependent Chapter because the enumerations are the same.

Conjoined Chapter

The Conjoined Chapter deals with mentality only and so all the 23 conditions have only 1 answer: (3–3). For this Chapter the text directs the reader to work with immateriality only.

Conditions: Negative

Dependent Chapter

Not-root, etc. 21. When the single enumerations of not-root condition and others are examined it will be found that, with the exception of not-mutuality, all contain great primaries and derived matter as conditioned states. As for not-mutuality, it contains only derived matter as conditioned states and great primaries as conditioning states. Therefore, all the 20 conditions have enumeration 21. From the single enumerations of the conditions concerned it can be known where "at the moment of conception" and "kamma-produced matter" are not included and so on.

Conditioned Chapter

In this Chapter classified answers must be given for the bases as was pointed out in the Positive conditions. Because of this there is no increase in the enumerations which are all 21.

Conjoined Chapter

In this Chapter only 10 conditions are expounded. From their single enumerations it will be seen that there can be only 1 answer: (3–3). Although the text is very brief, the details have to be known by applying the method above. The text always directs that everything be known in detail, never in brief.

Conditions: Positive-Negative

Root By Twos

Here not-kamma and not-dissociation conditions, which have different enumerations, will be considered.

Not kamma 1. The common states of root and not-kamma are faultless, faulty or rooted functional aggregates as conditioning states and faultless, faulty or rooted volitions as conditioned states. These are contained in section 3 and so there is only 1 answer: (3–3).

Not-dissociation 1. Here the common conditioning and conditioned states of root and not-dissociation conditions are the mental states of the immaterial plane contained in the single enumeration of not-dissociation. So there is only 1 answer: (3–3).

Conditions: Negative-Positive

Not-root By Twos

With not-root condition, path 1. This is the only thing to be noted here. The common states are 2 delusion-rooted consciousnesses as conditioning states and delusion from 2 delusion-rooted consciousnesses as conditioned state. So there is only 1 answer: (3–3).

Investigation Chapter

Root 7. The roots are included in section 3 and therefore the enumeration is 7, the answers being (3–3), (3–1) and so on. These are the answers whenever the enumeration is 7.

Object 3. The conditioned states of object condition are all mentality which is contained in section 3; the conditioning states are all mentality and materiality. Therefore there are only 3 answers: (1–3), (2–3), (3–3). The material states in sections 1, 2 and 3 are not conascent and so they cannot be taken together for answers.

Predominance 9. Object-predominance, like object, has 3 answers. Conascence-predominance, just like root, has 7 answers: (3-3) and so on. When the different kinds of answers are taken, the enumeration is 9.

Proximity, etc. 1. The conditioning and conditioned states of proximity, contiguity, repetition, association, absence and disappearance are mentality which is included in section 3. So there is only one answer: (3-3).

Conascence 21, Dependence 21. As shown in the Dependent Chapter each has enumeration 21.

Mutuality 6. As shown in the Dependent Chapter the enumeration is 6.

Strong-dependence 3. Although proximity-strong-dependence, like proximity, has only 1 answer: (3-3), object-strong-dependence and natural strong-dependence, like object-predominance, has 3 answers. So the enumeration is 3.

Prenascence 6. Here object-prenascence, like object, has 3 answers: (1-3), (2-3), (3-3); base-prenascence alone has 2 answers: (2-3), (3-3); mixed object-prenascence-base-prenascence has 3 answers: (1,3-3), (2,3-3), (1,2-3). When the different kinds of answers are taken, the enumeration is 6.

Faculty 9. Conascence-faculty, like root, has 7 answers; base-prenascence-faculty has 1 answer: (2-3); mixed conascence-prenascence-faculty has 1 answer: (2,3-3). So the total enumeration is 9. In the text, where it is stated that 7 answers are to be classified for section 3, it is directed that physical life-faculty be placed at the end. The reason for this is that, like the 7 kinds of delusion in the Applied Thought Triplet, there are 7 kinds of physical life-faculty.

Dissociation 8. The conditioning states of conascence-dissociation and postnascence-dissociation are mentality and so, like root, these mental states in section 3 give the same 7 answers for each; prenascence-dissociation has 2 answers: (2-3), (3-3). As (3-3) is already included, there is an extra answer: (2-3). So the enumeration is 8.

Presence 25. To conascence-presence 21 must be added the 3 answers: (1,3-3), (2,3-3), (1,2-3) obtained above for prenascence and another answer (1,2,3-3) for mixed conascence-object-prenascence-base-prenascence to give a total of 25. So the enumeration is 25.

Root: Common

In this last Triplet examples of common and combination are shown with root condition. Of course, the text directs that all the enumerations in the Enumeration Chapters be worked out. Never is there an occasion when the text directs that the matter be known briefly. It always directs that, based on the method in the Faultless Triplet, the details be known. Now that the method has been provided, wherever necessary, the reader who is interested must work out the details. Here it will be shown how the commons are determined.

The method of determining the commons in the 6 Chapters is different from that in the Investigation Chapter. In the 6 Chapters the commons are found by selecting the common states from the conditioning and conditioned states of the conditions. That is why the conditions have to be taken "By Twos", "By Threes" and so on in the Positive, Negative, Positive-Negative and Negative-Positive conditions.

In the Investigation Chapter, however, the commons are determined by selecting the common states from the conditioning and conditioned states of the conditions in the same group. There are 8 conditions in the object group, 15 in the conascence group and so forth. They can be found when Chart II (A) on p. liii of C.R. I is read vertically. (Moreover, the single enumerations of the conditions in the various groups are given in Charts II (B)–(H) in C.R. I facing p. lxiv.)

Root condition of this Triplet belongs to the conascence group and has 11 common conditions (C.R. I, p. 180, item 440 or Chart II (C) in C.R. I facing p. lxiv). Since root condition belongs to the Minor Conascence group its conditioning and conditioned states are included in the 4 Major Conascence group. So when the commons with the 4 Major Conascence group of conditions are determined, they are found to be the conditioning and conditioned states of root condition which has enumeration 7.

Predominance 7. When the conditioning and conditioned states of root and conascence-predominance are compared, it is found that investigating-wisdom predominance is the common conditioning state and associated aggregates together with predominant mind-produced matter are the common conditioned states. According to this Triplet, these states of section 3 give enumeration 7.

Faculty 7, *Path* 7. Non-delusion is the common conditioning state and associated aggregates together with rooted mind-produced matter and rooted rebirth kamma-produced matter are the common conditioned states. Here also these states of section 3 give enumeration 7 for each.

Resultant 7. The common conditioning states are the 3 resultant roots and the common conditioned states are like those given above. So the states of section 3 give enumeration 7.

Dissociation 7. Although the common conditioned states are materiality, the common conditioning states are the 6 roots and, here again, the enumeration is 7.

Mutuality 1, Association 1. With mutuality the common conditioning states are the 6 roots and the common conditioned states are the associated aggregates together with (heart-)base. These states of section 3 give only 1 answer: (3–3). With association the difference is that (heart-)base is not included.

A Commons Chart for this last Triplet is drawn up opposite, so that the reader will know the method of determining the enumerations and be able to reflect upon them. From the Commons chart it will be seen that the commons of all the conditions are given. The text gives root condition only and so the enumerations of the conditions common with it are shown in the chart with dashes over the figures. The rest of the enumerations which are elided, have been determined. They can be found by applying the method given in Guide to C.R., Part III (in preparation). It is in this way that all the innumerable elisions in the text can be known.

Root: Combination

The text gives only one of the combinations, i.e. ordinary 9, for root condition. The method by which these combinations are derived from the commons is illustrated below:

Without resultant 4

1. Here root is taken with the 4 Major conascence conditions to give enumeration 7. This combination is derived by taking together the commons given for root condition which are: "With root condition, conascence 7, dependence 7, presence 7, non-disappearance 7."

2. Here mutuality is included and so the enumeration is 1, which is that of the common of root and mutuality.

3. Here association is also included and so the enumeration is 1, which is that of the common of root and association.

4. Here only dissociation is included and so the enumeration is 7, which is that of the common of root and dissociation.

COMMONS CHART

	Ro	Ob	Pd	Px	Ct	Cn	Mu	Dp	S.D.	Prn	Pon	Rp	Kam	Rs	Nu	Fa	Jh	Pa	Ass	Dss	Ps	Ab	Dsp	N.D.
Ro	*		$\bar{7}$			$\bar{7}$	$\bar{1}$	$\bar{7}$						$\bar{7}$		$\bar{7}$		$\bar{7}$	$\bar{1}$	$\bar{7}$	$\bar{7}$			$\bar{7}$
Ob		*	3					1	3	3										1	3			3
Pd	7	3	*			7	1	7	3	3				7	7	7		7	1	7	9			9
Px				*	1				1			1	1									1	1	
Ct				1	*				1			1	1									1	1	
Cn	7		7			*	6	21					7	7	7	7	7	7	1	7	21			21
Mu	1		1			6	*	6					1	1	1	1	1	1	1	1	6			6
Dp	7	1	7			21	6	*	1	2			7	7	7	9	7	7	1	8	21			21
S.D.		1	3	1	1			1	*	3		1	1							1	3	1	1	3
Prn		3	3					2	3	*						1				2	6			6
Pon											*									7	7			7
Rp				1	1				1			*										1	1	
Kam				1	1	7	1	7	1				*	7	7				1	7	7	1	1	7
Rs	7		7			7	1	7					7	*	7	7	7	7	1	7	7			7
Nu			7			7	1	7					7	7	*	7			1	7	7			7
Fa	7		7			7	1	9		1				7	7	*	7	7	1	8	9			9
Jh						7	1	7						7		7	*	7	1	7	7			7
Pa	7		7			7	1	7						7		7	7	*	1	7	7			7
Ass	1		1			1	1	1					1	1	1	1	1	1	*		1			1
Dss	7	1	7			7	1	8	1	2	7		7	7	7	8	7	7		*	8			8
Ps	7	3	9			21	6	21	3	6	7		7	7	7	9	7	7	1	8	*			25
Ab				1	1				1			1	1									*	1	
Dsp				1	1				1			1	1									1	*	
N.D.	7	3	9			21	6	21	3	6	7		7	7	7	9	7	7	1	8	25			*

With resultant 5

1. Here resultant is included every time. The common of root and resultant is given as: "With root condition, resultant 7." So the enumeration for this combination is 7.

2 & 3. Here mutuality and association are respectively included and the enumeration for each of the combinations is 1.

4. With dissociation the enumeration for the combination is 7.

5. Here mutuality is again included and the enumeration for the combination is 1.

It is by this method that the enumerations for all the 415 combinations are to be known.

Selection of the Conditions for Negative

Here there are 6 different kinds of enumerations, namely: 25, 24, 23, 22, 12, 9. Not-root condition and others, which have all the 25, need not be considered. Only those conditions with the other enumerations are dealt with below. These will be clear only with the aid of the chart provided.

2. Conditions: Negative

By Ones

Not-object 22. (1,3–3) and (1,2–3) of item 10 and (1,2,3–3) of item 11 are solely of object condition and so, when these are excluded, the enumeration is 22.

Not-conascence 12. The answers which are obtained besides those of conascence are: (1–3), (2–3), 7 with R 3 and the 3 of item 10, i.e. 12. Those of items 9 and 11 are conascence and are, therefore, not obtained.

Not-mutuality, not-resultant, not-association 24. As (1,2,3–3) of item 11 is excluded, the enumeration is 24. (2,3–3) of item 9 is not excluded because it is included in item 10.

Not-dependence 9. (1–3) and (2–3) of object and strong-dependence and the 7 answers for kamma give enumeration 9. Whenever the enumeration is 9 these are the answers.

Not-prenascence, not-dissociation 22. They are the same as not-object.

Not-faculty 23. To the 21 of conascence add (1–3) and (1,2–3) to give enumeration 23. As for items 9 and 11 they are concerned with faculty.

SELECTION OF THE CONDITIONS FOR NEGATIVE 25

No.	Conditions	3 1	2 2	1 "	3 "	1,3 "	2,3 "	1,2 "	1,2,3 "	3 3	1 "	2 "	1,3 "	2,3 "	1,2 "	1,2,3 "	3 1,3	1 2,3	2 "	3 "	1,3 "	2,3 "	1,2 "	1,2,3 "	3 1,2	3 1,2,3	Enu
1	Object	"			"					"																	3
2	Conascence		"	"	"	"	"	"	"	"	"	"	"	"	"	"		"	"	"	"	"	"	"			21
3	Strong-dependence	"			"					"																	3
4	Prenascence				"					"																	2
5	Postnascence									"	"	"	"	"	"	"											7
6	Kamma									"	"	"	"	"	"	"											7
7	Nutriment									"	"	"	"	"	"	"											7
8	Faculty									"	"	"	"	"	"	"											7
9	Cn-Base-prn-Faculty																			"							1
10	Ob-Base-Prenascence																"			"					"		3
11	Cn-Ob-Base-Prenascence																									"	1

By Twos, By Threes

"By Twos" are not different from "By Ones". In "By Threes" not-object also becomes a reference condition and so the enumerations for them cannot be more than 22 which is that of not-object alone. Whenever the enumeration is 22 it is the same as not-object. Those with different enumerations are:

Not-conascence 9. (1-3) and (2-3) of strong-dependence and the 7 answers with R 3 give enumeration 9. It is the same for not-dependence 9.

Not-strong-dependence 21. They are the 21 of conascence.

Not-presence 9. They are the same 9 given above.

3. Conditions: Positive-Negative

Root By Twos

These are straightforward.

Root: Combination

They are given briefly. Not-dissociation is 1 because the conditioning and conditioned states are mentality included in section 3 and for which there is only 1 answer: (3-3), i.e. enumeration 1.

4. Conditions: Negative-Positive

Not-root By Twos

They are the same as "By Ones" of the Positive conditions.

END OF VISIBLE AND IMPINGING TRIPLET

END OF TRIPLET PAṬṬHĀNA, STATE: POSITIVE

CONCISE METHOD FOR C.R. VOL. II

Here in this Introduction to the second volume of Conditional Relations it has been shown, in some detail, (1) how the 17 Triplets expounded in the text are to be dealt with; (2) how the enumerations given in the text as well as those elided are to be obtained and so forth. Also, with the difficult Negative conditions of the Investigation Chapters, it has been shown how the enumerations are to be determined with the aid of the charts provided for the Selection of the Conditions for Negative.

In this volume there are 8 Triplets, namely: (1) the Applied Thought Triplet, (2) the Rapture Triplet, (3) the Limited Object Triplet, (4) the Path Object Triplet, (5) the Arisen Triplet, (6) the Past Triplet, (7) the Past Object Triplet, (8) the Internal Object Triplet, that do not contain certain states. These, being Triplet-freed, are not taken into account. The remaining Triplets contain all the ultimate realities.

Single Enumerations

The Triplet Paṭṭhāna cannot be understood without knowing the single enumerations, i.e. the conditioning and conditioned states of the conditions, of the Triplets concerned. So the first thing to do is to know what the single enumerations are. This can be done by applying the method given in the Faultless Triplet. How is this done? In each Triplet the states of the 3 sections of the Triplet are given and it is from these states—excluding Nibbāna for the 6 Chapters and including Nibbāna for the Investigation Chapters—that the single enumerations are found. In the case of the Triplets without Triplet-freed states, the conditioning and conditioned states of the conditions are the same as those contained in the single enumerations of the Faultless Triplet; but for those Triplets with Triplet-freed states, the freed states are simply excluded.

6 Chapters

After knowing what the single enumerations are, the states in the Triplets have to be examined, as has been repeatedly pointed out, to find (1) whether they are conascent or not for the Dependent and Conascent Chapters, (2) whether the 6 bases are involved for the Conditioned and Supported Chapters, (3) whether they are associated or not for the Conjoined and Associated Chapters. Then from the answers for the states so selected the enumerations of the single Positive and Negative conditions can be obtained. As for the Enumeration Chapters "By Twos", "By Threes" and so on, the common states of the Positive, Negative, Positive-Negative and Negative-Positive conditions are found and from them the enumerations for the Triplet concerned are determined. Although the method is given concisely, it will be seen, when it is applied, that everything is included for the 6 Chapters. Examples of the method were given in the Intr. to C.R. and summarized on p. xlvii.

Investigation Chapters

Classification Chapters

In these Chapters, also, the states of the Triplets concerned, as shown in the 6 Chapters, have to be examined to determine the single enumerations of the conditions of the Triplets concerned so as to know the direct and classified answers for root and the rest of the 24 conditions. Then, by reading the text along with the states of the Triplets that were tabulated above, it will be seen how the above answers are obtained. An example of the method was given in Intr. to C.R., pp. xlix–li.

Enumeration Chapters

In these Chapters there are, as in the 6 Chapters, 4 kinds of conditions, namely: (1) Positive, (2) Negative, (3) Positive-Negative and (4) Negative-Positive.

(1) Positive Conditions

Here the three kinds dealt with are: (a) "By Ones", (b) Common, (c) Combination. "By Ones" is given in all the Triplets but only in the Visible and Impinging Triplet are the commons and combinations given briefly. Wherever they are not given the text always directs that the commons and combinations be fully known as in the Faultless Triplet. But, beginning from the First Synod right up to the Sixth Synod, no country and no Sayadaw had ever given them fully. The reason for this was that they are difficult and, therefore, it requires deep knowledge to know what they are. The translator, however, with intense confidence and effort, put them down in black and white about thirty years ago. Although they are of great benefit they are not easily available nor easily known. That is why, with the belief that readers interested in the Great Book of Paṭṭhāna would want to know what the elisions are, there was a fervent desire that they should be able to do so.

My thanks are due to Dr. I. B. Horner for giving whole-hearted support and encouragement to undertake this translation and also to Dr. Thein Maung, the Abhidhamma Propagating Society, U Kyaw Sein and U Htoon Thwin, for assistance in many ways.

U NĀRADA
MŪLA PAṬṬHĀNA SAYADAW

PAGE

CONTENTS OF CONDITIONAL RELATIONS VOL. II

STATE: POSITIVE

CONDITIONAL RELATIONS OF TRIPLETS

ANSWERS

6. Applied Thought Triplet I. "DEPENDENT" CHAPTER

1. CONDITIONS: POSITIVE (i) CLASSIFICATION CHAPTER

1. CONDITIONS: POSITIVE (ii) ENUMERATION CHAPTER

2. CONDITIONS: NEGATIVE (i) CLASSIFICATION CHAPTER

2. CONDITIONS: NEGATIVE (ii) ENUMERATION CHAPTER

3. CONDITIONS: POSITIVE–NEGATIVE

4. CONDITIONS: NEGATIVE–POSITIVE

6. Applied Thought Triplet III. "CONDITIONED" CHAPTER

1. CONDITIONS: POSITIVE (i) CLASSIFICATION CHAPTER

2. CONDITIONS: NEGATIVE

---

*Those in brackets are not given in the Pali Text.

CONDITIONAL RELATIONS

STATE: POSITIVE

CONDITIONAL RELATIONS OF TRIPLETS (TIKA PAṬṬHĀNA)

Veneration to that Exalted One, the Arahat, the Enlightened Buddha

6. APPLIED THOUGHT TRIPLET[1] I. "DEPENDENT" CHAPTER

1. CONDITIONS: POSITIVE (i) CLASSIFICATION CHAPTER

Root 37

1. (i) Dependent on state with applied thought and sustained thought (savitakka-savicāraṁ dhammaṁ paṭicca), arises state with applied thought and sustained thought by root condition.

(*a*) Dependent on one aggregate with applied thought and sustained thought (savitakka-savicāraṁ ekaṁ khandhaṁ paṭicca), arise three aggregates; dependent on three aggregates, arises one aggregate; dependent on two aggregates, arise two aggregates;

(*b*) At the moment of conception (paṭisandhikkhaṇe), dependent on one aggregate with applied thought and sustained thought, arise three aggregates . . . dependent on two aggregates, arise two aggregates. (1)

(ii) Dependent on state with applied thought and sustained thought, arises state without applied thought but with sustained thought (avitakkavicāramatta) by root condition.

(*a*) Dependent on aggregates with applied thought and sustained thought, arises applied thought (vitakka);

---

[1] This comprises (1) States with applied thought and sustained thought, (2) States without applied thought but with sustained thought and (3) States without applied thought and sustained thought.

(*b*) At the moment of conception, dependent on aggregates with applied thought and sustained thought, arises applied thought. (2)

(iii) Dependent on state with applied thought and sustained thought, arises state without applied thought and sustained thought (avitakka-avicāra) by root condition.

(*a*) Dependent on aggregates with applied thought and sustained thought, arises mind-produced matter (cittasamuṭṭhānaṁ rūpaṁ);

(*b*) At the moment of conception, dependent on aggregates with applied thought and sustained thought, arises kamma-produced matter (kaṭattā rūpaṁ). (3)

(iv) Dependent on state with applied thought and sustained thought, arise states with applied thought and sustained thought and without applied thought and sustained thought by root condition.

(*a*) Dependent on one aggregate with applied thought and sustained thought, arise three aggregates and mind-produced matter . . . dependent on two aggregates, arise two aggregates and mind-produced matter;

(*b*) At the moment of conception, dependent on one aggregate with applied thought and sustained thought, arise three aggregates and kamma-produced matter . . . dependent on two aggregates, arise two aggregates and kamma-produced matter. (4)

(v) Dependent on state with applied thought and sustained thought, arise states without applied thought but with sustained thought and without applied thought and sustained thought by root condition.

(*a*) Dependent on aggregates with applied thought and sustained thought, arise applied thought and mind-produced matter;

(*b*) At the moment of conception, dependent on aggregates with applied thought and sustained thought, arise applied thought and kamma-produced matter. (5)

(vi) Dependent on state with applied thought and sustained thought, arise states with applied thought and sustained thought and without applied thought but with sustained thought by root condition.

(*a*) Dependent on one aggregate with applied thought and sustained thought, arise three aggregates and applied thought . . . dependent on two aggregates, arise two aggregates and applied thought;

(*b*) At the moment of conception, dependent on one aggregate with applied thought and sustained thought, arise three aggregates and applied thought . . . dependent on two aggregates, arise two aggregates and applied thought. (6)

(vii) Dependent on state with applied thought and sustained thought, arise states with applied thought and sustained thought, without applied thought but with sustained thought and without applied thought and sustained thought by root condition.

(*a*) Dependent on one aggregate with applied thought and sustained thought, arise three aggregates, applied thought and mind-produced matter . . . dependent on two aggregates, arise two aggregates, applied thought and mind-produced matter;

(*b*) At the moment of conception, dependent on one aggregate with applied thought and sustained thought, arise three aggregates, applied thought and kamma-produced matter . . . dependent on two aggregates, arise two aggregates, applied thought and kamma-produced matter. (7)

2. (viii) Dependent on state without applied thought but with sustained thought, arises state without applied thought but with sustained thought by root condition.

(*a*) Dependent on one aggregate without applied thought but with sustained thought, arise three aggregates . . . dependent on two aggregates, arise two aggregates;

(*b*) At the moment of conception, dependent on one aggregate without applied thought but with sustained thought, arise three aggregates . . . dependent on two aggregates, arise two aggregates. (1)

(ix) Dependent on state without applied thought but with sustained thought, arises state with applied thought and sustained thought by root condition.

(*a*) Dependent on applied thought, arise aggregates with applied thought and sustained thought;

(*b*) At the moment of conception, dependent on applied thought, arise aggregates with applied thought and sustained thought. (2)

(x) Dependent on state without applied thought but with sustained thought, arises state without applied thought and sustained thought by root condition.

(*a*) Dependent on aggregates without applied thought but with sustained thought, arise sustained thought and mind-produced matter; dependent on applied thought, arises mind-produced matter;

(*b*) At the moment of conception, dependent on aggregates without applied thought but with sustained thought, arise sustained thought and kamma-produced matter; at the moment of conception, dependent on applied thought, arises kamma-produced matter. (3)

(xi) Dependent on state without applied thought but with sustained thought, arise states with applied thought and sustained thought and without applied thought and sustained thought by root condition.

(*a*) Dependent on applied thought, arise aggregates with applied thought and sustained thought and mind-produced matter;

(*b*) At the moment of conception, dependent on applied thought, arise aggregates with applied thought and sustained thought and kamma-produced matter. (4)

(xii) Dependent on state without applied thought but with sustained thought, arise states without applied thought but with sustained thought and without applied thought and sustained thought by root condition.

(*a*) Dependent on one aggregate without applied thought but with sustained thought, arise three aggregates, sustained thought and mind-produced matter . . . dependent on two aggregates, arise two aggregates, sustained thought and mind-produced matter;

(*b*) At the moment of conception, dependent on one aggregate without applied thought but with sustained thought, arise three aggregates, sustained thought and kamma-produced matter . . . dependent on two aggregates, arise two aggregates, sustained thought and kamma-produced matter. (5)

3. (xiii) Dependent on state without applied thought and sustained thought, arises state without applied thought and sustained thought by root condition.

(*a*) Dependent on one aggregate without applied thought and sustained thought, arise three aggregates and mind-produced matter . . . dependent on two aggregates, arise two aggregates and mind-produced matter; dependent on sustained thought, arises mind-produced matter;

(*b*) At the moment of conception, dependent on one aggregate without applied thought and sustained thought, arise three aggregates and kamma-produced matter . . . dependent on two aggregates, arise two aggregates and kamma-produced matter; at the moment of conception, dependent on sustained thought, arises kamma-produced matter; dependent on aggregates, arises (heart-)base (khandhe paṭicca vatthu); dependent on (heart-)base, arise aggregates; dependent on sustained thought, arises (heart-)base; dependent on (heart-)base, arises sustained thought;

(*c*) Dependent on one great primary, arise three great primaries . . . dependent on great primaries (mahābhūte paṭicca), arise mind-produced and kamma-produced derived matter (upādārūpa). (1)

(xiv) Dependent on state without applied thought and sustained thought, arises state with applied thought and sustained thought by root condition.

At the moment of conception, dependent on (heart-)base, arise aggregates with applied thought and sustained thought. (2)

(xv) Dependent on state without applied thought and sustained thought, arises state without applied thought but with sustained thought by root condition.

(*a*) Dependent on sustained thought, arise aggregates without applied thought but with sustained thought;

(*b*) At the moment of conception, dependent on sustained thought, arise aggregates without applied thought but with sustained thought; at the moment of conception, dependent on (heart-)base, arise aggregates without applied thought but with sustained thought; at the moment of conception, dependent on (heart-)base, arises applied thought. (3)

(xvi) Dependent on state without applied thought and sustained thought, arise states with applied thought and sustained thought and without applied thought and sustained thought by root condition.

At the moment of conception, dependent on (heart-)base, arise aggregates with applied thought and sustained thought; dependent on great primaries, arises kamma-produced matter. (4)

(xvii) Dependent on state without applied thought and sustained thought, arise states without applied thought but with sustained thought and without applied thought and sustained thought by root condition.

(*a*) Dependent on sustained thought, arise aggregates without applied thought but with sustained thought and mind-produced matter;

(*b*) At the moment of conception, dependent on sustained thought, arise aggregates without applied thought but with sustained thought and kamma-produced matter; at the moment of conception, dependent on (heart-)base, arise aggregates without applied thought but with sustained thought; dependent on great primaries, arises kamma-produced matter; at the moment of conception, dependent on (heart-)base, arises applied thought; dependent on great primaries, arises kamma-produced matter; at the moment of conception, dependent on (heart-)base, arise aggregates without applied thought but with sustained thought, and sustained thought. (5)

(xviii) Dependent on state without applied thought and sustained thought, arise states with applied thought and sustained thought and without applied thought but with sustained thought by root condition.

At the moment of conception, dependent on (heart-)base, arise aggregates with applied thought and sustained thought, and applied thought. (6)

(xix) Dependent on state without applied thought and sustained thought, arise states with applied thought and sustained thought, without applied thought but with sustained thought and without applied thought and sustained thought by root condition.

At the moment of conception, dependent on (heart-)base, arise aggregates with applied thought and sustained thought, and applied thought; dependent on great primaries, arises kamma-produced matter. (7)

4. (xx) Dependent on state with applied thought and sustained thought and without applied thought and sustained thought, arises state with applied thought and sustained thought by root condition.

At the moment of conception, dependent on one aggregate with applied thought and sustained thought, and (heart-)base, arise three aggregates . . . dependent on two aggregates and (heart-)base, arise two aggregates. (1)

(xxi) Dependent on state with applied thought and sustained thought and without applied thought and sustained thought, arises state without applied thought but with sustained thought by root condition.

At the moment of conception, dependent on aggregates with applied thought and sustained thought, and (heart-)base, arises applied thought. (2)

(xxii) Dependent on state with applied thought and sustained thought and without applied thought and sustained thought, arises state without applied thought and sustained thought by root condition.

(*a*) Dependent on aggregates with applied thought and sustained thought, and great primaries, arises mind-produced matter;

(*b*) At the moment of conception, dependent on aggregates with applied thought and sustained thought, and great primaries, arises kamma-produced matter. (3)

(xxiii) Dependent on state with applied thought and sustained thought and without applied thought and sustained thought, arise states with applied thought and sustained thought and without applied thought and sustained thought by root condition.

At the moment of conception, dependent on one aggregate with applied thought and sustained thought, and (heart-)base, arise three aggregates . . . dependent on two aggregates and (heart-)base, arise two aggregates; dependent on aggregates with applied thought and sustained thought, and great primaries, arises kamma-produced matter. (4)

(xxiv) Dependent on state with applied thought and sustained thought and without applied thought and sustained thought, arise states without applied thought but with sustained thought and without applied thought and sustained thought by root condition.

At the moment of conception, dependent on aggregates with applied thought and sustained thought, and (heart-)base, arises applied thought; dependent on aggregates with applied thought and sustained thought, and great primaries, arises kamma-produced matter. (5)

(xxv) Dependent on state with applied thought and sustained thought and without applied thought and sustained thought, arise states with applied thought and sustained thought and without applied thought but with sustained thought by root condition.

At the moment of conception, dependent on one aggregate with applied thought and sustained thought, and (heart-)base, arise three aggregates and applied thought . . . dependent on two aggregates and (heart-)base, arise two aggregates and applied thought. (6)

(xxvi) Dependent on state with applied thought and sustained thought and without applied thought and sustained thought, arise states with applied thought and sustained thought, without applied thought but with sustained thought and without applied thought and sustained thought by root condition.

At the moment of conception, dependent on one aggregate with applied thought and sustained thought, and (heart-)base, arise three aggregates and applied thought . . . dependent on two aggregates and (heart-)base, arise two aggregates and applied thought; dependent on aggregates with applied thought and sustained thought, and great primaries, arises kamma-produced matter. (7)

5. (xxvii) Dependent on state without applied thought but with sustained thought and without applied thought and sustained thought, arises state with applied thought and sustained thought by root condition.

At the moment of conception, dependent on applied thought and (heart-)base, arise aggregates with applied thought and sustained thought. (1)

(xxviii) Dependent on state without applied thought but with sustained thought and without applied thought and sustained thought, arises state without applied thought but with sustained thought by root condition.

(*a*) Dependent on one aggregate without applied thought but with sustained thought, and sustained thought, arise three aggregates . . . dependent on two aggregates and sustained thought, arise two aggregates;

(*b*) At the moment of conception, dependent on one aggregate without applied thought but with sustained thought, and sustained thought, arise three aggregates . . . dependent on two aggregates and sustained thought, arise two aggregates; at the moment of conception, dependent on one aggregate without applied thought but with sustained thought, and (heart-)base, arise three aggregates . . . dependent on two aggregates and (heart-)base, arise two aggregates. (2)

(xxix) Dependent on state without applied thought but with sustained thought and without applied thought and sustained thought, arises state without applied thought and sustained thought by root condition.

(*a*) Dependent on aggregates without applied thought but with sustained thought, and sustained thought, arises mind-produced matter; dependent on aggregates without applied thought but with sustained thought, and great primaries, arises mind-produced matter; dependent on applied thought and great primaries, arises mind-produced matter;

(*b*) At the moment of conception, dependent on aggregates without applied thought but with sustained thought, and sustained thought, arises kamma-produced matter; at the moment of conception, dependent on aggregates without applied thought but with sustained thought, and great primaries, arises kamma-produced matter; at the moment of conception, dependent on applied thought and great primaries, arises kamma-produced matter; at the moment of conception, dependent on aggregates without applied thought but with sustained thought, and (heart-)base, arises sustained thought. (3)

(xxx) Dependent on state without applied thought but with sustained thought and without applied thought and sustained thought, arise states with applied thought and sustained thought and without applied thought and sustained thought by root condition.

At the moment of conception, dependent on applied thought and (heart-)base, arise aggregates with applied thought and sustained thought; dependent on applied thought and great primaries, arises kamma-produced matter. (4)

(xxxi) Dependent on state without applied thought but with sustained thought and without applied thought and sustained thought, arise states without applied thought but with sustained thought and without applied thought and sustained thought by root condition.

(*a*) Dependent on one aggregate without applied thought but with sustained thought, and sustained thought, arise three aggregates and mind-produced matter . . . dependent on two aggregates and sustained thought, arise two aggregates and mind-produced matter;

(*b*) At the moment of conception, dependent on one aggregate without applied thought buf with sustained thought, and sustained thought, arise three aggregates and kamma-produced matter . . . dependent on two aggregates and sustained thought, arise two aggregates and kamma-produced matter; at the moment of conception, dependent on one aggregate without applied thought but with sustained thought, and (heart-)base, arise three aggregates and sustained thought . . . dependent on two aggregates and (heart-)base, arise two aggregates and sustained thought. (5)

6. (xxxii) Dependent on state with applied thought and sustained thought and without applied thought but with sustained thought, arises state with applied thought and sustained thought by root condition.

(*a*) Dependent on one aggregate with applied thought and sustained thought, and applied thought, arise three aggregates . . . dependent on two aggregates and applied thought, arise two aggregates;

(*b*) At the moment of conception, dependent on one aggregate with applied thought and sustained thought, and applied thought, arise three aggregates . . . dependent on two aggregates and applied thought, arise two aggregates. (1)

(xxxiii) Dependent on state with applied thought and sustained thought and without applied thought but with sustained thought, arises state without applied thought and sustained thought by root condition.

(*a*) Dependent on aggregates with applied thought and sustained thought, and applied thought, arises mind-produced matter;

(*b*) At the moment of conception, dependent on aggregates with applied thought and sustained thought, and applied thought, arises kamma-produced matter. (2)

(xxxiv) Dependent on state with applied thought and sustained thought and without applied thought but with sustained thought, arise states with applied thought and sustained thought and without applied thought and sustained thought by root condition.

(*a*) Dependent on one aggregate with applied thought and sustained thought, and applied thought, arise three aggregates and mind-produced matter . . . dependent on two aggregates and applied thought, arise two aggregates and mind-produced matter;

(*b*) At the moment of conception, dependent on one aggregate with applied thought and sustained thought, and applied thought, arise three aggregates and kamma-produced matter . . . dependent on two aggregates and applied thought, arise two aggregates and kamma-produced matter. (3)

7. (xxxv) Dependent on state with applied thought and sustained thought, without applied thought but with sustained thought and without applied thought and sustained thought, arises state with applied thought and sustained thought by root condition.

At the moment of conception, dependent on one aggregate with applied thought and sustained thought, applied thought and (heart-)base, arise three aggregates . . . dependent on two aggregates, applied thought and (heart-)base, arise two aggregates. (1)

(xxxvi) Dependent on state with applied thought and sustained thought, without applied thought but with sustained thought and without applied thought and sustained thought, arises state without applied thought and sustained thought by root condition.

(*a*) Dependent on aggregates with applied thought and sustained thought, applied thought and great primaries, arises mind-produced matter;

(*b*) At the moment of conception, dependent on aggregates with applied thought and sustained thought, applied thought and great primaries, arises kamma-produced matter. (2)

(xxxvii) Dependent on state with applied thought and sustained thought, without applied thought but with sustained thought and without applied thought and sustained thought, arise states with applied thought and sustained thought and without applied thought and sustained thought by root condition.

At the moment of conception, dependent on one aggregate with applied thought and sustained thought, applied thought and (heart-) base, arise three aggregates; dependent on three aggregates, applied thought and (heart-)base, arises one aggregate; dependent on two aggregates, applied thought and (heart-)base, arise two aggregates; dependent on aggregates with applied thought and sustained thought, applied thought and great primaries, arises kamma-produced matter. (3)

Object 21

8. (i) Dependent on state with applied thought and sustained thought, arises state with applied thought and sustained thought by object condition.

(*a*) Dependent on one aggregate with applied thought and sustained thought, arise three aggregates . . . dependent on two aggregates, arise two aggregates;

(*b*) At the moment of conception . . . (1)

(ii) Dependent on state with applied thought and sustained thought, arises state without applied thought but with sustained thought by object condition.

(*a*) Dependent on aggregates with applied thought and sustained thought, arises applied thought;

(*b*) At the moment of conception . . . (2)

(iii) Dependent on state with applied thought and sustained thought, arise states with applied thought and sustained thought and without applied thought but with sustained thought by object condition.

(*a*) Dependent on one aggregate with applied thought and sustained thought, arise three aggregates and applied thought . . . dependent on two aggregates, arise two aggregates and applied thought;

(*b*) At the moment of conception . . . (3)

9. (iv) Dependent on state without applied thought but with sustained thought, arises state without applied thought but with sustained thought by object condition.

(*a*) Dependent on one aggregate without applied thought but with sustained thought, arise three aggregates . . . dependent on two aggregates, arise two aggregates;

(*b*) At the moment of conception . . . (1)

(v) Dependent on state without applied thought but with sustained thought, arises state with applied thought and sustained thought by object condition.

(*a*) Dependent on applied thought, arise aggregates with applied thought and sustained thought;

(*b*) At the moment of conception . . . (2)

(vi) Dependent on state without applied thought but with sustained thought, arises state without applied thought and sustained thought by object condition.

(*a*) Dependent on aggregates without applied thought but with sustained thought, arises sustained thought;

(*b*) At the moment of conception . . . (3)

(vii) Dependent on state without applied thought but with sustained thought, arise states without applied thought but with sustained thought and without applied thought and sustained thought by object condition.

(*a*) Dependent on one aggregate without applied thought but with sustained thought, arise three aggregates and sustained thought . . . dependent on two aggregates, arise two aggregates and sustained thought;

(*b*) At the moment of conception . . . (4)

10. (viii) Dependent on state without applied thought and sustained thought, arises state without applied thought and sustained thought by object condition.

(*a*) Dependent on one aggregate without applied thought and sustained thought, arise three aggregates . . . dependent on two aggregates, arise two aggregates;

(*b*) At the moment of conception, dependent on one aggregate without applied thought and sustained thought, arise three aggregates . . . dependent on two aggregates, arise two aggregates; at the moment of conception, dependent on (heart-)base, arise aggregates; dependent on (heart-)base, arises sustained thought. (1)

(ix) Dependent on state without applied thought and sustained thought, arises state with applied thought and sustained thought by object condition.

At the moment of conception, dependent on (heart-)base, arise aggregates with applied thought and sustained thought. (2)

(x) Dependent on state without applied thought and sustained thought, arises state without applied thought but with sustained thought by object condition.

(*a*) Dependent on sustained thought, arise aggregates without applied thought but with sustained thought;

(*b*) At the moment of conception, dependent on sustained thought, arise aggregates without applied thought but with sustained thought; at the moment of conception, dependent on (heart-)base, arise aggregates without applied thought but with sustained thought; at the moment of conception, dependent on (heart-)base, arises applied thought. (3)

(xi) Dependent on state without applied thought and sustained thought, arise states without applied thought but with sustained thought and without applied thought and sustained thought by object condition.

At the moment of conception, dependent on (heart-)base, arise aggregates without applied thought but with sustained thought, and sustained thought. (4)

(xii) Dependent on state without applied thought and sustained thought, arise states with applied thought and sustained thought and without applied thought but with sustained thought by object condition.

At the moment of conception, dependent on (heart-)base, arise aggregates with applied thought and sustained thought, and applied thought. (5)

11. (xiii) Dependent on state with applied thought and sustained thought and without applied thought and sustained thought, arises state with applied thought and sustained thought by object condition.

At the moment of conception, dependent on one aggregate with applied thought and sustained thought, and (heart-)base, arise three aggregates . . . dependent on two aggregates and (heart-)base, arise two aggregates. (1)

(xiv) Dependent on state with applied thought and sustained thought and without applied thought and sustained thought, arises state without applied thought but with sustained thought by object condition.

At the moment of conception, dependent on aggregates with applied thought and sustained thought, and (heart-)base, arises applied thought. (2)

(xv) Dependent on state with applied thought and sustained thought and without applied thought and sustained thought, arise states with applied thought and sustained thought and without applied thought but with sustained thought by object condition.

At the moment of conception, dependent on one aggregate with applied thought and sustained thought, and (heart-)base, arise three aggregates and applied thought . . . dependent on two aggregates and (heart-)base, arise two aggregates and applied thought. (3)

12. (xvi) Dependent on state without applied thought but with sustained thought and without applied thought and sustained thought, arises state with applied thought and sustained thought by object condition.

At the moment of conception, dependent on applied thought and (heart-)base, arise aggregates with applied thought and sustained thought. (1)

(xvii) Dependent on state without applied thought but with sustained thought and without applied thought and sustained thought, arises state without applied thought but with sustained thought by object condition.

(*a*) Dependent on one aggregate without applied thought but with sustained thought, and sustained thought, arise three aggregates . . . dependent on two aggregates and sustained thought, arise two aggregates;

(*b*) At the moment of conception, dependent on one aggregate without applied thought but with sustained thought, and sustained thought, arise three aggregates . . . dependent on two aggregates and sustained thought, arise two aggregates; at the moment of conception, dependent on one aggregate without applied thought but with sustained thought, and (heart-)base, arise three aggregates . . . dependent on two aggregates and (heart-)base, arise two aggregates. (2)

(xviii) Dependent on state without applied thought but with sustained thought and without applied thought and sustained thought, arises state without applied thought and sustained thought by object condition.

At the moment of conception, dependent on aggregates without applied thought but with sustained thought, and (heart-)base, arises sustained thought. (3)

(xix) Dependent on state without applied thought but with sustained thought and without applied thought and sustained thought, arise states without applied thought but with sustained thought and without applied thought and sustained thought by object condition.

At the moment of conception, dependent on one aggregate without applied thought but with sustained thought, and (heart-)base, arise three aggregates and sustained thought . . . dependent on two aggregates and (heart-)base, arise two aggregates and sustained thought. (4)

13. (xx) Dependent on state with applied thought and sustained thought and without applied thought but with sustained thought, arises state with applied thought and sustained thought by object condition.

(*a*) Dependent on one aggregate with applied thought and sustained thought, and applied thought, arise three aggregates . . . dependent on two aggregates and applied thought, arise two aggregates.

(*b*) At the moment of conception . . . (1)

(xxi) Dependent on state with applied thought and sustained thought, without applied thought but with sustained thought and without applied thought and sustained thought, arises state with applied thought and sustained thought by object condition.

At the moment of conception, dependent on one aggregate with applied thought and sustained thought, applied thought and (heart-) base, arise three aggregates . . . dependent on two aggregates, applied thought and (heart-)base, arise two aggregates. (1)

(Two conditions have been given in detail according to the way of recital. Likewise, the remaining twenty conditions should be given in detail.)

Dissociation 37

14. (i) Dependent on state with applied thought and sustained thought, arises state with applied thought and sustained thought by dissociation condition.

(*a*) Dependent on one aggregate with applied thought and sustained thought, arise three aggregates . . . (dependent on) (heart-)base, (arise aggregates) by dissociation condition (vatthuṁ vippayuttapaccayā);

(*b*) At the moment of conception, dependent on one aggregate with applied thought and sustained thought, arise three aggregates . . . (dependent on) (heart-)base, (arise aggregates) by dissociation condition. (1)

(ii) Dependent on state with applied thought and sustained thought, arises state without applied thought but with sustained thought by dissociation condition.

(*a*) Dependent on aggregates with applied thought and sustained thought, arises applied thought; (dependent on) (heart-)base, (arises applied thought) by dissociation condition;

(*b*) At the moment of conception . . . (2)

(iii) Dependent on state with applied thought and sustained thought, arises state without applied thought and sustained thought by dissociation condition.

(*a*) Dependent on aggregates with applied thought and sustained thought, arises mind-produced matter; (dependent on) aggregates, (arises mind-produced matter) by dissociation condition (khandhe vippayuttapaccayā);

(*b*) At the moment of conception . . . (3)

(iv) Dependent on state with applied thought and sustained thought, arise states with applied thought and sustained thought and without applied thought and sustained thought by dissociation condition.

(*a*) Dependent on one aggregate with applied thought and sustained thought, arise three aggregates and mind-produced matter . . . (dependent on six) bases, (arise) aggregates (khandhā vatthuṁ) by dissociation condition; (dependent on) aggregates, (arises) mind-produced matter (cittasamuṭṭhānaṁ rūpaṁ khandhe) by dissociation condition;

(*b*) At the moment of conception . . . (4)

(v) Dependent on state with applied thought and sustained thought, arise states without applied thought but with sustained thought and without applied thought and sustained thought by dissociation condition.

(*a*) Dependent on aggregates with applied thought and sustained thought, arise applied thought and mind-produced matter; (dependent on) (heart-)base, (arises) applied thought by dissociation condition; (dependent on) aggregates, (arises) mind-produced matter by dissociation condition;

(*b*) At the moment of conception . . . (5)

(vi) Dependent on state with applied thought and sustained thought, arise states with applied thought and sustained thought and without applied thought but with sustained thought by dissociation condition.

(*a*) Dependent on one aggregate with applied thought and sustained thought, arise three aggregates and applied thought . . . dependent on two aggregates, arise two aggregates and applied thought; (dependent on) (heart-)base, (arise aggregates) by dissociation condition;

(*b*) At the moment of conception . . . (6)

(vii) Dependent on state with applied thought and sustained thought, arise states with applied thought and sustained thought, without applied thought but with sustained thought and without applied thought and sustained thought by dissociation condition.

(*a*) Dependent on one aggregate with applied thought and sustained thought, arise three aggregates, applied thought and mind-produced matter . . . dependent on two aggregates, arise two aggregates, applied thought and mind-produced matter; (dependent on) (heart-)base, (arise) aggregates and applied thought by dissociation condition; (dependent on) aggregates, (arises) mind-produced matter by dissociation condition;

(*b*) At the moment of conception . . . (7)

15. (viii) Dependent on state without applied thought but with sustained thought, arises state without applied thought but with sustained thought . . .

(*a*) Dependent on one aggregate without applied thought but with sustained thought, arise three aggregates . . . (dependent on) two aggregates . . . (dependent on) (heart-)base, (arise aggregates) by dissociation condition;

(*b*) At the moment of conception . . . (1)

(ix) Dependent on state without applied thought but with sustained thought, arises state with applied thought and sustained thought by dissociation condition.

(*a*) Dependent on applied thought, arise aggregates with applied thought and sustained thought; (dependent on) (heart-)base, (arise aggregates) by dissociation condition;

(*b*) At the moment of conception . . . (2)

(x) Dependent on state without applied thought but with sustained thought, arises state without applied thought and sustained thought by dissociation condition.

(*a*) Dependent on aggregates without applied thought but with sustained thought, arise sustained thought and mind-produced matter; (dependent on) (heart-)base, (arises) sustained thought by dissociation condition; (dependent on) aggregates, (arises) mind-produced matter by dissociation condition; dependent on applied thought, arises mind-produced matter; (dependent on) applied thought, [arises (heart-)base] by dissociation condition;

(*b*) At the moment of conception . . . (3)

(xi) Dependent on state without applied thought but with sustained thought, arise states with applied thought and sustained thought and without applied thought and sustained thought by dissociation condition.

(*a*) Dependent on applied thought, arise aggregates with applied thought and sustained thought and mind-produced matter; (dependent on) (heart-)base, (arise) aggregates by dissociation condition; (dependent on) applied thought, (arises) mind-produced matter by dissociation condition;

(*b*) At the moment of conception . . . (4)

(xii) Dependent on state without applied thought but with sustained thought, arise states without applied thought but with sustained thought and without applied thought and sustained thought by dissociation condition.

(*a*) Dependent on one aggregate without applied thought but with sustained thought, arise three aggregates, sustained thought and mind-produced matter . . . dependent on two aggregates, arise two aggregates, sustained thought and mind-produced matter; (dependent on) (heart-) base, (arise) aggregates and sustained thought by dissociation condition; (dependent on) aggregates, (arises) mind-produced matter by dissociation condition;

(*b*) At the moment of conception . . . (5)

16. (xiii) Dependent on state without applied thought and sustained thought, arises state without applied thought and sustained thought

by dissociation condition.

(*a*) Dependent on one aggregate without applied thought and sustained thought, arise three aggregates and mind-produced matter . . . (dependent on) two aggregates . . . (dependent on six) bases, (arise) aggregates by dissociation conditions; (dependent on) aggregates, (arises) mind-produced matter by dissociation condition; dependent on sustained thought, arises mind-produced matter; [dependent on (heart-) base, arises] sustained thought by dissociation condition;

(*b*) At the moment of conception . . . at the moment of conception, dependent on sustained thought, arises kamma-produced matter; [dependent on (heart-)base, arises] sustained thought by dissociation condition; dependent on aggregates, arises (heart-)base; dependent on (heart-)base, (arise) aggregates; (dependent on) (heart-)base, (arise) aggregates by dissociation condition; (dependent on) aggregates, (arises) (heart-)base by dissociation condition; dependent on sustained thought, arises (heart-)base; dependent on (heart-)base, arises sustained thought; (dependent on) (heart-)base, (arises) sustained thought by dissociation condition; (dependent on) sustained thought, (arises) (heart-)base by dissociation condition;

(*c*) Dependent on one great primary, arise three great primaries . . . dependent on great primaries, arise mind-produced and kamma-produced derived matter; (dependent on) aggregates, (arises kamma-produced matter) by dissociation condition. (1)

(xiv) Dependent on state without applied thought and sustained thought, arises state with applied thought and sustained thought by dissociation condition.

At the moment of conception, dependent on (heart-)base, arise aggregates with applied thought and sustained thought; (dependent on) (heart-)base, (arise aggregates) by dissociation condition. (2)

(xv) Dependent on state without applied thought and sustained thought, arises state without applied thought but with sustained thought by dissociation condition.

(*a*) Dependent on sustained thought, arise aggregates without applied thought but with sustained thought; (dependent on) (heart-)base, (arise aggregates) by dissociation condition;

(*b*) At the moment of conception, dependent on sustained thought, arise aggregates without applied thought but with sustained thought; (dependent on) (heart-)base, (arise aggregates) by dissociation condition; at the moment of conception, dependent on (heart-)base, arise aggregates without applied thought but with sustained thought; (dependent on) (heart-)base, (arise aggregates) by dissociation condition; at the moment of conception, dependent on (heart-)base, arises applied thought; (dependent on) (heart-)base, (arises applied thought) by dissociation condition. (3)

(xvi) Dependent on state without applied thought and sustained thought, arise states with applied thought and sustained thought and without applied thought and sustained thought by dissociation condition.

At the moment of conception, dependent on (heart-)base, arise aggregates with applied thought and sustained thought; dependent on great primaries, arises kamma-produced matter; (dependent on) (heart-) base, (arise) aggregates by dissociation conditions; (dependent on) aggregates, (arises) kamma-produced matter by dissociation condition. (4)

(xvii) Dependent on state without applied thought and sustained thought, arise states without applied thought but with sustained thought and without applied thought and sustained thought by dissociation condition.

(*a*) Dependent on sustained thought, arise aggregates without applied thought but with sustained thought and mind-produced matter; (dependent on) (heart-)base, (arise) aggregates by dissociation condition; (dependent on) sustained thought, (arises) mind-produced matter by dissociation condition;

(*b*) At the moment of conception, dependent on sustained thought, arise aggregates without applied thought but with sustained thought and kamma-produced matter; (dependent on) (heart-)base, (arise) aggregates by dissociation condition; (dependent on) sustained thought, (arises) kamma-produced matter by dissociation condition; at the moment of conception, dependent on (heart-)base, arise aggregates without applied thought but with sustained thought; dependent on great primaries, arises kamma-produced matter; (dependent on) (heart-) base, (arise) aggregates by dissociation condition; (dependent on) aggregates, (arises) kamma-produced matter by dissociation condition; at the moment of conception, dependent on (heart-)base, arises applied thought; dependent on great primaries, arises kamma-produced matter; (dependent on) (heart-)base, (arises) applied thought by dissociation condition; (dependent on) aggregates, (arises) kamma-produced matter by dissociation condition; at the moment of conception, dependent on (heart-)base, arise aggregates without applied thought but with sustained thought, and sustained thought; (dependent on) (heart-)base, (arise aggregates) by dissociation condition. (5)

(xviii) Dependent on state without applied thought and sustained thought, arise states with applied thought and sustained thought and without applied thought but with sustained thought by dissociation condition.

At the moment of conception, dependent on (heart-)base, arise aggregates with applied thought and sustained thought, and applied thought; (dependent on) (heart-)base, (arise aggregates) by dissociation condition. (6)

(xix) Dependent on state without applied thought and sustained thought, arise states with applied thought and sustained thought, without applied thought but with sustained thought and without applied thought and sustained thought by dissociation condition.

At the moment of conception, dependent on (heart-)base, arise aggregates with applied thought and sustained thought, and applied thought; dependent on great primaries, arises kamma-produced matter; (dependent on) (heart-)base, (arise) aggregates and applied thought by dissociation condition; (dependent on) aggregates, (arises) kamma-produced matter by dissociation condition. (7)

17. (xx) Dependent on state with applied thought and sustained thought and without applied thought and sustained thought, arises state with applied thought and sustained thought by dissociation condition.

At the moment of conception, dependent on one aggregate with applied thought and sustained thought, and (heart-)base, arise three aggregates . . . (dependent on) (heart-)base, (arise aggregates) by dissociation condition. (1)

(xxi) Dependent on state with applied thought and sustained thought and without applied thought and sustained thought, (arises) state without applied thought but with sustained thought . . .

At the moment of conception, dependent on aggregates with applied thought and sustained thought, and (heart-)base, arises applied thought; (dependent on) (heart-)base, (arise aggregates) by dissociation condition. (2)

(xxii) Dependent on state with applied thought and sustained thought and without applied thought and sustained thought, (arises) state without applied thought and sustained thought . . .

(*a*) Dependent on aggregates with applied thought and sustained thought, and great primaries, arises mind-produced matter; (dependent on) aggregates, (arises mind-produced matter) by dissociation condition;

(*b*) At the moment of conception . . . (3)

(xxiii) Dependent on state with applied thought and sustained thought and without applied thought and sustained thought; (arise) states with applied thought and sustained thought and without applied thought and sustained thought . . .

At the moment of conception, dependent on one aggregate with applied thought and sustained thought, and (heart-)base, arise three aggregates . . . dependent on two aggregates and (heart-)base, arise two aggregates; dependent on aggregates with applied thought and sustained thought, and great primaries, arises kamma-produced matter; (dependent on) (heart-)base, (arise) aggregates by dissociation condition; (dependent on) aggregates, (arises) kamma-produced matter by dissociation condition. (4)

(xxiv) Dependent on state with applied thought and sustained thought and without applied thought and sustained thought, (arise) states without applied thought but with sustained thought and without applied thought and sustained thought . . .

At the moment of conception, dependent on aggregates with applied thought and sustained thought, and (heart-)base, arises applied thought; dependent on aggregates with applied thought and sustained thought, and great primaries, arises kamma-produced matter; (dependent on) (heart-)base, (arises) applied thought by dissociation condition; (dependent on) aggregates, (arises) kamma-produced matter by dissociation condition. (5)

(xxv) Dependent on state with applied thought and sustained thought and without applied thought and sustained thought, (arise) states with applied thought and sustained thought and without applied thought but with sustained thought . . .

At the moment of conception, dependent on one aggregate with applied thought and sustained thought, and (heart-)base, arise three aggregates and applied thought . . . dependent on two aggregates and (heart-)base, arise two aggregates and applied thought; (dependent on) (heart-)base, (arise aggregates) by dissociation condition. (6)

(xxvi) Dependent on state with applied thought and sustained thought and without applied thought and sustained thought, (arise) states with applied thought and sustained thought, without applied thought but with sustained thought and without applied thought and sustained thought . . .

At the moment of conception, dependent on one aggregate with applied thought and sustained thought, and (heart-)base, arise three aggregates and applied thought . . . dependent on two aggregates and (heart-)base, arise two aggregates and applied thought; dependent on aggregates with applied thought and sustained thought, and great primaries, arises kamma-produced matter; (dependent on) (heart-)base, (arise) aggregates and applied thought by dissociation condition; (dependent on) aggregates, (arises) kamma-produced matter by dissociation condition. (7)

18. (xxvii) Dependent on state without applied thought but with sustained thought and without applied thought and sustained thought, (arises) state with applied thought and sustained thought . . .

At the moment of conception, dependent on applied thought and (heart-)base, arise aggregates with applied thought and sustained thought; (dependent on) (heart-)base, (arise aggregates) by dissociation condition. (1)

(xxviii) Dependent on state without applied thought but with sustained thought and without applied thought and sustained thought, (arises) state without applied thought but with sustained thought . . .

(*a*) Dependent on one aggregate without applied thought but with sustained thought, and sustained thought, arise three aggregates . . . two aggregates and . . . (dependent on) (heart-)base, (arise aggregates) by dissociation condition;

(*b*) At the moment of conception, dependent on one aggregate without applied thought but with sustained thought, and sustained thought, arise three aggregates . . . two aggregates and . . . (dependent on) (heart-) base, (arise aggregates) by dissociation condition; at the moment of conception, dependent on one aggregate without applied thought but with sustained thought, and (heart-)base, arise three aggregates . . . two aggregates and . . . (dependent on) (heart-)base, (arise aggregates) by dissociation condition. (2)

(xxix) Dependent on state without applied thought but with sustained thought and without applied thought and sustained thought, (arises) state without applied thought and sustained thought . . .

(*a*) Dependent on aggregates without applied thought but with sustained thought, and sustained thought, arises mind-produced matter; (dependent on) aggregates and sustained thought, (arises mind-produced matter) by dissociation condition; dependent on aggregates without applied thought but with sustained thought, and great primaries, arises mind-produced matter; (dependent on) aggregates, (arises mind-produced matter) by dissociation condition; dependent on applied thought and great primaries, arises mind-produced matter; (dependent on) applied thought, (arises mind-produced matter) by dissociation condition;

(*b*) At the moment of conception, dependent on aggregates without applied thought but with sustained thought, and sustained thought, arises kamma-produced matter; (dependent on) aggregates and sustained thought, (arises kamma-produced matter) by dissociation condition; at the moment of conception, dependent on aggregates without applied thought but with sustained thought, and great primaries, arises kamma-produced matter; (dependent on) aggregates, (arises kamma-produced matter) by dissociation condition; at the moment of conception, dependent on applied thought and great primaries, arises kamma-produced matter; (dependent on) applied thought, (arises kamma-produced matter) by dissociation condition; at the moment of conception, dependent on aggregates without applied thought but with sustained thought, and (heart-)base, arises sustained thought; (dependent on) (heart-)base, (arise aggregates) by dissociation condition. (3)

(xxx) Dependent on state without applied thought but with sustained thought and without applied thought and sustained thought, arise states with applied thought and sustained thought and without applied thought and sustained thought by dissociation condition.

At the moment of conception, dependent on applied thought and (heart-)base, arise aggregates with applied thought and sustained thought; dependent on applied thought and great primaries, arises kamma-produced matter; (dependent on) (heart-)base, (arise) aggregates by dissociation condition; (dependent on) applied thought, (arises) kamma-produced matter by dissociation condition. (4)

(xxxi) Dependent on state without applied thought but with sustained thought and without applied thought and sustained thought, (arise) states without applied thought but with sustained thought and without applied thought and sustained thought . . .

(*a*) Dependent on one aggregate without applied thought but with sustained thought, and sustained thought, arise three aggregates and mind-produced matter . . . (dependent on) (heart-)base, (arise) aggregates by dissociation condition; (dependent on) aggregates and sustained thought, (arises) mind-produced matter by dissociation condition;

(*b*) At the moment of conception, dependent on one aggregate without applied thought but with sustained thought, and sustained thought, (arise) three aggregates and kamma-produced matter . . . (dependent on) (heart-)base, (arise) aggregates by dissociation condition; (dependent on) aggregates and sustained thought, (arises) kamma-produced matter by dissociation condition; at the moment of conception, dependent on one aggregate without applied thought but with sustained thought, and (heart-)base, arise three aggregates . . . two aggregates and . . . dependent on aggregates without applied thought but with sustained thought, and great primaries, arises kamma-produced matter; (dependent on) (heart-)base, (arise) aggregates by dissociation condition; (dependent on) aggregates, (arises) kamma-produced matter by dissociation condition; at the moment of conception, dependent on one aggregate without applied thought but with sustained thought, and (heart-)base, arise three aggregates and sustained thought . . . two aggregates and . . . (dependent on) (heart-)base, (arise aggregates) by dissociation condition. (5)

19. (xxxii) Dependent on state with applied thought and sustained thought and without applied thought but with sustained thought, arises state with applied thought and sustained thought . . .

(*a*) Dependent on one aggregate with applied thought and sustained thought, and applied thought, arise three aggregates . . . two aggregates and . . . (dependent on) (heart-)base, (arise aggregates) by dissociation condition;

(*b*) At the moment of conception . . . (dependent on) (heart-)base, (arise aggregates) by dissociation condition. (1)

(xxxiii) Dependent on state with applied thought and sustained thought and without applied thought but with sustained thought, arises state without applied thought and sustained thought . . .

(*a*) Dependent on aggregates with applied thought and sustained thought, and applied thought, arises mind-produced matter; (dependent on) aggregates and applied thought, (arises mind-produced matter) by dissociation condition;

(*b*) At the moment of conception . . . (dependent on) aggregates and applied thought, (arises kamma-produced matter) by dissociation condition. (2)

(xxxiv) Dependent on state with applied thought and sustained thought and without applied thought but with sustained thought, arise states with applied thought and sustained thought and without applied thought and sustained thought . . .

(*a*) Dependent on one aggregate with applied thought and sustained thought, and applied thought, arise three aggregates and mind-produced matter . . . two aggregates . . . (dependent on) (heart-)base, (arise) aggregates by dissociation condition; (dependent on) aggregates and applied thought, (arises) mind-produced matter by dissociation condition;

(*b*) At the moment of conception . . . (dependent on) (heart-)base, (arise) aggregates by dissociation condition; (dependent on) aggregates and applied thought, (arises) kamma-produced matter by dissociation condition. (3)

20. (xxxv) Dependent on state with applied thought and sustained thought, without applied thought but with sustained thought and without applied thought and sustained thought, arises state with applied thought and sustained thought . . .

At the moment of conception, dependent on one aggregate with applied thought and sustained thought, applied thought and (heart-)base, arise three aggregates . . . two aggregates . . . (dependent on) (heart-)base, (arise) aggregates by dissociation condition. (1)

(xxxvi) Dependent on state with applied thought and sustained thought, without applied thought but with sustained thought and without applied thought and sustained thought, arises state without applied thought and sustained thought . . .

(*a*) Dependent on aggregates with applied thought and sustained thought, applied thought and great primaries, arises mind-produced matter; (dependent on) aggregates and applied thought, (arises mind-produced matter) by dissociation condition;

(*b*) At the moment of conception . . . (dependent on) aggregates and applied thought, (arises kamma-produced matter) by dissociation condition. (2)

(xxxvii) Dependent on state with applied thought and sustained thought, without applied thought but with sustained thought and without applied thought and sustained thought, arise states with applied thought and sustained thought and without applied thought and sustained thought by dissociation condition.

At the moment of conception, dependent on one aggregate with applied thought and sustained thought, applied thought and (heart-) base, arise three aggregates . . . two aggregates and . . . dependent on aggregates with applied thought and sustained thought, applied thought and great primaries, arises kamma-produced matter; (dependent on) (heart-)base, (arise) aggregates by dissociation condition; (dependent on) aggregates and applied thought, (arises) kamma-produced matter by dissociation condition. (3)

Presence, Non-disappearance

21. Dependent on state with applied thought and sustained thought, arises state with applied thought and sustained thought by presence condition . . . by absence condition . . . by disappearance condition . . . by non-disappearance condition. (Abbreviated.)

1. CONDITIONS: POSITIVE (ii) ENUMERATION CHAPTER

By Ones

22. With root condition 37, object 21, predominance 23, proximity 21, contiguity 21, conascence 37, mutuality 28, dependence 37, strong-dependence 21, prenascence 11, repetition 11, kamma 37, resultant 37, nutriment, faculty, jhāna, path 37, association 21, dissociation 37, presence 37, absence 21, disappearance 21, non-disappearance 37.

By Twos

With root condition and object 21 . . . non-disappearance 37. (Abbreviated.)

(Enumerate in the same way as in Faultless Triplet.)

End of Positive

2. CONDITIONS: NEGATIVE (i) CLASSIFICATION CHAPTER

Not-root 33

23. (i) Dependent on state with applied thought and sustained thought, arises state with applied thought and sustained thought by not-root condition.

(*a*) Dependent on one rootless aggregate with applied thought and sustained thought (ahetukaṁ savitakka-savicāraṁ ekaṁ khandhaṁ), arise three aggregates . . . dependent on two aggregates, arise two aggregates;

(*b*) At the moment of rootless conception (ahetukapaṭisandhikkhaṇe) . . .

(*c*) Dependent on doubt-accompanied or restlessness-accompanied aggregates (vicikicchasahagate uddhaccasahagate khandhe), arises doubt-accompanied or restlessness-accompanied delusion. (1)

(ii) Dependent on state with applied thought and sustained thought, arises state without applied thought but with sustained thought by not-root condition.

(*a*) Dependent on rootless aggregates with applied thought and sustained thought, arises applied thought;

(*b*) At the moment of rootless conception . . . (2)

(iii) Dependent on state with applied thought and sustained thought, arises state without applied thought and sustained thought by not-root condition.

(*a*) Dependent on rootless aggregates with applied thought and sustained thought, arises mind-produced matter;

(*b*) At the moment of rootless conception . . . (3)

(iv) Dependent on state with applied thought and sustained thought, arise states with applied thought and sustained thought and without applied thought and sustained thought by not-root condition.

(*a*) Dependent on one rootless aggregate with applied thought and sustained thought, arise three aggregates and mind-produced matter . . . dependent on two aggregates, arise two aggregates and mind-produced matter;

(*b*) At the moment of rootless conception . . . (4)

(v) Dependent on state with applied thought and sustained thought, arise states without applied thought but with sustained thought and without applied thought and sustained thought by not-root condition.

(*a*) Dependent on rootless aggregates with applied thought and sustained thought, arise applied thought and mind-produced matter;

(*b*) At the moment of rootless conception . . . (5)

(vi) Dependent on state with applied thought and sustained thought, arise states with applied thought and sustained thought and without applied thought but with sustained thought by not-root condition.

(*a*) Dependent on one rootless aggregate with applied thought and sustained thought, arise three aggregates and applied thought . . . dependent on two aggregates, arise two aggregates and applied thought;

(*b*) At the moment of rootless conception . . . (6)

(vii) Dependent on state with applied thought and sustained thought, arise states with applied thought and sustained thought, without applied thought but with sustained thought and without applied thought and sustained thought by not-root condition.

(*a*) Dependent on one rootless aggregate with applied thought and sustained thought, arise three aggregates, applied thought and mind-produced matter . . .

(*b*) At the moment of rootless conception . . . (7)

24. (viii) Dependent on state without applied thought but with sustained thought, arises state with applied thought and sustained thought by not-root condition.

(*a*) Dependent on rootless applied thought, arise aggregates with applied thought and sustained thought;

(*b*) At the moment of rootless conception, dependent on applied thought, arise aggregates with applied thought and sustained thought;

(*c*) Dependent on doubt-accompanied or restlessness-accompanied applied thought, arises doubt-accompanied or restlessness-accompanied delusion. (1)

(ix) Dependent on state without applied thought but with sustained thought, arises state without applied thought and sustained thought by not-root condition.

(*a*) Dependent on rootless applied thought, arises mind-produced matter;

(*b*) At the moment of rootless conception, dependent on applied thought, arises kamma-produced matter. (2)

(x) Dependent on state without applied thought but with sustained thought, arise states with applied thought and sustained thought and without applied thought and sustained thought by not-root condition.

(*a*) Dependent on rootless applied thought, arise aggregates with applied thought and sustained thought and mind-produced matter;

(*b*) At the moment of rootless conception, dependent on applied thought, arise aggregates with applied thought and sustained thought and kamma-produced matter. (3)

(xi) Dependent on state without applied thought and sustained thought, arises state without applied thought and sustained thought by not-root condition.

(*a*) Dependent on one rootless aggregate without applied thought and sustained thought, arise three aggregates; dependent on three aggregates, arises one aggregate; dependent on two aggregates, arise two aggregates;

(*b*) Dependent on one great primary, arise three great primaries . . . dependent on great primaries, arise mind-produced and kamma-produced derived matter;

(*c*) External . . . nutriment-produced . . . temperature-produced . . . dependent on one great primary of non-percipient beings (asaññasatta) . . . dependent on great primaries, arises kamma-produced derived matter. (1)

(xii) Dependent on state without applied thought and sustained thought, arises state with applied thought and sustained thought by not-root condition.

At the moment of rootless conception, dependent on (heart-)base, arise aggregates with applied thought and sustained thought. (2)

(xiii) Dependent on state without applied thought and sustained thought, arises state without applied thought but with sustained thought by not-root condition.

At the moment of rootless conception, dependent on (heart-)base, arises applied thought. (3)

(xiv) Dependent on state without applied thought and sustained thought, arise states with applied thought and sustained thought and without applied thought and sustained thought by not-root condition.

At the moment of rootless conception, dependent on (heart-)base, arise aggregates with applied thought and sustained thought; dependent on great primaries, arises kamma-produced matter. (4)

(xv) Dependent on state without applied thought and sustained thought, arise states without applied thought but with sustained thought and without applied thought and sustained thought by not-root condition.

At the moment of rootless conception, dependent on (heart-)base, arises applied thought; dependent on great primaries, arises kamma-produced matter. (5)

(xvi) Dependent on state without applied thought and sustained thought, arise states with applied thought and sustained thought and without applied thought but with sustained thought by not-root condition.

At the moment of rootless conception, dependent on (heart-)base, arise aggregates with applied thought and sustained thought, and applied thought. (6)

(xvii) Dependent on state without applied thought and sustained thought, arise states with applied thought and sustained thought, without applied thought but with sustained thought and without applied thought and sustained thought by not-root condition.

At the moment of rootless conception, dependent on (heart-)base, arise aggregates with applied thought and sustained thought, and applied thought; dependent on great primaries, arises kamma-produced matter. (7)

25. (xviii) Dependent on state with applied thought and sustained thought and without applied thought and sustained thought, arises state with applied thought and sustained thought by not-root condition.

At the moment of rootless conception, dependent on one aggregate with applied thought and sustained thought, and (heart-)base, arise three aggregates . . . dependent on two aggregates and (heart-)base, arise two aggregates. (1)

(xix) Dependent on state with applied thought and sustained thought and without applied thought and sustained thought, arises state without applied thought but with sustained thought by not-root condition.

At the moment of rootless conception, dependent on aggregates with applied thought and sustained thought, and (heart-)base, arises applied thought. (2)

(xx) Dependent on state with applied thought and sustained thought and without applied thought and sustained thought, arises state without applied thought and sustained thought by not-root condition.

(*a*) Dependent on rootless aggregates with applied thought and sustained thought, and great primaries, arises mind-produced matter;

(*b*) At the moment of rootless conception, dependent on aggregates with applied thought and sustained thought, and great primaries, arises kamma-produced matter. (3)

(xxi) Dependent on state with applied thought and sustained thought and without applied thought and sustained thought, arise states with applied thought and sustained thought and without applied thought and sustained thought by not-root condition.

At the moment of rootless conception, dependent on one aggregate with applied thought and sustained thought, and (heart-)base, arise three aggregates . . . dependent on two aggregates and (heart-)base, arise two aggregates; dependent on aggregates with applied thought and sustained thought, and great primaries, arises kamma-produced matter. (4).

(xxii) Dependent on state with applied thought and sustained thought and without applied thought and sustained thought, arise states without applied thought but with sustained thought and without applied thought and sustained thought by not-root condition.

At the moment of rootless conception, dependent on aggregates with applied thought and sustained thought, and (heart-)base, arises applied thought; dependent on aggregates with applied thought and sustained thought, and great primaries, arises kamma-produced matter. (5)

(xxiii) Dependent on state with applied thought and sustained thought and without applied thought and sustained thought, arise states with applied thought and sustained thought and without applied thought but with sustained thought by not-root condition.

At the moment of rootless conception, dependent on one aggregate with applied thought and sustained thought, and (heart-)base, arise three aggregates and applied thought . . . dependent on two aggregates and (heart-)base, arise two aggregates and applied thought. (6)

(xxiv) Dependent on state with applied thought and sustained thought and without applied thought and sustained thought, arise states with applied thought and sustained thought, without applied thought but with sustained thought and without applied thought and sustained thought by not-root condition.

At the moment of rootless conception, dependent on one aggregate with applied thought and sustained thought, and (heart-)base, arise three aggregates and applied thought . . . dependent on two aggregates and (heart-)base, arise two aggregates and applied thought; dependent on aggregates with applied thought and sustained thought, and great primaries, arises kamma-produced matter. (7)

26. (xxv) Dependent on state without applied thought but with sustained thought and without applied thought and sustained thought, arises state with applied thought and sustained thought by not-root condition.

At the moment of rootless conception, dependent on applied thought and (heart-)base, arise aggregates with applied thought and sustained thought. (1)

(xxvi) Dependent on state without applied thought but with sustained thought and without applied thought and sustained thought, arises state without applied thought and sustained thought by not-root condition.

(*a*) Dependent on rootless applied thought and great primaries, arises mind-produced matter;

(*b*) At the moment of rootless conception, dependent on applied thought and great primaries, arises kamma-produced matter. (2)

(xxvii) Dependent on state without applied thought but with

sustained thought and without applied thought and sustained thought, arise states with applied thought and sustained thought and without applied thought and sustained thought by not-root condition.

At the moment of rootless conception, dependent on applied thought and (heart-)base, arise aggregates with applied thought and sustained thought; dependent on applied thought and great primaries, arises kamma-produced matter. (3)

27. (xxviii) Dependent on state with applied thought and sustained thought and without applied thought but with sustained thought, arises state with applied thought and sustained thought by not-root condition.

(*a*) Dependent on one rootless aggregate with applied thought and sustained thought, and applied thought, arise three aggregates . . . dependent on two aggregates and applied thought, arise two aggregates;

(*b*) At the moment of rootless conception, dependent on one aggregate with applied thought and sustained thought, and applied thought, arise three aggregates . . . dependent on two aggregates and applied thought, arise two aggregates;

(*c*) Dependent on doubt-accompanied or restlessness-accompanied aggregates and applied thought, arises doubt-accompanied or restlessness-accompanied delusion. (1)

(xxix) Dependent on state with applied thought and sustained thought and without applied thought but with sustained thought, arises state without applied thought and sustained thought by not-root condition.

(*a*) Dependent on rootless aggregates with applied thought and sustained thought, and applied thought, arises mind-produced matter;

(*b*) At the moment of rootless conception . . . (2)

(xxx) Dependent on state with applied thought and sustained thought and without applied thought but with sustained thought, arise states with applied thought and sustained thought and without applied thought and sustained thought by not-root condition.

(*a*) Dependent on one rootless aggregate with applied thought and sustained thought, and applied thought, arise three aggregates and mind-produced matter . . . dependent on two aggregates and applied thought, arise two aggregates and mind-produced matter;

(*b*) At the moment of rootless conception . . . (3)

28. (xxxi) Dependent on state with applied thought and sustained thought, without applied thought but with sustained thought and without applied thought and sustained thought, arises state with applied

thought and sustained thought by not-root condition.

At the moment of rootless conception, dependent on one aggregate with applied thought and sustained thought, applied thought and (heart-)base, arise three aggregates . . . dependent on two aggregates, applied thought and (heart-)base, arise two aggregates. (1)

(xxxii) Dependent on state with applied thought and sustained thought, without applied thought but with sustained thought and without applied thought and sustained thought, arises state without applied thought and sustained thought by not-root condition.

(*a*) Dependent on rootless aggregates with applied thought and sustained thought, applied thought and great primaries, arises mind-produced matter;

(*b*) At the moment of rootless conception . . . (2)

(xxxiii) Dependent on state with applied thought and sustained thought, without applied thought but with sustained thought and without applied thought and sustained thought, arise states with applied thought and sustained thought and without applied thought and sustained thought by not-root condition.

At the moment of rootless conception, dependent on one aggregate with applied thought and sustained thought, applied thought and (heart-)base, arise three aggregates . . . dependent on two aggregates, applied thought and (heart-)base, arise two aggregates; dependent on aggregates with applied thought and sustained thought, applied thought and great primaries, arises kamma-produced matter. (3)

Not-object 7

29. (i) Dependent on state with applied thought and sustained thought, arises state without applied thought and sustained thought by not-object condition.

(*a*) Dependent on aggregates with applied thought and sustained thought, arises mind-produced matter;

(*b*) At the moment of conception, dependent on aggregates with applied thought and sustained thought, arises kamma-produced matter. (1)

(ii) Dependent on state without applied thought but with sustained thought, arises state without applied thought and sustained thought by not-object condition.

(*a*) Dependent on aggregates without applied thought but with sustained thought, arises mind-produced matter; dependent on applied thought, arises mind-produced matter;

(*b*) At the moment of conception, dependent on aggregates without applied thought but with sustained thought, arises kamma-produced matter; at the moment of conception, dependent on applied thought, arises kamma-produced matter. (1)

(iii) Dependent on state without applied thought and sustained thought, arises state without applied thought and sustained thought by not-object condition.

(*a*) Dependent on aggregates without applied thought and sustained thought, arises mind-produced matter; dependent on sustained thought, arises mind-produced matter;

(*b*) At the moment of conception, dependent on aggregates without applied thought and sustained thought, arises kamma-produced matter; dependent on sustained thought, arises kamma-produced matter; dependent on aggregates, arises (heart-)base; dependent on sustained thought, arises (heart-)base;

(*c*) Dependent on one great primary . . .

(*d*) External . . . nutriment-produced . . . temperature-produced . . . dependent on one great primary of non-percipient beings . . . (1)

30. (iv) Dependent on state with applied thought and sustained thought and without applied thought and sustained thought, arises state without applied thought and sustained thought by not-object condition.

(*a*) Dependent on aggregates with applied thought and sustained thought and great primaries, arises mind-produced matter;

(*b*) At the moment of conception, dependent on aggregates with applied thought and sustained thought and great primaries, arises kamma-produced matter. (1)

(v) Dependent on state without applied thought but with sustained thought and without applied thought and sustained thought, arises state without applied thought and sustained thought by not-object condition.

(*a*) Dependent on aggregates without applied thought but with sustained thought, and sustained thought, arises mind-produced matter; dependent on aggregates without applied thought but with sustained thought, and great primaries, arises mind-produced matter; dependent on applied thought and great primaries, arises mind-produced matter;

(*b*) At the moment of conception, dependent on aggregates without applied thought but with sustained thought, and sustained thought . . . kamma-produced matter. (1)

(vi) Dependent on state with applied thought and sustained thought and without applied thought but with sustained thought, arises state without applied thought and sustained thought by not-object condition.

(*a*) Dependent on aggregates with applied thought and sustained thought, and applied thought, arises mind-produced matter;

(*b*) At the moment of conception . . . (1)

(vii) Dependent on state with applied thought and sustained thought, without applied thought but with sustained thought and without applied thought and sustained thought, arises state without applied thought and sustained thought by not-object condition.

(*a*) Dependent on aggregates with applied thought and sustained thought, applied thought and great primaries, arises mind-produced matter;

(*b*) At the moment of conception . . . kamma-produced matter. (1)

Not-predominance 37

31. (i)-(vii) Dependent on state with applied thought and sustained thought, arises state with applied thought and sustained thought by not-predominance condition . . . seven.

(viii) Dependent on state without applied thought but with sustained thought, arises state without applied thought but with sustained thought by not-predominance condition.

(*a*) Dependent on aggregates without applied thought but with sustained thought, arises predominance without applied thought but with sustained thought; dependent on one resultant aggregate without applied thought but with sustained thought, arise three aggregates . . .

(*b*) At the moment of conception . . . (1)

(ix) Dependent on state without applied thought but with sustained thought, arises state with applied thought and sustained thought by not-predominance condition.

(*a*) Dependent on applied thought, arise aggregates with applied thought and sustained thought;

(*b*) At the moment of conception . . . (2)

(x) Dependent on state without applied thought but with sustained thought, arises state without applied thought and sustained thought by not-predominance condition.

(*a*) Dependent on resultant aggregates without applied thought but with sustained thought, arise sustained thought and mind-produced matter;

(*b*) At the moment of conception . . . (3)

(xi) Dependent on state without applied thought but with sustained thought, arise states with applied thought and sustained thought and without applied thought and sustained thought by not-predominance condition.

(*a*) Dependent on applied thought, arise aggregates with applied thought and sustained thought and mind-produced matter;

(*b*) At the moment of conception . . . (4)

(xii) Dependent on state without applied thought but with sustained thought, arise states without applied thought but with sustained thought and without applied thought and sustained thought by not-predominance condition.

(*a*) Dependent on one resultant aggregate without applied thought but with sustained thought, arise three aggregates, sustained thought and mind-produced matter . . .

(*b*) At the moment of conception . . . (5)

32. (xiii) Dependent on state without applied thought and sustained thought, arises state without applied thought and sustained thought by not-predominance condition.

(*a*) Dependent on aggregates without applied thought and sustained thought, arises predominance without applied thought and sustained thought; dependent on one resultant aggregate without applied thought and sustained thought, arise three aggregates . . .

(*b*) At the moment of conception . . . (1)

(xiv) Dependent on state without applied thought and sustained thought, arises state with applied thought and sustained thought by not-predominance condition.

At the moment of conception, dependent on (heart-)base, arise aggregates with applied thought and sustained thought. (2)

(xv) Dependent on state without applied thought and sustained thought, arises state without applied thought but with sustained thought by not-predominance condition.

(*a*) Dependent on sustained thought, arises predominance without applied thought but with sustained thought; dependent on resultant sustained thought, arise aggregates without applied thought but with sustained thought;

(*b*) At the moment of conception . . . (3)

(xvi)–(xxii) Dependent on state without applied thought and sustained thought . . . seven.

33. (xxiii)–(xxix) Dependent on state with applied thought and sustained thought and without applied thought and sustained thought . . . seven. (Abbreviated.)

(xxx)–(xxxvii) Dependent on state without applied thought but with sustained thought and without applied thought and sustained thought, arises state with applied thought and sustained thought . . . arises state without applied thought but with sustained thought by not-predominance condition.

Dependent on aggregates without applied thought but with sustained thought, and sustained thought, arises predominance without applied thought but with sustained thought; dependent on one resultant aggregate without applied thought but with sustained thought, and sustained thought . . . (Abbreviated.)

Not-proximity, etc. 7

34. Dependent on state with applied thought and sustained thought, arises state without applied thought and sustained thought by not-proximity condition . . . by not-contiguity condition . . . by not-mutuality condition . . . by not-strong-dependence condition. (The same as not-object) . . .

Not-prenascence 37

35. (i)-(vii) Dependent on state with applied thought and sustained thought, arises state with applied thought and sustained thought by not-prenascence condition . . . seven.

(viii) Dependent on state without applied thought but with sustained thought, arises state without applied thought but with sustained thought by not-prenascence condition.

(*a*) In the immaterial plane (arūpe), dependent on one aggregate without applied thought but with sustained thought . . .

(*b*) At the moment of conception . . . (1)

(ix) Dependent on state without applied thought but with sustained thought, arises state with applied thought and sustained thought by not-prenascence condition.

(*a*) In the immaterial plane, dependent on applied thought, arise aggregates with applied thought and sustained thought;

(*b*) At the moment of conception . . . (2)

(x) Dependent on state without applied thought but with sustained thought, arises state without applied thought and sustained thought by not-prenascence condition.

(*a*) In the immaterial plane, dependent on aggregates without applied thought but with sustained thought, arises sustained thought; dependent on aggregates without applied thought but with sustained thought, arises mind-produced matter; dependent on applied thought, arises mind-produced matter;

(*b*) At the moment of conception . . . (3)

(xi) Dependent on state without applied thought but with sustained thought, arise states with applied thought and sustained thought and without applied thought and sustained thought by not-prenascence condition.

At the moment of conception, dependent on applied thought, arise aggregates with applied thought and sustained thought and kamma-produced matter. (4)

(xii) Dependent on state without applied thought but with sustained thought, arise states without applied thought but with sustained thought and without applied thought and sustained thought by not-prenascence condition.

(*a*) In the immaterial plane, dependent on one aggregate without applied thought but with sustained thought, arise three aggregates and sustained thought . . .

(*b*) At the moment of conception . . . (5)

36. (xiii) Dependent on state without applied thought and sustained thought, arises state without applied thought and sustained thought by not-prenascence condition.

(*a*) In the immaterial plane, dependent on one aggregate without applied thought and sustained thought, arise three aggregates . . . dependent on aggregates without applied thought and sustained thought, arises mind-produced matter; dependent on sustained thought, arises mind-produced matter;

(*b*) At the moment of conception . . . (1)

(xiv) Dependent on state without applied thought and sustained thought, arises state with applied thought and sustained thought by not-prenascence condition.

At the moment of conception, dependent on (heart-)base, arise aggregates with applied thought and sustained thought. (2)

(xv)-(xix) Dependent on state without applied thought and sustained thought, arises state without applied thought but with sustained thought by not-prenascence condition.

(*a*) In the immaterial plane, dependent on sustained thought, arise aggregates without applied thought but with sustained thought;

(*b*) At the moment of conception. (Abbreviated.) (7)

(xx)-(xxvi) Dependent on state with applied thought and sustained thought and without applied thought and sustained thought . . . seven.

37. (xxvii)–(xxxiii) Dependent on state without applied thought but with sustained thought and without applied thought and sustained thought, arises state without applied thought but with sustained thought by not-prenascence condition.

(*a*) In the immaterial plane, dependent on one aggregate without applied thought but with sustained thought, and sustained thought, arise three aggregates . . .

(*b*) At the moment of conception. (Abbreviated.) (7)

(xxxiv)–(xxxvii) Dependent on state without applied thought but with sustained thought and without applied thought and sustained thought, arise states without applied thought but with sustained thought and without applied thought and sustained thought . . .

At the moment of conception. (Abbreviated.)

(With not-prenascence as reference, there is purely the immaterial (plane). Likewise do the immaterial (here).)

Not-postnascence, etc. 37

38. Dependent on state with applied thought and sustained thought, arises state with applied thought and sustained thought by not-postnascence condition . . . by not-repetition condition . . . seven.

Dependent on state without applied thought but with sustained thought, arises state without applied thought but with sustained thought by not-repetition condition.

Dependent on one resultant aggregate without applied thought but with sustained thought. (Abbreviated.) (5)

Dependent on state without applied thought and sustained thought, arises state without applied thought and sustained thought by not-repetition condition.

Dependent on one resultant aggregate without applied thought and sustained thought. (Abbreviated.)

(With not-repetition as reference, resultant is to be taken in "without applied thought but with sustained thought" in the same way as in not-prenascence. In "without applied thought but with sustained thought" resultant is to be taken according to the nature of "without applied thought but with sustained thought".)

Not-kamma 7

39. (i) Dependent on state with applied thought and sustained thought, arises state with applied thought and sustained thought by not-kamma

condition.

Dependent on aggregates with applied thought and sustained thought, arises volition with applied thought and sustained thought. (1)

(ii) Dependent on state without applied thought but with sustained thought, arises state without applied thought but with sustained thought by not-kamma condition.

Dependent on aggregates without applied thought but with sustained thought, arises volition without applied thought but with sustained thought. (1)

(iii) Dependent on state without applied thought but with sustained thought, arises state with applied thought and sustained thought by not-kamma condition.

Dependent on applied thought, arises volition with applied thought and sustained thought. (2)

(iv) Dependent on state without applied thought and sustained thought, arises state without applied thought and sustained thought by not-kamma condition.

(*a*) Dependent on aggregates without applied thought and sustained thought, arises volition without applied thought and sustained thought;

(*b*) External . . . nutriment-produced . . . dependent on one temperature-produced (utusamuṭṭhāna) great primary . . . (1)

(v) Dependent on state without applied thought and sustained thought, arises state without applied thought but with sustained thought by not-kamma condition.

Dependent on sustained thought, arises volition without applied thought but with sustained thought. (2)

(vi) Dependent on state without applied thought but with sustained thought and without applied thought and sustained thought, arises state without applied thought but with sustained thought by not-kamma condition.

Dependent on aggregates without applied thought but with sustained thought, and sustained thought, arises volition without applied thought but with sustained thought. (1)

(vii) Dependent on state with applied thought and sustained thought and without applied thought but with sustained thought, arises state with applied thought and sustained thought by not-kamma condition.

Dependent on aggregates with applied thought and sustained thought, and applied thought, arises volition with applied thought and sustained thought. (1)

Not-resultant, etc.

40. Dependent on state with applied thought and sustained thought, arises state with applied thought and sustained thought by not-resultant condition . . . by not-nutriment condition. External . . . temperature-produced . . . by not-faculty condition. External . . . nutriment-produced . . . temperature-produced . . . dependent on great primaries of non-percipient beings, arises physical life-faculty . . . by not-jhāna condition. (Dependent on) one five-fold-consciousness-accompanied aggregate . . . External . . . nutriment-produced . . . temperature-produced . . . non-percipient beings . . . by not-path condition . . . by not-association condition . . .

Not-dissociation 11

41. (i) . . . by not-dissociation condition.

In the immaterial plane, dependent on one aggregate with applied thought and sustained thought, arise three aggregates . . . dependent on two aggregates, arise two aggregates. (1)

(ii) Dependent on state with applied thought and sustained thought, arises state without applied thought but with sustained thought by not-dissociation condition.

In the immaterial plane, dependent on aggregates with applied thought and sustained thought, arises applied thought. (2)

(iii) Dependent on state with applied thought and sustained thought, arise states with applied thought and sustained thought and without applied thought but with sustained thought by not-dissociation condition.

In the immaterial plane, dependent on one aggregate with applied thought and sustained thought, arise three aggregates and applied thought . . . dependent on two aggregates, arise two aggregates and applied thought. (3)

42. (iv) Dependent on state without applied thought but with sustained thought, arises state without applied thought but with sustained thought by not-dissociation condition.

In the immaterial plane, dependent on one aggregate without applied thought but with sustained thought, arise three aggregates . . . dependent on two aggregates, arise two aggregates. (1)

(v) Dependent on state without applied thought but with sustained thought, arises state with applied thought and sustained thought by not-dissociation condition.

In the immaterial plane, dependent on applied thought, arise aggregates with applied thought and sustained thought. (2)

(vi) Dependent on state without applied thought but with sustained thought, arises state without applied thought and sustained thought by not-dissociation condition.

In the immaterial plane, dependent on aggregates without applied thought but with sustained thought, arises sustained thought. (3)

(vii) Dependent on state without applied thought but with sustained thought, arise states without applied thought but with sustained thought and without applied thought and sustained thought by not-dissociation condition.

In the immaterial plane, dependent on one aggregate without applied thought but with sustained thought, arise three aggregates and sustained thought . . . dependent on two aggregates, arise two aggregates and sustained thought. (4)

(viii) Dependent on state without applied thought and sustained thought, arises state with applied thought and sustained thought by not-dissociation condition.

(*a*) In the immaterial plane, dependent on one aggregate without applied thought and sustained thought, arise three aggregates . . . dependent on two aggregates, arise two aggregates;

(*b*) External . . . nutriment-produced . . . temperature-produced . . . dependent on one great primary of non-percipient beings . . . (1)

(ix) Dependent on state without applied thought and sustained thought, arises state without applied thought but with sustained thought by not-dissociation condition.

In the immaterial plane, dependent on sustained thought, arise aggregates without applied thought but with sustained thought. (2)

(x) Dependent on state without applied thought but with sustained thought and without applied thought and sustained thought, arises state without applied thought but with sustained thought by not-dissociation condition.

In the immaterial plane, dependent on one aggregate without applied thought but with sustained thought, and sustained thought, arise three aggregates . . . dependent on two aggregates and sustained thought, arise two aggregates. (1)

(xi) Dependent on state with applied thought and sustained thought and without applied thought but with sustained thought, arises state with applied thought and sustained thought by not-dissociation condition.

In the immaterial plane, dependent on one aggregate with applied thought and sustained thought, and applied thought, arise three aggregates . . . dependent on two aggregates and applied thought, arise two aggregates. (1)

Not-absence 7, Not-disappearance 7

43. Dependent on state with applied thought and sustained thought, arises state without applied thought and sustained thought by not-absence condition . . . by not-disappearance condition . . . (Abbreviated.)

2. CONDITIONS: NEGATIVE (ii) ENUMERATION CHAPTER

Numbers (of Answers)

By Ones

44. With not-root 33, not-object 7, not-predominance 37, not-proximity 7, not-contiguity 7, not-mutuality 7, not-strong-dependence 7, not-prenascence 37, not-postnascence 37, not-repetition 37, not-kamma 7, not-resultant 23, not-nutriment 1, not-faculty 1, not-jhāna 1, not-path 33, not-association 7, not-dissociation 11, not-absence 7, not-disappearance 7 . . . (Abbreviated.)

(Enumerate in the same way as in the Negative Enumeration of the Faultless Triplet.)

End of Negative

3. CONDITIONS: POSITIVE-NEGATIVE

(Root By Twos)

45. With root condition, but not-object 7 . . . not-disappearance 7.

(Enumerate in the same way as in the Positive-Negative Enumeration of the Faultless Triplet.)

4. CONDITIONS: NEGATIVE-POSITIVE

Not-root By Twos

46. With not-root condition, object 14, proximity, contiguity 14, conascence 33, mutuality 22, dependence 33, strong-dependence 14, prenascence 6, repetition 5, kamma 33 . . . jhāna 33, path 3, association 14, dissociation 33 . . . not-disappearance 33 . . . (Abbreviated.)

(Enumerate in the same way as in the Negative-Positive enumeration of the Faultless Triplet.)

End of "DEPENDENT" CHAPTER

(The "Conascent" Chapter should also be done in the same way as the "Dependent" Chapter.)

6. APPLIED THOUGHT TRIPLET III. "CONDITIONED" CHAPTER

1. CONDITIONS: POSITIVE (i) CLASSIFICATION CHAPTER

Root 37

47. (i)-(vii) Conditioned by state with applied thought and sustained thought (savitakka-savicāraṁ dhammaṁ paccayā), arises state with applied thought and sustained thought by root condition.

Conditioned by one aggregate with applied thought and sustained thought, arise three aggregates . . . two aggregates . . . seven.

(viii)-(xii) Conditioned by state without applied thought but with sustained thought . . . five. (The same as in the "Dependent" Chapter.)

(xiii) Conditioned by state without applied thought and sustained thought, arises state without applied thought and sustained thought by root condition.

(*a*) Conditioned by one aggregate without applied thought and sustained thought, arise three aggregates and mind-produced matter . . . conditioned by two aggregates . . . conditioned by sustained thought, arises mind-produced matter;

(*b*) At the moment of conception . . . conditioned by (heart-)base, arise aggregates without applied thought and sustained thought; conditioned by (heart-)base, arises sustained thought. (1)

(xiv) Conditioned by state without applied thought and sustained thought, arises state with applied thought and sustained thought . . .

(*a*) Conditioned by (heart-)base, arise aggregates with applied thought and sustained thought;

(*b*) At the moment of conception . . . (2)

(xv) Conditioned by state without applied thought and sustained thought, arises state without applied thought but with sustained thought . . .

(*a*) Conditioned by sustained thought, arise aggregates without applied thought but with sustained thought; conditioned by (heart-)base, arise aggregates without applied thought but with sustained thought; conditioned by (heart-)base, arises applied thought;

(*b*) At the moment of conception . . . (3)

(xvi) Conditioned by state without applied thought and sustained thought, arise states with applied thought and sustained thought and without applied thought and sustained thought . . .

(*a*) Conditioned by (heart-)base, arise aggregates with applied thought and sustained thought; conditioned by great primaries, arises mind-produced matter;

(*b*) At the moment of conception . . . (4)

(xvii) Conditioned by state without applied thought and sustained thought, (arise) states without applied thought but with sustained thought and without applied thought and sustained thought . . .

(*a*) Conditioned by sustained thought, arise aggregates without applied thought but with sustained thought and mind-produced matter; conditioned by (heart-)base, arise aggregates without applied thought but with sustained thought; conditioned by great primaries, arises mind-produced matter; conditioned by (heart-)base, arises applied thought; conditioned by great primaries, arises mind-produced matter; conditioned by (heart-)base, arise aggregates without applied thought but with sustained thought, and sustained thought;

(*b*) At the moment of conception . . . (5)

(xviii) Conditioned by state without applied thought and sustained thought, (arise) states with applied thought and sustained thought and without applied thought but with sustained thought . . .

(*a*) Conditioned by (heart-)base, arise aggregates with applied thought and sustained thought, and applied thought;

(*b*) At the moment of conception . . . (6)

(xix) Conditioned by state without applied thought and sustained thought, (arise) states with applied thought and sustained thought, without applied thought but with sustained thought and without applied thought and sustained thought . . .

(*a*) Conditioned by (heart-)base, arise aggregates with applied thought and sustained thought, and applied thought; conditioned by great primaries, arises mind-produced matter;

(*b*) At the moment of conception . . . (7)

48. (xx)–(xxvi) Conditioned by state with applied thought and sustained thought and without applied thought and sustained thought, (arises) state with applied thought and sustained thought . . .

(*a*) Conditioned by one aggregate with applied thought and sustained thought, and (heart-)base, arise three aggregates . . . two aggregates . . .

(*b*) At the moment of conception . . .

Conditioned by state with applied thought and sustained thought and without applied thought and sustained thought, (arises) state without applied thought but with sustained thought . . . (Do seven questions for "during life" and "at the moment of conception" in the first examples.)

(xxvii) Conditioned by state without applied thought but with sustained thought and without applied thought and sustained thought, (arises) state with applied thought and sustained thought . . .

(*a*) Conditioned by applied thought and (heart-)base, arise aggregates with applied thought and sustained thought;

(*b*) At the moment of conception . . . (1)

(xxviii) Conditioned by state without applied thought but with sustained thought and without applied thought and sustained thought, (arises) state without applied thought but with sustained thought . . .

(*a*) Conditioned by one aggregate without applied thought but with sustained thought, and sustained thought, arise three aggregates . . . conditioned by one aggregate without applied thought but with sustained thought, and (heart-)base, arise three aggregates . . .

(*b*) At the moment of conception, conditioned by one aggregate without applied thought but with sustained thought, and sustained thought, arise three aggregates . . . at the moment of conception, conditioned by one aggregate without applied thought but with sustained thought, and (heart-)base, arise three aggregates . . . (2)

(xxix) Conditioned by state without applied thought but with sustained thought and without applied thought and sustained thought, arises state without applied thought and sustained thought . . .

(*a*) Conditioned by aggregates without applied thought but with sustained thought, and sustained thought, arises mind-produced matter; conditioned by aggregates without applied thought but with sustained thought, and great primaries, arises mind-produced matter; conditioned by applied thought and great primaries, arises mind-produced matter; conditioned by aggregates without applied thought but with sustained thought, and (heart-)base, arises sustained thought;

(*b*) [In the same way (there are) four (questions) for "at the moment of conception".] (3)

(xxx) Conditioned by state without applied thought but with

sustained thought and without applied thought and sustained thought, arise states with applied thought and sustained thought and without applied thought and sustained thought . . .

(*a*) Conditioned by applied thought and (heart-)base, arise aggregates with applied thought and sustained thought; conditioned by applied thought and great primaries, arises mind-produced matter;

(*b*) At the moment of conception . . . (4)

(xxxi)–(xxxv) Conditioned by state without applied thought but with sustained thought and without applied thought and sustained thought, arise states without applied thought but with sustained thought and without applied thought and sustained thought . . .

(*a*) Conditioned by one aggregate without applied thought but with sustained thought, and sustained thought, arise three aggregates and mind-produced matter . . . conditioned by one aggregate without applied but with sustained thought, and (heart-)base, arise three aggregates . . . conditioned by aggregates without applied thought but with sustained thought, and great primaries, arises mind-produced matter; conditioned by one aggregate without applied thought but with sustained thought, and (heart-)base, arise three aggregates and sustained thought . . .

(*b*) At the moment of conception . . . three aggregates . . . (5)

(xxxvi)–(xxxvii) Expand "during life" and "at the moment of conception" in the remaining two combinations.)

End of Root Condition

(Expand "Conditioned" Chapter after considering root condition. Enumerate in the same way as in the "Dependent" (Chapter). Predominance 37, prenascence and repetition 21. This is the difference here.)

2. CONDITIONS: NEGATIVE

49. In Negative—with not-root 33 questions; in seven places extract seven delusions in reference section only. Not-object 7; extract mind-produced matter.

Not-predominance 37

50. (i)–(vii) Do seven questions for not-predominance with the reference "with applied thought and sustained thought".

(viii)–(xii) Conditioned by state without applied thought but with sustained thought, arises state without applied thought but with sustained thought by not-predominance condition.

(*a*) Conditioned by aggregates without applied thought but with sustained thought, arises predominance without applied thought but with sustained thought; conditioned by one resultant aggregate without applied thought but with sustained thought, arise three aggregates . . .

(*b*) At the moment of conception . . . (1)

Conditioned by state without applied thought but with sustained thought . . . (As in the method of the "Dependent", so do 5 questions.)

51. (xiii) Conditioned by state without applied thought and sustained thought, arises state without applied thought and sustained thought . . .

(*a*) Conditioned by aggregates without applied thought and sustained thought, arises predominance without applied thought and sustained thought; conditioned by one resultant aggregate without applied thought and sustained thought, arise three aggregates and mind-produced matter . . . conditioned by resultant sustained thought, arises mind-produced matter;

(*b*) At the moment of conception . . . conditioned by (heart-)base, arises predominance without applied thought and sustained thought; conditioned by (heart-)base, arise resultant aggregates without applied thought and sustained thought, and sustained thought . . . (1)

(xiv) Conditioned by state without applied thought and sustained thought, (arises) state with applied thought and sustained thought . . .

(*a*) Conditioned by (heart-)base, arise aggregates with applied thought and sustained thought;

(*b*) At the moment of conception . . . (2)

(xv) Conditioned by state without applied thought and sustained thought, (arises) state without applied thought but with sustained thought . . .

(*a*) Conditioned by sustained thought, arises predominance without applied thought but with sustained thought; conditioned by (heart-) base, arises predominance without applied thought but with sustained thought; conditioned by resultant sustained thought, arise aggregates without applied thought but with sustained thought; conditioned by (heart-)base, arise resultant aggregates without applied thought but with sustained thought;

(*b*) At the moment of conception . . . (3)

(xvi) Conditioned by state without applied thought and sustained thought, (arise) states with applied thought and sustained thought and without applied thought and sustained thought . . .

(*a*) Conditioned by (heart-)base, arise aggregates with applied thought and sustained thought; conditioned by great primaries, arises mind-produced matter;

(*b*) At the moment of conception . . . (4)

(xvii) Conditioned by state without applied thought and sustained thought, (arise) states without applied thought but with sustained thought and without applied thought and sustained thought . . .

(*a*) Conditioned by resultant sustained thought, arise aggregates without applied thought but with sustained thought and mind-produced matter; conditioned by (heart-)base, arise resultant aggregates without applied thought but with sustained thought; conditioned by great primaries, arises mind-produced matter; conditioned by (heart-)base, arises applied thought; conditioned by great primaries, arises mind-produced matter; conditioned by (heart-)base, arise resultant aggregates without applied thought but with sustained thought, and sustained thought;

(*b*) At the moment of conception . . . (5)

(xviii)-(xix) Conditioned by state without applied thought and sustained thought, (arise) states with applied thought and sustained thought and without applied thought but with sustained thought . . .

(*a*) Conditioned by (heart-)base, arise aggregates with applied thought and sustained thought, and applied thought;

(*b*) At the moment of conception . . . (6) (Do seven questions in full in the first combination.)

52. (xx) Conditioned by state without applied thought but with sustained thought and without applied thought and sustained thought, arises state with applied thought and sustained thought . . .

(*a*) Conditioned by applied thought and (heart-)base, arise aggregates with applied thought and sustained thought;

(*b*) At the moment of conception . . .

(xxi)-(xxxvii) Conditioned by state without applied thought but with sustained thought and without applied thought and sustained thought, arises state without applied thought but with sustained thought . . .

(*a*) Conditioned by aggregates without applied thought but with sustained thought, and sustained thought, arises predominance without applied thought but with sustained thought; conditioned by aggregates without applied thought but with sustained thought, and (heart-)base, arises predominance without applied thought but with sustained thought; conditioned by one resultant aggregate without applied thought but with sustained thought, and sustained thought . . . conditioned by one resultant aggregate without applied thought but with sustained thought, and (heart-)base, arise three aggregates . . .

(Make five questions for "at the moment of conception". When it comes to "without applied thought but with sustained thought" take resultant there. Make 37 questions in not-predominance.)

Not-proximity, etc.

53. Also not-proximity, not-contiguity, not-mutuality and not-strong-dependence have seven questions with materiality only. Not-prenascence 37: the same as the Negative in the "Dependent" Chapter. Not-post-nascence 37; also in not-repetition it is the same. When it comes to "without applied thought but with sustained thought" also, take resultant.

Not-kamma 11

54. (i) Conditioned by state with applied thought and sustained thought, arises state with applied thought and sustained thought by not-kamma condition.

Conditioned by aggregates with applied thought and sustained thought, arises volition with applied thought and sustained thought. (1)

(ii) Conditioned by state without applied thought but with sustained thought, (arises) state without applied thought but with sustained thought . . .

Conditioned by aggregates without applied thought but with sustained thought, arises volition without applied thought but with sustained thought.

(iii) . . . state with applied thought and sustained thought . . .

Conditioned by applied thought, arises volition with applied thought and sustained thought. (2)

(iv) Conditioned by state without applied thought and sustained thought, (arises) state without applied thought and sustained thought . . .

. . . volition without applied thought and sustained thought. (Do completely.)

(v) . . . with applied thought and sustained thought . . .

Conditioned by (heart-)base, arises volition with applied thought and sustained thought.

(vi) . . . without applied thought but with sustained thought . . .

Conditioned by sustained thought, arises volition without applied thought but with sustained thought; conditioned by (heart-)base, arises volition without applied thought but with sustained thought. (3)

55. (vii) Conditioned by state with applied thought and sustained thought and without applied thought and sustained thought, (arises) state with applied thought and sustained thought . . .

Conditioned by aggregates with applied thought and sustained thought, and (heart-)base, arises volition with applied thought and sustained thought. (1)

(viii) Conditioned by state without applied thought but with sustained thought and without applied thought and sustained thought, (arises) state with applied thought and sustained thought . . .

Conditioned by applied thought and (heart-)base, arises volition with applied thought and sustained thought. (1)

(ix) Conditioned by state without applied thought but with sustained thought and without applied thought and sustained thought, (arises) state without applied thought but with sustained thought . . .

Conditioned by aggregates without applied thought but with sustained thought, and sustained thought, arises volition without applied thought but with sustained thought; conditioned by aggregates without applied thought but with sustained thought, and (heart-)base, arises volition without applied thought but with sustained thought. (2)

(x) Conditioned by state with applied thought and sustained thought and without applied thought but with sustained thought, (arises) state with applied thought and sustained thought . . .

Conditioned by aggregates with applied thought and sustained thought, and applied thought, arises volition with applied thought and sustained thought. (1)

(xi) Conditioned by state with applied thought and sustained thought, without applied thought but with sustained thought and without applied thought and sustained thought, arises state with applied thought and sustained thought by not-kamma condition.

Conditioned by aggregates with applied thought and sustained thought, applied thought and (heart-)base, arises volition with applied thought and sustained thought. (1)

(Make 37 questions in not-resultant. Expand not-nutriment, not-faculty, not-jhāna, not-path, not-association, not-dissociation, not-absence and not-disappearance conditions.)

2. CONDITIONS: NEGATIVE (ii) ENUMERATION CHAPTER

By Ones

56. With not-root 33, not-object 7, not-predominance 37, not-proximity, not-contiguity, not-mutuality, not-strong-dependence 7, not-prenascence, not-postnascence, not-repetition 37, not-kamma 11, not-resultant 37, not-nutriment 1, not-faculty 1, not-jhāna 1, not-path 33, not-association 7, not-dissociation 11, not-absence 7, not-disappearance 7.

3. CONDITIONS: POSITIVE-NEGATIVE

(Root by Twos)

57. With root condition, not-object 7 . . . not-disappearance 7 . . .

End of Positive-Negative

4. CONDITIONS: NEGATIVE-POSITIVE

(Not-root By Twos)

58. With not-root condition, object, proximity, contiguity 14, conascence 33, mutuality 22, dependence 33, strong-dependence, prenascence 14, repetition 13, kamma, resultant, nutriment, faculty, jhāna 33, path 5, association 14, dissociation, presence 33 . . . non-disappearance 33 . . .

End of Negative-Positive

End of "CONDITIONED" CHAPTER

(Also the "Supported" Chapter is the same.)

6. APPLIED THOUGHT TRIPLET V. "CONJOINED" CHAPTER

1. CONDITIONS: POSITIVE (i) CLASSIFICATION CHAPTER

Root 11

59. (i) Conjoined with state with applied thought and sustained thought (savitakka-savicāraṁ dhammaṁ saṁsaṭṭho), arises state with applied thought and sustained thought by root condition.

(*a*) Conjoined with one aggregate with applied thought and sustained thought, arise three aggregates . . . two aggregates . . .

(*b*) At the moment of conception . . . (1)

(ii) Conjoined with state with applied thought and sustained thought, (arises) state without applied thought but with sustained thought . . .

(*a*) Conjoined with aggregates with applied thought and sustained thought, arises applied thought;

(*b*) At the moment of conception . . . (2)

(iii) Conjoined with state with applied thought and sustained thought, (arise) states with applied thought and sustained thought and without applied thought but with sustained thought . . .

(*a*) Conjoined with one aggregate with applied thought and sustained thought, arise three aggregates and applied thought . . . two aggregates . . .

(*b*) At the moment of conception . . . (3)

60. (iv) Conjoined with state without applied thought but with sustained thought, arises state without applied thought but with sustained thought by root condition.

(*a*) Conjoined with one aggregate without applied thought but with sustained thought, arise three aggregates . . . two aggregates . . .

(*b*) At the moment of conception . . . (1)

(v) Conjoined with state without applied thought but with sustained thought, (arises) state with applied thought and sustained thought . . .

(*a*) Conjoined with applied thought, arise aggregates with applied thought and sustained thought;

(*b*) At the moment of conception . . . (2)

(vi) Conjoined with state without applied thought but with sustained thought, (arises) state without applied thought and sustained thought . . .

(*a*) Conjoined with aggregates without applied thought but with sustained thought, arises sustained thought;

(*b*) At the moment of conception, conjoined with aggregates without applied thought but with sustained thought, arises sustained thought. (3)

(vii) Conjoined with state without applied thought but with sustained thought, (arise) states without applied thought but with sustained thought and without applied thought and sustained thought . . .

(*a*) Conjoined with one aggregate without applied thought but with sustained thought, arise three aggregates and sustained thought . . .

two aggregates . . .

(*b*) At the moment of conception . . . (4)

61. (viii) Conjoined with state without applied thought and sustained thought, arises state without applied thought and sustained thought by root condition.

(*a*) Conjoined with one aggregate without applied thought and sustained thought, arise three aggregates . . . conjoined with two aggregates . . .

(*b*) At the moment of conception . . . (1)

(ix) Conjoined with state without applied thought and sustained thought, (arises) state without applied thought but with sustained thought . . .

(*a*) Conjoined with sustained thought, arise aggregates without applied thought but with sustained thought;

(*b*) At the moment of conception, conjoined with sustained thought . . . (2)

(x) Conjoined with state without applied thought but with sustained thought and without applied thought and sustained thought, (arises) state without applied thought but with sustained thought . . .

(*a*) Conjoined with one aggregate without applied thought but with sustained thought, and sustained thought, arise three aggregates . . . two aggregates . . .

(*b*) At the moment of conception . . . (1)

(xi) Conjoined with state with applied thought and sustained thought and without applied thought but with sustained thought, arises state with applied thought and sustained thought by root condition.

(*a*) Conjoined with one aggregate with applied thought and sustained thought, and applied thought, arise three aggregates . . . two aggregates and applied thought . . .

(*b*) At the moment of conception . . . (1)

(Expand all the conditions after considering root condition.)

1. CONDITIONS: POSITIVE (ii) ENUMERATION CHAPTER

By Ones

62. With root 11, object, predominance, proximity, contiguity, conascence, mutuality, dependence, strong-dependence, prenascence, repetition, kamma, resultant, nutriment, faculty, jhāna, path, association,

dissociation, presence, absence, disappearance and non-disappearance are all 11.

End of Positive

2. CONDITIONS: NEGATIVE (i) CLASSIFICATION CHAPTER

(Do the Negative without confusion.)

(2. CONDITIONS: NEGATIVE (ii) ENUMERATION CHAPTER)

(By Ones)

63. With not-root 6, not-predominance 11, not-prenascence 11, not-postnascence 11, not-repetition 11, not-kamma 7, not-resultant 11, not-jhāna 1, not-path 6, not-dissociation 11.

End of Negative

3. CONDITIONS: POSITIVE-NEGATIVE

(Root) By Twos

64. With root condition, not-predominance 11 . . . not-dissociation 11. (Abbreviated.)

End of Positive-Negative

4. CONDITIONS: NEGATIVE-POSITIVE

(Not-root By Twos)

65. With not-root condition, object 6 . . . prenascence 6, repetition 5, kamma 6 . . . jhāna 6, path 3, association 6 . . . non-disappearance 6.

(Expand the "Associated" Chapter also.)

6. APPLIED THOUGHT TRIPLET
VII. "INVESTIGATION" CHAPTER

1. CONDITIONS: POSITIVE (i) CLASSIFICATION CHAPTER

Root 11

66. (i) State with applied thought and sustained thought (savitakka-savicāro dhammo) is related to state with applied thought and sustained thought by root condition.

(*a*) Roots with applied thought and sustained thought (savitakka-savicārā hetū) are related to (their association aggregates by root condition;

(*b*) At the moment of conception . . . (1)

(ii) State with applied thought and sustained thought is related to state without applied thought but with sustained thought by root condition.

(*a*) Roots with applied thought and sustained thought are related to applied thought by root condition;

(*b*) At the moment of conception . . . (2)

(iii) State with applied thought and sustained thought is related to state without applied thought and sustained thought by root condition.

(*a*) Roots with applied thought and sustained thought are related to mind-produced matter by root condition;

(*b*) At the moment of conception, roots with applied thought and sustained thought are related to kamma-produced matter by root condition. (3)

(iv) State with applied thought and sustained thought is related to state with applied thought and sustained thought and without applied thought and sustained thought by root condition.

(*a*) Roots with applied thought and sustained thought are related to (their) associated aggregates and mind-produced matter by root condition;

(*b*) At the moment of conception, roots with applied thought and sustained thought are related to (their) associated aggregates and kamma-produced matter by root condition. (4)

(v) State with applied thought and sustained thought is related to state without applied thought but with sustained thought and without applied thought and sustained thought by root condition.

(*a*) Roots with applied thought and sustained thought are related to applied thought and mind-produced matter by root condition;

(*b*) At the moment of conception, roots with applied thought and sustained thought are related to applied thought and kamma-produced matter by root condition. (5)

(vi) State with applied thought and sustained thought is related to state with applied thought and sustained thought and without applied thought but with sustained thought by root condition.

(*a*) Roots with applied thought and sustained thought are related to (their) associated aggregates and applied thought by root condition;

(*b*) At the moment of conception, roots with applied thought and sustained thought are related to (their) associated aggregates and applied thought by root condition. (6)

(vii) State with applied thought and sustained thought is related to state with applied thought and sustained thought, without applied thought but with sustained thought and without applied thought and sustained thought by root condition.

(*a*) Roots with applied thought and sustained thought are related to (their) associated aggregates, applied thought and mind-produced matter by root condition;

(*b*) At the moment of conception, roots with applied thought and sustained thought are related to (their) associated aggregates, applied thought and kamma-produced matter by root condition. (7)

67. (viii) State without applied thought but with sustained thought is related to state without applied thought but with sustained thought by root condition.

(*a*) Roots without applied thought but with sustained thought are related to (their) associated aggregates by root condition;

(*b*) At the moment of conception, roots without applied thought but with sustained thought are related to (their) associated aggregates by root condition. (1)

(ix) State without applied thought but with sustained thought is related to state without applied thought and sustained thought by root condition.

(*a*) Roots without applied thought but with sustained thought are related to sustained thought and mind-produced matter by root condition;

(*b*) At the moment of conception, roots without applied thought but with sustained thought are related to sustained thought and kamma-produced matter by root condition. (2)

(x) State without applied thought but with sustained thought is related to state without applied thought but with sustained thought and without applied thought and sustained thought by root condition.

(*a*) Roots without applied thought but with sustained thought are related to (their) associated aggregates, sustained thought and mind-produced matter by root condition;

(*b*) At the moment of conception, roots without applied thought but with sustained thought are related to (their) associated aggregates, sustained thought and kamma-produced matter by root condition. (3)

68. (xi) State without applied thought and sustained thought is related to state without applied thought and sustained thought by root condition.

(*a*) Roots without applied thought and sustained thought are related to (their) associated aggregates and mind-produced matter by root condition;

(*b*) At the moment of conception, roots without applied thought and sustained thought are related to (their) associated aggregates and kamma-produced matter by root condition. (1)

Object 21

69. (i) State with applied thought and sustained thought is related to state with applied thought and sustained thought by object condition.

After having offered an offering (dāna), having undertaken precepts (sīla), having fulfilled the duty of observance (uposathakamma), (one) reviews that (taṁ paccavekkhati). (One) reviews (such acts) formerly well done (pubbe suciṇṇāni). Having emerged from jhāna with applied thought and sustained thought (savitakka-savicārā jhānā vuṭṭhahitvā), having emerged from Path (magga), having emerged from Fruition (phala), (one) reviews the Fruition.

The Noble persons review the eradicated defilements (pahīne kilese), review the uneradicated defilements (vikkhambhite kilese), know the defilements addicted to before (pubbe samudāciṇṇe). (They practise insight into the impermanence, suffering and impersonality of aggregates with applied thought and sustained thought (savitakkasavicāre khandhe aniccato dukkhato anattato vipassanti); enjoy and delight in (assādenti abhinandanti) (those aggregates). Taking that as object, arises lust (taṁ ārabbha rāgo uppajjati) . . . arises grief (domanassa). Taking the aggregates with applied thought and sustained thought as object, arise aggregates with applied thought and sustained thought. (1)

(ii) State with applied thought and sustained thought is related to state without applied thought but with sustained thought by object condition.

After having offered an offering, having undertaken precepts having fulfilled the duty of observance, (one) reviews that. Taking it as object, arises applied thought. (One) reviews (such acts) formerly well done. Having emerged from jhāna with applied thought and sustained thought, having emerged from Path, having emerged from Fruition, (one) reviews the Fruition. Taking it as object, arises applied thought.

The Noble persons review the eradicated defilements, review the uneradicated defilements, know the defilements addicted to before. (They) practise insight into the impermanence, suffering and impersonality of aggregates with applied thought and sustained thought; enjoy and delight in (those aggregates). Taking them as object, arises applied thought. Taking aggregates with applied thought and sustained thought as object, arises applied thought. (2)

(iii) State with applied thought and sustained thought is related to state without applied thought and sustained thought by object condition.

By the knowledge of penetration into others' minds (cetopariyañāṇa) (one) knows the other being's mind with applied thought and sustained thought (savitakka-savicāracittasamaṅgissa cittaṁ jānāti). Aggregates with applied thought and sustained thought are related to knowledge of penetration into others' minds, knowledge of remembrance of past existences (pubbenivāsānussatiñāṇa), knowledge of rebirths according to one's kamma (yathākammūpagañāṇa), knowledge of future existences (anāgataṁsañāṇa) by object condition. Taking aggregates with applied thought and sustained thought as object, arise aggregates without applied thought and sustained thought. (3)

(iv) State with applied thought and sustained thought is related to state with applied thought and sustained thought and without applied thought but with sustained thought by object condition.

After having offered an offering, having undertaken precepts, having fulfilled the duty of observance, (one) reviews that. Taking it as object, arise aggregates with applied thought and sustained thought, and applied thought. (One) reviews (such acts) formerly well done. Having emerged from jhāna with applied thought and sustained thought, having emerged from Path, having emerged from Fruition, (one) reviews the Fruition. Taking it as object, arise aggregates with applied thought and sustained thought, and applied thought.

The Noble persons review the eradicated defilements, review the uneradicated defilements, know the defilements addicted to before. (They) practise insight into the impermanence, suffering and impersonality of aggregates with applied thought and sustained thought; enjoy and delight in (those aggregates). Taking them as object, arise aggregates with applied thought and sustained thought, and applied thought. Taking the aggregates with applied thought and sustained thought as object, arise aggregates with applied thought and sustained thought, and applied thought. (4)

70. (v) State without applied thought but with sustained thought is related to state without applied thought but with sustained thought by object condition.

Having emerged from jhāna without applied thought but with sustained thought, having emerged from Path, having emerged from Fruition, (one) reviews the Fruition. Taking it as object, arises applied thought. (One) practises insight into the impermanence, suffering and impersonality of aggregates without applied thought but with sustained thought, and of applied thought; enjoys and delights in (them). Taking them as object, arises applied thought. Taking aggregates without applied thought but with sustained thought, and applied thought as object, arises applied thought. (1)

(vi) State without applied thought but with sustained thought is related to state with applied thought and sustained thought by object condition.

Having amerged from jhāna without applied thought but with sustained thought, having emerged from Path, having emerged from Fruition, (they) review the Fruition. Taking it as object, arise aggregates with applied thought and sustained thought.

(One) practises insight into the impermanence, suffering and impersonality of aggregates without applied thought but with sustained thought, and of applied thought; enjoys and delights in (them). Taking it as object, arises lust . . . arises grief. Taking aggregates without applied thought but with sustained thought, and applied thought as object, arise aggregates with applied thought and sustained thought. (2)

(vii) State without applied thought but with sustained thought is related to state without applied thought and sustained thought by object condition.

By the knowledge of penetration into others' minds, (one) knows the other being's mind without applied thought but with sustained thought. Aggregates without applied thought but with sustained thought are related to knowledge of penetration into others' minds, knowledge of remembrance of past existences, knowledge of rebirths according to one's kamma, knowledge of future existences by object condition. Taking aggregates without applied thought but with sustained thought, and applied thought as object, arise aggregates without applied thought and sustained thought. (3)

(viii) State without applied thought but with sustained thought is related to state with applied thought and sustained thought and without applied thought but with sustained thought by object condition.

Having emerged from jhāna without applied thought but with sustained thought, having emerged from Path, having emerged from Fruition, (one) reviews the Fruition. Taking it as object, arise aggregates with applied thought and sustained thought, and applied thought. (One) practises insight into the impermanence, suffering and impersonality of aggregates without applied thought but with sustained thought, and of applied thought; enjoys and delights in (them). Taking them as object, arise aggregates with applied thought and sustained thought, and applied thought. Taking aggregates without applied thought but with sustained thought, and applied thought as object, arise aggregates with applied thought and sustained thought, and applied thought. (4)

71. (ix) State without applied thought and sustained thought is related to state without applied thought and sustained thought by object condition.

Nibbāna is related to Path without applied thought and sustained thought, Fruition and sustained thought by object condition.

By the power of divine-eye (dibba-cakkhu), one sees a visible object. By the power of divine-ear element (dibbāya sota-dhātuyā), one hears a sound. By the knowledge of penetration into others' minds, one knows the other being's mind without applied thought and sustained thought.

"Infinity of space" (ākāsānañcāyatana) to "Infinity of consciousness" (viññāṇañcāyatana) . . . "Nothingness" (ākiñcaññāyatana) is related to "Neither-perception-nor-non-perception" (neva-saññā-nāsaññāyatana) by object condition.

Visible object-base to eye-consciousness . . . tangible object-base is related to body-consciousness by object condition.

Aggregates without applied thought and sustained thought are related to knowledge of supernormal power (iddhividhañāṇa), knowledge of penetration into others' minds, knowledge of remembrance of past existences, knowledge of rebirths according to one's kamma, knowledge of future existences by object condition. Taking aggregates without applied thought and sustained thought, and sustained thought as object, arise aggregates without applied thought and sustained thought. (1)

(x) State without applied thought and sustained thought is related to state with applied thought and sustained thought by object condition.

The Noble persons, having emerged from jhāna without applied thought and sustained thought, having emerged from Path, having emerged from Fruition, review the Fruition. Taking it as object, arise aggregates with applied thought and sustained thought. The Noble persons review Nibbāna. Nibbāna is related to change-of-lineage (gotrabhū), purification (vodāna), Path with applied thought and sustained thought, Fruition, (mind-door) advertence (āvajjanā) by object condition.

(One) practises insight into the impermanence, suffering and impersonality of the eye(-base); enjoys and delights in (it). Taking it as object, arises lust . . . arises grief . . . ear . . . nose . . . tongue . . . body . . . visible object . . . sound . . . smell . . . taste . . . tangible object . . . (heart-)base . . . One practises insight into the impermanence, suffering and impersonality of aggregates without applied thought and sustained thought, and of sustained thought; enjoys and delights in (them). Taking these as object, arises lust . . . arises grief. Taking aggregates without applied thought and sustained thought, and sustained thought as object, arise aggregates with applied thought and sustained thought. (2)

(xi) State without applied thought and sustained thought is related to state without applied thought but with sustained thought by object condition.

The Noble persons, having emerged from jhāna without applied thought and sustained thought, having emerged from Path, having emerged from Fruition, review the Fruition. Taking it as object, arises applied thought. The Noble persons review Nibbāna. Nibbāna is related to Path without applied thought but with sustained thought, Fruition and applied thought by object condition.

(One) practises insight into the impermanence, suffering and impersonality of the eye . . . (heart-)base . . . (One) practises insight into the impermanence, suffering and impersonality of the aggregates without applied thought and sustained thought, and of sustained thought; enjoys and delights in (them). Taking these as object, arises applied thought. Taking aggregates without applied thought and sustained thought, and sustained thought as object, arises applied thought. (3)

(xii) State without applied thought and sustained thought is related to state without applied thought but with sustained thought and without applied thought and sustained thought by object condition.

Nibbāna is related to Path without applied thought but with sustained thought, Fruition and sustained thought by object condition. (4)

(xiii) State without applied thought and sustained thought is related to state with applied thought and sustained thought and without applied thought but with sustained thought by object condition.

The Noble persons, having emerged from jhāna without applied thought and sustained thought, having emerged from Path, having emerged from Fruition, review the Fruition. Taking it as object, arise aggregates with applied thought and sustained thought, and applied thought. The Noble persons review Nibbāna. Nibbāna is related to change-of-lineage and applied thought; to purification and applied thought; to Path with applied thought and sustained thought, and applied thought; to Fruition with applied thought and sustained thought, and applied thought; to advertence and applied thought by object condition.

(One) practises insight into the impermanence, suffering and impersonality of the eye; enjoys and delights in (it). Taking it as object, arise aggregates with applied thought and sustained thought, and applied thought . . . ear . . . tangible object . . . (heart-)base . . . (One) practises insight into the impermanence, suffering and impersonality of aggregates without applied thought and sustained thought, and sustained thought; enjoys and delights in (them). Taking these as object, arise aggregates with applied thought and sustained thought, and applied thought. (5)

72. (xiv) States without applied thought but with sustained thought and without applied thought and sustained thought are related to state with applied thought and sustained thought by object condition.

Taking aggregates without applied thought but with sustained thought, and sustained thought as object, arise aggregates with applied thought and sustained thought. (1)

(xv) States without applied thought but with sustained thought and without applied thought and sustained thought are related to state without applied thought but with sustained thought by object condition.

Taking aggregates without applied thought but with sustained thought, and sustained thought as object, arises applied thought. (2)

(xvi) States without applied thought but with sustained thought and without applied thought and sustained thought are related to state without applied thought and sustained thought by object condition.

Aggregates without applied thought but with sustained thought, and sustained thought are related to knowledge of penetration into others' minds, knowledge of remembrance of past existences, knowledge of rebirths according to one's kamma, knowledge of future existences by object condition. Taking aggregates without applied thought but with sustained thought, and sustained thought as object, arise aggregates without applied thought and sustained thought. (3)

(xvii) States without applied thought but with sustained thought and without applied thought and sustained thought are related to state with applied thought and sustained thought and without applied thought but with sustained thought by object condition.

Taking aggregates without applied thought but with sustained thought, and sustained thought as object, arise aggregates with applied thought and sustained thought, and applied thought. (4)

73. (xviii) States with applied thought and sustained thought and without applied thought but with sustained thought are related to state with applied thought and sustained thought by object condition.

Taking aggregates with applied thought and sustained thought, and applied thought as object, arise aggregates with applied thought and sustained thought. (1)

(xix) States with applied thought and sustained thought and without applied thought but with sustained thought are related to state without applied thought but with sustained thought by object condition.

Taking aggregates with applied thought and sustained thought, and applied thought as object, arises applied thought. (2)

(xx) States with applied thought and sustained thought and without applied thought but with sustained thought are related to state without applied thought and sustained thought by object condition.

Aggregates with applied thought and sustained thought, and applied thought are related to knowledge of penetration into others' minds, knowledge of remembrance of past existences, knowledge of rebirths according to one's kamma, knowledge of future existences by object condition. Taking aggregates with applied thought and sustained thought, and applied thought as object, arise aggregates without applied thought and sustained thought. (3)

(xxi) States with applied thought and sustained thought and without applied thought but with sustained thought are related to state with applied thought and sustained thought and without applied thought but with sustained thought by object condition.

Taking aggregates with applied thought and sustained thought, and applied thought as object, arise aggregates with applied thought and sustained thought, and applied thought. (4)

Predominance 23

74. (i) State with applied thought and sustained thought is related to state with applied thought and sustained thought by predominance condition.

(It is of two kinds, namely:) (*a*) object-predominance (ārammaṇādhipati), (*b*) conascence-predominance (sahajātādhipati).

(*a*) *Object-predominance:* After having offered an offering, having undertaken precepts, having fulfilled the duty of observance, (one) esteems and reviews that (taṁ garuṁ katvā paccavekkhati). (One) esteems and reviews (such acts) formerly well done. Having emerged from jhāna with applied thought and sustained thought, having emerged from Path, having emerged from Fruition, (one) esteems and reviews the Fruition. (One) esteems, enjoys and delights in aggregates with applied thought and sustained thought. Taking these as estimable object, arises lust, arises wrong views.

(*b*) *Conascence-predominance:* Predominance with applied thought and sustained thought is related to (its) associated aggregates by predominance condition. (1)

(ii) State with applied thought and sustained thought is related to state without applied thought but with sustained thought by predominance condition.

(It is of two kinds, namely:) (*a*) object-predominance, (*b*) conascence-predominance.

(*a*) *Object-predominance:* After having offered an offering, having undertaken precepts, having fulfilled the duty of observance, (one) esteems and reviews that. Taking it as estimable object, arises applied thought. (One) esteems and reviews (such acts) formerly well done. Having emerged from jhāna with applied thought and sustained thought, having emerged from Path, having emerged from Fruition, (one) esteems and reviews the Fruition. Taking it as estimable object, arises applied thought. (One) esteems, enjoys and delights in aggregates with applied thought and sustained thought. Taking them as estimable object, arises applied thought.

(*b*) *Conascence-predominance:* Predominance with applied thought and sustained thought is related to applied thought by predominance condition. (2)

(iii) State with applied thought and sustained thought is related to state without applied thought and sustained thought by predominance condition.

Conascence-predominance: Predominance with applied thought and sustained thought is related to mind-produced matter by predominance condition. (3)

(iv) State with applied thought and sustained thought is related to state with applied thought and sustained thought and without applied thought and sustained thought by predominance condition.

Conascence-predominance: Predominance with applied thought and sustained thought is related to (its) associated aggregates and mind-produced matter by predominance condition. (4)

(v) State with applied thought and sustained thought is related to state without applied thought but with sustained thought and without applied thought and sustained thought by predominance condition.

Conascence-predominance: Predominance with applied thought and sustained thought is related to applied thought and mind-produced matter by predominance condition. (5)

(vi) State with applied thought and sustained thought is related to state with applied thought and sustained thought and without applied thought but with sustained thought by predominance condition.

(It is of two kinds, namely:) (*a*) object-predominance, (*b*) conascence-predominance.

(*a*) *Object-predominance:* After having offered an offering, having undertaken precepts, having fulfilled the duty of observance, (one) esteems and reviews that. Taking it as estimable object, arise aggregates with applied thought and sustained thought, and applied thought. (One) esteems and reviews (such acts) formerly well done. Having emerged from jhāna with applied thought and sustained thought, having emerged from Path, having emerged from Fruition, (one) esteems and reviews the Fruition. Taking it as estimable object, arise aggregates with applied thought and sustained thought, and applied thought. (One) esteems, enjoys and delights in aggregates with applied thought and sustained thought. Taking them as estimable object, arise aggregates with applied thought and sustained thought, and applied thought.

(*b*) *Conascence-predominance:* Predominance with applied thought and sustained thought is related to (its) associated aggregates and applied thought by predominance condition. (6)

(vii) State with applied thought and sustained thought is related to state with applied thought and sustained thought, without applied thought but with sustained thought and without applied thought and sustained thought by predominance condition.

Conascence-predominance: Predominance with applied thought and sustained thought is related to (its) associated aggregates, applied thought and mind-produced matter by predominance condition. (7)

75. (viii) State without applied thought but with sustained thought is related to state without applied thought but with sustained thought by predominance condition.

(It is of two kinds, namely:) (*a*) object-predominance, (*b*) conascence-predominance.

(*a*) *Object-predominance:* Having emerged from jhāna without applied thought but with sustained thought, having emerged from Path, having emerged from Fruition, (one) esteems and reviews the Fruition. Taking it as estimable object, arises applied thought. (One) esteems, enjoys and delights in aggregates without applied thought but with sustained thought, and applied thought. Taking these as estimable object, arises applied thought.

(*b*) *Conascence-predominance:* Predominance without applied thought but with sustained thought is related to (its) associated aggregates by predominance condition. (1)

(ix) State without applied thought but with sustained thought is related to state with applied thought and sustained thought by predominance condition.

Object-predominance: Having emerged from jhāna without applied thought but with sustained thought, having emerged from Path, having emerged from Fruition, (one) esteems and reviews the Fruition. Taking it as estimable object, arise aggregates with applied thought and sustained thought. (One) esteems, enjoys and delights in aggregates without applied thought but with sustained thought, and applied thought. Taking these as estimable object, arises lust, arises wrong views. (2)

(x) State without applied thought but with sustained thought is related to state without applied thought and sustained thought by predominance condition.

Conascence-predominance: Predominance without applied thought but with sustained thought is related to sustained thought and mind-produced matter by predominance condition. (3)

(xi) State without applied thought but with sustained thought is related to state without applied thought but with sustained thought and without applied thought and sustained thought by predominance condition.

Conascence-predominance: Predominance without applied thought but with sustained thought is related to (its) associated aggregates, sustained thought and mind-produced matter by predominance condition. (4)

(xii) State without applied thought but with sustained thought is related to state with applied thought and sustained thought and without applied thought but with sustained thought by predominance condition.

Object-predominance: Having emerged from jhāna without applied thought but with sustained thought, having emerged from Path, having emerged from Fruition, (one) esteems and reviews the Fruition. Taking it as estimable object, arise aggregates with applied thought and sustained thought, and applied thought. One esteems, enjoys and delights in aggregates without applied thought but with sustained thought, and applied thought. Taking these as estimable object, arise aggregates with applied thought and sustained thought, and applied thought. (5)

76. (xiii) State without applied thought and sustained thought is related to state without applied thought and sustained thought by predominance condition.

(It is of two kinds, namely:) (*a*) object-predominance, (*b*) conascence-predominance.

(*a*) *Object-predominance:* Nibbāna is related to Path without applied thought and sustained thought, Fruition and sustained thought by predominance condition.

(*b*) *Conascence-predominance:* Predominance without applied thought and sustained thought is related to (its) associated aggregates and mind-produced matter by predominance condition. (1)

(xiv) State without applied thought and sustained thought is related to state with applied thought and sustained thought by predominance condition.

Object-predominance: The Noble persons, having emerged from jhāna without applied thought and sustained thought, having emerged from Path, having emerged from Fruition, esteem and review the Fruition. Taking it as estimable object, arise aggregates with applied thought and sustained thought. The Noble persons esteem and review Nibbāna. Nibbāna is related to change-of-lineage, purification, Path with applied thought and sustained thought, Fruition by predominance condition.

(One) esteems, enjoys and delights in the eye. Taking it as estimable object, arises lust, arises wrong views . . . ear . . . nose . . . tongue . . . body . . . visible object . . . sound . . . smell . . . taste . . . tangible object . . . (heart-)base . . . (One) esteems, enjoys and delights in aggregates without applied thought and sustained thought, and sustained thought. Taking these as estimable object, arises lust, arises wrong views. (2)

(xv) State without applied thought and sustained thought is related to state without applied thought but with sustained thought by predominance condition.

Object-predominance: The Noble persons, having emerged from jhāna without applied thought and sustained thought, having emerged from Path, having emerged from Fruition, esteem and review the Fruition. Taking it as estimable object, arises applied thought. The Noble persons esteem and review Nibbāna. Nibbāna is related to Path without applied thought but with sustained thought, Fruition and applied thought by predominance condition.

Eye . . . (heart-)base . . . (One) esteems, enjoys and delights in aggregates without applied thought and sustained thought, and sustained thought. Taking these as estimable object, arises applied thought. (3)

(xvi) State without applied thought and sustained thought is related to state without applied thought but with sustained thought and without applied thought and sustained thought by predominance condition.

Object-predominance: Nibbāna is related to Path without applied thought but with sustained thought, Fruition and sustained thought by predominance condition. (4)

(xvii) State without applied thought and sustained thought is related to state with applied thought and sustained thought and without applied thought but with sustained thought by predominance condition.

Object-predominance: The Noble persons, having emerged from jhāna without applied thought and sustained thought, having emerged from Path, having emerged from Fruition, esteem and review the Fruition. Taking it as estimable object, arise aggregates with applied thought and sustained thought, and applied thought. The Noble persons esteem and review Nibbāna. Nibbāna is related to change-of-lineage and applied thought, purification and applied thought, Path with applied thought and sustained thought, and applied thought, Fruition with applied thought and sustained thought, and applied thought by predominance condition.

(One) esteems . . . the eye . . . (heart-)base . . . (One) esteems, enjoys and delights in aggregates without applied thought and sustained thought, and sustained thought. Taking these as estimable object, arise aggregates with applied thought and sustained thought, and applied thought. (5)

77. (xviii) States without applied thought but with sustained thought and without applied thought and sustained thought are related to state with applied thought and sustained thought by predominance condition.

Object-predominance: Taking aggregates without applied thought but with sustained thought, and sustained thought as estimable object, arise aggregates with applied thought and sustained thought. (1)

(xix) States without applied thought but with sustained thought and without applied thought and sustained thought are related to state without applied thought but with sustained thought by predominance condition.

Object-predominance: Taking aggregates without applied thought but with sustained thought, and sustained thought as estimable object, arises applied thought. (2)

(xx) States without applied thought but with sustained thought and without applied thought and sustained thought are related to state with applied thought and sustained thought and without applied thought but with sustained thought by predominance condition.

Object-predominance: Taking aggregates without applied thought but with sustained thought, and sustained thought as estimable object, arise aggregates with applied thought and sustained thought, and applied thought. (3)

78. (xxi) States with applied thought and sustained thought and without applied thought but with sustained thought are related to state with applied thought and sustained thought by predominance condition.

Object-predominance: Taking aggregates with applied thought and sustained thought, and applied thought as estimable object, arise aggregates with applied thought and sustained thought. (1)

(xxii) States with applied thought and sustained thought and without applied thought but with sustained thought are related to state without applied thought but with sustained thought by predominance condition.

Object-predominance: Taking aggregates with applied thought and sustained thought, and applied thought as estimable object, arises applied thought. (2)

(xxiii) States with applied thought and sustained thought and without applied thought but with sustained thought are related to state with applied thought and sustained thought and without applied thought but with sustained thought by predominance condition.

Object-predominance: Taking aggregates with applied thought and sustained thought, and applied thought as estimable object, arise aggregates with applied thought and sustained thought, and applied thought. (3)

Proximity 25

79. (i) State with applied thought and sustained thought is related to state with applied thought and sustained thought by proximity condition.

Preceding aggregates with applied thought and sustained thought are related to subsequent aggregates with applied thought and sustained thought by proximity condition. Adaptation (anuloma) to change-of-lineage (gotrabhū); adaptation to purification (vodāna); change-of-lineage to Path with applied thought and sustained thought; purification to Path with applied thought and sustained thought; Path with applied thought and sustained thought to Fruition with applied thought and sustained thought; Fruition with applied thought and sustained thought to Fruition with applied thought and sustained thought; adaptation is related to the attainment of Fruition (Phalasamāpatti) with applied thought and sustained thought by proximity condition. (1)

(ii) State with applied thought and sustained thought is related to state without applied thought but with sustained thought by proximity condition.

Preceding aggregates with applied thought and sustained thought are related to subsequent applied thought by proximity condition. Death-consciousness (cuti-citta) with applied thought and sustained thought to rebirth-consciousness (upapatti-citta) without applied thought but with sustained thought . . . aggregates with applied thought and sustained thought to emergence (vuṭṭhāna) without applied thought but with sustained thought, and applied thought . . .

The preparation (parikamma) for jhāna without applied thought but with sustained thought to jhāna without applied thought but with sustained thought; change-of-lineage to Path without applied thought but with sustained thought; purification to Path without applied thought but with sustained thought; adaptation is related to the attainment of Fruition without applied thought but with sustained thought, and applied thought by proximity condition. (2)

(iii) State with applied thought and sustained thought is related to state without applied thought and sustained thought by proximity condition.

Death-consciousness with applied thought and sustained thought is related to rebirth-consciousness without applied thought and sustained thought by proximity condition. Advertence (āvajjanā) is related to five-fold consciousness by proximity condition. Aggregates with applied thought and sustained thought to emergence without applied thought and sustained thought, and sustained thought . . .

The preparation for second jhāna is related to sustained thought (present) at second jhāna by proximity condition. The preparation for third jhāna . . . The preparation for fourth jhāna . . . The preparation for infinity of space . . . The preparation for infinity of consciousness . . . The preparation for nothingness . . . The preparation for neither-perception-nor-non-perception . . .

The preparation for divine-eye . . . The preparation for divine-ear element . . . The preparation for knowledge of supernormal power . . . The preparation for knowledge of penetration into others' minds . . . The preparation for knowledge of remembrance of past existences . . . The preparation for knowledge of rebirths according to one's kamma . . . The preparation for knowledge of future existences . . . Change-of-lineage to Path without applied thought and sustained thought, and sustained thought; purification to Path without applied thought and sustained thought, and sustained thought; adaptation is related to the attainment of Fruition without applied thought and sustained thought, and sustained thought by proximity condition. (3)

(iv) State with applied thought and sustained thought is related to state without applied thought but with sustained thought and without applied thought and sustained thought by proximity condition.

Death-consciousness with applied thought and sustained thought is related to rebirth-consciousness without applied thought but with sustained thought, and sustained thought by proximity condition. Aggregates with applied thought and sustained thought are related to emergence without applied thought but with sustained thought, and sustained thought by proximity condition.

The preparation for jhāna without applied thought but with sustained thought is related to jhāna without applied thought but with sustained thought, and sustained thought by proximity condition.

Change-of-lineage to Path without applied thought but with sustained thought, and sustained thought; purification to Path without applied thought but with sustained thought, and sustained thought; adaptation is related to the attainment of Fruition without applied thought but with sustained thought, and sustained thought by proximity condition. (4)

(v) State with applied thought and sustained thought is related to state with applied thought and sustained thought and without applied thought but with sustained thought by proximity condition.

Preceding aggregates with applied thought and sustained thought are related to subsequent aggregates with applied thought and sustained thought, and applied thought by proximity condition. Adaptation to change-of-lineage and applied thought; adaptation to purification and applied thought; change-of-lineage to Path with applied thought and sustained thought, and applied thought; purification to Path with applied thought and sustained thought, and applied thought; Path with applied thought and sustained thought to Fruition with applied thought and sustained thought, and applied thought; Fruition with applied thought and sustained thought to Fruition with applied thought and sustained thought, and applied thought; adaptation is related to the attainment of Fruition with applied thought and sustained thought, and applied thought by proximity condition. (5)

80. (vi) State without applied thought but with sustained thought is related to state without applied thought but with sustained thought by proximity condition.

Preceding applied thought is related to subsequent applied thought by proximity condition. Preceding aggregates without applied thought but with sustained thought are related to subsequent aggregates without applied thought but with sustained thought by proximity condition. Path without applied thought but with sustained thought to Fruition without applied thought but with sustained thought; Fruition without applied thought but with sustained thought is related to Fruition without applied thought but with sustained thought by proximity condition. (1)

(vii) State without applied thought but with sustained thought is related to state with applied thought and sustained thought by proximity condition.

Preceding applied-thought is related to subsequent aggregates with applied thought and sustained thought by proximity condition. Death-consciousness without applied thought but with sustained thought is related to rebirth-consciousness with applied thought and sustained thought by proximity condition. Life-continuum (bhavaṇga) without applied thought but with sustained thought is related to advertence by proximity condition. Aggregates without applied thought but with sustained thought are related to emergence with applied thought and sustained thought by proximity condition. (2)

(viii) State without applied thought but with sustained thought is related to state without applied thought and sustained thought by proximity condition.

Preceding aggregates without applied thought but with sustained thought are related to subsequent sustained thought by proximity condition. Death-consciousness without applied thought but with sustained thought, and applied thought are related to rebirth-consciousness without applied thought and sustained thought, and sustained thought by proximity condition. Aggregates without applied thought but with sustained thought, and applied thought are related to emergence without applied thought and sustained thought, and sustained thought by proximity condition. (3)

(ix) State without applied thought but with sustained thought is related to state without applied thought but with sustained thought and without applied thought and sustained thought by proximity condition.

Preceding aggregates without applied thought but with sustained thought are related to subsequent aggregates without applied thought but with sustained thought, and sustained thought by proximity condition. Path without applied thought but with sustained thought to Fruition without applied thought but with sustained thought, and sustained thought; Fruition without applied thought but with sustained thought is related to Fruition without applied thought but with sustained thought, and sustained thought by proximity condition. (4)

(x) State without applied thought but with sustained thought is related to state with applied thought and sustained thought and without applied thought but with sustained thought by proximity condition.

Preceding applied thought is related to subsequent aggregates with applied thought and sustained thought, and applied thought by proximity condition. Death-consciousness without applied thought but with sustained thought is related to rebirth-consciousness with applied thought and sustained thought, and applied thought by proximity condition. Life-continuum without applied thought but with sustained thought is related to advertence and applied thought by proximity condition. Aggregates without applied thought but with sustained thought are related to emergence with applied thought and sustained thought, and applied thought by proximity condition. (5)

81. (xi) State without applied thought and sustained thought is related to state without applied thought and sustained thought by proximity condition.

Preceding sustained thought is related to subsequent sustained thought by proximity condition. Preceding aggregates without applied thought and sustained thought are related to subsequent aggregates without applied thought and sustained thought by proximity condition. Path without applied thought and sustained thought to Fruition without applied thought and sustained thought; Fruition without applied thought and sustained thought is related to Fruition without applied thought and sustained thought by proximity condition. For one emerging from the attainment of Extinction (nirodhā vuṭṭhahantassa), neither-perception-nor-non-perception is related to the attainment of Fruition without applied thought and sustained thought, and sustained thought by proximity condition. (1)

(xii) State without applied thought and sustained thought is related to state with applied thought and sustained thought by proximity condition.

Death-consciousness without applied thought and sustained thought, and sustained thought are related to rebirth-consciousness with applied thought and sustained thought by proximity condition. Life-continuum without applied thought and sustained thought, and sustained thought are related to advertence by proximity condition. Aggregates without applied thought and sustained thought, and sustained thought are related to emergence with applied thought and sustained thought by proximity condition. For one emerging from the attainment of Extinction, neither-perception-nor-non-perception is related to the attainment of Fruition with applied thought and sustained thought by proximity condition. (2)

(xiii) State without applied thought and sustained thought is related to state without applied thought but with sustained thought by proximity condition.

Preceding sustained thought is related to subsequent aggregates without applied thought but with sustained thought by proximity condition. Death-consciousness without applied thought and sustained thought, and sustained thought are related to rebirth-consciousness without applied thought but with sustained thought, and applied thought by proximity condition. Aggregates without applied thought and sustained thought, and sustained thought are related to emergence without applied thought but with sustained thought, and applied thought by proximity condition. For one emerging from the attainment of Extinction, neither-perception-nor-non-perception is related to the attainment of Fruition without applied thought but with sustained thought, and applied thought by proximity condition. (3)

(xiv) State without applied thought and sustained thought is related to state without applied thought but with sustained thought and without applied thought and sustained thought by proximity condition.

Preceding sustained thought is related to subsequent aggregates without applied thought but with sustained thought, and sustained thought by proximity condition. Death-consciousness without applied thought and sustained thought is related to rebirth-consciousness without applied thought but with sustained thought, and sustained thought by proximity condition. Aggregates without applied thought and sustained thought are related to emergence without applied thought but with sustained thought, and sustained thought by proximity condition. For one emerging from the attainment of Extinction, neither-perception-nor-non-perception is related to the attainment of Fruition without applied thought but with sustained thought, and sustained thought by proximity condition. (4)

(xv) State without applied thought and sustained thought is related to state with applied thought and sustained thought and without applied thought but with sustained thought by proximity condition.

Death-consciousness without applied thought and sustained thought, and sustained thought are related to rebirth-consciousness with applied thought and sustained thought, and applied thought by proximity condition. Life-continuum without applied thought and sustained thought, and sustained thought are related to advertence and applied thought by proximity condition. Aggregates without applied thought and sustained thought, and sustained thought are related to emergence with applied thought and sustained thought, and applied thought by proximity condition. For one emerging from the attainment of Extinction, neither-perception-nor-non-perception is related to the attainment of Fruition with applied thought and sustained thought, and applied thought by proximity condition. (5)

82. (xvi) States without applied thought but with sustained thought and without applied thought and sustained thought are related to state with applied thought and sustained thought by proximity condition.

Death-consciousness without applied thought but with sustained thought, and sustained thought are related to rebirth-consciousness with applied thought and sustained thought by proximity condition. Life-continuum without applied thought but with sustained thought, and sustained thought are related to advertence by proximity condition. Aggregates without applied thought but with sustained thought, and sustained thought are related to emergence with applied thought and sustained thought by proximity condition. (1)

(xvii) States without applied thought but with sustained thought and without applied thought and sustained thought are related to state without applied thought but with sustained thought by proximity condition.

Preceding aggregates without applied thought but with sustained thought, and sustained thought are related to subsequent aggregates without applied thought but with sustained thought by proximity condition. Path without applied thought but with sustained thought, and sustained thought are related to Fruition without applied thought but with sustained thought by proximity condition. Fruition without applied thought but with sustained thought, and sustained thought are related to Fruition without applied thought but with sustained thought by proximity condition. (2)

(xviii) States without applied thought but with sustained thought and without applied thought and sustained thought are related to state without applied thought and sustained thought by proximity condition.

Preceding aggregates without applied thought but with sustained thought, and sustained thought are related to subsequent sustained thought by proximity condition. Death-consciousness without applied thought but with sustained thought, and sustained thought are related to rebirth-consciousness without applied thought and sustained thought by proximity condition. Aggregates without applied thought but with sustained thought, and sustained thought are related to emergence without applied thought and sustained thought by proximity condition. (3)

(xix) States without applied thought but with sustained thought and without applied thought and sustained thought are related to state without applied thought but with sustained thought and without applied thought and sustained thought by proximity condition.

Preceding aggregates without applied thought but with sustained thought, and sustained thought are related to subsequent aggregates without applied thought but with sustained thought, and sustained thought by proximity condition. Path without applied thought but with sustained thought, and sustained thought are related to Fruition without applied thought but with sustained thought, and sustained thought by proximity condition. Fruition without applied thought but with sustained thought, and sustained thought are related to Fruition without applied thought but with sustained thought, and sustained thought by proximity condition. (4)

(xx) States without applied thought but with sustained thought and without applied thought and sustained thought are related to state with applied thought and sustained thought and without applied thought but with sustained thought by proximity condition.

Death-consciousness without applied thought but with sustained thought, and sustained thought are related to rebirth-consciousness with applied thought and sustained thought, and applied thought by proximity condition. Life-continuum without applied thought but with sustained thought, and sustained thought are related to advertence and applied thought by proximity condition. Aggregates without applied thought but with sustained thought, and sustained thought are related to emergence with applied thought and sustained thought, and applied thought by proximity condition. (5)

83. (xxi) States with applied thought and sustained thought and without applied thought but with sustained thought are related to state with applied thought and sustained thought by proximity condition.

Preceding aggregates with applied thought and sustained thought, and applied thought are related to subsequent aggregates with applied thought and sustained thought by proximity condition. Adaptation and applied thought to change-of-lineage; adaptation and applied thought to purification; change-of-lineage and applied thought to Path with applied thought and sustained thought; purification and applied thought to Path with applied thought and sustained thought; Path with applied thought and sustained thought, and applied thought to Fruition with applied thought and sustained thought; Fruition with applied thought and sustained thought, and applied thought to Fruition with applied thought and sustained thought; adaptation and applied thought are related to the attainment of Fruition with applied thought and sustained thought by proximity condition. (1)

(xxii) States with applied thought and sustained thought and without applied thought but with sustained thought are related to state without applied thought but with sustained thought by proximity condition.

Preceding aggregates with applied thought and sustained thought, and applied thought are related to subsequent applied thought by proximity condition. Death-consciousness with applied thought and sustained thought, and applied thought are related to rebirth-consciousness without applied thought but with sustained thought by proximity condition. Aggregates with applied thought and sustained thought, and applied thought are related to emergence without applied thought but with sustained thought by proximity condition.

The preparation for jhāna without applied thought but with sustained thought, and applied thought are related to jhāna without applied thought but with sustained thought by proximity condition. Change-of-lineage and applied thought to Path without applied thought but with sustained thought; purification and applied thought to Path without applied thought but with sustained thought; adaptation and applied thought are related to the attainment of Fruition without applied thought but with sustained thought by proximity condition. (2)

(xxiii) States with applied thought and sustained thought and without applied thought but with sustained thought are related to state without applied thought and sustained thought by proximity condition.

Death-consciousness with applied thought and sustained thought, and applied thought are related to rebirth-consciousness without applied thought and sustained thought, and sustained thought by proximity condition. Advertence and applied thought are related to five-fold consciousness by proximity condition. Aggregates with applied thought and sustained thought, and applied thought are related to emergence without applied thought and sustained thought, and sustained thought by proximity condition.

The preparation for second jhāna and applied thought are related to sustained thought (present) at second jhāna by proximity condition. The preparation for third jhāna and applied thought . . . The preparation for fourth jhāna and applied thought . . . The preparation for infinity of space and applied thought . . . The preparation for infinity of consciousness and applied thought . . . The preparation for nothingness and applied thought . . . The preparation for neither-perception-nor-non-perception and applied thought . . .

The preparation for divine-eye and applied thought . . . The preparation for divine-ear element and applied thought . . . The preparation for knowledge of supernormal power and applied thought . . . The preparation for knowledge of penetration into others' minds and applied thought . . . The preparation for knowledge of remembrance of past existences and applied thought . . . The preparation for knowledge of rebirths according to one's kamma and applied thought . . . The preparation for knowledge of future existences and applied thought . . . Change-of-lineage and applied thought to Path without applied thought and sustained thought, and sustained thought; purification and applied thought to Path without applied thought and sustained thought, and sustained thought; adaptation and applied thought are related to the attainment of Fruition without applied thought and sustained thought, and sustained thought by proximity condition. (3)

(xxiv) States with applied thought and sustained thought and without applied thought but with sustained thought are related to state without applied thought but with sustained thought and without applied thought and sustained thought by proximity condition.

Death-consciousness with applied thought and sustained thought, and applied thought are related to rebirth-consciousness without applied thought but with sustained thought, and sustained thought by proximity condition. Aggregates with applied thought and sustained thought, and applied thought are related to emergence without applied thought but with sustained thought, and sustained thought by proximity condition.

The preparation for jhāna without applied thought but with sustained thought, and applied thought are related to jhāna without applied thought but with sustained thought, and sustained thought by proximity condition. Change-of-lineage and applied thought are related to Path without applied thought but with sustained thought, and sustained thought by proximity condition. Purification and applied thought to Path without applied thought but with sustained thought, and sustained thought; adaptation and applied thought are related to the attainment of Fruition without applied thought but with sustained thought, and sustained thought by proximity condition. (4)

(xxv) States with applied thought and sustained thought and without applied thought but with sustained thought are related to state with applied thought and sustained thought and without applied thought but with sustained thought by proximity condition.

Preceding aggregates with applied thought and sustained thought, and applied thought are related to subsequent aggregates with applied thought and sustained thought, and applied thought by proximity condition. Adaptation and applied thought to change-of-lineage and applied thought; adaptation and applied thought to purification and applied thought; change-of-lineage and applied thought to Path with applied thought and sustained thought, and applied thought; purification and applied thought are related to Path with applied thought and sustained thought, and applied thought by proximity condition. Path with applied thought and sustained thought, and applied thought to Fruition with applied thought and sustained thought, and applied thought; Fruition with applied thought and sustained thought, and applied thought to Fruition with applied thought and sustained thought, and applied thought; adaptation and applied thought are related to the attainment of Fruition with applied thought and sustained thought, and applied thought by proximity condition. (5)

Contiguity 25

84. State with applied thought and sustained thought is related to state with applied thought and sustained thought by contiguity condition.

(Proximity and contiguity conditions are the same.)

Conascence 30

85. (i) State with applied thought and sustained thought is related to state with applied thought and sustained thought by conascence condition.

(*a*) One aggregate with applied thought and sustained thought is related to three aggregates by conascence condition; three aggregates are related to one aggregate by conascence condition; two aggregates are related to two aggregates by conascence condition;

(*b*) At the moment of conception, one aggregate with applied thought and sustained thought to three aggregates . . . two aggregates to two aggregates . . . (1)

(ii) State with applied thought and sustained thought is related to state without applied thought but with sustained thought by conascence condition.

(*a*) Aggregates with applied thought and sustained thought are related to applied thought by conascence condition;

(*b*) At the moment of conception . . . (2)

(iii) State with applied thought and sustained thought is related to state without applied thought and sustained thought by conascence condition.

(*a*) Aggregates with applied thought and sustained thought are related to mind-produced matter by conascence condition;

(*b*) At the moment of conception . . . kamma-produced matter. (3)

(iv) State with applied thought and sustained thought is related to state with applied thought and sustained thought and without applied thought and sustained thought by conascence condition.

(*a*) One aggregate with applied thought and sustained thought is related to three aggregates and mind-produced matter by conascence condition . . . two aggregates are related to two aggregates and mind-produced matter by conascence condition;

(*b*) At the moment of conception . . . (4)

(v) State with applied thought and sustained thought is related to state without applied thought but with sustained thought and without applied thought and sustained thought by conascence condition.

(*a*) Aggregates with applied thought and sustained thought are related to applied thought and mind-produced matter by conascence condition;

(*b*) At the moment of conception . . . (5)

(vi) State with applied thought and sustained thought is related to state with applied thought and sustained thought and without applied thought but with sustained thought by conascence condition.

(*a*) One aggregate with applied thought and sustained thought is related to three aggregates and applied thought by conascence condition . . . two aggregates are related to two aggregates and applied thought by conascence condition;

(*b*) At the moment of conception . . . (6)

(vii) State with applied thought and sustained thought is related to state with applied thought and sustained thought, without applied thought but with sustained thought and without applied thought and sustained thought by conascence condition.

(*a*) One aggregate with applied thought and sustained thought is related to three aggregates, applied thought and mind-produced matter by conascence condition . . . two aggregates to two aggregates, applied thought and mind-produced matter . . .

(*b*) At the moment of conception . . . (7)

86. (viii) State without applied thought but with sustained thought is related to state without applied thought but with sustained thought by

conascence condition.

(*a*) One aggregate without applied thought but with sustained thought is related to three aggregates by conascence condition . . . two aggregates to two aggregates . . .

(*b*) At the moment of conception . . . (1)

(ix) State without applied thought but with sustained thought is related to state with applied thought and sustained thought by conascence condition.

(*a*) Applied thought is related to aggregates with applied thought and sustained thought by conascence condition;

(*b*) At the moment of conception . . . (2)

(x) State without applied thought but with sustained thought is related to state without applied thought and sustained thought by conascence condition.

(*a*) Aggregates without applied thought but with sustained thought are related to sustained thought and mind-produced matter by conascence condition; applied thought is related to mind-produced matter by conascence condition;

(*b*) At the moment of conception . . . (3)

(xi) State without applied thought but with sustained thought is related to state with applied thought and sustained thought and without applied thought and sustained thought by conascence condition.

(*a*) Applied thought is related to aggregates with applied thought and sustained thought and mind-produced matter by conascence condition;

(*b*) At the moment of conception . . . (4)

(xii) State without applied thought but with sustained thought is related to state without applied thought but with sustained thought and without applied thought and sustained thought by conascence condition.

(*a*) One aggregate without applied thought but with sustained thought is related to three aggregates, sustained thought and mind-produced matter by conascence condition . . . two aggregates to two aggregates, sustained thought and mind-produced matter . . .

(*b*) At the moment of conception . . . (5)

87. (xiii) State without applied thought and sustained thought is related to state without applied thought and sustained thought by conascence condition.

(*a*) One aggregate without applied thought and sustained thought is related to three aggregates and mind-produced matter by conascence condition . . . two aggregates are related to two aggregates and mind-produced matter by conascence condition; sustained thought to mind-produced matter . . .

(*b*) At the moment of conception, one aggregate without applied thought and sustained thought to three aggregates and kamma-produced matter . . . two aggregates to two aggregates and kamma-produced matter . . . sustained thought to kamma-produced matter . . . aggregates to (heart-)base . . . (heart-)base to aggregates . . . sustained thought to (heart-)base . . . (heart-)base to sustained thought . . .

(*c*) One great primary to three great primaries . . . great primaries to mind-produced and kamma-produced derived matter . . .

(*d*) External . . . nutriment-produced . . . temperature-produced . . . one great primary of non-percipient beings . . . great primaries are related to kamma-produced derived matter by conascence condition. (1)

(xiv) State without applied thought and sustained thought is related to state with applied thought and sustained thought by conascence condition.

At the moment of conception, (heart-)base is related to aggregates with applied thought and sustained thought by conascence condition. (2)

(xv) State without applied thought and sustained thought is related to state without applied thought but with sustained thought by conascence condition.

(*a*) Sustained thought is related to aggregates without applied thought but with sustained thought by conascence condition;

(*b*) At the moment of conception, sustained thought is related to aggregates without applied thought but with sustained thought by conascence condition; at the moment of conception, (heart-)base is related to aggregates without applied thought but with sustained thought by conascence condition; at the moment of conception, (heart-)base is related to applied thought by conascence condition. (3)

(xvi) State without applied thought and sustained thought is related to state without applied thought but with sustained thought and without applied thought and sustained thought by conascence condition.

(*a*) Sustained thought is related to aggregates without applied thought but with sustained thought and mind-produced matter by conascence condition;

(*b*) At the moment of conception, sustained thought to aggregates without applied thought but with sustained thought and kamma-produced matter . . . at the moment of conception, (heart-)base is related to aggregates without applied thought but with sustained thought, and sustained thought by conascence condition. (4)

(xvii) State without applied thought and sustained thought is related to state with applied thought and sustained thought and without applied thought but with sustained thought by conascence condition.

At the moment of conception, (heart-)base is related to aggregates with applied thought and sustained thought, and applied thought by conascence condition. (5)

88. (xviii) States with applied thought and sustained thought and without applied thought and sustained thought are related to state with applied thought and sustained thought by conascence condition.

At the moment of conception, one aggregate with applied thought and sustained thought, and (heart-)base are related to three aggregates by conascence condition . . . two aggregates and (heart-)base are related to two aggregates by conascence condition. (1)

(xix) States with applied thought and sustained thought and without applied thought and sustained thought are related to state without applied thought but with sustained thought by conascence condition.

At the moment of conception, aggregates with applied thought and sustained thought, and (heart-)base are related to applied thought by conascence condition. (2)

(xx) States with applied thought and sustained thought and without applied thought and sustained thought are related to state without applied thought and sustained thought by conascence condition.

(*a*) Aggregates with applied thought and sustained thought, and great primaries are related to mind-produced matter by conascence condition;

(*b*) At the moment of conception, aggregates with applied thought and sustained thought, and great primaries are related to kamma-produced matter by conascence condition. (3)

(xxi) States with applied thought and sustained thought and without applied thought and sustained thought are related to state with applied thought and sustained thought and without applied thought but with sustained thought by conascence condition.

At the moment of conception, one aggregate with applied thought and sustained thought, and (heart-)base to three aggregates and applied thought . . . two aggregates and (heart-)base are related to two aggregates and applied thought by conascence condition. (4)

89. (xxii) States without applied thought but with sustained thought and without applied thought and sustained thought are related to state with applied thought and sustained thought by conascence condition.

At the moment of conception, applied thought and (heart-)base are related to aggregates with applied thought and sustained thought by conascence condition. (1)

(xxiii) States without applied thought but with sustained thought and without applied thought and sustained thought are related to state without applied thought but with sustained thought by conascence condition.

(*a*) One aggregate without applied thought but with sustained thought, and sustained thought to three aggregates . . . two aggregates and sustained thought are related to two aggregates by conascence condition;

(*b*) At the moment of conception, one aggregate without applied thought but with sustained thought, and sustained thought to three aggregates . . . two aggregates and sustained thought to two aggregates . . . at the moment of conception, one aggregate without applied thought but with sustained thought, and (heart-)base are related to three aggregates by conascence condition . . . (2)

(xxiv) States without applied thought but with sustained thought and without applied thought and sustained thought are related to state without applied thought and sustained thought by conascence condition.

(*a*) Aggregates without applied thought but with sustained thought, and sustained thought are related to mind-produced matter by conascence condition; aggregates without applied thought but with sustained thought, and great primaries to mind-produced matter . . . applied thought and great primaries to mind-produced matter . . .

(*b*) At the moment of conception, aggregates without applied thought but with sustained thought, and sustained thought to kamma-produced matter . . . at the moment of conception, aggregates without applied thought but with sustained thought, and great primaries to kamma-produced matter . . . at the moment of conception, applied thought and great primaries to kamma-produced matter . . . at the moment of conception, aggregates without applied thought but with sustained thought, and (heart-)base are related to sustained thought by conascence condition. (3)

(xxv) States without applied thought but with sustained thought and without applied thought and sustained thought are related to state without applied thought but with sustained thought and without applied thought and sustained thought by conascence condition.

(*a*) One aggregate without applied thought but with sustained thought, and sustained thought are related to three aggregates and mind-produced matter by conascence condition; three aggregates and sustained thought are related to one aggregate and mind-produced matter by conascence condition; two aggregates and sustained thought are related to two aggregates and mind-produced matter by conascence condition;

(*b*) At the moment of conception, one aggregate without applied thought but with sustained thought, and sustained thought are related to three aggregates and kamma-produced matter by conascence condition . . . two aggregates . . . at the moment of conception, one aggregate without applied thought but with sustained thought, and (heart-)base are related to three aggregates and sustained thought by conascence condition . . . two aggregates and (heart-)base are related to two aggregates and sustained thought by conascence condition. (4)

90. (xxvi) States with applied thought and sustained thought and without applied thought but with sustained thought are related to state with applied thought and sustained thought by conascence condition.

(*a*) One aggregate with applied thought and sustained thought, and applied thought are related to three aggregates by conascence condition . . . two aggregates and applied thought are related to two aggregates by conascence condition;

(*b*) At the moment of conception . . . (1)

(xxvii) States with applied thought and sustained thought and without applied thought but with sustained thought are related to state without applied thought and sustained thought by conascence condition.

(*a*) Aggregates with applied thought and sustained thought, and applied thought are related to mind-produced matter by conascence condition;

(*b*) At the moment of conception . . . (2)

(xxviii) States with applied thought and sustained thought and without applied thought but with sustained thought are related to state with applied thought and sustained thought and without applied thought and sustained thought by conascence condition.

(*a*) One aggregate with applied thought and sustained thought, and applied thought are related to three aggregates and mind-produced matter by conascence condition . . . two aggregates and applied thought are related to two aggregates and mind-produced matter by conascence condition;

(*b*) At the moment of conception . . . (3)

91. (xxix) States with applied thought and sustained thought, without applied thought but with sustained thought and without applied thought and sustained thought are related to state with applied thought and sustained thought by conascence condition.

At the moment of conception, one aggregate with applied thought and sustained thought, applied thought and (heart-)base are related to three aggregates by conascence condition . . . two aggregates, applied thought and (heart-)base are related to two aggregates by conascence condition. (1)

(xxx) States with applied thought and sustained thought, without applied thought but with sustained thought and without applied thought and sustained thought are related to state without applied thought and sustained thought by conascence condition.

(*a*) Aggregates with applied thought and sustained thought, applied thought and great primaries are related to mind-produced matter by conascence condition;

(*b*) At the moment of conception, aggregates with applied thought and sustained thought, applied thought and great primaries are related to kamma-produced matter by conascence condition. (2)

Mutuality 28

92. (i) State with applied thought and sustained thought is related to state with applied thought and sustained thought by mutuality condition.

(*a*) One aggregate with applied thought and sustained thought is related to three aggregates by mutuality condition . . .

(*b*) At the moment of conception, one aggregate with applied thought and sustained thought is related to three aggregates by mutuality condition . . . two aggregates are related to two aggregates by mutuality condition. (1)

(ii) State with applied thought and sustained thought is related to state without applied thought but with sustained thought by mutuality condition.

(*a*) Aggregates with applied thought and sustained thought are related to applied thought by mutuality condition;

(*b*) At the moment of conception . . . (2)

(iii) State with applied thought and sustained thought is related to state without applied thought and sustained thought by mutuality condition.

At the moment of conception, aggregates with applied thought and sustained thought are related to (heart-)base by mutuality condition. (3)

(iv) State with applied thought and sustained thought is related to state with applied thought and sustained thought and without applied thought and sustained thought by mutuality condition.

At the moment of conception, one aggregate with applied thought and sustained thought is related to three aggregates and (heart-)base by mutuality condition . . . two aggregates are related to two aggregates and (heart-)base by mutuality condition. (4)

(v) State with applied thought and sustained thought is related to state without applied thought but with sustained thought and without applied thought and sustained thought by mutuality condition.

At the moment of conception, aggregates with applied thought and sustained thought are related to applied thought and (heart-)base by mutuality condition. (5)

(vi) State with applied thought and sustained thought is related to state with applied thought and sustained thought and without applied thought but with sustained thought by mutuality condition.

(*a*) One aggregate with applied thought and sustained thought is related to three aggregates and applied thought by mutuality condition . . . two aggregates are related to two aggregates and applied thought by mutuality condition;

(*b*) At the moment of conception (6)

(vii) State with applied thought and sustained thought is related to state with applied thought and sustained thought, without applied thought but with sustained thought and without applied thought and sustained thought by mutuality condition.

At the moment of conception, one aggregate with applied thought and sustained thought is related to three aggregates, applied thought and (heart-)base by mutuality condition . . . two aggregates are related to two aggregates, applied thought and (heart-)base by mutuality condition. (7)

93. (viii) State without applied thought but with sustained thought is related to state without applied thought but with sustained thought by mutuality condition.

(*a*) One aggregate without applied thought but with sustained thought is related to three aggregates by mutuality condition . . . two aggregates are related to two aggregates by mutuality condition;

(*b*) At the moment of conception . . . (1)

(ix) State without applied thought but with sustained thought is related to state with applied thought and sustained thought by mutuality condition.

(*a*) Applied thought is related to aggregates with applied thought and sustained thought by mutuality condition;

(*b*) At the moment of conception . . . (2)

(x) State without applied thought but with sustained thought is related to state without applied thought and sustained thought by mutuality condition.

(*a*) Aggregates without applied thought but with sustained thought are related to sustained thought by mutuality condition;

(*b*) At the moment of conception, aggregates without applied thought but with sustained thought are related to sustained thought and (heart-)base by mutuality condition; at the moment of conception, applied thought is related to (heart-)base by mutuality condition. (3)

(xi) State without applied thought but with sustained thought is related to state with applied thought and sustained thought and without applied thought and sustained thought by mutuality condition.

At the moment of conception, applied thought is related to aggregates with applied thought and sustained thought and (heart-)base by mutuality condition. (4)

(xii) State without applied thought but with sustained thought is related to state without applied thought but with sustained thought and without applied thought and sustained thought by mutuality condition.

(*a*) One aggregate without applied thought but with sustained thought is related to three aggregates and sustained thought by mutuality condition . . . two aggregates are related to two aggregates and sustained thought by mutuality condition;

(*b*) At the moment of conception, one aggregate without applied thought but with sustained thought is related to three aggregates, sustained thought and (heart-)base by mutuality condition . . . two aggregates are related to two aggregates, sustained thought and (heart-) base by mutuality condition. (5)

94. (xiii) State without applied thought and sustained thought is related to state without applied thought and sustained thought by mutuality condition.

(*a*) One aggregate without applied thought and sustained thought is related to three aggregates by mutuality condition . . . two aggregates are related to two aggregates by mutuality condition;

(*b*) At the moment of conception, one aggregate without applied thought and sustained thought is related to three aggregates and (heart-) base by mutuality condition . . . two aggregates are related to two aggregates and (heart-)base by mutuality condition; aggregates to (heart-)base . . . (heart-)base to aggregates . . . sustained thought to (heart-)base . . . (heart-)base to sustained thought . . .

(*c*) One great primary to three great primaries . . .

(*d*) External . . . nutriment-produced . . . temperature-produced . . . one great primary of non-percipient beings . . . (1)

(xiv) State without applied thought and sustained thought is related to state with applied thought and sustained thought by mutuality condition.

At the moment of conception, (heart-)base is related to aggregates with applied thought and sustained thought by mutuality condition. (2)

(xv) State without applied thought and sustained thought is related to state without applied thought but with sustained thought by mutuality condition.

(*a*) Sustained thought is related to aggregates without applied thought but with sustained thought by mutuality condition;

(*b*) At the moment of conception, sustained thought is related to aggregates without applied thought but with sustained thought by mutuality condition; at the moment of conception, (heart-)base is related to aggregates without applied thought but with sustained thought by mutuality condition; at the moment of conception, (heart-) base is related to applied thought by mutuality condition. (3)

(xvi) State without applied thought and sustained thought is related to state without applied thought but with sustained thought and without applied thought and sustained thought by mutuality condition.

At the moment of conception, sustained thought is related to aggregates without applied thought but with sustained thought and (heart-)base by mutuality condition; at the moment of conception, (heart-)base is related to aggregates without applied thought but with sustained thought, and sustained thought by mutuality condition. (4)

(xvii) State without applied thought and sustained thought is related to state with applied thought and sustained thought and without applied thought but with sustained thought by mutuality condition.

At the moment of conception, (heart-)base is related to aggregates with applied thought and sustained thought, and applied thought by mutuality condition. (5)

95. (xviii) States with applied thought and sustained thought and without applied thought and sustained thought are related to state with applied thought and sustained thought by mutuality condition.

At the moment of conception, one aggregate with applied thought and sustained thought, and (heart-)base to three aggregates . . . two aggregates and (heart-)base are related to two aggregates by mutuality condition. (1)

(xix) States with applied thought and sustained thought and without applied thought and sustained thought are related to state without applied thought but with sustained thought by mutuality condition.

At the moment of conception, aggregates with applied thought and sustained thought, and (heart-)base are related to applied thought by mutuality condition. (2)

(xx) States with applied thought and sustained thought and without applied thought and sustained thought are related to state with applied thought and sustained thought and without applied thought but with sustained thought by mutuality condition.

At the moment of conception, one aggregate with applied thought and sustained thought, and (heart-)base are related to three aggregates and applied thought by mutuality condition . . . two aggregates and (heart-)base are related to two aggregates and applied thought by mutuality condition. (3)

96. (xxi) States without applied thought but with sustained thought and without applied thought and sustained thought are related to state with applied thought and sustained thought by mutuality condition.

At the moment of conception, applied thought and (heart-)base are related to aggregates with applied thought and sustained thought by mutuality condition. (1)

(xxii) States without applied thought but with sustained thought and without applied thought and sustained thought are related to state without applied thought but with sustained thought by mutuality condition.

(*a*) One aggregate without applied thought but with sustained thought, and sustained thought are related to three aggregates by mutuality condition . . . two aggregates and sustained thought are related to two aggregates by mutuality condition;

(*b*) At the moment of conception, one aggregate without applied thought but with sustained thought, sustained thought and (heart-) base to three aggregates . . . two aggregates, sustained thought and (heart-)base are related to two aggregates by mutuality condition. (2)

(xxiii) States without applied thought but with sustained thought and without applied thought and sustained thought are related to state without applied thought and sustained thought by mutuality condition.

At the moment of conception, aggregates without applied thought but with sustained thought, and sustained thought are related to (heart-) base by mutuality condition; at the moment of conception, aggregates without applied thought but with sustained thought, and (heart-) base are related to sustained thought by mutuality condition. (3)

(xxiv) States without applied thought but with sustained thought and without applied thought and sustained thought are related to state without applied thought but with sustained thought and without applied thought and sustained thought by mutuality condition.

At the moment of conception, one aggregate without applied thought but with sustained thought, and sustained thought are related to three aggregates and (heart-)base by mutuality condition . . . two aggregates and sustained thought are related to two aggregates and (heart-)base by mutuality condition; at the moment of conception, one aggregate without applied thought but with sustained thought, and (heart-)base are related to three aggregates and sustained thought by mutuality condition . . . two aggregates and (heart-)base are related to two aggregates and sustained thought by mutuality condition. (4)

97. (xxv) States with applied thought and sustained thought and without applied thought but with sustained thought are related to state with applied thought and sustained thought by mutuality condition.

(*a*) One aggregate with applied thought and sustained thought, and applied thought are related to three aggregates by mutuality condition . . . two aggregates and applied thought are related to two aggregates by mutuality condition;

(*b*) At the moment of conception . . . (1)

(xxvi) States with applied thought and sustained thought and without applied thought but with sustained thought are related to state without applied thought and sustained thought by mutuality condition.

At the moment of conception, aggregates with applied thought and sustained thought, and applied thought are related to (heart-)base by mutuality condition. (2)

(xxvii) States with applied thought and sustained thought and without applied thought but with sustained thought are related to state with applied thought and sustained thought and without applied thought and sustained thought by mutuality condition.

At the moment of conception, one aggregate with applied thought and sustained thought, and applied thought are related to three aggregates and (heart-)base by mutuality condition . . . two aggregates and applied thought are related to two aggregates and (heart-)base by mutuality condition. (3)

(xxviii) States with applied thought and sustained thought, without applied thought but with sustained thought and without applied thought and sustained thought are related to state with applied thought and sustained thought by mutuality condition.

At the moment of conception, one aggregate with applied thought and sustained thought, applied thought and (heart-)base are related to three aggregates by mutuality condition . . . two aggregates, applied thought and (heart-)base are related to two aggregates by mutuality condition. (1)

Dependence 30

98. (i)–(vii) State with applied thought and sustained thought is related to state with applied thought and sustained thought by dependence condition.

One aggregate with applied thought and sustained thought to three aggregates . . . (Abbreviated.) . . . seven.

(viii)–(xii) State without applied thought but with sustained thought is related to state without applied thought but with sustained thought by dependence condition. (Abbreviated.) . . . five.

(xiii) State without applied thought and sustained thought is related to state without applied thought and sustained thought by dependence condition.

(*a*) One aggregate without applied thought and sustained thought is related to three aggregates and mind-produced matter by dependence condition . . . two aggregates are related to two aggregates and mind-produced matter by dependence condition; sustained thought is related to mind-produced matter by dependence condition;

(*b*) At the moment of conception, one aggregate without applied thought and sustained thought is related to three aggregates and kamma-produced matter by dependence condition . . . two aggregates to two aggregates . . .

(*c*) One great primary of non-percipient beings . . .

(*d*) Eye-base to eye-consciousness . . . body-base to body-consciousness . . . (heart-)base is related to aggregates without applied thought and sustained thought, and sustained thought by dependence condition. (1)

(xiv) State without applied thought and sustained thought is related to state with applied thought and sustained thought by dependence condition.

(*a*) (Heart-)base is related to aggregates with applied thought and sustained thought by dependence condition;

(*b*) At the moment of conception, (heart-)base . . . (2)

(xv) State without applied thought and sustained thought is related to state without applied thought but with sustained thought by dependence condition.

(*a*) Sustained thought is related to aggregates without applied thought but with sustained thought by dependence condition; (heart-) base is related to aggregates without applied thought but with sustained thought, and applied thought by dependence condition;

(*b*) At the moment of conception, sustained thought . . . (3)

(xvi) State without applied thought and sustained thought is related to state without applied thought but with sustained thought and without applied thought and sustained thought by dependence condition.

(*a*) Sustained thought to aggregates without applied thought but with sustained thought and mind-produced matter . . . (heart-)base is related to aggregates without applied thought but with sustained thought, and sustained thought by dependence condition;

(*b*) At the moment of conception, sustained thought . . . (4)

(xvii) State without applied thought and sustained thought is related to state with applied thought and sustained thought and without applied thought but with sustained thought by dependence condition.

(*a*) (Heart-)base is related to aggregates with applied thought and sustained thought, and applied thought by dependence condition;

(*b*) At the moment of conception, (heart-)base . . . (5)

99. (xviii) States with applied thought and sustained thought and without applied thought and sustained thought are related to state with applied thought and sustained thought by dependence condition.

(*a*) One aggregate with applied thought and sustained thought, and (heart-)base are related to three aggregates by dependence condition . . . (Make clear also "during life" and "at the moment of conception".) (1)

(xix) States with applied thought and sustained thought and without applied thought and sustained thought are related to state without applied thought but with sustained thought by dependence condition.

(*a*) Aggregates with applied thought and sustained thought, and (heart-)base to applied thought . . .

(*b*) At the moment of conception . . . (2)

(xx) States with applied thought and sustained thought, and without applied thought and sustained thought are related to state without applied thought and sustained thought by dependence condition.

(*a*) Aggregates with applied thought and sustained thought, and great primaries are related to mind-produced matter by dependence condition;

(*b*) At the moment of conception . . . (3)

(xxi) States with applied thought and sustained thought and without applied thought and sustained thought are related to state with applied thought and sustained thought and without applied thought but with sustained thought by dependence condition.

(*a*) One aggregate with applied thought and sustained thought, and (heart-)base are related to three aggregates and applied thought by dependence condition . . .

(*b*) At the moment of conception . . . (4)

100. (xxii) States without applied thought but with sustained thought and without applied thought and sustained thought are related to state with applied thought and sustained thought by dependence condition.

(*a*) Applied thought and (heart-)base to aggregates with applied thought and sustained thought . . .

(*b*) At the moment of conception . . . (1)

(xxiii) States without applied thought but with sustained thought and without applied thought and sustained thought are related to state without applied thought but with sustained thought by dependence condition.

(*a*) One aggregate without applied thought but with sustained thought, and sustained thought to three aggregates . . . one aggregate without applied thought but with sustained thought, and (heart-)base to three aggregates . . .

(*b*) At the moment of conception . . . (2)

(xxiv) States without applied thought but with sustained thought and without applied thought and sustained thought are related to state without applied thought and sustained thought by dependence condition.

(*a*) Aggregates without applied thought but with sustained thought, and sustained thought are related to mind-produced matter by dependence condition; aggregates without applied thought but with sustained thought, and great primaries to mind-produced matter . . . applied thought and great primaries to mind-produced matter . . . aggregates without applied thought but with sustained thought, and (heart-)base are related to sustained thought by dependence condition;

(*b*) (At conception 4. Abbreviated.) (3)

(xxv) States without applied thought but with sustained thought and without applied thought and sustained thought are related to state without applied thought but with sustained thought and without applied thought and sustained thought by dependence condition.

(*a*) One aggregate without applied thought but with sustained thought, and sustained thought are related to three aggregates and mind-produced matter by dependence condition . . . two aggregates and sustained thought are related to two aggregates and mind-produced matter by dependence condition; one aggregate without applied thought but with sustained thought, and (heart-)base to three aggregates and sustained thought . . . two aggregates and (heart-)base are related to two aggregates and sustained thought by dependence condition;

(*b*) At the moment of conception . . . (4)

101. (xxvi)–(xxviii) States with applied thought and sustained thought and without applied thought but with sustained thought to state with applied thought and sustained thought . . . to state without applied thought and sustained thought . . . to state with applied thought and sustained thought and without applied thought and sustained thought . . . three.

(xxix)–(xxx) States with applied thought and sustained thought, without applied thought but with sustained thought and without applied thought and sustained thought to state with applied thought and sustained thought . . . are related to state without applied thought and sustained thought by dependence condition.

(Expand the two combinations.)

Strong-dependence 25

102. (i) State with applied thought and sustained thought is related to state with applied thought and sustained thought by strong-dependence condition.

(It is of three kinds, namely:) (*a*) object-strong-dependence (ārammaṇūpanissaya), (*b*) proximity-strong-dependence (anantarūpanissaya), (*c*) natural strong-dependence (pakatūpanissaya) . . .

(*c*) *Natural strong-dependence:* By the strong-dependence of confidence (saddhaṁ upanissāya) with applied thought and sustained thought, (one) offers an offering, undertakes precepts, fulfils the duty of observance, develops (uppādeti) jhāna with applied thought and sustained thought, develops insight (vipassanā) . . . Path, develops attainment; arouses (jappeti) conceit, adopts (gaṇhāti) wrong views . . . precept with applied thought and sustained thought . . . learning (suta) . . . generosity (cāga) . . . wisdom (paññā) . . . lust (rāga) . . . hate (dosa) . . . delusion (moha) . . . conceit (māna) . . . wrong views (diṭṭhi) . . . By the strong-dependence of wish (patthanā), (one) offers an offering, undertakes precepts, fulfils the duty of observance, develops jhāna with applied thought and sustained thought, develops insight . . . Path . . . attainment; kills a living being . . . causes schism in the Saṅgha. Confidence with applied thought and sustained thought, precept, learning, generosity, wisdom, lust, hate, delusion, conceit, wrong views, wish is related to confidence with applied thought and sustained thought, precept, learning, generosity, wisdom, lust, hate, delusion, conceit, wrong views, wish by strong-dependence condition. (1)

(ii) State with applied thought and sustained thought is related to state without applied thought but with sustained thought by strong-dependence condition.

(It is of three kinds, namely:) (*a*) object-strong-dependence, (*b*) proximity-strong-dependence, (*c*) natural strong-dependence . . .

(*c*) *Natural strong-dependence:* By the strong-dependence of confidence with applied thought and sustained thought, (one) develops jhāna without applied thought but with sustained thought . . . Path

. . . attainment . . . precept with applied thought and sustained thought . . . By the strong-dependence of wish, (one) develops jhāna without applied thought but with sustained thought . . . Path . . . attainment. Confidence with applied thought and sustained thought . . . wish is related to confidence without applied thought but with sustained thought, precept, learning, generosity, wisdom and applied thought by strong-dependence condition. (2)

(iii) State with applied thought and sustained thought is related to state without applied thought and sustained thought by strong-dependence condition.

(It is of two kinds, namely:) (*a*) proximity-strong-dependence, (*b*) natural strong-dependence . . .

(*b*) *Natural strong-dependence:* By the strong-dependence of confidence with applied thought and sustained thought, (one) develops jhāna without applied thought and sustained thought . . . Path . . . superknowledge, develops attainment . . . precept with applied thought and sustained thought . . . By the strong-dependence of wish, (one) develops jhāna without applied thought and sustained thought . . . Path . . . superknowledge, develops attainment. Confidence with applied thought and sustained thought . . . wish is related to confidence without applied thought and sustained thought, precept, learning, generosity, wisdom and sustained thought, bodily happiness (sukha), bodily pain (dukkha) by strong-dependence condition. (3)

(iv) State with applied thought and sustained thought is related to state without applied thought but with sustained thought and without applied thought and sustained thought by strong-dependence condition.

(It is of two kinds, namely:) (*a*) proximity-strong-dependence, (*b*) natural strong-dependence . . .

(*b*) *Natural strong-dependence:* Confidence with applied thought and sustained thought . . . wish is related to confidence without applied thought but with sustained thought, precept, learning, generosity, wisdom and sustained thought by strong-dependence condition. (4)

(v) State with applied thought and sustained thought is related to state with applied thought and sustained thought and without applied thought but with sustained thought by strong-dependence condition.

(It is of three kinds, namely:) (*a*) object-strong-dependence, (*b*) proximity-strong-dependence, (*c*) natural strong-dependence . . .

(*c*) *Natural strong-dependence:* Confidence with applied thought and sustained thought . . . wish is related to confidence with applied thought and sustained thought . . . wish and applied thought by strong-dependence condition. (5)

103. (vi) State without applied thought but with sustained thought is related to state without applied thought but with sustained thought by strong-dependence condition.

(It is of three kinds, namely:) (*a*) object-strong-dependence, (*b*) proximity-strong-dependence, (*c*) natural strong-dependence . . .

(*c*) *Natural strong-dependence:* By the strong-dependence of confidence without applied thought but with sustained thought, (one) develops jhāna without applied thought but with sustained thought . . . Path, develops attainment . . . precept without applied thought but with sustained thought . . . learning . . . generosity . . . wisdom . . . By the strong-dependence of applied thought, (one) develops jhāna without applied thought but with sustained thought . . . Path, develops attainment. Confidence without applied thought but with sustained thought, precept, learning, generosity, wisdom and applied thought is related to confidence without applied thought but with sustained thought, precept, learning, generosity, wisdom and applied thought by strong-dependence condition. (1)

(vii) State without applied thought but with sustained thought is related to state with applied thought and sustained thought by strong-dependence condition.

(It is of three kinds, namely:) (*a*) object-strong-dependence, (*b*) proximity-strong-dependence, (*c*) natural strong-dependence . . .

(*c*) *Natural strong-dependence:* By the strong-dependence of confidence without applied thought but with sustained thought, (one) offers an offering, undertakes precepts, fulfils the duty of observance, develops jhāna with applied thought and sustained thought . . . insight . . . Path, develops attainment; arouses conceit, adopts wrong views . . . precept without applied thought but with sustained thought . . . learning . . . generosity . . . wisdom . . . By the strong-dependence of applied thought, (one) offers an offering, undertakes precepts, fulfils the duty of observance, develops jhāna with applied thought and sustained thought, develops insight, develops Path, develops attainment; kills a living being . . . causes schism in the Saṅgha. Confidence without applied thought but with sustained thought, precept, learning, generosity, wisdom and applied thought is related to confidence with applied thought and sustained thought . . . wish by strong-dependence condition. (2)

(viii) State without applied thought but with sustained thought is related to state without applied thought and sustained thought by strong-dependence condition.

(It is of two kinds, namely:) (*a*) proximity-strong-dependence, (*b*) natural strong-dependence . . .

(*b*) *Natural strong-dependence:* By the strong-dependence of confidence without applied thought but with sustained thought, (one) develops jhāna without applied thought and sustained thought . . . Path . . . superknowledge, develops attainment . . . precept without applied thought but with sustained thought . . . learning . . . generosity . . . wisdom . . . By the strong-dependence of applied thought, (one) develops jhāna without applied thought and sustained thought . . . Path . . . superknowledge, develops attainment. Confidence without applied thought but with sustained thought, precept, learning, generosity, wisdom and applied thought is related to confidence without applied thought and sustained thought, precept, learning, generosity, wisdom and sustained thought, bodily happiness, bodily pain by strong-dependence condition. (3)

(ix) State without applied thought but with sustained thought is related to state without applied thought but with sustained thought and without applied thought and sustained thought by strong-dependence condition.

(It is of two kinds, namely:) (*a*) proximity-strong-dependence, (*b*) natural strong-dependence . . .

(*b*) *Natural strong-dependence:* Confidence without applied thought but with sustained thought, precept, learning, generosity, wisdom and applied thought is related to confidence without applied thought but with sustained thought, precept, learning, generosity, wisdom and sustained thought by strong-dependence condition. (4)

(x) State without applied thought but with sustained thought is related to state with applied thought and sustained thought and without applied thought but with sustained thought by strong-dependence condition.

(It is of three kinds, namely:) (*a*) object-strong dependence, (*b*) proximity-strong-dependence, (*c*) natural strong-dependence . . .

(*c*) *Natural strong-dependence:* Confidence without applied thought but with sustained thought, precept, learning, generosity, wisdom and applied thought is related to confidence with applied thought and sustained thought . . . wish and applied thought by strong-dependence condition. (5)

104. (xi) State without applied thought and sustained thought is related to state without applied thought and sustained thought by strong-dependence condition.

(It is of three kinds, namely:) (*a*) object-strong-dependence, (*b*) proximity-strong-dependence, (*c*) natural strong-dependence . . .

(*c*) *Natural strong-dependence:* By the strong-dependence of confidence without applied thought and sustained thought, (one) develops jhāna without applied thought and sustained thought . . . Path . . . superknowledge, develops attainment . . . precept without applied thought and sustained thought . . . learning . . . generosity . . . wisdom . . . sustained thought . . . bodily happiness . . . bodily pain . . . temperature . . . food (bhojana) . . . By the strong-dependence of lodging-place (senāsana), (one) develops jhāna without applied thought and sustained thought . . . Path . . . superknowledge, develops attainment. Confidence without applied thought and sustained thought, precept, learning, generosity, wisdom, and sustained thought, bodily happiness, bodily pain, temperature, food, lodging-place is related to confidence without applied thought and sustained thought, precept, learning, generosity, wisdom, and sustained thought, bodily happiness, bodily pain by strong-dependence condition. (1)

(xii) State without applied thought and sustained thought is related to state with applied thought and sustained thought by strong-dependence condition.

(It is of three kinds, namely:) (*a*) object-strong dependence, (*b*) proximity-strong-dependence, (*c*) natural strong-dependence . . .

(*c*) *Natural strong-dependence:* By the strong-dependence of confidence without applied thought and sustained thought, (one) offers an offering, undertakes precepts, fulfils the duty of observance, develops jhāna with applied thought and sustained thought . . . insight . . . Path, develops attainment; arouses conceit, adopts wrong views . . . precept without applied thought and sustained thought . . . learning . . . generosity . . . wisdom . . . sustained thought . . . bodily happiness . . . bodily pain . . . temperature . . . food . . . By the strong-dependence of lodging-place, (one) offers an offering, undertakes precepts, fulfils the duty of observance, develops jhāna with applied thought and sustained thought . . . insight . . . Path, develops attainment; kills a living being . . . causes schism in the Saṅgha. Confidence without applied thought and sustained thought . . . lodging-place is related to confidence with applied thought and sustained thought, precept . . . wish by strong-dependence condition. (2)

(xiii) State without applied thought and sustained thought is related to state without applied thought but with sustained thought by strong-dependence condition.

(It is of three kinds, namely:) (*a*) object-strong-dependence, (*b*) proximity-strong-dependence, (*c*) natural strong-dependence . . .

(*c*) *Natural strong-dependence:* By the strong-dependence of confidence without applied thought and sustained thought, (one) develops jhāna without applied thought but with sustained thought . . . insight . . . Path, develops attainment . . . precept without applied thought and sustained thought . . . By the strong-dependence of lodging-place, (one) develops jhāna without applied thought but with sustained thought . . . insight . . . Path, develops attainment. Confidence without applied thought and sustained thought . . . lodging-place is related to confidence without applied thought but with sustained thought, precept, learning, generosity, wisdom and applied thought by strong-dependence condition. (3)

(xiv) State without applied thought and sustained thought is related to state without applied thought but with sustained thought and without applied thought and sustained thought by strong-dependence condition.

(It is of three kinds, namely:) (*a*) object-strong dependence, (*b*) proximity-strong-dependence, (*c*) natural strong-dependence . . .

(*c*) *Natural strong-dependence:* Confidence without applied thought and sustained thought . . . lodging-place is related to confidence without applied thought but with sustained thought, precept, learning, generosity, wisdom and sustained thought by strong-dependence condition. (4)

(xv) State without applied thought and sustained thought is related to state with applied thought and sustained thought and without applied thought but with sustained thought by strong-dependence condition.

(It is of three kinds, namely:) (*a*) object-strong-dependence, (*b*) proximity-strong-dependence, (*c*) natural strong-dependence . . .

(*c*) *Natural strong-dependence:* Confidence without applied thought and sustained thought . . . lodging-place is related to confidence with applied thought and sustained thought, precept . . . wish and applied thought by strong-dependence condition. (5)

105. (xvi) States without applied thought but with sustained thought and without applied thought and sustained thought are related to state with applied thought and sustained thought by strong-dependence condition.

(It is of three kinds, namely:) (*a*) object-strong-dependence, (*b*) proximity-strong-dependence, (*c*) natural strong-dependence . . .

(*c*) *Natural strong-dependence:* Confidence without applied thought but with sustained thought, precept, learning, generosity, wisdom and sustained thought is related to confidence with applied thought and sustained thought . . . wish by strong-dependence condition. (1)

(xvii) States without applied thought but with sustained thought and without applied thought and sustained thought are related to state without applied thought but with sustained thought by strong-dependence condition.

(It is of three kinds, namely:) (*a*) object-strong-dependence, (*b*) proximity-strong-dependence, (*c*) natural strong-dependence . . .

(*c*) *Natural strong-dependence:* Confidence without applied thought but with sustained thought, precept, learning, generosity, wisdom and sustained thought is related to confidence without applied thought but with sustained thought, precept, learning, generosity, wisdom and applied thought by strong-dependence condition. (2)

(xviii) States without applied thought but with sustained thought and without applied thought and sustained thought are related to state without applied thought and sustained thought by strong-dependence condition.

(It is of two kinds, namely:) (*a*) proximity-strong-dependence, (*b*) natural strong-dependence . . .

(*b*) *Natural strong-dependence:* Confidence without applied thought but with sustained thought, precept, learning, generosity, wisdom and sustained thought is related to confidence without applied thought and sustained thought, precept, learning, generosity, wisdom and sustained thought, bodily happiness, bodily pain by strong-dependence condition. (3)

(xix) States without applied thought but with sustained thought and without applied thought and sustained thought are related to state without applied thought but with sustained thought and without applied thought and sustained thought by strong-dependence condition.

(It is of two kinds, namely:) (*a*) proximity-strong-dependence, (*b*) natural strong-dependence . . .

(*b*) *Natural strong-dependence:* Confidence without applied thought but with sustained thought, precept, learning, generosity, wisdom and sustained thought is related to confidence without applied thought but with sustained thought, precept, learning, generosity, wisdom and sustained thought by strong-dependence condition. (4)

(xx) States without applied thought but with sustained thought and without applied thought and sustained thought are related to state with applied thought and sustained thought and without applied thought but with sustained thought by strong-dependence condition.

(It is of three kinds, namely:) (*a*) object-strong-dependence, (*b*) proximity-strong-dependence, (*c*) natural strong-dependence . . .

(*c*) *Natural strong-dependence:* Confidence without applied thought but with sustained thought, precept, learning, generosity, wisdom and sustained thought is related to confidence with applied thought and sustained thought, precept, learning, generosity, wisdom, lust, hate delusion, conceit, wrong views, wish and applied thought by strong-dependence condition. (5)

106. (xxi) States with applied thought and sustained thought and without applied thought but with sustained thought are related to state with applied thought and sustained thought by strong-dependence condition.

(It is of three kinds, namely:) (*a*) object-strong-dependence, (*b*) proximity-strong-dependence, (*c*) natural strong-dependence . . .

(*c*) *Natural strong-dependence:* Confidence with applied thought and sustained thought, precept, learning, generosity, wisdom, lust, hate, delusion, conceit, wrong views, wish and applied thought is related to confidence with applied thought and sustained thought, precept . . . wish by strong-dependence condition. (1)

(xxii) States with applied thought and sustained thought and without applied thought but with sustained thought are related to state without applied thought but with sustained thought by strong-dependence condition.

(It is of three kinds, namely:) (*a*) object-strong-dependence, (*b*) proximity-strong-dependence, (*c*) natural strong-dependence . . .

(*c*) *Natural strong-dependence:* Confidence with applied thought and sustained thought, precept . . . wish and applied thought is related to confidence without applied thought but with sustained thought, precept, learning, generosity, wisdom and applied thought by strong-dependence condition. (2)

(xxiii) States with applied thought and sustained thought and without applied thought but with sustained thought are related to state without applied thought and sustained thought by strong-dependence condition.

(It is of two kinds, namely:) (*a*) proximity-strong-dependence, (*b*) natural strong-dependence . . .

(*b*) *Natural strong-dependence:* Confidence with applied thought and sustained thought, precept, learning, generosity, wisdom . . . wish and applied thought is related to confidence without applied thought and sustained thought, precept, learning, generosity, wisdom and sustained thought, bodily happiness, bodily pain by strong-dependence condition. (3)

(xxiv) States with applied thought and sustained thought and without applied thought but with sustained thought are related to state without applied thought but with sustained thought and without applied thought and sustained thought by strong-dependence condition.

(It is of two kinds, namely:) (*a*) proximity-strong-dependence, (*b*) natural strong-dependence . . .

(*b*) *Natural strong-dependence:* Confidence with applied thought and sustained thought, precept, learning, generosity, wisdom . . . wish and applied thought is related to confidence without applied thought but with sustained thought, precept, learning, generosity, wisdom and sustained thought by strong-dependence condition. (4)

(xxv) States with applied thought and sustained thought and without applied thought but with sustained thought are related to state with applied thought and sustained thought and without applied thought but with sustained thought by strong-dependence condition.

(It is of three kinds, namely:) (*a*) object-strong-dependence, (*b*) proximity-strong-dependence, (*c*) natural strong-dependence . . .

(*c*) *Natural strong-dependence:* Confidence with applied thought and sustained thought, precept, learning, generosity, wisdom, lust, hate, delusion, conceit, wrong views, wish and applied thought is related to confidence with applied thought and sustained thought . . . wish and applied thought by strong-dependence condition. (5)

Prenascence 5

107. (i) State without applied thought and sustained thought is

related to state without applied thought and sustained thought by prenascence condition.

(It is of two kinds, namely:) (*a*) object-prenascence (ārammaṇa-purejāta), (*b*) base-prenascence (vatthu-purejāta).

(*a*) *Object-prenascence:* By the power of divine-eye, one sees a visible object. By the power of divine-ear element, one hears a sound. Visible object-base to eye-consciousness . . . tangible object-base is related to body-consciousness by prenascence condition.

(*b*) *Base-prenascence:* Eye-base to eye-consciousness . . . body-base to body-consciousness . . . (heart-)base is related to aggregates without applied thought and sustained thought, and sustained thought by prenascence condition. (1)

(ii) State without applied thought and sustained thought is related to state with applied thought and sustained thought by prenascence condition.

(It is of two kinds, namely:) (*a*) object-prenascence, (*b*) base-prenascence.

(*a*) *Object-prenascence:* (One) practises insight into the impermanence, suffering and impersonality of the eye . . . tangible object . . . (One) practises insight into the impermanence, suffering and impersonality of the (heart-)base; enjoys and delights in [the (heart-)base]. Taking it as object, arises lust . . . arises grief.

(*b*) *Base-prenascence:* (Heart-)base is related to aggregates with applied thought and sustained thought by prenascence condition. (2)

(iii) State without applied thought and sustained thought is related to state without applied thought but with sustained thought by prenascence condition.

(It is of two kinds, namely:) (*a*) object-prenascence, (*b*) base-prenascence.

(*a*) *Object-prenascence:* (One) practises insight into the impermanence, suffering and impersonality of the eye; enjoys and delights in (the eye). Taking it as object, arises applied thought . . . (One) practises insight into the impermanence, suffering and impersonality of the (heart-)base; enjoys and delights in [the (heart-)base]. Taking it as object, arises applied thought.

(*b*) *Base-prenascence:* (Heart-)base is related to aggregates without applied thought but with sustained thought, and applied thought by prenascence condition. (3)

(iv) State without applied thought and sustained thought is

related to state without applied thought but with sustained thought and without applied thought and sustained thought by prenascence condition.

Base-prenascence: (Heart-)base is related to aggregates without applied thought but with sustained thought, and sustained thought by prenascence condition. (4)

(v) State without applied thought and sustained thought is related to state with applied thought and sustained thought and without applied thought but with sustained thought by prenascence condition.

(It is of two kinds, namely:) (*a*) object-prenascence, (*b*) base-prenascence.

(*a*) *Object-prenascence:* (One) practises insight into the impermanence, suffering and impersonality of the eye; enjoys and delights in (the eye). Taking it as object, arise aggregates with applied thought and sustained thought, and applied thought, . . . ear . . . nose . . . tongue . . . body . . . visible object . . . sound . . . smell . . . taste . . . tangible object . . . (One) practises insight into the impermanence, suffering and impersonality of the (heart-)base; enjoys and delights in [the (heart-)base]. Taking it as object, arise aggregates with applied thought and sustained thought, and applied thought.

(*b*) *Base-prenascence:* (Heart-)base is related to aggregates with applied thought and sustained thought, and applied thought by prenascence condition. (5)

Postnascence 5

108. (i) State with applied thought and sustained thought is related to state without applied thought and sustained thought by postnascence condition.

Postnascent aggregates with applied thought and sustained thought are related to this prenascent (purejāta) body by postnascence condition. (1)

(ii) State without applied thought but with sustained thought is related to state without applied thought and sustained thought by postnascence condition.

Postnascent aggregates without applied thought but with sustained thought, and applied thought are related to this prenascent body by postnascence condition. (1)

(iii) State without applied thought and sustained thought is related to state without applied thought and sustained thought by postnascence condition.

Postnascent aggregates without applied thought and sustained thought, and sustained thought are related to this prenascent body by postnascence condition. (1)

(iv) States without applied thought but with sustained thought and without applied thought and sustained thought are related to state without applied thought and sustained thought by postnascence condition.

Postnascent aggregates without applied thought but with sustained thought, and sustained thought are related to this prenascent body by postnascence condition. (1)

(v) States with applied thought and sustained thought and without applied thought but with sustained thought are related to state without applied thought and sustained thought by postnascence condition.

Postnascent aggregates with applied thought and sustained thought, and applied thought are related to this prenascent body by postnascence condition. (1)

Repetition 21

109. (i) State with applied thought and sustained thought is related to state with applied thought and sustained thought by repetition condition.

Preceding aggregates with applied thought and sustained thought are related to subsequent aggregates with applied thought and sustained thought by repetition condition. Adaptation to change-of-lineage; adaptation to purification; change-of-lineage to Path with applied thought and sustained thought; purification is related to Path with applied thought and sustained thought by repetition condition. (1)

(ii) State with applied thought and sustained thought is related to state without applied thought but with sustained thought by repetition condition.

Preceding aggregates with applied thought and sustained thought are related to subsequent applied thought by repetition condition. The preparation for jhāna without applied thought but with sustained thought is related to jhāna without applied thought but with sustained thought by repetition condition. Change-of-lineage is related to Path without applied thought but with sustained thought by repetition condition. Purification is related to Path without applied thought but with sustained thought by repetition condition. (2).

(iii) State with applied thought and sustained thought is related to state without applied thought and sustained thought by repetition condition.

The preparation for second jhāna is related to sustained thought (present) at second jhāna by repetition condition. The preparation for third jhāna to third jhāna . . . The preparation for fourth jhāna to fourth jhāna . . . the preparation for infinity of space to infinity of space . . . the preparation for infinity of consciousness to infinity of consciousness . . . the preparation for nothingness to nothingness . . . the preparation for neither-perception-nor-non-perception to neither-perception-nor-non-perception . . .

The preparation for divine-eye to divine-eye . . . the preparation for divine-ear element to divine-ear element . . . the preparation for knowledge of supernormal power . . . the preparation for knowledge of penetration into others' minds . . . the preparation for knowledge of remembrance of past existences . . . the preparation for knowledge of rebirths according to one's kamma . . . the preparation for knowledge of future existences . . . Change-of-lineage to Path without applied thought and sustained thought, and sustained thought; purification is related to Path without applied thought and sustained thought, and sustained thought by repetition condition. (3)

(iv) State with applied thought and sustained thought is related to state without applied thought but with sustained thought and without applied thought and sustained thought by repetition condition.

The preparation for jhāna without applied thought but with sustained thought is related to jhāna without applied thought but with sustained thought, and sustained thought by repetition condition. Change-of-lineage to Path without applied thought but with sustained thought, and sustained thought; purification is related to Path without applied thought but with sustained thought, and sustained thought by repetition condition. (4)

(v) State with applied thought and sustained thought is related to state with applied thought and sustained thought and without applied thought but with sustained thought by repetition condition.

Preceding aggregates with applied thought and sustained thought are related to subsequent aggregates with applied thought and sustained thought, and applied thought by repetition condition. Adaptation to change-of-lineage and applied thought; adaptation to purification and applied thought; change-of-lineage to Path with applied thought and sustained thought, and applied thought; purification is related to Path with applied thought and sustained thought, and applied thought by repetition condition. (5)

110. (vi) State without applied thought but with sustained thought is related to state without applied thought but with sustained thought by repetition condition.

Preceding applied thought is related to subsequent applied thought by repetition condition. Preceding aggregates without applied thought but with sustained thought are related to subsequent aggregates without applied thought but with sustained thought by repetition condition. (1)

(vii) State without applied thought but with sustained thought is related to state with applied thought and sustained thought by repetition condition.

Preceding applied thought is related to subsequent aggregates with applied thought and sustained thought by repetition condition. (2)

(viii) State without applied thought but with sustained thought is related to state without applied thought and sustained thought by repetition condition.

Preceding aggregates without applied thought but with sustained thought are related to subsequent sustained thought by repetition condition. (3)

(ix) State without applied thought but with sustained thought is related to state without applied thought but with sustained thought and without applied thought and sustained thought by repetition condition.

Preceding aggregates without applied thought but with sustained thought are related to subsequent aggregates without applied thought but with sustained thought, and sustained thought by repetition condition. (4)

(x) State without applied thought but with sustained thought is related to state with applied thought and sustained thought and without applied thought but with sustained thought by repetition condition.

Preceding applied thought is related to subsequent aggregates with applied thought and sustained thought, and applied thought by repetition condition. (5)

111. (xi) State without applied thought and sustained thought is related to state without applied thought and sustained thought by repetition condition.

Preceding sustained thought is related to subsequent sustained thought by repetition condition. Preceding aggregates without applied thought and sustained thought are related to subsequent aggregates without applied thought and sustained thought by repetition condition. (1)

(xii) State without applied thought and sustained thought is related to state without applied thought but with sustained thought by repetition condition.

Preceding sustained thought is related to subsequent aggregates without applied thought but with sustained thought by repetition condition. (2)

(xiii) State without applied thought and sustained thought is related to state without applied thought but with sustained thought and without applied thought and sustained thought by repetition condition.

Preceding sustained thought is related to subsequent aggregates without applied thought but with sustained thought, and sustained thought by repetition condition. (3)

112. (xiv) States without applied thought but with sustained thought and without applied thought and sustained thought are related to state without applied thought but with sustained thought by repetition condition.

Preceding aggregates without applied thought but with sustained thought, and sustained thought are related to subsequent aggregates without applied thought but with sustained thought by repetition condition. (1)

(xv) States without applied thought but with sustained thought and without applied thought and sustained thought are related to state without applied thought and sustained thought by repetition condition.

Preceding aggregates without applied thought but with sustained thought, and sustained thought are related to subsequent sustained thought by repetition condition. (2)

(xvi) States without applied thought but with sustained thought and without applied thought and sustained thought are related to state without applied thought but with sustained thought and without applied thought and sustained thought by repetition condition.

Preceding aggregates without applied thought but with sustained thought, and sustained thought are related to subsequent aggregates without applied thought but with sustained thought, and sustained thought by repetition condition. (3)

113. (xvii) States with applied thought and sustained thought and without applied thought but with sustained thought are related to state with applied thought and sustained thought by repetition condition.

Preceding aggregates with applied thought and sustained thought, and applied thought are related to subsequent aggregates with applied thought and sustained thought by repetition condition. Adaptation and applied thought to change-of-lineage; adaptation and applied thought to purification; change-of-lineage and applied thought to Path with applied thought and sustained thought; purification and applied thought are related to Path with applied thought and sustained thought by repetition condition. (1)

(xviii) States with applied thought and sustained thought and without applied thought but with sustained thought are related to state without applied thought but with sustained thought by repetition condition.

Preceding aggregates with applied thought and sustained thought, and applied thought are related to subsequent applied thought by repetition condition. The preparation for jhāna without applied thought but with sustained thought, and applied thought are related to jhāna without applied thought but with sustained thought by repetition condition. Change-of-lineage and applied thought to Path without applied thought but with sustained thought; purification and applied thought are related to Path without applied thought but with sustained thought by repetition condition. (2)

(xix) States with applied thought and sustained thought and without applied thought but with sustained thought are related to state without applied thought and sustained thought by repetition condition.

The preparation for second jhāna and applied thought are related to sustained thought (present) at second jhāna by repetition condition . . . the preparation for neither-perception-nor-non-perception and applied thought . . . the preparation for divine-eye and applied thought . . . the preparation for knowledge of future existences and applied thought are related to knowledge of future existences by repetition condition. Change-of-lineage and applied thought are related to Path without applied thought and sustained thought, and sustained thought by repetition condition. Purification and applied thought are related to Path without applied thought and sustained thought, and sustained thought by repetition condition. (3)

(xx) States with applied thought and sustained thought and without applied thought but with sustained thought are related to state without applied thought but with sustained thought and without applied thought and sustained thought by repetition condition.

The preparation for jhāna without applied thought but with sustained thought, and applied thought to jhāna without applied thought but with sustained thought, and sustained thought; change-of-lineage and applied thought to Path without applied thought but with sustained thought, and sustained thought; purification and applied thought are related to Path without applied thought but with sustained thought, and sustained thought by repetition condition. (4)

(xxi) States with applied thought and sustained thought and without applied thought but with sustained thought are related to state with applied thought and sustained thought and without applied thought but with sustained thought by repetition condition.

Preceding aggregates with applied thought and sustained thought, and applied thought are related to subsequent aggregates with applied thought and sustained thought, and applied thought by repetition condition. Adaptation and applied thought to change-of-lineage and applied thought; adaptation and applied thought to purification and applied thought; change-of-lineage and applied thought to Path with applied thought and sustained thought, and applied thought; purification and applied thought are related to Path with applied thought and sustained thought, and applied thought by repetition condition. (5)

Kamma 11

114. (i) State with applied thought and sustained thought is related to state with applied thought and sustained thought by kamma condition.

(It is of two kinds, namely:) (*a*) conascence(-kamma), (*b*) asynchronous (kamma).

(*a*) (1) Conascent volition with applied thought and sustained thought (sahajātā savitakka-savicārā cetanā) is related to (its) associated aggregates by kamma condition;

(2) At the moment of conception, volition with applied thought and sustained thought is related to (its) associated aggregates by kamma condition.

(*b*) Asynchronous (nānākhaṇika) volition with applied thought and sustained thought is related to (its) resultant aggregates with applied thought and sustained thought by kamma condition. (1)

(ii) State with applied thought and sustained thought is related to state without applied thought but with sustained thought by kamma condition.

(It is of two kinds, namely:) (*a*) conascence(-kamma), (*b*) asynchronous (kamma).

(*a*) (1) Conascent volition with applied thought and sustained thought is related to applied thought by kamma condition;

(2) At the moment of conception, volition with applied thought and sustained thought is related to applied thought by kamma condition.

(*b*) Asynchronous volition with applied thought and sustained thought is related to (its) resultant applied thought by kamma condition. (2)

(iii) State with applied thought and sustained thought is related to state without applied thought and sustained thought by kamma condition.

(It is of two kinds, namely:) (*a*) conascence(-kamma), (*b*) asynchronous (kamma).

(*a*) (1) Conascent volition with applied thought and sustained thought is related to mind-produced matter by kamma condition;

(2) At the moment of conception, volition with applied thought and sustained thought is related to kamma-produced matter by kamma condition.

(*b*) Asynchronous volition with applied thought and sustained thought is related to (its) resultant aggregates without applied thought and sustained thought and kamma-produced matter by kamma condition. (3)

(iv) State with applied thought and sustained thought is related to state with applied thought and sustained thought and without applied thought and sustained thought by kamma condition.

(It is of two kinds, namely:) (*a*) conascence(-kamma), (*b*) asynchronous (kamma).

(*a*) (1) Conascent volition with applied thought and sustained thought is related to (its) associated aggregates and mind-produced matter by kamma condition;

(2) At the moment of conception, volition with applied thought and sustained thought is related to (its) associated aggregates and kamma-produced matter by kamma condition.

(*b*) Asynchronous volition with applied thought and sustained thought is related to (its) resultant aggregates with applied thought and sustained thought and kamma-produced matter by kamma condition. (4)

(v) State with applied thought and sustained thought is related to state without applied thought but with sustained thought and without applied thought and sustained thought by kamma condition.

(It is of two kinds, namely:) (*a*) conascence(-kamma), (*b*) asynchronous (kamma).

(*a*) (1) Conascent volition with applied thought and sustained thought is related to applied thought and mind-produced matter by kamma condition;

(2) At the moment of conception, volition with applied thought and sustained thought is related to applied thought and kamma-produced matter by kamma condition.

(*b*) Asynchronous volition with applied thought and sustained thought is related to (its) resultant applied thought and kamma-produced matter by kamma condition. (5)

(vi) State with applied thought and sustained thought is related to state with applied thought and sustained thought and without applied thought but with sustained thought by kamma condition.

(It is of two kinds, namely:) (*a*) conascence(-kamma), (*b*) asynchronous (kamma).

(*a*) (1) Conascent volition with applied thought and sustained thought is related to (its) associated aggregates and applied thought by kamma condition;

(2) At the moment of conception, volition with applied thought and sustained thought is related to (its) associated aggregates and applied thought by kamma condition.

(*b*) Asynchronous volition with applied thought and sustained thought is related to (its) resultant aggregates with applied thought and sustained thought, and applied thought by kamma condition. (6)

(vii) State with applied thought and sustained thought is related to state with applied thought and sustained thought, without applied thought but with sustained thought and without applied thought and sustained thought by kamma condition.

(It is of two kinds, namely:) (*a*) conascence(-kamma), (*b*) asynchronous (kamma).

(*a*) (1) Conascent volition with applied thought and sustained thought is related to (its) associated aggregates, applied thought and mind-produced matter by kamma condition;

(2) At the moment of conception, volition with applied thought and sustained thought is related to (its) associated aggregates, applied thought and kamma-produced matter by kamma condition.

(*b*) Asynchronous volition with applied thought and sustained thought is related to (its) resultant aggregates with applied thought and sustained thought, applied thought and kamma-produced matter by kamma condition. (7)

115. (viii) State without applied thought but with sustained thought is related to state without applied thought but with sustained thought by kamma condition.

(It is of two kinds, namely:) (*a*) conascence(-kamma), (*b*) asynchronous (kamma).

(*a*) (1) Conascent volition without applied thought but with sustained thought is related to (its) associated aggregates by kamma condition;

(2) At the moment of conception . . .

(*b*) Asynchronous volition without applied thought but with sustained thought is related to (its) resultant aggregates without applied thought but with sustained thought by kamma condition. (1)

(ix) State without applied thought but with sustained thought is related to state without applied thought and sustained thought by kamma condition.

(It is of two kinds, namely:) (*a*) conascence(-kamma), (*b*) asynchronous (kamma).

(*a*) (1) Conascent volition without applied thought but with sustained thought is related to sustained thought and mind-produced matter by kamma condition;

(2) At the moment of conception, volition without applied thought but with sustained thought is related to (its) resultant sustained thought and kamma-produced matter by kamma condition.

(*b*) Asynchronous volition without applied thought but with sustained thought is related to (its) resultant sustained thought and kamma-produced matter by kamma condition. (2)

(x) State without applied thought but with sustained thought is related to state without applied thought but with sustained thought and without applied thought and sustained thought by kamma condition.

(It is of two kinds, namely:) (*a*) conascence(-kamma), (*b*) asynchronous (kamma).

(*a*) (1) Conascent volition without applied thought but with sustained thought is related to (its) associated aggregates, sustained thought and mind-produced matter by kamma condition;

(2) At the moment of conception, volition without applied thought but with sustained thought is related to (its) associated aggregates, sustained thought and kamma-produced matter by kamma condition.

(*b*) Asynchronous volition without applied thought but with sustained thought is related to (its) resultant aggregates without applied thought but with sustained thought, sustained thought and kamma-produced matter by kamma condition. (3)

(xi) State without applied thought and sustained thought is related to state without applied thought and sustained thought by kamma condition.

(It is of two kinds, namely:) (*a*) conascence(-kamma), (*b*) asynchronous (kamma).

(*a*) (1) Conascent volition without applied thought and sustained thought is related to (its) associated aggregates and mind-produced matter by kamma condition;

(2) At the moment of conception, volition without applied thought and sustained thought is related to (its) associated aggregates and kamma-produced matter by kamma condition.

(*b*) Asynchronous volition without applied thought and sustained thought is related to (its) resultant aggregates without applied thought and sustained thought and kamma-produced matter by kamma condition. (1)

Resultant 21

116. (i) State with applied thought and sustained thought is related to state with applied thought and sustained thought by resultant condition.

(*a*) One resultant aggregate with applied thought and sustained thought is related to three aggregates by resultant condition . . .

(*b*) At the moment of conception, one resultant[1] aggregate with applied thought and sustained thought is related to three aggregates by resultant condition . . .

(ii)–(vii) State with applied thought and sustained thought is related to state without applied thought but with sustained thought by resultant condition.

(*a*) Resultant aggregates with applied thought and sustained thought are related to applied thought by resultant condition;

(*b*) At the moment of conception . . .

(7 questions for the reference "with applied thought and sustained thought" are to be completed.)

---

[1] Vipāka (resultant) has been omitted in the Pali Text. Also pa, the sign of elision, has been left out in both cases.

(viii)–(xii) State without applied thought but with sustained thought is related to state without applied thought but with sustained thought by resultant condition.

(*a*) One resultant aggregate without applied thought but with sustained thought is related to three aggregates by resultant condition . . . two aggregates . . .

(*b*) At the moment of conception, one resultant aggregate without applied thought but with sustained thought . . .

[Do 5 questions for the reference "without applied thought but with sustained thought"; remember (to take) resultant.]

117. (xiii) State without applied thought and sustained thought is related to state without applied thought and sustained thought by resultant condition.

(*a*) One resultant aggregate without applied thought and sustained thought is related to three aggregates and mind-produced matter by resultant condition . . . two aggregates . . . resultant sustained thought is related to mind-produced matter by resultant condition;

(*b*) At the moment of conception . . . aggregates are related to (heart-)base by resultant condition; sustained thought is related to (heart-)base by resultant condition. (1)

(xiv) State without applied thought and sustained thought is related to state without applied thought but with sustained thought by resultant condition.

(*a*) Resultant sustained thought is related to aggregates without applied thought but with sustained thought by resultant condition;

(*b*) At the moment of conception, resultant sustained thought is related to aggregates without applied thought but with sustained thought by resultant condition. (2)

(xv) State without applied thought and sustained thought is related to state without applied thought but with sustained thought and without applied thought and sustained thought by resultant condition.

(*a*) Resultant sustained thought is related to aggregates without applied thought but with sustained thought and mind-produced matter by resultant condition;

(*b*) At the moment of conception, resultant sustained thought is related to aggregates without applied thought but with sustained thought and kamma-produced matter by resultant condition. (3)

118. (xvi) States without applied thought but with sustained thought and without applied thought and sustained thought are related to state

without applied thought but with sustained thought by resultant condition.

(*a*) One resultant aggregate without applied thought but with sustained thought, and sustained thought are related to three aggregates by resultant condition . . . two aggregates . . .

(*b*) At the moment of conception . . . (1)

(xvii) States without applied thought but with sustained thought and without applied thought and sustained thought are related to state without applied thought and sustained thought by resultant condition.

(*a*) Resultant aggregates without applied thought but with sustained thought, and sustained thought are related to mind-produced matter by resultant condition;

(*b*) At the moment of conception, resultant aggregates without applied thought but with sustained thought, and sustained thought are related to kamma-produced matter by resultant condition. (2)

(xviii) States without applied thought but with sustained thought and without applied thought and sustained thought are related to state without applied thought but with sustained thought and without applied thought and sustained thought by resultant condition.

(*a*) One resultant aggregate without applied thought but with sustained thought, and sustained thought are related to three aggregates and mind-produced matter by resultant condition . . .

(*b*) At the moment of conception, one resultant aggregate without applied thought but with sustained thought, and sustained thought are related to three aggregates and kamma-produced matter by resultant condition . . . (3)

(xix) States with applied thought and sustained thought and without applied thought but with sustained thought are related to state with applied thought and sustained thought by resultant condition.

(*a*) One resultant aggregate with applied thought and sustained thought, and applied thought are related to three aggregates by resultant condition . . . two aggregates . . .

(*b*) At the moment of conception . . . (1)

(xx) States with applied thought and sustained thought and without applied thought but with sustained thought are related to state without applied thought and sustained thought by resultant condition.

(*a*) Resultant aggregates with applied thought and sustained thought, and applied thought are related to mind-produced matter by resultant condition;

(*b*) At the moment of conception . . . (2)

(xxi) States with applied thought and sustained thought and without applied thought but with sustained thought are related to state with applied thought and sustained thought and without applied thought and sustained thought by resultant condition.

(*a*) One resultant aggregate with applied thought and sustained thought, and applied thought are related to three aggregates and mind-produced matter by resultant condition . . .

(*b*) At the moment of conception . . . (3)

Nutriment 11

119. (i) State with applied thought and sustained thought is related to state with applied thought and sustained thought by nutriment condition.

(*a*) Nutriments (āhāra) with applied thought and sustained thought are related to (their) associated aggregates by nutriment condition;

(*b*) At the moment of conception . . . (1)

(ii)-(vii) State with applied thought and sustained thought is related to state without applied thought but with sustained thought by nutriment condition.

(*a*) Nutriments with applied thought and sustained thought are related to applied thought by nutriment condition;

(*b*) At the moment of conception . . .

(Classify 7 questions in this way for the reference "with applied thought and sustained thought".)

(viii) State without applied thought but with sustained thought is related to state without applied thought but with sustained thought by nutriment condition.

(*a*) Nutriments without applied thought but with sustained thought are related to (their) associated aggregates by nutriment condition;

(*b*) At the moment of conception . . . (1)

(ix) State without applied thought but with sustained thought is related to state without applied thought and sustained thought by nutriment condition.

(*a*) Nutriments without applied thought but with sustained thought are related to sustained thought and mind-produced matter by nutriment condition;

(*b*) At the moment of conception . . . (2)

(x) State without applied thought but with sustained thought is related to state without applied thought but with sustained thought and without applied thought and sustained thought by nutriment condition.

(*a*) Nutriments without applied thought but with sustained thought are related to (their) associated aggregates, sustained thought and mind-produced matter by nutriment condition;

(*b*) At the moment of conception . . . (3)

(xi) State without applied thought and sustained thought is related to state without applied thought and sustained thought by nutriment condition.

(*a*) Nutriments without applied thought and sustained thought are related to (their) associated aggregates and mind-produced matter by nutriment condition;

(*b*) At the moment of conception . . .

(*c*) Edible (kabalīkāra) food is related to this body by nutriment condition. (1)

Faculty 11

120. (i) State with applied thought and sustained thought is related to state with applied thought and sustained thought by faculty condition.

(*a*) Faculties (indriya) with applied thought and sustained thought are related to (their) associated aggregates by faculty condition;

(*b*) At the moment of conception . . . (1)

(ii)–(vii) State with applied thought and sustained thought is related to state without applied thought but with sustained thought by faculty condition.

(*a*) Faculties with applied thought and sustained thought are related to applied thought by faculty condition;

(*b*) At the moment of conception . . . (7)

(Classify 7 questions in this way for the reference "with applied thought and sustained thought".)

(viii) State without applied thought but with sustained thought is related to state without applied thought but with sustained thought by faculty condition.

(*a*) Faculties without applied thought but with sustained thought are related to (their) associated aggregates by faculty condition;

(*b*) At the moment of conception . . . (1)

(ix) State without applied thought but with sustained thought is related to state without applied thought and sustained thought by faculty condition.

(*a*) Faculties without applied thought but with sustained thought are related to sustained thought and mind-produced matter by faculty condition;

(*b*) At the moment of conception . . . (2)

(x) State without applied thought but with sustained thought is related to state without applied thought but with sustained thought and without applied thought and sustained thought by faculty condition.

(*a*) Faculties without applied thought but with sustained thought are related to (their) associated aggregates, sustained thought and mind-produced matter by faculty condition;

(*b*) At the moment of conception . . . (3)

(xi) State without applied thought and sustained thought is related to state without applied thought and sustained thought by faculty condition.

(*a*) Faculties without applied thought and sustained thought are related to (their) associated aggregates and mind-produced matter by faculty condition;

(*b*) At the moment of conception . . .

(*c*) Eye-faculty to eye-consciousness . . . body-faculty is related to body-consciousness by faculty condition;

(*d*) Physical life-faculty (rūpajīvitindriya) is related to kamma-produced matter by faculty condition. (1)

Jhāna 21

121. (i)–(vii) State with applied thought and sustained thought is related to state with applied thought and sustained thought by jhāna condition.

(*a*) Jhāna factors (jhānaṅga) with applied thought and sustained thought are related to (their) associated aggregates by jhāna condition;

(*b*) At the moment of conception . . . (7)

(Classify 7 questions in this way for the reference "with applied thought and sustained thought".)

(viii)–(xii) State without applied thought but with sustained thought is related to state without applied thought but with sustained thought by jhāna condition.

(*a*) Jhāna factors without applied thought but with sustained thought are related to (their) associated aggregates by jhāna condition;

(*b*) At the moment of conception . . . (5)

(Classify 5 questions in this way for the reference "without applied thought but with sustained thought".)

(xiii) State without applied thought and sustained thought is related to state without applied thought and sustained thought by jhāna condition.

(*a*) Jhāna factors without applied thought and sustained thought are related to (their) associated aggregates and mind-produced matter by jhāna condition; sustained thought is related to mind-produced matter by jhāna condition;

(*b*) At the moment of conception (. . . at the moment of conception,)* sustained thought is related to kamma-produced matter by jhāna condition; sustained thought is related to (heart-)base by jhāna condition. (1)

(xiv) State without applied thought and sustained thought is related to state without applied thought but with sustained thought by jhāna condition.

(*a*) Sustained thought is related to aggregates without applied thought but with sustained thought by jhāna condition;

(*b*) At the moment of conception, sustained thought is related to aggregates without applied thought but with sustained thought by jhāna condition. (2)

(xv) State without applied thought and sustained thought is related to state without applied thought but with sustained thought and without applied thought and sustained thought by jhāna condition.

(*a*) Sustained thought is related to aggregates without applied thought but with sustained thought and mind-produced matter by jhāna condition;

(*b*) At the moment of conception, sustained thought is related to aggregates without applied thought but with sustained thought and kamma-produced matter by jhāna condition. (3)

122. (xvi) States without applied thought but with sustained thought and without applied thought and sustained thought are related to state without applied thought but with sustained thought by jhāna condition.

(*a*) Jhāna factors without applied thought but with sustained thought, and sustained thought are related to (their) associated aggregates by jhāna condition;

---

* The bracketed portion is omitted in the Pali Text.

(*b*) At the moment of conception . . . (1)

(xvii) States without applied thought but with sustained thought and without applied thought and sustained thought are related to state without applied thought and sustained thought by jhāna condition.

(*a*) Jhāna factors without applied thought but with sustained thought, and sustained thought are related to mind-produced matter by jhāna condition;

(*b*) At the moment of conception . . . (2)

(xviii) States without applied thought but with sustained thought and without applied thought and sustained thought are related to state without applied thought but with sustained thought and without applied thought and sustained thought by jhāna condition.

(*a*) Jhāna factors without applied thought but with sustained thought, and sustained thought are related to (their) associated aggregates and mind-produced matter by jhāna condition;

(*b*) At the moment of conception, jhāna factors without applied thought but with sustained thought, and sustained thought are related to (their) associated aggregates and kamma-produced matter by jhāna condition. (3)

(xix) States with applied thought and sustained thought and without applied thought but with sustained thought are related to state with applied thought and sustained thought by jhāna condition.

(*a*) Jhāna factors with applied thought and sustained thought, and applied thought are related to (their) associated aggregates by jhāna condition;

(*b*) At the moment of conception . . . (1)

(xx) States with applied thought and sustained thought and without applied thought but with sustained thought are related to state without applied thought and sustained thought by jhāna condition.

(*a*) Jhāna factors with applied thought and sustained thought, and applied thought are related to mind-produced matter by jhāna condition;

(*b*) At the moment of conception . . . (2)

(xxi) States with applied thought and sustained thought and without applied thought but with sustained thought are related to state with applied thought and sustained thought and without applied thought and sustained thought by jhāna condition.

(*a*) Jhāna factors with applied thought and sustained thought, and applied thought are related to (their) associated aggregates and mind-produced matter by jhāna condition;

(*b*) At the moment of conception . . . (3)

Path 16

123. (i)–(vii) State with applied thought and sustained thought is related to state with applied thought and sustained thought by path condition.

(*a*) Path factors (maggaṅga) with applied thought and sustained thought are related to (their) associated aggregates by path condition;

(*b*) At the moment of conception . . .

(Classify 7 questions in this way for the reference "with applied thought and sustained thought".)

(viii)–(xii) State without applied thought but with sustained thought is related to state without applied thought but with sustained thought by path condition.

(*a*) Path factors without applied thought but with sustained thought are related to (their) associated aggregates by path condition;

(*b*) At the moment of conception . . .

(Classify 5 questions in this way for the reference "without applied thought but with sustained thought".)

(xiii) State without applied thought and sustained thought is related to state without applied thought and sustained thought by path condition.

(*a*) Path factors without applied thought and sustained thought are related to (their) associated aggregates and mind-produced matter by path condition;

(*b*) At the moment of conception . . . (1)

(xiv) States with applied thought and sustained thought and without applied thought but with sustained thought are related to state with applied thought and sustained thought by path condition.

(*a*) Path factors with applied thought and sustained thought, and applied thought are related to (their) associated aggregates by path condition;

(*b*) At the moment of conception . . . (1)

(xv) States with applied thought and sustained thought and without applied thought but with sustained thought are related to state without applied thought and sustained thought by path condition.

(*a*) Path factors with applied thought and sustained thought, and applied thought are related to mind-produced matter by path condition;

(*b*) At the moment of conception . . . (2)

(xvi) States with applied thought and sustained thought and without applied thought but with sustained thought are related to state with applied thought and sustained thought and without applied thought and sustained thought by path condition.

(*a*) Path factors with applied thought and sustained thought, and applied thought are related to (their) associated aggregates and mind-produced matter by path condition;

(*b*) At the moment of conception . . . (3)

Association 11

124. (i) State with applied thought and sustained thought is related to state with applied thought and sustained thought by association condition.

(*a*) One aggregate with applied thought and sustained thought is related to three aggregates by association condition . . . two aggregates to two aggregates . . .

(*b*) At the moment of conception . . . (1)

(ii) State with applied thought and sustained thought is related to state without applied thought but with sustained thought by association condition.

(*a*) Aggregates with applied thought and sustained thought are related to applied thought by association condition;

(*b*) At the moment of conception . . . (2)

(iii) State with applied thought and sustained thought is related to state with applied thought and sustained thought and without applied thought but with sustained thought by association condition.

(*a*) One aggregate with applied thought and sustained thought is related to three aggregates and applied thought by association condition . . . two aggregates to two aggregates and applied thought . . .

(*b*) At the moment of conception . . . (3)

125. (iv) State without applied thought but with sustained thought is related to state without applied thought but with sustained thought by association condition.

(*a*) One aggregate without applied thought but with sustained thought is related to three aggregates by association condition . . . two aggregates to two aggregates . . .

(*b*) At the moment of conception . . . (1)

(v) State without applied thought but with sustained thought is related to state with applied thought and sustained thought by association condition.

(*a*) Applied thought is related to aggregates with applied thought and sustained thought by association condition;

(*b*) At the moment of conception . . . (2)

(vi) State without applied thought but with sustained thought is related to state without applied thought and sustained thought by association condition.

(*a*) Aggregates without applied thought but with sustained thought are related to sustained thought by association condition;

(*b*) At the moment of conception . . . (3)

(vii) State without applied thought but with sustained thought is related to state without applied thought but with sustained thought and without applied thought and sustained thought by association condition.

(*a*) One aggregate without applied thought but with sustained thought is related to three aggregates and sustained thought by association condition . . . two aggregates to two aggregates and sustained thought . . .

(*b*) At the moment of conception . . . (4)

126. (viii) State without applied thought and sustained thought is related to state without applied thought and sustained thought by association condition.

(*a*) One aggregate without applied thought and sustained thought is related to three aggregates by association condition . . . two aggregates to two aggregates . . .

(*b*) At the moment of conception . . . (1)

(ix) State without applied thought and sustained thought is related to state without applied thought but with sustained thought by association condition.

(*a*) Sustained thought is related to aggregates without applied thought but with sustained thought by association condition;

(*b*) At the moment of conception . . . (2)

(x) States without applied thought but with sustained thought and without applied thought and sustained thought are related to state without applied thought but with sustained thought by association condition.

(*a*) One aggregate without applied thought but with sustained thought, and sustained thought are related to three aggregates by association condition . . . two aggregates and sustained thought to two aggregates . . .

(*b*) At the moment of conception . . . (1)

(xi) States with applied thought and sustained thought and without applied thought but with sustained thought are related to state with applied thought and sustained thought by association condition.

(*a*) One aggregate with applied thought and sustained thought, and applied thought are related to three aggregates by association condition . . . two aggregates and applied thought to two aggregates . . .

(*b*) At the moment of conception . . . (1)

Dissociation 9

127. (i) State with applied thought and sustained thought is related to state without applied thought and sustained thought by dissociation condition.

(It is of two kinds, namely:) (*a*) conascence, (*b*) postnascence.

(*a*) (1) Conascent aggregates with applied thought and sustained thought are related to mind-produced matter by dissociation condition;

(2) At the moment of conception, aggregates with applied thought and sustained thought are related to kamma-produced matter by dissociation condition.

(*b*) Postnascent aggregates with applied thought and sustained thought are related to this prenascent body by dissociation condition. (1)

(ii) State without applied thought but with sustained thought is related to state without applied thought and sustained thought by dissociation condition.

(It is of two kinds, namely:) (*a*) conascence, (*b*) postnascence.

(*a*) (1) Conascent aggregates without applied thought but with sustained thought are related to mind-produced matter by dissociation condition; applied thought is related to mind-produced matter by dissociation condition;

(2) At the moment of conception, aggregates without applied thought but with sustained thought are related to kamma-produced matter by dissociation condition; applied thought is related to kamma-produced matter by dissociation condition.

(*b*) Postnascent aggregates without applied thought but with sustained thought, and applied thought are related to this prenascent body by dissociation condition. (1)

128. (iii) State without applied thought and sustained thought is related to state without applied thought and sustained thought by dissociation condition.

(It is of three kinds, namely:) (*a*) conascence, (*b*) prenascence, (*c*) postnascence.

(*a*) (1) Conascent aggregates without applied thought and sustained thought are related to mind-produced matter by dissociation condition; sustained thought is related to mind-produced matter by dissociation condition;

(2) At the moment of conception, aggregates without applied thought and sustained thought are related to kamma produced matter by dissociation condition; sustained thought is related to kamma-produced matter by dissociation condition; aggregates are related to (heart-)base by dissociation condition; (heart-)base is related to aggregates by dissociation condition; sustained thought is related to (heart-)base by dissociation condition; (heart-)base is related to sustained thought by dissociation condition.

(*b*) Prenascent eye-base is related to eye-consciousness by dissociation condition . . . body-base is related to body-consciousness by dissociation condition; (heart-)base is related to aggregates without applied thought and sustained thought, and sustained thought by dissociation condition.

(*c*) Postnascent aggregates without applied thought and sustained thought, and sustained thought are related to this prenascent body by dissociation condition. (1)

(iv) State without applied thought and sustained thought is related to state with applied thought and sustained thought by dissociation condition.

(It is of two kinds, namely:) (*a*) conascence, (*b*) prenascence.

(*a*) *Conascence:* At the moment of conception, (heart-)base is related to aggregates with applied thought and sustained thought by dissociation condition.

(*b*) *Prenascence:* (Heart-)base is related to aggregates with applied thought and sustained thought by dissociation condition. (2)

(v) State without applied thought and sustained thought is related to state without applied thought but with sustained thought by dissociation condition.

(It is of two kinds, namely:) (*a*) conascence, (*b*) prenascence.

(*a*) *Conascence:* At the moment of conception, (heart-)base is related to aggregates without applied thought but with sustained thought, and applied thought by dissociation condition.

(*b*) *Prenascence:* (Heart-)base is related to aggregates without applied thought but with sustained thought, and applied thought by dissociation condition. (3)

(vi) State without applied thought and sustained thought is related to state without applied thought but with sustained thought and without applied thought and sustained thought by dissociation condition.

(It is of two kinds, namely:) (*a*) conascence, (*b*) prenascence.

(*a*) *Conascence:* At the moment of conception, (heart-)base is related to aggregates without applied thought but with sustained thought, and sustained thought by dissociation condition.

(*b*) *Prenascence:* (Heart-)base is related to aggregates without applied thought but with sustained thought, and sustained thought by dissociation condition. (4)

(vii) State without applied thought and sustained thought is related to state with applied thought and sustained thought and without applied thought but with sustained thought by dissociation condition.

(It is of two kinds, namely:) (*a*) conascence, (*b*) prenascence.

(*a*) *Conascence:* At the moment of conception, (heart-)base is related to aggregates with applied thought and sustained thought, and applied thought by dissociation condition.

(*b*) *Prenascence:* (Heart-)base is related to aggregates with applied thought and sustained thought, and applied thought by dissociation condition. (5)

129. (viii) States without applied thought but with sustained thought and without applied thought and sustained thought are related to state without applied thought and sustained thought by dissociation condition.

(It is of two kinds, namely:) (*a*) conascence, (*b*) postnascence.

(*a*) (1) Conascent aggregates without applied thought but with sustained thought, and sustained thought are related to mind-produced matter by dissociation condition;

(2) At the moment of conception, aggregates without applied thought but with sustained thought, and sustained thought are related to kamma-produced matter by dissociation condition.

(*b*) Postnascent aggregates without applied thought but with sustained thought, and sustained thought are related to this prenascent body by dissociation condition. (1)

(ix) States with applied thought and sustained thought and without applied thought but with sustained thought are related to state without applied thought and sustained thought by dissociation condition.

(It is of two kinds, namely:) (*a*) conascence, (*b*) postnascence.

(*a*) (1) Conascent aggregates with applied thought and sustained thought, and applied thought are related to mind-produced matter by dissociation condition;

(2) At the moment of conception, aggregates with applied thought and sustained thought, and applied thought are related to kamma-produced matter by dissociation condition.

(*b*) Postnascent aggregates with applied thought and sustained thought, and applied thought are related to this prenascent body by dissociation condition. (1)

Presence 30

130. (i) State with applied thought and sustained thought is related to state with applied thought and sustained thought by presence condition.

(*a*) One aggregate with applied thought and sustained thought is related to three aggregates by presence condition . . . two aggregates to two aggregates . . .

(*b*) At the moment of conception . . . (1)

(ii) State with applied thought and sustained thought is related to state without applied thought but with sustained thought by presence condition.

(*a*) Aggregates with applied thought and sustained thought are related to applied thought by presence condition;

(*b*) At the moment of conception . . . (2)

(iii)–(vii) State with applied thought and sustained thought is related to state without applied thought and sustained thought by presence condition.

(It is of two kinds, namely:) (*a*) conascence, (*b*) postnascence.

(*a*) (1) Conascent aggregates with applied thought and sustained thought are related to mind-produced matter by presence condition;

(2) At the moment of conception, aggregates with applied thought and sustained thought are related to kamma-produced matter by presence condition.

(*b*) Postnascent aggregates with applied thought and sustained thought are related to this prenascent body by presence condition. (3)

(For the reference "with applied thought and sustained thought", the remaining questions are the same as for conascence condition.)

131. (viii) State without applied thought but with sustained thought is related to state without applied thought but with sustained thought by presence condition.

(*a*) One aggregate without applied thought but with sustained thought is related to three aggregates by presence condition . . . two aggregates to two aggregates . . .

(*b*) At the moment of conception . . . (1)

(ix) State without applied thought but with sustained thought is related to state with applied thought and sustained thought by presence condition.

(*a*) Applied thought is related to aggregates with applied thought and sustained thought by presence condition;

(*b*) At the moment of conception . . . (2)

(x)-(xii) State without applied thought but with sustained thought is related to state without applied thought and sustained thought by presence condition.

(It is of two kinds, namely:) (*a*) conascence, (*b*) postnascence.

(*a*) (1) Conascent aggregates without applied thought but with sustained thought are related to sustained thought and mind-produced matter by presence condition; applied thought is related to mind-produced matter by presence condition;

(2) At the moment of conception, aggregates without applied thought but with sustained thought are related to sustained thought and kamma-produced matter by presence condition; applied thought is related to kamma-produced matter by presence condition.

(*b*) Postnascent aggregates without applied thought but with sustained thought, and applied thought are related to this prenascent body by presence condition. (3)

(For the reference "without applied thought but with sustained thought" there are five questions. The remaining ones are the same as for conascence condition.)

132. (xiii) State without applied thought and sustained thought is related to state without applied thought and sustained thought by presence condition.

(It is of five kinds, namely:) (*a*) conascence, (*b*) prenascence, (*c*) postnascence, (*d*) nutriment, (*e*) faculty.

(*a*) (1) One conascent aggregate without applied thought and sustained thought is related to three aggregates and mind-produced matter by presence condition ... two aggregates to two aggregates ... sustained thought is related to mind-produced matter by presence condition;

(2) At the moment of conception, one aggregate without applied thought and sustained thought is related to three aggregates and kamma-produced matter by presence condition . . . aggregates are related to (heart-)base by presence condition; (heart-)base is related to aggregates by presence condition; sustained thought is related to (heart-)base by presence condition; (heart-)base is related to sustained thought by presence condition;

(3) One great primary is related to three great primaries by presence condition . . . great primaries are related to mind-produced and kamma-produced derived matter by presence condition;

(4) External . . . nutriment-produced . . . temperature-produced . . . one great primary of non-percipient beings to three great primaries . . . great primaries are related to kamma-produced derived matter by presence condition.

(*b*) *Prenascence:* By the power of divine-eye, one sees a visible object. By the power of divine-ear element, one hears a sound. Visible object-base to eye-consciousness . . . tangible object-base is related to body-consciousness by presence condition; eye-base to eye-consciousness . . . body-base is related to body-consciousness by presence condition; (heart-)base is related to aggregates without applied thought and sustained thought, and sustained thought by presence condition.

(*c*) Postnascent aggregates without applied thought and sustained thought, and sustained thought are related to this prenascent body by presence condition.

(*d*) Edible food is related to this body by presence condition.

(*e*) Physical life-faculty is related to kamma-produced matter by presence condition. (1)

(xiv) State without applied thought and sustained thought is related to state with applied thought and sustained thought by presence condition.

(It is of two kinds, namely:) (*a*) conascence, (*b*) prenascence.

(*a*) *Conascence:* At the moment of conception, (heart-)base is related to aggregates with applied thought and sustained thought by presence condition.

(*b*) *Prenascence:* (One) practises insight into the impermanence, suffering and impersonality of the eye; enjoys and delights in (the eye). Taking it as object, arises lust . . . arises grief . . . ear . . . nose . . . tongue . . . body . . . visible object . . . sound . . . smell . . . taste . . . tangible object . . . (One) practises insight into the impermanence, suffering and impersonality of the (heart-)base . . . arises grief. (Heart-)base is related to aggregates with applied thought and sustained thought by presence condition. (2)

(xv) State without applied thought and sustained thought is related to state without applied thought but with sustained thought by presence condition.

(It is of two kinds, namely:) (*a*) conascence, (*b*) prenascence.

(*a*) (1) Conascent sustained thought is related to aggregates without applied thought but with sustained thought by presence condition;

(2) At the moment of conception, sustained thought is related to aggregates without applied thought but with sustained thought by presence condition; at the moment of conception, (heart-)base is related to aggregates without applied thought but with sustained thought, and applied thought by presence condition.

(*b*) *Prenascence:* (One) practises insight into the impermanence, suffering and impersonality of the eye; enjoys and delights in (the eye). Taking it as object, arises applied thought . . . ear . . . nose . . . tongue . . . body . . . visible object . . . sound . . . smell . . . taste . . . tangible object . . . (One) practises insight into the impermanence, suffering and impersonality of the (heart-)base; enjoys and delights in [the (heart-)base]. Taking it as object, arises applied thought. (Heart-)base is related to aggregates without applied thought but with sustained thought, and applied thought by presence condition. (3)

(xvi) State without applied thought and sustained thought is related to state without applied thought but with sustained thought and without applied thought and sustained thought by presence condition.

(It is of two kinds, namely:) (*a*) conascence, (*b*) prenascence.

(*a*) (1) Conascent sustained thought is related to aggregates without applied thought but with sustained thought and mind-produced matter by presence condition;

(2) At the moment of conception, sustained thought is related to aggregates without applied thought but with sustained thought and kamma-produced matter by presence condition; at the moment of conception, (heart-)base is related to aggregates without applied thought

but with sustained thought, and sustained thought by presence condition.

(*b*) Prenascent (heart-)base is related to aggregates without applied thought but with sustained thought, and sustained thought by presence condition. (4)

(xvii) State without applied thought and sustained thought is related to state with applied thought and sustained thought and without applied thought but with sustained thought by presence condition.

(It is of two kinds, namely:) (*a*) conascence, (*b*) prenascence.

(*a*) *Conascence:* At the moment of conception, (heart-)base is related to aggregates with applied thought and sustained thought, and applied thought by presence condition.

(*b*) *Prenascence:* (One) practises insight into the impermanence, suffering and impersonality of the eye; enjoys and delights in (the eye). Taking it as object, arise aggregates with applied thought and sustained thought, and applied thought . . . ear . . . nose . . . tongue . . . body . . . (One) practises insight into the impermanence, suffering and impersonality of the (heart-)base; enjoys and delights in [the (heart-)base]. Taking it as object, arise aggregates with applied thought and sustained thought, and applied thought by presence condition. (Heart-)base is related to aggregates with applied thought and sustained thought, and applied thought by presence condition. (5)

133. (xviii) States with applied thought and sustained thought and without applied thought and sustained thought are related to state with applied thought and sustained thought by presence condition.

Conascence-prenascence: One conascent aggregate with applied thought and sustained thought, and (heart-)base are related to three aggregates by presence condition . . . two aggregates and (heart-)base are related to two aggregates by presence condition;

At the moment of conception, one aggregate with applied thought and sustained thought, and (heart-)base are related to three aggregates by presence condition . . . two aggregates and (heart-)base are related to two aggregates by presence condition. (1)

(xix) States with applied thought and sustained thought and without applied thought and sustained thought are related to state without applied thought but with sustained thought by presence condition.

Conascence-prenascence: Conascent aggregates with applied thought and sustained thought, and (heart-)base are related to applied thought by presence condition;

At the moment of conception, aggregates with applied thought and sustained thought, and (heart-)base are related to applied thought by presence condition. (2)

(xx) States with applied thought and sustained thought and without applied thought and sustained thought are related to state without applied thought and sustained thought by presence condition.

(It is of three kinds, namely:) (*a*) conascence, (*b*) postnascence-nutriment, (*c*) (postnascence-)faculty.

(*a*) (1) Conascent aggregates with applied thought and sustained thought, and great primaries are related to mind-produced matter by presence condition;

(2) At the moment of conception, aggregates with applied thought and sustained thought, and great primaries are related to kamma-produced matter by presence condition.

(*b*) Postnascent aggregates with applied thought and sustained thought, and edible food are related to this prenascent body by presence condition.

(*c*) Postnascent aggregates with applied thought and sustained thought, and physical life-faculty are related to kamma-produced matter by presence condition. (3)

(xxi) States with applied thought and sustained thought and without applied thought and sustained thought are related to state with applied thought and sustained thought and without applied thought but with sustained thought by presence condition.

Conascence-prenascence: One conascent aggregate with applied thought and sustained thought, and (heart-)base are related to three aggregates and applied thought by presence condition . . . two aggregates and (heart-)base are related to two aggregates and applied thought by presence condition;

At the moment of conception . . . (4)

134. (xxii) States without applied thought but with sustained thought and without applied thought and sustained thought are related to state with applied thought and sustained thought by presence condition.

Conascence-prenascence: Conascent applied thought and (heart-) base are related to aggregates with applied thought and sustained thought by presence condition;

At the moment of conception, applied thought and (heart-)base are related to aggregates with applied thought and sustained thought by presence condition. (1)

(xxiii) States without applied thought but with sustained thought and without applied thought and sustained thought are related to state without applied thought but with sustained thought by presence condition.

(It is of two kinds, namely:) (*a*) conascence, (*b*) (conascence-)prenascence.

(*a*) *Conascence:* One aggregate without applied thought but with sustained thought, and sustained thought are related to three aggregates by presence condition . . . two aggregates and sustained thought to two aggregates . . .

(*b*) *(Conascence-)prenascence:* One conascent aggregate without applied thought but with sustained thought, and (heart-)base are related to three aggregates by presence condition . . . two aggregates and (heart-) base are related to two aggregates by presence condition;

At the moment of conception, one aggregate without applied thought but with sustained thought, and sustained thought are related to three aggregates by presence condition . . . two aggregates and sustained thought to two aggregates . . . at the moment of conception, one aggregate without applied thought but with sustained thought, and (heart-)base to three aggregates . . . two aggregates and (heart-)base are related to two aggregates by presence condition. (2)

(xxiv) States without applied thought but with sustained thought and without applied thought and sustained thought are related to state without applied thought and sustained thought by presence condition.

(It is of five kinds, namely:) (*a*) conascence, (*b*) (conascence-)prenascence, (*c*) postnascence, (*d*) postnascence-nutriment, (*e*) (postnascence-)faculty.

(*a*) Conascent aggregates without applied thought but with sustained thought, and sustained thought are related to mind-produced matter by presence condition; conascent aggregates without applied thought but with sustained thought, and great primaries are related to mind-produced matter by presence condition; conascent applied thought and great primaries are related to mind-produced matter by presence condition.

(*b*) *(Conascence-)prenascence:* Conascent aggregates without applied thought but with sustained thought, and (heart-)base are related to sustained thought by presence condition;

At the moment of conception, aggregates without applied thought but with sustained thought, and sustained thought are related to kamma-produced matter by presence condition; at the moment of conception, aggregates without applied thought but with sustained thought, and great primaries are related to kamma-produced matter by presence condition; at the moment of conception, applied thought and great primaries are related to kamma-produced matter by presence condition; at the moment of conception, aggregates without applied thought but with sustained thought, and (heart-)base are related to sustained thought by presence condition.

(*c*) Postnascent aggregates without applied thought but with sustained thought, and sustained thought are related to this prenascent body by presence condition.

(*d*) *Postnascence-nutriment:* Postnascent aggregates without applied thought but with sustained thought, applied thought and edible food are related to this prenascent body by presence condition.

(*e*) *(Postnascence-)faculty:* Postnascent aggregates without applied thought but with sustained thought, applied thought and physical life-faculty are related to kamma-produced matter by presence condition. (3)

(xxv) States without applied thought but with sustained thought and without applied thought and sustained thought are related to state without applied thought but with sustained thought and without applied thought and sustained thought by presence condition.

(It is of two kinds, namely:) (*a*) conascence, (*b*) (conascence-)prenascence.

(*a*) One conascent aggregate without applied thought but with sustained thought, and sustained thought are related to three aggregates and mind-produced matter by presence condition . . . two aggregates and sustained thought . . .

(*b*) *(Conascence-)prenascence:* One (conascent) aggregate without applied thought but with sustained thought, and (heart-)base are related to three aggregates and sustained thought by presence condition . . . two aggregates and (heart-)base . . .

At the moment of conception . . . (4)

135. (xxvi) States with applied thought and sustained thought and without applied thought but with sustained thought are related to state with applied thought and sustained thought by presence condition.

(*a*) One aggregate with applied thought and sustained thought, and applied thought are related to three aggregates by presence condition

. . . two aggregates and applied thought . . .

(*b*) At the moment of conception . . . (1)

(xxvii) States with applied thought and sustained thought and without applied thought but with sustained thought are related to state without applied thought and sustained thought by presence condition.

(It is of two kinds, namely:) (*a*) conascence, (*b*) postnascence.

(*a*) (1) Conascent aggregates with applied thought and sustained thought, and applied thought are related to mind-produced matter by presence condition;

(2) At the moment of conception, aggregates with applied thought and sustained thought, and applied thought are related to kamma-produced matter by presence condition.

(*b*) Postnascent aggregates with applied thought and sustained thought, and applied thought are related to this prenascent body by presence condition. (2)

(xxviii) States with applied thought and sustained thought and without applied thought but with sustained thought are related to state with applied thought and sustained thought and without applied thought and sustained thought by presence condition.

(*a*) One aggregate with applied thought and sustained thought, and applied thought are related to three aggregates and mind-produced matter by presence condition . . . two aggregates and applied thought to two aggregates . . .

(*b*) At the moment of conception . . . (3)

136. (xxix) States with applied thought and sustained thought, without applied thought but with sustained thought and without applied thought and sustained thought are related to state with applied thought and sustained thought by presence condition.

Conascence-prenascence: One conascent aggregate with applied thought and sustained thought, applied thought and (heart-)base are related to three aggregates by presence condition . . .

At the moment of conception . . . (1)

(xxx) States with applied thought and sustained thought, without applied thought but with sustained thought and without applied thought and sustained thought are related to state without applied thought and sustained thought by presence condition.

(It is of three kinds, namely:) (*a*) conascence, (*b*) postnascence-nutriment, (*c*) (postnascence-)faculty.

(*a*) (1) Conascent aggregates with applied thought and sustained thought, applied thought and great primaries are related to mind-produced matter by presence condition;

(2) At the moment of conception . . .

(*b*) *Postnascence–nutriment:* Postnascent aggregates with applied thought and sustained thought, applied thought and edible food are related to this prenascent body by presence condition.

(*c*) *(Postnascence-)faculty:* Postnascent aggregates with applied thought and sustained thought, applied thought and physical life-faculty are related to kamma-produced matter by presence condition. (2)

Absence, Disappearance and Non-disappearance

137. State with applied thought and sustained thought is related to state with applied thought and sustained thought by absence condition . . . by disappearance condition.

(Absence and disappearance conditions are the same as proximity; non-disappearance is the same as presence.)

1. CONDITIONS: POSITIVE (ii) ENUMERATION CHAPTER

By Ones

138. With root 11, object 21, predominance 23, proximity 25, contiguity 25, conascence 30, mutuality 28, dependence 30, strong-dependence 25, prenascence 5, postnascence 5, repetition 21, kamma 11, resultant 21, nutriment 11, faculty 11, jhāna 21, path 16, association 11, dissociation 9, presence 30, absence 25, disappearance 25, non-disappearance 30 . . .

(Combination is just the same as for the Faultless Triplet; enumerate the enumeration of the "Investigation Chapter" in the same way without confusion.)

End of Positive

2. SELECTION OF THE CONDITIONS FOR NEGATIVE 35

139. (i) State with applied thought and sustained thought is related to state with applied thought and sustained thought by object condition, conascence condition, strong-dependence condition, kamma condition. (1)

(ii) State with applied thought and sustained thought is related to state without applied thought but with sustained thought by object condition, conascence condition, strong-dependence condition, kamma condition. (2)

(iii) State with applied thought and sustained thought is related to state without applied thought and sustained thought by object condition, conascence condition, strong-dependence condition, postnascence condition, kamma condition. (3)

(iv) State with applied thought and sustained thought is related to state with applied thought and sustained thought and without applied thought and sustained thought by conascence condition, kamma condition. (4)

(v) State with applied thought and sustained thought is related to state without applied thought but with sustained thought and without applied thought and sustained thought by conascence condition, strong-dependence condition, kamma condition. (5)

(vi) State with applied thought and sustained thought is related to state with applied thought and sustained thought and without applied thought but with sustained thought by object condition, conascence condition, strong-dependence condition, kamma condition. (6)

(vii) State with applied thought and sustained thought is related to state with applied thought and sustained thought, without applied thought but with sustained thought and without applied thought and sustained thought by conascence condition, kamma condition. (7)

140. (viii) State without applied thought but with sustained thought is related to state without applied thought but with sustained thought by object condition, conascence condition, strong-dependence condition. (1)

(ix) State without applied thought but with sustained thought is related to state with applied thought and sustained thought by object condition, conascence condition, strong-dependence condition. (2)

(x) State without applied thought but with sustained thought is related to state without applied thought and sustained thought by object condition, conascence condition, strong-dependence condition, postnascence condition, kamma condition. (5)

(xi) State without applied thought but with sustained thought is related to state with applied thought and sustained thought and without applied thought and sustained thought by conascence condition. (4)

(xii) State without applied thought but with sustained thought is related to state without applied thought but with sustained thought and without applied thought and sustained thought by conascence condition, strong-dependence condition, kamma condition. (5)

(xiii) State without applied thought but with sustained thought is related to state with applied thought and sustained thought and without applied thought but with sustained thought by object condition, strong-dependence condition. (6)

141. (xiv) State without applied thought and sustained thought is related to state without applied thought and sustained thought by object condition, conascence condition, strong-dependence condition, prenascence condition, postnascence condition, kamma condition, nutriment condition, faculty condition. (1)

(xv) State without applied thought and sustained thought is related to state with applied thought and sustained thought by object condition, conascence condition, strong-dependence condition, prenascence condition. (2)

(xvi) State without applied thought and sustained thought is related to state without applied thought but with sustained thought by object condition, conascence condition, strong-dependence condition, prenascence condition. (3)

(xvii) State without applied thought and sustained thought is related to state without applied thought but with sustained thought and without applied thought and sustained thought by object condition, conascence condition, strong-dependence condition, prenascence condition. (4)

(xviii) State without applied thought and sustained thought is related to state with applied thought and sustained thought and without applied thought but with sustained thought by object condition, conascence condition, strong-dependence condition, prenascence condition. (5)

142. (xix) States with applied thought and sustained thought and without applied thought and sustained thought are related to state with applied thought and sustained thought by conascence-prenascence. (1)

(xx) States with applied thought and sustained thought and without applied thought and sustained thought are related to state without applied thought but with sustained thought by conascence-prenascence. (2)

(xxi) States with applied thought and sustained thought and without applied thought and sustained thought are related to state without applied thought and sustained thought by conascence, postnascence-nutriment-faculty. (3)

(xxii) States with applied thought and sustained thought and without applied thought and sustained thought are related to state with applied thought and sustained thought and without applied thought but with sustained thought by conascence-prenascence. (4)

143. (xxiii) States without applied thought but with sustained thought and without applied thought and sustained thought are related to state with applied thought and sustained thought by object condition, conascence condition, strong-dependence condition, prenascence condition. (1)

(xxiv) States without applied thought but with sustained thought and without applied thought and sustained thought are related to state without applied thought but with sustained thought by object condition, conascence condition, strong-dependence condition, prenascence condition. (2)

(xxv) States without applied thought but with sustained thought and without applied thought and sustained thought are related to state without applied thought and sustained thought by object condition, conascence condition, strong-dependence condition, prenascence condition, postnascence condition, nutriment condition, faculty condition. (3)

(xxvi) States without applied thought but with sustained thought and without applied thought and sustained thought are related to state without applied thought but with sustained thought and without applied thought and sustained thought by conascence condition, strong-dependence condition, prenascence condition. (4)

(xxvii) States without applied thought but with sustained thought and without applied thought and sustained thought are related to state with applied thought and sustained thought and without applied thought but with sustained thought by object condition, strong-dependence condition. (5)

144. (xxviii) States with applied thought and sustained thought and without applied thought but with sustained thought are related to state with applied thought and sustained thought by object condition, conascence condition, strong-dependence condition. (1)

(xxix) States with applied thought and sustained thought and without applied thought but with sustained thought are related to state without applied thought but with sustained thought by object condition, strong-dependence condition. (2)

(xxx) States with applied thought and sustained thought and

without applied thought but with sustained thought are related to state without applied thought and sustained thought by object condition, conascence condition, strong-dependence condition, postnascence condition. (3)

(xxxi) States with applied thought and sustained thought and without applied thought but with sustained thought are related to state with applied thought and sustained thought and without applied thought and sustained thought by conascence condition. (4)

(xxxii) States with applied thought and sustained thought and without applied thought but with sustained thought are related to state without applied thought but with sustained thought and without applied thought and sustained thought by strong-dependence condition. (5)

(xxxiii) States with applied thought and sustained thought and without applied thought but with sustained thought are related to state with applied thought and sustained thought and without applied thought but with sustained thought by object condition, strong-dependence condition. (6)

(xxxiv) States with applied thought and sustained thought, without applied thought but with sustained thought and without applied thought and sustained thought are related to state with applied thought and sustained thought by conascence-prenascence. (1)

(xxxv) States with applied thought and sustained thought, without applied thought but with sustained thought and without applied thought and sustained thought are related to state without applied thought and sustained thought by conascence, postnascence-nutriment-faculty. (2)

End of Selection of the Conditions for Negative

2. CONDITIONS: NEGATIVE (ii) ENUMERATION CHAPTER

By Ones

145. With not-root 35, not-object 35, not-predominance 35, not-proximity 35, not-contiguity 35, not-conascence 29, not-mutuality 29, not-dependence 29, not-strong-dependence 34, not-prenascence 35, not-postnascence, not-repetition, not-kamma, not-resultant, not-nutriment, not-faculty, not-jhāna, not-path 35, not-association 29, not-dissociation 27, not-presence 27, not-absence 35, not-disappearance 35, not-non-disappearance 27 . . .

(When the "Negative" is enumerated, enumerate by considering these items.)

End of Negative

3. CONDITIONS: POSITIVE-NEGATIVE

Root By Twos

146. With root condition, not-object 11, not-predominance 11, not-proximity, not-contiguity 11, not-mutuality 3, not-strong-dependence 11, not-prenascence, not-postnascence, not-repetition, not-kamma, not-resultant, not-nutriment, not-faculty, not-jhāna, not-path (are) all 11, not-association 3, not-dissociation 7, not-absence 11, not-disappearance 11 . . .

(Enumerate in this way the enumeration of Positive–Negative.)

End of Positive–Negative

4. CONDITIONS: NEGATIVE-POSITIVE

Not-root By Twos

147. With not-root condition, object 21, predominance 23, proximity 25, contiguity 25, conascence 30, mutuality 28, dependence 30, strong-dependence 25, prenascence 5, postnascence 5, repetition 21, kamma 11, resultant 21, nutriment 11, faculty 11, jhāna 21, path 16, association 11, dissociation 9, presence 30, absence 25, disappearance 25, non-disappearance 30 . . .

(Classify in this way the Negative–Positive.)

End of Negative–Positive

END OF APPLIED THOUGHT TRIPLET

7. RAPTURE TRIPLET[1] I. "DEPENDENT" CHAPTER

1. CONDITIONS: POSITIVE (i) CLASSIFICATION CHAPTER

Root 10

1. (i) Dependent on state accompanied by rapture (pītisahagata), arises state accompanied by rapture by root condition.

---

[1] This comprises (1) States accompanied by rapture, (2) States accompanied by pleasure, (3) States accompanied by indifference.

(*a*) Dependent on one aggregate accompanied by rapture, arise three aggregates; dependent on three aggregates, arises one aggregate; dependent on two aggregates, arise two aggregates;

(*b*) At the moment of conception, dependent on one aggregate accompanied by rapture, arise three aggregates . . . dependent on two aggregates, arise two aggregates. (1)

(ii) Dependent on state accompanied by rapture, arises state accompanied by pleasure (sukhasahagata) by root condition.

(*a*) Dependent on one aggregate accompanied by rapture, arise three aggregates accompanied by pleasure . . . dependent on two aggregates, arise two aggregates;

(*b*) At the moment of conception, dependent on one aggregate accompanied by rapture, arise three aggregates accompanied by pleasure . . . dependent on two aggregates, arise two aggregates. (2)

(iii) Dependent on state accompanied by rapture, arise states accompanied by rapture and accompanied by pleasure by root condition.

(*a*) Dependent on one aggregate accompanied by rapture, arise three aggregates accompanied by rapture and accompanied by pleasure . . . dependent on two aggregates, arise two aggregates;

(*b*) At the moment of conception, dependent on one aggregate accompanied by rapture, arise three aggregates accompanied by rapture and accompanied by pleasure . . . dependent on two aggregates, arise two aggregates. (3)

2. (iv) Dependent on state accompanied by pleasure, arises state accompanied by pleasure by root condition.

(*a*) Dependent on one aggregate accompanied by pleasure, arise two aggregates; dependent on two aggregates, arises one aggregate;

(*b*) At the moment of conception, dependent on one aggregate accompanied by pleasure, arise two aggregates; dependent on two aggregates, arises one aggregate. (1)

(v) Dependent on state accompanied by pleasure, arises state accompanied by rapture by root condition.

(*a*) Dependent on one aggregate accompanied by pleasure, arise three aggregates accompanied by rapture . . . dependent on two aggregates, arise two aggregates;

(*b*) At the moment of conception, dependent on one aggregate accompanied by pleasure, arise three aggregates accompanied by rapture . . . dependent on two aggregates, arise two aggregates. (2)

(vi) Dependent on state accompanied by pleasure, arise states accompanied by rapture and accompanied by pleasure by root condition.

(*a*) Dependent on one aggregate accompanied by pleasure, arise two aggregates accompanied by rapture and accompanied by pleasure; dependent on two aggregates, arises one aggregate;

(*b*) At the moment of conception, dependent on one aggregate accompanied by pleasure, arise two aggregates accompanied by rapture and accompanied by pleasure; dependent on two aggregates, arises one aggregate. (3)

3. (vii) Dependent on state accompanied by indifference (upekkhāsahagata), arises state accompanied by indifference by root condition.

(*a*) Dependent on one aggregate accompanied by indifference, arise two aggregates; dependent on two aggregates, arises one aggregate;

(*b*) At the moment of conception . . . (1)

(viii) Dependent on state accompanied by rapture and accompanied by pleasure, arises state accompanied by rapture by root condition.

(*a*) Dependent on one aggregate accompanied by rapture and accompanied by pleasure, arise three aggregates accompanied by rapture . . . dependent on two aggregates, arise two aggregates;

(*b*) At the moment of conception, dependent on one aggregate accompanied by rapture and accompanied by pleasure, arise three aggregates accompanied by rapture . . . dependent on two aggregates, arise two aggregates. (1)

(ix) Dependent on state accompanied by rapture and accompanied by pleasure, arises state accompanied by pleasure by root condition.

(*a*) Dependent on one aggregate accompanied by rapture and accompanied by pleasure, arise two aggregates accompanied by pleasure; dependent on two aggregates, arises one aggregate;

(*b*) At the moment of conception, dependent on one aggregate accompanied by rapture and accompanied by pleasure, arise two aggregates accompanied by pleasure; dependent on two aggregates, arises one aggregate. (2)

(x) Dependent on state accompanied by rapture and accompanied by pleasure, arise states accompanied by rapture and accompanied by pleasure by root condition.

(*a*) Dependent on one aggregate accompanied by rapture and accompanied by pleasure, arise two aggregates accompanied by rapture and accompanied by pleasure; dependent on two aggregates, arises one aggregate;

(*b*) At the moment of conception, dependent on one aggregate accompanied by rapture and accompanied by pleasure, arise two aggregates accompanied by rapture and accompanied by pleasure; dependent on two aggregates, arises one aggregate. (3)

Object, etc. 10

4. Dependent on state accompanied by rapture, arises state accompanied by rapture by object condition . . . by predominance condition. (No "at the moment of conception".) . . . by proximity condition . . . by contiguity condition . . . by conascence condition . . . by mutuality condition . . . by dependence condition . . . by strong-dependence condition . . . by prenascence condition. (No "at the moment of conception" in prenascence.) . . . by repetition condition. (No "resultant" in repetition.) . . . by kamma condition . . . by resultant condition . . . nutriment . . . faculty . . . jhāna . . . path . . . association . . . dissociation . . . presence . . . absence . . . disappearance . . . non-disappearance condition.

1. CONDITIONS: POSITIVE (ii) ENUMERATION CHAPTER

By Ones

5. With root condition 10, object 10, predominance 10, proximity, contiguity, conascence, mutuality, dependence, strong-dependence, prenascence, repetition, kamma, resultant, nutriment, faculty, jhāna, path, association, dissociation, presence, absence, disappearance, non-disappearance (are) all 10 . . .

(Thus enumerate the "Positive" enumerations.)

End of Positive

2. CONDITIONS: NEGATIVE (i) CLASSIFICATION CHAPTER

Not-root 10

6. (i) Dependent on state accompanied by rapture, arises state accompanied by rapture by not-root condition.

Dependent on one rootless aggregate accompanied by rapture (ahetukaṁ pītisahagataṁ ekaṁ khandhaṁ), arise three aggregates . . . dependent on two aggregates, arise two aggregates. (1)

(ii) Dependent on state accompanied by rapture, arises state accompanied by pleasure by not-root condition.

Dependent on one rootless aggregate accompanied by rapture, arise three aggregates accompanied by pleasure . . . dependent on two aggregates, arise two aggregates. (2)

(iii) Dependent on state accompanied by rapture, arise states accompanied by rapture and accompanied by pleasure by not-root condition.

Dependent on one rootless aggregate accompanied by rapture, arise three aggregates accompanied by rapture and accompanied by pleasure . . . dependent on two aggregates, arise two aggregates. (3)

7. (iv) Dependent on state accompanied by pleasure, arises state accompanied by pleasure by not-root condition.

Dependent on one rootless aggregate accompanied by pleasure, arise two aggregates; dependent on two aggregates, arises one aggregate. (1)

(v) Dependent on state accompanied by pleasure, arises state accompanied by rapture by not-root condition.

Dependent on one rootless aggregate accompanied by pleasure, arise three aggregates accompanied by rapture . . . dependent on two aggregates, arise two aggregates. (2)

(vi) Dependent on state accompanied by pleasure, arise states accompanied by rapture and accompanied by pleasure by not-root condition.

Dependent on one rootless aggregate accompanied by pleasure, arise two aggregates accompanied by rapture and accompanied by pleasure; dependent on two aggregates, arises one aggregate. (3)

8. (vii) Dependent on state accompanied by indifference, arises state accompanied by indifference by not-root condition.

(*a*) Dependent on one rootless aggregate accompanied by indifference, arise two aggregates; dependent on two aggregates, arises one aggregate;

(*b*) At the moment of rootless conception, dependent on one aggregate accompanied by indifference, arise two aggregates; dependent on two aggregates, arises one aggregate;

(*c*) Dependent on doubt-accompanied or restlessness-accompanied aggregates, arises doubt-accompanied or restlessness-accompanied delusion. (1)

9. (viii) Dependent on state accompanied by rapture and accompanied by pleasure, arises state accompanied by rapture by not-root condition.

Dependent on one rootless aggregate accompanied by rapture and accompanied by pleasure, arise three aggregates accompanied by rapture . . . dependent on two aggregates, arise two aggregates. (1)

(ix) Dependent on state accompanied by rapture and accompanied by pleasure, arises state accompanied by pleasure by not-root condition.

Dependent on one rootless aggregate accompanied by rapture and accompanied by pleasure, arise two aggregates accompanied by pleasure; dependent on two aggregates, arises one aggregate. (2)

(x) Dependent on state accompanied by rapture and accompanied by pleasure, arise states accompanied by rapture and accompanied by pleasure by not-root condition.

Dependent on one rootless aggregate accompanied by rapture and accompanied by pleasure, arise two aggregates accompanied by rapture and accompanied by pleasure; dependent on two aggregates, arises one aggregate. (3)

Not-predominance 10—Not-repetition 10

10. Dependent on state accompanied by rapture, arises state accompanied by rapture by not-predominance condition. (In not-predominance complete "at the moment of conception".) . . . by not-prenascence condition. [Remember (to take) immaterial and "at the moment of conception".] . . . by not-postnascence condition . . . by not-repetition condition.

Not-kamma 10

11. (i) Dependent on state accompanied by rapture, arises state accompanied by rapture by not-kamma condition.

Dependent on aggregates accompanied by rapture, arises volition accompanied by rapture.

(ii) Dependent on state accompanied by rapture, arises state accompanied by pleasure by not-kamma condition.

Dependent on aggregates accompanied by rapture, arises volition accompanied by pleasure.

(Expand in this way 10 questions.)

Not-resultant 10

12. (i) Dependent on state accompanied by rapture, arises state accompanied by rapture by not-resultant condition . . . (Complete. No conception.)

Not-jhāna 2, etc.

13. (i) Dependent on state accompanied by pleasure, arises state accompanied by pleasure by not-jhāna condition.

Dependent on one aggregate accompanied by pleasure-accompanied body-consciousness, arise two aggregates; dependent on two aggregates, arises one aggregate. (1)

(ii) Dependent on state accompanied by indifference, arises state accompanied by indifference by not-jhāna condition.

Dependent on one aggregate accompanied by four-fold consciousness, arise two aggregates; dependent on two aggregates, arises one aggregate. (2)

(Not-path condition is the same as not-root condition; no delusion. Complete by not-dissociation condition; only immaterial question.)

2. CONDITIONS: NEGATIVE (ii) ENUMERATION CHAPTER

By Ones

14. With not-root 10, not-predominance 10, not-prenascence, not-postnascence, not-repetition, not-kamma, not-resultant 10, not-jhāna 2, not-path 10, not-dissociation 10 . . . (Do Negative completely.)

End of Negative

3. CONDITIONS: POSITIVE-NEGATIVE

(Root) By Twos

15. With root condition, not-predominance 10, not-prenascence 10, not-postnascence, not-repetition, not-kamma, not-resultant, not-dissociation 10 . . .

(Enumerate Positive–Negative in detail.)

End of Positive–Negative

4. CONDITIONS: NEGATIVE-POSITIVE

(Not-root) By Twos

16. With not-root condition, object 10, proximity 10, contiguity 10, conascence, mutuality, dependence, strong-dependence, prenascence, repetition, kamma, resultant, nutriment, faculty, jhāna (are) all 10, path 1, association 10, dissociation, presence, absence, disappearance, non-disappearance (are) all 10 . . .

End of Negative–Positive

End of "DEPENDENT" CHAPTER

(The "Conascence", "Conditioned", "Supported", "Conjoined" and "Associated" Chapters are also the same as the "Dependent" Chapter.)

7. Rapture Triplet VII. "Investigation" Chapter

1. CONDITIONS: POSITIVE (i) CLASSIFICATION CHAPTER

Root 10

17. (i) State accompanied by rapture is related to state accompanied by rapture by root condition.

(*a*) Roots accompanied by rapture are related to (their) associated aggregates by root condition;

(*b*) At the moment of conception, roots accompanied by rapture are related to (their) associated aggregates by root condition. (1)

(ii) State accompanied by rapture is related to state accompanied by pleasure by root condition.

(*a*) Roots accompanied by rapture are related to (their) associated aggregates accompanied by pleasure by root condition;

(*b*) At the moment of conception . . . (2)

(iii) State accompanied by rapture is related to state accompanied by rapture and accompanied by pleasure by root condition.

(*a*) Roots accompanied by rapture are related to (their) associated aggregates accompanied by rapture and accompanied by pleasure by root condition;

(*b*) At the moment of conception . . . (3)

18. (iv)-(vi) State accompanied by pleasure to state accompanied by pleasure . . . to state accompanied by rapture . . . to state accompanied by rapture and accompanied by pleasure . . . (For the reference with "pleasure": three.)

(vii) State accompanied by indifference is related to state accompanied by indifference by root condition.

(*a*) Roots accompanied by indifference are related to (their) associated aggregates by root condition;

(*b*) At the moment of conception . . . (1)

(viii)-(x) States accompanied by rapture and accompanied by pleasure to state accompanied by rapture . . . to state accompanied by pleasure . . . are related to state accompanied by rapture and accompanied by pleasure by root condition.

(*a*) Roots accompanied by rapture and accompanied by pleasure are related to (their) associated aggregates accompanied by rapture and accompanied by pleasure by root condition;

(*b*) At the moment of conception . . . (1)

Object 16

19. (i) State accompanied by rapture is related to state accompanied by rapture by object condition.

After having offered an offering with the mind accompanied by rapture, having undertaken precepts, having fulfilled the duty of observance, (one) reviews it with the mind accompanied by rapture. Having emerged from jhāna accompanied by rapture, having emerged from Path, having emerged from Fruition, (one) reviews it with the mind accompanied by rapture.

The Noble persons, with the mind accompanied by rapture, review the eradicated defilements which were accompanied by rapture, review the uneradicated defilements, know the defilements addicted before.

(They) practise insight into the impermanence, suffering and impersonality of aggregates accompanied by rapture with the mind accompanied by rapture; enjoy and delight in (those aggregates). Taking them as object, arises lust accompanied by rapture, arise wrong views. Taking aggregates accompanied by rapture as object, arise aggregates accompanied by rapture. (1)

(ii) State accompanied by rapture is related to state accompanied by pleasure by object condition.

After having offered an offering with the mind accompanied by rapture, having undertaken precepts, having fulfilled the duty of observance, (one) reviews it with the mind accompanied by pleasure. Having emerged from jhāna accompanied by rapture, having emerged from Path, having emerged from Fruition, (one) reviews it with the mind accompanied by pleasure.

The Noble persons, with the mind accompanied by pleasure, review the eradicated defilements which were accompanied by rapture, review the uneradicated defilements, know the defilements addicted to before.

(They) practise insight into the impermanence, suffering and impersonality of aggregates accompanied by rapture with the mind accompanied by pleasure; enjoy and delight in (those aggregates). Taking them as object, arises lust accompanied by pleasure, arise wrong views. Taking aggregates accompanied by rapture as object, arise aggregates accompanied by pleasure. (2)

(iii) State accompanied by rapture is related to state accompanied by indifference by object condition.,

After having offered an offering with the mind accompanied by rapture, having undertaken precepts, having fulfilled the duty of observance, (one) reviews it with the mind accompanied by indifference. Having emerged from jhāna accompanied by rapture, having emerged from Path, having emerged from Fruition, (one) reviews it with the mind accompanied by indifference.

The Noble persons, with the mind accompanied by indifference, review the eradicated defilements which were accompanied by rapture, review the uneradicated defilements, know the defilements addicted to before.

(They) practise insight into the impermanence, suffering and impersonality of aggregates accompanied by rapture with the mind accompanied by indifference; enjoy and delight in (those aggregates). Taking them as object, arises lust accompanied by indifference, arise wrong views, arises doubt, arises restlessness.

By the knowledge of penetration into others' minds, (one) knows the other being's mind accompanied by rapture. Aggregates accompanied by rapture are related to knowledge of penetration into others' minds, knowledge of remembrance of past existences, knowledge of rebirths according to one's kamma, knowledge of future existences, advertence by object condition. Taking aggregates accompanied by rapture as object, arise aggregates accompanied by indifference. (3)

(iv) State accompanied by rapture is related to state accompanied by rapture and accompanied by pleasure by object condition.

After having offered an offering with the mind accompanied by rapture, having undertaken precepts, having fulfilled the duty of observance, (one) reviews it with the mind accompanied by rapture and accompanied by pleasure. Having emerged from jhāna with the mind accompanied by rapture, having emerged from Path, having emerged from Fruition, (one) reviews it with the mind accompanied by rapture and accompanied by pleasure.

The Noble persons, with the mind accompanied by rapture and accompanied by pleasure, review the eradicated defilements which were accompanied by rapture, review the uneradicated defilements, know the defilements addicted to before.

(They) practise insight into the impermanence, suffering and impersonality of aggregates accompanied by rapture with the mind accompanied by rapture and accompanied by pleasure; enjoy and delight in (those aggregates). Taking them as object, arises lust accompanied by rapture and accompanied by pleasure, arise wrong views. Taking aggregates accompanied by rapture as object, arise aggregates accompanied by rapture and accompanied by pleasure. (4)

20. (v)-(viii) State accompanied by pleasure is related to state accompanied by pleasure by object condition . . . state accompanied by pleasure to state accompanied by rapture . . . to state accompanied by indifference . . . to state accompanied by rapture and accompanied by pleasure by object condition.

Taking aggregates accompanied by pleasure as object, arise aggregates accompanied by rapture and accompanied by pleasure. (4)

(ix) State accompanied by indifference is related to state accompanied by indifference by object condition.

After having offered an offering with the mind accompanied by indifference, having undertaken precepts, having fulfilled the duty of observance, (one) reviews it with the mind accompanied by indifference. Having emerged from jhāna accompanied by indifference, having emerged from Path, having emerged from Fruition, (one) reviews it with the mind accompanied by indifference.

The Noble persons, with the mind accompanied by indifference, review the eradicated defilements which were accompanied by indifference, review the uneradicated defilements, know the defilements addicted to before.

(They) practise insight into the impermanence, suffering and impersonality of aggregates accompanied by indifference with the mind accompanied by indifference; enjoy and delight in (those aggregates). Taking them as object, arises lust accompanied by indifference, arise wrong views, arises doubt, arises restlessness.

By the knowledge of penetration into others' minds, (one) knows the other being's mind accompanied by indifference. Infinity of space is related to infinity of consciousness by object condition . . . Nothingness is related to neither-perception-nor-non-perception by object condition. Aggregates accompanied by indifference are related to knowledge of supernormal power, knowledge of penetration into others' minds, knowledge of remembrance of past existences, knowledge of rebirths according to one's kamma, knowledge of future existences, advertence by object condition. Taking aggregates accompanied by indifference as object, arise aggregates accompanied by indifference. (1)

(x)-(xii) State accompanied by indifference to state accompanied by rapture . . . to state accompanied by pleasure . . . is related to state accompanied by rapture and accompanied by pleasure by object condition.

After having offered an offering with the mind accompanied by indifference, having undertaken precepts, having fulfilled the duty of observance, (one) reviews it with the mind accompanied by rapture and accompanied by pleasure. Having emerged from jhāna accompanied by indifference, having emerged from Path, having emerged from Fruition, (one) reviews it with the mind accompanied by rapture and accompanied by pleasure.

The Noble persons, with the mind accompanied by rapture and accompanied by pleasure, review the eradicated defilements which were accompanied by indifference, review the uneradicated defilements, know the defilements addicted to before.

(They) practise insight into the impermanence, suffering and impersonality of aggregates accompanied by indifference with the mind accompanied by rapture and accompanied by pleasure; enjoy and delight in (those aggregates). Taking them as object, arises lust accompanied by rapture and accompanied by pleasure, arise wrong views. Taking aggregates accompanied by indifference as object, arise aggregates accompanied by rapture and accompanied by pleasure. (4)

21. (xiii)-(xv) States accompanied by rapture and accompanied by pleasure to state accompanied by rapture . . . to state accompanied by pleasure . . . is related to state accompanied by indifference by object condition.

After having offered an offering with the mind accompanied by rapture and accompanied by pleasure, having undertaken precepts, having fulfilled the duty of observance . . .

(One) practises insight into the impermanence, suffering and impersonality of aggregates accompanied by rapture and accompanied by pleasure with the mind accompanied by indifference; enjoys and delights in (those aggregates). Taking them as object, arises lust accompanied by indifference, arise wrong views, arises doubt, arises restlessness.

By the knowledge of penetration into others' minds, (one) knows the other being's mind accompanied by rapture and accompanied by pleasure. Aggregates accompanied by rapture and accompanied by pleasure are related to knowledge of penetration into others' minds, knowledge of remembrance of past existences, knowledge of rebirths according to one's kamma, knowledge of future existences, advertence by object condition. Taking aggregates accompanied by rapture and accompanied by pleasure as object, arise aggregates accompanied by indifference. (3)

(xvi) States accompanied by rapture and accompanied by pleasure are related to state accompanied by rapture and accompanied by pleasure by object condition. (Abbreviated.) (4)

Predominance 16

22. (i) State accompanied by rapture is related to state accompanied by rapture by predominance condition.

(It is of two kinds, namely:) (*a*) object-predominance, (*b*) conascence-predominance.

(*a*) *Object-predominance:* After having offered an offering with the mind accompanied by rapture, having undertaken precepts, having fulfilled the duty of observance, (one) esteems and reviews it with the mind accompanied by rapture. Having emerged from jhāna accompanied by rapture, having emerged from Path, having emerged from Fruition, (one) esteems and reviews it with the mind accompanied by rapture. (One) esteems, enjoys and delights in aggregates accompanied by rapture with the mind accompanied by rapture. Taking them as estimable object, arises lust accompanied by rapture, arise wrong views.

(*b*) *Conascence-predominance:* Predominance accompanied by rapture is related to (its) associated aggregates by predominance condition. (1)

(ii) State accompanied by rapture is related to state accompanied by pleasure by predominance condition.

(It is of two kinds, namely:) (*a*) object-predominance, (*b*) conascence-predominance.

(*a*) *Object-predominance:* After having offered an offering with the mind accompanied by rapture . . .

(*b*) *Conascence-predominance:* Predominance accompanied by rapture is related to (its) associated aggregates accompanied by pleasure by predominance condition. (2)

(iii) State accompanied by rapture is related to state accompanied by indifference by predominance condition.

Object-predominance: After having offered an offering with the mind accompanied by rapture . . . with the mind accompanied by indifference. (Abbreviated.) (3)

(iv) State accompanied by rapture is related to state accompanied by rapture and accompanied by pleasure by predominance condition.

(It is of two kinds, namely:) (*a*) object-predominance, (*b*) conascence-predominance.

(*a*) *Object-predominance:* After having offered an offering with the mind accompanied by rapture . . .

(*b*) *Conascence-predominance:* Predominance accompanied by rapture is related to (its) associated aggregates accompanied by rapture and accompanied by pleasure by predominance condition. (4)

23. (v) State accompanied by pleasure is related to state accompanied by pleasure by predominance condition.

(It is of two kinds, namely:) (*a*) object-predominance, (*b*) conascence-predominance.

(*a*) *Object-predominance:* After having offered the offering with the mind accompanied by pleasure . . .

(*b*) *Conascence-predominance:* Predominance accompanied by pleasure is related to (its) associated aggregates by predominance condition. (1)

(vi) State accompanied by pleasure is related to state accompanied by rapture by predominance condition.

(It is of two kinds, namely:) (*a*) object-predominance, (*b*) conascence-predominance . . .

(*b*) *Conascence-predominance:* Predominance accompanied by pleasure is related to (its) associated aggregates accompanied by rapture by predominance condition. (2)

(vii) State accompanied by pleasure is related to state accompanied by indifference by predominance condition.

Object-predominance: (Abbreviated.) (3)

(viii) State accompanied by pleasure is related to state accompanied by rapture and accompanied by pleasure by predominance condition.

(It is of two kinds, namely:) (*a*) object-predominance, (*b*) conascence-predominance . . .

(*b*) *Conascence-predominance:* Predominance accompanied by pleasure is related to (its) associated aggregates accompanied by rapture and accompanied by pleasure by predominance condition. (4)

24. (ix) State accompanied by indifference is related to state accompanied by indifference by predominance condition.

(It is of two kinds, namely:) (*a*) object-predominance, (*b*) conascence-predominance . . .

(*b*) *Conascence-predominance:* Predominance accompanied by indifference is related to (its) associated aggregates by predominance condition. (1)

(x) State accompanied by indifference is related to state accompanied by rapture by predominance condition.

Object-predominance: (Abbreviated.) (2)

(xi) State accompanied by indifference is related to state accompanied by pleasure by predominance condition.

Object-predominance: (Abbreviated.) (3)

(xii) State accompanied by indifference is related to state accompanied by rapture and accompanied by pleasure by predominance condition.

Object-predominance: (Abbreviated.) (4)

25. (xiii) States accompanied by rapture and accompanied by pleasure are related to state accompanied by rapture by predominance condition.

(It is of two kinds, namely:) (*a*) object-predominance, (*b*) conascence-predominance . . .

(*b*) *Conascence-predominance:* Predominance accompanied by rapture and accompanied by pleasure is related to (its) associated aggregates accompanied by rapture by predominance condition. (1)

(xiv) States accompanied by rapture and accompanied by pleasure are related to state accompanied by pleasure by predominance condition.

(It is of two kinds, namely:) (*a*) object-predominance, (*b*) conascence-predominance . . .

(*b*) *Conascence-predominance:* Predominance accompanied by rapture and accompanied by pleasure is related to (its) associated aggregates accompanied by pleasure by predominance condition. (2)

(xv) States accompanied by rapture and accompanied by pleasure are related to state accompanied by indifference by predominance condition.

Object-predominance: (Abbreviated.) (3)

(xvi) States accompanied by rapture and accompanied by pleasure are related to state accompanied by rapture and accompanied by pleasure by predominance condition.

(It is of two kinds, namely:) (*a*) object-predominance, (*b*) conascence-predominance . . .

(*b*) *Conascence-predominance:* Predominance accompanied by rapture and accompanied by pleasure is related to (its) associated aggregates accompanied by rapture and accompanied by pleasure by predominance condition. (4)

Proximity 16

26. (i) State accompanied by rapture is related to state accompanied by rapture by proximity condition.

Preceding aggregates accompanied by rapture are related to subsequent aggregates accompanied by rapture by proximity condition. Adaptation accompanied by rapture is related to change-of-lineage by proximity condition. (In this manner all the relations of the sections should be clearly shown.) Adaptation to purification; change-of-lineage to Path; purification to Path; Path to Fruition; Fruition to Fruition; adaptation is related to the attainment of Fruition accompanied by rapture by proximity condition. (1)

(ii) State accompanied by rapture is related to state accompanied by pleasure by proximity condition.

Preceding aggregates accompanied by rapture are related to subsequent aggregates accompanied by pleasure by proximity condition. Adaptation accompanied by rapture is related to change-of-lineage accompanied by pleasure by proximity condition; adaptation accompanied by rapture is related to purification accompanied by pleasure by proximity condition; adaptation accompanied by rapture is related to the attainment of Fruition accompanied by pleasure by proximity condition. (2)

(iii) State accompanied by rapture is related to state accompanied by indifference by proximity condition.

Death-consciousness accompanied by rapture is related to rebirth-consciousness accompanied by indifference by proximity condition. Life-continuum accompanied by rapture is related to advertence by proximity condition. Resultant mind-consciousness element accompanied by rapture is related to functional mind-consciousness element by proximity condition. Life-continuum accompanied by rapture is related to life-continuum accompanied by indifference by proximity condition. Faultless or faulty (consciousness) accompanied by rapture to emergence accompanied by indifference; functional to emergence; Fruition is related to emergence by proximity condition. (3)

(iv) State accompanied by rapture is related to state accompanied by rapture and accompanied by pleasure by proximity condition.

Preceding aggregates accompanied by rapture are related to subsequent aggregates accompanied by rapture and accompanied by pleasure by proximity condition. Adaptation accompanied by rapture is related to change-of-lineage accompanied by rapture and accompanied by pleasure by proximity condition . . . adaptation accompanied by rapture is related to the attainment of Fruition accompanied by rapture and accompanied by pleasure by proximity condition. (4)

27. (v) State accompanied by pleasure is related to state accompanied by pleasure by proximity condition.

Preceding aggregates accompanied by pleasure are related to subsequent aggregates accompanied by pleasure by proximity condition. Adaptation accompanied by pleasure is related to change-of-lineage accompanied by pleasure by proximity condition . . . adaptation accompanied by pleasure is related to the attainment of Fruition accompanied by pleasure by proximity condition. (1)

(vi) State accompanied by pleasure is related to state accompanied by rapture by proximity condition.

Preceding aggregates accompanied by pleasure are related to subsequent aggregates accompanied by rapture by proximity condition . . . adaptation accompanied by pleasure is related to the attainment of Fruition accompanied by rapture by proximity condition. (2)

(vii) State accompanied by pleasure is related to state accompanied by indifference by proximity condition.

Death-consciousness accompanied by pleasure is related to rebirth-consciousness accompanied by indifference by proximity condition. Life-continuum accompanied by pleasure is related to advertence by proximity condition. Body-consciousness accompanied by pleasure is related to resultant mind-element by proximity condition. Resultant mind-consciousness element accompanied by pleasure is related to functional mind-consciousness element by proximity condition. Life-continuum accompanied by pleasure is related to life-continuum accompanied by indifference by proximity condition. Faultless or faulty accompanied by pleasure to emergence accompanied by indifference; functional to emergence; Fruition is related to emergence by proximity condition. (3)

(viii) State accompanied by pleasure is related to state accompanied by rapture and accompanied by pleasure by proximity condition.

Preceding aggregates accompanied by pleasure are related to subsequent aggregates accompanied by rapture and accompanied by pleasure by proximity condition . . . adaptation accompanied by pleasure is related to the attainment of Fruition accompanied by rapture and accompanied by pleasure by proximity condition. (4)

28. (ix) State accompanied by indifference is related to state accompanied by indifference by proximity condition.

Preceding aggregates accompanied by indifference to subsequent aggregates accompanied by indifference . . . Advertence is related to four-fold consciousness by proximity condition. Adaptation accompanied by indifference to the attainment of Fruition accompanied by indifference; for one emerging from the attainment of Extinction, neither-perception-nor-non-perception is related to the attainment of Fruition accompanied by indifference by proximity condition. (1)

(x) State accompanied by indifference is related to state accompanied by rapture by proximity condition.

Death-consciousness accompanied by indifference to rebirth-consciousness accompanied by rapture . . . advertence to aggregates accompanied by rapture . . . resultant mind-element to resultant mind-consciousness element accompanied by rapture . . . life-continuum accompanied by indifference to life-continuum accompanied by rapture . . . faultless or faulty accompanied by indifference to emergence accompanied by rapture; functional to emergence; Fruition to emergence; for one emerging from the attainment of Extinction, neither-perception-nor-non-perception is related to the attainment of Fruition accompanied by rapture by proximity condition. (2)

(xi)–(xii) State accompanied by indifference to state accompanied by pleasure . . . is related to state accompanied by rapture and accompanied by pleasure by proximity condition. (4)

(Also remember to proceed with them in the same way.)

29. (xiii)–(xv) States accompanied by rapture and accompanied by pleasure to state accompanied by rapture . . . to state accompanied by pleasure . . . are related to state accompanied by indifference by proximity condition.

Death-consciousness accompanied by rapture and accompanied by pleasure to rebirth-consciousness accompanied by indifference . . . life-continuum accompanied by rapture and accompanied by pleasure to advertence . . . resultant mind-consciousness element accompanied by rapture and accompanied by pleasure to functional mind-consciousness element . . . life-continuum accompanied by rapture and accompanied by pleasure to life-continuum accompanied by indifference . . . faultless or faulty accompanied by rapture and accompanied by pleasure to emergence accompanied by indifference; functional to emergence; Fruition is related to emergence by proximity condition. (3)

(xvi) States accompanied by rapture and accompanied by pleasure are related to state accompanied by rapture and accompanied by pleasure by proximity condition.

Preceding aggregates accompanied by rapture and accompanied by pleasure to subsequent aggregates accompanied by rapture and accompanied by pleasure . . . adaptation accompanied by rapture and accompanied by pleasure are related to the attainment of Fruition accompanied by pleasure by proximity condition. (4)

Contiguity 16

30. State accompanied by rapture is related to state accompanied by rapture by contiguity condition. (The same as proximity condition.)

Conascence 10

31. State accompanied by rapture is related to state accompanied by rapture by conascence condition.

One aggregate accompanied by rapture is related to three aggregates by conascence condition . . . two aggregates are related to two aggregates by conascence condition . . . [The same as for the "Dependent" (Chapter). 10 questions in conascence.]

Mutuality, Dependence 10

32. State accompanied by rapture is related to state accompanied by rapture by mutuality condition . . . by dependence condition. (Do 10 questions.)

Strong-dependence 16

33. (i) State accompanied by rapture is related to state accompanied by rapture by strong-dependence condition.

(It is of three kinds, namely:) (*a*) object-strong-dependence, (*b*) proximity-strong-dependence, (*c*) natural strong-dependence . . .

(*c*) *Natural strong-dependence:* By the strong-dependence of confidence accompanied by rapture, with the mind accompanied by rapture, one offers an offering, undertakes precepts, fulfils the duty of observance, develops jhāna accompanied by rapture, develops insight, develops

Path, develops attainment; arouses conceit, adopts wrong views . . . precept accompanied by rapture . . . learning . . . generosity . . . By the strong-dependence of wisdom, (one), with the mind accompanied by rapture, offers an offering, undertakes precepts . . . arouses conceit, adopts wrong views . . . lust accompanied by rapture . . . delusion . . . conceit . . . wrong views . . . By the strong-dependence of wish, with the mind accompanied by rapture, one offers an offering, undertakes precepts, fulfils the duty of observance, develops jhāna accompanied by rapture . . . develops attainment; with the mind accompanied by rapture, one takes the property of others which has not been given to one, speaks untruth, slanders, babbles foolishly, breaks into a house, plunders the property of others, leaves behind only one house, lies in wait at the junction of highways, goes to other men's wives, plunders villages, plunders market-towns. Confidence accompanied by rapture, precept, learning, generosity, wisdom, lust, delusion, conceit, wrong views, wish is related to confidence accompanied by rapture, precept, learning, generosity, wisdom, lust, delusion, conceit, wrong views, wish by strong-dependence condition. (1)

(ii) State accompanied by rapture is related to state accompanied by pleasure by strong-dependence condition.

(It is of three kinds, namely:) (*a*) object-strong-dependence, (*b*) proximity-strong-dependence, (*c*) natural strong-dependence . . .

(*c*) *Natural strong-dependence:* By the strong-dependence of confidence accompanied by rapture, with the mind accompanied by pleasure, one offers an offering . . . develops attainment; arouses conceit, adopts wrong views . . . precept accompanied by rapture . . . learning . . . generosity . . . wisdom . . . lust . . . delusion . . . conceit . . . wrong views . . . By the strong-dependence of wish, with the mind accompanied by pleasure, one offers an offering . . . develops attainment; with the mind accompanied by pleasure, takes the property of others which has not been given to one . . . plunders market-towns. Confidence accompanied by rapture . . . wish is related to confidence accompanied by pleasure . . . wish, body-consciousness accompanied by pleasure by strong-dependence condition. (2)

(iii) State accompanied by rapture is related to state accompanied by indifference by strong-dependence condition.

(It is of three kinds, namely:) (*a*) object-strong-dependence, (*b*) proximity-strong-dependence, (*c*) natural strong-dependence . . .

(*c*) *Natural strong-dependence:* By the strong-dependence of confidence accompanied by rapture, with the mind accompanied by indifference, one offers an offering . . . develops superknowledge, develops attainment; arouses conceit, adopts wrong views . . . precept accompanied by rapture . . . By the strong-dependence of wish, with the mind accompanied by indifference, one offers an offering . . . plunders market-towns. Confidence accompanied by rapture . . . wish is related to confidence accompanied by indifference . . . wish by strong-dependence condition. (3)

(iv) State accompanied by rapture is related to state accompanied by rapture and accompanied by pleasure by strong-dependence condition.

(It is of three kinds, namely:) (*a*) object-strong-dependence, (*b*) proximity-strong-dependence, (*c*) natural strong-dependence . . .

(*c*) *Natural strong-dependence:* By the strong-dependence of confidence accompanied by rapture, with the mind accompanied by rapture and accompanied by pleasure, one offers an offering . . . adopts wrong views . . . precept accompanied by rapture . . . By the strong-dependence of wish, with the mind accompanied by rapture and accompanied by pleasure, one offers an offering . . . plunders market-towns. Confidence accompanied by rapture . . . wish is related to confidence accompanied by rapture and accompanied by pleasure . . . wish by strong-dependence condition. (4)

34. (v) State accompanied by pleasure is related to state accompanied by pleasure by strong-dependence condition.

(It is of three kinds, namely:) (*a*) object-strong-dependence, (*b*) proximity-strong-dependence, (*c*) natural strong-dependence . . .

(*c*) *Natural strong-dependence:* By the strong-dependence of confidence accompanied by pleasure, with the mind accompanied by pleasure one offers an offering . . . adopts wrong views . . . precept accompanied by pleasure . . . wish . . . By the strong-dependence of body-consciousness accompanied by pleasure, with the mind accompanied by pleasure, one offers an offering . . . plunders market-towns. Confidence accompanied by pleasure . . . wish, body-consciousness accompanied by pleasure is related to confidence accompanied by pleasure . . . wish, body-consciousness accompanied by pleasure by strong-dependence condition. (1)

(vi) State accompanied by pleasure is related to state accompanied by rapture by strong-dependence condition.

(It is of three kinds, namely:) (*a*) object-strong-dependence, (*b*) proximity-strong-dependence, (*c*) natural strong-dependence . . .

(*c*) *Natural strong-dependence:* By the strong-dependence of confidence accompanied by pleasure, with the mind accompanied by rapture, one offers an offering . . . adopts wrong views . . . precept accompanied by pleasure . . . wish . . . By the strong-dependence of body-consciousness accompanied by pleasure, with the mind accompanied by rapture, one offers an offering . . . plünders market-towns. Confidence accompanied by pleasure . . . wish, body-consciousness accompanied by pleasure is related to confidence accompanied by rapture . . . wish by strong-dependence condition. (2)

(vii) State accompanied by pleasure is related to state accompanied by indifference by strong-dependence condition.

(It is of three kinds, namely:) (*a*) object-strong-dependence, (*b*) proximity-strong-dependence, (*c*) natural strong-dependence . . .

(*c*) *Natural strong-dependence:* By the strong-dependence of confidence accompanied by pleasure, with the mind accompanied by indifference, one offers an offering . . . develops superknowledge . . . adopts wrong views . . . precept accompanied by pleasure . . . wish . . . By the strong-dependence of body-consciousness accompanied by pleasure, with the mind accompanied by indifference, one offers an offering . . . plunders market-towns. Confidence accompanied by pleasure . . . wish, body-consciousness accompanied by pleasure is related to confidence accompanied by indifference . . . wish by strong-dependence condition. (3)

(viii) State accompanied by pleasure is related to state accompanied by rapture and accompanied by pleasure by strong-dependence condition.

(It is of three kinds, namely:) (*a*) object-strong-dependence, (*b*) proximity-strong-dependence, (*c*) natural strong-dependence . . .

(*c*) *Natural strong-dependence:* By the strong-dependence of confidence accompanied by pleasure, with the mind accompanied by rapture and accompanied by pleasure, one offers an offering . . . adopts wrong views . . . precept accompanied by pleasure . . . wish . . . By the strong-dependence of body-consciousness accompanied by pleasure, with the mind accompanied by rapture and accompanied by pleasure, one offers an offering . . . plunders market-towns. Confidence accompanied by pleasure . . . wish, body-consciousness accompanied by pleasure is related to confidence accompanied by rapture and accompanied by pleasure . . . wish by strong-dependence condition. (4)

35. (ix) State accompanied by indifference is related to state accompanied by indifference by strong-dependence condition.

(It is of three kinds, namely:) (*a*) object-strong-dependence, (*b*) proximity-strong-dependence, (*c*) natural strong-dependence . . .

(*c*) *Natural strong-dependence:* By the strong-dependence of confidence accompanied by indifference, with the mind accompanied by indifference, one offers an offering . . . develops superknowledge . . . adopts wrong views . . . precept accompanied by indifference . . . By the strong-dependence of wish, with the mind accompanied by indifference, one offers an offering . . . plunders market-towns. Confidence accompanied by indifference . . . wish is related to confidence accompanied by indifference . . . wish by strong-dependence condition. (1)

(x) State accompanied by indifference is related to state accompanied by rapture by strong-dependence condition.

(It is of three kinds, namely:) (*a*) object-strong-dependence, (*b*) proximity-strong-dependence, (*c*) natural strong-dependence . . .

(*c*) *Natural strong-dependence:* By the strong-dependence of confidence accompanied by indifference, with the mind accompanied by rapture, one offers an offering . . . adopts wrong views . . . precept accompanied by indifference . . . By the strong-dependence of wish, with the mind accompanied by rapture, one offers an offering . . . plunders market-towns. Confidence accompanied by indifference . . . wish is related to confidence accompanied by rapture . . . wish by strong-dependence condition. (2)

(xi) State accompanied by indifference is related to state accompanied by pleasure by strong-dependence condition.

(It is of three kinds, namely:) (*a*) object-strong-dependence, (*b*) proximity-strong-dependence, (*c*) natural strong-dependence . . .

(*c*) *Natural strong-dependence:* By the strong-dependence of confidence accompanied by indifference, with the mind accompanied by pleasure, one offers an offering . . . adopts wrong views . . . precept accompanied by indifference . . . By the strong-dependence of wish, with the mind accompanied by pleasure, one offers an offering . . . plunders market-towns. Confidence accompanied by indifference . . . wish is related to confidence accompanied by pleasure . . . wish, body-consciousness accompanied by pleasure by strong-dependence condition. (3)

(xii) State accompanied by indifference is related to state accompanied by rapture and accompanied by pleasure by strong-dependence condition.

(It is of three kinds, namely:) (*a*) object-strong-dependence, (*b*) proximity-strong-dependence, (*c*) natural strong-dependence . . .

(*c*) *Natural strong-dependence:* By the strong-dependence of confidence accompanied by indifference, with the mind accompanied by rapture and accompanied by pleasure, one offers an offering . . . adopts wrong views . . . precept accompanied by indifference . . . By the strong-dependence of wish, with the mind accompanied by rapture and accompanied by pleasure, one offers an offering . . . plunders market-towns. Confidence accompanied by indifference . . . wish is related to confidence accompanied by rapture and accompanied by pleasure . . . wish by strong-dependence condition. (4)

36. (xiii) States accompanied by rapture and accompanied by pleasure are related to state accompanied by rapture by strong-dependence condition.

(It is of three kinds, namely:) (*a*) object-strong-dependence, (*b*) proximity-strong-dependence, (*c*) natural strong-dependence . . .

(*c*) *Natural strong-dependence:* By the strong-dependence of confidence accompanied by rapture and accompanied by pleasure, with the mind accompanied by rapture, one offers an offering . . . adopts wrong views . . . precept accompanied by rapture and accompanied by pleasure . . . By the strong-dependence of wish, with the mind accompanied by rapture, one offers an offering . . . plunders market-towns. Confidence accompanied by rapture and accompanied by pleasure . . . wish is related to confidence accompanied by rapture . . . wish by strong-dependence condition. (1)

(xiv) States accompanied by rapture and accompanied by pleasure are related to state accompanied by pleasure by strong-dependence condition.

(It is of three kinds, namely:) (*a*) object-strong-dependence, (*b*) proximity-strong-dependence, (*c*) natural strong-dependence . . .

(*c*) *Natural strong-dependence:* By the strong-dependence of confidence accompanied by rapture and accompanied by pleasure, with the mind accompanied by pleasure, one offers an offering . . . adopts wrong views . . . precept accompanied by rapture and accompanied by pleasure . . . By the strong-dependence of wish, with the mind accompanied by pleasure, one offers an offering . . . plunders market-towns. Confidence accompanied by rapture and accompanied by pleasure . . . wish is related to confidence accompanied by pleasure . . . wish, body-consciousness accompanied by pleasure by strong-dependence condition. (2)

(xv) States accompanied by rapture and accompanied by pleasure are related to state accompanied by indifference by strong-dependence condition.

(It is of three kinds, namely:) (*a*) object-strong-dependence, (*b*) proximity-strong-dependence, (*c*) natural strong-dependence . . .

(*c*) *Natural strong-dependence:* By the strong-dependence of confidence accompanied by rapture and accompanied by pleasure, with the mind accompanied by indifference, one offers an offering . . . develops superknowledge . . . adopts wrong views . . . precept accompanied by rapture and accompanied by pleasure . . . By the strong-dependence of wish, with the mind accompanied by indifference, one offers an offering . . . plunders market-towns. Confidence accompanied by rapture and accompanied by pleasure . . . wish is related to confidence accompanied by indifference . . . wish by strong-dependence condition. (3)

(xvi) States accompanied by rapture and accompanied by pleasure are related to state accompanied by rapture and accompanied by pleasure by strong-dependence condition.

(It is of three kinds, namely:) (*a*) object-strong-dependence, (*b*) proximity-strong-dependence, (*c*) natural strong-dependence . . .

(*c*) *Natural strong-dependence:* By the strong-dependence of confidence accompanied by rapture and accompanied by pleasure, with the mind accompanied by rapture and accompanied by pleasure, one offers an offering, undertakes precepts, fulfils the duty of observance, develops jhāna accompanied by rapture and accompanied by pleasure, develops insight, develops Path, develops attainment; arouses conceit, adopts wrong views . . . precept accompanied by rapture and accompanied by pleasure . . . learning . . . generosity . . . wisdom . . . lust . . . delusion . . . conceit . . . wrong views . . . By the strong-dependence of wish, with the mind accompanied by rapture and accompanied by pleasure, one offers an offering, undertakes precepts, fulfils the duty of observance, develops jhāna accompanied by rapture and accompanied by pleasure . . . develops attainment; with the mind accompanied by rapture and accompanied by pleasure, takes the property of others which has not been given to one, speaks untruth, slanders, babbles foolishly, breaks into a house, plunders the property of others, leaves behind only one house, lies in wait at the junction of highways, goes to other men's wives, plunders villages, plunders market-towns. Confidence accompanied by rapture and accompanied by pleasure . . . wish is related to confidence accompanied by rapture and accompanied by pleasure . . .

wish by strong-dependence condition. (4)

Repetition 10

37. (i) State accompanied by rapture is related to state accompanied by rapture by repetition condition.

Preceding aggregates accompanied by rapture are related to subsequent aggregates accompanied by rapture by repetition condition. Adaptation accompanied by rapture to change-of-lineage accompanied by rapture; adaptation to purification; change-of-lineage to Path; purification is related to Path by repetition condition. (1)

(ii) State accompanied by rapture is related to state accompanied by pleasure by repetition condition.

Preceding aggregates accompanied by rapture are related to subsequent aggregates accompanied by pleasure by repetition condition. Adaptation accompanied by rapture is related to change-of-lineage accompanied by pleasure by repetition condition; adaptation accompanied by rapture is related to purification accompanied by pleasure by repetition condition; change-of-lineage accompanied by rapture to Path accompanied by pleasure; purification accompanied by rapture is related to Path accompanied by pleasure by repetition condition. (2)

(iii) State accompanied by rapture is related to state accompanied by rapture and accompanied by pleasure by repetition condition.

Preceding aggregates accompanied by rapture are related to subsequent aggregates accompanied by rapture and accompanied by pleasure by repetition condition . . . purification accompanied by rapture is related to Path accompanied by rapture and accompanied by pleasure by repetition condition. (3)

38. (iv)–(vi) State accompanied by pleasure to state accompanied by pleasure . . . to state accompanied by rapture . . . is related to state accompanied by rapture and accompanied by pleasure by repetition condition. (Abbreviated.) (Proceed after looking at the method for rapture.)

(vii) State accompanied by indifference is related to state accompanied by indifference by repetition condition.

Preceding aggregates accompanied by indifference to subsequent aggregates accompanied by indifference . . . purification accompanied by indifference is related to Path accompanied by indifference by repetition condition. (1)

39. (viii)–(x) States accompanied by rapture and accompanied by

pleasure to state accompanied by rapture . . . to state accompanied by pleasure . . . are related to state accompanied by rapture and accompanied by pleasure by repetition condition.

Preceding aggregates accompanied by rapture and accompanied by pleasure are related to subsequent aggregates accompanied by rapture and accompanied by pleasure by repetition condition . . . purification accompanied by rapture and accompanied by pleasure is related to Path accompanied by rapture and accompanied by pleasure by repetition condition. (3)

Kamma 16

40. (i) State accompanied by rapture is related to state accompanied by rapture by kamma condition.

(It is of two kinds, namely:) (*a*) conascence(-kamma), (*b*) asynchronous (kamma).

(*a*) (1) Conascent volition accompanied by rapture is related to (its) associated aggregates by kamma condition;

(2) At the moment of conception, volition accompanied by rapture is related to (its) associated aggregates by kamma condition.

(*b*) Asynchronous volition accompanied by rapture is related to (its) resultant aggregates accompanied by rapture by kamma condition. (1)

(ii) State accompanied by rapture is related to state accompanied by pleasure by kamma condition.

(It is of two kinds, namely:) (*a*) conascence(-kamma), (*b*) asynchronous (kamma).

(*a*) (1) Conascent volition accompanied by rapture is related to (its) associated aggregates accompanied by pleasure by kamma condition;

(2) At the moment of conception, volition accompanied by rapture is related to (its) associated aggregates accompanied by pleasure by kamma condition.

(*b*) Asynchronous volition accompanied by rapture is related to (its) resultant aggregates accompanied by pleasure by kamma condition. (2)

(iii) State accompanied by rapture is related to state accompanied by indifference by kamma condition.

Asynchronous volition accompanied by rapture is related to (its) resultant aggregates accompanied by indifference by kamma condition. (3)

(iv) State accompanied by rapture is related to state accompanied by rapture and accompanied by pleasure by kamma condition.

(It is of two kinds, namely:) (*a*) conascence(-kamma), (*b*) asynchronous (kamma).

(*a*) (1) Conascent volition accompanied by rapture is related to (its) associated aggregates accompanied by rapture and accompanied by pleasure by kamma condition;

(2) At the moment of conception ....

(*b*) Asynchronous volition accompanied by rapture is related to (its) resultant aggregates accompanied by rapture and accompanied by pleasure by kamma condition. (4)

41. (v)–(viii) State accompanied by pleasure to state accompanied by pleasure . . . [Also proceed after looking at the four enumerations (above).]

42. (ix) State accompanied by indifference is related to state accompanied by indifference by kamma condition.

(It is of two kinds, namely:) (*a*) conascence(-kamma), (*b*) asynchronous (kamma) . . .

(x) State accompanied by indifference is related to state accompanied by rapture by kamma condition.

Asynchronous volition accompanied by indifference . . .

(xi) State accompanied by indifference is related to state accompanied by pleasure by kamma condition.

Asynchronous volition accompanied by indifference . . .

(xii) State accompanied by indifference is related to state accompanied by rapture and accompanied by pleasure by kamma condition.

Asynchronous volition accompanied by indifference . . . (4)

(xiii)–(xvi) States accompanied by rapture and accompanied by pleasure to state accompanied by rapture . . . (Do four. Classify after considering "accompanied by rapture".) (4)

Resultant 10

43. State accompanied by rapture is related to state accompanied by rapture by resultant condition.

(*a*) One resultant aggregate accompanied by rapture is related to three aggregates by resultant condition . . . two aggregates to two aggregates . . .

(*b*) At the moment of conception, one aggregate accompanied by rapture to three aggregates . . . two aggregates to two aggregates . . .

(Expand 10 questions in the same way as for root condition in the "Dependent" Chapter.)

Nutriment, etc. 10

44. State accompanied by rapture is related to state accompanied by rapture by nutriment condition . . . by faculty condition . . . by jhāna condition . . . by path condition . . . by association condition . . . by presence condition. (Expand 10 questions.) . . . by absence condition . . . by disappearance condition. (Absence and disappearance are also the same as proximity.) . . . by non-disappearance condition . . .

1. CONDITIONS: POSITIVE (ii) ENUMERATION CHAPTER

By Ones

45. With root 10, object 16, predominance 16, proximity 16, contiguity 16, conascence 10, mutuality 10, dependence 10, strong-dependence 16, repetition 10, kamma 16, resultant 10, nutriment, faculty, jhāna, path, association, presence 10, absence 16, disappearance 16, non-disappearance 10.

(Enumerate after considering the Positive in the Faultless Triplet.)

End of Positive

2. SELECTION OF THE CONDITIONS FOR NEGATIVE 16

46. (i) State accompanied by rapture is related to state accompanied by rapture by object condition, conascence condition, strong-dependence condition, kamma condition. (1)

(ii) State accompanied by rapture is related to state accompanied by pleasure by object condition, conascence condition, strong-dependence condition, kamma condition. (2)

(iii) State accompanied by rapture is related to state accompanied by indifference by object condition, strong-dependence condition, kamma condition. (3)

(iv) State accompanied by rapture is related to state accompanied by rapture and accompanied by pleasure by object condition, conascence condition, strong-dependence condition, kamma condition. (4)

47. (v) State accompanied by pleasure is related to state accompanied by pleasure by object condition, conascence condition, strong-dependence condition, kamma condition. (1)

(vi) State accompanied by pleasure is related to state accompanied by rapture by object condition, conascence condition, strong-dependence condition, kamma condition. (2)

(vii) State accompanied by pleasure is related to state accompanied by indifference by object condition, strong-dependence condition, kamma condition. (3)

(viii) State accompanied by pleasure is related to state accompanied by rapture and accompanied by pleasure by object condition, conascence condition, strong-dependence condition, kamma condition. (4)

48. (ix) State accompanied by indifference is related to state accompanied by indifference by object condition, conascence condition, strong-dependence condition, kamma condition. (1)

(x) State accompanied by indifference is related to state accompanied by rapture by object condition, strong-dependence condition, kamma condition. (2)

(xi) State accompanied by indifference is related to state accompanied by pleasure by object condition, strong-dependence condition, kamma condition. (3)

(xii) State accompanied by indifference is related to state accompanied by rapture and accompanied by pleasure by object condition, strong-dependence condition, kamma condition. (4)

49. (xiii) States accompanied by rapture and accompanied by pleasure are related to state accompanied by rapture by object condition, conascence condition, strong-dependence condition, kamma condition. (1)

(xiv) States accompanied by rapture and accompanied by pleasure are related to state accompanied by pleasure by object condition, conascence condition, strong-dependence condition, kamma condition. (2)

(xv) States accompanied by rapture and accompanied by pleasure are related to state accompanied by indifference by object condition, strong-dependence condition, kamma condition. (3)

(xvi) States accompanied by rapture and accompanied by pleasure are related to state accompanied by rapture and accompanied by pleasure by object condition, conascence condition, strong-dependence condition, kamma condition. (4)

2. CONDITIONS: NEGATIVE (ii) ENUMERATION CHAPTER

By Ones

50. With not-root 16, not-object, not-predominance, not-proximity, not-contiguity, not-conascence, not-mutuality, not-dependence, not-

strong-dependence, not-prenascence, not-postnascence, not-repetition, not-kamma, not-resultant, not-nutriment, not-faculty, not-jhāna, not-path, not-association, not-dissociation, not-presence, not-absence, not-disappearance, not-non-disappearance (are) all 16.

(Enumerate by considering the Negative.)

End of Negative

3. CONDITIONS: POSITIVE–NEGATIVE

(Root) By Twos

51. With root condition, not-object 10, not-predominance 10, not-proximity, not-contiguity, not-strong-dependence, not-prenascence, not-postnascence, not-repetition, not-kamma, not-resultant, not-nutriment, not-faculty, not-jhāna, not-path, not-dissociation, not-absence, not-disappearance (are) all 10.

(Enumerate by considering the Positive–Negative.)

End of Positive–Negative

4. CONDITIONS: NEGATIVE–POSITIVE

(Not-root) By Twos

52. With not-root condition, object 16, predominance, proximity, contiguity 16, conascence 10, mutuality 10, dependence 10, strong-dependence 16, repetition 10, kamma 16, resultant 10, nutriment 10, faculty 10, jhāna 10, path 10, association 10, presence 10, absence 16, disappearance 16, non-disappearance 10.

(Enumerate after considering the Negative–Positive.)

End of Negative–Positive

END OF RAPTURE TRIPLET

8. TRIPLET OF (STATE) ERADICATED BY FIRST PATH[1]
I. "DEPENDENT" CHAPTER

1. CONDITIONS: POSITIVE (i) CLASSIFICATION CHAPTER

Root 9

1. (i) Dependent on state eradicated by First Path (dassanena pahātabba), arises state eradicated by First Path by root condition.

Dependent on one aggregate eradicated by First Path, arise three aggregates . . . dependent on two aggregates, arise two aggregates. (1)

(ii) Dependent on state eradicated by First Path, arises state eradicated neither by First Path nor by Higher 3 Paths (neva dassanena na bhāvanāya pahātabba) by root condition.

Dependent on aggregates eradicated by First Path, arises mind-produced matter. (2)

(iii) Dependent on state eradicated by First Path, arise states eradicated by First Path and eradicated neither by First Path nor by Higher 3 Paths by root condition.

Dependent on one aggregate eradicated by First Path, arise three aggregates and mind-produced matter . . . dependent on two aggregates, arise two aggregates and mind-produced matter. (3)

2. (iv) Dependent on state eradicated by Higher 3 Paths (bhāvanāya pahātabba), arises state eradicated by Higher 3 Paths by root condition.

Dependent on one aggregate eradicated by Higher 3 Paths, arise three aggregates . . . dependent on two aggregates, arise two aggregates. (1)

(v) Dependent on state eradicated by Higher 3 Paths, arises state eradicated neither by First Path nor by Higher 3 Paths by root condition.

Dependent on aggregates eradicated by Higher 3 Paths, arises mind-produced matter. (2)

(vi) Dependent on state eradicated by Higher 3 Paths, arise states eradicated by Higher 3 Paths and eradicated neither by First Path nor by Higher 3 Paths by root condition.

Dependent on one aggregate eradicated by Higher 3 Paths, arise three aggregates and mind-produced matter . . . dependent on two aggregates, arise two aggregates and mind-produced matter. (3)

---

[1] This comprises (1) States eradicated by First Path, (2) States eradicated by Higher 3 Paths, (3) States eradicated neither by First Path nor by Higher 3 Paths.

3. (vii) Dependent on state eradicated neither by First Path nor by Higher 3 Paths, arises state eradicated neither by First Path nor by Higher 3 Paths by root condition.

(*a*) Dependent on one aggregate eradicated neither by First Path nor by Higher 3 Paths, arise three aggregates and mind-produced matter . . . dependent on two aggregates, arise two aggregates and mind-produced matter;

(*b*) At the moment of conception, dependent on one aggregate eradicated neither by First Path nor by Higher 3 Paths, arise three aggregates and kamma-produced matter . . . dependent on two aggregates, arise two aggregates and kamma-produced matter; dependent on aggregates, arises (heart-)base; dependent on (heart-)base, arise aggregates;

(*c*) Dependent on one great primary, arise three great primaries . . . dependent on two great primaries, arise two great primaries; dependent on great primaries, arise mind-produced and kamma-produced derived matter. (1)

4. (viii) Dependent on state eradicated by First Path and eradicated neither by First Path nor by Higher 3 Paths, arises state eradicated neither by First Path nor by Higher 3 Paths by root condition.

Dependent on aggregates eradicated by First Path and great primaries, arises mind-produced matter. (1)

(ix) Dependent on state eradicated by Higher 3 Paths and eradicated neither by First Path nor by Higher 3 Paths, arises state eradicated neither by First Path nor by Higher 3 Paths by root condition.

Dependent on aggregates eradicated by Higher 3 Paths and great primaries, arises mind-produced matter. (1)

Object 3

5. (i) Dependent on state eradicated by First Path, arises state eradicated by First Path by object condition.

Dependent on one aggregate eradicated by First Path, arise three aggregates . . . dependent on two aggregates, arise two aggregates. (1)

(ii) Dependent on state eradicated by Higher 3 Paths, arises state eradicated by Higher 3 Paths by object condition.

Dependent on one aggregate eradicated by Higher 3 Paths, arise three aggregates . . . dependent on two aggregates, arise two aggregates. (1)

(iii) Dependent on state eradicated neither by First Path nor by

Higher 3 Paths, arises state eradicated neither by First Path nor by Higher 3 Paths by object condition.

(*a*) Dependent on one aggregate eradicated neither by First Path nor by Higher 3 Paths, arise three aggregates . . . dependent on two aggregates, arise two aggregates;

(*b*) At the moment of conception, dependent on one aggregate eradicated neither by First Path nor by Higher 3 Paths, arise three aggregates . . . dependent on two aggregates, arise two aggregates; dependent on (heart-)base, arise aggregates. (1)

Predominance 9

6. (i)–(iii) Dependent on state eradicated by First Path, arises state eradicated by First Path by predominance condition . . . three.

(iv)–(vi) Dependent on state eradicated by Higher 3 Paths, arises state eradicated by Higher 3 Paths by predominance condition . . . three.

(vii) Dependent on state eradicated neither by First Path nor by Higher 3 Paths, arises state eradicated neither by First Path nor by Higher 3 Paths by predominance condition.

(*a*) Dependent on one aggregate eradicated neither by First Path nor by Higher 3 Paths, arise three aggregates and mind-produced matter . . . dependent on two aggregates, arise two aggregates and mind-produced matter;

(*b*) Dependent on one great primary, arise three great primaries . . . dependent on two great primaries, arise two great primaries; dependent on great primaries, arises mind-produced derived matter. (1)

7. (viii) Dependent on state eradicated by First Path and eradicated neither by First Path nor by Higher 3 Paths, arises state eradicated neither by First Path nor by Higher 3 Paths by predominance condition.

Dependent on aggregates eradicated by First Path and great primaries, arises mind-produced matter. (1)

(ix) Dependent on state eradicated by Higher 3 Paths and eradicated neither by First Path nor by Higher 3 Paths, arises state eradicated neither by First Path nor by Higher 3 Paths by predominance condition.

Dependent on aggregates eradicated by Higher 3 Paths and great primaries, arises mind-produced matter. (1)

Proximity, Contiguity 3

8. Dependent on state eradicated by First Path, arises state eradicated

by First Path by proximity condition . . . by contiguity condition. (The same as object.)

Conascence 9

9. (i)–(iii) Dependent on state eradicated by First Path, arises state eradicated by First Path by conascence condition . . . three.

(iv)–(vi) Dependent on state eradicated by Higher 3 Paths, arises state eradicated by Higher 3 Paths by conascence condition . . . three.

(vii) Dependent on state eradicated neither by First Path nor by Higher 3 Paths, arises state eradicated neither by First Path nor by Higher 3 Paths by conascence condition . . .

(*c*) Dependent on one great primary . . .

(*d*) External . . . nutriment-produced . . . temperature-produced . . . one great primary of non-percipient beings . . . (1)

10. (viii) Dependent on state eradicated by First Path and eradicated neither by First Path nor by Higher 3 Paths, arises state eradicated neither by First Path nor by Higher 3 Paths by conascence condition.

Dependent on aggregates eradicated by First Path and great primaries, arises mind-produced matter. (1)

(ix) Dependent on state eradicated by Higher 3 Paths and eradicated neither by First Path nor by Higher 3 Paths, arises state eradicated neither by First Path nor by Higher 3 Paths by conascence condition.

Dependent on aggregates eradicated by Higher 3 Paths and great primaries, arises mind-produced matter. (1)

Mutuality 3

11. (i) Dependent on state eradicated by First Path, arises state eradicated by First Path by mutuality condition . . . one.

(ii) Dependent on state eradicated by Higher 3 Paths, arises state eradicated by Higher 3 Paths by mutuality condition . . . one.

(iii) Dependent on state eradicated neither by First Path nor by Higher 3 Paths, arises state eradicated neither by First Path nor by Higher 3 Paths by mutuality condition.

(*a*) Dependent on one aggregate eradicated neither by First Path nor by Higher 3 Paths, arise three aggregates . . . dependent on two aggregates, arise two aggregates;

(*b*) At the moment of conception, dependent on one aggregate eradicated neither by First Path nor by Higher 3 Paths, arise three aggregates and (heart-)base . . . dependent on two aggregates, arise two aggregates and (heart-)base; dependent on aggregates, arises (heart-) base; dependent on (heart-)base, arise aggregates;

(*c*) Dependent on one great primary, arise three great primaries . . . dependent on two great primaries, arise two great primaries;

(*d*) External . . . nutriment-produced . . . temperature-produced . . . non-percipient beings . . . dependent on two great primaries, arise two great primaries.

Dependence, etc.

12. Dependent on state eradicated by First Path, arises state eradicated by First Path by dependence condition. (The same as root condition.) . . . by strong-dependence condition . . . three . . . by prenascence condition . . . three. (No conception.) . . . by repetition condition. (No resultant conception.) . . . by kamma condition. (Complete. Great primaries of internal and non-percipient beings.)

Resultant 1

13. Dependent on state eradicated neither by First Path nor by Higher 3 Paths, arises state eradicated neither by First Path nor by Higher 3 Paths by resultant condition.

(*a*) Dependent on one resultant aggregate, arise three aggregates and mind-produced matter . . .

(*b*) At the moment of conception . . . dependent on aggregates, arises (heart-)base; dependent on (heart-)base, arise aggregates;

(*c*) One great primary . . . dependent on great primaries, arise mind-produced and kamma-produced derived matter. (1)

Nutriment, etc.

14. Dependent on state eradicated by First Path, arises state eradicated by First Path by nutriment condition. (Complete. Internal great primaries and nutriment-produced.) . . . by faculty condition. (The same as kamma condition.) . . . by jhāna condition . . . by path condition. (The same as root condition.) . . . by association condition. (The same as object condition.) . . . by dissociation condition. (The same as dissociation condition in the Faultless Triplet.) . . . by presence condition. (The same as conascence condition.) . . . by absence condition . . . by disappearance condition . . . by non-disappearance condition . . .

1. CONDITIONS: POSITIVE (ii) ENUMERATION CHAPTER

By Ones

15. With root 9, object 3, predominance 9, proximity 3, contiguity 3, conascence 9, mutuality 3, dependence 9, strong-dependence 3, prenascence 3, repetition 3, kamma 9, resultant 1, nutriment 9, faculty 9, jhāna 9, path 9, association 3, dissociation 9, presence 9, absence 3, disappearance 3, non-disappearance 9.

(Enumerate the Positive after considering these sections.)

End of Positive

2. CONDITIONS: NEGATIVE (i) CLASSIFICATION CHAPTER

Not-root 3

16. (i) Dependent on state eradicated by First Path, arises state eradicated by First Path by not-root condition.

Dependent on doubt-accompanied aggregates, arises doubt-accompanied delusion. (1)

(ii) Dependent on state eradicated by Higher 3 Paths, arises state eradicated by Higher 3 Paths by not-root condition.

Dependent on restlessness-accompanied aggregates, arises restlessness-accompanied delusion. (1)

(iii) Dependent on state eradicated neither by First Path nor by Higher 3 Paths, arises state eradicated neither by First Path nor by Higher 3 Paths by not-root condition.

(*a*) Dependent on one rootless aggregate eradicated neither by First Path nor by Higher 3 Paths, arise three aggregates and mind-produced matter . . . dependent on two aggregates . . .

(*b*) At the moment of rootless conception, dependent on one aggregate eradicated neither by First Path nor by Higher 3 Paths, arise three aggregates and kamma-produced matter . . . dependent on two aggregates, arise two aggregates . . . dependent on aggregates, arises (heart-) base; dependent on (heart-)base, arise aggregates;

(*c*) Dependent on one great primary, arise three great primaries . . . dependent on great primaries, arise mind-produced and kamma-produced derived matter;

(*d*) External . . . nutriment-produced . . . temperature-produced . . . dependent on one great primary of non-percipient beings, arise three great primaries . . . dependent on great primaries, arises kamma-produced derived matter. (1)

Not-object 5

17. (i) Dependent on state eradicated by First Path, arises state eradicated neither by First Path nor by Higher 3 Paths by not-object condition.

Dependent on aggregates eradicated by First Path, arises mind-produced matter. (1)

(ii) Dependent on state eradicated by Higher 3 Paths, arises state eradicated neither by First Path nor by Higher 3 Paths by not-object condition.

Dependent on aggregates eradicated by Higher 3 Paths, arises mind-produced matter. (1)

(iii) Dependent on state eradicated neither by First Path nor by Higher 3 Paths, arises state eradicated neither by First Path nor by Higher 3 Paths by not-object condition.

(*a*) Dependent on aggregates eradicated neither by First Path nor by Higher 3 Paths, arises mind-produced matter;

(*b*) At the moment of conception, dependent on aggregates eradicated neither by First Path nor by Higher 3 Paths, arises kamma-produced matter; dependent on aggregates, arises (heart-)base;

(*c*) One great primary . . .

(*d*) External . . . nutriment-produced . . . temperature-produced . . . one great primary of non-percipient beings . . . (1)

18. (iv) Dependent on state eradicated by First Path and eradicated neither by First Path nor by Higher 3 Paths, arises state eradicated neither by First Path nor by Higher 3 Paths by not-object condition.

Dependent on aggregates eradicated by First Path and great primaries, arises mind-produced matter. (1)

(v) Dependent on state eradicated by Higher 3 Paths and eradicated neither by First Path nor by Higher 3 Paths, arises state eradicated neither by First Path nor by Higher 3 Paths by not-object condition.

Dependent on aggregates eradicated by Higher 3 Paths and great primaries, arises mind-produced matter. (1)

Not-predominance, etc.

19. Dependent on state eradicated by First Path, arises state eradicated by First Path by not-predominance condition. (Complete; the same as root condition.) . . . by not-proximity condition . . . by not-contiguity condition . . . by not-mutuality condition . . . by not-strong-dependence condition . . .

Not-prenascence 7

20. (i) Dependent on state eradicated by First Path, arises state eradicated by First Path by not-prenascence condition.

In the immaterial plane, dependent on one aggregate eradicated by First Path, arise three aggregates . . . (1)

(ii) Dependent on state eradicated by First Path, arises state eradicated neither by First Path nor by Higher 3 Paths by not-prenascence condition.

Dependent on aggregates eradicated by First Path, arises mind-produced matter. (2)

(iii) Dependent on state eradicated by Higher 3 Paths . . . eradicated by Higher 3 Paths . . .

In the immaterial plane, dependent on one aggregate eradicated by Higher 3 Paths, arise three aggregates . . . dependent on two aggregates, arise two aggregates. (1)

(iv) Dependent on state eradicated by Higher 3 Paths . . . eradicated neither by First Path nor by Higher 3 Paths . . .

Dependent on aggregates eradicated by Higher 3 Paths, arises mind-produced matter. (2)

21. (v) Dependent on state eradicated neither by First Path nor by Higher 3 Paths, arises state eradicated neither by First Path nor by Higher 3 Paths by not-prenascence condition.

(*a*) In the immaterial plane, dependent on one aggregate eradicated neither by First Path nor by Higher 3 Paths, arise three aggregates . . . dependent on two aggregates, arise two aggregates; dependent on aggregates eradicated neither by First Path nor by Higher 3 Paths, arises mind-produced matter;

(*b*) At the moment of conception, dependent on one aggregate eradicated neither by First Path nor by Higher 3 Paths, arise three aggregates and kamma-produced matter . . . dependent on two aggregates, arise two aggregates and kamma-produced matter; dependent on aggregates, arises (heart-)base; dependent on (heart-)base, arise aggregates;

(*c*) Dependent on one great primary, arise three great primaries . . .

(*d*) External . . . nutriment-produced . . . temperature-produced . . . one great primary of non-percipient beings . . . (1)

(vi) Dependent on state eradicated by First Path and eradicated neither by First Path nor by Higher 3 Paths . . . state eradicated neither by First Path nor by Higher 3 Paths . . .

Dependent on aggregates eradicated by First Path and great primaries, arises mind-produced matter. (1)

(vii) Dependent on state eradicated by Higher 3 Paths and eradicated neither by First Path nor by Higher 3 Paths, arises state eradicated neither by First Path nor by Higher 3 Paths by not-prenascence condition.

Dependent on aggregates eradicated by Higher 3 Paths and great primaries, arises mind-produced matter. (1)

Not-postnascence, etc.

22. Dependent on state eradicated by First Path, arises state eradicated by First Path by not-postnascence condition . . . by not-repetition condition . . .

Not-kamma 3

23. (i) Dependent on state eradicated by First Path, arises state eradicated by First Path by not-kamma condition.

Dependent on aggregates eradicated by First Path, arises volition eradicated by First Path. (1)

(ii) Dependent on state eradicated by Higher 3 Paths, arises state eradicated by Higher 3 Paths by not-kamma condition.

Dependent on aggregates eradicated by Higher 3 Paths, arises volition eradicated by Higher 3 Paths. (1)

(iii) Dependent on state eradicated neither by First Path nor by Higher 3 Paths, arises state eradicated neither by First Path nor by Higher 3 Paths by not-kamma condition.

(*a*) Dependent on aggregates eradicated neither by First Path nor by Higher 3 Paths, arises volition eradicated neither by First Path nor by Higher 3 Paths;

(*b*) External . . . nutriment-produced . . . temperature-produced . . . one great primary of non-percipient beings . . . (1)

Not-resultant 9

24. Dependent on state eradicated by First Path, arises state eradicated by First Path by not-resultant condition . . . (The same as not-predominance condition; no conception.)

Not-nutriment 1

25. Dependent on state eradicated neither by First Path nor by Higher 3 Paths, arises state eradicated neither by First Path nor by Higher 3 Paths by not-nutriment condition.

External . . . temperature-produced . . . one great primary of non-percipient beings . . .

Not-faculty 1

26. . . . eradicated neither by First Path nor by Higher 3 Paths . . . by not-faculty condition.

External . . . nutriment-produced . . . one temperature-produced great primary . . . dependent on great primaries of non-percipient beings, arises physical life-faculty.

Not-jhāna 1

27. . . . state eradicated neither by First Path nor by Higher 3 Paths . . . by not-jhāna condition.

(*a*) Dependent on one five-fold consciousness-accompanied aggregate, arise three aggregates . . . two aggregates . . .

(*b*) External . . . nutriment-produced . . . temperature-produced . . . one great primary of non-percipient beings . . .

Not-path 1

28. . . . eradicated neither by First Path nor by Higher 3 Paths . . . by not-path condition.

(*a*) . . . rootless . . . eradicated neither by First Path nor by Higher 3 Paths . . .

(*b*) At the moment of rootless conception . . .

(*c*) One great primary . . .

(*d*) External . . . nutriment-produced . . . temperature-produced . . . one great primary of non-percipient beings . . .

Not-association 5

29. Dependent on state eradicated by First Path, arises state eradicated neither by First Path nor by Higher 3 Paths by not-association condition. (The same as not-object.)

Not-dissociation 3

30. (i) . . . eradicated by First Path . . . by not-dissociation condition.

In the immaterial plane, dependent on one aggregate eradicated by First Path . . . (1)

(ii) . . . eradicated by Higher 3 Paths . . . by not-dissociation condition.

In the immaterial plane, dependent on one aggregate eradicated by Higher 3 Paths . . . (1)

(iii) . . . eradicated neither by First Path nor by Higher 3 Paths . . . by not-dissociation condition.

(*a*) In the immaterial plane, dependent on one aggregate eradicated neither by First Path nor by Higher 3 Paths . . .

(*b*) External . . . nutriment-produced . . . temperature-produced . . . non-percipient beings . . . (1)

Not-absence, Not-disappearance 5

31. Dependent on state eradicated by First Path . . . eradicated neither by First Path nor by Higher 3 Paths . . . by not-absence condition . . . by not-disappearance condition. (The same as not-object.) . . .

2. CONDITIONS: NEGATIVE (ii) ENUMERATION CHAPTER

(By Ones)

32. With not-root 3, not-object 5, not-predominance 9, not-proximity 5, not-contiguity 5, not-mutuality 5, not-strong-dependence 5, not-prenascence 7, not-postnascence 9, not-repetition 9, not-kamma 3, not-resultant 9, not-nutriment 1, not-faculty 1, not-jhāna 1, not-path 1, not-association 5, not-dissociation 3, not-absence 5, not-disappearance 5.

(Enumerate after knowing (the above).)

End of Negative

3. CONDITIONS: POSITIVE-NEGATIVE

Root By Twos

33. With root condition, not-object 5, not-predominance 9, not-proximity 5, not-contiguity 5, not-mutuality 5, not-strong-dependence 5, not-prenascence 7, not-postnascence 9, not-repetition 9, not-kamma 3, not-resultant 9, not-association 5, not-dissociation 3, not-absence 5, not-disappearance 5.

(Enumerate by considering thus.)

End of Positive-Negative

4. CONDITIONS: NEGATIVE-POSITIVE

Not-root By Twos

34. With not-root condition, object 3, proximity 3, contiguity 3, conascence 3, mutuality 3, dependence 3, strong-dependence 3, prenascence 3, repetition 3, kamma 3, resultant 1, nutriment 3, faculty 3, jhāna 3, path 2, association 3, dissociation 3, presence 3, absence 3, disappearance 3, non-disappearance 3.

(Enumerate by considering thus.)

End of Negative-Positive

End of "DEPENDENT" CHAPTER

8. TRIPLET OF (STATE) ERADICATED BY FIRST PATH
II. "CONASCENT" CHAPTER

1–4. CONDITIONS: POSITIVE, ETC.

35. Conascent with state eradicated by First Path, arises state eradicated by First Path by root condition.

Conascent with one aggregate eradicated by First Path, arise three aggregates . . . conascent with two aggregates . . .

(The "Conascent" Chapter is the same as the "Dependent" Chapter.)

8. TRIPLET OF (STATE) ERADICATED BY FIRST PATH
III. "CONDITIONED" CHAPTER

1. CONDITIONS: POSITIVE (i) CLASSIFICATION CHAPTER

Root 17

36. (i)–(iii) Conditioned by state eradicated by First Path, arises state eradicated by First Path by root condition . . . three.

(iv)–(vi) Conditioned by state eradicated by Higher 3 Paths . . . Higher 3 Paths . . . three.

37. (vii) Conditioned by state eradicated neither by First Path nor by Higher 3 Paths, arises state eradicated neither by First Path nor by Higher 3 Paths by root condition.

(*a*) Conditioned by one aggregate eradicated neither by First Path nor by Higher 3 Paths, arise three aggregates and mind-produced matter . . . two aggregates . . .

(*b*) At the moment of conception, conditioned by one aggregate eradicated neither by First Path nor by Higher 3 Paths, arise three aggregates and kamma-produced matter . . . conditioned by two aggregates, arise two aggregates . . . conditioned by aggregates, arises (heart-) base; conditioned by (heart-)base, arise aggregates;

(*c*) Conditioned by one great primary, arise three great primaries . . . conditioned by great primaries, arise mind-produced and kamma-produced derived matter;

(*d*) Conditioned by (heart-)base, arise aggregates eradicated neither by First Path nor by Higher 3 Paths. (1)

(viii) Conditioned by state eradicated neither by First Path nor by Higher 3 Paths, arises state eradicated by First Path by root condition.

Conditioned by (heart-)base, arise aggregates eradicated by First Path. (2)

(ix) Conditioned by state eradicated neither by First Path nor by Higher 3 Paths, arises state eradicated by Higher 3 Paths by root condition.

Conditioned by (heart-)base, arise aggregates eradicated by Higher 3 Paths. (3)

(x) Conditioned by state eradicated neither by First Path nor by Higher 3 Paths, arise states eradicated by First Path and eradicated neither by First Path nor by Higher 3 Paths by root condition.

Conditioned by (heart-)base, arise aggregates eradicated by First Path; conditioned by great primaries, arises mind-produced matter. (4)

(xi) Conditioned by state eradicated neither by First Path nor by Higher 3 Paths, arise states eradicated by Higher 3 Paths and eradicated neither by First Path nor by Higher 3 Paths by root condition.

Conditioned by (heart-)base, arise aggregates eradicated by Higher 3 Paths; conditioned by great primaries, arises mind-produced matter. (5)

38. (xii) Conditioned by state eradicated by First Path and eradicated neither by First Path nor by Higher 3 Paths, arises state eradicated by First Path by root condition.

Conditioned by one aggregate eradicated by First Path and (heart-) base, arise three aggregates . . . conditioned by two aggregates and (heart-)base, arise two aggregates. (1)

(xiii) Conditioned by state eradicated by First Path and eradicated neither by First Path nor by Higher 3 Paths, arises state eradicated neither by First Path nor by Higher 3 Paths by root condition.

Conditioned by aggregates eradicated by First Path and great primaries, arises mind-produced matter. (2)

(xiv) Conditioned by state eradicated by First Path and eradicated neither by First Path nor by Higher 3 Paths, arise states eradicated by First Path and eradicated neither by First Path nor by Higher 3 Paths by root condition.

Conditioned by one aggregate eradicated by First Path and (heart-)base, arise three aggregates . . . conditioned by two aggregates and (heart-)base, arise two aggregates; conditioned by aggregates eradicated by First Path and great primaries, arises mind-produced matter. (3)

39. (xv) Conditioned by state eradicated by Higher 3 Paths and eradicated neither by First Path nor by Higher 3 Paths, arises state eradicated by Higher 3 Paths by root condition.

Conditioned by one aggregate eradicated by Higher 3 Paths and (heart-)base, arise three aggregates . . . two aggregates and (heart-)base . . . (1)

(xvi) Conditioned by state eradicated by Higher 3 Paths and eradicated neither by First Path nor by Higher 3 Paths, arises state eradicated neither by First Path nor by Higher 3 Paths by root condition.

Conditioned by aggregates eradicated by Higher 3 Paths and great primaries, arises mind-produced matter. (2)

(xvii) Conditioned by state eradicated by Higher 3 Paths and eradicated neither by First Path nor by Higher 3 Paths, arise states eradicated by Higher 3 Paths and eradicated neither by First Path nor by Higher 3 Paths by root condition.

Conditioned by one aggregate eradicated by Higher 3 Paths and (heart-)base, arise three aggregates . . . two aggregates and (heart-)base . . . conditioned by aggregates eradicated by Higher 3 Paths and great primaries, arises mind-produced matter. (3)

Object 7

40. (i) Conditioned by state eradicated by First Path, arises state eradicated by First Path by object condition.

Conditioned by one aggregate eradicated by First Path, arise three aggregates . . . two aggregates . . . (1)

(ii) Conditioned by state eradicated by Higher 3 Paths, arises state eradicated by Higher 3 Paths by object condition.

Conditioned by one aggregate eradicated by Higher 3 Paths, arise three aggregates . . . (1)

(iii) Conditioned by state eradicated neither by First Path nor by Higher 3 Paths, arises state eradicated neither by First Path nor by Higher 3 Paths by object condition.

(*a*) Conditioned by one aggregate eradicated neither by First Path nor by Higher 3 Paths, arise three aggregates . . . two aggregates . . .

(*b*) At the moment of conception, conditioned by one aggregate eradicated neither by First Path nor by Higher 3 Paths, arise three aggregates . . . two aggregates . . . conditioned by (heart-)base, arise aggregates;

(*c*) Conditioned by eye-base, arises eye-consciousness . . . conditioned by body-base, arises body-consciousness; conditioned by (heart-) base, arise aggregates eradicated neither by First Path nor by Higher 3 Paths. (1)

(iv) Conditioned by state eradicated neither by First Path nor by Higher 3 Paths, arises state eradicated by First Path by object condition.

Conditioned by (heart-)base, arise aggregates eradicated by First Path. (2)

(v) Conditioned by state eradicated neither by First Path nor by Higher 3 Paths, arises state eradicated by Higher 3 Paths by object condition.

Conditioned by (heart-)base, arise aggregates eradicated by Higher 3 Paths. (3)

41. (vi) Conditioned by state eradicated by First Path and eradicated neither by First Path nor by Higher 3 Paths, arises state eradicated by First Path by object condition.

Conditioned by one aggregate eradicated by First Path and (heart-) base, arise three aggregates . . . conditioned by two aggregates and (heart-)base . . . (1)

(vii) Conditioned by state eradicated by Higher 3 Paths and eradicated neither by First Path nor by Higher 3 Paths, arises state eradicated by Higher 3 Paths by object condition.

Conditioned by one aggregate eradicated by Higher 3 Paths and (heart-)base, arise three aggregates . . . conditioned by two aggregates and (heart-)base, arise two aggregates. (1)

Predominance, etc.

42. Conditioned by state eradicated by First Path, arises state eradicated by First Path by predominance condition. (Complete; no conception.) . . . by proximity condition . . . by contiguity condition. (The same as object.) . . .

Conascence 17

43. (i)–(iii) Conditioned by state eradicated by First Path, arises state eradicated by First Path by conascence condition.

... one aggregate eradicated by First Path ... three.

(iv)–(vi) Conditioned by state eradicated by Higher 3 Paths ... three.

(vii) Conditioned by state eradicated neither by First Path nor by Higher 3 Paths, arises state eradicated neither by First Path nor by Higher 3 Paths by conascence condition.

(*a*) Conditioned by one aggregate eradicated neither by First Path nor by Higher 3 Paths, arise three aggregates and mind-produced matter ... conditioned by two aggregates, arise two aggregates ...

(*b*) At the moment of conception ... conditioned by aggregates, arises (heart-)base; conditioned by (heart-)base, arise aggregates;

(*c*) Conditioned by one great primary, arise three great primaries ... conditioned by great primaries ...

(*d*) External ... nutriment-produced ... temperature-produced ... one ... non-percipient beings ...

(*e*) Conditioned by eye-base, arises eye-consciousness ... conditioned by body-base, arises body-consciousness; conditioned by (heart-) base, arise aggregates eradicated neither by First Path nor by Higher 3 Paths.

(viii)–(xvii) Conditioned by state eradicated neither by First Path nor by Higher 3 Paths, arises state eradicated by First Path by conascence condition. (The rest are the same as for root condition.) ...

Mutuality, etc.

44. Conditioned by state eradicated by First Path, arises state eradicated by First Path by mutuality condition ... by dependence condition ... by strong-dependence condition ... by prenascence condition. (No conception.) ... by repetition condition. (No conception and resultant.) ... by kamma condition ... by resultant condition ... by nutriment condition ... by faculty condition ... by jhāna condition ... by path condition ... by association condition ... by dissociation condition ... by presence condition ... by absence condition ... by disappearance condition ... by non-disappearance condition ...

1. CONDITIONS: POSITIVE (ii) ENUMERATION CHAPTER

By Ones

45. With root 17, object 7, predominance 17, proximity 7, contiguity 7, conascence 17, mutuality 7, dependence 17, strong-dependence 7, prenascence 7, repetition 7, kamma 17, resultant 1, nutriment 17, faculty 17, jhāna 17, path 17, association 7, dissociation 17, presence 17, absence 7, disappearance 7, non-disappearance 17. (Enumerate thus.)

End of Positive

2. CONDITIONS: NEGATIVE (i) CLASSIFICATION CHAPTER

Not-root 7

46. (i) Conditioned by state eradicated by First Path, arises state eradicated by First Path by not-root condition.

Conditioned by doubt-accompanied aggregates, arises doubt-accompanied delusion. (1)

(ii) Conditioned by state eradicated by Higher 3 Paths, arises state eradicated by Higher 3 Paths by not-root condition.

Conditioned by restlessness-accompanied aggregates, arises restlessness-accompanied delusion. (1)

(iii) Conditioned by state eradicated neither by First Path nor by Higher 3 Paths, arises state eradicated neither by First Path nor by Higher 3 Paths by not-root condition.

(*a*) Conditioned by one rootless aggregate eradicated neither by First Path nor by Higher 3 Paths, arise three aggregates and mind-produced matter . . . two aggregates . . .

(*b*) At the moment of rootless conception . . . conditioned by aggregates, arises (heart-)base; conditioned by (heart-)base, arise aggregates;

(*c*), (*d*) One great primary . . . External . . . nutriment-produced . . . temperature-produced . . . non-percipient beings . . .

(*e*) Conditioned by eye-base, arises eye-consciousness . . . conditioned by body-base, arises body-consciousness; conditioned by (heart-) base, arise rootless aggregates eradicated neither by First Path nor by Higher 3 Paths. (1)

(iv) Conditioned by state eradicated neither by First Path nor by Higher 3 Paths, arises state eradicated by First Path by not-root condition.

Conditioned by (heart-)base, arises doubt-accompanied delusion. (2)

(v) Conditioned by state eradicated neither by First Path nor by Higher 3 Paths, arises state eradicated by Higher 3 Paths by not-root condition.

Conditioned by (heart-)base, arises restlessness-accompanied delusion. (3)

47. (vi) Conditioned by state eradicated by First Path and eradicated neither by First Path nor by Higher 3 Paths, arises state eradicated by First Path by not-root condition.

Conditioned by doubt-accompanied aggregates and (heart-)base, arises doubt-accompanied delusion. (1)

(vii) Conditioned by state eradicated by Higher 3 Paths and eradicated neither by First Path nor by Higher 3 Paths, arises state eradicated by Higher 3 Paths by not-root condition.

Conditioned by restlessness-accompanied aggregates and (heart-)base, arises restlessness-accompanied delusion. (1)

Not-object 5

48. (i) Conditioned by state eradicated by First Path, arises state eradicated neither by First Path nor by Higher 3 Paths by not-object condition.

Conditioned by aggregates eradicated by First Path, arises mind-produced matter. (1)

(ii) Conditioned by state eradicated by Higher 3 Paths, arises state eradicated neither by First Path nor by Higher 3 Paths by not-object condition.

Conditioned by aggregates eradicated by Higher 3 Paths, arises mind-produced matter. (1)

(iii) Conditioned by state eradicated neither by First Path nor by Higher 3 Paths, arises state eradicated neither by First Path nor by Higher 3 Paths by not-object condition.

(*a*) Conditioned by aggregates eradicated neither by First Path nor by Higher 3 Paths, arises mind-produced matter;

(*b*) At the moment of conception, conditioned by aggregates eradicated neither by First Path nor by Higher 3 Paths, arises kamma-produced matter; conditioned by aggregates, arises (heart-)base;

(*c*), (*d*) Conditioned by one great primary ... External ... nutriment-produced ... temperature-produced ... non-percipient beings ... (1)

49. (iv) Conditioned by state eradicated by First Path and eradicated neither by First Path nor by Higher 3 Paths, arises state eradicated

neither by First Path nor by Higher 3 Paths by not-object condition.

Conditioned by aggregates eradicated by First Path and great primaries, arises mind-produced matter. (1)

(v) Conditioned by state eradicated by Higher 3 Paths and eradicated neither by First Path nor by Higher 3 Paths, arises state eradicated neither by First Path nor by Higher 3 Paths by not-object condition.

Conditioned by aggregates eradicated by Higher 3 Paths and great primaries, arises mind-produced matter. (1)

Not-predominance, etc.

50. Conditioned by state eradicated by First Path, arises state eradicated by First Path by not-predominance condition. (The same as conascence.) . . . by not-proximity condition . . . by not-contiguity condition . . . by not-mutuality condition . . . by not-strong-dependence condition . . .

Not-prenascence 7

51. (i) Conditioned by state eradicated by First Path, arises state eradicated by First Path by not-prenascence condition.

In the immaterial plane, conditioned by one aggregate eradicated by First Path . . . (1)

(ii) Conditioned by state eradicated by First Path, arises state eradicated neither by First Path nor by Higher 3 Paths by not-prenascence condition.

Conditioned by aggregates eradicated by First Path, arises mind-produced matter. (2)

(iii) Conditioned by state eradicated by Higher 3 Paths, arises state eradicated by Higher 3 Paths, by not-prenascence condition.

In the immaterial plane, conditioned by one aggregate eradicated by Higher 3 Paths . . . (1)

(iv) Conditioned by state eradicated by Higher 3 Paths, arises state eradicated neither by First Path nor by Higher 3 Paths by not-prenascence condition.

Conditioned by aggregates eradicated by Higher 3 Paths, arises mind-produced matter. (2)

52. (v) Conditioned by state eradicated neither by First Path nor by Higher 3 Paths, arises state eradicated neither by First Path nor by Higher 3 Paths by not-prenascence condition.

(*a*) In the immaterial plane, conditioned by one aggregate eradicated neither by First Path nor by Higher 3 Paths, arise three aggregates . . . conditioned by aggregates eradicated neither by First Path nor by Higher 3 Paths, arises mind-produced matter;

(*b*) At the moment of conception . . . conditioned by aggregates, arises kamma-produced matter; conditioned by aggregates, arises (heart-)base; conditioned by (heart-)base, arise aggregates;

(*c*), (*d*) One great primary . . . External . . . nutriment-produced . . . temperature-produced . . . non-percipient beings . . . (1)

(vi) Conditioned by state eradicated by First Path and eradicated neither by First Path nor by Higher 3 Paths, arises state eradicated neither by First Path nor by Higher 3 Paths by not-prenascence condition.

Conditioned by aggregates eradicated by First Path and great primaries, arises mind-produced matter. (1)

(vii) Conditioned by state eradicated by Higher 3 Paths and eradicated neither by First Path nor by Higher 3 Paths, arises state eradicated neither by First Path nor by Higher 3 Paths by not-prenascence condition.

Conditioned by aggregates eradicated by Higher 3 Paths and great primaries, arises mind-produced matter. (1)

Not-postnascence, etc.

53. Conditioned by state eradicated by First Path, arises state eradicated by First Path by not-postnascence condition . . . by not-repetition condition . . .

Not-kamma 7

54. (i) Conditioned by state eradicated by First Path, arises state eradicated by First Path by not-kamma condition.

Conditioned by aggregates eradicated by First Path, arises volition eradicated by First Path. (1)

(ii) . . . state eradicated by Higher 3 Paths . . . by not-kamma condition.

Conditioned by aggregates eradicated by Higher 3 Paths, arises volition eradicated by Higher 3 Paths. (1)

(iii) . . . state eradicated neither by First Path nor by Higher 3 Paths . . . by not-kamma condition.

(*a*) Conditioned by aggregates eradicated neither by First Path nor by Higher 3 Paths, arises volition eradicated neither by First Path nor by Higher 3 Paths;

(*b*) External . . . nutriment-produced . . . temperature-produced . . . (1)

(iv) Conditioned by state eradicated neither by First Path nor by Higher 3 Paths, arises state eradicated by First Path by not-kamma condition.

Conditioned by (heart-)base, arises volition eradicated by First Path. (2)

(v) Conditioned by state eradicated neither by First Path nor by Higher 3 Paths, arises state eradicated by Higher 3 Paths by not-kamma condition.

Conditioned by (heart-)base, arises volition eradicated by Higher 3 Paths. (3)

55. (vi) Conditioned by state eradicated by First Path and eradicated neither by First Path nor by Higher 3 Paths, arises state eradicated by First Path by not-kamma condition.

Conditioned by aggregates eradicated by First Path and (heart-)base, arises volition eradicated by First Path. (1)

(vii) Conditioned by state eradicated by Higher 3 Paths and eradicated neither by First Path nor by Higher 3 Paths, arises state eradicated by Higher 3 Paths by not-kamma condition.

Conditioned by aggregates eradicated by Higher 3 Paths and (heart-) base, arises volition eradicated by Higher 3 Paths. (1)

Not-resultant, etc.

56. Conditioned by state eradicated by First Path, arises state eradicated by First Path by not-resultant condition. (Complete; no conception.) . . . by not-nutriment condition. External . . . temperature-produced . . . non-percipient beings . . . by not-faculty condition. External . . . nutriment-produced . . . temperature-produced . . . non-percipient beings . . . conditioned by great primaries, arises physical life-faculty . . . by not-jhāna condition. Five-fold consciousness . . . External . . . non-percipient beings . . . by not-path condition.

(*a*) Conditioned by one rootless aggregate eradicated neither by First Path nor by Higher 3 Paths, arise three aggregates and mind-produced matter . . .

(*b*) At the moment of rootless conception . . .

(*c*) One great primary . . . non-percipient beings . . . by not-association condition . . . by not-dissociation condition. In the immaterial plane, conditioned by one aggregate eradicated by First Path . . . In the immaterial plane, conditioned by one aggregate eradicated by Higher 3 Paths, arise three aggregates . . . Conditioned by state eradicated neither by First Path nor by Higher 3 Paths . . . neither by First Path . . .

(*d*) In the immaterial plane, conditioned by one aggregate eradicated neither by First Path nor by Higher 3 Paths, arise three aggregates . . . two aggregates . . .

(*e*) External . . . nutriment-produced . . . temperature-produced . . . non-percipient beings . . . by not-absence condition . . . by not-disappearance condition . . .

2. CONDITIONS: NEGATIVE (ii) ENUMERATION CHAPTER

(By Ones)

57. With not-root 7, not-object 5, not-predominance 17, not-proximity 5, not-contiguity 5, not-mutuality 5, not-strong-dependence 5, not-prenascence 7, not-postnascence 17, not-repetition 17, not-kamma 7, not-resultant 17, not-nutriment 1, not-faculty 1, not-jhāna 1, not-path 1, not-association 5, not-dissociation 3, not-absence 5, not-disappearance 5.

End of Negative

3. CONDITIONS: POSITIVE-NEGATIVE

(Root By Twos)

58. With root condition, not-object 5, not-predominance 17, not-proximity 5, not-contiguity 5, not-mutuality 5, not-strong-dependence 5, not-prenascence 7, not-postnascence 17, not-repetition 17, not-kamma 7, not-resultant 17, not-association 5, not-dissociation 3, not-absence 5, not-disappearance 5.

End of Positive–Negative

4. CONDITIONS: NEGATIVE-POSITIVE

(Not-root By Twos)

59. With not-root condition, object 7, proximity 7, contiguity 7, conascence 7, mutuality 7, dependence 7, strong-dependence 7, prenascence 7, repetition 7, kamma 7, resultant 1, nutriment 7, faculty 7, jhāna 7, path 6, association 7, dissociation 7, presence 7, absence 7,

disappearance 7, non-disappearance 7. (Enumerate thus.)

End of Negative-Positive

End of "CONDITIONED" CHAPTER

(Do the "Supported" Chapter in the same way as the "Conditioned" Chapter.)

8. TRIPLET OF (STATE) ERADICATED BY FIRST PATH
V. "CONJOINED" CHAPTER

1. CONDITIONS: POSITIVE (i) CLASSIFICATION CHAPTER

Root 3

60. (i) Conjoined with state eradicated by First Path, arises state eradicated by First Path by root condition.

Conjoined with one aggregate eradicated by First Path, arise three aggregates . . . conjoined with two aggregates, arise two aggregates. (1)

(ii) Conjoined with state eradicated by Higher 3 Paths, arises state eradicated by Higher 3 Paths by root condition.

Conjoined with one aggregate eradicated by Higher 3 Paths . . . (1)

(iii) Conjoined with state eradicated neither by First Path nor by Higher 3 Paths, arises state eradicated neither by First Path nor by Higher 3 Paths by root condition.

(*a*) Conjoined with one aggregate eradicated neither by First Path nor by Higher 3 Paths, arise three aggregates . . .

(*b*) At the moment of conception, conjoined with one aggregate eradicated neither by First Path nor by Higher 3 Paths . . . (1)

Object 3

61. Conjoined with state eradicated by First Path, arises state eradicated by First Path by object condition. (Expand all sections. Three, three.)

1. CONDITIONS: POSITIVE (ii) ENUMERATION CHAPTER

(By Ones)

62. With root 3, object 3, predominance 3, proximity 3, contiguity 3, conascence 3, mutuality 3, dependence 3, strong-dependence 3, prenascence 3, repetition 3, kamma 3, resultant 1, nutriment 3, faculty 3,

jhāna 3, path 3, association 3, dissociation 3, presence 3, absence 3, disappearance 3, non-disappearance 3.

End of Positive

2. CONDITIONS: NEGATIVE (i) CLASSIFICATION CHAPTER

Not-root 3

63. (i) Conjoined with state eradicated by First Path, arises state eradicated by First Path by not-root condition.

Conjoined with doubt-accompanied aggregates, arises doubt-accompanied delusion. (1)

(ii) Conjoined with state eradicated by Higher 3 Paths, arises state eradicated by Higher 3 Paths by not-root condition.

Conjoined with restlessness-accompanied aggregates, arises restlessness-accompanied delusion. (1)

(iii) Conjoined with state eradicated neither by First Path nor by Higher 3 Paths, arises state eradicated neither by First Path nor by Higher 3 Paths by not-root condition.

(*a*) Conjoined with one rootless aggregate eradicated neither by First Path nor by Higher 3 Paths, arise three aggregates . . .

(*b*) At the moment of rootless conception . . . (1)

Not-predominance, etc.

64. Conjoined with state eradicated by First Path, arises state eradicated by First Path by not-predominance condition . . . by not-prenascence condition . . . by not-postnascence condition . . . by not-repetition condition . . . by not-kamma condition . . . by not-resultant condition . . . eradicated neither by First Path nor by Higher 3 Paths by not-jhāna condition. Five-fold consciousness . . . by not-path condition. Rootless . . . eradicated neither by First Path nor by Higher 3 Paths . . . by not-dissociation condition . . . three.

2. CONDITIONS: NEGATIVE (ii) ENUMERATION CHAPTER

(By Ones)

65. With not-root 3, not-predominance 3, not-prenascence 3, not-postnascence 3, not-repetition 3, not-kamma 3, not-resultant 3, not-jhāna 1, not-path 1, not-dissociation 3.

End of Negative

3. CONDITIONS: POSITIVE-NEGATIVE

(Root By Twos)

66. With root condition, not-predominance 3, not-prenascence 3, not-postnascence 3, not-repetition 3, not-kamma 3, not-resultant 3, not-dissociation 3.

End of Positive-Negative

4. CONDITIONS: NEGATIVE-POSITIVE

(Not-root By Twos)

67. With not-root condition, object 3, proximity 3, contiguity 3, conascence 3, mutuality 3, dependence 3, strong-dependence 3, prenascence 3, repetition 3, kamma 3, resultant 1, nutriment 3, faculty 3, jhāna 3, path 2, association 3, dissociation 3, presence 3, absence 3, disappearance 3, non-disappearance 3.

End of Negative-Positive

End of "CONJOINED" CHAPTER

8. TRIPLET OF (STATE) ERADICATED BY FIRST PATH
VI. "ASSOCIATED" CHAPTER

1. CONDITIONS: POSITIVE, ETC.

68. Associated with state eradicated by First Path, arises state eradicated by First Path by root condition.

(The "Associated" Chapter is the same as the "Conjoined" Chapter.)

8. TRIPLET OF (STATE) ERADICATED BY FIRST PATH
VII. "INVESTIGATION" CHAPTER

1. CONDITIONS: POSITIVE (i) CLASSIFICATION CHAPTER

Root 7

69. (i) State eradicated by First Path is related to state eradicated by First Path by root condition.

Roots eradicated by First Path are related to (their) associated aggregates by root condition. (1)

(ii) State eradicated by First Path is related to state eradicated neither by First Path nor by Higher 3 Paths by root condition.

Roots eradicated by First Path are related to mind-produced matter by root condition. (2)

(iii) State eradicated by First Path is related to state eradicated by First Path and eradicated neither by First Path nor by Higher 3 Paths by root condition.

Roots eradicated by First Path are related to (their) associated aggregates and mind-produced matter by root condition. (3)

70. (iv) States eradicated by Higher 3 Paths . . . to state . . . by root condition.

Roots eradicated by Higher 3 Paths are related to (their) associated aggregates by root condition. (1)

(v) State eradicated by Higher 3 Paths to . . . eradicated neither by First Path nor by Higher 3 Paths . . .

Roots eradicated by Higher 3 Paths are related to mind-produced matter by root condition. (2)

(vi) State eradicated by Higher 3 Paths . . . to state eradicated by Higher 3 Paths and eradicated neither by First Path nor by Higher 3 Paths . . .

Roots eradicated by Higher 3 Paths are related to (their) associated aggregates and mind-produced matter by root condition. (3)

(vii) State eradicated neither by First Path nor by Higher 3 Paths . . . to state eradicated neither by First Path nor by Higher 3 Paths . . .

(*a*) Roots eradicated neither by First Path nor by Higher 3 Paths are related to (their) associated aggregates and mind-produced matter by root condition;

(*b*) At the moment of conception, roots eradicated neither by First Path nor by Higher 3 Paths are related to (their) associated aggregates and kamma-produced matter by root condition. (1)

Object 8

71. (i) State eradicated by First Path is related to state eradicated by First Path by object condition.

(One) enjoys and delights in lust eradicated by First Path. Taking it as object, arises lust eradicated by First Path, arise wrong views, arises doubt, arises grief eradicated by First Path. (One) enjoys and delights in wrong views. Taking it as object, arises lust eradicated by First Path, arise wrong views, arises doubt, arises grief eradicated by First Path. Taking doubt as object, arises doubt, arise wrong views, arises grief eradicated by First Path. Taking grief eradicated by First Path as object, arises grief eradicated by First Path, arise wrong views, arises doubt. (1)

(ii) State eradicated by First Path is related to state eradicated neither by First Path nor by Higher 3 Paths by object condition.

The Noble persons review the eradicated defilements eradicated by First Path, know the defilements addicted to before.

(They) practise insight into the impermanence, suffering and impersonality of aggregates eradicated by First Path. By the knowledge of penetration into others' minds, (they) know the other being's mind eradicated by First Path. Aggregates eradicated by First Path are related to knowledge of penetration into others' minds, knowledge of remembrance of past existences, knowledge of rebirths according to one's kamma, knowledge of future existences, advertence by object condition. (2)

72. (iii) State eradicated by Higher 3 Paths is related to state eradicated by Higher 3 Paths by object condition.

(One) enjoys and delights in lust eradicated by Higher 3 Paths. Taking it as object, arises lust eradicated by Higher 3 Paths, arises restlessness, arises grief eradicated by Higher 3 Paths. Taking restlessness as object, arises restlessness, arises grief eradicated by Higher 3 Paths. Taking grief eradicated by Higher 3 Paths as object, arises grief eradicated by Higher 3 Paths, arises restlessness. (1)

(iv) State eradicated by Higher 3 Paths is related to state eradicated by First Path by object condition.

(One) enjoys and delights in lust eradicated by Higher 3 Paths, Taking it as object, arises lust eradicated by First Path, arise wrong views, arises doubt, arises grief eradicated by First Path. Taking restlessness as object, arise wrong views, arises doubt, arises grief eradicated by First Path. Taking grief eradicated by Higher 3 Paths as object, arises grief eradicated by First Path, arise wrong views, arises doubt. (2)

(v) State eradicated by Higher 3 Paths is related to state eradicated neither by First Path nor by Higher 3 Paths by object condition.

The Noble persons review the eradicated defilements eradicated by Higher 3 Paths, review the uneradicated defilements, know the defilements addicted to before.

(They) practise insight into the impermanence, suffering and impersonality of aggregates eradicated by Higher 3 Paths. By the knowledge of penetration into others' minds, (they) know the other beings' mind eradicated by Higher 3 Paths. Aggregates eradicated by Higher 3 Paths are related to knowledge of penetration into others' minds, knowledge of remembrance of past existences, knowledge of rebirths according to one's kamma, knowledge of future existences, advertence by object condition. (3)

73. (vi) State eradicated neither by First Path nor by Higher 3 Paths is related to state eradicated neither by First Path nor by Higher 3 Paths by object condition.

After having offered an offering, having undertaken precepts, having fulfilled the duty of observance, (one) reviews it. (One) reviews (such acts) formerly well done. Having emerged from jhāna, (one) reviews the jhāna. The Noble persons, having emerged from Path, review the Path, review the Fruition, review Nibbāna. Nibbāna is related to change-of-lineage, purification, Path, Fruition, advertence by object condition.

(One) practises insight into the impermanence, suffering and impersonality of the eye; . . . ear . . . nose . . . tongue . . . body . . . visible object . . . sound . . . smell . . . taste . . . tangible object . . . (heart-)base; (one) practises insight into the impermanence, suffering and impersonality of aggregates eradicated neither by First Path nor by Higher 3 Paths.

By the power of divine-eye, one sees a visible object. By the power of divine-ear element, (one) hears a sound. By the knowledge of penetration into others' minds, (they) know the other being's mind eradicated neither by First Path nor by Higher 3 Paths.

Infinity of space to infinity of consciousness . . . nothingness to neither-perception-nor-non-perception . . . visible object-base is related to eye-consciousness by object condition . . . tangible object-base is related to body-consciousness by object condition.

Aggregates eradicated neither by First Path nor by Higher 3 Paths are related to knowledge of supernormal power, knowledge of penetration into others' minds, knowledge of remembrance of past existences, knowledge of rebirths according to one's kamma, knowledge of future existences, advertence by object condition. (1)

(vii) State eradicated neither by First Path nor by Higher 3 Paths is related to state eradicated by First Path by object condition.

After having offered an offering, having undertaken precepts, having fulfilled the duty of observance, (one) enjoys and delights in it. Taking it as object, arises lust eradicated by First Path, arise wrong views, arises doubt, arises grief eradicated by First Path. (One) enjoys and delights in (such acts) formerly well done . . . Having emerged from jhāna, (one) enjoys and delights in the jhāna. Taking it as object, (arises) lust eradicated by First Path . . . wrong views . . . doubt. When jhāna has disappeared, (one) regrets it and thereby arises grief eradicated by First Path.

(One) enjoys and delights in the eye . . . ear . . . nose . . . tongue . . . body . . . visible object . . . sound . . . smell . . . taste . . . tangible object . . . (heart-)base . . . (One) enjoys and delights in aggregates eradicated neither by First Path nor by Higher 3 Paths. Taking them as object, (arises) lust eradicated by First Path . . . wrong views . . . doubt, arises grief eradicated by First Path. (2)

(viii) State eradicated neither by First Path nor by Higher 3 Paths is related to state eradicated by Higher 3 Paths by object condition.

After having offered an offering, having undertaken precepts, having fulfilled the duty of observance, (one) enjoys and delights in it. Taking it as object, arises lust eradicated by Higher 3 Paths, arises restlessness, arises grief eradicated by Higher 3 Paths . . . formerly well done . . . Having emerged from jhāna . . . eye . . . (heart-)base . . . (One) enjoys . . . aggregates eradicated neither by First Path nor by Higher 3 Paths. Taking them as object, arises lust eradicated by Higher 3 Paths, arises restlessness, arises grief eradicated by Higher 3 Paths. (3)

Predominance 10

74. (i) State eradicated by First Path is related to state eradicated by First Path by predominance condition.

(It is of two kinds, namely:) (*a*) object-predominance, (*b*) conascence-predominance.

(*a*) *Object-predominance:* (One) esteems, enjoys and delights in lust eradicated by First Path. Taking it as estimable object, arises lust eradicated by First Path, arise wrong views. (One) esteems, enjoys and delights in wrong views. Taking them as estimable object, arises lust eradicated by First Path, arise wrong views.

(*b*) *Conascence-predominance:* Predominance eradicated by First Path is related to (its) associated aggregates by predominance condition. (1)

(ii) State eradicated by First Path is related to state eradicated neither by First Path nor by Higher 3 Paths by predominance condition.

Conascence-predominance: Predominance eradicated by First Path is related to mind-produced matter by predominance condition. (2)

(iii) State eradicated by First Path is related to state eradicated by First Path and eradicated neither by First Path nor by Higher 3 Paths by predominance condition.

Conascence-predominance: Predominance eradicated by First Path is related to (its) associated aggregates and mind-produced matter by predominance condition. (3)

75. (iv) State eradicated by Higher 3 Paths is related to state eradicated by Higher 3 Paths by predominance condition.

(It is of two kinds, namely:) (*a*) object-predominance, (*b*) conascence-predominance.

(*a*) *Object-predominance:* (One) esteems, enjoys and delights in lust eradicated by Higher 3 Paths. Taking it as estimable object, arises lust eradicated by Higher 3 Paths.

(*b*) *Conascence-predominance:* Predominance eradicated by Higher 3 Paths is related to (its) associated aggregates by predominance condition. (1)

(v) State eradicated by Higher 3 Paths is related to state eradicated by First Path by predominance condition.

Object-predominance: (One) esteems, enjoys and delights in lust eradicated by Higher 3 Paths. Taking it as estimable object, arises lust eradicated by First Path, arise wrong views. (2)

(vi) State eradicated by Higher 3 Paths is related to state eradicated neither by First Path nor by Higher 3 Paths by predominance condition.

Conascence-predominance: Predominance eradicated by Higher 3 Paths is related to mind-produced matter by predominance condition. (3)

(vii) State eradicated by Higher 3 Paths is related to state eradicated by Higher 3 Paths and eradicated neither by First Path nor by Higher 3 Paths by predominance condition.

Conascence-predominance: Predominance eradicated by Higher 3 Paths is related to (its) associated aggregates and mind-produced matter by predominance condition. (4)

76. (viii) State eradicated neither by First Path nor by Higher 3 Paths is related to state eradicated neither by First Path nor by Higher 3 Paths by predominance condition.

(It is of two kinds, namely:) (*a*) object-predominance, (*b*) conascence-predominance.

(*a*) *Object-predominance:* After having offered an offering, having undertaken precepts, having fulfilled the duty of observance, (one) esteems and reviews it . . . formerly well done . . . Having emerged from jhāna, (one) esteems and reviews the jhāna.

The Noble persons, having emerged from Path, esteem and review the Path, esteem and review the Fruition, esteem and review Nibbāna. Nibbāna is related to change-of-lineage, purification, Path, Fruition by predominance condition.

(*b*) *Conascence-predominance:* Predominance eradicated neither by First Path nor by Higher 3 Paths is related to (its) associated aggregates and mind-produced matter by predominance condition. (1)

(ix) State eradicated neither by First Path nor by Higher 3 Paths is related to state eradicated by First Path by predominance condition.

Object-predominance: After having offered an offering, having undertaken precepts, having fulfilled the duty of observance, (one) esteems, enjoys and delights in it. Taking it as estimable object, arises lust eradicated by First Path, arise wrong views. (One) esteems . . . formerly well done . . . Having emerged from jhāna, (one) esteems . . . the jhāna . . . eye . . . (heart-)base . . . (One) esteems, enjoys and delights in aggregates eradicated neither by First Path nor by Higher 3 Paths. Taking it as estimable object, arises lust eradicated by First Path, arise wrong views. (2)

(x) State eradicated neither by First Path nor by Higher 3 Paths is related to state eradicated by Higher 3 Paths by predominance condition.

Object-predominance: After having offered an offering, having undertaken precepts, having fulfilled the duty of observance, (one) esteems, enjoys and delights in it. Taking it as estimable object, arises lust eradicated by Higher 3 Paths . . . formerly . . . (One) esteems, enjoys and delights in aggregates eradicated neither by First Path nor by Higher 3 Paths. Taking them as estimable object, arises lust eradicated by Higher 3 Paths. (3)

Proximity 7

77. (i) State eradicated by First Path is related to state eradicated by First Path by proximity condition.

Preceding aggregates eradicated by First Path are related to subsequent aggregates eradicated by First Path by proximity condition. (1)

(ii) State eradicated by First Path is related to state eradicated neither by First Path nor by Higher 3 Paths by proximity condition.

Aggregates eradicated by First Path are related to emergence by proximity condition. (2)

(iii) State eradicated by Higher 3 Paths is related to state eradicated by Higher 3 Paths by proximity condition.

Preceding aggregates eradicated by Higher 3 Paths are related to subsequent aggregates eradicated by Higher 3 Paths by proximity condition. (1)

(iv) State eradicated by Higher 3 Paths is related to state eradicated neither by First Path nor by Higher 3 Paths by proximity condition.

Aggregates eradicated by Higher 3 Paths are related to emergence by proximity condition. (2)

(v) State eradicated neither by First Path nor by Higher 3 Paths is related to state eradicated neither by First Path nor by Higher 3 Paths by proximity condition.

Preceding aggregates eradicated neither by First Path nor by Higher 3 Paths are related to subsequent aggregates eradicated neither by First Path nor by Higher 3 Paths by proximity condition. Adaptation to change-of-lineage; adaptation to purification; change-of-lineage to Path; purification to Path; Path to Fruition; Fruition to Fruition; adaptation to the attainment of Fruition; for one emerging from the attainment of Extinction, neither-perception-nor-non-perception is related to the attainment of Fruition by proximity condition. (1)

(vi) State eradicated neither by First Path nor by Higher 3 Paths to state eradicated by First Path . . .

Advertence is related to aggregates eradicated by First Path by proximity condition. (2)

(vii) State eradicated neither by First Path nor by Higher 3 Paths is related to state eradicated by Higher 3 Paths by proximity condition.

Advertence is related to aggregates eradicated by Higher 3 Paths by proximity condition. (3)

Contiguity 7

78. State eradicated by First Path is related to state eradicated by First Path by contiguity condition. (The same as proximity.)

Conascence 9

79. (i)–(iii) State eradicated by First Path is related to state eradicated by First Path by conascence condition . . . three.

(iv)–(vi) State eradicated by Higher 3 Paths to state eradicated by Higher 3 Paths . . . three.

(vii) State eradicated neither by First Path nor by Higher 3 Paths is related to state eradicated neither by First Path nor by Higher 3 Paths by conascence condition.

(*a*) One aggregate eradicated neither by First Path nor by Higher 3 Paths is related to three aggregates and mind-produced matter by conascence condition . . . two aggregates . . .

(*b*) At the moment of conception . . . aggregates are related to (heart-)base by conascence condition; (heart-)base to aggregates . . .

(*c*) One great primary to three great primaries . . . great primaries to mind-produced matter . . .

(*d*) External . . . nutriment-produced . . . temperature-produced . . . non-percipient beings . . . (1)

(viii) States eradicated by First Path and eradicated neither by First Path nor by Higher 3 Paths are related to state eradicated neither by First Path nor by Higher 3 Paths by conascence condition.

Aggregates eradicated by First Path and great primaries are related to mind-produced matter by conascence condition. (1)

(ix) States eradicated by Higher 3 Paths and eradicated neither by First Path nor by Higher 3 Paths are related to state eradicated neither by First Path nor by Higher 3 Paths by conascence condition.

Aggregates eradicated by Higher 3 Paths and great primaries are related to mind-produced matter by conascence condition. (1)

Mutuality 3

80. (i) State eradicated by First Path is related to state eradicated by First Path by mutuality condition.

One aggregate eradicated by First Path to three aggregates . . . (1)

(ii) State eradicated by Higher 3 Paths to state eradicated by Higher 3 Paths . . .

One aggregate eradicated by Higher 3 Paths to three aggregates . . . (1)

(iii) State eradicated neither by First Path nor by Higher 3 Paths to state eradicated neither by First Path nor by Higher 3 Paths . . .

(*a*) One aggregate eradicated neither by First Path nor by Higher 3 Paths is related to three aggregates by mutuality condition . . . two aggregates . . .

(*b*) At the moment of conception, one aggregate eradicated neither by First Path nor by Higher 3 Paths is related to three aggregates and (heart-)base by mutuality condition . . . two aggregates . . . aggregates to (heart-)base . . . (heart-)base to aggregates . . .

(*c*) One great primary is related to three great primaries by mutuality condition . . . non-percipient beings . . . (1)

Dependence 13

81. (i)–(iii) State eradicated by First Path is related to state eradicated by First Path by dependence condition . . . three.

(iv)–(vi) State eradicated by Higher 3 Paths to state eradicated by Higher 3 Paths . . . three.

(vii) State eradicated neither by First Path nor by Higher 3 Paths is related to state eradicated neither by First Path nor by Higher 3 Paths by dependence condition.

(*a*) One aggregate eradicated neither by First Path nor by Higher 3 Paths to three aggregates and mind-produced matter . . . two aggregates . . .

(*b*) At the moment of conception . . . aggregates to (heart-)base . . . (heart-)base to aggregates . . .

(*c*), (*d*) One great primary . . . non-percipient beings . . .

(*e*) Eye-base to eye-consciousness . . . body-base to body-consciousness . . . (heart-)base . . . (1)

(viii) State eradicated neither by First Path nor by Higher 3 Paths is related to state eradicated by First Path by dependence condition.

(Heart-)base is related to aggregates eradicated by First Path by dependence condition. (2)

(ix) State eradicated neither by First Path nor by Higher 3 Paths is related to state eradicated by Higher 3 Paths by dependence condition.

(Heart-)base is related to aggregates eradicated by Higher 3 Paths by dependence condition. (3)

82. (x) States eradicated by First Path and eradicated neither by First Path nor by Higher 3 Paths are related to state eradicated by First Path by dependence condition.

One aggregate eradicated by First Path and (heart-)base are related to three aggregates by dependence condition . . . two aggregates . . . (1)

(xi) States eradicated by First Path and eradicated neither by First Path nor by Higher 3 Paths are related to state eradicated neither by First Path nor by Higher 3 Paths by dependence condition.

Aggregates eradicated by First Path and great primaries are related to mind-produced matter by dependence condition. (2)

(xii) States eradicated by Higher 3 Paths and eradicated neither by

First Path nor by Higher 3 Paths are related to state eradicated by Higher 3 Paths by dependence condition.

One aggregate eradicated by Higher 3 Paths and (heart-)base are related to three aggregates by dependence condition . . . two aggregates . . . (1)

(xiii) States eradicated by Higher 3 Paths and eradicated neither by First Path nor by Higher 3 Paths are related to state eradicated neither by First Path nor by Higher 3 Paths by dependence condition.

Aggregates eradicated by Higher 3 Paths and great primaries are related to mind-produced matter by dependence condition. (2)

Strong-dependence 8

83. (i) State eradicated by First Path is related to state eradicated by First Path by strong-dependence condition.

(It is of three kinds, namely:) (*a*) object-strong-dependence, (*b*) proximity-strong-dependence, (*c*) natural strong-dependence . . .

(*c*) *Natural strong-dependence:* By the strong-dependence of lust eradicated by First Path, (one) kills a living being, takes the property of others which has not been given to one . . . causes schism in the Saṅgha . . . hate eradicated by First Path . . . delusion . . . wrong views . . . By the strong-dependence of wish, (one) kills a living being . . . causes schism in the Saṅgha. Lust eradicated by First Path, hate, delusion, wrong views, wish is related to lust eradicated by First Path, hate, delusion, wrong views, wish by strong-dependence condition. (1)

(ii) State eradicated by First Path is related to state eradicated neither by First Path nor by Higher 3 Paths by strong-dependence condition.

(It is of two kinds, namely:) (*a*) proximity-strong-dependence, (*b*) natural strong-dependence . . .

(*b*) *Natural strong-dependence:* By the strong-dependence of lust eradicated by First Path, (one) offers an offering, undertakes precepts, fulfils the duty of observance . . . develops attainment . . . hate eradicated by First Path . . . By the strong-dependence of wish, (one) offers an offering . . . develops attainment. Lust eradicated by First Path, hate, delusion, wrong views, wish is related to confidence . . . wisdom, bodily happiness, bodily pain, attainment of Fruition by strong-dependence condition. (2)

84. (iii) State eradicated by Higher 3 Paths is related to state eradicated by Higher 3 Paths by strong-dependence condition.

(It is of three kinds, namely:) (*a*) object-strong-dependence, (*b*) proximity-strong-dependence, (*c*) natural strong-dependence . . .

(*c*) *Natural strong-dependence:* Lust eradicated by Higher 3 Paths, hate, delusion, conceit, wish is related to lust eradicated by Higher 3 Paths, hate, delusion, conceit, wish by strong-dependence condition. (1)

(iv) State eradicated by Higher 3 Paths is related to state eradicated by First Path by strong-dependence condition.

(It is of two kinds, namely:) (*a*) object-strong-dependence, (*b*) natural strong-dependence . . .

(*b*) *Natural strong-dependence:* By the strong-dependence of lust eradicated by Higher 3 Paths, (one) kills a living being . . . causes schism in the Saṅgha . . . hate eradicated by Higher 3 Paths . . . delusion . . . conceit . . . By the strong-dependence of wish, (one) kills a living being . . . causes schism in the Saṅgha. Lust eradicated by Higher 3 Paths, hate, delusion, conceit, wish is related to lust eradicated by First Path, hate, delusion, wrong views, wish by strong-dependence condition. Lustful desire for one's own property (sakabhaṇḍe chanda-rāgo) is related to lustful desire for other's property by strong-dependence condition; Lustful desire for one's own possessions (sakapariggaha) is related to lustful desire for other's possessions by strong-dependence condition. (2)

(v) State eradicated by Higher 3 Paths is related to state eradicated neither by First Path nor by Higher 3 Paths by strong-dependence condition.

(It is of two kinds, namely:) (*a*) proximity-strong-dependence, (*b*) natural strong-dependence . . .

(*b*) *Natural strong-dependence:* By the strong-dependence of lust eradicated by Higher 3 Paths, (one) offers an offering . . . develops attainment . . . hate eradicated by Higher 3 Paths . . . delusion . . . conceit . . . By the strong-dependence of wish, (one) offers an offering . . . develops attainment. Lust eradicated by Higher 3 Paths, hate, delusion, conceit, wish is related to confidence . . . attainment of Fruition by strong-dependence condition. (3)

85. (vi) State eradicated neither by First Path nor by Higher 3 Paths is related to state eradicated neither by First Path nor by Higher 3 Paths by strong-dependence condition.

(It is of three kinds, namely:) (*a*) object-strong-dependence, (*b*) proximity-strong-dependence, (*c*) natural strong-dependence . . .

(*c*) *Natural strong-dependence:* By the strong-dependence of confidence, (one) offers an offering . . . develops attainment . . . precept . . . learning . . . generosity . . . wisdom . . . bodily happiness . . . bodily pain . . . temperature . . . food . . . By the strong-dependence of lodging-place, (one) offers an offering . . . develops attainment. Confidence, precept, learning, generosity, wisdom, bodily happiness, bodily pain, temperature, food, lodging-place is related to confidence . . . wisdom, bodily happiness, bodily pain, attainment of Fruition by strong-dependence condition. (1)

(vii) State eradicated neither by First Path nor by Higher 3 Paths is related to state eradicated by First Path by strong-dependence condition.

(It is of three kinds, namely:) (*a*) object-strong-dependence, (*b*) proximity-strong-dependence, (*c*) natural strong-dependence . . .

(*c*) *Natural strong-dependence:* By the strong-dependence of confidence (one) adopts wrong views . . . precept . . . By the strong-dependence of lodging-place, (one) kills a living being . . . causes schism in the Saṅgha. Confidence . . . lodging-place is related to lust eradicated by First Path, hate, delusion, wrong views, wish by strong-dependence condition. (2)

(viii) State eradicated neither by First Path nor by Higher 3 Paths is related to state eradicated by Higher 3 Paths by strong-dependence condition.

(It is of three kinds, namely:) (*a*) object-strong-dependence, (*b*) proximity-strong-dependence, (*c*) natural strong-dependence . . .

(*c*) *Natural strong-dependence:* By the strong-dependence of confidence, (one) arouses conceit . . . precept . . . wisdom . . . bodily happiness . . . bodily pain . . . temperature . . . food . . . By the strong-dependence of lodging-place, (one) arouses conceit. Confidence . . . wisdom, bodily happiness, bodily pain, temperature, food, lodging-place is related to lust eradicated by Higher 3 Paths, hate, delusion, conceit, wish by strong-dependence condition. (3)

Prenascence 3

86. (i) State eradicated neither by First Path nor by Higher 3 Paths is related to state eradicated neither by First Path nor by Higher 3 Paths by prenascence condition.

(It is of two kinds, namely:) (*a*) object-prenascence, (*b*) base-prenascence.

(*a*) *Object-prenascence:* (One) practises insight into the impermanence, suffering and impersonality of the eye . . . ear . . . nose . . . tongue . . . body . . . visible object . . . sound . . . smell . . . taste . . . tangible object . . . (heart-)base. By the power of divine-eye, (one) sees a visible object. By the power of divine-ear element, (one) hears a sound. Visible object-base to eye-consciousness . . . tangible object-base is related to body-consciousness by prenascence condition.

(*b*) *Base-prenascence:* Eye-base to eye-consciousness . . . body-base to body-consciousness . . . (heart-)base is related to aggregates eradicated neither by First Path nor by Higher 3 Paths by prenascence condition. (1)

(ii) State eradicated neither by First Path nor by Higher 3 Paths is related to state eradicated by First Path by prenascence condition.

(It is of two kinds, namely:) (*a*) object-prenascence, (*b*) base-prenascence.

(*a*) *Object-prenascence:* (One) enjoys and delights in the eye. Taking it as object, arises lust eradicated by First Path, arise wrong views, arises doubt, arises grief eradicated by First Path . . . (One) enjoys and delights in the (heart-)base. Taking it as object, arises lust eradicated by First Path, arise wrong views, arises doubt, arises grief eradicated by First Path.

(*b*) *Base-prenascence:* (Heart-)base is related to aggregates eradicated by First Path by prenascence condition. (2)

(iii) State eradicated neither by First Path nor by Higher 3 Paths is related to state eradicated by Higher 3 Paths by prenascence condition.

(It is of two kinds, namely:) (*a*) object-prenascence, (*b*) base-prenascence.

(*a*) *Object-prenascence:* (One) enjoys and delights in the eye. Taking it as object, arises lust eradicated by Higher 3 Paths, arises restlessness, arises grief eradicated by Higher 3 Paths . . . ear . . . body . . . visible object . . . tangible object . . . (One) enjoys and delights in the (heart-)base. Taking it as object, arises lust eradicated by Higher 3 Paths, arises restlessness, arises grief eradicated by Higher 3 Paths.

(*b*) *Base-prenascence:* (Heart-)base is related to aggregates eradicated by Higher 3 Paths by prenascence condition. (3)

Postnascence 3

87. (i) State eradicated by First Path is related to state eradicated neither by First Path nor by Higher 3 Paths by postnascence condition.

Postnascent aggregates eradicated by First Path are related to this prenascent body by postnascence condition. (1)

(ii) State eradicated by Higher 3 Paths is related to state eradicated neither by First Path nor by Higher 3 Paths by postnascence condition.

Postnascent aggregates eradicated by Higher 3 Paths are related to this prenascent body by postnascence condition. (1)

(iii) State eradicated neither by First Path nor by Higher 3 Paths is related to state eradicated neither by First Path nor by Higher 3 Paths by postnascence condition.

Postnascent aggregates eradicated neither by First Path nor by Higher 3 Paths are related to this prenascent body by postnascence condition. (1)

Repetition 3

88. (i) State eradicated by First Path is related to state eradicated by First Path by repetition condition.

Preceding aggregates eradicated by First Path are related to subsequent . . . by repetition condition. (1)

(ii) State eradicated by Higher 3 Paths is related to state eradicated by Higher 3 Paths by repetition condition.

Preceding aggregates eradicated by Higher 3 Paths are related to subsequent . . . by repetition condition. (1)

(iii) State eradicated neither by First Path nor by Higher 3 Paths is related to state eradicated neither by First Path nor by Higher 3 Paths by repetition condition.

Preceding aggregates eradicated neither by First Path nor by Higher 3 Paths are related to subsequent . . . by repetition condition. Adaptation to change-of-lineage; adaptation to purification; change-of-lineage to Path; purification is related to Path by repetition condition. (1)

Kamma 7

89. (i) State eradicated by First Path is related to state eradicated by First Path by kamma condition.

Volition eradicated by First Path is related to (its) associated aggregates by kamma condition. (1)

(ii) State eradicated by First Path is related to state eradicated neither by First Path nor by Higher 3 Paths by kamma condition.

(It is of two kinds, namely:) (*a*) conascence(-kamma), (*b*) asynchronous (kamma).

(*a*) Conascent volition eradicated by First Path is related to mind-produced matter by kamma condition.

(*b*) Asynchronous volition eradicated by First Path is related to (its) resultant aggregates and kamma-produced matter by kamma condition. (2)

(iii) State eradicated by First Path is related to state eradicated by First Path and eradicated neither by First Path nor by Higher 3 Paths by kamma condition.

Volition eradicated by First Path is related to (its) associated aggregates and mind-produced matter by kamma condition. (3)

(iv) State eradicated by Higher 3 Paths is related to state eradicated by Higher 3 Paths by kamma condition.

Volition eradicated by Higher 3 Paths is related to (its) associated aggregates by kamma condition. (1)

(v) State eradicated by Higher 3 Paths is related to state eradicated neither by First Path nor by Higher 3 Paths by kamma condition.

Volition eradicated by Higher 3 Paths is related to mind-produced matter by kamma condition. (2)

(vi) State eradicated by Higher 3 Paths is related to state eradicated by Higher 3 Paths and eradicated neither by First Path nor by Higher 3 Paths by kamma condition.

Volition eradicated by Higher 3 Paths is related to (its) associated aggregates and mind-produced matter by kamma condition. (3)

(vii) State eradicated neither by First Path nor by Higher 3 Paths is related to state eradicated neither by First Path nor by Higher 3 Paths by kamma condition.

(It is of two kinds, namely:) (*a*) conascence(-kamma), (*b*) asynchronous (kamma).

(*a*) (1) Conascent volition eradicated neither by First Path nor by Higher 3 Paths is related to (its) associated aggregates and mind-produced matter by kamma condition;

(2) At the moment of conception, volition eradicated neither by First Path nor by Higher 3 Paths to (its) associated aggregates and kamma-produced matter . . .

(*b*) Asynchronous volition eradicated neither by First Path nor by Higher 3 Paths is related to (its) resultant aggregates and kamma-produced matter by kamma condition. (1)

Resultant 1

90. State eradicated neither by First Path nor by Higher 3 Paths is related to state eradicated neither by First Path nor by Higher 3 Paths by resultant condition.

(*a*) One resultant aggregate eradicated neither by First Path nor by Higher 3 Paths is related to three aggregates and mind-produced matter by resultant condition . . .

(*b*) At the moment of conception . . . aggregates are related to (heart-)base by resultant condition.

Nutriment, etc.

91. State eradicated by First Path is related to state eradicated by First Path by nutriment condition. (Abbreviated.) Edible food. 7 questions . . . by faculty condition. Eye-faculty . . . and physical life-faculty. 7 questions . . . by jhāna condition . . . by path condition . . . by association condition . . .

Dissociation 5

92. (i) State eradicated by First Path is related to state eradicated neither by First Path nor by Higher 3 Paths[1] by dissociation condition.

(It is of two kinds, namely:) (*a*) conascence, (*b*) postnascence.

(*a*) Conascent aggregates eradicated by First Path are related to mind-produced matter by dissociation condition.

(*b*) Postnascent aggregates eradicated by First Path are related to this prenascent body by dissociation condition. (1)

(ii) State eradicated by Higher 3 Paths is related to state eradicated neither by First Path nor by Higher 3 Paths by dissociation condition.

(It is of two kinds, namely:) (*a*) conascence, (*b*) postnascence.

(This is also like First Path.)

(iii) State eradicated neither by First Path nor by Higher 3 Paths is related to state eradicated neither by First Path nor by Higher 3 Paths by dissociation condition.

(It is of three kinds, namely:) (*a*) conascence, (*b*) prenascence, (*c*) postnascence.

(*a*) (1) Conascent aggregates eradicated neither by First Path nor by

---

[1] NOT "eradicated by First Path" as given in the Pali Text.

Higher 3 Paths are related to mind-produced matter by dissociation condition;

(2) At the moment of conception, aggregates eradicated neither by First Path nor by Higher 3 Paths are related to kamma-produced matter by dissociation condition; aggregates are related to (heart-)base by dissociation condition; (heart-)base is related to aggregates by dissociation condition.

(*b*) Prenascent eye-base to eye-consciousness . . . body-base to body-consciousness . . . (heart-)base is related to aggregates eradicated neither by First Path nor by Higher 3 Paths by dissociation condition.

(*c*) Postnascent aggregates eradicated neither by First Path nor by Higher 3 Paths are related to this prenascent body by dissociation condition. (1)

(iv) State eradicated neither by First Path nor by Higher 3 Paths is related to state eradicated by First Path by dissociation condition.

Prenascent (heart-)base is related to aggregates eradicated by First Path by dissociation condition. (2)

(*c*) State eradicated neither by First Path nor by Higher 3 Paths is related to state eradicated by Higher 3 Paths by dissociation condition.

Prenascent (heart-)base is related to aggregates eradicated by Higher 3 Paths by dissociation condition. (3)

Presence 13

93. (i) State eradicated by First Path is related to state eradicated by First Path by presence condition.

One aggregate eradicated by First Path is related to three aggregates by presence condition . . . two aggregates . . . (1)

(ii) State eradicated by First Path is related to state eradicated neither by First Path nor by Higher 3 Paths by presence condition.

(It is of two kinds, namely:) (*a*) conascence, (*b*) postnascence.

(*a*) Conascent aggregates eradicated by First Path are related to mind-produced matter by presence condition.

(*b*) Postnascent aggregates eradicated by First Path are related to this prenascent body by presence condition. (2)

(iii) State eradicated by First Path is related to state eradicated by First Path and eradicated neither by First Path nor by Higher 3 Paths by presence condition.

One aggregate eradicated by First Path to three aggregates and mind-produced matter . . . two aggregates . . . (3)

(iv)–(vi) State eradicated by Higher 3 Paths to state eradicated by Higher 3 Paths . . . three. (Proceed as for First Path.)

94. (vii) State eradicated neither by First Path nor by Higher 3 Paths is related to state eradicated neither by First Path nor by Higher 3 Paths by presence condition.

(It is of five kinds, namely:) (*a*) conascence, (*b*) prenascence, (*c*) postnascence, (*d*) nutriment, (*e*) faculty.

(*a*) (1) One conascent aggregate eradicated neither by First Path nor by Higher 3 Paths is related to three aggregates and mind-produced matter by presence condition . . .

(2) At the moment of conception . . . aggregates to (heart-)base . . . (heart-)base is related to aggregates by presence condition;

(3) One great primary . . . one great primary of non-percipient beings . . .

(*b*) *(Object-)prenascence:* (One) practises insight into the impermanence, suffering and impersonality of the eye . . . ear . . . body . . . visible object . . . tangible object. (One) practises insight into the impermanence, suffering and impersonality of the (heart-)base. By the power of divine-eye, (one) sees a visible object. By the power of divine-ear element, (one) hears a sound. Visible object-base to eye-consciousness . . . tangible object-base to body-consciousness . . .

(Base-)prenascence: Eye-base to eye-consciousness . . . body-base to body-consciousness . . . (heart-)base is related to aggregates eradicated neither by First Path nor by Higher 3 Paths by presence condition.

(*c*) Postnascent aggregates eradicated neither by First Path nor by Higher 3 Paths are related to this prenascent body by presence condition.

(*d*) Edible food to this body . . .

(*e*) Physical life-faculty is related to kamma-produced matter by presence condition. (1)

(viii) State eradicated neither by First Path nor by Higher 3 Paths is related to state eradicated by First Path by presence condition.

(Object-)prenascence: (One) enjoys and delights in the eye. Taking it as object, arises lust eradicated by First Path, arise wrong views, arises doubt, arises grief eradicated by First Path . . . ear . . . (One) enjoys . . . the (heart-)base . . .

(Base-)prenascence: (Heart-)base is related to aggregates eradicated by First Path by presence condition. (2)

(ix) State eradicated neither by First Path nor by Higher 3 Paths is related to state eradicated by Higher 3 Paths by presence condition.

(Object-)prenascence: (One) enjoys and delights in the eye. Taking it as object, arises lust eradicated by Higher 3 Paths, arises restlessness, arises grief eradicated by Higher 3 Paths . . . ear . . . (One) enjoys and delights in the (heart-)base . . .

(Base-)prenascence: (Heart-)base is related to aggregates eradicated by Higher 3 Paths by presence condition. (3)

95. (x) States eradicated by First Path and eradicated neither by First Path nor by Higher 3 Paths are related to state eradicated by First Path by presence condition.

Conascence-prenascence: One conascent aggregate eradicated by First Path and (heart-)base are related to three aggregates by presence condition . . . two aggregates and (heart-)base . . . (1)

(xi) States eradicated by First Path and eradicated neither by First Path nor by Higher 3 Paths are related to state eradicated neither by First Path nor by Higher 3 Paths by presence condition.

(It is of three kinds, namely:) (*a*) conascence, (*b*) postnascence-nutriment, (*c*) (postnascence-)faculty.

(*a*) Conascent aggregates eradicated by First Path and great primaries, are related to mind-produced matter by presence condition.

(*b*) Postnascent aggregates eradicated by First Path and edible food are related to this body by presence condition.

(*c*) Postnascent aggregates eradicated by First Path and physical life-faculty are related to kamma-produced matter by presence condition. (1)

(xii)–(xiii) States eradicated by Higher 3 Paths and eradicated neither by First Path nor by Higher 3 Paths . . . eradicated by Higher 3 Paths . . .

(Do two questions.)

Absence, Disappearance, Non-disappearance

96. State eradicated by First Path is related to state eradicated by First Path by absence condition . . . by disappearance condition . . . by non-disappearance condition . . .

1. CONDITIONS: POSITIVE (ii) ENUMERATION CHAPTER

(By Ones)

97. With root 7, object 8, predominance 10, proximity 7, contiguity 7,

conascence 9, mutuality 3, dependence 13, strong-dependence 8, prenascence 3, postnascence 3, repetition 3, kamma 7, resultant 1, nutriment 7, faculty 7, jhāna 7, path 7, association 3, dissociation 5, presence 13, absence 7, disappearance 7, non-disappearance 13. (Enumerate thus.)

End of Positive

2. SELECTION OF THE CONDITIONS FOR NEGATIVE 14

98. (i) State eradicated by First Path is related to state eradicated by First Path by object condition, conascence condition, strong-dependence condition. (1)

(ii) State eradicated by First Path is related to state eradicated neither by First Path nor by Higher 3 Paths by object condition, conascence condition, strong-dependence condition, postnascence condition, kamma condition. (2)

(iii) State eradicated by First Path is related to state eradicated by First Path and eradicated neither by First Path nor by Higher 3 Paths by conascence condition. (3)

99. (iv) State eradicated by Higher 3 Paths is related to state eradicated by Higher 3 Paths by object condition, conascence condition, strong-dependence condition. (1)

(v) State eradicated by Higher 3 Paths is related to state eradicated by First Path by object condition, strong-dependence condition. (2)

(vi) State eradicated by Higher 3 Paths is related to state eradicated neither by First Path nor by Higher 3 Paths by object condition, conascence condition, strong-dependence condition, postnascence condition. (3)

(vii) State eradicated by Higher 3 Paths is related to state eradicated by Higher 3 Paths and eradicated neither by First Path nor by Higher 3 Paths by conascence condition. (4)

100. (viii) State eradicated neither by First Path nor by Higher 3 Paths is related to state eradicated neither by First Path nor by Higher 3 Paths by object condition, conascence condition, strong-dependence condition, prenascence condition, postnascence condition, kamma condition, nutriment condition, faculty condition. (1)

(ix) State eradicated neither by First Path nor by Higher 3 Paths is related to state eradicated by First Path by object condition, strong-dependence condition, prenascence condition. (2)

(x) State eradicated neither by First Path nor by Higher 3 Paths is related to state eradicated by Higher 3 Paths by object condition, strong-dependence condition, prenascence condition. (3)

101. (xi) States eradicated by First Path and eradicated neither by First Path nor by Higher 3 Paths are related to state eradicated by First Path by conascence-prenascence. (1)

(xii) States eradicated by First Path and eradicated neither by First Path nor by Higher 3 Paths are related to state eradicated neither by First Path nor by Higher 3 Paths by conascence, postnascence-nutriment-faculty. (2)

(xiii) States eradicated by Higher 3 Paths and eradicated neither by First Path nor by Higher 3 Paths are related to state eradicated by Higher 3 Paths by conascence-prenascence. (1)

(xiv) States eradicated by Higher 3 Paths and eradicated neither by First Path nor by Higher 3 Paths are related to state eradicated neither by First Path nor by Higher 3 Paths by conascence, postnascence-nutriment-faculty. (2)

2. CONDITIONS: NEGATIVE (ii) ENUMERATION CHAPTER

(By Ones)

102. With not-root 14, not-object 14, not-predominance 14, not-proximity 14, not-contiguity 14, not-conascence 10, not-mutuality 10, not-dependence 10, not-strong-dependence 14, not-prenascence 12, not-postnascence 14, not-repetition 14, not-kamma 14, not-resultant 14, not-nutriment 14, not-faculty 14, not-jhāna 14, not-path 14, not-association 10, not-dissociation 8, not-presence 8, not-absence 14, not-disappearance 14, not-non-disappearance 8. (Enumerate thus.)

End of Negative

3. CONDITIONS: POSITIVE-NEGATIVE

(Root By Twos)

103. With root condition, not-object 7, not-predominance 7, not-proximity 7, not-contiguity 7, not-mutuality 3, not-strong-dependence 7, not-prenascence 7, not-postnascence 7, not-repetition 7, not-kamma 7, not-resultant 7, not-nutriment 7, not-faculty 7, not-jhāna 7, not-path 7, not-association 3, not-dissociation 3, not-absence 7, not-disappearance 7. (Enumerate thus.)

End of Positive–Negative

4. CONDITIONS: NEGATIVE–POSITIVE

(Not-root By Twos)

104. With not-root condition, object 8, predominance 10, proximity 7, contiguity 7, conascence 9, mutuality 3, dependence 13, strong-dependence 8, prenascence 3, postnascence 3, repetition 3, kamma 7, resultant 1, nutriment 7, faculty 7, jhāna 7, path 7, association 3, dissociation 5, presence 13, absence 7, disappearance 7, non-disappearance 13. (Enumerate thus.)

End of Negative–Positive

END OF TRIPLET OF (STATE) ERADICATED BY FIRST PATH

9. TRIPLET OF (STATE) TOGETHER WITH ROOT ERADICATED BY FIRST PATH[1] I. "DEPENDENT" CHAPTER

1. CONDITIONS: POSITIVE (i) CLASSIFICATION CHAPTER

Root 17

1. (i) Dependent on state together with root eradicated by First Path, arises state together with root eradicated by First Path by root condition.

Dependent on one aggregate together with root eradicated by First Path, arise three aggregates . . . two aggregates . . . (1)

(ii) Dependent on state together with root eradicated by First Path, arises state together with root eradicated neither by First Path nor by Higher 3 Paths by root condition.

Dependent on aggregates together with roots eradicated by First Path, arises mind-produced matter. (2)

(iii) Dependent on state together with root eradicated by First Path, arise states together with root eradicated by First Path and together with root eradicated neither by First Path nor by Higher 3 Paths by root condition.

Depndent on one aggregate together with root eradicated by First Path, arise three aggregates and mind-produced matter . . . two aggregates . . . (3)

---

[1] This comprises (1) States together with root eradicated by First Path, (2) States together with root eradicated by Higher 3 Paths, (3) States together with root eradicated neither by First Path nor by Higher 3 Paths.

2. (iv) Dependent on state together with root eradicated by Higher 3 Paths, arises state together with root eradicated by Higher 3 Paths by root condition.

Dependent on one aggregate together with root eradicated by Higher 3 Paths, arise three aggregates . . . two aggregates . . . (1)

(v) Dependent on state together with root eradicated by Higher 3 Paths, arises state together with root eradicated neither by First Path nor by Higher 3 Paths by root condition.

Dependent on aggregates together with root eradicated by Higher 3 Paths, arises mind-produced matter. (2)

(vi) Dependent on state together with root eradicated by Higher 3 Paths, arise states together with root eradicated by Higher 3 Paths and together with root eradicated neither by First Path nor by Higher 3 Paths by root condition.

Dependent on one aggregate together with root eradicated by Higher 3 Paths, arise three aggregates and mind-produced matter . . . two aggregates . . . (3)

3. (vii) Dependent on state together with root eradicated neither by First Path nor by Higher 3 Paths, arises state together with root eradicated neither by First Path nor by Higher 3 Paths by root condition.

(*a*) Dependent on one aggregate together with root eradicated neither by First Path nor by Higher 3 Paths, arise three aggregates and mind-produced matter . . . dependent on two aggregates, arise two aggregates and mind-produced matter; dependent on doubt-accompanied or restlessness-accompanied delusion, arises mind-produced matter;

(*b*) At the moment of conception, dependent on one aggregate together with root eradicated neither by First Path nor by Higher 3 Paths, arise three aggregates and kamma-produced matter . . . two aggregates . . . dependent on aggregates, arises (heart-)base; dependent on (heart-)base, arise aggregates;

(*c*) Dependent on one great primary . . . dependent on great primaries, arise mind-produced and kamma-produced derived matter. (1)

(viii) Dependent on state together with root eradicated neither by First Path nor by Higher 3 Paths, arises state together with root eradicated by First Path by root condition.

Dependent on doubt-accompanied delusion, arise associated aggregates. (2)

(ix) Dependent on state together with root eradicated neither by First Path nor by Higher 3 Paths, arises state together with root eradicated by Higher 3 Paths by root condition.

Dependent on restlessness-accompanied delusion, arise assocaited aggregates. (3)

(x) Dependent on state together with root eradicated neither by First Path nor by Higher 3 Paths, arise states together with root eradicated by First Path and together with root eradicated neither by First Path nor by Higher 3 Paths by root condition.

Dependent on doubt-accompanied delusion, arise associated aggregates and mind-produced matter. (4)

(xi) Dependent on state together with root eradicated neither by First Path nor by Higher 3 Paths, arise states together with root eradicated by Higher 3 Paths and together with root eradicated neither by First Path nor by Higher 3 Paths by root condition.

Dependent on restlessness-accompanied delusion, arise associated aggregates and mind-produced matter. (5)

4. (xii) Dependent on state together with root eradicated by First Path and together with root eradicated neither by First Path nor by Higher 3 Paths, arises state together with root eradicated by First Path by root condition.

Dependent on one doubt-accompanied aggregate and delusion, arise three aggregates . . . dependent on two aggregates and delusion, arise two aggregates. (1)

(xiii) Dependent on state together with root eradicated by First Path and together with root eradicated neither by First Path nor by Higher 3 Paths, arises state together with root eradicated neither by First Path nor by Higher 3 Paths by root condition.

Dependent on aggregates together with root eradicated by First Path and great primaries, arises mind-produced matter; dependent on doubt-accompanied aggregates and delusion, arises mind-produced matter. (2)

(xiv) Dependent on state together with root eradicated by First Path and together with root eradicated neither by First Path nor by Higher 3 Paths, arise states together with root eradicated by First Path and together with root eradicated neither by First Path nor by Higher 3 Paths by root condition.

Dependent on one doubt-accompanied aggregate and delusion, arise three aggregates and mind-produced matter . . . dependent on two aggregates and delusion, arise two aggregates . . . (3)

5. (xv) Dependent on state together with root eradicated by Higher 3

Paths and together with root eradicated neither by First Path nor by Higher 3 Paths, arises state together with root eradicated by Higher 3 Paths by root condition.

Dependent on one restlessness-accompanied aggregate and delusion, arise three aggregates . . . dependent on two aggregates and delusion, arise two aggregates. (1)

(xvi) Dependent on state together with root eradicated by Higher 3 Paths and together with root eradicated neither by First Path nor by Higher 3 Paths, arises state together with root eradicated neither by First Path nor by Higher 3 Paths by root condition.

Dependent on aggregates together with root eradicated by Higher 3 Paths and great primaries, arises mind-produced matter; dependent on restlessness-accompanied aggregates and delusion, arises mind-produced matter. (2)

(xvii) Dependent on state together with root eradicated by Higher 3 Paths and together with root eradicated neither by First Path nor by Higher 3 Paths, arise states together with root eradicated by Higher 3 Paths and together with root eradicated neither by First Path nor by Higher 3 Paths by root condition.

Dependent on one restlessness-accompanied aggregate and delusion, arise three aggregates and mind-produced matter . . . (3)

Object 11

6. (i) Dependent on state together with root eradicated by First Path, arises state together with root eradicated by First Path by object condition.

Dependent on one aggregate together with root eradicated by First Path, arise three aggregates . . . dependent on two aggregates, arise two aggregates. (1)

(ii) Dependent on state together with root eradicated by First Path, arises state together with root eradicated neither by First Path nor by Higher 3 Paths by object condition.

Dependent on doubt-accompanied aggregates, arises doubt-accompanied delusion. (2)

(iii) Dependent on state together with root eradicated by First Path, arise states together with root eradicated by First Path and together with root eradicated neither by First Path nor by Higher 3 Paths by object condition.

Dependent on one doubt-accompanied aggregate, arise three aggregates and delusion . . . dependent on two aggregates, arise two aggregates and delusion. (3)

(iv)–(vi) Dependent on state together with root eradicated by Higher 3 Paths, arises state together with root eradicated by Higher 3 Paths by object condition . . . three. (Classify like First Path.)

7. (vii) Dependent on state together with root eradicated neither by First Path nor by Higher 3 Paths, arises state together with root eradicated neither by First Path nor by Higher 3 Paths by object condition.

(*a*) Dependent on one aggregate together with root eradicated neither by First Path nor by Higher 3 Paths, arise three aggregates . . . dependent on two aggregates, arise two aggregates;

(*b*) At the moment of conception . . . dependent on (heart-)base, arise aggregates. (1)

(viii) Dependent on state together with root eradicated neither by First Path nor by Higher 3 Paths, arises state together with root eradicated by First Path by object condition.

Dependent on doubt-accompanied delusion, arise associated aggregates. (2)

(ix) Dependent on state together with root eradicated neither by First Path nor by Higher 3 Paths, arises state together with root eradicated by Higher 3 Paths by object condition.

Dependent on restlessness-accompanied delusion, arise associated aggregates. (3)

8. (x) Dependent on state together with root eradicated by First Path and together with root eradicated neither by First Path nor by Higher 3 Paths, arises state together with root eradicated by First Path by object condition.

Dependent on one doubt-accompanied aggregate and delusion, arise three aggregates . . . dependent on two aggregates and delusion, arise two aggregates. (1)

(xi) Dependent on state together with root eradicated by Higher 3 Paths and together with root eradicated neither by First Path nor by Higher 3 Paths, arises state together with root eradicated by Higher 3 Paths by object condition.

Dependent on one restlessness-accompanied aggregate and delusion, arise three aggregates . . . dependent on two aggregates and delusion, arise two aggregates. (1)

Predominance 9

9. (i)-(iii) Dependent on state together with root eradicated by First Path, arises state together with root eradicated by First Path by predominance condition . . . three. (The same as root.)

(iv)-(vi) Dependent on state together with root eradicated by Higher 3 Paths . . . three. (The same as root. No delusion in predominance.)

(vii) Dependent on state together with root eradicated neither by First Path nor by Higher 3 Paths, arises state together with root eradicated neither by First Path nor by Higher 3 Paths by predominance condition.

(*a*) Dependent on one aggregate together with root eradicated neither by First Path nor by Higher 3 Paths, arise three aggregates and mind-produced matter . . . two aggregates . . .

(*b*) Dependent on one great primary, arise three great primaries . . . dependent on great primaries, arises mind-produced derived matter. (1)

10. (viii) Dependent on state together with root eradicated by First Path and together with root eradicated neither by First Path nor by Higher 3 Paths, arises state together with root eradicated neither by First Path nor by Higher 3 Paths by predominance condition.

Dependent on aggregates together with root eradicated by First Path and great primaries, arises mind-produced matter. (1)

(ix) Dependent on state together with root eradicated by Higher 3 Paths and together with root eradicated neither by First Path nor by Higher 3 Paths, arises state together with root eradicated neither by First Path nor by Higher 3 Paths by predominance condition.

Dependent on aggregates together with root eradicated by Higher 3 Paths and great primaries, arises mind-produced matter. (1)

Proximity, Contiguity 11

11. Dependent on state together with root eradicated by First Path, arises state together with root eradicated by First Path by proximity condition . . . by contiguity condition . . . (The same as object.)

Conascence 17

12. (i) Dependent on state together with root eradicated by First Path, arises state together with root eradicated by First Path by conascence condition.

Dependent on one aggregate together with root eradicated by First Path, arise three aggregates . . . dependent on two aggregates, arise two aggregates. (1)

(ii) Dependent on state together with root eradicated by First Path, arises state together with root eradicated neither by First Path nor by Higher 3 Paths by conascence condition.

Dependent on aggregates together with root eradicated by First Path, arises mind-produced matter; dependent on doubt-accompanied aggregates, arise delusion and mind-produced matter. (2)

(iii) Dependent on state together with root eradicated by First Path, arise states together with root eradicated by First Path and together with root eradicated neither by First Path nor by Higher 3 Paths by conascence condition.

Dependent on one aggregate together with root eradicated by First Path, arise three aggregates and mind-produced matter . . . dependent on two aggregates, arise two aggregates and mind-produced matter; dependent on one doubt-accompanied aggregate, arise three aggregates, delusion and mind-produced matter . . . (3)

13. (iv) Dependent on state together with root eradicated by Higher 3 Paths, arises state together with root eradicated by Higher 3 Paths by conascence condition.

Dependent on one aggregate together with root eradicated by Higher 3 Paths, arise three aggregates . . . dependent on two aggregates, arise two aggregates. (1)

(v) Dependent on state together with root eradicated by Higher 3 Paths, arises state together with root eradicated neither by First Path nor by Higher 3 Paths by conascence condition.

Dependent on aggregates together with root eradicated by Higher 3 Paths, arises mind-produced matter; dependent on restlessness-accompanied aggregates, arise delusion and mind-produced matter. (2)

(vi) Dependent on state together with root eradicated by Higher 3 Paths, arise states together with root eradicated by Higher 3 Paths and together with root eradicated neither by First Path nor by Higher 3 Paths by conascence condition.

Dependent on one aggregate together with root eradicated by Higher 3 Paths, arise three aggregates and mind-produced matter . . . dependent on two aggregates, arise two aggregates and mind-produced matter; dependent on one restlessness-accompanied aggregate, arise three aggregates, delusion and mind-produced matter . . . (3)

14. (vii) Dependent on state together with root eradicated neither by First Path nor by Higher 3 Paths, arises state together with root eradicated neither by First Path nor by Higher 3 Paths by conascence condition.

(*a*) Dependent on one aggregate together with root eradicated neither by First Path nor by Higher 3 Paths, arise three aggregates and mind-produced matter . . . two aggregates . . . dependent on doubt-accompanied or restlessness-accompanied delusion, arises mind-produced matter;

(*b*) At the moment of conception . . . dependent on aggregates, arises (heart-)base; dependent on (heart-)base, arise aggregates;

(*c*) Dependent on one great primary, arise three great primaries . . . External . . . nutriment-produced . . . temperature-produced . . . one non-percipient being . . . (1)

(viii) Dependent on state together with root eradicated neither by First Path nor by Higher 3 Paths, arises state together with root eradicated by First Path by conascence condition.

Dependent on doubt-accompanied delusion, arise associated aggregates. (2)

(ix)-(xvii) Dependent on state together with root eradicated neither by First Path nor by Higher 3 Paths, arises state together with root eradicated by Higher 3 Paths by conascence condition . . . (Abbreviated.) (Proceed in the same way as for root.) (3)

Mutuality, etc.

15. Dependent on state together with root eradicated by First Path, arises state together with root eradicated by First Path by mutuality condition . . . by dependence condition . . . by strong-dependence condition . . . by prenascence condition . . . by repetition condition . . . by kamma condition . . . by resultant condition . . . by nutriment condition . . . by faculty condition . . . by jhāna condition . . . by path condition . . . by association condition . . . by dissociation condition . . . by presence condition . . . by absence condition . . . by disappearance condition . . . by non-disappearance condition . . .

1. CONDITIONS: POSITIVE (ii) ENUMERATION CHAPTER

By Ones

16. With root 17, object 11, predominance 9, proximity 11, contiguity 11, conascence 17, mutuality 11, dependence 17, strong-dependence 11,

prenascence 11, repetition 11, kamma 17, resultant 1, nutriment 17, faculty 17, jhāna 17, path 17, association 11, dissociation 17, presence 17, absence 11, disappearance 11, non-disappearance 17. (Enumerate thus.)

End of Positive

1. CONDITIONS: NEGATIVE (i) CLASSIFICATION CHAPTER

Not-root 3

17. (i) Dependent on state together with root eradicated by First Path, arises state together with root eradicated neither by First Path nor by Higher 3 Paths by not-root condition.

Dependent on doubt-accompanied aggregates, arises doubt-accompanied delusion. (1)

(ii) Dependent on state together with root eradicated by Higher 3 Paths, arises state together with root eradicated neither by First Path nor by Higher 3 Paths by not-root condition.

Dependent on restlessness-accompanied aggregates, arises restlessness-accompanied delusion. (1)

(iii) Dependent on state together with root eradicated neither by First Path nor by Higher 3 Paths, arises state together with root eradicated neither by First Path nor by Higher 3 Paths by not-root condition.

(*a*) Dependent on one rootless aggregate together with root eradicated neither by First Path nor by Higher 3 Paths, arise three aggregates and mind-produced matter . . . two aggregates . . .

(*b*) At the moment of rootless conception . . . dependent on aggregates, arises (heart-)base; dependent on (heart-)base, arise aggregates;

(*c*) Dependent on one great primary . . . External . . . nutriment-produced . . . temperature-produced . . . non-percipient beings . . . (1)

Not-object 5

18. (i) Dependent on state together with root eradicated by First Path, arises state together with root eradicated neither by First Path nor by Higher 3 Paths by not-object condition.

Dependent on aggregates together with root eradicated by First Path, arises mind-produced matter. (1)

(ii) Dependent on state together with root eradicated by Higher 3 Paths, arises state together with root eradicated neither by First Path nor by Higher 3 Paths by not-object condition.

Dependent on aggregates together with roots eradicated by Higher 3 Paths, arises mind-produced matter. (1)

(iii) Dependent on state together with root eradicated neither by First Path nor by Higher 3 Paths, arises state together with root eradicated neither by First Path nor by Higher 3 Paths by not-object condition.

(*a*) Dependent on aggregates together with root eradicated neither by First Path nor by Higher 3 Paths, arises mind-produced matter; dependent on doubt-accompanied or restlessness-accompanied delusion, arises mind-produced matter;

(*b*) At the moment of conception, dependent on aggregates together with root eradicated neither by First Path nor by Higher 3 Paths, arises kamma-produced matter; dependent on aggregates, arises (heart-)base . . .

(*c*) One great primary . . . non-percipient beings . . . (1)

19. (iv) Dependent on state together with root eradicated by First Path and together with root eradicated neither by First Path nor by Higher 3 Paths, arises state together with root eradicated neither by First Path nor by Higher 3 Paths by not-object condition.

Dependent on aggregates together with root eradicated by First Path and great primaries, arises mind-produced matter; dependent on doubt-accompanied aggregates and delusion, arises mind-produced matter. (1)

(v) Dependent on state together with root eradicated by Higher 3 Paths and together with root eradicated neither by First Path nor by Higher 3 Paths, arises state together with root eradicated neither by First Path nor by Higher 3 Paths by not-object condition.

Dependent on aggregates together with root eradicated by Higher 3 Paths and great primaries, arises mind-produced matter; dependent on restlessness-accompanied aggregates and delusion, arises mind-produced matter. (1)

Not-predominance, etc.

20. Dependent on state together with root eradicated by First Path, arises state together with root eradicated by First Path by not-predominance condition. (The same as conascence.) . . . by not-proximity condition . . . by not-contiguity condition . . . by not-mutuality condition . . . by not-strong-dependence condition . . .

Not-prenascence 13

21. (i) Dependent on state together with root eradicated by First Path, arises state together with root eradicated by First Path by not-prenascence condition.

In the immaterial plane, dependent on one aggregate together with root eradicated by First Path . . . (1)

(ii) Dependent on state together with root eradicated by First Path, arises state together with root eradicated neither by First Path nor by Higher 3 Paths by not-prenascence condition.

In the immaterial plane, dependent on doubt-accompanied aggregates, arises doubt-accompanied delusion; dependent on aggregates together with root eradicated by First Path, arises mind-produced matter. (2)

(iii) Dependent on state together with root eradicated by First Path, arise states together with root eradicated by First Path and together with root eradicated neither by First Path nor by Higher 3 Paths by not-prenascence condition.

In the immaterial plane, dependent on one doubt-accompanied aggregate, arise three aggregates and delusion . . . two aggregates . . . (3)

(iv)–(vi) State together with root eradicated by Higher 3 Paths . . . three. (Like First Path.)

22. (vii) Dependent on state together with root eradicated neither by First Path nor by Higher 3 Paths, arises state together with root eradicated neither by First Path nor by Higher 3 Paths by not-prenascence condition.

(*a*) In the immaterial plane, dependent on one aggregate together with root eradicated neither by First Path nor by Higher 3 Paths, arise three aggregates . . . two aggregates; dependent on aggregates together with root eradicated neither by First Path nor by Higher 3 Paths, arises mind-produced matter; dependent on doubt-accompanied or restlessness-accompanied delusion, arises mind-produced matter;

(*b*) At the moment of conception . . .

(*c*) . . . non-percipient beings . . . (1)

(viii) Dependent on state together with root eradicated neither by First Path nor by Higher 3 Paths, arises state together with root eradicated by First Path by not-prenascence condition.

In the immaterial plane, dependent on doubt-accompanied delusion, arise associated aggregates. (2)

(ix) Dependent on state together with root eradicated neither by First Path nor by Higher 3 Paths, arises state together with root eradicated by Higher 3 Paths by not-prenascence condition.

In the immaterial plane, dependent on restlessness-accompanied delusion, arise associated aggregates. (3)

23. (x) Dependent on state together with root eradicated by First Path and together with root eradicated neither by First Path nor by Higher 3 Paths, arises state together with root eradicated by First Path by not-prenascence condition.

In the immaterial plane, dependent on one doubt-accompanied aggregate and delusion, arise three aggregates . . . (1)

(xi) Dependent on state together with root eradicated by First Path and together with root eradicated neither by First Path nor by Higher 3 Paths, arises state together with root eradicated neither by First Path nor by Higher 3 Paths by not-prenascence condition.

Dependent on aggregates together with root eradicated by First Path and great primaries, arises mind-produced matter; dependent on doubt-accompanied aggregates and delusion, arises mind-produced matter. (2)

(xii)–(xiii) Dependent on state together with root eradicated by Higher 3 Paths and together with root eradicated neither by First Path nor by Higher 3 Paths, arises state together with root eradicated by Higher 3 Paths by not-prenascence condition. (Do these two also.)

Not-postnascence, etc.

24. Dependent on state together with root eradicated by First Path, arises state together with root eradicated by First Path by not-postnascence condition . . . by not-repetition condition . . .

Not-kamma 7

25. (i) Dependent on state together with root eradicated by First Path, arises state together with root eradicated by First Path by not-kamma condition.

Dependent on aggregates together with root eradicated by First Path, arises volition together with root eradicated by First Path. (1)

(ii) Dependent on state together with root eradicated by Higher 3 Paths, arises state together with root eradicated by Higher 3 Paths by not-kamma condition.

Dependent on aggregates together with root eradicated by Higher 3

Paths, arises volition together with root eradicated by Higher 3 Paths. (1)

(iii) Dependent on state together with root eradicated neither by First Path nor by Higher 3 Paths, arises state together with root eradicated neither by First Path nor by Higher 3 Paths by not-kamma condition.

(*a*) Dependent on aggregates together with root eradicated neither by First Path nor by Higher 3 Paths, arises volition together with root eradicated neither by First Path nor by Higher 3 Paths;

(*b*) External ... nutriment-produced ... temperature-produced ... (1)

(iv) Dependent on state together with root eradicated neither by First Path nor by Higher 3 Paths, arises state together with root eradicated by First Path by not-kamma condition.

Dependent on doubt-accompanied delusion, arises associated volition. (2)

(v) Dependent on state together with root eradicated neither by First Path nor by Higher 3 Paths, arises state together with root eradicated by Higher 3 Paths by not-kamma condition.

Dependent on restlessness-accompanied delusion, arises associated volition. (3)

26. (vi) Dependent on state together with root eradicated by First Path and together with root eradicated neither by First Path nor by Higher 3 Paths, arises state together with root eradicated by First Path by not-kamma condition.

Dependent on doubt-accompanied aggregates and delusion, arises associated volition. (1)

(vii) Dependent on state together with root eradicated by Higher 3 Paths and together with root eradicated neither by First Path nor by Higher 3 Paths, arises state together with root eradicated by Higher 3 Paths by not-kamma condition.

Dependent on restlessness-accompanied aggregates and delusion, arises associated volition. (1)

Not-resultant 17

27. Dependent on state together with root eradicated by First Path, arises state together with root eradicated by First Path by not-resultant condition. (No conception.) . . .

Not-nutriment, etc.

28. Dependent on state together with root eradicated neither by First

Path nor by Higher 3 Paths, arises state together with root eradicated neither by First Path nor by Higher 3 Paths by not-nutriment condition. External . . . temperature-produced . . . non-percipient beings . . . by not-faculty condition. External . . . nutriment-produced . . . temperature-produced . . . non-percipient beings . . . dependent on great primaries, arises physical life-faculty . . . by not-jhāna condition. Five-fold consciousness . . . (Include great primaries.) . . . by not-path condition. One rootless aggregate together with root eradicated neither by First Path nor by Higher 3 Paths . . . non-percipient beings . . . by not-association condition . . .

Not-dissociation, etc.

29. (i) Dependent on state together with root eradicated by First Path, arises state together with root eradicated by First Path by not-dissociation condition.

In the immaterial plane, dependent on one aggregate together with root eradicated by First Path, arise three aggregates . . . (1)

(ii) Dependent on state together with root eradicated by First Path, arises state together with root eradicated neither by First Path nor by Higher 3 Paths by not-dissociation condition.

In the immaterial plane, dependent on doubt-accompanied aggregates, arises doubt-accompanied delusion. (2)

(iii) Dependent on state together with root eradicated by First Path, arise states together with root eradicated by First Path and together with root eradicated neither by First Path nor by Higher 3 Paths by not-dissociation condition.

In the immaterial plane, dependent on one doubt-accompanied aggregate, arise three aggregates and delusion . . . two aggregates . . . (3)

(iv)–(vi) Dependent on state together with root eradicated by Higher 3 Paths, arises state together with root eradicated by Higher 3 Paths by not-dissociation condition.

In the immaterial plane . . . Higher 3 Paths . . . three.

30. (vii) Dependent on state together with root eradicated neither by First Path nor by Higher 3 Paths, arises state together with root eradicated neither by First Path nor by Higher 3 Paths by not-dissociation condition.

(*a*) In the immaterial plane, dependent on one aggregate together with root eradicated neither by First Path nor by Higher 3 Paths, arise three aggregates . . . dependent on two aggregates, arise two aggregates;

(*b*) External . . . nutriment-produced . . . temperature-produced . . . non-percipient beings . . . (1)

(viii) Dependent on state together with root eradicated neither by First Path nor by Higher 3 Paths, arises state together with root eradicated by First Path by not-dissociation condition.

In the immaterial plane, dependent on doubt-accompanied delusion, arise associated aggregates. (2)

(ix) Dependent on state together with root eradicated neither by First Path nor by Higher 3 Paths, arises state together with root eradicated by Higher 3 Paths by not-dissociation condition.

In the immaterial plane, dependent on restlessness-accompanied delusion, arise associated aggregates. (3)

31. (x) Dependent on state together with root eradicated by First Path and together with root eradicated neither by First Path nor by Higher 3 Paths, arises state together with root eradicated by First Path by not-dissociation condition.

In the immaterial plane, dependent on one doubt-accompanied aggregate and delusion, arise three aggregates . . . two aggregates. (1)

(xi) Dependent on state together with root eradicated by Higher 3 Paths and together with root eradicated neither by First Path nor by Higher 3 Paths, arises state together with root eradicated by Higher 3 Paths by not-dissociation condition.

In the immaterial plane, dependent on one restlessness-accompanied aggregate and delusion, arise three aggregates . . . two aggregates.

. . . by not-absence condition . . . by not-disappearance condition . . .

2. CONDITIONS: NEGATIVE (ii) ENUMERATION CHAPTER

By Ones

32. With not-root 3, not-object 5, not-predominance 17, not-proximity 5, not-contiguity 5, not-mutuality 5, not-strong-dependence 5, not-prenascence 13, not-postnascence 17, not-repetition 17, not-kamma 7, not-resultant 17, not-nutriment 1, not-faculty 1, not-jhāna 1, not-path 1, not-association 5, not-dissociation 11, not-absence 5, not-disappearance 5. (Enumerate thus.)

End of Negative

3. CONDITIONS: POSITIVE-NEGATIVE

(Root By Twos)

33. With root condition, not-object 5, not-predominance 17, not-proximity 5, not-contiguity 5, not-mutuality 5, not-strong-dependence 5, not-prenascence 13, not-postnascence 17, not-repetition 17, not-kamma 7, not-resultant 17, not-association 5, not-dissociation 11, not-absence 5, not-disappearance 5. (Enumerate thus.)

End of Positive-Negative

4. CONDITIONS: NEGATIVE-POSITIVE

(Not-root By Twos)

34. With not-root condition, object 3, proximity 3, contiguity 3, conascence 3, mutuality 3, dependence 3, strong-dependence 3, prenascence 3, repetition 3, kamma 3, resultant 1, nutriment 3, faculty 3, jhāna 3, path 2, association 3, dissociation 3, presence 3, absence 3, disappearance 3, non-disappearance 3. (Enumerate thus.)

End of Negative-Positive

End of "DEPENDENT" CHAPTER

(The "Conascent" Chapter is the same as the "Dependent" Chapter.)

9. TRIPLET OF (STATE) TOGETHER WITH ROOT ERADICATED BY FIRST PATH III. "CONDITIONED" CHAPTER

1. CONDITIONS: POSITIVE (i) CLASSIFICATION CHAPTER

Root 17

35. (i)-(iii) Conditioned by state together with root eradicated by First Path, arises state together with root eradicated by First Path by root condition . . . three. (The same as in the "Dependent" Chapter.)

(iv)-(vi) Conditioned by state together with root eradicated by Higher 3 Paths . . . three. (The same as in the "Dependent" Chapter.)

(vii) Conditioned by state together with root eradicated neither by First Path nor by Higher 3 Paths . . . neither by First Path nor by Higher 3 Paths . . . One . . . (The same as in the "Dependent" Chapter.); conditioned by (heart-)base, arise aggregates together with root eradicated neither by First Path nor by Higher 3 Paths. (1)

(viii) Conditioned by state together with root eradicated neither by First Path nor by Higher 3 Paths, arises state together with root eradicated by First Path by root condition.

Conditioned by (heart-)base, arise aggregates together with root eradicated by First Path; conditioned by doubt-accompanied delusion, arise associated aggregates. (2)

(ix) Conditioned by state together with root eradicated neither by First Path nor by Higher 3 Paths, arises state together with root eradicated by Higher 3 Paths by root condition.

Conditioned by (heart-)base, arise aggregates together with root eradicated by Higher 3 Paths; conditioned by restlessness-accompanied delusion, arise associated aggregates. (3)

(x) Conditioned by state together with root eradicated neither by First Path nor by Higher 3 Paths, arise states together with root eradicated by First Path and together with root eradicated neither by First Path nor by Higher 3 Paths by root condition.

Conditioned by (heart-)base, arise aggregates together with root eradicated by First Path; conditioned by great primaries, arises mind-produced matter; conditioned by doubt-accompanied delusion, arise associated aggregates and mind-produced matter. (4)

(xi) Conditioned by state together with root eradicated neither by First Path nor by Higher 3 Paths, arise states together with root eradicated by Higher 3 Paths and together with root eradicated neither by First Path nor by Higher 3 Paths by root condition.

Conditioned by (heart-)base, arise aggregates together with root eradicated by Higher 3 Paths; conditioned by great primaries, arises mind-produced matter; conditioned by restlessness-accompanied delusion, arise associated aggregates and mind-produced matter. (5)

36. (xii) Conditioned by state together with root eradicated by First Path and together with root eradicated neither by First Path nor by Higher 3 Paths, arises state together with root eradicated by First Path by root condition.

Conditioned by one aggregate together with root eradicated by First Path and (heart-)base, arise three aggregates . . . two aggregates . . . conditioned by one doubt-accompanied aggregate and delusion, arise three aggregates . . . conditioned by two aggregates and delusion, arise two aggregates. (1)

(xiii) Conditioned by state together with root eradicated by First Path and together with root eradicated neither by First Path nor by Higher 3 Paths, arises state together with root eradicated neither by

First Path nor by Higher 3 Paths by root condition.

Conditioned by aggregates together with root eradicated by First Path and great primaries, arises mind-produced matter; conditioned by doubt-accompanied aggregates and delusion, arises mind-produced matter. (2)

(xiv) Conditioned by state together with root eradicated by First Path and together with root eradicated neither by First Path nor by Higher 3 Paths, arise states together with root eradicated by First Path and together with root eradicated neither by First Path nor by Higher 3 Paths by root condition.

Conditioned by one aggregate together with root eradicated by First Path and (heart-)base, arise three aggregates . . . conditioned by two aggregates and (heart-)base, arise two aggregates; conditioned by aggregates together with root eradicated by First Path and great primaries, arises mind-produced matter; conditioned by one doubt-accompanied aggregate and delusion, arise three aggregates and mind-produced matter . . . (3)

(xv)–(xvii) Conditioned by state together with root eradicated by Higher 3 Paths and together with root eradicated neither by First Path nor by Higher 3 Paths, arises state together with root eradicated by Higher 3 Paths by root condition . . . three.

Object 17

37. (i)–(iii) Conditioned by state together with root eradicated by First Path, arises state together with root eradicated by First Path by object condition . . . three. (The same as object condition in the "Dependent" Chapter.)

(iv)–(vi) Conditioned by state together with root eradicated by Higher 3 Paths . . . three. (The same as in the "Dependent" Chapter.)

38. (vii) Conditioned by state together with root eradicated neither by First Path nor by Higher 3 Paths, arises state together with root eradicated neither by First Path nor by Higher 3 Paths by object condition.

(*a*) Conditioned by one aggregate together with root eradicated neither by First Path nor by Higher 3 Paths, arise three aggregates . . . two aggregates;

(*b*) At the moment of conception . . . conditioned by (heart-)base, arise aggregates;

(*c*) Conditioned by eye-base, arises eye-consciousness . . . conditioned by body-base, arise body-consciousness; conditioned by (heart-)

base, arise aggregates together with root eradicated neither by First Path nor by Higher 3 Paths. (1)

(viii) Conditioned by state together with root eradicated neither by First Path nor by Higher 3 Paths, arises state together with root eradicated by First Path by object condition.

Conditioned by (heart-)base, arise aggregates together with root eradicated by First Path; conditioned by doubt-accompanied delusion, arise associated aggregates. (2)

(ix) Conditioned by state together with root eradicated neither by First Path nor by Higher 3 Paths, arises state together with root eradicated by Higher 3 Paths by object condition.

Conditioned by (heart-)base, arise aggregates together with root eradicated by Higher 3 Paths; conditioned by restlessness-accompanied delusion, arise associated aggregates. (3)

(x) Conditioned by state together with root eradicated neither by First Path nor by Higher 3 Paths, arise states together with root eradicated by First Path and together with root eradicated neither by First Path nor by Higher 3 Paths by object condition.

Conditioned by (heart-)base, arise doubt-accompanied aggregates and delusion. (4)

(xi) Conditioned by state together with root eradicated neither by First Path nor by Higher 3 Paths, arise states together with root eradicated by Higher 3 Paths and together with root eradicated neither by First Path nor by Higher 3 Paths by object condition.

Conditioned by (heart-)base, arise restlessness-accompanied aggregates and delusion. (5)

39. (xii) Conditioned by state together with root eradicated by First Path and together with root eradicated neither by First Path nor by Higher 3 Paths, arises state together with root eradicated by First Path by object condition.

Conditioned by one aggregate together with root eradicated by First Path and (heart-)base, arise three aggregates . . . two aggregates; conditioned by one doubt-accompanied aggregate and delusion, arise three aggregates . . . conditioned by two aggregates and delusion, arise two aggregates. (1)

(xiii) Conditioned by state together with root eradicated by First Path and together with root eradicated neither by First Path nor by Higher 3 Paths, arises state together with root eradicated neither by First Path nor by Higher 3 Paths by object condition.

Conditioned by doubt-accompanied aggregates and (heart-)base, arises doubt-accompanied delusion. (2)

(xiv) Conditioned by state together with root eradicated by First Path and together with root eradicated neither by First Path nor by Higher 3 Paths, arise states together with root eradicated by First Path and together with root eradicated neither by First Path nor by Higher 3 Paths by object condition.

Conditioned by one doubt-accompanied aggregate and (heart-)base, arise three aggregates and delusion . . . two aggregates and (heart-)base . . . (3)

40. (xv) Conditioned by state together with root eradicated by Higher 3 Paths and together with root eradicated neither by First Path nor by Higher 3 Paths, arises state together with root eradicated by Higher 3 Paths by object condition.

Conditioned by one aggregate together with root eradicated by Higher 3 Paths and (heart-)base, arise three aggregates . . . two aggregates; conditioned by one restlessness-accompanied aggregate and delusion, arise three aggregates . . . two aggregates. (1)

(xvi) Conditioned by state together with root eradicated by Higher 3 Paths and together with root eradicated neither by First Path nor by Higher 3 Paths, arises state together with root eradicated neither by First Path nor by Higher 3 Paths by object condition.

Conditioned by restlessness-accompanied aggregates and (heart-) base, arises restlessness-accompanied delusion. (2)

(xvii) Conditioned by state together with root eradicated by Higher 3 Paths and together with root eradicated neither by First Path nor by Higher 3 Paths, arise states together with root eradicated by Higher 3 Paths and together with root eradicated neither by First Path nor by Higher 3 Paths by object condition.

Conditioned by one restlessness-accompanied aggregate and (heart-) base, arise three aggregates and delusion . . . two aggregates . . . (3)

Predominance, etc. 17

41. (i)–(iii) Conditioned by state together with root eradicated by First Path, arises state together with root eradicated by First Path by predominance condition . . . three.

(iv)–(vi) Conditioned by state together with root eradicated by Higher 3 Paths . . . three.

(vii) Conditioned by state together with root eradicated neither by First Path nor by Higher 3 Paths, arises state together with root eradicated neither by First Path nor by Higher 3 Paths by predominance condition.

. . . one . . . conditioned by (heart-)base, arise aggregates together with root eradicated neither by First Path nor by Higher 3 Paths. (1)

(viii) Conditioned by state together with root eradicated neither by First Path nor by Higher 3 Paths, arises state together with root eradicated by First Path by predominance condition.

Conditioned by (heart-)base, arise aggregates together with root eradicated by First Path. (2)

(ix) Conditioned by state together with root eradicated neither by First Path nor by Higher 3 Paths, arises state together with root eradicated by Higher 3 Paths by predominance condition.

Conditioned by (heart-)base, arise aggregates together with root eradicated by Higher 3 Paths. (3)

(x) Conditioned by state together with root eradicated neither by First Path nor by Higher 3 Paths, arise states together with root eradicated by First Path and together with root eradicated neither by First Path nor by Higher 3 Paths by predominance condition.

Conditioned by (heart-)base, arise aggregates together with root eradicated by First Path; conditioned by great primaries, arises mind-produced matter. (4)

(xi) Conditioned by state together with root eradicated neither by First Path nor by Higher 3 Paths, arise states together with root eradicated by Higher 3 Paths and together with root eradicated neither by First Path nor by Higher 3 Paths by predominance condition.

Conditioned by (heart-)base, arise aggregates together with root eradicated by Higher 3 Paths; conditioned by great primaries, arises mind-produced matter. (5)

42. (xii) Conditioned by state together with root eradicated by First Path and together with root eradicated neither by First Path nor by Higher 3 Paths, arises state together with root eradicated by First Path by predominance condition.

Conditioned by one aggregate together with root eradicated by First Path and (heart-)base, arise three aggregates . . . two aggregates and . . . (1)

(xiii) Conditioned by state together with root eradicated by First Path and together with root eradicated neither by First Path nor by Higher 3 Paths, arises state together with root eradicated neither by

First Path nor by Higher 3 Paths by predominance condition.

Conditioned by aggregates together with root eradicated by First Path and great primaries, arises mind-produced matter. (2)

(xiv) Conditioned by state together with root eradicated by First Path and together with root eradicated neither by First Path nor by Higher 3 Paths, arise states together with root eradicated by First Path and together with root eradicated neither by First Path nor by Higher 3 Paths by predominance condition.

Conditioned by one aggregate together with root eradicated by First Path and (heart-)base, arise three aggregates . . . two aggregates and . . . conditioned by aggregates together with root eradicated by First Path and great primaries, arises mind-produced matter. (3)

(xv)–(xvii) Conditioned by state together with root eradicated by Higher 3 Paths and together with root eradicated neither by First Path nor by Higher 3 Paths, arises state together with root eradicated by Higher 3 Paths by predominance condition.

Conditioned by one aggregate together with root eradicated by Higher 3 Paths and (heart-)base, arise three aggregates . . . three. (Like First Path.)

. . . by proximity condition . . . by contiguity condition . . .

Conascence 17

43. (i) Conditioned by state together with root eradicated by First Path, arises state together with root eradicated by First Path by conascence condition.

Conditioned by one aggregate together with root eradicated by First Path, arise three aggregates . . . (1)

(ii) Conditioned by state together with root eradicated by First Path, arises state together with root eradicated neither by First Path nor by Higher 3 Paths by conascence condition.

Conditioned by aggregates together with root eradicated by First Path, arises mind-produced matter; conditioned by doubt-accompanied aggregates, arise doubt-accompanied delusion and mind-produced matter. (2)

(iii) Conditioned by state together with root eradicated by First Path, arise states together with root eradicated by First Path and together with root eradicated neither by First Path nor by Higher 3 Paths by conascence condition.

Conditioned by one aggregate together with root eradicated by First

Path, arise three aggregates and mind-produced matter . . . conditioned by one doubt-accompanied aggregate, arise three aggregates, delusion and mind-produced matter . . . two aggregates . . . (3)

(iv)–(vi) Conditioned by state together with root eradicated by Higher 3 Paths . . . three. (Abbreviated.) (Like First Path.)

44. (vii) Conditioned by state together with root eradicated neither by First Path nor by Higher 3 Paths, arises state together with root eradicated neither by First Path nor by Higher 3 Paths by conascence condition.

(*a*) Conditioned by one aggregate together with root eradicated neither by First Path nor by Higher 3 Paths, arise three aggregates and mind-produced matter . . . conditioned by doubt-accompanied or restlessness-accompanied delusion, arises mind-produced matter;

(*b*) At the moment of conception . . . conditioned by aggregates, arises (heart-)base; conditioned by (heart-)base, arise aggregates;

(*c*) Conditioned by one great primary, arise three great primaries . . . non-percipient beings . . .

(*d*) Conditioned by eye-base, arises eye-consciousness . . . conditioned by body-base, arises body-consciousness; conditioned by (heart-) base, arise aggregates together with root eradicated neither by First Path nor by Higher 3 Paths. (1)

(viii) Conditioned by state together with root eradicated neither by First Path nor by Higher 3 Paths, arises state together with root eradicated by First Path by conascence condition.

Conditioned by (heart-)base, arise aggregates together with root eradicated by First Path; conditioned by doubt-accompanied delusion, arise associated aggregates. (2)

(ix) Conditioned by state together with root eradicated neither by First Path nor by Higher 3 Paths, arises state together with root eradicated by Higher 3 Paths by conascence condition.

Conditioned by (heart-)base, arise aggregates together with root eradicated by Higher 3 Paths; conditioned by restlessness-accompanied delusion, arise associated aggregates. (3)

(x) Conditioned by state together with root eradicated neither by First Path nor by Higher 3 Paths, arise states together with root eradicated by First Path and together with root eradicated neither by First Path nor by Higher 3 Paths by conascence condition.

Conditioned by (heart-)base, arise aggregates together with roots eradicated by First Path; conditioned by great primaries, arises mind-produced matter; conditioned by doubt-accompanied delusion, arise associated aggregates and mind-produced matter; conditioned by (heart-) base, arise doubt-accompanied aggregates and delusion. (4)

(xi) Conditioned by state together with root eradicated neither by First Path nor by Higher 3 Paths, arise states together with root eradicated by Higher 3 Paths and together with root eradicated neither by First Path nor by Higher 3 Paths by conascence condition.

Conditioned by (heart-)base, arise aggregates together with root eradicated by Higher 3 Paths; conditioned by great primaries, arises mind-produced matter; conditioned by restlessness-accompanied delusion, arise associated aggregates and mind-produced matter; conditioned by (heart-)base, arise restlessness-accompanied aggregates and delusion. (5)

45. (xii) Conditioned by state together with root eradicated by First Path and together with root eradicated neither by First Path nor by Higher 3 Paths, arises state together with root eradicated by First Path by conascence condition.

Conditioned by one aggregate together with root eradicated by First Path and (heart-)base, arise three aggregates . . . conditioned by one doubt-accompanied aggregate and delusion, arise three aggregates . . . (1)

(xiii) Conditioned by state together with root eradicated by First Path and together with root eradicated neither by First Path nor by Higher 3 Paths, arises state together with root eradicated neither by First Path nor by Higher 3 Paths by conascence condition.

Conditioned by aggregates together with root eradicated by First Path and great primaries, arises mind-produced matter; conditioned by doubt-accompanied aggregates and delusion, arises mind-produced matter; conditioned by doubt-accompanied aggregates and (heart-)base, arises doubt-accompanied delusion. (2)

(xiv) Conditioned by state together with root eradicated by First Path and together with root eradicated neither by First Path nor by Higher 3 Paths, arise states together with root eradicated by First Path and together with root eradicated neither by First Path nor by Higher 3 Paths by conascence condition.

Conditioned by one aggregate together with root eradicated by First Path and (heart-)base, arise three aggregates . . . two aggregates . . . conditioned by aggregates together with roots eradicated by First Path and great primaries, arises mind-produced matter; conditioned by one doubt-accompanied aggregate and delusion, arise three aggregates and mind-produced matter . . . two aggregates . . . conditioned by one doubt-accompanied aggregate and (heart-)base, arise three aggregates and delusion . . . conditioned by two aggregates and (heart-)base, arise two aggregates and delusion. (3)

(xv)–(xvii) Conditioned by state together with root eradicated by Higher 3 Paths and together with root eradicated neither by First Path nor by Higher 3 Paths, arises state together with root eradicated by Higher 3 Paths by conascence condition . . . three.

Mutuality, etc.

46. Conditioned by state together with root eradicated by First Path, arises state together with root eradicated by First Path by mutuality condition . . . by dependence condition . . . by strong-dependence condition . . . by prenascence condition . . . by repetition condition . . . by kamma condition . . . by resultant condition . . . by nutriment condition . . . by faculty condition . . . by jhāna condition . . . by path condition . . . by association condition . . .

Dissociation 17

47. (i) Conditioned by state together with root eradicated by First Path, arises state together with root eradicated by First Path by dissociation condition.

Conditioned by one aggregate together with root eradicated by First Path, arise three aggregates . . . two aggregates; (conditioned by) (heart-) base, (arise) aggregates by dissociation condition. (1)

(ii) Conditioned by state together with root eradicated by First Path, arises state together with root eradicated neither by First Path nor by Higher 3 Paths by dissociation condition.

Conditioned by aggregates together with root eradicated by First Path, arises mind-produced matter; (conditioned by) aggregates, (arises mind-produced matter) by dissociation condition; conditioned by doubt-accompanied aggregates, arise delusion and mind-produced matter; (conditioned by) (heart-)base, arises delusion by dissociation condition; (conditioned by) aggregates, arises mind-produced matter by dissociation condition. (2)

(iii) Conditioned by state together with root eradicated by First Path, arise states together with root eradicated by First Path and together with root eradicated neither by First Path nor by Higher 3 Paths by dissociation condition.

Conditioned by one aggregate together with root eradicated by First Path, arise three aggregates and mind-produced matter . . . two aggregates . . . (conditioned by) (heart-)base, arise aggregates by dissociation condition; (conditioned by) aggregates, arises mind-produced matter by dissociation condition; conditioned by one doubt-accompanied aggregate, arise three aggregates, delusion and mind-produced matter . . . two aggregates . . . (conditioned by) (heart-)base, arise aggregates and delusion by dissociation condition; (conditioned by) aggregates, arises mind-produced matter by dissociation condition. (3)

(iv)-(vi) Conditioned by state together with root eradicated by Higher 3 Paths, arises state together with root eradicated by Higher 3 Paths by dissociation condition . . . three. (Like First Path.)

48. (vii) Conditioned by state together with root eradicated neither by First Path nor by Higher 3 Paths, arises state together with root eradicated neither by First Path nor by Higher 3 Paths by dissociation condition.

(*a*) Conditioned by one aggregate together with root eradicated neither by First Path nor by Higher 3 Paths, arise three aggregates and mind-produced matter . . . two aggregates . . . (conditioned by) (heart-) base, arise aggregates by dissociation condition; (conditioned by) aggregates, arises mind-produced matter by dissociation condition; conditioned by doubt-accompanied or restlessness-accompanied delusion, arises mind-produced matter; (conditioned by) delusion, (arises mind-produced matter) by dissociation condition;

(*b*) At the moment of conception . . . conditioned by aggregates, arises (heart-)base; conditioned by (heart-)base, arise aggregates; (conditioned by) (heart-)base, arise aggregates by dissociation condition; (conditioned by) aggregates, arises (heart-)base by dissociation condition;

(*c*) Conditioned by one great primary, arise three great primaries . . . conditioned by great primaries, arise mind-produced and kamma-produced derived matter; (conditioned by) aggregates, (arises mind-produced matter) by dissociation condition;

(*d*) Conditioned by eye-base, arises eye-consciousness . . . conditioned by body-base, arises body-consciousness; conditioned by (heart-) base, arise aggregates together with root eradicated neither by First Path nor by Higher 3 Paths. (1)

(viii) Conditioned by state together with root eradicated neither by First Path nor by Higher 3 Paths, arises state together with root eradicated by First Path by dissociation condition.

Conditioned by (heart-)base, arise aggregates together with root eradicated by First Path; (conditioned by) (heart-)base, (arise aggregates) by dissociation condition; conditioned by doubt-accompanied delusion, arise associated aggregates; (conditioned by) (heart-)base, (arise aggregates) by dissociation condition. (2)

(ix) Conditioned by state together with root eradicated neither by First Path nor by Higher 3 Paths, arises state together with root eradicated by Higher 3 Paths by dissociation condition.

Conditioned by (heart-)base, arise aggregates together with root eradicated by Higher 3 Paths; (conditioned by) (heart-)base, (arise aggregates) by dissociation condition; conditioned by restlessness-accompanied delusion, arise associated aggregates; (conditioned by) (heart-)base, (arise aggregates) by dissociation condition. (3)

(x) Conditioned by state together with root eradicated neither by First Path nor by Higher 3 Paths, arise states together with root eradicated by First Path and together with root eradicated neither by First Path nor by Higher 3 Paths by dissociation condition.

Conditioned by (heart-)base, arise aggregates together with root eradicated by First Path; conditioned by great primaries, arises mind-produced matter; (conditioned by) (heart-)base, arise aggregates by dissociation condition; (conditioned by) aggregates, arises mind-produced matter by dissociation condition; conditioned by doubt-accompanied delusion, arise associated aggregates and mind-produced matter; (conditioned by) (heart-)base, arise aggregates by dissociation condition; (conditioned by) delusion, arises mind-produced matter by dissociation condition; conditioned by (heart-)base, arise doubt-accompanied aggregates and delusion; (conditioned by) (heart-)base, (arise aggregates) by dissociation condition. (4)

(xi) Conditioned by state together with root eradicated neither by First Path nor by Higher 3 Paths, arise states together with root eradicated by Higher 3 Paths and together with root eradicated neither by First Path nor by Higher 3 Paths by dissociation condition.

Conditioned by (heart-)base, arise aggregates together with root eradicated by Higher 3 Paths . . . (Like First Path.) (5)

49. (xii) Conditioned by state together with root eradicated by First Path and together with root eradicated neither by First Path nor by Higher 3 Paths, arises state together with root eradicated by First Path by dissociation condition.

Conditioned by one aggregate together with root eradicated by First Path and (heart-)base, arise three aggregates . . . two aggregates . . . (conditioned by) (heart-)base, (arise aggregates) by dissociation condition; conditioned by one doubt-accompanied aggregate and delusion, arise three aggregates . . . two aggregates . . . (conditioned by) (heart-) base, (arise aggregates) by dissociation condition. (1)

(xiii) Conditioned by state together with root eradicated by First Path and together with root eradicated neither by First Path nor by Higher 3 Paths, arises state together with root eradicated neither by First Path nor by Higher 3 Paths by dissociation condition.

Conditioned by aggregates together with root eradicated by First Path and great primaries, arises mind-produced matter; (conditioned by) aggregates, (arises mind-produced matter) by dissociation condition; conditioned by doubt-accompanied aggregates and delusion, arises mind-produced matter; (conditioned by) aggregates and delusion, (arises mind-produced matter) by dissociation condition; conditioned by doubt-accompanied aggregates and (heart-)base, arises doubt-accompanied delusion; (conditioned by) (heart-)base, (arises delusion) by dissociation condition. (2)

(xiv) Conditioned by state together with root eradicated by First Path and together with root eradicated neither by First Path nor by Higher 3 Paths, arise states together with root eradicated by First Path and together with root eradicated neither by First Path nor by Higher 3 Paths by dissociation condition.

Conditioned by one aggregate together with root eradicated by First Path and (heart-)base, arise three aggregates . . . two aggregates . . . conditioned by aggregates together with root eradicated by First Path and great primaries, arises mind-produced matter; (conditioned by) (heart-)base, arise aggregates by dissociation condition; (conditioned by) aggregates, arises mind-produced matter by dissociation condition; conditioned by one doubt-accompanied aggregate and delusion, arise three aggregates and mind-produced matter . . . two aggregates and . . . (conditioned by) (heart-)base, arise aggregates by dissociation condition; (conditioned by) aggregates and delusion, arises mind-produced matter by dissociation condition; conditioned by one doubt-accompanied aggregate and (heart-) base, arise three aggregates and delusion . . . two aggregates and . . . (conditioned by) (heart-)base, (arise aggregates) by dissociation condition. (3)

(xv)–(xvii) . . . eradicated by Higher 3 Paths . . . three. (Like First Path.)

Presence, etc. 17.

50. Conditioned by state together with root eradicated by First Path, arises state together with root eradicated by First Path by presence condition . . . by absence condition . . . by disappearance condition . . . by non-disappearance condition . . .

1. CONDITIONS: POSITIVE (ii) ENUMERATION CHAPTER

By Ones

51. With root 17, object 17, predominance 17, proximity 17, contiguity 17, conascence 17, mutuality 17, dependence 17, strong-dependence 17, prenascence 17, repetition 17, kamma 17, resultant 1, nutriment 17, faculty 17, jhāna 17, path 17, association 17, dissociation 17, presence, 17, absence 17, disappearance 17, non-disappearance 17. (Enumerate thus.)

End of Positive

2. CONDITIONS: NEGATIVE (i) CLASSIFICATION CHAPTER

Not-root 5

52. (i) Conditioned by state together with root eradicated by First Path, arises state together with root eradicated neither by First Path nor by Higher 3 Paths by not-root condition.

Conditioned by doubt-accompanied aggregates, arises doubt-accompanied delusion. (1)

(ii) Conditioned by state together with root eradicated by Higher 3 Paths, arises state together with root eradicated neither by First Path nor by Higher 3 Paths by not-root condition.

Conditioned by restlessness-accompanied aggregates, arises restlessness-accompanied delusion. (1)

(iii) Conditioned by state together with root eradicated neither by First Path nor by Higher 3 Paths, arises state together with root eradicated neither by First Path nor by Higher 3 Paths by not-root condition.

(*a*) Conditioned by one rootless aggregate together with root eradicated neither by First Path nor by Higher 3 Paths, arise three aggregates and mind-produced matter . . .

(*b*) At the moment of rootless conception . . . (Complete.)

(*c*) Conditioned by eye-base, arises eye-consciousness . . . conditioned by body-base, arises body-consciousness; conditioned by (heart-)base, arise rootless aggregates together with root eradicated neither by First Path nor by Higher 3 Paths; conditioned by (heart-)base, arises doubt-accompanied or restlessness-accompanied delusion. (1)

53. (iv) Conditioned by state together with root eradicated by First Path and together with root eradicated neither by First Path nor by Higher 3 Paths, arises state together with root eradicated neither by First Path nor by Higher 3 Paths by not-root condition.

Conditioned by doubt-accompanied aggregates and (heart-)base, arises doubt-accompanied delusion. (1)

(v) Conditioned by state together with root eradicated by Higher 3 Paths and together with root eradicated neither by First Path nor by Higher 3 Paths, arises state together with root eradicated neither by First Path nor by Higher 3 Paths by not-root condition.

Conditioned by restlessness-accompanied aggregates and (heart-) base, arises restlessness-accompanied delusion. (1)

Not-object 5

54. (i) Conditioned by state together with root eradicated by First Path, arises state together with root eradicated neither by First Path nor by Higher 3 Paths by not-object condition.

Conditioned by aggregates together with root eradicated by First Path, arises mind-produced matter. (1)

(ii) Conditioned by state together with root eradicated by Higher 3 Paths, arises state together with root eradicated neither by First Path nor by Higher 3 Paths by not-object condition.

Conditioned by aggregates together with root eradicated by Higher 3 Paths, arises mind-produced matter. (1)

(iii) Conditioned by state together with root eradicated neither by First Path nor by Higher 3 Paths, arises state together with root eradicated neither by First Path nor by Higher 3 Paths by not-object condition.

(*a*) Conditioned by aggregates together with root eradicated neither by First Path nor by Higher 3 Paths, arises mind-produced matter;

(*b*) At the moment of conception, conditioned by aggregates together with root eradicated neither by First Path nor by Higher 3 Paths, arises kamma-produced matter; conditioned by aggregates, arises (heart-)base;

(*c*) One great primary . . . External . . . nutriment-produced . . . temperature-produced . . . non-percipient beings . . . (1)

55. (iv) Conditioned by state together with root eradicated by First Path and together with root eradicated neither by First Path nor by Higher 3 Paths, arises state together with root eradicated neither by First Path nor by Higher 3 Paths by not-object condition.

Conditioned by aggregates together with root eradicated by First Path and great primaries, arises mind-produced matter; conditioned by doubt-accompanied aggregates and delusion, arises mind-produced matter. (1)

(v) Conditioned by state together with root eradicated by Higher 3 Paths and together with root eradicated neither by First Path nor by Higher 3 Paths, arises state together with root eradicated neither by First Path nor by Higher 3 Paths by not-object condition.

Conditioned by aggregates together with root eradicated by Higher 3 Paths and great primaries, arises mind-produced matter; conditioned by restlessness-accompanied aggregates and delusion, arises mind-produced matter. (1)

Not-predominance, etc.

56. Conditioned by state together with root eradicated by First Path, arises state together with root eradicated by First Path by not-predominance condition. (The same as conascence.) . . . by not-proximity condition . . . by not-contiguity condition . . . by not-mutuality condition . . . by not-strong-dependence condition . . . by not-prenascence condition. (The same as Negative in the "Dependent" Chapter. 13 questions. No difference.) . . . by not-postnascence condition . . . by not-repetition condition . . .

Not-kamma 7

57. (i) Conditioned by state together with root eradicated by First Path, arises state together with root eradicated by First Path by not-kamma condition.

Conditioned by aggregates together with root eradicated by First Path, arises volition together with root eradicated by First Path. (1)

(ii) Conditioned by state together with root eradicated by Higher 3 Paths, arises state together with root eradicated by Higher 3 Paths by not-kamma condition.

Conditioned by aggregates together with root eradicated by Higher 3 Paths, arises volition together with root eradicated by Higher 3 Paths. (1)

(iii) Conditioned by state together with root eradicated neither by First Path nor by Higher 3 Paths, arises state together with root eradicated neither by First Path nor by Higher 3 Paths by not-kamma condition.

(*a*) Conditioned by aggregates together with root eradicated neither by First Path nor by Higher 3 Paths, arises volition together with root eradicated neither by First Path nor by Higher 3 Paths;

(*b*) External . . . nutriment-produced . . . temperature-produced . . .

(*c*) Conditioned by (heart-)base, arises volition together with root eradicated neither by First Path nor by Higher 3 Paths. (1)

(iv) Conditioned by state together with root eradicated neither by First Path nor by Higher 3 Paths, arises state together with root eradicated by First Path by not-kamma condition.

Conditioned by (heart-)base, arises volition together with root eradicated by First Path; conditioned by doubt-accompanied delusion, arises associated volition. (2)

(v) Conditioned by state together with root eradicated neither by First Path nor by Higher 3 Paths, arises state together with root eradicated by Higher 3 Paths by not-kamma condition.

Conditioned by (heart-)base, arises volition together with root eradicated by Higher 3 Paths; conditioned by restlessness-accompanied delusion, arises associated volition. (3)

58. (vi) Conditioned by state together with root eradicated by First Path and together with root eradicated neither by First Path nor by Higher 3 Paths, arises state together with root eradicated by First Path by not-kamma condition.

Conditioned by aggregates together with root eradicated by First Path and (heart-)base, arises volition together with root eradicated by First Path; conditioned by doubt-accompanied aggregates and delusion, arises associated volition. (1)

(vii) Conditioned by state together with root eradicated by Higher 3 Paths and together with root eradicated neither by First Path nor by Higher 3 Paths, arises state together with root eradicated by Higher 3 Paths by not-kamma condition.

Conditioned by aggregates together with root eradicated by Higher 3 Paths and (heart-)base, arises volition together with root eradicated by Higher 3 Paths; conditioned by restlessness-accompanied aggregates and delusion, arises associated volition. (1)

Not-resultant, etc.

59. Conditioned by state together with root eradicated by First Path, arises state together with root eradicated by First Path by not-resultant condition. (Complete; no conception.) . . . by not-nutriment condition. External . . . temperature-produced . . . non-percipient beings . . . by not-faculty condition. External . . . nutriment-produced . . . temperature-produced . . . non-percipient beings . . . conditioned by great primaries, arises physical life-faculty . . . by not-jhāna condition . . . one five-fold consciousness-accompanied aggregate . . . External . . . nutriment-produced . . . temperature-produced . . . non-percipient beings . . . by not-path condition . . . one rootless . . . by not-association condition . . . by not-dissociation condition. (The same as not-dissociation in Negative of the "Dependent" Chapter; no difference. 11) . . . by not-absence condition . . . by not-disappearance condition . . .

2. CONDITIONS: NEGATIVE (ii) ENUMERATION CHAPTER

(By Ones)

60. With not-root 5, not-object 5, not-predominance 17, not-proximity 5, not-contiguity 5, not-mutuality 5, not-strong-dependence 5, not-prenascence 13, not-postnascence 17, not-repetition 17, not-kamma 7, not-resultant 17, not-nutriment 1, not-faculty 1, not-jhāna 1, not-path 1, not-association 5, not-dissociation 11, not-absence 5, not-disappearance 5. (Enumerate thus.)

End of Negative

3. CONDITIONS: POSITIVE–NEGATIVE

Root By Twos

61. With root condition, not-object 5, not-predominance 17, not-proximity 5, not-contiguity 5, not-mutuality 5, not-strong-dependence 5, not-prenascence 13, not-postnascence 17, not-repetition 17, not-kamma 7, not-resultant 17, not-association 5, not-dissociation 11, not-absence 5, not-disappearance 5. (Enumerate thus.)

End of Positive–Negative

4. CONDITIONS: NEGATIVE–POSITIVE

Not-root By Twos

62. With not-root condition, object 5, proximity 5, contiguity 5,

conascence 5, mutuality 5, dependence 5, strong-dependence 5, prenascence 5, repetition 5, kamma 5, resultant 1, nutriment 5, faculty 5, jhāna 5, path 5, association 5, dissociation 5, presence 5, absence 5, disappearance 5, non-disappearance 5. (Enumerate thus.)

End of Negative–Positive

End of "CONDITIONED" CHAPTER

(The "Supported" Chapter is the same as the "Conditioned" Chapter.)

9. TRIPLET OF (STATE) TOGETHER WITH ROOT ERADICATED BY FIRST PATH V. "CONJOINED" CHAPTER

1. CONDITIONS: POSITIVE (i) CLASSIFICATION CHAPTER

Root 7

63. (i) Conjoined with state together with root eradicated by First Path, arises state together with root eradicated by First Path by root condition.

Conjoined with one aggregate together with root eradicated by First Path, arise three aggregates . . . conjoined with two aggregates, arise two aggregates. (1)

(ii) Conjoined with state together with root eradicated by Higher 3 Paths, arises state together with root eradicated by Higher 3 Paths by root condition.

Conjoined with one aggregate together with root eradicated by Higher 3 Paths, arise three aggregates . . . conjoined with two aggregates, arise two aggregates. (1)

(iii) Conjoined with state together with root eradicated neither by First Path nor by Higher 3 Paths, arises state together with root eradicated neither by First Path nor by Higher 3 Paths by root condition.

(*a*) Conjoined with one aggregate together with root eradicated neither by First Path nor by Higher 3 Paths, arise three aggregates . . .

(*b*) At the moment of conception . . . (1)

(iv) Conjoined with state together with root eradicated neither by First Path nor by Higher 3 Paths, arises state together with root eradicated by First Path by root condition.

Conjoined with doubt-accompanied delusion, arise associated aggregates. (2)

(v) Conjoined with state together with root eradicated neither by

First Path nor by Higher 3 Paths, arises state together with root eradicated by Higher 3 Paths by root condition.

Conjoined with restlessness-accompanied delusion, arise associated aggregates. (3)

64. (vi) Conjoined with state together with root eradicated by First Path and together with root eradicated neither by First Path nor by Higher 3 Paths, arises state together with root eradicated by First Path by root condition.

Conjoined with one doubt-accompanied aggregate and delusion, arise three aggregates . . . two aggregates. (1)

(vii) Conjoined with state together with root eradicated by Higher 3 Paths and together with root eradicated neither by First Path nor by Higher 3 Paths, arises state together with root eradicated by Higher 3 Paths by root condition.

Conjoined with one restlessness-accompanied aggregate and delusion, arise three aggregates . . . two aggregates. (1)

Object 11

65. (i) Conjoined with state together with root eradicated by First Path, arises state together with root eradicated by First Path by object condition.

Conjoined with one aggregate together with root eradicated by First Path, arise three aggregates . . . two aggregates. (1)

(ii) Conjoined with state together with root eradicated by First Path, arises state together with root eradicated neither by First Path nor by Higher 3 Paths by object condition.

Conjoined with doubt-accompanied aggregates, arises doubt-accompanied delusion. (2)

(iii) Conjoined with state together with root eradicated by First Path, arise states together with root eradicated by First Path and together with root eradicated neither by First Path nor by Higher 3 Paths by object condition.

Conjoined with one doubt-accompanied aggregate, arise three aggregates and delusion . . . two aggregates . . . (3)

(iv)-(vi) Conjoined with state together with root eradicated by Higher 3 Paths . . . three.

66. (vii) Conjoined with state together with root eradicated neither by First Path nor by Higher 3 Paths, arises state together with root eradicated neither by First Path nor by Higher 3 Paths by object condition.

(*a*) Conjoined with one aggregate together with root eradicated neither by First Path nor by Higher 3 Paths, arise three aggregates . . . conjoined with two aggregates, arise two aggregates;

(*b*) At the moment of conception . . . (1)

(viii) Conjoined with state together with root eradicated neither by First Path nor by Higher 3 Paths, arises state together with root eradicated by First Path by object condition.

Conjoined with doubt-accompanied delusion, arise associated aggregates. (2)

(ix) Conjoined with state together with root eradicated neither by First Path nor by Higher 3 Paths, arises state together with root eradicated by Higher 3 Paths by object condition.

Conjoined with restlessness-accompanied delusion, arise associated aggregates. (3)

(x) Conjoined with state together with root eradicated by First Path and together with root eradicated neither by First Path nor by Higher 3 Paths, arises state together with root eradicated by First Path by object condition.

Conjoined with one doubt-accompanied aggregate and delusion, arise three aggregates . . . conjoined with two aggregates and delusion, arise two aggregates. (1)

(ix) Conjoined with state together with root eradicated by Higher 3 Paths and together with root eradicated neither by First Path nor by Higher 3 Paths, arises state together with root eradicated by Higher 3 Paths by object condition.

Conjoined with one restlessness-accompanied aggregate and delusion, arise three aggregates . . . two aggregates. (1)

Predominance, etc.

67. (i) Conjoined with state together with root eradicated by First Path, arises state together with root eradicated by First Path by predominance condition.

Conjoined with one aggregate together with root eradicated by First Path, arise three aggregates . . . two aggregates. (1)

(ii) Conjoined with state together with root eradicated by Higher 3 Paths . . . one.

(iii) Conjoined with state together with root eradicated neither by First Path nor by Higher 3 Paths, arises state together with root eradicated neither by First Path nor by Higher 3 Paths by predominance condition.

Conjoined with one aggregate together with root eradicated neither by First Path nor by Higher 3 Paths, arise three aggregates . . . two aggregates . . . by proximity condition . . . by contiguity condition . . .

Conascence, etc.

68. Conjoined with state together with root eradicated by First Path, arises state together with root eradicated by First Path by conascence condition . . . by mutuality condition . . . by dependence condition . . . by strong-dependence condition . . . by prenascence condition . . . by repetition condition . . . by kamma condition . . . by resultant condition . . . by nutriment condition . . . by faculty condition . . . by jhāna condition . . . by path condition . . . by association condition . . . by dissociation condition . . . by presence condition . . . by absence condition . . . by disappearance condition . . . by non-disappearance condition . . .

1. CONDITIONS: POSITIVE (ii) ENUMERATION CHAPTER

(By Ones)

69. With root 7, object 11, predominance 3, proximity 11, contiguity 11, conascence 11, mutuality 11, dependence 11, strong-dependence 11, prenascence 11, repetition 11, kamma 11, resultant 1, nutriment 11, faculty 11, jhāna 11, path 11, association 11, dissociation 11, presence 11, absence 11, disappearance 11, non-disappearance 11. (Enumerate thus.)

End of Positive

2. CONDITIONS: NEGATIVE (i) CLASSIFICATION CHAPTER

Not-root 3

70. (i) Conjoined with state together with root eradicated by First Path, arises state together with root eradicated neither by First Path nor by Higher 3 Paths by not-root condition.

Conjoined with doubt-accompanied aggregates, arises doubt-accompanied delusion. (1)

(ii) Conjoined with state together with root eradicated by Higher 3 Paths, arises state together with root eradicated neither by First Path nor by Higher 3 Paths by not-root condition.

Conjoined with restlessness-accompanied aggregates, arises restlessness-accompanied delusion. (1)

(iii) Conjoined with state together with root eradicated neither by First Path nor by Higher 3 Paths, arises state together with root eradicated neither by First Path nor by Higher 3 Paths by not-root condition.

(*a*) Conjoined with one rootless aggregate together with root eradicated neither by First Path nor by Higher 3 Paths, arise three aggregates . . . conjoined with two aggregates, arise two aggregates;

(*b*) At the moment of rootless conception . . . (1)

Not-predominance, etc.

71. Conjoined with state together with root eradicated by First Path . . . by not-predominance condition. (The same as conascence.) . . . by not-prenascence condition . . . by not-postnascence condition . . . by not-repetition condition . . . by not-kamma condition . . . 7 . . . by not-resultant condition . . . by not-jhāna condition . . . by not-path condition . . . by not-dissociation condition . . .

2. CONDITIONS: NEGATIVE (ii) ENUMERATION CHAPTER

(By Ones)

72. With not-root 3, not predominance 11, not-prenascence 11, not-postnascence 11, not-repetition 11, not-kamma 7, not-resultant 11, not-jhāna 1, not-path 1, not-dissociation 11. (Enumerate thus.)

End of Negative

3. CONDITIONS: POSITIVE-NEGATIVE

(Root By Twos)

73. With root condition, not-predominance 7, not-prenascence 7, not-postnascence 7, not-repetition 7, not-kamma 7, not-resultant 7, not-dissociation 7. (Enumerate thus.)

End of Positive–Negative

4. CONDITIONS: NEGATIVE-POSITIVE

(Not-root By Twos)

74. With not-root condition, object 3, proximity 3, contiguity 3, conascence 3, mutuality 3, dependence 3, strong-dependence 3, prenascence 3, repetition 3, kamma 3, resultant 1, nutriment 3, faculty 3,

jhāna 3, path 2, association 3, dissociation 3, presence 3, absence 3, disappearance 3, non-disappearance 3. (Enumerate thus.)

End of Negative–Positive

End of "CONJOINED" CHAPTER

(The "Associated" Chapter is the same as the "Conjoined" Chapter.)

9. TRIPLET OF (STATE) TOGETHER WITH ROOT ERADICATED BY FIRST PATH VII. "INVESTIGATION" CHAPTER

1. CONDITIONS: POSITIVE (i) CLASSIFICATION CHAPTER

Root 11

75. (i) State together with root eradicated by First Path is related to state together with root eradicated by First Path by root condition.

Roots together with root eradicated by First Path are related to (their) associated aggregates by root condition. (1)

(ii) State together with root eradicated by First Path is related to state together with root eradicated neither by First Path nor by Higher 3 Paths by root condition.

Roots together with root eradicated by First Path are related to mind-produced matter by root condition. (2)

(iii) State together with root eradicated by First Path is related to state together with root eradicated by First Path and together with root eradicated neither by First Path nor by Higher 3 Paths by root condition.

Roots together with root eradicated by First Path are related to (their) associated aggregates and mind-produced matter by root condition. (3)

(iv)–(vi) State together with root eradicated by Higher 3 Paths . . . three.

76. (vii) State together with root eradicated neither by First Path nor by Higher 3 Paths is related to state together with root eradicated neither by First Path nor by Higher 3 Paths by root condition . . . (1)

(viii) State together with root eradicated neither by First Path nor by Higher 3 Paths is related to state together with root eradicated by First Path by root condition.

Doubt-accompanied delusion is related to (its) associated aggregates by root condition. (2)

(ix) State together with root eradicated neither by First Path nor by Higher 3 Paths is related to state together with root eradicated by Higher 3 Paths by root condition.

Restlessness-accompanied delusion is related to (its) associated aggregates by root condition. (3)

(x) State together with root eradicated neither by First Path nor by Higher 3 Paths is related to state together with root eradicated by First Path and together with root eradicated neither by First Path nor by Higher 3 Paths by root condition.

Doubt-accompanied delusion is related to (its) associated aggregates and mind-produced matter by root condition. (4)

(xi) State together with root eradicated neither by First Path nor by Higher 3 Paths is related to state together with root eradicated by Higher 3 Paths and together with root eradicated neither by First Path nor by Higher 3 Paths by root condition.

Restlessness-accompanied delusion is related to (its) associated aggregates and mind-produced matter by root condition. (5)

Object 21

77. (i) State together with root eradicated by First Path is related to state together with root eradicated by First Path by object condition.

(One) enjoys and delights in lust together with root eradicated by First Path. Taking it as object, arises lust together with root eradicated by First Path, arise wrong views, arises doubt, arises grief together with root eradicated by First Path. (One) enjoys and delights in wrong views. Taking them as object, arises lust together with root eradicated by First Path, arise wrong views, arises doubt, arises grief together with root eradicated by First Path. Taking doubt as object, arises doubt, arise wrong views, arises grief together with root eradicated by First Path. Taking grief together with root eradicated by First Path as object, arises grief together with root eradicated by First Path, arise wrong views, arises doubt. (1)

(ii) State together with root eradicated by First Path is related to state together with root eradicated neither by First Path nor by Higher 3 Paths by object condition.

The Noble persons review the eradicated defilements together with root eradicated by First Path, know the defilements addicted to before.

(They) . . . into the impermanence . . . of aggregates together with root eradicated by First Path.

By the knowledge of penetration into others' minds . . . Aggregates together with root eradicated by First Path are related to knowledge of penetration into others' minds, knowledge of remembrance of past existences, knowledge of rebirths according to one's kamma, knowledge of future existences, (mind-door) advertence and delusion by object condition. (2)

(iii) State together with root eradicated by First Path is related to state together with root eradicated by First Path and together with root eradicated neither by First Path nor by Higher 3 Paths by object condition.

Taking aggregates together with root eradicated by First Path as object, arise doubt-accompanied aggregates and delusion. (3)

78. (iv) State together with root eradicated by Higher 3 Paths is related to state together with root eradicated by Higher 3 Paths by object condition.

(One) enjoys and delights in lust together with root eradicated by Higher 3 Paths. Taking it as object, arises lust together with root eradicated by Higher 3 Paths, arises restlessness, arises grief together with root eradicated by Higher 3 Paths. Taking restlessness as object, arises restlessness, arises grief together with root eradicated by Higher 3 Paths. Taking grief together with root eradicated by Higher 3 Paths as object, arises grief together with root eradicated by Higher 3 Paths, arises restlessness. (1)

(v) State together with root eradicated by Higher 3 Paths is related to state together with root eradicated by First Path by object condition.

(One) enjoys and delights in lust together with root eradicated by Higher 3 Paths. Taking it as object, arises lust together with root eradicated by First Path, arise wrong views, arises doubt, arises grief together with root eradicated by First Path. Taking restlessness as object, arise wrong views, arises doubt, arises grief together with root eradicated by First Path. Taking grief together with root eradicated by Higher 3 Paths as object, arises grief together with root eradicated by First Path, arise wrong views, arises doubt. (2)

(vi) State together with root eradicated by Higher 3 Paths is related to state together with root eradicated neither by First Path nor by Higher 3 Paths by object condition.

The Noble persons review the eradicated defilements together with root eradicated by Higher 3 Paths, review the uneradicated defilements, know the defilements addicted to before.

(They) . . . into the impermanence . . . of aggregates together with root eradicated by Higher 3 Paths.

By the knowledge of penetration into others' minds . . . Aggregates together with root eradicated by Higher 3 Paths are related to knowledge of penetration into others' minds, knowledge of remembrance of past existences, knowledge of rebirths according to one's kamma, knowledge of future existences, advertence and delusion by object condition. (3)

(vii) State together with root eradicated by Higher 3 Paths is related to state together with root eradicated by First Path and together with root eradicated neither by First Path nor by Higher 3 Paths by object condition.

Taking aggregates together with root eradicated by Higher 3 Paths as object, arise doubt-accompanied aggregates and delusion. (4)

(viii) State together with root eradicated by Higher 3 Paths is related to state together with root eradicated by Higher 3 Paths and together with root eradicated neither by First Path nor by Higher 3 Paths by object condition.

Taking aggregates together with root eradicated by Higher 3 Paths as object, arise restlessness-accompanied aggregates and delusion. (5)

79. (ix) State together with root eradicated neither by First Path nor by Higher 3 Paths is related to state together with root eradicated neither by First Path nor by Higher 3 Paths by object condition.

After having offered an offering . . . [Expand. The same as First Path Triplet.] . . . advertence and delusion by object condition. (1)

(x) State together with root eradicated neither by First Path nor by Higher 3 Paths is related to state together with root eradicated by First Path by object condition.

After having offered an offering . . . (Similar to First Path Triplet.) (2)

(xi) State together with root eradicated neither by First Path nor by Higher 3 Paths is related to state together with root eradicated by Higher 3 Paths by object condition.

After having offered an offering . . . (Similar to First Path Triplet.) (3)

(xii) State together with root eradicated neither by First Path nor by Higher 3 Paths is related to state together with root eradicated by First Path and together with root eradicated neither by First Path nor by Higher 3 Paths by object condition.

Taking the eye as object, arise doubt-accompanied aggregates and delusion . . . ear . . . (heart-)base . . . Taking aggregates together with root eradicated neither by First Path nor by Higher 3 Paths as object, arise doubt-accompanied aggregates and delusion. (4)

(xiii) State together with root eradicated neither by First Path nor by Higher 3 Paths is related to state together with root eradicated by Higher 3 Paths and together with root eradicated neither by First Path nor by Higher 3 Paths by object condition.

The eye . . . (heart-)base . . . Taking aggregates together with root eradicated neither by First Path nor by Higher 3 Paths as object, arise restlessness-accompanied aggregates and delusion. (5)

80. (xiv) States together with root eradicated by First Path and together with root eradicated neither by First Path nor by Higher 3 Paths are related to state together with root eradicated by First Path by object condition.

Taking doubt-accompanied aggregates and delusion as object, arise aggregates together with root eradicated by First Path. (1)

(xv) States together with root eradicated by First Path and together with root eradicated neither by First Path nor by Higher 3 Paths are related to state together with root eradicated neither by First Path nor by Higher 3 Paths by object condition.

Taking doubt-accompanied aggregates and delusion as object, arise aggregates together with root eradicated neither by First Path nor by Higher 3 Paths and delusion. (2)

(xvi) States together with root eradicated by First Path and together with root eradicated neither by First Path nor by Higher 3 Paths are related to state together with root eradicated by First Path and together with root eradicated neither by First Path nor by Higher 3 Paths by object condition.

Taking doubt-accompanied aggregates and delusion as object, arise doubt-accompanied aggregates and delusion. (3)

81. (xvii) States together with root eradicated by Higher 3 Paths and together with root eradicated neither by First Path nor by Higher 3 Paths are related to state together with root eradicated by First Path by object condition.

Taking restlessness-accompanied aggregates and delusion as object, arise aggregates together with root eradicated by First Path. (1)

(xviii) States together with root eradicated by Higher 3 Paths and together with root eradicated neither by First Path nor by Higher 3 Paths are related to state together with root eradicated by Higher 3 Paths by object condition.

Taking restlessness-accompanied aggregates and delusion as object, arise aggregates together with root eradicated by Higher 3 Paths. (2)

(xix) States together with root eradicated by Higher 3 Paths and together with root eradicated neither by First Path nor by Higher 3 Paths are related to state together with root eradicated neither by

First Path nor by Higher 3 Paths by object condition.

Taking restlessness-accompanied aggregates and delusion as object, arise aggregates together with root eradicated neither by First Path nor by Higher 3 Paths and delusion. (3)

(xx) States together with root eradicated by Higher 3 Paths and together with root eradicated neither by First Path nor by Higher 3 Paths are related to state together with root eradicated by First Path and together with root eradicated neither by First Path nor by Higher 3 Paths by object condition.

Taking restlessness-accompanied aggregates and delusion as object, arise doubt-accompanied aggregates and delusion. (4)

(xxi) States together with root eradicated by Higher 3 Paths and together with root eradicated neither by First Path nor by Higher 3 Paths are related to state together with root eradicated by Higher 3 Paths and together with root eradicated neither by First Path nor by Higher 3 Paths by object condition.

Taking restlessness-accompanied aggregates and delusion as object, arise restlessness-accompanied aggregates and delusion. (5)

Predominance 10

82. State together with root eradicated by First Path is related to state together with root eradicated by First Path by predominance condition. (The same as First Path Triplet; 10 questions.)

Proximity 17

83. (i) State together with root eradicated by First Path is related to state together with root eradicated by First Path by proximity condition.

Preceding aggregates together with root eradicated by First Path are related to subsequent aggregates together with root eradicated by First Path by proximity condition. (1)

(ii) State together with root eradicated by First Path is related to state together with root eradicated neither by First Path nor by Higher 3 Paths by proximity condition.

Preceding doubt-accompanied aggregates are related to subsequent delusion by proximity condition. Aggregates together with root eradicated by First Path are related to emergence by proximity condition. (2)

(iii) State together with root eradicated by First Path is related to state together with root eradicated by First Path and together with root eradicated neither by First Path nor by Higher 3 Paths by proximity condition.

Preceding doubt-accompanied aggregates are related to subsequent doubt-accompanied aggregates and delusion by proximity condition. (3)

84. (iv) State together with root eradicated by Higher 3 Paths is related to state together with root eradicated by Higher 3 Paths by proximity condition.

Preceding aggregates together with root eradicated by Higher 3 Paths are related to subsequent aggregates together with root eradicated by Higher 3 Paths by proximity condition. (1)

(v) State together with root eradicated by Higher 3 Paths is related to state together with root eradicated neither by First Path nor by Higher 3 Paths by proximity condition.

Preceding restlessness-accompanied aggregates are related to subsequent delusion by proximity condition. Aggregates together with root eradicated by Higher 3 Paths are related to emergence by proximity condition. (2)

(vi) State together with root eradicated by Higher 3 Paths is related to state together with root eradicated by Higher 3 Paths and together with root eradicated neither by First Path nor by Higher 3 Paths by proximity condition.

Preceding restlessness-accompanied aggregates are related to subsequent restlessness-accompanied aggregates and delusion by proximity condition. (3)

85. (vii) State together with root eradicated neither by First Path nor by Higher 3 Paths is related to state together with root eradicated neither by First Path nor by Higher 3 Paths by proximity condition.

Preceding doubt-accompanied or restlessness-accompanied delusion is related to subsequent doubt-accompanied or restlessness-accompanied delusion by proximity condition. Preceding aggregates together with root eradicated neither by First Path nor by Higher 3 Paths are related to subsequent aggregates together with root eradicated neither by First Path nor by Higher 3 Paths by proximity condition. Adaptation to change-of-lineage; adaptation to purification . . . For one emerging from the attainment of Extinction, neither-perception-nor-non-perception is related to the attainment of Fruition by proximity condition. (1)

(viii) State together with root eradicated neither by First Path nor by Higher 3 Paths is related to state together with root eradicated by First Path by proximity condition.

Preceding doubt-accompanied delusion is related to subsequent doubt-accompanied aggregates by proximity condition. Advertence is related to aggregates together with root eradicated by First Path by proximity condition. (2)

(ix) State together with root eradicated neither by First Path nor by Higher 3 Paths is related to state together with root eradicated by Higher 3 Paths by proximity condition.

Preceding restlessness-accompanied delusion is related to subsequent restlessness-accompanied aggregates by proximity condition. Advertence is related to aggregates together with root eradicated by Higher 3 Paths by proximity condition. (3)

(x) State together with root eradicated neither by First Path nor by Higher 3 Paths is related to state together with root eradicated by First Path and together with root eradicated neither by First Path nor by Higher 3 Paths by proximity condition.

Preceding doubt-accompanied delusion is related to subsequent doubt-accompanied aggregates and delusion by proximity condition. Advertence is related to doubt-accompanied aggregates and delusion by proximity condition. (4)

(xi) State together with root eradicated neither by First Path nor by Higher 3 Paths is related to state together with root eradicated by Higher 3 Paths and together with root eradicated neither by First Path nor by Higher 3 Paths by proximity condition.

Preceding restlessness-accompanied delusion is related to subsequent restlessness-accompanied aggregates and delusion by proximity condition. Advertence is related to restlessness-accompanied aggregates and delusion by proximity condition. (5)

86. (xii) States together with root eradicated by First Path and together with root eradicated neither by First Path nor by Higher 3 Paths are related to state together with root eradicated by First Path by proximity condition.

Preceding doubt-accompanied aggregates and delusion are related to subsequent doubt-accompanied aggregates by proximity condition. (1)

(xiii) States together with root eradicated by First Path and together with root eradicated neither by First Path nor by Higher 3 Paths are related to state together with root eradicated neither by First Path nor by Higher 3 Paths by proximity condition.

Preceding doubt-accompanied aggregates and delusion are related to subsequent delusion by proximity condition. Doubt-accompanied aggregates and delusion are related to emergence by proximity condition. (2)

(xiv) States together with root eradicated by First Path and together with root eradicated neither by First Path nor by Higher 3 Paths are related to state together with root eradicated by First Path and together with root eradicated neither by First Path nor by Higher 3 Paths by proximity condition.

Preceding doubt-accompanied aggregates and delusion are related to subsequent doubt-accompanied aggregates and delusion by proximity condition. (3)

(xv)–(xvii) States together with root eradicated by Higher 3 Paths and together with root eradicated neither by First Path nor by Higher 3 Paths are related to state together with root eradicated by Higher 3 Paths by proximity condition . . . three. (Proceed like First Path.)

Contiguity, etc.

87. State together with root eradicated by First Path is related to state together with root eradicated by First Path by contiguity condition. (The same as proximity.) . . . by conascence condition. (Abbreviated. The same as conascence in the "Dependent" Chapter.) . . . by mutuality condition. (Abbreviated. The same as mutuality in the "Dependent" Chapter.) . . . by dependence condition. (Abbreviated. The same as supported in the "Conditioned" Chapter. No separate combination.) . . .

Strong-dependence 21

88. (i) State together with root eradicated by First Path is related to state together with root eradicated by First Path by strong-dependence condition.

(It is of three kinds, namely:) (*a*) object-strong-dependence, (*b*) proximity-strong dependence, (*c*) natural strong-dependence . . .

(*c*) *Natural strong-dependence:* By the strong-dependence of lust together with root eradicated by First Path, (one) kills a living being . . . causes schism in the Saṅgha . . . hate together with root eradicated by First Path . . . delusion . . . wrong views . . . By the strong-dependence of wish, (one) kills a living being . . . causes schism in the Saṅgha. Lust together with root eradicated by First Path, hate, delusion, wrong views, wish is related to lust together with root eradicated by First Path . . . wish by strong-dependence condition. (1)

(ii) State together with root eradicated by First Path is related to state together with root eradicated neither by First Path nor by Higher 3 Paths by strong-dependence condition.

(It is of two kinds, namely:) (*a*) proximity-strong-dependence, (*b*) natural strong-dependence . . .

(*b*) *Natural strong-dependence:* By the strong-dependence of lust together with root eradicated by First Path, (one) offers an offering . . . develops attainment . . . hate together with root eradicated by First Path . . . delusion . . . wrong views . . . By the strong-dependence of wish, (one) offers an offering . . . develops attainment. Lust together with root eradicated by First Path . . . wish is related to confidence . . . wisdom, bodily happiness, bodily pain, the attainment of Fruition and delusion by strong-dependence condition. (2)

(iii) State together with root eradicated by First Path is related to state together with root eradicated by First Path and together with root eradicated neither by First Path nor by Higher 3 Paths by strong-dependence condition.

(It is of two kinds, namely:) (*a*) proximity-strong-dependence, (*b*) natural strong-dependence . . .

(*b*) *Natural strong-dependence:* Lust together with root eradicated by First Path, hate, delusion, wrong views, wish is related to doubt-accompanied aggregates and delusion by strong-dependence condition. (3)

89. (iv) State together with root eradicated by Higher 3 Paths is related to state together with root eradicated by Higher 3 Paths by strong-dependence condition.

(It is of three kinds, namely:) (*a*) object-strong-dependence, (*b*) proximity-strong-dependence, (*c*) natural strong-dependence . . .

(*c*) *Natural strong-dependence:* Lust together with root eradicated by Higher 3 Paths, hate, delusion, conceit, wish is related to lust together with root eradicated by Higher 3 Paths, hate, delusion, conceit, wish by strong-dependence condition. (1)

(v) State together with root eradicated by Higher 3 Paths is related to state together with root eradicated by First Path by strong-dependence condition.

(It is of two kinds, namely:) (*a*) object-strong-dependence, (*b*) natural strong-dependence . . .

(*b*) *Natural strong-dependence:* By the strong-dependence of lust together with root eradicated by Higher 3 Paths, (one) kills a living being . . . causes schism in the Saṅgha . . . hate together with root eradicated by Higher 3 Paths . . . delusion . . . conceit . . . By the strong-dependence of wish, (one) kills a living being . . . cause schism in the Saṅgha. Lust together with root eradicated by Higher 3 Paths . . . wish is related to lust together with root eradicated by First Path, hate, delusion, wrong views, wish by strong-dependence condition. Lustful desire for one's own property is related to lustful desire for others' property by strong-dependence condition. Lustful desire for one's own possessions is related to lustful desire for others' possessions by strong-dependence condition. (2)

(vi) State together with root eradicated by Higher 3 Paths is related to state together with root eradicated neither by First Path nor by Higher 3 Paths by strong-dependence condition.

(It is of two kinds, namely:) (*a*) proximity-strong-dependence, (*b*) natural strong-dependence . . .

(*b*) *Natural strong-dependence:* By strong-dependence of lust together with root eradicated by Higher 3 Paths, (one) offers an offering . . . develops attainment . . . hate together with root eradicated by Higher 3 Paths . . . delusion . . . conceit . . . By the strong-dependence of wish, (one) offers an offering . . . develops attainment. Lust together with root eradicated by Higher 3 Paths . . . wish is related to confidence . . . wisdom, bodily happiness, bodily pain, the attainment of Fruition and delusion by strong-dependence condition. (3)

(vii) State together with root eradicated by Higher 3 Paths is related to state together with root eradicated by First Path and together with root eradicated neither by First Path nor by Higher 3 Paths by strong-dependence condition.

Natural strong-dependence: Lust together with root eradicated by Higher 3 Paths . . . wish is related to doubt-accompanied aggregates and delusion by strong-dependence condition. (4)

(viii) State together with root eradicated by Higher 3 Paths is related to state together with root eradicated by Higher 3 Paths and together with root eradicated neither by First Path nor by Higher 3 Paths by strong-dependence condition.

(It is of two kinds, namely:) (*a*) proximity-strong-dependence, (*b*) natural strong-dependence . . .

(*b*) *Natural strong-dependence:* Lust together with root eradicated by Higher 3 Paths . . . wish is related to restlessness-accompanied aggregates and delusion by strong-dependence condition. (5)

90. (ix) State together with root eradicated neither by First Path nor

by Higher 3 Paths is related to state together with root eradicated neither by First Path nor by Higher 3 Paths by strong-depedence condition.

(It is of three kinds, namely:) (*a*) object-strong-dependence, (*b*) proximity-strong-dependence, (*c*) natural strong-dependence . . .

(*c*) *Natural strong-dependence:* By the strong-dependence of confidence, (one) offers an offering . . . develops attainment . . . precept . . . wisdom . . . bodily happiness . . . bodily pain . . . temperature . . . food . . . lodging-place . . . By the strong-dependence of delusion, (one) offers an offering . . . Confidence . . . delusion is related to confidence . . . the attainment of Fruition and delusion by strong-dependence condition. (1)

(x) State together with root eradicated neither by First Path nor by Higher 3 Paths is related to state together with root eradicated by First Path by strong-dependence condition.

(It is of three kinds, namely:) (*a*) object-strong-dependence, (*b*) proximity-strong-dependence, (*c*) natural strong-dependence . . .

(*c*) *Natural strong-dependence:* By the strong-dependence of confidence, (one) adopts wrong views . . . precept . . . wisdom . . . bodily happiness . . . bodily pain . . . lodging-place . . . By the strong-dependence of delusion, (one) kills a living being . . . causes schism in the Saṅgha. Confidence . . . lodging-place and delusion is related to lust together with root eradicated by First Path . . . wish by strong-dependence condition. (2)

(xi) State together with root eradicated neither by First Path nor by Higher 3 Paths is related to state together with root eradicated by Higher 3 Paths by strong-dependence condition.

(It is of three kinds: namely:) (*a*) object-strong-dependence, (*b*) proximity-strong-dependence, (*c*) natural strong-dependence . . .

(*c*) *Natural strong-dependence:* By the strong-dependence of confidence, (one) arouses conceit . . . By the strong-dependence of delusion, (one) arouses conceit. Confidence . . . lodging-place and delusion is related to lust together with root eradicated by Higher 3 Paths . . . wish by strong-dependence condition. (3)

(xii) State together with root eradicated neither by First Path nor by Higher 3 Paths is related to state together with root eradicated by First Path and together with root eradicated neither by First Path nor by Higher 3 Paths by strong-dependence condition.

(It is of two kinds, namely:) (*a*) proximity-strong-dependence, (*b*) natural strong-dependence . . .

(*b*) *Natural strong-dependence:* Confidence . . . wisdom, bodily happiness, bodily pain . . . lodging-place and delusion is related to doubt-accompanied aggregates and delusion by strong-dependence condition. (4)

(xiii) State together with root eradicated neither by First Path nor by Higher 3 Paths is related to state together with root eradicated by Higher 3 Paths and together with root eradicated neither by First Path nor by Higher 3 Paths by strong-dependence condition.

(It is of two kinds, namely:) (*a*) proximity-strong-dependence, (*b*) natural strong-dependence . . .

(*b*) *Natural strong-dependence:* Confidence . . . lodging-place and delusion is related to restlessness-accompanied aggregates and delusion by strong-dependence condition. (5)

91. (xiv) States together with root eradicated by First Path and together with root eradicated neither by First Path nor by Higher 3 Paths are related to state together with root eradicated by First Path by strong-dependence condition.

(It is of two kinds, namely:) (*a*) proximity-strong-dependence, (*b*) natural strong-dependence . . .

(*b*) *Natural strong-dependence:* Doubt-accompanied aggregates and delusion are related to lust together with root eradicated by First Path . . . wish by strong-dependence condition. (1)

(xv) States together with root eradicated by First Path and together with root eradicated neither by First Path nor by Higher 3 Paths are related to state together with root eradicated neither by First Path nor by Higher 3 Paths by strong-dependence condition.

(It is of two kinds, namely:) (*a*) proximity-strong-dependence, (*b*) natural strong-dependence . . .

(*b*) *Natural strong-dependence:* Doubt-accompanied aggregates and delusion are related to confidence . . . wisdom, bodily happiness, bodily pain, the attainment of Fruition and delusion by strong-dependence condition. (2)

(xvi) States together with root eradicated by First Path and together with root eradicated neither by First Path nor by Higher 3 Paths are related to state together with root eradicated by First Path and together with root eradicated neither by First Path nor by Higher 3 Paths by strong-dependence condition.

(It is of two kinds, namely:) (*a*) proximity-strong-dependence, (*b*) natural strong-dependence . . .

(*b*) *Natural strong-dependence:* Doubt-accompanied aggregates and delusion are related to doubt-accompanied aggregates and delusion by strong-dependence condition. (3)

92. (xvii) States together with root eradicated by Higher 3 Paths and together with root eradicated neither by First Path nor by Higher 3 Paths are related to state together with root eradicated by First Path by strong-dependence condition.

Natural strong-dependence: Restlessness-accompanied aggregates and delusion are related to lust together with root eradicated by First Path . . . wish by strong-dependence condition. (1)

(xviii) States together with root eradicated by Higher 3 Paths and together with root eradicated neither by First Path nor by Higher 3 Paths are related to state together with root eradicated by Higher 3 Paths by strong-dependence condition.

(It is of two kinds, namely:) (*a*) proximity-strong-dependence, (*b*) natural strong-dependence . . .

(*b*) *Natural strong-dependence:* Restlessness-accompanied aggregates and delusion are related to lust together with root eradicated by Higher 3 Paths . . . wish by strong-dependence condition. (2)

(xix) States together with root eradicated by Higher 3 Paths and together with root eradicated neither by First Path nor by Higher 3 Paths are related to state together with root eradicated neither by First Path nor by Higher 3 Paths by strong-dependence condition.

(It is of two kinds, namely:) (*a*) proximity-strong-dependence, (*b*) natural strong-dependence . . .

(*b*) *Natural strong-dependence:* Restlessness-accompanied aggregates and delusion are related to confidence . . . the attainment of Fruition and delusion by strong-dependence condition. (3)

(xx) States together with root eradicated by Higher 3 Paths and together with root eradicated neither by First Path nor by Higher 3 Paths are related to state together with root eradicated by First Path and together with root eradicated neither by First Path nor by Higher 3 Paths by strong-dependence condition.

Natural strong-dependence: Restlessness-accompanied aggregates and delusion are related to doubt-accompanied aggregates and delusion by strong-dependence condition. (4)

(xxi) States together with root eradicated by Higher 3 Paths and together with root eradicated neither by First Path nor by Higher 3 Paths are related to state together with root eradicated by Higher 3

Paths and together with root eradicated neither by First Path nor by Higher 3 Paths by strong-dependence condition.

(It is of two kinds, namely:) (*a*) proximity-strong-dependence, (*b*) natural strong-dependence . . .

(*b*) *Natural strong-dependence:* Restlessness-accompanied aggregates and delusion are related to restlessness-accompanied aggregates and delusion by strong-dependence condition. (5)

Prenascence 5

93. (i) State together with root eradicated neither by First Path nor by Higher 3 Paths is related to state together with root eradicated neither by First Path nor by Higher 3 Paths by prenascence condition.

(It is of two kinds, namely:) (*a*) object-prenascence, (*b*) base-prenascence.

(*a*) *Object-prenascence:* (One) practises insight into the impermanence . . . of the eye . . . ear . . . (One) practises insight into the impermanence . . . of the (heart-)base. By the power of divine-eye, (one) sees a visible object. By the power of divine-ear element, (one) hears a sound. Visible object-base to eye-consciousness . . . tangible object-base is related to body-consciousness by prenascence condition.

(*b*) *Base-prenascence:* Eye-base to eye-consciousness . . . body-base to body-consciousness . . . (heart-)base is related to aggregates together with root eradicated neither by First Path nor by Higher 3 Paths and delusion by prenascence condition. (1)

(ii) State together with root eradicated neither by First Path nor by Higher 3 Paths is related to state together with root eradicated by First Path by prenascence condition.

(It is of two kinds, namely:) (*a*) object-prenascence, (*b*) base-prenascence.

(*a*) *Object-prenascence:* Eye . . . (One) enjoys and delights in the (heart-)base. Taking it as object, (arises) lust together with root eradicated by First Path . . . wrong views . . . doubt, arises grief together with root eradicated by First Path.

(*b*) *Base-prenascence:* (Heart-)base is related to aggregates together with root eradicated by First Path by prenascence condition. (2)

(iii) State together with root eradicated neither by First Path nor by Higher 3 Paths is related to state together with root eradicated by Higher 3 Paths by prenascence condition.

(It is of two kinds, namely:) (*a*) object-prenascence, (*b*) base-prenascence.

(*a*) *Object-prenascence:* Eye . . . (One) enjoys and delights in the (heart-)base. Taking it as object, arises lust together with root eradicated by Higher 3 Paths, arises restlessness, arises grief together with root eradicated by Higher 3 Paths.

(*b*) *Base-prenascence:* (Heart-)base is related to aggregates together with root eradicated by Higher 3 Paths by prenascence condition. (3)

(iv) State together with root eradicated neither by First Path nor by Higher 3 Paths is related to state together with root eradicated by First Path and together with root eradicated neither by First Path nor by Higher 3 Paths by prenascence condition.

(It is of two kinds, namely:) (*a*) object-prenascence, (*b*) base-prenascence.

(*a*) *Object-prenascence:* Eye . . . Taking (heart-)base as object, arise doubt-accompanied aggregates and delusion.

(*b*) *Base-prenascence:* (Heart-)base is related to doubt-accompanied aggregates and delusion by prenascence condition. (4)

(v) State together with root eradicated neither by First Path nor by Higher 3 Paths is related to state together with root eradicated by Higher 3 Paths and together with root eradicated neither by First Path nor by Higher 3 Paths by prenascence condition.

(It is of two kinds, namely:) (*a*) object-prenascence, (*b*) base-prenascence.

(*a*) *Object-prenascence:* Eye . . . Taking (heart-)base as object, arise restlessness-accompanied aggregates and delusion.

(*b*) *Base-prenascence:* (Heart-)base is related to restlessness-accompanied aggregates and delusion by prenascence condition. (5)

Postnascence 5

94. (i) State together with root eradicated by First Path is related to state together with root eradicated neither by First Path nor by Higher 3 Paths by postnascence condition.

Postnascent aggregates together with root eradicated by First Path are related to this prenascent body by postnascence condition. (1)

(ii) State together with root eradicated by Higher 3 Paths is related to state together with root eradicated neither by First Path nor by Higher 3 Paths by postnascence condition.

Postnascent aggregates together with root eradicated by Higher 3 Paths are related to this prenascent body by postnascence condition. (1)

(iii) State together with root eradicated neither by First Path nor by Higher 3 Paths is related to state together with root eradicated neither by First Path nor by Higher 3 Paths by postnascence condition.

Postnascent aggregates together with root eradicated neither by First Path nor by Higher 3 Paths are related to this prenascent body by postnascence condition. (1)

(iv) States together with root eradicated by First Path and together with root eradicated neither by First Path nor by Higher 3 Paths are related to state together with root eradicated neither by First Path nor by Higher 3 Paths by postnascence condition.

Postnascent doubt-accompanied aggregates and delusion are related to this prenascence body by postnascence condition. (1)

(v) States together with root eradicated by Higher 3 Paths and together with root eradicated neither by First Path nor by Higher 3 Paths are related to state together with root eradicated neither by First Path nor by Higher 3 Paths by postnascence condition.

Postnascent restlessness-accompanied aggregates and delusion are related to this prenascent body by postnascence condition. (1)

Repetition 17

95. (i) State together with root eradicated by First Path is related to state together with root eradicated by First Path by repetition condition.

Preceding aggregates together with root eradicated by First Path are related to subsequent aggregates together with root eradicated by First Path by repetition condition. (1)

(ii) State together with root eradicated by First Path is related to state together with root eradicated neither by First Path nor by Higher 3 Paths by repetition condition.

Preceding doubt-accompanied aggregates are related to subsequent delusion by repetition condition. (2)

(iii) State together with root eradicated by First Path is related to state together with root eradicated by First Path and together with root eradicated neither by First Path nor by Higher 3 Paths by repetition condition.

Preceding doubt-accompanied aggregates are related to subsequent doubt-accompanied aggregates and delusion by repetition condition. (3)

(iv)–(vi) State together with root eradicated by Higher 3 Paths to state together with root eradicated by Higher 3 Paths . . . (Abbreviated.) three.

(vii)–(xvii) State together with root eradicated neither by First Path nor by Higher 3 Paths . . . (In repetition as reference, exclude emergence as well as advertence; 17 questions are to be completed; the same as proximity.)

Kamma 7

96. (i) State together with root eradicated by First Path is related to state together with root eradicated by First Path by kamma condition.

Volition together with root eradicated by First Path is related to (its) associated aggregates by kamma condition. (1)

(ii) State together with root eradicated by First Path is related to state together with root eradicated neither by First Path nor by Higher 3 Paths by kamma condition.

(It is of two kinds, namely:) (*a*) conascence(-kamma), (*b*) asynchronous (kamma).

(*a*) Conascent volition together with root eradicated by First Path is related to delusion and mind-produced matter by kamma condition.

(*b*) Asynchronous volition together with root eradicated by First Path is related to (its) resultant aggregates and kamma-produced matter by kamma condition. (2)

(iii) State together with root eradicated by First Path is related to state together with root eradicated by First Path and together with root eradicated neither by First Path nor by Higher 3 Paths by kamma condition.

Volition together with root eradicated by First Path is related to (its) associated aggregates, delusion and mind-produced matter by kamma condition. (3)

97. (iv) State together with root eradicated by Higher 3 Paths is related to state together with root eradicated by Higher 3 Paths by kamma condition.

Volition together with root eradicated by Higher 3 Paths is related to (its) associated aggregates by kamma condition. (1)

(v) State together with root eradicated by Higher 3 Paths is related to state together with root eradicated neither by First Path nor by Higher 3 Paths by kamma condition.

Volition together with root eradicated by Higher 3 Paths is related to delusion and mind-produced matter by kamma condition. (2)

(vi) State together with root eradicated by Higher 3 Paths is related to state together with root eradicated by Higher 3 Paths and together with root eradicated neither by First Path nor by Higher 3 Paths by kamma condition.

Volition together with root eradicated by Higher 3 Paths is related to (its) associated aggregates, delusion and mind-produced matter by kamma condition. (3)

98. (vii) State together with root eradicated neither by First Path nor by Higher 3 Paths is related to state together with root eradicated neither by First Path nor by Higher 3 Paths by kamma condition.

(It is of two kinds, namely:) (*a*) conascence(-kamma), (*b*) asynchronous (kamma).

(*a*) (1) Conascent volition together with root eradicated neither by First Path nor by Higher 3 Paths is related to (its) associated aggregates and mind-produced matter by kamma condition;

(2) At the moment of conception . . .

(*b*) Asynchronous volition together with root eradicated neither by First Path nor by Higher 3 Paths is related to (its) resultant aggregates and kamma-produced matter by kamma condition. (1)

Resultant 1

99. State together with root eradicated neither by First Path nor by Higher 3 Paths is related to state together with root eradicated neither by First Path nor by Higher 3 Paths by resultant condition.

(During life and conception) resultant aggregates to (heart-)base . . .

Nutriment 7

100. (i) State together with root eradicated by First Path is related to state together with root eradicated by First Path by nutriment condition.

Nutriments together with root eradicated by First Path are related to (their) associated aggregates by nutriment condition. (1)

(ii) State together with root eradicated by First Path is related to state together with root eradicated neither by First Path nor by Higher 3 Paths by nutriment condition.

Nutriments together with root eradicated by First Path are related to delusion and mind-produced matter by nutriment condition. (2)

(iii) State together with root eradicated by First Path is related to state together with root eradicated by First Path and together with root eradicated neither by First Path nor by Higher 3 Paths by nutriment condition.

Nutriments together with root eradicated by First Path are related to (their) associated aggregates, delusion and mind-produced matter by nutriment condition. (3)

(iv)–(vi) State together with root eradicated by Higher 3 Paths . . . three. (Like First Path.)

(vii) State together with root eradicated neither by First Path nor by Higher 3 Paths is related to state together with root eradicated neither by First Path nor by Higher 3 Paths by nutriment condition.

(*a*) Nutriments together with root eradicated neither by First Path nor by Higher 3 Paths are related to (their) associated aggregates and mind-produced matter by nutriment condition;

(*b*) At the moment of conception . . .

(*c*) Edible food is related to this body by nutriment condition. (1)

Faculty, etc. 7

101. (i)–(iii) State together with root eradicated by First Path is related to state together with root eradicated by First Path by faculty condition . . . three. (The same as nutriment. Include delusion.)

(iv)–(vi) State together with root eradicated by Higher 3 Paths . . . three.

(vii) State together with root eradicated neither by First Path nor by Higher 3 Paths is related to state together with root eradicated neither by First Path nor by Higher 3 Paths by faculty condition.

(*a*) Faculties together with root eradicated neither by First Path nor by Higher 3 Paths to (their) associated aggregates . . .

(*b*) Eye-faculty to eye-consciousness . . . body-faculty to body-consciousness . . .

(*c*) Physical life-faculty is related to kamma-produced matter by faculty condition.

. . . by jhāna condition . . . by path condition. (Take these as rooted.) . . . by association condition. (The same as association in the "Dependent" Chapter.)

Dissociation 9

102. (i) State together with root eradicated by First Path is related to state together with root eradicated neither by First Path nor by

Higher 3 Paths by dissociation condition.

(It is of two kinds, namely:) (*a*) conascence, (*b*) postnascence.

(The same as First Path Triplet.)

(ii) State together with root eradicated by Higher 3 Paths is related to state together with root eradicated neither by First Path nor by Higher 3 Paths by dissociation condition.

(It is of two kinds, namely:) (*a*) conascence, (*b*) postnascence.

(The same as First Path Triplet.)

(iii) State together with root eradicated neither by First Path nor by Higher 3 Paths is related to state together with root eradicated neither by First Path nor by Higher 3 Paths by dissociation condition.

(It is of three kinds, namely:) (*a*) conascence, (*b*) prenascence, (*c*) postnascence.

(*a*), (*b*) (The same as First Path Triplet.)

(*c*) Postnascent aggregates together with root eradicated neither by First Path nor by Higher 3 Paths and delusion to this prenascent body . . . (1)

(iv) State together with root eradicated neither by First Path nor by Higher 3 Paths is related to state together with root eradicated by First Path by dissociation condition.

Prenascent (heart-)base to aggregates together with root eradicated by First Path . . . (2)

(v) State together with root eradicated neither by First Path nor by Higher 3 Paths is related to state together with root eradicated by Higher 3 Paths by dissociation condition.

Prenascent (heart-)base to aggregates together with root eradicated by Higher 3 Paths . . . (3)

(vi) State together with root eradicated neither by First Path nor by Higher 3 Paths is related to state together with root eradicated by First Path and together with root eradicated neither by First Path nor by Higher 3 Paths by dissociation condition.

Prenascent (heart-)base is related to doubt-accompanied aggregates and delusion by dissociation condition. (4)

(vii) State together with root eradicated neither by First Path nor by Higher 3 Paths is related to state together with root eradicated by Higher 3 Paths and together with root eradicated neither by First Path nor by Higher 3 Paths by dissociation condition.

Prenascent (heart-)base is related to restlessness-accompanied aggregates and delusion by dissociation condition. (5)

103. (viii) States together with root eradicated by First Path and together with root eradicated neither by First Path nor by Higher 3 Paths are related to state together with root eradicated neither by First Path nor by Higher 3 Paths by dissociation condition.

(It is of two kinds, namely:) (*a*) conascence, (*b*) postnascence.

(*a*) Conascent doubt-accompanied aggregates and delusion are related to mind-produced matter by dissociation condition.

(*b*) Postnascent doubt-accompanied aggregates and delusion are related to this prenascent body by dissociation condition. (1)

(ix) States together with root eradicated by Higher 3 Paths and together with root eradicated neither by First Path nor by Higher 3 Paths are related to state together with root eradicated neither by First Path nor by Higher 3 Paths by dissociation condition.

(It is of two kinds, namely:) (*a*) conascence, (*b*) postnascence.

(*a*) Conascent restlessness-accompanied aggregates and delusion to mind-produced matter . . .

(*b*) Postnascent restlessness-accompanied aggregates and delusion are related to this prenascent body by dissociation condition. (1)

Presence, etc. 17

104. (i) State together with root eradicated by First Path is related to state together with root eradicated by First Path by presence condition.

One aggregate together with root eradicated by First Path to three aggregates . . . (1)

(ii) State together with root eradicated by First Path is related to state together with root eradicated neither by First Path nor by Higher 3 Paths by presence condition.

(It is of two kinds, namely:) (*a*) conascence, (*b*) postnascence.

(*a*) Conascent aggregates together with root eradicated by First Path are related to mind-produced matter by presence condition; conascent doubt-accompanied aggregates are related to delusion and mind-produced matter by presence condition.

(*b*) Postnascent aggregates together with root eradicated by First Path are related to this prenascent body by presence condition. (2)

(iii) State together with root eradicated by First Path is related to state together with root eradicated by First Path and together with root eradicated neither by First Path nor by Higher 3 Paths by presence condition.

One aggregate together with root eradicated by First Path is related to three aggregates and mind-produced matter by presence condition . . . One doubt-accompanied aggregate is related to three aggregates, delusion and mind-produced matter by presence condition . . . (3)

(iv)–(vi) State together with root eradicated by Higher 3 Paths . . . three.

105. (vii) State together with root eradicated neither by First Path nor by Higher 3 Paths is related to state together with root eradicated neither by First Path nor by Higher 3 Paths by presence condition.

(It is of five kinds, namely:) (*a*) conascence, (*b*) prenascence, (*c*) postnascence, (*d*) nutriment, (*e*) faculty.

(*a*) (1) One conascent aggregate together with root eradicated neither by First Path nor by Higher 3 Paths is related to three aggregates and mind-produced matter by presence condition . . . doubt-accompanied or restlessness-accompanied delusion is related to mind-produced matter by presence condition;

(2) At the moment of conception . . .

(3) . . . non-percipient beings . . .

(*b*) *(Object-)prenascence:* Eye . . . impermanence . . . of the (heart-) base. By the power of divine-eye, (one) sees a visible object. By the power of divine-ear element, (one) hears a sound. Visible object-base to eye-consciousness . . . tangible object-base to body-consciousness . . .

(Base-)prenascence: Eye-base . . . body-base . . . (heart-)base is related to aggregates together with root eradicated neither by First Path nor by Higher 3 Paths and delusion by presence condition.

(*c*) Postnascent aggregates together with root eradicated neither by First Path nor by Higher 3 Paths and delusion are related to this prenascent body by presence condition.

(*d*) Edible food to this body . . .

(*e*) Physical life-faculty to kamma-produced matter . . . (1)

(viii) State together with root eradicated neither by First Path nor by Higher 3 Paths is related to state together with root eradicated by First Path by presence condition.

(It is of two kinds, namely:) (*a*) conascence, (*b*) prenascence.

(*a*) Conascent doubt-accompanied delusion is related to (its) associated aggregates by presence condition.

(*b*) *(Object-)prenascence:* Eye . . . (One) enjoys and delights in the (heart-)base. Taking it as object, arises lust together with root eradicated by First Path, arise wrong views, arises doubt, arises grief together with root eradicated by First Path.

(Base-)prenasence: (Heart-)base is related to aggregates together with root eradicated by First Path by presence condition. (2)

(ix) State together with root eradicated neither by First Path nor by Higher 3 Paths is related to state together with root eradicated by Higher 3 Paths by presence condition.

(It is of two kinds, namely:) (*a*) conascence, (*b*) prenascence.

(*a*) Conascent restlessness-accompanied delusion is related to (its) associated aggregates by presence condition.

(*b*) *(Object-)prenascence:* Eye . . . (One) enjoys and delights in the (heart-)base . . .

(Base-)prenascence: (Heart-)base is related to aggregates together with root eradicated by Higher 3 Paths by presence condition. (3)

(x) State together with root eradicated neither by First Path nor by Higher 3 Paths is related to state together with root eradicated by First Path and together with root eradicated neither by First Path nor by Higher 3 Paths by presence condition.

(It is of two kinds, namely:) (*a*) conascence, (*b*) prenascence.

(*a*) Conascent doubt-accompanied delusion is related to (its) associated aggregates and mind-produced matter by presence condition.

(*b*) *(Object-)prenascence:* Taking eye as object, arise doubt-accompanied aggregates and delusion . . . Taking (heart-)base as object . . .

(Base-)prenascence: (Heart-)base is related to doubt-accompanied aggregates and delusion by presence condition. (4)

(xi) State together with root eradicated neither by First Path nor by Higher 3 Paths is related to state together with root eradicated by Higher 3 Paths and together with root eradicated neither by First Path nor by Higher 3 Paths by presence condition.

(It is of two kinds, namely:) (*a*) conascence, (*b*) prenascence.

(*a*) Conascent restlessness-accompanied delusion is related to (its) associated aggregates and mind-produced matter by presence condition.

(*b*) *(Object-)prenascence:* Taking eye as object, arise restlessness-accompanied aggregates and delusion . . . Taking (heart-)base as object . . .

(Base-)prenascence: (Heart-)base is related to restlessness-accompanied aggregates and delusion by presence condition. (5)

106. (xii) States together with root eradicated by First Path and together with root eradicated neither by First Path nor by Higher 3

Paths are related to state together with root eradicated by First Path by presence condition.

(It is of two kinds, namely:) (*a*) conascence-prenascence, (*b*) (conascence).

Conascence-prenascence: One conascent aggregate together with root eradicated by First Path and (heart-)base are related to three aggregates . . . two aggregates . . .

(Conascence): One doubt-accompanied aggregate and delusion are related to three aggregates by presence condition . . . two aggregates . . . (1)

(xiii) States together with root eradicated by First Path and together with root eradicated neither by First Path nor by Higher 3 Paths are related to state together with root eradicated neither by First Path nor by Higher 3 Paths by presence condition.

(It is of five kinds, namely:) (*a*) conascence, (*b*) (conascence-)prenascence, (*c*) postnascence, (*d*) (postnascence-)nutriment, (*e*) (postnascence-)faculty.

(*a*) Conascent aggregates together with root eradicated by First Path and great primaries are related to mind-produced matter by presence condition. Conascent doubt-accompanied aggregates and delusion are related to mind-produced matter by presence condition.

(*b*) *(Conascence-)prenascence:* Doubt-accompanied aggregates and (heart-)base are related to delusion by presence condition.

(*c*) Postnascent doubt-accompanied aggregates and delusion are related to this prenascent body by presence condition.

(*d*) Postnascent aggregates together with root eradicated by First Path and edible food are related to this body by presence condition.

(*e*) Postnascent aggregates together with root eradicated by First Path and physical life-faculty are related to kamma-produced matter by presence condition. (2)

(xiv) States together with root eradicated by First Path and together with root eradicated neither by First Path nor by Higher 3 Paths are related to state together with root eradicated by First Path and together with root eradicated neither by First Path nor by Higher 3 Paths by presence condition.

(It is of two kinds, namely:) (*a*) conascence-prenascence, (*b*) (conascence).

(*a*) *Conascence-prenascence:* One doubt-accompanied aggregate and (heart-)base are related to three aggregates and delusion by presence condition . . . two aggregates . . .

(*b*) *(Conascence):* One doubt-accompanied aggregate and delusion are related to three aggregates and mind-produced matter by presence condition . . . two aggregates and delusion . . . (3)

(xv)-(xvii) States together with root eradicated by Higher 3 Paths and together with root eradicated neither by First Path nor by Higher 3 Paths are related to state together with root eradicated by Higher 3 Paths by presence condition. [Abbreviated. Three questions. Classify according to the method of First Path. Remember (to take) restlessness.]

. . . by absence condition . . . by disappearance condition . . . by non-disappearance condition . . .

1. CONDITIONS: POSITIVE (ii) ENUMERATION CHAPTER

By Ones

107. With root 11, object 21, predominance 10, proximity 17, contiguity 17, conascence 17, mutuality 11, dependence 17, strong-dependence 21, prenascence 5, postnascence 5, repetition 17, kamma 7, resultant 1, nutriment 7, faculty 7, jhāna 7, path 7, association 11, dissociation 9, presence 17, absence 17, disappearance 17, non-disappearance 17. (Enumerate thus.)

End of Positive

2. SELECTION OF THE CONDITIONS FOR NEGATIVE 21

108. (i) State together with root eradicated by First Path is related to state together with root eradicated by First Path by object condition, conascence condition, strong-dependence condition. (1)

(ii) State together with root eradicated by First Path is related to state together with root eradicated neither by First Path nor by Higher 3 Paths by object condition, conascence condition, strong-dependence condition, postnascence condition, kamma condition. (2)

(iii) State together with root eradicated by First Path is related to state together with root eradicated by First Path and together with root eradicated neither by First Path nor by Higher 3 Paths by object condition, conascence condition, strong-dependence condition. (3)

109. (iv) State together with root eradicated by Higher 3 Paths is related to state together with root eradicated by Higher 3 Paths by

object condition, conascence condition, strong-dependence condition. (1)

(v) State together with root eradicated by Higher 3 Paths is related to state together with root eradicated by First Path by object condition, strong-dependence condition. (2)

(vi) State together with root eradicated by Higher 3 Paths is related to state together with root eradicated neither by First Path nor by Higher 3 Paths by object condition, conascence condition, strong-dependence condition, postnascence condition. (3)

(vii) State together with root eradicated by Higher 3 Paths is related to state together with root eradicated by First Path and together with root eradicated neither by First Path nor by Higher 3 Paths by object condition, strong-dependence condition. (4)

(viii) State together with root eradicated by Higher 3 Paths is related to state together with root eradicated by Higher 3 Paths and together with root eradicated neither by First Path nor by Higher 3 Paths by object condition, conascence condition, strong-dependence condition. (5)

110. (ix) State together with root eradicated neither by First Path nor by Higher 3 Paths is related to state together with root eradicated neither by First Path nor by Higher 3 Paths by object condition, conascence condition, strong-dependence condition, prenascence condition, postnascence condition, kamma condition, nutriment condition, faculty condition. (1)

(x) State together with root eradicated neither by First Path nor by Higher 3 Paths is related to state together with root eradicated by First Path by object condition, conascence condition, strong-dependence condition, prenascence condition. (2)

(xi) State together with root eradicated neither by First Path nor by Higher 3 Paths is related to state together with root eradicated by Higher 3 Paths by object condition, conascence condition, strong-dependence condition, prenascence condition. (3)

(xii) State together with root eradicated neither by First Path nor by Higher 3 Paths is related to state together with root eradicated by First Path and together with root eradicated neither by First Path nor by Higher 3 Paths by object condition, conascence condition, strong-dependence condition, prenascence condition. (4)

(xiii) State together with root eradicated neither by First Path nor by Higher 3 Paths is related to state together with root eradicated by Higher 3 Paths and together with root eradicated neither by First Path nor by Higher 3 Paths by object condition, conascence condition, strong-dependence condition, prenascence condition. (5)

111. (xiv) States together with root eradicated by First Path and together with root eradicated neither by First Path nor by Higher 3 Paths are related to state together with root eradicated by First Path by object condition, conascence condition, strong-dependence condition. (1)

(Here there is mixed conascence-prenascence. Fill in the Text. As for the enumeration, enumerate it after investigation.)

(xv) States together with root eradicated by First Path and together with root eradicated neither by First Path nor by Higher 3 Paths are related to state together with root eradicated neither by First Path nor by Higher 3 Paths by conascence-prenascence, postnascence-nutriment-faculty. (2)

(Here also there are "by object condition, by strong-dependence condition", but they are not given in the Text. The enumerator should enumerate after investigation.)

(xvi) States together with root eradicated by First Path and together with root eradicated neither by First Path nor by Higher 3 Paths are related to state together with root eradicated by First Path and together with root eradicated neither by First Path nor by Higher 3 Paths by object condition, conascence condition, strong-dependence condition. (3)

(Here also there is a question on mixed conascence-prenascence. Fill in the Text.)

112. (xvii) States together with root eradicated by Higher 3 Paths and together with root eradicated neither by First Path nor by Higher 3 Paths are related to state together with root eradicated by First Path by object condition, strong-dependence condition. (1)

(xviii) States together with root eradicated by Higher 3 Paths and together with root eradicated neither by First Path nor by Higher 3 Paths are related to state together with root eradicated by Higher 3 Paths by object condition, conascence condition, strong-dependence condition. (2)

(Here also there is a question on mixed conascence-prenascence.)

(xix) States together with root eradicated by Higher 3 Paths and together with root eradicated neither by First Path nor by Higher 3 Paths are related to state together with root eradicated neither by First Path nor by Higher 3 Paths by conascence-prenascence, postnascence-nutriment-faculty. (3)

(Here also there are object and strong-dependence.)

(xx) States together with root eradicated by Higher 3 Paths and together with root eradicated neither by First Path nor by Higher 3 Paths are related to state together with root eradicated by First Path and together with root eradicated neither by First Path nor by Higher 3 Paths by object condition, strong-dependence condition. (4)

(xxi) States together with root eradicated by Higher 3 Paths and together with root eradicated neither by First Path nor by Higher 3 Paths are related to state together with root eradicated by Higher 3 Paths and together with root eradicated neither by First Path nor by Higher 3 Paths by object condition, conascence condition, strong-dependence condition. (5)

(Here also there is mixed conascence-prenascence. These questions (on the mixed conditions) are not given. But when enumerated (without these conditions) the figures obtained do not agree with those in the Text. Therefore, although they (the mixed conditions) are not given in the Text, it is clear that their enumerations must be determined. If there be any doubt, see presence condition in the Positive.)

2. CONDITIONS: NEGATIVE (ii) ENUMERATION CHAPTER

By Ones

113. With not-root 21, not-object, not-predominance, not-proximity, not-contiguity, not-conascence, not-mutuality, not-dependence, not-strong-dependence, not-prenascence, not-postnascence, not-repetition, not-kamma, not-resultant, not-nutriment, not-faculty, not-jhāna, not-path, not-association, not-dissociation, not-presence, not-absence, not-disappearance, not-non-disappearance (are) all 21. (Enumerate thus.)

End of Negative

3. CONDITIONS: POSITIVE-NEGATIVE

Root By Twos

114. With root condition, not-object 11, not-predominance, not-proximity, not-contiguity 11, not-mutuality 3, not-strong-dependence, not-prenascence, not-postnascence, not-repetition, not-kamma, not-resultant, not-nutriment, not-faculty, not-jhāna, not-path 11, not-association 3, not-dissociation 5, not-absence 11, not-disappearance 11. (Enumerate thus.)

End of Positive-Negative

4. CONDITIONS: NEGATIVE-POSITIVE

Not-root By Twos

115. With not-root condition, object 21, predominance 10, proximity 17, contiguity 17, conascence 17, mutuality 11, dependence 17, strong-dependence 21, prenascence 5, postnascence 5, repetition 17, kamma 7, resultant 1, nutriment 7, faculty 7, jhāna 7, path 7, association 11, dissociation 9, presence 17, absence 17, disappearance 17, non-disappearance 17. (Enumerate thus.)

End of Negative–Positive

End of "INVESTIGATION" CHAPTER

END OF TRIPLET OF (STATE) TOGETHER WITH ROOT ERADICATED BY FIRST PATH

10. TRIPLET OF (STATE) LEADING TO REBIRTH AND DEATH[1]

I. "DEPENDENT" CHAPTER

1. CONDITIONS: POSITIVE (i) CLASSIFICATION CHAPTER

Root 9

1. (i) Dependent on state leading to rebirth and death (ācayagāmin), arises state leading to rebirth and death by root condition.

Dependent on one aggregate leading to rebirth and death, arise three aggregates . . . dependent on two aggregates, arise two aggregates. (1)

(ii) Dependent on state leading to rebirth and death, arises state leading neither to rebirth and death nor to Nibbāna by root condition.

Dependent on aggregates leading to rebirth and death, arises mind-produced matter. (2)

(iii) Dependent on state leading to rebirth and death, arise states leading to rebirth and death and leading neither to rebirth and death nor to Nibbāna by root condition.

Dependent on one aggregate leading to rebirth and death, arise three aggregates and mind-produced matter . . . dependent on two aggregates, arise two aggregates and mind-produced matter. (3)

2. (iv) Dependent on state leading to Nibbāna (apacayagāmin), arises state leading to Nibbāna by root condition.

---

[1] This comprises (1) States leading to rebirth and death, (2) States leading to Nibbāna, (3) States leading neither to rebirth and death nor to Nibbāna.

Dependent on one aggregate leading to Nibbāna, arise three aggregates . . . dependent on two aggregates, arise two aggregates. (1)

(v) Dependent on state leading to Nibbāna, arise state leading neither to rebirth and death nor to Nibbāna by root condition.

Dependent on aggregates leading to Nibbāna, arises mind-produced matter. (2)

(vi) Dependent on state leading to Nibbāna, arise states leading to Nibbāna and leading neither to rebirth and death nor to Nibbāna by root condition.

Dependent on one aggregate leading to Nibbāna, arise three aggregates and mind-produced matter . . . dependent on two aggregates, arise two aggregates and mind-produced matter. (3)

3. (vii) Dependent on state leading neither to rebirth and death nor to Nibbāna (nevācayagāmi-nāpacayagāmin), arises state leading neither to rebirth and death nor to Nibbāna by root condition.

(*a*) Dependent on one aggregate leading neither to rebirth and death nor to Nibbāna, arise three aggregates and mind-produced matter . . . two aggregates . . .

(*b*) At the moment of conception, dependent on one aggregate leading neither to rebirth and death nor to Nibbāna, arise three aggregates and kamma-produced matter . . . two aggregates . . . dependent on aggregates, arises (heart-)base; dependent on (heart-)base, arise aggregates;

(*c*) Dependent on one great primary, arise three great primaries . . . dependent on two great primaries, arise two great primaries; dependent on great primaries, arise mind-produced and kamma-produced derived matter. (1)

(viii) Dependent on state leading to rebirth and death and leading neither to rebirth and death nor to Nibbāna, arises state leading neither to rebirth and death nor to Nibbāna by root condition.

Dependent on aggregates leading to rebirth and death and great primaries, arises mind-produced matter. (1)

(ix) Dependent on state leading to Nibbāna and leading neither to rebirth and death nor to Nibbāna, arises state leading neither to rebirth and death nor to Nibbāna by root condition.

Dependent on aggregates leading to Nibbāna and great primaries, arises mind-produced matter. (1)

Object 3

4. (i) Dependent on state leading to rebirth and death, arises state leading to rebirth and death by object condition.

Dependent on one aggregate leading to rebirth and death, arise three aggregates . . . two aggregates . . . (1)

(ii) Dependent on state leading to Nibbāna, arises state leading to Nibbāna by object condition.

Dependent on one aggregate leading to Nibbāna, arise three aggregates . . . two aggregates . . . (1)

(iii) Dependent on state leading neither to rebirth and death nor to Nibbāna, arises state leading neither to rebirth and death nor to Nibbāna by object condition.

(*a*) Dependent on one aggregate leading neither to rebirth and death nor to Nibbāna, arise three aggregates . . . dependent on two aggregates, arise two aggregates;

(*b*) At the moment of conception . . . dependent on (heart-)base, arise aggregates. (1)

Predominance 9

5. (i)–(iii) Dependent on state leading to rebirth and death, arises state leading to rebirth and death by predominance condition . . . three.

(iv)–(vi) Dependent on state leading to Nibbāna, arises state leading to Nibbāna by predominance condition . . . three.

(vii) Dependent on state leading neither to rebirth and death nor to Nibbāna . . . state leading neither to rebirth and death nor to Nibbāna . . .

(*a*) . . . one . . . (No conception.)

(*b*) Dependent on one great primary, arise three great primaries . . . dependent on great primaries, arises mind-produced derived matter. (1)

(viii) Dependent on state leading to rebirth and death and leading neither to rebirth and death nor to Nibbāna, arises state leading neither to rebirth and death nor to Nibbāna by predominance condition.

Dependent on aggregates leading to rebirth and death and great primaries, arises mind-produced matter. (1)

(ix) Dependent on state leading to Nibbāna and leading neither to rebirth and death nor to Nibbāna, arises state leading neither to rebirth and death nor to Nibbāna by predominance condition.

Dependent on aggregates leading to Nibbāna and great primaries, arises mind-produced matter. (1)

Proximity, etc.

6. Dependent on state leading to rebirth and death, arises state leading to rebirth and death by proximity condition . . . by contiguity condition . . . by conascence condition. (Include all great primaries.) . . . by mutuality condition. (No mind-produced and kamma-produced derived matter.) . . . by dependence condition . . . by strong-dependence condition . . . by prenascence condition . . . by repetition condition . . . by kamma condition . . . by resultant condition . . . by nutriment condition . . . by faculty condition . . . by jhāna condition . . . by path condition . . . by association condition . . . by dissociation condition . . . by presence condition . . . by absence condition . . . by disappearance condition . . . by non-disappearance condition . . .

1. CONDITIONS: POSITIVE (ii) ENUMERATION CHAPTER

By Ones

7. With root 9, object 3, predominance 9, proximity 3, contiguity 3, conascence 9, mutuality 3, dependence 9, strong-dependence 3, prenascence 3, repetition 3, kamma 9, resultant 1, nutriment 9, faculty 9, jhāna 9, path 9, association 3, dissociation 9, presence 9, absence 3, disappearance 3, non-disappearance 9. (Enumerate thus.)

End of Positive

2. CONDITIONS: NEGATIVE (i) CLASSIFICATION CHAPTER

Not-root 2

8. (i) Dependent on state leading to rebirth and death, arises state leading to rebirth and death by not-root condition.

Dependent on doubt-accompanied or restlessness-accompanied aggregates, arises doubt-accompanied or restlessness-accompanied delusion. (1)

(ii) Dependent on state leading neither to rebirth and death nor to Nibbāna, arises state leading neither to rebirth and death nor to Nibbāna by not-root condition.

(*a*) Dependent on one rootless aggregate leading neither to rebirth and death nor to Nibbāna, arise three aggregates and mind-produced matter . . . two aggregates . . .

(*b*) At the moment of rootless conception . . . dependent on aggregates, arises (heart-)base; dependent on (heart-)base, arise aggregates;

(*c*) One great primary . . . External . . . nutriment-produced . . . temperature-produced . . . one great primary of non-percipient beings . . . (1)

Not-object 5

9. (i) Dependent on state leading to rebirth and death, arises state leading neither to rebirth and death nor to Nibbāna by not-object condition.

Dependent on aggregates leading to rebirth and death, arises mind-produced matter. (1)

(ii) Dependent on state leading to Nibbāna, arises state leading neither to rebirth and death nor to Nibbāna by not-object condition.

Dependent on aggregates leading to Nibbāna, arises mind-produced matter. (1)

(iii) Dependent on state leading neither to rebirth and death nor to Nibbāna, arises state leading neither to rebirth and death nor to Nibbāna by not-object condition.

(*a*) Dependent on aggregates leading neither to rebirth and death nor to Nibbāna, arises mind-produced matter;

(*b*) At the moment of conception . . . dependent on aggregates, arises (heart-)base . . .

(*c*) One great primary . . . External . . . nutriment-produced . . . temperature-produced . . . non-percipient beings . . . (1)

(iv) Dependent on state leading to rebirth and death and leading neither to rebirth and death nor to Nibbāna, arises state leading neither to rebirth and death nor to Nibbāna by not-object condition.

Dependent on aggregates leading to rebirth and death and great primaries, arises mind-produced matter. (1)

(v) Dependent on state leading to Nibbāna and leading neither to rebirth and death nor to Nibbāna, arises state leading neither to rebirth and death nor to Nibbāna by not-object condition.

Dependent on aggregates leading to Nibbāna and great primaries, arises mind-produced matter. (1)

Not-predominance 6

10. (i)–(iii) Dependent on state leading to rebirth and death, arises state leading to rebirth and death by not-predominance condition . . . three.

(iv) Dependent on state leading to Nibbāna, arises state leading to Nibbāna by not-predominance condition.

Dependent on aggregates leading to Nibbāna, arises predominance leading to Nibbāna. (1)

(v) Dependent on state leading neither to rebirth and death nor to Nibbāna, arises state leading neither to rebirth and death nor to Nibbāna by not-predominance condition.

(*a*) Dependent on one aggregate leading neither to rebirth and death nor to Nibbāna, arise three aggregates and mind-produced matter . . . two aggregates . . .

(*b*) At the moment of conception . . . dependent on aggregates, arises (heart-)base; dependent on (heart-)base, arise aggregates;

(*c*) One great primary . . . External . . . nutriment-produced . . . temperature-produced . . . one great primary of non-percipient beings . . . (1)

(vi) Dependent on state leading to rebirth and death and leading neither to rebirth and death nor to Nibbāna, arises state leading neither to rebirth and death nor to Nibbāna by not-predominance condition.

Dependent on aggregates leading to rebirth and death and great primaries, arises mind-produced matter. (1)

Not-proximity, etc.

11. Dependent on state leading to rebirth and death, arises state leading neither to rebirth and death nor to Nibbāna by not-proximity condition . . . by not-contiguity condition . . . by not-mutuality condition . . . by not-strong-dependence condition . . . by not-prenascence condition. [As for the Faultless Triplet (there are) 7 questions.] . . . by not-postnascence condition . . .

Not-repetition 7

12. (i)-(iii) Dependent on state leading to rebirth and death, arises state leading to rebirth and death by not-repetition condition . . . three.

(iv) Dependent on state leading to Nibbāna, arises state leading neither to rebirth and death nor to Nibbāna by not-repetition condition.

Dependent on aggregates leading to Nibbāna, arises mind-produced matter. (1)

(v) Dependent on state leading neither to rebirth and death nor to Nibbāna, arises state leading neither to rebirth and death nor to Nibbāna by not-repetition condition.

(One question. Include all great primaries.)

(vi) Dependent on state leading to rebirth and death and leading neither to rebirth and death nor to Nibbāna, arises state leading neither to rebirth and death nor to Nibbāna by not-repetition condition.

Dependent on aggregates leading to rebirth and death and great primaries, arises mind-produced matter. (1)

(vii) Dependent on state leading to Nibbāna and leading neither to rebirth and death nor to Nibbāna, arises state leading neither to rebirth and death nor to Nibbāna by not-repetition condition.

Dependent on aggregates leading to Nibbāna and great primaries, arises mind-produced matter. (1)

Not-kamma 3

13. (i) Dependent on state leading to rebirth and death, arises state leading to rebirth and death by not-kamma condition.

Dependent on aggregates leading to rebirth and death, arises volition leading to rebirth and death. (1)

(ii) Dependent on state leading to Nibbāna, arises state leading to Nibbāna by not-kamma condition.

Dependent on aggregates leading to Nibbāna, arises volition leading to Nibbāna. (1)

(iii) Dependent on state leading neither to rebirth and death nor to Nibbāna, arises state leading neither to rebirth and death nor to Nibbāna by not-kamma condition.

(*a*) Dependent on aggregates leading neither to rebirth and death nor to Nibbāna, arises volition leading neither to rebirth and death nor to Nibbāna;

(*b*) External . . . nutriment-produced . . . one great primary of temperature-produced . . . (1)

Not-resultant, etc.

14. Dependent on state leading to rebirth and death, arises state leading to rebirth and death by not-resultant condition. (Complete. No conception.) . . . by not-nutriment condition . . . by not-faculty condition . . . by not-jhāna condition . . . by not-path condition . . . by not-association condition . . . by not-dissociation condition. (Three.) . . . by not-absence condition . . . by not-disappearance condition . . .

2. CONDITIONS: NEGATIVE (ii) ENUMERATION CHAPTER

By Ones

15. With not-root 2, not-object 5, not-predominance 6, not-proximity

5, not-contiguity 5, not-mutuality 5, not-strong-dependence 5, not-prenascence 7, not-postnascence 9, not-repetition 7, not-kamma 3, not-resultant 9, not-nutriment 1, not-faculty 1, not-jhāna 1, not-path 1, not-association 5, not-dissociation 3, not-absence 5, not-disappearance 5 (Enumerate thus.)

End of Negative

3. CONDITIONS: POSITIVE-NEGATIVE

Root By Twos

16. With root condition, not-object 5, not-predominance 6, not-proximity 5, not-contiguity 5, not-mutuality 5, not-strong-dependence 5, not-prenascence 7, not-postnascence 9, not-repetition 7, not-kamma 3, not-resultant 9, not-association 5, not-dissociation 3, not-absence 5, not-disappearance 5. (Enumerate thus.)

End of Positive–Negative

4. CONDITIONS: NEGATIVE-POSITIVE

Not-root By Twos

17. With not-root condition, object 2, proximity 2, contiguity 2, co-nascence 2, mutuality, dependence, strong-dependence, prenascence, repetition, kamma 2, resultant 1, nutriment 2, faculty 2, jhāna 2, path 1, association 2, dissociation, presence, absence, disappearance, non-disappearance 2. (Enumerate thus.)

End of Negative–Positive

End of "DEPENDENT" CHAPTER

(The "Conascent" Chapter is the same as the "Dependent" Chapter.)

10. TRIPLET OF (STATE) LEADING TO REBIRTH AND DEATH
III. "CONDITIONED" CHAPTER

1. CONDITIONS: POSITIVE (i) CLASSIFICATION CHAPTER

Root 17

18. (i) Conditioned by state leading to rebirth and death, arises state leading to rebirth and death by root condition.

Conditioned by one aggregate leading to rebirth and death, arise three aggregates . . . conditioned by two aggregates, arise two aggregates. (1)

(ii) Conditioned by state leading to rebirth and death, arises state leading neither to rebirth and death nor to Nibbāna by root condition.

Conditioned by aggregates leading to rebirth and death, arises mind-produced matter. (2)

(iii) Conditioned by state leading to rebirth and death, arise states leading to rebirth and death and leading neither to rebirth and death nor to Nibbāna by root condition.

Conditioned by one aggregate leading to rebirth and death, arise three aggregates and mind-produced matter . . . two aggregates . . . (3)

(iv)–(vi) Conditioned by state leading to Nibbāna, (arises) state leading to Nibbāna . . . three.

19. (vii) Conditioned by state leading neither to rebirth and death nor to Nibbāna, arises state leading neither to rebirth and death nor to Nibbāna by root condition.

(*a*) Conditioned by one aggregate leading neither to rebirth and death nor to Nibbāna, arise three aggregates and mind-produced matter . . . two aggregates . . .

(*b*) At the moment of conception . . . conditioned by aggregates, arises (heart-)base; conditioned by (heart-)base, arise aggregates;

(*c*) Conditioned by one great primary . . .

(*d*) Conditioned by (heart-)base, arise aggregates leading neither to rebirth and death nor to Nibbāna. (1)

(viii) Conditioned by state leading neither to rebirth and death nor to Nibbāna, arises state leading to rebirth and death by root condition.

Conditioned by (heart-)base, arise aggregates leading to rebirth and death. (2)

(ix) Conditioned by state leading neither to rebirth and death nor to Nibbāna, arises state leading to Nibbāna by root condition.

Conditioned by (heart-)base, arise aggregates leading to Nibbāna. (3)

(x) Conditioned by state leading neither to rebirth and death nor to Nibbāna, arise states leading to rebirth and death and leading neither to rebirth and death nor to Nibbāna by root condition.

Conditioned by (heart-)base, arise aggregates leading to rebirth and death; conditioned by great primaries, arises mind-produced matter. (4)

(xi) Conditioned by state leading neither to rebirth and death nor to Nibbāna, arise states leading to Nibbāna and leading neither to rebirth and death nor to Nibbāna by root condition.

Conditioned by (heart-)base, arise aggregates leading to Nibbāna; conditioned by great primaries, arises mind-produced matter. (5)

20. (xii) Conditioned by state leading to rebirth and death and leading neither to rebirth and death nor to Nibbāna, arises state leading to rebirth and death by root condition.

Conditioned by one aggregate leading to rebirth and death and (heart-)base, arise three aggregates . . . two aggregates . . . (1)

(xiii) Conditioned by state leading to rebirth and death and leading neither to rebirth and death nor to Nibbāna, arises state leading neither to rebirth and death nor to Nibbāna by root condition.

Conditioned by aggregates leading to rebirth and death and great primaries, arises mind-produced matter. (2)

(xiv) Conditioned by state leading to rebirth and death and leading neither to rebirth and death nor to Nibbāna, arise states leading to rebirth and death and leading neither to rebirth and death nor to Nibbāna by root condition.

Conditioned by one aggregate leading to rebirth and death and (heart-)base, arise three aggregates . . . two aggregates . . . conditioned by aggregates leading to rebirth and death and great primaries, arises mind-produced matter. (3)

(xv)-(xvii) Conditioned by state leading to Nibbāna and leading neither to rebirth and death nor to Nibbāna, (arises) state leading to Nibbāna . . . three.

Object 7

21. (i) Conditioned by state leading to rebirth and death, arises state leading to rebirth and death by object condition.

Conditioned by one aggregate leading to rebirth and death . . . (1)

(ii) Conditioned by state leading to Nibbāna, (arises) state leading to Nibbāna . . . one.

(iii) Conditioned by state leading neither to rebirth and death nor to Nibbāna, arises state leading neither to rebirth and death nor to Nibbāna by object condition.

(*a*) Conditioned by one aggregate leading neither to rebirth and death nor to Nibbāna, arise three aggregates . . . two aggregates . . .

(*b*) At the moment of conception . . . conditioned by (heart-)base, arise aggregates;

(*c*) Conditioned by eye-base, arises eye-consciousness . . . conditioned by body-base, arises body-consciousness; conditioned by (heart-)base, arise aggregates leading neither to rebirth and death nor to Nibbāna. (1)

(iv) Conditioned by state leading neither to rebirth and death nor to Nibbāna, arises state leading to rebirth and death by object condition.

Conditioned by (heart-)base, arise aggregates leading to rebirth and death. (2)

(v) Conditioned by state leading neither to rebirth and death nor to Nibbāna, arises state leading to Nibbāna by object condition.

Conditioned by (heart-)base, arise aggregates leading to Nibbāna. (3)

(vi) Conditioned by state leading to rebirth and death and leading neither to rebirth and death nor to Nibbāna, arises state leading to rebirth and death by object condition.

Conditioned by one aggregate leading to rebirth and death and (heart-)base, arise three aggregates . . . two aggregates . . . (1)

(vii) Conditioned by state leading to Nibbāna and leading neither to rebirth and death nor to Nibbāna, arises state leading to Nibbāna by object condition.

Conditioned by one aggregate leading to Nibbāna and (heart-)base, arise three aggregates . . . two aggregates . . . (1)

Predominance 17

22. (i)-(iii) Conditioned by state leading to rebirth and death, arises state leading to rebirth and death by predominance condition . . . three.

(iv)-(vi) Conditioned by state leading to Nibbāna, (arises) state leading to Nibbāna . . . three.

(vii) Conditioned by state leading neither to rebirth and death nor to Nibbāna, (arises) state leading neither to rebirth and death nor to Nibbāna . . .

One . . . conditioned by (heart-)base, arise aggregates leading neither to rebirth and death nor to Nibbāna.

(viii)-(xvii) Conditioned by state leading neither to rebirth and death nor to Nibbāna, (arises) state leading to rebirth and death . . . (Here also the combinations are the same as root.)

Proximity, etc.

23. (i)-(iii) Conditioned by state leading to rebirth and death, arises state leading to rebirth and death by proximity condition . . . by contiguity condition . . . by conascence condition . . . three.

(iv)-(vi) Conditioned by state leading to Nibbāna, (arises) state leading to Nibbāna . . . three.

(vii) Conditioned by state leading neither to rebirth and death nor to Nibbāna, arises state leading neither to rebirth and death nor to Nibbāna by conascence condition.

(*a*) Conditioned by one aggregate leading neither to rebirth and death nor to Nibbāna, arise three aggregates and mind-produced matter . . . two aggregates . . .

(*b*) At the moment of conception . . .

(*c*) One great primary of non-percipient beings . . .

(*d*) Conditioned by eye-base, arises eye-consciousness . . . conditioned by body-base, arises body-consciousness; conditioned by (heart-) base . . . (1)

(viii) Conditioned by state leading neither to rebirth and death nor to Nibbāna, arises state leading to rebirth and death by conascence condition. (Abbreviated. Do all combinations.)

Mutuality, etc.

24. Conditioned by state [1]leading to Nibbāna, arises state [1]leading to Nibbāna by mutuality condition . . . by dependence condition . . . by strong-dependence condition . . . by prenascence condition . . . by repetition condition . . . by kamma condition . . . by resultant condition . . . by nutriment condition . . . by faculty condition . . . by jhāna condition . . . by path condition . . . by association condition . . . by dissociation condition . . . by presence condition . . . by absence condition . . . by disappearance condition . . . by non-disappearance condition . . .

1. CONDITIONS: POSITIVE (ii) ENUMERATION CHAPTER

By Ones

25. With root 17, object 7, predominance 17, proximity 7, contiguity 7, conascence 17, mutuality 7, dependence 17, strong-dependence 7, prenascence 7, repetition 7, kamma 17, resultant 1, nutriment 17, faculty, jhāna, path 17, association 7, dissociation 17, presence 17, absence 7, disappearance 7, non-disappearance 17. (Enumerate thus.)

End of Positive

---

[1] Should be "leading to rebirth and death" in both cases.

2. CONDITIONS: NEGATIVE (i) CLASSIFICATION CHAPTER

Not-root 4

26. (i) Conditioned by state leading to rebirth and death, arises state leading to rebirth and death by not-root condition.

Conditioned by doubt-accompanied or restlessness-accompanied aggregates, arises doubt-accompanied or restlessness-accompanied delusion. (1)

(ii) Conditioned by state leading neither to rebirth and death nor to Nibbāna, arises state leading neither to rebirth and death nor to Nibbāna by not-root condition.

(*a*) Conditioned by one rootless aggregate leading neither to rebirth and death nor to Nibbāna, arise three aggregates and mind-produced matter . . . two aggregates . . .

(*b*) At the moment of rootless conception . . .

(*c*) One great primary of non-percipient beings . . .

(*d*) Conditioned by eye-base, arises eye-consciousness . . . conditioned by body-base, arises body-consciousness; conditioned by (heart-) base, arise rootless aggregates leading neither to rebirth and death nor to Nibbāna. (1)

(iii) Conditioned by state leading neither to rebirth and death nor to Nibbāna, arises state leading to rebirth and death by not-root condition.

Conditioned by (heart-)base, arises doubt-accompanied or restlessness-accompanied delusion. (2)

(iv) Conditioned by state leading to rebirth and death and leading neither to rebirth and death nor to Nibbāna, arises state leading to rebirth and death by not-root condition.

Conditioned by doubt-accompanied or restlessness-accompanied aggregates and (heart-)base, arises doubt-accompanied or restlessness-accompanied delusion. (1)

Not-object 5

27. Conditioned by state leading to rebirth and death, arises state leading neither to rebirth and death nor to Nibbāna by not-object condition. (Abbreviated. The same as in the "Dependent" Chapter.)

Not-predominance 12

28. (i)–(iii) Conditioned by state leading to rebirth and death, arises

state leading to rebirth and death by not-predominance condition . . . three.

(iv) Conditioned by state leading to Nibbāna, arises state leading to Nibbāna by not-predominance condition.

Conditioned by aggregates leading to Nibbāna, arises predominance leading to Nibbāna. (1)

(v) Conditioned by state leading neither to rebirth and death nor to Nibbāna, arises state leading neither to rebirth and death nor to Nibbāna by not-predominance condition.

(*a*) . . . non-percipient beings . . .

(*b*) Conditioned by eye-base, arises eye-consciousness . . . conditioned by body-base, arises body-consciousness; conditioned by (heart-)base, arise aggregates leading neither to rebirth and death nor to Nibbāna. (1)

(vi) Conditioned by state leading neither to rebirth and death nor to Nibbāna, arises state leading to rebirth and death by not-predominance condition.

Conditioned by (heart-)base, arise aggregates leading to rebirth and death. (2)

(vii) Conditioned by state leading neither to rebirth and death nor to Nibbāna, arises state leading to Nibbāna by not-predominance condition.

Conditioned by (heart-)base, arises predominance. (3)

(viii) Conditioned by state leading neither to rebirth and death nor to Nibbāna, arise states leading to rebirth and death and leading neither to rebirth and death nor to Nibbāna by not-predominance condition.

Conditioned by (heart-)base, arise aggregates leading to rebirth and death; conditioned by great primaries, arises mind-produced matter. (4)

29. (ix) Conditioned by state leading to rebirth and death and leading neither to rebirth and death nor to Nibbāna, arises state leading to rebirth and death by not-predominance condition.

Conditioned by one aggregate leading to rebirth and death and (heart-)base, arise three aggregates . . . two aggregates . . . (1)

(x) Conditioned by state leading to rebirth and death and leading neither to rebirth and death nor to Nibbāna, arises state leading neither to rebirth and death nor to Nibbāna by not-predominance condition.

Conditioned by aggregates leading to rebirth and death and great primaries, arises mind-produced matter. (2)

(xi) Conditioned by state leading to rebirth and death and leading neither to rebirth and death nor to Nibbāna, arise states leading to rebirth and death and leading neither to rebirth and death nor to Nibbāna by not-predominance condition.

Conditioned by one aggregate leading to rebirth and death and (heart-)base, arise three aggregates . . . two aggregates . . . conditioned by aggregates leading to rebirth and death and great primaries, arises mind-produced matter. (3)

(xii) Conditioned by state leading to Nibbāna and leading neither to rebirth and death nor to Nibbāna, arises state leading to Nibbāna by not-predominance condition.

Conditioned by aggregates leading to Nibbāna and (heart-)base, arises predominance leading to Nibbāna. (1)

Not-proximity, etc.

30. . . . by not-proximity condition . . . by not-contiguity condition . . . by not-mutuality condition . . . by not-strong-dependence condition . . . by not-prenascence condition. (The same as for the "Dependent" Chapter. 7 questions.) . . . by not-postnascence condition. (Complete.) . . .

Not-repetition 11

31. (i)-(iii) Conditioned by state leading to rebirth and death, arises state leading to rebirth and death by not-repetition condition . . . three.

(iv) Conditioned by state leading to Nibbāna, arises state leading neither to rebirth and death nor to Nibbāna by not-repetition condition.

Conditioned by aggregates leading to Nibbāna, arises mind-produced matter. (1)

(v) Conditioned by state leading neither to rebirth and death nor to Nibbāna, arises state leading neither to rebirth and death nor to Nibbāna by not-repetition condition.

(*a*) . . . non-percipient beings . . .

(*b*) Conditioned by eye-base, arises eye-consciousness . . . conditioned by body-base, arises body-consciousness; conditioned by (heart-) base, arise aggregates leading neither to rebirth and death nor to Nibbāna. (1)

(vi) Conditioned by state leading neither to rebirth and death nor to Nibbāna, arises state leading to rebirth and death by not-repetition condition.

Conditioned by (heart-)base, arise aggregates leading to rebirth and death. (2)

(vii) Conditioned by state leading neither to rebirth and death nor to Nibbāna, arise states leading to rebirth and death and leading neither to rebirth and death nor to Nibbāna by not-repetition condition.

Conditioned by (heart-)base, arise aggregates leading to rebirth and death; conditioned by great primaries, arises mind-produced matter. (3)

(viii) Conditioned by state leading to rebirth and death and leading neither to rebirth and death nor to Nibbāna, arises state leading to rebirth and death by not-repetition condition.

Conditioned by one aggregate leading to rebirth and death and (heart-)base, arise three aggregates . . . two aggregates . . . (1)

(ix) Conditioned by state leading to rebirth and death and leading neither to rebirth and death nor to Nibbāna, arises state leading neither to rebirth and death nor to Nibbāna by not-repetition condition.

Conditioned by aggregates leading to rebirth and death and great primaries, arises mind-produced matter. (2)

(x) Conditioned by state leading to rebirth and death and leading neither to rebirth and death nor to Nibbāna, arise states leading to rebirth and death and leading neither to rebirth and death nor to Nibbāna by not-repetition condition.

Conditioned by one aggregate leading to rebirth and death and (heart-)base, arise three aggregates . . . two aggregates . . . conditioned by aggregates leading to rebirth and death and great primaries, arises mind-produced matter. (3)

(xi) Conditioned by state leading to Nibbāna and leading neither to rebirth and death nor to Nibbāna, arises state leading neither to rebirth and death nor to Nibbāna by not-repetition condition.

Conditioned by aggregates leading to Nibbāna and great primaries, arises mind-produced matter. (1)

Not-kamma 7

32. (i) Conditioned by state leading to rebirth and death, arises state leading to rebirth and death by not-kamma condition.

Conditioned by aggregates leading to rebirth and death, arises volition leading to rebirth and death. (1)

(ii) Conditioned by state leading to Nibbāna, arises state leading to Nibbāna by not-kamma condition.

Conditioned by aggregates leading to Nibbāna, arises volition leading to Nibbāna. (1)

(iii) Conditioned by state leading neither to rebirth and death nor to Nibbāna, arises state leading neither to rebirth and death nor to Nibbāna by not-kamma condition.

(*a*) Conditioned by aggregates leading neither to rebirth and death nor to Nibbāna, arises volition leading neither to rebirth and death nor to Nibbāna;

(*b*) External . . . nutriment-produced . . . temperature-produced . . .

(*c*) Conditioned by (heart-)base, arises volition leading neither to rebirth and death nor to Nibbāna. (1)

(iv) Conditioned by state leading neither to rebirth and death nor to Nibbāna, arises state leading to rebirth and death by not-kamma condition.

Conditioned by (heart-)base, arises volition leading to rebirth and death. (2)

(v) Conditioned by state leading neither to rebirth and death nor to Nibbāna, arises state leading to Nibbāna by not-kamma condition.

Conditioned by (heart-)base, arises volition leading to Nibbāna. (3)

(vi) Conditioned by state leading to rebirth and death and leading neither to rebirth and death nor to Nibbāna, arises state leading to rebirth and death by not-kamma condition.

Conditioned by aggregates leading to rebirth and death and (heart-)base, arises volition leading to rebirth and death. (1)

(vii) Conditioned by state leading to Nibbāna and leading neither to rebirth and death nor to Nibbāna, arises state leading to Nibbāna by not-kamma condition.

Conditioned by aggregates leading to Nibbāna and (heart-)base, arises volition leading to Nibbāna. (1)

Not-resultant, etc.

33. Conditioned by state leading to rebirth and death, arises state leading to rebirth and death by not-resultant condition. (Do completely. No "at the moment of conception".)

Conditioned by state leading neither to rebirth and death nor to Nibbāna, arises state leading neither to rebirth and death nor to Nibbāna by not-nutriment condition.

External . . . temperature-produced . . . non-percipient beings . . .

. . . by not-faculty condition.

External . . . nutriment-produced . . . temperature-produced . . . non-percipient beings . . . conditioned by great primaries, arises physical life-faculty.

. . . by not-jhāna condition.

. . . five-fold consciousness . . . External . . . nutriment-produced . . . temperature-produced . . . non-percipient beings . . . conditioned by eye-base, arises eye-consciousness . . . conditioned by body-base, arises body-consciousness . . .

. . . by not-path condition.

. . . rootless (aggregates) leading neither to rebirth and death nor to Nibbāna . . . one great primary of non-percipient beings . . . conditioned by eye-base, arises eye-consciousness . . . conditioned by body-base, arises body-consciousness; conditioned by (heart-)base, arise rootless (aggregates) leading neither to rebirth and death nor to Nibbāna.

. . . by not-association condition . . . by not-dissociation condition. (The same as in the "Dependent" Chapter. Three.) . . . by not-absence condition . . . by not-disappearance condition . . .

2. CONDITIONS: NEGATIVE (ii) ENUMERATION CHAPTER

By Ones

34. With not-root 4, not-object 5, not-predominance 12, not-proximity 5, not-contiguity, not-mutuality, not-strong-dependence 5, not-prenascence 7, not-postnascence 17, not-repetition 11, not-kamma 7, not-resultant 17, not-nutriment, not-faculty, not-jhāna, not-path 1, not-association 5, not-dissociation 3, not-absence, not disappearance 5. (Enumerate thus.)

End of Negative

3. CONDITIONS: POSITIVE-NEGATIVE

Root By Twos

35. With root condition, not-object 5, not-predominance 12, not-proximity, not-contiguity, not-mutuality, not-strong-dependence 5, not-prenascence 7, not-postnascence 17, not-repetition 11, not-kamma 7, not-resultant 17, not-association 5, not-dissociation 3, not-absence, not-disappearance 5. (Enumerate thus.)

End of Positive-Negative

4. CONDITIONS: NEGATIVE-POSITIVE

Not-root By Twos

36. With not-root condition, object 4, proximity, contiguity, conascence, mutuality, dependence, strong-dependence, prenascence, repetition, kamma 4, resultant 1, nutriment 4, faculty, jhāna 4, path 3, association, dissociation, presence, absence, disappearance 4, non-disappearance 4. (Enumerate thus.)

End of Negative-Positive

End of "CONDITIONED" CHAPTER

(The "Supported" Chapter is the same as the "Conditioned" Chapter.)

10. TRIPLET OF (STATE) LEADING TO REBIRTH AND DEATH
V. "CONJOINED" CHAPTER

1. CONDITIONS: POSITIVE (i) CLASSIFICATION CHAPTER

Root 3

37. (i) Conjoined with state leading to rebirth and death, arises state leading to rebirth and death by root condition.

Conjoined with one aggregate leading to rebirth and death, arise three aggregates . . . conjoined with two aggregates, arise two aggregates. (1)

(ii) Conjoined with state leading to Nibbāna, arises state leading to Nibbāna by root condition.

Conjoined with one aggregate leading to Nibbāna, arise three aggregates . . . two aggregates . . . (1)

(iii) Conjoined with state leading neither to rebirth and death nor to Nibbāna, arises state leading neither to rebirth and death nor to Nibbāna by root condition.

(*a*) Conjoined with one aggregate leading neither to rebirth and death nor to Nibbāna, arise three aggregates . . . two aggregates . . .

(*b*) At the moment of conception . . . (1)

Object, etc.

38. Conjoined with state leading to rebirth and death, arises state leading to rebirth and death by object condition . . . by predominance condition . . . by proximity condition . . . by contiguity condition . . .

by conascence condition . . . by mutuality condition . . . by dependence condition . . . by strong-dependence condition . . . by prenascence condition . . . by repetition condition . . . by kamma condition . . . by resultant condition . . . by nutriment condition . . . by faculty condition . . . by jhāna condition . . . by path condition . . . by association condition . . . by dissociation condition . . . by presence condition . . . by absence condition . . . by disappearance condition . . . by non-disappearance condition . . .

1. CONDITIONS: POSITIVE (ii) ENUMERATION CHAPTER

By Ones

39. With root 3, object, predominance, proximity, contiguity, conascence, mutuality, dependence, strong-dependence, prenascence, repetition, kamma (are) all 3, resultant 1, nutriment 3, faculty, jhāna, path, association, dissociation, presence, absence, disappearance, non-disappearance 3. (Enumerate thus.)

End of Positive

2. CONDITIONS: NEGATIVE (i) CLASSIFICATION CHAPTER

Not-root 2

40. (i) Conjoined with state leading to rebirth and death, arises state leading to rebirth and death by not-root condition.

Conjoined with doubt-accompanied or restlessness-accompanied aggregates, arises doubt-accompanied or restlessness-accompanied delusion. (1)

(ii) Conjoined with state leading neither to rebirth and death nor to Nibbāna, arises state leading neither to rebirth and death nor to Nibbāna by not-root condition.

(*a*) Conjoined with one rootless aggregate leading neither to rebirth and death nor to Nibbāna, arise three aggregates . . . two aggregates . . .

(*b*) At the moment of rootless conception . . . (1)

Not-predominance, etc.

41. (i) Conjoined with state leading to rebirth and death, arises state leading to rebirth and death by not-predominance condition . . . by not-prenascence condition . . . by not-postnascence condition . . . by not-repetition condition.

Conjoined with one aggregate leading to rebirth and death, arise three aggregates . . . two aggregates . . .

(ii) Conjoined with state leading neither to rebirth and death nor to Nibbāna, arises state leading neither to rebirth and death nor to Nibbāna by not-repetition condition.

(*a*) Conjoined with one aggregate leading neither to rebirth and death nor to Nibbāna . . .

(*b*) At the moment of conception . . .

. . . by not-kamma condition . . . by not-resultant condition . . . by not-jhāna condition . . . by not-path condition . . . by not-dissociation condition . . .

2. CONDITIONS: NEGATIVE (ii) ENUMERATION CHAPTER

By Ones

42. With not-root 2, not-predominance 3, not-prenascence 3, not-postnascence 3, not-repetition 2, not-kamma 3, not-resultant 3, not-jhāna 1, not-path 1, not-dissociation 3. (Enumerate thus.)

End of Negative

3. CONDITIONS: POSITIVE–NEGATIVE

(Root By Twos)

43. With root condition, not-predominance 3, not-prenascence 3, not-postnascence 3, not-repetition 2, not-kamma 3, not-resultant 3, not-dissociation 3. (Enumerate thus.)

End of Positive–Negative

4. CONDITIONS: NEGATIVE–POSITIVE

(Not-root By Twos)

44. With not-root condition, object 2, proximity, contiguity, conascence, mutuality, dependence, strong-dependence, prenascence, repetition, kamma (are) all 2, resultant 1, nutriment 2, faculty 2, jhāna 2, path 1, association 2, dissociation, presence, absence, disappearance, non-disappearance 2. (Enumerate thus.)

End of Negative–Positive

End of "CONJOINED" CHAPTER

(The "Associated" Chapter is the same as the "Conjoined" Chapter.)

10. TRIPLET OF (STATE) LEADING TO REBIRTH AND DEATH
VII. "INVESTIGATION" CHAPTER

1. CONDITIONS: POSITIVE (i) CLASSIFICATION CHAPTER

Root 7

45. (i) State leading to rebirth and death is related to state leading to rebirth and death by root condition.

Roots leading to rebirth and death are related to (their) associated aggregates by root condition. (1)

(ii) State leading to rebirth and death is related to state leading neither to rebirth and death nor to Nibbāna by root condition.

Roots leading to rebirth and death are related to mind-produced matter by root condition. (2)

(iii) State leading to rebirth and death is related to state leading to rebirth and death and leading neither to rebirth and death nor to Nibbāna by root condition.

Roots leading to rebirth and death are related to (their) associated aggregates and mind-produced matter by root condition. (3)

(iv)-(vi) State leading to Nibbāna is related to state leading to Nibbāna by root condition . . . three.

(vii) State leading neither to rebirth and death nor to Nibbāna is related to state leading neither to rebirth and death nor to Nibbāna by root condition.

(*a*) Roots leading neither to rebirth and death nor to Nibbāna are related to (their) associated aggregates and mind-produced matter by root condition;

(*b*) At the moment of conception, roots leading neither to rebirth and death nor to Nibbāna are related to (their) associated aggregates and kamma-produced matter by root condition. (1)

Object 7

46. (i) State leading to rebirth and death is related to state leading to rebirth and death by object condition.

After having offered an offering, having undertaken precepts, having fulfilled the duty of observance, (one) reviews it. (One) reviews (such acts) formerly well done. Having emerged from jhāna, (one) reviews the jhāna.

Learners review the eradicated defilements, review the uneradicated defilements, know the defilements addicted to before. Learners or common worldlings practise insight into the impermanence, suffering and impersonality of aggregates leading to rebirth and death; enjoy and delight in (those aggregates). Taking them as object, arises lust . . . wrong views . . . doubt . . . restlessness, arises grief. By the knowledge of penetration into others' minds, (they) know the other being's mind leading to rebirth and death.

Faultless "infinity of space" is related to faultless "infinity of consciousness" by object condition. Faultless "nothingness" to faultless "neither-perception-nor-non-perception" . . . Aggregates leading to rebirth and death are related to knowledge of supernormal power, knowledge of penetration into others' minds, knowledge of remembrance of past existences, knowledge of rebirths according to one's kamma, knowledge of future existences by object condition. (1)

(ii) State leading to rebirth and death is related to state leading neither to rebirth and death nor to Nibbāna by object condition.

The Arahat reviews the eradicated defilements, knows the defilements addicted to before. (He) practises insight into the impermanence, suffering and impersonality of aggregates leading to rebirth and death. By the knowledge of penetration into others' minds, (He) knows the other being's mind leading to rebirth and death.

Learners or common worldlings practise insight into the impermanence, suffering and impersonality of aggregates leading to rebirth and death. When faultless (state) has ceased, the resultant (state) arises as registering (consciousness). (They) enjoy and delight in the aggregates leading to rebirth and death. Taking them as object, arises lust . . . arises grief. When faulty (state) has ceased, the resultant arises as registering.

Faultless "infinity of space" is related to resultant or functional "infinity of consciousness" by object condition. Faultless "nothingness" is related to resultant or functional "neither-perception-nor-non-perception" by object condition. Aggregates leading to rebirth and death are related to knowledge of penetration into others' minds, knowledge of remembrance of past existences, knowledge of rebirths according to one's kamma, knowledge of future existences, (mind-door) advertence by object condition. (2)

40. (iii) State leading to Nibbāna is related to state leading to rebirth and death by object condition.

Learners, having emerged from Path, review the Path. By the knowledge of penetration into others' minds, (they) know the other being's mind leading to Nibbāna. Aggregates leading to Nibbāna are related to knowledge of penetration into others' minds, knowledge of remembrance of past existences, knowledge of future existences by object condition. (1)

(iv) State leading to Nibbāna is related to state leading neither to rebirth and death nor to Nibbāna by object condition.

The Arahat, having emerged from (Arahatta) Path, reviews the Path. By the knowledge of penetration into others' minds, (He) knows the other being's mind leading to Nibbāna. Aggregates leading to Nibbāna are related to knowledge of penetration into others' minds, knowledge of remembrance of past existence, knowledge of future existences, advertence by object condition. (2)

48. (v) State leading neither to rebirth and death nor to Nibbāna is related to state leading neither to rebirth and death nor to Nibbāna by object condition.

The Arahat reviews (Arahatta) Fruition, reviews Nibbāna. Nibbāna is related to Fruition, advertence by object condition.

The Arahat practises insight into the impermanence, suffering and impersonality of the eye(-base); . . . ear . . . (heart-)base; (He) practises insight into the impermanence, suffering and impersonality of aggregates leading neither to rebirth and death nor to Nibbāna.

By the power of divine-eye, (the Arahat) sees a visible object. By the power of divine-ear element, (He) hears a sound. By the knowledge of penetration into others' minds, (He) knows the other being's mind leading neither to rebirth and death nor to Nibbāna.

Functional "infinity of space" is related to functional "infinity of consciousness" by object condition. Functional "nothingness" to functional "neither-perception-nor-non-perception" . . .

Visible object-base to eye-consciousness . . . tangible object-base to body-consciousness . . . Aggregates leading neither to rebirth and death nor to Nibbāna are related to knowledge of supernormal power, knowledge of penetration into others' minds, knowledge of remembrance of past existences, knowledge of future existences, advertence by object condition. (1)

(vi) State leading neither to rebirth and death nor to Nibbāna is related to state leading to rebirth and death by object condition.

Learners review (lower) Fruition, review Nibbāna. Nibbāna is related to change-of-lineage, purification by object condition.

Learners or common worldlings practise insight into the impermanence, suffering and impersonality of the eye; enjoy and delight in (the eye). Taking it as object, arises lust . . . arises grief . . . ear . . . (heart-) base . . . (they) practise insight into the impermanence, suffering and impersonality of aggregates leading neither to rebirth and death nor to Nibbāna; enjoy and delight in (those aggregates). Taking them as object, arises lust, arise wrong views, . . . doubt . . . restlessness . . . grief.

By the power of divine-eye, (they) see a visible object. By the power of divine-ear element, (they) hear a sound. By the knowledge of penetration into others' minds, (they) know the other being's mind leading neither to rebirth and death nor to Nibbāna. Aggregates leading neither to rebirth and death nor to Nibbāna are related to knowledge of supernormal power, knowledge of penetration into others' minds, knowledge of remembrance of past existences, knowledge of future existences by object condition. (2)

(vii) State leading neither to rebirth and death nor to Nibbāna is related to state leading to Nibbāna by object condition.

Nibbāna is related to Path by object condition. (3)

Predominance 10

49. (i) State leading to rebirth and death is related to state leading to rebirth and death by predominance condition.

(It is of two kinds, namely:) (*a*) object-predominance, (*b*) conascence-predominance.

(*a*) *Object-predominance:* After having offered an offering, having undertaken precepts, having fulfilled the duty of observance, (one) esteems and reviews it. (One) esteems and reviews (such acts) formerly well done. Having emerged from jhāna, (one) esteems and reviews the jhāna. (One) esteems, enjoys and delights in aggregates leading to re-rebirth and death. Taking them as estimable object, arises lust, arise wrong views.

(*b*) *Conascence-predominance:* Predominance leading to rebirth and death is related to (its) associated aggregates by predominance condition. (1)

(ii) State leading to rebirth and death is related to state leading neither to rebirth and death nor to Nibbāna by predominance condition.

Conascence-predominance: Predominance leading to rebirth and death is related to mind-produced matter by predominance condition. (2)

(iii) State leading to rebirth and death is related to state leading to rebirth and death and leading neither to rebirth and death nor to

Nibbāna by predominance condition.

Conascence-predominance: Predominance leading to rebirth and death is related to (its) associated aggregates and mind-produced matter by predominance condition. (3)

50. (iv) State leading to Nibbāna is related to state leading to Nibbāna by predominance condition.

Conascence-predominance: Predominance leading to Nibbāna is related to (its) associated aggregates by predominance condition. (1)

(v) State leading to Nibbāna is related to state leading to rebirth and death by predominance condition.

Object-predominance: Learners, having emerged from Path, esteem and review the Path. (2)

(vi) State leading to Nibbāna is related to state leading neither to rebirth and death nor to Nibbāna by predominance condition.

(It is of two kinds, namely:) (*a*) object-predominance, (*b*) conascence-predominance.

(*a*) *Object-predominance:* Having emerged from (Arahatta) Path, the Arahat esteems and reviews the Path.

(*b*) *Conascence-predominance:* Predominance leading to Nibbāna is related to mind-produced matter by predominance condition. (3)

(vii) State leading to Nibbāna is related to state leading to Nibbāna and leading neither to rebirth and death nor to Nibbāna by predominance condition.

Conascence-predominance: Predominance leading to Nibbāna is related to (its) associated aggregates and mind-produced matter by predominance condition. (4)

51. (viii) State leading neither to rebirth and death nor to Nibbāna is related to state leading neither to rebirth and death nor to Nibbāna by predominance condition.

(It is of two kinds, namely:) (*a*) object-predominance, (*b*) conascence-predominance.

(*a*) *Object-predominance:* The Arahat esteems and reviews (Arahatta) Fruition, esteems and reviews Nibbāna. Nibbāna is related to Fruition by predominance condition.

(*b*) *Conascence-predominance:* Predominance leading neither to rebirth and death nor to Nibbāna is related to (its) associated aggregates and mind-produced matter by predominance condition. (1)

(ix) State leading neither to rebirth and death nor to Nibbāna is related to state leading to rebirth and death by predominance condition.

Object-predominance: Learners esteem and review (lower) Fruition, esteem and review Nibbāna. Nibbāna is related to change-of-lineage, purification by predominance condition.

(One) esteems, enjoys . . . in the eye . . . (heart-)base . . . (One) esteems, enjoys and delights in aggregates leading neither to rebirth and death nor to Nibbāna. Taking them as estimable object, arises lust, arise wrong views. (2)

(x) State leading neither to rebirth and death nor to Nibbāna is related to state leading to Nibbāna by predominance condition.

Object-predominance: Nibbāna is related to Path by predominance condition. (3)

Proximity 6

52. (i) State leading to rebirth and death is related to state leading to rebirth and death by proximity condition.

Preceding aggregates leading to rebirth and death are related to subsequent aggregates leading to rebirth and death by proximity condition. Adaptation to change-of-lineage; adaptation is related to purification by proximity condition. (1)

(ii) State leading to rebirth and death is related to state leading to Nibbāna by proximity condition.

Change-of-lineage to Path; purification is related to Path by proximity condition. (2)

(iii) State leading to rebirth and death is related to state leading neither to birth and death nor to Nibbāna by proximity condition.

Aggregates leading to rebirth and death are related to emergence by proximity condition. Adaptation of the Learners to the attainment of Fruition; for one emerging from the attainment of Extinction, faultless neither-perception-nor-non-perception is related to the attainment of Fruition by proximity condition. (3)

(iv) State leading to Nibbāna is related to state leading to Nibbāna by proximity condition.

Path is related to Fruition by proximity condition. (1)

(v) State leading neither to rebirth and death nor to Nibbāna is related to state leading neither to rebirth and death nor to Nibbāna by proximity condition.

Preceding aggregates leading neither to rebirth and death nor to Nibbāna are related to subsequent aggregates leading neither to rebirth and death nor to Nibbāna by proximity condition. Life-continuum to advertence; functional to emergence; adaptation of the Arahat to the attainment of Fruition; for one emerging from the attainment of Extinction, functional neither-perception-nor-non-perception is related to the attainment of Fruition by proximity condition. (1)

(vi) State leading neither to rebirth and death nor to Nibbāna is related to state leading to rebirth and death by proximity condition.

Advertence is related to aggregates leading to rebirth and death by proximity condition. (2)

Contiguity, etc.

53. State leading to rebirth and death is related to state leading to rebirth and death by contiguity condition. (The same as proximity.) . . . (For conascence condition, it is the same as conascence in the "Dependent" Chapter. 9 questions. For mutuality condition, it is the same as mutuality in the "Dependent" Chapter. Three. For dependence condition, it is the same as dependence in the "Conditioned" Chapter. No separate combinations for four questions. 13 questions.)

Strong-dependence 9

54. (i) State leading to rebirth and death is related to state leading to rebirth and death by strong-dependence condition.

(It is of three kinds, namely:) (*a*) object-strong-dependence, (*b*) proximity-strong-dependence, (*c*) natural strong-dependence . . .

(*c*) *Natural strong-dependence:* By the strong-dependence of confidence leading to rebirth and death, (one) offers an offering . . . precepts . . . duty of observance . . . jhāna . . . insight . . . superknowledge, develops attainment; arouses conceit, adopts wrong views . . . precept leading to rebirth and death . . . learning . . . generosity . . . wisdom . . . lust . . . hate . . . delusion . . . conceit . . . wrong views . . . By the strong-dependence of wish, (one) offers an offering . . . precepts . . . duty of observance . . . jhāna . . . insight . . . superknowledge . . . attainment, kills a living being . . . causes schism in the Saṅgha. Confidence leading to rebirth and death . . . wisdom, lust . . . wish is related to confidence leading to rebirth and death . . . wisdom, lust . . . wish by strong-dependence condition.

The preparation for first jhāna is related to first jhāna by strong-dependence condition . . . the preparation for neither-perception-nor-non-perception is related to neither-perception-nor-non-perception by strong-dependence condition. First jhāna to second jhāna . . . nothingness is related to neither-perception-nor-non-perception by strong-dependence condition. (1)

(ii) State leading to rebirth and death is related to state leading to Nibbāna by strong-dependence condition.

(It is of two kinds, namely:) (*a*) proximity-strong-dependence, (*b*) natural strong-dependence . . .

(*b*) *Natural strong-dependence:* The preparation for first Path to first Path . . . the preparation for fourth Path is related to fourth Path by strong-dependence condition. (2)

(iii) State leading to rebirth and death is related to state leading neither to rebirth and death nor to Nibbāna by strong-dependence condition.

(It is of two kinds, namely:) (*a*) proximity-strong-dependence, (*b*) natural strong-dependence . . .

(*b*) *Natural strong-dependence:* By the strong-dependence of confidence leading to rebirth and death, (one) tortures oneself (attānaṁ ātāpeti), tortures oneself fully (paritāpeti), experiences the suffering caused by searching (pariyiṭṭhimūlakaṁ dukkhaṁ paccanubhoti) . . . precept leading to rebirth and death . . . wisdom . . . lust . . . By the strong-dependence of wish, (one) tortures oneself, tortures oneself fully, experiences the suffering caused by searching. Confidence leading to rebirth and death . . . wisdom, lust . . . wish is related to bodily happiness, bodily pain, attainment of Fruition by strong-dependence condition. Faultless or faulty kamma is related to (its) resultant by strong-dependence condition. (3)

55. (iv) State leading to Nibbāna is related to state leading to Nibbāna by strong-dependence condition.

Natural strong-dependence: First Path to second Path . . . third Path is related to fourth Path by strong-dependence condition. (1)

(v) State leading to Nibbāna is related to state leading to rebirth and death by strong-dependence condition.

(It is of two kinds, namely:) (*a*) object-strong-dependence, (*b*) natural strong-dependence . . .

(*b*) *Natural strong-dependence:* Learners, by the strong-dependence of the Path, generate a faultless attainment which has not yet arisen (anuppannaṁ kusalasamāpattiṁ uppādenti), enter (samāpajjanti) an attainment which has arisen. (They) practise insight into the impermanence, suffering and impersonality of the formations (saṅkhāra). The (lower) Path is related to the Learner's analytical knowledge of meaning (atthappaṭisambhidā) . . . analytical knowledge of the above three (paṭibhānappaṭisambhidā), knowledge of correct and faulty conclusion (ṭhānāṭhānakosalla) by strong-dependence condition. (2)

(vi) State leading to Nibbāna is related to state leading neither to rebirth and death nor to Nibbāna by strong-dependence condition.

(It is of three kinds, namely:) (*a*) object-strong-dependence, (*b*) proximity-strong-dependence, (*c*) natural strong-dependence . . .

(*c*) *Natural strong-dependence:* The Arahat, by the strong-dependence of the Path, generates a functional attainment which has not yet arisen, enters an attainment which has arisen . . . knowledge of correct and faulty conclusion by strong-dependence condition. Path is related to the attainment of Fruition by strong-dependence condition. (3)

56. (vii) State leading neither to rebirth and death nor to Nibbāna is related to state leading neither to rebirth and death nor to Nibbāna by strong-dependence condition.

(It is of three kinds, namely:) (*a*) object-strong-dependence, (*b*) proximity-strong-dependence, (*c*) natural strong-dependence . . .

(*c*) *Natural strong-dependence:* By the strong-dependence of bodily happiness, (one) tortures oneself, tortures oneself fully, experiences the suffering caused by searching . . . bodily pain . . . temperature . . . food . . . By the strong-dependence of lodging-place, (one) tortures oneself, tortures oneself fully . . . Bodily happiness, bodily pain, temperature, food, lodging-place is related to bodily happiness, bodily pain, attainment of Fruition by strong-dependence condition.

The Arahat, by the strong-dependence of bodily happiness, generates a functional attainment which has not yet arisen . . . practises insight . . . bodily pain . . . temperature . . . food . . . By the strong-dependence of lodging-place . . . practises insight. (1)

(viii) State leading neither to rebirth and death nor to Nibbāna is related to state leading to rebirth and death by strong-dependence condition.

(It is of three kinds, namely:) (*a*) object-strong-dependence, (*b*) proximity-strong-dependence, (*c*) natural strong-dependence . . .

(*c*) *Natural strong-dependence:* By the strong-dependence of bodily happiness, (one) offers an offering . . . develops attainment, kills a living being . . . causes schism in the Saṅgha . . . bodily pain . . . temperature . . . food . . . By the strong-dependence of lodging-place, (one) offers an offering . . . causes schism in the Saṅgha. Bodily happiness . . . lodging-place is related to confidence leading to rebirth and death . . .

wisdom, lust . . . wish by strong-dependence condition. (2)

(ix) State leading neither to rebirth and death nor to Nibbāna is related to state leading to Nibbāna by strong-dependence condition.

(It is of two kinds, namely:) (*a*) object-strong-dependence, (*b*) natural strong-dependence . . .

(*b*) *Natural strong-dependence:* By the strong-dependence of bodily happiness, (one) develops Path . . . bodily pain . . . By the strong-dependence of lodging-place, (one) develops Path. Bodily happiness, bodily pain . . . lodging-place is related to Path by strong-dependence condition. (3)

Prenascence 3

57. (i) State leading neither to rebirth and death nor to Nibbāna is related to state leading neither to rebirth and death nor to Nibbāna by prenascence condition.

(It is of two kinds, namely:) (*a*) object-prenascence, (*b*) base-prenascence.

(*a*) *Object-prenascence:* The Arahat . . . eye . . . practises insight into the impermanence, suffering and impersonality of the (heart-)base. (The Arahat), by the power of divine-eye, sees a visible object. By the power of divine-ear element, (He) hears a sound. Visible object-base to eye-consciousness . . . tangible object-base is related to body-consciousness by prenascence condition.

(*b*) *Base-prenascence:* Eye-base to eye-consciousness . . . body-base to body-consciousness . . . (heart-)base is related to aggregates leading neither to rebirth and death nor to Nibbāna by prenascence condition. (1)

(ii) State leading neither to rebirth and death nor to Nibbāna is related to state leading to rebirth and death by prenascence condition.

(It is of two kinds, namely:) (*a*) object-prenascence, (*b*) base-prenascence.

(*a*) *Object-prenascence:* Learners or common worldlings . . . eye . . . practise insight into the impermanence, suffering and impersonality of the (heart-)base; enjoy and delight in it. Taking it as object, arises lust . . . arises grief. By the power of divine-eye, (one) sees a visible object. By the power of divine-ear element, (one) hears a sound.

(*b*) *Base-prenascence:* (Heart-)base is related to aggregates leading to rebirth and death by prenascence condition. (2)

(iii) State leading neither to rebirth and death nor to Nibbāna is related to state leading to Nibbāna by prenascence condition.

Base-prenascence: (Heart-)base is related to aggregates leading to Nibbāna by prenascence condition. (3)

Postnascence 3

58. (i) State leading to rebirth and death is related to state leading neither to rebirth and death nor to Nibbāna by postnascence condition.

Postnascent aggregates leading to rebirth and death are related to this prenascent body by postnascence condition. (1)

(ii) State leading to Nibbāna is related to state leading neither to rebirth and death nor to Nibbāna by postnascence condition.

Postnascent aggregates leading to Nibbāna are related to this prenascent body by postnascence condition. (1)

(iii) State leading neither to rebirth and death nor to Nibbāna is related to state leading neither to rebirth and death nor to Nibbāna by postnascence condition.

Postnascent aggregates leading neither to rebirth and death nor to Nibbāna are related to this prenascent body by postnascence condition. (1)

Repetition 3

59. (i) State leading to rebirth and death is related to state leading to rebirth and death by repetition condition.

Preceding aggregates leading to rebirth and death are related to subsequent aggregates leading to rebirth and death by repetition condition. Adaptation to change-of-lineage; adaptation is related to purification by repetition condition. (1)

(ii) State leading to rebirth and death is related to state leading to Nibbāna by repetition condition.

Change-of-lineage to Path; purification is related to Path by repetition condition. (2)

(iii) State leading neither to rebirth and death nor to Nibbāna is related to state leading neither to rebirth and death nor to Nibbāna by repetition condition.

Preceding aggregates leading neither to rebirth and death nor to Nibbāna are related to subsequent aggregates leading neither to rebirth and death nor to Nibbāna by repetition condition. (1)

Kamma 7

60. (i) State leading to rebirth and death is related to state leading to rebirth and death by kamma condition.

Volition leading to rebirth and death is related to (its) associated aggregates by kamma condition. (1)

(ii) State leading to rebirth and death is related to state leading neither to rebirth and death nor to Nibbāna by kamma condition.

(It is of two kinds, namely:) (*a*) conascence(-kamma), (*b*) asynchronous (kamma).

(*a*) Conascent volition leading to rebirth and death is related to mind-produced matter by kamma condition.

(*b*) Asynchronous volition leading to rebirth and death is related to (its) resultant aggregates and kamma-produced matter by kamma condition. (2)

(iii) State leading to rebirth and death is related to state leading to rebirth and death and leading neither to rebirth and death nor to Nibbāna by kamma condition.

Volition leading to rebirth and death is related to (its) associated aggregates and mind-produced matter by kamma condition. (3)

61. (iv) State leading to Nibbāna is related to state leading to Nibbāna by kamma condition.

Volition leading to Nibbāna is related to (its) associated aggregates by kamma condition. (1)

(v) State leading to Nibbāna is related to state leading neither to rebirth and death nor to Nibbāna by kamma condition.

(It is of two kinds, namely:) (*a*) conascence(-kamma), (*b*) asynchronous (kamma).

(*a*) Conascent volition leading to Nibbāna is related to mind-produced matter by kamma condition.

(*b*) Asynchronous volition leading to Nibbāna is related to (its) resultant aggregates by kamma condition. (2)

(vi) State leading to Nibbāna is related to state leading to Nibbāna and leading neither to rebirth and death nor to Nibbāna by kamma condition.

Volition leading to Nibbāna is related to (its) associated aggregates and mind-produced matter by kamma condition. (3)

(vii) State leading neither to rebirth and death nor to Nibbāna is related to state leading neither to rebirth and death nor to Nibbāna by kamma condition.

(*a*) Volition leading neither to rebirth and death nor to Nibbāna is related to (its) associated aggregates and mind-produced matter by kamma condition.

(*b*) At the moment of conception, volition leading neither to rebirth and death nor to Nibbāna is related to (its) associated aggregates and kamma-produced matter by kamma condition. (1)

Resultant 1

62. State leading neither to rebirth and death nor to Nibbāna is related to state leading neither to rebirth and death nor to Nibbāna by resultant condition.

(*a*) One resultant aggregate leading neither to rebirth and death nor to Nibbāna to three aggregates . . .

(*b*) At the moment of conception . . . aggregates are related to (heart-)base by resultant condition. (1)

Nutriment, etc.

63. State leading to rebirth and death is related to state leading to rebirth and death by nutriment condition . . . by faculty condition . . . by jhāna condition . . . by path condition . . . by association condition . . .

Dissociation 5

64. (i) State leading to rebirth and death is related to state leading neither to rebirth and death nor to Nibbāna by dissociation condition.

(It is of two kinds, namely:) (*a*) conascence, (*b*) postnascence.

(*a*) Conascent aggregates leading to rebirth and death are related to mind-produced matter by dissociation condition.

(*b*) Postnascent aggregates leading to rebirth and death are related to this prenascent body by dissociation condition. (1)

(ii) State leading to Nibbāna is related to state leading neither to rebirth and death nor to Nibbāna by dissociation condition.

(It is of two kinds, namely:) (*a*) conascence, (*b*) postnascence.

(*a*) Conascent aggregates leading to Nibbāna are related to mind-produced matter by dissociation condition.

(*b*) Postnascent aggregates leading to Nibbāna are related to this prenascent body by dissociation condition. (1)

(iii) State leading neither to rebirth and death nor to Nibbāna is related to state leading neither to rebirth and death nor to Nibbāna by dissociation condition.

(It is of three kinds, namely:) (*a*) conascence, (*b*) prenascence, (*c*) postnascence.

(*a*) (1) Conascent aggregates leading neither to rebirth and death nor to Nibbāna are related to mind-produced matter by dissociation condition.

(2) At the moment of conception, aggregates leading neither to rebirth and death nor to Nibbāna are related to kamma-produced matter by dissociation condition; aggregates are related to (heart-)base by dissociation condition; (heart-)base is related to aggregates by dissociation condition.

(*b*) Prenascent eye-base to eye-consciousness . . . body-base to body-consciousness . . . (heart-)base is related to aggregates leading neither to rebirth and death nor to Nibbāna by dissociation condition.

(*c*) Postnascent aggregates leading neither to rebirth and death nor to Nibbāna to this prenascent body . . . (1)

(iv) State leading neither to rebirth and death nor to Nibbāna is related to state leading to rebirth and death by dissociation condition.

Prenascent (heart-)base is related to aggregates leading to rebirth and death by dissociation condition. (2)

(v) State leading neither to rebirth and death nor to Nibbāna is related to state leading to Nibbāna by dissociation condition.

Prenascent (heart-)base is related to aggregates leading to Nibbāna by dissociation condition. (3)

Presence 13, etc.

65. (i) State leading to rebirth and death is related to state leading to rebirth and death by presence condition.

One aggregate leading to rebirth and death to three aggregates . . . (1)

(ii) State leading to rebirth and death is related to state leading neither to rebirth and death nor to Nibbāna by presence condition.

(It is of two kinds, namely:) (*a*) conascence, (*b*) postnascence.

(*a*) Conascent aggregates leading to rebirth and death are related to mind-produced matter by presence condition.

(*b*) Postnascent aggregates leading to rebirth and death are related to this prenascent body by presence condition. (2)

(iii) State leading to rebirth and death is related to state leading to rebirth and death and leading neither to rebirth and death nor to Nibbāna by presence condition.

One aggregate leading to rebirth and death is related to three aggregates and mind-produced matter by presence condition . . . two aggregates . . . (3)

(iv)-(vi) State leading to Nibbāna . . . three. (Do according to the method of "leading to rebirth and death".)

66. (vii) State leading neither to rebirth and death nor to Nibbāna is related to state leading neither to rebirth and death nor to Nibbāna by presence condition.

(It is of five kinds, namely:) (*a*) conascence, (*b*) prenascence, (*c*) postnascence, (*d*) nutriment, (*e*) faculty.

(*a*) (1) One conascent aggregate leading neither to rebirth and death nor to Nibbāna is related to three aggregates and mind-produced matter by presence condition . . . two aggregates . . .

(2) At the moment of conception . . . aggregates are related to (heart-)base by presence condition; (heart-)base is related to aggregates by presence condition;

(3) One great primary . . . External . . . nutriment-produced . . . temperature-produced . . . non-percipient beings . . .

(*b*) *(Object-)prenascence:* The Arahat . . . eye . . . practises insight into the impermanence, suffering and impersonality of the (heart-)base. (The Arahat), by the power of divine-eye, sees a visible object. By the power of divine-ear element, (He) hears a sound. Visible object-base to eye-consciousness . . . tangible object-base to body-consciousness . . .

(Base-)prenascence: Eye-base to eye-consciousness . . . body-base to body-consciousness . . . (heart-)base is related to aggregates leading neither to rebirth and death nor to Nibbāna by presence condition.

(*c*) Postnascent aggregates leading neither to rebirth and death nor to Nibbāna are related to this prenascent body by presence condition.

(*d*) Edible food to this body . . .

(*e*) Physical life-faculty to kamma-produced matter . . . (1)

(viii) State leading neither to rebirth and death nor to Nibbāna is related to state leading to rebirth and death by presence condition.

(Object-)prenascence: Learners or common worldlings practise insight into the impermanence, suffering and impersonality of the eye; enjoy and delight in it. Taking it as object, arises lust . . . arises grief . . . ear . . . practise insight into the impermanence . . . of the (heart-) base; enjoy and delight in it. Taking it as object, arises lust . . . arises grief. By the power of divine-eye, (one) sees a visible object. By the power of divine-ear element, (one) hears a sound.

(Base-)prenascence: (Heart-)base is related to aggregates leading to rebirth and death by presence condition. (2)

(ix) State leading neither to rebirth and death nor to Nibbāna is related to state leading to Nibbāna by presence condition.

(Base-)prenascence: (Heart-)base is related to aggregates leading to Nibbāna by presence condition. (3)

67. (x) States leading to rebirth and death and leading neither to rebirth and death nor to Nibbāna are related to state leading to rebirth and death by presence condition.

Conascence-prenascence: One conascent aggregate leading to rebirth and death and (heart-)base are related to three aggregates by presence condition . . . two aggregates . . . (1)

(xi) States leading to rebirth and death and leading neither to rebirth and death nor to Nibbāna are related to state leading neither to rebirth and death nor to Nibbāna by presence condition.

(It is of three kinds, namely:) (*a*) conascence, (*b*) postnascence-nutriment, (*c*) (postnascence-)faculty.

(*a*) Conascent aggregates leading to rebirth and death and great primaries are related to mind-produced matter by presence condition.

(*b*) Postnascent aggregates leading to rebirth and death and edible food are related to this body by presence condition.

(*c*) Postnascent aggregates leading to rebirth and death and physical life-faculty are related to kamma-produced matter by presence condition. (2)

(xii)-(xiii) States leading to Nibbāna and leading neither to rebirth and death nor to Nibbāna are related to state leading to Nibbāna by presence condition. (Do two by the method shown above.)

. . . by absence condition . . . by disappearance condition . . . by non-disappearance condition . . .

1. CONDITIONS: POSITIVE (ii) ENUMERATION CHAPTER

By Ones

68. With root 7, object 7, predominance 10, proximity 6, contiguity 6, conascence 9, mutuality 3, dependence 13, strong-dependence 9, prenascence 3, postnascence 3, repetition 3, kamma 7, resultant 1, nutriment 7, faculty 7, jhāna 7, path 7, association 3, dissociation 5, presence 13, absence 6, disappearance 6, non-disappearance 13. (Enumerate thus.)

End of Positive

2. SELECTION OF THE CONDITIONS FOR NEGATIVE 15

69. (i) State leading to rebirth and death is related to state leading to rebirth and death by object condition, conascence condition, strong-dependence condition. (1)

(ii) State leading to rebirth and death is related to state leading to Nibbāna by strong-dependence condition. (2)

(iii) State leading to rebirth and death is related to state leading neither to rebirth and death nor to Nibbāna by object condition, conascence condition, strong-dependence condition, postnascence condition, kamma condition. (3)

(iv) State leading to rebirth and death is related to state leading to rebirth and death and leading neither to rebirth and death nor to Nibbāna by conascence condition. (4)

70. (v) State leading to Nibbāna is related to state leading to Nibbāna by conascence condition, strong-dependence condition. (1)

(vi) State leading to Nibbāna is related to state leading to rebirth and death by object condition, strong-dependence condition. (2)

(vii) State leading to Nibbāna is related to state leading neither to rebirth and death nor to Nibbāna by object condition, conascence condition, strong-dependence condition, postnascence condition. (3)

(viii) State leading to Nibbāna is related to state leading to Nibbāna and leading neither to rebirth and death nor to Nibbāna by conascence condition. (4)

71. (ix) State leading neither to rebirth and death nor to Nibbāna is related to state leading neither to rebirth and death nor to Nibbāna by object condition, conascence condition, strong-dependence condition, prenascence condition, postnascence condition, nutriment condition, faculty condition. (1)

(x) State leading neither to rebirth and death nor to Nibbāna is related to state leading to rebirth and death by object condition, strong-dependence condition, prenascence condition. (2)

(ix) State leading neither to rebirth and death nor to Nibbāna is related to state leading to Nibbāna by strong-dependence condition, prenascence condition. (3)

72. (xii) States leading to rebirth and death and leading neither to rebirth and death nor to Nibbāna are related to state leading to rebirth and death by conascence-prenascence. (1)

(xiii) States leading to rebirth and death and leading neither to birth and death nor to Nibbāna are related to state leading neither to rebirth and death nor to Nibbāna by conascence, postnascence-nutriment-faculty. (2)

(xiv) States leading to Nibbāna and leading neither to rebirth and death nor to Nibbāna are related to state leading to Nibbāna by conascence-prenascence. (1)

(xv) States leading to Nibbāna and leading neither to rebirth and death nor to Nibbāna are related to state leading neither to rebirth and death nor to Nibbāna by conascence, postnascence-nutriment-faculty. (2)

2. CONDITIONS: NEGATIVE (ii) ENUMERATION CHAPTER

By Ones

73. With not-root 15, not-object, not-predominance, not-proximity, not-contiguity 15, not-conascence 11, not-mutuality 11, not-dependence 11, not-strong-dependence 14 (na upanissaya cuddassa), not-prenascence 13, not-postnascence 15, not-repetition, not-kamma, not-resultant, not-nutriment, not-faculty, not-jhāna, not-path 15, not-association 11, not-dissociation 9, not-presence 9, not-absence 15, not-disappearance 15, not-non-disappearance 9. (Enumerate thus.)

End of Negative

3. CONDITIONS: POSITIVE-NEGATIVE

Root By Twos

74. With root condition, not-object 7, not-predominance, not-proximity, not-contiguity 7, not-mutuality 3, not-strong-dependence 7, not-prenascence, not-postnascence, not-repetition, not-kamma, not-resultant, not-nutriment, not-faculty, not-jhāna, not-path 7, not-association 3, not-dissociation 3, not-absence 7, not-disappearance 7. (Enumerate thus.)

End of Positive-Negative

4. CONDITIONS: NEGATIVE-POSITIVE

Not-root By Twos

75. With not-root condition, object 7, predominance 10, proximity 6, contiguity 6, conascence 9, mutuality 3, dependence 13, strong-dependence 9, prenascence 3, postnascence 3, repetition 3, kamma 7, resultant

1, nutriment 7, faculty, jhāna, path 7, association 3, dissociation 5, presence 13, absence 6, disappearance 6, non-disappearance 13. (Enumerate thus.)

End of Negative-Positive

END OF TRIPLET OF (STATE) LEADING TO REBIRTH AND DEATH

11. LEARNERS TRIPLET[1] I. "DEPENDENT" CHAPTER

1. CONDITIONS: POSITIVE (i) CLASSIFICATION CHAPTER

Root 9

1. (i) Dependent on state appertaining to Learners (sekkhaṁ dhammaṁ paticca), arises state appertaining to Learners by root condition.

Dependent on one aggregate appertaining to Learners, arise three aggregates . . . two aggregates . . . (1)

(ii) Dependent on state appertaining to Learners, arises state appertaining neither to Learners nor to Arahatta (nevasekkha-nāsekkha) by root condition.

Dependent on aggregates appertaining to Learners, arises mind-produced matter. (2)

(iii) Dependent on state appertaining to Learners, arise states appertaining to Learners and appertaining neither to Learners nor to Arahatta by root condition.

Dependent on one aggregate appertaining to Learners, arise three aggregates and mind-produced matter . . . two aggregates . . . (3)

2. (iv) Dependent on state appertaining to Arahatta (asekkha), arises state appertaining to Arahatta by root condition.

Dependent on one aggregate appertaining to Arahatta, arise three aggregates . . . (1)

(v) Dependent on state appertaining to Arahatta, arises state appertaining neither to Learners nor to Arahatta by root condition.

Dependent on aggregates appertaining to Arahatta, arises mind-produced matter. (2)

(vi) Dependent on state appertaining to Arahatta . . . states apper-

---

[1] This comprises (1) States appertaining to Learners, (2) States appertaining to Arahatta, (3) States appertaining neither to Learners nor to Arahatta.

taining to Arahatta and appertaining neither to Learners nor to Arahatta . . .

Dependent on one aggregate appertaining to Arahatta, arise three aggregates and mind-produced matter . . . two aggregates . . . (3)

3. (vii) Dependent on state appertaining neither to Learners nor to Arahatta (nevasekkha-nāsekkha), arises state appertaining neither to Learners nor to Arahatta by root condition.

(*a*) Dependent on one aggregate appertaining neither to Learners nor to Arahatta, arise three aggregates and mind-produced matter . . . two aggregates . . .

(*b*) At the moment of conception . . . dependent on aggregates, arises (heart-)base; dependent on (heart-)base, arise aggregates;

(*c*) Dependent on one great primary, arise three great primaries . . . dependent on two great primaries, arise two great primaries; dependent on great primaries, arise mind-produced and kamma-produced derived matter. (1)

(viii) Dependent on state appertaining to Learners and appertaining neither to Learners nor to Arahatta, arises state appertaining neither to Learners nor to Arahatta by root condition.

Dependent on aggregates appertaining to Learners and great primaries, arises mind-produced matter. (1)

(ix) Dependent on state appertaining to Arahatta and appertaining neither to Learners nor to Arahatta, arises state appertaining neither to Learners nor to Arahatta by root condition.

Dependent on aggregates appertaining to Arahatta and great primaries, arises mind-produced matter. (1)

Object, etc.

4. Dependent on state appertaining to Learners, arises state appertaining to Learners by object condition . . . by predominance condition. (No conception.) . . . by proximity condition . . . by contiguity condition . . . by conascence condition. (Include all great primaries.) . . . by mutuality condition . . . by dependence condition . . . by strong-dependence condition . . . by prenascence condition . . . by repetition condition.

Dependent on one aggregate appertaining to Learners, arise three aggregates . . . two aggregates . . .

Dependent on state appertaining neither to Learners nor to Arahatta, arises state appertaining neither to Learners nor to Arahatta by repetition condition.

Dependent on one aggregate appertaining neither to Learners nor to Arahatta, arise three aggregates . . . two aggregates . . .

. . . by kamma condition . . . (i)–(iii) by resultant condition.

Dependent on one resultant aggregate appertaining to Learners, arise three aggregates . . . two aggregates . . . (Three. Complete.)

(iv)–(vi) Dependent on state appertaining to Arahatta, arises state appertaining to Arahatta by resultant condition.

Dependent on one aggregate appertaining to Arahatta . . . three.

(vii) Dependent on state appertaining neither to Learners nor to Arahatta, arises state appertaining neither to Learners nor to Arahatta by resultant condition.

(*a*) Dependent on one resultant aggregate appertaining neither to Learners nor to Arahatta, arise three aggregates and mind-produced matter . . . two aggregates . . .

(*b*) At the moment of conception . . . dependent on aggregates, arises (heart-)base; dependent on (heart-)base, arise aggregates;

(*c*) One great primary . . . (1)

(viii) Dependent on state appertaining to Learners and appertaining neither to Learners nor to Arahatta, arises state appertaining neither to Learners nor to Arahatta by resultant condition.

Dependent on resultant aggregates appertaining to Learners and great primaries, arises mind-produced matter. (1)

(ix) Dependent on state appertaining to Arahatta and appertaining neither to Learners nor to Arahatta, arises state appertaining neither to Learners nor to Arahatta by resultant condition.

Dependent on aggregates appertaining to Arahatta and great primaries, arises mind-produced matter. (1)

Nutriment, etc.

5. Dependent on state appertaining to Learners, arises state appertaining to Learners by nutriment condition . . . by faculty condition . . . by jhāna condition . . . by path condition . . . by association condition . . . by dissociation condition . . . by presence condition . . . by absence condition . . . by disappearance condition . . . by non-disappearance condition . . .

1. CONDITIONS: POSITIVE (ii) ENUMERATION CHAPTER

By Ones

6. With root 9, object 3, predominance 9, proximity 3, contiguity 3, conascence 9, mutuality 3, dependence 9, strong-dependence 3, prenascence 3, repetition 2 (āsevane dve), kamma 9, resultant (vipāke), nutriment, faculty, jhāna, path 9, association 3, dissociation 9, presence 9, absence 3, disappearance 3, non-disappearance 9. (Enumerate thus.)

End of Positive

2. CONDITIONS: NEGATIVE (i) CLASSIFICATION CHAPTER

Not-root 1

7. (i) Dependent on state appertaining neither to Learners nor to Arahatta, arises state appertaining neither to Learners nor to Arahatta by not-root condition.

(*a*) Dependent on one rootless aggregate appertaining neither to Learners nor to Arahatta, arise three aggregates and mind-produced matter . . . two aggregates . . .

(*b*) At the moment of rootless conception . . . dependent on aggregates, arises (heart-)base; dependent on (heart-)base, arise aggregates;

(*c*) One great primary . . . External . . . nutriment-produced . . . temperature-produced . . . one great primary of non-percipient beings . . .

(*d*) Dependent on doubt-accompanied or restlessness-accompanied aggregates, arises doubt-accompanied or restlessness-accompanied delusion. (1)

Not-object 5

8. (i) Dependent on state appertaining to Learners, arises state appertaining neither to Learners nor to Arahatta by not-object condition.

Dependent on aggregates appertaining to Learners, arises mind-produced matter. (1)

(ii) Dependent on state appertaining to Arahatta, arises state appertaining neither to Learners nor to Arahatta by not-object condition.

Dependent on aggregates appertaining to Arahatta, arises mind-produced matter. (1)

(iii) Dependent on state appertaining neither to Learners nor to Arahatta, arises state appertaining neither to Learners nor to Arahatta by not-object condition.

(*a*) Dependent on aggregates appertaining neither to Learners nor to Arahatta, arises mind-produced matter;

(*b*) At the moment of conception . . . dependent on aggregates, arises (heart-)base . . .

(*c*) One great primary . . . non-percipient beings . . . (1)

(iv) Dependent on state appertaining to Learners and appertaining neither to Learners nor to Arahatta, arises state appertaining neither to Learners nor to Arahatta by not-object condition.

Dependent on aggregates appertaining to Learners and great primaries, arises mind-produced matter. (1)

(v) Dependent on state appertaining to Arahatta and appertaining neither to Learners nor to Arahatta, arises state appertaining neither to Learners nor to Arahatta by not-object condition.

Dependent on aggregates appertaining to Arahatta and great primaries, arises mind-produced matter. (1)

Not-predominance, etc.

9. (i) Dependent on state appertaining to Learners, arises state appertaining to Learners by not-predominance condition.

Dependent on aggregates appertaining to Learners, arises predominance appertaining to Learners. (1)

(ii) Dependent on state appertaining to Arahatta, arises state appertaining to Arahatta by not-predominance condition.

Dependent on aggregates appertaining to Arahatta, arises predominance appertaining to Arahatta. (1)

(iii) Dependent on state appertaining neither to Learners nor to Arahatta, arises state appertaining neither to Learners nor to Arahatta by not-predominance condition. [Complete. (Include) all conceptions and great primaries.] . . .

. . . by not-proximity condition . . . by not-contiguity condition . . . by not-mutuality condition . . . by not-strong-dependence condition . . . by not-prenascence condition. 7. (As for the Faultless Triplet.) . . . by not-postnascence condition . . . by not-repetition condition.

10. (i) Dependent on one resultant aggregate appertaining to Learners, arise three aggregates . . . two aggregates . . . (1)

(ii) Dependent on state appertaining to Learners, arises state appertaining neither to Learners nor to Arahatta by not-repetition condition.

Dependent on aggregates appertaining to Learners, arises mind-produced matter. (2)

(iii) Dependent on state appertaining to Learners, arise states appertaining to Learners and appertaining neither to Learners nor to Arahatta by not-repetition condition.

Dependent on one resultant aggregate appertaining to Learners, arise three aggregates and mind-produced matter . . . two aggregates . . . (3)

(iv)–(vi) Dependent on state appertaining to Arahatta . . . state appertaining to Arahatta . . . three.

(vii) Dependent on state appertaining neither to Learners nor to Arahatta, arises state appertaining neither to Learners nor to Arahatta by not-repetition condition.

Appertaining neither to Learners nor to Arahatta . . . (One; complete; appertaining to Learners and appertaining neither to Learners nor to Arahatta . . . Combinations are to be completed. Do two questions. 9.)

. . . by not-kamma condition.

Dependent on aggregates appertaining to Learners, arises volition appertaining to Learners.

Dependent on state appertaining neither to Learners nor to Arahatta, arises state appertaining neither to Learners nor to Arahatta by not-kamma condition.

Dependent on aggregates appertaining neither to Learners nor to Arahatta, arises volition appertaining neither to Learners nor to Arahatta;

External . . . nutriment-produced . . . one great primary of temperature-produced . . .

Not-resultant 5

11. (i) Dependent on state appertaining to Learners, arises state appertaining to Learners by not-resultant condition.

Dependent on one aggregate appertaining to Learners, arise three aggregates . . . (1)

(ii) Dependent on state appertaining to Learners, arises state appertaining neither to Learners nor to Arahatta by not-resultant condition.

Dependent on aggregates appertaining to Learners, arises mind-produced matter. (2)

(iii) Dependent on state appertaining to Learners, arise states appertaining to Learners and appertaining neither to Learners nor to Arahatta by not-resultant condition.

Dependent on one aggregate appertaining to Learners, arise three aggregates and mind-produced matter . . . (3)

12. (iv) Dependent on state appertaining neither to Learners nor to Arahatta, arises state appertaining neither to learners nor to Arahatta by not-resultant condition. (Complete. No conception.)

(v) Dependent on state appertaining to Learners and appertaining neither to Learners nor to Arahatta, arises state appertaining neither to Learners nor to Arahatta by not-resultant condition.

Dependent on aggregates appertaining to Learners and great primaries, arises mind-produced matter. (1)

Not-nutriment, etc.

13. Dependent on state appertaining neither to Learners nor to Arahatta, arises state appertaining neither to Learners nor to Arahatta by not-nutriment condition . . . by not-faculty condition . . . by not-jhāna condition . . . by not-path condition . . .

Not-association 5

14. Dependent on state appertaining to Learners, arises state appertaining neither to Learners nor to Arahatta by not-association condition. (The same as not-object condition.)

Not-dissociation, etc.

(i) Dependent on state appertaining to Learners, arises state appertaining to Learners by not-dissociation condition.

In the immaterial plane, dependent on one aggregate appertaining to Learners, arise three aggregates . . . (1)

(ii) Dependent on state appertaining to Arahatta, arises state appertaining to Arahatta by not-dissociation condition.

In the immaterial plane, dependent on one aggregate appertaining to Arahatta, arise three aggregates . . . (1)

(iii) Dependent on state appertaining neither to Learners nor to Arahatta, arises state appertaining neither to Learners nor to Arahatta by not-dissociation condition.

(*a*) In the immaterial plane, dependent on one aggregate appertaining neither to Learners nor to Arahatta, arise three aggregates . . .

(*b*) External . . . nutriment-produced . . . temperature-produced . . . non-percipient beings . . .

. . . by not-absence condition . . . by not-disappearance condition . . .

2. CONDITIONS: NEGATIVE (ii) ENUMERATION CHAPTER

By Ones

15. With not-root 1, not-object 5, not-predominance 3, not-proximity, not-contiguity, not-mutuality, not-strong-dependence 5, not-prenascence 7, not-postnascence 9, not-repetition 9, not-kamma 2, not-resultant 5, not-nutriment 1, not-faculty 1, not-jhāna 1, not-path 1, not-association 5, not-dissociation 3, not-absence 5, not-disappearance 5. (Enumerate thus.)

End of Negative

3. CONDITIONS: POSITIVE–NEGATIVE

Root By Twos

16. With root condition, not-object 5, not-predominance 3, not-proximity, not-contiguity, not-mutuality, not-strong-dependence 5, not-prenascence 7, not-postnascence, not-repetition 9, not-kamma 2, not-resultant 5, not-association 5, not-dissociation 3, not-absence 5, not-disappearance 5. (Enumerate thus.)

End of Positive–Negative

4. CONDITIONS: NEGATIVE–POSITIVE

Not-root By Twos

17. With not-root condition, object 1, proximity, contiguity, conascence, mutuality, dependence, strong-dependence, prenascence, repetition, kamma, resultant, nutriment, faculty, jhāna, path, association, dissociation, presence, absence, disappearance, non-disappearance 1. (Enumerate thus.)

End of Negative–Positive

End of "DEPENDENT" CHAPTER

(The "Conascent" Chapter is the same as the "Dependent" Chapter.)

11. LEARNERS TRIPLET III. "CONDITIONED" CHAPTER

1. CONDITIONS: POSITIVE (i) CLASSIFICATION CHAPTER

Root 17

18. (i)–(iii) Conditioned by state appertaining to Learners, arises state

appertaining to Learners by root condition . . . three. (The same as in the "Dependent" Chapter.)

(iv)-(vi) Conditioned by state appertaining to Arahatta, arises state appertaining to Arahatta by root condition . . . three. (The same as in the "Dependent" Chapter.)

19. (vii) Conditioned by state appertaining neither to Learners nor to Arahatta, arises state appertaining neither to Learners nor to Arahatta by root condition. (Complete.) . . .

Conditioned by great primaries, arise mind-produced and kamma-produced derived matter;

Conditioned by (heart-)base, arise aggregates appertaining neither to Learners nor to Arahatta. (1)

(viii) Conditioned by state appertaining neither to Learners nor to Arahatta, arises state appertaining to Learners by root condition.

Conditioned by (heart-)base, arise aggregates appertaining to Learners. (2)

(ix) Conditioned by state appertaining neither to Learners nor to Arahatta, arises state appertaining to Arahatta by root condition.

Conditioned by (heart-)base, arise aggregates appertaining to Arahatta. (3)

(x) Conditioned by state appertaining neither to Learners nor to Arahatta, arise states appertaining to Learners and appertaining neither to Learners nor to Arahatta by root condition.

Conditioned by (heart-)base, arise aggregates appertaining to Learners; conditioned by great primaries, arises mind-produced matter. (4)

(xi) Conditioned by state appertaining neither to Learners nor to Arahatta, arise states appertaining to Arahatta and appertaining neither to Learners nor to Arahatta by root condition.

Conditioned by (heart-)base, arise aggregates appertaining to Arahatta; conditioned by great primaries, arises mind-produced matter. (5)

20. (xii) Conditioned by state appertaining to Learners and appertaining neither to Learners nor to Arahatta, arises state appertaining to Learners by root condition.

Conditioned by one aggregate appertaining to Learners and (heart-) base, arise three aggregates . . . two aggregates. (1)

(xiii) Conditioned by state appertaining to Learners and appertaining neither to Learners nor to Arahatta, arises state appertaining neither to Learners nor to Arahatta by root condition.

Conditioned by aggregates appertaining to Learners and great primaries, arises mind-produced matter. (2)

(xiv) Conditioned by state appertaining to Learners and appertaining neither to Learners nor to Arahatta, arise states appertaining to Learners and appertaining neither to Learners nor to Arahatta by root condition.

Conditioned by one aggregate appertaining to Learners and (heart-) base, arise three aggregates . . . two aggregates; conditioned by aggregates appertaining to Learners and great primaries, arises mind-produced matter. (3)

(xv)-(xvii) Conditioned by state appertaining to Arahatta and appertaining neither to Learners nor to Arahatta . . . three. (The same as Learners.)

Object 7

21. (i) Conditioned by state appertaining to Learners, arises state appertaining to Learners by object condition . . . one.

(ii) Conditioned by state appertaining to Arahatta . . . state appertaining to Arahatta . . . one.

(iii) Conditioned by state appertaining neither to Learners nor to Arahatta, arises state appertaining neither to Learners nor to Arahatta by object condition . . . one.

(At the moment of conception . . .)[1] conditioned by (heart-)base, arise aggregates appertaining neither to Learners nor to Arahatta;

Conditioned by eye-base, arises eye-consciousness . . . conditioned by body-base, arises body-consciousness; conditioned by (heart-)base, arise aggregates appertaining neither to Learners nor to Arahatta. (1)

(iv) Conditioned by state appertaining neither to Learners nor to Arahatta, arises state appertaining to Learners by object condition.

Conditioned by (heart-)base, arise aggregates appertaining to Learners. (2)

(v) Conditioned by state appertaining neither to Learners nor to Arahatta, arises state appertaining to Arahatta by object condition.

Conditioned by (heart-)base, arise aggregates appertaining to Arahatta. (3)

(vi) Conditioned by state appertaining to Learners and appertaining neither to Learners nor to Arahatta, arises state appertaining to Learners by object condition.

---

[1] Omitted in the Pali Text.

Conditioned by one aggregate appertaining to Learners and (heart-) base, arise three aggregates . . . two aggregates. (1)

(vii) Conditioned by state appertaining to Arahatta and appertaining neither to Learners nor to Arahatta, arises state appertaining to Arahatta by object condition.

Conditioned by one aggregate appertaining to Arahatta and (heart-) base, arise three aggregates . . . two aggregates. (1)

Predominance, etc.

22. Conditioned by state appertaining to Learners, arises state appertaining to Learners by predominance condition . . . by proximity condition . . . by contiguity condition . . . by conascence condition . . . by mutuality condition . . . by dependence condition . . . by strong-dependence condition . . . by prenascence condition . . . by repetition condition.

Conditioned by one aggregate appertaining to Learners, arise three aggregates . . .

Conditioned by state appertaining neither to Learners nor to Arahatta, arises state appertaining neither to Learners nor to Arahatta by repetition condition.

Conditioned by one aggregate appertaining neither to Learners nor to Arahatta . . . conditioned by (heart-)base, arise aggregates appertaining neither to Learners nor to Arahatta. (1)

Conditioned by state appertaining neither to Learners nor to Arahatta, arises state appertaining to Learners by repetition condition.

Conditioned by (heart-)base, arise aggregates appertaining to Learners. (2)

Conditioned by state appertaining to Learners and appertaining neither to Learners nor to Arahatta, arises state appertaining to Learners by repetition condition.

Conditioned by one aggregate appertaining to Learners and (heart-) base, arise three aggregates . . . two aggregates. (1)

Kamma, etc.

23. Conditioned by state appertaining to Learners, arises state appertaining to Learners by kamma condition . . . by resultant condition. (Conditioned by) one resultant aggregate appertaining to Learners . . . by nutriment condition . . . by faculty condition . . . by jhāna condition . . . by path condition . . . by association condition . . . by dissociation

condition . . . by presence condition . . . by absence condition . . . by disappearance condition . . . by non-disappearance condition . . .

1. CONDITIONS: POSITIVE (ii) ENUMERATION CHAPTER

By Ones

24. With root 17, object 7, predominance 17, proximity 7, contiguity 7, conascence 17, mutuality 7, dependence 17, strong-dependence 7, prenascence 7, repetition 4, kamma 17, resultant 17, nutriment 17, faculty, jhāna, path 17, association 7, dissociation 17, presence 17, absence 7, disappearance 7, non-disappearance 17. (Enumerate thus.)

End of Positive

2. CONDITIONS: NEGATIVE (i) CLASSIFICATION CHAPTER

Not-root 1

25. Conditioned by state appertaining neither to Learners nor to Arahatta, arises state appertaining neither to Learners nor to Arahatta by not-root condition.

(*a*) Conditioned by one rootless aggregate appertaining neither to Learners nor to Arahatta, arise three aggregates and mind-produced matter . . . two aggregates . . .

(*b*) At the moment of rootless conception . . . conditioned by aggregates, arises (heart-)base; conditioned by (heart-)base, arise aggregates;

(*c*) Conditioned by one great primary . . . External . . . nutriment-produced . . . temperature-produced . . . non-percipient beings . . .

(*d*) Conditioned by eye-base, arises eye-consciousness . . . conditioned by body-base, arises body-consciousness; conditioned by (heart-)base, arise rootless aggregates appertaining neither to Learners nor to Arahatta;

(*e*) Conditioned by doubt-accompanied or restlessness-accompanied aggregates and (heart-)base, arises doubt-accompanied or restlessness-accompanied delusion. (1)

Not-object, etc.

26. (i) Conditioned by state appertaining to Learners, arises state appertaining neither to Learners nor to Arahatta by not-object condition . . . (1)

(i) Conditioned by state appertaining to Learners, arises state appertaining to Learners by not-predominance condition.

Conditioned by aggregates appertaining to Learners, arises predominance appertaining to Learners. (1)

(ii) Conditioned by state appertaining to Arahatta, arises state appertaining to Arahatta by not-predominance condition.

Conditioned by aggregates appertaining to Arahatta, arises predominance appertaining to Arahatta. (1)

(iii) Conditioned by state appertaining neither to Learners nor to Arahatta, arises state appertaining neither to Learners nor to Arahatta by not-predominance condition. (Complete.) . . . non-percipient beings . . . eye-base . . . conditioned by (heart-)base, arise aggregates appertaining neither to Learners nor to Arahatta. (1)

(iv) Conditioned by state appertaining neither to Learners nor to Arahatta, arises state appertaining to Learners by not-predominance condition.

Conditioned by (heart-)base, arises predominance appertaining to Learners. (2)

(v) Conditioned by state appertaining neither to Learners nor to Arahatta, arises state appertaining to Arahatta by not-predominance condition.

Conditioned by (heart-)base, arises predominance appertaining to Arahatta. (3)

(vi) Conditioned by state appertaining to Learners and appertaining neither to Learners nor to Arahatta, arises state appertaining to Learners by not-predominance condition.

Conditioned by aggregates appertaining to Learners and (heart-)base, arises predominance appertaining to Learners. (1)

(vii) Conditioned by state appertaining to Arahatta and appertaining neither to Learners nor to Arahatta, arises state appertaining to Arahatta by not-predominance condition.

Conditioned by aggregates appertaining to Arahatta and (heart-)base, arises predominance appertaining to Arahatta. (1)

Not-proximity, etc.

27. Conditioned by state appertaining to Learners, arises state appertaining neither to Learners nor to Arahatta by not-proximity condition . . . by not-contiguity condition . . . by not-mutuality condition . . . by not-strong-dependence condition . . . by not-prenascence condition. (Seven.)[1]

---

[1] Not for Not-postnascence as given in the Pali Text.

. . . by not-postnascence condition . . . by not-repetition condition . . . by not-kamma condition.

(i) Conditioned by aggregates appertaining to Learners, arises volition appertaining to Learners.

(ii) Conditioned by state appertaining neither to Learners nor to Arahatta, arises state appertaining neither to Learners nor to Arahatta by not-kamma condition.

(*a*) Conditioned by aggregates appertaining neither to Learners nor to Arahatta, arises volition appertaining neither to Learners nor to Arahatta;

(*b*) External . . . nutriment-produced . . . temperature-produced . . .

(*c*) Conditioned by (heart-)base, arises volition appertaining neither to Learners nor to Arahatta. (1)

(iii) Conditioned by state appertaining neither to Learners nor to Arahatta, arises state appertaining to Learners by not-kamma condition.

Conditioned by (heart-)base, arises volition appertaining to Learners. (2)

(iv) Conditioned by state appertaining to Learners and appertaining neither to Learners nor to Arahatta, arises state appertaining to Learners by not-kamma condition.

Conditioned by aggregates appertaining to Learners and (heart-)base, arises volition appertaining to Learners. (1)

Not-resultant 9

28. (i)-(iii) Conditioned by state appertaining to Learners, arises state appertaining to Learners by not-resultant condition. (For the reference with Learners, three.)

(iv)-(vi) Conditioned by state appertaining neither to Learners nor to Arahatta, arises state appertaining neither to Learners nor to Arahatta by not-resultant condition. (For the reference with "appertaining neither to Learners nor to Arahatta", three.)

(vii)-(ix) Conditioned by state appertaining to Learners and appertaining neither to Learners nor to Arahatta, arises state appertaining to Learners by not-resultant condition. (For the combinations with Learners, three.)

Not-nutriment, etc.

29. Conditioned by state appertaining neither to Learners nor to Arahatta, arises state appertaining neither to Learners nor to Arahatta by

not-nutriment condition . . . by not-faculty condition . . . by not-jhāna condition . . . by not-path condition . . . by not-association condition . . . by not-dissociation condition . . . by not-absence condition . . . by not-disappearance condition . . .

2. CONDITIONS: NEGATIVE (ii) ENUMERATION CHAPTER

By Ones

30. With not-root 1, not-object 5, not-predominance 7, not-proximity 5, not-contiguity 5, not-mutuality 5, not-strong-dependence 5, not-prenascence 7, not-postnascence 17, not-repetition 17, not-kamma 4, not-resultant 9, not-nutriment 1, not-faculty 1, not-jhāna 1, not-path 1, not-association 5, not-dissociation 3, not-absence 5, not-disappearance 5. (Enumerate thus.)

End of Negative

3. CONDITIONS: POSITIVE-NEGATIVE

Root By Twos

31. With root condition, not-object 5, not-predominance 7, not-proximity, not-contiguity, not-mutuality, not-strong-dependence 5, not-prenascence 7, not-postnascence 17, not-repetition 17, not-kamma 4, not-resultant 9, not-association 5, not-dissociation 3, not-absence 5, not-disappearance 5. (Enumerate thus.)

End of Positive-Negative

4. CONDITIONS: NEGATIVE-POSITIVE

(Not-root By Twos)

32. With not-root condition, object 1, proximity, contiguity, conascence, mutuality 1 . . . non-disappearance 1. (Enumerate thus.)

End of Negative-Positive

End of "CONDITIONED" CHAPTER

(The "Supported" Chapter is the same as the "Conditioned" Chapter.)

11. Learners Triplet V. "Conjoined" Chapter

1. CONDITIONS: POSITIVE (i) CLASSIFICATION CHAPTER

Root 3

33. (i) Conjoined with state appertaining to Learners, arises state appertaining to Learners by root condition.

Conjoined with one aggregate appertaining to Learners, arise three aggregates . . . two aggregates . . . (1)

(ii) Conjoined with state appertaining to Arahatta, arises state appertaining to Arahatta by root condition.

Conjoined with one aggregate appertaining to Arahatta, arise three aggregates . . . two aggregates . . . (1)

(iii) Conjoined with state appertaining neither to Learners nor to Arahatta, arises state appertaining neither to Learners nor to Arahatta by root condition.

(*a*) Conjoined with one aggregate appertaining neither to Learners nor to Arahatta, arise three aggregates . . . two aggregates . . .

(*b*) At the moment of conception . . . (1)

Object, etc.

34. Conjoined with state appertaining to Learners, arises state appertaining to Learners by object condition . . . by predominance condition . . . by prenascence condition . . . by repetition condition. [Do two (questions.)] . . . by non-disappearance condition . . .

1. CONDITIONS: POSITIVE (ii) ENUMERATION CHAPTER

(By Ones)

35. With root 3, object 3, predominance 3, proximity, contiguity, conascence, mutuality, dependence, strong-dependence, prenascence 3, repetition 2, kamma 3 . . . non-disappearance 3. (Enumerate thus.)

End of Positive

2. CONDITIONS: NEGATIVE (i) CLASSIFICATION CHAPTER

Not-root 1

36. Conjoined with state appertaining neither to Learners nor to Arahatta, arises state appertaining neither to Learners nor to Arahatta by not-root condition.

(*a*) Conjoined with one rootless aggregate appertaining neither to Learners nor to Arahatta, arise three aggregates . . . two aggregates . . .

(*b*) At the moment of rootless conception . . .

(*c*) Conjoined with doubt-accompanied or restlessness-accompanied aggregates, arises doubt-accompanied or restlessness-accompanied delusion. (1)

Not-predominance 3

37. (i) Conjoined with state appertaining to Learners, arises state appertaining to Learners by not-predominance condition.

Conjoined with aggregates appertaining to Learners, arises predominance appertaining to Learners. (1)

(ii) Conjoined with state appertaining to Arahatta, arises state appertaining to Arahatta by not-predominance condition.

Conjoined with aggregates appertaining to Arahatta, arises predominance appertaining to Arahatta. (1)

(iii) Conjoined with state appertaining neither to Learners nor to Arahatta, arises state appertaining neither to Learners nor to Arahatta by not-predominance condition. (Complete. One.)

Not-prenascence, etc.

38. Conjoined with state appertaining to Learners, arises state appertaining to Learners by not-prenascence condition . . . by not-postnascence condition . . . by not-repetition condition . . . by not-kamma condition. [Do two (questions.)] . . . by not-resultant condition. [Do two (questions.)] . . . by not-jhāna condition . . . by not-path condition . . . by not-dissociation condition . . .

2. CONDITIONS: NEGATIVE (ii) ENUMERATION CHAPTER

(By Ones)

39. With not-root 1, not-predominance 3, not-prenascence 3, not-postnascence 3, not-repetition 3, not-kamma 2, not-resultant 2, not-jhāna 1, not-path 1, not-dissociation 3. (Enumerate thus.)

End of Negative

3. CONDITIONS: POSITIVE-NEGATIVE

(Root By Twos)

40. With root condition, not-predominance 3, not-prenascence 3,

not-postnascence, not-repetition 3, not-kamma 2, not-resultant 2, not-dissociation 3. (Enumerate thus.)

End of Positive-Negative

4. CONDITIONS: NEGATIVE-POSITIVE

(Not root By Twos)

41. With not-root condition, object 1, proximity, contiguity, co-nascence, mutuality, dependence, strong-dependence, prenascence, repetition, kamma, resultant, nutriment, faculty, jhāna, path, association, dissociation, presence, absence, disappearance, non-disappearance 1. (Enumerate thus.)

End of Negative-Positive

End of "CONJOINED" CHAPTER

(The "Associated" Chapter is the same as the "Conjoined" Chapter.)

11. LEARNERS TRIPLET VII. "INVESTIGATION" CHAPTER

1. CONDITIONS: POSITIVE (i) CLASSIFICATION CHAPTER

Root 7

42. (i) State appertaining to Learners (sekkho dhammo) is related to state appertaining to Learners by root condition.

Roots appertaining to Learners are related to (their) associated aggregates by root condition. (1)

(ii) State appertaining to Learners is related to state appertaining neither to Learners nor to Arahatta by root condition.

Roots appertaining to Learners are related to mind-produced matter by root condition. (2)

(iii) State appertaining to Learners is related to state appertaining to Learners and appertaining neither to Learners nor to Arahatta by root condition.

Roots appertaining to Learners are related to (their) associated aggregates and mind-produced matter by root condition. (3)

(iv)-(vi) State appertaining to Arahatta (asekkha) to state appertaining to Arahatta . . . (Three.)

(vii) State appertaining neither to Learners nor to Arahatta is related to state appertaining neither to Learners nor to Arahatta by root condition.

(*a*) Roots appertaining neither to Learners nor to Arahatta are related to (their) associated aggregates and mind-produced matter by root condition;

(*b*) At the moment of conception . . . (1)

Object 5

43. (i) State appertaining to Learners is related to state appertaining neither to Learners nor to Arahatta by object condition.

The Noble persons, having emerged from Path, review the Path, review the Fruition appertaining to Learners. By the knowledge of penetration into others' minds, (they) know the other being's mind appertaining to Learners. Aggregates appertaining to Learners are related to knowledge of penetration into others' minds, knowledge of remembrance of past existences, knowledge of future existences, advertence by object condition. (1)

(ii) State appertaining to Arahatta is related to state appertaining neither to Learners nor to Arahatta by object condition.

The Arahat reviews the Fruition appertaining to Arahatta. By the knowledge of penetration into others' minds, (he) knows the other being's mind appertaining to Arahatta. Aggregates appertaining to Arahatta are related to knowledge of penetration into others' minds, knowledge of remembrance of past existences, knowledge of future existences, advertence by object condition. (1)

44. (iii) State appertaining neither to Learners nor to Arahatta is related to state appertaining neither to Learners nor to Arahatta by object condition.

After having offered an offering, having undertaken precepts, having fulfilled the duty of observance, (one) reviews it . . . formerly well done. Having emerged from jhāna, (one) reviews the jhāna. The Noble persons review Nibbāna. Nibbāna is related to change-of-lineage, purification, advertence by object condition.

The Noble persons review the eradicated defilements, review the uneradicated defilements, know the defilements addicted to before. (They) practise insight into the impermanence, suffering and impersonality of the eye; enjoy and delight in (the eye). Taking it as object, arises lust . . . arises grief . . . ear . . . (heart-)base . . . (They) practise insight into the impermanence, suffering and impersonality of aggregates appertaining neither to Learners nor to Arahatta . . . enjoy . . . arises grief.

By the power of divine-eye, (one) sees a visible object. By the power of divine-ear element, (one) hears a sound. By the knowledge of penetration into others' minds, (one) knows the other being's mind appertaining neither to Learners nor to Arahatta.

Infinity of space to infinity of consciousness . . . nothingness is related to neither-perception-nor-non-perception by object condition. Visible object-base to eye-consciousness . . . tangible object-base to body-consciousness . . .

Aggregates appertaining neither to Learners nor to Arahatta are related to knowledge of supernormal power, knowledge of penetration into others' minds, knowledge of remembrance of past existences, knowledge of rebirths according to one's kamma, knowledge of future existences, advertence by object condition. (1)

(iv) State appertaining neither to Learners nor to Arahatta is related to state appertaining to Learners by object condition.

Nibbāna is related to Path, Fruition appertaining to Learners by object condition. (2)

(v) State appertaining neither to Learners nor to Arahatta is related to state appertaining to Arahatta by object condition.

Nibbāna is related to Fruition appertaining to Arahatta by object condition. (3)

Predominance 9

45. (i) State appertaining to Learners is related to state appertaining to Learners by predominance condition.

Conascence-predominance: Predominance appertaining to Learners is related to (its) associated aggregates by predominance condition. (1)

(ii) State appertaining to Learners is related to state appertaining neither to Learners nor to Arahatta by predominance condition.

(It is of two kinds, namely:) (*a*) object-predominance, (*b*) conascence-predominance.

(*a*) *Object-predominance:* The Noble persons, having emerged from Path, esteem and review the Path, esteem and review the Fruition appertaining to Learners.

(*b*) *Conascence-predominance:* Predominance appertaining to Learners is related to mind-produced matter by predominance condition. (2)

(iii) State appertaining to Learners is related to state appertaining to Learners and appertaining neither to Learners nor to Arahatta by predominance condition.

Conascence-predominance: Predominance appertaining to Learners is related to (its) associated aggregates and mind-produced matter by predominance condition. (3)

46. (iv) State appertaining to Arahatta is related to state appertaining to Arahatta by predominance condition.

Conascence-predominance: Predominance appertaining to Arahatta is related to (its) associated aggregates by predominance condition. (1)

(v) State appertaining to Arahatta is related to state appertaining neither to Learners nor to Arahatta by predominance condition.

(It is of two kinds, namely:) (*a*) object-predominance, (*b*) conascence-predominance.

(*a*) *Object-predominance:* The Arahat esteems and reviews the Fruition appertaining to Arahatta.

(*b*) *Conascence-predominance:* Predominance appertaining to Arahatta is related to mind-produced matter by predominance condition. (2)

(vi) State appertaining to Arahatta is related to state appertaining to Arahatta and appertaining neither to Learners nor to Arahatta by predominance condition.

Conascence-predominance: Predominance appertaining to Arahatta is related to (its) associated aggregates and mind-produced matter by predominance condition. (3)

47. (vii) State appertaining neither to Learners nor to Arahatta is related to state appertaining neither to Learners nor to Arahatta by predominance condition.

(It is of two kinds, namely:) (*a*) object-predominance, (*b*) conascence-predominance.

(*a*) *Object-predominance:* After having offered an offering, having undertaken precepts, having fulfilled the duty of observance, (one) esteems and reviews it. (One) esteems and reviews (such acts) formerly well done. Having emerged from jhāna, one esteems and reviews the jhāna. The Noble persons esteem and review Nibbāna. Nibbāna is related to change-of-lineage, purification by predominance condition.

(One) esteems, enjoys and delights in the eye. Taking it as estimable object, arises lust, arise wrong views . . . ear . . . (heart-)base . . . (One) esteems, enjoys and delights in aggregates appertaining neither to Learners nor to Arahatta. Taking them as estimable object, arises lust, arise wrong views.

(*b*) *Conascence-predominance:* Predominance appertaining neither to Learners nor to Arahatta is related to (its) associated aggregates and mind-produced matter by predominance condition. (1)

(viii) State appertaining neither to Learners nor to Arahatta is related to state appertaining to Learners by predominance condition.

Object-predominance: Nibbāna is related to Path, Fruition appertaining to Learners by predominance condition. (2)

(ix) State appertaining neither to Learners nor to Arahatta is related to state appertaining to Arahatta by predominance condition.

Object-predominance: Nibbāna is related to Fruition appertaining to Arahatta by predominance condition. (3)

Proximity 8

48. (i) State appertaining to Learners is related to state appertaining to Learners by proximity condition.

Preceding aggregates appertaining to Learners are related to subsequent aggregates appertaining to Learners by proximity condition. Path to Fruition appertaining to Learners; Fruition appertaining to Learners is related to Fruition appertaining to Learners by proximity condition. (1)

(ii) State appertaining to Learners is related to state appertaining to Arahatta by proximity condition.

Path is related to Fruition appertaining to Arahatta by proximity condition. (2)

(iii) State appertaining to Learners is related to state appertaining neither to Learners nor to Arahatta by proximity condition.

Fruition appertaining to Learners is related to emergence by proximity condition. (3)

49. (iv) State appertaining to Arahatta is related to state appertaining to Arahatta by proximity condition.

Preceding aggregates appertaining to Arahatta are related to subsequent aggregates appertaining to Arahatta by proximity condition. Fruition appertaining to Arahatta is related to Fruition appertaining to Arahatta by proximity condition. (1)

(v) State appertaining to Arahatta is related to state appertaining neither to Learners nor to Arahatta by proximity condition.

Fruition appertaining to Arahatta is related to emergence by proximity condition. (2)

50. (vi) State appertaining neither to Learners nor to Arahatta is related to state appertaining neither to Learners nor to Arahatta by

proximity condition.

Preceding aggregates appertaining neither to Learners nor to Arahatta to subsequent aggregates appertaining neither to Learners nor to Arahatta . . . Adaptation to change-of-lineage; adaptation to purification; advertence is related to aggregates appertaining neither to Learners nor to Arahatta by proximity condition. (1)

(vii) State appertaining neither to Learners nor to Arahatta is related to state appertaining to Learners by proximity condition.

Change-of-lineage to Path; purification to Path; adaptation to the attainment of Fruition appertaining to Learners; for one emerging from the attainment of Extinction, faultless neither-perception-nor-non-perception is related to the attainment of Fruition appertaining to Learners by proximity condition. (2)

(viii) State appertaining neither to Learners nor to Arahatta is related to state appertaining to Arahatta by proximity condition.

Adaptation to the attainment of Fruition appertaining to Arahatta; for one emerging from the attainment of Extinction, functional neither-perception-nor-non-perception is related to the attainment of Fruition appertaining to Arahatta by proximity condition. (3)

Contiguity 8

51. State appertaining to Learners is related to state appertaining to Learners by contiguity condition . . . (The same as proximity; 8 questions.)

Conascence, etc.

52. State appertaining to Learners is related to state appertaining to Learners by conascence condition. (The same as conascence in the "Dependent" Chapter: 9 questions.) . . . by mutuality condition. (The same as mutuality in the "Dependent" Chapter; three. In dependence condition it is the same as dependence condition in the Faultless Triplet: 13 questions.)

Strong-dependence 8

53. (i) State appertaining to Learners is related to state appertaining to Learners by strong-dependence condition.

(It is of two kinds, namely:) (*a*) proximity-strong-dependence, (*b*) natural strong-dependence . . .

(*b*) *Natural strong-dependence:* First Path is related to second Path by strong-dependence condition; second Path is related to third Path by strong-dependence condition; third Path is related to fourth Path by strong-dependence condition. Path is related to the attainment of Fruition appertaining to Learners by strong-dependence condition. (1)

(ii) State appertaining to Learners is related to state appertaining to Arahatta by strong-dependence condition.

(It is of two kinds, namely:) (*a*) proximity-strong-dependence, (*b*) natural strong-dependence . . .

(*b*) *Natural strong-dependence:* Path is related to the attainment of Fruition appertaining to Arahatta by strong-dependence condition. (2)

(iii) State appertaining to Learners is related to state appertaining neither to Learners nor to Arahatta by strong-dependence condition.

(It is of three kinds, namely:) (*a*) object-strong-dependence, (*b*) proximity-strong-dependence, (*c*) natural strong-dependence . . .

(*c*) *Natural strong-dependence:* The Noble persons, by the strong-dependence of the Path, generate a faultless attainment which has not yet arisen, enter an attainment which has arisen. They practise insight into the impermanence . . . of the formations. Path is related to the Noble person's analytical knowledge of meaning . . . analytical knowledge of the above three, knowledge of correct and faulty conclusion by strong-dependence condition. The attainment of Fruition appertaining to Learners is related to bodily happiness by strong-dependence condition. (3)

54. (iv) State appertaining to Arahatta is related to state appertaining to Arahatta by strong-dependence condition.

Proximity-strong-dependence: Preceding aggregates appertaining to Arahatta to subsequent aggregates appertaining to Arahatta . . . Fruition appertaining to Arahatta is related to Fruition appertaining to Arahatta by strong-dependence condition. (1)

(v) State appertaining to Arahatta is related to state appertaining neither to Learners nor to Arahatta by strong-dependence condition.

(It is of three kinds, namely:) (*a*) object-strong-dependence, (*b*) proximity-strong-dependence, (*c*) natural strong-dependence . . .

(*c*) *Natural strong-dependence:* The attainment of Fruition appertaining to Arahatta is related to bodily happiness by strong-dependence condition. (2)

55. (vi) State appertaining neither to Learners nor to Arahatta is related to state appertaining neither to Learners nor to Arahatta by strong-dependence condition.

(It is of three kinds, namely:) (*a*) object-strong-dependence, (*b*) proximity-strong-dependence, (*c*) natural strong-dependence . . .

(*c*) *Natural strong-dependence:* By the strong-dependence of confidence appertaining neither to Learners nor to Arahatta, (one) offers an offering . . . precepts . . . duty of observance . . . jhāna . . . insight . . . superknowledge, develops attainment; arouses conceit, adopts wrong views . . . precept appertaining neither to Learners nor to Arahatta . . . wisdom . . . lust . . . wish . . . bodily happiness . . . temperature . . . food . . . By the strong-dependence of lodging-place, (one) offers an offering . . . precepts . . . develops attainment, kills a living being . . . causes schism in the Saṅgha. Confidence appertaining neither to Learners nor to Arahatta . . . wisdom, lust . . . wish, bodily happiness . . . lodging-place is related to confidence appertaining neither to Learners nor to Arahatta . . . wisdom, lust . . . wish, bodily happiness, bodily pain by strong-dependence condition.

The preparation for first jhāna is related to first jhāna by strong-dependence condition . . . the preparation for neither-perception-nor-non-perception to neither-perception-nor-non-perception . . . First jhāna is related to second jhāna by strong-dependence condition . . . nothingness is related to neither-perception-nor-non-perception by strong-dependence condition. (1)

(vii) State appertaining neither to Learners nor to Arahatta is related to state appertaining to Learners by strong-dependence condition.

(It is of three kinds, namely:) (*a*) object-strong-dependence, (*b*) proximity-strong-dependence, (*c*) natural strong-dependence . . .

(*c*) *Natural strong-dependence:* The preparation for first Path is related to first Path by strong-dependence condition . . . the preparation for fourth Path is related to fourth Path by strong-dependence condition. (2)

(viii) State appertaining neither to Learners nor to Arahatta is related to state appertaining to Arahatta by strong-depdence condition.

(It is of three kinds, namely:) (*a*) object-strong-dependence, (*b*) proximity-strong-dependence, (*c*) natural strong-dependence . . .

(*c*) *Natural strong-dependence:* Bodily happiness, bodily pain, temperature, food, lodging-place is related to the attainment of Fruition appertaining to Arahatta by strong-dependence condition. (3)

Prenascence 3

56. (i) State appertaining neither to Learners nor to Arahatta is related to state appertaining neither to Learners nor to Arahatta by prenascence condition.

(It is of two kinds, namely:) (*a*) object-prenascence, (*b*) base-prenascence.

(*a*) *Object-prenascence:* (One practises insight into the impermanence . . . of the eye; enjoys and delights in (the eye). Taking it as object, arises lust . . . arises grief . . . ear . . . (One) practises insight into the impermanence, suffering and impersonality of the (heart-)base . . . arises grief. By the power of divine-eye, (one) sees a visible object. By the power of divine-ear element, (one) hears a sound. Visible object-base to eye-consciousness . . . tangible object-base is related to body-consciousness by prenascence condition.

(*b*) *Base-prenascence:* Eye-base to eye-consciousness . . . body-base to body-consciousness . . . (heart-)base is related to aggregates appertaining neither to Learners nor to Arahatta by prenascence condition. (1)

(ii) State appertaining neither to Learners nor to Arahatta is related to state appertaining to Learners by prenascence condition.

Base-prenascence: (Heart-)base is related to aggregates appertaining to Learners by prenascence condition. (2)

(iii) State appertaining neither to Learners nor to Arahatta is related to state appertaining to Arahatta by prenascence condition.

Base-prenascence: (Heart-)base is related to aggregates appertaining to Arahatta by prenascence condition. (3)

Postnascence 3

57. (i) State appertaining to Learners is related to state appertaining neither to Learners nor to Arahatta by postnascence condition.

Postnascent aggregates appertaining to Learners are related to this prenascent body by postnascence condition. (1)

(ii) State appertaining to Arahatta is related to state appertaining neither to Learners nor to Arahatta by postnascence condition.

Postnascent aggregates appertaining to Arahatta are related to this prenascent body by postnascence condition. (1)

(iii) State appertaining neither to Learners nor to Arahatta is related to state appertaining neither to Learners nor to Arahatta by postnascence condition.

Postnascent aggregates appertaining neither to Learners nor to Arahatta are related to this prenascent body by postnascence condition. (1)

Repetition 2

58. (i) State appertaining neither to Learners nor to Arahatta is related to state appertaining neither to Learners nor to Arahatta by repetition condition.

Preceding aggregates appertaining neither to Learners nor to Arahatta are related to subsequent aggregates appertaining neither to Learners nor to Arahatta by repetition condition. Adaptation to change-of-lineage; adaptation is related to purification by repetition condition. (1)

(ii) State appertaining neither to Learners nor to Arahatta is related to state appertaining to Learners by repetition condition.

Change-of-lineage to Path; purification is related to Path by repetition condition. (2)

Kamma 8

59. (i) State appertaining to Learners is related to state appertaining to Learners by kamma condition.

(It is of two kinds, namely:) (*a*) conascence(-kamma), (*b*) asynchronous (kamma).

(*a*) Conascent volition appertaining to Learners is related to (its) associated aggregates by kamma condition.

(*b*) Asynchronous volition appertaining to Learners is related to (its) resultant aggregates appertaining to Learners by kamma condition. (1)

(ii) State appertaining to Learners is related to state appertaining to Arahatta by kamma condition.

Asynchronous volition appertaining to Learners is related to the aggregates appertaining to Arahatta by kamma condition. (2)

(iii) State appertaining to Learners is related to state appertaining neither to Learners nor to Arahatta by kamma condition.

Conascent volition appertaining to Learners is related to mind-produced matter by kamma condition. (3)

(iv) State appertaining to Learners is related to state appertaining to Learners and appertaining neither to Learners nor to Arahatta by kamma condition.

Volition appertaining to Learners is related to (its) associated aggregates and mind-produced matter by kamma condition. (4)

60. (v) State appertaining to Arahatta is related to state appertaining

to Arahatta by kamma condition.

Volition appertaining to Arahatta is related to (its) associated aggre gates by kamma condition. (1)

(vi) State appertaining to Arahatta is related to state appertaining neither to Learners nor to Arahatta by kamma condition.

Volition appertaining to Arahatta is related to mind-produced matter by kamma condition. (2)

(vii) State appertaining to Arahatta is related to state appertaining to Arahatta and appertaining neither to Learners nor to Arahatta by kamma condition.

Volition appertaining to Arahatta is related to (its) associated aggregates and mind-produced matter by kamma condition. (3)

61. (viii) State appertaining neither to Learners nor to Arahatta is related to state appertaining neither to Learners nor to Arahatta by kamma condition.

(It is of two kinds, namely:) (*a*) conascence(-kamma), (*b*) asynchronous (kamma).

(*a*) (1) Conascent volition appertaining neither to Learners nor to Arahatta is related to (its) associated aggregates and mind-produced matter by kamma condition;

(2) At the moment of conception . . .

(*b*) Asynchronous volition appertaining neither to Learners nor to Arahatta is related to (its) resultant aggregates appertaining neither to Learners nor to Arahatta and kamma-produced matter by kamma condition. (1)

Resultant 7

62. (i)–(iii) State appertaining to Learners is related to state appertaining to Learners by resultant condition.

One resultant aggregate appertaining to Learners to three aggregates . . . (For the reference with "appertaining to Learners": three.)

(iv)–(vi) State appertaining to Arahatta is related to state appertaining to Arahatta by resultant condition.

One aggregate appertaining to Arahatta to three aggregates . . . (For the reference with "appertaining to Arahatta": three.)

(vii) State appertaining neither to Learners nor to Arahatta is related to state appertaining neither to Learners nor to Arahatta by resultant condition.

(*a*) One resultant aggregate appertaining neither to Learners nor to

Arahatta to three aggregates . . .

(*b*) At the moment of conception . . . aggregates are related to (heart-)base by resultant condition. (1)

Nutriment, etc.

63. State appertaining to Learners is related to state appertaining to Learners by nutriment condition . . . by faculty condition . . . by jhāna condition . . . by path condition . . . by association condition . . .

Dissociation 5

64. (i) State appertaining to Learners is related to state appertaining neither to Learners nor to Arahatta by dissociation condition.

(It is of two kinds, namely:) (*a*) conascence, (*b*) postnascence.

(*a*) Conascent aggregates appertaining to Learners are related to mind-produced matter by dissociation condition.

(*b*) Postnascent aggregates appertaining to Learners are related to this prenascent body by dissociation condition. (1)

(ii) State appertaining to Arahatta is related to state appertaining neither to Learners nor to Arahatta by dissociation condition.

(It is of two kinds, namely:) (*a*) conascence, (*b*) postnascence. (Like Learners.)

(iii) State appertaining neither to Learners nor to Arahatta is related to state appertaining neither to Learners nor to Arahatta by dissociation condition.

(It is of three kinds, namely:) (*a*) conascence, (*b*) prenascence, (*c*) postnascence.

(*a*) (1) Conascent aggregates appertaining neither to Learners nor to Arahatta are related to mind-produced matter by dissociation condition;

(2) At the moment of conception, aggregates appertaining neither to Learners nor to Arahatta are related to kamma-produced matter by dissociation condition; aggregates are related to (heart-)base by dissociation condition; (heart-)base is related to aggregates by dissociation condition.

(*b*) Prenascent eye-base to eye-consciousness . . . body-base to body-consciousness . . . (heart-)base is related to aggregates appertaining neither to Learners nor to Arahatta by dissociation condition.

(*c*) Postnascent aggregates appertaining neither to Learners nor to Arahatta are related to this prenascent body by dissociation condition. (1)

(iv) State appertaining neither to Learners nor to Arahatta is related to state appertaining to Learners by dissociation condition.

Prenascent (heart-)base is related to aggregates appertaining to Learners by dissociation condition. (2)

(v) State appertaining neither to Learners nor to Arahatta is related to state appertaining to Arahatta by dissociation condition.

Prenascent (heart-)base is related to aggregates appertaining to Arahatta by dissociation condition. (3)

Presence 13

65. (i) State appertaining to Learners is related to state appertaining to Learners by presence condition.

One aggregate appertaining to Learners to three aggregates . . . (1)

(ii) State appertaining to Learners is related to state appertaining neither to Learners nor to Arahatta by presence condition.

(It is of two kinds, namely:) (*a*) conascence, (*b*) postnascence.

(*a*) Conascent aggregates appertaining to Learners are related to mind-produced matter by presence condition.

(*b*) Postnascent aggregates appertaining to Learners are related to this prenascent body by presence condition. (2)

(iii) State appertaining to Learners is related to state appertaining to Learners and appertaining neither to Learners nor to Arahatta by presence condition.

One aggregate appertaining to Learners is related to three aggregates and mind-produced matter by presence condition . . . two aggregates . . . (3)

(iv)-(vi) State appertaining to Arahatta is related to state appertaining to Arahatta by presence condition . . . three. (Like Learners.)

66. (vii) State appertaining neither to Learners nor to Arahatta is related to state appertaining neither to Learners nor to Arahatta by presence condition.

(It is of five kinds, namely:) (*a*) conascence, (*b*) prenascence, (*c*) postnascence, (*d*) nutriment, (*e*) faculty.

(*a*) (1) One conascent aggregate appertaining neither to Learners nor to Arahatta is related to three aggregates and mind-produced matter by presence condition . . . two aggregates . . .

(2) At the moment of conception . . . aggregates are related to (heart-)base by presence condition; (heart-)base is related to aggregates by presence condition;

(3) One great primary . . . External . . . non-percipient beings . . .

(*b*) *(Object-)prenascence:* (One) practises insight into the impermanence, suffering and impersonality of the eye; enjoys and delights in (the eye). Taking it as object, arises lust . . . arises grief . . . ear . . . (One) practises insight into the impermanence . . . of the (heart-)base . . . By the power of divine-eye, (one) sees a visible object. By the power of divine-ear element, (one) hears a sound. Visible object-base to eye-consciousness . . . tangible object-base to body-consciousness . . .

(Base-)prenascence: Eye-base to eye-consciousness . . . body-base to body-consciousness . . . (heart-)base is related to aggregates appertaining neither to Learners nor to Arahatta by presence condition.

(*c*) Postnascent aggregates appertaining neither to Learners nor to Arahatta are related to this prenascent body by presence condition.

(*d*) Edible food is related to this body by presence condition.

(*e*) Physical life-faculty is related to kamma-produced matter by presence condition. (1)

(viii) State appertaining neither to Learners nor to Arahatta is related to state appertaining to Learners by presence condition.

(Base-)prenascence: (Heart-)base is related to aggregates appertaining to Learners by presence condition. (2)

(ix) State appertaining neither to Learners nor to Arahatta is related to state appertaining to Arahatta by presence condition.

(Base-)prenascence: (Heart-)base is related to aggregates appertaining to Arahatta by presence condition. (3)

67. (x) States appertaining to Learners and appertaining neither to Learners nor to Arahatta are related to state appertaining to Learners by presence condition.

Conascence-prenascence: One conascent aggregate appertaining to Learners and (heart-)base are related to three aggregates by presence condition . . . two aggregates . . . (1)

(xi) States appertaining to Learners and appertaining neither to Learners nor to Arahatta are related to state appertaining neither to Learners nor to Arahatta by presence condition.

(It is of three kinds, namely:) (*a*) conascence, (*b*) postnascence-nutriment, (*c*) (postnascence-)faculty.

(*a*) Conascent aggregates appertaining to Learners and great primaries are related to mind-produced matter by presence condition.

(*b*) Postnascent aggregates appertaining to Learners and edible food are related to this body by presence condition.

(*c*) Postnascent aggregates appertaining to Learners and physical life-faculty are related to kamma-produced matter by presence condition. (2)

(xii)-(xiii) States appertaining to Arahatta and appertaining neither to Learners nor to Arahatta are related to state appertaining to Arahatta by presence condition . . . [Do two (questions:) like Learners.] . . .

1. CONDITIONS: POSITIVE (ii) ENUMERATION CHAPTER

By Ones

68. With root 7, object 5, predominance 9, proximity 8, contiguity 8, conascence 9, mutuality 3, dependence 13, strong-dependence 8, prenascence 3, postnascence 3, repetition 2, kamma 8, resultant, nutriment, faculty, jhāna, path 7, association 3, dissociation 5, presence 13, absence 8, disappearance 8, non-disappearance 13. (Enumerate thus.)

End of Positive

2. SELECTION OF THE CONDITIONS FOR NEGATIVE 14

69. (i) State appertaining to Learners is related to state appertaining to Learners by conascence condition, strong-dependence condition. (1)

(ii) State appertaining to Learners is related to state appertaining to Arahatta by strong-dependence condition. (2)

(iii) State appertaining to Learners is related to state appertaining neither to Learners nor to Arahatta by object condition, conascence condition, strong-dependence condition, postnascence condition. (3)

(iv) State appertaining to Learners is related to state appertaining to Learners and appertaining neither to Learners nor to Arahatta by conascence condition. (4)

70. (v) State appertaining to Arahatta is related to state appertaining to Arahatta by conascence condition, strong-dependence condition. (1)

(vi) State appertaining to Arahatta is related to state appertaining neither to Learners nor to Arahatta by object condition, conascence condition, strong-dependence condition, postnascence condition. (2)

(vii) State appertaining to Arahatta is related to state appertaining to Arahatta and appertaining neither to Learners nor to Arahatta by conascence condition. (3)

71. (viii) State appertaining neither to Learners nor to Arahatta is related to state appertaining neither to Learners nor to Arahatta by object condition, conascence condition, strong-dependence condition, prenascence condition, postnascence condition, kamma condition, nutriment condition, faculty condition. (1)

(ix) State appertaining neither to Learners nor to Arahatta is related to state appertaining to Learners by strong-dependence condition, prenascence condition. (2)

(x) State appertaining neither to Learners nor to Arahatta is related to state appertaining to Arahatta by strong-dependence condition, prenascence condition. (3)

72. (xi) States appertaining to Learners and appertaining neither to Learners nor to Arahatta are related to state appertaining to Learners by conascence-prenascence. (1)

(xii) States appertaining to Learners and appertaining neither to Learners nor to Arahatta are related to state appertaining neither to Learners nor to Arahatta by conascence, postnascence-nutriment-faculty. (2)

(xiii) States appertaining to Arahatta and appertaining neither to Learners nor to Arahatta are related to state appertaining to Arahatta by conascence-prenascence. (1)

(xiv) States appertaining to Arahatta and appertaining neither to Learners nor to Arahatta are related to state appertaining neither to Learners nor to Arahatta by conascence, postnascence-nutriment-faculty. (2)

2. CONDITIONS: NEGATIVE (ii) ENUMERATION CHAPTER

(By Ones)

73. With not-root 14, not-object, not-predominance, not-proximity, not-contiguity 14, not-conascence 10, not-mutuality 10, not-dependence 10, not-strong-dependence 13, not-prenascence 12, not-postnascence 14, not-repetition, not-kamma 14, not-resultant 12, not-nutriment, not-faculty, not-jhāna, not-path 14, not-association 10, not-dissociation 8, not-presence 8, not-absence 14, not-disappearance 14, not-non-disappearance 8. (Enumerate thus.)

End of Negative

3. CONDITIONS: POSITIVE-NEGATIVE

Root By Twos

74. With root condition, not-object 7, not-predominance 7, not-proximity 7, not-contiguity 7, not-mutuality 3, not-strong-dependence, not-prenascence, not-postnascence, not-repetition, not-kamma 7, not-resultant 4, not-nutriment, not-faculty, not-jhāna, not-path 7, not-association 3, not-dissociation 3, not-absence 7, not-disappearance 7. (Enumerate thus.)

End of Positive-Negative

4. CONDITIONS: NEGATIVE-POSITIVE

Not-root By Twos

75. With not-root condition, object 5, predominance 9, proximity 8, contiguity 8, conascence 9, mutuality 3, dependence 13, strong-dependence 8, prenascence 3, postnascence 3, repetition 2, kamma 8, resultant, nutriment, faculty, jhāna, path 7, association 3, dissociation 5, presence 13, absence 8, disappearance 8, non-disappearance 13. (Enumerate thus.)

End of Negative-Positive

End of "INVESTIGATION" CHAPTER

END OF LEARNERS TRIPLET

12. LIMITED TRIPLET[1] I. "DEPENDENT" CHAPTER

1. CONDITIONS: POSITIVE (i) CLASSIFICATION CHAPTER

Root 13

1. (i) Dependent on limited (paritta) state, arises limited state by root condition.

(*a*) Dependent on one limited aggregate, arise three aggregates and mind-produced matter . . . two aggregates . . .

(*b*) At the moment of conception, dependent on one limited aggregate, arise three aggregates and kamma-produced matter . . . two aggregates . . . dependent on aggregates, arises (heart-)base; dependent on (heart-)base arise aggregates;

(*c*) Dependent on one great primary, arise three great primaries . . .

[1] This comprises (1) Limited states, (2) Lofty states, (3) Incomparable states.

two . . . dependent on great primaries, arises mind-produced (derived) matter. (1)

(ii) Dependent on limited state, arises Lofty state by root condition.

At the moment of conception, dependent on (heart-)base, arise Lofty aggregates. (2)

(iii) Dependent on limited state, arise limited and Lofty states by root condition.

At the moment of conception, dependent on (heart-)base, arise Lofty aggregates; dependent on great primaries, arises kamma-produced matter. (3)

2. (iv) Dependent on Lofty (Mahaggata) state, arises Lofty state by root condition.

(*a*) Dependent on one Lofty aggregate, arise three aggregates . . . two aggregates . . .

(*b*) At the moment of conception . . . (1)

(v) Dependent on Lofty state, arises limited state by root condition.

(*a*) Dependent on Lofty aggregates, arises mind-produced matter;

(*b*) At the moment of conception, dependent on Lofty aggregates, arises kamma-produced matter. (2)

(vi) Dependent on Lofty state, arise limited and Lofty states by root condition.

(*a*) Dependent on one Lofty aggregate, arise three aggregates and mind-produced matter . . .

(*b*) At the moment of conception, dependent on one Lofty aggregate, arise three aggregates and kamma-produced matter . . . two aggregates . . . (3)

3. (vii) Dependent on Incomparable (appamāṇa) state, arises Incomparable state by root condition.

Dependent on one Incomparable aggregate, arise three aggregates . . . two aggregates . . . (1)

(viii) Dependent on Incomparable state, arises limited state by root condition.

Dependent on Incomparable aggregates, arises mind-produced matter. (2)

(ix) Dependent on Incomparable state, arise limited and Incomparable states by root condition.

Dependent on one Incomparable aggregate, arise three aggregates and mind-produced matter . . . two aggregates . . . (3)

4. (x) Dependent on limited and Incomparable state, arises limited state by root condition.

Dependent on Incomparable aggregates and great primaries, arises mind-produced matter. (1)

(xi) Dependent on limited and Lofty state, arises limited state by root condition.

(*a*) Dependent on Lofty aggregates and great primaries, arises mind-produced matter;

(*b*) At the moment of conception . . . (1)

(xii) Dependent on limited and Lofty state, arises Lofty state by root condition.

At the moment of conception, dependent on one Lofty aggregate and (heart-)base, arise three aggregates . . . two aggregates . . . (2)

(xiii) Dependent on limited and Lofty state, arise limited and Lofty states by root condition.

At the moment of conception, dependent on one Lofty aggregate and (heart-)base, arise three aggregates . . . two aggregates . . . dependent on Lofty aggregates and great primaries, arises kamma-produced matter. (3)

Object 5

5. (i) Dependent on limited state, arises limited state by object condition.

(*a*) Dependent on one limited aggregate, arise three aggregates . . . two aggregates . . .

(*b*) At the moment of conception . . . dependent on (heart-)base, arise aggregates. (1)

(ii) Dependent on limited state, arises Lofty state by object condition.

At the moment of conception, dependent on (heart-)base, arise Lofty aggregates. (2)

(iii) Dependent on Lofty state, arises Lofty state by object condition.

(*a*) Dependent on one Lofty aggregate, arise three aggregates . . . two aggregates . . .

(*b*) At the moment of conception . . . (1)

(iv) Dependent on Incomparable state, arises Incomparable state by object condition.

Dependent on one Incomparable aggregate, arise three aggregates . . . two aggregates . . . (1)

(v) Dependent on limited and Lofty state, arises Lofty state by object condition.

At the moment of conception, dependent on one Lofty aggregate and (heart-)base, arise three aggregates . . . two aggregates . . . (1)

Predominance 9

6. (i) Dependent on limited state, arises limited state by predominance condition.

(*a*) Dependent on one limited aggregate, arise three aggregates and mind-produced matter . . . two aggregates . . .

(*b*) Dependent on one great primary, arise three great primaries . . . dependent on great primaries, arises mind-produced derived matter. (1)

(ii) Dependent on Lofty state, arises Lofty state by predominance condition.

Dependent on one Lofty aggregate, arise three aggregates . . . two aggregates . . . (1)

(iii) Dependent on Lofty state, arises limited state by predominance condition.

Dependent on Lofty aggregates, arises mind-produced matter. (2)

(iv) Dependent on Lofty state, arise limited and Lofty states by predominance condition.

Dependent on one Lofty aggregate, arise three aggregates and mind-produced matter . . . two aggregates . . . (3)

(v) Dependent on Incomparable state, arises Incomparable state by predominance condition.

Dependent on one Incomparable aggregate, arise three aggregates . . . two aggregates . . . (1)

(vi) Dependent on Incomparable state, arises limited state by predominance condition.

Dependent on Incomparable aggregates, arises mind-produced matter. (2)

(vii) Dependent on Incomparable state, arise limited and Incomparable states by predominance condition.

Dependent on one Incomparable aggregate, arise three aggregates and mind-produced matter . . . two aggregates . . . (3)

7. (viii) Dependent on limited and Incomparable state, arises limited state by predominance condition.

Dependent on Incomparable aggregates and great primaries, arises mind-produced matter. (1)

(ix) Dependent on limited and Lofty state, arises limited state by predominance condition.

Dependent on Lofty aggregates and great primaries, arises mind-produced matter. (1)

Proximity, etc.

8. Dependent on limited state, arises limited state by proximity condition . . . by contiguity condition . . . by conascence condition. (Include all great primaries.) . . . by mutuality condition . . . by dependence condition . . . by strong-dependence condition . . . by prenascence condition. (Do three questions.) . . . by repetition condition. (Do three questions.) . . . by kamma condition . . . by resultant condition. (13 questions.) . . . by nutriment condition . . . by faculty condition . . . by jhāna condition . . . by path condition . . . by association condition . . . by dissociation condition . . . by presence condition . . . by absence condition . . . by disappearance condition . . . by non-disappearance condition . . .

1. CONDITIONS: POSITIVE (ii) ENUMERATION CHAPTER

(By Ones)

9. With root 13, object 5, predominance 9, proximity 5, contiguity 5, conascence 13, mutuality 7, dependence 13, strong-dependence 5, prenascence 3, repetition 3, kamma 13, resultant 13, nutriment, faculty, jhāna, path 13, association 5, dissociation 13, presence 13, absence 5, disappearance 5, non-disappearance 13. (Enumerate thus.)

End of Positive

2. CONDITIONS: NEGATIVE (i) CLASSIFICATION CHAPTER

Not-root 1

10. Dependent on limited state, arises limited state by not-root condition.

(*a*) Dependent on one rootless limited aggregate, arise three aggregates and mind-produced matter . . . two aggregates . . .

(*b*) At the moment of rootless conception . . . dependent on aggregates, arises (heart-)base; dependent on (heart-)base, arise aggregates;

(*c*) One great primary . . . External . . . nutriment-produced . . . temperature-produced . . . one great primary of non-percipient beings . . .

(*d*) Dependent on doubt-accompanied or restlessness-accompanied aggregates, arises doubt-accompanied or restlessness-accompanied delusion. (1)

Not-object 5

11. (i) Dependent on limited state, arises limited state by not-object condition.

(*a*) Dependent on limited aggregates, arises mind-produced matter;

(*b*) At the moment of conception, dependent on limited aggregates, arises kamma-produced matter; dependent on aggregates, arises (heart-) base . . .

(*c*) One great primary . . . External . . . nutriment-produced . . . temperature-produced . . . one great primary of non-percipient beings . . . (1)

(ii) Dependent on Lofty state, arises limited state by not-object condition.

(*a*) Dependent on Lofty aggregates, arises mind-produced matter;

(*b*) At the moment of conception, dependent on Lofty aggregates, arises kamma-produced matter. (1)

(iii) Dependent on Incomparable state, arises limited state by not-object condition.

Dependent on Incomparable aggregates, arises mind-produced matter. (1)

(iv) Dependent on limited and Incomparable state, arises limited state by not-object condition.

Dependent on Incomparable aggregates and great primaries, arises mind-produced matter. (1)

(v) Dependent on limited and Lofty state, arises limited state by not-object condition.

(*a*) Dependent on Lofty aggregates and great primaries, arises mind-produced matter;

(*b*) At the moment of conception, dependent on Lofty aggregates and great primaries, arises kamma-produced matter. (1)

Not-predominance 10

12. (i) Dependent on limited state, arises limited state by not-predominance condition.

(*a*) Dependent on one limited aggregate, arise three aggregates . . .

(*b*) At the moment of conception . . . dependent on aggregates, arises (heart-)base; dependent on (heart-)base, arise aggregates;

(*c*) One great primary . . . non-percipient beings . . . (1)

(ii) Dependent on limited state, arises Lofty state by not-predominance condition.

At the moment of conception, dependent on (heart-)base, arise Lofty aggregates. (2)

(iii) Dependent on limited state, arise limited and Lofty states by not-predominance condition.

At the moment of conception, dependent on (heart-)base, arise Lofty aggregates; dependent on great primaries, arises kamma-produced matter. (3)

13. (iv) Dependent on Lofty state, arises Lofty state by not-predominance condition.

(*a*) Dependent on Lofty aggregates, arises Lofty predominance; dependent on one resultant Lofty aggregate . . .

(*b*) At the moment of conception . . . (1)

(v) Dependent on Lofty state, arises limited state by not-predominance condition.

(*a*) Dependent on resultant Lofty aggregates, arises mind-produced matter;

(*b*) At the moment of conception, dependent on Lofty aggregates, arises kamma-produced matter. (2)

(vi) Dependent on Lofty state, arise limited and Lofty states by not-predominance condition.

(*a*) Dependent on one resultant Lofty aggregate, arise three aggregates and mind-produced matter . . . two aggregates . . .

(*b*) At the moment of conception . . . (3)

14. (vii) Dependent on Incomparable state, arises Incomparable state by not-predominance condition.

Dependent on Incomparable aggregates, arises Incomparable predominance. (1)

(viii) Dependent on limited and Lofty state, arises limited state by not-predominance condition.

(*a*) Dependent on resultant Lofty aggregates and great primaries, arises mind-produced matter;

(*b*) At the moment of conception, dependent on Lofty aggregates and great primaries, arises kamma-produced matter. (1)

(ix) Dependent on limited and Lofty state, arises Lofty state by not-predominance condition.

At the moment of conception, dependent on one Lofty aggregate and (heart-)base, arise three aggregates . . . two aggregates . . . (2)

(x) Dependent on limited and Lofty state, arise limited and Lofty states by not-predominance condition.

At the moment of conception, dependent on one Lofty aggregate and (heart-)base, arise three aggregates . . . two aggregates . . . dependent on Lofty aggregates and great primaries, arises kamma-produced matter. (3)

Not-proximity, etc. 5

15. Dependent on limited state, arises limited state by not-proximity condition . . . by not-contiguity condition . . . by not-mutuality condition . . . by not-strong-dependence condition . . .

Not-prenascence 12

16. (i)–(iii) Dependent on limited state, arises limited state by not-prenascence condition.

In the immaterial plane, dependent on one limited aggregate, arise three aggregates . . . two aggregates . . . dependent on limited aggregates, arises mind-produced matter;

At the moment of conception, dependent on one limited aggregate, arise three aggregates and kamma-produced matter . . . two aggregates . . . [Expand all great primaries. In the immaterial plane, there are three questions for the reference with "limited (state)".]

(iv) Dependent on Lofty state, arises Lofty state by not-prenascence condition.

(*a*) One Lofty aggregate . . .

(*b*) At the moment of conception . . . (1)

(v) Dependent on Lofty state, arises limited state by not-prenascence condition.

(*a*) Dependent on Lofty aggregates, arises mind-produced matter;

(*b*) At the moment of conception, dependent on Lofty aggregates, arises kamma-produced matter. (2)

(vi) Dependent on Lofty state, arise limited and Lofty states by not-prenascence condition.

At the moment of conception, dependent on one Lofty aggregate, arise three aggregates and kamma-produced matter . . . two aggregates . . . (3)

17. (vii) Dependent on Incomparable state, arises Incomparable state by not-prenascence condition.

In the immaterial plane, one Incomparable aggregate . . . (1)

(viii) Dependent on Incomparable state, arises limited state by not-prenascence condition.

Dependent on Incomparable aggregates, arises mind-produced matter. (2)

(ix) Dependent on limited and Incomparable state, arises limited state by not-prenascence condition.

Dependent on Incomparable aggregates and great primaries, arises mind-produced matter. (1)

(x) Dependent on limited and Lofty state, arises limited state by not-prenascence condition.

(*a*) Dependent on Lofty aggregates and great primaries, arises mind-produced matter;

(*b*) At the moment of conception . . . (1)

(xi) Dependent on limited and Lofty state, arises Lofty state by not-prenascence condition.

At the moment of conception, dependent on one Lofty aggregate and (heart-)base, arise three aggregates . . . (2)

(xii) Dependent on limited and Lofty state, arise limited and Lofty states by not-prenascence condition.

At the moment of conception, dependent on one Lofty aggregate and (heart-)base, arise three aggregates . . . two aggregates . . . dependent on Lofty aggregates and great primaries, arises kamma-produced matter. (3)

Not-postnascence, etc. 13

18. (i) Dependent on limited state, arises limited state by not-postnascence condition . . . by not-repetition condition.

(*a*) Dependent on one limited aggregate, arise three aggregates and mind-produced matter . . . two aggregates . . .

(*b*) At the moment of conception . . . dependent on aggregates, arises (heart-)base; dependent on (heart-)base, arise aggregates;

(*c*) One great primary . . . one great primary of non-percipient beings . . . (1)

(ii) Dependent on limited state, arises Lofty state by not-repetition condition.

At the moment of conception, dependent on (heart-)base, arise Lofty aggregates. (2)

(iii) Dependent on limited state, arise limited and Lofty states by not-repetition condition.

At the moment of conception, dependent on (heart-)base, arise Lofty aggregates; dependent on great primaries, arises kamma-produced matter. (3)

19. (iv) Dependent on Lofty state, arises Lofty state by not-repetition condition.

(*a*) Dependent on one resultant Lofty aggregate, arise three aggregates . . . two aggregates . . .

(*b*) At the moment of conception, dependent on one Lofty aggregate, arise three aggregates . . . (1)

(v) Dependent on Lofty state, arises limited state by not-repetition condition.

(*a*) Dependent on Lofty aggregates, arises mind-produced matter;

(*b*) At the moment of conception . . . (2)

(vi) Dependent on Lofty state, arise limited and Lofty states by not-repetition condition.

(*a*) Dependent on one resultant Lofty aggregate, arise three aggregates and mind-produced matter . . . two aggregates . . .

(*b*) At the moment of conception . . . one Lofty aggregate . . . (3)

20. (vii) Dependent on Incomparable state, arises Incomparable state by not-repetition condition.

Dependent on one resultant Incomparable aggregate, arise three aggregates . . . dependent on two aggregates, arise two aggregates. (1)

(viii) Dependent on Incomparable state, arises limited state by not-repetition condition.

Dependent on Incomparable aggregates, arises mind-produced matter. (2)

(ix) Dependent on Incomparable state, arise limited and Incomparable states by not-repetition condition.

Dependent on one resultant Incomparable aggregate, arise three aggregates and mind-produced matter . . . (3)

21. (x) Dependent on limited and Incomparable state, arises limited state by not-repetition condition.

Dependent on Incomparable aggregates and great primaries, arises mind-produced matter. (1)

(xi) Dependent on limited and Lofty state, arises limited state by not-repetition condition.

(*a*) Dependent on Lofty aggregates and great primaries, arises mind-produced matter;

(*b*) At the moment of conception, dependent on Lofty aggregates and great primaries, arises kamma-produced matter. (1)

(xii) Dependent on limited and Lofty state, arises Lofty state by not-repetition condition.

At the moment of conception, dependent on one Lofty aggregate and (heart-)base, arise three aggregates . . . two aggregates . . . (2)

(xiii) Dependent on limited and Lofty state, arise limited and Lofty states by not-repetition condition.

At the moment of conception, dependent on one Lofty aggregate and (heart-)base, arise three aggregates . . . two aggregates . . . dependent on Lofty aggregates and great primaries, arises kamma-produced matter. (3)

Not-kamma 3

22. (i) Dependent on limited state, arises limited state by not-kamma condition.

(*a*) Dependent on limited aggregates, arises limited volition;

(*b*) External . . . nutriment-produced . . . one great primary of temperature-produced . . . (1)

(ii) Dependent on Lofty state, arises Lofty state by not-kamma condition.

Dependent on Lofty aggregates, arises Lofty volition. (1)

(iii) Dependent on Incomparable state, arises Incomparable state by not-kamma condition.

Dependent on faultless Incomparable aggregates, arises Incomparable volition. (1)

Not-resultant 9

23. (i) Dependent on limited state, arises limited state by not-resultant condition.

(*a*) Dependent on one limited aggregate, arise three aggregates and mind-produced matter . . . two aggregates . . .

(*b*) Dependent on one great primary, arise three great primaries . . . dependent on great primaries, arises mind-produced derived matter;

(*c*) External . . . nutriment-produced . . . temperature-produced . . .

one great primary of non-percipient beings . . . (1)

(ii) Dependent on Lofty state, arises Lofty state by not-resultant condition.

Dependent on one Lofty aggregate, arise three aggregates . . . two aggregates . . . (1)

(iii) Dependent on Lofty state, arises limited state by not-resultant condition.

Dependent on Lofty aggregates, arises mind-produced matter. (2)

(iv) Dependent on Lofty state, arise limited and Lofty states by not-resultant condition.

Dependent on one Lofty aggregate, arise three aggregates and mind-produced matter . . . two aggregates . . . (3)

(v) Dependent on Incomparable state, arises Incomparable state by not-resultant condition.

Dependent on one faultless Incomparable aggregate, arise three aggregates . . . (1)

(vi) Dependent on Incomparable state, arises limited state by not-resultant condition.

Dependent on faultless Incomparable aggregates, arises mind-produced matter. (2)

(vii) Dependent on Incomparable state, arise limited and Incomparable states by not-resultant condition.

Dependent on one faultless Incomparable aggregate, arise three aggregates and mind-produced matter . . . two aggregates . . . (3)

(viii) Dependent on limited and Incomparable state, arises limited state by not-resultant condition.

Dependent on faultless Incomparable aggregates and great primaries, arises mind-produced matter. (1)

(ix) Dependent on limited and Lofty state, arises limited state by not-resultant condition.

Dependent on Lofty aggregates and great primaries, arises mind-produced matter. (1)

Not-nutriment, etc.

24. Dependent on limited state, arises limited state by not-nutriment condition. External . . . temperature-produced . . . non-percipient beings (Expand.) . . .

. . . by not faculty condition. External . . . nutriment-produced . . . temperature-produced . . . non-percipient beings . . . dependent on great primaries, arises physical life-faculty.

. . . by not-jhāna condition . . . one five-fold consciousness-accompanied aggregate . . . External . . . one great primary of non-percipient beings . . . (Include all great primaries.)

. . . by not-path condition . . . one rootless limited aggregate . . . At the moment of rootless conception, one . . . (Include all great primaries.)

. . . by not-association condition . . .

(i) . . . by not-dissociation condition.

In the immaterial plane, dependent on one limited aggregate, arise three aggregates . . . two aggregates . . .

External . . . nutriment-produced . . . temperature-produced . . . non-percipient beings . . .

(ii) Dependent on Lofty state, arises Lofty state by not-dissociation condition.

In the immaterial plane, one Lofty aggregate . . . (1)

(iii) Dependent on Incomparable state, arises Incomparable state by not-dissociation condition.

In the immaterial plane, one Incomparable aggregate . . . (1)

. . . by not-absence condition . . . by not-disappearance condition . . .

2. CONDITIONS: NEGATIVE (ii) ENUMERATION CHAPTER

(By Ones)

25. With not-root 1, not-object 5, not-predominance 10, not-proximity 5, not-contiguity 5, not-mutuality, not-strong-dependence 5, not-prenascence 12, not-postnascence 13, not-repetition 13, not-kamma 3, not-resultant 9, not-nutriment 1, not-faculty, not-jhāna, not-path 1, not-association 5, not-dissociation 3, not-absence 5, not-disappearance 5. (Enumerate thus.)

End of Negative

3. CONDITIONS: POSITIVE–NEGATIVE

(Root By Twos)

26. With root condition, not-object 5, not-predominance 10, not-proximity 5, not-contiguity, not-mutuality, not-strong-dependence 5, not-prenascence 12, not-postnascence 13, not-repetition 13, not-kamma 3, not-resultant 9, not-association 5, not-dissociation 3, not-absence 5, not-disappearance 5. (Enumerate thus.)

End of Positive–Negative

4. CONDITIONS: NEGATIVE–POSITIVE

(Not-root By Twos)

27. With not-root condition, object 1, proximity 1 . . . disappearance 1, non-disappearance 1. (Enumerate thus.)

End of Negative–Positive

End of "DEPENDENT" CHAPTER

(The "Conascent" Chapter is the same as the "Dependent" Chapter.)

12. LIMITED TRIPLET III. "CONDITIONED" CHAPTER

1. CONDITIONS: POSITIVE (i) CLASSIFICATION CHAPTER

Root 17

28. (i) Conditioned by limited state, arises limited state by root condition.

(*a*) Conditioned by one limited aggregate, arise three aggregates and mind-produced matter . . . two aggregates . . .

(*b*) At the moment of conception . . . conditioned by aggregates, arises (heart-)base; conditioned by (heart-)base, arise aggregates;

(*c*) Conditioned by one great primary . . . derived matter;

(*d*) Conditioned by (heart-)base, arise limited aggregates. (1)

(ii) Conditioned by limited state, arises Lofty state by root condition.

(*a*) Conditioned by (heart-)base, arise Lofty aggregates;

(*b*) At the moment of conception, conditioned by (heart-)base, arise Lofty aggregates. (2)

(iii) Conditioned by limited state, arises Incomparable state by root condition.

Conditioned by (heart-)base, arise Incomparable aggregates. (3)

(iv) Conditioned by limited state, arise limited and Incomparable states by root condition.

Conditioned by (heart-)base, arise Incomparable aggregates; conditioned by great primaries, arises mind-produced matter. (4)

(v) Conditioned by limited state, arise limited and Lofty states by root condition.

(*a*) Conditioned by (heart-)base, arise Lofty aggregates; conditioned by great primaries, arises mind-produced matter;

(*b*) At the moment of conception, conditioned by (heart-)base, arise Lofty aggregates . . . (5)

29. (vi) Conditioned by Lofty state, arises Lofty state by root condition.

(*a*) Conditioned by one Lofty aggregate, arise three aggregates . . .

(*b*) At the moment of conception, . . . one Lofty aggregate . . . (1)

(vii) Conditioned by Lofty state, arises limited state by root condition.

(*a*) Conditioned by Lofty aggregates, arises mind-produced matter;

(*b*) At the moment of conception . . . (2)

(viii) Conditioned by Lofty state, arise limited and Lofty states by root condition.

(*a*) Conditioned by one Lofty aggregate, arise three aggregates and mind-produced matter . . . two aggregates . . .

(*b*) At the moment of conception, . . . one Lofty aggregate . . . (3)

(ix)-(xi) Conditioned by Incomparable state, arises Incomparable state by root condition. In Incomparable . . . three.

30. (xii) Conditioned by limited and Incomparable state, arises limited state by root condition.

Conditioned by Incomparable aggregates and great primaries, arises mind-produced matter. (1)

(xiii) Conditioned by limited and Incomparable state, arises Incomparable state by root condition.

Conditioned by one Incomparable aggregate and (heart-)base, arise three aggregates . . . (2)

(xiv) Conditioned by limited and Incomparable state, arise limited and Incomparable states by root condition.

Conditioned by one Incomparable aggregate and (heart-)base, arise three aggregates . . . two aggregates . . . conditioned by Incomparable aggregates and great primaries, arises mind-produced matter. (3)

(xv)-(xvii) Conditioned by limited and Lofty state, arises limited state by root condition . . . three. (For "at the moment of conception" do three also.)

Object, etc.

31. Conditioned by limited state, arises limited state by object condition.

(*a*) Conditioned by one limited aggregate, arise three aggregates . . . two aggregates . . .

(*b*) At the moment of conception . . . conditioned by (heart-)base, arise aggregates;

(*c*) Conditioned by eye-base, arises eye-consciousness . . . conditioned by body-base, arises body-consciousness; conditioned by (heart-)base, arise limited aggregates. (The remaining six questions are the same as for root condition. Do 7.)

. . . by predominance condition. (No conception. Complete 17 questions.) . . . by proximity condition . . . by non-disappearance condition . . .

1. CONDITIONS: POSITIVE (ii) ENUMERATION CHAPTER

(By Ones)

32. With root 17, object 7, predominance 17, proximity 7, contiguity 7, conascence 17, mutuality 9, dependence 17, strong-dependence 7, prenascence 7, repetition 7, kamma 17, resultant 17, nutriment 17, faculty, jhāna, path 17, association 7, dissociation 17, presence 17, absence 7, disappearance 7, non-disappearance 17. (Enumerate thus.)

End of Positive

2. CONDITIONS: NEGATIVE (i) CLASSIFICATION CHAPTER

Not-root 1

33. Conditioned by limited state, arises limited state by not-root condition.

(*a*) Conditioned by one rootless limited aggregate, arise three aggregates and mind-produced matter . . . two aggregates . . .

(*b*) At the moment of rootless conception . . . conditioned by aggregates, arises (heart-)base; conditioned by (heart-)base, arise aggregates;

(*c*) One great primary . . . non-percipient beings . . .

(*d*) Conditioned by eye-base, arises eye-consciousness . . . conditioned by body-base, arises body-consciousness; conditioned by (heart-)base, arise rootless limited aggregates;

(*e*) Conditioned by doubt-accompanied or restlessness-accompanied aggregates and (heart-)base, arises doubt-accompanied or restlessness-accompanied delusion. (1)

Not-object 5

34. Conditioned by limited state, arises limited state by not-object condition. (The same as in the "Dependent" Chapter. Five.)

Not-predominance 12

35. (i) Conditioned by limited state, arises limited state by not-predominance condition.

(*a*) Conditioned by one limited aggregate, arise three aggregates and mind-produced matter . . . two aggregates . . .

(*b*) At the moment of conception . . .

(*c*) . . . non-percipient beings . . .

(*d*) . . . eye-base . . . body-base . . . conditioned by (heart-)base, arise limited aggregates. (1)

(ii) Conditioned by limited state, arises Lofty state by not-predominance condition.

(*a*) Conditioned by (heart-)base, arises Lofty predominance; conditioned by (heart-)base, arise resultant Lofty aggregates;

(*b*) At the moment of conception, conditioned by (heart-)base, arise Lofty aggregates. (2)

(iii) Conditioned by limited state, arises Incomparable state by not-predominance condition.

Conditioned by (heart-)base, arises Incomparable predominance. (3)

(iv) Conditioned by limited state, arise limited and Lofty states by not-predominance condition.

(*a*) Conditioned by (heart-)base, arise resultant Lofty aggregates; conditioned by great primaries, arises mind-produced matter;

(*b*) At the moment of conception . . . (4)

36. (v) Conditioned by Lofty state, arises Lofty state by not-predominance condition.

(*a*) Conditioned by Lofty aggregates, arises Lofty predominance; conditioned by one resultant Lofty aggregate, arise three aggregates . . . two aggregates . . .

(*b*) At the moment of conception . . . (1)

(vi) Conditioned by Lofty state, arises limited state by not-predominance condition.

(*a*) Conditioned by resultant Lofty aggregates, arises mind-produced matter;

(*b*) At the moment of conception . . . (2)

(vii) Conditioned by Lofty state, arise limited and Lofty states by not-predominance condition.

(*a*) Conditioned by one resultant Lofty aggregate, arise three aggregates and mind-produced matter . . . two aggregates . . .

(*b*) At the moment of conception . . . (3)

(viii) Conditioned by Incomparable state, arises Incomparable state by not-predominance condition.

Conditioned by Incomparable aggregates, arises Incomparable predominance. (1)

37. (ix) Conditioned by limited and Incomparable state, arises Incomparable state by not-predominance condition.

Conditioned by Incomparable aggregates and (heart-)base, arises Incomparable predominance. (1)

(x) Conditioned by limited and Lofty state, arises limited state by not-predominance condition.

(*a*) Conditioned by resultant Lofty aggregates and great primaries, arises mind-produced matter;

(*b*) At the moment of conception . . . (1)

(xi) Conditioned by limited and Lofty state, arises Lofty state by not-predominance condition.

(*a*) Conditioned by Lofty aggregates and (heart-)base, arises Lofty predominance; conditioned by one resultant Lofty aggregate and (heart-)base, arise three aggregates . . . two aggregates . . .

(*b*) At the moment of conception . . . (2)

(xii) Conditioned by limited and Lofty state, arise limited and Lofty states by not-predominance condition.

(*a*) Conditioned by one resultant Lofty aggregate and (heart-)base, arise three aggregates . . . two aggregates . . . conditioned by resultant Lofty aggregates and great primaries, arises mind-produced matter;

(*b*) At the moment of conception, conditioned by one resultant Lofty aggregate and (heart-)base, arise three aggregates . . . two aggregates . . . conditioned by resultant Lofty aggregates and great primaries, arises kamma-produced matter. (3)

Not-proximity, etc.

38. Conditioned by limited state, arises limited state by not-proximity condition . . . by not-contiguity condition . . . by not-mutuality condition . . . by not-strong-dependence condition . . . by not-prenascence condition. (The same as in the "Dependent" Chapter: 12 questions.) . . . by not-postnascence condition . . . by not-repetition condition. (Complete: point out resultant and include mind-produced matter with resultant.) . . . by not-kamma condition . . . by not-resultant condition. (No resultant conception.) . . . by not-nutriment condition . . . by not-faculty condition . . . by not-jhāna condition . . . by not-path condition

. . . by not-association condition . . . by not-dissociation condition . . . by not-absence condition . . . by not-disappearance condition . . .

2. CONDITIONS: NEGATIVE (ii) ENUMERATION CHAPTER

(By Ones)

39. With not-root 1, not-object 5, not-predominance 12, not-proximity 5, not-contiguity, not-mutuality, not-strong-dependence 5, not-prenascence 12, not-postnascence 17, not-repetition 17, not-kamma 7, not-resultant 17, not-nutriment, not-faculty, not-jhāna, not-path 1, not-association 5, not-dissociation 3, not-absence 5, not-disappearance 5. (Enumerate thus.)

End of Negative

3. CONDITIONS: POSITIVE–NEGATIVE

(Root By Twos)

40. With root condition, not-object 5, not-predominance 12, not-proximity 5, not-contiguity 5, not-mutuality 5, not-strong-dependence 5, not-prenascence 12, not-postnascence 17, not-repetition 17, not-kamma 7, not-resultant 17, not-association 5, not-dissociation 3, not-absence 5, not-disappearance 5. (Enumerate thus.)

End of Positive–Negative

4. CONDITIONS: NEGATIVE–POSITIVE

(Not-root By Twos)

41. With not-root condition, object 1, proximity, contiguity, conascence . . . disappearance, non-disappearance 1. (Enumerate thus.)

End of Negative–Positive

End of "CONDITIONED" CHAPTER

(The "Supported" Chapter is the same as the "Conditioned" Chapter.)

12. Limited Triplet V. "Conjoined" Chapter

1. CONDITIONS: POSITIVE (i) CLASSIFICATION CHAPTER

Root 3

42. (i) Conjoined with limited state, arises limited state by root condition.

(*a*) Conjoined with one limited aggregate, arise three aggregates . . . two aggregates . . .

(*b*) At the moment of conception . . . (1)

(ii) Conjoined with Lofty state, arises Lofty state by root condition.

(*a*) Conjoined with one Lofty aggregate, arise three aggregates . . . two aggregates . . .

(*b*) At the moment of conception . . . (1)

(iii) Conjoined with Incomparable state, arises Incomparable state by root condition.

Conjoined with one Incomparable aggregate, arise three aggregates . . . two aggregates . . . (1)

Object, etc.

43. Conjoined with limited state, arises limited state by object condition . . . by predominance condition. (No conception.) . . . by proximity condition . . . by contiguity condition . . . by conascence condition . . . by mutuality condition . . . by dependence condition . . . by strong-dependence condition . . . by prenascence condition. (No conception.) . . . by repetition condition. (Also no resultant and conception.) . . . by kamma condition . . . by resultant condition . . . by nutriment condition . . . by faculty condition . . . by jhāna condition . . . by path condition . . . by association condition . . . by dissociation condition . . . by presence condition . . . by absence condition . . . by disappearance condition . . . by non-disappearance condition . . .

1. CONDITIONS: POSITIVE (ii) ENUMERATION CHAPTER

(By Ones)

44. With root 3, object 3, predominance 3 . . . non-disappearance 3. (Enumerate thus.)

End of Positive

2. CONDITIONS: NEGATIVE (i) CLASSIFICATION CHAPTER

Not-root 1

45. Conjoined with limited state, arises limited state by not-root condition.

(*a*) Conjoined with one rootless limited aggregate, arise three aggregates . . . two aggregates . . .

(*b*) At the moment of rootless conception . . .

(*c*) Conjoined with doubt-accompanied or restlessness-accompanied aggregates, arises doubt-accompanied or restlessness-accompanied delusion. (1)

Not-predominance 3

46. (i) Conjoined with limited state, arises limited state by not-predominance condition.

(*a*) Conjoined with one limited aggregate, arise three aggregates . . . two aggregates . . .

(*b*) At the moment of conception . . . (1)

(ii) Conjoined with Lofty state, arises Lofty state by not-predominance condition.

(*a*) Conjoined with Lofty aggregates, arises Lofty predominance; conjoined with one resultant Lofty aggregate . . .

(*b*) At the moment of conception . . . (1)

(iii) Conjoined with Incomparable state, arises Incomparable state by not-predominance condition.

Conjoined with Incomparable aggregates, arises Incomparable predominance. (1)

Not-prenascence 3

47. (i) Conjoined with limited state, arises limited state by not-prenascence condition.

(*a*) In the immaterial plane, conjoined with one limited aggregate, arise three aggregates . . .

(*b*) At the moment of conception . . . (1)

(ii) Conjoined with Lofty state, arises Lofty state by not-prenascence condition.

(*a*) In the immaterial plane, conjoined with one Lofty aggregate, arise three aggregates . . .

(*b*) At the moment of conception . . . (1)

(iii) Conjoined with Incomparable state, arises Incomparable state by not-prenascence condition.

In the immaterial plane, conjoined with one Incomparable aggregate, arise three aggregates . . . (1)

Not-postnascence 3, Not-repetition 3

48. (i) Conjoined with limited state, arises limited state by not-postnascence condition . . . by not-repetition condition.

(*a*) Conjoined with one limited aggregate, arise three aggregates . . .

(*b*) At the moment of conception . . . (1)

(ii) Conjoined with Lofty state, arises Lofty state by not-repetition condition.

(*a*) Conjoined with one resultant Lofty aggregate, arise three aggregates . . .

(*b*) At the moment of conception . . . (1)

(iii) Conjoined with Incomparable state, arises Incomparable state by not-repetition condition.

Conjoined with one resultant Incomparable aggregate, arise three aggregates . . . (1)

Not-kamma 3

49. (i) Conjoined with limited state, arises limited state by not-kamma condition.

Conjoined with limited aggregates, arises limited volition. (1)

(ii) Conjoined with Lofty state, arises Lofty state by not-kamma condition.

Conjoined with Lofty aggregates, arises Lofty volition. (1)

(iii) Conjoined with Incomparable state, arises Incomparable state by not-kamma condition.

Conjoined with faultless Incomparable aggregates, arises Incomparable volition. (1)

Not-resultant 3

50. (i) Conjoined with limited state, arises limited state by not-

resultant condition.

Conjoined with one limited aggregate, arise three aggregates . . . (1)

(ii) Conjoined with Lofty state, arises Lofty state by not-resultant condition.

Conjoined with one Lofty aggregate, arise three aggregates . . . (1)

(iii) Conjoined with Incomparable state, arises Incomparable state by not-resultant condition.

Conjoined with one faultless Incomparable aggregate, arise three aggregates . . . (1)

Not-jhāna, etc.

51. (i) Conjoined with limited state, arises limited state by not-jhāna condition . . . by not-path condition . . . by not-dissociation condition.

In the immaterial plane, conjoined with one limited aggregate, arise three aggregates . . . (1)

(ii) Conjoined with Lofty state, arises Lofty state by not-dissociation condition.

In the immaterial plane, conjoined with one Lofty aggregate, arise three aggregates . . . (1)

(iii) Conjoined with Incomparable state, arises Incomparable state by not-dissociation condition.

In the immaterial plane, conjoined with one Incomparable aggregate, arise three aggregates . . . (1)

2. CONDITIONS: NEGATIVE (ii) ENUMERATION CHAPTER

(By Ones)

52. With not-root 1, not-predominance 3, not-prenascence 3, not-postnascence 3, not-repetition 3, not-kamma 3, not-resultant 3, not-jhāna 1, not-path 1, not-dissociation 3. (Enumerate thus.)

End of Negative

3. CONDITIONS: POSITIVE–NEGATIVE

(Root By Twos)

53. With root condition, not-predominance 3, not-prenascence, not-postnascence, not-repetition, not-kamma, not-resultant, not-dissociation 3. (Enumerate thus.)

End of Positive–Negative

4. CONDITIONS: NEGATIVE-POSITIVE

(Not-root By Twos)

54. With not-root condition, object 1, proximity 1 . . . non-disappearance 1. (Enumerate thus.)

End of Negative-Positive

End of "CONJOINED" CHAPTER

(The "Associated" Chapter is the same as the "Conjoined" Chapter.)

12. LIMITED TRIPLET VII. "INVESTIGATION" CHAPTER

1. CONDITIONS: POSITIVE (i) CLASSIFICATION CHAPTER

Root 7

55. (i) Limited state is related to limited state by root condition.

(*a*) Limited roots are related to (their) associated aggregates and mind-produced matter by root condition;

(*b*) At the moment of conception . . . (1)

(ii)–(iv) Lofty state is related to Lofty state by root condition . . . three. (Do "during life" and "at conception".)

(v)–(vii) Incomparable state is related to Incomparable state by root condition . . . three.

Object 7

56. (i) Limited state is related to limited state by object condition.

After having offered an offering, having undertaken precepts, having fulfilled the duty of observance, (one) reviews it. (One) reviews (such acts) formerly well done. The Noble persons review change-of-lineage, review purification, review the eradicated defilements, review the uneradicated defilements, know the defilements addicted to before.

Eye . . . (heart-)base . . . (They) practise insight into the impermanence, suffering and impersonality of limited aggregates; enjoy and delight in (those aggregates). Taking them as object, arises lust . . . arises grief. Visible object-base to eye-consciousness . . . tangible object-base is related to body-consciousness by object condition. (1)

(ii) Limited state is related to Lofty state by object condition.

By the power of divine-eye, (one) sees a visible object. By the power of divine-ear element, (one) hears a sound. By the knowledge of penetration into others' minds, (one) knows the other being's limited mind.

Limited aggregates are related to knowledge of supernormal power, knowledge of penetration into others' minds, knowledge of remembrance of past existences, knowledge of rebirths according to one's kamma, knowledge of future existences by object condition. (2)

57. (iii) Lofty state is related to Lofty state by object condition.

By the knowledge of penetration into others' minds, (one) knows the other being's Lofty mind. Infinity of space to infinity of consciousness . . . nothingness is related to neither-perception-nor-non-perception by object condition. Lofty aggregates are related to knowledge of supernormal power, knowledge of penetration into others' minds, knowledge of remembrance of past existences, knowledge of rebirths according to one's kamma, knowledge of future existences by object condition. (1)

(iv) Lofty state is related to limited state by object condition.

(One) reviews first jhāna . . . reviews neither-perception-nor-non-perception, reviews divine-eye, reviews divine-ear element, reviews knowledge of supernormal power, reviews knowledge of penetration into others' minds, reviews knowledge of remembrance of past existences, reviews knowledge of rebirths according to one's kamma, reviews knowledge of future existences.

(One) practices insight into the impermanence . . . of Lofty aggregates; enjoys and delights in (those aggregates). Taking them as object, arises lust . . . arises grief. (2)

58. (v) Incomparable state is related to Incomparable state by object condition.

Nibbāna is related to Path, Fruition by object condition. (1)

(vi) Incomparable state is related to limited state by object condition.

The Noble persons, having emerged from Path, review the Path, review Fruition, review Nibbāna. Nibbāna is related to change-of-lineage, purification, advertence by object condition. (2)

(vii) Incomparable state is related to Lofty state by object condition.

The Noble persons, by the knowledge of penetration into others' minds, know the other being's Incomparable mind. Incomparable aggregates are related to knowledge of penetration into others' minds, knowledge of remembrance of past existences, knowledge of future existences by object condition. (3)

Predominance 7

59. (i) Limited state is related to limited state by predominance condition.

(It is of two kinds, namely:) (*a*) object-predominance, (*b*) conascence-predominance.

(*a*) *Object-predominance:* After having offered an offering, having undertaken precepts, having fulfilled the duty of observance, (one) esteems and reviews it. (One) esteems and reviews (such acts) formerly well done. Learners esteem and review change-of-lineage, esteem and review purification. Eye . . . (heart-)base . . . (they) esteem, enjoy and delight in limited aggregates. Taking them as estimable object, arises lust, arise wrong views.

(*b*) *Conascence-predominance:* Limited predominance is related to (its) associated aggregates and mind-produced matter by predominance condition. (1)

(ii) Lofty state is related to Lofty state by predominance condition.

Conascence-predominance: Lofty predominance is related to (its) associated aggregates by predominance condition. (1)

(iii) Lofty state is related to limited state by predominance condition.

(It is of two kinds, namely:) (*a*) object-predominance, (*b*) conascence-predominance.

(*a*) *Object-predominance:* (One) esteems and (reviews) first jhāna . . . neither-perception-nor-non-perception . . . divine-eye . . . (One) esteems and reviews knowledge of future existences. (One) esteems, enjoys and delights in Lofty aggregates. Taking them as estimable object, arises lust, arise wrong views.

(*b*) *Conascence-predominance:* Lofty predominance is related to mind-produced matter by predominance condition. (2)

(iv) Lofty state is related to limited and Lofty state by predominance condition.

Conascence-predominance: Lofty predominance is related to (its) associated aggregates and mind-produced matter by predominance condition. (3)

60. (v) Incomparable state is related to Incomparable state by predominance condition.

(It is of two kinds, namely:) (*a*) object-predominance, (*b*) conascence-predominance.

(*a*) *Object-predominance:* Nibbāna is related to Path, Fruition by predominance condition.

(*b*) *Conascence-predominance:* Incomparable predominance is related to (its) associated aggregates by predominance condition. (1)

(vi) Incomparable state is related to limited state by predominance condition.

(It is of two kinds, namely:) (*a*) object-predominance, (*b*) conascence-predominance.

(*a*) *Object-predominance:* The Noble persons, having emerged from Path, esteem and review the Path, esteem and review Fruition, esteem and review Nibbāna. Nibbāna is related to change-of-lineage, purification by predominance condition.

(*b*) *Conascence-predominance:* Incomparable predominance is related to mind-produced matter by predominance condition. (2)

(vii) Incomparable state is related to limited and Incomparable state by predominance condition.

Conascence-predominance: Incomparable predominance is related to (its) associated aggregates and mind-produced matter by predominance condition. (3)

Proximity 9, Contiguity 9

61. (i) Limited state is related to limited state by proximity condition.

Preceding limited aggregates are related to subsequent limited aggregates by proximity condition. Adaptation to change-of-lineage; adaptation to purification; advertence is related to limited aggregates by proximity condition. (1)

(ii) Limited state is related to Lofty state by proximity condition.

Limited death-consciousness is related to Lofty rebirth-consciousness by proximity condition. Limited aggregates are related to Lofty emergence by proximity condition. The preparation for first jhāna . . . the preparation for neither-perception-nor-non-perception . . . the preparation for divine-eye . . . the preparation for knowledge of future existences is related to knowledge of future existences by proximity condition. (2)

(iii) Limited state is related to Incomparable state by proximity condition.

Change-of-lineage to Path; purification to Path; adaptation is related to the attainment of Fruition by proximity condition. (3)

62. (iv) Lofty state is related to Lofty state by proximity condition.

Preceding Lofty aggregates are related to subsequent Lofty aggregates by proximity condition. (1)

(v) Lofty state is related to limited state by proximity condition.

Lofty death-consciousness is related to limited rebirth-consciousness by proximity condition. Lofty life-continuum is related to advertence by proximity condition. Lofty aggregates are related to limited emergence by proximity condition. (2)

(vi) Lofty state is related to Incomparable state by proximity condition.

For one emerging from the attainment of Extinction, neither-perception-nor-non-perception is related to the attainment of Fruition by proximity condition. (3)

63. (vii) Incomparable state is related to Incomparable state by proximity condition.

Preceding Incomparable aggregates are related to subsequent Incomparable aggregates by proximity condition. Path to Fruition; Fruition is related to Fruition by proximity condition. (1)

(viii) Incomparable state is related to limited state by proximity condition.

Fruition is related to limited emergence by proximity condition. (2)

(ix) Incomparable state is related to Lofty state by proximity condition.

Fruition is related to Lofty emergence by proximity condition. (3)
(Contiguity condition is the same as proximity condition.)

Conascence 11

64. (i) Limited state is related to limited state by conascence condition.

(*a*) One limited aggregate is related to three aggregates and mind-produced matter by conascence condition . . . two aggregates . . .

(*b*) At the moment of conception . . . aggregates to (heart-)base; (heart-)base is related to aggregates by conascence condition;

(*c*) One great primary . . . non-percipient beings . . . (1)

(ii) Limited state is related to Lofty state by conascence condition.

At the moment of conception, (heart-)base is related to Lofty aggregates by conascence condition. (2)

65. (iii) Lofty state is related to Lofty state by conascence condition.

(*a*) One Lofty aggregate to three aggregates . . . two aggregates . . .

(*b*) At the moment of conception . . . (1)

(iv) Lofty state is related to limited state by conascence condition.

(*a*) Lofty aggregates are related to mind-produced matter by conascence condition.

(*b*) At the moment of conception, Lofty aggregates are related to kamma-produced matter by conascence condition. (2)

(v) Lofty state is related to limited and Lofty state by conascence condition.

(*a*) One Lofty aggregate is related to three aggregates and mind-produced matter by conascence condition . . . two aggregates . . .

(*b*) At the moment of conception . . . (3)

66. (vi) Incomparable state is related to Incomparable state by conascence condition.

One Incomparable aggregate is related to three aggregates by conascence condition . . . (1)

(vii) Incomparable state is related to limited state by conascence condition.

Incomparable aggregates are related to mind-produced matter by conascence condition. (2)

(viii) Incomparable state is related to limited and Incomparable state by conascence condition.

One Incomparable aggregate is related to three aggregates and mind-produced matter by conascence condition . . . (3)

67. (ix) Limited and Incomparable states are related to limited state by conascence condition.

Incomparable aggregates and great primaries are related to mind-produced matter by conascence condition. (1)

(x) Limited and Lofty states are related to limited state by conascence condition.

(*a*) Lofty aggregates and great primaries are related to mind-produced matter by conascence condition;

(*b*) At the moment of conception, Lofty aggregates and great primaries are related to kamma-produced matter by conascence condition. (1)

(xi) Limited and Lofty states are related to Lofty state by conascence condition.

At the moment of conception, one Lofty aggregate and (heart-)base are related to three aggregates by conascence condition . . . (2)

Mutuality 7

68. (i) Limited state is related to limited state by mutuality condition.

(*a*) One limited aggregate is related to three aggregates by mutuality condition . . .

(*b*) At the moment of conception . . . aggregates to (heart-)base; (heart-)base is related to aggregates by mutuality condition;

(*c*) One great primary . . . non-percipient beings . . . (1)

(ii) Limited state is related to Lofty state by mutuality condition. At the moment of conception, (heart-)base is related to Lofty aggregates by mutuality condition. (2)

(iii) Lofty state is related to Lofty state by mutuality condition.

(*a*) One Lofty aggregate is related to three aggregates by mutuality condition . . .

(*b*) At the moment of conception . . . (1)

(iv) Lofty state is related to limited state by mutuality condition. At the moment of conception, Lofty aggregates are related to (heart-) base by mutuality condition. (2)

(v) Lofty state is related to limited and Lofty state by mutuality condition.

At the moment of conception, one Lofty aggregate is related to three aggregates and (heart-)base by mutuality condition . . . (3)

(vi) Incomparable state is related to Incomparable state by mutuality condition.

One Incomparable aggregate is related to three aggregates by mutuality condition . . . two aggregates . . . (1)

(vii) Limited and Lofty states are related to Lofty state by mutuality condition.

At the moment of conception, one Lofty aggregate and (heart-)base are related to three aggregates by mutuality condition . . . (1)

Dependence 13

69. (i) Limited state is related to limited state by dependence condition.

(*a*) One limited aggregate is related to three aggregates and mind-produced matter by dependence condition . . . two aggregates . . .

(*b*) At the moment of conception . . . aggregates to (heart-)base; (heart-)base is related to aggregates by dependence condition;

(*c*) One great primary . . . one great primary of non-percipient beings . . .

(*d*) Eye-base to eye-consciousness . . . body-base to body-consciousness . . . (heart-)base is related to limited aggregates by dependence condition. (1)

(ii) Limited state is related to Lofty state by dependence condition.

(*a*) (Heart-)base is related to Lofty aggregates by dependence condition.

(*b*) At the moment of conception, (heart-)base is related to Lofty aggregates by dependence condition. (2)

(iii) Limited state is related to Incomparable state by dependence condition.

(Heart-)base is related to Incomparable aggregates by dependence condition. (3)

70. (iv) Lofty state is related to Lofty state by dependence condition.

(*a*) One Lofty aggregate to three aggregates . . . two aggregates . . .

(*b*) At the moment of conception . . . (1)

(v) Lofty state is related to limited state by dependence condition.

(*a*) Lofty aggregates are related to mind-produced matter by dependence condition;

(*b*) At the moment of conception, Lofty aggregates are related to kamma-produced matter by dependence condition. (2)

(vi) Lofty state is related to limited and Lofty state by dependence condition.

(*a*) One Lofty aggregate is related to three aggregates and mind-produced matter by dependence condition . . . two aggregates . . .

(*b*) At the moment of conception . . . (3)

71. (vii) Incomparable state is related to Incomparable state by dependence condition.

One Incomparable aggregate is related to three aggregates by dependence condition . . . (1)

(viii) Incomparable state is related to limited state by dependence condition.

Incomparable aggregates are related to mind-produced matter by dependence condition. (2)

(ix) Incomparable state is related to limited and Incomparable state by dependence condition.

One Incomparable aggregate is related to three aggregates and mind-produced matter by dependence condition . . . (3)

(x) Limited and Incomparable states are related to limited state by dependence condition.

Incomparable aggregates and great primaries are related to mind-produced matter by dependence condition. (1)

(xi) Limited and Incomparable states are related to Incomparable state by dependence condition.

One Incomparable aggregate and (heart-)base are related to three aggregates by dependence condition . . . two aggregates . . . (2)

(xii) Limited and Lofty states are related to limited state by dependence condition.

(*a*) Lofty aggregates and great primaries are related to mind-produced matter by dependence condition;

(*b*) At the moment of conception, Lofty aggregates and great primaries are related to kamma-produced matter by dependence condition. (1)

(xiii) Limited and Lofty states are related to Lofty state by dependence condition.

(*a*) One Lofty aggregate and (heart-)base are related to three aggregates by dependence condition . . .

(*b*) At the moment of conception, one Lofty aggregate and (heart-) base are related to three aggregates by dependence condition . . . two aggregates . . . (2)

Strong-dependence 9

72. (i) Limited state is related to limited state by strong-dependence condition.

(It is of three kinds, namely:) (*a*) object-strong-dependence, (*b*) proximity-strong-dependence, (*c*) natural strong-dependence . . .

(*c*) *Natural strong-dependence:* By the strong-dependence of limited confidence, (one) offers an offering, undertakes precepts, fulfils the duty of observance, develops insight; arouses conceit, adopts wrong views . . . limited precept . . . wisdom . . . lust . . . wish . . . bodily happiness . . . By the strong-dependence of lodging-place, (one) offers an offering . . . precepts . . . duty of observance, develops insight, kills a living being . . . causes schism in the Saṅgha. Limited confidence . . . wisdom, lust . . . wish, bodily happiness . . . lodging-place is related to limited confidence . . . wisdom, lust . . . wish, bodily happiness, bodily pain by strong-dependence condition.

Faultless or faulty kamma is related to (its) resultant by strong-dependence condition. Killing is related to killing by strong-dependence condition. (Perform the cycle.) Matricide is related to matricide by strong-dependence condition. (Perform the cycle. It is the same as in the Faultless Triplet.) (1)

(ii) Limited state is related to Lofty state by strong-dependence condition.

(It is of two kinds, namely:) (*a*) proximity-strong-dependence, (*b*) natural strong-dependence . . .

(*b*) *Natural strong-dependence:* By the strong-dependence of limited confidence, (one) develops Lofty jhāna, develops superknowledge, develops attainment . . . limited precept . . . wisdom . . . lust . . . By the strong-dependence of lodging-place, (one) develops Lofty jhāna, develops superknowledge, develops attainment. Limited confidence . . . lodging-place is related to Lofty confidence . . . wisdom by strong-dependence condition.

The preparation for first jhāna . . . the preparation for neither-perception-nor-non-perception is related to neither-perception-nor-non-perception by strong-dependence condition. The preparation for divine-eye . . . the preparation for knowledge of future existences . . . (2)

(iii) Limited state is related to Incomparable state by strong-dependence condition.

(It is of two kinds, namely:) (*a*) proximity-strong-dependence, (*b*) natural strong-dependence . . .

(*b*) *Natural strong-dependence:* By the strong-dependence of limited confidence, (one) develops Incomparable jhāna, develops Path, develops the attainment of Fruition . . . limited precept . . . wisdom . . . lust . . . wish . . . bodily happiness . . . By the strong-dependence of lodging-place, (one) develops Incomparable jhāna, develops Path, develops the attainment of Fruition. Limited confidence . . . lodging-place is related to Incomparable confidence . . . wisdom, Path, the attainment of Fruition by strong-dependence condition.

The preparation for first Path to first Path . . . the preparation for fourth Path is related to fourth Path by strong-dependence condition. (3)

73. (iv) Lofty state is related to Lofty state by strong-dependence condition.

(It is of two kinds, namely:) (*a*) proximity-strong-dependence, (*b*) natural strong-dependence . . .

(*b*) *Natural strong-dependence:* By the strong-dependence of Lofty confidence, (one) develops Lofty jhāna, develops superknowledge, develops attainment . . . Lofty precept . . . By the strong-dependence of wisdom, (one) develops Lofty jhāna, develops superknowledge, develops attainment. Lofty confidence . . . wisdom is related to Lofty confidence . . . wisdom by strong-dependence condition.

First jhāna to second jhāna . . . nothingness is related to neither-perception-nor-non-perception by strong-dependence condition. (1)

(v) Lofty state is related to limited state by strong-dependence condition.

(It is of three kinds, namely:) (*a*) object-strong-dependence, (*b*) proximity-strong-dependence, (*c*) natural strong-dependence . . .

(*c*) *Natural strong-dependence:* By the strong-dependence of Lofty confidence, (one) offers an offering, undertakes precepts, fulfils the duty of observance, develops insight; arouses conceit, adopts wrong views . . . Lofty precept . . . By the strong-dependence of wisdom, (one) offers an offering . . . develops insight . . . Lofty confidence . . . wisdom is related to limited confidence . . . wisdom . . . bodily happiness, bodily pain by strong-dependence condition. (2)

(vi) Lofty state is related to Incomparable state by strong-dependence condition.

(It is of two kinds, namely:) (*a*) proximity-strong-dependence, (*b*) natural strong-dependence . . .

(*b*) *Natural strong-dependence:* By the strong-dependence of Lofty confidence, (one) develops Incomparable jhāna, develops Path, develops the attainment of Fruition . . . Lofty precept . . . By the strong-dependence of wisdom, (one) develops Incomparable jhāna, develops Path, develops the attainment of Fruition. Lofty confidence . . . wisdom is related to Incomparable confidence . . . wisdom, Path, the attainment of Fruition by strong-dependence condition. (3)

74. (vii) Incomparable state is related to Incomparable state by strong-dependence condition.

(It is of three kinds, namely:) (*a*) object-strong-dependence, (*b*) proximity-strong-dependence, (*c*) natural strong-dependence . . .

(*c*) *Natural strong-dependence:* By the strong-dependence of Incomparable confidence, (one) develops Incomparable jhāna, develops Path, develops the attainment of Fruition . . . Incomparable precept . . . By the strong-dependence of wisdom, (one) develops Incomparable jhāna, develops Path, develops the attainment of Fruition. Incomparable confidence . . . wisdom is related to Incomparable confidence . . . wisdom by strong-dependence condition.

First Path to second Path . . . third Path to fourth Path . . . Path is related to the attainment of Fruition by strong-dependence condition. (1)

(viii) Incomparable state is related to limited state by strong-dependence condition.

(It is of three kinds, namely:) (*a*) object-strong-dependence, (*b*) proximity-strong-dependence, (*c*) natural strong-dependence . . .

(*c*) *Natural strong-dependence:* By the strong-dependence of Incomparable confidence, (one) offers an offering . . . precepts . . . duty of observance, develops insight . . . Incomparable precept . . . By the strong-dependence of wisdom (one) offers an offering . . . precepts . . . duty of observance . . . insight. Incomparable confidence . . . wisdom is related to limited confidence . . . wisdom . . . bodily happiness, bodily pain by strong-dependence condition. The attainment of Fruition is related to bodily happiness by strong-dependence condition.

The Noble persons, by the strong-dependence of the Path, practise insight into the impermanence . . . of the formations. Path is related to the Noble person's analytical knowledge of meaning . . . analytical knowledge of the above three, knowledge of correct and faulty conclusion by strong-dependence condition. (2)

(ix) Incomparable state is related to Lofty state by strong-dependence condition.

(It is of two kinds, namely:) (*a*) proximity-strong-dependence, (*b*) natural strong-dependence . . .

(*b*) *Natural strong-dependence:* By the strong-dependence of Incomparable confidence, (one) develops Lofty jhāna, develops superknowledge, develops attainment . . . Incomparable precept . . . By the strong-dependence of wisdom, (one) develops Lofty jhāna, develops superknowledge, develops attainment. Incomparable confidence . . . wisdom is related to Lofty confidence . . . wisdom by strong-dependence condition.

The Noble persons, by the strong-dependence of Path, generate an attainment which has not yet arisen, enter an attainment which has arisen. (3)

Prenascence 3

75. (i) Limited state is related to limited state by prenascence condition.

(It is of two kinds, namely:) (*a*) object-prenascence, (*b*) base-prenascence.

(*a*) *Object-prenascence:* (One) practises insight into the impermanence . . . of the eye; enjoys and delights in (the eye). Taking it as object, arises lust . . . arises grief . . . ear . . . into the impermanence . . . of the (heart-)base . . . arises grief. Visible object-base to eye-consciousness . . . tangible object-base is related to body-consciousness by prenascence condition.

(*b*) *Base-prenascence:* Eye-base to eye-consciousness . . . body-base to body-consciousness . . . (heart-)base is related to limited aggregates by prenascence condition. (1)

(ii) Limited state is related to Lofty state by prenascence condition.

(It is of two kinds, namely:) (*a*) object-prenascence, (*b*) base-prenascence.

(*a*) *Object-prenascence:* By the power of divine-eye, (one) sees a visible object. By the power of divine-ear element, (one) hears a sound.

(*b*) *Base-prenascence:* (Heart-)base is related to Lofty aggregates by prenascence condition. (2)

(iii) Limited state is related to Incomparable state by prenascence condition.

Base-prenascence: (Heart-)base is related to Incomparable aggregates by prenascence condition. (3)

Postnascence 3

76. (i) Limited state is related to limited state by postnascence condition.

Postnascent limited aggregates are related to this prenascent body by postnascence condition. (1)

(ii) Lofty state is related to limited state by postnascence condition.

Postnascent Lofty aggregates are related to this prenascent body by postnascence condition. (1)

(iii) Incomparable state is related to limited state by postnascence condition.

Postnascent Incomparable aggregates are related to this prenascent body by postnascence condition. (1)

Repetition 4

77. (i) Limited state is related to limited state by repetition condition.

Preceding limited aggregates to subsequent limited aggregates . . . Adaptation to change-of-lineage; adaptation is related to purification by repetition condition. (1)

(ii) Limited state is related to Lofty state by repetition condition. The preparation for first jhāna is related to this first jhāna by repetition condition . . . the preparation for neither-perception-nor-non-perception is related to this neither-perception-nor-non-perception by repetition condition. The preparation for divine-eye . . . the preparation for knowledge of future existences is related to knowledge of future existences by repetition condition. (2)

(iii) Limited state is related to Incomparable state by repetition condition.

Change-of-lineage to Path; purification is related to Path by repetition condition. (3)

(iv) Lofty state is related to Lofty state by repetition condition.

Preceding Lofty aggregates are related to subsequent Lofty aggregates by repetition condition. (1)

Kamma 7

78. (i) Limited state is related to limited state by kamma condition.

(It is of two kinds, namely:) (*a*) conascence(-kamma), (*b*) asynchronous (kamma).

(*a*) (1) Conascent limited volition is related to (its) associated aggregates and mind-produced matter by kamma condition;

(2) At the moment of conception, limited volition is related to (its) associated aggregates and kamma-produced matter by kamma condition.

(*b*) Asynchronous limited volition is related to (its) resultant limited aggregates and kamma-produced matter by kamma condition. (1)

(ii) Lofty state is related to Lofty state by kamma condition.

(It is of two kinds, namely:) (*a*) conascence(-kamma), (*b*) asynchronous (kamma).

(*a*) (1) Conascent Lofty volition is related to (its) associated aggregates by kamma condition;

(2) At the moment of conception, Lofty volition is related to (its) associated aggregates by kamma condition.

(*b*) Asynchronous Lofty volition is related to (its) resultant Lofty aggregates by kamma condition. (1)

(iii) Lofty state is related to limited state by kamma condition.

(It is of two kinds, namely:) (*a*) conascence(-kamma), (*b*) asynchronous (kamma).

(*a*) (1) Conascent Lofty volition is related to mind-produced matter by kamma condition;

(2) At the moment of conception, Lofty volition is related to kamma-produced matter by kamma condition.

(*b*) Asynchronous Lofty volition is related to kamma-produced matter by kamma condition. (2)

(iv) Lofty state is related to limited and Lofty state by kamma condition.

(It is of two kinds, namely:) (*a*) conascence(-kamma), (*b*) asynchronous (kamma).

(*a*) (1) Conascent Lofty volition is related to (its) associated aggregates and mind-produced matter by kamma condition;

(2) At the moment of conception, Lofty volition is related to (its) associated aggregates and kamma-produced matter by kamma condition.

(*b*) Asynchronous Lofty volition is related to (its) resultant Lofty aggregates and kamma-produced matter by kamma condition. (3)

79. (v) Incomparable state is related to Incomparable state by kamma condition.

(It is of two kinds, namely:) (*a*) conascence(-kamma), (*b*) asynchronous (kamma).

(*a*) Conascent Incomparable volition is related to (its) associated aggregates by kamma condition.

(*b*) Asynchronous Incomparable volition is related to (its) resultant Incomparable aggregates by kamma condition. (1)

(vi) Incomparable state is related to limited state by kamma condition.

Incomparable volition is related to mind-produced matter by kamma condition. (2)

(vii) Incomparable state is related to limited and Incomparable state by kamma condition.

Incomparable volition is related to (its) associated aggregates and mind-produced matter by kamma condition. (3)

Resultant 7

80. (i) Limited state is related to limited state by resultant condition.

(*a*) One resultant limited aggregate is related to three aggregates and mind-produced matter by resultant condition . . .

(*b*) At the moment of conception . . . aggregates are related to (heart-)base by resultant condition. (1)

(ii)–(iv) Lofty state is related to Lofty state by resultant condition . . . (Three questions. Include "during life" and "conception".) (3)

(v)–(vii) Incomparable state is related to Incomparable state by resultant condition . . . three. (Only "during life".)

Nutriment, etc.

81. (i) Limited state is related to limited state by nutriment condition . . . by faculty condition . . . by jhāna condition . . . by path condition . . . by association condition . . . by dissociation condition.

(It is of three kinds, namely:) (*a*) conascence, (*b*) prenascence, (*c*) postnascence.

(*a*) (1) Conascent limited aggregates are related to mind-produced matter by dissociation condition;

(2) At the moment of conception, limited aggregates are related to kamma-produced matter by dissociation condition; aggregates to (heart-)base . . . (heart-)base is related to aggregates by dissociation condition.

(*b*) Prenascent eye-base is related to eye-consciousness by dissociation . . . body-base is related to body-consciousness by dissociation condition; (heart-)base is related to limited aggregates by dissociation condition.

(*c*) Postnascent limited aggregates are related to this prenascent body by dissociation condition. (1)

(ii) Limited state is related to Lofty state by dissociation condition.

(It is of two kinds, namely:) (*a*) conascence, (*b*) prenascence.

(*a*) *Conascence:* At the moment of conception, (heart-)base is related to Lofty aggregates by dissociation condition.

(*b*) Prenascent (heart-)base is related to Lofty aggregates by dissociation condition. (2)

(iii) Limited state is related to Incomparable state by dissociation condition.

Prenascent (heart-)base is related to Incomparable aggregates by dissociation condition. (3)

82. (iv) Lofty state is related to limited state by dissociation condition.

(It is of two kinds, namely:) (*a*) conascence, (*b*) postnascence.

(*a*) (1) Conascent Lofty aggregates are related to mind-produced matter by dissociation condition;

(2) At the moment of conception . . .

(*b*) Postnascent Lofty aggregates are related to this prenascent body by dissociation condition. (1)

(v) Incomparable state is related to limited state by dissociation condition.

(It is of two kinds, namely: (*a*) conascence, (*b*) postnascence.

(*a*) Conascent Incomparable aggregates are related to mind-produced matter by dissociation condition.

(*b*) Postnascent Incomparable aggregates are related to this prenascent body by dissociation condition. (1)

Presence 13, etc.

83. (i) Limited state is related to limited state by presence condition.

(It is of five kinds, namely:) (*a*) conascence, (*b*) prenascence, (*c*) postnascence, (*d*) nutriment, (*d*) faculty.

(*a*) (1) One conascent limited aggregate is related to three aggregates and mind-produced matter by presence condition . . . two aggregates . . .

(2) At the moment of conception . . . aggregates are related to (heart-)base by presence condition; (heart-)base is related to aggregates by presence condition;

(3) One great primary . . . non-percipient beings . . .

(*b*) *(Object-)prenascence:* Eye . . . (One) practises insight into the impermanence . . . of the (heart-)base; enjoys and delights in [the (heart-)base]. Taking it as object, arises lust . . . arises grief. Visible object-base to eye-consciousness . . . tangible object-base is related to body-consciousness by presence condition.

(Base-)prenascence: Eye-base is related to eye-consciousness by presence condition . . . body-base to body-consciousness . . . (heart-) base is related to limited aggregates by presence condition.

(*c*) Postnascent limited aggregates are related to this prenascent body by presence condition.

(*d*) Edible food is related to this body by presence condition.

(*e*) Physical life-faculty is related to kamma-produced matter by presence condition. (1)

(ii) Limited state is related to Lofty state by presence condition.

(It is of two kinds, namely:) (*a*) conascence, (*b*) prenascence.

(*a*) *Conascence:* At the moment of conception, (heart-)base is related to Lofty aggregates by presence condition.

(*b*) *(Object-)prenascence:* By the power of divine-eye, (one) sees a visible object. By the power of divine-ear element, (one) hears a sound.

(Base-)presence: (Heart-)base is related to Lofty aggregates by presence condition. (2)

(iii) Limited state is related to Incomparable state by presence condition.

Prenascent (heart-)base is related to Incomparable aggregates by presence condition. (3)

84. (iv) Lofty state is related to Lofty state by presence condition.

(*a*) One Lofty aggregate to three aggregates . . . two aggregates . . .

(*b*) At the moment of conception . . . (1)

(v) Lofty state is related to limited state by presence condition.

(It is of two kinds, namely:) (*a*) conascence, (*b*) postnascence.

(*a*) (1) Conascent Lofty aggregates are related to mind-produced matter by presence condition;

(2) At the moment of conception, Lofty aggregates are related to kamma-produced matter by presence condition.

(*b*) Postnascent Lofty aggregates are related to this prenascent body by presence condition. (2)

(vi) Lofty state is related to limited and Lofty state by presence condition.

(*a*) One Lofty aggregate is related to three aggregates and mind-produced matter by presence condition . . . two aggregates . . .

(*b*) At the moment of conception . . . (3)

85. (vii) Incomparable state is related to Incomparable state by presence condition.

One Incomparable aggregate to three aggregates . . . (1)

(viii) Incomparable state is related to limited state by presence condition.

(It is of two kinds, namely:) (*a*) conascence, (*b*) postnascence.

(*a*) Conascent Incomparable aggregates are related to mind-produced matter by presence condition.

(*b*) Postnascent Incomparable aggregates are related to this prenascent body by presence condition. (2)

(ix) Incomparable state is related to limited and Incomparable state by presence condition.

One Incomparable aggregate is related to three aggregates and mind-produced matter by presence condition . . . (3)

86. (x) Limited and Incomparable states are related to limited state by presence condition.

(It is of three kinds, namely:) (*a*) conascence, (*b*) postnascence-nutriment, (*c*) (postnascence-)faculty.

(*a*) Conascent Incomparable aggregates and great primaries are related to mind-produced matter by presence condition.

(*b*) Postnascent Incomparable aggregates and edible food are related to this body by presence condition.

(*c*) Postnascent Incomparable aggregates and physical life-faculty are related to kamma-produced matter by presence condition. (1)

(xi) Limited and Incomparable states are related to Incomparable state by presence condition.

Conascence-prenascence: One conascent Incomparable aggregate and (heart-)base are related to three aggregates by presence condition . . . two aggregates . . . (2)

(xii) Limited and Lofty states are related to limited state by presence condition.

(It is of three kinds, namely:) (*a*) conascence, (*b*) postnascence-nutriment, (*c*) (postnascence-)faculty.

(*a*) (1) Conascent Lofty aggregates and great primaries are related to mind-produced matter by presence condition;

(2) At the moment of conception, Lofty aggregates and great primaries are related to kamma-produced matter by presence condition.

(*b*) Postnascent Lofty aggregates and edible food are related to this body by presence condition.

(*c*) Postnascent Lofty aggregates and physical life-faculty are related to kamma-produced matter by presence condition. (1)

(xiii) Limited and Lofty states are related to Lofty state by presence condition.

(*a*) *Conascence-prenascence:* One conascent Lofty aggregate and (heart-)base are related to three aggregates by presence condition . . . two aggregates . . .

(*b*) At the moment of conception, one Lofty aggregate and (heart-) base are related to three aggregates by presence condition . . . two aggregates and (heart-)base . . . (2)

. . . by absence condition . . . by disappearance condition . . . by non-disappearance condition . . .

1. CONDITIONS: POSITIVE (ii) ENUMERATION CHAPTER

(By Ones)

87. With root 7, object 7, predominance 7, proximity 9, contiguity 9, conascence 11, mutuality 7, dependence 13, strong-dependence 9, prenascence 3, postnascence 3, repetition 4, kamma 7, resultant, nutriment, faculty, jhāna, path 7, association 3, dissociation 5, presence 13, absence 9, disappearance 9, non-disappearance 13. (Enumerate thus.)

End of Positive

2. SELECTION OF THE CONDITIONS FOR NEGATIVE 15

88. (i) Limited state is related to limited state by object condition, conascence condition, strong-dependence condition, prenascence condition, postnascence condition, kamma condition, nutriment condition, faculty condition. (1)

(ii) Limited state is related to Lofty state by object condition, conascence condition, strong-dependence condition, prenascence condition. (2)

(iii) Limited state is related to Incomparable state by strong-dependence condition, prenascence condition. (3)

(iv) Lofty state is related to Lofty state by object condition, conascence condition, strong-dependence condition. (1)

(v) Lofty state is related to limited state by object condition, conascence condition, strong-dependence condition, postnascence condition, kamma condition. (2)

(vi) Lofty state is related to Incomparable state by strong-dependence condition. (3)

(vii) Lofty state is related to limited and Lofty state by conascence condition, kamma condition. (4)

89. (viii) Incomparable state is related to Incomparable state by object condition, conascence condition, strong-dependence condition. (1)

(ix) Incomparable state is related to limited state by object condition, conascence condition, strong-dependence condition, postnascence condition. (2)

(x) Incomparable state is related to Lofty state by object condition, strong-dependence condition. (3)

(xi) Incomparable state is related to limited and Incomparable state by conascence condition. (4)

(xii) Limited and Incomparable states are related to limited state by conascence, postnascence-nutriment-faculty. (1)

(xiii) Limited and Incomparable states are related to Incomparable state by conascence-prenascence. (2)

(xiv) Limited and Lofty states are related to limited state by conascence, postnascence-nutriment-faculty. (1)

(xv) Limited and Lofty states are related to Lofty state by conascence-prenascence. (2)

2. CONDITIONS: NEGATIVE (ii) ENUMERATION CHAPTER

(By Ones)

90. With not-root 15, not-object 15, not-predominance, not-proximity, not-contiguity 15, not-conascence 12, not-mutuality 12, not-dependence 12, not-strong-dependence 14, not-prenascence 14, not-postnascence 15, not-repetition 15 . . . not-path 15, not-association 12, not-dissociation 10, not-presence 10, not-absence 15, not-disappearance 15, not-non-disappearance 10. (Enumerate thus.)

End of Negative

3. CONDITIONS: POSITIVE-NEGATIVE

Root By Twos

91. With root condition, not-object 7, not-predominance, not-proximity, not-contiguity 7, not-mutuality 3, not-strong-dependence 7, not-prenascence 7 . . . not-path 7, not-association 3, not-dissociation 3, not-absence 7, not-disappearance 7. (Enumerate thus.)

End of Positive-Negative

4. CONDITIONS: NEGATIVE-POSITIVE

Not-root By Twos

92. With not-root condition, object 7, predominance 7, proximity 9, contiguity 9, conascence 11, mutuality 7, dependence 13, strong-dependence 9, prenascence 3, postnascence 3, repetition 4, kamma 7 . . . path 7, association 3, dissociation 5, presence 13, absence 9, disappearance 9, non-disappearance 13. (Enumerate thus.)

End of Negative-Positive

END OF LIMITED TRIPLET

13. LIMITED OBJECT TRIPLET[1] I. "DEPENDENT" CHAPTER

1. CONDITIONS: POSITIVE (i) CLASSIFICATION CHAPTER

Root 3

1. (i) Dependent on state with limited object (parittārammaṇa), arises state with limited object by root condition.

(*a*) Dependent on one aggregate with limited object, arise three aggregates . . . two aggregates;

(*b*) At the moment of conception, dependent on one aggregate with limited object, arise three aggregates . . . two aggregates. (1)

(ii) Dependent on state with Lofty object, arises state with Lofty object by root condition.

(*a*) Dependent on one aggregate with Lofty object, arise three aggregates . . . two aggregates;

(*b*) At the moment of conception . . . with Lofty object . . . (1)

(iii) Dependent on state with Incomparable object, arises state with Incomparable object by root condition.

Dependent on one aggregate with Incomparable object, arise three aggregates . . . two aggregates. (1)

Object, etc.

2. Dependent on state with limited object, arises state with limited object by object condition . . . by predominance condition. (Abbreviated.) . . . by non-disappearance condition . . .

1. CONDITIONS: POSITIVE (ii) ENUMERATION CHAPTER

(By Ones)

3. With root 3, object 3, predominance 3 . . . non-disappearance 3. (Enumerate thus.)

End of Positive

2. CONDITIONS: NEGATIVE (i) CLASSIFICATION CHAPTER

Not-root 3

4. (i) Dependent on state with limited object, arises state with limited object by not-root condition.

---

[1] This comprises (1) States with limited object, (2) States with Lofty object, (3) States with Incomparable object.

(*a*) Dependent on one rootless aggregate with limited object, arise three aggregates . . . two aggregates;

(*b*) At the moment of rootless conception, dependent on one aggregate with limited object, arise three aggregates . . . two aggregates;

(*c*) Dependent on doubt-accompanied or restlessness-accompanied aggregates, arises doubt-accompanied or restlessness-accompanied delusion. (1)

(ii) Dependent on state with Lofty object, arises state with Lofty object by not-root condition.

Dependent on one rootless aggregate with Lofty object, arise three aggregates . . . two aggregates;

Dependent on doubt-accompanied or restlessness-accompanied aggregates, arises doubt-accompanied or restlessness-accompanied delusion. (1)

(iii) Dependent on state with Incomparable object, arises state with Incomparable object by not-root condition.

Dependent on one rootless aggregate with Incomparable object, arise three aggregates . . . two aggregates. (1)

Not-predominance 3

5. (i) Dependent on state with limited object, arises state with limited object by not-predominance condition.

(*a*) Dependent on one aggregate with limited object, arise three aggregates . . . two aggregates;

(*b*) At the moment of conception . . . (1)

(ii) Dependent on state with Lofty object, arises state with Lofty object by not-predominance condition.

(*a*) Dependent on one aggregate with Lofty object, arise three aggregates . . . two aggregates;

(*b*) At the moment of conception . . . (1)

(iii) Dependent on state with Incomparable object, arises state with Incomparable object by not-predominance condition.

Dependent on one aggregate with Incomparable object, arise three aggregates . . . two aggregates. (1)

Not-prenascence, etc.

6. (i) Dependent on state with limited object, arises state with limited object by not-prenascence condition.

(*a*) In the immaterial plane, dependent on one aggregate with limited object, arise three aggregates . . .

(*b*) At the moment of conception . . . (1)

(ii) Dependent on state with Lofty object, arises state with Lofty object by not-prenascence condition.

In the immaterial plane, dependent on one aggregate with Lofty object, arise three aggregates . . . two aggregates. (No "conception" for Lofty object.) (1)

(iii) Dependent on state with Incomparable object, arises state with Incomparable object by not-prenascence condition.

In the immaterial plane, dependent on one aggregate with Incomparable object, arise three aggregates . . . two aggregates.

(Not-postnascence condition and not-repetition condition are the same as not-predominance.)

Not-kamma 3

7. (i) Dependent on state with limited object, arises state with limited object by not-kamma condition.

Dependent on aggregates with limited object, arises volition with limited object. (1)

(ii) Dependent on state with Lofty object, arises state with Lofty object by not-kamma condition.

Dependent on aggregates with Lofty object, arises volition with Lofty object. (1)

(iii) Dependent on state with Incomparable object, arises state with Incomparable object by not-kamma condition.

Dependent on aggregates with Incomparable object, arises volition with Incomparable object. (1)

Not-resultant, etc.

8. Dependent on state with limited object, arises state with limited object by not-resultant condition. (No conception.) . . . by not-jhāna condition.

Dependent on one five-fold consciousness-accompanied aggregate, arise three aggregates . . . two aggregates.

(i) . . . by not-path condition.

(*a*) Dependent on one rootless aggregate with limited object, arise three aggregates . . . two aggregates;

(*b*) At the moment of rootless conception . . . two aggregates . . . (1)

(ii) Dependent on state with Lofty object, arises state with Lofty object by not-path condition.

Dependent on one rootless aggregate with Lofty object, arise three aggregates . . . two aggregates. (1)

(iii) Dependent on state with Incomparable object, arises state with Incomparable object by not-path condition.

Dependent on one rootless aggregate with Incomparable object, arise three aggregates . . . two aggregates. (1)

Not-dissociation 3

9. (i) Dependent on state with limited object, arises state with limited object by not-dissociation condition.

In the immaterial plane, dependent on one aggregate with limited object, arise three aggregates . . . (1)

(ii) Dependent on state with Lofty object, arises state with Lofty object by not-dissociation condition.

In the immaterial plane, dependent on one aggregate with Lofty object, arise three aggregates . . . (1)

(iii) Dependent on state with Incomparable object, arises state with Incomparable object by not-dissociation condition.

In the immaterial plane, dependent on one aggregate with Incomparable object, arise three aggregates . . . two aggregates. (1)

2. CONDITIONS: NEGATIVE (ii) ENUMERATION CHAPTER

(By Ones)

10. With not-root 3, not-predominance 3 . . . not-prenascence 3, not-postnascence 3, not-repetition 3, not-kamma 3, not-resultant 3, not-jhāna 1, not-path 3, not-dissociation 3. (Enumerate thus.)

End of Negative

3. CONDITIONS: POSITIVE–NEGATIVE

(Root By Twos)

11. With root condition, not-predominance 3, not-prenascence 3, not-postnascence 3, not-repetition 3, not-kamma 3, not-resultant 3, not-dissociation 3. (Enumerate thus.)

End of Positive–Negative

4. CONDITIONS: NEGATIVE–POSITIVE

Not-root By Twos

12. With not-root condition, object 3, proximity 3, contiguity 3, conascence 3, mutuality 3, dependence 3, strong-dependence 3, prenascence 3, repetition 2, kamma 3, resultant 1, nutriment 3, faculty 3, jhāna 3, path 2, association 3, dissociation 3, presence 3, absence 3, disappearance 3, non-disappearance 3. (Enumerate thus.)

End of Negative-Positive

End of "DEPENDENT" CHAPTER

(The "Conascent", "Conditioned", "Supported", "Conjoined" and "Associated" Chapters are also the same as the "Dependent" Chapter.)

13. LIMITED OBJECT TRIPLET

VII. "INVESTIGATION" CHAPTER

1. CONDITIONS: POSITIVE (i) CLASSIFICATION CHAPTER

Root 3

13. (i) State with limited object is related to state with limited object by root condition.

(*a*) Roots with limited object are related to (their) associated aggregates by root condition;

(*b*) At the moment of conception, roots with limited object are related to (their) associated aggregates by root condition. (1)

(ii) State with Lofty object is related to state with Lofty object by root condition.

(*a*) Roots with Lofty object are related to (their) associated aggregates by root condition;

(*b*) At the moment of conception . . . (1)

(iii) State with Incomparable object is related to state with Incomparable object by root condition.

Roots with Incomparable object are related to (their) associated aggregates by root condition.

Object 7

14. (i) State with limited object is related to state with limited object by object condition.

After having offered an offering, having undertaken precepts, having fulfilled the duty of observance, (one) reviews it. (One) reviews (such acts) formerly well done. The Noble persons review the eradicated defilements with limited object, review the uneradicated defilements, know the defilements addicted to before.

(One) practises insight into the impermanence, suffering and impersonality of limited aggregates with limited object; enjoys and delights in (those aggregates). Taking them as object, arises lust with limited object . . . arises grief. By the knowledge of penetration into others' minds, (one) knows the other being's limited mind with limited object. Limited aggregates with limited object are related to knowledge of penetration into others' minds, knowledge of remembrance of past existences, knowledge of rebirths according to one's kamma, knowledge of future existences, advertence by object condition. (1)

(ii) State with limited object is related to state with Lofty object by object condition.

(One) reviews divine-eye, reviews divine-ear element, reviews knowledge of supernormal power with limited object . . . knowledge of penetration into others' minds . . . knowledge of remembrance of past existences . . . knowledge of rebirths according to one's kamma, reviews knowledge of future existences.

(One) practises insight into the impermanence . . . of Lofty aggregates with limited object; enjoys and delights in (those aggregates). Taking them as object, arises lust with Lofty object . . . arises grief. By the knowledge of penetration into others' minds, (one) knows the other being's Lofty mind with limited object. Lofty aggregates with limited object are related to knowledge of penetration into others' minds, knowledge of remembrance of past existences, knowledge of future existences, advertence by object condition. (2)

15. (iii) State with Lofty object is related to state with Lofty object by object condition.

(One) reviews infinity of consciousness, reviews neither-perception-nor-non-perception, reviews knowledge of supernormal power with Lofty object . . . knowledge of penetration into others' minds . . . knowledge of remembrance of past existences . . . knowledge of rebirths according to one's kamma, reviews knowledge of future existences.

(One) practises insight into the impermanence . . . of Lofty aggregates with Lofty object; enjoys and delights in (those aggregates). Taking them as object, arises lust with Lofty object . . . arises grief. By the knowledge of penetration into others' minds, (one) knows the other being's Lofty mind with Lofty object. Lofty aggregates with Lofty object are related to knowledge of penetration into others' minds, knowledge of remembrance of past existences, knowledge of rebirths according to one's kamma, knowledge of future existences, advertence by object condition. (1)

(iv) State with Lofty object is related to state with limited object by object condition.

(One) reviews the reviewal of first jhāna (paṭhamajjhāna-paccavekkhaṇaṁ paccavekkhati) . . . reviews the reviewal of neither-perception-nor-non-perception, reviews the reviewal of divine-eye, reviews the reviewal of divine-ear element . . . the reviewal of knowledge of supernormal power . . . the reviewal of knowledge of penetration into others' minds . . . the reviewal of knowledge of remembrance of past existences . . . the reviewal of knowledge of rebirths according to one's kamma, reviews the reviewal of knowledge of future existences. The Noble persons review the eradicated defilements with Lofty object, review the uneradicated defilements, know the defilements addicted to before.

(One) practises insight into the impermanence . . . of limited aggregates with Lofty object; enjoys and delights in (those aggregates). Taking them as object, arises lust with limited object . . . arises grief. By the knowledge of penetration into others' minds, (one) knows the other being's limited mind with Lofty object. Limited aggregates with Lofty object are related to knowledge of penetration into others' minds, knowledge of remembrance of past existences, knowledge of rebirths according to one's kamma, knowledge of future existences, advertence by object condition. (2)

16. (v) State with Incomparable object is related to state with Incomparable object by object condition.

The Noble persons, having emerged from Path, review the Path, review the Fruition. By the knowledge of penetration into others' minds, (one) knows the other being's Incomparable mind with Incomparable object. Incomparable aggregates with Incomparable object are related to knowledge of penetration into others' minds, knowledge of remembrance of past existences, knowledge of future existences, advertence by object condition. (1)

(vi) State with Incomparable object is related to state with limited object by object condition.

The Noble persons review change-of-lineage, review purification, review the reviewal of the Path, review the reviewal of the Fruition, review the reviewal of Nibbāna.

(One) practises insight into the impermanence . . . of limited aggregates with Incomparable object. By the knowledge of penetration into others' minds, (one) knows the other being's limited mind with Incomparable object. Limited aggregates with Incomparable object are related to knowledge of penetration into others' minds, knowledge of remembrance of past existences, knowledge of rebirths according to one's kamma, knowledge of future existences, advertence by object condition. (2)

(vii) State with Incomparable object is related to state with Lofty object by object condition.

The Noble persons review the knowledge of penetration into others' minds with Incomparable object, review the knowledge of remembrance of past existences, review the knowledge of future existences. By the knowledge of penetration into others' minds, (they) know the other being's Lofty mind with Incomparable object. Lofty aggregates with Incomparable object are related to knowledge of penetration into others' minds, knowledge of remembrance of past existences, knowledge of future existences, advertence by object condition. (3)

Predominance 7

17. (i) State with limited object is related to state with limited object by predominance condition.

(It is of two kinds, namely:) (*a*) object-predominance, (*b*) conascence-predominance.

(*a*) *Object-predominance:* After having offered an offering, having undertaken precepts, having fulfilled the duty of observance, (one) esteems and reviews it. (One) esteems and reviews (such acts) formerly well done. (One) esteems, enjoys and delights in limited aggregates with limited object. Taking them as estimable object, arises lust with limited object, arise wrong views.

(*b*) *Conascence-predominance:* Predominance with limited object is related to (its) associated aggregates by predominance condition. (1)

(ii) State with limited object is related to state with Lofty object by predominance condition.

Object-predominance: (One) esteems and reviews divine-eye . . . divine-ear element . . . knowledge of supernormal power with limited object . . . knowledge of penetration into others' minds . . . knowledge of remembrance of past existences . . . knowledge of rebirths according to one's kamma; (one) esteems and reviews knowledge of future existences. (One) esteems, enjoys and delights in Lofty aggregates with limited object. Taking them as estimable object, arises lust with Lofty object, arise wrong views. (2)

18. (iii) State with Lofty object is related to state with Lofty object by predominance condition.

(It is of two kinds, namely:) (*a*) object-predominance, (*b*) conascence-predominance.

(*a*) *Object-predominance:* (One) esteems and reviews infinity of consciousness . . . neither-perception-nor-non-perception . . . knowledge of supernormal power with Lofty object . . . knowledge of penetration into others' minds . . . knowledge of remembrance of past existences . . . knowledge of rebirths according to one's kamma; (one) esteems and reviews knowledge of future existences. (One) esteems, enjoys and delights in Lofty aggregates with Lofty object. Taking them as estimable object, arises lust with Lofty object, arise wrong views.

(*b*) *Conascence-predominance:* Predominance with Lofty object is related to (its) associated aggregates by predominance condition. (1)

(iv) State with Lofty object is related to state with limited object by predominance condition.

Object-predominance: (One) esteems and reviews the reviewal of first jhāna . . . esteems and reviews the reviewal of knowledge of future existences. (One) esteems, enjoys and delights in limited aggregates with Lofty object. Taking them as estimable object, arises lust with limited object, arise wrong views. (2)

19. (v) State with Incomparable object is related to state with Incomparable object by predominance condition.

(It is of two kinds, namely:) (*a*) object-predominance, (*b*) conascence-predominance.

(*a*) *Object-predominance:* The Noble persons, having emerged from Path, esteem and review the Path, esteem and review the Fruition.

(*b*) *Conascence-predominance:* Predominance with Incomparable object is related to (its) associated aggregates by predominance condition. (1)

(vi) State with Incomparable object is related to state with limited object by predominance condition.

Object-predominance: Learners esteem and review change-of-lineage, esteem and review purification, esteem and review the reviewal of the

Path, esteem and review the reviewal of the Fruition, esteem and review the reviewal of Nibbāna. (2)

(vii) State with Incomparable object is related to state with Lofty object by predominance condition.

Object-predominance: Learners esteem and review knowledge of penetration into others' minds with Incomparable object . . . knowledge of remembrance of past existences, esteem and review knowledge of future existences. (3)

Proximity 9

20. (i) State with limited object is related to state with limited object by proximity condition.

Preceding aggregates with limited object are related to subsequent aggregates with limited object by proximity condition. (1)

(ii) State with limited object is related to state with Lofty object by proximity condition.

Death-consciousness with limited object is related to rebirth-consciousness with Lofty object by proximity condition. Life-continuum with limited object is related to advertence with Lofty object by proximity condition. Aggregates with limited object are related to emergence with Lofty object by proximity condition. (2)

(iii) State with limited object is related to state with Incomparable object by proximity condition.

Life-continuum with limited object is related to advertence with Incomparable object by proximity condition. Adaptation with limited object to change-of-lineage; adaptation to purification; adaptation is related to the attainment of Fruition by proximity condition. (3)

21. (iv) State with Lofty object is related to state with Lofty object by proximity condition.

Preceding aggregates with Lofty object are related to subsequent aggregates with Lofty object by proximity condition. (1)

(v) State with Lofty object is related to state with limited object by proximity condition.

Death-consciousness with Lofty object is related to rebirth-consciousness with limited object by proximity condition. Life-continuum with Lofty object is related to advertence with limited object by proximity condition. Aggregates with Lofty object are related to emergence with limited object by proximity condition. (2)

(vi) State with Lofty object is related to state with Incomparable object by proximity condition.

Life-continuum with Lofty object is related to advertence with Incomparable object by proximity condition. Adaptation with Lofty object to change-of-lineage; adaptation to purification; adaptation to the attainment of Fruition; for one emerging from the attainment of Extinction, neither-perception-nor-non-perception is related to the attainment of Fruition by proximity condition. (3)

22. (vii) State with Incomparable object is related to state with Incomparable object by proximity condition.

Preceding aggregates with Incomparable object are related to subsequent aggregates with Incomparable object by proximity condition. Change-of-lineage to Path; purification to Path; Path to Fruition; Fruition is related to Fruition by proximity condition. (1)

(viii) State with Incomparable object is related to state with limited object by proximity condition.

Reviewal of Path to emergence with limited object; reviewal of Fruition to emergence with limited object; reviewal of Nibbāna to emergence with limited object; knowledge of penetration into others' minds with Incomparable object to emergence with limited object; knowledge of remembrance of past existences to emergence with limited object; Fruition is related to emergence with limited object by proximity condition. (2)

(ix) State with Incomparable object is related to state with Lofty object by proximity condition.

Reviewal of Path to emergence with Lofty object; reviewal of Fruition to emergence with Lofty object; reviewal of Nibbāna to emergence with Lofty object; Fruition is related to emergence with Lofty object by proximity condition. (3)

Contiguity 9

23. State with limited object is related to state with limited object by contiguity condition. (The same as proximity.)

Conascence, etc. 3

24. State with limited object is related to state with limited object by conascence condition . . . by mutuality condition . . . by dependence condition . . . three. (Proceed as in the "Dependent" Chapter.)

Strong-dependence 9

25. (i) State with limited object is related to state with limited object by strong-dependence condition.

(It is of three kinds, namely:) (*a*) object-strong-dependence, (*b*) proximity-strong-dependence, (*c*) natural strong-dependence . . .

(*c*) *Natural strong-dependence:* By the strong-dependence of confidence with limited object, (one) offers an offering . . . precepts . . . duty of observance, develops jhāna with limited object . . . insight . . . superknowledge, develops attainment; arouses conceit, adopts wrong views . . . precept with limited object . . . wisdom . . . lust . . . hate . . . delusion . . . conceit . . . wrong views . . . wish . . . bodily happiness . . . By the strong-dependence of bodily pain, (one) offers an offering . . . precepts . . . duty of observance, develops jhāna with limited object . . . insight . . . superknowledge, develops attainment, kills a living being . . . causes schism in the Saṅgha. Confidence with limited object . . . wisdom, lust . . . wish, bodily happiness, bodily pain is related to confidence with limited object . . . wisdom, lust . . . wish, bodily happiness, bodily pain by strong-dependence condition. (1)

(ii) State with limited object is related to state with Lofty object by strong-dependence condition.

(It is of three kinds, namely:) (*a*) object-strong-dependence, (*b*) proximity-strong-dependence, (*c*) natural strong-dependence . . .

(*c*) *Natural strong-dependence:* By the strong-dependence of confidence with limited object, (one) develops jhāna with Lofty object . . . insight . . . superknowledge, develops attainment; arouses conceit, adopts wrong views . . . precept with limited object . . . wisdom . . . lust . . . wish . . . bodily happiness . . . By the strong-dependence of bodily pain, (one) develops jhāna with Lofty object . . . insight . . . superknowledge, develops attainment; arouses conceit, adopts wrong views. Confidence with limited object . . . bodily happiness, bodily pain is related to confidence with Lofty object . . . wisdom, lust . . . wish by strong-dependence condition. (2)

(iii) State with limited object is related to state with Incomparable object by strong-dependence condition.

(It is of two kinds, namely:) (*a*) proximity-strong-dependence, (*b*) natural strong-dependence . . .

(*b*) *Natural strong-dependence:* By the strong-dependence of confidence with limited object, (one) develops jhāna with Incomparable object . . . Path . . . superknowledge, develops attainment . . . precept with limited object . . . wisdom . . . lust . . . bodily happiness . . . By the strong-dependence of bodily pain, (one) develops jhāna with Incomparable object . . . Path . . . superknowledge, develops attainment. Confidence with limited object . . . bodily happiness, bodily pain is related to confidence with Incomparable object . . . wisdom by strong-dependence condition. (3)

26. (iv) State with Lofty object is related to state with Lofty object by strong-dependence condition.

(It is of three kinds, namely:) (*a*) object-strong-dependence, (*b*) proximity-strong-dependence, (*c*) natural strong-dependence . . .

(*c*) *Natural strong-dependence:* By the strong-dependence of confidence with Lofty object, (one) develops jhāna with Lofty object . . . insight . . . superknowledge, develops attainment; arouses conceit, adopts wrong views . . . precept with Lofty object . . . wisdom . . . lust . . . By the strong-dependence of wish, (one) develops jhāna with Lofty object . . . adopts wrong views. Confidence with Lofty object . . . wisdom, lust . . . wish is related to confidence with Lofty object . . . wish by strong-dependence condition. (1)

(v) State with Lofty object is related to state with limited object by strong-dependence condition.

(It is of three kinds, namely:) (*a*) object-strong-dependence, (*b*) proximity-strong-dependence, (*c*) natural strong-dependence . . .

(*c*) *Natural strong-dependence:* By the strong-dependence of confidence with Lofty object, (one) offers an offering, undertakes precepts, fulfils the duty of observance, develops jhāna with limited object . . . insight . . . superknowledge, develops attainment; arouses conceit, adopts wrong views . . . precept with Lofty object . . . By the strong-dependence of wish, (one) offers an offering . . . adopts wrong views. Confidence with Lofty object . . . wish is related to confidence with limited object . . . wish, bodily happiness, bodily pain by strong-dependence condition. (2)

(vi) State with Lofty object is related to state with Incomparable object by strong-dependence condition.

(It is of two kinds, namely:) (*a*) proximity-strong-dependence, (*b*) natural strong-dependence . . .

(*b*) *Natural strong-dependence:* By the strong-dependence of confidence with Lofty object, (one) develops jhāna with Incomparable object . . . Path . . . superknowledge, develops attainment . . . precept with Lofty object . . . By the strong-dependence of wish, (one) develops jhāna with Incomparable object . . . develops attainment. Confidence with Lofty object . . . wish is related to confidence with Incomparable object . . . wisdom by strong-dependence condition. (3)

27. (vii) State with Incomparable object is related to state with Incomparable object by strong-dependence condition.

(It is of three kinds, namely:) (*a*) object-strong-dependence, (*b*) proximity-strong-dependence, (*c*) natural strong-dependence . . .

(*c*) *Natural strong-dependence:* By the strong-dependence of confidence with Incomparable object, (one) develops jhāna with Incomparable object . . . Path . . . superknowledge, develops attainment . . . precept with Incomparable object . . . By the strong-dependence of wisdom, (one) develops jhāna with Incomparable object . . . Path . . . superknowledge, develops attainment. Confidence with Incomparable object . . . wisdom is related to confidence with Incomparable object . . . wisdom, Path, the attainment of Fruition by strong-dependence condition. (1)

(viii) State with Incomparable object is related to state with limited object by strong-dependence condition.

(It is of three kinds, namely:) (*a*) object-strong-dependence, (*b*) proximity-strong-dependence, (*c*) natural strong-dependence . . .

(*c*) *Natural strong-dependence:* By the strong-dependence of confidence with Incomparable object, (one) offers an offering, undertakes precepts, fulfils the duty of observance, develops jhāna with limited object . . . insight . . . superknowledge, develops attainment . . . precept with Incomparable object . . . By the strong-dependence of wisdom, (one) offers an offering . . . develops attainment. Confidence with Incomparable object . . . wisdom is related to confidence with limited object . . . wisdom, bodily happiness, bodily pain by strong-dependence condition. (2)

(ix) State with Incomparable object is related to state with Lofty object by strong-dependence condition.

(It is of three kinds, namely:) (*a*) object-strong-dependence, (*b*) proximity-strong-dependence, (*c*) natural strong-dependence . . .

(*c*) *Natural strong-dependence:* By the strong-dependence of confidence with Incomparable object, (one) develops jhāna with Lofty object . . . insight . . . superknowledge, develops attainment . . . precept with Incomparable object . . . By the strong-dependence of wisdom, (one) develops jhāna with Lofty object . . . insight . . . superknowledge, develops attainment. Confidence with Incomparable object . . . wisdom is related to confidence with Lofty object . . . wisdom by strong-dependence condition. (3)

Repetition 5

28. (i) State with limited object is related to state with limited object by repetition condition.

Preceding aggregates with limited object are related to subsequent aggregates with limited object by repetition condition. (1)

(ii) State with limited object is related to state with Incomparable object by repetition condition.

Adaptation with limited object to change-of-lineage; adaptation is related to purification by repetition condition. (2)

29. (iii) State with Lofty object is related to state with Lofty object by repetition condition.

Preceding aggregates with Lofty object are related to subsequent aggregates with Lofty object by repetition condition. (1)

(iv) State with Lofty object is related to state with Incomparable object by repetition condition.

Adaptation with Lofty object to change-of-lineage; adaptation is related to purification by repetition condition. (2)

30. (v) State with Incomparable object is related to state with Incomparable object by repetition condition.

Preceding aggregates with Incomparable object are related to subsequent aggregates with Incomparable object by repetition condition. Change-of-lineage to Path; purification is related to Path by repetition condition. (1)

Kamma 5

31. (i) State with limited object is related to state with limited object by kamma condition.

(It is of two kinds, namely:) (*a*) conascence(-kamma), (*b*) asynchronous (kamma).

(*a*) (1) Conascent volition with limited object is related to (its) associated aggregates by kamma condition;

(2) At the moment of conception . . .

(*b*) Asynchronous volition with limited object is related to (its) resultant aggregates with limited object by kamma condition. (1)

(ii) State with Lofty object is related to state with Lofty object by kamma condition.

(It is of two kinds, namely:) (*a*) conascence(-kamma), (*b*) asynchronous (kamma).

(*a*) (1) Conascent volition with Lofty object is related to (its) associated aggregates by kamma condition;

(2) At the moment of conception . . .

(*b*) Asynchronous volition with Lofty object is related to (its) resultant aggregates with Lofty object by kamma condition. (1)

(iii) State with Lofty object is related to state with limited object by kamma condition.

Asynchronous volition with Lofty object is related to (its) resultant aggregates with limited object by kamma condition. (2)

32. (iv) State with Incomparable object is related to state with Incomparable object by kamma condition.

(It is of two kinds, namely:) (*a*) conascence(-kamma), (*b*) asynchronous (kamma).

(*a*) Conascent volition with Incomparable object is related to (its) associated aggregates by kamma condition.

(*b*) Asynchronous volition with Incomparable object is related to (its) resultant aggregates with Incomparable object by kamma condition. (1)

(v) State with Incomparable object is related to state with limited object by kamma condition.

Asynchronous volition with Incomparable object is related to (its) resultant aggregates with limited object by kamma condition. (2)

Resultant, etc.

33. State with limited object is related to state with limited object by resultant condition . . . by nutriment condition . . . by faculty condition . . . by jhāna condition . . . by path condition . . . by association condition . . . by presence condition . . . by absence condition . . . by disappearance condition . . . by non-disappearance condition . . .

1. CONDITIONS: POSITIVE (ii) ENUMERATION CHAPTER

(By Ones)

34. With root 3, object 7, predominance 7, proximity 9, contiguity 9, conascence 3, mutuality 3, dependence 3, strong-dependence 9,

repetition 5, kamma 5, resultant 3, nutriment 3, faculty, jhāna, path, association, presence 3, absence 9, disappearance 9, non-disappearance 3. (Enumerate thus.)

End of Positive

2. SELECTION OF THE CONDITIONS FOR NEGATIVE 9

35. (i) State with limited object is related to state with limited object by object condition, conascence condition, strong-dependence condition, kamma condition. (1)

(ii) State with limited object is related to state with Lofty object by object condition, strong-dependence condition. (2)

(iii) State with limited object is related to state with Incomparable object by strong-dependence condition. (3)

36. (iv) State with Lofty object is related to state with Lofty object by object condition, conascence condition, strong-dependence condition. (1)

(v) State with Lofty object is related to state with limited object by object condition, strong-dependence condition, kamma condition. (2)

(vi) State with Lofty object is related to state with Incomparable object by strong-dependence condition. (3)

37. (vii) State with Incomparable object is related to state with Incomparable object by object condition, conascence condition, strong-dependence condition. (1)

(viii) State with Incomparable object is related to state with limited object by object condition, strong-dependence condition, kamma condition. (2)

(ix) State with Incomparable object is related to state with Lofty object by object condition, strong-dependence condition. (3)

2. CONDITIONS: NEGATIVE (ii) ENUMERATION CHAPTER

(By Ones)

38. With not-root 9, not-object 9, not-predominance 9, not-proximity 9, not-contiguity 9, not-conascence 9, not-mutuality 9, not-dependence 9, not-strong-dependence 7, not-prenascence 9, not-postnascence 9, not-repetition 9 . . . not-path 9, not-association 9, not-dissociation 9,

not-presence 9, not-absence 9, not-disappearance 9, not-non-disappearance 9. (Enumerate thus.)

End of Negative

3. CONDITIONS: POSITIVE-NEGATIVE

Root By Twos

39. With root condition, not-object 3, not-predominance, not-proximity, not-contiguity, not-strong-dependence, not-prenascence, not-postnascence, not-repetition 3 . . . not path, not-dissociation, not-absence, not-disappearance 3. (Enumerate thus.)

End of Positive-Negative

4. CONDITIONS: NEGATIVE-POSITIVE

Not-root By Twos

40. With not-root condition, object 7, predominance 7, proximity 9, contiguity 9, conascence 3, mutuality 3, dependence 3, strong-dependence 9, repetition 5, kamma 5, resultant 3 . . . association 3, presence 3, absence 9, disappearance 9, non-disappearance 3. (Enumerate thus.)

End of Negative-Positive

End of "INVESTIGATION" CHAPTER

END OF LIMITED OBJECT TRIPLET

14. LOW TRIPLET[1] I. "DEPENDENT" CHAPTER

1. CONDITIONS: POSITIVE (i) CLASSIFICATION CHAPTER

Root 9

1. (i) Dependent on low state, arises low state by root condition.

Dependent on one low aggregate, arise three aggregates . . . dependent on two aggregates, arise two aggregates. (1)

(ii) Dependent on low state, arises medium state by root condition.

Dependent on low aggregates, arises mind-produced matter. (2)

(iii) Dependent on low state, arise low and medium states by root condition.

[1] This comprises (1) Low states, (2) Medium states, (3) Exalted states.

Dependent on one low aggregate, arise three aggregates and mind-produced matter . . . two aggregates . . . (3)
2. (iv) Dependent on medium state, arises medium state by root condition.

(*a*) Dependent on one medium aggregate, arise three aggregates and mind-produced matter . . . two aggregates . . .

(*b*) At the moment of conception . . . dependent on aggregates, arises (heart-)base; dependent on (heart-)base, arise aggregates;

(*c*) One great primary . . . dependent on great primaries, arise mind-produced and kamma-produced derived matter. (1)
3. (v)–(vii) Dependent on Exalted state, arises Exalted state by root condition . . . three.
4. (viii) Dependent on medium and Exalted state, arises medium state by root condition.

Dependent on Exalted aggregates and great primaries, arises mind-produced matter. (1)
5. (ix) Dependent on low and medium state, arises medium state by root condition.

Dependent on low aggregates and great primaries, arises mind-produced matter. (1)

(The Low Triplet is the same as the Corrupt Triplet. Expand completely.)

END OF LOW TRIPLET

15. Triplet of (State) with Fixed Destiny due to Wrong Views[1] I. "Dependent" Chapter

1. Conditions: Positive (i) Classification Chapter

Root 9

1. (i) Dependent on state with fixed destiny due to wrong views (micchattaniyata), arises state with fixed destiny due to wrong views by root condition.

Dependent on one aggregate with fixed destiny due to wrong views, arise three aggregates . . . two aggregates. (1)

---

[1] This comprises (1) States with fixed destiny due to wrong views, (2) States with fixed destiny due to right views, (3) States with no fixed destiny.

(ii) Dependent on state with fixed destiny due to wrong views, arises state with no fixed destiny by root condition.

Dependent on aggregates with fixed destiny due to wrong views, arises mind-produced matter. (2)

(iii) Dependent on state with fixed destiny due to wrong views, arise states with fixed destiny due to wrong views and with no fixed destiny by root condition.

Dependent on one aggregate with fixed destiny due to wrong views, arise three aggregates and mind-produced matter . . . two aggregates . . . (3)

2. (iv)–(vi) Dependent on state with fixed destiny due to right views (sammattaniyata), arises state with fixed destiny due to right views by root condition . . . three.

3. (vii) Dependent on state with no fixed destiny (aniyata), arises state with no fixed destiny by root condition.

(*a*) Dependent on one aggregate with no fixed destiny, arise three aggregates and mind-produced matter . . . two aggregates . . .

(*b*) At the moment of conception, dependent on one aggregate with no fixed destiny, arise three aggregates and kamma-produced matter . . . two aggregates . . . dependent on aggregates, arises (heart-)base; dependent on (heart-)base, arise aggregates;

(*c*) Dependent on one great primary, arise three great primaries . . . two great primaries; dependent on great primaries, arise mind-produced and kamma-produced derived matter. (1)

4. (viii) Dependent on state with fixed destiny due to wrong views and with no fixed destiny, arises state with no fixed destiny by root condition.

Dependent on aggregates with fixed destiny due to wrong views and great primaries, arises mind-produced matter. (1)

(ix) Dependent on state with fixed destiny due to right views and with no fixed destiny, arises state with no fixed destiny by root condition.

Dependent on aggregates with fixed destiny due to right views and great primaries, arises mind-produced matter. (1)

Object 3, etc.

5. (i) Dependent on state with fixed destiny due to wrong views, arises state with fixed destiny due to wrong views by object condition.

Dependent on one aggregate with fixed destiny due to wrong views, arise three aggregates . . . two aggregates . . . (1)

(ii) Dependent on state with fixed destiny due to right views, arises state with fixed destiny due to right views by object condition.

Dependent on one aggregate with fixed destiny due to right views, arise three aggregates . . . two aggregates . . . (1)

(iii) Dependent on state with no fixed destiny, arises state with no fixed destiny by object condition.

(*a*) Dependent on one aggregate with no fixed destiny, arise three aggregates . . . two aggregates . . .

(*b*) At the moment of conception, dependent on one aggregate with no fixed destiny, arise three aggregates . . . two aggregates . . . dependent on (heart-)base, arise aggregates.

(Expand all conditions in this way. Abbreviated.)

1. CONDITIONS: POSITIVE (ii) ENUMERATION CHAPTER

(By Ones)

6. With root 9, object 3, predominance 9, proximity 3, contiguity 3, conascence 9, mutuality 3, dependence 9, strong-dependence 3, prenascence 3, repetition 3, kamma 9, resultant 1, nutriment 9, faculty 9, jhāna 9, path 9, association 3, dissociation 9, presence 9, absence 3, disappearance 3, non-disappearance 9. (Enumerate thus.)

End of Positive

2. CONDITIONS: NEGATIVE (i) CLASSIFICATION CHAPTER

Not-root 1

7. (i) Dependent on state with no fixed destiny, arises state with no fixed destiny by not-root condition.

(*a*) Dependent on one rootless aggregate with no fixed destiny, arise three aggregates and mind-produced matter . . . two aggregates . . .

(*b*) At the moment of rootless conception . . .

(*c*) Dependent on one great primary . . . External . . . nutriment-produced . . . temperature-produced . . . non-percipient beings . . .

(*d*) Dependent on doubt-accompanied or restlessness-accompanied aggregates, arises doubt-accompanied or restlessness-accompanied delusion. (1)

Not-object 5

8. Dependent on state with fixed destiny due to wrong views, arises state with no fixed destiny by not-object condition.

Dependent on aggregates with fixed destiny due to wrong views, arises mind-produced matter. (Abbreviated.)

Not-predominance 3

9. (i) Dependent on state with fixed destiny due to wrong views, arises state with fixed destiny due to wrong views by not-predominance condition.

Dependent on aggregates with fixed destiny due to wrong views, arises predominance with fixed destiny due to wrong views. (1)

(ii) Dependent on state with fixed destiny due to right views, arises state with fixed destiny due to right views by not-predominance condition.

Dependent on aggregates with fixed destiny due to right views, arises predominance with fixed destiny due to right views. (1)

(iii) Dependent on state with no fixed destiny, arises state with no fixed destiny by not-predominance condition.

(*a*) Dependent on one aggregate with no fixed destiny, arise three aggregates and mind-produced matter . . . two aggregates . . .

(*b*) At the moment of conception . . . dependent on aggregates, arises (heart-)base; dependent on (heart-)base, arise aggregates;

(*c*) One great primary . . . non-percipient beings . . . (1)

Not-proximity, etc.

10. Dependent on state with fixed destiny due to wrong views, arises state with no fixed destiny by not-proximity condition. (Abbreviated. Expand all conditions.)

2. CONDITIONS: NEGATIVE (ii) ENUMERATION CHAPTER

(By Ones)

11. With not-root 1, not-object 5, not-predominance 3, not-proximity 5, not-contiguity 5, not-mutuality 5, not-strong-dependence 5, not-prenascence 6, not-postnascence 9, not-repetition 5, not-kamma 3, not-resultant 9, not-nutriment 1, not-faculty 1, not-jhāna 1, not-path 1,

not-association 5, not-dissociation 2, not-absence 5, not-disappearance 5. (Enumerate thus.)

End of Negative

3. CONDITIONS: POSITIVE–NEGATIVE

Root By Twos

12. With root condition, not-object 5, not-predominance 3, not-proximity, not-contiguity, not-mutuality, not-strong-dependence 5, not-prenascence 6, not-postnascence 9, not-repetition 5, not-kamma 3, not-resultant 9, not-association 5, not-dissociation 2, not-absence 5, not-disappearance 5. (Enumerate thus.)

End of Positive–Negative

4. CONDITIONS: NEGATIVE–POSITIVE

Not-root By Twos

13. With not-root condition, object 1, proximity 1, contiguity 1, conascence 1 . . . non-disappearance 1. (Enumerate thus.)

End of Negative–Positive

End of "DEPENDENT" CHAPTER

(The "Conascent" Chapter is the same as the "Dependent" Chapter.)

15. TRIPLET OF (STATE) WITH FIXED DESTINY DUE TO WRONG VIEWS III. "CONDITIONED" CHAPTER

1. CONDITIONS: POSITIVE (i) CLASSIFICATION CHAPTER

Root 17

14. (i)–(iii) Conditioned by state with fixed destiny due to wrong views, arises state with fixed destiny due to wrong views by root condition . . . three.

(iv)–(vi) Conditioned by state with fixed destiny due to right views, arises state with fixed destiny due to right views by root condition . . . three.

15. (vii) Conditioned by state with no fixed destiny, arises state with no fixed destiny by root condition.

(*a*) Conditioned by one aggregate with no fixed destiny, arise three aggregates and mind-produced matter . . . two aggregates . . .

(*b*) At the moment of conception . . . conditioned by aggregates, arises (heart-)base; conditioned by (heart-)base, arise aggregates;

(*c*) Conditioned by one great primary . . .

(*d*) Conditioned by (heart-)base, arise aggregates with no fixed destiny. (1)

(viii) Conditioned by state with no fixed destiny, arises state with fixed destiny due to wrong views by root condition.

Conditioned by (heart-)base, arise aggregates with fixed destiny due to wrong views. (2)

(ix) Conditioned by state with no fixed destiny, arises state with fixed destiny due to right views by root condition.

Conditioned by (heart-)base, arise aggregates with fixed destiny due to right views. (3)

(x) Conditioned by state with no fixed destiny, arise states with fixed destiny due to wrong views and with no fixed destiny by root condition.

Conditioned by (heart-)base, arise aggregates with fixed destiny due to wrong views; conditioned by great primaries, arises mind-produced matter. (4)

(xi) Conditioned by state with no fixed destiny, arise states with fixed destiny due to right views and with no fixed destiny by root condition.

Conditioned by (heart-)base, arise aggregates with fixed destiny due to right views; conditioned by great primaries, arises mind-produced matter. (5)

16. (xii) Conditioned by state with fixed destiny due to wrong views and with no fixed destiny, arises state with fixed destiny due to wrong views by root condition.

Conditioned by one aggregate with fixed destiny due to wrong views and (heart-)base, arise three aggregates . . . two aggregates . . . (1)

(xiii) Conditioned by state with fixed destiny due to wrong views and with no fixed destiny, arises state with no fixed destiny by root condition.

Conditioned by aggregates with fixed destiny due to wrong views and great primaries, arises mind-produced matter. (2)

(xiv) Conditioned by state with fixed destiny due to wrong views and with no fixed destiny, arise states with fixed destiny due to wrong views and with no fixed destiny by root condition.

Conditioned by one aggregate with fixed destiny due to wrong views and (heart-)base, arise three aggregates . . . two aggregates . . . conditioned by aggregates with fixed destiny due to wrong views and great primaries, arises mind-produced matter. (3)

(xv)–(xvii) Conditioned by state with fixed destiny due to right views and with no fixed destiny, arises state with fixed destiny due to right views by root condition. (Three questions. The same as those due to wrong views.)

Object, etc.

17. Conditioned by state with fixed destiny due to wrong views, arises state with fixed destiny due to wrong views by object condition. (Abbreviated. Classify in the same way as the "Conditioned" Chapter in the Faultless Triplet.) . . . by non-disappearance condition . . .

1. CONDITIONS: POSITIVE (ii) ENUMERATION CHAPTER

(By Ones)

18. With root 17, object 7, predominance 17, proximity 7, contiguity 7, conascence 17, mutuality 7, dependence 17, strong-dependence 7, prenascence 7, repetition 7, kamma 17, resultant 1, nutriment 17, faculty 17, jhāna 17, path 17, association 7, dissociation 17, presence 17, absence 7, disappearance 7, non-disappearance 17. (Enumerate thus.)

End of Positive

2. CONDITIONS: NEGATIVE (i) CLASSIFICATION CHAPTER

Not-root 1

19. Conditioned by state with no fixed destiny, arises state with no fixed destiny by not-root condition.

(*a*) Conditioned by one rootless aggregate with no fixed destiny, arise three aggregates and mind-produced matter . . . two aggregates . . .

(*b*) At the moment of rootless conception . . . conditioned by aggregates, arises (heart-)base; conditioned by (heart-)base, arise aggregates;

(*c*) One great primary . . . non-percipient beings . . .

(*d*) Conditioned by eye-base, arises eye-consciousness . . . conditioned by body-base, arises body-consciousness; conditioned by (heart-)base, arise rootless aggregates with no fixed destiny; conditioned by doubt-accompanied or restlessness-accompanied aggregates and (heart-)base, arises doubt-accompanied or restlessness-accompanied delusion. (1)

Not-object 5

20. (i) Conditioned by state with fixed destiny due to wrong views, arises state with no fixed destiny by not-object condition.

Conditioned by aggregates with fixed destiny due to wrong views, arises mind-produced matter. (Like Faultless Triplet. Do 5.)

Not-predominance 7

21. (i) Conditioned by state with fixed destiny due to wrong views, arises state with fixed destiny due to wrong views by not-predominance condition.

Conditioned by aggregates with fixed destiny due to wrong views, arises predominance with fixed destiny due to wrong views. (1)

(ii) Conditioned by state with fixed destiny due to right views, arises state with fixed destiny due to right views by not-predominance condition.

Conditioned by aggregates with fixed destiny due to right views, arises predominance with fixed destiny due to right views. (1)

(iii) Conditioned by state with no fixed destiny, arises state with no fixed destiny by not-predominance condition.

(*a*) Conditioned by one aggregate with no fixed destiny, arise three aggregates and mind-produced matter . . . two aggregates . . .

(*b*) At the moment of conception . . .

(*c*) . . . non-percipient beings . . .

(*d*) Conditioned by eye-base, arises eye-consciousness . . . conditioned by body-base, arises body-consciousness; conditioned by (heart-)base, arise aggregates with no fixed destiny. (1)

(iv) Conditioned by state with no fixed destiny, arises state with fixed destiny due to wrong views by not-predominance condition.

Conditioned by (heart-)base, arises predominance with fixed destiny due to wrong views. (2)

(v) Conditioned by state with no fixed destiny, arises state with fixed destiny due to right views by not-predominance condition.

Conditioned by (heart-)base, arises predominance with fixed destiny due to right views. (3)

(vi) Conditioned by state with fixed destiny due to wrong views and with no fixed destiny, arises state with fixed destiny due to wrong views by not-predominance condition.

Conditioned by aggregates with fixed destiny due to wrong views and (heart-)base, arises predominance with fixed destiny due to wrong views. (1)

(vii) Conditioned by state with fixed destiny due to right views and with no fixed destiny, arises state with fixed destiny due to right views by not-predominance condition.

Conditioned by aggregates with fixed destiny due to right views and (heart-)base, arises predominance with fixed destiny due to right views. (1)

Not-proximity, etc.

22. Conditioned by state with fixed destiny due to wrong views, arises state with no fixed destiny by not-proximity condition . . . by not-absence condition . . . by not-disappearance condition . . .

2. CONDITIONS: NEGATIVE (ii) ENUMERATION CHAPTER

(By Ones)

23. With not-root 1, not-object 5, not-predominance 7, not-proximity 5, not-contiguity 5, not-mutuality 5, not-strong-dependence 5, not-prenascence 6, not-postnascence 17, not-repetition 5, not-kamma 7, not-resultant 17, not-nutriment 1, not-faculty, not-jhāna, not-path 1, not-association 5, not-dissociation 2, not-absence 5, not-disappearance 5. (Enumerate thus.)

End of Negative

3. CONDITIONS: POSITIVE–NEGATIVE

Root By Twos

24. With root condition, not-object 5, not-predominance 7, not-proximity 5, not-contiguity, not-mutuality, not-strong-dependence 5, not-prenascence 6, not-postnascence 17, not-repetition 5, not-kamma 7, not-resultant 17, not-association 5, not-dissociation 2, not-absence 5, not-disappearance 5. (Enumerate thus.)

End of Positive–Negative

4. CONDITIONS: NEGATIVE-POSITIVE

Not-root By Twos

25. With not-root condition, object 1, proximity 1 (Abbreviated.) . . . non-disappearance 1. (Enumerate thus.)

End of Negative-Positive

End of "CONDITIONED" CHAPTER

(The "Supported" Chapter is the same as the "Conditioned" Chapter.)

15. TRIPLET OF (STATE) WITH FIXED DESTINY DUE TO WRONG VIEWS V. "CONJOINED" CHAPTER

1. CONDITIONS: POSITIVE (i) CLASSIFICATION CHAPTER

Root 3

26. (i) Conjoined with state with fixed destiny due to wrong views, arises state with fixed destiny due to wrong views by root condition.

Conjoined with one aggregate with fixed destiny due to wrong views, arise three aggregates . . . two aggregates . . . (1)

(ii) Conjoined with state with fixed destiny due to right views, arises state with fixed destiny due to right views by root condition.

Conjoined with one aggregate with fixed destiny due to right views, arise three aggregates . . . two aggregates . . . (1)

(iii) Conjoined with state with no fixed destiny, arises state with no fixed destiny by root condition.

(*a*) Conjoined with one aggregate with no fixed destiny, arise three aggregates . ... two aggregates . . .

(*b*) At the moment of conception . . . (1)

Object, etc.

27. Conjoined with state with fixed destiny due to wrong views, arises state with fixed destiny due to wrong views by object condition . . . by non-disappearance condition . . .

1. CONDITIONS: POSITIVE (ii) ENUMERATION CHAPTER

(By Ones)

28. With root 3, object 3 . . . kamma 3, resultant 1, nutriment 3 . . . non-disappearance 3. (Enumerate thus.)

End of Positive

2. CONDITIONS: NEGATIVE (i) CLASSIFICATION CHAPTER

Not-root 1

29. Conjoined with state with no fixed destiny, arises state with no fixed destiny by not-root condition.

(*a*) Conjoined with one rootless aggregate with no fixed destiny, arise three aggregates . . . two aggregates . . .

(*b*) At the moment of rootless conception . . . (1)

Not-predominance 3

30. (i) Conjoined with state with fixed destiny due to wrong views, arises state with fixed destiny due to wrong views by not-predominance condition.

Conjoined with aggregates with fixed destiny due to wrong views, arises predominance with fixed destiny due to wrong views. (1)

(ii) Conjoined with state with fixed destiny due to right views, arises state with fixed destiny due to right views by not-predominance condition.

Conjoined with aggregates with fixed destiny due to right views; arises predominance with fixed destiny due to right views. (1)

(iii) Conjoined with state with no fixed destiny, arises state with no fixed destiny by not-predominance condition.

(*a*) Conjoined with one aggregate with no fixed destiny, arises three aggregates . . . two aggregates . . .

(*b*) At the moment of conception . . . (1)

Not-prenascence, etc.

31. (i) Conjoined with state with fixed destiny due to right views, arises state with fixed destiny due to right views by not-prenascence condition.

In the immaterial plane, conjoined with one aggregate with fixed destiny due to right views, arise three aggregates . . . two aggregates . . . (1)

(ii) Conjoined with state with no fixed destiny, arises state with no fixed destiny by not-prenascence condition.

(*a*) In the immaterial plane, conjoined with one aggregate with no fixed destiny, arise three aggregates . . . two aggregates . . .

(*b*) At the moment of conception . . . (1)

Conjoined with state with fixed destiny due to wrong views, arises state with fixed destiny due to wrong views by not-postnascence condition . . . (Complete.)

Not-repetition, etc.

32. Conjoined with state with no fixed destiny, arises state with no fixed destiny by not-repetition condition.

(*a*) Conjoined with one aggregate with no fixed destiny, arise three aggregates . . . two aggregates . . .

(*b*) At the moment of conception . . . (1)

Conjoined with state with fixed destiny due to wrong views, arises state with fixed destiny due to wrong views by not-kamma condition . . . by not-resultant condition . . . (Abbreviated.)

Conjoined with state with no fixed destiny, arises state with no fixed destiny by not-jhāna condition. Five-fold consciousness . . . by not-path condition. Rootless with no fixed destiny . . .

(i) Conjoined with state with fixed destiny due to right views, arises state with fixed destiny due to right views by not-dissociation condition.

In the immaterial plane, conjoined with one aggregate with fixed destiny due to right views, arise three aggregates . . . two aggregates . . . (1)

(ii) Conjoined with state with no fixed destiny, arises state with no fixed destiny by not-dissociation condition.

In the immaterial plane, conjoined with one aggregate with no fixed destiny, arise three aggregates . . . two aggregates . . . (1)

2. CONDITIONS: NEGATIVE (ii) ENUMERATION CHAPTER

(By Ones)

33. With not-root 1, not-predominance 3, not-prenascence 2, not-postnascence 3, not-repetition 1, not-kamma 3, not-resultant 3, not-jhāna 1, not-path 1, not-dissociation 2. (Enumerate thus.)

End of Negative

3. CONDITIONS: POSITIVE-NEGATIVE

(Root By Twos)

34. With root condition, not-predominance 3, not-prenascence 2,

not-postnascence 3, not-repetition 1, not-kamma 3, not-resultant 3, not-dissociation 2. (Enumerate thus.)

End of Positive-Negative

4. CONDITIONS: NEGATIVE-POSITIVE

(Not-root By Twos)

35. With not-root condition, object 1, proximity 1 (Abbreviated.) . . . non-disappearance 1. (Enumerate thus.)

End of Negative-Positive

End of "CONJOINED" CHAPTER

(The "Associated" Chapter is the same as the "Conjoined" Chapter.)

15. TRIPLET OF (STATE) WITH FIXED DESTINY DUE TO WRONG VIEWS VII. "INVESTIGATION" CHAPTER

1. CONDITIONS: POSITIVE (i) CLASSIFICATION CHAPTER

Root 7

36. (i) State with fixed destiny due to wrong views (micchattaniyata) is related to state with fixed destiny due to wrong views by root condition.

Roots with fixed destiny due to wrong views are related to (their) associated aggregates by root condition. (1)

(ii) State with fixed destiny due to wrong views is related to state with no fixed destiny by root condition.

Roots with fixed destiny due to wrong views are related to mind-produced matter by root condition. (2)

(iii) State with fixed destiny due to wrong views is related to state with fixed destiny due to wrong views and with no fixed destiny by root condition.

Roots with fixed destiny due to wrong views are related to (their) associated aggregates and mind-produced matter by root condition. (3)

(iv)–(vi) State with fixed destiny due to right views is related to state with fixed destiny due to right views by root condition . . . three.

(vii) State with no fixed destiny is related to state with no fixed destiny by root condition.

(*a*) Roots with no fixed destiny are related to (their) associated aggregates and mind-produced matter by root condition;

(*b*) At the moment of conception . . . (1)

Object 5

37. (i) State with fixed destiny due to wrong views is related to state with no fixed destiny by object condition.

The Noble persons review the eradicated defilements with fixed destiny due to wrong views, know the defilements addicted to before. (They) practise insight into the impermanence . . . of the aggregates with fixed destiny due to wrong views. By the knowledge of penetration into others' minds, (they) know the other being's mind with fixed destiny due to wrong views. Aggregates with fixed destiny due to wrong views are related to knowledge of penetration into others' minds, knowledge of remembrance of past existences, knowledge of rebirths according to one's kamma, knowledge of future existences, advertence by object condition. (1)

(ii) State with fixed destiny due to right views is related to state with no fixed destiny by object condition.

The Noble persons, having emerged from Path, review the Path. By the knowledge of penetration into others' minds, (they) know the other being's mind with fixed destiny due to right views. Aggregates with fixed destiny due to right views are related to knowledge of penetration into others' minds, knowledge of remembrance of past existences, knowledge of future existences, advertence by object condition. (1)

38. (iii) State with no fixed destiny is related to state with no fixed destiny by object condition.

After having offered an offering, having undertaken precepts, having fulfilled the duty of observance, (one) reviews it. (One) reviews (such acts) formerly well done. Having emerged from jhāna, (one) reviews the jhāna. The Noble persons review the Fruition, review Nibbāna. Nibbāna is related to change-of-lineage, purification, Fruition, advertence by object condition.

The Noble persons review the eradicated defilements with no fixed destiny, review the uneradicated defilements, know the defilements addicted to before. Eye . . . (heart-)base . . . (They) practise insight into the impermanence, suffering and impersonality of aggregates with no fixed destiny; enjoy and delight in (those aggregates). Taking them as object, arises lust with no fixed destiny . . . arises grief.

By the power of divine-eye, (one) sees a visible object. By the power of divine-ear element, (one) hears a sound. By the knowledge of penetration into others' minds, (one) knows the other being's mind with no fixed destiny. Infinity of space to infinity of consciousness . . . nothingness is related to neither-perception-nor-non-perception by object condition. Visible object-base to eye-consciousness . . . tangible object-base is related to body-consciousness by object condition. Aggregates with no fixed destiny are related to knowledge of supernormal power, knowledge of penetration into others' minds, knowledge of remembrance of past existences, knowledge of rebirths according to one's kamma, knowledge of future existences, advertence by object condition. (1)

(iv) State with no fixed destiny is related to state with fixed destiny due to wrong views by object condition.

Physical life-faculty is related to matricide (mātughāti-kamma), patricide (pitughāti-kamma), killing an Arahat (arahantaghāti-kamma), wounding a Buddha (ruhiruppāda-kamma) by object condition. When in misapprehending (parāmasantassa) something, (there) arise aggregates with fixed destiny due to wrong views, that thing (vatthu) is related to aggregates with fixed destiny due to wrong views by object condition. (2)

(v) State with no fixed destiny is related to state with fixed destiny due to right views by object condition.

Nibbāna is related to Path by object condition. (3)

Predominance 8

39. (i) State with fixed destiny due to wrong views is related to state with fixed destiny due to wrong views by predominance condition.

Conascence-predominance: Predominance with fixed destiny due to wrong views is related to (its) associated aggregates by predominance condition. (1)

(ii) State with fixed destiny due to wrong views is related to state with no fixed destiny by predominance condition.

Conascence-predominance: Predominance with fixed destiny due to wrong views is related to mind-produced matter by predominance condition. (2)

(iii) State with fixed destiny due to wrong views is related to state with fixed destiny due to wrong views and with no fixed destiny by predominance condition.

Conascence-predominance: Predominance with fixed destiny due to wrong views is related to (its) associated aggregates and mind-produced matter by predominance condition. (3)

40. (iv) State with fixed destiny due to right views is related to state with fixed destiny due to right views by predominance condition.

Conascence-predominance: Predominance with fixed destiny due to right views is related to (its) associated aggregates by predominance condition. (1)

(v) State with fixed destiny due to right views is related to state with no fixed destiny by predominance condition.

(It is of two kinds, namely:) (*a*) object-predominance, (*b*) conascence-predominance.

(*a*) *Object-predominance:* The Noble persons, having emerged from Path, esteem and review the Path.

(*b*) *Conascence-predominance:* Predominance with fixed destiny due to right views is related to mind-produced matter by predominance condition. (2)

(vi) State with fixed destiny due to right views is related to state with fixed destiny due to right views and with no fixed destiny by predominance condition.

Conascence-predominance: Predominance with fixed destiny due to right views is related to (its) associated aggregates and mind-produced matter by predominance condition. (3)

41. (vii) State with no fixed destiny is related to state with no fixed destiny by predominance condition.

(It is of two kinds, namely:) (*a*) object-predominance, (*b*) conascence-predominance.

(*a*) *Object-predominance:* After having offered an offering, having undertaken precepts, having fulfilled the duty of observance, (one) esteems and reviews it. (One) esteems and reviews (such acts) formerly well done . . . jhāna . . . The Noble persons esteem and review the Fruition, esteem and review Nibbāna. Nibbāna is related to change-of-lineage, purification, Fruition by predominance condition.

Eye . . . (heart-)base . . . (One) esteems, enjoys and delights in aggregates with no fixed destiny. Taking them as estimable object, arises lust with no fixed destiny, arise wrong views.

(*b*) *Conascence-predominance:* Predominance with no fixed destiny is related to (its) associated aggregates and mind-produced matter by predominance condition. (1)

(viii) State with no fixed destiny is related to state with fixed destiny due to right views by predominance condition.

Object-predominance: Nibbāna is related to Path by predominance condition. (2)

Proximity 5

42. (i) State with fixed destiny due to wrong views is related to state with no fixed destiny by proximity condition.

Aggregates with fixed destiny due to wrong views are related to emergence by proximity condition. (1)

(ii) State with fixed destiny due to right views is related to state with no fixed destiny by proximity condition.

Path is related to Fruition by proximity condition. (1)

43. (iii) State with no fixed destiny is related to state with no fixed destiny by proximity condition.

Preceding aggregates with no fixed destiny are related to subsequent aggregates with no fixed destiny by proximity condition. Adaptation to change-of-lineage; adaptation to purification; Fruition to Fruition; adaptation to the attainment of Fruition; for one emerging from the attainment of Extinction, neither-perception-nor-non-perception is related to the attainment of Fruition by proximity condition. (1)

(iv) State with no fixed destiny is related to state with fixed destiny due to wrong views by proximity condition.

Grief with no fixed destiny is related to grief with fixed destiny due to wrong views by proximity condition. Wrong views with no fixed destiny are related to wrong views with fixed destiny by proximity condition. (2)

(v) State with no fixed destiny is related to state with fixed destiny due to right views by proximity condition.

Change-of-lineage to Path; purification is related to Path by proximity condition. (3)

Contiguity, etc.

44. State with fixed destiny due to wrong views is related to state with no fixed destiny by contiguity condition. (The same as proximity.) . . . by conascence condition. (The same as in the "Dependent" Chapter. 9 questions.) . . . by mutuality condition. (The same as in the "Dependent" Chapter. 3 questions.) . . . by dependence condition. (The same as in the Faultless Triplet. 13 questions.)

Strong-dependence 7

45. (i) State with fixed destiny due to wrong views is related to state with fixed destiny due to wrong views by strong-dependence condition.

Natural strong-dependence: Matricide is related to matricide by strong-dependence condition. Matricide . . . patricide . . . killing an Arahat . . . wounding a Buddha . . . causing schism in the Saṅgha . . . is related to wrong views with fixed destiny by strong-dependence condition. (Perform the cycle.) Wrong views with fixed destiny are related to wrong views with fixed destiny by strong-dependence condition. Wrong views with fixed destiny to matricide . . . are related to causing schism in the Saṅgha by strong-dependence condition. (1)

(ii) State with fixed destiny due to wrong views is related to state with no fixed destiny by strong-dependence condition.

(It is of two kinds, namely:) (*a*) proximity-strong-dependence, (*b*) natural strong-dependence . . .

(*b*) *Natural strong-dependence:* After having committed matricide, (one) offers an offering, undertakes precepts, fulfils the duty of observance, to counteract it (tassa paṭighātatthāya). After having committed patricide . . . killed an Arahat . . . drawn blood from the body of a Buddha with evil intent (duṭṭhena cittena) . . . After having caused schism in the Saṅgha (saṁghaṁ bhinditvā), (one) offers an offering, undertakes precepts, fulfils the duty of observance, to counteract it. (2)

46. (iii) State with fixed destiny due to right views is related to state with fixed destiny due to right views by strong-dependence condition.

Natural strong-dependence: First Path is related to second Path by strong-dependence condition . . . third Path is related to fourth Path by strong-dependence condition. (1)

(iv) State with fixed destiny due to right views is related to state with no fixed destiny by strong-dependence condition.

(It is of three kinds, namely:) (*a*) object-strong-dependence, (*b*) proximity-strong-dependence, (*c*) natural strong-dependence . . .

(*c*) *Natural strong-dependence:* The Noble persons, by the strong-dependence of the Path, generate an attainment which has not yet arisen, enter an attainment which has arisen. (They) practise insight into the impermanence, suffering and impersonality of the formations. The Path is related to the Noble person's analytical knowledge of meaning . . . knowledge of correct and faulty conclusion by strong-dependence condition. Path is related to the attainment of Fruition by strong-dependence condition. (2)

47. (v) State with no fixed destiny is related to state with no fixed destiny by strong-dependence condition.

(It is of three kinds, namely:) (*a*) object-strong-dependence, (*b*) proximity-strong-dependence, (*c*) natural strong-dependence . . .

(*c*) *Natural strong-dependence:* By the strong-dependence of confidence with no fixed destiny, (one) offers an offering, undertakes precepts . . . duty of observance, develops jhāna . . . insight . . . super-knowledge, develops attainment; arouses conceit, adopts wrong views . . . precept with no fixed destiny . . . learning . . . generosity . . . wisdom . . . lust . . . wish . . . bodily happiness . . . bodily pain . . . temperature . . . food . . . By the strong-dependence of lodging-place, (one) offers an offering . . . plunders market-towns. Confidence with no fixed destiny . . . wisdom, lust . . . lodging-place is related to confidence with no fixed destiny . . . bodily happiness, bodily pain, the attainment of Fruition by strong-dependence condition.

The preparation for first jhāna to the same (jhāna) (tasseva) . . . the preparation for neither-perception-nor-non-perception to the same (jhāna) . . . first jhāna to second jhāna . . . nothingness to neither-perception-nor-non-perception . . . killing is related to killing by strong-dependence condition . . . (Perform the cycle.) (1)

(vi) State with no fixed destiny is related to state with fixed destiny due to wrong views by strong-dependence condition.

(It is of two kinds, namely:) (*a*) proximity-strong-dependence, (*b*) natural strong-dependence . . .

(*b*) *Natural strong-dependence:* By the strong-dependence of lust with no fixed destiny, (one) commits matricide . . . causes schism in the Saṅgha . . . hate with no fixed destiny . . . wish . . . bodily happiness . . . by the strong-dependence of lodging-place, (one) commits matricide . . . causes schism in the Saṅgha. Lust with no fixed destiny . . . lodging-place is related to matricide, patricide, killing an Arahat, wounding a Buddha, causing schism in the Saṅgha, wrong views with fixed destiny by strong-dependence condition. (2)

(vii) State with no fixed destiny is related to state with fixed destiny due to right views by strong-dependence condition.

(It is of three kinds, namely:) (*a*) object-strong-dependence, (*b*) proximity-strong-dependence, (*c*) natural strong-dependence . . .

(*c*) *Natural strong-dependence:* The preparation for first Path to first Path . . . the preparation for fourth Path is related to fourth Path by strong-dependence condition. (3)

Prenascence 3

48. (i) State with no fixed destiny is related to state with no fixed destiny by prenascence condition.

(It is of two kinds, namely:) (*a*) object-prenascence, (*b*) base-prenascence.

(*a*) *Object-prenascence:* Eye . . . (One) practises insight into the impermanence . . . of the (heart-)base; enjoys and delights in [the (heart-)base]. Taking it as object, arises lust with no fixed destiny . . . arises grief.

By the power of divine-eye, (one) sees a visible object. By the power of divine-ear element, (one) hears a sound. Visible object-base to eye-consciousness . . . tangible object-base is related to body-consciousness by prenascence condition.

(*b*) *Base-prenascence:* Eye-base to eye-consciousness . . . body-base to body-consciousness . . . (heart-)base is related to aggregates with no fixed destiny by prenascence condition. (1)

(ii) State with no fixed destiny is related to state with fixed destiny due to wrong views by prenascence condition.

(It is of two kinds, namely:) (*a*) object-prenascence, (*b*) base-prenascence.

(*a*) *Object-prenascence:* Physical life-faculty is related to matricide, patricide, killing an Arahat, wounding a Buddha by prenascence condition.

(*b*) *Base-prenascence:* (Heart-)base is related to aggregates with fixed destiny due to wrong views by prenascence condition. (2)

(iii) State with no fixed destiny is related to state with fixed destiny due to right views by prenascence condition.

Base-prenascence: (Heart-)base is related to aggregates with fixed destiny due to right views by prenascence condition. (3)

Postnascence 3

49. (i) State with fixed destiny due to wrong views is related to state with no fixed destiny by postnascence condition.

Postnascent aggregates with fixed destiny due to wrong views are related to this prenascent body by postnascence condition. (1)

(ii) State with fixed destiny due to right views is related to state with no fixed destiny by postnascence condition.

Postnascent aggregates with fixed destiny due to right views are related to this prenascent body by postnascence condition. (1)

(iii) State with no fixed destiny is related to state with no fixed destiny by postnascence condition.

Postnascent aggregates with no fixed destiny are related to this prenascent body by postnascence condition. (1)

Repetition 3

50. (i) State with no fixed destiny is related to state with no fixed destiny by repetition condition.

Preceding aggregates with no fixed destiny are related to subsequent aggregates with no fixed destiny by repetition condition. Adaptation to change-of-lineage; adaptation is related to purification by repetition condition. (1)

(ii) State with no fixed destiny is related to state with fixed destiny due to wrong views by repetition condition.

Grief with no fixed destiny is related to grief with fixed destiny due to wrong views by repetition condition. Wrong views with no fixed destiny are related to wrong views with fixed destiny by repetition condition. (2)

(iii) State with no fixed destiny is related to state with fixed destiny due to right views by repetition condition.

Change-of-lineage to Path; purification is related to Path by repetition condition. (3)

Kamma 7

51. (i) State with fixed destiny due to wrong views is related to state with fixed destiny due to wrong views by kamma condition.

Volition with fixed destiny due to wrong views is related to (its) associated aggregates by kamma condition. (1)

(ii) State with fixed destiny due to wrong views is related to state with no fixed destiny by kamma condition.

(It is of two kinds, namely:) (*a*) conascence(-kamma), (*b*) asynchronous (kamma).

(*a*) Conascent volition with fixed destiny due to wrong views is related to mind-produced matter by kamma condition.

(*b*) Asynchronous volition with fixed destiny due to wrong views is related to (its) resultant aggregates and kamma-produced matter by kamma condition. (2)

(iii) State with fixed destiny due to wrong views is related to state with fixed destiny due to wrong views and with no fixed destiny by kamma condition.

Volition with fixed destiny due to wrong views is related to (its) associated aggregates and mind-produced matter by kamma condition. (3)

52. (iv) State with fixed destiny due to right views is related to state with fixed destiny due to right views by kamma condition.

Volition with fixed destiny due to right views is related to (its) associated aggregates by kamma condition. (1)

(v) State with fixed destiny due to right views is related to state with no fixed destiny by kamma condition.

(It is of two kinds, namely:) (*a*) conascence(-kamma), (*b*) asynchronous (kamma).

(*a*) Conascent volition with fixed destiny due to right views is related to mind-produced matter by kamma condition.

(*b*) Asynchronous volition with fixed destiny due to right views is related to (its) resultant aggregates by kamma condition. (2)

(vi) State with fixed destiny due to right views is related to state with fixed destiny due to right views and with no fixed destiny by kamma condition.

Volition with fixed destiny due to right views is related to (its) associated aggregates and mind-produced matter by kamma condition. (3)

(vii) State with no fixed destiny is related to state with no fixed destiny by kamma condition.

(It is of two kinds, namely:) (*a*) conascence(-kamma), (*b*) asynchronous (kamma).

(*a*) (1) Conascent volition with no fixed destiny is related to (its) associated aggregates and mind-produced matter by kamma condition.

(2) At the moment of conception . . .

(*b*) Asynchronous volition with no fixed destiny is related to (its) resultant aggregates and kamma-produced matter by kamma condition. (1)

Resultant 1

53. State with no fixed destiny is related to state with no fixed destiny by resultant condition.

(*a*) One resultant aggregate with no fixed destiny is related to three aggregates and mind-produced matter by resultant condition . . .

(*b*) At the moment of conception . . . aggregates to (heart-)base . . .

Nutriment, etc.

54. State with fixed destiny due to wrong views is related to state with fixed destiny due to wrong views by nutriment condition . . . by faculty condition . . . by jhāna condition . . . by path condition . . . by associated condition . . .

Dissociation 5

55. (i) State with fixed destiny due to wrong views is related to state with no fixed destiny by dissociation condition.

(It is of two kinds, namely:) (*a*) conascence, (*b*) postnascence.

(*a*) Conascent aggregates with fixed destiny due to wrong views are related to mind-produced matter by dissociation condition.

(*b*) Postnascent aggregates with fixed destiny due to wrong views are related to this prenascent body by dissociation condition. (1)

(ii) State with fixed destiny due to right views is related to state with no fixed destiny by dissociation condition.

(It is of two kinds, namely:) (*a*) conascence, (*b*) postnascence.

(*a*) Conascent aggregates with fixed destiny due to right views are related to mind-produced matter by dissociation condition.

(*b*) Postnascent aggregates with fixed destiny due to right views are related to this prenascent body by dissociation condition. (1)

(iii) State with no fixed destiny is related to state with no fixed destiny by dissociation condition.

(It is of three kinds, namely:) (*a*) conascence, (*b*) prenascence, (*c*) postnascence.

(*a*) (1) Conascent aggregates with no fixed destiny are related to mind-produced matter by dissociation condition;

(2) At the moment of conception . . . aggregates are related to (heart-)base by dissociation condition; (heart-)base is related to aggregates by dissociation condition.

(*b*) Prenascent eye-base to eye-consciousness . . . body-base to body-consciousness . . . (heart-)base is related to aggregates with no fixed destiny by dissociation condition.

(*c*) Postnascent aggregates with no fixed destiny are related to this prenascent body by dissociation condition. (1)

(iv) State with no fixed destiny is related to state with fixed destiny due to wrong views by dissociation condition.

Prenascent (heart-)base is related to aggregates with fixed destiny due to wrong views by dissociation condition. (2)

(v) State with no fixed destiny is related to state with fixed destiny due to right views by dissociation condition.

Prenascent (heart-)base is related to aggregates with fixed destiny due to right views by dissociation condition. (3)

Presence 13

56. (i) State with fixed destiny due to wrong views is related to state with fixed destiny due to wrong views by presence condition.

One aggregate with fixed destiny due to wrong views to three aggregates . . . two aggregates are related to two aggregates by presence condition. (1)

(ii) State with fixed destiny due to wrong views is related to state with no fixed destiny by presence condition.

(It is of two kinds, namely:) (*a*) conascence, (*b*) postnascence.

(*a*) Conascent aggregates with fixed destiny due to wrong views are related to mind-produced matter by presence condition.

(*b*) Postnascent aggregates with fixed destiny due to wrong views are related to this prenascent body by presence condition. (2)

(iii) State with fixed destiny due to wrong views is related to state with fixed destiny due to wrong views and with no fixed destiny by presence condition.

One aggregate with fixed destiny due to wrong views is related to three aggregates and mind-produced matter by presence condition . . . two aggregates . . . (3)

(iv)–(vi) State with fixed destiny due to right views is related to state with fixed destiny due to right views by presence condition . . . (Three questions.)

(vii) State with no fixed destiny is related to state with no fixed destiny by presence condition.

(It is of five kinds, namely:) (*a*) conascence, (*b*) prenascence, (*c*) postnascence, (*d*) nutriment, (*e*) faculty.

(*a*) (1) One conascent aggregate with no fixed destiny is related to three aggregates and mind-produced matter by presence condition . . . two aggregates . . .

(2) At the moment of conception . . . aggregates are related to

(heart-)base by presence condition; (heart-)base is related to aggregates by presence condition;

(3) One great primary . . . one great primary of non-percipient beings . . .

(*b*) *(Object-)prenascence:* Eye . . . (One) practises insight into the impermanence, suffering and impersonality of the (heart-)base; enjoys and delights in [the (heart-)base]. Taking it as object, arises lust . . . arises grief. By the power of divine-eye, (one) sees a visible object. By the power of divine-ear element, (one) hears a sound. Visible object-base to eye-consciousness . . . tangible object-base to body-consciousness . . .

(Base-)prenascence: Eye-base to eye-consciousness . . . body-base to body-consciousness . . . (heart-)base is related to aggregates with no fixed destiny by presence condition.

(*c*) Postnascent aggregates with no fixed destiny are related to this prenascent body by presence condition.

(*d*) Edible food is related to this body by presence condition.

(*e*) Physical life-faculty is related to kamma-produced matter by presence condition. (1)

(viii) State with no fixed destiny is related to state with fixed destiny due to wrong views by presence condition.

(Object-)prenascence: Physical life-faculty is related to matricide . . . wounding a Buddha by presence condition.

(Base-)prenascence: (Heart-)base is related to aggregates with fixed destiny due to wrong views by presence condition. (2)

(ix) State with no fixed destiny is related to state with fixed destiny due to right views by presence condition.

(Base-)prenascence: (Heart-)base is related to aggregates with fixed destiny due to right views by presence condition. (3)

57. (x) States with fixed destiny due to wrong views and with no fixed destiny are related to state with fixed destiny due to wrong views by presence condition.

Conascence-prenascence: One conascent aggregate with fixed destiny due to wrong views and (heart-)base to three aggregates . . . two aggregates and . . . (1)

(xi) States with fixed destiny due to wrong views and with no fixed destiny are related to state with no fixed destiny by presence condition.

(It is of three kinds, namely:) (*a*) conascence, (*b*) postnascence-nutriment, (*c*) (postnascence-)faculty.

(*a*) Conascent aggregates with fixed destiny due to wrong views and great primaries are related to mind-produced matter by presence condition.

(*b*) Postnascent aggregates with fixed destiny due to wrong views and edible food are related to this body by presence condition.

(*c*) Postnascent aggregates with fixed destiny due to wrong views and physical life-faculty are related to kamma-produced matter by presence condition. (2)

(xii)–(xiii) States with fixed destiny due to right views and with no fixed destiny are related to state with fixed destiny due to right views by presence condition . . . (Like the 2 questions with fixed destiny due to wrong views.)

1. CONDITIONS: POSITIVE (ii) ENUMERATION CHAPTER

(By Ones)

58. With root 7, object 5, predominance 8, proximity 5, contiguity 5, conascence 9, mutuality 3, dependence 13, strong-dependence 7, prenascence 3, postnascence 3, repetition 3, kamma 7, resultant 1, nutriment 7, faculty 7, jhāna 7, path 7, association 3, dissociation 5, presence 13, absence 5, disappearance 5, non-disappearance 13. (Enumerate thus.)

End of Positive

2. SELECTION OF THE CONDITIONS FOR NEGATIVE 13

59. (i) State with fixed destiny due to wrong views is related to state with fixed destiny due to wrong views by conascence condition, strong-dependence condition. (1)

(ii) State with fixed destiny due to wrong views is related to state with no fixed destiny by object condition, conascence condition, strong-dependence condition, postnascence condition, kamma condition. (2)

(iii) State with fixed destiny due to wrong views is related to state with fixed destiny due to wrong views and with no fixed destiny by conascence condition. (3)

(iv) State with fixed destiny due to right views is related to state with fixed destiny due to right views by conascence condition, strong-dependence condition. (1)

(v) State with fixed destiny due to right views is related to state with no fixed destiny by object condition, conascence condition, strong-dependence condition, postnascence condition. (2)

(vi) State with fixed destiny due to right views is related to state with fixed destiny due to right views and with no fixed destiny by conascence condition. (3)

60. (vii) State with no fixed destiny is related to state with no fixed destiny by object condition, conascence condition, strong-dependence condition, prenascence condition, postnascence condition, kamma condition, nutriment condition, faculty condition. (1)

(viii) State with no fixed destiny is related to state with fixed destiny due to wrong views by object condition, strong-dependence condition, prenascence condition. (2)

(ix) State with no fixed destiny is related to state with fixed destiny due to right views by strong-dependence condition, prenascence condition. (3)

(x) States with fixed destiny due to wrong views and with no fixed destiny are related to state with fixed destiny due to wrong views by conascence-prenascence. (1)

(xi) States with fixed destiny due to wrong views and with no fixed destiny are related to state with no fixed destiny by conascence, postnascence-nutriment-faculty. (2)

(xii) States with fixed destiny due to right views and with no fixed destiny are related to state with fixed destiny due to right views by conascence-prenascence. (1)

(xiii) States with fixed destiny due to right views and with no fixed destiny are related to state with no fixed destiny by conascence, postnascence-nutriment-faculty. (2)

2. CONDITIONS: NEGATIVE (ii) ENUMERATION CHAPTER

(By Ones)

61. With not-root 13, not-object, not-predominance, not-proximity, not-contiguity 13, not-conascence 9, not-mutuality 9, not-dependence 9, not-strong-dependence 13, not-prenascence 11, not-postnascence 13, not-repetition 13, not-kamma, not-resultant, not-nutriment 13 . . . not-path 13, not-association 9, not-dissociation 7, not-presence 7, not-absence 13, not-disappearance 13, not-non-disappearance 7. (Enumerate thus.)

End of Negative

3. CONDITIONS: POSITIVE-NEGATIVE

Root By Twos

62. With root condition, not-object 7, not-predominance 7, not-proximity 7, not-contiguity 7, not-mutuality 3, not-strong-dependence 7 . . . not-path 7, not-association 3 not-dissociation 3, not-absence 7, not-disappearance 7. (Enumerate thus.)

End of Positive-Negative

4. CONDITIONS: NEGATIVE-POSITIVE

Not-root By Twos

63. With not-root condition, object 5, predominance 8, proximity 5, contiguity 5, conascence 9, mutuality 3, dependence 13, strong-dependence 7, prenascence 3, postnascence 3, repetition 3, kamma 7, resultant 1, nutriment 7, faculty, jhāna, path 7, association 3, dissociation 5, presence 13, absence 5, disappearance 5, non-disappearance 13. (Enumerate thus.)

End of Negative-Positive

END OF TRIPLET OF (STATE) WITH FIXED DESTINY DUE TO WRONG VIEWS

16. PATH OBJECT TRIPLET[1] I. "DEPENDENT" CHAPTER

1. CONDITIONS: POSITIVE (i) CLASSIFICATION CHAPTER

Root 17

1. (i) Dependent on state with Path object (Maggārammaṇa), arises state with Path object by root condition.

Dependent on one aggregate with Path object, arise three aggregates . . . two aggregates (1)

(ii) Dependent on state with Path object, arises state dominated by the Path by root condition.

Dependent on one aggregate with Path object, arise three aggregates dominated by the Path; dependent on three aggregates, arises one aggregate . . . two aggregates . . . (2)

---

[1] This comprises (1) States with Path object, (2) States conditioned by the Path, (3) States dominated by the Path.

(iii) Dependent on state with Path object, arise states with Path object and dominated by the Path by root condition.

Dependent on one aggregate with Path object, arise three aggregates with Path object and dominated by the Path . . . two aggregates . . . (3)

2. (iv) Dependent on state conditioned by the Path (Maggahetuka), arises state conditioned by the Path by root condition.

Dependent on one aggregate conditioned by the Path, arise three aggregates . . . two aggregates . . . (1)

(v) Dependent on state conditioned by the Path, arises state dominated by the Path by root condition.

Dependent on one aggregate conditioned by the Path, arise three aggregates dominated by the Path . . . two aggregates . . . (2)

(vi) Dependent on state conditioned by the Path, arise states conditioned by the Path and dominated by the Path by root condition.

Dependent on one aggregate conditioned by the Path, arise three aggregates conditioned by the Path and dominated by the Path . . . two aggregates . . . (3)

3. (vii) Dependent on state dominated by the Path (Maggādhipati), arises state dominated by the Path by root condition.

Dependent on one aggregate dominated by the Path, arise three aggregates . . . two aggregates . . . (1)

(viii) Dependent on state dominated by the Path, arises state with Path object by root condition.

Dependent on one aggregate dominated by the Path, arise three aggregates with Path object . . . two aggregates . . . (2)

(ix) Dependent on state dominated by the Path, arises state conditioned by the Path by root condition.

Dependent on one aggregate dominated by the Path, arise three aggregates conditioned by the Path . . . two aggregates . . . (3)

(x) Dependent on state dominated by the Path, arise states with Path object and dominated by the Path by root condition.

Dependent on one aggregate dominated by the Path, arise three aggregates with Path object and dominated by the Path . . . two aggregates . . . (4)

(xi) Dependent on state dominated by the Path, arise states conditioned by the Path and dominated by the Path by root condition.

Dependent on one aggregate dominated by the Path, arise three aggregates conditioned by the Path and dominated by the Path . . . two aggregates . . . (5)

4. (xii) Dependent on state with Path object and dominated by the Path, arises state with Path object by root condition.

Dependent on one aggregate with Path object and dominated by the Path, arise three aggregates with Path object . . . two aggregates . . . (1)

(xiii) Dependent on state with Path object and dominated by the Path, arises state dominated by the Path by root condition.

Dependent on one aggregate with Path object and dominated by the Path, arise three aggregates dominated by the Path . . . two aggregates (2)

(xiv) Dependent on state with Path object and dominated by the Path, arise states with Path object and dominated by the Path by root condition.

Dependent on one aggregate with Path object and dominated by the Path, arise three aggregates with Path object and dominated by the Path . . . two aggregates . . . (3)

5. (xv) Dependent on state conditioned by the Path and dominated by the Path, arises state conditioned by the Path by root condition.

Dependent on one aggregate conditioned by the Path and dominated by the Path, arise three aggregates conditioned by the Path . . . two aggregates . . . (1)

(xvi) Dependent on state conditioned by the Path and dominated by the Path, arises state dominated by the Path by root condition.

Dependent on one aggregate conditioned by the Path and dominated by the Path, arise three aggregates dominated by the Path . . . two aggregates . . . (2)

(xvii) Dependent on state conditioned by the Path and dominated by the Path, arise states conditioned by the Path and dominated by the Path by root condition.

Dependent on one aggregate conditioned by the Path and dominated by the Path, arise three aggregates conditioned by the Path and dominated by the Path . . . two aggregates . . . (3)

Object, etc.

6. Dependent on state with Path object, arises state with Path object by object condition . . . by predominance condition . . . by proximity condition . . . by contiguity condition . . . by conascence condition . . . by mutuality condition . . . by dependence condition . . . by strong-dependence condition . . . by prenascence condition . . . by repetition condition . . . by kamma condition . . . by nutriment condition . . . by faculty condition . . . by jhāna condition . . . by path condition . . . by

association condition . . . by dissociation condition . . . by presence condition . . . by absence condition . . . by disappearance condition . . . by non-disappearance condition . . .

1. CONDITIONS: POSITIVE (ii) ENUMERATION CHAPTER

(By Ones)

7. With root 17, object, predominance, proximity, contiguity, conascence, mutuality, dependence, strong-dependence, prenascence, repetition, kamma, nutriment, faculty, jhāna, path, association, dissociation, presence, absence, disappearance, non-disappearance 17. (Enumerate thus.)

End of Positive

2. CONDITIONS: NEGATIVE (i) CLASSIFICATION CHAPTER

Not-root 1

8. Dependent on state with Path object, arises state with Path object by not-root condition.

Dependent on one rootless aggregate with Path object, arise three aggregates . . . two aggregates . . . (1)

Not-predominance 17

9. (i) Dependent on state with Path object, arises state with Path object by not-predominance condition.

Dependent on one aggregate with Path object, arise three aggregates . . . two aggregates . . . (1)

(ii) Dependent on state with Path object, arises state dominated by the Path by not-predominance condition.

Dependent on one aggregate with Path object, arise three aggregates dominated by the Path . . . two aggregates . . . (2)

(iii) Dependent on state with Path object, arise states with Path object and dominated by the Path by not-predominance condition.

Dependent on one aggregate with Path object, arise three aggregates with Path object and dominated by the Path . . . two aggregates . . . (3)

10. (iv) Dependent on state condition by the Path, arises state conditioned by the Path by not-predominance condition.

Dependent on aggregates conditioned by the Path, arises predominance conditioned by the Path. (1)

(v) Dependent on state conditioned by the Path, arises state dominated by the Path by not-predominance condition.

Dependent on aggregates conditioned by the Path, arises predominance dominated by the Path. (2)

(vi) Dependent on state conditioned by the Path, arise states conditioned by the Path and dominated by the Path by not-predominance condition.

Dependent on aggregates conditioned by the Path, arises predominance conditioned by the Path and dominated by the Path. (3)

11. (vii) Dependent on state dominated by the Path, arises state dominated by the Path by not-predominance condition.

Dependent on aggregates dominated by the Path, arises predominance dominated by the Path; dependent on one aggregate dominated by the Path, arise three aggregates . . . two aggregates . . . (1)

(viii) Dependent on state dominated by the Path, arises state with Path object by not-predominance condition.

Dependent on one aggregate dominated by the Path, arise three aggregates with Path object . . . two aggregates . . . (2)

(ix) Dependent on state dominated by the Path, arises state conditioned by the Path by not-predominance condition.

Dependent on aggregates dominated by the Path, arises predominance conditioned by the Path. (3)

(x) Dependent on state dominated by the Path, arise states with Path object and dominated by the Path by not-predominance condition.

Dependent on one aggregate dominated by the Path, arise three aggregates with Path object and dominated by the Path . . . two aggregates . . . (4)

(xi) Dependent on state dominated by the Path, arise states conditioned by the Path and dominated by the Path by not-predominance condition.

Dependent on aggregates dominated by the Path, arises predominance conditioned by the Path and dominated by the Path. (5)

12. (xii) Dependent on state with Path object and dominated by the Path, arises state with Path object by not-predominance condition.

Dependent on one aggregate with Path object and dominated by the Path, arise three aggregates with Path object . . . two aggregates . . . (1)

(xiii) Dependent on state with Path object and dominated by the Path, arises state dominated by the Path by not-predominance condition.

Dependent on one aggregate with Path object and dominated by the Path, arise three aggregates dominated by the Path . . . two aggregates . . . (2)

(xiv) Dependent on state with Path object and dominated by the Path, arise states with Path object and dominated by the Path by not-predominance condition.

Dependent on one aggregate with Path object and dominated by the Path, arise three aggregates with Path Object and dominated by the Path . . . two aggregates . . . (3)

13. (xv) Dependent on state conditioned by the Path and dominated by the Path, arises state conditioned by the Path by not-predominance condition.

Dependent on aggregates conditioned by the Path and dominated by the Path, arises predominance conditioned by the Path. (1)

(xvi) Dependent on state conditioned by the Path and dominated by the Path, arises state dominated by the Path by not-predominance condition.

Dependent on aggregates conditioned by the Path and dominated by the Path, arises predominance dominated by the Path. (2)

(xvii) Dependent on state conditioned by the Path and dominated by the Path, arise states conditioned by the Path and dominated by the Path by not-predominance condition.

Dependent on aggregates conditioned by the Path and dominated by the Path, arises predominance conditioned by the Path and dominated by the Path. (3)

Not-prenascence, etc. 17

14. Dependent on state with Path object, arises state with Path object by not-prenascence condition . . . by not-postnascence condition . . . (Complete two also.)

Not-repetition 9

15. (i) Dependent on state with Path object, arises state with Path object by not-repetition condition.

Dependent on one aggregate with Path object, arise three aggregates . . . two aggregates . . . (1)

(ii) Dependent on state with Path object, arises state dominated by the Path by not-repetition condition.

Dependent on one aggregate with Path object, arise three aggregates dominated by the Path . . . two aggregates . . . (2)

(iii) Dependent on state with Path object, arise states with Path object and dominated by the Path by not-repetition condition.

Dependent on one aggregate with Path object, arise three aggregates with Path object and dominated by the Path . . . two aggregates . . . (3)

16. (iv) Dependent on state dominated by the Path, arises state dominated by the Path by not-repetition condition.

Dependent on one aggregate dominated by the Path, arise three aggregates . . . two aggregates . . . (1)

(v) Dependent on state dominated by the Path, arises state with Path object by not-repetition condition.

Dependent on one aggregate dominated by the Path, arise three aggregates with Path object . . . two aggregates . . . (2)

(vi) Dependent on state dominated by the Path, arise states with Path object and dominated by the Path by not-repetition condition.

Dependent on one aggregate dominated by the Path, arise three aggregates with Path object and dominated by the Path . . . two aggregates . . . (3)

17. (vii) Dependent on state with Path object and dominated by the Path, arises state with Path object by not-repetition condition.

Dependent on one aggregate with Path object and dominated by the Path, arise three aggregates with Path object . . . two aggregates . . . (1)

(viii) Dependent on state with Path object and dominated by the Path, arises state dominated by the Path by not-repetition condition.

Dependent on one aggregate with Path object and dominated by the Path, arise three aggregates dominated by the Path . . . two aggregates . . . (2)

(ix) Dependent on state with Path object and dominated by the Path, arise states with Path object and dominated by the Path by not-repetition condition.

Dependent on one aggregate with Path object and dominated by the Path, arise three aggregates with Path object and dominated by the Path . . . two aggregates . . . (3)

Not-kamma 17

18. (i) Dependent on state with Path object, arises state with Path object by not-kamma condition.

Dependent on aggregates with Path object, arises volition with Path object. (1)

(ii) Dependent on state with Path object, arises state dominated by the Path by not-kamma condition.

Dependent on aggregates with Path object, arises volition dominated by the Path. (2)

(iii) Dependent on state with Path object, arise states with Path object and dominated by the Path by not-kamma condition.

Dependent on aggregates with Path object, arises volition with Path object and dominated by the Path. (3)

19. (iv) Dependent on state conditioned by the Path, arises state conditioned by the Path by not-kamma condition.

Dependent on aggregates conditioned by the Path, arises volition conditioned by the Path. (1)

(v) Dependent on state conditioned by the Path, arises state dominated by the Path by not-kamma condition.

Dependent on aggregates conditioned by the Path, arises volition dominated by the Path. (2)

(vi) Dependent on state conditioned by the Path, arise states conditioned by the Path and dominated by the Path by not-kamma condition.

Dependent on aggregates conditioned by the Path, arises volition conditioned by the Path and dominated by the Path. (3)

20. (vii)-(xi) Dependent on state dominated by the Path, arises state dominated by the Path by not-kamma condition.

Dependent on aggregates dominated by the Path, arises volition dominated by the Path . . . (5 questions.)

(xii)-(xiv) Dependent on state with Path object and dominated by the Path, arises state with Path object by not-kamma condition . . . (Three in the first combination.)

(xv)-(xvii) Dependent on state conditioned by the Path and dominated by the Path, arises state conditioned by the Path by not-kamma condition . . . (Three questions in the second combination.)

Not-resultant 17

21. Dependent on state with Path object, arises state with Path object by not-resultant condition . . . (Complete.)

Not-path 1

22. Dependent on state with Path object, arises state with Path object by not-path condition.

Dependent on one rootless aggregate with Path object, arise three aggregates . . . two aggregates . . . (1)

Not-dissociation 17

23. Dependent on state with Path object, arises state with Path object by not-dissociation condition . . . [Complete. Remember (to take) immaterial.]

2. CONDITIONS: NEGATIVE (ii) ENUMERATION CHAPTER

(By Ones)

24. With not-root 1, not-predominance 17, not-prenascence 17, not-postnascence 17, not-repetition 9, not-kamma 17, not-resultant 17, not-path 1, not-dissociation 17. (Enumerate thus.)

End of Negative

3. CONDITIONS: POSITIVE-NEGATIVE

Root By Twos

25. With root condition, not-predominance 17, not-prenascence 17, not-postnascence 17, not-repetition 9, not-kamma 17, not-resultant, not-dissociation 17. (Enumerate thus.)

End of Positive-Negative

4. CONDITIONS: NEGATIVE-POSITIVE

Not-root By Twos

26. With not-root condition, object 1, proximity 1, contiguity 1, . . . jhāna, association, dissociation, presence, absence, disappearance, non-disappearance 1. (Enumerate thus.)

End of Negative-Positive

End of "DEPENDENT" CHAPTER

(The "Conascent", "Conditioned", "Supported", "Conjoined" and "Associated' Chapters are also the same as the "Dependent" Chapter.)

16. PATH OBJECT TRIPLET VII. "INVESTIGATION" CHAPTER

1. CONDITIONS: POSITIVE (i) CLASSIFICATION CHAPTER

Root 17

27. (i) State with Path object is related to state with Path object by root condition.

Roots with Path object are related to (their) associated aggregates by root condition. (1)

(ii) State with Path object is related to state dominated by the Path by root condition.

Roots with Path object are related to (their) associated aggregates dominated by the Path by root condition. (2)

(iii) State with Path object is related to state with Path object and dominated by the Path by root condition . . . (Do 17 questions in this way.)

Object 9

28. (i) State conditioned by the Path is related to state with Path object by object condition.

The Noble persons, having emerged from Path, review the Path. By the knowledge of penetration into others' minds, (they) know the other being's mind conditioned by the Path. Aggregates conditioned by the Path are related to knowledge of penetration into others' minds, knowledge of remembrance of past existences, knowledge of future existences, advertence by object condition. (1)

(ii) State conditioned by the Path is related to state dominated by the Path by object condition.

The Noble persons, having emerged from Path, esteem and review the Path. (2)

(iii) State conditioned by the Path is related to state with Path object and dominated by the Path by object condition.

The Noble persons, having emerged from Path, esteem and review the Path. (3)

29. (iv) State dominated by the Path is related to state dominated by the Path by object condition.

The Noble persons, having emerged from Path, esteem and review the Path. (1)

(v) State dominated by the Path is related to state with Path object by object condition.

The Noble persons, having emerged from Path, review the Path. By the knowledge of penetration into others' minds, (they) know the other being's mind dominated by the Path. The aggregates dominated by the Path are related to knowledge of penetration into others' minds, knowledge of remembrance of past existences, knowledge of future existences, advertence by object condition. (2)

(vi) State dominated by the Path is related to state with Path object and dominated by the Path by object condition.

The Noble persons, having emerged from Path, esteem and review the Path. (3)

30. (vii) States conditioned by the Path and dominated by the Path are related to state with Path object by object condition.

The Noble persons, having emerged from Path, review the Path. By the knowledge of penetration into others' minds, (they) know the other being's mind conditioned by the Path and dominated by the Path. Aggregates conditioned by the Path and dominated by the Path are related to knowledge of penetration into others' minds, knowledge of remembrance of past existences, knowledge of future existences, advertence by object condition. (1)

(viii) States conditioned by the Path and dominated by the Path are related to state dominated by the Path by object condition.

The Noble persons, having emerged from Path, esteem and review the Path. (2)

(ix) States conditioned by the Path and dominated by the Path are related to state with Path object and dominated by the Path by object condition.

The Noble persons, having emerged from Path, esteem and review the Path. (3)

Predominance 21

31. (i) State with Path object is related to state with Path object by predominance condition.

Conascence-predominance: Predominance with Path object is related to (its) associated aggregates by predominance condition. (1)

(ii) State with Path object is related to state dominated by the Path by predominance condition.

Conascence-predominance: Predominance with Path object is related to (its) associated aggregates dominated by the Path by predominance condition. (2)

(iii) State with Path object is related to state with Path object and dominated by the Path by predominance condition.

Conascence-predominance: Predominance with Path object is related to (its) associated aggregates with Path object and dominated by the Path by predominance condition. (3)

32. (iv) State conditioned by the Path is related to state conditioned

by the Path by predominance condition.

Conascence-predominance: Predominance conditioned by the Path is related to (its) associated aggregates by predominance condition. (1)

(v) State conditioned by the Path is related to state with Path object by predominance condition.

Object-predominance: The Noble persons, having emerged irom Path, esteem and review the Path. (2)

(vi) State conditioned by the Path is related to state dominated by the Path by predominance condition.

(It is of two kinds, namely:) (*a*) object-predominance, (*b*) conascence-predominance.

(*a*) *Object-predominance:* The Noble persons, having emerged from Path, esteem and review the Path.

(*b*) *Conascence-predominance:* Predominance conditioned by the Path is related to (its) associated aggregates dominated by the Path by predominance condition. (3)

(vii) State conditioned by the Path is related to state with Path object and dominated by the Path by predominance condition.

Object-predominance: The Noble persons, having emerged from Path, esteem and review the Path. (4)

(viii) State conditioned by the Path is related to state conditioned by the Path and dominated by the Path by predominance condition.

Conascence-predominance: Predominance conditioned by the Path is related to (its) associated aggregates conditioned by the Path and dominated by the Path by predominance condition. (5)

33. (ix) State dominated by the Path is related to state dominated by the Path by predominance condition.

(It is of two kinds, namely:) (*a*) object-predominance, (*b*) conascence-predominance.

(*a*) *Object-predominance:* The Noble persons, having emerged from Path, esteem and review the Path.

(*b*) *Conascence-predominance:* Predominance dominated by the Path is related to (its) associated aggregates by predominance condition. (1)

(x) State dominated by the Path is related to state with Path object by predominance condition.

(It is of two kinds, namely:) (*a*) object-predominance, (*b*) conascence-predominance.

(*a*) *Object-predominance:* The Noble persons, having emerged from Path, esteem and review the Path.

(*b*) *Conascence-predominance:* Predominance dominated by the Path is related to (its) associated aggregates with Path object by predominance condition. (2)

(xi) State dominated by the Path is related to state conditioned by the Path by predominance condition.

Conascence-predominance: Predominance dominated by the Path is related to (its) associated aggregates conditioned by the Path by predominance condition. (3)

(xii) State dominated by the Path is related to state with Path object and dominated by the Path by predominance condition.

(It is of two kinds, namely:) (*a*) object-predominance, (*b*) conascence-predominance.

(*a*) *Object-predominance:* The Noble persons, having emerged from Path, esteem and review the Path.

(*b*) *Conascence-predominance:* Predominance dominated by the Path is related to (its) associated aggregates with Path object and dominated by the Path by predominance condition. (4)

(xiii) State dominated by the Path is related to state conditioned by the Path and dominated by the Path by predominance condition.

Conascence-predominance: Predominance dominated by the Path is related to (its) associated aggregates conditioned by the Path and dominated by the Path by predominance condition. (5)

34. (xiv) States with Path object and dominated by the Path are related to state with Path object by predominance condition.

Conascence-predominance: Predominance with Path object and dominated by the Path is related to (its) associated aggregates with Path object by predominance condition. (1)

(xv) States with Path object and dominated by the Path are related to state dominated by the Path by predominance condition.

Conascence-predominance: Predominance with Path object and dominated by the Path is related to (its) associated aggregates dominated by the Path by predominance condition. (2)

(xvi) States with Path object and dominated by the Path are related to state with Path object and dominated by the Path by predominance condition.

Conascence-predominance: Predominance with Path object and dominated by the Path is related to (its) associated aggregates with Path object and dominated by the Path by predominance condition. (3)

35. (xvii) States conditioned by the Path and dominated by the Path

are related to state with Path object by predominance condition.

Object-predominance: The Noble persons, having emerged from Path, esteem and review the Path. (1)

(xviii) States conditioned by the Path and dominated by the Path are related to state conditioned by the Path by predominance condition.

Conascence-predominance: Predominance conditioned by the Path and dominated by the Path is related to (its) associated aggregates conditioned by the Path by predominance condition. (2)

(xix) States conditioned by the Path and dominated by the Path are related to state dominated by the Path by predominance condition.

(It is of two kinds, namely:) (*a*) object-predominance, (*b*) conascence-predominance.

(*a*) *Object-predominance:* The Noble persons, having emerged from Path, esteem and review the Path.

(*b*) *Conascence-predominance:* Predominance conditioned by the Path and dominated by the Path is related to (its) associated aggregates dominated by the Path by predominance condition. (3)

(xx) States conditioned by the Path and dominated by the Path are related to state with Path object and dominated by the Path by predominance condition.

Object-predominance: The Noble persons, having emerged from Path, esteem and review the Path. (4)

(xxi) States conditioned by the Path and dominated by the Path are related to state conditioned by the Path and dominated by the Path by predominance condition.

Conascence-predominance: Predominance conditioned by the Path and dominated by the Path is related to (its) associated aggregates conditioned by the Path and dominated by the Path by predominance condition. (5)

Proximity 9

36. (i) State with Path object is related to state with Path object by proximity condition.

Preceding aggregates with Path object are related to subsequent aggregates with Path object by proximity condition. Advertence is related to aggregates with Path object by proximity condition. (1)

(ii) State with Path object is related to state dominated by the Path by proximity condition.

Preceding aggregates with Path object are related to subsequent aggregates dominated by the Path by proximity condition. Advertence is related to aggregates dominated by the Path by proximity condition. (2)

(iii) State with Path object is related to state with Path object and dominated by the Path by proximity condition.

Preceding aggregates with Path object are related to subsequent aggregates with Path object and dominated by the Path by proximity condition. Advertence is related to aggregates with Path object and dominated by the Path by proximity condition. (3)

37. (iv) State dominated by the Path is related to state dominated by the Path by proximity condition.

Preceding aggregates dominated by the Path are related to subsequent aggregates dominated by the Path by proximity condition. (1)

(v) State dominated by the Path is related to state with Path object by proximity condition.

Preceding aggregates dominated by Path are related to subsequent aggregates with Path object by proximity condition. (2)

(vi) State dominated by the Path is related to state with Path object and dominated by the Path by proximity condition.

Preceding aggregates dominated by the Path are related to subsequent aggregates with Path object and dominated by the Path by proximity condition. (3)

38. (vii) States with Path object and dominated by the Path are related to state with Path object by proximity condition.

Preceding aggregates with Path object and dominated by the Path are related to subsequent aggregates with Path object by proximity condition. (1)

(viii) States with Path object and dominated by the Path are related to state dominated by the Path by proximity condition.

Preceding aggregates with Path object and dominated by the Path are related to subsequent aggregates dominated by the Path by proximity condition. (2)

(ix) States with Path object and dominated by the Path are related to state with Path object and dominated by the Path by proximity condition.

Preceding aggregates with Path object and dominated by the Path are related to subsequent aggregates with Path object and dominated by the Path by proximity condition. (3)

Contiguity, etc.

39. State with Path object is related to state with Path object by contiguity condition. (The same as proximity.) . . . by conascence condition . . . by mutuality condition . . . by dependence condition . . . (Do 17 questions for these three also.)

Strong-dependence 21

40. (i) State with Path object is related to state with Path object by strong-dependence condition.

(It is of two kinds, namely:) (*a*) proximity-strong-dependence, (*b*) natural strong-dependence . . .

(*b*) *Natural strong-dependence:* Reviewing is related to reviewing by strong-dependence condition. (1)

(ii) State with Path object is related to state dominated by the Path by strong-dependence condition.

(It is of two kinds, namely:) (*a*) proximity-strong-dependence, (*b*) natural strong-dependence . . .

(*b*) *Natural strong-dependence:* Reviewing is related to reviewing by strong-dependence condition. (2)

(iii) State with Path object is related to state with Path object and dominated by the Path by strong-dependence condition.

(It is of two kinds, namely:) (*a*) proximity-strong-dependence, (*b*) natural strong-dependence . . .

(*b*) *Natural strong-dependence:* Reviewing is related to reviewing by strong-dependence condition. (3)

41. (iv) State conditioned by the Path is related to state conditioned by the Path by strong-dependence condition.

Natural strong-dependence: First Path is related to second Path by strong-dependence condition . . . third Path is related to fourth Path by strong-dependence condition. (1)

(v) State conditioned by the Path is related to state with Path object by strong-dependence condition.

Object-strong-dependence: The Noble persons, having emerged from Path, esteem and review the Path. (2)

(vi) State conditioned by the Path is related to state dominated by the Path by strong-dependence condition.

(It is of two kinds, namely:) (*a*) object-strong-dependence, (*b*) natural strong-dependence . . .

(*b*) *Natural strong-dependence:* First Path to second Path . . . third Path is related to fourth Path by strong-dependence condition. (3)

(vii) State conditioned by the Path is related to state with Path object and dominated by the Path by strong-dependence condition.

Object-strong-dependence: The Noble persons, having emerged from Path, esteem and review the Path. (4)

(viii) State conditioned by the Path is related to state conditioned by the Path and dominated by the Path by strong-dependence condition.

Natural strong-dependence: First Path to second Path . . . third Path is related to fourth Path by strong-dependence condition. (5)

42. (ix) State dominated by the Path is related to state dominated by the Path by strong-dependence condition.

(It is of three kinds, namely:) (*a*) object-strong-dependence, (*b*) proximity-strong-dependence, (*c*) natural strong-dependence . . .

(*c*) *Natural strong-dependence:* First Path to second Path . . . third Path is related to fourth Path by strong-dependence condition. Reviewing is related to reviewing by strong-dependence condition. (1)

(x) State dominated by the Path is related to state with Path object by strong-dependence condition.

(It is of three kinds, namely:) (*a*) object-strong-dependence, (*b*) proximity-strong-dependence, (*c*) natural strong-dependence . . .

(*c*) *Natural strong-dependence:* Reviewing is related to reviewing by strong-dependence condition. (2)

(xi) State dominated by the Path is related to state conditioned by the Path by strong-dependence condition.

Natural strong-dependence: First Path to second Path . . . third Path is related to fourth Path by strong-dependence condition. (3)

(xii) State dominated by the Path is related to state with Path object and dominated by the Path by strong-dependence condition.

(It is of three kinds, namely:) (*a*) object-strong-dependence, (*b*) proximity-strong-dependence, (*c*) natural strong-dependence . . .

(*c*) *Natural strong-dependence:* Reviewing is related to reviewing by strong-dependence condition. (4)

(xiii) State dominated by the Path is related to state conditioned by the Path and dominated by the Path by strong-dependence condition.

Natural strong-dependence: First Path to second Path . . . third Path is related to fourth Path by strong-dependence condition. (5)

43. (xiv) States with Path object and dominated by the Path are related to state with Path object by strong-dependence condition.

(It is of two kinds, namely:) (*a*) proximity-strong-dependence, (*b*) natural strong-dependence . . .

(*b*) *Natural strong-dependence:* Reviewing is related to reviewing by strong-dependence condition. (1)

(xv) States with Path object and dominated by the Path are related to state dominated by the Path by strong-dependence condition.

(It is of two kinds, namely:) (*a*) proximity-strong-dependence, (*b*) natural strong-dependence . . .

(*b*) *Natural strong-dependence:* Reviewing is related to reviewing by strong-dependence condition. (2)

(xvi) States with Path object and dominated by the Path are related to state with Path object and dominated by the Path by strong-dependence condition.

(It is of two kinds, namely:) (*a*) proximity-strong-dependence, (*b*) natural strong-dependence . . .

(*b*) *Natural strong-dependence:* Reviewing is related to reviewing by strong-dependence condition. (3)

44. (xvii) States conditioned by the Path and dominated by the Path are related to state with Path object by strong-dependence condition.

Object-strong-dependence: The Noble persons, having emerged from Path, esteem and review the Path. (1)

(xviii) States conditioned by the Path and dominated by the Path are related to state conditioned by the Path by strong-dependence condition.

Natural strong-dependence: First Path to second Path . . . third Path is related to fourth Path by strong-dependence condition. (2)

(xix) States conditioned by the Path and dominated by the Path are related to state dominated by the Path by strong-dependence condition.

(It is of two kinds, namely:) (*a*) object-strong-dependence, (*b*) natural strong-dependence . . .

(*b*) *Natural strong-dependence:* First Path to second Path . . . third Path is related to fourth Path by strong-dependence condition. (3)

(xix) States conditioned by the Path and dominated by the Path are related to state with Path object and dominated by the Path by strong-dependence condition.

Object-strong-dependence: The Noble persons, having emerged from

Path, esteem and review the Path. (4)

(xxi) States conditioned by the Path and dominated by the Path are related to state conditioned by the Path and dominated by the Path by strong-dependence condition.

Natural strong-dependence: First Path to second Path . . . third Path is related to fourth Path by strong-dependence condition. (5)

Repetition 9

45. (i) State with Path object is related to state with Path object by repetition condition.

Preceding aggregates with Path object are related to subsequent aggregates with Path object by repetition condition. (1)

(ii) State with Path object is related to state dominated by the Path by repetition condition . . . (The same as proximity: do 9 questions: do not include advertence.)

Kamma 17

46. State with Path object is related to state with Path object by kamma condition.

Conascent . . . (No asynchronous: do 17 questions.)

Nutriment, etc.

47. State with Path object is related to state with Path object by nutriment condition . . . by faculty condition . . . by jhāna condition . . . by path condition . . . by association condition . . . by presence condition. (These 6[1] conditions have 17 questions as with root.) . . . by absence condition . . . by disappearance condition. (The same as proximity.) . . . by non-disappearance condition . . . (17 questions.)

1. CONDITIONS: POSITIVE (ii) ENUMERATION CHAPTER

(By Ones)

48. With root 17, object 9, predominance 21, proximity 9, contiguity 9, conascence 17, mutuality 17, dependence 17, strong-dependence 21, repetition 9, kamma 17, nutriment, faculty, jhāna, path, association 17,

[1] Not 7 as given in the Pali Text.

presence 17, absence 9, disappearance 9, non-disappearance 17. (Enumerate thus.)

End of Positive

2. SELECTION OF THE CONDITIONS FOR NEGATIVE 21

49. (i) State with Path object is related to state with Path object by conascence condition, strong-dependence condition. (1)

(ii) State with Path object is related to state dominated by the Path by conascence condition, strong-dependence condition. (2)

(iii) State with Path object is related to state with Path object and dominated by the Path by conascence condition, strong-dependence condition. (3)

50. (iv) State conditioned by the Path is related to state conditioned by the Path by conascence condition, strong-dependence condition. (1)

(v) State conditioned by the Path is related to state with Path object by object condition, strong-dependence condition. (2)

(vi) State conditioned by the Path is related to state dominated by the Path by object condition, conascence condition, strong-dependence condition. (3)

(vii) State conditioned by the Path is related to state with Path object and dominated by the Path by object condition, strong-dependence condition. (4)

(viii) State conditioned by the Path is related to state conditioned by the Path and dominated by the Path by conascence condition, strong-dependence condition. (5)

51. (ix) State dominated by the Path is related to state dominated by the Path by conascence condition, strong-dependence condition. (1)

(x) State dominated by the Path is related to state with Path object by object condition, conascence condition, strong-dependence condition. (2)

(xi) State dominated by the Path is related to state conditioned by the Path by conascence condition, strong-dependence condition. (3)

(xii) State dominated by the Path is related to state with Path object and dominated by the Path by conascence condition, strong-dependence condition. (4)

(xiii) State dominated by the Path is related to state conditioned by the Path and dominated by the Path by conascence condition, strong-dependence condition. (5)

52. (xiv) States with Path object and dominated by the Path are related to state with Path object by conascence condition, strong-dependence condition. (1)

(xv) States with Path object and dominated by the Path are related to state dominated by the Path by conascence condition, strong-dependence condition. (2)

(xvi) States with Path object and dominated by the Path are related to state with Path object and dominated by the Path by conascence condition, strong-dependence condition. (3)

53. (xvii) States conditioned by the Path and dominated by the Path are related to state with Path object by object condition, strong-dependence condition. (1)

(xviii) States conditioned by the Path and dominated by the Path are related to state conditioned by the Path by conascence condition, strong-dependence condition. (2)

(xix) States conditioned by the Path and dominated by the Path are related to state dominated by the Path by conascence condition, strong-dependence condition. (3)

(xx) States conditioned by the Path and dominated by the Path are related to state with Path object and dominated by the Path by strong-dependence condition. (4)

(xxi) States conditioned by the Path and dominated by the Path are related to state conditioned by the Path and dominated by the Path by conascence condition, strong-dependence condition. (5)

2. CONDITIONS: NEGATIVE (ii) ENUMERATION CHAPTER

By Ones

54. With not-root 21, not-object 17 (when not-object is taken, both natural object and strong-dependence object are excluded), not-predominance 21, not-proximity, not-contiguity, not-conascence, not-mutuality, not-dependence, not-strong-dependence, not-prenascence, not-postnascence, not-repetition, not-kamma, not-resultant, not-nutriment, not-faculty, not-jhāna, not-path, not-association, not-dissociation, not-presence, not-absence, not-disappearance, not-non-disappearance 21. (Enumerate thus.)

End of Negative

3. CONDITIONS: POSITIVE-NEGATIVE

Root By Twos

55. With root condition, not-object 17, not-predominance, not-proximity, not-contiguity, not-strong-dependence, not-prenascence, not-postnascence, not-repetition, not-kamma, not-resultant, not-nutriment, not-faculty, not-jhāna, not-path, not-dissociation, not-absence, not-disappearance 17. (Enumerate thus.)

End of Positive-Negative

4. CONDITIONS: NEGATIVE-POSITIVE

Not-root By Twos

56. With not-root condition, object 9, predominance 21, proximity 9, contiguity 9, conascence 17, mutuality 17, dependence 17, strong-dependence 21, repetition 9, kamma 17, nutriment 17, faculty, jhāna, path, association 17, presence 17, absence 9, disappearance 9, non-disappearance 17. (Enumerate thus.)

End of Negative-Positive

END OF PATH OBJECT TRIPLET

17. ARISEN TRIPLET[1] VII. "INVESTIGATION" CHAPTER

1. CONDITIONS: POSITIVE (i) CLASSIFICATION CHAPTER

Root 1

1. (i) Arisen (uppanna) state is related to arisen state by root condition.

(*a*) Arisen roots are related to (their) associated aggregates and mind-produced matter by root condition;

(*b*) At the moment of conception, arisen roots are related to (their) associated aggregates and kamma-produced matter by root condition. (1)

Object 3

2. (i) Arisen state is related to arisen state by object condition.

---

[1] This comprises (1) Arisen states, (2) States not arisen, (3) States bound to arise.

(One) practises insight into the impermanence, suffering and impersonality of the arisen eye; enjoys and delights in (the eye). Taking it as object, arises lust, arise wrong views . . . doubt . . . restlessness, arises grief . . . arisen ear . . . nose . . . tongue . . . body . . . visible object . . . sound . . . smell . . . taste . . . tangible object . . . (heart-)base . . . (One) practises insight into the impermanence, suffering and impersonality of arisen aggregates . . . arises grief.

By the power of divine-eye, (one) sees a visible object. By the power of divine-ear element, (one) hears a sound. Visible object-base to eye-consciousness . . . tangible object-base to body-consciousness . . . Arisen aggregates are related to knowledge of supernormal power, advertence by object condition. (1)

3. (ii) State not arisen (anuppanna) is related to arisen state by object condition.

Visible object not arisen . . . sound . . . smell . . . taste . . . tangible object . . . (One) practises insight into the impermanence, suffering and impersonality of aggregates not arisen . . . arises grief. Aggregates not arisen are related to knowledge of supernormal power, knowledge of penetration into others' minds, knowledge of future existences, advertence by object condition. (1)

4. (iii) State bound to arise (uppādin) is related to arisen state by object condition.

Eye bound to arise . . . body . . . visible object . . . smell . . . taste . . . tangible object . . . (heart-)base . . . into the impermanence, suffering and impersonality of aggregates bound to arise . . . arises grief. Aggregates bound to arise are related to knowledge of supernormal power, knowledge of penetration into others' minds, knowledge of future existences, advertence by object condition. (1)

Predominance 3

5. (i) Arisen state is related to arisen state by predominance condition. (It is of two kinds, namely:) (*a*) object-predominance, (*b*) conascence-predominance.

(*a*) *Object-predominance:* (One) esteems, enjoys and delights in the arisen eye. Taking it as estimable object, arises lust, arise wrong views . . . arisen ear . . . nose . . . tongue . . . body . . . visible object . . . sound . . . smell . . . taste . . . tangible object . . . (heart-)base . . . (One) esteems, enjoys and delights in arisen aggregates. Taking them as estimable object, arises lust . . .

(*b*) *Conascence-predominance:* Arisen predominance is related to (its) associated aggregates and mind-produced matter by predominance condition. (1)

(ii) State not arisen is related to arisen state by predominance condition.

Object-predominance: Visible object not arisen . . . sound . . . smell . . . taste . . . tangible object . . . (One) esteems, enjoys and delights in aggregates not arisen. Taking them as estimable object, arises lust, arise wrong views. (1)

(iii) State bound to arise is related to arisen state by predominance condition.

Object-predominance: Eye bound to arise . . . body . . . visible object . . . tangible object . . . (heart-)base . . . (One) esteems, enjoys and delights in aggregates bound to arise. Taking them as estimable object, arises lust, arise wrong views. (1)

Conascence 1

6. (i) Arisen state is related to arisen state by conascence condition.

(*a*) One arisen aggregate is related to three aggregates and mind-produced matter by conascence condition . . . two aggregates are related to two aggregates and mind-produced matter by conascence condition;

(*b*) At the moment of conception, one arisen aggregate is related to three aggregates and kamma-produced matter by conascence condition . . . two aggregates are related to two aggregates and kamma-produced matter by conascence condition; aggregates are related to (heart-)base by conascence condition; (heart-)base is related to aggregates by conascence condition;

(*c*) One great primary is related to three great primaries by conascence condition . . . two great primaries . . . great primaries are related to mind-produced and kamma-produced derived matter by conascence condition;

(*d*) External . . . nutriment-produced . . . temperature-produced . . . one great primary of non-percipient beings . . . two great primaries . . . great primaries are related to kamma-produced derived matter by conascence condition. (1)

Mutuality 1

7. (i) Arisen state is related to arisen state by mutuality condition.

(*a*) One arisen aggregate is related to three aggregates by mutuality condition . . . two aggregates . . .

(*b*) At the moment of conception, one arisen aggregate is related to three aggregates and (heart-)base by mutuality condition . . . two aggregates . . . aggregates are related to (heart-)base by mutuality condition; (heart-)base is related to aggregates by mutuality condition;

(*c*) One great primary . . . External . . . nutriment-produced . . . temperature-produced . . . one great primary of non-percipient beings is related to three great primaries by mutuality condition . . . two great primaries . . . (1)

Dependence 1

8. (i) Arisen state is related to arisen state by dependence condition.

(*a*) One arisen aggregate is related to three aggregates and mind-produced matter by dependence condition . . . two aggregates . . .

(*b*) At the moment of conception . . . aggregates to (heart-)base . . . (heart-)base to aggregates . . .

(*c*) One great primary . . . External . . . nutriment-produced . . . temperature-produced . . . one great primary of non-percipient beings . . . great primaries to kamma-produced[1] derived matter . . .

(*d*) Eye-base to eye-consciousness . . . body-base to body-consciousness . . . (heart-)base is related to arisen aggregates by dependence condition. (1)

Strong-dependence 3

9. (i) Arisen state is related to arisen state by strong-dependence condition.

(It is of two kinds, namely:) (*a*) object-strong-dependence, (*b*) natural strong-dependence . . .

(*b*) *Natural strong-dependence:* By the strong-dependence of arisen temperature (uppannaṁ utuṁ upanissāya), (one) develops jhāna . . . insight . . . Path . . . superknowledge, develops attainment; arouses conceit, adopts wrong views . . . arisen food . . . By the strong-dependence of lodging-place, (one) develops jhāna . . . insight . . . Path . . . superknowledge, develops attainment; arouses conceit, adopts wrong views. Arisen temperature, food, lodging-place is related to arisen confidence

---

[1] "Mind-produced", given in the Pali Text, is left out because it is not concerned with non-percipient beings.

. . . wisdom, bodily happiness, bodily pain, Path, the attainment of Fruition by strong-dependence condition. (1)

(ii) State not arisen is related to arisen state by strong-dependence condition.

(It is of two kinds, namely:) (*a*) object-strong-dependence, (*b*) natural strong-dependence . . .

(*b*) *Natural strong-dependence:* Wishing for the fullness of colour not arisen (anuppannaṁ vaṇṇasampadaṁ patthayamāno), (one) offers an offering, undertakes precepts, fulfils the duty of observance. Wishing for the fullness of sound not arisen . . . fullness of smell . . . fullness of taste . . . fullness of tangible object . . . Wishing for aggregates not arisen, (one) offers an offering, undertakes precepts, fulfils the duty of observance. Fullness of colour not arisen . . . aggregates not arisen is related to arisen confidence . . . wisdom, bodily happiness, bodily pain, Path, the attainment of Fruition by strong-dependence condition. (1)

(iii) State bound to arise is related to arisen state by strong-dependence condition.

(It is of two kinds, namely:) (*a*) object-strong-dependence, (*b*) natural strong-dependence . . .

(*b*) *Natural strong-dependence:* Wishing for the fullness of eye bound to arise (uppādiṁ cakkhusampadaṁ patthayamāno), (one) offers an offering, undertakes precepts, fulfils the duty of observance . . . fullness of ear bound to arise . . . fullness of body . . . fullness of colour . . . fullness of smell . . . fullness of taste . . . fullness of tangible object . . . Wishing for aggregates bound to arise, (one) offers an offering, undertakes precepts, fulfils the duty of observance. Fullness of eye bound to arise . . . fullness of body, fullness of colour . . . fullness of tangible object, aggregates bound to arise is related to arisen confidence . . . wisdom, bodily happiness, bodily pain, Path, the attainment of Fruition by strong-dependence condition. (1)

Prenascence 1

10. (i) Arisen state is related to arisen state by prenascence condition.

(It is of two kinds, namely:) (*a*) object-prenascence, (*b*) base-prenascence.

(*a*) *Object-prenascence:* Eye . . . (One) practises insight into the impermanence, suffering and impersonality of the (heart-)base; enjoys and delights in [the (heart-)base]. Taking it as object, arises lust . . . arises grief. By the power of divine-eye, (one) sees a visible object. By the power of divine-eye, (one) sees a visible object. By the power of divine-ear element, (one) hears a sound. Visible object-base to eye-consciousness . . . tangible object-base is related to body-consciousness by prenascence condition.

(*b*) *Base-prenascence:* Eye-base to eye-consciousness . . . (heart-)base is related to arisen aggregates by prenascence condition. (1)

Postnascence 1

11. (i) Arisen state is related to arisen state by postnascence condition.

Postnascent arisen aggregates are related to this prenascent body by postnascence condition. (1)

Kamma 1

12. (i) Arisen state is related to arisen state by kamma condition.

(*a*) Arisen volition is related to (its) associated aggregates and mind-produced matter by kamma condition;

(*b*) At the moment of conception, arisen volition is related to (its) associated aggregates and kamma-produced matter by kamma condition. (1)

Resultant 1

13. (i) Arisen state is related to arisen state by resultant condition.

(*a*) One resultant arisen aggregate is related to three aggregates and mind-produced matter by resultant condition . . . two aggregates . . .

(*b*) At the moment of conception, one arisen aggregate to three aggregates and kamma-produced matter . . . two aggregates . . . aggregates are related to (heart-)base by resultant condition. (1)

Nutriment 1

14. (i) Arisen state is related to arisen state by nutriment condition.

(*a*) Arisen nutriments are related to (their) associated aggregates and mind-produced matter by nutriment condition;

(*b*) At the moment of conception . . .

(*c*) Edible food is related to this body by nutriment condition. (1)

Faculty 1

15. (i) Arisen state is related to arisen state by faculty condition.

(*a*) Arisen faculties are related to (their) associated aggregates and mind-produced matter by faculty condition;

(*b*) At the moment of conception . . .

(*c*) Eye-faculty to eye-consciousness . . . body-faculty to body-consciousness . . .

(*d*) Physical life-faculty is related to kamma-produced matter by faculty condition. (1)

Jhāna, etc. 1

16. Arisen state is related to arisen state by jhāna condition . . . by path condition . . . by association condition . . . by dissociation condition.

(It is of three kinds, namely:) (*a*) conascence, (*b*) prenascence, (*c*) postnascence.

(*a*) (1) Conascent arisen aggregates are related to mind-produced matter by dissociation condition;

(2) At the moment of conception, arisen aggregates are related to kamma-produced matter by dissociation condition; aggregates to (heart-)base; (heart-)base is related to aggregates by dissociation condition;

(*b*) Prenascent eye-base to eye-consciousness . . . body-base to body-consciousness . . . (heart-)base is related to arisen aggregates by dissociation condition;

(*c*) Postnascent arisen aggregates are related to this prenascent body by dissociation condition. (1)

Presence 1

17. (i) Arisen state is related to arisen state by presence condition.

(It is of five kinds, namely:) (*a*) conascence, (*b*) prenascence, (*c*) postnascence, (*d*) nutriment, (*e*) faculty.

(*a*) (1) One conascent arisen aggregate is related to three aggregates and mind-produced matter by presence condition . . . two aggregates . . .

(2) At the moment of conception . . .

(3) One great primary . . . External . . . nutriment-produced . . . temperature-produced . . . non-percipient beings . . .

(*b*) *(Object-)prenascence:* Impermanence . . . of eye(-base) . . . impermanence . . . of (heart-)base . . . arises grief. By the power of divine-eye, (one) sees a visible object. By the power of divine-ear element, (one) hears a sound. Visible object-base to eye-consciousness . . . tangible object-base is related to body-consciousness by presence condition.

(Base-)prenascence: Eye-base to eye-consciousness . . . body-base to body-consciousness . . . (heart-)base is related to arisen aggregates by presence condition.

(*c*) Postnascent arisen aggregates are related to this prenascent body by presence condition.

(*d*) Edible food is related to this body by presence condition.

(*e*) Physical life-faculty is related to kamma-produced matter by presence condition. (1)

Non-disappearance 1

18. Arisen state is related to arisen state by non-disappearance condition . . .

1. CONDITIONS: POSITIVE (ii) ENUMERATION CHAPTER

(By Ones)

19. With root 1, object 3, predominance 3, conascence 1, mutuality 1, dependence 1, strong-dependence 3, prenascence 1, postnascence, kamma, resultant, nutriment, faculty, jhāna, path, association, dissociation, presence, non-disappearance 1. (Enumerate thus.)

End of Positive

2. SELECTION OF THE CONDITIONS FOR NEGATIVE 3

20. (i) Arisen state is related to arisen state by object condition, conascence condition, strong-dependence condition, prenascence condition, postnascence condition, nutriment condition, faculty condition. (1)

(ii) State not arisen is related to arisen state by object condition, strong-dependence condition. (1)

(iii) State bound to arise is related to arisen state by object condition, strong-dependence condition. (1)

2. CONDITIONS: NEGATIVE (ii) ENUMERATION CHAPTER

(By Ones)

21. With not-root 3, not-object 3, not-predominance 3 . . . not-dissociation 3, not-presence 2, not-absence 3, not-disappearance 3, not-non-disappearance 2. (Enumerate thus.)

End of Negative

3. CONDITIONS: POSITIVE-NEGATIVE

(Root By Twos)

22. With root condition, not-object 1 . . . not-absence, not-disappearance 1. (Enumerate thus.)

End of Positive-Negative

4. CONDITIONS: NEGATIVE-POSITIVE

(Not-root By Twos)

23. With not-root condition, object 3, predominance 3, conascence 1, mutuality 1, dependence 1, strong-dependence 3, prenascence 1, postnascence 1, kamma, resultant, nutriment, faculty, jhāna, path, association, dissociation, presence, non-disappearance 1. (Enumerate thus.)

End of Negative-Positive

END OF ARISEN TRIPLET

18. PAST TRIPLET[1] VII. "INVESTIGATION" CHAPTER

1. CONDITIONS: POSITIVE (i) CLASSIFICATION CHAPTER

Root 1

1. (i) Present state is related to present state by root condition.

(*a*) Present roots are related to (their) associated aggregates and mind-produced matter by root condition;

(*b*) At the moment of conception . . . (1)

Object 3

2. (i) Past state is related to present state by object condition.

After having offered an offering, having undertaken precepts . . . the duty of observance, (one) reviews it. (One) reviews (such acts) formerly well done. Having emerged from jhāna, (one) reviews the jhāna. The Noble persons, having emerged from Path, review the Path, review the Fruition, review the eradicated defilements, review the uneradicated defilements, know the defilements addicted to before.

(One) practises insight into the impermanence, suffering and impersonality of the past eye . . . arises grief . . . past ear . . . nose . . . tongue

---

[1] This comprises (1) Past states, (2) Future states, (3) Present states.

. . . body . . . visible object . . . sound . . . smell . . . taste . . . tangible object . . . (heart-)base . . . (One) practises insight into the impermanence, suffering and impersonality of past aggregates; enjoys and delights in (those aggregates). Taking them as object, arises lust, arise wrong views . . . doubt . . . restlessness, arises grief.

Infinity of space is related to infinity of consciousness by object condition. Nothingness is related to neither-perception-nor-non-perception by object condition. Past aggregates are related to knowledge of supernormal power, knowledge of penetration into others' minds, knowledge of remembrance of past existences, knowledge of rebirths according to one's kamma, advertence by object condition. (1)

3. (ii) Future state is related to present state by object condition.

Future eye . . . (heart-)base . . . into the impermanence . . . of future aggregates . . . arises grief. Future aggregates are related to knowledge of supernormal power, knowledge of penetration into others' minds, knowledge of future existences, advertence by object condition. (1)

(iii) Present state is related to present state by object condition.

Present eye . . . body . . . visible object . . . sound . . . smell . . . taste . . . tangible object . . . (heart-)base . . . into the impermanence . . . of present aggregates . . . arises grief. By the power of divine-eye, (one) sees a visible object. By the power of divine-ear element, (one) hears a sound. Visible object-base to eye-consciousness . . . tangible object-base to body-consciousness . . . Present aggregates are related to knowledge of supernormal power, advertence by object condition. (1)

Predominance 3

4. (i) Past state is related to present state by predominance condition.

Object-predominance: After having offered an offering, having undertaken precepts . . . (One) esteems and reviews (such acts) formerly well done. Having emerged from jhāna, (one) esteems and reviews the jhāna. The Noble persons, having emerged from Path, esteem and review the Path, esteem and review the Fruition. Past eye . . . body . . . visible object . . . sound . . . smell . . . taste . . . tangible object . . . (heart-)base . . . (One) esteems, enjoys and delights in past aggregates. Taking them as estimable object, arises lust, arise wrong views. (1)

(ii) Future state is related to present state by predominance condition.

Object-predominance: Future eye . . . (heart-)base . . . (One) esteems, enjoys and delights in future aggregates. Taking them as estimable object, arises lust, arise wrong views. (1)

(iii) Present state is related to present state by predominance condition.

(It is of two kinds, namely:) (*a*) object-predominance, (*b*) conascence-predominance.

(*a*) *Object-predominance:* Present eye . . . (heart-)base . . . (One) esteems, enjoys and delights in present aggregates. Taking them as estimable object, arises lust, arise wrong views.

(*b*) *Conascence-predominance:* Present predominance is related to (its) associated aggregates and mind-produced matter by predominance condition. (1)

Proximity 1

5. (i) Past state is related to present state by proximity condition.

Preceding past aggregates are related to subsequent present aggregates by proximity condition. Adaptation to change-of-lineage; adaptation to purification; change-of-lineage to Path; purification to Path; Path to Fruition; Fruition to Fruition; adaptation to the attainment of Fruition; for one emerging from the attainment of Extinction, neither-perception-nor-non-perception is related to the attainment of Fruition by proximity condition. (1)

Contiguity 1

6. (i) Past state is related to present state by contiguity condition. (The same as proximity.) (1)

Conascence, etc. 1

7. (i) Present state is related to present state by conascence condition . . . by mutuality condition . . . by dependence condition . . . (Abbreviated.) (1)

Strong-dependence 3

8. (i) Past state is related to present state by strong-dependence condition.

(It is of three kinds, namely:) (*a*) object-strong-dependence, (*b*) proximity-strong-dependence, (*c*) natural strong-dependence . . .

(*c*) *Natural strong-dependence:* By the strong-dependence of past confidence, (one) offers an offering, undertakes precepts, fulfils the duty of observance, develops jhāna . . . insight . . . Path . . . super-knowledge, develops attainment; arouses conceit, adopts wrong views . . . past precept . . . wisdom . . . lust . . . wish . . . bodily happiness . . . By the strong-dependence of bodily pain, (one) offers an offering, undertakes precepts . . . the duty of observance . . . develops attainment, kills a living being . . . causes schism in the Saṅgha. Past confidence . . . wisdom, lust . . . wish, bodily happiness, bodily pain is related to present confidence . . . wisdom, lust . . . wish . . . the attainment of Fruition by strong-dependence condition. (1)

(ii) Future state is related to present state by strong-dependence condition.

(It is of two kinds, namely:) (*a*) object-strong-dependence, (*b*) natural strong-dependence . . .

(*b*) *Natural strong-dependence:* Wishing for fullness of future eye . . . fullness of ear . . . fullness of nose . . . fullness of tongue . . . fullness of body . . . fullness of colour . . . fullness of sound . . . fullness of smell . . . fullness of taste . . . Wishing for the fullness of tangible object . . . Wishing for future aggregates, (one) offers an offering, undertakes precepts . . . the duty of observance. Fullness of future eye . . . fullness of colour . . . fullness of tangible object, future aggregates is related to present confidence . . . wisdom, bodily happiness, bodily pain, Path, the attainment of Fruition by strong-dependence condition. (1)

(iii) Present state is related to present state by strong-dependence condition.

(It is of two kinds, namely:) (*a*) object-strong-dependence, (*b*) natural strong-dependence . . .

(*b*) *Natural strong-dependence:* By the strong-dependence of present temperature, (one) develops jhāna . . . insight . . . present food . . . By the strong-dependence of lodging-place, (one) develops jhāna . . . develops attainment. Present temperature, food, lodging-place is related to present confidence . . . wisdom, bodily . . . the attainment of Fruition by strong-dependence condition. (1)

Prenascence 1

9. (i) Present state is related to present state by prenascence condition.

(It is of two kinds, namely:) (*a*) object-prenascence, (*b*) base-prenascence.

(*a*) *Object-prenascence:* Eye . . . into the impermanence . . . of the (heart-)base . . . arises grief. By the power of divine-eye, (one) sees a visible object. By the power of divine-ear element, (one) hears a sound. Visible object-base to eye-consciousness . . . tangible object-base is related to body-consciousness by prenascence condition.

(*b*) *Base-prenascence:* Eye-base to eye-consciousness . . . body-base to body-consciousness . . . (heart-)base is related to present aggregates by prenascence condition. (1)

Postnascence 1

10. (i) Present state is related to present state by postnascence condition.

Postnascent present aggregates are related to this prenascent body by postnascence condition. (1)

Repetition 1

11. (i) Past state is related to present state by repetition condition.

Preceding past aggregates are related to subsequent present aggregates by repetition condition. Adaptation to change-of-lineage; adaptation to purification; change-of-lineage to Path; purification is related to Path by repetition condition. (1)

Kamma 2

12. (i) Past state is related to present state by kamma condition.

Asynchronous past volition is related to present resultant aggregates and kamma-produced matter by kamma condition. (1)

(ii) Present state is related to present state by kamma condition.

(*a*) Present volition is related to (its) associated aggregates and mind-produced matter by kamma condition;

(*b*) At the moment of conception, present volition is related to (its) associated aggregates and kamma-produced matter by kamma condition. (1)

Resultant 1

13. (i) Present state is related to present state by resultant condition.

(*a*) One present resultant aggregate is related to three aggregates and mind-produced matter by resultant condition . . . two aggregates . . .

(*b*) At the moment of conception . . . aggregates are related to (heart-)base by resultant condition. (1)

Nutriment, etc. 1

14. (i) Present state is related to present state by nutriment condition . . . by faculty condition . . . by jhāna condition . . . by path condition . . . by association condition . . . by dissociation condition.

(It is of three kinds, namely:) (*a*) conascence, (*b*) prenascence, (*c*) postnascence.

(*a*) (1) Conascent present aggregates are related to mind-produced matter by dissociation condition;

(2) At the moment of conception, present aggregates are related to kamma-produced matter by dissociation condition; aggregates are related to (heart-)base by dissociation condition; (heart-)base is related to aggregates by dissociation condition.

(*b*) Prenascent eye-base to eye-consciousness . . . body-base to body-consciousness . . . (heart-)base is related to present aggregates by dissociation condition.

(*c*) Postnascent present aggregates are related to this prenascent body by dissociation condition. (1)

Presence 1

15. (i) Present state is related to present state by presence condition. [The same as presence (condition) in the Arisen Triplet.] (1)

Absence, Disappearance, Non-disappearance 1

16. Past state is related to present state by absence condition . . . by disappearance condition . . .

Present state is related to present state by non-disappearance condition . . .

1. CONDITIONS: POSITIVE (ii) ENUMERATION CHAPTER

(By Ones)

17. With root 1, object 3, predominance 3, proximity 1, contiguity 1, conascence, mutuality, dependence 1, strong-dependence 3, prenascence, postnascence, repetition 1, kamma 2, resultant, nutriment 1 . . . non-disappearance 1. (Enumerate thus.)

End of Positive

2. SELECTION OF THE CONDITIONS FOR NEGATIVE 3

18. (i) Past state is related to present state by object condition, strong-dependence condition, kamma condition. (1)

(ii) Future state is related to present state by object condition, strong-dependence condition. (1)

(iii) Present state is related to present state by object condition, conascence condition, strong-dependence condition, prenascence condition, postnascence condition, nutriment condition, faculty condition. (1)

2. CONDITIONS: NEGATIVE (ii) ENUMERATION CHAPTER

(By Ones)

19. With not-root 3, not-object 3, not-predominance 3, not-proximity 3 . . . not-association 3, not-dissociation 3, not-presence 2, not-absence 3, not-disappearance 3, not-non-disappearance 2. (Enumerate thus.)

End of Negative

3. CONDITIONS: POSITIVE-NEGATIVE

(Root By Twos)

20. With root condition, not-object 1, not-predominance, not-proximity, not-contiguity, not-mutuality, not-strong-dependence . . . not-association, not-dissociation, not-absence, not-disappearance 1. (Enumerate thus.)

End of Positive-Negative

4. CONDITIONS: NEGATIVE-POSITIVE

(Not-root By Twos)

21. With not-root condition, object 3, predominance 3, proximity, contiguity, conascence, mutuality, dependence 1, strong-dependence 3, prenascence 1, postnascence, repetition 1, kamma 2, resultant 1. (For these sections it is only 1.) . . . non-disappearance 1. (Enumerate thus.)

End of Negative-Positive

End of "INVESTIGATION" CHAPTER

END OF PAST TRIPLET

19. Past Object Triplet[1] I. "Dependent" Chapter

1. CONDITIONS: POSITIVE (i) CLASSIFICATION CHAPTER

Root 3

1. (i) Dependent on state with past object (atītārammana), arises state with past object by root condition.

(*a*) Dependent on one aggregate with past object, arise three aggregates . . . dependent on two aggregates, arise two aggregates;

(*b*) At the moment of conception, dependent on one aggregate with past object, arise three aggregates . . . dependent on two aggregates, arise two aggregates. (1)

2. (ii) Dependent on state with future object (anāgatārammaṇa), arises state with future object by root condition.

Dependent on one aggregate with future object, arise three aggregates . . . two aggregates. (1)

3. (iii) Dependent on state with present object (paccuppannārammaṇa), arises state with present object by root condition.

(*a*) Dependent on one aggregate with present object, arise three aggregates . . . two aggregates;

(*b*) At the moment of conception, dependent on one aggregate with present object, arise three aggregates . . . two aggregates. (1)

Object, etc. 3

4. Dependent on state with past object, arises state with past object by object condition . . . by predominance condition. (No conception in predominance.) . . . by proximity condition . . . by contiguity condition . . . by conascence condition . . . by mutuality condition . . . by dependence condition . . . by strong-dependence condition . . . by prenascence condition . . . by repetition condition. (No conception in prenascence and repetition.) . . . by kamma condition . . . by resultant condition. (One resultant aggregate with past object; complete three questions also. Include both "during life" and "conception".) . . . by nutriment condition . . . by faculty condition . . . by jhāna condition . . . by path condition . . . by association condition . . . by dissociation condition . . . by presence condition . . . by absence condition . . . by disappearance condition . . . by non-disappearance condition . . .

---

[1] This comprises (1) States with past object, (2) States with future object, (3) States with present object.

1. CONDITIONS: POSITIVE (ii) ENUMERATION CHAPTER

(By Ones)

5. With root 3, object 3, predominance 3 . . . (all three) . . . disappearance 3, non-disappearance 3. (Enumerate thus.)

End of Positive

2. CONDITIONS: NEGATIVE (i) CLASSIFICATION CHAPTER

Not-root 3

6. (i) Dependent on state with past object, arises state with past object by not-root condition.

(*a*) Dependent on one rootless aggregate with past object, arise three aggregates . . . two aggregates . . .

(*b*) At the moment of rootless conception . . .

(*c*) Dependent on doubt-accompanied or restlessness-accompanied aggregates, arises doubt-accompanied or restlessness-accompanied delusion. (1)

7. (ii) Dependent on state with future object, arises state with future object by not-root condition.

Dependent on one rootless aggregate with future object, arise three aggregates . . . two aggregates . . . Dependent on doubt-accompanied or restlessness-accompanied aggregates, arises doubt-accompanied or restlessness-accompanied delusion. (1)

8. (iii) Dependent on state with present object, arises state with present object by not-root condition.

(*a*) Dependent on one rootless aggregate with present object, arise three aggregates . . . two aggregates . . .

(*b*) At the moment of rootless conception . . .

(*c*) Dependent on doubt-accompanied or restlessness-accompanied aggregates, arises doubt-accompanied or restlessness-accompanied delusion. (1)

Not-predominance 3

9. (i) Dependent on state with past object, arises state with past object by not-predominance condition. (The same as conascence in Positive.)

Not-prenascence 3

10. (i) Dependent on state with past object, arises state with past object by not-prenascence condition.

(*a*) In the immaterial plane, dependent on one aggregate with past object . . . two aggregates . . .

(*b*) At the moment of conception . . . (1)

(ii) Dependent on state with future object, arises state with future object by not-prenascence condition.

In the immaterial plane, dependent on one aggregate with future object, arise three aggregates . . . two aggregates . . . (1)

(iii) Dependent on state with present object, arises state with present object by not-prenascence condition.

At the moment of conception, dependent on one aggregate with present object . . . two aggregates . . . (1)

Not-postnascence, etc. 3

11. (i) Dependent on state with past object, arises state with past object by not-postnascence condition . . . by not-repetition condition. (The same as not-predominance.) . . . by not-kamma condition.

Dependent on aggregates with past object, arises volition with past object. (1)

(ii) Dependent on state with future object, arises state with future object by not-kamma condition.

Dependent on aggregates with future object, arises volition with future object. (1)

(iii) Dependent on state with present object, arises state with present object by not-kamma condition.

Dependent on aggregates with present object, arises volition with present object. (1)

Not-resultant 3

12. Dependent on state with past object, arises state with past object by not-resultant condition . . . (No conception in not-resultant.)

Not-jhāna 1

13. Dependent on state with present object, arises state with present object by not-jhāna condition.

Dependent on one five-fold consciousness-accompanied aggregate, arise three aggregates . . . two aggregates . . . (1)

Not-path 3

14. Dependent on state with past object, arises state with past object by not-path condition.

Dependent on one rootless aggregate with past object, arise three aggregates . . . (The same as not-root. Three questions. No delusion.)

Not-dissociation 2

15. (i) Dependent on state with past object, arises state with past object by not-dissociation condition.

In the immaterial plane, dependent on one aggregate with past object, arise three aggregates . . . two aggregates . . . (1)

(ii) Dependent on state with future object, arises state with future object by not-dissociation condition.

In the immaterial plane, dependent on one aggregate with future object, arise three aggregates . . . two aggregates . . . (1)

2. CONDITIONS: NEGATIVE (ii) ENUMERATION CHAPTER

(By Ones)

16. With not-root 3, not-predominance, not-prenascence, not-postnascence, not-repetition, not-kamma, not-resultant 3, not-jhāna 1, not-path 3, not-dissociation 2. (Enumerate thus.)

End of Negative

3. CONDITIONS: POSITIVE–NEGATIVE

Root By Twos

17. With root condition, not-predominance 3, not-prenascence, not-postnascence, not-repetition, not-kamma, not-resultant 3, not-dissociation 2. (Enumerate thus.)

End of Positive–Negative

4. CONDITIONS: NEGATIVE-POSITIVE

(Not-root By Twos)

18. With not-root condition, object 3 . . . (All three.) . . . non-disappearance 3. (Enumerate thus.)

End of Negative-Positive

End of "DEPENDENT" CHAPTER

(The "Conascent", "Conditioned", "Supported", "Conjoined" and "Associated" Chapters are also the same as the "Dependent" Chapter.)

19. PAST OBJECT TRIPLET VII. "INVESTIGATION" CHAPTER

1. CONDITIONS: POSITIVE (i) CLASSIFICATION CHAPTER

Root 3

19. (i) State with past object (atītārammana) is related to state with past object by root condition.

(*a*) Roots with past object are related to (their) associated aggregates by root condition;

(*b*) At the moment of conception, roots with past object are related to (their) associated aggregates by root condition. (1)

(ii) State with future object is related to state with future object by root condition.

Roots with future object are related to (their) associated aggregates by root condition. (1)

(iii) State with present object is related to state with present object by root condition.

(*a*) Roots with present object are related to (their) associated aggregates by root condition;

(*b*) At the moment of conception, roots with present object are related to (their) associated aggregates by root condition. (1)

Object 9

20. (i) State with past object is related to state with past object by object condition.

(One) reviews past infinity of consciousness, reviews neither-perception-nor-non-perception. (One) reviews past knowledge of supernormal power with past object . . . knowledge of penetration into others' minds . . . knowledge of remembrance of past existences, reviews knowledge of rebirths according to one's kamma. The Noble persons review the eradicated defilements with past object, review the uneradicated defilements, know the defilements addicted to before.

(One) practises insight into the impermanence, suffering and impersonality of past aggregates with past object; enjoys and delights in (those aggregates). Taking them as object, arises lust with past object . . . wrong views . . . doubt . . . restlessness, arises grief. Past aggregates with past object are related to knowledge of penetration into others' minds, knowledge of remembrance of past existences, knowledge of rebirths according to one's kamma, advertence by object condition. (1)

(ii) State with past object is related to state with future object by object condition.

(One) reviews future infinity of consciousness, reviews neither-perception-nor-non-perception. (One) reviews future knowledge of supernormal power with past object . . . knowledge of penetration into others' minds . . . knowledge of remembrance of past existences, reviews knowledge of rebirths according to one's kamma.

(One) practises insight into the impermanence . . . of future aggregates with past object; enjoys and delights in (those aggregates). Taking them as object, arises lust with future object . . . arises grief. Future aggregates with past object are related to knowledge of penetration into others' minds, knowledge of future existences, advertence by object condition. (2)

(iii) State with past object is related to state with present object by object condition.

By the knowledge of penetration into others' minds, (one) knows the other being's present mind with past object. Present aggregates with past object are related to knowledge of penetration into others' minds, advertence by object condition. (3)

21. (iv) State with future object is related to state with future object by object condition.

(One) reviews future knowledge of supernormal power with future object . . . knowledge of penetration into others' minds . . . knowledge of future existences. (One) practises insight into the impermanence . . . of future aggregates with future object; enjoys and delights in (those aggregates). Taking them as object, arises lust with future object . . . arises grief. Future aggregates with future object are related to knowledge of penetration into others' minds, knowledge of future existences, advertence by object condition. (1)

(v) State with future object is related to state with past object by object condition.

(One) reviews past knowledge of supernormal power with future object . . . knowledge of penetration into others' minds . . . knowledge of future existences. The Noble persons review the eradicated defilements with future object, review the uneradicated defilements, know the defilements addicted to before.

(One) practises insight into the impermanence . . . of past aggregates with future object; enjoys and delights in (those aggregates). Taking them as object, arises lust with past object . . . arises grief. Past aggregates with future object are related to knowledge of penetration into others' minds, knowledge of remembrance of past existences, knowledge of rebirths according to one's kamma, advertence by object condition. (2)

(vi) State with future object is related to state with present object by object condition.

By the knowledge of penetration into others' minds, (one) knows the other being's present mind with future object. Present aggregates with future object are related to knowledge of penetration into others' minds, advertence by object condition. (3)

22. (vii) State with present object is related to state with present object by object condition.

By the knowledge of penetration into others' minds, (one) knows the other being's present mind with present object. Present aggregates with present object are related to knowledge of penetration into others' minds, advertence by object condition. (1)

(viii) State with present object is related to state with past object by object condition.

(One) reviews past divine-eye, reviews divine-ear element, reviews past knowledge of supernormal power with present object, reviews knowledge of penetration into others' minds. The Noble persons review the eradicated defilements with present object, review the uneradicated defilements, know the defilements addicted to before.

(One) practises insight into the impermanence . . . of past aggregates with present object; enjoys and delights in (those aggregates). Taking them as object, arises lust with past object . . . arises grief. Past aggregates with present object are related to knowledge of penetration into others' minds, knowledge of remembrance of past existences, knowledge of rebirths according to one's kamma, advertence by object condition. (2)

(ix) State with present object is related to state with future object by object condition.

(One) reviews future divine-eye, reviews divine-ear element, reviews future knowledge of supernormal power with present object . . . knowledge of penetration into others' minds.

(One) practises insight into the impermanence . . . of future aggregates with present object . . . Taking them as object, arises lust with future object . . . arises grief. Future aggregates with present object are related to knowledge of penetration into others' minds, knowledge of future existences, advertence by object condition. (3)

Predominance 7

23. (i) State with past object is related to state with past object by predominance condition.

(It is of two kinds, namely:) (*a*) object-predominance, (*b*) conascence-predominance.

(*a*) *Object-predominance:* (One) esteems and reviews past infinity of consciousness, esteems and reviews neither-perception-nor-non-perception. (One) esteems and reviews past knowledge of supernormal power with past object . . . knowledge of penetration into others' minds . . . knowledge of remembrance of past existences, esteems and reviews knowledge of rebirths according to one's kamma. (One) esteems, enjoys and delights in past aggregates with past object. Taking them as estimable object, arises lust with past object, arise wrong views.

(*b*) *Conascence-predominance:* Predominance with past object is related to (its) associated aggregates by predominance condition. (1)

(ii) State with past object is related to state with future object by predominance condition.

Object-predominance: (One) esteems and . . . future infinity of consciousness . . . neither-perception-nor-non-perception. (One) esteems and . . . future knowledge of supernormal power with past object . . . knowledge of penetration into others' minds . . . knowledge of remembrance of past existences . . . knowledge of rebirths according to one's kamma. (One) esteems, enjoys and delights in future aggregates with past object. Taking them as estimable object, arises lust with future object, arise wrong views. (2)

24. (iii) State with future object is related to state with future object by predominance condition.

(It is of two kinds, namely:) (*a*) object-predominance, (*b*) conascence-predominance.

(*a*) *Object-predominance:* (One) esteems and . . . future knowledge of supernormal power with future object . . . knowledge of penetration into others' minds, esteems and reviews knowledge of future existences. (One) esteems, enjoys and delights in future aggregates with future object. Taking them as estimable object, arises lust with future object, arise wrong views.

(*b*) *Conascence-predominance:* Predominance with future object is related to (its) associated aggregates by predominance condition. (1)

(iv) State with future object is related to state with past object by predominance condition.

Object-predominance: (One) esteems and . . . past knowledge of supernormal power with future object . . . knowledge of penetration into others' minds, esteems and . . . knowledge of future existences. (One) esteems, enjoys and delights in past aggregates with future object. Taking them as estimable object, arises lust with past object, arise wrong views. (2)

25. (v) State with present object is related to state with present object by predominance condition.

Conascence-predominance: Predominance with present object is related to (its) associated aggregates by predominance condition. (1)

(vi) State with present object is related to state with past object by predominance condition.

Object-predominance: (One) esteems and reviews past divine-eye, esteems and reviews divine-ear element, esteems and . . . past knowledge of supernormal power with present object, esteems and . . . knowledge of penetration into others' minds. (One) esteems, enjoys and delights in past aggregates with present object. Taking them as estimable object, arises lust with past object, arise wrong views. (2)

(vii) State with present object is related to state with future object by predominance condition.

Object-predominance: (One) esteems and reviews future divine-eye, esteems and . . . divine-ear element, esteems and . . . future knowledge of supernormal power with present object, esteems and . . . knowledge of penetration into others' minds. (One) esteems, enjoys and delights in future aggregates with present object. Taking them as estimable object, arises lust with future object, arise wrong views. (3)

Proximity 7

26. (i) State with past object is related to state with past object by proximity condition.

Preceding aggregates with past object are related to subsequent aggregates with past object by proximity condition. (1)

(ii) State with past object is related to state with future object by proximity condition.

Life-continuum with past object is related to advertence with future object by proximity condition. (2)

(iii) State with past object is related to state with present object by proximity condition.

Death-consciousness with past object is related to rebirth-consciousness with present object by proximity condition. Life-continuum with past object is related to advertence with present object by proximity condition. (3)

27. (iv) State with future object is related to state with future object by proximity condition.

Preceding aggregates with future object are related to subsequent aggregates with future object by proximity condition. (1)

(v) State with future object is related to state with past object by proximity condition.

Knowledge of supernormal power with future object to emergence with past object . . . knowledge of penetration into others' minds to emergence with past object . . . knowledge of future existences to emergence with past object . . . aggregates with future object are related to emergence with past object by proximity condition. (2)

28. (vi) State with present object is related to state with present object by proximity condition.

Preceding aggregates with present object are related to subsequent aggregates with present object by proximity condition. Rebirth-consciousness with present object to life-continuum with present object . . . life-continuum with present object is related to life-continuum with present object by proximity condition. (1)

(vii) State with present object is related to state with past object by proximity condition.

Rebirth-consciousness with present object to life-continuum with past object . . . life-continuum with present object to life-continuum with past object . . . aggregates with present object are related to emergence with past object by proximity condition. (2)

Contiguity 7

29. State with past object is related to state with past object by contiguity condition. (The same as proximity.)

Conascence, etc. 3

30. State with past object is related to state with past object by conascence condition . . . by mutuality condition . . . by dependence condition. [The three conditions are also the same as (those) in the "Dependent" Chapter.]

Strong-dependence 9

31. (i) State with past object is related to state with past object by strong-dependence condition.

(It is of three kinds, namely:) (*a*) object-strong-dependence, (*b*) proximity-strong-dependence, (*c*) natural strong dependence . . .

(*c*) *Natural strong-dependence:* Contemplation of impermanence, suffering and impersonality of past object is related to contemplation of impermanence, suffering and impersonality of past object by strong-dependence condition. (1)

(ii) State with past object is related to state with future object by strong-dependence condition.

(It is of three kinds, namely:) (*a*) object-strong-dependence, (*b*) proximity-strong-dependence, (*c*) natural strong-dependence . . .

(*c*) *Natural strong-dependence:* Contemplation of impermanence, suffering and impersonality of past object is related to contemplation of impermanence, suffering and impersonality of future object by strong-dependence condition. (2)

(iii) State with past object is related to state with present object by strong-dependence condition.

(It is of two kinds, namely:) (*a*) proximity-strong-dependence, (*b*) natural strong-dependence . . .

(*b*) *Natural strong-dependence:* Contemplation of impermanence, suffering and impersonality of past object is related to contemplation of impermanence, suffering and impersonality of present object by strong-dependence condition. (3)

32. (iv) State with future object is related to state with future object by strong-dependence condition.

(It is of three kinds, namely:) (*a*) object-strong-dependence, (*b*) proximity-strong-dependence, (*c*) natural strong-dependence . . .

(*c*) *Natural strong-dependence:* Contemplation of impermanence, suffering and impersonality of future object is related to contemplation of impermanence, suffering and impersonality of future object by strong-dependence condition. (1)

(v) State with future object is related to state with past object by strong-dependence condition.

(It is of three kinds, namely:) (*a*) object-strong-dependence, (*b*) proximity-strong-dependence, (*c*) natural strong-dependence . . .

(*c*) *Natural strong-dependence:* Contemplation of impermanence, suffering and impersonality of future object is related to contemplation of impermanence, suffering and impersonality of past object by strong-dependence condition. (2)

(vi) State with future object is related to state with present object by strong-dependence condition.

Natural strong-dependence: Contemplation of impermanence, suffering and impersonality of future object is related to contemplation of impermanence, suffering and impersonality of present object by strong-dependence condition. (3)

33. (vii) State with present object is related to state with present object by strong-dependence condition.

(It is of two kinds, namely:) (*a*) proximity-strong-dependence, (*b*) natural strong-dependence . . .

(*b*) *Natural strong-dependence:* Contemplation of impermanence, suffering and impersonality of present object is related to contemplation of impermanence, suffering and impersonality of present object by strong-dependence condition. (1)

(viii) State with present object is related to state with past object by strong-dependence condition.

(It is of three kinds, namely:) (*a*) object-strong-dependence, (*b*) proximity-strong-dependence, (*c*) natural strong-dependence . . .

(*c*) *Natural strong-dependence:* Contemplation of impermanence, suffering and impersonality of present object is related to contemplation of impermanence, suffering and impersonality of past object by strong-dependence condition. (2)

(ix) State with present object is related to state with future object by strong-dependence condition.

(It is of two kinds, namely:) (*a*) object-strong-dependence, (*b*) natural strong-dependence . . .

(*b*) *Natural strong-dependence:* Contemplation of impermanence, suffering and impersonality of present object is related to contemplation of impermanence, suffering and impersonality of future object by strong-dependence condition. (3)

Repetition 3

34. (i) State with past object is related to state with past object by repetition condition.

Preceding aggregates with past object are related to subsequent aggregates with past object by repetition condition. (1)

(ii) State with future object is related to state with future object by repetition condition.

Preceding aggregates with future object are related to subsequent aggregates with future object by repetition condition. (1)

(iii) State with present object is related to state with present object by repetition condition.

Preceding aggregates with present object are related to subsequent aggregates with present object by repetition condition. (1)

Kamma 9

35. (i) State with past object is related to state with past object by kamma condition.

(It is of two kinds, namely:) (*a*) conascence(-kamma), (*b*) asynchronous (kamma).

(*a*) (1) Conascent volition with past object is related to (its) associated aggregates by kamma condition;

(2) At the moment of conception . . .

(*b*) Asynchronous volition with past object is related to (its) resultant aggregates with past object by kamma condition. (1)

(ii) State with past object is related to state with future object by kamma condition.

Asynchronous volition with past object is related to (its) resultant aggregates with future object by kamma condition. (2)

(iii) State with past object is related to state with present object by kamma condition.

Asynchronous volition with past object is related to (its) resultant aggregates with present object by kamma condition. (3)

36. (iv) State with future object is related to state with future object by kamma condition.

(It is of two kinds, namely:) (*a*) conascence(-kamma), (*b*) asynchronous (kamma).

(*a*) Conascent volition with future object is related to (its) associated aggregates by kamma condition.

(*b*) Asynchronous volition with future object is related to (its) resultant aggregates with future object by kamma condition. (1)

(v) State with future object is related to state with past object by kamma condition.

Asynchronous volition with future object is related to (its) resultant aggregates with past object by kamma condition. (2)

(vi) State with future object is related to state with present object by kamma condition.

Asynchronous volition with future object is related to (its) resultant aggregates with present object by kamma condition. (3)

37. (vii) State with present object is related to state with present object by kamma condition.

(It is of two kinds, namely:) (*a*) conascence(-kamma), (*b*) asynchronous (kamma).

(*a*) (1) Conascent volition with present object is related to (its) associated aggregates by kamma condition.

(2) At the moment of conception . . .

(*b*) Asynchronous volition with present object is related to (its) resultant aggregates with present object by kamma condition. (1)

(viii) State with present object is related to state with past object by kamma condition.

Asynchronous volition with present object is related to (its) resultant aggregates with past object by kamma condition. (2)

(ix) State with present object is related to state with future object by kamma condition.

Asynchronous volition with present object is related to (its) resultant aggregates with future object by kamma condition. (3)

Resultant, etc.

38. State with past object is related to state with past object by resultant condition . . . by nutriment condition . . . by faculty condition . . . by jhāna condition . . . by path condition . . . by association condition . . . by presence condition . . . by absence condition . . . by disappearance condition . . . by non-disappearance condition . . .

1. CONDITIONS: POSITIVE (ii) ENUMERATION CHAPTER

By Ones

39. With root 3, object 9, predominance 7, proximity 7, contiguity 7, conascence, mutuality, dependence 3, strong-dependence 9, repetition 3, kamma 9, resultant 3, nutriment 3, faculty, jhāna, path, association 3, presence 3, absence 7, disappearance 7, non-disappearance 3. (Enumerate thus.)

End of Positive

2. SELECTION OF THE CONDITIONS FOR NEGATIVE 9

40. (i) State with past object is related to state with past object by object condition, conascence condition, strong-dependence condition, kamma condition. (1)

(ii) State with past object is related to state with future object by object condition, strong-dependence condition, kamma condition. (2)

(iii) State with past object is related to state with present object by object condition, strong-dependence condition, kamma condition. (3)

41. (iv) State with future object is related to state with future object by object condition, conascence condition, strong-dependence condition, kamma condition. (1)

(v) State with future object is related to state with past object by object condition, strong-dependence condition, kamma condition. (2)

(vi) State with future object is related to state with present object by object condition, strong-dependence condition, kamma condition. (3)

42. (vii) State with present object is related to state with present object by object condition, conascence condition, strong-dependence condition, kamma condition. (1)

(viii) State with present object is related to state with past object by object condition, strong-dependence condition, kamma condition. (2)

(ix) State with present object is related to state with future object by object condition, strong-dependence condition, kamma condition. (3)

2. CONDITIONS: NEGATIVE (ii) ENUMERATION CHAPTER

(By Ones)

43. With not-root 9, not-object 9, not-predominance 9, not-proximity 9, not-contiguity 9 . . . (Abbreviated. All 9.) . . . not-disappearance 9, not-non-disappearance 9. (Enumerate thus.)

End of Negative

3. CONDITIONS: POSITIVE–NEGATIVE

Root By Twos

44. With root condition, not-object 3, not-predominance, not-proximity, not-contiguity, not-strong-dependence, not-prenascence, not-postnascence, not-repetition, not-kamma, not-resultant 3 . . . (All 3. Abbreviated.) . . . not-absence, not-disappearance 3. (Enumerate thus.)

End of Positive–Negative

4. CONDITIONS: NEGATIVE–POSITIVE

Not-root By Twos

45. With not-root condition, object 9, predominance 7, proximity 7, contiguity 7, conascence 3, mutuality 3, dependence 3, strong-dependence 9, repetition 3, kamma 9, resultant 3, nutriment, faculty, jhāna, path, association, presence 3, absence 7, disappearance 7, non-disappearance 3. (Enumerate thus.)

End of Negative–Positive

End of "INVESTIGATION" CHAPTER

END OF PAST OBJECT TRIPLET

20. INTERNAL TRIPLET[1] I. "DEPENDENT" CHAPTER

1. CONDITIONS: POSITIVE (i) CLASSIFICATION CHAPTER

Root 2

1. (i) Dependent on internal (ajjhatta) state, arises internal state by root condition.

---

[1] This comprises (1) Internal states, (2) External states, (3) Internal and External states.

(*a*) Dependent on one internal aggregate, arise three aggregates and mind-produced matter . . . two aggregates . . .

(*b*) At the moment of conception, dependent on one internal aggregate, arise three aggregates and kamma-produced matter . . . two aggregates . . . dependent on aggregates, arises (heart-)base; dependent on (heart-)base, arise aggregates;

(*c*) Dependent on one great primary, arise three great primaries . . . dependent on great primaries, arise mind-produced and kamma-produced derived matter. (1)

(ii) Dependent on external (bahiddhā) state, arises external state by root condition.

(*a*) Dependent on one external aggregate, arise three aggregates and mind-produced matter . . . two aggregates . . .

(*b*) At the moment of conception, dependent on one external aggregate, arise three aggregates and kamma-produced matter . . . dependent on two aggregates, arise two aggregates . . . dependent on aggregates, arises (heart-)base; dependent on (heart-)base, arise aggregates;

(*c*) Dependent on one great primary, arise three great primaries . . . dependent on great primaries, arise mind-produced and kamma-produced derived matter. (1)

Object 2

2. (i) Dependent on internal state, arises internal state by object condition.

(*a*) Dependent on one internal aggregate, arise three aggregates . . . dependent on two aggregates . . .

(*b*) At the moment of conception, dependent on one internal aggregate, arise three aggregates . . . dependent on (heart-)base, arise aggregates. (1)

(ii) Dependent on external state, arises external state by object condition.

(*a*) Dependent on one external aggregate, arise three aggregates . . . two aggregates . . .

(*b*) At the moment of conception . . . dependent on (heart-)base, arise aggregates. (1)

Predominance 2

3. (i) Dependent on internal state, arises internal state by predominance condition.

(*a*) Dependent on one internal aggregate, arise three aggregates and mind-produced matter . . . two aggregates . . .

(*b*) Dependent on one great primary . . . dependent on great primaries, arises mind-produced derived matter. (1)

(ii) Dependent on external state, arises external state by predominance condition.

(*a*) Dependent on one external aggregate, arise three aggregates and mind-produced matter . . . two aggregates . . .

(*b*) Dependent on one great primary . . . dependent on great primaries, arises mind-produced derived matter. (1)

Proximity, etc. 2

4. (i) Dependent on internal state, arises internal state by proximity condition . . . by contiguity condition . . . by conascence condition.

(*a*) Dependent on one internal aggregate, arise three aggregates and mind-produced matter . . . two aggregates . . .

(*b*) At the moment of conception, dependent on one internal aggregate, arise three aggregates and kamma-produced matter . . . two aggregates . . . dependent on aggregates, arises (heart-)base; dependent on (heart-)base, arise aggregates;

(*c*) Dependent on one great primary, arise three great primaries . . . dependent on great primaries, arise mind-produced and kamma-produced derived matter;

(*d*) Nutriment-produced . . . temperature-produced . . . dependent on one great primary of non-percipient beings . . . dependent on great primaries, arises kamma-produced derived matter. (1)

(ii) Dependent on external state, arises external state by conascence condition.

(*a*) Dependent on one external aggregate, arise three aggregates and mind-produced matter . . . two aggregates . . .

(*b*) At the moment of conception, dependent on one external aggregate, arise three aggregates and kamma-produced matter . . . two aggregates . . . dependent on aggregates, arises (heart-)base; dependent on (heart-)base, arise aggregates;

(*c*) Dependent on one great primary . . . dependent on great primaries, arise mind-produced and kamma-produced derived matter;

(*d*) External . . . nutriment-produced . . . temperature-produced . . . dependent on one great primary of non-percipient beings . . . dependent on great primaries, arises kamma-produced derived matter. (1)

Mutuality, etc.

5. Dependent on internal state, arises internal state by mutuality condition . . . by dependence condition . . . by strong-dependence condition . . . by prenascence condition . . . by repetition condition. (No conception in prenascence and repetition also.) . . . by kamma condition . . . by resultant condition . . . by nutriment condition . . . by faculty condition . . . by jhāna condition . . . by path condition . . . by association condition . . . by dissociation condition . . . by presence condition . . . by absence condition . . . by disappearance condition . . . by non-disappearance condition . . .

1. CONDITIONS: POSITIVE (ii) ENUMERATION CHAPTER

(By Ones)

6. With root 2, object 2 . . . non-disappearance 2. (Enumerate thus.)

End of Positive

2. CONDITIONS: NEGATIVE (i) CLASSIFICATION CHAPTER

Not-root 2

7. (i) Dependent on internal state, arises internal state by not-root condition.

(*a*) Dependent on one rootless internal aggregate, arise three aggregates and mind-produced matter . . . two aggregates . . .

(*b*) At the moment of rootless conception . . . dependent on aggregates, arises (heart-)base; dependent on (heart-)base, arise aggregates;

(*c*) One great primary . . .

(*d*) Nutriment-produced . . . temperature-produced . . . dependent on one great primary of non-percipient beings . . . dependent on great primaries, arises kamma-produced derived matter;

(*e*) Dependent on doubt-accompanied or restlessness-accompanied aggregates, arises doubt-accompanied or restlessness-accompanied delusion. (1)

(ii) Dependent on external state, arises external state by not-root condition.

(*a*) Dependent on one rootless external aggregate, arise three aggregates and mind-produced matter . . . two aggregates . . .

(*b*) At the moment of rootless conception . . . dependent on aggregates, arises (heart-)base; dependent on (heart-)base, arise aggregates;

(*c*) Dependent on one great primary . . .

(*d*) External . . . nutriment-produced . . . temperature-produced . . . dependent on one great primary of non-percipient beings . . .

(*e*) Dependent on doubt-accompanied or restlessness-accompanied aggregates, arises doubt-accompanied or restlessness-accompanied delusion. (1)

Not-object 2

8. (i) Dependent on internal state, arises internal state by not-object condition.

(*a*) Dependent on internal aggregates, arises mind-produced matter;

(*b*) At the moment of conception, dependent on internal aggregates, arises kamma-produced matter; dependent on aggregates, arises (heart-) base;

(*c*) Dependent on one great primary . . .

(*d*) Nutriment-produced . . . temperature-produced . . . dependent on one great primary of non-percipient beings . . . (1)

(ii) Dependent on external state, arises external state by not-object condition.

(*a*) Dependent on external aggregates, arises mind-produced matter;

(*b*) At the moment of conception, dependent on external aggregates, arises kamma-produced matter; dependent on aggregates, arises (heart-) base . . .

(*c*) One great primary . . .

(*d*) External . . . nutriment-produced . . . temperature-produced . . . non-percipient beings . . . (1)

Not-predominance, etc. 2

9. (i) Dependent on internal state, arises internal state by not-predominance condition. (The same as conascence in Positive; make no difference.) . . . by not-proximity condition . . . by not-contiguity condition . . . by not-mutuality condition . . . by not-strong-dependence condition . . . by not-prenascence condition.

(*a*) In the immaterial plane, dependent on one internal aggregate . . . dependent on internal aggregates, arises mind-produced matter;

(*b*) At the moment of conception, dependent on one internal aggregate, arise three aggregates and kamma-produced matter . . . two aggregates . . . dependent on aggregates, arises (heart-)base; dependent on (heart-)base, arise aggregates;

(*c*) Dependent on one great primary . . .

(*d*) Nutriment-produced . . . temperature-produced . . . non-percipient beings . . . (1)

10. (ii) Dependent on external state, arises external state by not-prenascence condition.

(*a*) In the immaterial plane, dependent on one external aggregate . . . two aggregates . . . dependent on external aggregates, arises mind-produced matter;

(*b*) At the moment of conception. (Complete.) . . .

(*c*) One great primary . . .

(*d*) External . . . nutriment-produced . . . temperature-produced . . . non-percipient beings . . . (1)

Not-postnascence, etc. 2

11. (i) Dependent on internal state, arises internal state by not-postnascence condition . . . by not-repetition condition . . . by not-kamma condition.

(*a*) Dependent on internal aggregates, arises internal volition;

(*b*) Nutriment-produced . . . temperature-produced . . . (1)

(ii) Dependent on external state, arises external state by not-kamma condition.

(*a*) Dependent on external aggregates, arises external volition;

(*b*) External . . . nutriment-produced . . . temperature produced . . . (1)

Not-resultant, etc. 2

12. (i) Dependent on internal state, arises internal state by not-resultant condition. (No conception.) . . . by not-nutriment condition.

Temperature-produced . . . non-percipient beings . . . (1)

(ii) Dependent on external state, arises external state by not-nutriment condition.

External . . . temperature-produced . . . non-percipient beings . . . (1)

12(A). (i) Dependent on internal state, arises internal state by not-faculty condition.

Nutriment-produced . . . temperature-produced . . . dependent on great primaries of non-percipient beings, arises physical life-faculty. (1)

(ii) Dependent on external state, arises external state by not-faculty condition.

External . . . nutriment-produced . . . temperature-produced . . .

dependent on great primaries of non-percipient beings, arises physical life-faculty. (1)

Not-jhāna 2

13. (i) Dependent on internal state, arises internal state by not-jhāna condition.

(*a*) Five-fold consciousness-accompanied . . .

(*b*) Nutriment-produced . . . temperature-produced . . . non-percipient beings . . . (1)

(ii) Dependent on external state, arises external state by not-jhāna condition.

(*a*) Five-fold consciousness-accompanied . . .

(*b*) External . . . nutriment-produced . . . temperature-produced . . . non-percipient beings . . . (1)

Not-path, etc. 2

14. (i) Dependent on internal state, arises internal state by not-path condition. (The same as not-root. No delusion.) . . . by not-association condition . . . by not-dissociation condition.

(*a*) In the immaterial plane . . .

(*b*) Nutriment-produced . . . temperature-produced . . . non-percipient beings . . . (1)

(ii) Dependent on external state, arises external state by not-dissociation condition.

(*a*) In the immaterial plane . . .

(*b*) External . . . nutriment-produced . . . temperature-produced . . . non-percipient beings . . .

by not-absence condition . . . by not-disappearance condition . . .

2. CONDITIONS: NEGATIVE (ii) ENUMERATION CHAPTER

(By Ones)

15. With not-root 2, not-object 2, not-predominance 2, not-proximity 2, not-contiguity 2 (Abbreviated. All 2.) . . . not-disappearance 2. (Enumerate thus.)

End of Negative

3. CONDITIONS: POSITIVE–NEGATIVE

(Root By Twos)

16. With root condition, not-object 2 . . . not-resultant, not-association, not-dissociation, not-absence, not-disappearance 2. (Enumerate thus.)

End of Positive–Negative

4. CONDITIONS: NEGATIVE–POSITIVE

(Not-root By Twos)

17. With not-root condition, object 2, proximity 2 . . . path 2 . . . non-disappearance 2. (Enumerate thus.)

End of Negative–Positive

End of "DEPENDENT" CHAPTER

(The "Conascent" Chapter is the same as the "Dependent" Chapter.)

20. INTERNAL TRIPLET III. "CONDITIONED" CHAPTER

1. CONDITIONS: POSITIVE (i) CLASSIFICATION CHAPTER

Root 2

18. (i) Conditioned by internal state, arises internal state by root condition.

(*a*) Conditioned by one internal aggregate, arise three aggregates and mind-produced matter . . . two aggregates . . .

(*b*) At the moment of conception. (Complete.) . . .

(*c*) One great primary . . .

(*d*) Conditioned by (heart-)base, arise internal aggregates. (1)

(ii) Conditioned by external state, arises external state by root condition.

(*a*) Conditioned by one external aggregate, arise three aggregates . . .

(*b*) At the moment of conception . . .

(*c*) One great primary . . .

(*d*) Conditioned by (heart-)base, arise external aggregates. (1)

Object 2

19. (i) Conditioned by internal state, arises internal state by object condition. (The same as in the "Dependent" Chapter.)

Conditioned by eye-base, arises eye-consciousness . . . conditioned by body-base, arises body-consciousness; conditioned by (heart-)base, arise internal aggregates. (1)

(ii) Conditioned by external state, arises external state by object condition. (The same as in the "Dependent" Chapter.)

Eye-base . . . body-base . . . conditioned by (heart-)base, arise external aggregates. (1)

Predominance, etc. 2

20. Conditioned by internal state, arises internal state by predominance condition. [Base is extra (atirekaṁ); the same as in the "Dependent" Chapter.] . . . by proximity condition . . . by contiguity condition . . . by conascence condition. (Complete as in the "Conascent" Chapter.) Conditioned by great primaries . . . [Do five bases and (heart-)base after great primaries and aggregates.] . . . by mutuality condition . . . by dependence condition . . . by non-disappearance condition . . .

1. CONDITIONS: POSITIVE (ii) ENUMERATION CHAPTER

(By Ones)

21. With root 2, object . . . non-disappearance 2. (Enumerate thus.)

End of Positive

2. CONDITIONS: NEGATIVE (i) CLASSIFICATION CHAPTER

Not-root 2

22. (i) Conditioned by internal state, arises internal state by not-root condition.

(*a*) Conditioned by one rootless internal aggregate, arise three aggregates . . .

(*b*) At the moment of rootless conception . . . conditioned by aggregates, arises (heart-)base; conditioned by (heart-)base, arise aggregates;

(*c*) One great primary . . . nutriment-produced . . . temperature-produced . . . non-percipient beings . . .

(*d*) Eye-base . . . body-base . . . conditioned by (heart-)base, arise rootless internal aggregates;

(*e*) Conditioned by doubt-accompanied or restlessness-accompanied aggregates and (heart-)base, arises doubt-accompanied or restlessness-accompanied delusion. (1)

(ii) Conditioned by external state, arises external state by not-root condition.

(Do also during life, conception and great primaries.) Eye-base . . . body-base . . . conditioned by (heart-)base, arise rootless external aggregates;

Conditioned by doubt-accompanied or restlessness-accompanied aggregates and (heart-)base, arises doubt-accompanied or restlessness-accompanied delusion. (1)

Not-object, etc. 2

23. By not-object condition . . . by not-predominance condition. (The same as conascence.) . . . by not-proximity condition . . . by not-contiguity condition . . . by not-mutuality condition . . . by not-strong-dependence condition . . . by not-prenascence condition. (The same as in the "Dependent" Chapter.) . . . by not-postnascence condition . . . by not-repetition condition . . . by not-kamma condition . . . by not-dissociation condition. [The same as dissociation (condition) in Negative of the "Dependent" Chapter.] . . . by not-absence condition . . . by not-disappearance condition . . .

2. CONDITIONS: NEGATIVE (ii) ENUMERATION CHAPTER

(By Ones)

24. With not-root 2, not-object 2 . . . not-disappearance 2.

End of Negative

3. CONDITIONS: POSITIVE–NEGATIVE

(Root By Twos)

25. With root condition, not-object 2, not-predominance 2 . . . not-resultant, not association, not dissociation, not-absence, not-disappearance 2.

End of Positive–Negative

4. CONDITIONS: NEGATIVE–POSITIVE

(Not-root By Twos)

26. With not-root condition, object 2 . . . non-disappearance 2.

End of Negative–Positive

(The "Supported" Chapter is the same as "Conditioned" Chapter. Expand the "Conjoined" Chapter and the "Associated" Chapter.)

20. INTERNAL TRIPLET VII. "INVESTIGATION" CHAPTER

1. CONDITIONS: POSITIVE (i) CLASSIFICATION CHAPTER

Root 2

27. (i) Internal state is related to internal state by root condition.

(*a*) Internal roots are related to (their) associated aggregates and mind-produced matter by root condition;

(*b*) At the moment of conception . . . (1)

(ii) External state is related to external state by root condition.

(*a*) External roots are related to (their) associated aggregates and mind-produced matter by root condition.

(*b*) At the moment of conception . . . (1)

Object 4

28. (i) Internal state is related to internal state by object condition.

After having offered an offering, having undertaken precepts, having fulfilled the duty of observance, (one) reviews it . . . formerly well done. Having emerged from jhāna . . . The Noble persons, having emerged from Path, review the Path, review the Fruition, review the eradicated defilements, review the uneradicated defilements, know the defilements addicted to before.

Internal eye . . . body . . . visible object . . . tangible object . . . (heart-)base . . . (One) practises insight into the impermanence, suffering and impersonality of internal aggregates; enjoys and delights in (those aggregates). Taking them as object, arises lust . . . arises grief.

By the power of divine-eye, (one) sees a visible object. By the power of divine-ear element, (one) hears a sound. Infinity of space is related to infinity of consciousness by object condition. Nothingness is related to neither-perception-nor-non-perception by object condition.

Visible object-base . . . tangible object-base is related to body-consciousness by object condition. Internal aggregates are related to knowledge of supernormal power, knowledge of remembrance of past existences, knowledge of rebirths according to one's kamma, knowledge of future existences, advertence by object condition. (1)

(ii) Internal state is related to external state by object condition.

The other person's (paro) internal eye . . . (heart-)base . . . (One) practises insight into the impermanence, suffering and impersonality of internal aggregates; enjoys and delights in (those aggregates). Taking them as object, arises lust . . . arises grief.

By the power of divine-eye, (one) sees a visible object. By the power of divine-ear element, (one) hears a sound. By the knowledge of penetration into others' minds, (one) knows the other being's internal mind.

Internal visible object-base to external eye-consciousness . . . internal tangible object-base is related to external body-consciousness by object condition. Internal aggregates are related to knowledge of supernormal power, knowledge of penetration into others' minds, knowledge of remembrance of past existences, knowledge of rebirths according to one's kamma, knowledge of future existences, advertence by object condition. (2)

29. (iii) External state is related to external state by object condition.

The other person, after having offered an offering, having undertaken precepts, having fulfilled the duty of observance, reviews it. (He) reviews (such acts) formerly well done. Having emerged from jhāna . . . The Noble persons, having emerged from Path, review the Path, review the Fruition, review Nibbāna. Nibbāna is related to change-of-lineage, purification, Path, Fruition, advertence by object condition. The Noble persons review the eradicated defilements, review the uneradicated defilements . . . addicted to before.

The other person's external eye . . . (heart-)base . . . into the impermanence . . . of external aggregates . . . arises grief.

By the power of divine-eye, (the other person) sees a visible object. By the power of divine-ear element, (he) hears a sound. By the knowledge of penetration into others' minds . . . the other being's external mind. Infinity of space is related to infinity of consciousness by object condition. Nothingness is related to neither-perception-nor-non-perception by object condition.

External visible object-base to external eye-consciousness . . . external tangible object-base to external body-consciousness . . . External aggregates are related to knowledge of supernormal power, knowledge of penetration into others' minds, knowledge of remembrance of past existences, knowledge of rebirths according to one's kamma, knowledge of future existences, advertence by object condition. (1)

(iv) External state is related to internal state by object condition.

The Noble persons review Nibbāna. Nibbāna is related to change-of lineage, purification, Path, Fruition, advertence by object condition.

External eye . . . (heart-)base . . . (One) . . . into the impermanence . . . of external aggregates . . . arises grief.

By the power of divine-eye, (one) sees a visible object. By the power of divine-ear element, (one) hears a sound. By the knowledge of penetration into others' minds, (one) knows the other being's external mind.

External visible object-base to internal eye-consciousness . . . external tangible object-base to internal body-consciousness . . . External aggregates are related to knowledge of supernormal power, knowledge of penetration into others' minds, knowledge of remembrance of past existences, knowledge of rebirths according to one's kamma, knowledge of future existences, advertence by object condition. (2)

Predominance 4

30. (i) Internal state is related to internal state by predominance condition.

(It is of two kinds, namely:) (*a*) object-predominance, (*b*) conascence-predominance.

(*a*) *Object-predominance:* After having offered an offering, having undertaken precepts, having fulfilled the duty of observance, (one) esteems and reviews it. (One) esteems and . . . (such acts) formerly well done. Having emerged from jhāna, (one) esteems and . . . jhāna. The Noble persons, having emerged from Path, esteem and . . . the Path, esteem and review the Fruition.

Internal eye . . . (heart-)base . . . (One) esteems, enjoys and delights in internal aggregates. Taking them as estimable object, arises lust, arise wrong views.

(*b*) *Conascence-predominance:* Internal predominance is related to (its) associated aggregates and mind-produced matter by predominance condition. (1)

(ii) Internal state is related to external state by predominance condition.

Object-predominance: The other person's internal eye . . . (heart-) base . . . (One) esteems, enjoys and delights in internal aggregates. Taking them as estimable object, arises lust, arise wrong views. (2)

31. (iii) External state is related to external state by predominance condition.

(It is of two kinds, namely:) (*a*) object-predominance, (*b*) conascence-predominance.

(*a*) *Object-predominance:* The other person, after having offered an offering, having undertaken precepts, having fulfilled the duty of observance, esteems and reviews it. (He) esteems and . . . (such acts) formerly well done. Having emerged from jhāna . . . The Noble persons, having emerged from Path, esteem and . . . the Path, esteem and . . . the Fruition, esteem and review Nibbāna. Nibbāna is related to change-of-lineage, purification, Path, Fruition by predominance condition.

External eye . . . (heart-)base . . . (One) esteems, enjoys and delights in external aggregates. Taking them as estimable object, arises lust, arise wrong views.

(*b*) *Conascence-predominance:* External predominance is related to (its) associated aggregates and mind-produced matter by predominance condition. (1)

(iv) External state is related to internal state by predominance condition.

Object-predominance: The Noble persons esteem and review Nibbāna. Nibbāna is related to change-of-lineage, purification, Path, Fruition by predominance condition.

External eye . . . (heart-)base . . . (One) esteems, enjoys and delights in external aggregates. Taking them as estimable object, . . . lust, arise wrong views. (2)

Proximity 2

32. (i) Internal state is related to internal state by proximity condition.

Preceding internal aggregates are related to subsequent internal aggregates by proximity condition. Adaptation to change-of-lineage; adaptation to purification; change-of-lineage to Path; purification to Path; Path to Fruition; Fruition to Fruition; adaptation to the attainment of Fruition; for one emerging from the attainment of Extinction, neither-perception-nor-non-perception is related to the attainment of Fruition by proximity condition. (1)

(ii) External state is related to external state by proximity condition.

("Preceding external" is the only difference. This proceeds in the same way.) (1)

Contiguity, etc. 2

33. Internal state is related to internal state by contiguity condition. (The same as proximity.) . . . by conascence condition . . . by mutuality condition . . . by dependence condition . . .

Strong-dependence 4

34. (i) Internal state is related to internal state by strong-dependence condition.

(It is of three kinds, namely:) (*a*) object-strong-dependence, (*b*) proximity-strong-dependence, (*c*) natural strong-dependence . . .

(*c*) *Natural strong-dependence:* By the strong-dependence of internal confidence, (one) offers an offering, undertakes precepts . . . duty of observance . . . jhāna . . . insight . . . Path . . . superknowledge, develops attainment; arouses conceit, adopts wrong views . . . internal precept . . . wisdom . . . lust . . . wish . . . bodily happiness . . . bodily pain . . . temperature . . . food . . . By the strong-dependence of lodging-place, (one) offers an offering . . . develops attainment, kills a living being . . . causes schism in the Saṅgha. Internal confidence . . . wisdom, lust . . . wish, bodily happiness, bodily pain . . . lodging-place is related to internal confidence . . . wisdom, lust . . . wish, bodily happiness, bodily pain, Path, the attainment of Fruition by strong-dependence condition. (1)

(ii) Internal state is related to external state by strong-dependence condition.

(It is of two kinds, namely:) (*a*) object-strong-dependence, (*b*) natural strong-dependence . . .

(*b*) *Natural strong-dependence:* The other person, by the strong-dependence of internal confidence, offers an offering . . . arouses conceit, adopts wrong views. The other person . . . internal precept . . . by the strong-dependence of lodging-place, offers an offering . . . kills a living being . . . causes schism in the Saṅgha. Internal confidence . . . lodging-place is related to external confidence . . . Path, the attainment of Fruition by strong-dependence condition. (2)

35. (iii) External state is related to external state by strong-dependence condition.

(It is of three kinds, namely:) (*a*) object-strong-dependence, (*b*) proximity-strong-dependence, (*c*) natural strong-dependence . . .

(*c*) *Natural strong-dependence:* The other person . . . external confidence . . . wish . . . bodily happiness . . . by the strong-dependence of lodging-place, offers an offering . . . causes schism in the Saṅgha. External confidence . . . lodging-place is related to external confidence . . . the attainment of Fruition by strong-dependence condition. (1)

(iv) External state is related to internal state by strong-dependence condition.

(It is of two kinds, namely:) (*a*) object-strong-dependence, (*b*) natural strong-dependence . . .

(*b*) *Natural strong-dependence:* External confidence . . . by the strong-dependence of lodging-place, offers an offering . . . causes schism in the Saṅgha. External confidence . . . lodging-place is related to internal confidence . . . the attainment of Fruition by strong-dependence condition. (2)

Prenascence 6

36. (i) Internal state is related to internal state by prenascence condition.

(It is of two kinds, namely:) (*a*) object-prenascence, (*b*) base-prenascence.

(*a*) *Object-prenascence:* Internal eye . . . (One) practises insight into the impermanence, suffering and impersonality of the (heart-)base . . . arises grief.

By the power of divine-eye, (one) sees a visible object. By the power of divine-ear element, (one) hears a sound. Visible object-base to eye-consciousness . . . tangible object-base is related to body-consciousness by prenascence condition.

(*b*) *Base-prenascence:* Eye-base to eye-consciousness . . . body-base to body-consciousness . . . (heart-)base is related to internal aggregates by prenascence condition. (1)

(ii) Internal state is related to external state by prenascence condition.

Object-prenascence: The other person's internal eye . . . into the impermanence . . . of the (heart-)base . . . arises grief. By the power of divine-eye, (one) sees a visible object. By the power of divine-ear element, (one) hears a sound. Internal visible object-base to external eye-consciousness . . . internal tangible object-base is related to external body-consciousness by prenascence condition. (2)

37. (iii) External state is related to external state by prenascence condition.

(It is of two kinds, namely:) (*a*) object-prenascence, (*b*) base-prenascence.

(*a*) *Object-prenascence:* The other person's external eye . . . into the impermanence . . . of the (heart-)base . . . By the power of divine-eye, (the other person) sees a visible object. By the power of divine-ear element, (he) hears a sound. External visible object-base to external eye-consciousness . . . external tangible object-base to external body-consciousness . . .

(*b*) *Base-prenascence:* External eye-base . . . body-base . . . (heart-) base is related to external aggregates by prenascence condition. (1)

(iv) External state is related to internal state by prenascence condition.

Object-prenascence: External eye . . . into the impermanence . . . of the (heart-)base . . . arises grief. By the power of divine-eye, (the other person) sees a visible object. By the power of divine-ear element, (he) hears a sound. External visible object-base to internal eye-consciousness . . . external tangible object-base is related to internal body-consciousness by prenascence condition. (2)

38. (v) Internal state and external state are related to internal state by prenascence condition.

Object-prenascence–base-prenascence: External visible object-base and internal eye-base are related to internal eye-consciousness by prenascence condition . . . external tangible object-base and internal body-base to internal body-consciousness . . . External visible object-base and internal (heart-)base . . . external tangible object-base and internal (heart-) base are related to internal aggregates by prenascence condition. (1)

(vi) Internal state and external state are related to external state by prenascence condition.

Object-prenascence–base-prenascence: Internal visible object-base and external eye-base are related to external eye-consciousness by prenascence condition . . . internal tangible object-base and external body-base are related to external body-consciousness by prenascence condition. Internal visible object-base and external (heart-)base . . . internal tangible object-base and external (heart-)base are related to external aggregates by prenascence condition. (2)

Postnascence 2

39. (i) Internal state is related to internal state by postnascence condition.

Postnascent internal aggregates are related to this prenascent body by postnascence condition. (1)

(ii) External state is related to external state by postnascence condition.

Postnascent external aggregates are related to this prenascent body by postnascence condition. (1)

Repetition 2

40. (i) Internal state is related to internal state by repetition condition.

Preceding internal aggregates are related to subsequent internal aggregates by repetition condition. Adaptation to change-of-lineage; adaptation to purification; change-of-lineage to Path; purification is related to Path by repetition condition. (1)

(ii) External state is related to external state by repetition condition.

Preceding . . . (In the same way as internal.)

Kamma 2

41. (i) Internal state is related to internal state by kamma condition.

(It is of two kinds, namely:) (*a*) conascence(-kamma), (*b*) asynchronous (kamma).

(*a*) (1) Conascent internal volition is related to (its) associated aggregates and mind-produced matter by kamma condition;

(2) At the moment of conception . . .[1]

(*b*) Asynchronous internal volition is related to (its) internal resultant aggregates and kamma-produced matter by kamma condition. (1)

(ii) External state is related to external state by kamma condition.

(It is of two kinds, namely:) (*a*) conascence(-kamma), (*b*) asynchronous (kamma).

(*a*) (1) Conascent external volition is related to (its) associated aggregates and mind-produced matter by kamma condition;

(2) At the moment of conception . . .[1]

(*b*) Asynchronous external volition is related to (its) external resultant aggregates and kamma-produced matter by kamma condition. (1)

---

[1] Left out in the Pali Text.

Resultant 2

42. Internal state is related to internal state by resultant condition ... (Complete. The same as for the "Dependent" Chapter.)

Nutriment 6

43. (i) Internal state is related to internal state by nutriment condition.

(*a*) Internal nutriments are related to (their) associated aggregates and mind-produced matter by nutriment condition;

(*b*) At the moment of conception ...

(*c*) Internal edible food is related to internal body by nutriment condition. (1)

(ii) Internal state is related to external state by nutriment condition.

Internal edible food is related to external body by nutriment condition. (2)

(iii) External state is related to external state by nutriment condition.

(During life and conception.)

External edible food is related to external body by nutriment condition. (1)

(iv) External state is related to internal state by nutriment condition.

External edible food is related to internal body by nutriment condition. (2)

44. (v) Internal state and external state are related to internal state by nutriment condition.

Internal edible food and external edible food are related to internal body by nutriment condition. (1)

(vi) Internal state and external state are related to external state by nutriment condition.

Internal edible food and external edible food are related to external body by nutriment condition. (2)

Faculty, etc. 2

45. (i) Internal state is related to internal state by faculty condition.

Internal faculties . . . (Also expand physical life-faculty.) . . . by jhāna condition . . . by path condition . . . by association condition . . . by dissociation condition.

(It is of three kinds, namely:) (*a*) conascence, (*b*) prenascence, (*c*) postnascence.

[Expand after considering the matrix (mātikā) section (of Dhammasaṅganī).]

(ii) External state is related to external state by dissociation condition.

(It is of three kinds, namely:) (*a*) conascence, (*b*) prenascence, (*c*) postnascence. (Abbreviated.)

Presence 6

46. (i) Internal state is related to internal state by presence condition.

(It is of five kinds, namely:) (*a*) conascence, (*b*) prenascence, (*c*) postnascence, (*d*) nutriment, (*e*) faculty.

(*a*) (1) One conascent internal aggregate to three aggregates and mind-produced matter . . . two aggregates . . .

(2) At the moment of conception . . . aggregates to (heart-)base . . . (heart-)base to aggregates . . .

(3) One great primary . . . one great primary of non-percipient beings to three great primaries . . .

(*b*) Prenascent eye . . . (heart-)base . . . (The same as prenascence.) (Heart-)base is related to internal aggregates by presence condition.

(*c*) Postnascent internal aggregates are related to this prenascent body by presence condition.

(*d*) Internal edible food to internal body . . .

(*e*) Physical life-faculty to kamma-produced matter . . . (1)

(ii) Internal state is related to external state by presence condition.

(It is of two kinds, namely:) (*a*) prenascence, (*b*) nutriment.

(*a*) *Prenascence:* The other person's internal eye . . . practises insight into the impermanence . . . of the (heart-)base. By the power of divine-eye, (the other person) sees a visible object. By the power of divine-ear element, (he) hears a sound. Internal visible object-base . . . tangible object-base is related to external body-consciousness by presence condition.

(*b*) Internal edible food is related to external body by presence condition. (2)

47. (iii) External state is related to external state by presence condition.

(It is of five kinds, namely:) (*a*) conascence, (*b*) prenascence, (*c*) postnascence, (*d*) nutriment, (*e*) faculty.

(The only difference is external: expand matrix section.) (1)

(iv) External state is related to internal state by presence condition.

(It is of two kinds, namely:) (*a*) prenascence, (*b*) nutriment.

(*a*) Prenascent external eye . . . (heart-)base . . . By the power of divine-eye, (one) sees a visible object. By the power of divine-ear element, (one) hears a sound. External visible object-base . . . tangible object-base is related to internal body-consciousness by presence condition.

(*b*) External edible food is related to internal body by presence condition. (2)

48. (v) Internal state and external state are related to internal state by presence condition.

(It is of two kinds, namely:) (*a*) prenascence, (*b*) nutriment.

(*a*) *Prenascence:* External visible object-base and internal eye(-base) to internal eye-consciousness . . . external tangible object-base and internal body-base are related to internal body-consciousness by presence condition. External visible object-base and internal (heart-) base . . . external tangible object-base and internal (heart-)base are related to internal aggregates by presence condition.

(*b*) *Nutriment:* Internal edible food and external edible food are related to internal body by presence condition. (1)

(vi) Internal state and external state are related to external state by presence condition.

(It is of two kinds, namely:) (*a*) prenascence, (*b*) nutriment.

(*a*) *Prenascence:* Internal visible object-base and external eye-base are related to external eye-consciousness by presence condition . . . internal tangible object-base and external body-base are related to external body-consciousness by presence condition. Internal visible object-base and external (heart-)base are related to external aggregates by presence condition . . . internal tangible object-base and external (heart-)base are related to external aggregates by presence condition.

(*b*) *Nutriment:* Internal edible food and external edible food are related to external body by presence condition. (2)

Absence, Disappearance, Non-disappearance

49. Internal state is related to internal state by absence condition . . . by disappearance condition . . . by non-disappearance condition . . .

1. CONDITIONS: POSITIVE (ii) ENUMERATION CHAPTER

By Ones

50. With root 2, object 4, predominance 4, proximity 2, contiguity 2, conascence, mutuality, dependence 2, strong-dependence 4, prenascence 6, postnascence, repetition, kamma, resultant 2, nutriment 6, faculty 2, jhāna, path, association, dissociation 2, presence 6, absence 2, disappearance 2, non-disappearance 6. (Enumerate thus.)

End of Positive

2. SELECTION OF THE CONDITIONS FOR NEGATIVE 6

51. (i) Internal state is related to internal state by object condition, conascence condition, strong-dependence condition, prenascence condition, postnascence condition, kamma condition, nutriment condition, faculty condition. (1)

(ii) Internal state is related to external state by object condition, strong-dependence condition, prenascence condition, nutriment condition. (2)

52. (iii) External state is related to external state by object condition, conascence condition, strong-dependence condition, prenascence condition, postnascence condition, kamma condition, nutriment condition, faculty condition. (1)

(iv) External state is related to internal state by object condition, strong-dependence condition, prenascence condition, nutriment condition. (2)

53. (v) Internal state and external state are related to internal state by prenascence, nutriment. (1)

(vi) Internal state and external state are related to external state by prenascence, nutriment. (2)

2. CONDITIONS: NEGATIVE (ii) ENUMERATION CHAPTER

(By Ones)

54. With not-root 6, not-object 6, not-predominance 6. (Abbreviated. Take 6 for all.) . . . not-dissociation 6, not-presence 4, not-absence 6, not-disappearance 6, not-non-disappearance 4. (Enumerate thus.)

End of Negative

3. CONDITIONS: POSITIVE-NEGATIVE

Root By Twos

55. With root condition, not-object 2, not-predominance, not-proximity, not-contiguity, not-mutuality, not-strong-dependence 2. (Abbreviated. All 2.) . . . not-association, not-dissociation, not-absence, not-disappearance 2. (Enumerate thus.)

End of Positive-Negative

4. CONDITIONS: NEGATIVE-POSITIVE

(Not-root By Twos)

56. With not-root condition, object 4, predominance 4. (Enumerate Positive sections.) . . . non-disappearance 6. (Enumerate thus.)

End of Negative-Positive

End of "INVESTIGATION" CHAPTER

END OF INTERNAL TRIPLET

21. INTERNAL OBJECT TRIPLET[1] I. "DEPENDENT" CHAPTER

1. CONDITIONS: POSITIVE (i) CLASSIFICATION CHAPTER

Root 2

1. (i) Dependent on state with internal object (ajjhattārammaṇa), arises state with internal object by root condition.

(*a*) Dependent on one aggregate with internal object, arise three aggregates . . . two aggregates . . .

(*b*) At the moment of conception, dependent on one aggregate with internal object, arise three aggregates . . . two aggregates . . . (1)

(ii) Dependent on state with external object (bahiddhārammaṇa), arises state with external object by root condition.

(*a*) Dependent on one aggregate with external object, arise three aggregates . . . two aggregates . . .

(*b*) At the moment of conception, dependent on one aggregate with external object, arise three aggregates . . . two aggregates . . . (1)

---

[1] This comprises (1) States with internal object, (2) States with external object, (3) States with internal and external object.

Object, etc. 2

2. Dependent on state with internal object, arises state with internal object by object condition . . . by non-disappearance condition. (Abbreviated.)

1. CONDITIONS: POSITIVE (ii) ENUMERATION CHAPTER

(By Ones)

3. With root 2, object 2.[1] (Abbreviated. All 2.) . . . non-disappearance 2. (Enumerate thus.)

End of Positive

2. CONDITIONS: NEGATIVE (i) CLASSIFICATION CHAPTER

Not-root 2

4. (i) Dependent on state with internal object, arises state with internal object by not-root condition.

(*a*) Dependent on one rootless aggregate with internal object, arise three aggregates . . . two aggregates . . .

(*b*) At the moment of rootless conception, dependent on one aggregate with internal object, arise three aggregates . . . two aggregates . . .

(*c*) Dependent on doubt-accompanied or restlessness-accompanied aggregates, arises doubt-accompanied or restlessness-accompanied delusion. (1)

(ii) Dependent on state with external object, arises state with external object by not-root condition.

(*a*) Dependent on one rootless aggregate with external object, arise three aggregates . . . two aggregates . . .

(*b*) At the moment of rootless conception . . .

(*c*) Dependent on doubt-accompanied or restlessness-accompanied aggregates, arises doubt-accompanied or restlessness-accompanied delusion. (1)

Not-predominance, etc. 2

5. (i) Dependent on state with internal object, arises state with internal object by not-predominance condition. (The same as conascence in Positive. No difference.) . . . by not-prenascence condition.

---

[1] Not as in the Pali Text.

(*a*) In the immaterial plane, dependent on one aggregate with internal object . . .

(*b*) At the moment of conception . . . (1)

6. (ii) Dependent on state with external object, arises state with external object by not-prenascence condition.

(*a*) In the immaterial plane, dependent on one aggregate with external object, arise three aggregates . . .

(*b*) At the moment of conception . . .

(iii) . . . by not-postnascence condition . . . by not-repetition condition. (The same as conascence.) . . . by not-kamma condition.

Dependent on aggregates with internal object, arises volition with internal object. (1)

(ii) Dependent on state with external object, arises state with external object by not-kamma condition.

Dependent on aggregates with external object, arises volition with external object. (1)

Not-resultant, etc. 2

7. (i) Dependent on state with internal object, arises state with internal object by not-resultant condition. (No conception.) . . . by not-jhāna condition.

One five-fold consciousness-accompanied (aggregate) with internal object . . . (1)

(ii) Dependent on state with external object, arises state with external object by not-jhāna condition.

Dependent on one five-fold consciousness-accompanied aggregate with external object, arise three aggregates . . .

(i) . . . by not-path condition. (The same as not-root. No delusion.) . . . by not-dissociation condition.

In the immaterial plane, dependent on one aggregate with internal object, arise three aggregates . . . (1)

(ii) Dependent on state with external object, arises state with external object by not-dissociation condition.

In the immaterial plane, dependent on one aggregate with external object, arise three aggregates . . . (1)

2: CONDITIONS: NEGATIVE (ii) ENUMERATION CHAPTER

(By Ones)

8. With not-root 2, not-predominance 2, not-prenascence 2, not-postnascence 2, not-repetition, not-kamma, not-resultant, not-jhāna, not-path, not-dissociation 2. (Enumerate thus.)

End of Negative

3. CONDITIONS: POSITIVE-NEGATIVE

(Root By Twos)

9. With root condition, not-predominance 2 . . . not-resultant 2, not-dissociation 2. (Enumerate thus.)

End of Positive-Negative

4. CONDITIONS: NEGATIVE-POSITIVE

(Not-root By Twos)

10. With not-root condition, object 2, proximity 2, contiguity 2 . . . path 2 . . . non-disappearance 2. (Enumerate thus.)

End of Negative-Positive

End of "DEPENDENT" CHAPTER

(The "Conascent", "Conditioned", "Supported", "Conjoined" and "Associated" Chapters are also the same as the "Dependent" Chapter.)

21. INTERNAL OBJECT TRIPLET
VII. "INVESTIGATION" CHAPTER

1. CONDITIONS: POSITIVE (i) CLASSIFICATION CHAPTER

Root 2

11. (i) State with internal object is related to state with internal object by root condition.

(*a*) Roots with internal object are related to (their) associated aggregates by root condition;

(*b*) At the moment of conception, roots with internal object are related to (their) associated aggregates by root condition. (1)

(ii) State with external object is related to state with external object by root condition.

(*a*) Roots with external object to associated aggregates . . .
(*b*) At the moment of conception . . . (1)

Object 4

12. (i) State with internal object is related to state with internal object by object condition.

(One) reviews internal infinity of consciousness, reviews neither-perception-nor-non-perception, reviews internal divine-eye with internal object . . . divine-ear element . . . knowledge of supernormal power . . . knowledge of remembrance of past existences . . . knowledge of rebirths according to one's kamma, reviews knowledge of future existences. The Noble persons review the eradicated defilements with internal object, review the uneradicated defilements, know the defilements addicted to before.

(One) practises insight into the impermanance . . . of internal aggregates with internal object; enjoys and delights in (those aggregates). Taking them as object, arises lust with internal object . . . arises grief. Internal aggregates with internal object are related to knowledge of remembrance of past existences, knowledge of rebirths according to one's kamma, knowledge of future existences, advertence by object condition. (1)

(ii) State with internal object is related to state with external object by object condition.

(One) reviews external infinity of consciousness, reviews neither-perception-nor-non-perception, reviews external divine-eye with internal object . . . divine-ear element . . . knowledge of supernormal power . . . knowledge of remembrance of past existences . . . knowledge of rebirths according to one's kamma, reviews knowledge of future existences.

(One) practises insight into the impermanence, suffering and impersonality of external aggregates with internal object . . . By the knowledge of penetration into others' minds, (one) knows the other being's external mind with internal object. External aggregates with internal object are related to knowledge of penetration into others' minds, knowledge of remembrance of past existences, knowledge of rebirths according to one's kamma, knowledge of future existences, advertence by object condition. (2)

13. (iii) State with external object is related to state with external object by object condition.

(One) reviews external divine-eye with external object, reviews divine-ear element . . . knowledge of supernormal power . . . knowledge of penetration into others' minds . . . knowledge of remembrance of past existences . . . knowledge of rebirths according to one's kamma, reviews knowledge of future existences.

(One) practises insight into the impermanence, suffering and impersonality of external aggregates with external object . . . By the knowledge of penetration into others' minds, (one) knows the other being's external mind with external object. External aggregates with external object are related to knowledge of penetration into others' minds, knowledge of remembrance of past existences, knowledge of rebirths according to one's kamma, knowledge of future existences, advertence by object condition. (1)

(iv) State with external object is related to state with internal object by object condition.

After having offered an offering, having undertaken precepts, having fulfilled the duty of observance, (one) reviews it. (One) reviews (such acts) formerly well done. Having emerged from jhāna, (one) reviews the jhāna. The Noble persons, having emerged from Path, review the Path, review the Fruition, review the eradicated defilements with external object, review the uneradicated defilements, know the defilements addicted to before.

(One) reviews internal divine-eye with external object . . . divine-ear element . . . knowledge of supernormal power . . . knowledge of penetration into others' minds . . . knowledge of remembrance of past existences . . . knowledge of rebirths according to one's kamma . . . knowledge of future existences.

(One) practises insight into the impermanence . . . of internal aggregates with external object; enjoys and delights in (those aggregates). Taking them as object, arises lust with internal object . . . arises grief. Internal aggregates with external object are related to knowledge of supernormal power, knowledge of remembrance of past existences, knowledge of rebirths according to one's kamma, knowledge of future existences, advertence by object condition. (2)

Predominance 3

14. (i) State with internal object is related to state with internal object by predominance condition.

(It is of two kinds, namely:) (*a*) object-predominance, (*b*) conascence-predominance.

(*a*) *Object-predominance:* (One) esteems and reviews internal infinity of consciousness, esteems and reviews neither-perception-nor-non-perception, esteems and . . . internal divine-eye with internal object . . . divine-ear element . . . knowledge of supernormal power . . . knowledge of remembrance of past existences . . . knowledge of rebirths according to one's kamma, esteems and . . . knowledge of future existences. (One) esteems, enjoys and delights in internal aggregates with internal object. Taking them as estimable object, arises lust with internal object, arise wrong views.

(*b*) *Conascence-predominance:* Predominance with internal object is related to (its) associated aggregates by predominance condition. (1)

15. (ii) State with external object is related to state with external object by predominance condition.

Conascence-predominance: Predominance with external object is related to (its) associated aggregates by predominance condition. (1)

(iii) State with external object is related to state with internal object by predominance condition.

Object-predominance: After having offered an offering, having undertaken precepts, having fulfilled the duty of observance, (one) esteems and reviews it. (One) esteems and reviews (such acts) formerly well done. Having emerged from jhāna . . . The Noble persons, having emerged from Path . . . the Path, esteem and review the Fruition.

(One) esteems and . . . internal divine-eye with external object . . . divine-ear element . . . knowledge of supernormal power . . . knowledge of penetration into others' minds . . . knowledge of remembrance of past existences . . . knowledge of rebirths according to one's kamma, esteems and reviews knowledge of future existences. (One) esteems, enjoys and delights in internal aggregates with external object. Taking them as estimable object, arises lust with internal object, arise wrong views. (2)

Proximity 4

16. (i) State with internal object is related to state with internal object by proximity condition.

Preceding aggregates with internal object are related to subsequent aggregates with internal object by proximity condition. (1)

(ii) State with internal object is related to state with external object by proximity condition.

Death-consciousness with internal object is related to rebirth-consciousness with external object by proximity condition. Life-continuum with internal object is related to advertence with external object by proximity condition. Aggregates with internal object are related to emergence with external object by proximity condition.

Adaptation with internal object to change-of-lineage; adaptation to purification; adaptation to the attainment of Fruition; for one emerging from the attainment of Extinction, neither-perception-nor-non-perception is related to the attainment of Fruition by proximity condition. (2)

17. (iii) State with external object is related to state with external object by proximity condition.

Preceding aggregates with external object are related to subsequent aggregates with external object by proximity condition. Adaptation with external object to change-of-lineage; adaptation to purification; change-of-lineage to Path; purification to Path; Path to Fruition; Fruition to Fruition; adaptation is related to the attainment of Fruition by proximity condition. (1)

(iv) State with external object is related to state with internal object by proximity condition.

Death-consciousness with external object is related to rebirth-consciousness with internal object by proximity condition. Life-continuum with external object is related to advertence with internal object by proximity condition. Aggregates with external object are related to emergence with internal object by proximity condition. (2)

Contiguity, etc.

18. State with internal object is related to state with internal object by contiguity condition . . . by conascence condition . . . by mutuality condition . . . by dependence condition . . .

Strong-dependence 4

19. (i) State with internal object is related to state with internal object by strong-dependence condition.

(It is of three kinds, namely:) (*a*) object-strong-dependence, (*b*) proximity-strong-dependence, (*c*) natural strong-dependence . . .

(*c*) *Natural strong-dependence:* Contemplation of impermanence, suffering and impersonality of internal object is related to contemplation of impermanence, suffering and impersonality of internal object by strong-dependence condition. (1)

(ii) State with internal object is related to state with external object by strong-dependence condition.

(It is of two kinds, namely:) (*a*) proximity-strong-dependence, (*b*) natural strong-dependence . . .

(*b*) *Natural strong-dependence:* Contemplation of impermanence, suffering and impersonality of internal object is related to contemplation of impermanence, suffering and impersonality of external object by strong-dependence condition. (2)

20. (iii) State with external object is related to state with external object by strong-dependence condition.

(It is of two kinds, namely:) (*a*) proximity-strong-dependence, (*b*) natural strong-dependence . . .

(*b*) *Natural strong-dependence:* Contemplation of impermanence, suffering and impersonality of external object is related to contemplation of impermanence, suffering and impersonality of external object by strong-dependence condition. (1)

(iv) State with external object is related to state with internal object by strong-dependence condition.

(It is of three kinds, namely:) (*a*) object-strong-dependence, (*b*) proximity-strong-dependence, (*c*) natural strong-dependence . . .

(*c*) *Natural strong-dependence:* Contemplation of impermanence, suffering and impersonality of external object is related to contemplation of impermanence, suffering and impersonality of internal object by strong-dependence condition. (2)

Repetition 3

21. (i) State with internal object is related to state with internal object by repetition condition.

Preceding aggregates with internal object are related to subsequent aggregates with internal object by repetition condition. (1)

(ii) State with internal object is related to state with external object by repetition condition.

Adaptation with internal object to change-of-lineage; adaptation is related to purification by repetition condition. (2)

(iii) State with external object is related to state with external object by repetition condition.

Preceding aggregates with external object are related to subsequent aggregates with external object by repetition condition. Adaptation with external object to change-of-lineage; adaptation to purification; change-of-lineage to Path; purification is related to Path by repetition condition. (1)

Kamma 4

22. (i) State with internal object is related to state with internal object by kamma condition.

(It is of two kinds, namely:) (*a*) conascence(-kamma), (*b*) asynchronous (kamma).

(*a*) (1) Conascent volition with internal object is related to (its) associated aggregates by kamma condition.

(2) At the moment of conception . . .

(*b*) Asynchronous volition with internal object is related to (its) resultant aggregates with internal object by kamma condition. (1)

(ii) State with internal object is related to state with external object by kamma condition.

Asynchronous volition with internal object is related to (its) resultant aggregates with external object by kamma condition. (2)

(iii) State with external object is related to state with external object by kamma condition.

(It is of two kinds, namely:) (*a*) conascence(-kamma), (*b*) asynchronous (kamma).

(*a*) (1) Conascent volition with external object is related to (its) associated aggregates by kamma condition;

(2) At the moment of conception . . .

(*b*) Asynchronous volition with external object is related to (its) resultant aggregates with external object by kamma condition. (1)

(iv) State with external object is related to state with internal object by kamma condition.

Asynchronous volition with external object is related to (its) resultant aggregates with internal object by kamma condition. (2)

Resultant, etc.

23. State with internal object is related to state with internal object by resultant condition . . . by nutriment condition . . . by faculty condition . . . by jhāna condition . . . by path condition . . . by association

condition . . . by presence condition . . . by absence condition . . . by disappearance condition . . . by non-disappearance condition . . .

1. CONDITIONS: POSITIVE (ii) ENUMERATION CHAPTER

By Ones

24. With root 2, object 4, predominance 3, proximity 4, contiguity 4, conascence 2, mutuality 2, dependence 2, strong-dependence 4, repetition 3, kamma 4, resultant 2 (all 2) . . . association 2, presence 2, absence 4, disappearance 4, non-disappearance 2. (Enumerate thus.)

End of Positive

2. SELECTION OF THE CONDITIONS FOR NEGATIVE 4

25. (i) State with internal object is related to state with internal object by object condition, conascence condition, strong-dependence condition, kamma condition. (1)

(ii) State with internal object is related to state with external object by object condition, strong-dependence condition, kamma condition. (2)

(iii) State with external object is related to state with external object by object condition, conascence condition, strong-dependence condition, kamma condition. (1)

(iv) State with external object is related to state with internal object by object condition, strong-dependence condition, kamma condition. (2)

2. CONDITIONS: NEGATIVE (ii) ENUMERATION CHAPTER

(By Ones)

26. With not-root 4, not-object 4, not-predominance 4, not-proximity 4. (Abbreviated. All 4.) . . . not-prenascence, not-postnascence, not-repetition . . . not-dissociation 4 . . . not-non-disappearance 4. (Enumerate thus.)

End of Negative

3. CONDITIONS: POSITIVE-NEGATIVE

(Root By Twos)

27. With root condition, not-object 2, not-predominance 2, not-proximity, not-contiguity, not-strong-dependence, not-repetition, not-kamma . . . not-absence, not-disappearance 2. (All 2.) (Enumerate thus.)

End of Positive-Negative

4. CONDITIONS: NEGATIVE-POSITIVE

(Not-root By Twos)

28. With not-root condition, object 4, predominance 3, proximity 4, contiguity 4, conascence, mutuality, dependence 2, strong-dependence 4, repetition 3, kamma 4, resultant 2 . . . association 2, presence 2, absence 4, disappearance 4, non-disappearance 2. (Enumerate thus.)

End of Negative-Positive

End of "INVESTIGATION" CHAPTER

END OF INTERNAL OBJECT TRIPLET

22. VISIBLE AND IMPINGING TRIPLET[1]

I. "DEPENDENT" CHAPTER

1. CONDITIONS: POSITIVE (i) CLASSIFICATION CHAPTER

Root 21

1. (i) Dependent on state (which is) invisible but impinging (anidassana-sappaṭigha), arises invisible but impinging state by root condition.

Dependent on one invisible but impinging great primary, arise two great primaries; dependent on two great primaries, arises one great primary; dependent on invisible but impinging great primaries, arises mind-produced and kamma-produced invisible but impinging derived matter; dependent on tangible object-base, arises eye-base . . . taste-base . . . (1)

(ii) Dependent on invisible but impinging state, arises both visible and impinging (sanidassana-sappaṭigha) state by root condition.

Dependent on invisible but impinging great primaries, arises mind-

[1] This comprises (1) States both visible and impinging, (2) States invisible but impinging, (3) States not visible and not impinging.

produced and kamma-produced derived matter both visible and impinging; dependent on tangible object-base, arises visible object-base. (2)

(iii) Dependent on invisible but impinging state, arises not visible and not impinging (anidassana-appaṭigha) state by root condition.

Dependent on invisible but impinging great primaries, arise mind-produced and kamma-produced not visible and not impinging derived matter; dependent on tangible object-base, arises cohesion element, femininity-faculty . . . edible food. (3)

(iv) Dependent on invisible but impinging state, arise both visible and impinging and not visible and not impinging states by root condition.

Dependent on invisible but impinging great primaries, arise mind-produced and kamma-produced derived matter both visible and impinging and not visible and not impinging; dependent on tangible object-base, arises visible object-base, cohesion element, femininity-faculty . . . edible food. (4)

(v) Dependent on invisible but impinging state, arise invisible but impinging and not visible and not impinging states by root condition.

Dependent on invisible but impinging great primary, arise two great primaries and cohesion element; dependent on two great primaries, arise one great primary and cohesion element; dependent on invisible but impinging great primaries, arise mind-produced and kamma-produced derived matter invisible but impinging and not visible and not impinging; dependent on tangible object-base, arises eye-base . . . taste-base, cohesion element, femininity-faculty . . . edible food. (5)

(vi) Dependent on invisible but impinging state, arise both visible and impinging and invisible but impinging states by root condition.

Dependent on invisible but impinging great primaries, arise mind-produced and kamma-produced derived matter both visible and impinging and invisible but impinging; dependent on tangible object-base, arises visible object-base, eye-base . . . taste-base. (6)

(vii) Dependent on invisible but impinging state, arise both visible and impinging, invisible but impinging and not visible and not impinging states by root condition.

Dependent on invisible but impinging great primaries, arise mind-produced and kamma-produced derived matter both visible and impinging, invisible but impinging and not visible and not impinging; dependent on tangible object-base, arises visible object-base, eye-base . . . taste-base, cohesion element, femininity-faculty . . . edible food. (7)

2. (viii) Dependent on not visible and not impinging state, arises not visible and not impinging state by root condition.

(*a*) Dependent on one not visible and not impinging aggregate, arise three aggregates and mind-produced matter not visible and not impinging . . . dependent on two aggregates, arise two aggregates and mind-produced matter not visible and not impinging;

(*b*) At the moment of conception, dependent on one not visible and not impinging aggregate, arise three aggregates and kamma-produced matter not visible and not impinging . . . two aggregates . . . dependent on aggregates, arises (heart-)base; dependent on (heart-)base, arise aggregates;

(*c*) Dependent on cohesion element, arise mind-produced and kamma-produced not visible and not impinging derived matter; dependent on cohesion element, arises femininity-faculty . . . edible food. (1)

(ix) Dependent on not visible and not impinging state, arises both visible and impinging state by root condition.

(*a*) Dependent on not visible and not impinging aggregates, arises mind-produced both visible and impinging matter;

(*b*) At the moment of conception, dependent on not visible and not impinging aggregates, arises kamma-produced both visible and impinging matter;

(*c*) Dependent on cohesion element, arise mind-produced and kamma-produced both visible and impinging derived matter; dependent on cohesion element, arises visible object-base. (2)

(x) Dependent on not visible and not impinging state, arises invisible but impinging state by root condition.

(*a*) Dependent on not visible and not impinging aggregates, arises mind-produced invisible but impinging matter;

(*b*) At the moment of conception, dependent on not visible and not impinging aggregates, arises kamma-produced invisible but impinging matter;

(*c*) Dependent on cohesion element, arise mind-produced and kamma-produced invisible but impinging derived matter; dependent on cohesion element, arises eye-base . . . taste-base. (3)

(xi) Dependent on not visible and not impinging state, arise both visible and impinging and not visible and not impinging states by root condition.

(*a*) Dependent on one not visible and not impinging aggregate, arise three aggregates and mind-produced matter both visible and impinging and not visible and not impinging . . . two aggregates . . .

(*b*) At the moment of conception, dependent on one not visible and not impinging aggregate, arise three aggregates and kamma-produced matter both visible and impinging and not visible and not impinging . . . two aggregates . . .

(*c*) Dependent on cohesion element, arise mind-produced and kamma-produced derived matter both visible and impinging and not visible and not impinging; dependent on cohesion element, arises visible object-base, femininity-faculty . . . edible food. (4)

(xii) Dependent on not visible and not impinging state, arise states invisible but impinging and not visible and not impinging by root condition.

(*a*) Dependent on one not visible and not impinging aggregate, arise three aggregates and mind-produced matter invisible but impinging and not visible and not impinging . . . two aggregates . . .

(*b*) At the moment of conception, dependent on one not visible and not impinging aggregate, arise three aggregates and kamma-produced matter invisible but impinging and not visible and not impinging . . . two aggregates . . .

(*c*) Dependent on cohesion element, arise mind-produced and kamma-produced derived matter invisible but impinging and not visible and not impinging; dependent on cohesion element, arises eye-base . . . taste-base, femininity-faculty . . . edible food. (5)

(xiii) Dependent on not visible and not impinging state, arise states both visible and impinging and invisible but impinging by root condition.

(*a*) Dependent on not visible and not impinging aggregates, arises mind-produced matter both visible and impinging and invisible but impinging;

(*b*) At the moment of conception, dependent on not visible and not impinging aggregates, arises kamma-produced matter both visible and impinging and invisible but impinging;

(*c*) Dependent on cohesion element, arise mind-produced and kamma-produced derived matter both visible and impinging and invisible but impinging; dependent on cohesion element, arises visible object-base, eye-base . . . taste-base. (6)

(xiv) Dependent on not visible and not impinging state, arise states both visible and impinging, invisible but impinging and not visible and not impinging by root condition.

(*a*) Dependent on one not visible and not impinging aggregate, arise three aggregates and mind-produced matter both visible and impinging, invisible but impinging and not visible and not impinging . . . two aggregates . . .

(*b*) At the moment of conception, dependent on one not visible and not impinging aggregate, arise three aggregates and kamma-produced matter both visible and impinging, invisible but impinging and not visible and not impinging . . . two aggregates . . .

(*c*) Dependent on cohesion element, arise mind-produced and kamma-produced derived matter both visible and impinging, invisible but impinging and not visible and not impinging; dependent on cohesion element, arises visible object-base, eye-base . . . taste-base, femininity-faculty . . . edible food. (7)

3. (xv) Dependent on invisible but impinging state and not visible and not impinging state, arises both visible and impinging state by root condition.

(*a*) Dependent on not visible and not impinging aggregates and great primaries, arises both visible and impinging mind-produced matter;

(*b*) At the moment of conception, dependent on not visible and not impinging aggregates and great primaries, arises both visible and impinging kamma-produced matter;

(*c*) Dependent on invisible but impinging great primaries and cohesion element, arise mind-produced and kamma-produced both visible and impinging derived matter; dependent on tangible object-base and cohesion element, arises visible object-base. (1)

(xvi) Dependent on invisible but impinging and not visible and not impinging state, arises state invisible but impinging by root condition.

(*a*) Dependent on not visible and not impinging aggregates and great primaries, arises invisible but impinging mind-produced matter;

(*b*) At the moment of conception, dependent on not visible and not impinging aggregates and great primaries, arises invisible but impinging kamma-produced matter;

(*c*) Dependent on one invisible but impinging great primary and cohesion element, arise two great primaries; dependent on two great primaries and cohesion element, arises one great primary; dependent on invisible but impinging great primaries and cohesion element, arise mind-produced and kamma-produced invisible but impinging derived matter; dependent on tangible object-base and cohesion element, arises eye-base . . . taste-base. (2)

(xvii) Dependent on invisible but impinging and not visible and not impinging state, arises not visible and not impinging state by root condition.

(*a*) Dependent on not visible and not impinging aggregates and great primaries, arises not visible and not impinging mind-produced matter;

(*b*) At the moment of conception, dependent on not visible and not impinging aggregates and great primaries, arises not visible and not impinging kamma-produced matter;

(*c*) Dependent on invisible but impinging great primaries and cohesion element, arise mind-produced and kamma-produced not visible and not impinging derived matter; dependent on tangible object-base and cohesion element, arises femininity-faculty . . . edible food. (3)

(xviii) Dependent on invisible but impinging and not visible and not impinging state, arise both visible and impinging and not visible and not impinging states by root condition.

(*a*) Dependent on not visible and not impinging aggregates and great primaries, arises both visible and impinging and not visible and not impinging mind-produced matter;

(*b*) At the moment of conception, dependent on not visible and not impinging aggregates and great primaries, arises both visible and impinging and not visible and not impinging kamma-produced matter;

(*c*) Dependent on invisible but impinging great primaries and cohesion element, arise mind-produced and kamma-produced derived matter both visible and impinging and not visible and not impinging; dependent on tangible object-base and cohesion element, arises visible object-base, femininity-faculty . . . edible food. (4)

(xix) Dependent on invisible but impinging and not visible and not impinging state, arise invisible but impinging and not visible and not impinging states by root condition.

(*a*) Dependent on not visible and not impinging aggregates and great primaries, arises invisible but impinging and not visible and not impinging mind-produced matter;

(*b*) At the moment of conception, dependent on not visible and not impinging aggregates and great primaries, arises invisible but impinging and not visible and not impinging kamma-produced matter;

(*c*) Dependent on invisible but impinging great primaries and cohesion element, arise mind-produced and kamma-produced derived matter invisible but impinging and not visible and not impinging; dependent on tangible object-base and cohesion element, arises eye-base . . . taste-base, femininity-faculty . . . edible food. (5)

(xx) Dependent on invisible but impinging and not visible and not impinging state, arise both visible and impinging and invisible but impinging states by root condition.

(*a*) Dependent on not visible and not impinging aggregates and great primaries, arises both visible and impinging and invisible but impinging mind-produced matter;

(*b*) At the moment of conception, dependent on not visible and not impinging aggregates and great primaries, arises both visible and impinging and invisible but impinging kamma-produced matter;

(*c*), Dependent on invisible but impinging great primaries and cohesion element, arise mind-produced and kamma-produced derived matter both visible and impinging and invisible but impinging; dependent on tangible object-base and cohesion element, arises visible object-base, eye-base . . . taste-base. (6)

(xxi) Dependent on invisible but impinging and not visible and not impinging state, arise both visible and impinging, invisible but impinging and not visible and not impinging states by root condition.

(*a*) Dependent on not visible and not impinging aggregates and great primaries, arises both visible and impinging, invisible but impinging and not visible and not impinging mind-produced matter;

(*b*) At the moment of conception, dependent on not visible and not impinging aggregates and great primaries, arises kamma-produced matter both visible and impinging, invisible but impinging and not visible and not impinging;

(*c*) Dependent on invisible but impinging great primaries and cohesion element, arise mind-produced and kamma-produced derived matter both visible and impinging, invisible but impinging and not visible and not impinging; dependent on tangible object-base and cohesion element, arises visible object-base, eye-base . . . taste-base, femininity-faculty . . . edible food. (7)

Object 1

4. (i) Dependent on not visible and not impinging state, arises not visible and not impinging state by object condition.

(*a*) Dependent on one not visible and not impinging aggregate, arise three aggregates . . . two aggregates . . .

(*b*) At the moment of conception, dependent on one not visible and not impinging aggregate, arise three aggregates . . . two aggregates . . . dependent on (heart-)base, arise aggregates. (1)

Predominance 21

5. (i)-(vii) Dependent on invisible but impinging state, arises invisible but impinging state by predominance condition.

Dependent on one invisible but impinging great primary, arise two great primaries; dependent on two great primaries, arises one great primary; dependent on invisible but impinging great primaries, arises mind-produced derived matter. (1)

(Classify seven questions in this way with "invisible but impinging" as reference. No final section.)

6. (viii)-(xiv) Dependent on not visible and not impinging state, arises not visible and not impinging state by predominance condition.

(*a*) Dependent on one not visible and not impinging aggregate, arise three aggregates and mind-produced matter not visible and not impinging . . . two aggregates . . .

(*b*) Dependent on cohesion element, arises mind-produced not visible and not impinging derived matter.

(Classify seven questions in this way with "not visible and not impinging" as reference. No last section.)

7. (xv)-(xxi) Dependent on invisible but impinging and not visible and not impinging state, arises both visible and impinging state by predominance condition.

(*a*) Dependent on not visible and not impinging aggregates and great primaries, arises both visible and impinging mind-produced matter;

(*b*) Dependent on invisible but impinging great primaries and cohesion element, arises mind-produced both visible and impinging derived matter.

(Classify seven questions also in this way.)

Proximity, Contiguity 1

8. Dependent on not visible and not impinging state, arises not visible and not impinging state by proximity condition . . . by contiguity condition . . . (The same as object.)

Conascence 21

9. (i)-(vii) Dependent on invisible but impinging state, arises invisible but impinging state by conascence condition.

(*a*) Dependent on one invisible but impinging great primary, arise two great primaries; dependent on two great primaries, arises one great primary; dependent on invisible but impinging great primaries, arise mind-produced and kamma-produced invisible but impinging derived matter;

(*b*) Dependent on tangible object-base, arises eye-base . . . taste-base;

(*c*) External . . . nutriment-produced . . . temperature-produced . . . dependent on one great primary of non-percipient beings, arise two great primaries . . .

(Classify seven questions in this way with "invisible but impinging" as reference.)

10. (viii)-(xiv) Dependent on not visible and not impinging state, arises not visible and not impinging state by conascence condition.

(*a*) Dependent on one not visible and not impinging aggregate, arise three aggregates and not visible and not impinging mind-produced matter . . . two aggregates . . .

(*b*) At the moment of conception, dependent on one not visible and not impinging aggregate, arise three aggregates and kamma-produced matter not visible and not impinging . . . two aggregates . . . dependent on aggregates, arises (heart-)base; dependent on (heart-)base, arise aggregates;

(*c*) Dependent on cohesion element, arise mind-produced and kamma-produced not visible and not impinging derived matter; dependent on cohesion element, arises femininity-faculty . . . edible food;

(*d*) External . . . nutriment-produced . . . temperature-produced . . . dependent on cohesion element of non-percipient beings, arises kamma-produced not visible and not impinging derived matter.

(Classify seven questions in this way with "not visible and not impinging" as reference.)

11. (xv)-(xxi) Dependent on invisible but impinging and not visible and not impinging state, arises both visible and impinging state by conascence condition.

(*a*) Dependent on not visible and not impinging aggregates and great primaries, arises mind-produced both visible and impinging matter;

(*b*) At the moment of conception, dependent on not visible and not impinging aggregates and great primaries, arises kamma-produced both visible and impinging matter;

(*c*) Dependent on invisible but impinging great primaries and cohesion element, arise mind-produced and kamma-produced both visible and impinging derived matter; dependent on tangible object-base and cohesion element, arises visible object-base;

(*d*) External . . . nutriment-produced . . . temperature-produced . . . dependent on invisible but impinging great primaries of non-percipient beings and cohesion element, arises kamma-produced both visible and impinging derived matter.

(Classify seven questions in this way.)

Mutuality 6

12. (i) Dependent on invisible but impinging state, arises invisible but impinging state by mutuality condition.

Dependent on one invisible but impinging great primary, arise two great primaries; dependent on two great primaries, arises one great primary. (1)

(ii) Dependent on invisible but impinging state, arises not visible and not impinging state by mutuality condition.

Dependent on invisible but impinging great primaries, arises cohesion element. (2)

(iii) Dependent on invisible but impinging state, arise invisible but impinging and not visible and not impinging states by mutuality condition.

(*a*) Dependent on one invisible but impinging great primary, arise two great primaries and cohesion element; dependent on two great primaries, arise one great primary and cohesion element;

(*b*) External . . . (3)

13. (iv) Dependent on not visible and not impinging state, arises not visible and not impinging state by mutuality condition.

(*a*) Dependent on one not visible and not impinging aggregate, arise three aggregates . . . two aggregates . . .

(*b*) At the moment of conception, dependent on one not visible and not impinging aggregate, arise three aggregates and (heart-)base . . . two aggregates . . . dependent on aggregates, arises (heart-)base; dependent on (heart-)base, arise aggregates. (1)

(v) Dependent on not visible and not impinging state, arises invisible but impinging state by mutuality condition.

(*a*) Dependent on cohesion element, arise invisible but impinging great primaries;

(*b*) External . . . (2)

14. (vi) Dependent on invisible but impinging and not visible and not impinging state, arises invisible but impinging state by mutuality condition.

(*a*) Dependent on one invisible but impinging great primary and cohesion element, arise two great primaries; dependent on two great primaries and cohesion element, arises one great primary;

(*b*) External . . . (1)

Dependence, etc.

15. Dependent on invisible but impinging state, arises invisible but impinging state by dependence condition . . . by strong-dependence condition . . . by prenascence condition . . . by repetition condition . . . by kamma condition . . . by resultant condition . . . by nutriment condition . . . by faculty condition . . . by jhāna condition . . . by path condition . . . by association condition . . . by dissociation condition . . . by presence condition . . . by absence condition . . . by disappearance condition . . . by non-disappearance condition . . .

1. CONDITIONS: POSITIVE (ii) ENUMERATION CHAPTER

By Ones

16. With root 21, object 1, predominance 21, proximity 1, contiguity 1, conascence 21, mutuality 6, dependence 21, strong-dependence 1, prenascence 1, repetition 1, kamma 21, resultant, nutriment 21, faculty 21, jhāna, path 21, association 1, dissociation 21, presence 21, absence 1, disappearance 1, non-disappearance 21. (Enumerate thus.)

End of Positive

2. CONDITIONS: NEGATIVE (i) CLASSIFICATION CHAPTER

Not-root 21

17. (i)-(vii) Dependent on invisible but impinging state, arises invisible but impinging state by not-root condition.

(*a*) Dependent on one invisible but impinging great primary, arise two great primaries; dependent on two great primaries, arises one great primary; dependent on invisible but impinging great primaries, arise mind-produced and kamma-produced invisible but impinging derived matter;

(*b*) Dependent on tangible object-base, arises eye-base . . . taste-base;

(*c*) External . . . nutriment-produced . . . temperature-produced . . . dependent on one invisible but impinging great primary of non-percipient beings, arise two great primaries; dependent on two great primaries, arises one great primary; dependent on great primaries . . .

(Classify seven questions also in this way with "invisible but impinging" as reference.)

18. (viii)–(xiv) Dependent on not visible and not impinging state, arises not visible and not impinging state by not-root condition.

(*a*) Dependent on one rootless not visible and not impinging aggregate, arise three aggregates and mind-produced not visible and not impinging matter . . . two aggregates . . .

(*b*) At the moment of rootless conception, dependent on one not visible and not impinging aggregate, arise three aggregates and kamma-produced not visible and not impinging matter . . . dependent on aggregates, arises (heart-)base; dependent on (heart-)base, arise aggregates;

(*c*) Dependent on cohesion element, arise mind-produced and kamma-produced not visible and not impinging derived matter; dependent on cohesion element, arises femininity-faculty . . . edible food;

(*d*) External . . . nutriment-produced . . . temperature-produced . . . dependent on cohesion element of non-percipient beings, arises kamma-produced not visible and not impinging derived matter;

(*e*) Dependent on doubt-accompanied or restlessness-accompanied aggregates, arises doubt-accompanied or restlessness-accompanied delusion.

(Classify seven questions in this way with "not visible and not impinging" as reference.)

19. (xv)–(xxi) Dependent on invisible but impinging and not visible and not impinging state, arise both visible and impinging state by not-root condition.

(*a*) Dependent on rootless not visible and not impinging aggregates and great primaries, arises mind-produced both visible and impinging matter;

(*b*) At the moment of rootless conception, dependent on not visible and not impinging aggregates and great primaries, arises kamma-produced both visible and impinging matter;

(*c*) Dependent on invisible but impinging great primaries and cohesion element, arise mind-produced and kamma-produced both visible and impinging derived matter; dependent on tangible object-base and cohesion element, arises visible object-base;

(*d*) External . . . nutriment-produced . . . temperature-produced . . . dependent on invisible but impinging great primaries of non-percipient beings and cohesion element, arises kamma-produced both visible and impinging derived matter.

(Expand seven questions in this way without confusion.)

Not-object 21

20. Dependent on invisible but impinging state, arises invisible but impinging state by not-object condition.

(*a*) Dependent on one invisible but impinging great primary, arise two great primaries; dependent on two great primaries, arises one great primary; dependent on invisible but impinging great primaries, arise mind-produced and kamma-produced invisible but impinging derived matter;

(*b*) Dependent on tangible object-base, arises eye-base . . . taste-base;

(*c*) External . . . nutriment-produced . . . temperature-produced . . . dependent on one invisible but impinging great primary of non-percipient beings, arise two great primaries; dependent on two great primaries, arises one great primary . . .

(Expand seven questions also in this way with "invisible but impinging" as reference.)

21. Dependent on not visible and not impinging state, arises not visible and not impinging state by not-object condition.

(*a*) Dependent on not visible and not impinging aggregates, arises mind-produced not visible and not impinging matter;

(*b*) At the moment of conception, dependent on not visible and not impinging aggregates, arises kamma-produced not visible and not impinging matter; dependent on aggregates, arises (heart-)base . . .

(*c*) Dependent on cohesion element, arise mind-produced and kamma-produced not visible and not impinging derived matter; dependent on cohesion element, arises femininity-faculty . . . edible food;

(*d*) External . . . nutriment-produced . . . temperature-produced . . . dependent on cohesion element of non-percipient beings, arises kamma-produced not visible and not impinging derived matter.

(Expand seven questions also in this way with "not visible and not impinging" as reference.)

22. Dependent on invisible but impinging and not visible and not impinging state, arises both visible and impinging state by not-object condition.

(*a*) Dependent on not visible and not impinging aggregates and great primaries, arises mind-produced both visible and impinging matter;

(*b*) At the moment of conception, dependent on not visible and not impinging aggregates and great primaries, arises kamma-produced both visible and impinging matter;

(*c*) Dependent on invisible but impinging great primaries and cohesion element, arise mind-produced and kamma-produced both visible and impinging derived matter; dependent on tangible object-base and cohesion element, arises visible object-base;

(*d*) External . . . nutriment-produced . . . temperature-produced . . . dependent on invisible but impinging great primaries of non-percipient beings and cohesion element, arises kamma-produced both visible and impinging derived matter.

(Classify seven questions also in this way for the combination.)

Not-predominance, etc. 21

23. Dependent on invisible but impinging state, arises invisible but impinging state by not-predominance condition. (The same as conascence.) . . . by not-proximity condition . . . by not-contiguity condition . . . by not-mutuality condition.

(*a*) Dependent on invisible but impinging great primaries, arise mind-produced and kamma-produced invisible but impinging derived matter;

(*b*) Dependent on tangible object-base, arises eye-base . . . taste-base;

(*c*) External . . . nutriment-produced . . . temperature-produced . . . dependent on great primaries of non-percipient beings, arises kamma-produced invisible but impinging derived matter.

(Classify twenty-one questions in this way.)

. . . by not-strong-dependence condition . . . by not-prenascence condition . . . by not-postnascence condition . . . by not-repetition condition . . . by not-kamma condition.

External . . . nutriment-produced . . . dependent on one temperature-produced invisible but impinging great primary, arise two great primaries; dependent on two great primaries, arises one great primary; dependent on invisible but impinging great primaries, arises invisible but impinging derived matter. (Having classified kamma, do twenty-one questions for not-kamma.)

. . . by not-resultant condition. (No conception and kamma-produced matter. Do it only for the five-aggregate planes.) . . . by not-nutriment condition.

External . . . temperature-produced . . . non-percipient beings . . . (Classify twenty-one also in this way.)

Not-faculty, etc. 21

24. Dependent on invisible but impinging state, arises invisible but impinging state by not-faculty condition.

External . . . nutriment-produced . . . temperature-produced . . . dependent on one invisible but impinging great primary . . . dependent on great primaries of non-percipient beings, arises physical life-faculty. (Abbreviated. Classify all questions.) . . . by not-jhāna condition.

External . . . nutriment-produced . . . temperature-produced . . . one great primary of non-percipient beings . . . (Abbreviated. Classify seven questions also.)

Dependent on not visible and not impinging state, arises not visible and not impinging state by not-jhāna condition.

Dependent on one five-fold consciousness-accompanied aggregate, arise three aggregates . . . two aggregates . . .

External . . . nutriment-produced . . . temperature-produced . . . dependent on cohesion element of non-percipient beings, arises kamma-produced not visible and not impinging derived matter.

(Thus classify seven questions also.)

25. Dependent on invisible but impinging and not visible and not impinging state, arises both visible and impinging state by not-jhāna condition.

External . . . nutriment-produced . . . temperature-produced . . . non-percipient beings . . . dependent on invisible but impinging great primaries and cohesion element, arises kamma-produced both visible and impinging derived matter.

(Thus classify seven questions also.)

. . . by not-path condition. (Do as for not-root. Complete. No delusion.) . . . by not-association condition . . . by not-dissociation condition. (Complete.) . . . by not-absence condition . . . by not-disappearance condition.

2. CONDITIONS: NEGATIVE (ii) ENUMERATION CHAPTER

By Ones

26. With not-root 21, not-object 21, not-predominance 21. (Abbreviated. All 21.) . . . not-absence 21, not-disappearance 21. (Enumerate thus.)

End of Negative

3. CONDITIONS: POSITIVE-NEGATIVE

Root By Twos

27. With root condition, not-object 21, not-predominance 21 . . . not-kamma 1, not-resultant 21, not-association 21, not-dissociation 1, not-absence 21, not-disappearance 21. (Enumerate thus.)

End of Positive-Negative

4. CONDITIONS: NEGATIVE-POSITIVE

Not-root By Twos

28. With not-root condition, object 1, proximity 1, contiguity 1, conascence 21 . . . jhāna 21, path 1, association 1, dissociation 21, presence 21, absence 1, disappearance 1, non-disappearance 21. (Enumerate thus.)

End of Negative-Positive

End of "DEPENDENT" CHAPTER

(The "Conascent", "Conditioned" and "Supported" Chapters are also the same as the "Dependent" Chapter. Do the "Conjoined" Chapter and the "Associated" Chapter with immateriality only.)

22. VISIBLE AND IMPINGING TRIPLET
VII. "INVESTIGATION" CHAPTER

1. CONDITIONS: POSITIVE (i) CLASSIFICATION CHAPTER

Root 7

29. (i) Not visible and not impinging state is related to not visible and not impinging state by root condition.

(*a*) Not visible and not impinging roots are related to (their) associated aggregates and mind-produced not visible and not impinging matter by root condition;

(*b*) At the moment of conception, not visible and not impinging roots are related to (their) associated aggregates and kamma-produced not visible and not impinging matter by root condition. (1)

(ii) Not visible and not impinging state is related to both visible and impinging state by root condition.

(*a*) Not visible and not impinging roots are related to mind-produced both visible and impinging matter by root condition;

(*b*) At the moment of conception . . . (2)

(Classify seven questions in this way with "not visible and not impinging" as reference.)

Object 3

30. (i) Both visible and impinging state is related to not visible and not impinging state by object condition.

(One) practises insight into the impermanence, suffering and impersonality of a visible object; enjoys and delights in (that visible object). Taking it as object, arises lust, arise wrong views, arises doubt, arises restlessness, arises grief.

By the power of divine-eye, (one} sees a visible object. Visible object-base is related to eye-consciousness by object condition. Both visible and impinging aggregates are related to knowledge of supernormal power, knowledge of remembrance of past existences, knowledge of future existences, advertence by object condition. (1)

(ii) Invisible but impinging state is related to not visible and not impinging state by object condition.

Eye . . . body . . . sound . . . smell . . . taste . . . into the impermanence . . . of tangible object . . . arises grief. By the power of divine-ear element, (one) hears a sound. Sound-base to ear-consciousness . . . tangible object-base to body-consciousness . . . Invisible but impinging aggregates are related to knowledge of supernormal power, knowledge of remembrance of past existences, knowledge of future existences, advertence by object condition. (1)

31. (iii) Not visible and not impinging state is related to not visible and not impinging state by object condition.

After having offered an offering, having undertaken precepts, having fulfilled the duty of observance, (one) reviews it. (One) reviews (such acts) formerly well done . . . jhāna . . .

The Noble persons, having emerged from Path, review the Path, review the Fruition, review Nibbāna. Nibbāna is related to change-of-lineage, purification, Path, Fruition, advertence by object condition. The Noble persons review the eradicated defilements, review the uneradicated defilements, know the defilements addicted to before.

(Heart-)base . . . femininity-faculty . . . masculinity-faculty . . . physical life-faculty . . . cohesion element . . . edible food . . . into the impermanence . . . of not visible and not impinging aggregates . . . arises grief.

By the knowledge of penetration into others' minds, (one) knows the other being's not visible and not impinging mind. Infinity of space is related to infinity of consciousness by object condition. Nothingness to neither-perception-nor-non-perception . . . Not visible and not impinging aggregates are related to knowledge of supernormal power, knowledge of penetration into others' minds, knowledge of remembrance of past existences, knowledge of rebirths according to one's kamma, knowledge of future existences, advertence by object condition. (1)

Predominance 9

32. (i) Both visible and impinging state is related to not visible and not impinging state by predominance condition.

Object-predominance: (One) esteems, enjoys and delights in visible object. Taking it as estimable object, arises lust, arise wrong views. (1)

(ii) Invisible but impinging state is related to not visible and not impinging state by predominance condition.

Object-predominance: Eye . . . body . . . sound . . . smell . . . taste . . . (One) esteems, enjoys and delights in tangible object. Taking it as estimable object, arises lust, arise wrong views. (1)

33. (iii) Not visible and not impinging state is related to not visible and not impinging state by predominance condition.

(It is of two kinds, namely:) (*a*) object-predominance, (*b*) conascence-predominance.

(*a*) *Object-predominance:* After having offered an offering, having undertaken precepts, having fulfilled the duty of observance, (one) esteems . . . it. Having emerged from jhāna . . . The Noble persons, having emerged from Path . . . having emerged from Fruition, esteem and . . . Fruition, esteem and . . . Nibbāna. Nibbāna is related to change-of-lineage, purification, Path, Fruition by predominance condition.

(Heart-)base . . . femininity-faculty . . . masculinity-faculty . . . physical life-faculty . . . cohesion element . . . edible food . . . (One) esteems, enjoys and delights in not visible and not impinging aggregates. Taking them as estimable object, arises lust, arise wrong views.

(*b*) *Conascence-predominance:* Not visible and not impinging predominance is related to (its) associated aggregates and mind-produced not visible and not impinging matter by predominance condition. (1)

(iv)–(ix) Not visible and not impinging state is related to both visible and impinging state by predominance condition.

Conascence-predominance: Not visible and not impinging predominance is related to mind-produced both visible and impinging matter by predominance condition.

(Classify seven questions also with "not visible and not impinging" as reference. Include three kinds of matter in predominance.)

Proximity 1

34. Not visible and not impinging state is related to not visible and not impinging state by proximity condition.

Preceding not visible and not impinging aggregates are related to subsequent not visible and not impinging aggregates by proximity condition. Adaptation to change-of-lineage; adaptation to purification; change-of-lineage to Path; purification to Path; Path to Fruition; Fruition to Fruition; adaptation to the attainment of Fruition; for one emerging from the attainment of Extinction, neither perception-nor-non-perception is related to the attainment of Fruition by proximity condition. (1)

Contiguity 1

35. Not visible and not impinging state is related to not visible and not impinging state by contiguity condition. (The same as proximity.)

Conascence, etc.

36. Invisible but impinging state is related to invisible but impinging state by conascence condition. (Make it thoroughly the same as in the "Dependent" Chapter. In mutuality condition it is the same as mutuality in the "Dependent" Chapter. In dependence condition it is the same as in the "Dependent" Chapter.)

Strong-dependence 3

37. (i) Both visible and impinging state is related to not visible and not impinging state by strong-dependence condition.

(It is of two kinds, namely:) (*a*) object-strong-dependence, (*b*) natural strong-dependence . . .

(*b*) *Natural strong-dependence:* Wishing for fullness of colour, (one) offers an offering, undertakes precepts . . . duty of observance. Fullness of colour is related to confidence . . . wisdom, lust . . . wish, bodily happiness, bodily pain, Path, the attainment of Fruition by strong-dependence condition. (1)

(ii) Invisible but impinging state is related to not visible and not impinging state by strong-dependence condition.

(It is of two kinds, namely:) (*a*) object-strong-dependence, (*b*) natural strong-dependence . . .

(*b*) *Natural strong-dependence:* Wishing for fullness of the eye . . . fullness of the body . . . fullness of sound . . . wishing for the fullness of tangible object, (one) offers an offering, undertakes precepts . . . duty of observance . . . temperature . . . By the strong-dependence of lodging-place, (one) offers an offering, undertakes precepts . . . duty of observance . . . jhāna . . . insight . . . Path . . . superknowledge, develops attainment, kills a living being . . . causes schism in the Saṅgha. Fullness of the eye . . . fullness of tangible object, temperature, lodging-place is related to confidence . . . wisdom, lust . . . wish, bodily happiness, bodily pain, Path, the attainment of Fruition by strong-dependence condition. (1)

38. (iii) Not visible and not impinging state is related to not visible and not impinging state by strong-dependence condition.

(It is of three kinds, namely:) (*a*) object-strong-dependence, (*b*) proximity-strong-dependence, (*c*) natural strong-dependence . . .

(*c*) *Natural strong-dependence:* By the strong-dependence of confidence, (one) offers an offering, undertakes precepts . . . duty of observance . . . jhāna . . . develops attainment; arouses conceit, adopts wrong views . . . precept . . . wisdom . . . lust . . . wish . . . bodily happiness . . . bodily pain . . . By the strong-dependence of edible food, (one) offers an offering . . . causes schism in the Saṅgha. Confidence . . . wisdom, lust . . . wish, bodily happiness, bodily pain, edible food is related to confidence . . . wisdom . . . Path, the attainment of Fruition by strong-dependence condition. (1)

Prenascence 6

39. (i) State both visible and impinging is related to state not visible and not impinging by prenascence condition.

Object-prenascence: (One) practises insight into the impermanence, suffering and impersonality of visible object; enjoys and delights in (that visible object). Taking it as object, arises lust . . . wrong views . . . doubt . . . restlessness, arises grief. By the power of divine-eye, (one) sees the visible object. Visible object-base is related to eye-consciousness by prenascence condition. (1)

(ii) Invisible but impinging state is related to not visible and not impinging state by prenascence condition.

(It is of two kinds, namely:) (*a*) object-prenascence, (*b*) base-prenascence.

(*a*) *Object-prenascence:* Eye . . . body . . . sound . . . into the impermanence . . . of tangible object . . . arises grief. By the power of divine-ear element, (one) hears a sound. Sound-base to ear-consciousness . . . tangible object-base is related to body-consciousness by prenascence condition.

(*b*) *Base-prenascence:* Eye-base to eye-consciousness . . . body-base is related to body-consciousness by prenascence condition. (1)

(iii) Not visible and not impinging state is related to not visible and not impinging state by prenascence condition.

(It is of two kinds, namely:) (*a*) object-prenascence, (*b*) base-prenascence.

(*a*) *Object-prenascence:* (Heart-)base . . . femininity-faculty . . . masculinity-faculty . . . physical life-faculty . . . cohesion element . . . into the impermanence . . . of edible food . . . arises grief.

(*b*) *Base-prenascence:* (Heart-)base is related to not visible and not impinging aggregates by prenascence condition. (1)

40. (iv) Both visible and impinging and not visible and not impinging states are related to not visible and not impinging state by prenascence condition.

Object-prenascence–base-prenascence: Visible object-base and (heart-)base are related to not visible and not impinging aggregates by prenascence condition. (1)

(v) Invisible but impinging and not visible and not impinging states are related to not visible and not impinging state by prenascence condition.

Object-prenascence–base-prenascence: Eye-base and (heart-)base . . . tangible object-base and (heart-)base are related to not visible and not impinging aggregates by prenascence condition. (1)

(vi) Both visible and impinging and invisible but impinging states are related to not visible and not impinging state by prenascence condition.

Object-prenascence–base-prenascence: Visible object-base and eye-base are related to eye-consciousness by prenascence condition. (1)

Postnascence 7

41. (i) Not visible and not impinging state is related to not visible and not impinging state by postnascence condition.

Postnascent not visible and not impinging aggregates are related to this prenascent not visible and not impinging body by postnascence condition. (1)

(ii) Not visible and not impinging state is related to both visible and impinging state by postnascence condition.

Postnascent not visible and not impinging aggregates are related to this prenascent both visible and impinging body by postnascence condition. (2)

(Thus classify for seven questions. Include 3 kinds of matter.) (7)

Repetition 1

42. (i) Not visible and not impinging state is related to not visible and not impinging state by repetition condition.

Preceding not visible and not impinging aggregates are related to subsequent not visible and not impinging aggregates by repetition condition. Adaptation to change-of-lineage; adaptation to purification; change-of-lineage to Path; purification is related to Path by repetition condition. (1)

Kamma 7

43. (i) Not visible and not impinging state is related to not visible and not impinging state by kamma condition.

(It is of two kinds, namely:) (*a*) conascence(-kamma), (*b*) asynchronous (kamma).

(*a*) (1) Conascent not visible and not impinging volition is related to (its) associated aggregates and mind-produced not visible and not impinging matter by kamma condition;

(2) At the moment of conception . . .

(*b*) Asynchronous not visible and not impinging volition is related to (its) resultant aggregates and kamma-produced not visible and not impinging matter by kamma condition. (1)

(ii) Not visible and not impinging state is related to both visible and impinging state by kamma condition.

(It is of two kinds, namely:) (*a*) conascence(-kamma), (*b*) asynchronous (kamma).

(*a*) (1) Conascent not visible and not impinging volition is related to mind-produced both visible and impinging matter by kamma condition;

(2) At the moment of conception . . .

(*b*) Asynchronous not visible and not impinging volition is related to kamma-produced both visible and impinging matter by kamma condition. (2)

[Thus classify seven questions in this way for (both) conascence and asynchronous. Include 3 kinds of matter.] (7)

Resultant 7

44. (i) Not visible and not impinging state is related to not visible and not impinging state by resultant condition.

(*a*) One resultant not visible and not impinging aggregate is related to three aggregates and mind-produced not visible and not impinging matter by resultant condition . . . two aggregates . . .

(*b*) At the moment of conception, one not visible and not impinging aggregate is related to three aggregates and kamma-produced not visible and not impinging matter by resultant condition . . . aggregates are related to (heart-)base by resultant condition. (1)

(ii) Not visible and not impinging state is related to both visible and impinging state by resultant condition.

(*a*) Resultant not visible and not impinging aggregates are related to mind-produced both visible and impinging matter by resultant condition;

(*b*) At the moment of conception, not visible and not impinging aggregates are related to kamma-produced both visible and impinging matter by resultant condition. (2)

(Thus expand seven questions for during life and conception.)

Nutriment 7

45. (i) Not visible and not impinging state is related to not visible and not impinging state by nutriment condition.

(*a*) Not visible and not impinging nutriments are related to (their) associated aggregates and mind-produced not visible and not impinging matter by nutriment condition;

(*b*) At the moment of conception, not visible and not impinging nutriments are related to (their) associated aggregates and kamma-produced not visible and not impinging matter by nutriment condition;

(*c*) Edible food is related to this not visible and not impinging body by nutriment condition. (1)

(ii) Not visible and not impinging state is related to both visible and impinging state by nutriment condition.

(*a*) Not visible and not impinging nutriments are related to mind-produced both visible and impinging matter by nutriment condition;

(*b*) At the moment of conception, not visible and not impinging nutriments are related to kamma-produced both visible and impinging matter by nutriment condition;

(*c*) Edible food is related to this both visible and impinging body by nutriment condition. (2)

[Thus classify seven questions for (both) during life and conception; include edible food in all seven also.] (7)

Faculty 9

46. (i) Invisible but impinging state is related to not visible and not impinging state by faculty condition.

Eye-faculty to eye-consciousness . . . body-faculty is related to body-consciousness by faculty condition. (1)

(ii) Not visible and not impinging state is related to not visible and not impinging state by faculty condition.

(*a*) Not visible and not impinging faculties are related to (their) associated aggregates and mind-produced not visible and not impinging matter by faculty condition;

(*b*) At the moment of conception, not visible and not impinging faculties are related to (their) associated aggregates and kamma-produced not visible and not impinging matter by faculty condition;

(*c*) Physical life-faculty is related to kamma-produced not visible and not impinging matter by faculty condition. (1)

(iii)–(viii) Not visible and not impinging state is related to both visible and impinging state by faculty condition.

(*a*) Not visible and not impinging faculties are related to mind-produced both visible and impinging matter by faculty condition;

(*b*) At the moment of conception, not visible and not impinging faculties are related to kamma-produced both visible and impinging matter by faculty condition;

(*c*) Physical life-faculty is related to kamma-produced both visible and impinging matter by faculty condition. (2)

[Thus classify seven questions for (both) during life and conception; physical life-faculty at the end.] (7)

47. (ix) Invisible but impinging and not visible and not impinging states are related to not visible and not impinging state by faculty condition.

Eye-faculty and eye-consciousness are related to eye-consciousness-accompanied aggregates by faculty condition . . . body-base and body-consciousness are related to body-consciousness-accompanied aggregates by faculty condition. (1)

Jhāna, etc.

48. Not visible and not impinging state is related to not visible and not impinging state by jhāna condition . . . by path condition . . . by association condition.

(*a*) One not visible and not impinging aggregate is related to three aggregates by association condition . . . two aggregates . . .

(*b*) At the moment of conception . . .

Dissociation 8

49. (i) Invisible but impinging state is related to not visible and not impinging state by dissociation condition.

Prenascent eye-base to eye-consciousness . . . body-base is related to body-consciousness by dissociation condition. (1)

(ii) Not visible and not impinging state is related to not visible and not impinging state by dissociation condition.

(It is of three kinds, namely:) (*a*) conascence, (*b*) prenascence, (*c*) postnascence.

(*a*) (1) Conascent not visible and not impinging aggregates are related to mind-produced not visible and not impinging matter by dissociation condition;

(2) At the moment of conception, not visible and not impinging aggregates are related to kamma-produced not visible and not impinging matter by dissociation condition; aggregates are related to (heart-)base by dissociation condition; (heart-)base is related to aggregates by dissociation condition.

(*b*) Prenascent (heart-)base is related to not visible and not impinging aggregates by dissociation condition.

(*c*) Postnascent not visible and not impinging aggregates are related to this prenascent not visible and not impinging body by dissociation condition. (1)

(iii) Not visible and not impinging state is related to both visible and impinging state by dissociation condition.

(It is of two kinds, namely:) (*a*) conascence, (*b*) postnascence.

(*a*) (1) Conascent not visible and not impinging aggregates are related to mind-produced both visible and impinging matter by dissociation condition;

(2) At the moment of conception, not visible and not impinging aggregates are related to kamma-produced both visible and impinging matter by dissociation condition.

(*b*) Postnascent not visible and not impinging aggregates are related to this prenascent both visible and impinging body by dissociation condition. (2)

(Expand the remaining five questions in this way as: conascence, postnascence.)

Presence 25

50. (i) Both visible and impinging state is related to not visible and not impinging state by presence condition.

Prenascence: . . . into the impermanence . . . of the visible object . . . arises grief. By the power of divine-eye, (one) sees a visible object. Visible object-base is related to eye-consciousness by presence condition. (1)

51. (ii) Invisible but impinging state is related to invisible but impinging state by presence condition.

(*a*) One invisible but impinging great primary is related to two great primaries by presence condition; two great primaries are related to one great primary by presence condition; invisible but impinging great primaries are related to mind-produced and kamma-produced invisible but impinging derived matter by presence condition.

(*b*) Tangible object-base to eye-base . . . taste-base by presence condition.

(*c*) External . . . nutriment-produced . . . one temperature-produced great primary is related to two great primaries by presence condition; two great primaries are related to one great primary by presence condition;

temperature-produced great primaries are related to invisible but impinging derived matter by presence condition; one invisible but impinging great primary of non-percipient beings is related to two great primaries by presence condition . . . two great primaries . . . (1)

(iii) Invisible but impinging state is related to both visible and impinging state by presence condition. (2) (The same as dependence condition in the "Dependent" Chapter.)

(iv)–(viii) Invisible but impinging state is related to not visible and not impinging state by presence condition.

(It is of two kinds, namely:) (*a*) conascence, (*b*) prenascence.

(*a*) Conascent invisible but impinging great primaries are related to mind-produced and kamma-produced not visible and not impinging derived matter by presence condition. (Expand up to non-percipient beings.)

(*b*) Prenascent eye . . . body . . . sound . . . into the impermanence . . . of tangible object . . . arises grief. Eye-base to eye-consciousness . . . tangible object-base is related to body-consciousness by presence condition. (3)

(Expand the remaining four questions. The same as conascence condition in the "Dependent" Chapter. No difference.) (7)

52. (ix)–(xv) Not visible and not impinging state is related to not visible and not impinging state by presence condition.

(It is of five kinds, namely:) (*a*) conascence, (*b*) prenascence, (*c*) postnascence, (*d*) nutriment, (*e*) faculty.

(*a*) (1) One conascent not visible and not impinging aggregate is related to three aggregates and mind-produced not visible and not impinging matter by presence condition . . . two aggregates . . .

(2) At the moment of conception . . .

(3) Cohesion element to mind-produced and kamma-produced not visible and not impinging derived matter . . . cohesion element is related to femininity-faculty . . . edible food by presence condition;

(4) External . . . nutriment-produced . . . temperature-produced . . . cohesion element of non-percipient beings is related to kamma-produced not visible and not impinging derived matter by presence condition.

(*b*) *(Object-)prenascence:* (Heart-)base . . . femininity-faculty . . . masculinity-faculty . . . physical life-faculty . . . cohesion element . . . into the impermanence . . . of edible food . . . arises grief.

(Base-)prenascence: (Heart-)base is related to not visible and

not impinging aggregates by presence condition.

(*c*) Postnascent not visible and not impinging aggregates are related to this prenascent not visible and not impinging body by presence condition.

(*d*) Edible food is related to this not visible and not impinging body by presence condition.

(*e*) Physical life-faculty is related to kamma-produced not visible and not impinging matter by presence condition.

(Classify the remaining six questions in this way. Do conascence, postnascence, nutriment and faculty.) (7)

53. (xvi) Both visible and impinging and not visible and not impinging states are related to not visible and not impinging state by presence condition.

Prenascent visible object-base and (heart-)base are related to not visible and not impinging aggregates by presence condition. (1)

(xvii) Invisible but impinging and not visible and not impinging states are related to both visible and impinging state by presence condition.

(*a*) Not visible and not impinging aggregates and great primaries are related to mind-produced both visible and impinging matter by presence condition.

(*b*) At the moment of conception . . . (Abbreviated. Include non-percipient beings also.) (1)

(xviii) Invisible but impinging and not visible and not impinging states are related to invisible but impinging state by presence condition. (Abbreviated.) (2)

54. (xix)–(xxiii) Invisible but impinging and not visible and not impinging states are related to not visible and not impinging state by presence condition.

(It is of two kinds, namely:) (*a*) conascence, (*b*) prenascence.

(*a*) Conascent not visible and not impinging aggregates and great primaries to mind-produced not visible and not impinging matter . . . (Do up to non-percipient beings.)

(*b*) Prenascent eye-base and (heart-)base . . . tangible object-base and (heart-)base are related to not visible and not impinging aggregates by presence condition. (3)

(Classify the remaining four questions.) (7)

55. (xxiv) Both visible and impinging and invisible but impinging states are related to not visible and not impinging state by presence condition.

Prenascent visible object-base and eye-base are related to eye-consciousness by presence condition. (1)

(xxv) Both visible and impinging, invisible but impinging and not visible and not impinging states are related to not visible and not impinging state by presence condition.

Conascence-prenascence: Visible object-base, eye-base and eye-consciousness are related to eye-consciousness-accompanied aggregates by presence condition. (1)

(Absence and disappearance conditions are the same as proximity. Non-disappearance condition is the same as presence.)

1. CONDITIONS: POSITIVE (ii) ENUMERATION CHAPTER

By Ones

56. With root 7, object 3, predominance 9, proximity 1, contiguity 1, conascence 21, mutuality 6, dependence 21, strong-dependence 3, prenascence 6, postnascence 7, repetition 1, kamma 7, resultant 7, nutriment 7, faculty 9, jhāna 7, path 7, association 1, dissociation 8, presence 25, absence 1, disappearance 1, non-disappearance 25.

Root

Common 11

57. With root condition and predominance (there are) 7 (answers), conascence 7, mutuality 1, dependence 7, resultant 7, faculty 7, path 7, association 1, dissociation 7, presence 7, non-disappearance 7.

Root

Ordinary Combinations 9

Without Resultant 4

58. 1. Combination of root, conascence, dependence, presence and non-disappearance (has) 7 (answers);

2. Of root, conascence, mutuality, dependence, presence and non-disappearance 1;

3. Of root, conascence, mutuality, dependence, association, presence and non-disappearance 1;

4. Of root, conascence, dependence, dissociation, presence and non-disappearance 7.

With Resultant 5

5. Combination of root, conascence, dependence, resultant, presence and non-disappearance 7;

6. Of root, conascence, mutuality, dependence, resultant, presence and non-disappearance 1;

7. Of root, conascence, mutuality, dependence, resultant, association, presence and non-disappearance 1;

8. Of root, conascence, dependence, resultant, dissociation, presence and non-disappearance 7;

9. Of root, conascence, mutuality, dependence, resultant, dissociation, presence and non-disappearance 1.

(Enumerate all the Enumeration Chapters in this way.)

End of Positive

2. SELECTION OF THE CONDITIONS FOR NEGATIVE 25

59. (i) Both visible and impinging state is related to not visible and not impinging state by object condition, strong-dependence condition, prenascence condition. (1)

(ii) Invisible but impinging state is related to invisible but impinging state by conascence condition. (1)

(iii) Invisible but impinging state is related to both visible and impinging state by conascence condition. (2)

(iv) Invisible but impinging state is related to not visible and not impinging state by object condition, conascence condition, strong-dependence condition, prenascence condition. (3)

(v) Invisible but impinging state is related to both visible and impinging and not visible and not impinging state by conascence condition. (4)

(vi) Invisible but impinging state is related to invisible but impinging and not visible and not impinging state by conascence condition. (5)

(vii) Invisible but impinging state is related to both visible and impinging and invisible but impinging state by conascence condition. (6)

(viii) Invisible but impinging state is related to both visible and impinging, invisible but impinging and not visible and not impinging state by conascence condition. (7)

60. (ix) Not visible and not impinging state is related to not visible and not impinging state by object condition, conascence condition,

strong-dependence condition, prenascence condition, postnascence condition, kamma condition, nutriment condition, faculty condition. (1)

(x) Not visible and not impinging state is related to both visible and impinging state by conascence condition, postnascence condition, kamma condition, nutriment condition, faculty condition. (2)

(xi) Not visible and not impinging state is related to invisible but impinging state by conascence condition, postnascence condition, kamma condition, nutriment condition, faculty condition. (3)

(xii) Not visible and not impinging state is related to both visible and impinging and not visible and not impinging state by conascence condition, postnascence condition, kamma condition, nutriment condition, faculty condition. (4)

(xiii) Not visible and not impinging state is related to invisible but impinging and not visible and not impinging state by conascence condition, postnascence condition, kamma condition, nutriment condition, faculty condition. (5)

(xiv) Not visible and not impinging state is related to both visible and impinging and invisible but impinging state by conascence condition, postnascence condition, kamma condition, nutriment condition, faculty condition. (6)

(xv) Not visible and not impinging state is related to both visible and impinging, invisible but impinging and not visible and not impinging state by conascence condition, postnascence condition, kamma condition, nutriment condition, faculty condition. (7)

61. (xvi) Both visible and impinging and not visible and not impinging states are related to not visible and not impinging state by prenascence. (1)

(xvii) Invisible but impinging and not visible and not impinging states are related to both visible and impinging state by conascence condition. (1)

(xviii) Invisible but impinging and not visible and not impinging states are related to invisible but impinging state by conascence condition. (2)

(xix) Invisible but impinging and not visible and not impinging states are related to not visible and not impinging state by conascence-prenascence. (3)

(xx) Invisible but impinging and not visible and not impinging states are related to both visible and impinging and not visible and not impinging state by conascence condition. (4)

(xxi) Invisible but impinging and not visible and not impinging states are related to invisible but impinging and not visible and not impinging state by conascence condition. (5)

(xxii) Invisible but impinging and not visible and not impinging states are related to both visible and impinging and invisible but impinging state by conascence condition. (6)

(xxiii) Invisible but impinging and not visible and not impinging states are related to both visible and impinging, invisible but impinging and not visible and not impinging state by conascence condition. (7)

62. (xxiv) Both visible and impinging and invisible but impinging states are related to not visible and not impinging state by prenascence. (1)

(xxv) Both visible and impinging, invisible but impinging and not visible and not impinging states are related to not visible and not impinging state by conascence condition, prenascence condition. (1)

2. CONDITIONS: NEGATIVE (ii) ENUMERATION CHAPTER

By Ones

63. With not-root 25, not-object 22, not-predominance 25, not-proximity 25, not-contiguity 25, not-conascence 12, not-mutuality 24, not-dependence 9, not-strong-dependence 25, not-prenascence 22, not-postnascence 25, not-repetition 25, not-kamma 25, not-resultant 24, not-nutriment 25, not-faculty 23, not-jhāna 25, not-path 25, not-association 24, not-dissociation 22, not-presence 9, not-absence 25, not-disappearance 25, not-non-disappearance 9.

Not-root By Twos

With not-root condition, not-object 22. (It proceeds in the same way as the first.) . . . not-non-disappearance 9.

Not-root By Threes

With not-root, not-object condition and not-predominance 22, not-proximity 22, not-contiguity 22, not-conascence 9, not-mutuality 22, not-dependence 9, not-strong-dependence 21, not-prenascence 22, not-postnascence 22 . . . not-association 22, not-dissociation 22, not-presence 9, not-absence 22, not-disappearance 22, not-non-disappearance 9. (Enumerate thus.)

End of Negative

3. CONDITIONS: POSITIVE-NEGATIVE

Root By Twos

64. With root condition, not-object 7, not-predominance 7, not-proximity 7, not-contiguity 7, not-mutuality 7, not-strong-dependence 7, not-prenascence 7, not-postnascence 7 . . . not-association 7, not-dissociation 1, not-absence 7, not-disappearance 7.

Root

Ordinary Combinations

65. Combinations of root, conascence, dependence, presence and non-disappearance conditions, not-object (condition) 7 . . . not-proximity 7, not-contiguity 7, not-mutuality 7. (Also abbreviated here.) . . . not-association 7, not-dissociation 1, not-absence 7, not-disappearance 7.

Of root, conascence, mutuality, dependence, presence and non-disappearance conditions, not-object 1. (All 1.) . . . not-disappearance 1. (Enumerate thus.)

End of Positive-Negative

4. CONDITIONS: NEGATIVE-POSITIVE

Not-root By Twos

66. With not-root condition, object 3, predominance 9, proximity 1, contiguity 1, conascence 21, mutuality 6, dependence 21, strong-dependence 3, prenascence 6, postnascence 7, repetition 1, kamma 7, resultant 7, nutriment 7, faculty 9, jhāna 7, path 7, association 1, dissociation 8, presence 25, absence 1, disappearance 1, non-disappearance 25. (Enumerate thus.)

End of Negative-Positive

End of "INVESTIGATION" CHAPTER

END OF VISIBLE AND IMPINGING TRIPLET

END OF TRIPLET PAṬṬHĀNA, STATES: POSITIVE

INDEX OF FIRST OCCURRENCES

PALI-ENGLISH

This Glossary includes Pali words and phrases of Paṭṭhāna Vols. I & II. Many of these words and phrases recur frequently throughout these texts. Therefore, only the first reference—by volume and page of Conditional Relations—is given for each of them. The Pali and English names of the twenty-four conditions are given in the Chapter on Enumeration of the Conditions (C.R. I, p. 1).

Kāmesu micchācāra: unlawful intercourse with the other sex I,161
Kāya: body I,2
Kāya-viññāṇa-dhātu: body-consciousness element I,2
Kāya-viññāṇa-sahagata: accompanied by body-consciousness I,319
Kāyāyatana: body-base I,6
Kāyika: bodily I,160
Kāyika-dukkha: bodily pain I,160
Kāyika-sukha: bodily happiness I,160
Kāy-indriya: body-faculty I,9
Kiñcikāle: sometimes I,5
Kiriya: functional I,8
Kiriya-mano-viññāṇa-dhātu: functional mind-consciousness element I,339
Kiriya-samāpatti: functional attainment I,164
Kiriyābyākatā: functional indeterminate I,8
Kiliṭṭha: corrupt I,502
Kilesa: defilement; corruption I,144
Kusala: faultless I,3
Kusala-citta-samaṅgissa: faultless mind of the other being I,142
Kusala-pada: faultless section I,13
Kusalattika: faultless triplet I,22
Kusalākusala-kamma: faultless and faulty kamma I,8
Kusalākusala-pada: faultless and faulty section I,15
Kusalābyākata: faultless and indeterminate I,14
Kusalābyākata-pada: faultless and indeterminate section I,15
Kusalākusalābyākata: faultless, faulty and indeterminate I,15
Kusalākusalābyākata-pada: faultless, faulty and indeterminate section I,15
Kusale niruddhe: when faultless (state) has ceased I,143
Kesañci: some I,6
Kosalla: knowledge; proficiency I,159

Khandha: aggregate I,22
Khandhe paṭicca vatthu: dependent on aggregates, (arises) (heart-)base I,23

Gacchati: goes to (other men's wives) I,161
Gacchantena: to be taken II, 39
Gaṇanā: numbers (of answers) I,35
Gaṇetabba: enumeration should be done I,38
Gaṇhāti: adopts I,159
Gandha: smell; odour I,2
Gandhāyatana: odour-base I,2
Gamana: proceed II, 163
Gambhīra: profound I,18
Garu: esteemed I,3
Garuṁ katvā: taking as estimable object I,3
Gaheta: taken II, 471
Gāma: village I,161
Gāmaghāta: one who plunders villages I,161
Gāmaghātaṁ karoti: plunders villages I,161
Gotrabhu: change-of-lineage I,142
Gotrabhuṁ paccavekkhati: reviews change-of-lineage I,142

Ghaṭanā: combinations I,180
Ghāna: nose I,2
Ghāna-viññāṇa-dhātu: nose-consciousness element I,2
Ghānāyatana: nose-base I,6
Ghān-indriya: nose-faculty I,9

Cakka: cycle I,161
Cakkaṁ kātabbaṁ: perform the cycle I,162
Cakkaṁ bandhitabbaṁ: bind the cycle I,161
Cakkhāyatana: eye-base I,6
Cakkhu: eye I,2
Cakkhu-ndriya: eye-faculty I,9
Cakkhu-viññāṇa-dhātu: eye-consciousness element I,2
Cakkhu-viññāṇa-sahagato eko khandho: one eye-consciousness-accompanied aggregate I,410
Catukka: by fours I,49
Catuttiṁsa: thirty-four II, 145
Catuttha-jhāna: fourth jhāna I,158
Catumūlaka: "by fours" as reference I,17
Catu-viññāṇa-sahagata: four-fold consciousness-accompanied I,323
Catuvīsaka: by twenty-four I,360
Catuvīsati: twenty-four I,501
Cattāri: four I,97

Ye ye dhammā uppajjanti: these states arise I,2
Yeva: only II, 47; just II, 141
Yeva gamanaṁ: proceeds in the same way II, 515

Rasa: taste I,145
Rasāyatana: taste-base I,2
Rāga: lust I,142
Rāgo uppajjati: arises lust I,142
Ruhira: blood I,161
Ruhiruppāda-kamma: wounding a Buddha I,161
Rūpa: matter, materiality I,6; visible object I,145
Rūpaṁ passati: sees the visible object I,145
Rūpaṁ yeva: materiality only II, 50
Rūpa-jīvit-indriya: physical life-faculty I,9
Rūpāyatana: visible object-base I,2
Rūpino dhammā: material states I,5

Labbhati: obtained I,341
Likhitā: given II, 289
Lohita: blood I,161
Lohitaṁ uppādeti: draws blood I,161

Vattanti: arise I,6
Vatthu: base I,23
Vatthu-purejāta: base-prenascence I,166
Vatthuṁ paṭicca khandhā: dependent on (heart-)base, (arise) aggregates I,23
Vaṇṇa: colour II, 476
Vaṇṇa-sampadā: fullness of colour II, 476
Vara: excellent, supreme I,18
Vācā: speech I,161
Vācanā-maggena: by way of recitation I,16
Vāra: chapter I,22
Vikkhambhite: uneradicated/suppressed I,144
Vikkhambhite kilese: uneradicated/suppressed defilements I,144
Vicāra: sustained thought II, 3
Vicikicchā: doubt I,142
Vicikicchā uppajjati: arises doubt I,142
Vicikicchā-sahagata: doubt-accompanied I,38
Viññāṇa: consciousness I,2
Viññāṇa-dhātu: consciousness element I,2
Viññāṇañcāyatana: infinity of consciousness I,142
Vitakka: applied thought II, 3
Vitakkattika: applied thought triplet II, 1
Vitthārito: has been fully expanded I,16
Vitthāretabba: should be expanded I,16
Vitthārena: in detail II, 152
Vipassati: practises insight I,143
Vipassanaṁ uppādeti: develops insight I,157
Vipāka: resultant I,362
Vipākattika: resultant triplet I,362
Vipākadhamma-dhammaṁ: state producing resultant state I,362
Vipāka-mano-dhātu: resultant mind-element I,339
Vipāka-mano-viññāṇa-dhātu: resultant mind-consciousness element I,339
Vipākā cattāro khandhā: four resultant aggregates I,8
Vipākābyākata: resultant indeterminate I,23
Vipāko tadārammaṇatā uppajjati: resultant (state) arises as registering I,143
Vippaṭisārissa: regrets I,143
Vibhaṅga-vāra: classification chapter I,22
Vibhajitabba: classify I,504
Vibhatta: as classified I,504
Visesa: difference II, 47
Visuṁ ghaṭanā natthi: no separate combination II, 269
Vīmaṁsā: investigating-wisdom I,2
Vīmaṁsa-sampayuttakānaṁ: associated with investigating-wisdom I,2
Vīmaṁsādhipati: predominant investigating-wisdom I,2
Vīriya: effort I,2
Vīriya sampayuttakānaṁ: associated with effort I,2
Vīriyādhipati: predominant effort I,2
Vīsaka: by twenty I,49
Vīsati: twenty I,501
Vuṭṭhāna: emergence I,149
Vuṭṭhahantassa (nirodhā): having emerged/emerging from (the attainment of Extinction) I,149

Savitakka-savicāra: with applied thought and sustained thought II, 1
Savicāra: with sustained thought II, 1
Savipāka: with resultant I,55
Saha gacchantena: to be taken with II, 39
Sahajāta-ghaṭanā: conascence combinations I,186
Sahajāta-vāra: conascent chapter I,73
Sahajātādhipati: conascence-predominance I,146
Sahajāto: conascent with I,73
Sādhukaṁ: thoroughly II, 553
Sāmañña: ordinary I,180
Sāmañña-ghaṭanā: ordinary combinations I,180
Sāsevana: with repetition I,55
Siyā: may I,13
Sīla: precept I,142
Sīlaṁ samādiyati: undertakes the precept I,157
Sīlaṁ samādiyitvā: having undertaken the precept I,142
Sukha: pleasant I,318; pleasure I,323
Sukha-sahagata: accompanied by pleasure II, 147
Sukha-sahagata-kāya-viññāṇa: pleasure-accompanied body-consciousness I,323
Sukhāya vedanāya sampayutta: associated with pleasant feeling I,318
Sugambhīrā ti: are profound I,18
Suciṇṇāni: well done I,142
Suṇāti: hears I,145
Suta: learning I,157
Suddha: by ones I,35
Suddhikaṁ arūpaṁ: purely immaterial (plane) II, 39
Sekkha: appertaining to learners II, 329
Sekkhattika: learners triplet II, 329
Sekkhā: learners I,142
Sekkhā vā puthujjana vā: learners or common worldlings I,142
Senāsana: lodging-place I,7
Sota: ear I,6
Sota-dhātu: ear element I,146
Sota-viññāṇa-dhātu: ear-consciousness element I,2
Sotāyatana: ear-base I,6
Sot-indriya: ear-faculty I,9
Soḷasa: sixteen I,427
Soḷasaka: by sixteens I,220

Hanati: kills I,161
Hantvā: after having killed I,162
Harati: plunders I,161
Haritvā: after having plundered I,162
Hīna: low II, 423
Hīnattika: low triplet II, 423
Hetu-paccayā ārammaṇe: with root condition and object I,35
Hetu-paccayena paccayo: related by root condition I,2
Hetu-sampayuttakānaṁ dhammānaṁ: to the states associated with roots I,2
Hetuyā nava: with root 9 I,35
Hetū: roots I,2
Honti: are I,65

APPENDIX

COMBINATIONS

With regard to the combinations which have to be given in detail, Guide to C.R., Part III, which treats of them in this manner, is under preparation. Therefore it will be difficult to understand what is now given briefly by means of charts. The Faultless Triplet is taken as example so that, based on what is given here, the combinations in the other Triplets can be understood. If the combinations are understood the commons can be found from them. On the other hand, if the commons are understood the combinations can be found from them. The combinations in the Faultless Triplet will now be examined.

CHART A

MIXED COMBINATION (MISSAKA-GHAṬANA) 39

	1	2	3	4	5	6	7	8	9	10	11	
Conditions	9 Kinds of Ps	4 Kinds of Dp	Ob-prn-pd* Cn-pd	Ba-ob-prn-pd* Cn-pd	Mental nu Physical nu	3 Kinds of Fa	Cn-fa Ba-prn-fa	4 Kinds of Dss	Ba-ob-prn Cn-dss Ba-prn-dss	Ba-ob-prn-pd Cn-pd-dss	Cn-fa-dss Ba-prn-fa	Total
1. Pd			"	"						"		3
2. Dp		"		"			"		"	"	"	6
3. Nu					"							1
4. Fa						"	"				"	3
5. Dss								"	"	"	"	4
6. Ps	"	"	"	"	"	"	"	"	"	"	"	11
7. N.D.	"	"	"	"	"	"	"	"	"	"	"	11
Enu	13	13	8	8	7	7	7	5	5	4	3	(39)

*See chart II(B) facing p. lxiv in Intr. to C.R. I

Note. The combinations can be easily explained by dealing with them in the following order: Mixed, Miscellaneous and Conascence taking all the conditions concerned in each case. But in the text, where the conditions are taken in the usual order, the combination or combinations are dealt with under each condition. So once these combinations are known they can then be taken according to the text.

A Short Explanation of the Chart

Headings

1. *9 Kinds of Presence.* For these see Ps in Chart II(A) given in Intr. to C.R. I, p. liii. They represent the conditioning and conditioned states of presence condition.
2. *4 Kinds of Dependence.* For these see Dp in the chart.
3. Predominance and presence are common.
4. Predominance and dependence are common.
5. See the nutriment (nu) heading in the chart.
6. See the faculty (fa) heading in the chart.
7. Dependence and faculty are common.
8. As in the dissociation (dss) heading.
9. Dependence and dissociation are common.
10. Predominance and dissociation are common.
11. Faculty and dissociation are common.

How they are common and how the combinations are obtained is given fully in Guide to C.R., Part III.

How to Read Chart A

It will be seen from the chart that in mixed combination there are only 7 conditions. Why only these 7 conditions, taken in that serial order, are chosen is explained in Guide to C.R., Part III.

When the "ditto" signs under the headings against predominance and the other conditions are read off, i.e. when the chart is read horizontally, it will be found that predominance has 3 mixed combinations, dependence has 6 and so on and that there is a total of 39 mixed combinations.

When the chart is read off vertically it gives the conditions contained in that particular mixed combination and also the enumeration.

These mixed combinations may be compared with those given for the 7 conditions in the following items (in brackets) under each of them in C.R. I. These are: 3 for predominance (447); 6 for dependence (462); 1 for nutriment (479); 3 for faculty (485); 4 for dissociation (512); 11 for presence (516); 11 for non-disappearance (524).

The 7 conditions and their 39 mixed combinations of the Faultless Triplet are all contained under one line of headings in the chart and when those for the 22 Triplets are dealt with they will be given under the same line of headings. This is the method by which the enumerations of the Triplets concerned can be determined. Then, based on this method, one can draw up detailed charts for each of the other Triplets.

How the Commons are Obtained from the Combinations (in brief)

How the commons are obtained from the combinations will now be dealt with briefly. When dealing with the headings of the chart it was shown under headings Nos. 3, 4, 7, 9, 10 and 11 how the commons are obtained from the combinations. As for the other headings, No. 1 shows that presence and non-disappearance are common; No. 2 that dependence, presence and non-disappearance are common; No. 5 that nutriment and presence are common (when presence is mentioned non-disappearance is also included); No. 6 that faculty and presence are common; No. 8 that dissociation and presence are common. The common conditioning and conditioned states of the common conditions concerned have to be selected to determine the enumerations. The single enumerations of the conditions are given in Charts II (B)–(H) facing p. lxiv in the Intr. to C.R. I.

The Miscellaneous combination chart that follows will be dealt with in a similar way.

Miscellaneous Combination (Pakiṇṇaka-Ghaṭanā) 64

Chart B

The chart contains all the enumerations and common conditions which were provided in Charts II (B)–(H) referred to above. The conditioning and conditioned states given there must be known. The only special thing here is heading No. 2 where there are two conditions. The enumeration for both object-prenascence and base-prenascence is 3. Object-prenascence has 4 common conditions and base-prenascence has 5 common conditions. But when the common of these conditions are taken there are only 3 as given in the chart.

Comparison with C.R. I

The Miscellaneous combinations of the conditions read off by reading the chart vertically can be compared with those given for the 16 conditions in the following items (in brackets) under each of them in C.R. I. These are: (1) 5 for object (445); (2) 3 for predominance (448); (3) 3 for proximity (454); (4) 3 for contiguity (456); (5) 4 for dependence (463); (6) 7 for strong-dependence (466); (7) 7 for prenascence (468); (8) 1 for postnascence (470); (9) 1 for repetition (472); (10) 2 for kamma (474); (11) 1 for faculty (486); (12) 5 for dissociation (513); (13) 8 for presence (517); (14) 3 for absence (520); (15) 3 for disappearance (522); (16) 8 for non-disappearance (525).

The method of finding the commons should be known by now. With the commons only 2 conditions are taken but with the combinations all that are possible.

The above 16 conditions must be noted. Here the 64 miscellaneous combinations of the Faultless Triplet are worked out under one line of headings. Those of the 22 Triplets will also be given under the same line of headings.

CHART B

MISCELLANEOUS COMBINATION (PAKIṆṆAKA–GHAṬANĀ) 64

	Conditions	1 Pon	2 Ob-prn Ba-prn	3 Ba-prn	4 Ob-pd	5 Ob-prn	6 Ba-ob-prn	7 Ob-prn-pd	8 Ba-ob-pd	9 Ba-prn-fa	10 Px	11 Rp	12 Asy-kam	13 Px-kam	Total
1	Ob				"	"	"	"	"						5
2	Pd				"			"	"						3
3	Px										"	"		"	3
4	Ct										"	"		"	3
5	Dp			"			"		"	"					4
6	S.D.				"			"	"		"	"	"	"	7
7	Prn		"	"		"	"	"	"	"					7
8	Pon	"													1
9	Rp											"			1
10	Kam												"	"	2
11	Fa									"					1
12	Dss	"		"			"		"	"					5
13	Ps	"	"	"		"	"	"	"	"					8
14	Ab										"	"		"	3
15	Dsp										"	"		"	3
16	N.D.	"	"	"		"	"	"	"	"					8
Enu		3	3	3	7	3	3	1	1	1	7	3	2	1	(64)

Conascence Combinations

Major and Medium Conascence Combination 57
(Mahā-Catukka-, Majjhima-Catukka-Ghaṭanā)

Chart C

Here conascence, mutuality, association, conascence-dissociation and resultant represent their single enumerations.

CHART C

MAJOR AND MEDIUM CONASCENCE COMBINATION 57
(MAHĀ-CATTUKKA-, MAJJHIMA-CATUKKA-GHAṬANĀ)

		Without resultant 5					With resultant 5					
		1	2	3	4	5	1	2	3	4	5	
Conditions		Cn	Mu	Ass	Cn-dss	Mu-dss	Rs	Rs-mu	Rs-ass	Rs-dss	Rs-mu dss	Total
1	Cn	"	"	"	"	"	"	"	"	"	"	10
2	Mu		"	"		"		"	"		"	6
3	Dp	"	"	"	"	"	"	"	"	"	"	10
4	Rs						"	"	"	"	"	5
5	Ass			"					"			2
6	Dss				"	"				"	"	4
7	Ps	"	"	"	"	"	"	"	"	"	"	10
8	N.D.	"	"	"	"	"	"	"	"	"	"	10
	Enu	9	3	3	3	1	1	1	1	1	1	(57)

Without Resultant 5. In heading No. 5 mutuality-dissociation shows that mutuality and conascence-dissociation are common. Their conditioning states are 4 mental aggregates and (heart-)base at the moment of conception in five-aggregate planes and their conditioned states are 4 mental aggregates and (heart-)base (mutually). They are given in mutuality (c) and conascence-dissociation (b) in Chart II (D) in Intr. to C.R. I already referred to. The enumeration for each of them is 1.

With Resultant 5. In heading No. 2 resultant-mutuality shows that resultant and mutuality are common; No. 3 resultant-association that resultant and association are common; No. 4 resultant-dissociation that resultant and dissociation are common; No. 5 resultant-mutuality-dissociation shows that these 3 conditions are common. For the latter the common states are the single enumeration given for resultant condition (b) in Chart II (D) referred to above. As for the commons given above they can be found from the single enumerations in the same chart.

The 57 combinations are included under one line of headings and those of the 22 Triplets will also be given under the same line of headings.

Comparison with C.R. I

The combinations of the conditions read off by reading the chart vertically can be compared with those given for the 8 conditions in the following items (in brackets) under each of them in C.R. I. These are: (1) 10 conascence combinations (458); (2) 6 mutuality combinations (460); (3) 10 dependence combinations (464); (4) 5 resultant combinations (477); (5) 2 association combinations (510); (6) 4 dissociation combinations (514); (7) 10 presence combinations (518); (8) 10 non-disappearance combinations (526).

Minor Conascence Combination 255
(Khuddaka-Sahajāta-Ghaṭanā)

Chart D (pp. 588–9)

A Short Explanation of Chart D

Chart D (i) on p. 588 gives the conditioning states and Chart D (ii) on p. 589 the conditioned states. Root and the rest of the 5 conditions, shown with asterisks, are ordinary combinations given as item 1. Here only 1 condition each has to be taken. As for item 2 and the others, 2 conditions have to be taken when there are 2 of them and 3 conditions when there are 3 and so on.

Enumerations. The enumerations for items 1–10 are always 7, 3, 3, 3 respectively for the 4 combinations without resultant and always 1 each for the 5 combinations with resultant. The conditioning and conditioned states of root and the rest of the 5 conditions are those given in the Single Enumeration charts in Intr. to C.R. I so often referred to. As for items 2–10, where there are 16 conditioning states, the conditions to be taken are those shown against them in the chart. Except for

CHART D (i)

MINOR CONASCENCE COMBINATION 255 (KHUDDAKA-SAHAJĀTA-GHAṬANĀ)

	Conditioning States	Names of Combinations							Total	Enu
		Ro	Pd	Kam	Nu	Fa	Jh	Pa		
1	Ordinary	* ,,			* ,,	* ,,	* ,,	* ,,	9 each	
2	Effort, mindfulness, one-pointedness, knowledge					,,		,,	,,	
3	Feeling, one-pointedness					,,	,,		,,	
4	Applied thought, one-pointedness						,,	,,	,,	
5	One-pointedness					,,	,,	,,	,,	7
6	Volition			,,	,,				,,	3
7	Consciousness				,,	,,			,,	3
8	Predominant desire		,,						6	3
9	Predominant consciousness		,,		,,	,,			6 each	
10	Predominant effort		,,			,,		,,	,,	
11	Non-delusion	,,				,,		,,	9 each	4 2
12	Investigating-wisdom predominance	,,	,,			,,		,,	6 each	2 2
	Total	24	24	9	33	72	36	57	(255)	

CHART D (ii)

CONDITIONED STATES

	Associated aggregates	Mind-produced matter	Rebirth kamma produced matter	Additional Conditions			Enu	Without resultant	With resultant
1	"	"	"	Major 4			7		
2*	"		heart-base	"	Mu		3		
3	"			"	Mu	Ass	3	4	5
4		"	Rebirth kamma	"		Dss	3		
5*			heart-base	"	Mu	Dss	1		1*

the 4 conditioning states of predominance (items 8, 9, 10 & 12), all the conditioning states of the other 8 items give 4 combinations without resultant and 5 with resultant, i.e. a total of 9 each. As for the conditioning states of predominance, which occur during life only, there are 3 combinations without resultant and 3 with resultant, i.e. a total of 6 each. In these cases items 2 and 5 of the conditioned states in the second part of the chart, shown with asterisks, are not included.

Additional Conditions. They are given in the second part of the chart (above). The 4 Major conascence conditions, as the leaders, are always included as additional conditions in any combination. For (a) item 2 mutuality is also added; (b) item 3 mutuality and association are added and (c) item 4 dissociation is added. These are the 4 combinations without resultant. For item 5, 2 conditions, mutuality and dissociation are added to give 5 combinations with resultant. Items 11 and 12 are wisdom and, therefore, the 3 answers for the faulty are excluded. So the enumerations with the conditions shown against them in the facing part of the chart for the 4 combinations without resultant are respectively 4, 2, 2, 2 and with resultant are all 1.

How to Read Chart D

Root: Ordinary 9

Without Resultant 4

1. Combination of root, conascence, dependence, presence and non-

disappearance (has) 7 (answers) when 6 roots are related to their associated aggregates, rooted mind-produced matter and rebirth kamma-produced matter;

2. Of root, conascence, mutuality, dependence, presence and non-disappearance 3 when 6 roots are related to their associated aggregates and (heart-)base;

3. Of root, conascence, mutuality, dependence, association, presence and non-disappearance 3 when 6 roots are related to their associated aggregates;

4. Of root, conascence, dependence, dissociation, presence and non-disappearance 3 when 6 roots are related to rooted mind-produced matter and rooted rebirth kamma-produced matter.

With Resultant 5

5. Combination of root, conascence, dependence, resultant, presence and non-disappearance 1 when 3 resultant roots are related to their associated aggregates, rooted mind-produced matter and rooted rebirth kamma-produced matter;

6. Of root, conascence, mutuality, dependence, resultant, presence and non-disappearance 1 when 3 resultant roots are related to their associated aggregates and (heart-)base;

7. Of root, conascence, mutuality, dependence, resultant, association, presence and non-disappearance 1 when 3 resultant roots are related to their associated aggregates;

8. Of root, conascence, dependence, resultant, dissociation, presence and non-disappearance 1 when 3 resultant roots are related to rooted mind-produced matter and rooted rebirth kamma-produced matter;

9. Of root, conascence, mutuality, dependence, resultant, dissociation, presence and non-disappearance 1 when 3 resultant roots at 13 rooted rebirth-consciousnesses in five-aggregate planes are related to (heart-)base.

Then root is taken with faculty and path of item 11 to give 9 combinations and with predominance, faculty and path of item 12 to give 6 combinations. In this way the rest of the combinations can be read off from the chart.

Comparison with C.R. I

The combinations of conditions read off from the chart in the above manner can be compared with those given for the 7 conditions in the following items (in brackets) under each of them in C.R. I. These are: (1) Root with 24 conascence combinations (441–443); (2) Predominance with 24 conascence combinations (449–452); (3) Kamma with 9 conascence combinations (475); (4) Nutriment with 33 conascence combinations (480–483); (5) Faculty with 72 conascence combinations (487–495); (6) Jhāna with 36 conascence combinations (497–500); (7) Path with 57 conascence combinations (502–508).

It will be found from both the chart and the text that there is a total of 255 Minor conascence combinations. Here also they are given under one line of headings. Those of the 22 Triplets will also be given under the same line of headings. How the commons are obtained from these combinations is fully explained in Guide to C.R., Part III.

As mentioned earlier the conditions are not taken in the usual order to explain the 3 kinds of combinations. As this is different from the text, another chart is provided giving the commons and combinations for the conditions taken in the usual order for the reader who desires to follow the text.

Serial Order of Common Conditions and 415 Combinations

Chart E (p. 592)

Now, the combinations with their enumerations in the 22 Triplet Paṭṭhānas, most of which are elided in the text, are given in charts.

Combinations for 22 Triplets

1. Mixed Combinations for 16 Triplets

Chart F (p. 593)

The Triplets are itemized according to their serial order, i.e. 1 is the Faultless Triplet, 2 is the Feeling Triplet, 3 is the Resultant Triplet and so on. In Mixed Combinations, the Feeling Triplet and the rest of the 6 Triplets (items 2, 7, 13, 16, 19, 21), which do not contain materiality, are excluded and that is why there are only 16 Triplets here. The enumerations under the headings Nos. 1, 2, 5, 6 and 8 are the same as for the "By Ones" of the Triplets concerned. The other enumerations have to be determined from the states of the Triplets concerned.

CHART E

SERIAL ORDER OF COMMON CONDITIONS AND 415 COMBINATIONS

	Common Conditions		Combinations		Conascence			Total
			Mixed	Miscel-laneous	Major	Medium	Minor	
1.	Ro	11					24	24
2.	Ob	7		5				5
3.	Pd	15	3	3			24	30
4.	Px	6		3				3
5.	Ct	6		3				3
6.	Cn	14			10			10
7.	Mu	14				6		6
8.	Dp	17	6	4	10			20
9.	S.D.	13		7				7
10.	Prn	8		7				7
11.	Pon	3		1				1
12.	Rp	5		1				1
13.	Kam	14		2			9	11
14.	Rs	14				5		5
15.	Nu	11	1				33	34
16.	Fa	14	3	1			72	76
17.	Jh	10					36	36
18.	Pa	12					57	57
19.	Ass	13				2		2
20.	Dss	17	4	5		4		13
21.	Ps	18	11	8	10			29
22.	Ab	6		3				3
23.	Dsp	6		3				3
24.	N.D.	18	11	8	10			29
	Total		39	64	40	17	255	(415)

CHART F

COMBINATIONS FOR 22 TRIPLETS
MIXED COMBINATIONS FOR 16 TRIPLETS

	1	2	3	4	5	6	7	8	9	10	11
Triplets	9 Kinds of Ps	4 Kinds of Dp	Ob-prn-pd Cn-pd	Ba-ob-prn-pd Cn-pd	Mental nu Physical nu	3 Kinds of Fa	Cn-Fa Ba-prn-fa	4 Kinds of Dss	Ba-ob-prn Cn-dss	Ba-prn-dss Ba-ob-prn-pd Cn-pd-dss	Cn-fa-dss Ba-prn-fa
1	13	13	8	8	7	7	7	5	5	4	3
3	13	13	8	8	7	9	9	5	5	4	4
4	23	11	5	5	12	7	7	10	5	3	4
5,14	13	13	8	8	7	7	7	5	5	4	3
6	30	30	14	14	11	11	11	9	9	6	3
8	13	13	9	9	7	7	7	5	5	5	3
9	17	17	9	9	7	7	7	9	9	5	3
10	13	13	8	8	7	7	7	5	5	4	3
11	13	13	7	7	7	7	7	5	5	3	3
12	13	13	7	7	7	7	7	5	5	3	3
15	13	13	7	7	7	7	7	5	5	3	3
17	1	1	1	1	1	1	1	1	1	1	1
18	1	1	1	1	1	1	1	1	1	1	1
20	6	2	4	2	6	2	2	2	2	2	2
22	25	21	9	7	7	9	9	8	8	7	8

2. Miscellaneous Combinations for 22 Triplets

Chart G (opposite)

The 6 Triplets mentioned above, items Nos. 2, 7, 13, 16, 19, 21 (the Feeling, Rapture and 4 Object Triplets), do not contain materiality and so the conditions like postnascence and others, which have only materiality as conditioning or conditioned states, are excluded. That is why only the conditions under headings Nos. 4, 10, 11, 12 and 13, which have mentality as conditioning and conditioned states, are included under these 6 Triplets. As for Triplet No. 16, the Path Object Triplet, it will be seen from its states that the conditions under headings Nos. 12 and 13 are excluded. Also, for Triplet No. 19, the Past Object Triplet, the condition under heading No. 13 is excluded. So the conditions have to be taken according to the states of the Triplets. All that is given briefly in this single chart should be expanded into 21 charts (Triplets Nos. 5 and 14 being the same) for the 22 Triplets in the way that was given for the Faultless Triplet.

3(a). Major and Medium Conascence Combinations for the 22 Triplets

Chart H (p. 596)

Just as with the Miscellaneous Combinations given above, the 5 Triplets Nos. 2, 7, 13, 19, 21, which do not contain materiality, have only 1 combination without resultant and 1 with resultant. The other combinations are not obtained because the conditioning and conditioned states of the conditions are mixed with materiality. In the case of the other Triplet No. 16, resultant is not included because it is not contained in the states of that Triplet and so there is only 1 combination without resultant.

3(b). Minor Conascence Combinations for 22 Triplets

Chart I (pp. 598–9)

With regard to the headings: (1) Ordinary, etc. 7. These are the 7 conditions given for Minor Conascence Combinations of the Faultless Triplet; (2) Predominant desire, etc. 3. The other 2 are predominant consciousness and predominant effort. When taken with the other 2

CHART G

MISCELLANEOUS COMBINATIONS FOR 22 TRIPLETS

	1	2	3	4	5	6	7	8	9	10	11	12	13
Triplets	Pon	Ob-prn Ba-prn	Ba-prn	Ob-pd	Ob-prn	Ba-ob-prn	Ob-prn-pd	Ba-ob-pd	Ba-prn-fa	Px	Rp	Asy-kam	Px-kam
1	3	3	3	7	3	3	1	1	1	7	3	2	1
2				4						7	3	8	2
3	3	3	3	7	3	3	1	1	1	7	2	1	1
4	9	7	3	4	4	2	2	1	1	7	2	2	1
5,14	3	3	3	5	2	2	1	1	1	7	3	3	1
6	5	5	5	17	4	3	3	3	1	25	21	8	7
7				16						16	10	16	10
8	3	3	3	6	3	3	2	2	1	7	3	2	1
9	5	5	5	6	5	5	2	2	1	17	17	2	1
10	3	3	3	6	2	2	1	1	1	6	3	2	1
11	3	3	3	5	1	1	1	1	1	8	2	3	2
12	3	3	3	4	2	1	1	1	1	9	4	3	1
13				7						9	5	5	1
15	3	3	3	3	2	1	1	1	1	5	3	3	1
16				9						9	9		
17	1	1	1	3	1	1	1	1	1				
18	1	1	1	3	1	1	1	1	1	1	1	1	1
19				6						7	3	9	
20	2	6	2	4	4	2	4	2	2	2	2	2	2
21			2							4	3	4	1
22	7	6	2	3	3	1	3	1	1	1	1	1	1

CHART H

MAJOR AND MEDIUM CONASCENCE COMBINATIONS FOR 22 TRIPLETS

Triplets	Without resultant 5					With resultant 5				
	1	2	3	4	5	1	2	3	4	5
	Con	Mu	Ass	Con-dss	Mu-dss	Rs	Rs-mu	Rs-ass	Rs-dss	Rs-mu-dss
1	9	3	3	3	1	1	1	1	1	1
2	3					3				
3	11	7	3	4	2	3	3	1	1	1
4	9	3	3	4	1	6	2	2	3	1
5,14	9	3	3	3	1	4	2	2	2	1
6	30	28	11	9	9	21	21	11	5	5
7	10					10				
8	9	3	3	3	1	1	1	1	1	1
9	17	11	11	5	1	1	1	1	1	1
10	9	3	3	3	1	1	1	1	1	1
11	9	3	3	3	1	7	3	3	3	1
12	11	7	3	4	3	7	5	3	3	2
13	3					3				
15	9	3	3	3	1	1	1	1	1	1
16	17									
17	1	1	1	1	1	1	1	1	1	1
18	1	1	1	1	1	1	1	1	1	1
19	3					3				
20	2	2	2	2	2	2	2	2	2	2
21	2					2				
22	21	6	1	7	1	7	1	1	7	1

headings there are 12 conditioning states. Those that are the same have been taken together.

So the Enumeration Chapters of the Investigation Chapters of (1) Positive conditions of Faultless Triplet in detail and the other 21 Triplets in brief, have been given. As for (2) Negative, (3) Positive-Negative and (4) Negative-Positive conditions, they cannot be given because it would make this book very lengthy.

CHART I (i)

MINOR CONASCENCE COMBINATIONS FOR 22 TRIPLETS

Triplets	Ordinary, etc. 7		Predominant desire, etc. 3		Non-delusion		Investigating-wisdom predominance	
	Without rs	With rs	Without rs	With rs	Without rs	With rs	Without rs	With rs
1	7 3 3 3	1 1 1 1 1	7 3 3	1 1 1	4 2 2 2	1 1 1 1 1	4 2 2	1 1 1
2	3	3	3	3	2	2	2	2
3	7 5 3 3	3 3 1 1 1	4 3 3	3 1 1	7 5 3 3	3 3 1 1 1	7 3 3	3 1 1
4	7 3 3 4	6 2 2 3 1	4 2 2	3 1 1	7 3 3 4	6 2 2 3 1	4 2 2	3 1 1
5,14	7 3 3 3	4 2 2 2 1	7 3 3	3 1 1	4 2 2 2	4 2 2 2 1	4 2 2	3 1 1
6	11 11 7 3	11 11 7 3 3	11 7 3	11 7 3	11 11 7 3	11 11 7 3 3	11 7 3	11 7 3
7	10	10	10	10	10	10	10	10
8	7 3 3 3	1 1 1 1 1	7 3 3	1 1 1	1 1 1 1	1 1 1 1 1	1 1 1	1 1 1
9	7 3 3 3	1 1 1 1 1	7 3 3	1 1 1	1 1 1 1	1 1 1 1 1	1 1 1	1 1 1
10	7 3 3 3	1 1 1 1 1	7 3 3	1 1 1	7 3 3 3	1 1 1 1 1	7 3 3	1 1 1
11	7 3 3 3	7 3 3 3 1	7 3 3	6 2 2	7 3 3 3	7 3 3 3 1	7 3 3	6 2 2
12	7 5 3 3	7 5 3 3 2	7 3 3	3 1 1	7 5 3 3	7 5 3 3 2	7 3 3	3 1 1
13	3	3	3	1	3	3	3	1

15	7	3	3	3	1	1	1	1	1	7	3	3	1	1	1	4	2	2	2	1	1	1	1	1	4	2	2	1	1	1
16	17									17						17									17					
17	1	1	1	1	1	1	1	1	1	1	1	1	1	1	1	1	1	1	1	1	1	1	1	1	1	1	1	1	1	1
18	1	1	1	1	1	1	1	1	1	1	1	1	1	1	1	1	1	1	1	1	1	1	1	1	1	1	1	1	1	1
19	3				3					3			3			3				3					3			3		
20	2	2	2	2	2	2	2	2	2	2	2	2	2	2	2	2	2	2	2	2	2	2	2	2	2	2	2	2	2	2
21	2				2					2			2			2				2					2			2		
22	7	1	1	7	7	1	1	7	1	7	1	7	7	1	7	7	1	1	7	7	1	1	7	1	7	1	7	7	1	7

CHART I (ii)

DIFFERENT ENUMERATIONS OF MINOR CONASCENCE COMBINATIONS

	Ordinary Jhāna									Ordinary Path, Applied thought, One-pointedness									Feeling, One-pointedness		Ordinary root								
	Without rs				With rs					Without rs				With rs					Without rs	With rs	Without rs				With rs				
6	21	21	11	5	21	21	11	5	5	16	16	9	4	16	16	9	4	4											
7																			3	3									
9																					11	5	5	3	1	1	1	1	1